Lecture Notes in Computer Science 4523

Yann-Hang Lee Heung-Nam Kim
Jong Kim Yongwan Park
Laurence T. Yang Sung Won Kim (Eds.)

Embedded Software and Systems

Third International Conference, ICESS 2007
Daegu, Korea, May 14-16, 2007
Proceedings

Springer

Volume Editors

Yann-Hang Lee
Arizona State University, Department of Computer Science and Engineering
699 S. Mill Av., Tempe, AZ 85287, USA
E-mail: yhlee@asu.edu

Heung-Nam Kim
Embedded S/W Research Division 161
Gajeong-Dong, Yuseong-Gu, Daejeon, 305-700, Korea
E-mail: hnkim@etri.re.kr

Jong Kim
Pohang University of Science and Technology
Department of Computer Science and Engineering (POSTECH)
San 31, Hyoja-dong, Nam-gu, Pohang 790-784, Korea
E-mail: jkim@postech.ac.kr

Yongwan Park
Sung Won Kim
Yeungnam University, School of Electrical Engineering and Computer Science
214-1 Dae-Dong, Gyeongsan City, Gyeongbuk, 712-749, Korea
E-mail: {ywpark, swon}@yu.ac.kr

Laurence T. Yang
St. Francis Xavier University, Department of Computer Science
Antigonish, NS, B2G 2W5, Canada
E-mail: lyang@stfx.ca

Library of Congress Control Number: 2007926910

CR Subject Classification (1998): C.3, C.2, C.5.3, D.2, D.4, H.4

LNCS Sublibrary: SL 2 – Programming and Software Engineering

ISSN 0302-9743
ISBN-10 3-540-72684-5 Springer Berlin Heidelberg New York
ISBN-13 978-3-540-72684-5 Springer Berlin Heidelberg New York

Springer is a part of Springer Science+Business Media

springer.com

Printed in Germany

Typesetting: Camera-ready by author, data conversion by Scientific Publishing Services, Chennai, India
Printed on acid-free paper SPIN: 12068289 06/3180 5 4 3 2 1 0

Preface

Embedded systems, i.e., computers inside products, have been adopted widely in many domains, including traditional control systems, medical instruments, wired and wireless communication devices, aerospace equipment, human-computer interfaces, and sensor networks. Two significant trends have recently been observed due to the increasing computation power and communication bandwidth. The first is that embedded systems are getting connected and are cooperating as distributed systems. The other is the extensive software in middleware and embedded applications. These trends are apparent in academic and industrial research and in the papers submitted to the International Conference on Embedded Software and Systems.

The 3rd International Conference on Embedded Software and Systems (ICESS 2007), to be held in Daegu, Republic of Korea, on May 14-16, aims to advance embedded software and systems research, development, and design competence, and to enhance international communication and collaboration. It consists of the traditional core area of embedded systems infrastructure in architecture, software, hardware, real-time computing, and testing and verification, as well as additional areas of special emphasis: pervasive/ubiquitous computing and sensor networks, HW/SW co-design and SoC, wireless communications, power-aware computing, security and dependability, and multimedia and HCI. In addition, tutorial sessions on the broad fields of embedded computing, a panel discussion session and keynote addresses are included in the conference. Based on the 387 submitted manuscripts and the 77 accepted papers, we expect that the forum will be full of high quality presentations and productive discussions.

ICESS 2007 has been made possible by the hard work of a number of people, to whom we are very grateful. They include the members of the organization committees and the vice chairs of the technical tracks in the technical program committee. Recognition is warranted for the commendable job of all members of the technical program committee, who, in the short paper reviewing period, have accomplished the significant workload of evaluating, on average, 9 papers and providing constructive comments.

We are particularly thankful to Laurence T. Yang for his guidance and effort in continuing the ICESS series. In addition, we thank all authors who submitted their outstanding work; without them the conference would not have been possible. Finally, we gratefully acknowledge the support from our sponsors.

April 2007 Yann-Hang Lee and Heung Nam Kim

Organization

Organizers

ICESS-07 was organized by the Institute of Embedded Engineering of Korea (IEMEK).

Sponsors

Daegu GyeoungBuk Institute of Science & Technology (DGIST), Korea
Embedded Technology Education Center (EmTEC), New University for Regional Innovation (NURI), Korea
ETNEWS, Korea
Daegu Digital Industry Promotion agency (DIP), Korea
R&DB Center for Embedded System Industry, Korea
The Federation of Korea Information Industries, Korea
SK Telecom, Korea
SAMSUNG, Korea
DAEGU Convention & Visitors Bureau, Korea
Gyeongsangbuk-Do, Korea
Lecture Notes in Computer Science (LNCS), Springer

Executive Committee

General Chairs	Kyu-Suk Chung, President of IEMEK and DGIST, Korea
	Peter Marwedel, University of Dortmund and ICD, Germany
Program Chairs	Yann-Hang Lee, Arizona State University, USA
	Heung Nam Kim, ETRI, Korea
Steering Chairs	Zhaohui Wu, Zhejiang University, China
	Laurence T. Yang, St. Francis Xavier University, Canada
Program Vice-Chairs	Zonghua Gu, Hong Kong University of Science and Technology,Hong Kong, China
	Kenneth Ricks, The University of Alabama, USA
	Chanik Park, Pohang University of Science and Technology, Korea
	Byoungchul Ahn, YeungNam University, Korea
	Seong-dong Kim, ETRI, Korea
	Karam Chatha, Arizona State University, USA

	Mohamed Younis, University of Maryland Baltimore County, USA
	Christian W. Probst, Technical University of Denmark, Denmark
	Farn Wong, National Taiwan University, Taiwan
	Liudong Xing, University of Massachusetts - Dartmouth, USA
	Sangwook Kim, Kyungpook National University, Korea
Publicity Chairs	Young Jin Nam, Daegu University, Korea
	Wei Zhang, Southern Illinois University, USA
	Yu Hua, HuaZhong University of Science and Technology, China
	Yongxin Zhu, Shanghai Jiaotong University, China
Publication Chair	Sung Won Kim, YeungNam University, Korea
	Tony Li Xu, St. Francis Xavier University, Canada
Finance Chair	Yongwan Park, Yeungnam University, Korea
Local Chair	Dong Ha Lee, DGIST, Korea
Organization Chair	Jong Kim, Pohang University of Science and Technology, Korea

Program/Technical Committee

Ayman Abdel-Hamid	Arab Academy for Science and Technology, Egypt
Kemal Akkaya	Southern Illinois University, USA
Fatih Alagoz	Bogazici University, Turkey
Suprasad Amari	Relex Software Corporation, USA
Kwang-Seon Ahn	Kyungpook National University, Korea
Beongku An	Hongik University, Korea
Adel Youssef	Google, USA
Li Bai	Temple University, USA
Iain Bate	University of York, UK
Jalel Ben-Othman	Université de Versailles, France
Elaheh Bozorgzadeh	University of California, Irvine, USA
Hasan Cam	Arizona State University, USA
Erdal Cayirci	University of Stavanger, Norway
Samarjit Chakraborty	National University of Singapore, Singapore
Naehyuck Chang	Seoul National University, Korea
Changsik Cho	ETRI, Korea
Tae-Young Choe	Kumoh National Institute of Technology, Korea
Byung-Jae Choi	Daegu University, Korea
Tae Yoon Chung	Kangnung National University, Korea
Yuanshun Dai	Purdue University, Indianapolis, USA

Susan K. Donohue	University of Virginia, USA
Sameh Elsharkawy	Catholic University of America, USA
Mohammed Ferdjallah	The University of Tennessee, USA
Diana Franklin	Cal Poly, San Luis Obispo, USA
Xinwen Fu	Dakota State University, USA
Masahiro Fujita	University of Tokyo, Japan
Gernot Heiser	The University of New South Wales, Sydney, Australia
Dieter Hogrefe	Universität Göttingen, Germany
Jerry Hom	Rutgers University, USA
Seongsoo Hong	Seoul National University, Korea
Harry Hsieh	University of California, Riverside, USA
Pao-Ann Hsiung	National Chung Cheng University, Taiwan
Chung-Hsing Hsu	Los Alamos National Laboratory, USA
Yu Hua	HUST, China
Huadong Ma	Beijing University of Post and Telecommunication, China
Chung-Yang (Ric) Huang	National Taiwan University, Taiwan
Dijiang Huang	Arizona State University, USA
Jae Doo Huh	ETRI, Korea
Claude Jard	IRISA, France
Jie-Hong Roland Jiang	National Taiwan University, Taiwan
SoonKi Jung	Kyungpook National University, Korea
Woo Young Jung	Daegu Gyeongbuk Institute of Science and Technology, Korea
Ibrahim Kamel	Sharjah University, UAE
Sooyong Kang	Hanyang University, Korea
Kevin Kassner	Dynetics Corporation, Huntsville, Alabama, USA
Srinivas Katkoori	University of Southern Florida, USA
Cheon Shik Kim	Anyang University, Korea
Daeyoung Kim	Information and Communication University, Korea
Heesun Kim	Andong National University, Korea
Jeein Kim	Konkuk University, Korea
Jeonggon Kim	Hansei University, Korea
Moonzoo Kim	KAIST, Korea
Munchurl Kim	ICU, Korea
Myungchul Kim	Information and Communications University, Korea
Namchul Kim	Kyungpook National University, Korea
Christos Kloukinas	City University London, UK
Turgay Korkmaz	University of Texas at San Antonio, USA
Ibrahim Korpeoglu	Bilkent University, Turkey
Uli Kremer	Rutgers University, USA
Kiryong Kwon	Pukyong National University, Korea

Ben Lee	Oregon State University, USA
Bong Gyu Lee	Yonsei University, Korea
Gangsoo Lee	Hannam University, Korea
Insup Lee	University of Pennsylvania, USA
Seunghwan Lee	Samsung Electronics, Korea
Seungjoon Lee	ATT Research, USA
Xiaolin Li	Oklahoma State University, USA
Huan Li	Beihang University, China
Xue Liu	McGill University, Canada
Sin Ming Loo	Boise State University, USA
Roman Lysecky	University of Arizona, USA
Pyeongsoo Mah	ETRI, Korea
Viswanathan Mahesh	University of Illinois at Urbana-Champaign, USA
Marc St-Hilaire	Carleton University, Canada
Nicholas McGuire	Lanzhou University, China
Abdelhamid Mellouk	University of Paris XII, France
Leila Meshkat	Jet Propulsion Laboratory, USA
Ahmed Mostefaoui	Laboratoire d'Informatique de Franche-Comté, France
Tamer Nadeem	Siemens Corporate Research, USA
Farid Nait-Abdesselam	University of Lille, France
Sang Yep Nam	Kyungmoon University, Korea
Alberto Nannarelli	Technical University of Denmark, Denmark
Yang Ni	Intel, USA
Hoon Oh	Ulsan University, Korea
Ossamma Younis	University of Arizona, USA
Soo Hyun Park	Kookmin University, Korea
Filip Perich	Shared Spectrum Company, USA
Daji Qiao	Iowa State University, USA
Srivaths Ravi	Texas Instruments, India
Binoy Ravindran	Virginia Tech, USA
Karim Seada	Nokia Research, USA
Szili Shao	Hong Kong Polytechnic University, China
Chi-Sheng (Daniel) Shih	National Taiwan University, Taiwan
Oliver Sinnen	University of Auckland, New Zealand
Sang H. Son	University of Virginia, USA
Christian Steger	Technical University Graz, Austria
William Stapleton	The University of Alabama, USA
Sooyong Kang	Hanyang University, Korea
Tarek Bejaoui	University of Carthage, Tunisia
Hiroyuki Tomiyama	Nagoya University, Japan
Damla Turgut	University of Central Florida, USA

Kuang-Ching Wang	Clemson University, USA
Shige Wang	General Motors, USA
Xiaorui Wang	University of Tennessee, USA
Earl Wells	The University of Alabama in Huntsville, USA
Youjip Won	Hanyang University, Korea
Woontack Woo	GIST, Korea
Haruo Yokoda	Tokyo Institute of Technology, Japan
Youngwoo Yoon	Yeungnam University, Korea
Adel Youssef	Google, USA
Moustafa Youssef	University of Maryland College Park, USA
Zhen Yu	Iowa State University, USA
Wenhui Zhang	Chinese Academy of Sciences, China
Wenbing Zhao	Cleveland State University, USA
Lin Zhong	Rice University, USA
Dakai Zhu	University of Texas at San Antonio, USA
Yongxin Zhu	Shanghai Jiaotong University, China
Cliff Zou	University of Central Florida, USA
Xukai Zou	Purdue University, Indianapolis, USA

Table of Contents

Track 1: Embedded Architecture

Track 2: Embedded Hardware

Track 3: Embedded Software

Track 4: HW-SW Co-design and SoC

Track 5: Multimedia and HCI

Track 6: Pervasive/Ubiquitos Computing and Sensor Network:

Track 7: Power-Aware Computing

Track 8: Real-Time Systems

Track 9: Security and Dependability

Track 10: Wireless Communication

Object-Orientation Is Evil to Mobile Game: Experience from Industrial Mobile RPGs

Weishan Zhang[1], Dong Han[2], and Thomas Kunz[3]

[1] School of Software Engineering, Tongji University
No. 1239 Siping Road, Shanghai, 200092, China
zhangws@mail.tongji.edu.cn
[2] Department of Computer Science
Anhui Vocational College of Electronics &Information Technology
Bengbu University Park, Anhui Province, 233030, China
handongavceit@gmail.com
[3] Department of Systems and Computer Engineering, Carleton University
1125 Colonel By Drive, Ottawa, Canada K1S 5B6
tkunz@sce.carleton.ca

Abstract. Mobile gaming is playing an important role in the entertainment industry. Good performance is a critical requirement for mobile games in order to achieve acceptable running speed although mobile devices are limited by scarce resources. Object-oriented programming is the prevalent programming paradigm and this is true for mobile game development as well. As the origin of object-orientation (OO) is not targeting the embedded software domain, there is suspicion as to OO's usability for embedded software, especially with respect to mobile games. Questions arise like how OO and to what degree OO will affect the performance, executable file size, and how optimization strategies can improve the qualities of mobile game software. In this paper we investigate these questions within the mobile Role-Playing-Game (RPG) domain using five industrial mobile games developed with OO. We re-implemented these five RPGs with a structural programming style, by reducing the inheritance relationships, removing excessive classes and interfaces. Some additional optimizations are also applied during the re-implementation, such as the tackling of performance bottleneck methods, using more efficient algorithms. New games after optimizations run on average almost 25% faster than the corresponding original games, with a maximum of 34.62% improvement; the memory usage is decreased by more than 10% on average and 17.56% as a maximum; we also achieved a 59% code reduction and a 71% Jar file decrease after optimization. Therefore if developers are aiming for mobile game performance, we conclude that they should use as few OO features as possible. Structural programming can be a very competitive alternative.

1 Introduction

Mobile games are one of the primary entertainment applications at present. Good performance is one of the top requirements for mobile games in spite of scarce resources on the mobile devices, such as low battery life, small memory and screen size, etc [1]. By performance we mean not only arithmetic operation time, but also memory

Y.-H. Lee et al. (Eds.): ICESS 2007, LNCS 4523, pp. 1–12, 2007.

consumption of the game, how long it will take for the game to start, and finally the size of the executable program.

Currently Object-Oriented Programming (OOP) is the mainstream programming paradigm, and this is true for mobile game development as well. OOP is using abstractions where a collection of objects interact with each other, which is beneficial for achieving encapsulation and polymorphism. But every object will incur resource consumption which may lead to poor performance for embedded software [2], although this may not be a problem for desktop applications. And also there are shortcomings to the inheritance-based reuse, for example code redundancy and extra complexity [3].

Now it naturally comes to the questions of how OO affects the performance of the mobile games and to what degree, and how to optimize the performance. How and to what extent should we use the current OO languages for mobile game development? At present there is scarce published work to answer these questions with comprehensive case studies and convincing figures, especially in the mobile game domain. This kind of research is vital in order to help make decisions on what strategies should be used to improve the performance during the development of mobile games.

In this paper, we address these issues within the mobile RPG domain using five industrial mobile games developed with OO. We re-implemented these five RPGs using a more structural programming style, by reducing the inheritance relationships, removing excessive classes and interfaces and the tackling of performance bottleneck methods, using more efficient algorithms. With all these optimization strategies the performance of new games are improved significantly and the size of the final Jar file is reduced greatly. We conclude that application developers should use object orientation sparsely for mobile game development if performance is vital, and if one uses the OO language in a Structural Programming way, it could help boost the performance!

The rest of the paper is structured as follows: In the next section, we will briefly introduce the five RPGs and explain their implementation; then optimization strategies and techniques are discussed in Section 3. Section 4 illustrates the usage of these optimizations by re-implementing and re-structuring these five RPGs, mainly focusing on the shift to using structural programming. In Section 5, we evaluate the performance including the memory usage, loading time, Jar file size and Line of Code (LOC) metric. This is followed by a section to evaluate the design of these games using OO metrics. The concluding remarks and future work end the paper.

2 Introduction to the Five Mobile RPGs

2.1 Basic Information of the Five Mobile RPGs

The five mobile games named Dig (a), Climb (b), Hunt (c), Feeding (d) and Kongfu (e) are shown in Fig. 1 respectively. In Dig Gem, a hero digs around the map to look for gems. Different scores for different gems are added to the total and displayed in the upper left corner of the screen as shown in Fig. 1 (a). In Climb (Fig. 1 (b)) the hero walks and jumps on the floor to avoid falling down to the mountain. In Hunt (Fig. 1 (c)), the hero shoots animals and monsters with arrows and different scores will be added to the total for shooting different targets. In Feeding (Fig. 1 (d)), the hero tries to pick up as much food as possible, with different scores for eating different types of food. In Kongfu (Fig. 1 (e)) we have two heroes and a 'learner' learns Kongfu skills from his 'master'.

(a) Dig gem (b) Climb (c) Hunt (d) Feeding (e) Kongfu

Fig. 1. Five mobile RPGs

2.2 Design and Implementation of the Mobile RPGs

In order to improve the productivity of game development, a game engine is designed (Fig. 2) and used with all the five games. The game engine has components to abstract all common issues of game development. Package 'engine.view' is used for game view management. In 'engine' package there is a PlayCanvas class inheriting GameCanvas from the J2ME [4] system library, layer management class Nlayer and NlayerManager, GameScreen etc. Package 'engine.viewlayer' realized the basic map operations where a three dimensional array is used to manage the map. Package 'engine.event' is used for event and message handling. All games and the game engine are developed with MIDP2.0 [4] where a new 'game' package is added to the system library after MIDP1.0 in order to facilitate game development with necessary APIs.

Because all games are based on the MIDP profile, the execution scenario and its control flow are similar: There is a main class that extends MIDlet (for example Dig class in Fig. 3), as required by MIDP. In the constructor of the main class, an instance of the game Canvas (for example DigCanvas) is created. Using a getInitialScreen() method, this instance creates a game starting screen object (for example DigScreen). In the starting screen, all initialization data are loaded, including map, sound, etc. The constructor of the game Canvas (for example DigCanvas) will call its super class constructor (PlayCanvas in 'engine' package), where the game thread is created and started. The thread then loops to monitor the input of the keyboard, to update the game screen in order to handle game logic, and to paint the canvas for the game.

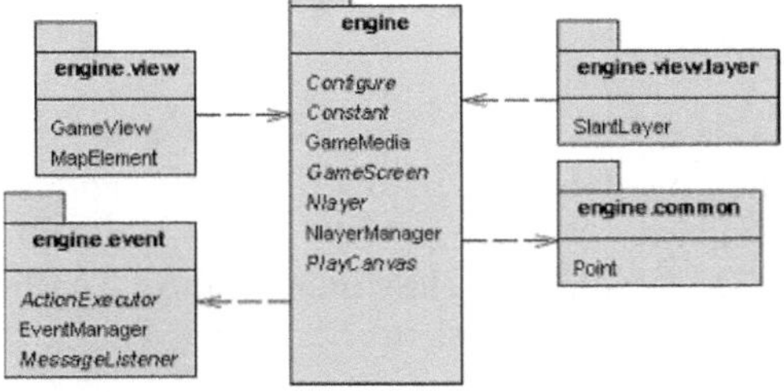

Fig. 2. Package diagram for game engine

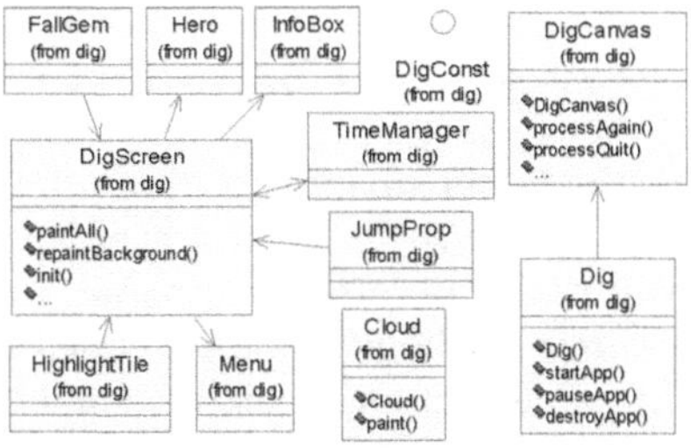

Fig. 3. Class diagram of Dig Gem

3 Performance Optimization Strategies and Techniques

3.1 Evaluation of the Game Engine and Original RPGs

In this section we will first evaluate the design qualities of the game engine and all RPGs and then decide how to optimize them, using typical OO metrics [5]. These metrics are shown in later sections to facilitate the metrics comparisons between original games and the final optimized games. We used Together Architect 2006 [6] to collect the actual figures and used its default threshold for these metrics.

Table 1. OO metrics used for design quality evaluation

OO Basic Metrics	OO Coupling Metrics	Inheritance based coupling
CIW-Class Interface Width NAM-Number Of Accessor Methods NOA-Number Of Attributes NOC-Number Of Classes NOCON-Number Of Constructors NOIS-Number Of Import Statements NOM-Number Of Members NOO-Number Of Operations PIS-Package Interface Size PS-Package Size	AOFD-Access Of Foreign Data CBO-Coupling Between Objects CM-Changing Methods DAC-Data Abstraction Coupling DD-Dependency Dispersion FO-FanOut MIC-Method Invocation Coupling NCC-Number Of Client Classes NOCP-Number Of Client Packages NOED-Number Of External Dependicies PUR-Package Usage Ratio VOD-Violations Of Demeters Law	DOIH-Depth Of Inheritance Hierarchy NOCC-Number Of Child Classes TRAp-Total Reuse of Ancestor percentage TRAu-Total Reuse of Ancestor unitary TRDp-Total Reuse in Descendants percentage TRDu-Total Reuse in Descendants unitary

We also measured the polymorphism with Number Of Added Methods (NOAM), Number Of Overridden Methods (NOOM) and Polymorphism Factor (PF). All of them are fine except that 'engine.view.layer.Slantlayer' has NOOM of 5, which is still ok but we do think that there is potential to improve this as subclasses should generally extend the functionality of the parent classes rather than overriding them. And after the optimizations all NOOM are 1 if there is NOOM. Because the polymorphism measurements are not significant, we are not showing them in the paper.

The OO metrics measurement shows that the original five games are designed as normal OO programs, with inheritance-based reuse as main design objective. This provides us with a good opportunity to simplify the class relationships and re-implementing these games to check how the usage of object-oriented language in a structural programming way affects the performance, and to what degree.

3.2 Optimization Strategies and Techniques

Methodological optimization

An object is the basic abstraction building block of OO, but more objects and classes will result in higher resource consumption. We try to solve this problem by minimizing the possible generated objects, simplifying class relationships. That is to say, we design our mobile game based on the traditional structural programing style and we check how this benefits the performance.

Some optimizations resulting from this choice are:

a. **Remove the constant interface.** There are some constant interfaces, one for every game. But interfaces should be used solely for type definitions [7], therefore we should remove all constant interfaces for all the five games.
b. **Remove redundant inheritance relationships.** In some cases, some classes that had very little in common were related by inheritance. We removed this kind of inheritance relationship along with unnecessary class members and methods.
c. **Remove unnecessary classes.** We re-allocated functionalities so that some classes, especially those with very few methods, could be removed.
d. **Remove obsolete class methods.** In some cases, we found that we never used certain class methods. We removed such obsolete methods.
e. **Find the performance bottleneck.** For example, use WTK to inspect which method is the one that consumes most of the CPU and memory and then optimize it.

Code optimization
The objective is to minimize memory consumption and prevent memory leaks. Code optimization may include:

f. Do not initialize all objects in the constructor and initialize it when first used.
g. Change class members to local variables.
h. Declare methods and variables final/static for faster access.
i. Set an object to null if it isn't used any more which accelerates memory recycle.

Algorithm optimization
j. Iterate loops down to zero as comparing against zero is faster.
k. Move the arithmetic operation in a loop outside the loop body.
l. Use bitwise operators (left shift/right shift) instead of multiplication and division.

Exception handling
m. Return a null object instead of throwing exceptions wherever possible, or use if/then/else to handle different situation.
n. Reuse an existing exception object rather than generating a new exception object.

Datatype optimization
Datatype optimization is an efficient way for improving performance as different data types use different resources.

o. Replace resizable Vectors with arrays, if possible.
p. Use primitive data type instead of the object type whenever possible.
q. Minimize the usage of string concatenation and comparison, use StringBuffer instead.

4 Re-implement the Five Mobile RPGs Using Optimizations

4.1 Optimization on Inheritance, Class and Interface

Our main optimization approach is the shifting from the object-orientation style of implementation to the structural programming style, where we simplify the class relationships by reducing inheritance hierarchies, cut the number of classes and interfaces, and add new responsities to classes where his parent has been removed.

Remove the constant interface
For Dig gem, there is a DigConst interface. And the game engine package has two constant interfaces, Configure and Constant. All of them are removed and all the constants are defined in class DigScreen. The other four games are handled in the same way.

Remove unnecessary/redundant inheritance
We know PlayCancas inherits GameCanvas and DigCanvas inherits PlayCanvas. And also from Fig. 8 we know that the DOIH of the original game and engine is 5 which exceeds the default upper threshold. Therefore our first optimization is to reduce the DOIH by simplifying the inheritance relationship. The three layer relationship can be simplified with DigCancas inheriting from GameCanvas directly. Therefore PlayCanvas is removed and DigCanvas is extended to take care of the responsibilities of PlayCanvas. Other usage of PlayCanvas will also be replaced with DigCanvas.

For the same reason and in the say way the GameScreen class in the engine package can also be removed and DigScreen can assume its responsibilities.

As we intended to remove all packages of the game engine, the inheritance between the 'dig.Hero' class and the 'engine.role.GameRole' class can be removed and replaced with the following new GameRole class (Fig. 4) by inheriting directly from J2ME system game library class Sprite.

```
public class GameRole extends Sprite {
  public GameRole(){
  super(DigScreen.loadImage
  ("dig/man.png"),32,30);
   setRoleName("Hero");
   this.setScrollView(true);
   ...// set action interval, speed }
   public void doAction(int keyStates)
   { ...... }
   }
```

Fig. 4. Redefined GameRole class

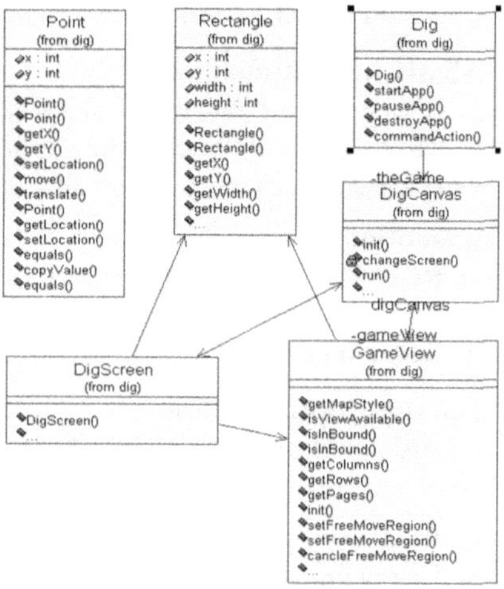

Fig. 5. Class diagram for Redesigned Dig gem

Remove unnecessary/redundant class and interface

- The 'engine.media.GameMedia' only defines some methods, and can be removed. The image related methods are now in the DigScreen class.
- Interface 'engine.view.layer.GroundMap' is only used by 'engine. view. layer.SlantLayer' and can be removed. All the contained methods are moved to SlantLayer.

- 'engine.view.GameScene' and 'engine.view.GameRole' form a GameView and therefore GameScene can be removed, all attributes and methods are now defined in GameView.
- Class 'engine.role.Motion' can be removed, and all attributes and methods are now defined in GameRole.

Remove obsolete class methods
For example in the GameMedia class, there are two methods for loading data from file or input stream, remaining from previous implementation, but never used in the current implementation. We remove such obsolete methods.

Other unnecessary classes include Menu, Color, Action, Event, EventManager, HotSpot, Message, Trigger, SoundCenter, MapElement; and unnecessary interfaces ActionExecutor, MessageListenable, MessageListener. All of them are removed. The class diagram for the redesigned Dig gem is shown in Fig. 5.

4.2 Further Optimizations

Spotting the performance bottleneck
Method Profiler provided by WTK2.2 can be used to find which method(s) dominate the running time. We found that method paintGround() in 'dig.SlantLayer' takes 80.75% of Dig gem running time. Therefore optimization to this method would bring the biggest benefits. In the same way, other runtime-intensive methods of the other four games could be handled. For example, paintAll() in 'hunt.HuntScreen' which takes 81.03% of the running time of Hunt and should be optimized.

Take paintGround(Graphics g) as an example. We use the following techniques for optimization:

- declaring the method to be 'final';
- multiplication and division are replaced with bitwise operators;
- control variable in 'for' loop is compared with 0;
- arithmetic operations in loop body are moved out;

After these optimizations, the paintGround(Graphics g) method takes 71.38% of the running time, a decrease of 9.37%.

Change class members to local variables
For example, the following buffer size is defined in class GameMedia:
public final static int BUFFER_SIZE = 1024;
But BUFFER_SIZE is used only in method LoadData() and it should be defined as a LoadData() local variable.

Declare method and variable as final/static for faster access
For example, in the DigScreen class the following code is used to make the access of the variable faster: public final static int MOTION_FACE_DOWN = 1; // ↓

Using obfuscator
We use ProGuard2.7 [8] to obfuscate the five games. After obfuscation the Jar file decreases from 357KB to 326KB.

Other optimizations include setting objects to null if they are not used anymore, using a string buffer, etc.

5 Evaluation with Typical OO Metrics

In this section, we will evalue the design of the original games and also the new games after optimization with typical OO metrics. We will first compare the results with packages, and then show the situation with Dig gem.

Evaluation with OO basic metrics

The Midlet suite name before optimization is MMMMM, and named MyGame_Final after optimization. From Fig. 6, we could see that in myGame_Final, NOM, NOO, NOA and NOCON are larger than the corresponding values in MMMMM. NOC, PS in MyGame_Final are less than the corresponding values in MMMMM. This is because we have simplified the class relationships, which leads to an increase in the number of attributes and therefore results in bigger classes.

Resource	NOA	NOC	NOCON	NOIS	NOM	NOO	PIS	PS
− MMMMM	• 37	47	2	23	53	23		
+ feeding	19	7	1	11	32	13	0	7
+ dig	• 37	12	1	17	53	16	3	12
+ hunt	29	11	1	23	52	23	0	11
+ climb	22	9	2	13	38	16	0	9
+ kongfu	23	8	2	12	33	13	0	8
− MyGame_Final	• 41	22	3	11	69	35		
+ kongfu	29	4	3	7	48	25	0	4
+ climb	28	3	2	6	55	27	0	3
+ dig	• 41	6	3	9	69	31	0	6
+ hunt	• 33	5	3	11	65	35	0	5
+ feeding	25	4	3	5	47	25	0	4

(a) OO basic metrics comparisons for packages

Resource	CIY	NAM	NOA	NOIS	NOM	NOO	PS
− MMMMM			• 37	17	53	16	
− dig			• 37	17	53	16	12
+ DigScreen	12	2	• 37	17	53	16	
+ HighlightTile	1	0	5	5	6	1	
+ Hero	2	0	0	6	4	4	
+ DigCanvas	6	0	4	10	13	9	
DigConst	40	0	0	0	0	0	
+ InfoBox	7	1	13	10	21	8	
+ Menu	5	3	8	7	13	5	
+ JumpProp	2	0	11	7	13	2	
+ Dig	3	0	2	2	5	3	
+ FallGem	1	0	6	6	7	1	
+ Cloud	1	0	7	6	8	1	
+ TimeManager	8	3	13	9	21	8	
− MyGame_Final			• 41	9	69	31	
− dig			• 41	9	69	31	6
+ DigCanvas	18	2	17	4	38	21	
+ Dig	4	0	5	5	9	4	
+ Rectangle	25	4	4	0	25	21	
+ Point	12	2	2	0	12	10	
+ GameView	20	7	8	6	28	20	
+ DigScreen	54	3	• 41	9	69	31	

(b) OO basic metrics comparisons for Dig gem

Fig. 6. OO basic metrics comparison

OO Coupling Metrics

Fig. 7 shows OO coupling metrics of the game packages and also Dig gem. We can see that before optimization, package 'dig' and 'hunt' have high degree of coupling. The DAC value of package 'climb', 'kongfu' and 'feeding' exceed the default threshold. Although not shown here, the values of DAC and FO of package 'engine.view' also exceed the upper default limit. This means that the original design of the 'engine' package was focusing on reuse but was not caring much about coupling.

After optimization we actually lower some of the coupling metrics, and leave the others at the same level. Big differences happened to package 'dig' before and after optimization, where we lower all metrics except the FO, which is not a problem as Digscreen deliberately is assigned more responsibilities during our re-implementation.

Resource	CBO	DAC	FO	MIC	NCC	NOCP	PUR	VOD
− MMMMMM	• 35	• 14	• 20	50				12
+ climb	20	• 9	12	24	0	0	0	5
+ dig	• 33	• 12	• 16	50	1	1	25	12
+ feeding	17	• 7	10	22	0	0	0	4
+ hunt	• 35	• 14	• 20	48	0	0	0	11
+ kongfu	17	• 7	10	20	0	0	0	4
− MyGame Final	22	• 12	• 22	14				7
+ climb	15	• 10	13	10	0	0	0	5
+ dig	21	• 11	• 19	14	0	0	0	7
+ feeding	12	• 8	12	14	0	0	0	4
+ hunt	22	• 12	• 22	14	0	0	0	7
+ kongfu	12	• 8	12	14	0	0	0	4

(a) OO coupling metrics comparison for packages

Resource	AOFD	CBO	CM	DAC	DD	FO	MIC	NOED	VOD
− MMMMMM		• 33		• 12		• 16	209		12
− dig		• 33		• 12		• 16	209		12
+ Cloud	1	5	1	3	3	4	9	6	1
+ Dig	0	4	1	2	3	2	9	4	1
+ DigCanvas	2	12	0	4	6	6	82	13	4
DigConst	0	0	14	0	1	0	0	0	0
+ DigScreen	7	• 33	3	• 12	12	• 16	209	26	12
+ FallGem	2	8	1	3	3	4	18	6	2
+ Hero	3	6	2	0	4	0	36	6	1
+ HighlightTile	2	7	2	2	3	4	18	6	2
+ InfoBox	3	9	3	3	5	4	27	10	2
+ JumpProp	2	7	1	3	3	4	27	7	1
+ Menu	2	7	1	3	4	4	9	8	2
+ TimeManager	2	6	4	3	3	4	18	5	1
− MyGame_Final		21		• 11		• 19	60		7
− dig		21		• 11		• 19	60		7
+ Dig	1	5	1	3	2	4	40	5	1
+ DigCanvas	1	7	8	• 5	4	6	60	3	4
+ DigScreen	4	21	15	• 11	4	• 19	60	5	7
+ GameView	0	10	13	• 5	3	9	40	3	3
+ Point	0	0	13	0	0	0	0	0	0
+ Rectangle	1	1	2	0	0	1	20	0	0

(a) OO coupling metrics comparison for Dig gem

Fig. 7. OO coupling metrics comparisons

Resource	DOIH	NOCC	TRAp	TRAu	TRDp	TRDu
− MMMMMM	• 5	28	27	100	287	859
+ engine.view	1	1	4	33	3	17
+ climb	• 5	0	11	80	0	0
+ engine.event	0	11	0	0	3	100
+ guessdual	• 5	0	20	90	0	0
+ sanjie	4	12	0	0	0	0
+ engine.common	0	0	0	0	0	0
+ engine	4	28	0	0	287	859
+ hunt	• 5	0	27	100	0	0
+ kongfu	• 5	0	8	80	0	0
+ dig	• 5	0	27	100	0	0
+ feeding	• 5	0	9	80	0	0
+ engine.view.layer	1	1	2	18	0	0
+ engine.role	3	4	0	0	29	138
+ engine.media	0	0	0	0	0	0
− MyGame_Final	2	0	0	0	0	0
+ feeding	2	0	0	0	0	0
+ kongfu	2	0	0	0	0	0
+ hunt	2	0	0	0	0	0
+ climb	2	0	0	0	0	0
+ dig	2	0	0	0	0	0

Fig. 8. Inheritance based coupling comparisons

OO Inheritance Metrics

Fig. 8 shows the OO inheritance-based coupling measurement. Before optimization, DOIH of games in MMMMM is 5, which is a bit high, exceeding the upper default bound, which motivates us to simplify the design and reduce the inheritance hierarchy. The DOIH becomes 2 after re-implementation. It is obvious that the original game design makes good use of inheritance-based reuse, while we are not using this at all as intended.

6 Experimental Results and Discussion

We compared the performance before and after optimizations shown in Table 2 and Table 3. The figures were obtained with Wireless Toolkit 2.2 (with memory monitor and profiler turned on in order to slow the running of these games to facilitate all measurements) on Windows 2000 Server service pack 3, 256M RAM, x86 Family 6 Model 8 Stepping 1 Authentic AMD 1499Mhz.

Table 2. Maximum memory usage comparison

		1	2	3	Average	Improvements
Dig gem	Before	263624	279436	264052	269037	17.56%
	After	220460	220764	224152	221792	
Hunt	Before	139296	145278	143662	142745	16.30%
	After	118800	120240	119398	119479	
Climb	Before	337612	333864	334523	335333	4.80%
	After	318975	321827	316958	319253	
Feeding	Before	345232	354532	354396	351387	5.85%
	After	328791	336948	326743	330827	
Kongfu	Before	350420	350000	333992	344781	7.51%
	After	31068	327263	318689	318877	

Table 3. Loading time comparisons

		1	2	3	Average	Improvements
Dig gem	Before	Before	79.37	79.86	79.28	22.73%
	After	After	61.10	61.84	61.36	
Hunt	Before	Before	6.17	5.68	6.77	34.62%
	After	After	4.15	3.64	4.39	
Climb	Before	Before	4.70	5.19	5.23	25.79%
	After	After	3.89	3.22	4.10	
Feeding	Before	Before	3.63	3.53	3.55	24.65%
	After	After	2.80	2.39	2.88	
Kongfu	Before	Before	5.29	5.19	5.32	16.70%
	After	After	4.34	4.87	3.96	

From Table 2 we can see that the new games, after optimizations, have better memory usage, with a maximum of almost 18% less memory and minimum reduction of almost 5%. This decrease is due to the fact that we are using less classes and interfaces and save heap usage during execution. We also improved the loading time

(Table 3) significantly after optimization, and the loading time of each optimized game decreases 22.73%, 34.62%, 25.79%, 24.65% and 16.70% respectively.

We also checked the LOC differences before and after optimizations. The LOC has been reduced from 21597 LOC to 8868, a 59% decrease. The Jar file decreased from 1.12MB to 326KB, and we obtained a 71% reduction after optimization.

These performance improvements are due to applying optimization strategies across all the games, mainly motivated by the usage of a more structural programming style.

7 Related Work

Mobile games are very popular and there are a number of online resources discussing the optimization of mobile games, e.g. [9]. They discuss various optimization techniques that could be used and also have been (or can be) incorporated in our work. Books like [7] also contain valuable suggestions for writing good Java programs that are not restricted to J2ME. But none of them provides us with convincing figures and a comprehensive case study to shown the actual impact of such optimizations.

There are company-specific guide-lines for the development of mobile games [10]. While they are very important and if possible, the usage of company-specific libraries usually is a wise option for improve the performance of the mobile games, we tried to be company-neutral in our research, which could be universal to all available devices.

Klingauf et al. [11] present a radical shift from the conventional approach to a native programming language like C to implement the whole system library and a high-level C-to-Java interface. This is very good in case this strategy is adopted by companies. We doubt though that this is a practical way for the companies who deliver mobile phones and mobile games. We present our optimizations and show how they affect the performance and all of them are very practical and useful.

There is an automatic J2ME games optimization tool called mBooster [12], designed mainly to minimize JAR file size. It can perform automatic class and interface merging and other low-level optimizations. But there are obvious limitations for its usage, for example it cannot perform class merging if the two candidate classes are in different packages. There is no mention on what criteria it uses to do class merging. But it does give us some ideas for implementing our own tool for optimizations.

8 Conclusions and Future Work

Mobile gaming is playing a more and more important role in the entertainment industry. Although object-oriented programming is the prevalent programming paradigm and OO is used widely for mobile game development, it is very doubtful to use object orientation in the embedded software domain because of its intrinsic problems. There arise questions like how OO and to what degree OO will affect the performance, executable file size, and how optimization strategies can improve the qualities of mobile game software. In this paper we investigated these questions using five industrial mobile games developed with OO.

We re-implemented these five RPGs with the style of structural programming, by reducing the inheritance relationships, removing excessive classes and interfaces. And also some other optimizations are used during the re-implementation, such as the tackling of performance bottleneck methods, using more efficient algorithms. After optimization, the loading time is significantly improved, on average almost 25% faster than loading the corresponding original games, and a maximum of 34.62% improvement; the memory usage is decreased by more than 10% on average and 17.56% as a maximum; we also achieved a 59% code reduction and a 71% Jar file decrease after optimization.

Therefore we conclude that if developers are going for mobile game performance, they should use as few OO features as possible because of the footprint of objects. Structural programming can be a very competitive alternative. It may seem strange to advocate using object oriented language with a structural programming style, but we found that this is a promising way to improve performance.

We will continue our work in two directions, the first is to explore the reuse based mobile game development using Frame concepts and technologies where we have expertise [13], the second is to design and implement an automatic tool support for Frame based and optimized mobile game development which is inspired by mBooster.

Acknowledgements

Thanks to Liu Wei and other authors from Meitong Co. Ltd. who have implemented the original games. We also owe our great thanks to Prof. Klaus Marius Hansen from University of Aarhus, and the generous support from the EU HYDRA project.

References

1. Blow J. Game Development: Harder Than You Think. Game DevelopmentVol. 1, No. 10, February 2004
2. Maarten Boasson. Embedded systems unsuitable for object orientation. 7th Ada-Europe International Conference on Reliable Software Technologies, Vienna, Austria, June 2002. pp.1-12
3. Object Oriented Programming Oversold. http://www.geocities.com/tablizer/oopbad.htm. 2007-3-10
4. J2ME homepage. http://java.sun.com/javame/index.jsp. 2007-3-10
5. Marinescu R. An Object Oriented Metrics Suite on Coupling. Master's thesis, Polytechnic University of Timisoara, 1998
6. Borland together Architect homepage http://www.borland.com/ downloads/ download_ together.html. 2007-3-10
7. Michael C. Daconta, et al. More java pitfalls. Wiley, 2003
8. Proguard homepage. http://proguard.sourceforge.net/. 2007-3-10
9. Supremej2me website. http://supremej2me.bambalam.se/. 2007-3-10
10. Nokia. Designing MIDP applications for optimization. http://sw.nokia.com/id/ 89527700c7ff/. 2007-3-10
11. W. Klingauf, L. Witte, U. Golze. Performance Optimization of Embedded Java Applications by a C/Java-hybrid Architecture. Global Signal Processing Conference, Santa Clara, CA, Sept. 2004
12. mBooster homepage. http://innaworks.com/mBooster.html. 2007-3-10
13. W. Zhang, S. Jarzabek. Reuse without Compromising Performance: Industrial Experience from RPG Software Product Line for Mobile Devices. Proc. of SPLC2005. Rennes, Sept. 2005, LNCS3714, pp. 57-69

Device-Aware Cache Replacement Algorithm for Heterogeneous Mobile Storage Devices

Young-Jin Kim and Jihong Kim

School of Computer Science & Engineering, Seoul National University,
San 56-1 Shillim-dong, Kwanak-gu, Seoul, Korea, 151-742
{youngjk,jihong}@davinci.snu.ac.kr

Abstract. Hard disks, most prevalent mass-storage devices, have high power consumption and high response time for random I/O requests. Recent remarkable technology improvement of flash memory has made it a rising secondary storage device but flash memory still has high cost per bit. Usage of heterogeneous storage devices such as a pair of a hard disk and a flash memory can provide reasonable cost, relatively acceptable response time, and low-power consumption. In this paper, we propose a novel buffer cache replacement algorithm which targets a mobile computing system with a heterogeneous storage pair of a hard disk and a flash memory. The algorithm partitions the cache per each device and adjusts the size of each partition based on the performance indices of the devices, and manages each partition according to workload patterns. Simulations show that the proposed algorithm yields a hit rate up to two times higher than LRU on the typical mobile traces according to the cache size and achieves also better system I/O response time and energy consumption.

Keywords: Heterogeneous storage, mobile systems, device-aware, workload-aware, cache replacement.

1 Introduction

As the mobile and ubiquitous computing technology progresses, end-users tend to want that they can use high-performance and high I/O load applications such as games and MPEG players. In the last decade, the innovational development of processors, memories, network devices, and secondary storage devices has enabled this. These days mobile computing systems with high-capacity storage devices are popular, such as PDAs, PMPs, and MP3 players. Since hard disk drives are widely adopted for mobile computing platforms, the demand for hard disk drives with a small form-factor (2.5″ or less), embedded in or connected to such systems, is also incrementally rising [1]. Concurrently, due to recent remarkable technology improvement of flash memory, it appears a rising secondary storage device.

However, despite attractive low cost per bit, hard disks are big power consumers and have poor performance for random I/O requests. Flash memory still

Y.-H. Lee et al. (Eds.): ICESS 2007, LNCS 4523, pp. 13–24, 2007.

has relatively high cost per bit. For example, NAND flash memory is said to be at least several times more expensive than disk drives with the same capacities [2]. Therefore, complementary storage architectures or techniques have been emerging. Several researchers have proposed combined storage techniques with a flash memory and a hard disk, which can be categorized into two: 1) using a flash memory as a non-volatile cache [3,4,5,6,7,8,9]; 2) using a flash memory as a secondary storage device [10]. Specially, [10] studied the potential of heterogeneous secondary storage by employing these two devices together with data concentration techniques. The heterogeneous storage solution in this work is expected to yield more energy saving in that it employs a flash memory as a secondary storage device directly and can maintain a larger set of energy-hungry blocks altogether on it compared with other work. However, the authors did not investigate performance improvement or load balancing problems deeply.

In case of using heterogeneous devices generally, file systems require caching algorithms that take into account the different miss penalties across file blocks depending on which devices they belong to. But, the most commonly used cache replacement algorithm, LRU is not aware of such different cost and treats all cache blocks as if they have the same replacement costs. In the web cache communities, there have been abundant research results on cost-aware cache replacement algorithms, which consider different file size, network latency during re-fetch due to a cache miss, file access frequency, etc. Recent web cache algorithms may be based on or enhance the *GreedyDual-Size* algorithm [11], which incorporates locality with miss penalty and file size concerns, generalizing the LRU algorithm. In disk-based storage systems, [12] studied storage-aware cache management algorithms using different costs on heterogeneous disks. This work maintained one partition per each disk and adjusted partition sizes based on the time spent per each disk (they call this *wait time*) over a period of device requests, and controlled the blocks within each partition similarly to the GreedyDual-Size algorithm. But, the authors did not take into account minutely the case of there being a number of sequential accesses, which may be problematic in their algorithms. This is because if a considerable number of sequential accesses are requested to a disk its wait time can be lengthened and the corresponding partition size will increase filling this partition with less valuable blocks. Consequently, in the worst case this algorithm may fail in obtaining good load balance.

In this paper, we build a novel cache replacement algorithm to overcome such limit, which targets mobile storage systems exploiting a pair of a hard disk and a flash memory as secondary storage. Our algorithm intends to enhance the system performance through both device-aware and workload-aware load balancing. For the former we use cache miss counts and access time per device and for the latter we have our algorithm manage the cache in the direction of exploiting the fast sequential performance feature of a hard disk. To the best of our knowledge, our work is the first attempt to design and incorporate a cost-aware cache management algorithm on the heterogeneous combination of a hard disk and a flash memory.

Our first goal is to investigate how our device-aware cache replacement algorithm can balance the I/O load between two heterogeneous devices on typical mobile workloads when the target system employs a hard disk and a flash memory as mass storage, compared with LRU. Second goal is to study how well our cache algorithm avoids cache pollution incurred by sequential block requests while balancing the I/O load.

We first tackle the design of a workload-aware cache replacement algorithm (in short, WAC) by introducing different cost per workload pattern similarly to the GreedyDual-Size algorithm. Then, we propose our re-partitioning policy on the total cache based on the cache miss counts at a fixed period and finally complete to embody our device-aware cache replacement algorithm (in short, DAC) combining these.

The rest of this paper is organized as follows. In Section 2, we review the features of a hard disk and a NAND flash memory to compose heterogeneous storage on mobile platforms and describe requirements for designing a device-aware cache replacement algorithm briefly. In Section 3, we describe our both workload-aware and device-aware algorithms in detail. Section 4 presents our simulation framework and simulation results. Related work is given in Section 5. Finally, we conclude in Section 6.

2 Motivation

2.1 Device Bandwidth and Sequentiality

Since our research targets heterogeneous storage systems with the configuration of a hard disk and a flash memory, it is necessary to examine the features of a hard disk and a flash memory. For this purpose, we simply take two typical devices as shown in Table 1, which are appropriate for mobile storage. Fujitsu MHT060BH has a 2.5″ form factor, a 60 GB capacity, and 5,400 RPM while Samsung K9K1208U is a NAND flash memory and has a 64 MB capacity, a block size of 16 KB, and a page size of 512 B. The throughputs of the flash memory were from [13] and those of the hard disk were obtained on our Sony VAIO laptop computer which embeds this disk using DiskSpd [14], which can measure disk I/O performance with various configurations including whether I/Os are sequential or random on Windows XP.

Table 1. Throughputs of a laptop disk and a NAND flash memory

Device			Hard disk	Flash memory
			MHT2060BH	K9K1208U
Throughput (MB/s)	Sequential	Read	30.47	14.3
		Write	30.47	1.78
	Random	Read	6.6	14.3
		Write	6.6	1.78

In Table 1, the disk shows a pretty good throughput for sequential I/Os and the value is about 5 times larger than that for random I/Os irrespective of the I/O type. In contrast to the disk, the flash memory doesn't concern sequentiality of I/Os and exhibits poor performance for write I/Os compared with reads. Therefore, when we design and use a heterogeneous storage system with such devices we surely need to meet performance imbalance which is likely to occur due to distinctly separable characteristics of these devices. This is because realistic workloads on mobile platforms often exhibit mixed patterns of sequential and random I/O operations like the case of concurrent execution of MP3 playing and program compiling. In addition, the conventional operating systems might not be designed well for I/O sequentiality coupled with this new and unfamiliar configuration of heterogeneous devices. For example, it seems that adequate management of sequentiality and I/O type for block requests across these heterogeneous devices in the viewpoint of performance may beyond the capability of the LRU algorithm as previously remarked.

2.2 Mobile Workloads and Sequentiality

Recent studies on mobile storage systems collected and utilized traces on applications typically used in mobile computing environments under feasible execution scenarios [5,10]. Among these, [10] gathered traces while executing real applications which can be used for a PDA immediately on an evaluation board similar to a PDA. The used execution scenario was repetition of *file transfer, email, file search, and sleep* (no operation). We examined the behavior of this mobile workload (hereafter, we will call *PDA trace*).

Since *file transfer* gives rise to disk reads (or writes) when files are sent to (or from) a network, the access pattern will be shown to be long sequential. The other applications except *sleep* are likely to exhibit random accesses (in this paper, a random access type means non-sequential one). Figure 1 shows the access pattern of the PDA trace, where x axis is *virtual time* (i.e., index of arriving requests) and y axis is *logical block address*. We notice that there are mixed accesses of a large number of sequential accesses, big and small loop-type accesses, and a small amount of temporal accesses. Similar access patterns can be found in the plots of traces gathered under programming and networking scenarios for mobile computing platforms in [5], though there is a different level of sequentiality compared with the PDA trace. Such observations drive us to need to deal with frequent sequential I/O operations together with random I/Os because if they weren't coped with adequately at the operating system software level there might occur critical performance degradation of the overall system.

3 Device-Aware Cache Replacement Algorithm

3.1 Workload-Aware Cache Algorithm

As was described in the previous section, it is requisite to deal with mixed access patterns which may frequently occur on generic mobile computing platforms

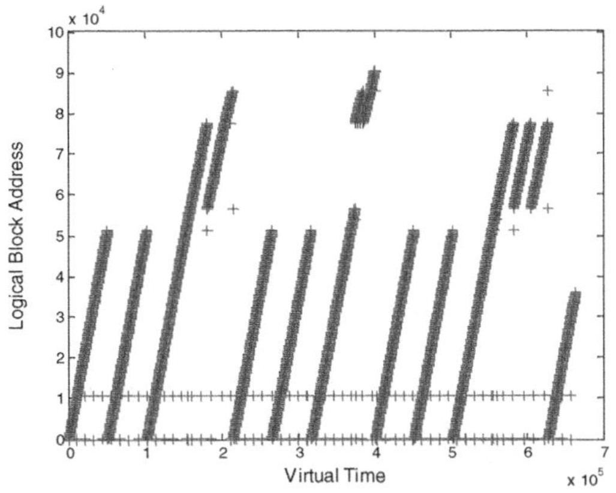

Fig. 1. Plot of the logical block address of each arriving IO request to its virtual time for the mobile trace used in [10]

as well as in our heterogeneous storage system with a hard disk and a flash memory. As a first step towards a solution, we first tackle the design of WAC, our workload-aware cache replacement algorithm using different cost per block according to workload patterns similarly to the GreedyDual-Size algorithm.

Figure 2 describes the overall algorithm of *WAC*. WAC combines different replacement cost and locality based on LRU. At the reference of a block x, when a cache miss occurs and it should be fetched to the cache WAC sets *L* to x's *H*. If there is no free block and block eviction is needed the cache block with the lowest H value is evicted and L is reset to this H value. If a cache hit occurs in the cache x's H is restored to L. How WAC updates the H values is shown in the subroutine *H_update*.

```
VARIABLE INITIALIZATION
L ← 0
C_SEQ ← α, C_RAND ← β (0<α < β)

MAIN ALGORITHM
At the reference of block x,
If x is hit in the cache
      H_update(x.H)
else
      If there is no free block in the cache
            L ← min{G| p∈T, G ← p.H}
            Evict p such that G = L
      Fetch x to the cache
      H_update(x.H)
```

```
SUBROUTINE H_update(x)
If x.pattern = SEQ
      x.H ← L + C_SEQ
else
      x.H ← L + C_RAND
```

Fig. 2. Proposed workload-aware cache replacement algorithm (WAC). In WAC, sequenitial I/O blocks have the most chances to stay in the cache, and random I/O blocks vice versa.

In designing the WAC algorithm, we tried to reflect the need that frequent and a large amount of sequential I/O requests which can be found in typical mobile workloads should be considered. Though there may be various ways in determining cost of each block in the cache while realizing this need, we simply divided the attribute, which each block can have in the cache, into 2: sequential and random. In the algorithm, the attribute is concreted by adding *C_SEQ* or *C_RAND* to the L value when the accessed block does take on sequentiality or not. Since when a block is sequential evicting it is more beneficial, we assign C_SEQ to a small positive value (in an actual implementation, we used 1). We expect more cache hits by keeping random blocks longer than those with sequentiality and thus C_RAND is assigned to a larger value than C_SEQ. Therefore, H values of cache blocks will be maintained relatively large if they are accessed recently or randomly and there will be more chances for such blocks to remain in the cache rather than blocks with little locality or sequentiality. This can be thought of a generalized version of LRU. In this paper, since we want to weight sequentiality for cache block replacement rather than I/O type, we do not consider more separated attributes like sequential and read accesses, random and write accesses, etc. Schemes using such more complex attributes will remain future work.

3.2 Evaluation: WAC and LRU

We evaluated performances of WAC and LRU in terms of cache hit rate using the PDA trace. For this, we built a trace-based cache simulator which implements WAC and LRU, and concatenated it and the simulator in [10] (Refer to subsection 4.1).

Figure 3 shows the hit rates of WAC and LRU, which were simulated for the PDA trace when the cache size varied from 5 to 60 MB with an incremental step of 5 MB except 55 MB (since the hit rate is already saturated around this size, we omitted it). We can notice that WAC outperformed LRU for all the cache sizes. This results apparently reflects the fact that WAC better maintains valuable (that is, causing more cache hits) blocks in the cache, which were not if they had been evicted early, and efficiently evicts less valuable blocks quickly, compared with LRU. Since we ascertain our workload-ware cache algorithm shows effectiveness for the mixed I/O request pattern of mobile workloads, our next task is to augment WAC such that it can be effective under mobile workloads in heterogeneous storage systems rather than single-device based storage systems (in this evaluation, a single disk was used).

3.3 Device-Aware Cache Replacement Algorithm

Our device-aware cache replacement algorithm (i.e., DAC) is mainly composed of 1) adjusting the sizes of partitions for a hard disk and a flash memory dynamically based on the performance index per device; 2) managing each partition according to the pattern of workloads by applying the WAC policy.

In designing the DAC algorithm, we took required cache management rules as follows: 1) the size of each partition should be adjusted so that the overall

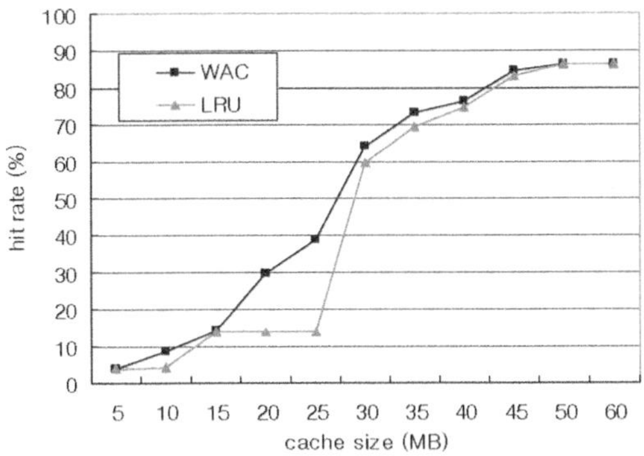

Fig. 3. Hit rates of WAC and LRU for the PDA trace when the cache size varies

load is balanced considering cache miss counts as well as different miss penalties between a hard disk and a flash memory. 2) sequential I/O requests should be managed to be evicted earlier by applying WAC to cache blocks within each partition.

Detailed DAC's algorithm is shown in Figure 4. DAC has two LRU lists *T1* and *T2*, each of which represents a partition assigned to cache blocks for either of heterogeneous devices (in this paper, T1 is used for a hard disk and T2 for a flash memory). *T1_req* (*T2_req*) is the target size of the T1 (T2) partition and c is the total cache size. *PR* is the access time ratio between a hard disk and a flash memory. W represents a partition-adjusting period, which is compared with cumulated reference counts (*cumulated_ref_count*) for re-partitioning.

DAC largely consists of 1) a cache replacement algorithm executed at every block reference; 2) a cache partitioning algorithm executed at W block references. At each block access, DAC determines the access pattern and whether the block is missed or hit. If a hit occurs in T1 (or T2), the block is moved to the MRU position of T1 (or T2). If there occurs a miss, the subroutine *List_update* is invoked with *miss_flag* which indicates in which device the missed block resides. Briefly, the mechanism of List_update is to control T1 and T2 so that their sizes follow T1_req and T2_req well, respectively. This is quite important process because good control of each partition size is based on the harmony of adjustment issuing and its follow-up. During such operations, we employ the subroutine H_update, which was seen in WAC, for the purpose of setting values to the cache blocks within each partition. In a period of W block references, the algorithm re-partitions the cache depending on miss counts of random-type blocks multiplied by PR. Multiplying PR is needed because two devices have different miss penalties (i.e., access times).

The strong points of the DAC algorithm come from its being device-aware as well as workload-aware: it adjusts the partition sizes based on performance skewness and manages cache blocks according to worth in the aspect of performance

```
VARIABLE INITIALIZATION
x : referenced block
c: cache size
W: partition-adjusting period
PR: performance ratio
|T1| ← 0, |T2| ← 0, T1_req ←c/2, T2_req ← c/2
T1.rand_misses ← 0, T2.rand_misses ← 0
T1.L ← 0, T2.L ← 0
miss_flag ← 0
cumulated_ref_count ← 0


MAIN ALGORITHM
At every reference of blocks,
Find the access pattern:
    x.pattern ← SEQ or RAND
Increase cumulated_ref_count
If  a cache hit  occurs in T1
    Move x to the MRU in T1
else if a cache hit  occurs in T2
    Move x to the MRU in T2
else
    If x resides in the disk
        miss_flag ← 1 (a cache miss in T1 is set)
    else
        miss_flag ← 2 (a cache miss in T2 is set)
    List_update (miss_flag, T1, T2)

At a period of W references,
    If cumulated_ref_count = W
        If T1.rand_misses* PR > T2.rand_misses
            delta ← T1.rand_misses – T2.rand_misses
            If  T1_req + delta > c
                T1_req ← c
            else
                T1_req ← T1_req + delta
                T2_req ← c – T1_req
        else
            delta ← T2.rand_misses – T1.rand_misses
            If T2_req + delta > c
                T2_req ← c
            else
                T2_req ← T2_req + delta
                T1_req ← c – T2_req
```

```
SUBROUTINE List_update ( miss_flag, T1, T2 )
If miss_flag = 1
    If |T1| > |T1_req| and |T1| is not zero
        T1.L ← min{y.H| y ∈ T1}
        Evict y which satisfies y.H = in T1.L
        Decrease |T1|
    Fetch x to the cache and move it to the MRU
    position in T1
    H_update(x, T1)
    Increase |T1|
    If |T1|+|T2|>= c and |T2| >= T2_req
    and |T2| is not 0
        T2.L ← min{y.H| y ∈ T2}
        Evict y which satisfies y.H = in T2.L
        Decrease |T2|
    Increase T1.rand_miss_times
else
    If |T2| > T2_req and |T2| is not zero
        T1.L ← min{y.H| y ∈ T1}
        Evict y which satisfies y.H = in T2.L
        Decrease |T2|
    Fetch x to the cache and move it to the MRU
    position in T2
    H_update(x, T2)
    Increase |T2|
    If |T1|+|T2|>= c and |T1| >= T1_req
    and |T1| is not 0
        T1.L ← min{y.H| y ∈ T1}
        Evict y which satisfies y.H = in T1.L
        Decrease |T1|
    Increase T2.rand_miss_times
miss_flag ← 0
```

```
SUBROUTINE H_update ( x, Ti ),  i= 1 or 2
If x.pattern = SEQ
    x.H ← Ti.L + C_SEQ
else
    x.H ← Ti.L + C_RAND
```

Fig. 4. Proposed device-aware cache replacement algorithm (DAC)

by taking into account the access pattern. Thus, we expect that it may improve the system performance better by dealing with performance imbalance efficiently in heterogeneous storage systems, compared with LRU. We also expect that DAC may be more helpful in enhancing the performance by evicting sequential blocks early.

There are several challenges in the DAC algorithm. First, we found that the value of PR can vary according to the degree of temporal locality through experiments in the viewpoint of the overall system performance. Therefore, in the experiments we simply (not optimally) changed the value of PR statically in order to obtain a better performance. Second, when we calculate *delta* we also found that it was sometimes more beneficial to weight the larger value of two random miss counts of T1 and T2 depending on the degree of temporal locality. We simulated while varying this value statically. Finally, the period of W affected the overall performance and needs to vary depending on workload patterns. However, building a fully automatically-tunable DAC to maintain optimal parameters is a problem rather beyond the scope of this paper and will remain future work.

4 Simulation and Results

4.1 Simulation Environment

We developed a trace-based cache simulator which incorporates LRU, WAC, and finally DAC. In order to link cache simulation with the operation of a heterogeneous storage system, we augmented the multi-device power and performance simulator in [10]. The hard disk model we used is the MK4004GAH with a 1.8″ form factor and 4,200 RPM [10] and the flash model is the K9K1208U shown in Table 1.

We also built a synthetic trace generator, which can generate three types of traces by controlling sequentiality and temporal locality: SEQUENTIAL, TEMPORAL, and COMPOUND. Our synthetic trace generator can also control various parameters such as control request rate, read/write ratio, file size, and request size. We ran our trace generator, varying default parameters. Default parameter setting is as follows: average interval time between I/O requests = 70 (ms), trace time = 80 (min), maximum file size = 5 (MB), total file size = 350 (MB), and write ratio = 0.5. Default I/O access pattern is set to COMPOUND (i.e., mixed of sequentiality and temporal locality).

For simulation, we used the PDA trace and two synthetic traces (we call *trace1* and *trace2*): trace1 uses the default parameters and trace2 also does except that the average interval time and the maximum file size are set to 20 ms and 1 MB, respectively. The PDC trace, trace1, and trace2 have working set sizes of 44, 23, and 57 MB and trace file sizes of 30, 2.8, and 9.6 MB, respectively. We evaluated the cache hit rate and average system I/O response time for DAC and LRU as metrics. We assumed that the overheads of re-partitioning and handling blocks per partition in DAC are acceptable in comparison with LRU and set W to 200 and PR to 35.

4.2 Simulation Results

In Figure 5, plots (a) and (b) show the hit rates of DAC and LRU and average system I/O response times and energy consumptions of DAC normalized over LRU, respectively, for the PDA trace with the cache size varied. In the plot (a), DAC has higher hit rates than LRU in all cases. The higher hit rates of DAC affected the average I/O response times and these values of DAC appeared smaller than those of LRU overall, as shown in the plot (b).

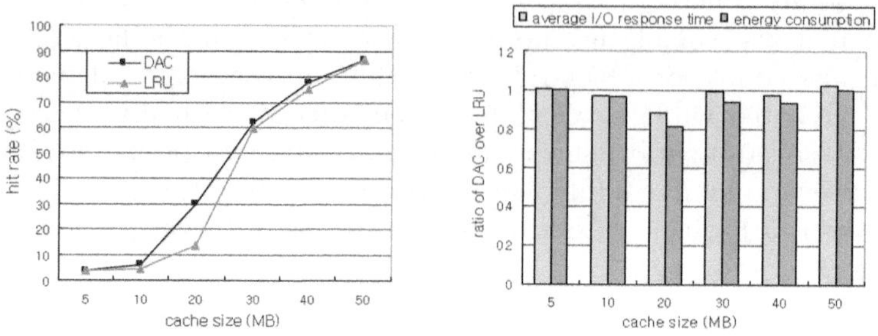

(a) (b)

Fig. 5. Simulation results of DAC and LRU for the PDA trace when the cache size varies: (a) Hit rates of DAC and LRU (b) Average system I/O response times and energy consumptions of DAC, which are normalized over LRU

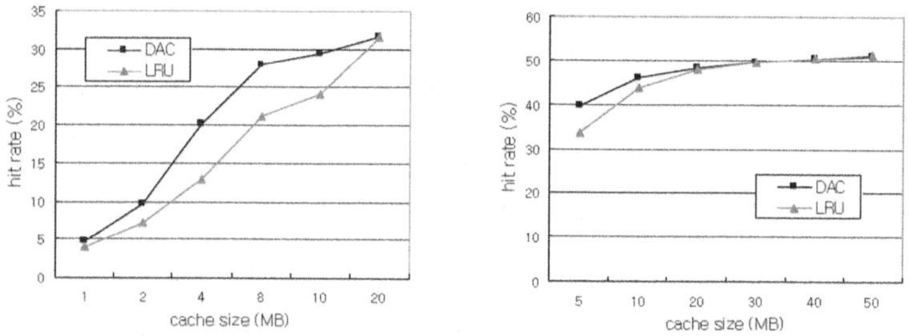

(a) (b)

Fig. 6. Simulation results of DAC and LRU for synthetic traces when the cache size varies: (a) Hit rates of DAC and LRU for the trace1 (b) Hit rates of DAC and LRU for the trace2

Two exceptions are when the cache sizes are 5 and 50 MB. We found that though there occurred the same device accesses for DAC and LRU the degree of clustering in the device (exactly, disk) queue was lower for DAC, that is, a little more non-sequential accesses occurred and they caused more seek time. This phenomenon rather seems to be related with adjustment of parameters described in subsection 3.3 for the case of two extremes of the cache sizes. We also notice that there were more chances for power-down in the devices. Consequently, the energy consumption of DAC was observed to be smaller than that of LRU almost always.

Figure 6 shows the hit rates of DAC and LRU for two synthetic traces with the cache size varied: (a) for the trace1 and (b) for the trace2. We notice that DAC showed almost equal or better results in hit rates for both traces. Comparing the hit rates in the plots (a) and (b) depending on working set sizes and varying cache sizes, we can notice that the trace2 has more temporal I/O accesses. This means that DAC might be effective regardless of the amount of sequentiality. To examine this, we evaluated two more synthetic traces with temporal access patterns, which have the same parameters of trace1 and trace2 except that the I/O access pattern is set to TEMPORAL (we call these traces *trace1_temp* and *trace2_temp*). For the trace1_temp, we found that the hit rates of DAC and LRU with a 4 MB cache were 53.0% and 54.1% (actually, with different setting of W and PR, we could obtain the almost same hit rate). For the trace2_temp, the hit rates were 97.1% for both DAC and LRU with a 10 MB cache. We omitted the average system I/O response time and energy consumption due to the space limit, but we found that DAC has better performance in these two metrics than LRU similarly to the results of the PDA trace.

5 Related Work

[3,4,5,9] have all proposed using flash memory as a non-volatile cache, maintaining blocks which are likely to be accessed in the near future, and thus allowing a hard disk to spin down for longer time. [4] focused on the use of a flash memory as a write buffer cache, while [5] has recently studied a technique of partitioning a flash memory into a cache, a prefetch buffer, and a write buffer to save energy. [9] mainly considered reducing the power consumption of a main memory by using a flash memory as a second-level buffer cache. Hybrid HDD solution co-developed by Samsung and MS uses a flash memory as an on-board non-volatile cache in addition to a hard disk, which aims at performance boosting, low power, and high reliability on mobile computers [6,7].

Our work is distinct from the above research in that it studies performance improvement in a heterogeneous storage system which uses a flash memory together with a hard disk as secondary storage. Our approach suggests an effective buffer cache management algorithm aiming at performance improvement, depending on both device-awareness and workload-awareness.

6 Conclusions

We have proposed a novel buffer cache replacement algorithm which targets a mobile computing system with a heterogeneous storage pair of a hard disk and a flash memory. The proposed algorithm partitions the cache per each device and adjusts the size of each partition based on the performance indices of the devices, and manages each partition according to workload patterns.

Trace-based simulations showed that the proposed technique can lead to up to a two times higher hit rate than LRU according to the cache size with a pair of a 1.8″ hard disk and a NAND flash memory on realistic mobile traces. In addition, our algorithm reduced the average system I/O response time and energy consumption by up to 12% and 19%, respectively, compared with LRU.

As future work, we plan to study software techniques including cache algorithms in order to mitigate the write/erase cycles of a flash memory while maintaining the performance. We also plan to research the performance and energy consumption using DAC under various data layouts.

Acknowledgments. This research was supported by the MIC (Ministry of Information and Communication), Korea, under the ITRC (Information Technology Research Center) support program supervised by the IITA (Institute of Information Technology Assessment). And the ICT at Seoul National University provided research facilities for this study.

References

1. L. D. Paulson. Will hard drives finally stop shrinking? *IEEE Computer*, Vol. 38., No. 5. pp.14–16, 2005.
2. G. Lawton. Improved flash memory grows in popularity. *IEEE Computer*, Vol. 39., No. 1. pp.16–18, 2006.
3. B. Marsh, F. Douglis, and P. Krishnan. Flash memory file caching for mobile computers. in *Proc. of the 27th Hawaii International Conference on System Sciences*, Hawaii, USA, pp.451–460, Jan. 1994.
4. T. Bisson and S. Brandt. Reducing energy consumption with a non-volatile storage cache. in *Proc. of International Workshop on Software Support for Portable Storage (IWSSPS)*, held in conjunction with *the IEEE Real-Time and Embedded Systems and Applications Symposium (RTAS 2005)*, San Francisco, California, March, 2005.
5. F. Chen, S. Jiang, and X. Zhang. SmartSaver: turning flash drive into a disk energy saver for mobile computers. in *Proc. of the 11th ACM/IEEE International Symposium on Low Power Electronics and Design (ISLPED'06)*, Tegernsee, Germany, October 4-6, 2006.
6. Microsoft, ReadyDrive and Hybrid Disk. `http://www.microsoft.com/whdc/device/storage/hybrid.mspx`.
7. `http://www.samsung.com/Products/HardDiskDrive/news/HardDiskDrive_20050425_0000117556.htm`.
8. R. Panabaker. Hybrid Hard Disk & ReadyDrive^{TM} Technology: Improving Performance and Power for Windows Vista Mobile PCs. in *Proc. of Microsoft WinHEC 2006*, June 2003. `http://www.microsoft.com/whdc/winhec/pres06.mspx`.
9. T. Kgil and T. Mudge. FlashCache: A NAND flash memory file cache for low power web servers. in *Proc. of 2006 International Conference on Compilers, Architecture and Synthesis for Embedded Systems (CASES '06)*, Seoul, Korea, October 22-25 2006.
10. Y.-J. Kim, K.-T. Kwon, and J. Kim. Energy-efficient file placement techniques for heterogeneous mobile storage systems. in *Proc. of the 6th ACM & IEEE Conference on Embedded Software (EMSOFT)*, Seoul, Korea, October 22-25 2006.
11. P. Cao and S. Irani. Cost-aware WWW proxy caching algorithms. in *Proc. of USENIX Symposium on Internet Technology and Systems*, December, 1997.
12. B. Forney, A. C. Arpaci-Dusseau, and R. H. Arpaci-Dusseau. Storage-aware caching: revisiting caching for heterogeneous storage systems. in *Proc. of the 1st. USENIX Conference on File and Storage Technologies (FAST)*, Jan. 2002.
13. H. G. Lee and N. Chang. Low-energy heterogeneous non-volatile memory systems for mobile systems. *Journal of Low Power Electronics*, Vol. 1, Number 1, pp. 52–62, April, 2005.
14. `http://research.microsoft.com/BARC/Sequential_IO/`.

The Lightweight Runtime Engine of the Wireless Internet Platform for Mobile Devices

Yong-Duck You, Choong-Bum Park, and Hoon Choi

Department of Computer Engineering, Chungnam National University, 220 Gung-dong, Yuseong-gu, Daejeon 305-764, Korea
{yyd7724,here4you,hc}@cnu.ac.kr

Abstract. This paper proposes a lightweight runtime engine that is the core part of the wireless Internet platform of mobiles devices such as cellular phones or PDAs. The proposed lightweight runtime engine downloads and executes mobile applications in the binary form. Its memory footprint is less than 100 Kbytes and consists of the lightweight scheduler module, memory management module, dynamic reconfiguration module, event handler module, and timer module. The lightweight scheduler can process events 13% faster than a competitive technique which is the widely used thread-based scheduler. The memory management module works 6 $\sim$ 10 times faster than other memory management algorithms, and the proposed dynamic reconfiguration module also shows a good performance in reconfiguring the platform software.

1 Introduction

Thanks to the mobile communication technology, wireless Internet access using a cellular phone or a PDA, is getting popular and users' demand for wireless Internet service has become more diversified. Thus, service providers develop differentiated services with new features to stay competitive in the market. In order to manage and execute various applications on a hand-held device, a flexible and scalable software platform [1] plays an essential role in coping with the rapidly changing wireless Internet applications. A wireless Internet platform is a sort of system software, like an operating system or a middleware of the computer that executes application programs. Examples of the wireless Internet platform for cellular phones include GVM (General Virtual Machine), XVM (eXtended Virtual Machine), BREW (Binary Runtime Environment Wireless) and WIPI (Wireless Internet Platform for Interoperability). The currently used wireless internet platforms use a java virtual machine to execute java applications, and a binary runtime environment for executing binary applications. However, java virtual machines require a large amount of memory and a high processor execution performance for executing java bytecodes, resulting in a decrease of performance in execution environments with limited resources such as mobile devices. In addition, existing binary runtime environments provide a lighter execution environment compared to java virtual machines, but because it doesn't consider mobile application execution characteristics and doesn't provide the

Y.-H. Lee et al. (Eds.): ICESS 2007, LNCS 4523, pp. 25–36, 2007.

self reconfiguration of middleware, it is not an effective solution for executing applications in resource-restricted execution environments.

This paper proposes the lightweight runtime engine that is included in wireless Internet platforms for binary runtime environment and consists of the lightweight scheduler module, memory management module, dynamic reconfiguration module, event handler module, and timer for mobile application's efficient execution. To verify the proposed runtime engine, we implemented the WIPI software platform that consists of the proposed runtime engine and WIPI APIs as shown in Fig. 1 [1, 2].

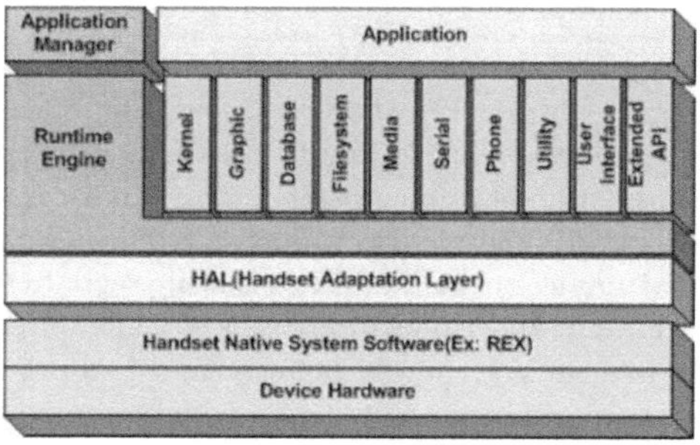

Fig. 1. WIPI Software Platform

We also implemented an emulation software for the cellular phone environment. The emulator, the CNU WIPI Emulator, measures the performance of the proposed runtime engine [3]. The emulator includes the implemented WIPI software platform and supports the development and execution of "C applications" on a desktop computer. The emulator passed the formal correctness test under the PCT (Platform Certification Toolkit) from EXEmobile Inc. [4]. From the experimental results, our scheduler processes events 13% faster than the thread-based scheduler and the proposed memory management module has worked 6.5 times, 10.5 times and 2.5 times faster than the Linked List algorithm [5], Brent algorithm [6], Doug. Lea's algorithm [7, 8], respectively. The proposed dynamic reconfiguration module shows a good performance in reconfiguring the platform. It takes 624.8μs for installations, and 65μs for deletions.

The rest of the paper is organized as follows: Section 2 describes the proposed runtime engine, Section 3 analyzes the performance of the proposed runtime engine through different tests; Finally, Section 4 presents the conclusion.

2 Proposed Runtime Engine

A mobile device is generally equipped with low performance CPU, small amount of memory, and system software consisting of basic functions for running an application. For example, typical CDMA (Code Division Multiple Access) mobile devices using QUALCOMM's Mobile Station Modem (MSM) chipsets use REX Operating Systems. REX operating systems only support essential functionalities such as task management scheduling, interrupt handling, timer, and signal. Therefore, a mobile device needs software called the runtime engine that supports the functions which are not supported by the phone's native system software to ensure the efficient execution of the application programs. This paper proposes the lightweight runtime engine that consists of the lightweight scheduler module, memory management module, dynamic reconfiguration module, event handler module, and timer.

2.1 Lightweight Scheduler Module

Because applications are developed in various forms depending on the intensions of the developers, it is difficult to manage these applications and results in a large management overhead. Therefore, in resource-restricted environments such as mobile devices, the system should be aware of the applications' architecture in order to man-age them efficiently. The application's life-cycle management APIs should be defined to solve this problem. In REX, a widely used operating system for mobile devices, a multi-thread feature, supporting parallel processing of applications, is not provided. Therefore, existing wireless internet platforms use user-level threads to provide these features. To manage user-level threads, current thread-based schedulers initially create an application thread, and life-cycle interfaces are called in the application thread. Because platform threads and application threads are executed and access the event handler module concurrently in thread-based scheduling techniques, a synchronization mechanism is needed, and there is a large context switching time overhead for processing platform events. In addition, it is difficult to apply this technique to re-source-restricted environments such as mobile devices, because of the large amount of resources it requires.

The lightweight scheduler proposed in this paper calls life-cycle management APIs to execute an application, rather than creating a thread. In addition, reference information for life-cycle management APIs are managed within the scheduler; when an application is executed, the API of the corresponding application is called according to the occurring events to execute the application. When events occur during the execution of the applications, the light-weight scheduler receives the event that must be process first, from the management module. If the received event is a platform event the platform itself processes it, and if it is an application event, the platform calls an event-handler function to execute the application. As a result, our lightweight scheduler has a small overhead compared to the thread based scheduler because there is no need for synchronizing threads, and context-switching for processing platform events is not required. In addition, applications can be executed quickly with small system resources because threads are not used.

2.2 Memory Management Module

Performance of the mobile devices greatly depends on the efficient resource management because they are usually resource-restricted. In particular, the dynamic storage allocation algorithm is very important part of the mobile device's operating system and OS-like software platform. The existing dynamic storage allocation algorithms did not consider application's execution style and the type, life-time, and characteristics of memory objects that the application uses. Those algorithms, as a result, could not manage memory efficiently [9, 10, 11]. Therefore, this paper analyzes the mobile application's execution characteristics and proposes a new dynamic storage allocation algorithm which saves the memory space and improves mobile application's execution speed.

Table 1. Execution characteristics of mobile application

Object type	MP3 player		Address Book		ICQ	
	Used memory (Byte)	percentage	Used memory (Byte)	percentage	Used memory (Byte)	percentage
int	231,000	17%	0	0%	1,248	1%
float	73,000	5%	0	0%	0	0%
char	215,000	16%	1,520	41%	76,000	40%
Byte	780,000	57%	0	0%	128	0%
double	0	0%	0	0%	0	0%
object	23,000	2%	260	7%	21,000	11%
string	16,000	1%	1,512	40%	58,000	31%
AccessControlContext	108	0%	180	5%	0	0%
Hashtable Entry	0	0%	108	3%	24,000	13%
class	23,000	2%	156	4%	8,424	4%
stringbuffer	3,836	0%	0	0%	28	0%
total	1,364,944	100%	3,736	100%	188,828	100%

Table 1 shows the object types and the amount of memory allocated by Java applications such as MP3 players [12], Address Books [13], and ICQ [14] applications. The MP3 application in Table 1, is an application that plays music files for 3-5minutes. In this application, the *int* object used for decoding, and the *char* and *byte* objects used for generating audio signals, make up 90% of all allocated objects. The Address Book application records and displays personal information, and the *char* and *string* type objects for storing each individual's name, address, and phone number make up 81% of all allocated objects. Finally, for the ICQ program, the window object for generating windows for instant messaging, and the *string* and *char* objects for messages make up 82% of all allocated objects.

The proposed memory management module considers this characteristics; the method divides the total memory provided by mobile systems into two Banks, and economizes memory use and enhances the execution speed of applications by apply-ing algorithms that accommodate the lifetime, size, type, and distribution characteristics of the objects in use [15].

Bank 1: This bank 1 considers the characteristics of mobile applications and applies a dynamic storage allocation technique for objects that occupy over 60% of the memory allocation/deallocation when an application is executed. Unlike the conventional memory pool allocation techniques, the suggested dynamic memory allocation method separately manages the linked lists by class according to the exact size of free memory, and the number of free memory blocks connected to each linked list varies depending on the applications that are executed.

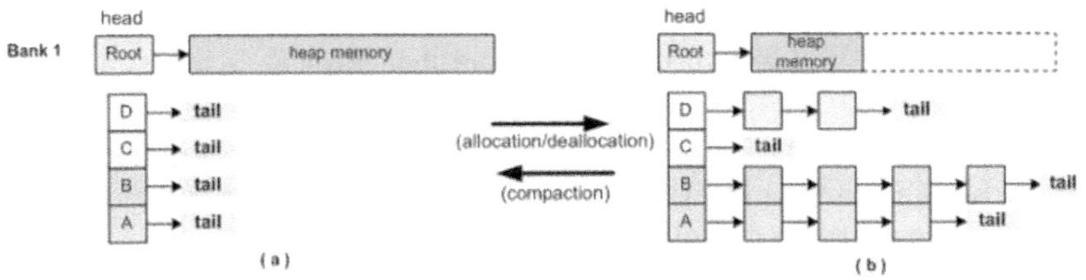

Fig. 2. Bank 1 memory management

In Fig. 2, the single linked list header values ($A \sim D$) represent the size of the memory block that each class manages. For example, class is determined by the size appropriate for frequently used objects such as *char*, *int*, *string*, and *object* from Table 1. (a) in Fig. 2 is the initialized status of the memory, and the entire memory consists of a single large memory. When the allocation of memory begins, the linked list of the class corresponding to the size of the object is first searched; then, if unused memory blocks are found they are allocated. If unused memory blocks are unavailable, memory is allocated from the linked list of upper classes according to the Best-Fit method, and if that is not available, memory is allocated from the Root list. When memory in use is deallocated, the deallocated memory block is connected to the corresponding class list, not the Root list ((b) in Fig. 2). Therefore, if the memory pool is dynamically reconfigured according to the characteristics of the applications, such as Bank 1, a greater performance for mobile applications can be expected($O(1)$).

Bank 2: The runtime libraries used until now, uses a technique that implements a linked list to manage memory during the allocation and deallocation of memory blocks of various sizes. However, the linked list allocation technique has many problems. This Bank 2 consists of a number of segments to solve those problems. The size of each segment is logically dependent on the initial configurators set through the segment boundary, but the size becomes variable depending on the applications that are executed. A memory block that is allocated near a boundary may let the size of the segment beyond the boundary value. This idea of flexible boundary size decreases memory fragmentation in boundary areas, and does not limit the size of the memory block to be allocated in a segment. In this Bank 2, when there is a request for memory allocation, the average value of unused memory block size is examined for each segment and the segment with the largest average value is selected. When a memory block in use is released, free memory blocks that are adjacent to this released memory block are merged to form a bigger unused memory block. Memory compression is performed in a

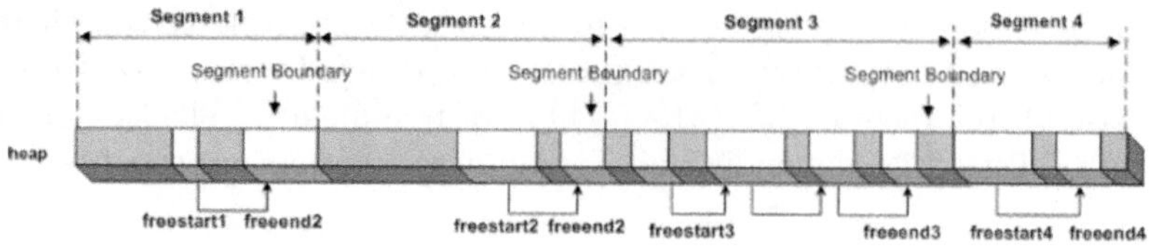

Fig. 3. Bank 2 memory management

segment. It is carried out by consecutively moving the corresponding segment's memory blocks, starting from the start memory block and ending at the memory block adjacent to the segment boundary as shown in Fig. 3.

2.3 Dynamic Reconfiguration

EJB (Enterprise Java Beans) [16], CCM (CORBA Component Model) [17] and COM (Component Object Model) [18] are examples of the component-based software framework that allows dynamic reconfiguration. EJB is a component based distributed object model that is supported by Sun Microsystems Inc. and J2EE is executed in the JVM; thus it requires ample computing power and resources. CCM is an expansion of the CORBA object model, which offers a set of CORBA services that are widely used in standard environments; it has a high performance in distributed server environments, but is inapplicable for individual distributed computing in resource restricted environments such as mobile devices. In addition, it does not offer fault-tolerance in case a component of a system runs into a problem. This section will describe the proposed component-based dynamic reconfiguration module which makes up the lightweight runtime engine. The dynamic reconfiguration module is designed to conserve system resources, and offer extensibility and stability in middleware by providing a dynamic reconfiguration feature through the upgrade and addition of new service components that compose the middleware, and by providing a self-healing feature through monitoring log messages.

Dynamic Reconfiguration: The component is represented as a single object and it provides specific services to applications. Each component consists of the Component Implementation part and the SAL (System Adaptation Layer) part that makes the Component Implementation part be independent from the underlying software. It is necessary to keep records of the numerous services and information about the various versions of applications and components in order to select and manage the components which are required and appropriate for the system. This paper proposes keeping records of component and application installation information in the CDF (Component Description File), which can be downloaded to the system along with the corresponding component through the network. The Component Controller within the Dynamic Reconfiguration Module manages the API reference information, which is provided by the component when the component is loaded to the memory, using the APIRT (API Reference Table). The APIRT consists of the names of the APIs within the Component Implementation,

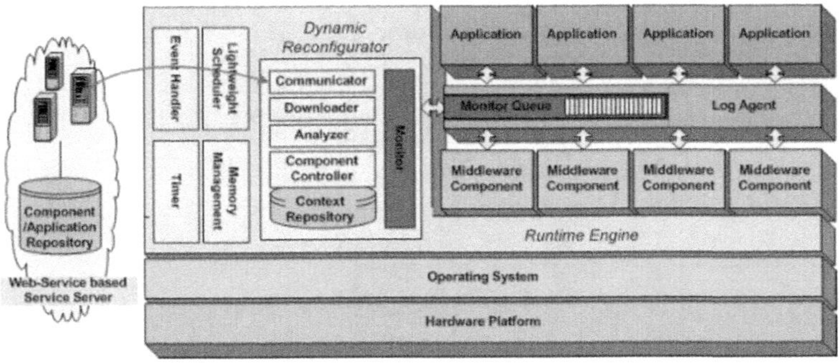

Fig. 4. Dynamic Reconfiguration Module in the Runtime Engine

and the addresses of the APIs loaded on the memory. When a component is inserted/deleted/updated, the APIRT is updated, and the updated information is sent to the components and applications referencing the APIRT using a message queue method that uses shared memory.

Self-Healing: The Self-Healing feature is augmented with reconfiguration of middleware and the re-installation of applications in case of failure. IBM has implemented an Autonomic Manager that performs automated computing for server-level computers [19], and they also proposed the autonomic personal computing that is suited for personal computing environment [20, 21]. However, autonomous computing technology requires a large amount of resources and computer power for intelligent reasoning. Therefore, this paper proposes a simple Self-Healing technique that is suited for resource-restricted environments such as mobile devices. As shown in Fig. 4, the proposed Dynamic Reconfiguration Module is consisted of the Monitor, Context Repository, Analyzer, Component Controller, and the Downloader modules. The Monitor module monitors component and application executions using a Monitor Queue and stores the collected information in the Context Repository module, then reports any error symptom to the Analyzer. The Context Repository module is a storage place for the Context collected by the Monitor module, as is used as history information which is required for system management. The Analyzer module performs analysis and diagnostics on the error symptoms reported by the Monitor and decides an appropriate treatment, and the Component Controller module treats the corresponding component or application according to the instructions sent by the Analyzer. The Log Messages which are records of the errors occurred during the execution of components or applications, is a good basis for figuring out the condition of the targets being observed.

The Log Agent in Fig. 4, 5 is a module that asynchronously sends the Available Log Message to the Monitor. The Log Agent process is described in the following: it collects the Log Messages created by components or applications (①), then using the State Mapping Table in Fig. 6 as a reference, the log code and log values of the Log Messages are checked to verify whether any status value exist for the values being mapped; if the status value exists, the Log Message is verified

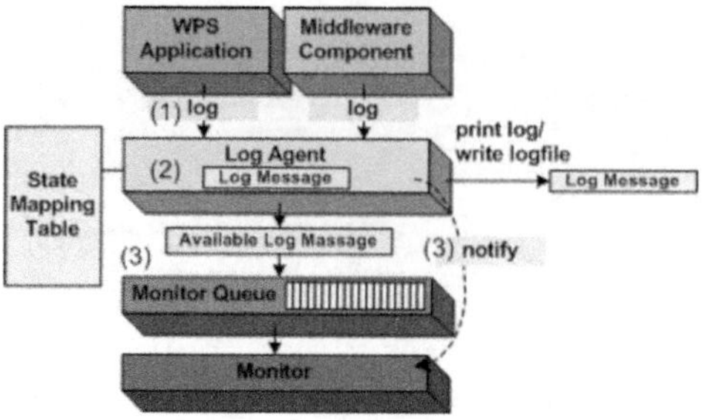

Fig. 5. Dynamic Reconfiguration Module in the Runtime Engine

State Mapping Table

Log Table

Log code	value	description	Status Value
WPS_ERROR	-1	Other Error	-6
WPS_BADFD	-2	Illegal ID	-
WPS_BADFILENAME	-3	Illegal File Name	-
⋮	⋮	⋮	⋮
WPS_NOTSUP	-16	Not Support	-5
WPS_NOMEMORY	-17	Insufficient Memory	-1
WPS_SHORTBUF	-18	Insufficient Buffer	-1
⋮	⋮	⋮	⋮
WPS_NORESOURCE	-25	Insufficient Resource	-1
⋮	⋮	⋮	⋮

Fig. 6. State Mapping Table

as a valid Log Message(②). The Available Log Messages are then stored in the Monitor Queue, and the creation of Available Log Messages is reported to the monitor(③). Depending on the Status Value, the middleware is reconfigured or the corresponding application is re-installed using the Component Controller.

3 Verification and Performance Analysis

3.1 Verification Using Platform Certification Toolkit

To verify the proposed runtime engine, we implemented an emulator, the CNU WIPI Emulator, which includes our WIPI software platform. The CNU WIPI Emulator supports the development and execution of "WIPI C application" on a desktop computer. To verify correctness of the WIPI software platform including the proposed runtime engine, PCT from EXEmobile Inc. was used. Except six test cases (LED, vibration, etc) that are not applicable to the emulator environment, all of the tests (328 test cases) passed successfully. The kernel API test is the test to verify the proposed runtime engine. So, the proposed runtime engine supports mobile application's execution.

3.2 Scheduler Performance

To evaluate the performance of the proposed scheduler, a test application generating WIPI emulator's button events and inserting the events into the event-handler module is used. The events generated and inserted in the test application are events related to executing WIPI applications. This experiment measures the speed of processing the events inserted into the event-handler module to analyze the performance for switching between applications, switching between the platform and application, and for the continuous execution of applications.

The result of the experiments show that the CNU WIPI Emulator embedded with the proposed scheduler processes events 13% more quickly than the Emulator embedded with the thread-based scheduler.

3.3 Memory Management Performance

To show the performance of the proposed memory management, experiment has been performed in an environment with Windows XP, 3.2GHz CPU, and 512MB of RAM with the heap memory size of the emulator set to 866Kbyte.

In this experiment, we measured allocation and deallocation speed by our memory management methods (Bank 1: dynamic memory pool, Bank 2: segmented linked list), and by other widely used memory management methods such as Linked List algorithm [5], Brent algorithm [6], Doug. Lea's algorithm [7, 8]. The test application used for the experiment allocates and deallocates memory blocks of random sizes of between 8 and 512 Bytes; during this process, the merging and compression of memory occurs. The results show that the proposed algorithm works 6.5 times faster than the Linked List algorithm, 10.5 times faster than the Brent algorithm and 2.5 times faster better than the Doug. Lea's algorithm as shown in Fig. 7. Therefore, when designing a memory allocation technique for mobile devices, considering the characteristic of the applications used for the mobile devices can result in an increase of performance when executing these applications in mobile devices.

3.4 Dynamic Reconfiguration Performance

Although the dynamic reconfiguration feature provides extensibility and flexibility of the middleware, the overall system performance can be lowered and the feature nay cause inconvenience to users if the delay is large or the time that it takes for reconfiguration cannot be predicted. Components were installed and deleted for this experiment, which was designed to measure the time required for dynamic reconfiguration, and to figure out the items that cause delays. Because the downloading time in the network depends on the media type of the network and traffic situation, therefore it varies each times, we measured the delay caused inside of the system, i.e., delay when the components already downloaded to the system. The experimental results and information of the components used in

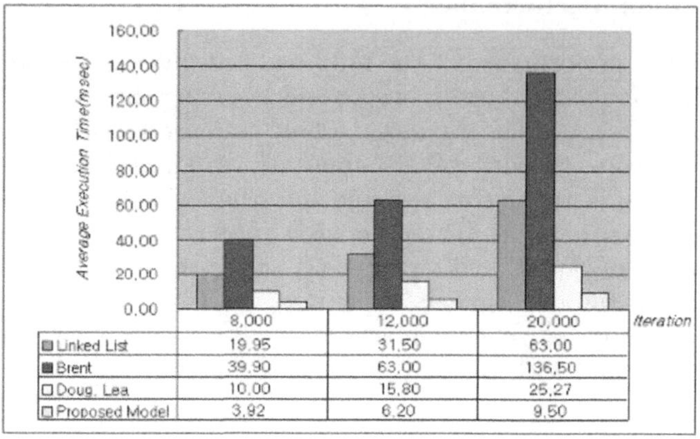

Fig. 7. Memory allocation/deallocation speed

Table 2. Execution characteristics of mobile application

	Component Size(Unit:byte)	# of APIs	Average Installation Time(Unit:μs)	Average Deletion Time(Unit:μs)
File system	42,182	15	310.5	45
Utility	16,625	6	151	35
Database	25,313	14	194	24.4
Kernel	86,709	48	624.8	65
Media	34,676	23	410	15
Serial	23,187	8	194	25.4

the experiment is provided in the following table 2; the experiment was repeated 90 times for each component in order to obtain an average value. The average installation time and average deletion time shown in Table 2 is the average of the time it takes to load or unload the component on the memory plus the time it takes to update the API reference information on the APIRT. Experimental results showed that the proposed dynamic reconfiguration is greatly affected by the code size of the component and is barely affected by the number of APIs.

4 Conclusions

In this paper, we proposed the runtime engine for a wireless Internet platform and implemented the WIPI software platform along with its emulator to verify the pro-posed runtime engine. The correctness of the implemented platform has been tested using the CNU WIPI Emulator and the PCT toolkit developed by EXEmobile Inc.. From the experimental results, the memory management capability of the developed runtime engine shows better performance compared with the widely used memory management algorithms. The proposed scheduler processes events 13% more quickly than the Emulator embedded with the thread-based scheduler. The proposed dynamic reconfiguration module showed a fast performance of platform reconfiguration, 624.8μs for installations and 65μs for deletions on the average.

References

1. TTA, Wireless Internet Platform for Interoperability TTAS.KO-06.0036/R3, 2004.6, www.tta.or.kr
2. S.Y. Lee, S.J. Kim and H. N. Kim, "Standardization status and development prospect of Korea Wireless Internet Platform for Interoperability," Korean Information Science Soci-ety, Vol. 22 No. 1, pp.16- 23, Jan. 2004.
3. CNU (Chungnam National University) WIPI Emulator, http://strauss.cnu.ac.kr/research/wipi/research.html, 2006.9.
4. PCT Toolkit: http://www.exemobile.com, Sep. 2006.
5. A.C.K. Lau, N.H.C. Yung, Y.S. Cheung, "Performance analysis of the doubly-linked list protocol family for distributed shared memory systems," Proceedings of ICAPP 96, IEEE Second International Conference on Algorithms and Architectures for Parallel Processing, pp. 365-372, Jun. 1996.
6. R. P. Brent, "Efficient Implementation of the First-Fit Strategy for Dynamic Storage Allo-cation," ACM Transactions on Programming Languages and Systems, Vol. 11, No. 3, Jul. 1989.
7. Doug. Lea' Algorithm, http://rtportal.upv.es/rtmalloc/allocators/dlmalloc/index.shtml, Jul. 2006.
8. M. Masmano, I. Ripoll, A. Crespo, J. Real, "TLSF: a new dynamic memory allocator for real-time systems," Proceedings of ECRTS, 16th Euromicro Conference on Real-Time Sys-tems, pp. 79-88, Jul. 2004.
9. M. S. Johnstone and P. R. Wilson, "The Memory Fragmentation Problem: Solved ?," In Proceedings of the International Symposium on Memory Management(ISMM'98), Van-couver, Canada. ACM Press, 1998.
10. Henry Lieberman and Carl Hewitt,"A Real-Time Garbage Collector Based on the Lifetimes of Objects," Communications of the ACM, Vol. 26, No. 6, pp. 419-429, Jun. 1983.
11. R. C. Krapf, G. Spellmeier and L. Carro, "A Study on a Garbage Collector for Embedded Applications," Proceedings of the 15 the Symposium on Integrated Circuits and Systems Design (SBCCI'02), pp. 127-132, 2002.
12. Javaplayer, Java MP3 Player, http://www.javazoom.net/javalayer/sources.html, 2006
13. Brenneman, Todd R. Java Address Book (ver. 1.1.1). Available at http://www.geocities.com/SiliconValley/2272/, Jan. 2002.
14. ICQ Inc., ICQ Lite, http://lite.icq.com, Aug. 2006.
15. Y. D. You, S. H. Park, H. Choi, "Dynamic storage management for mobile platform based on the characteristics of mobile application," Korea Information Processing Society Jour-nal, Vol. 13-1, No. 7, pp. 561-572, Dec. 2006.
16. Sun Microsystems, Enterprise Javabeans, http://java.sun.com/products/ejb/, 2000.
17. S. Landis and S. Maffeis, "Building Reliable Distributed Systems with CORBA," Theory and Practice of Object Systems, John Wiley, New York, Apr. 1997.

18. Microsoft Company, "Component Object Model," http://www.microsoft.com/com/, 2000.
19. Horn, Paul, "Autonomic Computing: IBM's Perspective on the State of Information Technology", available form the IBM Corporation at http://www.research.ibm.com/autonomic/manifesto/autonomiccomputing.pdf
20. Bantz D, Frank D, "Autonomic personal computing," available form the IBM Corpora-tion at http://researchweb.watson.ibm.com/journal/sj/421/bantz.html
21. Sterritt R, Bantz D, "Personal autonomic computing reflex reactions and self-healing," IEEE Transactions on Systems, Man and Cybernetics, Part C, VOL.36, No. 3, pp. 304-314, May 2006.

Product Line Based Reuse Methodology for Developing Generic ECU*

Si Won Choi, Jin Sun Her, Hyun Koo Kang, and Soo Dong Kim

Department of Computer Science, Soongsil University
511 Sangdo-dong, Dongjak-Ku, Seoul, Korea 156-734
{swchoi,jsher,h9kang}@otlab.ssu.ac.kr, sdkim@ssu.ac.kr

Abstract. As an important application domain of embedded software, automotive software is playing a more important role within automotive industry. There are some essential issues to be resolved; managing software complexity, reducing software cost, and shortening time-to-market. An effective solution to these issues is to reuse generic Electronic Control Units (ECUs) in building various ECUs rather than building every piece from scratch. *Generic ECU* is an ECU level reuse unit which consists of automotive components and embeds variability. Among the reuse approaches, Product Line Engineering (PLE) can be effectively applied in developing generic ECUs. However, current PLE methodologies do not effectively support developing generic ECUs. Hence, in this paper, we first define a meta-model of generic ECUs. Then, we define variability types and variation points for generic ECUs. Based on the meta-model and variability types, we propose a product line process for developing ECUs. To assess the applicability of the proposed meta-model and the PLE process, we present the case study of developing an automotive ECU for Window Control System (WCS).

1 Introduction

As automotive software is playing a more important role within automotive industry, the demands on managing software complexity, shortening time-to-market, and facilitating cost-effective development have increased more in automotive software engineering area [1][2]. An effective solution to these demands is to maximize reuse in building automotive software. There have been several efforts to promote reuse in automotive industry such as applying *Model driven development (MDD)* and developing a standard architecture AUTOSAR [3][4]. However, well defined methodology is not yet provided and the reuse unit is limited to component level. In this paper, we extend the unit of reusability to the level of ECU which is larger grained than component. We suggest that ECU is an appropriate unit for reuse since it is a cohesive control unit that monitors and controls various automobile components. In addition, we embed variability into ECU so that one ECU can be tailored for specific needs of the numerous automobile models and we call this *generic ECU*.

* This work was supported by the Korea Science and Engineering Foundation(KOSEF) grant funded by the Korea government(MOST) (No. R01-2005-000-11215-0).

Y.-H. Lee et al. (Eds.): ICESS 2007, LNCS 4523, pp. 37–45, 2007.

Among the few reuse technologies, we find that PLE is effective for developing generic ECU in terms of granularity of the reuse unit, applicable technique, and familiarity. A core asset in PLE can be mapped to generic ECU and techniques in PLE can be effectively applied in developing a generic ECU.

However, current PLE methodologies need adaptation to effectively support developing generic ECUs. Hence, in this paper, we first define a meta-model and variability types for generic ECUs. Based on the meta-model and the variability model, we propose an effective product line development process for developing ECUs. To assess the applicability of the proposed PLE process, we present the case study of developing an automotive ECU for Window Control System (WCS).

2 Related Works

Thiel's work presents a product line process for developing automotive systems [5]. Commonality and variability (C&V) among automotive components is first captured by the feature model and then realized by the product line architecture. They apply their architecture design framework "Quality-Driven Software Architecting" (QUASAR) and their architectural variability metamodel to Car Periphery Supervision systems and show how variability is realized in the architecture.

Eklund's work presents a motivation and a development process for applying reference architectures in developing automotive electronic systems at Volvo Cars [6]. This work presents a reference architecture based development process which consists of five steps; analyzing the design prerequisites, designing, verifying, disseminating, and maintaining the reference architecture.

Hardung's work proposes a framework for reusing application software components in automotive systems [7]. The proposed framework is divided into three parts; a process for developing modularized components, a definition of the function repository, and a process for developing ECUs with a standard software core, *SSC*.

However, these approaches need to be elaborated in terms of reuse unit, activities and instructions, and types of variation points.

3 Generic ECU

A generic ECU consists of a generic ECU architecture, software components, and a decision model as shown in Fig. 1. *Generic ECU architecture* is a generic structure for a family of ECUs, and it consists of software components and their relationship. *Software Components* implement the functionality of ECU specified in pre-defined *Component Interfaces. Logic Component* implements the control logic of the ECU, *Sensor Component* acquires various signals and data through hardware sensor elements, and *Actuator Component* delivers decisions made and controlling commands to various hardware actuators. *Setpoint Generator Component* is to acquire input from hardware setpoint generators.

Decision Model is a specification of variability in generic ECUs and is defined in terms of *variation points, variants, resolution tasks,* and *post-conditions. Resolution task* specifies activities to perform to resolve a variation point (VP) for a given variant.

Post-condition specifies a condition that must be true after setting the variant. *Affected decision* specifies a range of relationships among VPs and it is represented with dependencies or conflicts among variability. We also identify seven places where ECU variability may occur. Each variability place is marked with «V» in Fig. 1.

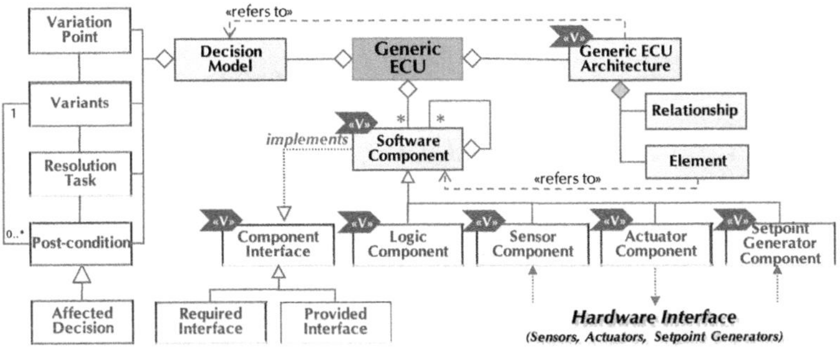

Fig. 1. Meta Model of Generic ECU with Variability Types

Variability on Generic ECU Architecture: Variability on architecture is classified into *architectural driver variability* and *architectural component variability* which respectively denotes the occurrence of VPs on the architectural drivers and architectural components. Architectural component variability includes variability on logic, sensor, actuator, and setpoint generator component.

Variability on Software Component: As the super class, SW components may have *attribute variability* which denotes occurrences of VPs on the set of attributes needed by components such as different number and/or data types of attributes. For example, attributes of Antilock Brake System (ABS) components for automobile X can be the road surface roughness and speed of the car's wheel. And automobile Y can additionally include the throttle condition to the two attributes.

Variability on Logic Component: Logic components implement the ECU logic and workflow. Hence, the variability can occur on logics and workflows. *Logic variability* denotes occurrences of VPs on the algorithm or logic of methods in a component. For example, logics for *computeParkingPath( )* method of *Automatic Parking System (APS)* varies according to automobile models such as sedan, SUV, and Van. *Workflow Variability* denotes occurrences of VPs on the sequence of method invocations. For APS, sequences of invoking *applyBrake( ), applyAccelerator( ); setForward( ); setBackward( ); turnLeft( )* and *turnRight( )* methods varies depending on the automobile models.

Variability on Sensor Component: *Variability on Sensor components* denotes occurrence of VP on the types of sensors needed. For example, the vehicle can sense the distance to the obstacle using an infrared sensor or ultrasonic sensor.

Variability on Actuator Component: *Variability on Actuator components* denotes occurrence of VP on the types of actuators needed. For example, HID lamp or halogen lamp can be used in providing light features of automobile.

Variability on Setpoint Generator Component: *Variability on Setpoint Generator Components* denotes occurrence of VP on the types of setpoint generators such as brake pedal, steering wheel and parking brake.

Variability on Component Interface: *Variability on Component Interface* denotes occurrences of VPs on the method signatures of the component interface. For the same functionality, each ECU may have its own convenient form of API, i.e. method name, orders and types of parameters, and its return type.

4 Product Line Process for ECUs

In this section, we present a product line process which consists of two engineering processes; *core asset engineering* for developing a generic ECU and *ECU engineering* for developing a specific ECU based on the generic ECU. Fig. 2 shows the activities with the input/output of each engineering process. To show the applicability of the process, we conduct a case study of developing a generic ECU for *Window Control System (WCS)*.

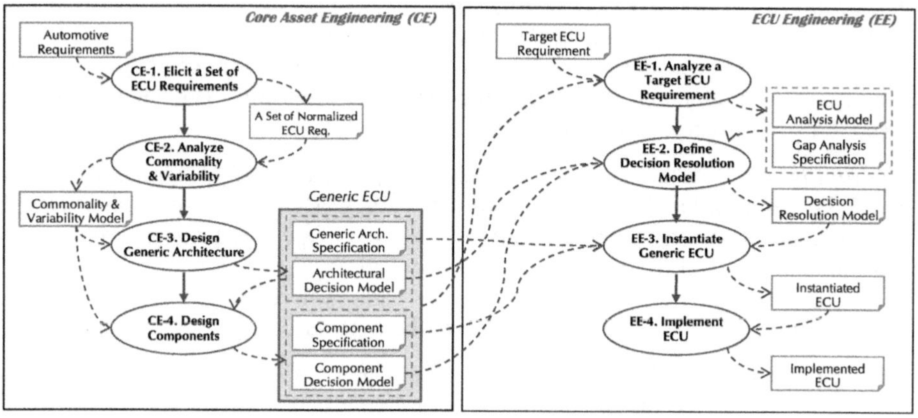

Fig. 2. PL Process for Developing Generic ECUs

4.1 Core Asset Engineering (CE)

CE-1. Elicit a Set of ECU Requirements: This activity is to elicit a set of ECU requirements for potential ECUs in a domain. First, we acquire a set of ECU requirement specifications. Especially for a ECU, we categorize the requirement into *functional requirement*, *non-functional requirement*, and *design constraints* on the ECU. Then we normalize the collected requirements since the requirements are all described in different forms. In our case study, we normalized three requirement specifications on WCS.

CE-2. Analyze Commonality & Variability: This activity is to analyze common and variable features among the normalized requirements. The extracted commonality is further designed into generic architecture and reusable components.

The first step is to identify common features. We suggest three factors to consider for determining common features; *degree of commonality*, *market demand*, and *potential value*. *Degree of commonality* can be computed as; *Number of ECUs Requiring the Feature / Total Number of ECUs*. The remaining two factors, *market demand* and *potential value,* are especially important for ECU software since development cost is higher than conventional applications. In our case study, we identified 19 common features among 25 features by applying the three factors.

Table 1. Variability Model of WCS

CF ID	VP	Type	Scope	Variants	Dependency
CF09	Automatic Lift-up of FL Window	Behavioral Variability	Optional	Lift-up FL Window Automatically	If variant is not selected, don't select the variant of CF11, CF13, and CF15.
CF16	Automatic Lift-down of RR Window	Behavioral Variability	Optional	Lift-down FL Window Automatically	
...	...	...	...	...	

The second step is to identify variability within the common features. Since concrete design elements are not designed yet, we first identify abstract level variability; *software variability (structural variability* and *behavioral variability)* and *hardware variability*. These variability can be further refined in CE-3 and CE-4. *Variability model* is specified as Table 1. *Dependency* here specifies the propagated constraints to the other VPs or variants caused by the current resolution and the constraints that have to be satisfied by other VPs or variants to resolve this VP [8]. For example, the VP on CF09 has dependency with VP on CF11, CF13, and CF15. If the FL window does not use the automatic lift-up feature then the other windows do not usually use the automatic lift-up features.

CE-3. Design Generic Architecture: This activity is to design an architecture common to a family of ECUs. Using the commonality & variability model as the

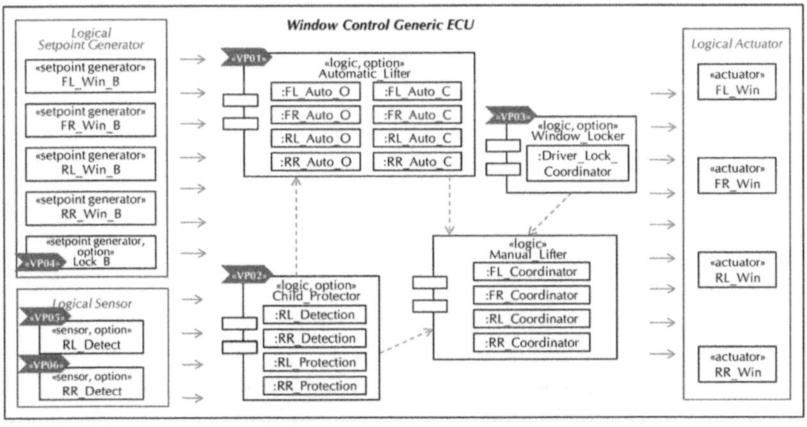

Fig. 3. Generic Architecture of WCS

input, we produce a *generic architecture specification* and an *architectural decision model* specifying the architectural variability.

The first step is to define a generic architecture by identifying software components and inter-connection between them. Architecture can be specified using a component diagram, class diagram, or a block diagram. We suggest using stereotypes, «logic», «sensor», «actuator», and «setpoint generator», to specify the types of a component. From the common features of WCSs, we designed a generic architecture as shown in Fig. 3. Two types of sensor components are to detect if there are obstacles when closing the window and five setpoint generator components let the driver to initiate the movement of the four windows and to lock the window. Four logic components are to manually lift the windows, to automatically lift the windows, to handle the windows for protecting a child, and to lock the windows.

The second step is to identify architectural variability based on the variability model. Dependency identified in CE-2 can be clarified with concrete design elements and new dependency can be identified which are only identifiable at the level of architectural design.

Table 2. Architectural Decision Model

VP ID	VP	Type	Scope	Variant	Resolution Task	Dependency
VP 03	Component 'Window_ Locker'	Arch. Comp.	Opt.	Locking All Windows	(a) Preserve 'Window_Locker'. (b) Preserve relationships related to 'Window_Locker'.	Select the variant of VP04
VP 04	Component 'Lock_B'	Arch. Comp.	Opt.	Keeping Locking Setpoint Generator	(a) Preserve 'Lock_B'. (b) Preserve relationships related to 'Lock_B'. (c) Verify if 'Window_Locker' is preserved.	
...						

In Fig. 3, the arrow sign depicts architectural VP and we mark the variability into the diagram using stereotypes, «option» and «selection». Especially for VP03 and VP04 from Fig. 3, Table 2 specifies the details. Dependency here is a newly identified one since the VPs are newly identified in this activity. If the variant is selected for VP03 then the variant is selected for VP04, that is, the 'Lock_B' must be preserved if the 'Window_Locker' is preserved.

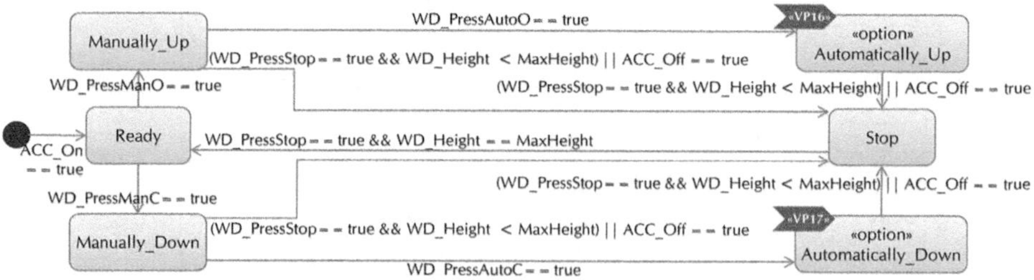

Fig. 4. State Transition Diagram of Window Behavior

CE-4. Design Components: This activity is to design the internal details of each component in terms of interface, data model, and behavioral model. The first step is to define the interfaces and operations of the identified components. Interface variability is also identified in this step by considering the pre-defined naming conventions. We identified interface variability in *Automatic-Lifter* component. Some requirements use the naming convention of *Com_XXX* and some used *Auto_XXX.*

The second step is to design a data model which defines the data that is to be processed by the software component. As identified in Table 1, there is VP on the automatic lifting features of the four windows, thus there exist variability on the input signals and output signals of the *Automatic_Lifter* Component.

The third step is to design a behavioral model in terms of data flow and control flow. Data flow is represented by control-specific modeling method on the basis of block diagrams and state machine. Fig. 4 shows the state machine of the behavior of a window. Since there is variability in the automatic lifting features of the window, states 'Automatically_Up' and 'Automatically_Down' embed variability. Control flow is designed in order to control the execution of instructions. Well-known notations for representing the control flow are structograms according to Nassi-Shneiderman [9].

4.2 ECU Engineering (EE)

EE-1. Analyze a Target ECU Requirement: This activity is to analyze the requirement of a target ECU and to identify the gap between the generic ECU and the target ECU. First, we elicit the software requirement of a target ECU from vehicle requirement. Secondly, we analyze the software requirement of target ECU to help distinguishing features supported from the generic ECU. Thirdly, we compare the target ECU analysis model with the generic ECU. Gap analysis specification is produced which specifies features supported from the generic ECU and features that have to be newly developed. In our case study, we reused the generic ECU to develop a WCS for *Picanto-SLX*. Fig. 5 illustrates the requirement specification and the major gap is the feature of locking windows; *Picanto-SLX* does not require this feature.

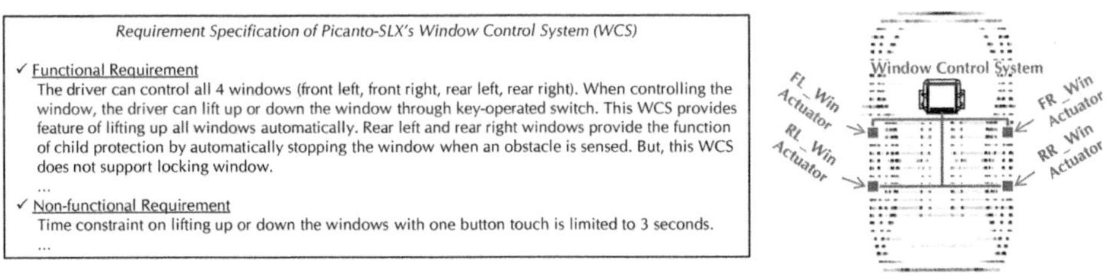

Fig. 5. Requirement Specification of WCS in *Picanto-SLX*

EE-2. Define Decision Resolution Model (DRM): This activity is to define a *DRM* which contains the variants specific to the target ECU. The first step is to identify the features containing variability from the overlapped features. When variable features are identified, we first identify architectural VPs from the decision model since the decisions on the architecture affect the software components. And then, we identify

VPs within the component. The second step is to define an appropriate variant for each VP. In our case study, WCS of *Picanto-SLX* does not support the feature for locking window. Hence variants are not selected for VP03 and VP04.

EE-3. Instantiate Generic ECU: In this activity, we resolve variability by setting the variants into the VPs and by modifying the parts of the generic ECU which are not required from the target ECU according to the decisions defined in the DRM. The first step is to instantiate the generic architecture according to resolution task of the architectural DRM. The second step is to instantiate the generic component model according to the resolution task of the component DRM. Since variants for VP03 and VP04 were not selected in the architectural DRM, *Lock_B* and *Window_Locker* are eliminated in the instantiated architecture.

EE-4. Implement ECU: This activity is to implement the instantiated ECU for the target platform. For the implementation, we should consider the programming language, class library, automotive operating system such as OSEK, bus architecture, architectural constraints imposed by certain standards such as AUTOSAR, and the whole domain (i.e. powertrain, chassis, body, etc.) architecture adopted for the target automobile model. Once a ECU software is implemented, it is integrated onto appropriate memory such as ROM, flash RAM of the ECU, and software components are interfaced to hardware sensors, actuators and setpoint generators.

5 Conclusion

There are several issues to be resolved in automotive software engineering area; managing software complexity, and reducing software cost and time-to-market. Product line development (PLE) can provide an effective solution to these issues.

In this paper, we first defined the key elements of generic ECUs. To handle the variability, we identified seven places where the variability may occur in the generic ECU. Based on the meta-model and variability types, we proposed a product line development process for developing ECUs. The process consists of two sub-processes; *Core Asset Engineering* and *ECU Engineering*. In the process, we especially dealt with the dependency between variability. We conducted a case study project for implementing a *Window Control System*. Through the case study, it has been shown that with our framework of ECU meta model and the development process, various ECUs can be cost-effectively developed by instantiating generic ECUs.

References

1. Simonot-Lion, F. and Song, Y., "Design and Validation Process of In-Vehicle Embedded Electronic Systems," *Chapter 41 of Embedded Systems Handbook*, Zurawski, R., ed., CRC, 2005.
2. Broy, M., "Challenges in Automotive Software Engineering," *Proceeding of the 28th International Conference on Software Engineering*, pp.33-42, 2006.

3. Ziegenbein, D., Braun, P., Freund, U., Bauer, A., Romberg, J., and Schatz, B., "AutoMoDe - Model-Based Development of Automotive Software," *Proceedings of the conference on Design, Automation and Test in Europe (DATE '05)*, Vol. 3, pp. 171-177, 2005.
4. AUTOSAR, Automotive Open System Architecture, http://www.autosar.org, June 2006.
5. Thiel, S. and Hein, A., "Modeling and Using Product Line Variability in Automotive Systems," *IEEE Software*, pp. 66-72, July 2002.
6. Eklund, U., Askerdal, O, Granholm, J., Alminger, A., and Axelsson, J., "Experience of introducing reference architectures in the development of automotive electronic systems," *Proceedings of the second international workshop on SEAS*, 2005.
7. Hardung, B., Kölzow, T., and Krüger, A., "Reuse of software in distributed embedded automotive systems," *Proceedings of the 4th ACM International Conference on Embedded software*, pp. 203-210, 2004.
8. Jaring, M. and Bosch, J., "Variability Dependencies in Product Line Engineering," *LNCS 3014, In Proceedings of the PFE 2003*, pp.81-97, 2004.
9. Schauffele, J., *Automotive Software Engineering: Principles, Processes, Methods, and Tools*, SAE International, 2005.

The Object-Oriented Protocol for Data Exchange and Control in Computational-Diverse Embedded Systems

Bogusław Cyganek

AGH - University of Science and Technology
Al. Mickiewicza 30, 30-059 Kraków, Poland
cyganek@uci.agh.edu.pl

Abstract. One of the key functionality of embedded-computer systems is control and data exchange among its building modules. Different size terminal sensors, microprocessor sub-systems, specialized devices, etc. should be able to smoothly exchange data and control notifications. This is often a difficult and time consuming task for a designer, mostly due to diversity of components. Usually the protocols and their realizations have to be implemented separately for each specific case. Therefore it would be desirable to have a definition of a protocol for data exchange and control that fits a certain class of such systems. In this paper we propose a solution to this problem which can be easily applied to different computer platforms. We start with the definition of the proposed DXC protocol. Then we present its object-oriented implementation. This way our proposition can be re-used on different platforms. The presented solution was employed with success to the suite of embedded systems for communication measurements and showed robustness and flexibility.

1 Introduction

In this paper we address the problem of control and data exchange among components of embedded computer systems [5][9][13]. The main problem encountered in such systems is a great diversity of their building blocks which most often than not differ in hardware, computational power, programming facilities and also networking capabilities. Actually many such systems are composed of few different computer platforms, quite often endowed with its own microprocessor and controlled by different operating system. Additionally, there can be dedicated hardware programmable devices (FPGA) and many intelligent sensors (e.g. based on the ARM, '51, HC, etc.). Connecting such components together is a challenging task. This is caused mostly by two factors: quite different programming facilities (C++ with mega-bytes of memory vs. assembly and kB) and data level networking (USB, Ethernet vs. RS232 or I2C). The main purpose of the DXC protocol (Data and eXChange), presented in this paper, is to facilitate the interconnection task for embedded systems.

We describe DXC providing its definition, sequence diagrams, and number of assumptions, among which the most important is placement of the DXC on top of a transport layer. The DXC protocol is characterized by five main groups of commands and their acknowledge counterparts. Compared with other protocols we can state that DXC is a complete system that can operate on a set of lower level protocols providing

Y.-H. Lee et al. (Eds.): ICESS 2007, LNCS 4523, pp. 46–58, 2007.

basic data networking, such as RS232 and USB, I2C, etc. On the other hand, it can operate also on the networks with such protocols as Bluetooth [3], Beep [10] or ZigBee [15]. Thus the main area of DXC applications constitute embedded systems consisting of many microprocessor-based components characterized by great dynamics of their computational and networking capabilities.

In this paper we present also an object-oriented framework for generation of user defined versions of DXCs. This allows very fast creation of new DXC protocols that are tailored to a given system. Although we assume an object-oriented approach, the presented solution can be implemented on almost any microprocessor system (in C, C++ or assembly) due to its simplicity and modular architecture. DXC was used in the series of embedded systems for telecommunication measurements and showed great robustness and flexibility.

2 The Protocol for Data Exchange and Control (DXC)

2.1 Definition of the DXC Protocol

It is not possible to define a protocol that would comply with all requirements for data exchange and control in computer (embedded) systems. However, based on the analysis of many embedded systems – starting from 8-bits up to 64-bits devices – we noticed that it is possible to define a minimal set of commands that can fulfil around 80% of the needs for moderate data exchange and control (DXC) in such systems. For a suitable DXC protocol we set the following assumptions:

1. The DXC protocol operates on some lower-level data protocol capable of connecting peer-to-peer components for data exchange.
2. Each message must be acknowledged by a recipient before another message of that type is sent again to recipients.
3. There are preset constraints on response latency for each type of a message.
4. The protocol is designated for moderate amounts of data exchange.

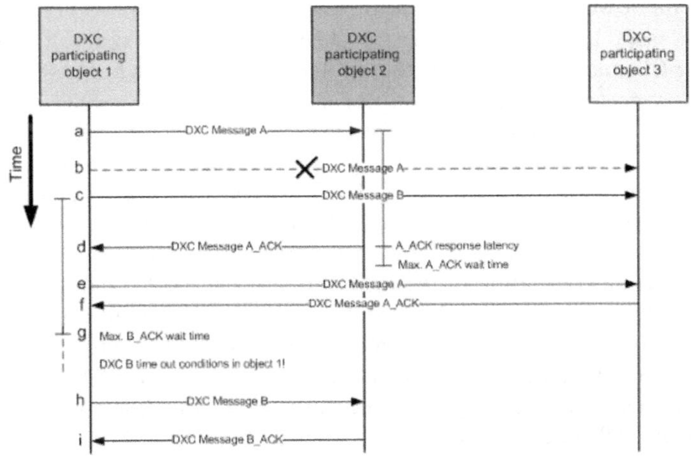

Fig. 1. Sequence diagram of the DXC protocol

The first condition places the DXC protocol in a certain hierarchy of protocols. It means that the protocol has precisely defined role in a system and relies on some other basic means of data communication and addressing among participants. On the other hand, it is possible to build other upper layers of protocols based on the DXC.

The second condition assures certain means of system robustness and protection against message stalling if, for instance, a recipient is not able to respond (conditions that are frequently encountered in the embedded systems).

The third condition imposes some timing constraints on message delivery – this is a very important feature if the protocol is to be applied in a real-time systems. The last condition places some constraints on amount of data to be sent based on this protocol. Although precise amount of allowable payload is system dependant it precludes sending data for example in a burst mode, etc.

The rules of the DXC protocol are explained by the sequence diagram in Fig. 1. A DXC message 'A' is sent from a DXC object 1 at event 'a'. Now the object 1 gets blocked from sending messages of type 'A' – event 'b' – until it receives 'A_ACK', what happens at a time event 'd'. However, before event 'd' commences, it is still possible for the object 1 to send other messages – by this token a message 'B' is sent at instant 'c'. An object 2 sends an 'A_ACK' message at event 'd' which finds itself in an allowable time-out period (preset in the object 1) for the acknowledge messages 'A_ACK'. Another message 'A' can be sent again from the object 1 only after it receives 'A_ACK'. Such situation happens at event 'e' with acknowledge received at 'f' in an allowable time.

A message 'B' was sent out from the object 1 to the object 3 at event 'c'. However, the latter has not responded with 'B_ACK' and therefore the object 1, after being blocked for sending another 'B' messages, enters time-out conditions for the 'B' message. After handling this time-out conditions, the object 1 is able again to send 'Bs' to other objects – this takes place at event 'h' with received acknowledge at 'i'.

2.2 Structure of the DXC Protocol

Based on the already presented assumptions (2.1), the DXC protocol is assumed to rely on some lower-level protocol with basic transport facilities [7][2], i.e. it should provide message addressing and data exchange. In our realization it was the Control Messaging Channel [4], although other protocols can be used here as well.

The other protocol layers, i.e. an upper and lower to the DXC layer, are totally transparent. The layered model with the DXC protocol is presented in Fig. 2.

The hardware communication network in Fig. 2 can be any lowest level media of communication. It is separated from DXC by the transport layers. Based on this architecture, each DXC message is embedded into lower level messages as shown in Fig. 3.

Table 1 presents definition of the main group of the DXC commands. Each row of this table contains a name and detailed description of a message, as well as the same information for its acknowledge counterpart messages. This proposition is based on many years of experience in implementations of the computer platforms. We believe that it is sufficient for majority of the common control and data exchange operations in most of the embedded systems.

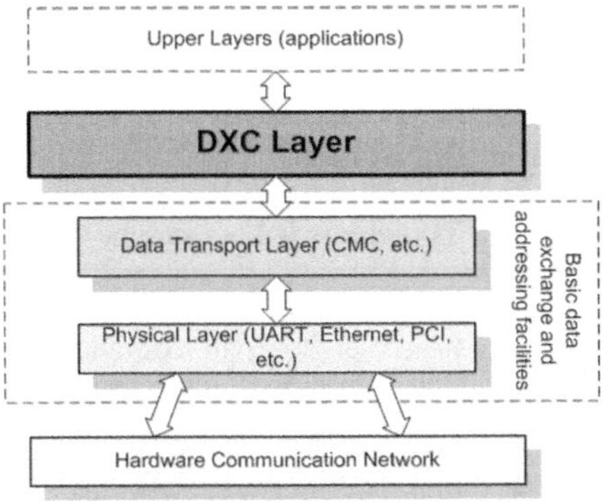

Fig. 2. The DXC protocol in the layered protocol model

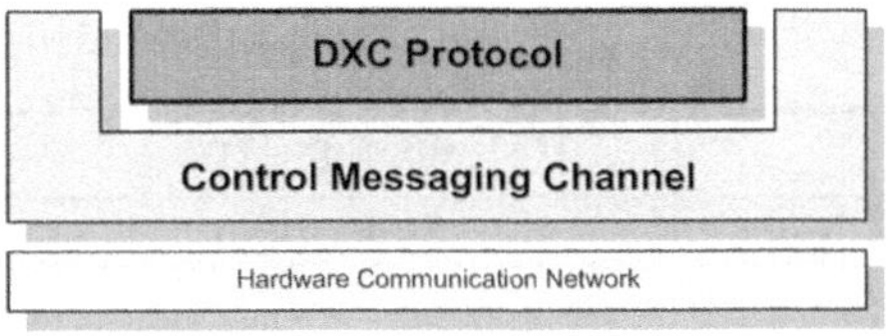

Fig. 3. A DXC frame embedded into a CMC frame

As alluded to previously (2.1), each DXC message has an acknowledge counterpart. This is achieved *automatically* without separate definition of the latter group of messages. This way the DXC messages can be actually taught of as pairs, consisting of a message and its acknowledge companion (i.e. a single row in Table 1). These features provide desirable properties of the protocol, such as responsiveness and simple error handling. They help also to maintain system correctness and robustness. At the same time the protocol is kept as minimal as possible. These attributes are especially important in case of real-time embedded systems [5][13].

Fig. 4. Structure of an exemplary DXC message. The first field contains message encoding (for example on 2×4-bits). The second field conveys a payload (potentially next layer message, etc.).

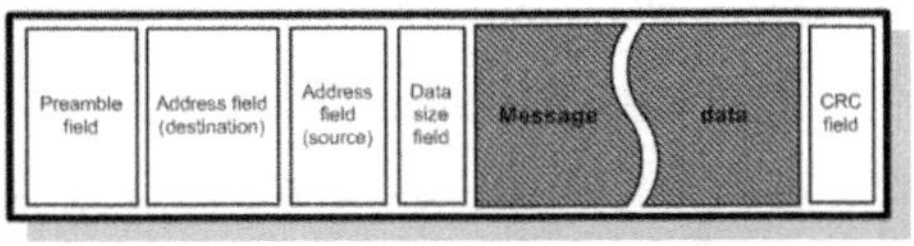

Fig. 5. Structure of a CMC message. Data field (green) is used to convey frames of upper layer protocols (DXC in this case).

Definition of the DXC presented in Table 1 is an open standard and new message groups can be easily added. However, it is highly recommended to keep this main group (Table 1) untouched and if necessary define sub-commands, i.e. specialized commands relating only to one command from the main group. In practice, this can be easily achieved by special message encoding format. Fig. 4 depicts structure of a DXC message. The first field contains message encoding – in this case it is composed of two fields, one for main message and the second for a sub-command. In practice we used eight bits for the DXC message encoding, a nibble for the main and the second nibble for the sub-command.

The last field in Fig. 4 conveys a payload (e.g. messages of a next layer, etc.).

Table 1. Definition of the main DXC commands

DXC message type		DXC acknowledge message type	
Name	**Description**	**Name**	**Description**
DXC_INIT	This type of message is sent for initialization of a receiving part. This message contains all required parameters.	DXC_INIT_ACK	A receiving part responds with this message upon successful reception of the initialize message DXC_INIT (and after initialization process, if required). Optionally, this type of message can contain the error code.
DXC_RESET	This type of message is sent to place a receiving part in a reset state. This type of message can contain some additional parameters.	DXC_RESET_ACK	A receiving part responds with this message upon successful reception and execution of the reset message (DXC_RESET). This type of message contains the error code to inform transmitter of reset state.
DXC_START	This type of message is sent to start an action on a receiving part (e.g.. a measurement). The action should have been already initialized. This type of message can convey some additional parameters.	DXC_START_ACK	A receiving part responds with this message upon successful reception and execution of the start message (DXC_START). This message can contain an error code to inform a transmitting part of an operation status.
DXC_STOP	This type of message is sent to stop an action on a receiving part. This type of message can contains some additional parameters.	DXC_STOP_ACK	A receiving part responds with this message upon successful reception and execution of the stop message (DXC_STOP). This message can contain an error code to inform a transmitting part of an operation status.
DXC_DATA_EXCH	This type of message is sent to exchange data with a receiving part. That action should be initialized previously. This type of message can convey some additional parameters.	DXC_DATA_ EXCH_ACK	A receiving part responds with this message upon successful reception and execution of the data exchange message (DXC_DATA_EXCH). This message can contain an error code to inform a transmitting part of an operation status.

2.3 The Base Protocol Layer

It was already mentioned that the DXC protocol relies on some lower-level protocol with basic message addressing and data exchange mechanisms. In our realization this layer was realized by means of the simple CMC protocol, which details can be found in [4]. This protocol relies on short messages, transferred over fixed channels. Fig. 5 presents the structure of a CMC message. Again, the data field of a massage can be used to convey frames of the upper layer protocols, i.e. the DXC messages in our case – see Fig. 3.

Each CMC message is identified by a constant preamble field used for proper message alignment. Then two address fields follow, the first for a destination, the second to identify a sender of that message. Each address field, in turn, is divided into two partitions:

1. System address.
2. Local address.

The first part of an address uniquely identifies a CMC system. The second identifies a client within a system [4].

Data is conveyed in the message data field of potentially different length which is placed in the data size field. This field contains number of bytes in the data part of a message. The CMC traffic is governed by a system of message dispatchers, working on different levels of a system [4].

3 Object-Oriented Implementation of the DXC Based Protocols

The functionality of the proposed design pattern for generation of DXC protocols can be summarized as follows:

1. There are two groups of messages:
   - Main commands.
   - Acknowledge counterpart commands (ACK).
2. For each "main" command there is *automatically* generated its counterpart in the "acknowledge" group. Therefore, there is only a need to explicitly define "main" commands.
3. There is exactly one entry for each command from each group. For each command it is possible to register an unlimited number of handlers that will be called (notified) on reception of a command they registered to.
4. In addition, for each command of the "main" group, it is possible to register an unlimited number of handlers that will be called on acknowledge time-out. This happens if after sending a given command there is no acknowledge in a predefined time for that "main" command.
5. Sending a subsequent "main" command is possible *only* after reception of the acknowledge message for this command or if *time-out* conditions have been met, i.e. after calling the special time-out handlers to handle this situation. Note however, that it is an error if we receive an acknowledge message while the corresponding command is not blocked at that time. In such a situation we do *not* call the registered handlers.

6. All actions of the protocol are handled by means of the specialized handlers (and time-out handlers) that are orphaned [12] to the protocol generator object.
7. A multi-platform implementation is assumed. However, some actions are by definition platform specific, e.g. time measurement or thread security. For those operations a separation is necessary (e.g. a handle/body and factories can be used here [6][1]).

Fig. 6 presents structure of a framework for generation of DXC protocols that realizes the stated functionality. It consists of the four main components:

1. The DXC commands policy.
2. Base data and addressing protocol.
3. Thread security policy.
4. Containers for DXC message handlers.

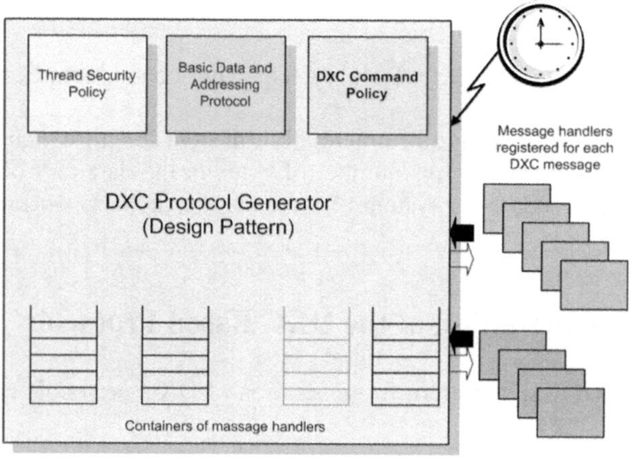

Fig. 6. Structure of the DXC protocol generator design pattern

The most important are the two first components. The role of the DXC commands policy is to define a group of DXC commands. This can be done e.g. in accordance with the specification given in Table 1.

The base data and addressing protocol provides basic transport facilities to the DXC layer. Although it is presented in Fig. 6 as an inherent block, actually it can be an external module.

The last component of the DXC generating pattern is actual storage for externally supplied handlers that are notified on messages they had been registered for.

Additionally, the DXC generator requires access to the system clock. This is used for example to control message latency and to fire time-out conditions if necessary. Thanks to this feature the system can cope with unexpected situations, e.g. when a recipient is not responding for some reasons – not unusual situation in embedded systems. Details of implementation with full C++ code can be found in [8].

Massage handling is accomplished by registering number of external objects to the DXC generator object. Handlers are notified on messages they registered for. It is possible that a single handler is registered to many DXC messages. It is also possible that no handler is registered for a message. The second group consists of handlers registered to be notified only on time-out conditions. This can happen if required acknowledge message is not received in a predefined period of time (which can be set dynamically). We should notice also that next message can be sent if such a message has been already acknowledged. Otherwise, sending of this message type is prohibited and the message sending mechanism stays in a blocked state.

3.1 Implementation Issues

Presenting implementation for embedded systems is always problematic due to many different programming platforms and system specifics. However, throughout recent years programming embedded computers with high level languages and object-oriented methods became more frequent. This is very desirable since such languages and programming environments allow faster development, quick debugging, and easy maintenance. These development methods lead to the multiplatform design, resulting with the good quality code, which allows easy upgrades, modifications, as well as reusability. In this section we present details of implementation of the proposed pattern for generation of the DXC protocols. This implementation was done in C++ on three platforms: Microsoft® Embedded 4.0 for Windows CE, Metrowerk's CodeWarrior® 6.0 for PowerPC embedded platforms, and reference implementation on Microsoft Visual C++ 6.0 for Windows. Full version of the latter can be downloaded from [8]. In addition this project contains complete implementation of the CMC protocol [4], timer adapter, and thread security mechanisms for Windows.

Design of a specific DXC should start with a list of the DXC commands and their encoding. Exemplary proposition of message encoding presents Table 2. A main command occupies the higher nibble, a sub-command is encoded on the lower nibble.

Table 2. Exemplary encoding scheme for the suite of the DXC commands. The main commands are encoded on the four MSBs. The sub-commands on the 2nd nibble ('x' bits).

Main DXC commands	DXC command encoding (higher nibble)
DXC_INIT	0000xxxx
DXC _INIT_ACK	0001xxxx
DXC _RESET	0010xxxx
DXC _RESET_ACK	0011xxxx
DXC _START	0100xxxx
DXC _START_ACK	0101xxxx
DXC _STOP	0110xxxx
DXC _STOP_ACK	0111xxxx
DXC _DATA_EXCH	1000xxxx
DXC _DATA_EXCH _ACK	1001xxxx
Reserved	11110000
x – a "don't care" value (these fields can be use to define sub-messages)	

In Fig. 7 the class hierarchy of the design pattern for generation of the DXC protocols is presented (UML and Taligent notations [12]). A practical implementation can be done in any available language on a given system, however. It has only to comply with the already defined functionality and semantics.

The *T_DXC_ProtocolGenerator* template class in Fig. 7 constitutes a core of the pattern for generation of a user defined DXC protocols. The presented implementation follows directly definition of the pattern given in (3) – see also Fig. 6 and [8]. It is derived from three classes – two of them are its template parameters at the same time. This programming techniques allows very flexible generations of

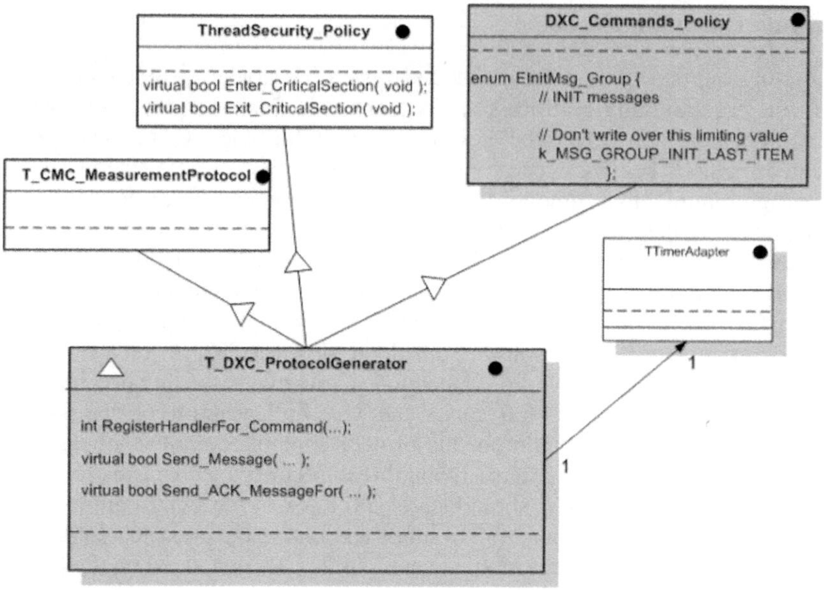

Fig. 7. Hierarchy of the pattern for generation of the user defined DXC protocols. The pattern consists of the main *T_DXC_ProtocolGenerator* template class which is derived from three classes. The *DXC_Command_Policy* base class defines user DXC commands. At the same time it is a template parameter of the *T_DXC_ProtocolGenerator* class.

compound hierarchies with class policies [1][14]. The *DXC_Command_Policy* base class defines such a policy which is a set up by DXC commands defined by a user.

The second (optional) policy is the thread security policy, defined here in the *ThreadSecurity_Policy* base class. The third *T_CMC_MeasurementProtocol* base class provides base protocol layers necessary for the DXC operations.

The *T_DXC_ProtocolGenerator* allows a designer to generate his/her own measurement protocol, given a specific policy. The key issue then is to define a specific policy in a form of command definitions that will be used by this protocol. The following list constitutes a user's guide for creation of the user's DXC protocols:

1. Copy the example class *DefaultCommands_Policy* [8], name it *User_Policy*, and define your "normal" commands in the appropriate enumerated types. Remember to keep the special *enums*, such as k_DXC_GROUP_INIT_LAST_ITEM intact. Remember also that the corresponding "*ack*" commands will be created automatically.
2. Create your own instantiation of the template *T_DXC_ProtocolGenerator*; As a template supply your *User_Policy*, e.g.:

   typedef TMeasurementProtocolGenerator< User_Policy > MyProtocol;

3. Write your own handlers, derived from the *THandler* (see [8]) and register them to the *MyProtocol*.

An example of the user defined DXC policy is the *InterSystemCommands_Policy* class which was defined for one of our measurement systems for the inter-system management [8].

4 Experimental Results

The DXC protocol was implemented in a form of a test platform that consists of the board with the ARM processor running Microsoft Windows CE and the slave-measurement boards with the PowerPC 8260 processors. The communication and data channels are implemented in a form of the CMC protocol [4]. The inter system connections were done by the local RS232 links, as well as the dual-ported RAM.

The obvious question pertinent to the communication protocol is its throughput, reliability and channel efficiency. The answer can put light onto the influence of the header overhead, retransmission rate, number of bits devoted to the data and CRC fields and the ACK message length, etc. on the performance criteria. It is not always easy to measure those data, however. This is due to the fact that the underlying protocols contain hidden (or not published) mechanisms which latencies are not known beforehand. Therefore when performing a quantitative analysis of the DXC protocol we measured the throughput of the whole chain of protocols with DXC on top and system mechanisms. The justification for such an approach comes from the fact the in practice the DXC protocol is not used alone, although different underlying protocols can significantly change the experimental results.

In the first group of our experiments we measured the channel utilization factor U, given by the following measure [2]:

$$U = \frac{1}{1+a}, \text{ with } a = \frac{r_b \cdot \tau_{pd}}{N_D} \tag{1}$$

where r_b is data bit rate [bits/s], τ_{pd} is a worst-case propagation delay [s], N_D stands for maximum frame length [bits]. In our experiments we set the echo mode, i.e. a transmission chain was set among three participating systems, as presented in Fig. 8.

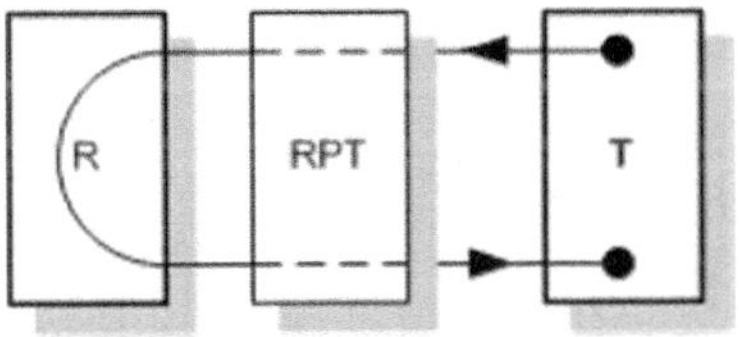

Fig. 8. The system set-up for measurement of the DXC performance parameters: T – a transmitter, RPT – a repeating system, R – a receiver

Since the data protocol was a very slow medium, we set the r_b as the maximum possible data rate for this channel, i.e. to 112.5 kB/s in our system. Absolute values of the τ_{pd} parameter in (1) were unknown, but they were increased by adding number Q of participating objects in the whole communication chain.

Fig. 9 shows two plots visualizing the measured performance parameters of the DXC protocol in the set-up in Fig. 8. The channel utilization parameter U versus number of protocol participating objects Q and for different lengths of a frame N_D = *80, 800*, and *2080* bits/frame (the latter is the maximal size determined by the underlying CMC layer) depicts Fig. 9a. It is visible that despite significant increase of the frame length and number of participants of this DXC system, the average channel utilization factor is quite similar in the three cases. This means that the throughput of the underlying data layer (CMC in our case) dominates, which is not a surprise for the RS232 protocol. This thesis is also acknowledged by the measurements of an average delay time τ_{pd} for different values of Q*'s* and N_D*'s* – visible in Fig. 9b.

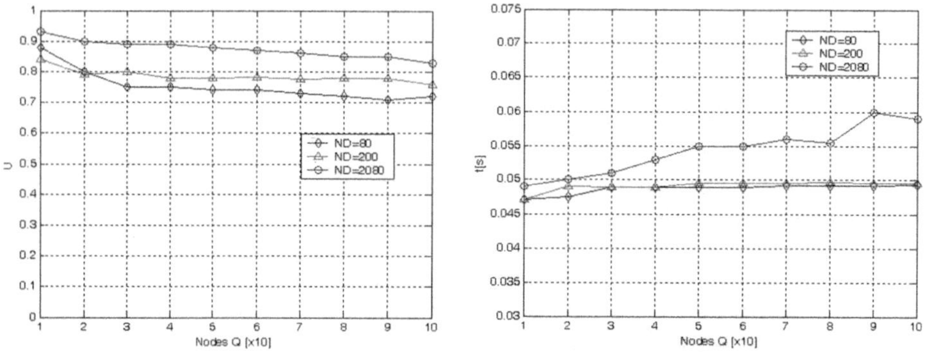

a b

Fig. 9. The DXC performance measurement for different N_D*=(10*8, 25*8, 260*8)*: (a) – the channel utilization parameter U vs. number of clients Q, (b) – the average delay time τ_{pd} vs. Q

Fig. 10a depicts another type of tests which consisted in measuring an average relative data rate of the system set-up shown in Fig. 8 for increased data rate of the

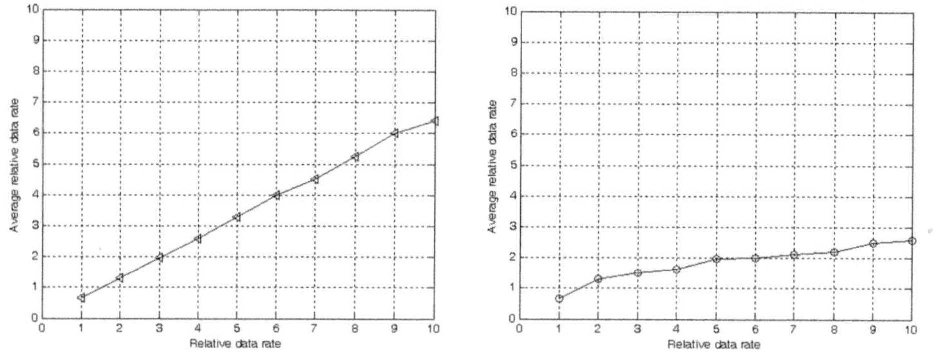

a b

Fig. 10. The average data rate vs. relative data rate of the data channel set in ten quantum steps for RS232 (*300-230400 bit/s*), N_D*=2080*, Q*=100* of the DXC protocol: (a) – all recipients responding, (b) – 10% of recipients not responding (ACK stall conditions) underlying data channel (in discrete steps from 300-230400 bits/s). These results show once again that the prominent factor for DXC is performance of the data link.

The situation gets quite different if 10% of randomly selected participating objects were not responding – Fig. 10b. In this case significant amount of service time was spent waiting for the ACK messages (the ACK stall conditions).

5 Conclusions

In this paper we address the problem of control and data exchange in embedded systems. We provide the complete definition of a versatile DXC protocol which is characterized by five groups of main and acknowledge commands. We also present a design framework for generation of user defined versions of this protocol. The object-oriented development technique allows code reuse and generation of DXC protocols tailored to specific embedded platforms.

The main areas of applications of the DXC protocol constitute embedded systems composed of many peer programmable modules that need to be connected together. DXC allows connection of systems characterized by extremely different programming and networking capabilities. The advantageous is its ability of using any lower level data connection of the sub-systems, which can be for instance RS232, USB, etc.

The DXC protocol showed its robustness and flexibility in our implementation on the test platforms (4). Based on experimental results and achieved performance in our realisation of the presented protocol, it can be especially recommended for multi processor and multi system embedded designs. This is due to the fact that the universal definition of DXC allows its operation on any different lower communication layers and operating systems. Thanks to the acknowledge policy, message blocking and time-out mechanisms, DXC joins them seamlessly allowing reliable control and data exchange even in a case of sub-system failures.

Finally, the multiplatform paradigm undertaken for implementation allows easy porting of the DXC protocol to other platforms. The C++ source code with full version of the presented patterns and protocols is also provided [8].

Acknowledgement. This work was supported by the Polish funds for the scientific research in 2007.

References

1. Alexandrescu A.: Modern C++ Design. Addison Wesley (2001)
2. Baker, D.G.: Monomode Fiber-Optic Design. Van Nostrand Reinhold (1987)
3. Bluetooth Specifications. Bluetooth SIG at http://www.bluetooth.com/ (2005)
4. Cyganek, B., Borgosz, J.: Control Messaging Channel for Distributed Computer Systems, Proceedings of the ICCSA 2004, Assisi, Italy, Springer LNCS No. 3046 (2004) 261 - 270
5. Douglass B.P.: Doing Hard Time. Developing Real-Time Systems with UML, Objects, Frameworks, and Patterns. Addison-Wesley (1999)
6. Gamma, E., E., Helm, R., Johnson, R.: Design Patterns. Addison-Wesley (1995)
7. Halsal, F.: Data Communications, Addison-Wesley (1995)
8. http://home.agh.edu.pl/~cyganek/DXC_Protocol.zip

9. Labrosse, J.J: Embedded Systems Building Blocks. R&D Books (2000)
10. RFC 3081: The Blocks Extensible Exchange Protocol Core (2001)
11. Stroustrup B.: The C++ Programming Language. Addison-Wesely (1998)
12. Taligent Inc.: Taligent's Guide to Designing Programs. Addison-Wesley (1994)
13. Yaghmour, K.: Building Embedded Linux Systems. O'Reilly (2003)
14. Vandervoorde D., Josuttis N.M.: C++ Templates. Addison Wesley (2003)
15. ZigBee Alliance: ZigBee Specification (2005)

A Link-Load Balanced Low Energy Mapping and Routing for NoC

ZhouWenbiao[1,2], ZhangYan[1], and MaoZhigang[2]

[1] Harbin Institute of Technology Shenzhen Graduate School, Shenzhen, China
[2] Harbin Institute of Technology Harbin, Harbin, China

Abstract. The paper presents a novel mapping and routing technique for the mesh based NoC design problem with an objective of minimizing the energy consumption and normalized worst link-load. The proposed algorithm is a particle swarm optimization (PSO) based two phases process, one is mapping core onto NoC, and another is the allocation of routing path. The proposed algorithm uses a novel representation for PSO particle. Experimental results show that the proposed technique can reduce the normalized worst link-load by 20% on average while guarantee a low energy consumption.

1 Introduction

New technologies allow many millions transistors integrated onto a single chip and thus the implementation of complex SoC that need special communication resources to handle very tight design requirement. System architecture design is shifting towards a more communication-centric methodology [1]. Meanwhile, with the chip size's growing, the global clock closure is also a problem. The Network-on-Chip [2,3], which plays a pivotal role in future SoCs, is one of a solution for these challenges. It integrates some heterogeneous resource (for example, CPU, ASIC, DSP, etc) in a homogeneous on chip network environment. The mapping and routing are two key steps for the NoC based system's design and implementation [4]. The whole design process of NoCs includes several processes, such as application decomposing, task assignment, topology selection, mapping IP cores onto title, and routing strategy. NoC design for a specific application offers an opportunity for optimizing the mapping of cores to different titles that act as the placeholder in the architecture, and the style of routing greatly affects the system performance and power consumption. For example, a specific application composed by a set of existing cores must be mapped onto the on-chip physical network structure, as shown in Fig.1, an application characteristic graph (APCG) that consists of 6 IP cores is mapped onto a 2x3 two-dimensional mesh NoC. Different mapping algorithms will map the IP cores onto various position. Meanwhile, after a core has been mapped the coordinate title, the next step is to determine how to route packets. In Fig.1, the core (a) is mapped onto title-1 and core (e) is mapped onto title-6, then the shortest routing path between core (a) and core (e) has three choices:$S1 \rightarrow S2 \rightarrow S3 \rightarrow S6$,$S1 \rightarrow S2 \rightarrow S5 \rightarrow S6$, $S1 \rightarrow S4 \rightarrow S5 \rightarrow S6$.The selection of routing path will greatly affect the link-load balance of system, and other performance parameter, such as the bandwidth, delay, jitter, and resource utilization.

Y.-H. Lee et al. (Eds.): ICESS 2007, LNCS 4523, pp. 59–66, 2007.

These lead us to find an optimized mapping position and select a custom routing path to satisfy the link-load-balance requirement of system while minimizing the NoC communication power consumption. The remainder of the paper is organized as follows.

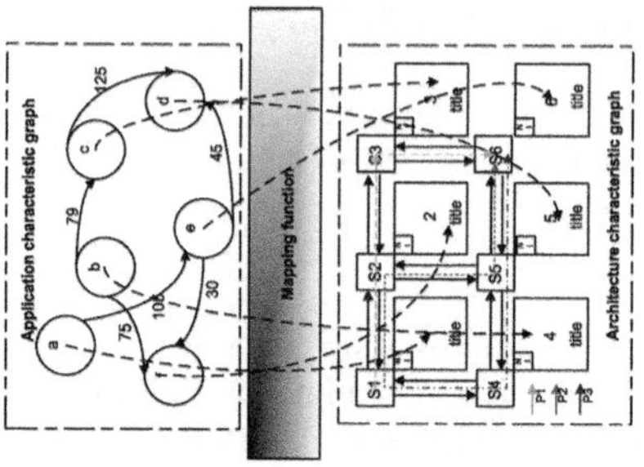

Fig. 1. A NOC mapping and routing allocation instance

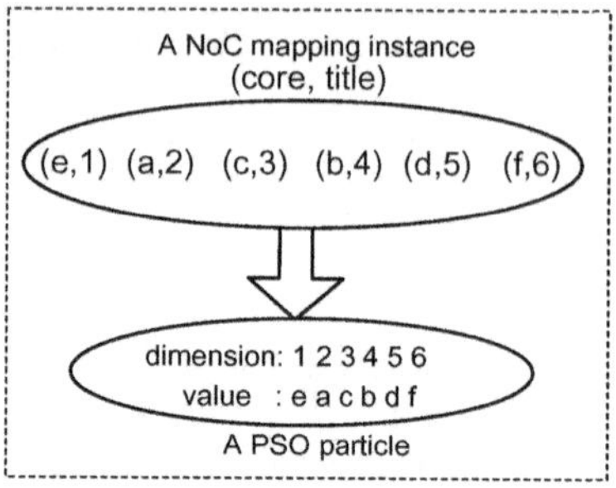

Fig. 2. particle of NoC mapping

Section 2 discusses previous work. Section 3 presents the formation of mapping and routing problem. Section 4 proposed our new technique for the mapping and routing problem. Section 5 is the experimental results and finally section 6 concludes the paper.

2 Previous Work

The design of regular NoC architecture has been proposed in [5,6]. In [7], Lei et al. proposed a two-step genetic algorithm that finds a mapping of cores onto NoC architecture such that the overall execution time is minimized, the first step is assigning the task onto different IP cores, and the second is mapping the IP cores onto the title of NoC. Krishnan Srinivasa et al. [8] utilized the GA for the custom NoC mapping process. And a BB algorithm is used to map cores onto a mesh-based NoC architecture and find a flexible routing path with the objective of minimizing energy and satisfying the bandwidth constraints [9]. In [10], an algorithm NMAP under different routing functions and bandwidth constraints is presented. Chan-Eun Rhee et al. [11] proposed a MILP algorithm for the many-to-many core-switch mapping for the NoC architecture with optimizing the power consumption.However, no methodologies can involve the design of link-load balance in the course of mapping and routing selection, and in this paper, we propose a PSO based design methodology to minimize the energy consumption of NoC while guaranteeing the balance of link-load.

3 Problem Formation

The NoC mapping problem is to determine how to topologically map the selected cores onto on chip network and select a routing path for different communication flows, such that certain metrics of performance are optimized. In our formulation, a periodic real-time application that already bounded and scheduled on a list of selected cores is characterized by an application characterization graph (APCG) $G(\mathbf{V}, E_C)$,it is a directed graph, where each vertex $v_i \in \mathbf{V}$represents a selected IP core, and each directed edge $e_{i,j} \in E_C$ models a communication flow between core v_i and core v_j. The edge weight $e_{i,j}$ is a 2-turples $v(e_{i,j}), w(e_{i,j})$ where $v(e_{i,j})$ denotes the information exchange volume between cores v_i and core v_j, $w(e_{i,j})$ indicates the bandwidth requirement. The communication volume, bandwidth requirement can be obtained through the set of concurrent tasks' performance and the respect deadline. In our paper, we assume that the value of $v(e_{i,j}), w(e_{i,j})$ has been computed in advance. The underling NoC is represented by an architecture characterization graph (ARCG) $G(T, L)$, it is also a directed graph, where each vertex $t_i \in \mathbf{T}$ represents one title in the architecture, and each directed edge $l_i \in \mathbf{L}$ represents a physical link, all links are assumed to have the same length and width B. A routing path $p(t_{v_i}, t_{v_j}) \in P$ indicates that map core v_i onto title i and core v_j onto title j, it is a set of several links $\{l_j, l_{j+1}, \ldots\}$, where P is a set of all routing path. In addition, for the same time, the link bandwidth cannot be processed by two or more communication flows. In our paper, we define the link-load function as follows:

$$U(l_j) = \sum_{\forall e_{i,j}} w(e_{i,j}) \times f(l_j, p(t_{v_i}, t_{v_j}) \tag{1}$$

where

$$f(l_j, p(t_{v_i}, t_{v_j})) = \begin{cases} 0 & l_j \in p(t_{v_i}, t_{v_j}) \\ 1 & l_j \notin p(t_{v_i}, t_{v_j}) \end{cases}$$

Moreover, we use the normalized worst link-load γ to evaluate the link-load-balance. For every core's mapping position MAP and its source and destination routing path P set, the normalized worst link-load γ:

$$\gamma(MAP, P) = \frac{\max\limits_{\forall i \in L} U(l_i)}{2WNK_m} \tag{2}$$

Where the denominator in the Eq.(2) is the bisection bandwidth of 2D mesh NoC, W is the link bandwidth,N is the node number of NoC, and the k_m is the max radix of 2D mesh.And we defined the energy consumption as follows. For the whole application, the energy consumption $Energy_{E_c}$:

$$Energy_{E_C} = \sum_{e_{i,j} \in E_C} v(e_{i,j}) \times \{(|p(t_{v_i}, t_{v_j})| + 1) \times E_R + (|p(t_{v_i}, t_{v_j})|) \times E_L\} \tag{3}$$

Where $|p(t_{v_i}, t_{v_j})|$ is the hop of path $p(t_{v_i}, t_{v_j})$, and E_R is the energy consumption of single router,E_L is the energy consumption of one link. After given above the definition, the objective of the NoC mapping and routing is as follows: 'Finding a mapping instance MAP and a set of routing path P, such that total energy consumption of the whole NoC (not include the IP core's energy consumption) is minimized and the value of $\gamma(MAP, P)$ is minimized'

That is:

$$\min\{Energy(MAP)\} \quad \text{and} \quad \min\{\gamma(MAP, P)\} \tag{4}$$

Such that:

$$\forall v_i \in \mathbf{V}, \qquad MAP(v_i) \in T \tag{5}$$

$$\forall v_i \neq v_i \in \mathbf{V}, \qquad MAP(v_i) \neq MAP(v_i) \tag{6}$$

$$\forall link\ l_k, W \geq \sum b(v_{i,j}) \times f(l_k, p(t_{v_i}, t_{v_j})) \tag{7}$$

4 Particle Swarm Optimization and NoC Mapping Problem

The mapping IP cores onto NoC architecture is a NP problem [9]. Our attempt is to try to develop an algorithm that can give near optimal results within the reasonable time, or, an algorithm with the best trade-off between result quality and computation time. Particle Swarm Optimization (PSO) has shown the potential to achieve this dual goal quite well [12,13]. We have developed a two-phase PSO based algorithm for NoC mapping problem. This section presents the process for the PSO based load balance mapping and routing in NoC architecture, therefore called PLBMR. PLBMR is a two-phase particle optimization algorithm. In the first phase, we use the PSO to map IP core onto the title on the NoC architecture to minimize the energy consumption, and the second phase is to find all routing path for every mapping pair to satisfy the link-load balance.

4.1 PLBMR Phase 1-Mapping Core onto Title

Particle Swarm Optimization. PSO is an algorithm proposed by Kennedy and Eberhart in 1995 [12].Kennedy and Eberhart explore several models to manipulate these factors to accurately resemble the dynamic of the social behavior of birds, before reaching to the following equations that amazingly achieve good performance on optimization problems [14]:

$$V_{id} = v_{id} \times (p_{id} - x_{id}) + c_2 \times Rand() \times (p_{gd} - x_{id}) \tag{8}$$

$$X_{id} = X_{id} + V_{id} \tag{9}$$

Eq.(9) is used to calculate the particle's new velocity according to its previous velocity and to the distances of its current position from both its own best historical position and its neighbors' best position. Then the particle flies toward a new position according to Eq.(10). The performance of each particle is measured according to a pre-defined fitness function, which is usually proportional to the cost function associated with the problem. This process is repeated until user-defined stopping criteria are satisfied. Two versions of PSO exist, gbest and lbest. T he difference is in the neighborhood topology used to exchange experience among particles. In the gbest model, the neighborhood of the particle is the whole swarm . In the lbest model, a swarm is divided into overlapping neighborhoods of particles. This best particle is called the neighborhood best particle. Next, we present a gbest-model PSO algorithm for the problem at-hand: NoC mapping problem.

Core Mapping's Particle Encoding Solution. Because NoC mapping has the constraint that different IP core cannot be mapped the same title, some randomly generated particle will violate the constraint. In order to represent a particle containing the mapping of N IP cores onto $2D$ mesh to satisfy the constraint, a convenient particle representation scheme is suggested here. Assuming the mapped $2D$ mesh NoC is represented by $1D$ array by using a left to right scan performing in a top-to-down fashion. This way an N-elements string of integers represents N different IP cores. In the proposed representation, at the ith position from the left of the string, an integer between 1 and i is allowed. The string is decoded to obtain the mapping as follows. The ith position denotes the mapping of IP cores i in the permutation. The decoding starts from the leftmost position and proceeds serially toward the right. While decoding the ith position, the first $i - 1$ IP cores are already mapped, thereby providing with the i placeholders to position the ith IP core. This decoding procedure is illustrated with an example having 6 IP cores $(a{\sim}f)$ to be mapped onto a 2×3 $2D$ mesh: $\{1 \quad 2 \quad 1 \quad 3 \quad 3 \quad 6\}$. In the above coding, the first integer is used to map a; the second integer is used to map b, and so on. All solutions will have a 1 in the first position. The coding actually starts from the second integer. The second IP cores b can be mapped onto two places:1)Before the IP core a;2)After the IP core a. The first case is represented by a value '1' and the second case is represented by a value '2'. Since the second integer is '2' in the above string, the IP core 'b' appears after the IP core 'a'. Similarly, with the first two IP cores mapped as $(a \ b)$, there are three placeholders for the IP core 'c':1) Before a (with a value 1);2) Between a and b (with a value 2);3) After b (with a value 3). Since the string has a value $'1'$ in the third place, the IP core is mapped before a, thereby constructing a partial mapping. Continuing in this fashion, the following permutation of the six alphabets is obtained:$\{c \quad a \quad e \quad d \quad b \quad f\}$. Next, this $1{-}D$ permutation is converted into 2×3 2D Mesh of alphabets representing components, as Utilizing this representing scheme for the particle, it can easily deal with the violated particle after update the particle velocity.

Data flow	a→e	b→c	b→f	c→d	e→d	e→f
Particle 1	0 0 1	1 0 0	0 1	0 1	0	1 0
Particle 2	0 1 0	1 0 0	0 1	0 1	0	1 0
Particle 3	0 0 1	0 0 1	1 0	0 1	0	1 0

Fig. 3. PSO particles of routing path

PSO Optimization for Core Mapping Problem. In our mapping IP cores onto NoC phase, we setup a search space of M dimension for an M cores mapping problem. Each dimension has a discrete set of possible values limited to $s = \{T_i : 1 \leq i \leq N\}(M \leq N)$; such that N is the number of titles in the NoC system under consideration. For example, consider the problem to map 6 cores in Fig.1 onto a 2×3 $2D$ NoC architecture. Fig.2 shows an instance between possible mappings to a particle position coordinates in the PSO domain. Using such particle representation, the PSO population is represented as a $P \times M$ two-dimensional array consisting of N particles, each represented as a vector of M cores. Thus, a particle flies in an M-dimensional search space. A core is internally represented as an integer value indicating the title number to which this core is mapped to during the course of PSO. Also, the minimum routing algorithm is used, but we still don't obtain the information which links the routing path contains, therefore, the bandwidth constraints is not considered in the PLBMR phase-1, and we only minimize the energy consumption. In the followed phase, we minimize the value of Eq.(2) while considering the link bandwidth constraints.

4.2 PLBMR Phase 2-Routing Path Selection

In the first phase of PLBMR, a core mapping position with minimizing the NoC power consumption is obtained. In the second phase of PLBMR, we aim to allocate a proper routing path for every communication flows, the purpose is to make a link-load balance of NoC with satisfying the link bandwidth constraints. Because the minimum-path routing algorithm is used, the IP core's mapping position determines the unique routing path length. As shown in Fig.1, IP core 'a' is mapped onto title '1', and IP core 'e' is mapped onto title '6', then the hop number of communication flow between 'a' and 'e' is fixed. We randomly allocate any path among the three paths, and the number of hop is 3. In our NoC, the routing information is represented by a binary number. Each bit of the binary number represents routing direction, i.e. bits '1' and '0' correspond to move along the X-direction and Y-direction respectively. The hop number between source tile and destination title determines the bit number of routing information, i.e. the three routing path $P1$, $P2$, $P3$ between 'a' and 'e' is respectively $\{0\ \ 0\ \ 1\}$, $\{0\ \ 1\ \ 0\}$, $\{1\ \ 0\ \ 0\}$.

Routing Path's Particle Encoding Solution. The particle of routing path in the PLBMR is represented by one-dimensional arrays of binary numbers. Each binary array represents one combination of all communication routing path set P in the APCG. For example, Fig.3 shows three particles of communication flow in the APCG which is shown in Fig. 1. The particle's representing way is shown in Fig.3. For example, the communication flow $\{(a\rightarrow e),(b\rightarrow c),(b\rightarrow f),(c\rightarrow d),(e\rightarrow d),(e\rightarrow f)\}$ routing path in particle '1' is respectively $\{0\ \ 0\ \ 1\ \ 1\ \ 0\ \ 0\ \ 0\ \ 1\ \ 0\ \ 1\ \ 0\}$. By representing the particle with this method, we can effectively generate the initial population size of PSO algorithm. However, the number of '1' and '0' is restricted for every communication flow. When the X-hop and the Y-hop of a communication flow are 'n' and 'm' respectively, the randomly generated binary numbers must assure 'n'-number of $1s$ and 'm'-number of $0s$. Thus, this method generates the combination of all communication flow's binary number, which forms a valid particle.

PSO Optimization for Routing Path Selection. After having the particle, the PSO based routing path allocating process is almost the same as the phase '1'. Because of the space limitation, we don't list the algorithm code. In the course of the position updating, the new particle's values will not be a binary number, it violates the routing path representing principle. Therefore, in the algorithm, we must round these numbers to the '0' or '1'; the greater value is rounded to the binary value '1' according with a communication flow's Y-distance. The effects of converting from real number to binary number should be determined further.

5 Experimental Results

We first compute the model parameters that used to evaluate the energy consumption. Assuming $0.18um$ technology and the link length between two switches is $2mm$, the

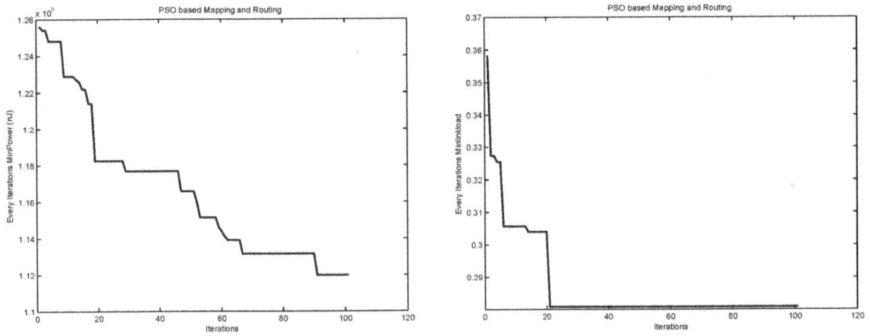

(a) Phase One (b) Phase Two

Fig. 4. PLBMR Optimization for 6×6 NoC

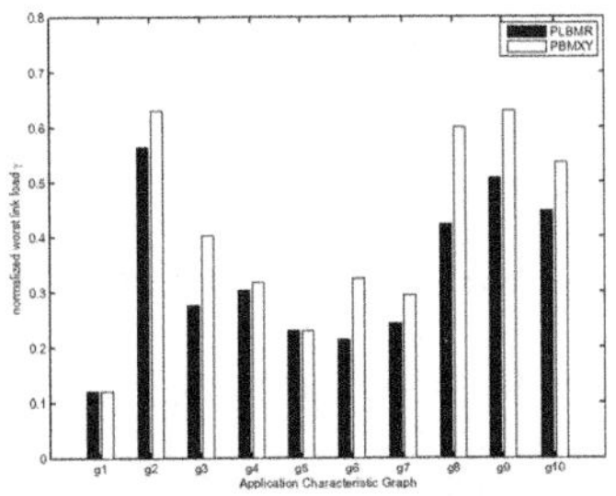

Fig. 5. Performance comparisons between PLBMR and PMXY

	Energy(nJ)			NormalWorstLoad		
	PLBMR	BnB	MOCA	PLBMR	BnB	MOCA
G0	54.56	54.56	54.56	0.120	0.120	0.120
G1	256.7	255.2	285.7	0.564	0.587	0.634
G2	156.7	156.5	176.8	0.276	0.395	0.403
G3	189.6	178.7	198.3	0.303	0.323	0.346
G4	168.2	156.1	180.9	0.230	0.296	0.305
G5	130.8	112.9	140.2	0.214	0.325	0.387
G6	178.5	160.4	189.6	0.243	0.356	0.402
G7	567.6	530.2	599.5	0.422	0.576	0.600
G8	356.7	349.2	390.6	0.507	0.613	0.634
G9	367.5	350.1	399.7	0.448	0.568	0.597
G10	298.9	278.2	321.0	0.345	0.456	0.499

Fig. 6. Comparsion of BnB, MOCA and PLBMR

capacitance of a wire is $0.56Ff/um$, the voltage swing is $3.3v$, then the energy consumption of the link is $6.115pJ$, and the bit energy value of 6×6 switches is $0.56pJ$. Given the bit-energy values and the mapping optimization results, the energy consumed in the NoC architecture can be obtained. At the same time, a minimum-path routing is used in the $2D$ mesh NoC and we assume the maximum link bandwidth of NoC is $1000Mb/s$. We started by estimating the efficiency of the PLBMR optimization algorithm. For our experimental, we generated random application characteristic graph. Fig.4 respectively shows the PLBMR algorithm optimization process for the 6×6 NoC.Fig.4(a) and Fig.4(b) shows the energy consumption and link-balance optimization process for 6×6 NoC. In order to show the impact of PLBMR algorithm for the link-load balance, we compare the PLBMR with the PSO based mapping algorithm for XY dimensional routing (we denote it as the PBMXY). We generated random application characteristic graph $g1$ to $g10$ for different parameter. Fig.5 shows the comparison results.

We also compared PLBMR algorithm with previous algorithm that related with path allocation: Hu's BnB [9] and Krishnan's MOCA [12]. For MOCA, we only consider no latency constraints. Table 3 presents the comparison of PLBMR with BnB and MOCA for g1 to g10 random APCG. As is shown in the table, the energy consumption has low discrepancies, but for the normalized worst link-load, PLBMR performed within 9% of MOCA, and 7% of BnB. Moreover, for a NoC with 36 node, our algorithm's running time is only 7 minutes with Pentium 4 $2.0G$ and $256M$ memory machine.

6 Conclusion

A novel PSO based heuristic algorithm called PLBMR is proposed for the design of link-load balance and low energy mesh based NoC architecture. We use particle swarm optimization algorithm to explore the large search space of NoC design effectively. The proposed algorithm optimizes the NoC energy consumption in the IP mapping phase, and guarantee the link-load balance in the routing path-allocating phase. The performance of PLBMR is evaluated in comparison with other proposed mapping and routing algorithm BnB and MOCA for a number of randomly generated applications.

References

1. A. Jantsch, H. Tenhunen,: Nonlinear oscillations and Network on Chip. Kluwer. (2003)
2. Luca. Benini, G.D.Micheli,: Networks on Chips: A New SoC Paradigm. IEEE Computer **1** (2002) 70-78
3. P. Wielage, K. Goossens: Networks on silicon: Blessing or Nightmare?. DSD'02, Dortmund, Germany, (2002) 196
4. U. Y. Ogras, J. Hu, and R. Marculescu: Key Research Problems in NoC Design: A Holistic Perspective. CODES+ISSS'05, Jersey City, NJ, (2005) 69-74
5. W. J. Dally ,B. Towles: Route Packets, Not Wires: On-Chip Interconnection Networks. DAC'01, (2001) 69-74
6. S. Kumar, A. Jantsch: A Network on Chip Architecture and Design Methodology. VLSI'02, (2002) 105-112
7. Tang Lei, Shashi Kumar: A Two Genetic Algorithm for Mapping Task Graphs to a Network on Chip Architecture. Antalya, Turkey, (2003) 180-187.
8. Krishnan Srinivasa, Karam and S. Chatha: ISIS: A Genetic Algorithm. based Technique for Custom On-Chip Interconnection Network Synthesis. VLSID'05, Kolkata, India, (2005) 623-628
9. J.Hu, R. Marculescu: Exploiting the Routing Flexibility for Energy/Performance Aware Mapping of Regular NoC architecture. DAT'03, (2003) 10688-10693
10. S. Murali, G. De Micheli: Bandwidth-constrained mapping of cores onto NoC architectures. DATE'04,Paris,France, (2004) 896-901.
11. Chan-Eun Rhee, Han-You Jeong, Soonhoi Ha: Many-to-Many Core-Switch Mapping in 2-D Mesh NoC Architectures. ICCD'04, San Jose, CA, USA, (2004) 438-443
12. J. Kennedy, R.C. Eberhart: Particle swarm optimization. ICNN, (1995) 1942-1948.
13. Y. Shi, R. Eberhart: Empirical Study of Particle Swarm Optimization. CEC'99, Washington, DC, USA, (1999) 1945-1950

Scheduling for Combining Traffic of On-Chip Trace Data in Embedded Multi-core Processor

Xiao Hu, Pengyong Ma, and Shuming Chen

School of Computer, National University of Defense Technology,
Changsha, Hunan, P.R. of China, 410073
xiaohu@nudt.edu.cn

Abstract. On-chip trace data contains run-time information of embedded multi-core processors for software debug. Trace data are transferred through special data path and output pins. Scheduling for combining the traffic of multi-source trace data is one of key issues that affect performance of the on-chip trace system. By analyzing features of trace traffic combination, a lazy scheduling algorithm based on the service threshold and the minimum service granularity is proposed. The queue length distribution is constrained by configurable service threshold of each queue, and switching overheads are reduced by lazy scheduling and configurable minimum service granularity. Two metrics of buffer utilizations on overflowing are presented to evaluate the efficacy of queue priority assignment. Simulation results show that the algorithm controls the overflow rate of each queue effectively and utilizes the buffer capacity according to the queues priority assigned sufficiently. The algorithm is realized in Verilog-HDL. Comparing with a leading method, the overflow rate is reduced 30% with additional 2,015um^2 in area.

1 Introduction

With widely use of SoC (System-on-Chip) and cache in embedded systems, the on-chip data and instructions are hard to be captured by out-chip instruments for debug. The real-time visibility of embedded processors has to be solved by additional silicon area [9]. The leading vendors of embedded processor cores provide on-chip solutions [1][2][4][5]. The IEEE-ISTO NEXUS 5001 STD also includes protocols to support on-chip trace [6]. The on-chip trace system non-intrusively records real-time information such as program path and data access by special hardware. These information are compressed to trace data and transferred to the Debug Host PC through special data path, output port and the out-chip emulator. The software tools in the host PC decompress trace data and recover run-time information for debug and optimization.

YHFT-QDSP is a multi-core processor with one RISC core and four DSP cores of YHFT-DSP/700[8]. To support real-time visibility of DSP cores for debug and optimization, an on-chip trace system named TraceDo (Trace for Debug and Optimization) is designed, as shown in Fig. 1. Trace data of each DSP core is buffered in its Trace Module and transferred to Trace Port by Trace Bus Arbitrator.

To reduce pins used, only one output port is used by on-chip trace system currently. The data path of the port is often 4bits~16bits currently. The output port is

Y.-H. Lee et al. (Eds.): ICESS 2007, LNCS 4523, pp. 67–79, 2007.

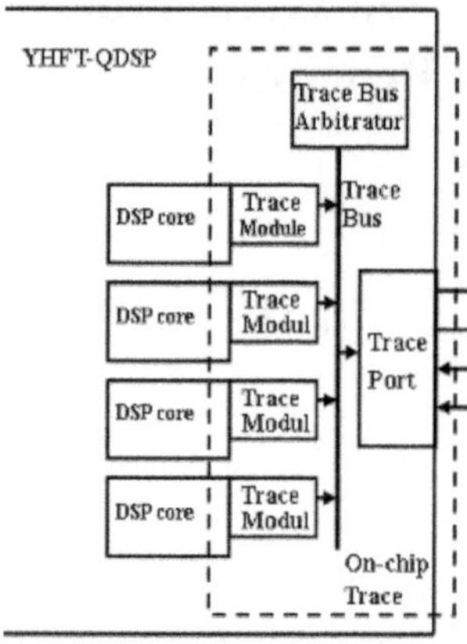

Fig. 1. Structure of the on-chip trace system in YHFT-QDSP (TraceDo)

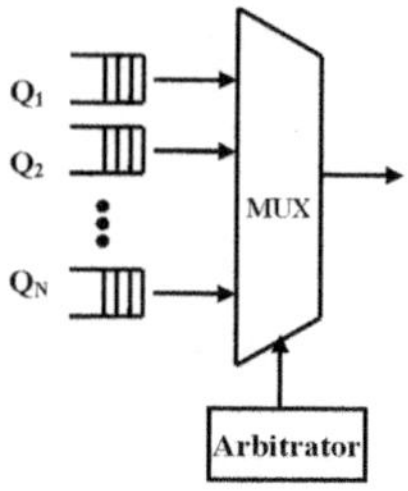

Fig. 2. Scheduling system for trace data combination

the bottleneck and an on-chip buffer is required for trace data traffic. For multi-source trace data in a multi-core trace system, a scheduling algorithm is required to combine trace data from multiple queue buffers to single output port.

Features of trace traffic combination, evaluation metrics and scheduling schemes are analyzed in this paper. A novel queue scheduling algorithm (TraceDo algorithm) with Service Require Threshold (SRH) and Minimum Service Granularity (MSG) is presented. Setting a SRH to each queue, queue switching is controlled by the comparing the queue length with the threshold level of SRH. Users can control queue length distributions and overflow rates according to overflow costs, buffer capacities and burst characteristics of trace traffic. Using MSG and Lazy Switching together, the minimum number of consumers served in a queue between two switchovers is promised and such service granularity will be increased when other queues have marginal capacity of buffer. Therefore switchover counts are reduced and overflow probabilities along with such gains are constrained by SRH. Simulation results show TraceDo algorithm can control queue length distributions effectively and reduce overflows of one buffer by utilizing other buffers sufficiently. The hardware realization of the algorithm meets timing constraints with reasonable area cost.

The remainder of this paper is organized as follows. Section 2 introduces background and related works. This is followed in Section 3 by describing the scheduling method. Section 4 discusses the realization in VLSI. Section 5 presents experimental results of benchmark programs. Section 6 concludes the paper.

2 Background and Related Works

The scheduling features for combining traffics of on-chip trace data from multiple cores are listed:

- Overflow Rate First

  The trace system records real-time information of processors, trace data will be lost when buffer overflows. Therefore, the overflow rate should be considered firstly. Constrained by cost and power, the size of on-chip trace buffer is less than one hundred bytes currently. The data volume of each transfer is within dozens of bytes. Therefore the relatively limited transfer delay can be ignored.

- Configurable Priority
  The service priority of trace buffers should be configurable because of different overflow costs, different buffer capacities and different burst characteristics of trace traffic. Capacity of buffer is fixed at the time of designing hardware by estimating the applications traffic. Characteristics of trace traffic are fixed at the time of developing software. Overflow costs are also known before program runs. Therefore users can tune buffer performance influenced by above three factors by configuring the service priority of each queue buffer before running program each time.
- Switchover Time
  For identifying the source of trace data after combination, an ID of each trace source should be inserted when queue switching. The IDs reduce the bandwidth of Trace Port for trace data and increase out-chip overheads of transfer and storage. The approach of reducing ID costs is to decrease queue switchover counts and increase the volume of consumers served at a switching interval. But such approach also increases the waiting time of other queues for getting service, and so the probability of overflow increases.
- Area and Timing Constraints
  The scheduling algorithm is realized by hardware, the strict constraints of silicon area and computing cycles require the algorithm should be simple and efficient.

The problem of trace scheduling in this paper is, in a multi-queue system with single server as shown in Fig. 2, to design a scheduling algorithm with reasonable cost that can reduce buffer overflows with configurable service priority, and make a good tradeoff between queue switchover counts and the probability of buffer overflow.

All on-chip trace systems that support multicores or multipipelines have to solve the same problem as TraceDo: how to combine trace data from multiple buffers to a single output port. ARC never reveals architecture details of its trace system [1], PDtrace [4] and Freescale's solutions [5] do not describe their scheduling methods, and neither configuration about scheduling in their program models can be found.

CoreSight of ARM is the leading solution of multi-core trace [3]. The module of Trace Funnel in CoreSight disposes trace scheduling. The scheduling scheme used in CoreSight is named as Funnel algorithm in this paper. It assigned different priority to each queue and a shared minimum service granularity[1] (MSG) to all queues. Both the priorities and MSG can be configured by users. Funnel is an exhaustive service system with non-preemptive priority. After serving the current queue with the MSG volume of customers, the server switches to the non-empty queue with higher priority if such queue exists. If such queue does not exist, the server keeps on serving the current queue until it is empty, and then the server switches to next non-empty queue with lower priority. This method has low hardware costs, but the exhaustive service

[1] It is called HTC in CoreSight, HoldTimeCycle.

policy often brings such condition that the buffers of high-priority queues are not utilized sufficiently while the lowest-priority queue overflows seriously. This is confirmed by experiments in section 5.2.1.

Trace scheduling system is a polling system [10]. Exhaustive service, gated service and limited service are three basic service policies. In LBF algorithm [11], the highest priority is given to the queue with max normalized queue length (the ratio of queue length to buffer capacity), but division operations for normalization increase hardware costs and comparing operations of all queues decrease the scalability. There are neither configurable priorities nor switchover times in LBF. Queues with different priorities are served in different probabilities [12], but generating random numbers and related operations require high hardware costs. Lackman uses the most similar method to this paper [13]. High priority is given to real-time traffic unless the queue length of non-real-time traffic is over a threshold. Lackman's method does not give a threshold to each queue and switchover time is not considered.

3 Algorithm

Definitions and explanations.

N: the number of queues in the scheduling system
Q_i: the ith queue
L_i: buffer capacity of Q_i
t: the system time, cycle unit of the processor clock
$b_i(t)$: queue length of Q_i at time t
$a_i(t)$: normalized queue length of Q_i at time t, $a_i(t) = b_i(t)/L_i$
A customer: one byte of trace data
Current queue: the queue on serving
Queue service time: the total serving time between two switchovers for a queue
Service granularity: the number of all customers served in a queue service time
ServCnt: the number of customers that have been served in current queue service time
Overflow Rate: the ratio of rejected customers to arriving customers
Overflowing Time: the time when overflow of any queue occurs

Trace buffers dose not overflow frequently, therefore average queue length is not a good metric for buffer utilizations when bandwidth is limited. A new metric named Overflow Buffer Utilization (OFBU) is present:

(1) Overflow Buffer Utilization of Q_i (OFBU_Q_i): average of $a_i(t)$, t includes all Overflowing Time. This metric gives the validity of queue priority assignment. Low value of this metric means high priority.
(2) Overflow Buffer Utilization of all queues (OFBU_All): average of all OFBU_Q_i. This metric gives the utilizations of all buffers by scheduling algorithms.

A lazy scheduling algorithm with Service Require Threshold and Minimum Service Granularity (TraceDo algorithm) is presented, as shown in Fig. 3 and Fig. 4.

Configurations:

SRH: Service Require Threshold of each queue
MSG: Minimum Service Granularity, shared by all queues
Order Priority: each queue is assigned to a priority, and no queues share the same priority

State definitions of each queue:

SRH_State: $b>SRH$, not on serving
Accu_State: $SRH \geq b>0$, not on serving
Null_State: $b = 0$, not on serving
MSG_State: $MSG \geq ServCnt>0$, on serving
Lazy_State: $ServCnt>MSG$, on serving

Switching Policies:

Lazy Switch: switching is permitted only when current queue is in **Lazy_State** and there is another queue in **SRH_State**, or the current queue is served to be its **Null_State**.

Order Priority arbitration: when switching, the queue to be served is selected according to Order Priority when multiple queues are in **SRH_States** or none of them is in **SRH_State**. The latter condition only occurs when current queue go to **Null_State**.

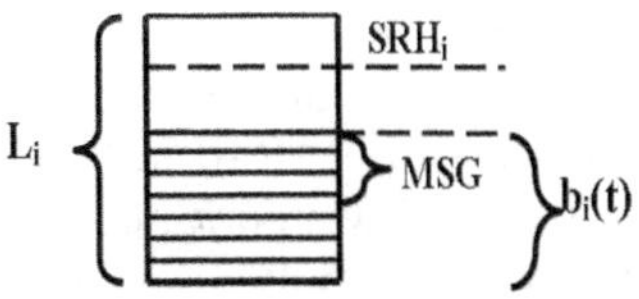

Fig. 3. Logical structure of Q_i. L_i is capacity of buffer. $b_i(t)$ is queue length at t time. SRH_i is the service require threshold. MSG is the minimum service granularity. Above parameters are in byte units

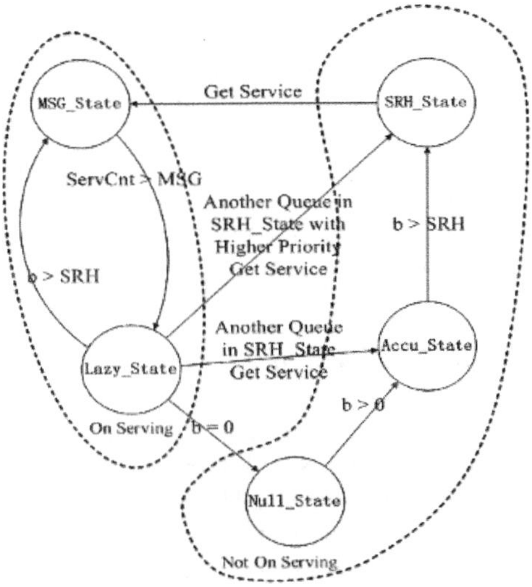

Fig. 4. States graph of a queue in TraceDo algorithm

Frequently switchings are avoided by setting MSG when several queue lengths are around their SRHs. The service granularity of the queue on serving is increased by Lazy Switch when other queues have marginal capacity of buffer. Above two approaches achieve a good trade off between switching and overflows. SRH acts as the actual assignments of the queue priority. SRH defines that a queue should be served imperatively when its length over the threshold level. Two type queues should be set to lower value of SRH: one is queues with high overflow costs; another is queues with small buffer leading to high overflow probabilities. TraceDo algorithm is equivalent to Funnel algorithm when all SRHs are set to zeros.

Similar to Funnel algorithm, Order Priority has to be assigned to each queue even if all queues should be served without priority difference factually. Experiments show, overflows will concentrate to the queue with lowest Order Priority when buffers of all queues are exhausted. Such circumstances about queues with factual same priority can be avoided by polling or random switching, however high hardware costs come from the configuration complexities of all potential priorities. Furthermore, there is even no harm for overflow concentrations among queues with same priority. Assigning a different MSG for each queue does not improve performance much except for the queue with lowest Order Priority discussed above.

4 Realization in VLSI

TraceDo algorithm and Funnel algorithm are realized by Verilog-HDL. There are four queues and the capacity of each queue buffer is 64 Bytes. Fine-tuning of SHR does not improve performance, so a 4-bit register is used for SRH and it is compared with only highest 4-bits of queue length. Such approach reduces half of hardware costs of SRH registers and comparators. A shared MSG register uses 4 bits, the same as that of Funnel.

Synthesized using standard cells in 0.18um CMOS process, the area of TraceDo algorithm is 3,844um^2 and the longest path is 1.82ns. Comparing with Funnel algorithm (1,829um^2), the additional area (2,015um^2) comes from SRH registers and comparators. The area is acceptable because the additional area for scheduling is less than 1% of all buffer area[2]. TraceDo algorithm has good scalability: the number of queues (*N*) hardly affects the critical path delay and area complexity is *O(N)*.

5 Evaluation

In this section, TraceDo algorithm and Funnel algorithm are evaluated by queue length distributions and queue switchover counts. Various configurations of SRH and MSG are sued in tests. Then Overflow Rate and Overflow Buffer Utilization (OFBU) with best configurations of the above two algorithms and LBF-w algorithm are tested. The results show TraceDo algorithm can reduce overflows efficiently.

5.1 Environments

For efficiency of testing and analyzing experimental results, emulation models of four queues and three algorithms (TraceDo, Funnel and LBF-w) are made by MATLAB

[2] The capacity of one buffer (FIFO structure) is 64 Bytes. All area of four buffers is 233,472um^2.

tools [14]. Each queue has a coefficient Qwi in LBF-w and the queue with max (ai(t)×Qwi) is always served at t time.

The trace traffic is related with program behaviors and compression methods of trace data, therefore benchmark programs are used to evaluate performance. Benchmarks include eight programs (e.g., MP3 decoder, Mpeg4 decoder, Mpeg4 encoder, jpeg encoder, FFT and LPC etc.) of YHFT-QDSP. When simulating the RTL (Register-Transfer Level) model of YHFT-QDSP by a simulation tool, trace data generated by TraceDo are recorded into Trace Files. Trace Files are the input traffic of emulation models.

5.2 Evaluate Configurations with Queue Length Distributions

Four tests are designed to evaluate the influence of SRH and MSG to the queue length distribution, and each test has three configurations, as listed in Table 1. Infinite buffer are used in this section for the convenience of queue length distribution. The switchover time is not considered in section 5.2 for isolating the influence of SRH and MSG, except the section 5.2.4. Results of experiments include $b_i(t)$, $D_i(b)$ and $AD_i(L_0)$. $D_i(b)$ is the distribution of $b_i(t)$. $AD_i(L_0)$ is the accumulation of $D_i(b)$:

Table 1. Configurations in experiments, all Byte units. From left to right in the table, four tests are MSG_F (MSG in Funnel), SRH with uniform priority, SRH with ununiform priority and MSG_T (MSG in TraceDo).

	Funnel: MSG_F	TraceDo: $SRH_1/SRH_2/SRH_3/SRH_4/MSG_T$ Uni-Priority	Priority	MSG_T
Config1	**14×4**	**56/56/56/56/**2×4	24/**56**/56/56/2×4	32/32/32/32/**7×4**
Config2	**7×4**	**32/32/32/32/**2×4	24/**16**/56/56/2×4	32/32/32/32/**4×4**
Config3	**2×4**	**16/16/16/16/**2×4	24/**8**/56/56/2×4	32/32/32/32/**1×4**

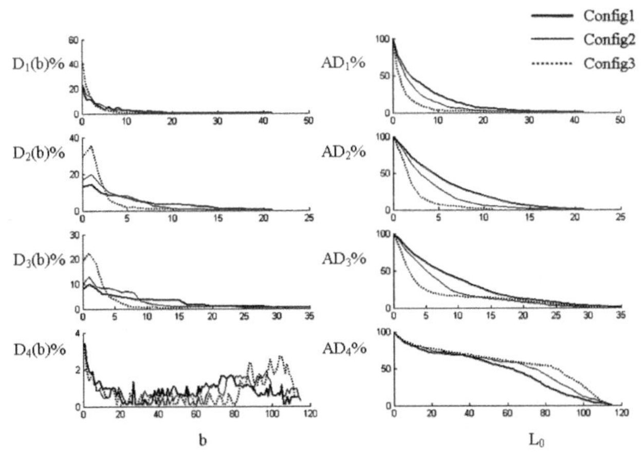

Fig. 5. $D_i(b)$ and $AD_i(L_0)$ in Funnel, in percentage

$AD_i(L_0)=\sum_{b=L_0}^{+\infty} D_i(b)$. A section with 80000 cycles in the Trace File of the jpeg benchmark is used in this section. The Order Priorities of four queues in TraceDo and Funnel are both set to 1234 (from high priority to low priority).

5.2.1 MSG_F in Funnel

There are sixteen configurations (*1×4~16×4*) supported by MSG_F, and three of them are tested and shown in Fig. 5. The results show the adjustability of MSG_F is limited. Q_1 is served sufficiently and the queue length of Q_4 is always large. When the Order Priority changes to 4123, the queue length distribution of Q_3 is the same as the original distribution of Q_4. The queue buffers with high priorities are unable to be utilized sufficiently. Increasing buffers of Q_1~Q_3 can not improves the overflow of Q_4 and increasing MSG_F improves weakly. Such scheduling is not fair for queues with factual uniform priority.

5.2.2 SRH in Uni-Priority

Assigning uniform priority to all queues in TraceDo by setting uniform values of SRHs, the curves of $D_i(b)$ and $AD_i(L_0)$ are shown in Fig. 6. The results of Config1 and Config2 show that queue length distribution has a cut-off at the threshold of SRH. When the SRH is so small in Config3 that the burst data is unable to be buffered under the threshold, TraceDo algorithm tries to satisfy high-priority queues firstly. Therefore overflow of buffer is tuned by SRH that controls the cut-off region of $D_i(b)$ and $AD_i(L_0)$.

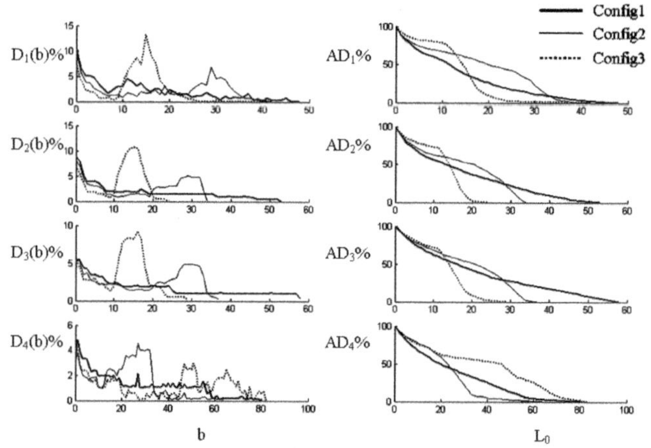

Fig. 6. $D_i(b)$ and $AD_i(L_0)$ in TraceDo, the test of Uni-Priority

5.2.3 SRH in Priority

By configurating different SRHs in this test, Q_1 is given the high priority, Q_3 and Q_4 are always given the low priorities, and the priority of Q_2 is changed from low to high, as shown in Table 1. When SRH_2 decreases, there are no visible changes on other queues'

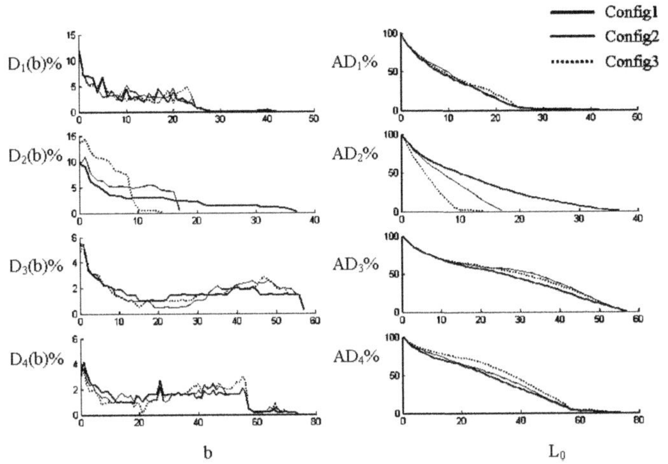

Fig. 7. $D_i(b)$ and $AD_i(L_0)$ in TraceDo, the test of Priority

distributions that over thresholds of SRHs. While the buffer under the threshold of SRH of each other queues is utilized more sufficiently, as shown in Fig. 7. Therefore a queue's priority is able to be changed independently in TraceDo algorithm and it does not worsen other queues' distributions to a certain extent.

5.2.4 MSG_T in TraceDo

When decreasing the service granularity that is connected with MSG_T tightly, switchover counts increase and queue length distributions decrease more sharply at thresholds of SRHs, as shown in Fig. 8.

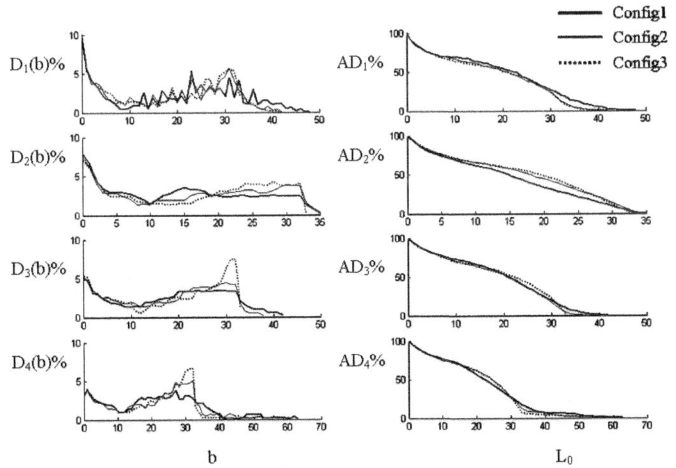

Fig. 8. Di(b) and ADi(L0) in TraceDo, the test of MSGT, no ID overheads

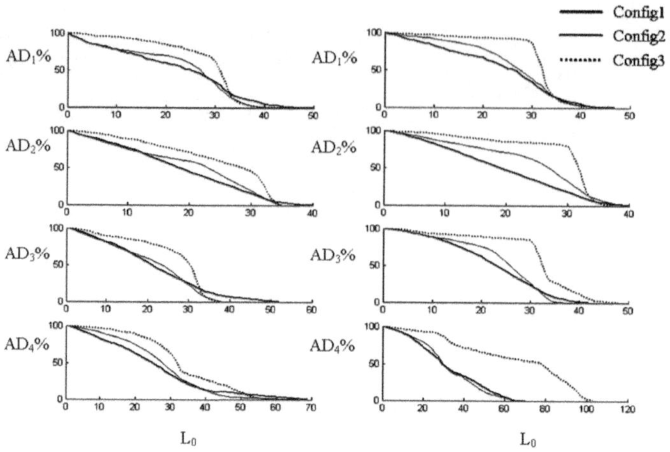

Fig. 9. $AD_i(L_0)$ in TraceDo, the test of MSG_T. ID_overhead is 0.5 Byte (left) and 1 Byte (right).

Considering switchover time, a queue ID inserted by Trace Bus Arbitrator consumes ID_Overhead bytes. Curves of $AD_i(L_0)$ are shown in Fig. 9 when ID_Overhead is set to 0.5 Byte and 1 Byte separately. The results show that TraceDo algorithm works well with switchover time. Small MSG_T increases traffic with more queue IDs and worsens queue length distributions greatly.

5.2.5 Queue Switchover Counts

Without the influence of switchover time, the queue switchover counts are shown in Fig. 10. MSGs of three Configs are listed in Table 1. Lazy Switch and SRH used in TraceDo algorithm much reduced queue switchover counts, especially when setting small MSGs.

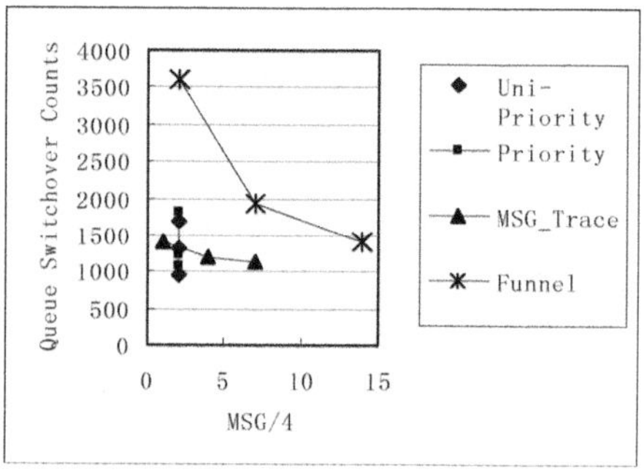

Fig. 10. Queue switchover counts

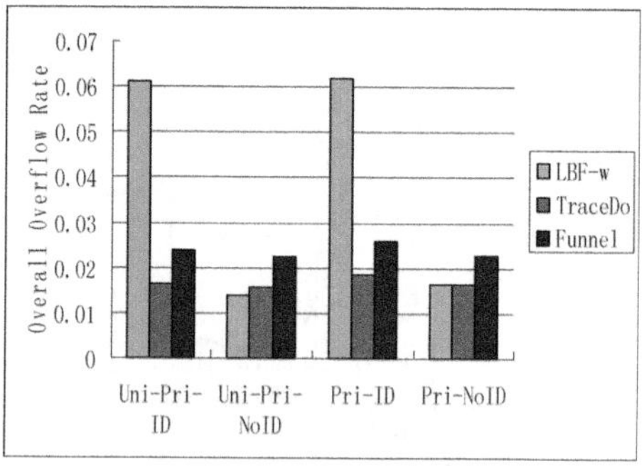

Fig. 11. Overall Overflow Rate

5.3 Evaluation of Overflow Rate

Overall Overflow Rate is the ratio of rejected customers of all queues and arriving customers of all queues, but not the average of the Overflow Rate of each queue. To evaluate Overall Overflow Rate and Overflow Buffer Utilization (OFBU) of the three algorithms (LBF-w, TraceDo and Funnel), finite buffers and random sections of Trace Files are used. For each algorithm, its best result in all its configurations is the final result. The final result of each algorithm is compared with others. Trace data of 10000 cycles are taken from each Trace File randomly and the final result is the average of eight Trace Files of benchmarks. The configuration of best result is the best configuration, listed in Table 2. The criterions of the best configuration are different according to the priority schemes. It is the configuration with the lowest Overall Overflow Rate in uniform-priority tests (Uni-Pri) with the same buffer size of all queues. In ununiform-priority tests (Pri) that Q_1 is assigned to high priority with small buffer size and Q_2~Q_4 are assigned to low priority with large buffer sizes, the best configuration is the configuration with the lowest Overall Overflow Rate and without overflow of Q_1.

Table 2. Best configurations in experiments for overflow rates

	Config (Byte)		LBF-w $Qw_1/Qw_2/Qw_3/Qw_4$	TraceDo (Byte) $SRH_1/SRH_2/SRH_3/SRH_4$ $-MSG_T$	Funnel MSG_F (Byte)
	Buffer size $L_1/L_2/L_3/L_4$	ID_ Overhead			
Uni-Pri-ID	64/64/64/64	0.5	**1/1/1/1**	**56/56/56/56 -24**	**16×4**
Uni-Pri-NoID	64/64/64/64	0	**1/1/1/1**	**56/56/56/56 -8**	**11×4**
Pri-ID	32/64/64/64	0.5	**1.7/1/1/1**	**24/56/56/56 -12**	**5×4**
Pri-NoID	32/64/64/64	0	**1.2/1/1/1**	**24/56/56/56 -4**	**7×4**

Overall Overflow Rates of three algorithms are shown in Fig. 11. Comparing with Funnel algorithm, there are 28% ~32% improvements in TraceDo algorithm. Not considering switchover time, Overall Overflow Rates of TraceDo are 14% and 1% higher than that of LBF-w algorithm. Without approaches in LBF-w for reducing queue switchover counts, results of LBF-w are two times larger than others when considering switchover time.

OFBU_Q_i and OFBU_All are shown in Fig. 12. A final OFBU of eight benchmarks is computed by averaging *(OR_j×$OFBU_j$)*. OR_j is the percentage of the Overflow Rate

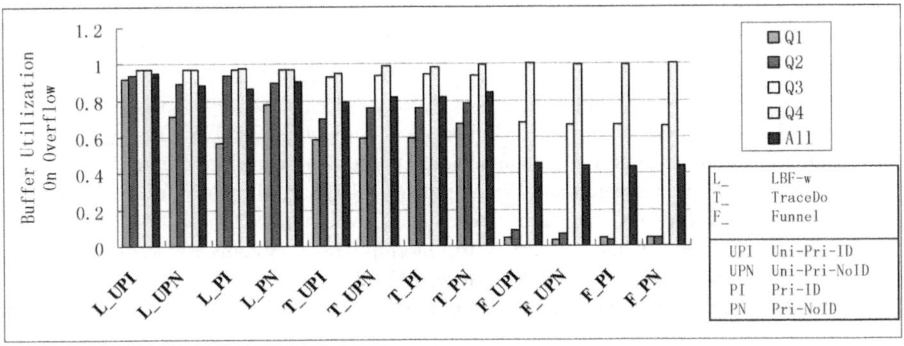

Fig. 12. Buffer Utilization On Overflow (OFBU)

of the jth benchmark to total Overflow Rates of eight benchmarks (Overall Overflow Rate for OFBU_All), and $OFBU_j$ is the OFBU of the jth benchmark. As an algorithm satisfying realization constraints, TraceDo algorithm improves impartiality and reduces OFBU_All comparing with Funnel algorithm, though there is a weak gap to LBF-w algorithm.

6 Conclusion

Solving the problem of combining on-chip trace data in a multi-core processor, this paper presents a lazy scheduling algorithm with Service Require Threshold (SRH) and Minimum Service Granularity (MSG). Simulations of variant configurations show, queue length distributions are constrained by SRH effectively and queue buffers are utilized sufficiently. All overflow rates decrease and the overflow rate of each queue is able to be tuned by users. The queue switching overheads are also reduced. The algorithm pays reasonable costs of realization and provides good scalability. Future work includes analyzing the algorithm in mathematical models.

Acknowledgements. This work is supported by the National Natural Science Foundation of China (60473079), SRFDP (No.20059998026).

References

1. ARC International Ltd. ARC International Provides New Configurable Trace and Debug Extensions to the ARC™ 600 and 700 Core Families. http://www.arc.com/news/PressRelease.html?id=227, 2005-11-29
2. ARM Ltd. CoreSight Flyer. http://www.arm.com/products/solutions/CoreSight.html
3. ARM Ltd. CoreSight™ Components Technical Reference Manual, http://www.arm.com/pdfs/DDI0314C_coresight_component_trm.pdf, 2006-7-31
4. MIPS Technologies Inc. The PDtrace™ Interface and Trace Control Block Specification. http://www.mips.com/content/Docmentation/MIPSDocumentation/ProcessorArchitecture/doclibrary#ArchitectureSetExtensions, 2005-7-4
5. Freescale Ltd. MPC565 Reference Manual. http://www.freescale.com/webapp/sps/site/prod_summary.jsp?code=MPC565, 2005-11
6. IEEE-ISTO 5001™-2003, The Nexus 5001 Forum™ Standard for a Global Embedded Processor Debug Interface v2.0. http://www.nexus5001.org/standard2.html, 2003-11
7. Hopkins, ABT, McDonald-Maier, KD. Debug Support Strategy for Systems-on-Chips with Multiple Processor Cores, IEEE Trans. on Computers, 2006, 55(2)
8. Shuming Chen, Zhentao Li, Jianghua Wan, Dinglei Hu, Yang Guo, Dong Wang, Xiao Hu and Shuwei Sun. "Research and Development of High Performance YHFT Digital Signal Processor", Journal of Computer Research and Development, 2006, 43(6)
9. Xiao Hu, Shuming Chen. A Survey to On-chip Trace Systems for Real-time Debug in Embedded Processors, NCCET'06, Guilin, 2006-8
10. TAGAGI H. Queuing analysis of polling models [J]. ACM Computing Surveys, 1988, 20 (1):5-28

11. LI Wan-lin, TIAN Chang, ZHANG Shao-ren. Performance AnaIysis of Output-Queued Two-Stage Packet Buffer Structure for Optical Bus Switching Network, ACTA ELECTRONICA SINICA, 2003, 31 (4):1-4
12. T. D. Lagkas, Georgios I. Papadimitriou, Petros Nicopolitidis, Andreas S. Pomportsis. Priority Oriented Adaptive Polling for wireless LANs. ISCC'06, 2006: 719-724
13. Robert A. Lackman, Jian Xu. Laxity Threshold Polling for Scalable Real-Time/Non-Real-Time Scheduling, ICCNMC'03, 2003
14. http://www.mathworks.com/

Memory Offset Assignment for DSPs

Jinpyo Hong[1] and J. Ramanujam[2]

[1] School of Internet-Media Engineering
Korea University of Technology and Education, Cheonan, Korea
jphong1@kut.ac.kr
[2] Dept. of Electrical and Computer Engineering
Louisiana State University, Baton Rouge, LA, USA
jxr@ece.lsu.edu

Abstract. Compact code generation is very important for an embedded system that has to be implemented on a chip with a severely limited amount of size. Even though on-chip data memory optimization technique has been given more attention, on-chip instruction memory optimization should not be neglected. We propose in this paper some algorithms for a memory offset assignment for embedded DSP processors in order to minimize the number of instructions for address register operations. Extensive experimental results demonstrate the efficacy of our solution.

1 Introduction

Embedded DSP processors contain an *address generation unit* (AGU) that enables the processor to compute the address of an operand of the next instruction while executing the current instruction. An AGU has auto-increment and auto-decrement capability, which can be done in the same clock of execution of a current instruction. It is very important to take advantage of AGUs in order to generate high-quality compact code. In this paper, we propose heuristics for the *single offset assignment with modify registers* (SOA-MR) problem and the *general offset assignment* (GOA) problem in order to exploit AGUs effectively. Experimental results show that our proposed methods can reduce address operation cost and in turn lead to compact code. The storage assignment problem was first studied by Bartley [6] and Liao [8,9,10]. Liao showed that the offset assignment problem even for a single address register is NP-complete and proposed a heuristic that uses the *access graph,* which can be constructed from a given access sequence. The access graph has one vertex per variable and edges between two vertices in the access graph indicate that the variables corresponding to the vertices are accessed consecutively; the weight of an edge is the number of times such consecutive access occurs. Liao's solution picks edges in the access graph in decreasing order of weight as long as they do not violate the assignment requirement. Liao also generalizes the storage assignment problem to include any number of address registers. Leupers and Marwedel [11] proposed a tie-breaking function to handle the same weighted edges, and a variable partitioning strategy to minimize GOA costs. They also show that the storage assignment cost can be reduced by utilizing modify registers. In [1,2,3,14], the interaction between instruction selection and scheduling is considered in order to improve code size. Rao and Pande [13] apply algebraic transformations to find a better

Y.-H. Lee et al. (Eds.): ICESS 2007, LNCS 4523, pp. 80–87, 2007.

access sequence. They define the least cost access sequence problem (LCAS), and propose heuristics to solve the LCAS problem. Other work on transformations for offset assignment includes those of Atri et al. [4,5] and Ramanujam et al. [12]. Recently, Choi and Kim [7] presented a technique that generalizes the work of Rao and Pande [13].

The remainder of this paper is organized as follows. In Section 2 and 3, we propose our heuristics for SOA with modify registers, and GOA problems. We also explain the basic concepts of our approach. In Section 4, we present experimental results. Finally, Section 5 provides a summary.

2 Our Approach to the SOA-MR Problem

2.1 The Single Offset Assignment (SOA) Problem

Given a variable set $V = \{v_0, v_1, \cdots, v_{n-1}\}$, the single offset assignment (SOA) problem is to find the offset of each variable $v_i, 0 \le i \le n-1$ so as to minimize the number of instructions needed only for memory address operations. In order to do that, it is very critical to maximize auto-increment/auto-decrement operations of an address register that can eliminate the explicit use of memory address instructions.

Liao [8] proposed a heuristic that finds a path cover of an access graph $G(V, E)$ by choosing edges in decreasing order of the number of transitions in an access sequence while avoiding cycles, but he does not say how to handle edges that have the same weight. Leupers and Marwedel [11] introduced a tie-breaking function to handle such edges. Their result is better than Liao's as expected.

2.2 Our Algorithm for SOA with an MR

Definition 1. *An edge $e = (v_i, v_j)$ is called an* uncovered edge *when variables that correspond to vertices v_i and v_j are not assigned adjacently in a memory.*

After applying the existing SOA heuristic to an access graph $G(V, E)$, we may have several paths. If there is a Hamiltonian path and SOA luckily finds it, then memory assignment is done, but we cannot expect that situation all the time. We prefer to call those paths partitions because each path is disjoint with others.

Definition 2. *An uncovered edge $e = (v_i, v_j)$ is called an intra-uncovered edge when variables v_i and v_j belong to the same partition. Otherwise, it is called an inter-uncovered edge. These are also referred to as intra-edge and an inter-edge respectively.*

Definition 3. *Each intra-edge and inter-edge contributes to an address operation cost. We call these the intra-cost and the inter-cost respectively.*

Uncovered edges account for cost if they are not subsumed by an MR register. Our goal is to maximize the number of uncovered edges that are subsumed by an MR register. The cost can be expressed by the following cost equation.

$$cost = \sum_{e_i \in intra\_edge} intra\_cost(e_i) + \sum_{e_j \in inter\_edge} inter\_cost(e_j).$$

It is clear that a set of intra-edges and a set of inter-edges are disjoint because from Definition 2, an uncovered edge e cannot be an intra-edge and an inter-edge at the same time. First, we want to maximize the number of intra-edges that are subsumed by an MR register. After that, we will try to maximize the number of inter-edges that will be subsumed by an MR register. We think this approach is reasonable because when the memory assignment is fixed by a SOA heuristic, there is no flexibility of intra-edges in such a sense that we cannot rearrange them. So, we want to recover as many intra-edges as possible with an MR register first. Then, with the observation that we can change the distances of inter-edges by rearranging partitions, we will try to recover inter-edges with an MR register.

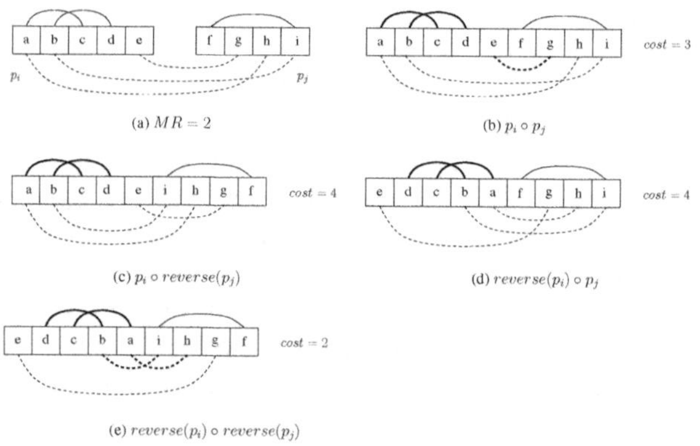

Fig. 1. Merging combinations

There are four possible merging combinations of two partitions. Figure 1 shows those four merging combinations. Intra-edges are represented by a solid line, and inter-edges by a dotted line. In Figure 1-(a), there are 6 uncovered edges among which there are 3 intra-edges and 3 inter-edges. So, the AR cost is 6. First, we try to find the most frequently appearing distance of intra-edges. In this example, distance 2 is the one because $distance(a, c)$ and $distance(b, d)$ are 2 and $distance(f, i)$ is 3. By assigning 2 to an MR register, we can recover two out of three intra-edges, which reduces the cost by 2. When an uncovered edge is recovered by an MR register, the corresponding line is depicted by a thick line. Next, we want to recover as many inter-edges as possible by making the distance of inter-edges 2 by applying proper merging combination. In Figure 1-(b), the two partitions are concatenated. One inter-edge,$e = (e, g)$ will be recovered, because $distance(e, g)$ in a merged partition is 2. So, the cost is 3. In Figure 1-(c), the first partition is concatenated with the reversed second one. No inter-edge will be recovered. The cost is 4. In Figure 1-(d), the reversed first partition is concatenated with the second one. No inter-edge will be recover, either. The cost is 4. In Figure 1-(e), the two partitions are reversed and concatenated. It is actually equal to exchanging the two partitions. Two inter-edges will be recovered. In this case, we recover four out of six uncovered edges by applying our method. Figure 2 shows our MR optimization algorithm.

```
Procedure SOA_mr
begin
  G_partition(V_par, E_par) ← Apply SOA to G(V, E);
  Φ_m_sorted ← sort m values of edges (v1, v2) by frequency in descending order;
  M ← the first m of Φ_m_sorted;
  optimizedSOA ← φ;

  for each partition pair of p_i and p_j do
    Find the number, m_(p_i,p_j) of edges, e = (v1, v2), e ∈ E, v1 ∈ p_i, v2 ∈ p_j
    such that their distance (m value) = M from four possible merging combinations,
    and assign a rule number that can generate m = M most frequently to (p_i, p_j);
  enddo

  Ψ_sorted_par_pair ← Sort partition pairs (p_i, p_j) by m_(p_i,p_j) in descending order;

  while (Ψ_sorted_par_pair ≠ φ) do
    (p_i, p_j) ← choose the first pair from Ψ_sorted_par_pair;
    Ψ_sorted_par_pair ← Ψ_sorted_par_pair − {(p_i, p_j)};
    if (p_i ∉ optimizedSOA and p_j ∉ optimizedSOA)
      optimizedSOA ← (optimizedSOA ∘ merge_by_rule(p_i, p_j));
      V_par ← V_par − {p_i, p_j};
    endif
  enddo

  while (V_par ≠ φ) do
    Choose p from V_par;
    V_par ← V_par − {p};
    optimizedSOA ← (optimizedSOA ∘ p);
  enddo

  return optimizedSOA;
end
```

Fig. 2. Heuristic for SOA with MR

3 General Offset Assignment (GOA)

The general offset assignment problem is, given a variable set $V = \{v_0, v_1, \cdots, v_{n-1}\}$ and an AGU that has k ARs, $k > 1$, to find a partition set $\mathcal{P} = \{p_0, p_1, \cdots, p_{l-1}\}$, where $p_i \cap p_j = \phi, i \neq j, 0 \leq i, j \leq l-1$, subject to minimize GOA cost $\sum_{i=0}^{l-1} SOA\_cost(p_i)$ $+l$, where l is the number of partitions, $l \leq k$. The second term l is the initialization cost of l ARs. Our GOA heuristic consists of two phases. In the first phase, we sort variables in descending order of their appearance frequencies in an access sequence, i.e., the number of accesses to a particular variable. Then, we construct a partition set $\mathcal{P}$ by selecting the two most frequently appearing variables, which will reduce the length of the remaining access sequence most, and making them a partition, $p_i, 0 \leq i \leq l-1$. After the first phase, the way we construct a partition set $\mathcal{P}$, we will have $l, l \leq k$, partitions that consist of only 2 variables each. Those partitions have zero SOA cost, and we have the shortest access sequence that consists of $(|V| - 2l)$ variables. In the second phase, we pick a variable v from the remaining variables in the descending order of frequency, and choose a partition p_i such that $SOA\_cost(p_i \cup \{v\})$ is increased minimally, which means that merging a variable v into that partition increases the GOA cost minimally. This process will be repeated $(|V| - 2l)$ times, till every variable is assigned to some partition.

4 Experimental Results

We generated access sequences randomly and apply our heuristics, Leupers' and Liao's. We repeated the simulation 1000 times on several problem sizes. Our experiments show that introducing an MR can improve the AGU performance and that an optimization heuristic for an MR register is needed to maximize a performance gain. Our experiments show that the results of 2-AR AGU are alway better than 1AR_1MR's and even ARmr_op's. It is because even if we apply a MR optimization heuristic, which is naturally to be more conservative than GOA heuristic of 2-AR in such a sense that only after several path partitions are generated by SOA heuristic on entire variables, a MR optimization heuristic would try to recover uncovered edges whose occurrences heavily depend on SOA heuristic. A GOA heuristic can exploit a better chance by partitioning variables into two sets and applying SOA heuristic on each partitioned set. However, GOA's gain over ARmr_op does not come for free. The cost of the partitioning of variables might not be negligible as it was shown in section 3. However, from the perspective of performance of an embedded system, our experiment shows that it is better to pay that cost to get performance gain of AGU. The gain of 2-AR GOA over ARmr_op is noticeable enough to justify our opinion. When an AGU has several pairs of a AR and an MR, in which AR[i] is coupled with MR[i], our path partition optimization heuristic can be used for each partitioned variable set. Then, the result of each pair of the AGU will be improved as we observed in Figure 3. Figures 3 shows bar graphs based on the results of randomly generated access sequences. When an access graph is dense, two heuristics perform similarly as shown in Figure 3-(a). In this case, introducing a mr

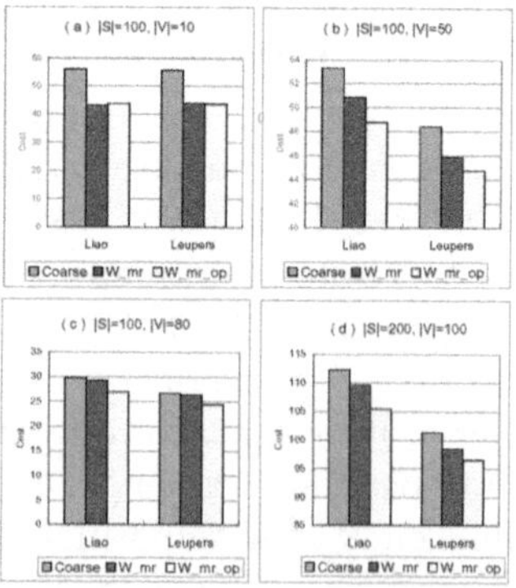

Fig. 3. Results for SOA and SOA_mr

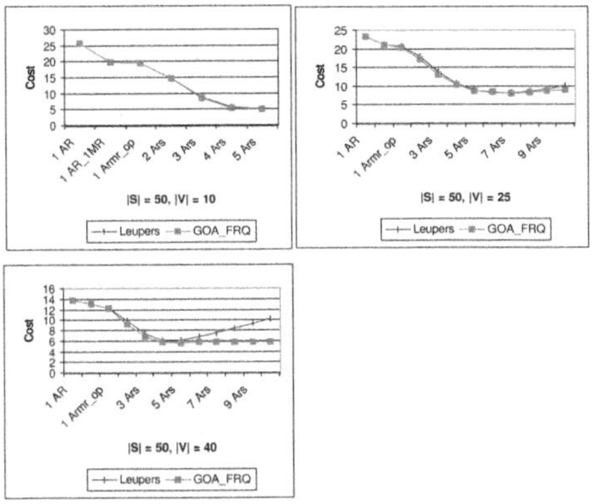

Fig. 4. Results for GOA_FRQ

optimization technique does not improve performance much. Figure 3-(b), 3-(d) show that when the number of variables is 50% of th length of an access sequence, introducing optimization technique can reduce the costs. Figure 3-(c) shows that when the access graph becomes sparse, the amount of improvement becomes smaller than when the graph is dense, but it is still reduce the costs noticeably. Except the case when an access graph is very dense like in Figure 3-(a), applying our mr optimization technique is beneficial in all heuristics including Liao's and Leupers'. Figure 4 shows that our GOA_FRQ algorithm outperforms Leupers' in many cases. Especially in Figure 4, we can witness that beyond certain threshold, our algorithm keeps its performance stable. However, Leupers' algorithm tries to use as many ARs as possible, which makes performance of his algorithm deteriorated as the number of ARs grows. Line graphs in Figure 4 shows that our mr optimization technique is beneficial, and that 2 ARs configuration always outperforms ar_mr_op as we mentioned earlier.

We experiment DSP benchmarks like BIQUAD_ONE, COMP (Complex multiplication), and ELLIP (Elliptical wave filter) and also numerical analysis algorithms like GAULEG (Gauss-Legendre weights and abscissas), GAUHER (Gauss-Laguerre weights and abscissas) and GAUJAC (Gauss-Jacobi weights and abscissas) from [15]. We also use several programs such as CHENDCT, CHENIDCT, LEEDCT and LEEIDCT from JPEG-MPEG package. Figure 5 shows the improvements of results of 1AR_1MR, ARmr_op, and 2 ARs to 1 AR. Improvement is computed as ($\frac{1AR-x}{1AR} \times 100$), where x is one of the above three AGUs. Except COMP which is too simple to show a meaningful result, introducing extra resource (MR) in AGU is always beneficial. The average improvement of rest 5 algorithms of including MR is 18.5%. With the same amount of resources (1 AR and 1 MR), we achieve more gains by applying our MR optimization technique. The average improvement of our MR optimization is 25.4%. The average improvement of 2 ARs is 44.2%. MR takes a supplemental role to recover edges that were not included in path covers. With understanding such a role of MR, superiority of the result of 2ARs over MR and MR_OP is understandable. However, we believe that improvement of our MR optimization technique shows that more

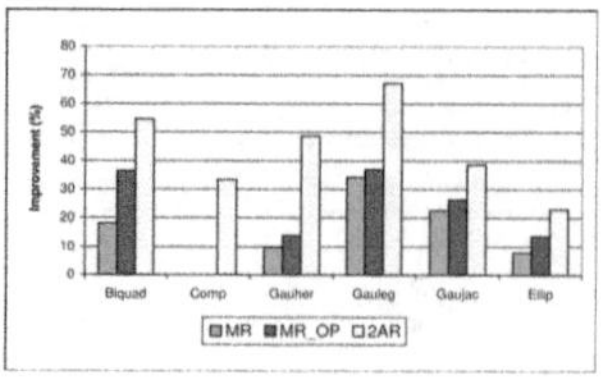

Fig. 5. Improvements of 1AR_1MR, MR_OP and 2ARs to 1 AR

aggressive method for MR optimization should be enforced and that MR be given more attention in a sense that setting value 1 to MR has an exactly same effect as AR's auto-increment/-decrement, which means MR has more flexibility than `AR++` and `AR--`. Our MR optimization technique can be used to exploit $m \geq 1$ pairs of (AR,MR) in AGU.

5 Summary

We have found that several fragmented paths are generated as the SOA algorithm trys to find a path cover. We have proposed a new optimization technique of handling these fragmented paths. As the SOA algorithm generates several fragmented paths, we show that our optimization technique of these path partitions is crucial to achieve an extra gain, which is clearly captured by our experimental results. We also have proposed usage of frequencies of variables in a GOA problem. Our experimental results show that this straightforward method is better than the previous research works.

Acknowledgments. This work is supported in part by the US National Science Foundation through awards 0073800, 0103933, 0121706, 0508245, 0509442 and 0541409.

References

1. G. Araujo. Code Generation Algorithms for Digital Signal Processors. PhD thesis, Princeton Department of EE, June 1997.
2. G. Araujo, S. Malik, and M. Lee. Using Register-Transfer Paths in Code Generation for Heterogeneous Memory-Register Architectures. In *Proceedings of 33rd ACM/IEEE Design Automation Conference*, pages 591-596, June 1996.
3. G. Araujo, A. Sudarsanam, and S. Malik. Instruction Set Design and Optimization for Address Computation in DSP Architectures. In *Proceedings of the 9th International Symposium on System Synthesis*, pages 31-37, November 1997.
4. S. Atri, J. Ramanujam, and M. Kandemir. Improving offset assignment on embedded processors using transformations. In *Proc. High Performance Computing–HiPC 2000,* pp. 367–374, December 2000.
5. Sunil Atri, J. Ramanujam, and M. Kandemir. Improving variable placement for embedded processors. In *Languages and Compilers for Parallel Computing,* (S. Midkiff et al. Eds.), Lecture Notes in Computer Science, vol. 2017, pp. 158–172, Springer-Verlag, 2001.
6. D. Bartley. Optimization Stack Frame Accesses for Processors with Restricted Addressing Modes. *Software Practice and Experience,* 22(2):101-110, February 1992.

7. Y. Choi and T. Kim. Address assignment combined with scheduling in DSP code generation. in *Proc. 39th Design Automation Conference,* June 2002.
8. S. Liao. Code Generation and Optimization for Embedded Digital Signal Processors. PhD thesis, MIT Department of EECS, January 1996.
9. S. Liao et al. Storage Assignment to Decrease Code Size. In *Proceedings of the ACM SIGPLAN '95 Conference on Programming Language Design and Implementation,* pages 186–196, 1995. (This is a preliminary version of [10].)
10. S. Liao, S. Devadas, K. Keutzer, S. Tjiang, and A. Wang. Storage assignment to decrease code size. *ACM Transactions on Programming Languages and Systems,* 18(3):235–253, May 1996.
11. R. Leupers and P. Marwedel. Algorithms for Address Assignment in DSP Code Generation. In *Proceedings of International Conference on Computer-Aided Design,* pages 109-112, 1996.
12. J. Ramanujam, J. Hong, M. Kandemir, and S. Atri. Address register-oriented optimizations for embedded processors. In *Proc. 9th Workshop on Compilers for Parallel Computers (CPC 2001),* pp. 281–290, Edinburgh, Scotland, June 2001.
13. A. Rao and S. Pande. Storage Assignment Optimizations to Generate Compact and Efficient Code on Embedded Dsps. *SIGPLAN '99, Atlanta, GA, USA*, pages 128-138, May 1999.
14. A. Sudarsanam and S. Malik. Memory Bank and Register Allocation in Software Synthesis for ASIPs. In *Proceedings of International Conference on Computer Aided Design*, pages 388-392, 1995.
15. W. H. Press, S. A. Teukolsky, W. T. Vetterling and B. P. Flannery (Editors), *Numerical Recipes in C: The Art of Science Computing,* Cambridge University Press, pages 152-155, 1993.

A Subsection Storage Policy in Intelligent RAID-Based Object Storage Device

Dan Feng, Qiang Zou, Lei Tian, Ling-fang Zeng, and Ling-jun Qin

College of Computer, Huazhong University of Science and Technology
Wuhan National Laboratory For Optoelectronics, China
dfeng@hust.edu.cn, hustmathcs@gmail.com

Abstract. With the development of network storage technology, some massive storage system architectures have exposed some drawbacks. How to remove the server bottleneck and decrease the loss rate of I/O requests have become an issue of increasing importance in the designing of network storage systems. In this paper, object-based storage system (OBSS) and RAID-based object storage device (RAID-based OSD) are briefly presented. Based on RAID-based OSD, an object subsection storage policy for the hot object files is put forward to increase the acceptance rate of I/O requests and improve the I/O performance of OBSS. Analytical and experimental results show that it is reasonable and effective.

1 Introduction

With the exponential growth of information, the first generation of massive storage system architectures such as network attached storage (NAS) for file storage, storage area networks (SANs) for block storage, have exposed some of their own advantages and drawbacks [1]. As a much higher level of abstraction for networked storage, object-based storage (OBS) has combined the advantages of SAN and NAS, and becomes the forefront of the next wave of storage technology and devices [2].

Object storage was first proposed by CMU as an academic research project [3] and continues to be a hot research topic. Version 1 of the T10 standard was publicly reviewed and approved in late 2004. The OSD standard proposes a standard interface for the object-based storage device, by which devices evolve from being relatively unintelligent and externally managed to being intelligent, self-managed, aware of the storage applications they serve and of high compatibility in the object-based storage system.

As a building block of OBS, object-based storage devices (OSDs) play an important role in OBS and have great impacts on the overall performance of the storage systems. Many efforts have been made to improve the performance of OSDs. ORAID (Object RAID), a novel object-based device, which consolidates disk space of individual disk into a single storage pool and implements object-sharing and fault-tolerance through the object-interface, is introduced in [4] and has the ability to implement online data re-layout and online capacity expansion. The design

Y.-H. Lee et al. (Eds.): ICESS 2007, LNCS 4523, pp. 88–97, 2007.

of the intelligent RAID-based object storage device and the methods to shorten the access latency and increase the intelligence for OSDs are described in [5].

In this paper, based on RAID-based OSD, we present a subsection storage strategy to improve the acceptance rate of I/O requests. Hot object files can be shared by several storage units, which can independently provide services for I/O requests. In this way, the loss rate of I/O requests decreases significantly and the I/O bandwidth of OBSS improves noticeably. Analytical and experimental results show that it is a reasonable and effective policy.

This paper is organized as follows. Section 2 is a short introduction to OBSS architecture and RAID-Based OSD. In section 3 we present an object subsection storage policy (OSSP)in brief. In section 4, mathematically we analyze the loss rate of I/O requests and the I/O bandwidth under OSSP, and the analytical results are given to suppport OSSP. Section 5 presents the experimental results that are consistent with the analytical results in section 4. Finally, we conclude this paper and discuss the future work in section 6.

2 Object-Based Storage System Architecture

2.1 OBSS Overview

In the OBSS, objects are primitive, logical units of storage that can be directly accessed on an OSD. An OBSS built from OSDs and other components is shown in Fig. 1. Metadata server (MDS) provides the information (global object metadata) necessary to directly access objects, along with other information about data including its extended attributes, security keys, and permissions (authentication). For example, MDS stores higher-level information about the object, such as OID (Object ID), object name, object type (e.g. file, device, database table) and storage map (e.g. OSD1, partition1, OID1, OSD2, partition2, OID2, stripe unit size of 64KB), which are not directly interpreted by OSD. OSDs export object-based interface, with the access/storage unit being an object, such as a file, a database table, a medical image or a video stream. It operates in a mode in which data is organized and accessed as objects rather than as an ordered sequence of sectors. OSDs manage local object metadata (data organization in

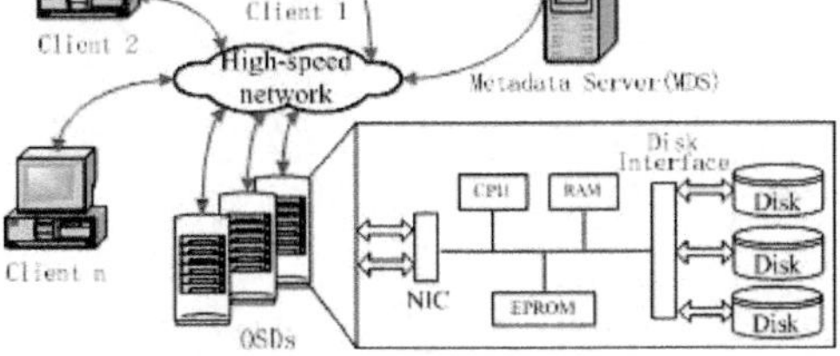

Fig. 1. Object-based storage system architecture

disks). Clients contact MDS to get information about the objects in which they are interested and send requests directly to OSDs. OSDs receive and process these requests based on some policies.

2.2 RAID-Based OSD

The RAID-based OSD architecture is shown in Figure 2. An OSD consists of a processor, RAM memory, disks and Ethernet interface. The RAID-Based OSD subsystem is an embedded system built on commodity hardware at a low cost but with a TERABYTE-scale massive storage capacity to make it more cost-effective for the general users. We add the ISCSI Target control layer and OSD command interface to the RAID control software to make the EIDE RAID an intelligent OSD. The software is running under the embedded Linux operating system.

As an embedded system, OSD is the core of the object-based storage system. It is an intelligent, self-managed device, which provides an object interface for clients to access data stored in it. Every OSD has its own globally unique ID. The new OSD command set describes the operations available on OSDs. The result is a group of intelligent disks (OSDs) attached to a switched network fabric (ISCSI over Ethernet) providing storage that is directly accessible by the clients. Unlike conventional SAN configurations, OSDs can be directly addressed in parallel, allowing extremely high aggregate data throughputs.

As an embedded system, OSD has its own CPU and memory to run the control software itself and executes self-managing functions to become an intelligent device. With a Gigabyte Ethernet interface OSD can provide high throughput as a network storage subsystem to process and store data from the network.

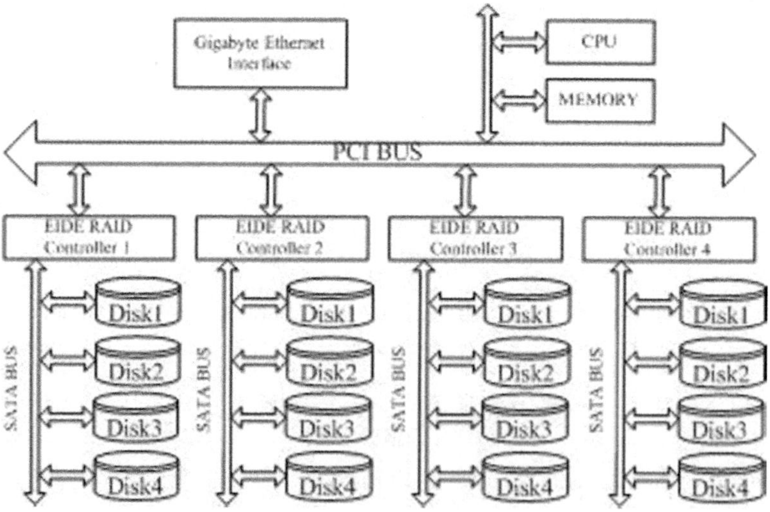

Fig. 2. RAID-based OSD architecture

Furthermore, it's also very easy to upgrade to serve the next generation of networks by upgrading the network protocol. In our previous work [5], the software architecture and extended attributes of the OSD are described in detail.

The RAID-based OSD design (see Fig.2) provides an object interface to every client according to the latest T10 standard, the standard interface focusing on integrating low-level storage, space management, and security functions into OSD from MDS.

Block-based file systems can be viewed to contain roughly two main components, namely, the user component and the storage component. The former is responsible for presenting user applications with logical data structures, such as files and directories, and an interface for accessing these data structures; whereas the latter maps the data structures to the physical storage. This separation of responsibilities makes it easy to offload management task to the storage device, which is the intended effect of the object-based storage.

It is safe to say that OBSS is more facile to set up mass storage system than NAS and SAN. In OBSS, there are three facets for load balancing. First, the global policies are initiated by MDS and clients interact with MDS. Second, OSD has better knowledge of its own load than MDS. Therefore, it is reasonable that local policy is initiated by OSD. Third, the storage object is encapsulated with data, attributes and methods. These attributes can be set or obtained as objects are accessed, and object attribute values are as good as policy threshold. Furthermore, object methods also can be triggered according to a policy as follows.

3 Object Subsection Storage Policy (OSSP)

As a resource manager, all of the data requests are monitored by MDS, and MDS records the correlative information about all OSDs such as total capacity, used space, available space, optional striping requirement among OSDs, total I/O bandwidth and IP address.

Santa Barbara's Active disks in University of California [8], and IDISK in University of California at Berkeley [9] are typical smart storage devices. Just like those devices, local intelligence is achieved in OSD and becomes the basis of the whole storage system. Therefore, OSD has better knowledge of its own load than MDS.

As we know, object sharing policy can be divided into two categories: long-term decision and short-term decision. The former makes a decision according to the history of object access, and the latter generally makes a decision according to the load state of current metadata server. Therefore, a special threshold should be devised to identify whether the hot object file belongs to long-term decision or short-term decision. If I/O load of one OSD reach the local threshold, OSD may initiate object subsection policy to enforce load balance, and OSD is able to decide the OSDs where the hot object file should be shared into, this interaction process is performed by the cooperation between MDS and OSD. With the overall resource information, MDS deals with subsection request from OSD and sends some tips to OSDs. At the same time, MDS records those metadata that has been modified (added or moved), and updates management parameters. Then, with the help of MDS, a hot object file can be divided into more than one object and mapped to different OSDs. The client can communicate with different OSDs in parallel to access the file to make good use of the I/O bandwidth and improve the throughput of the system.

OSSP is a real-time policy, and based on high-speed network with the high bandwidth and low delay. With the rapid development of network technology, a real-time OSSP is feasible. Of course, there are also some additional system cost and the minimum cost is expected while the hot object file is shared from the congested OSD into other OSDs. The additional system cost due to OSSP in each OSD can be denoted as $\Delta t(i)$, and the average is $E[\Delta t(i)]$. Furthermore, the cost due to the data conformity in Client is neglectable.

The advantages of OSSP will be shown in the following sections by means of mathematical analysis and experiments.

4 System Performance Analysis

4.1 Mathematical Description of OBS

Consider a simple object storage system that includes only one OSD in which there is only one disk that can sustains N I/O requests simultaneously. In the disk there is only one program whose transmission length is T. The I/O requests arrive stochastically, with a service time of T. Suppose that the ith I/O request time is $t_i, i = 1, 2, ...$, then the first N requests can be immediately serviced as soon as the server receives them. The $(N+1)th$ request will be serviced upon its arrival if the first request has been completed before the $(N+1)th$ request arrives, i.e. $t_1 + T \leq t_{N+1}$; Otherwise, i.e. $t_1 + T > t_{N+1}$, the requests that arrive in the interval $(t_N, t_1 + T)$ will be refused. At the moment $t_1 + T$, the first I/O request has been completed so that the system is able to respond to new requests.

The service time for each request is a constant T, so that the requests arriving in the interval $[0, t_N]$ should be accepted, and the requests arriving in the interval $(t_N, t_1 + T]$ are rufused. Requests arrive with a probability of λ in the interval $[2t_1 + T, t_1 + t_N + T]$, requests arriving in the interval $[t_1 + t_N, t_1 + t_N + T]$ will be accepted. Similarly, requests arriving in the interval $[t_1 + t_N + T, 2t_1 + 2T]$ will be refused. Therefore, using the same methods as above we know that requests arriving in the interval $[it_1 + iT, it_1 + t_N + iT]$ will be accepted, and requests arriving in the interval $[it_1 + t_N + iT, (i+1)t_1 + (i+1)T]$ will be refused (see Fig.3).

From the above analysis, we can draw a conclusion that the I/O request response time is composed of a continuous cycle that can be devided into two different phases of "accept" and "refuse", and the cycle length is $t_1 + T$, where the length of the "accept" phase is t_N and the length of the "refuse" phase is $t_1 + T - t_N$.

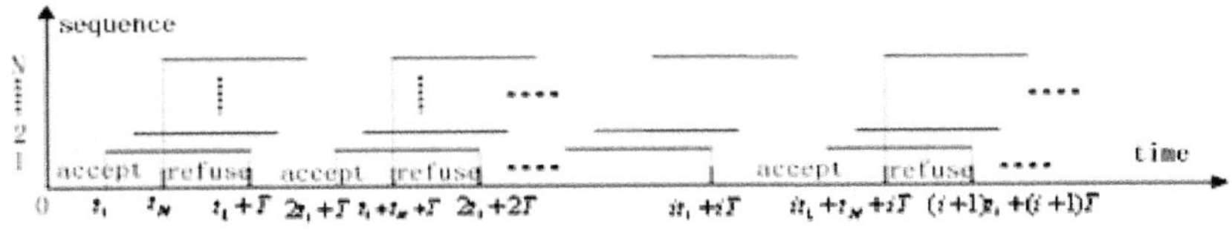

Fig. 3. The respondence sequence of I/O requests

Definitions and notations:

NRR— the number of refused requests;
TNR— the total number of requests;
LRP— the length of the "refuse" phase;
TTL— the total length;
OFS— the object filesize;
THR— the transmission rate.

According to the properties of Poisson distribution, the average of I/O requests during the time length of t_i is λt_i. The average value of t_i is i/λ. Therefore, the loss rate of I/O requests can be expressed as relation (1), which presents that T(=OFS/THR) should be decreased first in order to minimize the loss rate of I/O requests (i.e. to decrease OFS or to increase THR).

$$\begin{aligned}\eta_{loss} &= \frac{NRR}{TNR} = \frac{\lambda LRP}{\lambda TTL} = \frac{t_1 - t_N + T}{t_1 + T} \\ &= \frac{1 - N + \lambda T}{1 + \lambda T} = 1 - \frac{N \cdot THR}{THR + \lambda \cdot OFS}\end{aligned} \tag{1}$$

In general RAID-based OSD is scalable so that an object storage system is composed of several RAID-based OSDs. Every OSD includes k storage units and there are several files in each object. In order to express the loss rate of I/O requests, we assume that the storage system is composed of k RAID-based OSDs that constitute one RAID0, and the ith OSD (RAID0) is composed of n_i disks. Therefore, there are m_{ij} files that are stored in the jth disk. The lth file length in the jth disk belonging to the ith RAID0 is T_{ijl} and the probability of that file being requested by an I/O request is $r_{ijl}, i = 1, 2, \cdots, k; j = 1, 2, \cdots, n_i; l = 1, 2, \cdots, m_{ij}, \sum_{i=1}^{k}\sum_{j=1}^{n_i}\sum_{l=1}^{m_{ij}} r_{ijl} = 1$. It is easy to express the loss rate of I/O requests as follows:

$$\eta'_{loss} = \sum_{i=1}^{k}\{(\sum_{j=1}^{n_i}\sum_{l=1}^{m_{ij}} r_{ijl}) \cdot [1 - \frac{N}{1 + \lambda \cdot \sum_{j=1}^{n_i}\sum_{l=1}^{m_{ij}} r_{ijl} \cdot T_{ijl}}]\} \tag{2}$$

4.2 The Formulation of OSSP

In the presence of hot data, subsection storage is an effective method to storage hot data in RAID-based OSD. In other words, the data is divided into k subsections with each subsection being stored in a different object. Suppose that the length of the ith subsection is $T(i), i = 1, 2, ..., k$, and the system cost due to subsection strategy is $\Delta t(i)$,$E[\Delta t(i)] = t$, then the loss rate of I/O requests is

$$\eta_{loss} = 1 - \frac{N}{1 + \lambda kt + \lambda max[T(i)]}, i = 1, 2, ..., k \tag{3}$$

As $T(i) = T(i+1) = T/k = E[T(i)], i = 1, ..., k-1$, relation (3) can be expressed as:

$$\begin{aligned}\eta_{loss} &= 1 - \frac{N}{1 + \lambda kt + \lambda T/k} \\ &= 1 - \frac{k \cdot N \cdot THR}{k \cdot THR + k^2 \cdot THR \cdot \lambda t + \lambda \cdot OFS}\end{aligned} \tag{4}$$

According to relation (4), we know that these performance values such as THR (i.e. the I/O bandwidth), the number of OSDs (i.e. k), system cost $\Delta t(i)$ and the loss rate of I/O requests, are interactional. Due to $\lambda kt + \lambda T/k \geq 2\lambda\sqrt{Tt}$, η_{loss} get the minimum as $\lambda kt + \lambda T/k = 2\lambda\sqrt{Tt}$. The figure corresponding to relation (4) can be described as Fig.4 where the abscissa shows the number of OSDs that the hot object files are divided into, and the ordinate shows the loss rate of I/O requests. Obviously, hotter is the object file, higher is the arrive rate of I/O request, and higher is the loss rate of I/O request. According to Fig.4, the value of η_{loss} arrives the minimum at one of the inflexions that exist evidently on each curve. As a result, there is an optimum value $k_{opt} = \sqrt{T/t}$ in which the system cost sway the improvement of performance values least. According

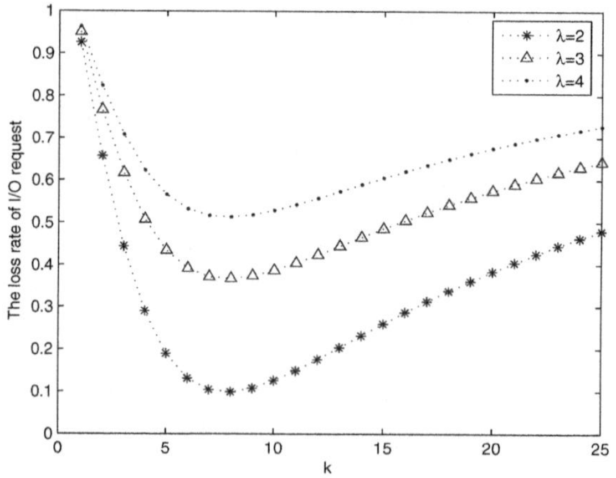

Fig. 4. The relationship can be mined from relation (4)

to relation (4), there is a close relationship between η_{loss} and THR. Higher is THR, less is the relevant η_{loss} as other factors are invariable.

Some experimental results are used to show that analytical results is a reasonable and effective in the following section.

5 Analysis and Discussion of Experimental Results

All of the experiments were executed on an OBSS with a 3.00GHZ Intel Xeon CPU, Super-Micro mainboard, 200GB(Maxtor, 7200RPM) disk and 512MB of RAM, running Linux AS3, kernel version 2.4.21. Fig.5 and Fig.6 show the experimental results with 2 OSDs and several OSDs.

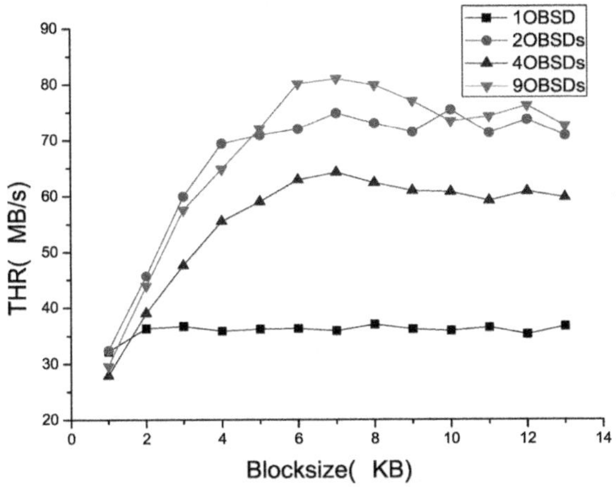

Fig. 5. The relationship between blocksize, the transmission rate (I/O bandwidth) and the number of OSDs where the hot object file is divided into

As a beginning, a hot object file whose filesize is 2 GB is separately divided into 2 OSDs, 4 OSDs and 9 OSDs. As can be seen from Fig.5, on the one hand, the value of THR in the case of 2 OSDs is much bigger than the case of single OSD, and the loss rate of I/O request decreases by a long way because of the less system cost. On the other hand, it is evident that the viewpoint to argue that more subsections the hot object file is divided into, better value system performance will achieve, is ivory-towered. As descriped in Fig.5, the I/O bandwidth improves enormously after the object file has been divided into 2 OSDs. However, the improvement ratio of I/O bandwidth after the object file has been divided into 4 OSDs is lower than the case of 2 OSDs. Even the I/O bandwidth after the object file has been divided into 9 OSDs is only near the case of 2 OSDs. The main reason for this phenomena is that the system cost due to the policy enhances rapidly so as to affect the improvement of system performance.

Moreover, the size of hot object file is also a important factor which effects the value of THR and the loss rate of I/O request. Fig.6 describes the variational I/O bandwidth as the hot object files with variational filesize are divided into several OSDs. As can be seen from Fig.5, the improvement ratio of I/O bandwidth will be evidently affected when the hot object filesize is very large (e.g. more than 1GB). While object filesize is no less than 100MB and the object file is divided into 3 OSDs and 4 OSDs, system cost enhances rapidly so as to the I/O bandwidth is less than the case of 2 OSDs, and then affect the improvement of the loss rate of I/O requests. The loss rate of I/O requests doesn't decrease enough to arrive in the expected goal, so that the anticipative effect of the subsection storage policy will be limited.

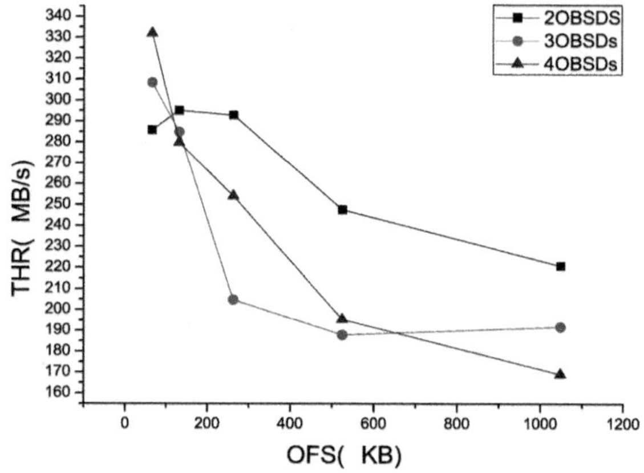

Fig. 6. The relationship between filesize, the transmission rate (I/O bandwidth) and the number of OSDs where the hot object file is divided into

The analytical and experimental results above show that OSSP is reasonable and effective. However, there are also some instance needed to be drawn attention. For an example, the I/O bandwidth improves enormously after the object file has been divided into 2 OSDs, and the system cost sway the system performance less than other cases. As a result, the loss rate of I/O requests arrives the minimum. Furthermore, the improvement of the loss rate of I/O requests is not so evident due to the impact of the increasing system cost. These experimental results inosculate entirely with the analytical result in section 4.

6 Conclusions and Future Work

With the exponential growth of information, how to remove the I/O bottleneck and increase the acceptance rate of I/O request come into being a challenging subject. In this paper, an object-based storage system (OBSS) is briefly presented. Based on RAID-based OSD that is composed of RAID0, an object subsection storage policy for hot object files is put forward to increase the acceptance rate of I/O request and improve the I/O bandwidth of OBSS. Analytical and experimental results show that it is reasonable and effective. As the future work, for more complex storage objects such as RAID3 and so on, a similar object storage policy which should be proved by experiment results will be provided to solve the problem of server bottleneck.

Acknowledgments

This work was supported by the National Basic Research Program of China (973 Program) under Grant No. 2004CB318201, and the National Science Foundation of China under Grant No. 60603048.

References

1. Alain Azagury, Vladimir Dreizin, Michael Factor, Ealan Henis, Dalit Naor, Noam Rinetzky, Ohad Rodeh, Julian Satran and Ami Tavory. Towards an Object Store. 20th IEEE/11th NASA Goddard Conference on Mass Storage Systems and Techologies (MSST'03), 2003.
2. P. J. Braam. The Lustre storage architecture. Technical report, Cluster File Systems. Inc., January 2004, available at http://www.lustre.org/docs/ lustre.pdf
3. G. Gibson, D. Nagle, K. Amiri, F. chang, H. Gobioff, E. Riedel, D. Rochberg and J. Zelenka. File systems for network-attached secure disks. Technical Report CMU-CS-97-112, CMU, 1997.
4. Dan Feng, Lingfang Zeng, Fang Wang and Shunda Zhang. ORAID: an intelligent and fault-tolerant object storage device. EUC Workshops 2005, LNCS 3823, pp.403-412, 2005.
5. Fang Wang, Song lv, Dan Feng and Shunda Zhang. A general-purpose, intelligent RAID-based object storage device. ICESS 2005, LNCS 3820, pp.747-756, 2005.
6. Lin-Wen Lee, Scheuermann P. and Vingralek R.. File assignment in parallel I/O systems with minimal variance of service time. IEEE Transactions on Computers. Vol 49, No.2, (2000) 136-143.
7. Kavitha Ranganathan and Ian Foster. Design and Evaluation of Dynamic Replication Strategies for a High-Performance Data Grid.
8. Acharya, M. Uysal, and J. Saltz. Active disks: programming model, algorithms and evaluation. In: Proceedings of the 8th Conference on Architectural Support for Programming Languages and Operating System (ASPLOS VIII), pp. 81-91, Oct. 1998.
9. K. Keeton, D. A. Patterson, and J. M. Hellerstein. A case for intelligent disks (IDISKs), SIGMOD Record, 27(3), Sept. 1998.

Joint Source-Channel Decoding ASIP Architecture for Sensor Networks*

Pablo Ituero[1], Gorka Landaburu[2], Javier Del Ser[3], Marisa López-Vallejo[1], Pedro M. Crespo[3], Vicente Atxa[2], and Jon Altuna[2]

[1] ETSIT, Universidad Politécnica de Madrid
{pituero,marisa}@die.upm.es
[2] Mondragon Unibertsitatea
{glandaburu,batxa,jaltuna}@eps.mondragon.edu
[3] CEIT and TECNUN, University of Navarra
{jdelser,pcrespo}@ceit.es

Abstract. In a sensor network, exploiting the correlation among different sources allows a significant reduction of the transmitted energy at the cost of a complex decoder scheme. This paper introduces the first hardware implementation for joint source-channel decoding of correlated sources. Specifically, a dual-clustered VLIW processor with a highly optimized datapath is presented.

Keywords: ASIP, DSC, Factor Graphs, Joint Source-Channel Coding, Sensor Networks, Turbo Codes, VLIW.

1 Introduction

During the last decade the research interest for sensor networks has risen sharply in the scientific community. Such networks consist of densely deployed sensors spread across a certain geographical area. Data is transmitted to either neighboring nodes or a common destination, which collects the information from all the existing sensors. This work focuses on the latter scenario, i.e. a centralized sensor network.

In this context, the high density of nodes in these networks and, consequently, their physical proximity may incur the appearance of correlation among the data collected by the different sensors. This correlation can be exploited, for instance, to reduce the required transmitted energy for a certain level of performance and complexity. Even if there is no communication among sources, the Slepian and Wolf Theorem reveals that distributed compression can be performed as long as the decoder is aware of the correlation among the sources.

However, when the channels from the sensors to the common receiver are noisy, each node has to add controlled redundancy (equivalently, apply forward

* This work was funded by the projects OPTIMA (TEC2006-00739) and MIMESIS (TEC2004-06451-C05-04/TCM) of the Spanish Ministry of Education and Science and TECMAR (IBA/PI2004-3) of the Basque Government Ministry of Industry.

Y.-H. Lee et al. (Eds.): ICESS 2007, LNCS 4523, pp. 98–108, 2007.

error correcting or *channel coding* techniques) to the transmitted data in order to combat the errors introduced by the channel. Under these circumstances, the separate design of source (compression) and channel coding schemes is an optimal solution whenever the complexity is not an issue (Separation Theorem).

The sensors of these networks are examples of complex embedded systems. Small, low-power, low-cost transceiver, sensing and processing units need to be designed. Actually, communication becomes one of the most power and area consuming elements in the hardware of a sensor network node. Thus, efficient hardware strategies are essential to obtain a good implementation. On the one hand, the power hungry general purpose processors do not satisfy the constraints given by such wireless systems. On the other hand, the high cost and low design productivity of new submicron technologies have turned ASIC designs into extremely expensive solutions. Therefore, special architectures that match the architecture to the application are required. Application Specific Instruction Set Processors (ASIPs) provide an attractive solution to this kind of problems: First, several applications can be run on it, and different generations of the same application are allowed. Second, for the application developer that uses an ASIP instead of an ASIC the time to market is reduced, it is cheaper and there is lower risk. Furthermore, the power overhead related to programmability (standard processors) can be mitigated by ASIPs architectures, especially if they are very dedicated.

In this paper we present a novel application specific processor architecture for centralized sensor networks. Specifically, we present a dual-clustered VLIW processor that implements a joint source-channel SISO decoder within an iterative scheme. To the best of our knowledge, the ASIP described here, based on [1], is the first hardware architecture for distributed coding of correlated sources. A customized datapath allows very high efficiency while providing enough flexibility to execute all the operations involved in the joint source-channel turbo decoding.

The remainder of the paper is outlined as follows. In the next section, an overview of the source data generating process is provided. Section 3 analyzes the proposed iterative joint source-channel turbo-decoder ASIP structure. In Sect. 4 the most important results of the design are presented. Finally Sect. 5 draws some concluding remarks.

2 State of the Art and Signal Processing Foundations

The research activity on the potential of the Slepian-Wolf Theorem for DSC (Distributed Source Coding), through noisy communication networks has gravitated around two different scenarios. On the one hand, for an asymmetric scenario consisting of two nodes (i.e. when only one of the channels is noisy), the authors in [2] proposed a joint source-channel coding scheme for a BSC channel based on turbo codes. Using Irregular Repeat Accumulate codes, the authors in [3] followed the same approach for BSC, AWGN and Rayleigh fading channels. On the other hand, the case of symmetric (i.e. both channels are noisy) joint

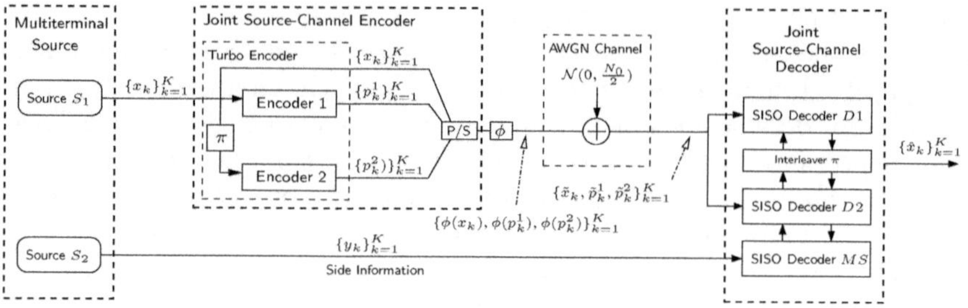

Fig. 1. Turbo joint source-channel decoding scheme with side information from [7]

source-channel coding with AWGN channels has been analyzed using turbo [4] and Low Density Generator Matrix [5] codes. Joint turbo equalization and decoding in asymmetric scenarios with correlated sources was also proposed in [6]. In [7] it was shown that the correlation parameters can be iteratively estimated at the decoder.

Following the system proposed in [7], the communication setup for the proposed VLIW based decoder is shown in Fig. 1. The source block $\{X_k\}_{k=1}^{M}$ produced by source S_1 is interleaved with a permutation function τ, and then processed by a binary rate $R_j = 1/3$ turbo code [8] with two identical constituent convolutional encoders C_1 and C_2 of constraint length L, giving rise to a set of $S^c = 2^{L-1}$ possible states. The encoded binary sequence is denoted by $\{X_k, P_k^1, P_k^2\}_{k=1}^{K}$, where we assume that P_k^1 and P_k^2 are the redundant symbols produced for input bit X_k by C_1, C_2, respectively. The input to the AWGN channel (with average energy per symbol E_c and noise variance $\sigma^2 = N_0/2$) is denoted as $\{\phi(X_k), \phi(P_k^1), \phi(P_k^2)\}_{k=1}^{K}$, where $\phi : \{0,1\} \to \{-\sqrt{E_c}, +\sqrt{E_c}\}$ denotes the BPSK transformation performed by the modulator. Finally, the received corresponding sequence will be denoted by $\{\tilde{X}_k, \tilde{P}_k^1, \tilde{P}_k^2\}_{k=1}^{K}$. The main idea behind the scheme in Fig. 1 hinges on the fact that, in order to estimate the original source symbols as $\{\hat{X}_k\}_{k=1}^{K}$, the joint decoder utilizes, not only the controlled redundancy $\{P_k^1, P_k^2\}_{k=1}^{K}$ added by the encoding stage, but also the side information $\{Y_k\}_{k=1}^{K}$ available at the decoder. A brief explanation of the HMM (Hidden Markov Model) based multiterminal source model and the designed decoding algorithm followed in [7] is next provided.

2.1 Adopted Model for the Correlated Multiterminal Source

As stated previously, we consider the general case where the random variable pairs (X_i, Y_i) and (X_j, Y_j) $\forall i \neq j$ at the output of the multiterminal source are not independent, i.e. the correlation among the sources represented by such a multiterminal source has memory. This class of multiterminal source may model, for instance, either temperature monitoring or video capture sensors. To emphasize the distributed nature of such modeled sources we will further assume that the random processes $\{X_k\}$ and $\{Y_k\}$ are binary, i.i.d.[1] and equiprobable.

[1] The term *i.i.d.* stands for *independent and identically distributed.*

The following generation model fulfills these requirements: the first component $\{X_k\}_{k=1}^{K}$ is a sequence of i.i.d. equiprobable binary random variables, while the second component $\{Y_k\}_{k=1}^{\infty}$ is produced by bitwise modulus-2 addition (hereafter denoted $\oplus$) of X_k and E_k, where $\{E_k\}$ is a binary stationary random process generated by a HMM. This model has often been utilized in the related literature [9,10]. The HMM is characterized by the set of parameters $\lambda_{HMM} = \{S_\lambda, \underline{A}, \underline{B}, \underline{\Pi}\}$, where S_λ is the number of states, $\underline{A} = [a_{s',s}]$ is a $S_\lambda \times S_\lambda$ state transition probability matrix, $\underline{B} = [b_{s,j}]$ is a $S_\lambda \times 2$ output distribution probability matrix, and $\underline{\Pi} = [\pi_s]$ is a $S_\lambda \times 1$ initial state probability vector. By changing these parameters of the HMM, different degrees of correlation can be obtained.

As shown in [7], this model can be reduced to an equivalent HMM that directly outputs the pair (X_k, Y_k) without any reference to E_k. Its Trellis diagram has S_λ states and $4S_\lambda$ branches arising from each state, one for each possible output (X_k, Y_k) combination. The associated branch transition probabilities are easily derived from the set of parameters λ_{HMM} of the original HMM and the marginal probability $P(x_k)$, yielding

$$T_k^{MS}(S_{k-1}^{MS} = s', S_k^{MS} = s, X_k = q, Y_k = v) \triangleq \begin{cases} a_{s',s}\, b_{s',0}\, 0.5 \text{ if } q = v, \\ a_{s',s}\, b_{s',1}\, 0.5 \text{ if } q \neq v, \end{cases} \quad (1)$$

where again $s, s' \in \{1, \ldots, S_\lambda\}$ and $q, v \in \{0, 1\}$. The label MS for the branch functions $T_k^{MS}(\cdot)$ and the state variables S_k^{MS} stands for *Multiterminal Source.*

2.2 Joint Source-Channel MAP Receiver Based on SISO Decoders

The tasks of source (compression) and channel coding of $\{X_k\}_{k=1}^{K}$ are jointly performed by means of a turbo code. The corresponding turbo decoder must be modified to take into account the correlated data $\{Y_k\}_{k=1}^{K}$ available at the receiver in order to decrease the required transmit energy. Such a joint decoder will estimate the original source sequence $\{X_k\}_{k=1}^{K}$ as $\{\widehat{X}_k\}_{k=1}^{K}$ under the MAP (Maximum a Posteriori) rule

$$\widehat{x}_k = \underset{x_k \in \{0,1\}}{\arg\max}\, P\left(x_k | \{\tilde{x}_k, \tilde{p}_k^1, \tilde{p}_k^2, y_k\}_{k=1}^{K}\right), \quad (2)$$

where $P(\cdot|\cdot)$ denotes conditional probability, and $k = 1, \ldots, K$. This can be achieved by applying the Sum-Product Algorithm (SPA) over the factor graph that jointly describes the two constituent recursive convolutional encoders and the statistical structure of the two correlated sources [11]. This factor graph is plotted in Fig. 2. Observe that such a graph is composed of 3 subgraphs (SISO decoders) corresponding to both convolutional decoders ($D1$ and $D2$) and the multiterminal source (MS), all of them describing Trellis diagrams with different parameters. Notice that variable nodes X_k and Y_k are related via T_k^{MS}, where $T_k^{MS}(\cdot)$ is given in expression (1). Also note the local functions $I_{Y_k}(y_k)$, which are indicator functions taking value 1 when $Y_k = y_k$, i.e. when the variable Y_k equals the known value y_k.

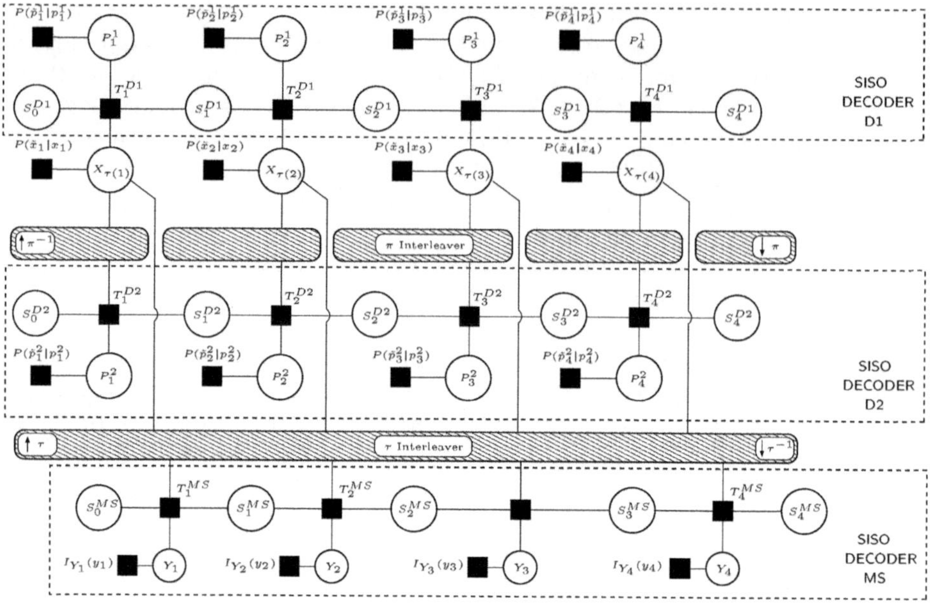

Fig. 2. Factor graph of the turbo joint source-channel decoder proposed in [7]

The SPA, when applied to cycle-free graphs, comprises a finite number of steps and provides the exact values for the computed marginalization [11]. However, the factor graph shown in Fig. 2 has cycles, and hence the algorithm has no natural termination. To overcome this issue, the SPA is separately applied to each subgraph — which, in turn, reduces to the Forward Backward (FBA) or BCJR algorithm — in the order $MS \rightarrow D1 \rightarrow D2$.

In practice, the forward and backward recursions are computed in the logarithmic domain to reduce complexity (Log-MAP and Max-Log-MAP). Let us be more concise and propose the notation:

- $L_{in}^{e,i}(x_k)$: extrinsic LLR (log-likelihood ratio) coming from Di ($i \in \{1,2\}$).
- $L_{in}^{s}(x_k)$: extrinsic LLR coming from SISO decoder MS.
- $L_{out}^{e}(x_k)$: *a posteriori* LLR generated at a certain SISO decoder.
- $t_p(s', s, x_k, y_k) \triangleq log\left(T_k^{MS}(s', s, x_k, y_k)\right)$: Logarithmic version of $T_k^{MS}(\cdot)$.

With the above notation, the Max-Log-MAP FBA recursions for SISO decoder $D1$ result in (similar expressions can be obtained for $D2$):

$$\overline{\gamma}_k(s', s) = \frac{1}{2}x_k\left(L_{in}^{e,2}(x_k) + L_{in}^{s}(x_k) + L_c\tilde{x}_k\right) + \frac{1}{2}L_c\tilde{p}_k^1 p_k^1, \tag{3}$$

$$\overline{\alpha}_k(s) = \max_{s' \in \{1,\ldots,S^c\}}^{*}\{\overline{\alpha}_{k-1}(s') + \overline{\gamma}_{k-1}(s', s)\}, \tag{4}$$

$$\overline{\beta}_{k-1}(s') = \max_{s \in \{1,\ldots,S^c\}}^{*}\{\overline{\beta}_k(s) + \overline{\gamma}_{k-1}(s', s)\}, \tag{5}$$

$$L_{out}^{e}(x_k) = max^*{}_{(s',s) \in S^+} \left\{ \overline{\alpha}_k(s') + \frac{1}{2} L_c \tilde{p}_k^1 p_k^1 + \overline{\beta}_{k+1}(s) \right\} - \underset{(s',s) \in S^-}{max^*} \left\{ \overline{\alpha}_k(s') + \frac{1}{2} L_c \tilde{p}_k^1 p_k^1 + \overline{\beta}_{k+1}(s) \right\}, \quad (6)$$

where $L_c \triangleq 2\sqrt{E_c}/\sigma^2$, $s', s \in \{1, \ldots, S^c\}$, and S^+ and S^- are the set of Trellis branches (s', s) with output $x_k = 1$ and $x_k = 0$, respectively. For the the SISO decoder MS, the recursions are:

$$\overline{\gamma}_k(s', s) = \frac{1}{2} x_k \left(L_{in}^{e,1}(x_k) + L_{in}^{e,2}(x_k) + L_c \tilde{x}_k \right) + t_p(s', s, x_k, y_k) \quad (7)$$

$$\overline{\alpha}_k(s) = \underset{s' \in \{1,\ldots,S_\lambda\}}{max^*} \{\overline{\alpha}_{k-1}(s') + \overline{\gamma}_{k-1}(s', s)\} \quad (8)$$

$$\overline{\beta}_{k-1}(s') = \underset{s \in \{1,\ldots,S_\lambda\}}{max^*} \{\overline{\beta}_k(s) + \overline{\gamma}_{k-1}(s', s)\} \quad (9)$$

$$L_{out}^{e}(x_k) = \underset{(s',s) \in S^+}{max^*} \{\overline{\alpha}_k(s') + t_p(s', s, x_k, y_k) + \overline{\beta}_{k+1}(s)\} - \underset{(s',s) \in S^-}{max^*} \{\overline{\alpha}_k(s') + t_p(s', s, x_k, y_k) + \overline{\beta}_{k+1}(s)\}. \quad (10)$$

Finally, the overall LLR for the source symbols X_k $(k = 1, \ldots, K)$ will be given by the sum of all LLR values arriving at variable node X_k, i.e. $LLR(x_k) = L_{out}^{e}(x_k) + L_{in}^{e,1}(x_k) + L_{in}^{e,2}(x_k) + L_c \tilde{x}_k$, over which a *hard decision* is carried out to provide the estimate $\widehat{X}_k$.

3 Hardware Architecture

The process of iterative joint source-channel turbo decoding described before has been implemented by means of a clustered VLIW ASIP. This kind of processor provides the best trade-off between area, performance and power in most signal processing applications.

The whole processor is meticulously optimized for the implementation of the convolutional SISO decoders *D1* and *D2* as well as for the implementation of SISO decoder *MS*. In a general perspective, the architecture comprises a master controller, a datapath and memory elements that store separately the data and the program.

The master controller consists of the instruction memory, the instruction decoder and the address generation unit. Following the approach exposed in [1], our controller is microprogrammed to direct each stage of the pipeline. This provides it with a higher flexibility and optimizes the resources utilization ratio, although complicates the labor of the programmer who is in charge of maintaining the pipeline [12].

All the computations of the system are performed in the Datapath of the processor, therefore the main design effort was carried out on it. This module is responsible for the frequency and latency of the whole decoder. Table 1 shows the computational needs of the datapath. The number of inputs, outputs and necessary hardware resources — adders, multipliers and Add Compare Select (ACS)

Table 1. SISO decoders computational needs

Operation	Inputs	Outputs	Add.	Mult.	ACS
SISOs D1 D2 *Gamma*	5	3	3	1	0
SISOs D1 D2 *Alpha Beta*	10	8	0	0	16
SISOs D1 D2 L^e_{out}	17	1	8	0	32
SISO MS *Gamma*	7	9	10	1	0
SISO MS *Alpha Beta*	10	2	0	0	8
SISO MS L^e_{out}-*LLR*	13	2	9	0	16

structures — are displayed. The Datapath is composed of two FUs (Functional Units), one for the *gamma* operations, which will be referred to as *gamma* FU, and another one for the *alpha, beta, LLR* and L^e_{out} operations which will be referred to as *ABLE* FU.

3.1 *ABLE* FU

The *ABLE* FU must be able to compute six operations that have different amounts of inputs — up to 17 — and outputs and different hardware resources needs. Based on [1] and in order to reduce the connectivity necessities, the number of registers inside the FU and improve the throughput, the serialization of the fetching and asserting of data was considered in the design.

Departing from equations 7 to 10 and 11 to 14 and Table 1 we came up with the design that is depicted in Fig. 3. The figure includes ACS (Add-Compare-Select) structures that implement the Jacobian algorithm approximation in the maximization, i.e. the *max** operator; there are also CSA (Compare Select Accumulate) structures that are used to compute many comparisons throughout several

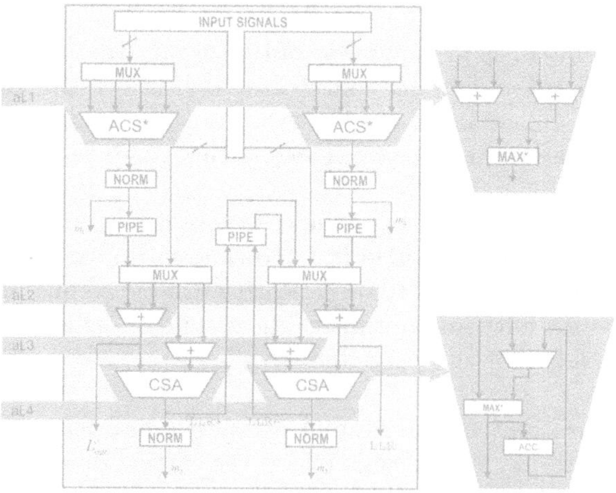

Fig. 3. *ABLE* Unit Implementation

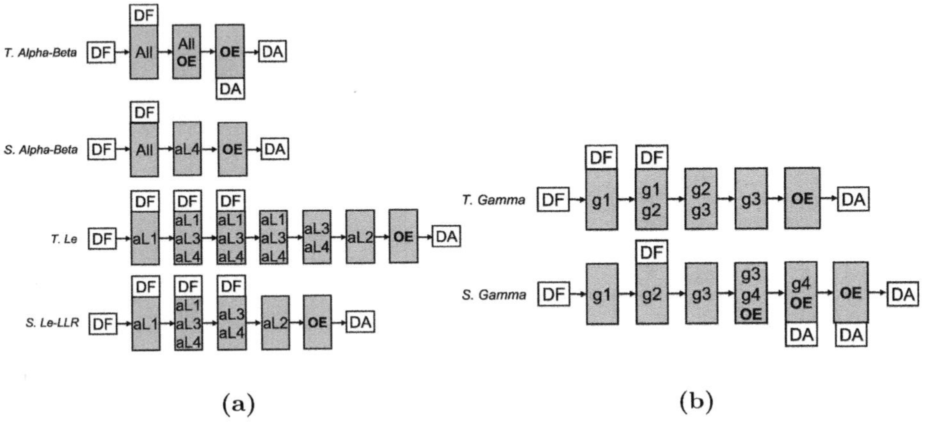

Fig. 4. (a) Pipelined execution of the *ABLE* Unit Operations.(b) Pipelined execution of the *Gamma* Unit Operations.

cycles. Pipeline registers (PIPE) divide the system into two halves comprising add-$max*$-norm structures which yields a design that is both well-balanced and independent of the max^* module implementation. The figure is segmented into four hardware blocks, aL1 to aL4, that will serve to explain each of the pipeline stages of each operation.

The execution of each operation of the *ABLE* Unit is described in Fig. 4.a. All the operations start with a data fetch (DF) and end with a data assert (DA), in between they use different hardware blocks and also fetch and assert data. Note that, since the outputs of the system are registered, these are always asserted one cycle later than produced, requiring an output enable (OE) signal.

As far as the operations of SISO decoders *D1* and *D2* are concerned, in the case of the *alpha-beta* computations, the unit in the first cycle half the *state metrics* and one *gamma* are fetched and in the second cycle the rest of the data is input, moreover in the second cycle the first set of four *state metrics* is produced and the remaining four *state metrics* are computed in a third cycle, all this entails a throughput of two cycles/symbol. Concerning the L^e_{out} operation, at each of the first four cycles the *state metrics* of a butterfly, which share the same *gamma*, are fetched and subsequently processed, a throughput of four cycles/symbol is achieved.

Regarding the operations of SISO decoder *MS*, the *alpha-beta* computations process all the branches arising from one *state metric* — i.e. *alpha* or *beta* — each cycle so that the number of inputs is reduced. Therefore in the first cycle one *state metric* is fetched along with the corresponding four *gammas*, and in the second cycle the other *state metric* and the rest of the *gammas* are fetched. In the case of the L^e_{out}-*LLR* operations, the procedure is similar to that of the other decoders, but taking in consideration the new trellis section constraints. These two previous operations achieve a throughput of two cycles/symbol.

Table 2. Latencies and throughputs of the datapath operations

Operation	Latency	Throughput
SISOs D1 D2 *Alpha Beta*	3	2
SISOs D1 D2 *LLR* L^{e}_{out}	7	4
SISO MS *Alpha Beta*	3	2
SISO MS *LLR* L^{e}_{out}	5	2
SISOs D1 D2 *Gamma*	5	2
SISO MS *Gamma*	6	2

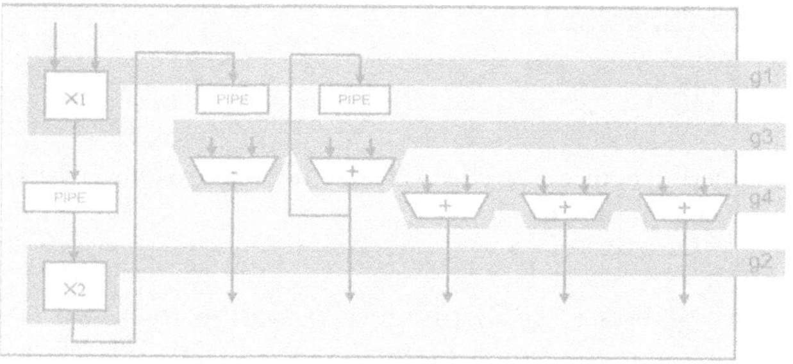

Fig. 5. *Gamma* Unit Implementation

Finally, Table 2 summarizes the latencies and throughputs of all the operations in the *ABLE* FU. Since these computations take their inputs from the *gamma* FU, the *gamma* computations of all the SISO decoders will have to achieve a throughput of two cycles/symbol.

3.2 *Gamma* FU

The *gamma* FU must be able to compute the *gamma* operations of the log-MAP algorithm and the source decoding. At first glance the only remarkable difference between equations 7 and 11 are the terms $\frac{1}{2}L_c\tilde{p}^k_k p^i_k$ — which can take two values, depending on p^i_k — and $t_p(u_k, z_k, s', s)$ — which can take eight different values that are prestored in a look-up table. Taking this into account, along with the figures in Table 1 and the throughput constraint of two cycles/symbol, we devised the structure displayed in Fig. 5. Here, the symbols $X1$ and $X2$ represent the first and second stages of a pipelined multiplier, respectively. Again, the unit is divided into four hardware blocks to ease the comprehension of the operations execution, shown in Fig. 4.b.

The *gamma* operation for SISOs *D1 D2* has to yield three outputs — two *gammas* and $\frac{1}{2}L_c y^p_k x^p_k$ — and achieves this with a latency of five cycles and throughput of two cycles continuously using every block except for "g4" that is left unused. In contrast the *gamma* operation in the source decoding yields nine outputs — eight *gammas* along with $L^{e,1}_{in} + L^{e,2}_{in} + L_c\tilde{x}_k$ — allowing a throughput of two cycles/symbol and a latency of six cycles, in this case all the blocks are used continuously except for "g1" that is used once every two cycles. Table 2 summarizes all these figures.

4 Synthesis Results

Considering that each symbol has to undergo one *alpha*, one *beta* and one L^e_{out} computation at each of the three decoders, and having in mind the figures from Table 2 the following results are yielded. The Datapath achieves a throughput of 8 cycles/symbol when implementing decoders *D1* and *D2* and a throughput of 6 cycles/symbol when decoder *SC* is implemented, thus a whole iteration through the three decoders entails a throughput of 22 cycles/symbol.

The design was prototyped in a Xilinx VirtexII 4000 FPGA. The whole system takes up 728 slices which is a very reduced area and makes the system attractive for embedded applications. The ABLE FU takes up 353 slices, almost half of the whole system, whereas the gamma FU takes up 42 slices, a relatively small portion. The maximum frequency of the system was fixed at 73.6 MHz which entails a data throughput of 3.3 MSym/sec for each complete iteration.

5 Concluding Remarks

Exploiting the correlation among different sources in a sensor network has drawn the attention of the research community due to its promising reduction of the transmitted energy. In this work, we have presented a dual-clustered VLIW architecture that supposes the first implementation of a turbo joint source-channel decoder for spatially correlated multiterminal sources with memory. The most critical aspects of the system design have been thoroughly described, especially the complex datapath that embodies two pipelined multioperand functional units. The approach combines the benefits of programmable solutions along with the characteristics of very dedicated designs, resulting highly appropriate for an embedded solution.

References

1. Ituero, P., Lopez-Vallejo, M.: New Schemes in Clustered VLIW Processors Applied to Turbo Decoding. In: 17th IEEE International Conference on Application-Specific Systems, Architecture Processors. (2006)
2. Aaron, A., Girod, B.: Compression with Side Information using Turbo Codes. In: Proceedings of the IEEE Data Compression Conference. (2002) 252–261
3. Liveris, A.D., Xiong, Z., Georghiades, C.N.: Joint Source-Channel Coding of Binary Sources with Side Information at the Decoder using IRA Codes. In: Proceedings of the IEEE International Workshop on Multimedia Signal. (2002) 440–442
4. Garcia-Frias, J.: Joint Source-Channel Decoding of Correlated Sources over Noisy Channels. In: Proceedings of the IEEE Data Compression Conference. (2001) 283–292

5. Zhong, W., Lou, H., Garcia-Frias, J.: LDGM Codes for Joint Source-Channel Coding of Correlated Sources. In: Proceedings of the IEEE International Conference on Image Processing. Volume 1. (2003) 593–596
6. Del Ser, J., Munoz, A., Crespo, P.M.: Joint source-channel decoding of correlated sources over ISI channels. In: Proceedings of the IEEE Vehicular Technology Conference. Volume 1. (2005) 625–629
7. Del Ser, J., Crespo, P.M., Galdos, O.: Asymmetric Joint Source-Channel Coding for Correlated Sources with Blind HMM Estimation at the Receiver. Eurasip Journal on Wireless Communications and Networking, Special Issue on Wireless Sensor Networks **4** (2005) 483–492
8. Berrou, C., Glavieux, A., Thitimajshima, P.: Near Shannon Limit Error-Correcting Coding and Decoding: Turbo Codes. In: Proceedings of the IEEE International Conference on Communications (ICC). (1993) 1064–1070
9. Tian, T., García-Frías, J., Zhong, W.: Compression of Correlated Sources Using LDPC Codes. In: Proceedings of the IEEE Data Compression Conference. (2003) 450
10. Garcia-Frias, J., Zhong, W.: LDPC Codes for Compression of Multi-Terminal Sources with Hidden Markov Correlation. IEEE Communication Letters **7** (2003) 115–117
11. Kschischang, F.R., Frey, B.J., Loeliger, H.A.: Factor Graphs and the Sum-Product Algorithm. IEEE Transactions on Information Theory **47** (2001) 498–519
12. Jacome, M.F., de Veciana, G.: Design challenges for new application-specific processors. Design&Test of computers **17** (2000) 40–50

Theory and Practice of Probabilistic Timed Game for Embedded Systems

Satoshi Yamane

Graduate School of Natural Science, Kanazawa University
syamane@is.t.kanazawa-u.ac.jp

Abstract. Recent embedded systems are composed of many components, and each component is an open system, and it has both real-time properties and uncertainties. We specify each component using timing constraints and probabilities, and compose systems from all the components. In order to treat them, we develop the followings: First we develop probabilistic timed game automata based on a probabilistic timed game as a computational model. Next we develop probabilistic timed game verification.

Keyword: formal specification, formal verification, game-theoretic approach, probabilistic timed game automaton, reachability game.

1 Introduction

Recently, 99 percent or more of the microprocessor is used for embedded systems from control systems to information appliances. Also, embedded systems are increasingly deployed in safety-critical situations [1]. This calls for systematic design and verification methodologies that cope with the following three major sources of complexity [2] :

1. Embedded systems have reactivity, and various components concurrently behave as open systems [3]
2. Embedded systems have real-time properties [4]
3. Embedded systems behave in an uncertain environment [5]

In order to resolve these sources, the following techniques have been studied.

1. A.Pnueli and his colleague have modeled reactivity by the game theory between system and environment [6].
2. In order to specify timing constraints, R.Alur and his colleagues have developed timed automata and hybrid automata [7,8].
3. In order to specify uncertainty, R.Segala and N.Lynch have studied probabilistic automata [9], and M. Kwiatkowska and her colleagues have developed probabilistic timed automata [10].

Especially, L. de Alfaro and T.A. Henzinger have notably developed interface theories for componentware of reactive systems [11,12,13]. They have guaranteed the validity of systems by weak game-theoretic foundations.

Y.-H. Lee et al. (Eds.): ICESS 2007, LNCS 4523, pp. 109–120, 2007.

In this paper, we propose probabilistic timed game theory by combining game theory and timed automata with probabilities as follows:

1. First, we propose probabilistic game automaton, and define its game-theoretic semantics.
2. Next, we propose verification method of probabilistic timed game.

The paper is organized as follows: In section 2, we define probabilistic timed game automaton. In section 3, we define verification method of probabilistic timed reachability game. In section 4, we specify wireless LAN protocol using probabilistic timed game automata. Finally, in section 5, we present conclusions.

2 Probabilistic Timed Game Automaton

We assume embedded systems consist of many components, which concurrently behave. We specify each component by probabilistic timed game automaton.

First we define probabilistic timed game automaton, and define its semantics by probabilistic timed game theory.

2.1 Probabilistic Timed Game Automaton

First we define the discrete probability distribution.

Definition 1 (Discrete probability distribution)
We denote the set of discrete probability distributions over a set Q by $\mu(Q)$. Therefore, each $p \in \mu(Q)$ is a function $p : Q \to [0,1]$ such that $\sum_{q \in Q} p(q) = 1$. ■

Next, we define clock constraints.

Definition 2 (Clock constraint and clock valuations)
Let χ be a set of clock variables over $\mathbf{R}$.

A constraint over χ is an expression of the form $x \prec c$ or $x - y \prec c$, where $c \in \mathbf{N} \cup \{\infty\}$, $x, y \in \chi$, $\prec \in \{<, \leq\}$. We denote a set of clock constraints over χ by $\Xi[\chi]$.

Let $v : \chi \to \mathbf{R}$ be a function assigning a real value to each of the clocks. We write $\mathbf{0}_\chi$ for the valuation that assigns 0 to each clock. We write $\mathcal{V}(\chi)$ for all the valuations in χ. We denote $v + \Delta$ for $\Delta \in \mathbf{R}$ the valuation such that for $x \in \chi$, $(v + \Delta)(x) = v(x) + \Delta$. For some $r \subseteq \chi$, we write $v[r := 0]$ for the clock valuation that assigns 0 to all clocks in r, and agrees with v for all clocks in $\chi \setminus r$. For $\varphi \in \Xi[\chi]$, we write $v \models \varphi$ if v satisfies φ. It clearly holds $v[r := 0]$ iff $v \models \varphi[r := 0]$. ■

Next we define probabilistic timed game automaton.

Definition 3 (Probabilistic timed game automaton)
A probabilistic timed game automaton is a tuple

$\mathbf{A} = (Q_A, q_A{}^{init}, \chi_A, Acts_A{}^I, Acts_A{}^O, Inv_A, \rho_A)$ *, where*

1. *Q_A is a finite set of locations*
2. *${q_A}^{init}$ is an initial location*
3. *χ_A is a finite set of clock variables*
4. *${Acts_A}^I$ is a set of input actions, and ${Acts_A}^O$ is a set of output actions, $Acts_A = {Acts_A}^I \cup {Acts_A}^O \cup D$, where D is the set of time delays and $\Delta \in D$. Input actions are generated by environment, and are not controlled by probabilistic timed game automaton. On the other hand, output actions are generated by probabilistic timed game automaton, and are controlled by probabilistic timed game automaton.*
5. *$Inv_A : Q_A \rightarrow \Xi[\chi_A]$ associates to each location its invariant.*
6. *$\rho_A \subseteq Q_A \times \Xi[\chi_A] \times \{{Acts_A}^I \cup {Acts_A}^O\} \times 2^{\chi_A} \times \mu(Q_A)$ is a finite set of transitions.*
   For $(q_A, g_A, a_A, r_A, p_A) \in \rho_A$, $q_A \in Q_A$ is a source location, $g_A \in \Xi[\chi]$ is a clock constraint, $a_A \in {Acts_A}^I \cup {Acts_A}^O$ is an action, $r_A \subseteq 2^{\chi_A}$ is a set of reset variables, $p_A \in \mu(Q_A)$ is a discrete probability distribution over a set of locations. ■

Our proposed probabilistic timed game automaton is quite different from M. Kwiatkowska's probabilistic timed automaton [10] as follows:

1. Probabilistic timed game automaton distinguishs between input actions and output actions. Input actions are generated by environment, and are not controlled by probabilistic timed game automaton. On the other hand, output actions are generated by probabilistic timed game automaton, and are controlled by probabilistic timed game automaton.
2. In order to simplify models, we define the discrete probability distribution over a set of locations. On the other hand, M. Kwiatkowska defines the discrete probability distribution over a set of locations and a powerset of reset variables.
3. We define game theoretic semantics of probabilistic timed game automaton.

Example 1 (Example of probabilistic timed game automaton)
Example of probabilistic timed game automaton is shown in Figure 1. The solid arrows denote controllable actions, and the dotted arrows denote uncontrollable actions. Now we consider a reachability game, and verify whether the goal is reachable from $< {q_A}^{init}, x \geq 2 >$ the probability by 0.8 or more. The reachability game consists in finding a strategy for a controller, i.e. when to take the controllable transitions that will guarantee that the system, regardless of when and if the opponent chooses to take uncontrollable transitions, will eventually end up some probability in the location the goal. In Figure 1, for all initial location with $x > 1$ there is no winning strategy. On the other hand, for all initial location with $x \leq 1$ there is such a winning strategy. ■

2.2 Theory of Probabilistic Timed Game

Probabilistic timed games are classified into **reachability game**, **safety game**, **infinite game**. In this paper, we consider reachability game. Given a probabilistic timed game automaton **A** and a reachability condition K such as a pair

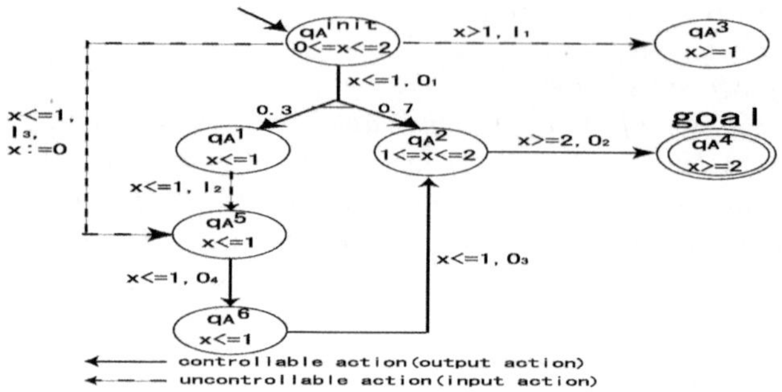

Fig. 1. Example of a probabilistic timed game automaton

$(G \subseteq Q_A \times \mathbf{R}, \geq p)$, the reachability game $(\mathbf{A}, K)$ consists in finding a strategy f such that $\mathbf{A}$ supervised by f enforces K.

A state of a $\mathbf{A}$ is a pair $< q_A, v_A > \in Q_A \times \mathbf{R}$, where $v_A \in \mathcal{V}(\chi_A)$. We denote a set of finite or infinite nonZeno runs from $< {q_A}^{init}, \mathbf{0}_{\chi_A} >$ by $\mathbf{Runs}(< {q_A}^{init}, \mathbf{0}_{\chi_A} >, \mathbf{A})$. ρ in $\mathbf{Runs}(< {q_A}^{init}, \mathbf{0}_{\chi_A} >, \mathbf{A})$ is as follows [14] :

$\rho =$

$< {q_A}^{init}, \mathbf{0}_{\chi_A} > \xrightarrow{\Delta_0}$

$< {q_A}^{init}, \mathbf{0}_{\chi_A} + \Delta_0 > \xrightarrow{g_0, i_0, r_0, p_0}$

$< q_{A1}, \mathbf{0}_{\chi_A} + \Delta_0[r_0 := 0] > \xrightarrow{\Delta_1}$

$< q_{A1}, \mathbf{0}_{\chi_A} + \Delta_0[r_0 := 0] + \Delta_1 > \xrightarrow{g_1, o_0, r_1, p_1}$

$< q_{A2}, \mathbf{0}_{\chi_A} + (\Delta_0[r_0 := 0] + \Delta_1)[r_1 := 0] > \xrightarrow{\Delta_2}$

$< q_{A2}, \mathbf{0}_{\chi_A} + (\Delta_0[r_0 := 0] + \Delta_1)[r_1 := 0] + \Delta_2 > \xrightarrow{g_2, i_1, r_2, p_2}$

....

We can compute the probability of ρ as follows:

$p_0(q_{A1}) \times p_1(q_{A2}) \times \ldots\ldots$

Let $(G \subseteq Q_A \times \mathbf{R}, \geq p)$ be a reachability condition.

The runs are winning if $\sum_k \{p_0(q_{A1}) \times p_1(q_{A2}) \times \ldots \times p_{k-1}(q_{Ak})\} \geq p$ holds true for any k which satisfies $< q_{Ak}, v_{Ak} > \in G$. The set of winning runs in $\mathbf{A}$ from $< {q_A}^{init}, \mathbf{0}_{\chi_A} >$ is denoted $\mathbf{WinRuns}(< {q_A}^{init}, \mathbf{0}_{\chi_A} >, \mathbf{A})$.

Basically actions of probabilistic timed game are determined by the following rule. An infinite run is assumed to have no infinite sequence of delay transitions of duration 0. We define rule based on timed game by O. Maler, A.Pnueli, J.Sifakis [15]. But we define the asymmetric setting between environment and system, as actions of environment have a priority over those of system.

Definition 4 (Rule of probabilistic timed game)
Actions of probabilistic timed game are determined by the following rule.

1. *First, in location q_A, action α is determined according to the following rule. Here $\alpha \in \mathbf{R}$ is passage of time to have stayed in the location, and $\alpha \in Acts_A$ generates the state transition.*
   (a) *If $\alpha_I, \alpha_O \in \mathbf{R}$, $\alpha = min\{\alpha_I, \alpha_O\}$ is chosen. Namely, if $\alpha_I < \alpha_O$ then α_I, otherwise α_O, where I is an input player(environment), and O is an output player(automaton).*
   (b) *If $\alpha_I \in {Acts_A}^I$ and $\alpha_O \in \mathbf{R}$, $\alpha = \alpha_I$ is chosen.*
   (c) *If $\alpha_O \in {Acts_A}^O$ and $\alpha_I \in \mathbf{R}$, $\alpha = \alpha_O$ is chosen.*
   (d) *If $\alpha_I \in {Acts_A}^I$ and $\alpha_O \in {Acts_A}^O$, $\alpha = \alpha_I$ is chosen.*
   (e) *If $\alpha_I, \alpha_{I'} \in {Acts_A}^I$, $\alpha = \alpha_I$ or $\alpha = \alpha_{I'}$ is nondeterministically chosen.*
   (f) *If $\alpha_O, \alpha_{O'} \in {Acts_A}^O$, $\alpha = \alpha_O$ or $\alpha = \alpha_{O'}$ is nondeterministically chosen.*
2. *Next, by α, a probability distribution p is solely determined.* ■

In the following, we define strategies and outcomes of probabilistic timed game.

First we define a strategy of probabilistic timed game by extending a strategy of timed game (proposed by O. Maler, A.Pnueli, J.Sifakis [15,16]). A strategy of probabilistic timed game is a function that during the course of the game constantly gives information as to what the controller should do in order to win the game.

Definition 5 (A strategy of probabilistic timed game)
Let $\mathbf{A} = (Q_A, {q_A}^{init}, \chi_A, {Acts_A}^O, {Acts_A}^I, Inv_A, \rho_A)$ be a probabilistic timed game automaton. A strategy f over $\mathbf{A}$ is a partial function from $\mathbf{Runs}(({q_A}^{init}, \mathbf{0}_{\chi_\mathbf{A}}), \mathbf{A})$ to ${Acts_A}^O \cup D$ such that for every finite run ρ, if $f(\rho) \in {Acts_A}^O$ then $last(\rho) \xrightarrow{f(\rho)} < q_{A'}, v_{A'} >$ for some $< q_{A'}, v_{A'} >$, where we denote $last(\rho)$ the last state of the run ρ. ■

Moreover, Luca de Alfaro, Thomas A. Henzinger, Rupak Majumdar [17] have proposed the idea such that the run controlled with some strategy f is defined by the notion of outcome. Here the runs of a probabilistic timed game automaton $\mathbf{A}$ controlled with some strategy f is the subset of all the runs. Using Luca de Alfaro's idea [17], we define the run controlled with some strategy f as outcome.

Definition 6 (Outcome of probabilistic timed game)
Let $\mathbf{A} = (Q_A, {q_A}^{init}, \chi_A, {Acts_A}^I, {Acts_A}^O, Inv_A, \rho_A)$ be a probabilistic timed game automaton and f be a strategy over $\mathbf{A}$. The outcome $\mathbf{Outcome}(< q_A, v_A >, f)$ of f from (q_A, v_A) is the subset of $\mathbf{Runs}(< q_A, v_A >, \mathbf{A})$ defined inductively by:

1. *$< q_A, v_A > \in \mathbf{Outcome}(< q_A, v_A >, f)$,*
2. *if $\rho \in \mathbf{Outcome}(< q_A, v_A >, f)$ then $\rho' = \rho \xrightarrow{e_A} < q_{A'}, v_{A'} >$ if $\rho' \in \mathbf{Runs}(< q_A, v_A >, \mathbf{A})$ and one of the following three conditions hold:*
   (a) *$e_A = (g, i, r, p)$,*
   (b) *$e_A = (g, o, r, p)$ and $o = f(\rho)$,*
   (c) *$e_A = \Delta \in \mathbf{R}$ and $\forall \Delta' \leq \Delta$, $\exists < q_{A''}, v_{A''} >$ such that $last(\rho) \xrightarrow{\Delta'} < q_{A''}, v_{A''} > \wedge f(\rho \xrightarrow{\Delta'} < q_{A''}, v_{A''} >) = \Delta'$.*

3. *for an infinite run ρ, $\rho \in$ **Outcome**$(< q_A, v_A >, f)$ if all the finite prefixes of ρ are in **Outcome**$(< q_A, v_A >, f)$.* ■

We assume that uncontrollable actions(input actions) can only spoil the game and the controller has to do some controllable action (output action) to win [15]. In this sense, we compute the minimal probability. A run may end in a state where only uncontrollable actions(input actions) can be taken. Here we define a maximal run ρ of probabilistic timed game by borrowing the maximal run of timed game from K.G.Larsen [18] as follows: A maximal run ρ is either an infinite NonZeno run [19] or a finite run ρ that satisfies either (1)$last(\rho) \in G$ or (2)if $\rho \stackrel{(g,a,r,p)}{\longrightarrow}$ then $a \in {Acts_A}^I$.

A strategy f is winning from $< q_A, v_A >$ if maximal runs in **Outcome**$(< q_A, v_A >, f)$ satisfy a reachability condition K. Also they are in **WinRuns**$(< q_A, v_A >, \mathbf{A})$. A state $< q_A, v_A >$ is winning if there exists a winning strategy f from $< q_A, v_A >$ in **A**.

3 Verification of Probabilistic Timed Reachability Game

3.1 Basic Idea

In famous existing timed game [15,17,18], they define controllable predecessors operator and compute a set of winning states by controllable predecessors operator. But in our probabilistic timed game, in order to compute probabilities, we apply M. Kwiatkowska's idea [10] into our verification of probabilistic timed reachability game. Therefore, as in existing timed game [15,17,18], we constrcut zone graph using controllable predecessors operator, and moreover compute probabilities over zone graph using linear equation systems [10].

3.2 Controllable Predecessors Operator

Let **A**$= (Q_A, {q_A}^{init}, \chi_A, {Acts_A}^I, {Acts_A}^O, Inv_A, \rho_A)$ be a probabilistic timed game automaton. First we define a symbolic state [10], and next define controllable predecessors operator [18].

Definition 7 (symbolic state)
A symbolic state is a pair of the form $< q_A, \zeta_A >$, where $q_A \in Q_A$ and $\zeta_A \in Z_A$. Z_A is a set of valuations satisfying the followingF

$$\bigwedge\nolimits_{0 \le i \ne j \le n} x_i - x_j \prec_{ij} c_{ij},$$

where $\chi = \{x_0, x_1, \ldots, x_n\}$ and $x_0 = 0$, $c_{ij} \in \mathbf{Z} \cup \{\infty\}$, $\prec_{ij} \in \{<, \le\}$. ■

Definition 8 (Discrete-successors and time-successors)
We define discrete-successors and time-successors as follows:

1. **Discrete-successors***:*
   For $a_A \in Acts_A$, we define discrete-successors $\mathbf{Post}_a(X)$ *as follows:*

$\mathbf{Post_a}(X) = \{< q_{A'}, \zeta_{A'} > | \exists < q_A, \zeta_A > \in X, < q_A, \zeta_A > \overset{(g_A, a_A, r_A, p_A)}{\longrightarrow} < q_{A'}, \zeta_{A'} >\}$,
where $p_A(q_{A'}) > 0$, $\zeta_{A'} = ((\zeta_A \cap g_A)[r_A := 0]) \cap Inv_A(q_{A'})$.

2. **Time-successors**:
We define controllable timed successors $\mathbf{Suc_t}(X)$ *as folllows:*
$\mathbf{Suc_t}(X) = \{< q_A, (\nearrow \zeta_A) \cap Inv_A(q_A) > | < q_A, \zeta_A > \in X\}$,
where $\nearrow \zeta_A = \{v | \exists \Delta > 0 \, . \, (v - \Delta \models \zeta_A \wedge \forall \Delta\prime \leq \Delta.(v - \Delta\prime \models \zeta_A))\}$. ■

Definition 9 (Discrete-predecessors and time-predecessors)
We define discrete-predecessors and time-predecessors as follows:

1. **Discrete-predecessors**:
For an $a_A \in Acts_A$, *we define discrete-predecessors* $\mathbf{Pred}_a(X)$ *as follows:*
$\mathbf{Pred_a}(X) = \{< q_A, \zeta_A > | \exists < q_{A'}, \zeta_{A'} > \in X, < q_A, \zeta_A > \overset{(g_A, a_A, r_A, p_A)}{\longrightarrow} < q_{A'}, \zeta_{A'} >\}$,
where $p_A(q_{A'}) > 0$, $\zeta_{A'} = ((\zeta_A \cap g_A)[r_A := 0]) \cap Inv_A(q_{A'})$.
2. **Time-predecessors**:
We define controllable timed predecessors $\mathbf{Pred_t}(X)$ *as folllows:*
$\mathbf{Pred_t}(X) = \{< q_A, (\swarrow \zeta_A) \cap Inv_A(q_A) > | < q_A, \zeta_A > \in X\}$,
where $\swarrow \zeta_A = \{v | \exists \Delta > 0 \, . \, (v + \Delta \models \zeta_A \wedge \forall \Delta\prime \leq \Delta.(v + \Delta\prime \models \zeta_A))\}$. ■

Finally we define controllable predecessorsF

Definition 10 (Controllable predecessors operator)
We define controllable predecessors operation $\mathbf{Pred_t}(X, Y)$ *as follows:*

$\mathbf{Pred_t}(X, Y) = \{< q_A, \zeta_A > \in Q_A \times Z_A | \exists \Delta \in \mathbf{R}$ *s.t.* $< q_A, \zeta_A > \overset{\Delta}{\longrightarrow} < q_A, \zeta_{A'} >, < q_A, \zeta_{A'} > \in X$ *and* $\mathbf{Post_{[0,\Delta]}}(< q_A, \zeta_A >) \subseteq \overline{Y}\}$,
where $\mathbf{Post_{[0,\Delta]}}(< q_A, \zeta_A >) = \{< q_A, \zeta_{A'} > \in Q_A \times Z_A | \exists t \in [0, \Delta]$*s.t.* $< q_A, \zeta_A > \overset{\Delta}{\longrightarrow} < q_A, \zeta_{A'} >\}$ *and* $\overline{Y} = (Q_A \times Z_A) \setminus Y$. *The controllable predecessors operator* π *is defined as follows:*
$\pi(X) = \mathbf{Pred_t}(X \cup \bigcup_{o \in Acts_A{}^O} \mathbf{Pred_a}(X), \bigcup_{i \in Acts_A{}^I} \mathbf{Pred_a}(\overline{X}))$. ■

3.3 Construction of Zone Graph

Let $(G \subseteq Q_A \times \mathbf{R}, \geq p)$ be the condition of a reachability game, where G_A is a set of target locations and G is a set of target symbolic states. We use zone graph construction method developed by K.G.Larsen' SOTFTR algorithm [18] based on controllable predecessors operation. The SOTFTR algorithm is viewed as an interleaved combination of forward computation of the probabilistic timed game automaton together with back-propagation of information of winning states, and finally construct zone graph, which consists of only winning states. In M. Kwiatkowska's method [10], as probabilistic timed automaton is nondeterministic with respect to probability distributions, zone graph is Markov decision process. On the other hand, probabilistic timed game automaton is deterministic with respect to probability distributions, zone graph is Markov process.

Definition 11 (Zone graph)
The zone graph $\mathbf{M_A}^{\mathbf{G_A}}$ *of the probabilistic timed game automaton* $\mathbf{A}= (Q_A, q_A{}^{init}, \chi_A, Acts_A{}^I, Acts_A{}^O, Inv_A, \rho_A)$ *with respect to* G_A *is the Markov process* $\mathbf{M_A}^{\mathbf{G_A}} = (S_A{}^{G_A}, < q_A{}^{init}, \zeta_A{}^{init} >, p_A{}^{G_A})$*, where*

1. $S_A{}^{G_A}$*: a set of winning symbolic states,*
2. $< q_A{}^{init}, \zeta_A{}^{init} >$ *is an initial symbolic state, where* $q_A{}^{init}$ *is an initial location and* $\zeta_A{}^{init}$ *is its initial zone,*
3. *For all* $< q_A, \zeta_A > \in S_A{}^{G_A}$ *and* $p_A \in \mu(Q_A)$*, there exists* $p_A{}^{G_A} \in \mu(S_A{}^{G_A})$*, such that, for each* $< q_A\prime, \zeta_A\prime > \in S_A{}^{G_A}$*,* $p_A{}^{G_A}(< q_A\prime, \zeta_A\prime >) = p_A(q_A\prime, r)$*, where* $< q_A, \zeta_A > \stackrel{(g_A, a_A, r_A, p_A)}{\longrightarrow} < q_A, \zeta_A\prime >$*. Here the probability (that Markov process will make a transition to a location* $q_A\prime$*, and reset all the clocks in* r *to 0,) is given by* $p_A(q_A\prime, r)$ ■

Now we define $P_A{}^{G_A}$ instead of $p_A{}^{G_A}$ as the standard form in Markov process.

$$P_A{}^{G_A}(< q_A, \zeta_A >, < q_A\prime, \zeta_A\prime >) = p_A(q_A\prime, r)$$

Namely, the zone graph is Markov process $\mathbf{M_A}^{\mathbf{G_A}} = (S_A{}^{G_A}, < q_A{}^{init}, \zeta_A{}^{init} >, P_A{}^{G_A})$.

3.4 Computing Probabilities over Zone Graph

We verify whether $(G \subseteq Q_A \times \mathbf{R}, \geq p)$ is satisfiable or not over Markov process $\mathbf{M_A}^{\mathbf{G_A}} = (S_A{}^{G_A}, < q_A{}^{init}, \zeta_A{}^{init} >, P_A{}^{G_A})$. First, we compute the total of probabilities such that all the states in G are reached from an intial $< q_A{}^{init}, \zeta_A{}^{init} >$. Second, if the total of probabilities satisfy $\geq p$, the probabilistic timed game automaton is winning. Here we compute the total of probabilities using C. Courcoubetis and M. Yannakakis's method [20,21,22] as follows.

Definition 12 (Method of computing the total of probability)
We verify whether $(G \subseteq Q_A \times \mathbf{R}, \geq p)$ *is satisfiable or not over Markov process* $\mathbf{M_A}^{\mathbf{G_A}} = (S_A{}^{G_A}, < q_A{}^{init}, \zeta_A{}^{init} >, P_A{}^{G_A})$ *according to the following steps:*

1. *First we divide* $S_A{}^{G_A}$ *into the following three sets by depth-first search.*
   (a) *All states in* G *are in* $S_A{}^{G_A{}^{YES}}$
   (b) *All states, which do not reach* G*, are in* $S_A{}^{G_A{}^{NO}}$
   (c) $S_A{}^{G_A{}^?} = S_A{}^{G_A} \setminus (S_A{}^{G_A{}^{YES}} \cup S_A{}^{G_A{}^{NO}})$
2. *Next we solve the regular linear equation system* $\mathbf{x} = \mathbf{A} \cdot \mathbf{x} + \mathbf{b}$*, where*
   (a) $\mathbf{x} = (x_s)_{s \in S_A{}^{G_A{}^?}}$.
   (b) $\mathbf{b} = (b_s)_{s \in S_A{}^{G_A{}^?}}$ *, where* $b_s = P_A{}^{G_A}(s, S_A{}^{G_A{}^{YES}})$.
   (c) $\mathbf{A} = (P_A{}^{G_A}(s,t))_{s,t \in S_A{}^{G_A{}^?}}$.

   We can easily solve this linear equation system using Gauss-Seidel method [23]. ■

3.5 Example

First we show probabilistic timed game automaton **A** in Figure 2. This automaton has the reachability condition $(< Goal, x = y >, \geq 0.90)$.

Next we construct zone graph $\mathbf{M_A}^{\mathbf{G_A}}$ shown in Figure 3 from probabilistic timed game automaton **A** in Figure 2.

If the total of probabilities of the runs from an initial state q_0 to *Goal* satisfies ≥ 0.90, the runs are in $\mathbf{WinRuns}(< q_0, \mathbf{0}_{\{x,y\}} >, \mathbf{A})$. The runs are classified into two categories, and the probabilities of candidates of $\mathbf{WinRuns}(< q_0, \mathbf{0}_{\{x,y\}} >, \mathbf{A})$ as follows:

1. Path without loops$(< q_0, x = y \leq 3 > \rightarrow < q_2, x = y \leq 3 > \rightarrow < Goal, x = y >)$:
   (a) $0.05 \times 0.8 = 0.04$
2. Paths with loops$(< q_0, x = y \leq 3 > \rightarrow (< q_1, x = y \leq 2 >)^{\omega} \rightarrow < Goal, x = y >)$:
   (a) $0.95 \times 0.9 = 0.855$
   (b) $0.95 \times 0.9 \times (0.1 \times 0.9)^1$

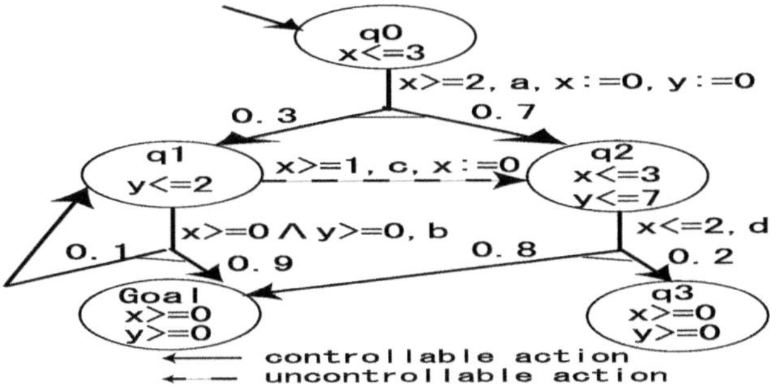

Fig. 2. Probabilistic timed game automaton **A**

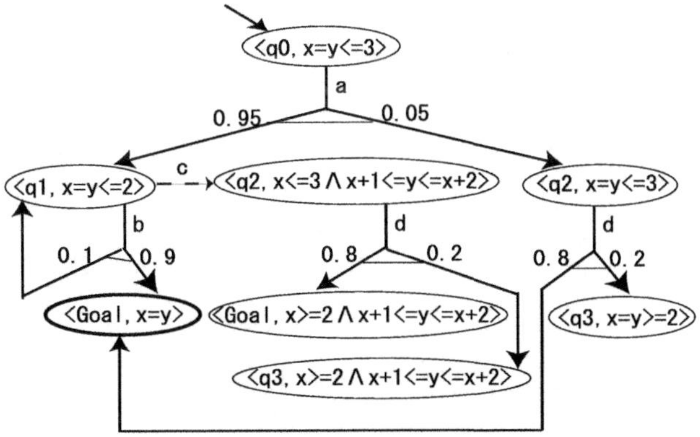

Fig. 3. Zone graph

(c) $0.95 \times 0.9 \times (0.1 \times 0.9)^2$
(d) $0.95 \times 0.9 \times (0.1 \times 0.9)^3$
....
....

We compute the total of probabilities of paths with loops by solving the following linear equation system. Here ${S_A}^{{G_A}^{YES}} = \{Goal\}$, ${S_A}^{{G_A}^{NO}} = \emptyset$, ${S_A}^{{G_A}^{?}} = \{q_0, q_1\}$.

1. $x_0 = 0.95 \times x_1$
2. $x_1 = 0.1 \times x_1 + 0.9 \times x_G$
3. $x_G = 1.0$,

where x_0 is the probability to reach *Goal* from q_0, x_1 is the probability to reach *Goal* from q_1, x_G is the probability to reach *Goal* from *Goal*. By solving the linear equation system, $x_0 = 0.95$ is computed. Therefore, the total of probabilities is $0.95 + 0.04 = 0.99$. Then we conclude this probabilistic timed game automaton is winning. Namely, the above runs are in **WinRuns**($< q_0, \mathbf{0}_{\{x,y\}} >, \mathbf{A}$). As **WinRuns**($< q_0, \mathbf{0}_{\{x,y\}} >, \mathbf{A}$) is not empty, a strategy f is winning from $< q_0, \mathbf{0}_{\{x,y\}} >$. Moreover, as there exists a winning strategy f from $< q_0, \mathbf{0}_{\{x,y\}} >$ of $\mathbf{A}$, $< q_0, \mathbf{0}_{\{x,y\}} >$ is winning.

4 Specifying IEEE802.11 Protocol

In this section, we model and specify DCF components of ad hoc network of the IEEE802.11 [24] using probabilistic timed game automatonD The model consists

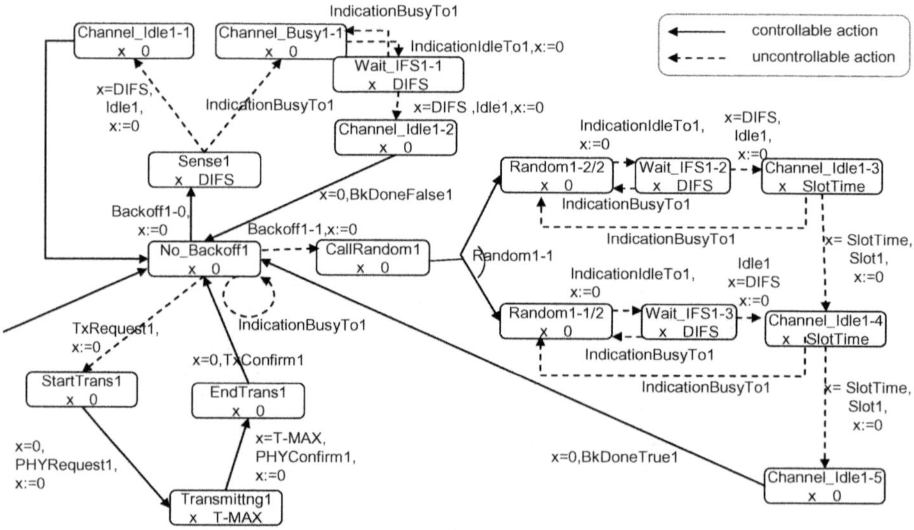

Fig. 4. $TRANSMISSION_1^{(S)}$

of $\mathrm{Send}_1 \mathrm{C} \mathrm{Send}_2$, $RECIEVE_1^{(S)} \mathrm{C} RECIEVE_2^{(S)}$C Wireless Media $WM^{(S)}$. Here Send_1 consists of $CONTROL_1^{(S)}$ and $TRANSMISSION_1^{(S)}$. The components concurrently behave. We show only $TRANSMISSION_1^{(S)}$ in Figure 4 because of lack of spaces. Here Ramdom1-1 means 1/16-probability distribution.

We easily specify each component in ad hoc network using probabilistic timed game automaton. Also, we can compose all the components into one embedded system described in probabilistic timed game automaton. In this experience, it is most important that we could easily specify systems using probabilistic timed game automaton.

5 Conclusion

In this paper, we propose both probabilistic timed game automaton and the verification method of probabilistic timed reachability game. Also, it is shown that we easily specify embedded systems using probabilistic timed game automaton. We are now planning to study the followings:

1. First we effectively implement verifier by on-the-fly method, and apply our proposed method into real systems.
2. Next we develop infinite probabilistic timed game theory.

References

1. T.A. Henzinger, C.M. Kirsch. Embedded Software: Proceedings of the First International Workshop, EMSOFT '01. *LNCS 2211*, P.504, Springer-Verlag, 2001.
2. T. A. Henzinger. Games, time, and probability: Graph models for system design and analysis. *LNCS*, 2007ito appearj.
3. D. Harel, A. Pnueli. On the Development of Reactive Systems. *NATO ASI Series F, Vol. 13*, pp.477-498, SpringerVerlag, 1985.
4. M.K. Inan, R.P. Kurshan. Verification of Digital and Hybrid Systems. *NATO ASI Series F: Computer and Systems Sciences*, Vol. 170, Springer-Verlag, 2000
5. H.A. Hansson. Time and Probability in Formal Design of Distributed Systems. *PhD thesis, Uppsala University*, 1991.
6. A. Pnueli, R. Rosner A Framework for the Synthesis of Reactive Modules. *LNCS 335*, pp.4-17, Springer 1988.
7. R. Alur, D.L. Dill. A theory of timed automata. *TCS*,Vol.126, pp.183-235, 1994.
8. R. Alur, et al. The Algorithmic Analysis of Hybrid Systems. *TCS*, Vol.138, No.1, pp. 3-34, 1995.
9. R. Segala, N.A. Lynch. Probabilistic Simulations for Probabilistic Processes. *Nordic Journal of Computing*, Vol.2, No.2, pp.250-273, 1995.
10. M. Kwiatkowska, et al. Automatic verication of real-time systems with discrete probability distributions. *TCS 282*, pp 101-150, 2002
11. L. de Alfaro, T.A. Henzinger. Interface Theories for Component-Based Design. *LNCS 2211*, pp.148-165. Springer-Verlag, 2001.
12. L. de Alfaro, T.A. Henzinger. Interface Automata. *FSE* ,pp. 109-120, ACM Press, 2001.

13. L. de Alfaro, T.A. Henzinger, M. Stoelinga. Timed interfaces. *LNCS 2491*, pp. 108-122, 2002.
14. S. Yamane Probabilistic Timed Simulation Verification and Its Application to Stepwise Refinement of Real-Time Systems. *LNCS 2896*, pp.276-290, 2003.
15. O. Maler, A.Pnueli, J.Sifakis. On the Synthesis of Discrete Controllers for Timed Systems. *LNCS 900*, pp.229-242, 1995.
16. R. Alur, T. A. Henzinger. Modularity for timed and hybrid systems. *LNCS 1243*, Springer, 1997, pp. 74-88.
17. Luca de Alfaro, Thomas A. Henzinger, and Rupak Majumdar. Symbolic algorithms for infinite-state games. *LNCS 2154*, pp. 536-550, 2001.
18. F. Cassez, A. David, E. Fleury, K.G. Larsen, D. Lime: Efficient On-the-Fly Algorithms for the Analysis of Timed Games. *LNCS 3653*, pp.66-80, 2005.
19. M. Abadi, L. Lamport. An Old-Fashioned Recipe for Real Time. *ACM TOPLAS*, No. 16, Vol.5, pp.1543-1571, 1994.
20. C. Courcoubetis, M. Yannakakis. Verifying Temporal Properties of Finite-State Probabilistic Programs. *29th FOCS*, pp.338-345, 1988.
21. H. Hansson, B. Jonsson. A Logic for Reasoning about Time and Reliability. *Formal Aspects of Computing*, 6(5), pp.512-535, 1994.
22. C. Courcoubetis, M. Yannakakis. The Complexity of Probabilistic Verification. *Journal of ACM*, 42(4), pp.857-907, 1995.
23. William J. Stewart. Introduction to the Numerical Solution of Markov Chains. *Princeton University Press.*, 1994.
24. Wireless LAN Medium Access Control(MAC) and Physical Layer(PHY) Specifications . ANSI/IEEE Std 802.11, 1999 Edition.

A Design Method for Heterogeneous Adders

Jeong-Gun Lee[1], Jeong-A Lee[2], Byeong-Seok Lee[2], and Milos D. Ercegovac[3]

[1] Computer Laboratory, University of Cambridge, UK
Jeong-Gun.Lee@cl.cam.ac.uk
[2] Department of Computer Engineering, Chosun University, Republic of Korea
[3] Dept. of Computer Science, University of California Los Angeles, US

Abstract. The performance of existing adders varies widely in their speed and area requirements, which in turn sometimes makes designers pay a high cost in area especially when the delay requirements exceeds the fastest speed of a specific adder, no matter how small the difference is. To expand the design space and manage delay/area tradeoffs, we propose new adder architecture and a design methodology. The proposed adder architecture, named *heterogeneous adder*, decomposes an adder into blocks (sub-adders) consisting of carry-propagate adders of different types and precision. The flexibility in selecting the characteristics of sub-adders is the basis in achieving adder designs with desirable characteristics.

We consider the area optimization under delay constraints and the delay optimization under area constraints by determining the bit-width of sub-adders using Integer Linear Programming. We demonstrate the effectiveness of the proposed architecture and the design method on 128-bit operands.

1 Introduction

Embedded system design recently has attracted much attention from academia and industry for its great demand in market. The demand in applications is very wide and the diversity covers from the very high-performance real-time embedded systems to the very simple micro-controller based embedded systems. In consequence, design requirements and constraints varies a lot according to applications, and cost-effective optimization has to be applied to reduce their cost. Especially the cost-effectiveness is very important in the hardware parts of the embedded systems.

In this paper, we propose a cost-effective optimization of adder architecture. Addition is an essential operation in a digital embedded hardware/system and many adders such as a ripple carry adder (RCA), a carry skip adder (CSKA), a carry lookahead adder (CLA), and a parallel prefix adder (PA) have been developed utilizing different carry generation schemes to provide tradeoffs in speed, area and power consumption [1,2]. To date, these single type (homogeneous) adders were mixed in a multi-level architecture by adopting a different scheme for carry and sum generation, e.g., a carry lookahead scheme in the carry generation network and a carry select scheme for the sum generation, as in the case of a hybrid carry-lookahead/carry-select adder [3].

Y.-H. Lee et al. (Eds.): ICESS 2007, LNCS 4523, pp. 121–132, 2007.

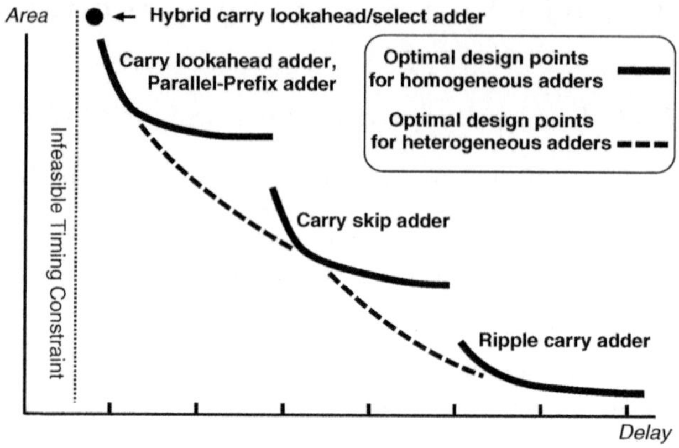

Fig. 1. Conceptual design space of adder design

For non-uniform input bit arrivals, adders consisting of sub-adders of different types have been proposed [4,5] and are typically used in the design of parallel multipliers. We do not consider here adders with non-uniform input arrivals. It is noteworthy that the hybrid adder in [3] improves the delay performance at the increased cost of area.

However, for a certain delay requirement, the additional area cost might be very big due to the characteristic of delay-area curves shown in Fig. 1. Solid lines in Fig. 1 are delay-area curves and correspond to a set of optimal design points for given conventional adder architectures [1,6]. The individual solid line is typically banana-shaped but the overall delay-area curve formed by these solid lines is not banana-shaped. Some of work [7,8] have tried to tradeoff area/delay through sparsing computational circuit and changing the amount of internal wiring/the fanout of intermediate nodes on the carry generation network in a parallel prefix adder.

In this paper, we propose a heterogeneous adder architecture, which corresponds to a pareto-optimal delay-area curve as denoted by the dashed lines in Fig. 1. The heterogeneous adder architecture permits better design tradeoffs in terms of area and delay. The same approach is expected to provide better tradeoffs when considering power consumption. The heterogeneous adder can be described as an n-bit adder where various bit-width blocks of carry propagation adders such as RCA, CSKA and CLA are connected iteratively using carry-in and carry-out signals of block adders. We will describe in this paper an Integer Linear Programming (ILP) based methodology to configure a heterogeneous adder. Our formulated ILP produces the best choice of types and precisions of sub-adders for two cases: (i) area-constrained delay optimization, and (ii) delay-constrained area optimization. Compared to the work [7,8], our approach provide more high-level view of arithmetic optimization without considering low-level circuit issues such as fanout size and wiring complexity. In addition, our formulation provide a more systematic optimization method through '*mathematically*' modelled adder delay and area.

The remainder of this paper is organized as follows. Heterogeneous adder architecture and its characteristics are explained in detail in Section II. In Section III, we address the mathematical modeling of the heterogeneous adder for its optimization. Experimental results are presented in Section IV to show the effectiveness of the proposed method. Finally, in Section V, we conclude this paper with summary of work and possible future work.

2 Proposed Architecture and Advantage

The architecture of a heterogeneous adder allows to combine different types of adder implementations with various precision to form a single heterogeneous adder. While the conventional implementation selects only one implementation in a given library, the proposed bit-level implementations with different sub-adders can explore an extended design space allowing more find-grained area-delay tradeoffs.

For example, in the Synopsis design library [12], many sub-adders of different precision are available and we can use those sub-adders to make an adder to satisfy design constraints manually which is quite laborious and inefficient. The proposed method provides an automated procedure for determining a best configuration of sub-adders and their precisions under given design constraints. The procedure is fast and allows efficient design exploration.

Definition [**Heterogeneous Adder**]. A ***S***ub ***A***dder $SA_i(n_i)$ is an n-bit sub-adder whose carry propagating scheme is denoted by SA_i. When the number of available sub-adders is I, an n-bit heterogeneous adder is defined as an n-bit adder which concatenates $SA_i(n_i)$ where $1 \leq i \leq I$. $SA_i(n_i)$ uses the carry-out signal of $SA_{i-1}(n_{i-1})$ as its carry-in signal. The sum of all n_i should be equal to n.

In Fig. 2 we show an n-bit heterogeneous adder with three different sub-adders, i.e., $I = 3$ with $n_1 + n_2 + n_3 = n$. In general, I can be any number according to the available adder designs. For better understanding, in this paper, we use three sub-adders for our example of heterogeneous adder. As we explore design space of a heterogeneous adder with at most three different sub-adders under either delay constraint or area constraint condition, it produces a solution with one, two sub-adders or three sub-adders. If the heterogeneous adder has two sub-adder components, this can be denoted as zero for a certain i in n_i.

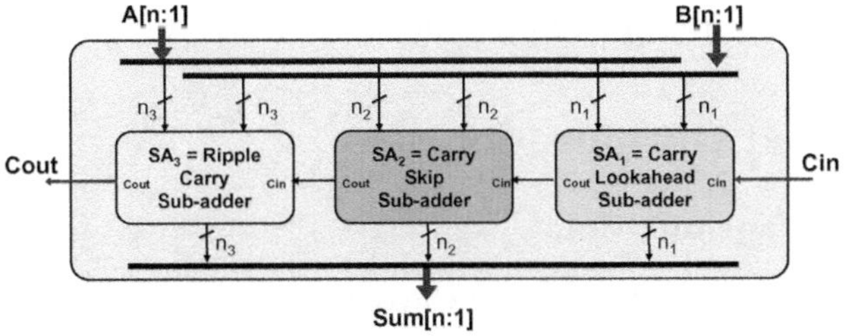

Fig. 2. A heterogeneous adder example

If n_i is found to be zero by the optimization procedures, then it means that SA_i type is not allocated to a heterogeneous adder and, in this case $SA_i(n_i)$ is simply a wire conveying a carry signal from $SA_{i-1}(n_{i-1})$ to $SA_{i+1}(n_{i+1})$. In this point of view, it is obvious that $SA_0(n_0)$ and $SA_{I+1}(n_{I+1})$ are carry-in and carry-out ports, respectively.

- **Property of Heterogeneous Adder:** First, the heterogeneous adder always has a lower cost (a lower delay) than a single type homogeneous adder for a given total delay (cost). Homogeneous adder is a subset of heterogeneous adder according to our definition. Consequently, in the worst case, the heterogeneous adder is implemented by a single homogeneous adder and, in other cases, a mix of different types of sub-adders implements the heterogeneous adder. Heterogeneous adder covers a bigger design space which in turn results a lower cost (delay) design for a given total delay (cost).

Second, the order of sub-adders has an impact on the delay of a heterogeneous adder. The processing delay of the heterogeneous adder is determined by finding a maximum value among the completion times of all sub-adders. In general, there is a time difference between carry generation delay and sum generation delay in each sub-adder. Depending on the order of sub-adders, the carry generation of sub-adders positioned at a MSB part can overlap sum generation of sub-adders at a LSB part.

Now, the question, "How to allocate bits for each sub-adder optimally and efficiently?" becomes an important design problem for a heterogeneous adder architecture. Here, 'optimal' means the minimum area under a delay constraint or minimum delay under an area constraint. The 'efficiency' relates to the efficiency of the automated procedure of finding optimal solutions.

To consider the advantages of the heterogeneous adder, which is optimized at the bit level, consider Fig. 3 showing the delays of three single type adders synthesized using Synopsis tools with $0.25\mu m$ CMOS library [11,12]. Even though there are timing variations, which can be controlled by the circuit or synthesis optimization, in general, there will be delay ranges falling between delay curves of various single type adders. This can be seen in Fig. 1.

When specific timing constraints fall into the uncovered delay ranges, a designer considering the design space consisting of single type homogeneous adders has no choice but to select another adder producing speed higher than necessary at an extra unavoidable cost. When an expanded design space provided by a heterogeneous adder is used, one can explore design points in the uncovered delay ranges, marked by a shadow region in Fig. 3, and select faster designs with smaller area.

3 ILP Based Optimization

3.1 Problem Formulation

With the target adder architecture, delay-constrained area optimization problem can be written as "find the bit widths, $n_1, n_2, \ldots, n_I$ of sub-adders to minimize

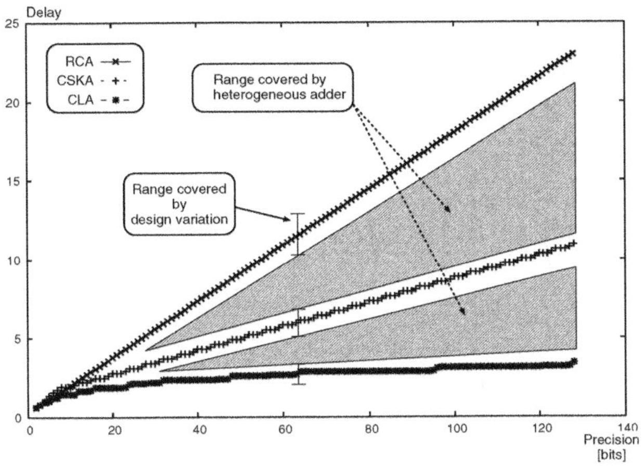

Fig. 3. Delay plot for three different types of adders

the area of n-bit heterogeneous adder, while satisfying a constraint that the total adder delay should be less than ub", where ub denote the upper bound of the total delay of the heterogeneous adder. The area-constrained delay optimization can be specified in a similar manner.

3.2 ILP Formulation

A direct formulation of the delay-constrained area optimization can be described by the following equations:

$$\underset{(n_1, n_2, \ldots, n_I)}{\textit{Minimize}} \ \text{AREA(Heterogeneous Adder)}$$

with Constraints

1: DELAY(Heterogeneous Adder) $\leq ub$

2: Bit-Width Sum of Sub-Adders $= n$

In these equations, 'AREA' and 'DELAY' are functions computing area and delay. To model these 'AREA' and 'DELAY', we use Integer Linear Programming (ILP) method [10]. Current ILP model assumes that the order of sub-adders allocated to a heterogeneous adder is fixed. Within an ILP formula, according to the assumption, 'I' types of sub-adders (SA_i, $1 \leq i \leq I$) are placed from the least significant bit (LSB) to the most significant bit (MSB).

In the proposed ILP formulation, an integer variable, $x_{ni}^{SA_i}$, denotes the number of $SA_i(n_i)$ which is used in a heterogeneous adder. Three constants, $D_{n_i,s}^{SA_i}$, $D_{n_i,c}^{SA_i}$ and $A_{n_i}^{SA_i}$, are the sum generation/carry generation delays and area of $SA_i(n_i)$, respectively. Here, 'c' denotes carry generation and 's' stands for sum generation. More precisely, $D_{n_i,s}^{SA_i}$ and $D_{n_i,c}^{SA_i}$ are worst-case delays from the carry-in signal arrival to the output of the sum and carry-out signals, respectively.

Basically, 'i' of n_i determines the type, SA_i, so we do not need to put 'SA_i' in the notations of these variable and constants. However, for better understaning, we put 'SA_i' to their notation.

- **Area Modelling:** For a specific i-th type of sub-adder, AREA $(SA_i(n_i))$ can be derived by the linear combination of $x_{ni}^{SA_i}$ and $A_{n_i}^{SA_i}$ as follows.

$$\sum_{n_i=0}^{n} A_{n_i}^{SA_i} \times x_{n_i}^{SA_i}, \text{ where } \sum_{n_i=0}^{n} x_{n_i}^{SA_i} \leq 1.$$

The equation, '$\sum_{n_i=0}^{n} x_{n_i}^{SA_i} \leq 1$', means at most one bit-width is selected for each type of sub-adder. This equation, however, can be removed in the constraint list to allow multiple instances of each sub-adder. When $n_1, n_2, \ldots, n_I$ are given, the area of a heterogeneous adder, (sum of the sub-adder areas), can be expressed as $\sum_{i=1}^{I}$ AREA$(SA_i(n_i))$ and, finally, in the following form:

$$\sum_{i=1}^{I} \sum_{n_i=0}^{n} A_{n_i}^{SA_i} \times x_{n_i}^{SA_i}, \text{ where } \sum_{n_i=0}^{n} x_{n_i}^{SA_i} \leq 1.$$

In this paper we assume that the area of a heterogeneous adder is described by the summation of areas of its sub-adders. Since sub-adders are linearly combined to make a heterogeneous adder by connecting carry signals, we believe that this assumption is reasonable.

- **Delay Modelling:** Compared to area modeling, 'DELAY (Heterogeneous Adder)' is more complex to model because the completion delay is not simply a sum of delays of sub-adders. The DELAY of a heterogeneous adder is a maximum propagation delay between many possible data propagation paths from the input signals and carry-in signal to the sum and carry-out signals of the heterogeneous adder.

Fig. 4 shows one possible timing path of a heterogeneous adder with three different sub-adders. There are three possible completion times for each sub-adder, (1) $D_{n_1,s}^{CLA}$, (2) $D_{n_1,c}^{CLA} + D_{n_2,s}^{CSKA}$ or (3) $D_{n_1,c}^{CLA} + D_{n_2,c}^{CSKA} + D_{n_3,s}^{RCA}$. The final completion time is evaluated by finding the maximum delay of those three different path delays. With the assumption that I sub-adders are allocated from LSB to MSB in the predefined order, the DELAY of a heterogeneous adder can be formulated in the following way.

$$\begin{aligned} \text{DELAY} &= \text{Max}\{T_{Pass_1}, T_{Pass_2}, \ldots, T_{Pass_I}\} \\ T_{Pass_1} &= D_{n_1,s}^{SA_1} \\ T_{Pass_i} &= \sum_{k=2}^{i} D_{n_{k-1},c}^{SA_{k-1}} + D_{n_i,s}^{SA_i}, \; 1 < i \leq I \end{aligned}$$

Since n_i can be varied from 0 to n, the constant values, $D_{n_i,s}^{SA_i}$ and $D_{n_i,c}^{SA_i}$ in this equations, can be derived from $\sum_{n_i=0}^{n} D_{n_i,s}^{SA_i} \times x_{n_i}^{SA_i}$ and $\sum_{n_i=0}^{n} D_{n_i,c}^{SA_i} \times x_{n_i}^{SA_i}$ with an additional constraint, $\sum_{n_i=0}^{n} x_{n_i}^{SA_i} \leq 1$, respectively, as in the AREA modeling.

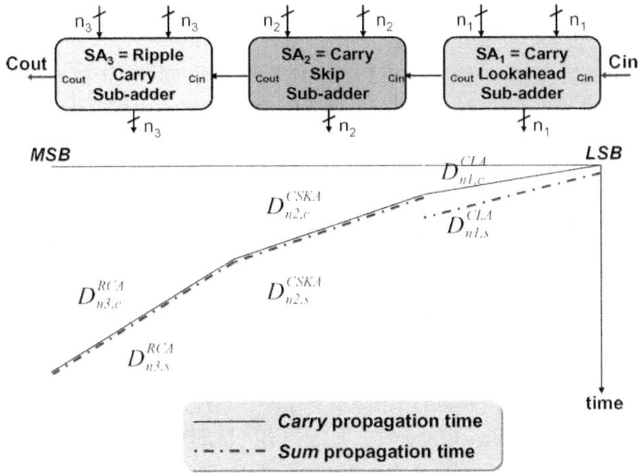

Fig. 4. Delay modeling of a heterogeneous adder

With the mathematically modeled delay and area, finally, the ILP formulation of our delay-constrained area optimization problem is described below.

$$\underset{(n_1,n_2,\ldots,n_I)}{Minimize} \sum_{i=1}^{I}\sum_{n_i=0}^{n} A_{n_i}^{SA_i} \times x_{n_i}^{SA_i}$$

with Constraints

1: $\sum_{n_i=0}^{n} D_{n_i,s}^{SA_i} \times x_{n_i}^{SA_i} \leq ub_{delay}$ for all SA_i, $(1 \leq i \leq I)$

2: $\sum_{k=2}^{i}\sum_{n_{k-1}=0}^{n} D_{n_{k-1},c}^{SA_{k-1}} \times x_{n_{k-1}}^{SA_{k-1}} + \sum_{n_i=0}^{n} D_{n_i,s}^{SA_i} \times x_{n_i}^{SA_i} \leq ub_{delay}, \quad 1 < i \leq I$

3: $\sum_{n_i=0}^{n} x_{n_i}^{SA_i} \leq 1$ for all SA_i

4: $\sum_{i=1}^{I}\sum_{n_i=0}^{n} n_i \times x_{n_i}^{SA_i} = n$

Similarly, area-constrained delay optimization is formulated as.

$$\underset{(n_1,n_2,\ldots,n_I)}{Minimize} d_{max}$$

with Constraints

1: $\sum_{n_i=0}^{n} D_{n_i,s}^{SA_i} \times x_{n_i}^{SA_i} \leq d_{max}$ for all SA_i, $(1 \leq i \leq I)$

2: $\sum_{k=2}^{i}\sum_{n_{k-1}=0}^{n} D_{n_{k-1},c}^{SA_{k-1}} \times x_{n_{k-1}}^{SA_{k-1}} + \sum_{n_i=0}^{n} D_{n_i,s}^{SA_i} \times x_{n_i}^{SA_i} \leq d_{max}, \quad 1 < i \leq I$

3: $\sum_{i=1}^{I}\sum_{n_i=0}^{n} A_{n_i}^{SA_i} \times x_{n_i}^{SA_i} \leq ub_{area}$

4: $\sum_{n_i=0}^{n} x_{n_i}^{SA_i} \leq 1$ for all SA_i

5: $\sum_{i=1}^{I}\sum_{n_i=0}^{n} n_i \times x_{n_i}^{SA_i} = n$

4 Experiments

As an experiment, we consider the three types of sub-adders, RCA, CSKA, and CLA, in the design a 128-bit heterogeneous adder. In addition, possible bit-widths of sub-adders are restricted to the bit-widths from 2 to 128 bits. In this paper, variations caused by actual implementation are not considered since our focus is on bit-level optimization strategies. In actual implementation, some physical design issues including layout and interconnect will lead to alterations of the optimized design produced by our method. However, the structurally optimized design obtained from our method makes the actual physical optimization more efficient.

For experiment, we calculate the constant delay and area estimates, $D^{SA_i}_{n_i,s}$, $D^{SA_i}_{n_i,c}$ and $A^{SA_i}_{n_i}$ which are estimated from synthesized designs using Synopsis with $0.25\mu m$ CMOS technology [11,12]. The ILP formulation is solved using a public domain LP solver called "lp_solve" [10].

Fig. 5 depicts the advantage of the proposed adder architecture, which shows the area-delay curve of the 128-bit heterogeneous adder obtained through the LP solver. While changing delay (or area) boundary, *ub*, optimal heterogeneous adder configurations are searched to minimize area (or delay). Fig. 5(a) shows the case of "Delay-constrained area optimization problem" and Fig. 5(b) shows the case of "Area-constrained delay optimization problem". In this experiment, the constraint '$\sum_{n_i=0}^{n} x^{SA_i}_{n_i} \leq 1$' is removed from the constraint list to allow multiple instances of each sub-adder to get more room for optimization.

We considered all possible combination of ordering of sub-adders, that is 15 configurations of a heterogeneous adder out of 3 sub-adders, RCA, CSKA, and CLA. For better illustration purposes, in Fig. 5, we show configurations of some design points marked with their delay/area values. In the figures, two values in parentheses are 'delay' and 'area' pairs of the corresponding heterogeneous adders.

LP solver produced a three sub-adder concatenation such as RCA || CSKA || CLA as a solution (here, we use a symbol, '||', to denote a linear carry connection between sub-adders. For example, in the case of RCA || CSKA || CLA, a CLA is located to a LBS part and CSKA is used in a middle part, and RCA is located to a MSB part). However, the difference of delay (or area) between RCA || CSKA || CLA and CSKA || CLA was so small, we eliminate this 3 sub-adder solution in the design space and keep only one or two sub-adder configurations for the heterogeneous adder design space.

The design space we obtained, as indicated in Fig. 5(a) and 5(b), shows that RCA, RCA || CSKA, CSKA, CSKA || CLA, RCA || CLA are good candidate orderings for the solution space. The design space covered by CSKA || CLA in Fig. 5 contains many solutions with various precision of CSKA and CLA sub-adders. The precision of each sub-adder shown in the Fig. 5 explains clearly that heterogeneous adder indeed allows time-area tradeoffs much better than the conventional adder design. The solutions with RCA || CSKA, CSKA || CLA, RCA || CLA are newly introduced design points. Those newly introduced

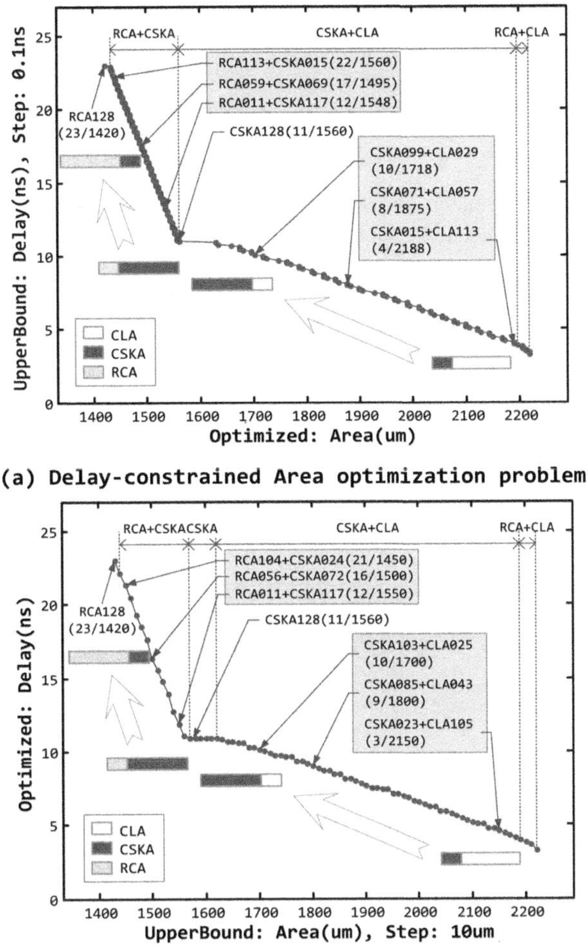

(a) Delay-constrained Area optimization problem

(b) Area-constrained Delay optimization problem

Fig. 5. A delay-area curve for a 128-bit heterogeneous adder

pareto-optimal points in these regions cannot be obtained without using heterogeneous adder architecture.

Finally, Fig. 6 shows the delay/area reduction rate obtained from the use of a heterogeneous adder. Delay/area reduction is observed in the interval where a heterogeneous adder interpolates a new design point effectively between two homogeneous adders. In these intervals, unless the heterogeneous adder is used, we have to use a homogeneous adder with extra cost. These intervals where delay/area reduction is observed are corresponding to the region covered by a heterogeneous adder in Fig. 3 given in Section 2. In this experiment, up to near 70% delay reduction and around 30% area reduction are obtained. However, we would like to note the improvement numbers are not absolute since this improvement

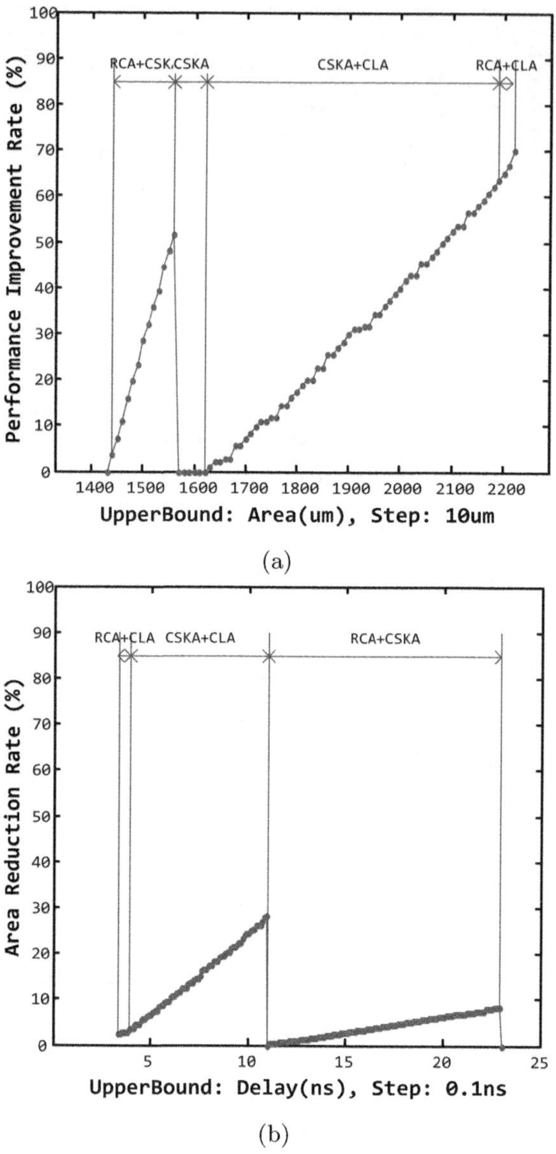

Fig. 6. Delay/area reduction rate by a 128-bit heterogeneous adder (a) Delay reduction rate, (b) Area reduction rate

is based on the assumption that the area/delay cost of a homogeneous adder we use is fixed. The improvement would be changed relatively if other circuit level optimizations like a transistor sizing are applied to homogeneous adders. Those area/delay variations of homogeneous adders are also shown in Fig. 4 as "range covered by design variations".

5 Conclusions and Future Work

For designing delay-area efficient adders, we have proposed a heterogeneous adder architecture, which consists of sub-adders of various sizes and different carry propagation schemes. The proposed decomposition into heterogeneous sub-adders allows more design tradeoffs in delay-area optimization. We also developed an ILP based technique and applied it iteratively to find an optimal configuration in selecting the type and bit-width of sub-adders as components of the heterogeneous adder.

Considering a 128-bit adder, we showed that many delay-area efficient designs could be found with the extended design space of heterogeneous adder architecture, which were not possible in a conventional, homogeneous adder design space using the proposed method with tools like Synopsis. Currently we are developing power modeling of heterogeneous adders using ILP and extending the design method to allow tradeoffs between delay, area, and power.

Acknowledgement

This work was supported in part by research funds from Chosun University, 2004 and by the Korea Research Foundation Grant funded by Korean Government (KRF-2005-D00026). The work of Jeong-Gun Lee was supported in part by IT Scholarship Program supervised by IITA & MIC, Republic of Korea.

References

1. C. Nagendra, M.J. Irwin, R.M. Owens, "Area-time-power tradeoffs in parallel adders," *In IEEE Trans. on Circuits and Systems II: Analog and Digital Signal Processing*, vol. 43, pp. 689-702, Oct. 1996
2. V. Oklobdzija, B. Zeydel, S. Mathew, and R. Krishnamurthy, "Energy-Delay Estimation Technique for High-Performance Microprocessor VLSI Adders," *In Prod. IEEE Symposium on Computer Arithmetic*, pp. 272- 279, Jun. 2003
3. Y. Wang, C. Pai, X. Song, "The design of hybrid carry-lookahead/carry-select adders," *In IEEE Trans. on Circuits and Systems II: Analog and Digital Signal Processing*, vol. 49, Jan. 2002
4. V. Oklobdzija and D. Villeger, "Improving Multiplier Design by Using Column Compression Tree and Optimized Final Adder in CMOS Technology," *IEEE Trans. on VLSI*, 3(2):292-301, 1995.
5. P. F. Stelling and V. Oklobdzija, "Design Strategies for Optimal Hybrid Final Adders in a Parallel Multiplier," *Journal of VLSI Signal Processing*, Vol. 14(3) pp.321-31, 1996.
6. M.D. Ercegovac and T. Lang, "Digital Arithmetic," *Morgan Kaufmann Publishers*, 2004
7. R. Zimmermann, "Binary Adder Architectures for Cell-Based VLSI and their Synthesis," *PhD thesis*, Swiss Federal Institute of Technology (ETH) Zurich, Hartung-Gorre Verlag, 1998
8. Simon Knowles, "A Family of Adders," *In Prod. IEEE Symposium on Computer Arithmetic*, pp. 30-34, 1999

9. H.P. Williams, "Model Building in Mathematical Programming," *4th Ed., John Wiley*, New York, 1999
10. M. Berkelaar, "lp_solve - version 4.0," *Eindhoven University of Technology*, ftp://ftp.ics.ele.tue.nl/pub/lp_solve/, 2003
11. "IDEC-C221: IDEC Cell Library Data Book," *IC Design Education Center*, 2000
12. "DesignWare IP Family Reference Guide," *Synopsis Corporation*, September 12, 2005

FPGA Based Implementation of Real-Time Video Watermarking Chip

Yong-Jae Jeong, Kwang-Seok Moon, and Jong-Nam Kim

Division of Electronic Computer and Telecommunication Engineering
Pukyong National University Busan, Korea
jy034@pknu.ac.kr

Abstract. In this paper, we propose a real-time video watermarking chip and system which is hardware based watermark embedding system of SD/HD (standard definition/high definition) video with STRATIX2 FPGA device from ALTERA. There was little visual artifact due to watermarking in subjective quality evaluation between the original video and the watermarked one. Embedded watermark was all extracted after a robustness test called natural video attacks such as A/D (analog/digital) conversion and MPEG compression. Our implemented watermarking hardware system can be useful in movie production and broadcasting companies that requires real-time based copyright protection system.

1 Introduction

The recent development of computing and communication technologies enabled high definition video (HDV) applications. In today's computing environment, the end users can easily perform storing, editing, reproducing, and or distributing HDV scripts. Copyright protection has therefore been increasingly important to protect HDV data against illegal copy and reproduction and copy right infringement.

Digital watermarking technology has been actively investigated to solve the copyright protection problem of HDV media data by hiding injected watermark information into original digital contents. To be effective, a watermarking scheme must satisfy two important technical requirements: invisibility and robustness [1]. To satisfy the invisibility (or transparency) requirement, the watermark should be injected into the original media contents in such a way that human beings cannot visually recognize the watermark. The effective watermarking scheme should also be robust against possible attacks such as translation, rotation, and/or scaling. In addition a watermarking scheme for HDV applications should be robust against natural attacks such as analog/digital conversion and/or MPEG compression.

The applications of HDV broadcast monitoring and on-air live broadcasting need fast real-time watermarking solution. To enable fast real-time watermarking, chip level implementations of watermarking algorithms have been investigated [2, 3]. VLSI implementations of watermarking algorithms, which are robust against analog/digital conversion and JPEG compression, for still digital images were reported in the literature [4, 5]. These research works focused on single chip implementations of watermarking algorithms but did not address system level studies on the effectiveness and efficiency of underlying watermarking schemes.

Y.-H. Lee et al. (Eds.): ICESS 2007, LNCS 4523, pp. 133–141, 2007.

In this paper, we present a hardware system that enables fast real-time watermarking for SD/HD applications. The presented hardware system has an embedded watermarking processor implemented based on the STRATIX II FPGA device family from ALTERA®. The embedded watermarking processor is based on our novel watermarking algorithm suitable for optimal hardware implementation. Our system can embed user information such as video meta-data to any selected video frames, so that we can extract the injected watermark data at any frame of the watermarked video. The presented hardware watermarking system for SD/HD real-time applications satisfies invisibility and robustness that are essential requirements for practical watermarking. The presented hardware system can not only be used for live broadcasting with real-time SD/HD watermarking but also used for mass production video watermarking such as movies or DVDs.

In Section 2, we describe the implementation of the proposed watermarking embedder which includes watermarking algorithm and hardware chip implementation. Section 3 explains the configuration of the proposed watermarking system with practical hardware equipments and experimental results. Finally, we conclude the paper in Section 4.

2 Implementation of Watermark Embedding Chip

This section explains hardware implementation of watermark embedder. To implement an efficient watermark embedder, a novel watermarking algorithm was developed based on the Kutter's algorithm [6] [7]. This algorithm is based on multiple embedding the same watermark at several times at horizontally and vertically shifted locations in the image. The watermark can be made by using the spread-spectrum manner between the binary signature and the modulation function. The proposed novel watermarking algorithm is suitable for optimal hardware implementation, and has strong robustness against known natural and hostile attacks.

Kutter et al. proposed an efficient watermark embedding algorithm using Eq. (1) and (2). The watermark $w(x, y)$ is consist of three factors: watermark strength from image characteristics and binary signature as the input message and finally modulation function that is generated from pseudo-random function. More specifically, watermark strength $\alpha(x, y)$ is calculated based on video characteristics which include variance, gradient, and spatial complexity of the pixels on a frame. In addition, the watermark strength calculation considers inter-frame motion speed. The novel proposed watermarking algorithm for optimal hardware implementation was devised by improving the modulation function and watermark strength of the Kutter's algorithm.

$$\hat{I}(x, y) = I(x, y) + w(x, y) \tag{1}$$

$$w(x, y) = \sum_{i=0}^{N-1} (-1)^{b_i} s_i(x, y)\alpha(x, y) \tag{2}$$

$I(x,y)$: original contents	$\hat{I}(x,y)$: watermarked contents
$\alpha(x,y)$: watermark strength	$w(x,y)$: watermark
$s_i(x,y)$: modulation function	b^i : binary signature

Our target is to embed not the binary signature but the string in the image. The watermark generates to spreading at the modulation function the code that mapping the string to the ASCII code. In the previous watermarking algorithms, modulation function has been realized by pseudo-random function. In general, when pseudo-random function size increases, the watermark detection ratio increases while embeddable watermark data decreases. In the proposed algorithm, Hadamard sequence [8] was employed to increase the detection ratio without increasing the pseudo-random sequence size (therefore without decreasing the embeddable watermark payload).

Watermark embedding strength in general affects invisibility of the watermark and robustness of the watermarking. When the embedding strength increases, the robustness increases; whereas, the invisibility property decreases. In our proposed algorithm, the watermark strength $\alpha(x, y)$ is calculated based on filtered image obtained by high pass filter such as Cross Shape Filter (CSF). Since the watermark strength is represented by a floating point number, obtaining watermark data needs computationally expensive floating point calculations as shown in Eq. (2). Watermark is injected into the plain areas of the image with relatively lower watermark strength. Image areas with contours (or edges) are considered as detailed areas into which watermark is injected with higher strength. In our proposed scheme, in order to accelerate the watermark data calculation, the floating point calculation is replaced by integer calculations. To enable integer calculation, the value of $\alpha(x, y)$ of Eq. (2) in our algorithm should be an integer value. To get integral watermark strength, the high pass filtered image is first quantized into different floating point intervals. Any floating number in an interval is then mapped into an integer value, which is called a quantization index. Using the Hadamard sequence as pseudo-random function and achieving integer calculations for watermark strength are the basis for the proposed algorithm.

The schematic diagram of the watermark embedder chip is shown in the Figure 1. The watermark embedder is implemented based on the STRATIX®II FPGA device family from ALTERA®. Watermark is injected into each frame of the video scripts. The original video signal is in the format of SDI from SMPTE [9]. The watermark data is embedded into only Y component of each pixel of the SDI format YCbCr.

As the diagram shows, the original video frame extract the TRS(Time Reference Signal) by the synchronize signal in the SDI format YCbCr. and then this frame is filtered by the high pass filter Cross Shape Filter (CSF) module which detects the edge of the original video. The CSF has N×N matrix window to detect edges, and the matrix window is a register of N^2 bytes. The video input signal is buffered into the video input buffer register. The buffer register can hold by N rows of the image pixels. In the case of HD video signal processing, the buffer size is 1920 * N bytes. The buffer is structured as a queue by shift registers, so that image rows are replaced in First In First Out (FIFO) manner. The buffer registers and arithmetic logic unit for the CSF are implemented by the STRATIX®II FPGA chip.

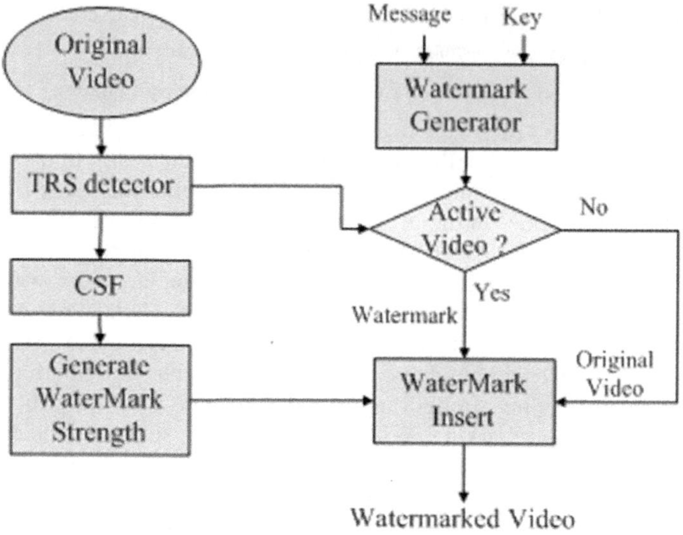

Fig. 1. Schematic diagram of the watermark embedding chip

The output signal of the CSF (i.e., detected edge of the video) is fed into Watermark Strength Generator (WSG). As explained in the previous section, WSG generates watermark strength value for each pixel of the filtered image. The WSG is realized as a simple lookup table which maps one byte Y component value into an integer value in the range of {0,..,M}. The mapping rule (i.e., the scalar quantization rule) was devised by empirical data obtained by a series of simulations.

The Watermark Generator generates watermark signals according user information which is mapped into appropriate Hadamard sequences according to the key. That is, the Watermark generator selects a proper Hadamard sequence according to the user information and the key. N-dimensional Hadamard matrix is stored in ROM of FPGA and selected in the fashion of lookup table.

Actually, SDI (Serial Digital Interface) signal format includes TRS(Time Reference Signal) which is composed of start of active video(SAV), end of active video(EAV), vertical flag(V) and field flag(F) and used to search the active video area in video signal [9]. By using the TRS, we seek the active video area in SDI signal, then add the scaled watermark to original video after scaling watermark signal according to the calculated watermark strength. The watermarked video has no any difference in the sense of appeared visual quality compared with the original video. According to the procedure described above, we implemented the watermarking chip based on VHDL and the STRATIX®II FPGA device family from ALTERA®. In our implementation, we used 720*487 video frame size specified by SD format. Video input signal is SDI format, which is composed of Y, C, and TRS signal. The Y and C are 10bit's signal individually, and TRS is composed of 3 bits. 256×256 sized Hadamard matrix is used, and the strength of watermark is adjusted with 6 levels.

Figure 2. shows that the RTL schematic of the synthesized embedder.

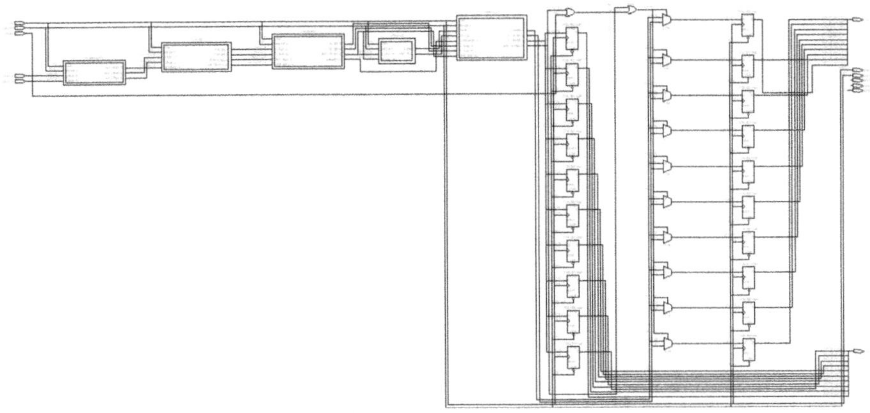

Fig. 2. RTL view result with the Quartus II

Figure 3 shows VHDL simulation waveform of the implementation of video watermark embedder on ALTERA Quartus II. In the figure 3, the signal ORGOUT is the output of original video and the signal WMOUT is the output of watermark embedding result. The original video and the watermark embedded video signals can be identified easily in the figure. The embedded watermark signals are in the range of -6 and +6 and are calculated according to complexity of the video signal. If we compare WMOUT with ORGOUT at 79.15us in the figure, ORGOUT has hexadecimal digit 167 and WMOUT has hexadecimal digit 16D. According to the simulation result, we can see that the implemented VHDL code is operated properly.

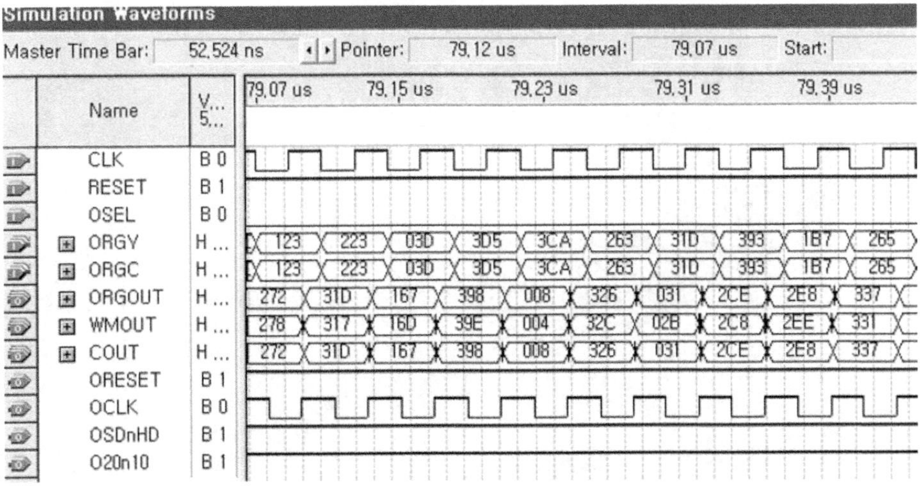

Fig. 3. VHDL simulation result with the Quartus II

3 System Configuration

We configured the overall real-time watermarking system as shown in Figure 4. Video source is from DVD player and the signal format of the video source is YPbPr. The YPbPr signal from the DVD player must be converted to be connected to the watermark embedder because the watermark embedder processes only SDI signal. A video signal converter from TV-Logic® is used and converts the YPbPr to SDI format. After embedding watermarks in the watermark embedder, the output signal of

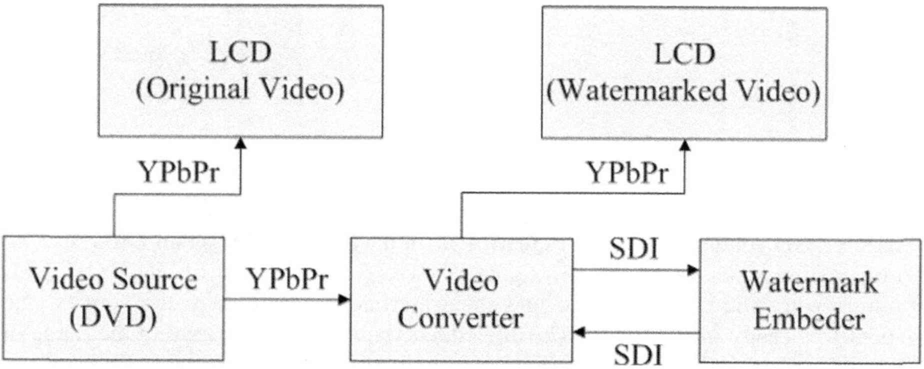

Fig. 4. Overall operation of watermark embedding system

Fig. 5. Original video (right) and watermark embed video (left)

the embedder must be converted to YPbPr from SDI for the watermarked video to be displayed in a LCD screen. Of course, the original DVD video signal is connected to LCD to compare the original video and watermarked one.

According to the figure 3, we practically made up a real-time video watermarking system as shown in figure 5. The most right things represent DVD player and the original video on a LCD monitor from the DVD player. The next left part shows the real-time video embedder and the watermarked video, and the most left small module is video format converter which converts YPbPr to SDI format or inversely for each other.

Figure 6 shows that our test of the real-time watermark embedder. there was little visual difference between the original video and the watermarked video.

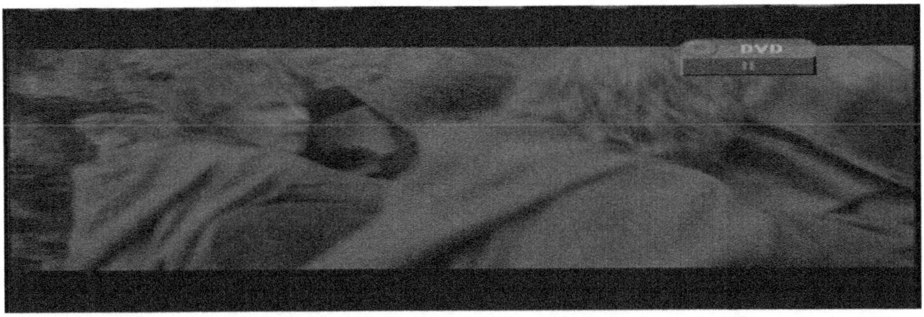

(a)

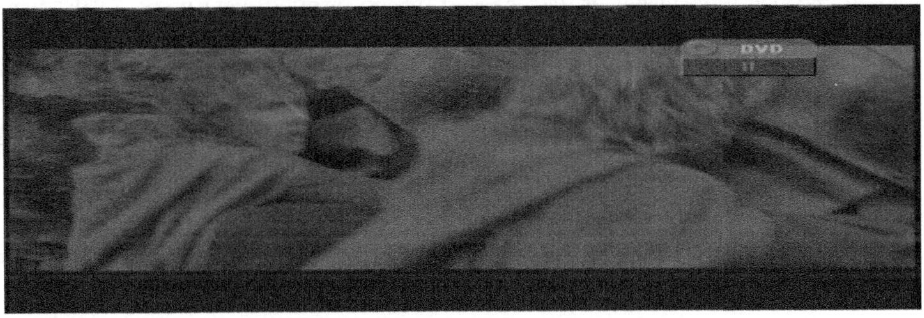

(b)

Fig. 6. Original video (a) and watermark embed video (b)

Table 1 shows the result of subject video quality test by five people who observe the original video and the watermarked video at the same time. In the experiment, five DVD contents are used as shown in Table 1, which shows various video characteristics such as brightness, motion, and texture. We measured subjective video quality instead of objective quality such as PSNR because the subject quality test measures actual video quality well than the objective quality test. The test distances between observers and LCD are 30 cm, 70 cm, 1m, 2m respectively, which is a 17 inch wide LCD monitor from LG®. There is no difference in video quality except for 30 cm

Table 1. Experimental result of watermark embedding

Distance / Video seq.	30(cm)	70(cm)	1 (m)	2(m)
The Lord of the Ling 3	2	1	1	1
Forrest Gump	2	1	1	1
Star Wars 3	2	1	1	1
Saving Private Ryan	2	1	1	1
Matrix 3	2	1	1	1

1. Imperceptible 2. Almost imperceptible 3. Perceptible 4. Very perceptible

between the original video and the watermarked video as shown in Table 1. For 30 cm, the video artifact from watermark is almost imperceptible, which can be negligible in practical applications

4 Conclusions

In this paper, we designed and implemented a real-time video watermark embedder chip by using STRATIX2 FPGA device from ALTER® and configured the embedder system. Our video watermarking system embeds watermarks into spatial domain of video, and has little visual artifact caused by the inserted watermark. In the watermarking chip, we modified and improved Kutter's algorithm for optimal hardware implementation. The presented hardware watermarking system satisfies invisibility and robustness that are essential requirements for practical watermarking applications. The implemented hardware watermarking system can be useful for real-time SD/HD video watermarking system, which requires the function of copyright protection in broadcasting or movie production.

References

1. Cox, M. Miller, and J. Bloom, "Digital Watermarking," Press of Morgan Faukmann, 2002.
2. L. Strycker, P. Termont, J. Vandewege, J. Haitsma, A. Kalker, M. Maes, and G. Depovere, "Implementation of a Real-Time Digital Watermarking Process for Broadcast Monitoring on Trimedia VLIW Processor," *IEE Proc. on Vision, Image and Signal Processing*, vol. 147, no. 4, pp. 371–376, Aug. 2000.
3. N. Mathai, A. Sheikholeslami, and D. Kundur, "VLSI Implementation of a Real-Time Video Watermark Embedder and Detector," *Proc. IEEE International Symposium on Circuits and Systems*, vol. 2, pp II-772 - II-775, May 2003.
4. Garimella, M. Satyanarayana, P. Murugesh, and U. Niranjan, "ASIC for digital color image watermarking," *IEEE Signal Processing Education Workshop* pp. 292-296 Aug. 2004.
5. S. Mohanty, N. Ranganathan, and R. Namball, "VLSI implementation of invisible digital watermarking algorithms towards the development of a secure JPEG encoder," *IEEE Workshop on Signal Processing Systems*, pp 183-188, Aug, 2003.

6. M. Kutter "Watermarking resisting to translation, rotation, and scaling," Proc. SPIE, vol. 3528, pp. 523-531, Nov. 1998.
7. M. Kutter and S. Winkler, "A Vision-Based Masking Model for Spread-Spectrum Image Watermarking", *IEEE Trans. on Image Processing*, vol. 11, pp. 16-25, Jan. 2002.
8. P. Shlichta, "Higher-dimensional Hadamard matrices," *IEEE Trans. on Information Theory,* 1979.
9. "Component Video Signal 4:2:2 Bit-Parallel Digital Interface," American National Standard, ANSI/SMPTE 125M, Sept, 1995.

A Unified Compressed Cache Hierarchy Using Simple Frequent Pattern Compression and Partial Cache Line Prefetching*

Xinhua Tian and Minxuan Zhang

Department of Computer Science, National University of Defense Technology, Changsha, Hunan, 410073, China
tianxinhua71@163.com, xhtian@nudt.edu.cn

Abstract. In this paper, we propose a novel compressed cache hierarchy that uses a unified compression algorithm in both L1 data cache and L2 cache, called Simple Frequent Pattern Compression(S-FPC). This scheme can increase the cache capacity of L1 data cache and L2 cache without any sacrifice of the L1 cache access latency. The layout of compressed data in L1 data cache enables partial cache line prefetching and does not introduce prefetch buffers or increase cache pollution and memory traffic. Compared to a baseline cache hierarchy not supporting data compression in cache, on average, our cache hierarchy design increases the average L1 cache capacity(in terms of the average number of valid words in cache per cycle) by about 33%, reduces the data cache miss rate by 21%, and speeds up program execution by 13%.

1 Introduction

Modern processors use two or more levels of cache memories to reduce memory latency and bandwidth. Effectively using the limited on-chip cache resources becomes more and more important as memory latencies continues to increase relative to processor speeds[1]. Cache compression[2,3] has previously been proposed to improve performance, since compressing data stored in on-chip caches can increase their effective capacity, potentially reducing misses and transmit bandwidth requirement between levels of memory hierarchy. However, current compression techniques[2,3,9] mainly proposed to compress the data in main memory or L2 cache can not be applied to the L1 cache because of rigorous restriction in L1 cache access latency.

In this paper, we propose a novel compressed cache hierarchy that uses a unified compression scheme in both L1 data cache and L2 cache, called Simple Frequent Pattern Compression (S-FPC). This compression algorithm is a simpler version of FPC (Frequent Pattern Compression) encode scheme [11], proposed by Alaa and applied to compressing data in L2 cache and main memory. Because FPC compression scheme needs 5 cycles decompression latency, it can not be directly applied to the L1 cache. To solve this problem, the decompression process of compressed cache line is

* This work was supported by National Natural Science Foundation of China, grant No. 60376018.

Y.-H. Lee et al. (Eds.): ICESS 2007, LNCS 4523, pp. 142–153, 2007.

divided into two stages: in the first stage, a compressed cache line in L2 cache is unpacked to separate encoded words and an encoded word is decoded in the second stage. The intermediate results produced by unpacking simultaneously two address-contiguous compressed cache lines from L2 cache in the first stage will be stored in one cache line in L1 D-cache, so the latency of the first stage is added to the access latency of L2 cache; In the second stage, the intermediate results stored in L1 D-cache are decoded and the latency of the second stage can be hidden when processor accesses L1 D-cache in our design, so the access latency of L1 D-cache will not increase. Because of the layout of compressed data in L1 D-cache, compressing two address-contiguous cache lines from L2 cache into one cache line in L1 D-cache will trigger to prefetch partially the cache line adjacent to the cache line requested normally by a cache miss. Because the prefeched partial cache line and normally requested cache line share a physical cache line space, the prefetching caused by L1 D-cache compression does not introduce prefetch buffers or increase the cache pollution and memory traffic relative to common sequential prefetch technology.

Compared to tradition cache hierarchy not supporting data compression in cache, our cache hierarchy design can apparently increase the effective cache capacity of L1 D-cache and L2 cache. In addition, our cache hierarchy design combines partial cache line prefetching and data compression, which can improve the performance and decrease cache miss rate significantly. We have evaluated our design through executing a set of SPEC benchmarks on SimpleScalar. Initial experimental results show that, on average, our cache hierarchy design can increase the average L1 cache capacity(in terms of the average number of valid words in cache per cycle) by about 33%, reduce the L1 D-cache miss rate by 21%, and speed up program execution by 13%.

The rest of this paper is organized as follow. Section 2 discusses the motivation behind our design and the related works. The compressed cache hierarchy design details presented in section 3. Section 4 evaluates our cache hierarchy design and gives experiment results. Section 5 concludes this paper.

2 Motivation and Related Works

2.1 Motivation

Cache compression is one way to improve the effectiveness of cache memories [4,5,6,7]. Storing compressed lines in the cache increases the effective cache capacity and reduces cache misses, thereby reduces the time spent to long off-chip miss penalties. However, compression increases the cache hit time, since the decompression overhead lies on the critical access path. Therefore, for some applications, cache compression can improve performance, but for other applications, cache compression can degrade performance. To solve this issue, some researchers proposed adaptive compression technique[2,7]. In this paper, we proposed a unified compression cache hierarchy. The motivation derived from the performance analysis of compressed cache hierarchy as follow:

The average memory access time of a conventional memory system ($AMAT_{conv}$) can be represented as in (1), in which T_{L1}, T_{L2}, M_{L1} and M_{L2} denote the L1 and L2 cache access times and their cache miss rate, respectively. T_{mem} is the main memory access latency classified into four timing components such as bus arbitration time, RAS latency, memory read overhead and data transfer time. For the convenience of analysis, the variety of data transfer time caused by the changing of the cache line size of the L2 compressed cache is ignored. So the T_{mem} is fixed.

$$AMAT_{conv} = T_{L1} + M_{L1} \times (T_{L2} + M_{L2} \times T_{mem}) \quad (1)$$

$$AMAT_{L2\_comp} = T_{L1} + M_{L1} \times (T_{L2} + T_{de} + \tilde{M}_{L2} \times (T_{mem} + T_{de})) \quad (2)$$

Equation (2) represents the average memory access time ($AMAT_{L2\_comp}$) when compression technique is applied to L2 cache. $\tilde{M}_{L2}$ is the L2 cache miss rate when compression technique is applied to L2 cache and T_{de} is the decompression latency. So the upper bounds of decompression latency for performance improvement are calculated as:

$$T_{de} < \frac{(M_{L2} - \tilde{M}_{L2})T_{mem}}{1 + \tilde{M}_{L2}} \quad (3)$$

Define *decompression latency balance point* D_{th} to be the point where the average memory access time of a conventional memory system ($AMAT_{conv}$) is equal to the average memory access time when compression technique is applied to the memory system. So when compression technique is applied to L2 cache, equation (3) can be written as:

$$T_{de} < D_{th} \quad (4)$$

in this case, $$D_{th} = \frac{(M_{L2} - \tilde{M}_{L2})T_{mem}}{1 + \tilde{M}_{L2}} \quad (5)$$

From (4), we can know that there are two ways to improve performance of compressed cache hierarchy, one is to decrease the decompression latency of compressed cache T_{de}, the other is to increase the decompression latency balance point D_{th}. The motivation of this paper is rooted in the second way, the compressed cache hierarchy proposed by this paper can increase the decompression latency balance point D_{th}. In our compressed cache hierarchy, data compression technique is applied in L1 D-cache and L2 cache, and the decompression latency of L1 D-cache can be hidden when the processor accesses L1 D-cache. So the decompression latency of L1 D-cache is zero. The average memory access time in our cache hierarchy can be calculated as:

$$AMAT_{L1\_L2\_comp} = T_{L1} + \tilde{M}_{L1} \times (T_{L2} + T_{de} + \tilde{M}_{L2} \times (T_{mem} + T_{de})) \quad (6)$$

$AMAT_{L1\_L2\_comp}$ represents the average memory access time in our cache hierarchy. $\tilde{M}_{L1}$ is the L1 D-cache miss rate when the compression technique is applied to L1 D-cache. In this case, according to equation $AMAT_{conv} = AMAT_{L1\_L2\_comp}$, the decompression latency balance point can be calculated as:

$$D_{th} = \frac{(\alpha - 1)T_{L2} + (\alpha M_{L2} - \tilde{M}_{L2})T_{mem}}{1 + \tilde{M}_{L2}} \quad (7)$$

In equation (7), $\alpha = \frac{M_{L1}}{\tilde{M}_{L1}}$. Because our cache hierarchy design combines partial cache line prefetching and data compression, L1 cache miss rate will decrease relative to conventional cache hierarchy, so $\alpha > 1$ will be satisfied. From equation (7) and (5), we can know that our design makes the decompression latency balance point growing. So our compressed cache hierarchy will improve performance significantly.

2.2 Related Works

Several researchers proposed hardware cache compression implementations that aimed at increasing the effective cache capacity and reducing cache miss rate. These implementations apply known hardware compression algorithms mainly to the L2 cache[2,3,18] or main memory[16,17,19]. More sophisticated compression techniques (such as XRL compression[12], and parallel compression with dictionary construction[8]) can only be applied to main memory and L2 cache as they are more tolerant to increase in hit times. Only a few simple compression algorithms[6,13,14,20] (such as frequent value compression, and sign-bit extension removing compression) can be applied to L1 cache.

Yang and Gupta designed L1 data compressed cache[6,13] based on frequent value compression. However, their compression technique needs to obtain frequent value table from value profile, and the compression scheme is not adaptable to program behavior. In addition, their technique increases L1 cache hit latency.

P.Pujara and A.Aggarwal proposed restrictive compression technique[14] for L1 data cache. Their compression scheme is based on the observation that most data types (e.g, 32-bit integers) can be stored in half of their original size through removing high 16 bits sign-bit extension. When all words (32 bits) in a cache line can be stored in half of their original size, the cache line is called a narrow cache line. Two narrow cache lines in the same set can be compressed to share one physical cache line. So their compression scheme will degrade compressibility of cache line when cache line size increase because the probability that a cache line is a narrow cache line will decrease.

Our work is inspired by frequent pattern compression algorithm shown by Alaa R. Alameldeen et al. [11] and partial cache line prefetching shown by Youtao Zhang et al. [15].

Alaa R. Alameldeen and David A. Wood developed frequent pattern compression (FPC) scheme for L2 cache. Their compression scheme is based on the observation that some data patterns are frequent and also compressible to a fewer number of bits. For example, many small-value integers can be stored in 4, 8 or 16 bits, but are normally stored in a full 32-bit word. In their compressed cache design, cache line decompression occurs when data is read from the L2 to L1 cache and needs 5 cycles decompression latency. So FPC can not directly be applied to L1 cache.

Youtao Zhang and Rajiv Gupta proposed a partial cache line prefetching scheme[15] through data compression. The layout of compressed data in their cache design is similar to our design, but their compressed algorithm will produce more cache block resource conflict than our compressed algorithm, thereby decrease the effective cache capacity of compressed cache.

3 Cache Design Details

3.1 Simple Frequent Pattern Compression (S-FPC) Encode

The compression encode algorithm used by our compressed cache hierarchy is called simple frequent pattern compression (S-FPC). Each word in the cache line is encoded into a compressed format if it matches any of the patterns in the first three rows in Table1. A word that doesn't match any of these patterns is stored in its original 32-bit format. All prefix values are stored at the beginning of the line to speed up decompression.

Table 1. Simple Frequent Pattern Encoding

Prefix	Pattern Encoded	Data Size
00	Zero Run	0 bit
01	One byte sign-extended	8 bits
10	Halfword sign-extended	16 bits
11	Uncompressed word	32 bits

3.2 Unified Compressed Cache Hierarchy

Our proposed unified compressed cache hierarchy has two levels on-chip cache, as shown in Fig.1. L1 I-cache stores instructions in uncompressed format. When data is written to L1 D-cache by processor, data will be encoded on a word basis at first, and then be placed to the corresponding location of L1 cache line according to its word offset. All encoded words in a L1 cache line will be packed to a compressed cache line when data is written back from L1 D-cache to L2 cache. In L2 cache, data and instruction are stored in compressed and uncompressed format respectively. When L1 D-cache miss occurs, L2 compressed cache line will be unpacked to separate encoded words, and then these encoded words will be placed into corresponding location of L1 cache line according to their word offset respectively.

3.3 L1 Data Cache Organization

In our compressed cache hierarchy, every physical cache line in L1 D-cache can hold content from two consecutive encoded cache lines, identified as the *primary* cache line and the *affiliated* cache line. As shown in Fig. 2, block *Prefix*0 and *Prefix*1 hold the prefixes of all words in primary and affiliated cache line respectively. The primary cache line is defined as the line mapped to physical cache line/set by a normal cache of the same size and associativity. Its affiliated cache line is the unique line that is calculated through the following formulas:

$$Tag_{affiliated} = Tag_{primary}$$
$$Set_{affiliated} = Set_{primary} + 1$$

The encoded data layout of L1 compressed D-cache enables a cache miss triggering next line partial prefetching. When a referenced cache line *x* causes a L1 cache miss, it will be loaded from L2 cache. In our S-FPC compression scheme, every word

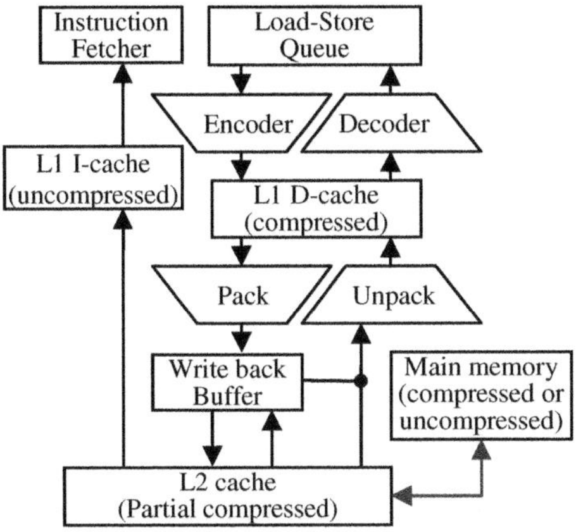

Fig. 1. Compressed Cache Hierarchy

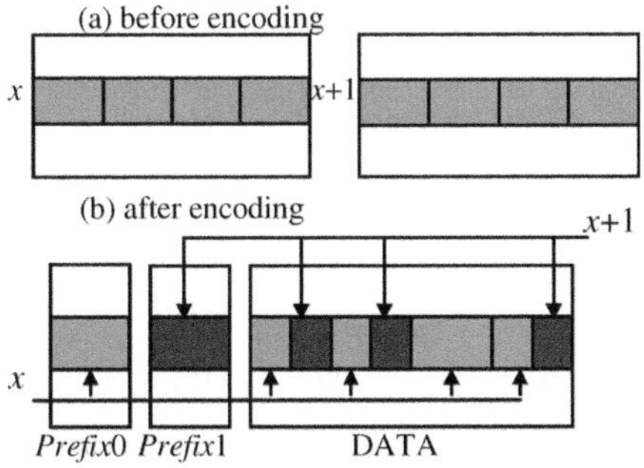

Fig. 2. Encoded Data Layout of L1 Data

(32-bit) can be encoded and occupy 0, 16 or 32 bits according its matching pattern (the word matching one byte sign-extended pattern occupies 16 bits in L1 D-cache). If the i-th word in the primary line x is compressible, as shown in Fig.2(b), the space freed up by the encoded i-th word can be used to store the i-th encoded word in the affiliated line $x+1$. Thus, when all words in primary line x are fetched into the cache, some of the words in affiliated line $x+1$ are also simultaneously prefetched into the cache. Let $prefix_x(i)$ represents the encode prefix of the i-th word in primary line x, $prefix_{x+1}(i)$ represents the encode prefix of the i-th word in affiliated line $x+1$. The condition that the i-th encoded word from line $x+1$ can be prefetched into the cache is that this word together with the i-th word in line x can be accommodated in one 32-bit word space, i.e. the encode prefix of the two words should satisfied the following inequation:

$$prefix_x(i) + prefix_{x+1}(i) < 4 \qquad (*)$$

Fig.3 illustrates the L1 compressed cache organization. This cache is composed of tag array, data array, primary prefix array and affiliated prefix array. When a read request is sent from the processor, there are two possible places that the requested word can reside in. So the primary cache line is accessed and its affiliated line is accessed at next cycle (with one extra cycle latency). If the requested word is found in the primary line, we return the data item in the next cycle, and so as found in the affiliated line. A encoded word is decompressed and sent back to processor. In the case of writing a value to L1 cache, a write hit in the affiliated cache will bring the line to its primary place and invalidate the affiliated one.

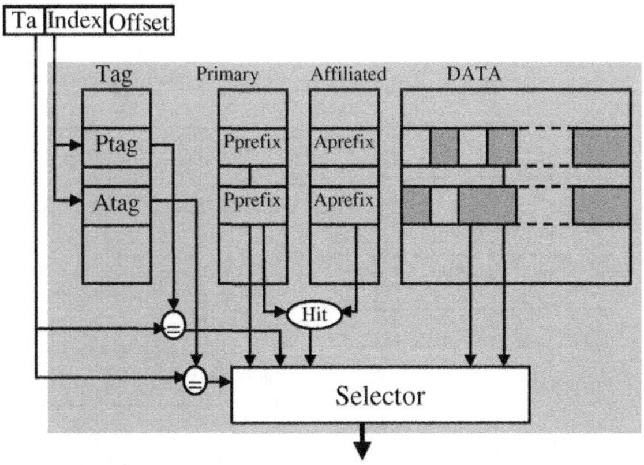

Fig. 3. L1 Compressed Cache Orgnization

When a new cache line arrives to the L1 D-cache from

L2 cache, the prefetched affiliated line is discarded if it is already in the cache (it must be in its primary place in this situation). On the other hand, before discarding a replaced cache line, we check to see if it is possible to put the line into its affiliated place. If the dirty bit is set, we still write back its contents and keep a clean partial copy in its affiliated place. In short, the cache access and replacement policy ensure that at most one copy of a cache line is kept in the cache at any time.

It is critical to quickly decompress an encoded word which is associated with a read instruction. To decompress an encoded word, determining primary or affiliated place and selecting one of four pattern are required. The total delay of critical path of decoding encoded word is a 8-to-1 multiplexer. This delay can be hidden in write back stage of the processor pipeline, so there is no decompression overhead in L1 access latency.

Compared to traditional cache, our compressed cache adds 4 bits for every 32-bit word. It is about 12.5% cache size increase. However, it enables next line partial prefetching, completely removes the prefetch buffer, and does not increase cache pollution and memory traffic between L1 D-cache and L2 cache (the sum of the line size of the primary and affiliated encoded cache line is equal to one physical cache line size). So it can distinctly reduce cache miss rate and improve performance of compressed cache hierarchy.

3.4 L2 Cache Organization

We show L2 compressed cache organization in our compressed cache hierarchy in Fig. 4. S-FPC compression algorithm compresses / decompresses on a cache line basis in L2 cache. L2 cache line size is 64 bytes, so its encode prefix has 32 bits (4-byte) after compression. In L2 cache, each set is 8-way set associative, with a compress information tag stored with each address tag. The data array is broken into 4-byte segments, with 64 segments statically allocated to each cache set. Thus, each set can hold no more than four uncompressed 64-byte lines, or no more than eight compressed cache lines. So compression can at most double the effective capacity. Each line is compressed into 1-16 4-byte segments, with 16 segments being the uncompressed form. The compression tag indicates i) the compressed size of the line (CSize) and ii) the form that the line is stored (Compress Flag), iii) the start segment of the compressed cache line (segments offset). The cache is split into banks for even and odd set index, in order that two address-consecutive cache lines can simultaneously be fetched per cycle and be used as primary and affiliated cache lines in L1 D-cache.

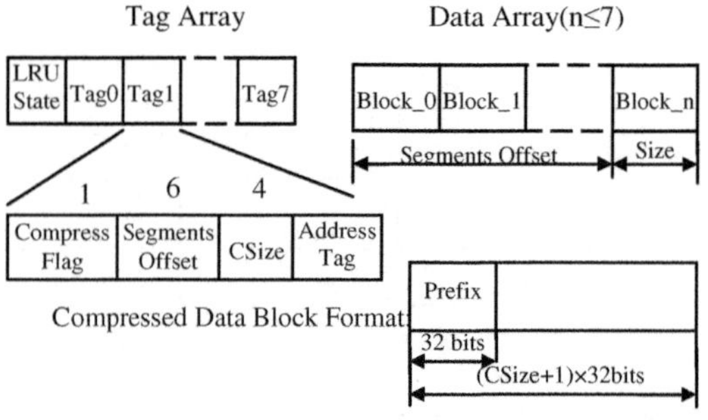

Fig. 4. L2 Compressed Cache Organization

Consider a 4-way, 1MB uncompressed cache with 64-byte lines, each set has 2048 date bits, in addition to four tags. Each tag includes a 14-bit address tag, a 2-bit LRU state, a valid bit and a dirty bit, for a total of 4*(14+2+1+1) =72 bits per set. Our compressed cache design adds four extra tags, increases the LRU state to three bits and adds a 6-bit segments offset, a 4-bit CSize and a 1-bit compress flag each tag, for a total of 8*(14+3+1+1+6+4+1)=240 bits tag overhead per set. This increases the total cache storage by approximately 8%.

3.5 Unpacking L2 Cache Line

In L2 cache, all encoded words of a cache line are packed together. So when a L1 D-cache miss occurs, two address-consecutive L2 compressed cache line will be simultaneously fetched into L1 D-cache, one is identified as primary cache line and the other is identified as affiliated cache line. Fig.5 shows the unpack pipeline of L2 compressed cache. Each prefix is used to determine the length of its corresponding encoded word and the starting location of all the subsequent compressed words. Both prefixes also is used to determine if to place encoded word at some word offset from the affiliated cache line to the corresponding location of the L1 affiliated line. Unpacking L2 cache latency is critical since it is directly added to the L2 hit latency, which is on the critical path. In our compressed design, unpack latency is 4 cycles.

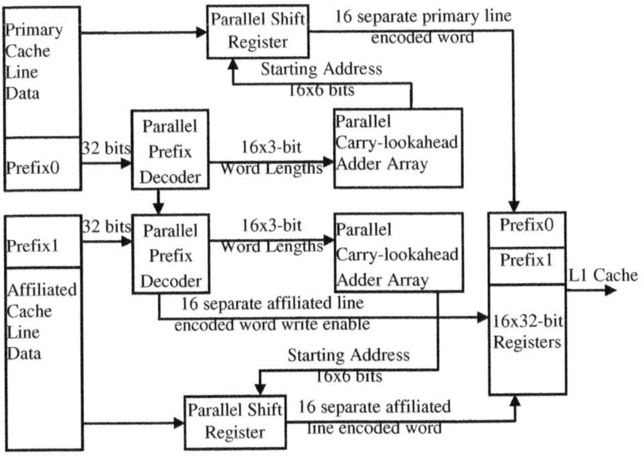

Fig. 5. Unpack Pipeline of L2 Compressed Cache

Cache line packing occurs when data is written back from L1 D-cache to L2 cache. A write back buffer that contains several entries can be used to hide the packing latency on L1 writebacks, as shown in Fig.1. However, since packing cache line is off the critical path, we do not consider pack latency as design constraint. An L2 fill caused by L1 writebacks or L2 cache miss can replace a line in L2 cache. If the new line's compressed size is the same as the replaced line (or small), this replacement is trivial. However, if the new line is larger, the cache controller has to allocate space in the set. This may entail replacing one or more L2 lines or compacting invalid lines to make space. More than one line may have to be replaced if the newly allocated line is larger than the LRU line plus the unused segments. In this case, wereplace at most two lines by replacing the LRU line and searching the LRU list to find the least-recently-used that ensures enough space is available. Compacting a set requires moving tags and data segments to maintain the contiguous storage invariant. With a large write-back buffer, compaction can have a negligible impact on performance.

4 Experimental Results

4.1 Experimental Setup

We implemented our unified compressed cache hierarchy and enabled partial cache line prefetching in L1 D-cache using Simplescalar 3.0[10], simulating alpha binary. The baseline processor is a four issue superscalar with two levels of on-chip cache (Table 2). Except the basic cache configuration, we use the same parameters for implementations of all different cache designs.

Table 2. Baseline experimental set up

Parameter	Value	Parameter	Value
Issue width	4 issue, OO	I-cache hit latency	2 cycles
IFQ size	16 instr.	I-cache miss latency	20 cycles
Branch Predictor	8 entry	L1 D-cache hit latency	2 cycles
Memory access latency	150 cycles	L1 D-cache miss latency	20 cycles
Func. units	4 ALUs, 1 Mult/Div, 2 Mem ports, 4 FALU, 1FMult/FDiv		

We chose a collection of 6 integer (vpr, mcf, parser, bzip2, gcc and twolf), and 6 FP (equake, ammp, art, swim, wupwise and mesa) from SPEC CPU 2000 benchmark suite, using *ref* inputs. The statistics are collected for 300M instructions after skipping the first 1 billion instructions. Firstly, we evaluated the increase of the L1 D-cache effective capacity with varying the cache line size. And then, we compared the performance of cache configurations described below. The comparisons are made in terms of IPC and miss rates.

- **Baseline Cache (BC):** The L1 D-cache and L1 I-cache are 32K 4-way set-associative and 64B/line. The L2 cache is 1MB 4-way associative and 64B/line.
- **Baseline cache with L2 compressed cache (BL2C):** The L1 D-cache and L1 I-cache are same as BC, and the L2 cache is 1MB 8-way associative and 64B/line, as described in the paper. The access latency of L2 compressed cache is 24 cycles.
- **Unified Compressed Cache Hierarchy (UCCH):** The L1 I-cache is same as BC, the L1 D-cache is compressed cache, 32K 4-way set-associative and 64B/line, combining partial cache line prefetching, 2 cycles primary cache line hit latency, 3 cycles affiliated cache line hit latency, and the L2 cache is 1MB 8-way associative and 64B/line, as described in the paper.
- **Higher Capacity Cache (HCC):** The L1 D-cache and L1 I-cache is uncompressed 64K 4-way set-associative and 64B/line. The L2 cache is uncompressed 2M 8-way set-associative and 64B/line.

4.2 Result

In this section, we evaluated the increase of the L1 D-cache effective capacity with varying the cache line size. For each simulation run, we computed the increase of effective capacity every 10000 cycles. In this paper, the increase rate of the effective capacity in L1 D-cache equal to the ratio of the number of all valid words in the L1 D-cache and the number of all words in all primary lines. Fig. 6 shows the percentage increase in cache capacity for 32KB 4-way set-associative L1 D-cache with varying cache line size from 32B to128B.

In our compressed cache design, the effective capacity of L1 compressed D-cache increase 33% for 64B cache line size, on average. When cache line size growing, the effective capacity of the L1 compressed D-cache decreases. This is because the possibility of a store instruction writing a value to a cache line will increase, when cache line size growing. Writing a value to affiliated cache line will make it move to its primary location, this decreasing the increase rate of effective capacity of L1 D-cache consequently.

The L1 D-cache and L2 cache miss rate comparisons of four different cache configurations, normalized with respect to BC, are shown in Fig.7 and Fig.8 respectively. The performance comparisons of these cache configurations, normalized with respect to BC, are shown in Fig.9. From Fig.9, we can see that BL2C configuration (i.e. storing compression data only in L2 cache) can improve the performance for some benchmarks (vpr, parser, bzip2, twolf and art), but for the other benchmarks, BL2C will hurt the performance. Because for some benchmarks such as vpr, parser, bzip2, twolf and art, their data working sets size during simulation is between 1MB and

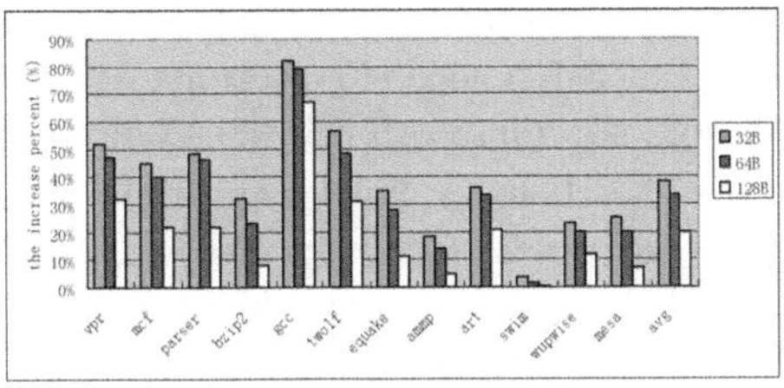

Fig. 6. The increase percent of L1 D-cache capacity for different cache line size

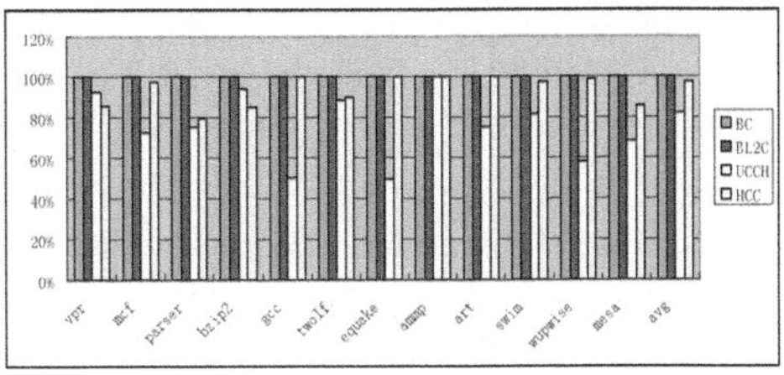

Fig. 7. Percentage reduction in L1 D-cache miss rate for four different cache configure

2MB, compression can decrease distinctly cache misses. But for the other benchmarks, compression can not decrease distinctly cache misses, decompression latency increase the hit latency, so compression hurts the performance of these benchmarks. Our unified compressed cache hierarchy can increase decompression latency balance point D_{th}, so for almost all benchmarks but ammp, our compressed cache can improve the performance. This is because our compressed cache hierarchy can benefit from both compression and partial cache line prefetching. For vpr, art, parser, bzip2, and twolf, as shown in Fig. 8, the L2 cache miss rate of HCC is far less than that of BC, so increasing cache capacity can distinctly decrease L2 cache miss, our scheme can benefit from compression. For mcf, equake, swim, wupwise, mesa, gcc and so on, our scheme can benefit from partial cache line prefetching. Only for ammp, the benefit from compression and partial cache line prefetching can not compensate the overhead caused by decompression latency, so performance is degraded by 2.5%. But partial cache line prefetching can reduce the importance of cache misses, so the performance of UCCH is better than BL2C for ammp.

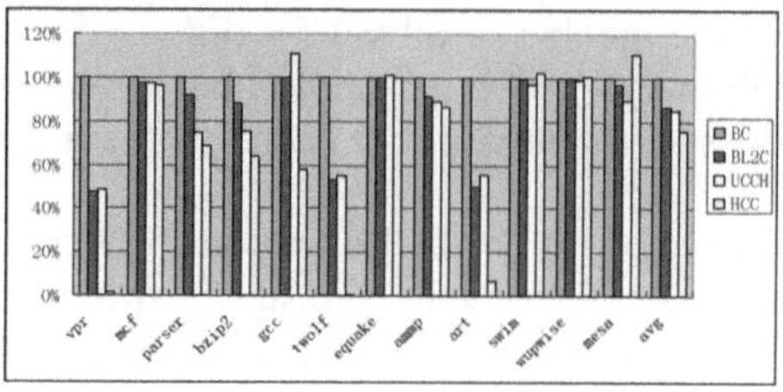

Fig. 8. Percentage Reduction in L2 cache for four different cache configure

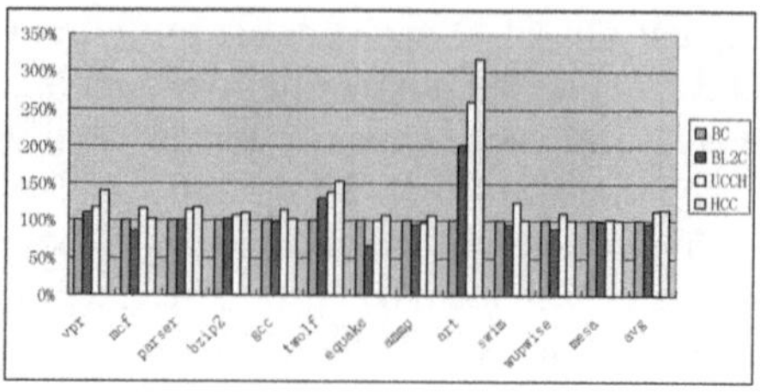

Fig. 9. Performance (IPC) Comparison of four different cache configure

In short, relative to a baseline cache hierarchy that does not support data compression in cache, on average, our cache hierarchy design increases the average L1 cache capacity(in terms of the average number of valid words in cache per cycle) by about 33%, reduces the data cache miss rate by 21%, and speeds up program execution by 13%, with the performance degraded by less than 2.5%.

5 Conclusion

in this paper, we propose a unified compressed cache hierarchy which holds compressed data in L1 D-cache and L2 cache based on S-FPC encoding scheme. We propose to combine partial cache line prefetching and compression in L1 compressed cache in order to increase decompression latency balance point D_{th} of the compressed cache hierarchy. We show that our unified compressed cache design, on average, increases the average L1 cache capacity(in terms of the average number of valid words in cache per cycle) by about 33%, reduces the data cache miss rate by 21%, and speeds up program execution by 13%, with the performance degraded by less than 2.5%.

References

1. John Hennessy and David Patterson, "Computer Architecture: A Quantitative Approach". Morgan Kaufmann Publishers, 1996.
2. A. Alameldeen and D. Wood, "Adaptive Cache Compression for High-Performance Processor", Proc. ISCA-31, 2004.
3. David Chen, Enoch Peserico, and Larry Rudolph. "A Dynamically Partitionable Compressed Cache." In Proceeding of the Singapore-MIT Alliance Symposium, January 2003.
4. Jang-Soo Lee, Won-Kee Hong, and Shin-Dug Kim. "Design and Evaluation of a Selective Compressed Memory System." In proceedings of International Conference on Computer Design (ICCD'99), pages 184-191, October 1999.
5. Jang-Soo Lee, Won-Kee Hong, and Shin-Dug Kim. "Adaptive Methods to Minimize Decompression Overhead for Compressed On-chip Cache." International Journal of Computers and Application, 25(2), January 2003.

6. Jun Yang, Youtao Zhang, and Rajiv Gupta. "Frequent Value Compression in Data Caches." In Proceedings of the 33rd Annual IEEE/ACM International Symposium on Microarchitecture, pages 258-265, December 2000.
7. E. Hallnor, S. Reinhardt, "A Unified Compressed Memory Hierarchy", Proceedings of the 11th Int'l Symposium on High-Performance Computer Architecture (HPCA-11 2005)
8. P. Franaszek, J. Robinson, and J. Thomas, "Parallel Compression with Cooperative Dictionary Construction", Proc. Data Compression Conf., 1996, pp. 200–209.
9. B. Abali, H. Franke, S. Xiaowei, et.al., "Performance of Hardware Compressed Main Memory", Proc. 7th Int'l Symp. on High-Performance Computer Architecture, 2001, pp. 73-81.
10. D. Burger and T. M. Austin, "The SimpleScalar Tool Set, Version 2.0," Computer Arch. News, 1997.
11. Alameldeen A. R. and Wood D. A. "Frequent Pattern Compression: A Significance-Based Compression Scheme for L2 Caches". Technical Report 1500, Computer Sciences Department, University of Wisconsin-Madison, April 2004.
12. M. Kjelso, et. al., "Design and Performance of a Main Memory Hardware Data Compressor", Proc. EUROMICRO Conference, 1996.
13. Y. Zhang, et. al., "Frequent Value Locality and Value Centric Data Cache Design", Proc. ASPLOS, 2000.
14. P. Pujara and A. Aggarwal. Restrictive Compression Techniques to Increase Level 1 Cache Capacity. International Conference on Computer Design, 2005.
15. Youtao Zhang, Rajiv Gupta: Enabling Partial Cache Line Prefetching Through Data Compression. ICPP 2003: 277-285
16. Jang-Soo Lee, Won-Kee Hong, and Shin-Dug Kim. Design and Evaluation of a Selective Compressed Memory System. In Proceedings of International Conference on Computer Design (ICCD'99), pages 184–191, October 1999.
17. S. Arramreddy, D. Har, K. Mak, et al., "IBM X-Press Memory Compression Technology Debuts in a ServerWorks NorthBridge", Hot Chips 12, 2000.
18. J.S. Lee, W.K. Hong, and S. D. Kim, "An on-chip cache compression technique to reduce decompression overhead and design complexity," Journal of Systems Architecture, vol. 46, Dec. 2000, pp. 1365-1382.
19. S. Roy, R. Kumar, and M. Prvulovic, "Improving System Performance with Compressed Memory", Proc. 15th Int'l Parallel and Distributed Processing Symp., Apr 2001, pp. 630–636.
20. S. Kumar, et. al., "Bit-Sliced Datapath for Energy-Efficient High Performance Microprocessors", Workshop on Power-Aware Computer Systems(PACS'04), 2004.

Function Inlining in Embedded Systems with Code Size Limitation

Xinrong Zhou[1], Lu Yan[2], and Johan Lilius[3]

[1] ZTE Corp., Zhongxing Telecom, Shenzhen, China
[2] University College London, Dept. of Computer Science, London, UK
[3] Åbo Akademi University, Dept. of Information Technologies, Turku, Finland

Abstract. Function inlining is a widely known technique that has been adopted in compiler optimization research domain. Inlining functions can eliminate the overhead resulted from function calls, but with inlining, the code size also grows unpredictably; this is not suitable for embedded processors whose memory size is relatively small. In this paper, we introduce a novel function inlining approach using the heuristic rebate_ratio, functions to be inlined are selected according to their rebate_ratios in a descending way. This kind of code optimization operation works at the source code level. Comparing with other algorithms, it is easier to implement. Our target is to get an optimal result of function inlining which can achieve the maximum performance improvement while keeping the code size within a defined limit.

1 Introduction

Nowadays, more and more people prefer to use C compiler rather than assembly one for programming embedded processors. Every C program is made of at least one function, the most frequently accessed parts are often put together into functions, it makes the programs more dependent and more readable, but an excessive use of functions may degrade program performance. When calling a function, the system should save all the values of current registers, pass the parameters and allocate stack for local variables. In processors which support pipeline, the actual function call and return may result a significant number of instruction pipeline stalls.

Function inlining replaces a function call with the body of function; it has the effect of removing all the overheads mentioned above. [2,3,4,8] Obviously, the performance of the system can be improved in some ways, but inlining functions does not come for free, one of its negative effects is the unpredictable code size, this is intolerable for embedded processors whose memory space is limited.

During the past years, lots of code optimization techniques have been developed. Many of them are low level optimizations, which are dependent on processor architecture. For example, code selection, register allocation [7, 10], and memory access optimization [12]. These works focus on how to get a performance enhancement, less attention was put on the code size. Leupers brought out a machine-independent source-level code optimization algorithm, named OptinlineVector, which aims at embedded processors and employs function inlining to achieve higher performance [7, 9]. In OptinlineVector algorithm the element b_i in the inline vector IV is used to

Y.-H. Lee et al. (Eds.): ICESS 2007, LNCS 4523, pp. 154–161, 2007.

indicate whether function f_i is inlined or not, all the functions in program are checked. OptinlineVector algorithm can find the optimal solution of function inlining, but the time and memory space it needs are huge. The worse case complexity of OptinlineVector algorithm is exponential to N, where N is the total number of functions in a program. In this paper, we present a new approach to function inlining which works at the source code level as well. The time and memory space needed in worst case is the cube of N.

The remainder of this paper is organized as follows. Section 2 illustrates the system model of function inlining, our new algorithm is explained in detail in section 3. Section 4 makes a brief analysis of our algorithm; the last section concludes this paper and points out our future work.

2 System Model for Function Inlining

In normal systems, performance enhancement is the main target, the negative effect code expansion which is brought by function inlining does not attract more attention, but in embedded processors, code expansion becomes a serious problem. An oversized code is intolerable. In order to control the code bloating problem of inlining, we should inline selectively. Leupers used branch-and-bound algorithm to determine which function to inline [3]. Although the result they got is an optimal one, the time and space the algorithm needs are too huge. In our method, we use heuristic to do the same job. The benefit using heuristic depends on the execution frequency of the inlined function. The more it is called, the better improvement it will achieve. We introduce a concept, named rebate_ratio, it is used as an inlining heuristic variable. Inlining a function with a high rebate_ratio will get a better performance than inlining a low rebate_ratio function.

The definition of rabate_ratio is:

$$rebate\_ratio = \frac{function\_calling\_frequency}{code\_size\_increased} \tag{1}$$

The function calling frequency is direct proportion to performance improvement while code size expansion is the other way round. Note that, in some case, code_size_increased may equal to zero, which means when inlining that function, the code size does not change. We assign a maximum value to the rebate_ratio of this function and inline them before inlining other functions.

The system model of function inlining is described as follows:

For a given C program, we use a graph $G=(V,E)$ to represent the function call structure inside it. Each node in V represents one function f_i and each edge $e=(v_i,v_j) \in E$ means function f_i calls f_j. Each node v_i has a two-tuple attributes v_i: (B_i, R_i), B_i denotes the real size of function f_i, R_i is the rebate_ratio of function f_i. Attribute R_i is used as a priority indicator of our queue operating, the smaller R_i is the higher possibility it will be at the head of a queue, which means the higher possibility to be inlined. Each edge e_i has a weight w_i which denotes the times f_i calls f_j.

The total sum of all the nodes' weight in V is the estimation of total code size of the given C program. As you can see, the code size calculated in this way is not precise since the detailed code size is only known after code generation. Algorithms using similar method to calculate code size have already shown that this estimation appears to be sufficiently accurate in practice. [7, 8, 9] The function inlining problem is now translated to a graph operation problem, what we will do is to present a method to realize the following work:

Input: $G=(V,E)$ and a global code size limit L

Output: $G'=(V',E')$ which $|V'|$ reaches its minimum value while $\sum_{i=1}^{|V'|} B(v_i) \leq L$,

where $|V'|$ is the number of nodes in Graph G'.

3 Minimizing Function Calls

As the number of function calls in a program decreases, the performance increases. Once a function is inlined, the corresponding operation in graph is that the node representing that function is deleted. When the code size of the inlining function increases, the change in graph is that the weight of deleted node's parent node increases also. Since the code size has an upper bound and we wish to inline as many function calls as possible, the operation to the graph is trying to delete as many nodes as possible while keeping the total sum of all the remained nodes' weight not larger than the limit value.

We inline the function calls in a rebate_ratio decreasing way, in another word, we inline first the function whose rebate_ratio is the largest and then inline the second largest and so on. When no more function call can be inlined with the total code size smaller than the upper bound, the work is done.

Before we start inlining functions, there are some preparation works to do. First, we must use a source code tool to find out the number of calls $w(e(v_i,v_j))$ from function f_i to f_j. Next, to compile the source code without function inlining to determine the code size $B(v_i)$ of each function.

Usually there are lots of loops in a program, if an inlined function is in a loop, the amount of code size increased is equal to the code size of this inlined function, not n times of code size (suppose n is the number of loop repetition), i.e. rebate_ratio is *n/code_size* not *n/(n*code_size)*.

The benefit of inlining a function in the loop is the same as inlining n times of a function whose code size is n times smaller. So in our algorithm, we assign an equal priority to the two functions, which means their rebate_ratios are the same.

If a function calls another one f_k both in loops and outside loops, we derive a new node v_n, where $B(v_n)=B(v_k)$, $R(v_n)=R(v_k)/n$, here n is the iteration of the loops, the new node is connect with all of node v_k's parent and child nodes. The weights of the new derived edges are defined as follows.

$$\forall v_p \in parent(v_k) \qquad \forall v_c \in child(v_k)$$
$$w(e(v_p, v_n)) = 1 \qquad w(e(v_n, v_c)) = w(e(v_k, v_c))$$

where the function that the new node represents is a copy of the function in loops. The weight $w(e(v_p,v_k))$ is also reduced to the number of calls outside loop. Thus, we change the nodes for functions in loops into normal ones. Figure 1 is an example of node deriving for functions in loop. Function f_1 calls $f_3 w_3$ times, $w'_3 = w_3 - n$ times are not in loops, the algorithm derives a new node v'_3, derives also an edge $e(v_1,v'_3)$, the edge's weight is 1.

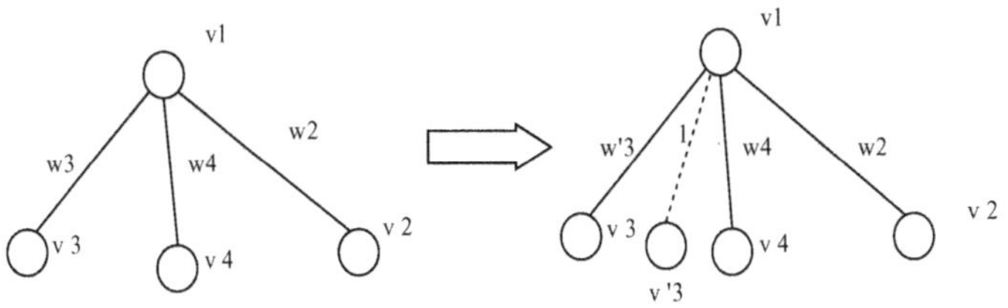

Fig. 1. Node deriving for functions in loops

There are two different situations when function f_i inlines function f_j, first, v_j is a leaf in the graph shown in figure 2, we delete both the node v_j and the edge $e(v_i,v_j)$, the weight of node v_i changes to a new value $B'(v_i) = B(v_i) + W(e(v_i,v_j)) * B(v_j)$, if more than two functions call f_j, the weight values of all these functions should also be modified and the edges be deleted.

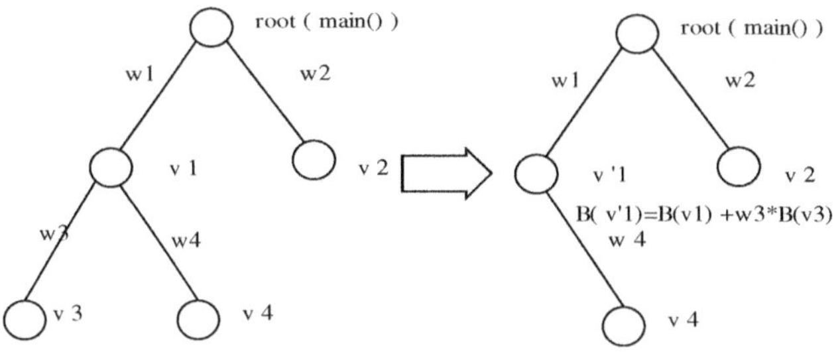

Fig. 2. Deleting a leaf node

Second, function f_j is not a leaf in the graph, node v_j is deleted, all its parent nodes' weights are also updated, the edges connected with v_j are deleted, v_j's parent nodes are connected with v_j's children nodes. The newly appeared edges also have new weights. For example, when root function inlines f_1, , as shown in figure 3, node v_1 is deleted, so do all the edges connecting with v_1, node v_3,v_4's parents are changed to the root, two new edges are derived, the weight values are w_1*w_3 and w_1*w_4 respectively.

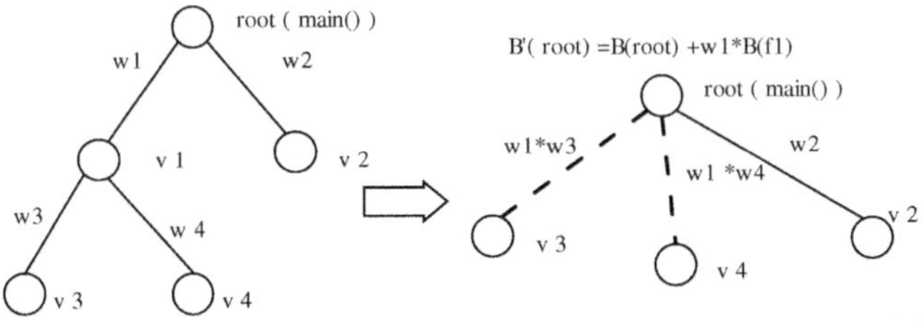

Fig. 3. Deleting a non-leaf node

Our method to inline functions consists of two steps. First, we process the functions in loops using algorithm Loop_Node_Process. We search the whole program and find out the functions in loops, and then change the corresponding nodes to new ones which are the same as the nodes representing outside loop functions, when the changing work finishes, we set up a queue and sort the queue.

Second, we inline the functions according to algorithm Mini_Func_Call. Since the queue has already been sorted in a rebate_ratio decending way, the most suitable function to be inlined is the one which is represented by the node in the head of the queue. We inline the function and delete the node from the queue. After inlining, the rebate_ratio values of its parent nodes are also changed, so we sort the queue again and ensure the first node in the queue has the largest rebate_ratio. When all the nodes in the queue are deleted, the operation finishes.

Algorithm Loop_Node_Process (V,E)

```
V' ← Find_Nodes_in_Loop(V)
for (v_i in V') do
   create a new node v_k
   B(v_k) ← B(v_i)
   R(v_k) ← R(v_i)/n  {increase the rebate_ratio of the new node}
   insert_queue (Q, v_i)  {insert the new node into queue Q}
   for ( v_j in child (v_i)) do
     E ← E + e(v_k, v_j)   {add edge e(v_k, v_j) to E}
     w(e(v_k, v_j)) ← w(e(v_i, v_j))
   end for
   for ( v_j in parent (v_i)) do
     E ← E + e(v_j, v_k)
     w(e(v_j, v_k)) ← 1
     w(e(v_j, v_i)) ← w(e(v_j, v_i)) – n
          {update the number v_j, calls v_i }
     update R(v_i)
     if ( w(e(v_j, v_i)) = 0 ) then
       V ← V -v_i
            {delete node v_i from the graph}
       delete_queue (Q, v_i)
            {get rid of the node from queue Q}
       for (v_c in child (v_i)) do
          E ← E - e(v_i, v_c) {delete edges connected to the child nodes}
       end for
     end if
   end for
end for
sort_queue (Q)
return (V+V',E)
```

```
Algorithm Mini_Func_Call (V, E, L)
    G(V,E) ← Loop_Node_Process(V,E)
    Q ← create a queue, {queue Q(v1,v2,...vn), vi ∈ V, |V| = n}
  sort_queue (Q), {∀vi, vj ∈ Q, (i<j), R(vi) > R(vj)}
    while (Q is not empty) ) do
     vi ← first element in Q
     delete vi from Q
     if
          ( Σ_{k=1}^{|V-vi|} B(vk) + Σ_{vp ∈ parent(vi)} (w(e(vp, vi)) × B(vi)) ≤ L )
        then
          {if code size is within constraint after inlining function fi}
      V ← V - vi {delete node vi from the graph}
      for (vc in child (vi)) do
        E ← E - e(vi, vc) {delete edges connected to the child nodes}
      end for
      for (vp in parent(vi)) do
        B(vp) ← B(vp) + w(e(vp, vi))*B(vi);
                 { modify parent node's code size}
        update R(vp)
        for (vc in child (vc)) do
          E ← E + e(vp, vc) { derive new edges}
          w(e(vp, vc)) ← w(e(vp, vi))* w(e(vi, vc))
         update R(vc)
        end for
      end for
      sort_queue(Q)
     end if
    end while
    return (V,E)
```

4 Algorithm Analysis

Although we also use heuristics aiding to find the optimal result of function inlining, unlike other ones, the value of the heuristic parameter – rebate_ratio in our algorithm is not fixed. When we inline a function call, the benefit we get is that we eliminate the overhead which is brought by setting up the call stack, passing parameter etc. The side-effect is the expansion of code size. Heuristic parameter – rebate_ratio is an indicator of the combination of the benefit and the side-effect. As shown in the algorithm, when we inline a function call, we select the one whose rebate_ratio value is the largest, it means we can get more performance improvement than inlining other function calls. If a function call has inlined other function calls, its code size changes, which means the side-effect of being inlined enlarges, so it is wise to alter its rebate_ratio to a smaller value, gives the priority of selection to other function calls.

Inside our algorithm, n represents the number of function calls. There are 3 level iteration inside our algorithm, the worst case of the time and space complexity of our algorithm is $O(n^3)$, if there are no circles in the graph, i.e. the graph is a family tree , the numbers of parent and child nodes are $O(\log n)$, the time we need reduces to $O(n\log^2 n)$. In most ideal situation, when the graph degenerates to a line, the complexity is equal to $\Theta(n)$.

The exception of our algorithm is described as following.

If there exists two adjacent nodes v_i and v_j in queue Q, function f_i has a larger rebate_ratio, when inlining function f_i, the code size is over the limit,

$$\text{i.e.} \sum_{k=1}^{|V-vi|} B(v_k) + \sum_{v_p \in parent(v_i)} (w(e(v_p, v_i)) \times B(v_i)) > L \quad (2)$$

so we give up function f_i and select function f_j , and we go on running until it reaches the final, but the total performance enhancement gained from inlining function f_j to end is not as good as inlining function f_i in part of its parent nodes' calls, this phenomena may occur in nest. One solution to this problem is that we derive as many sibling nodes as possible when the above situation is detected, the newly born nodes have a same rebate_ratio, and they join the queue Q waiting for selection.

5 Conclusion and Future Work

The small memory space of embedded processors requires applications keep a sophisticated tradeoff between the program code size and system performance. Nowadays' heuristics inlining techniques do not meet such a demand. In this paper we present a code optimization technique which works at the source level, it can minimize the number of function calls by inlining proper subset of functions under a code size constraint.

Like other algorithms, we need profiling to get the exact number of functions to inline. The repetition times in recursive loops, *repeat/until* and *while* statements are uncertain, when processing these loops, we give a rough estimation. Sometimes inlining functions in these loops can give significant savings; one of our future works is to handle this situation precisely. Some functions which are small in size but have many local variables may have a negative effect on the execution time when inlined, more work will also need to focus on solving these problems in the near future.

References

1. Araujo G. and Malik S., "Timal Code Generation for Embedded Memory Non-Homogenerous Register Architecture." Proc. 8th Int. Symp. On Synthesis, pp.36-41, 1995
2. Ayers A., Gottlieb R. and Schooler, "Aggressive inlining. " In ACM SIGPLAN Conf. on Programming Language Design and Implementation, May, 1997
3. Davidson J.W. and Holler A.M., "Subprogram inlining:A study of its effects on program execution time" *IEEE Transanctions on Software Engineering,* vol. 18 no.2, pp. 89-102, 1992.
4. Davidson J.W. and Holler A.M., "A Study of a C Function Inliner" *Software Practice Experience*, pp. 775-790, 1988.
5. Liao S., Devadas S., Keutzer K. and TJiang S. "Instruction Selection Using Binate Covering for Code Size Optimization" *Int. Conf. on Compuer-Aided Design*, pp.393-399, 1995.
6. Liao S., Devadas S., Keutzer K., Tjiang S. and Wang A. "Storage Assignment to Decrease Code Size", *In Proc. Programming Language Design and Implementation,* 1995.
7. Leupers R., *Code Optimization Techniques for Embedded Processors,* Kluwer Academic Publishers, 2000.
8. Leupers R. and Marwedel P. "Algorithms for Address Assignment in DSP Code Generation" *Proc. IEEE/ACM Int. Conf. On Computer-Aided Design,* 1996
9. Leupers R. and Marwedel P. "Function Inlining under Code Size Constraints for Embedded Processors" *Proc. IEEE/ACM Int. Conf. On Computer-Aided Design*, 1999
10. Liem C., May T. and Paulin P. "Instruction-Set Matching and Selection for DSP and ASIP Code Generation" *European Design and Test Conference*,pp. 31-37, 1994.
11. Muchnik S.S. *Advanced Compiler Design and Implementation*, Morgan Kaufmann Publishers, 1997
12. Sudarsanam A. and Malik S. "Memory Bank and Register Allocation in Software Synthesis for ASIPs", *Int. Conf. on Computer-Aided Design*, pp.388-392, 1995

Performance Characteristics of Flash Memory: Model and Implications*,**

Seungjae Baek[1], Jongmoo Choi[1], Donghee Lee[2], and Sam H. Noh[3]

[1] Division of Information and Computer Science, Dankook University, Korea,
Hannam-Dong, Yongsan-Gu, Seoul, 140-714 Korea, +82-2-799-1367
{ibanez1383,choijm}@dankook.ac.kr

[2] Department of Computer Science, University of Seoul, Korea,
Jeonnong-Dong, Dongdaemun-Gu, Seoul, 130-743 Korea +82-2-2210-5615
dhlee@venus.uos.ac.kr

[3] School of Computer and Information Engineering, Hongik University, Korea,
Sangsu-Dong, Mapo-Gu, Seoul, 121-791, Korea, +82-2-320-1470
samhnoh@hongik.ac.kr

Abstract. In this paper, we propose a model to identify the cost of block cleaning of Flash memory. The model defines three performance parameters, namely, utilization, invalidity, and uniformity and presents a formula for estimating the block cleaning cost based on these parameters. Then, we design a new modification-aware (MODA) page allocation scheme which can improve the block cleaning cost by enhancing uniformity of Flash memory. Real implementation experiments conducted on an embedded system show that the MODA scheme can reduce block cleaning time by up to 43 seconds (with an average of 10.2 seconds) compared to the traditional sequential allocation scheme that is used in YAFFS.

1 Introduction

Characteristics of storage media have been the key driving force behind the development of file systems. The introduction of cylinder groups in Fast File System (FFS) and the log-unit large sequential writes in Log-structured File System (LFS) were, essentially, to reduce seek time, which is the key bottleneck for user perceived disk performance [1, 2]. Similarly, various scheduling algorithms that consider physical characteristics of MEMS devices such as the disparity of seek distances in the x and y dimensions have been suggested [3].

In this paper, we explore and identify the characteristics of Flash memory and analyze how they influence the latency of data access. We identify the cost of block cleaning as the key characteristic that influences latency. A performance model for analyzing the cost of block cleaning is presented based on three parameters that we derive, namely, utilization, invalidity, and uniformity, which we define clearly later.

* This work was supported in part by grant No. R01-2004-000-10188-0 from the Basic Research Program of the Korea Science & Engineering Foundation.

** This work was supported in part by MIC & IITA through IT Leading R&D Support Project.

Y.-H. Lee et al. (Eds.): ICESS 2007, LNCS 4523, pp. 162–173, 2007.

The model reveals that the cost of block cleaning is strongly influenced by uniformity just like seek is a strong influence for disk based storage. We observe that most previous algorithms that try to improve block cleaning time in Flash memory are, essentially, trying to maintain high uniformity of Flash memory. Our model gives the upper bound on the performance gain expected by developing a new algorithm. To validate the model and to analyze our observations in real environments, we design a new **mod**ification-**a**ware (MODA) page allocation scheme that strives to maintain high uniformity by grouping files based on their update frequencies.

We implement the MODA page allocation scheme on an embedded system that has 64MB of NAND Flash memory running the Linux kernel 2.4.19. The NAND Flash memory is managed by YAFFS (Yet Another Flash File System) [4] supported in Linux. We modify the page allocation scheme in YAFFS to MODA and compare its performance with the original scheme. Experimental results show that, by enhancing uniformity, the MODA scheme can reduce block cleaning time up to 43 seconds with an average of 10.2 seconds for the benchmarks considered.

The rest of the paper is organized as follows. In Section 2, we elaborate on the characteristics of Flash memory and explain the need for cleaning, which is the key issue that we deal with. Then, we present a model for analyzing the cost of block cleaning in Section 3. In Section 4, we present the new page allocation scheme, which we refer to as MODA, in detail. The implementation details and the performance evaluation results are discussed in Section 5. We conclude the paper with a summary and directions for future works in Section 6.

2 Flash Memory and Block Cleaning

2.1 General Characteristics of Flash Memory

Flash memory as a storage medium has characteristics that are different from traditional disk storage. These characteristics can be summarized as follows .

- Access time in Flash memory is location independent similar to RAM. There is no "seek time" involved.
- Overwrite is not possible in Flash memory. Flash memory is a form of EEPROM (Electrically Erasable Programmable Read Only Memory), so it needs to be erased before new data can be overwritten.
- Execution time for the basic operations in Flash memory is asymmetric. Traditionally, three basic operations, namely, read, write, and erase, are supported. An erase operation is used to clean used pages so that the page may be written to again. In general, a write operation takes an order of magnitude longer than a read operation, while an erase operation takes another order or more magnitudes longer than a write operation [5].
- The unit of operation is also different for the basic operations. While the erase operation is performed in block units, read/write operations are performed in page units.
- The number of erasures possible on each block is limited, typically, to 100,000 or 1,000,000 times.

These characteristics make designing software for Flash memory challenging and interesting [6].

2.2 The Need for Block Cleaning

Reading data or writing totally new data into Flash memory is simply like reading/writing to disk. A page in Flash is referenced/allocated for the data and data is read/written from/to that particular page. The distinction from a disk is that all reads/writes take a (much shorter) constant amount of time (though writes take longer than reads).

However, for updates of existing data, the story is totally different. As overwriting updated pages is not possible, various mechanisms for non-in-place update have been developed [4, 7, 8, 9]. Though specific details differ, the basic mechanism is to allocate a new page, write the updated data onto the new page, and then, invalidate the original page that holds the (now obsolete) original data. The original page now becomes a dead or invalid page.

Note that from the above discussions a page can be in three different states. That is, a page can be holding legitimate data making it a valid page; we will say that a page is in a valid state if the page is valid. If the page no longer holds valid data, that is, it was invalidated by being deleted or by being updated, then the page is a dead/invalid page, and the page is in an invalid state. Note that a page in this state cannot be written to until the block it resides in is first erased. Finally, if the page has not been written to in the first place or the block in which the page resides has just been erased, then the page is clean. In this case, we will say that the page is in a clean state. Note that only pages that are in a clean state may be written to. Figure 1 shows the state transition diagram of pages in Flash memory. Recall that in disks, there is no notion of an invalid state as in-place overwrites to sectors is always possible.

Note from the tri-state characteristics that the number of clean pages diminishes not only as new data is written, but also as existing data is updated. In order to store more data and even to make updates to existing data, it is imperative that invalid pages be continually cleaned. Since cleaning is done via erase operation, which is done in block units, valid pages in the block to be erased must be copied to a clean block. This exacerbates the already large overhead incurred by the erase operation needed for cleaning a block.

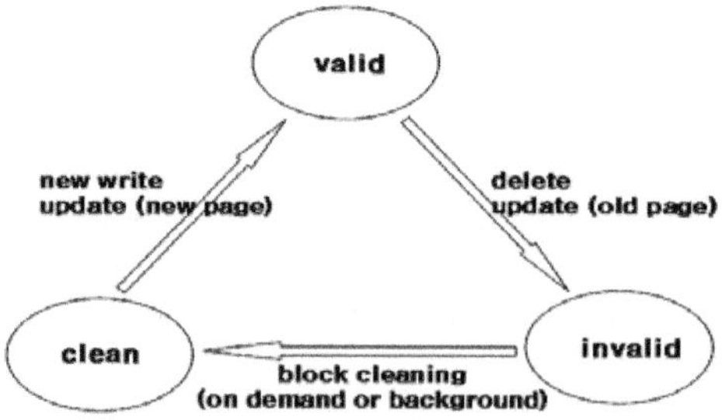

Fig. 1. Page state transition

3 Analysis of Block Cleaning Cost

3.1 Performance Parameters

Two types of block cleaning are possible in Flash memory. The first is when valid and invalid pages coexist within the block that is to be cleaned. Here, the valid pages must first be copied to a clean page in a different block before the erase operation on the block can happen. We shall refer to this type of cleaning as 'copy-erase cleaning'. The other kind of cleaning is where there are no valid pages in the block to be erased. All pages in this block are either invalid or clean. This cleaning imposes only a single erase operation, and we shall refer to this type of cleaning as 'erase-only cleaning'. Note that for the same number of cleaning attempts, more erase-only cleaning will result in lower cleaning cost.

Observe that for copy-erase cleaning the number of valid pages in the block to be cleaned is a key factor that affects the cost of cleaning. The more valid pages there are in the block to be cleaned, more copy operations need to be performed. Also observe that for more erase-only cleaning to happen, the way in which the invalid pages are distributed plays a key role. Distribution of invalid pages skewed towards particular blocks will increase the chance of having only invalid pages in blocks, increasing the possibility of erase-only cleaning.

From these observations, we identify three parameters that affect the cost of block cleaning. They are defined as follows:

- Utilization (u): the fraction of valid pages in Flash memory
- Invalidity (i): the fraction of invalid pages in Flash memory
- Uniformity (p): the fraction of blocks that are uniform in Flash memory, where a uniform block is a block that does *not* contain both valid and invalid blocks simultaneously.

Figure 2 shows three page allocation situations where utilization and invalidity are the same, but uniformity is different. Since there are eight valid pages and eight invalid pages among the 20 pages for all three cases, utilization and invalidity are both 0.4. However, there is one, three, and five uniform blocks in Figure 2(a), (b), and (c), respectively, hence uniformity is 0.2, 0.6, and 1, respectively.

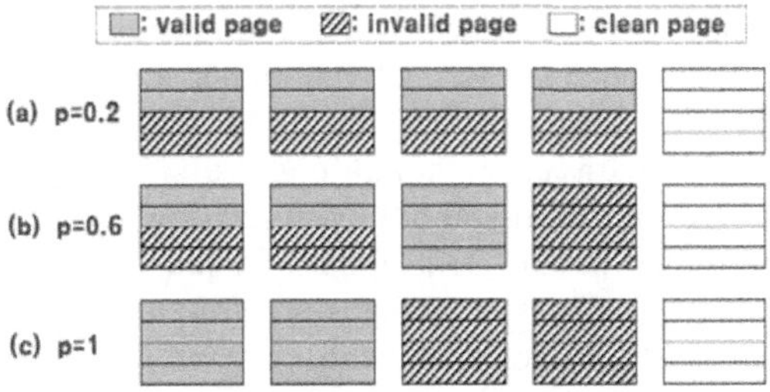

Fig. 2. Situation where utilization (u=0.4) and invalidity (i=0.4) remains unchanged, while uniformity (p) changes (a) p = 0.2 (b) p = 0.6 (c) p = 1

Utilization determines, on average, the number of valid pages that need to be copied for copy-erase cleaning. Invalidity determines the number of blocks that are candidates for cleaning. Finally, uniformity refers to the fraction of blocks that are uniform blocks. A uniform block is a block with zero or more clean pages and the remainder of the pages in the block are uniformly valid or uniformly invalid pages. Another definition of uniformity would be "1 – the fraction of blocks that have both valid and invalid pages." Of all the uniform blocks, only those blocks containing invalid pages are candidates for erase-only cleaning.

From these observations, we can formulate the cost of block cleaning as follows:

Cost of Block Cleaning
= Cost of copy-erase cleaning + Cost of erase-only cleaning
= (# of non-uniform blocks * e_t)+(# of valid pages in non-uniform blocks * (r_t + w_t)) +
(# of uniform blocks with invalid pages * e_t)
where
r_t : read operation execution time
w_t: write operation execution time
e_t : erase operation execution time

# of non-uniform blocks = (1 - p) * B
# of valid pages in non-uniform blocks
= # of non-uniform blocks * # of valid pages in a block
= (1 - p) * B * (P/B) * (u /(u + i))
# of uniform blocks with invalid pages
= (# of invalid pages - # of invalid pages in non-uniform blocks) / (# of pages in a block)
= ((i * P) – ((1 - p) * B * (P/B) * (i /(u + i)))) / (P/B)
where
u: utilization ($0 \le u \le 1$)
i : invalidity ($0 \le i \le 1 - u$)
p: uniformity ($0 \le p \le 1$)
P: # of pages in Flash memory (P=capacity/size of page)
B: # of blocks in Flash memory (P/B: # of pages in a block)

3.2 Implication of the Parameters on Block Cleaning Costs

Figure 3 shows the analytic results of the cost of block cleaning based on the derived model. In the figure, the x-axis is utilization, the y-axis is uniformity, and the z-axis is the cost of block cleaning. For this graph, we set invalidity as 0.1 and use the raw data of a small block 64MB NAND Flash memory [10]. The execution times for the read, write, and erase operation is 15us, 200us, and 2000us, respectively.

The main observation from Figure 3 is that the cost of cleaning increases dramatically when utilization is high and uniformity is low. We also conduct analysis with different values of invalidity and with the raw data of a large block 1GB NAND Flash memory[10], which shows similar trends observed in Figure 3.

We now discuss the implication of each parameter. Utilization is determined by the amount of useful data that the user stores. From the file system's point of view, this is almost an uncontrollable parameter, though compression techniques with a hardware accelerator [11] may be used to maintain low utilization.

Invalidity is determined by the data update frequency and cleaning frequency. If updates (including deletions of stored data) are frequent, invalidity will rise. However, since invalidity will be decreased with each block cleaning, frequent cleaning will keep invalidity low. Update frequency is controllable by delaying the updates using the buffer cache. However, mobile appliances such as cellular phones, MP3 players, and digital cameras that use Flash memory as its storage device are prone to sudden power failures. Hence, delayed writes can be applied only if some form of

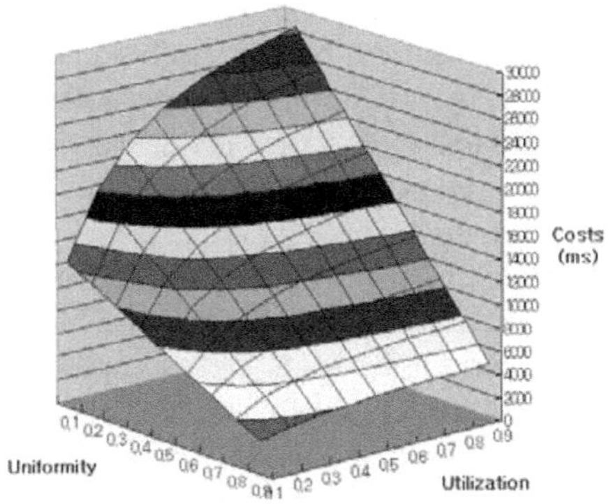

Fig. 3. Block cleaning costs

power failure recovery mechanism is present. Cleaning frequency is also controllable, but we need to consider carefully how to balance the benefit caused by decreasing invalidity and the cost caused by frequent cleaning.

Finally, uniformity is a parameter that may be controlled by the file system as the file system is in charge of allocating particular pages upon a write request. The redistribution policy that determines where the valid data in reclaimed blocks should be written out to also influences this parameter. By judiciously allocating and reorganizing pages, we may be able to maintain high uniformity.

4 Page Allocation Scheme That Strives for Uniformity

In the previous section, we found that among the three parameters, uniformity is a parameter that strongly influences the cost of block cleaning. In this section, we present a new page allocation scheme that strives to maintain high uniformity so that the cost of block cleaning may be kept low.

4.1 Modification-Aware Allocation Scheme

When pages are requested in file systems, in general, pages are allocated sequentially [4, 8]. Flash file systems tend to follow this approach and simply allocate the next available clean page when a page is requested, not taking into account any of the characteristics of the storage media.

We propose an allocation scheme that takes into account the file modification characteristics such that uniformity may be maximized. The allocation scheme is **mod**ification-**a**ware (MODA) as it distinguishes data that are hot-modified, that is, modified frequently and data that are cold-modified, that is, modified infrequently. Allocation of pages for the distinct type of data is done from distinct blocks.

The motivation behind this scheme is that by classifying hot-modified pages and allocating them to the same block, we will eventually turn the block into a uniform block filled with invalid pages. Likewise, by classifying cold-modified pages and allocating them together, we will turn this block into a uniform block filled with valid pages. Pages that are neither hot-modified nor cold-modified are sequestered so that they may not corrupt the uniformity of blocks that hold hot and cold modified pages.

Specifically, two levels of modification-aware classifications are used in MODA to classify hot/cold-modified data. At the first level, we make use of static properties, and dynamic properties are used at the second level. This classification is based on the skewness in page modification distribution [14, 15].

As static property, we distinguish system data and user data as the modification characteristics of the two are quite different. The superblock and inodes are examples of system data, while data written by users are examples of user data. We know that inodes are modified more intensively than user data, since any change to the user data in a file causes changes to its associated inode.

User data is further classified at the second level, where its dynamic property is used. In particular, we make use of the modification count. Keeping the modification count for each page, however, may incur considerable overhead. Therefore, we choose to monitor at a much larger granularity and keep a modification count for each file, which is updated when the modification time is updated.

For classification with the modification count, we adopt the MQ (Multi Queue) algorithm [12]. Specifically, it uses multiple LRU queues numbered Q_0, Q_1,..., Q_{m-1}. Each file stays in a queue for a given *lifetime*. When a file is first written (created), it is inserted into Q_0. If a file is modified within its *lifetime*, it is promoted from Q_i to Q_{i+1}.On the other hand, if a file is not modified within its *lifetime*, it is demoted from Q_i to Q_{i-1}. Then, we classify a file promoted from Q_{m-1} as hot-modified data, while a file demoted from Q_0 as cold-modified data. Files within queues are defined as unclassified data. In our experiments, we set m as 2 and *lifetime* as 100 times (time is virtual that ticks at each modification request). In other words, a file modified more than 2 is classified as hot, while a file that has not been modified within the recent 100 modification requests is classified as cold. We find that MODA with different values of $m = 3$ and/or *lifetime* = 500 show similar behavior.

Figure 4 shows the structure of the MODA scheme. There are 4 managers, each named the hot block, cold block, unclassified block and clean block manager. The first three managers govern hot-classified files, cold- classified files, and unclassified

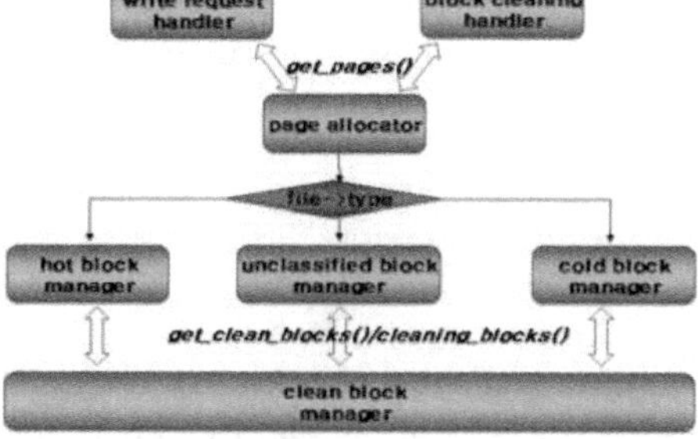

Fig. 4. Managing mechanism for MODA

files, respectively. When blocks are reclaimed, they are given to the clean block manager, while clean blocks are requested by the other three managers dynamically to serve write requests.

5 Implementation and Performance Evaluation

5.1 Platform and Implementation

We have implemented the MODA scheme on an embedded system. Hardware components of the system include a 400MHz XScale PXA CPU, 64MB SDRAM, 64MB NAND Flash memory, 0.5MB NOR Flash memory, and embedded controllers [16]. The same NAND Flash memory that was used to analyze the cost of block cleaning in Figure 3 is used here.

The Linux kernel 2.4.19 was ported on the hardware platform and YAFFS is used to manage the NAND Flash memory [4]. We modify the page allocation scheme in YAFFS and compare the performance with the native YAFFS. We will omit a detailed discussion regarding YAFFS, but only describe the relevant parts below. Interested readers are directed to [4] for details of YAFFS.

The default page allocation scheme in YAFFS is the sequential allocation scheme. We implemented the MODA scheme in YAFFS and will refer to this version of YAFFS, the MODA-YAFFS or simply MODA. In MODA-YAFFS, we modified functions such as *yaffs_WriteChunkDataToObject()*, *yaffs_UpdateObjectHeader()*, *yaffs_FlushFile()* in yaffs_guts.c and *init_yaffs_fs()*, *exit_yaffs_fs()* in yaffs_fs.c.

The block cleaning scheme in YAFFS is invoked at each write request. There are two modes of cleaning: normal and aggressive. In normal mode, YAFFS chooses the block that has the largest number of invalid pages among the predefined number of blocks (default setting is 200). If the chosen block has less than 3 valid pages, it reclaims the block. Otherwise, it gives up on the reclaiming. If the number of clean blocks is lower than a predefined number (default setting is 6), the mode is converted to aggressive. In aggressive mode, YAFFS chooses a block that has invalid pages and reclaims the block without checking the number of valid pages in it. The block cleaning scheme in MODA-YAFFS is exactly the same. We do add a new interface for block cleaning that may be invoked at the user level for ease of measurement.

5.2 The Workload

To gather sufficient workloads for evaluating our scheme, we survey Flash memory related papers as many as possible and choose the following 7 benchmarks for our implementation experiments, namely, Camera, Movie, Phone, Recorder, Fax, Postmark and Andrew benchmark [9].

These benchmarks can be grouped into three categories: sequential read/write intensive workloads, update intensive workloads, and multiple files intensive workloads. The first group includes Camera and Movie benchmark that access large files sequentially. Phone and Recorder benchmark are typical examples of the update intensive workloads that manipulate a small number of files and update them intensively. The Fax, Postmark and Andrew benchmark are embraced as the final category that accesses multiple files with different access probabilities.

5.3 Performance Evaluation

5.3.1 Performance Results

Table 1 shows performance results both measured by executing benchmarks and estimated by the model. Before each execution the utilization of Flash memory is set to 0, that is, the Flash memory is reset completely. Then, we execute each benchmark on YAFFS and MODA-YAFFS and measure its execution time reported in the 'Benchmark Running Time' column. Note that the only difference between YAFFS and MODA-YAFFS is the page allocation scheme. Also, after executing the benchmark, we measure the performance parameters, namely utilization, invalidity, and uniformity of Flash memory denoted as 'U', 'I', 'P' in the Table 1.

Using the measured performance parameters and the model proposed in Section 3.1, we can estimate the number of erase and copy operations required to reclaim all the invalid pages. Also, the model gives us the expected cleaning time. These estimated results are reported in the 'Estimated Results' column. Finally, we actually measure the number of erase and copy operations and cleaning times to reclaim all invalid pages, which are reported in the 'Measured Results' column. The measured results reported are averages of three executions for each case unless otherwise stated.

5.3.2 Model Validation

Table 1 shows that the number of erase and copy operations estimated by the model are similar to those measured in the real implementation, though the model tends to overestimate the copy operations when invalidity is low. These similarities imply that the model is fairly effective in predicting how many operations are required under a given status of Flash memory.

However, there are noticable differences between the measured and estimated block cleaning times. Through sensitive analysis, we find two main reasons behind these differences. The first reason is that the model requires the read, write, and erase

Table 1. Performance comparison of YAFFS and MODA-YAFFS for the benchmarks when utilization at start of execution is 0 (The unit of time measurement is in seconds)

Benchmark	Scheme	Bench mark Running Time	Performance Parameters			Estimated Results			Measured Results		
			U	I	P	# of Erase	# of Copy	Cleaing Time	# of Erase	# of Copy	Cleaning Time
Camera	YAFFS	37	0.3	0.0006	0.98	62	1916	2.46	60	1504	9.97
	MODA	37	0.3	0.0006	0.99	7	159	0.20	5	62	7.58
Movie	YAFFS	564	0.99	0.0001	0.99	10	319	0.41	10	17	24.64
	MODA	564	0.99	0.0001	0.99	1	31	0.04	1	3	24.54
Phone	YAFFS	88	0.05	0.32	0.62	1398	6047	9.87	1398	6047	13.40
	MODA	88	0.05	0.22	0.72	1010	6052	9.20	1011	6063	12.08
Recorder	YAFFS	31	0.005	0.16	0.83	626	692	1.94	626	699	2.17
	MODA	31	0.005	0.08	0.90	233	692	1.44	344	690	1.91
Fax machine	YAFFS	97	0.86	0.0087	0.73	1023	31710	40.78	1001	30996	67.50
	MODA	97	0.86	0.0087	0.97	107	2407	3.14	76	1383	23.47
Postmark	YAFFS	16	0.08	0.0107	0.90	357	10158	13.11	357	10147	18.39
	MODA	16	0.08	0.0107	0.93	260	7057	9.13	248	6652	12.84
Andrew	YAFFS	33	0.09	0.0008	0.90	348	10174	13.12	345	10060	18.51
	MODA	32	0.09	0.0008	0.98	87	1828	2.40	62	1004	3.86

times to estimate the block cleaning time. The simplest way to determine these values is by using the data sheet provided by the Flash memory chip vendor. However, through experiments we observe that the values reported in the datasheet and the actual time seen at various levels of the system differ considerably. The second reason is that block cleaning causes not only copy and erase overheads, but also software manipulating overheads. Specifically, YAFFS does not manage block and page status information in main memory to minimize RAM footprint. Hence, it needs to read Flash memory to detect blocks and pages to be cleaned. Due to this overhead, there are gaps between the measured and estimated cleaning times.

5.3.3 Effects of Uniformity

By comparing the results of YAFFS and those of MODA, we make the following observations.

- The benchmark execution time is the same for YAFFS and MODA. This implies that there is minimal overhead for the additional computation that may be incurred for data classification.
- The MODA scheme maintains high uniformity, which reduces the block cleaning time up to 43 seconds (for Fax machine benchmark) with an average of 10.2 seconds for the benchmarks considered.
- The performance gains of MODA for Movie and Camera benchmarks are trivial. Our model reveals that the original sequential page allocation scheme used in YAFFS also keeps high uniformity, makes making it difficult to obtain considerable gains.
- The gains of MODA for the Phone and Recorder benchmarks are also trivial, even though there is still room for enhancing uniformity. Careful analysis shows that MODA classifies hot/cold data on the file-level granularity, but these benchmarks access a small number of files; six files for Phone and two files for Recorder. These experiments disclose the limitation of the MODA scheme and suggest that page-level classification may be used effectively for the benchmarks.

We also perform experiments with two or more benchmarks running simultaneously by combining benchmarks, such as 'Camera + Phone' simulating recent cellular phones with digital camera capabilities and 'Movie + Recorder + Postmark' simulating a PMP player that uses an embedded database to maintain movie titles, actor library and digital rights. Experiments show that the trends of multiple benchmark executions are similar to those of the Postmark benchmark as reported in Table 1. For example, for 'Movie + Recorder + Postmark', the block cleaning time of YAFFS and MODA are 34.82 and 22.58 seconds, while uniformity are 0.73 and 0.84, respectively. We also find that interferences among benchmarks drive uniformity low, even for large sequential multimedia files.

5.3.4 Effects of Utilization

In real life, utilization of Flash memory will rarely be 0. Hence, we conduct similar measurements as was done for Table 1, but varying the initial utilization value. Figure 5 shows the results of executing Postmark under the various initial utilization values. Utilization was artificially increased by executing the Andrew benchmark before each

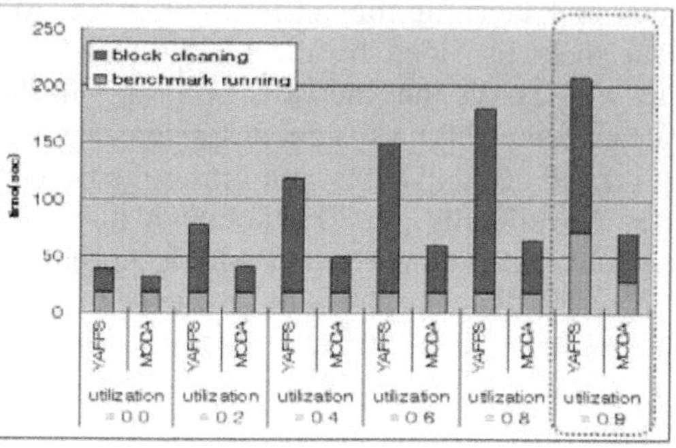

Fig. 5. Results reported under various initial utilization values

of the measurements. Exact same experiments were conducted with utilization adjusted by pre-executing the Postmark benchmark, but the result trend is similar, hence we only report one set of these results.

For the moment, ignore the results reported when utilization is 0.9, which shows somewhat different behavior. We come back to discuss these results shortly. The results in Figure 5 show that block cleaning time increases as utilization increases. Our model predicts, as shown in Figure 3, that when utilization is high, improved uniformity results in greater reduction of cleaning time. Figure 5 substantiates the expectation by showing that the difference in block cleaning time between YAFFS and MODA-YAFFS increases as utilization increases.

Let us now discuss results reported when the initial utilization is 0.9. Observe that the results are different from the results with lower utilization values, in that the benchmark running time is much higher, more so for YAFFS. This is because YAFFS is confronted with a lack of clean blocks during execution, and hence, turns the block cleaning mode to aggressive. As a result, on-demand block cleaning occurs frequently increasing the benchmark running time to 72 seconds, four times the running time compared to when utilization is lower. Note that in MODA-YAFFS, the running time does increase, but not as significantly. This is because the MODA allocation scheme allows for more blocks to be kept uniform, and hence aggressive on-demand block cleaning is invoked less.

6 Conclusion

Two contributions are made in this paper. First, we identify the cost of block cleaning as the key performance bottleneck for Flash memory analogous to the seek time in disk storage. We derive three performance parameters from features of Flash memory and present a formula for block cleaning cost based on these parameters. We show that, of these parameters, uniformity is the key controllable parameter that has a strong influence on the cost. This leads us to our second contribution, which is a new **mod**ification-**a**ware (MODA) page allocation scheme that strives to maintain high uniformity. Using the MODA scheme, we validate our model and evaluate the performance characteristics in light of uniformity, utilization and periodic cleaning.

References

[1] M. McKusick, W. Joy, S. Leffler, and R. Fabry, "A Fast File System for UNIX", ACM Transactions on Computer Systems, 2(3), pp. 181-197, Aug., 1984.

[2] M. Rosenblum and J. K. Ousterhout, "The design and implementation of a log-structured file system", ACM Transactions on Computer Systems, vol. 10, no. 1, pp. 26-52, 1992.

[3] H. Yu, D. Agrawal, and A. E. Abbadi, "Towards optimal I/O scheduling for MEMS-based storage," Proceedings of the 20th IEEE/11th NASA Goddard Conference on Mass Storage Systems and Technologies (MSS'03), 2003.

[4] Aleph One, "YAFFS: Yet another Flash file system", www.aleph1.co.uk/yaffs/.

[5] J. Kim, J. M. Kim, S. H. Noh, S. L. Min, Y. Cho, "A space-efficient Flash translation layer for CompactFlash systems", IEEE Transactions on Consumer Electronics, vol. 48, no. 2, pp. 366-375, 2002.

[6] E. Gal and S. Toledo, "Algorithms and Data Structures for Flash Memories", ACM Computing Surveys, vol. 37, no. 2, pp 138-163, 2005.

[7] D. Woodhouse, "JFFS: The journaling Flash file system", Ottawa Linux Symposium, 2001, http://source.redhat.com/jffs2/jffs2.pdf.

[8] A. Kawaguchi, S. Nishioka and H. Motoda, "A Flash-memory based file system", Proceedings of the 1995 USENIX Annual Technical Conference, pp. 155-164, 1995.

[9] E. Gal and S. Toledo, "A transactions Flash file system for microcontrollers", Proceedings of the 2005 USENIX Annual Technical Conference, pp. 89-104, 2005.

[10] Samsung Electronics, "NAND Flash Data Sheet", www.samsung. com/Products/Semiconductor/NANDFlash.

[11] K. Yim, H. Bahn, and K. Koh "A Flash Compression Layer for SmartMedia Card Systems", IEEE Transactions on Consumer Electronics, Vol. 50, No. 1, pp. 192-197, Feb. 2004.

[12] Y. Zhou, P. M. Chen, and K. Li, "The Multi-Queue Replacement Algorithm for Second-Level Buffer Caches, Proceeding of the 2001 USENIX Annual Technical Conference, June, 2001.

[13] J. Wang and Y. Hu, "WOLF - a novel reordering write buffer to boost the performance of log-structured file system", Proceedings of the USENIX Conference on File and Storage Technologies (FAST), pp. 46-60, 2002.

[14] W. Wang, Y. Zhao, and R. Bunt, "HyLog: A High Performance Approach to Managing Disk Layout", Proceedings of the USENIX Conference on File and Storage Technologies (FAST), pp. 145-158, 2004.

[15] M-L. Chiang, P. C. H. Lee, and R-C. Chang, "Using data clustering to improve cleaning performance for Flash memory", Software: Practice and Experience, vol. 29, no. 3, pp. 267-290, 1999.

[16] EZ-X5, www.falinux.com/zproducts.

A New Type of Embedded File System Based on SPM

Tianzhou Chen, Feng Sha, Wei Hu, and Qingsong Shi

College of Computer Science, Zhejiang University, Hangzhou, Zhejiang, China, 310027
{tzchen,zhaoyi,ehu,zjsqs}@zju.edu.cn

Abstract. Commonly, embedded file systems reside in main memory to manage the external memory such as flash memory in embedded systems. With the progress of hardware of embedded systems, the gap of speed between main memory and CPU is becoming larger and larger. The traditional embedded file systems can not be able to support real-time response enough for their main memory management policy. A new type of embedded file system is presented to provide more real-time performance. This new embedded file system, SPM file system, is based on the internal SRAM on chip and is able to reduce response time.

Keywords: Embedded System, File System, Scratched-Pad Memory.

1 Introduction

Scratch-pad Memory (SPM) has played an important role in embedded systems by collaborating with cache. SPM has many advantages for embedded systems such as lower energy consumption. Though the size of SPM is much smaller compared with the DRAM, it has been used in many high-end embedded microprocessors. The Intel PXA 27x family is the processor covered this new feature. The performance of the whole embedded systems can be improved by using SPM when developing systems. SPM has more potential than DRAM. SPM is at least 10 times faster than the normal DRAM. And the speed of SPM will be increased faster than DRAM: the speed of SPM is increasing by 60% a year versus only 7% a year for DRAM [1].

Embedded systems have to provide real-time, fast speed and power-aware features to the users. But the memory references in the embedded system are always bottleneck of the whole systems. Though Cache has been popular in embedded systems, the only use of cache is not sufficient. Programmers can not utilize Cache unrestricted to improve the performance because of the security of the systems. The utilization of SPM can provide performance improvement to the embedded systems. A detailed recent study compares the tradeoffs of a cache as compared to a SPM. Their results show that a SPM has 34% smaller area and 40% lower power consumption than a cache memory of the same capacity [2].

In tradition, the embedded file systems, which are mostly based on flash memory, do not care the SPM on chip. Commonly the main target of embedded file systems is to manage a large capacity flash memory. eNVy [2] proposed a large non-volatile main memory storage system built primarily with Flash memory. eNVy uses a copy-on-write scheme, page remapping, a small amount of battery backed SRAM, and high

Y.-H. Lee et al. (Eds.): ICESS 2007, LNCS 4523, pp. 174–180, 2007.

bandwidth parallel data transfers for Flash memory. A hybrid cleaning algorithm (combining FIFO and greedy algorithms) for large Flash arrays is used to reclaim space. The algorithm is designed to evenly wear the array, thereby extending its life time. And more other excellent works have been done on Flash memory [4-7]. These are all static table-driven schemes and operate on Flash arrays and it is not efficient to manage large-scale flash memory.

As we know from above, there are no embedded file systems concerning the use of SPM to improve the performance of response time. SOC [9] is also the direction of embedded systems in the future. Thus the software for embedded systems should be more efficient. In this paper, we present a new type of embedded file system named SPMFS (SPM File System) to take advantage of the SPM on chip.

The rest of the paper is organized as follows. Section 2 describes the architecture of SPMFS. Section 3 covers the experimental results. Section 4 concludes.

2 Architecture of SPM File System

Commonly the embedded file systems are stored in the flash or some other external storage according to the storage hierarchy. These embedded file systems have many functions to manage the flash, provide access response and so on. Thus these file systems do not need to take their size into accounts. The SPMFS is designed for SOC chip to improve the performance of the file system.

The traditional embedded file systems integrate many functions together. The SPMFS is not same to these file systems. It has to be fit for the size of the SPM on chip. The SPM can not hold so many data and instructions simultaneously for its small size. Thus we design a MFSC (Micro File System Component) for our new file system architecture.

MFSC is main component of the SPMFS. It will run in SPM from the start of the system. There are many other functions, which are reduced from MFSC and should be provided by file system. They will reside in main memory. In our design, SPMFS consists of three parts: MFSC, BFSM (Basic File System Management) and ComM (Communication Management). The architecture is shown in Figure 1.

MFSC: this part is stored in internal Flash memory on chip. To get short response time, MFSC will be not altered to avoiding writing to flash memory. If and only if the MFSC has been a new version, the MFSC in internal Flash memory will be updated. When the system starts, the MFSC will execute with the whole file system. When the MFSC executes, it will maintain an open file table for files used continually and the data area for these files. The data area can be considered as a buffer of the data in main memory.

SPMFS must ensure that this MFSC can run in SPM. Because of the size limitation of SPM, the MFSC has to be designed as small as possible. Thus some parts in traditional embedded file system must be taken from the MFSC and the remainders have to be cut down or modified in order to make all necessary functionalities of SPMFS can be able to be contained in SPM. The most design principle is minimum and optimal. According to the foregoing design principle, we only provide necessary functions in MFSC to manage SPM.

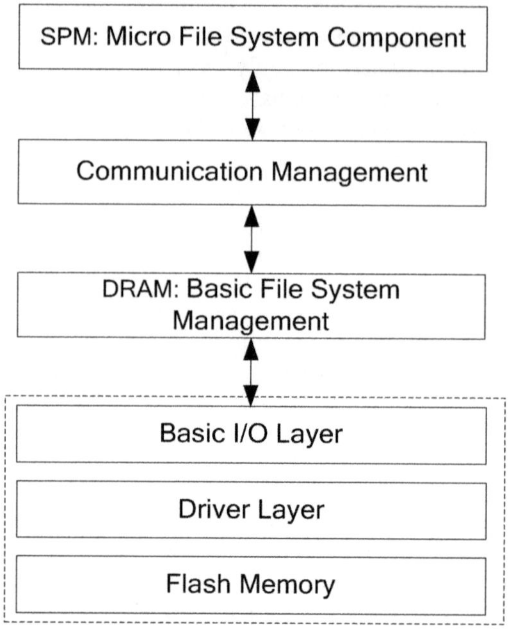

Fig. 1. Architecture of SPMFS

ComM: this part has a buffer in which data is provided by BFSM. The requested data will be stored in this buffer and when MFSC needs, it will fetch data block to SPM. And ComM should provide security such as data protection, data synchronization, concurrent control, mutual exclusion and so on to this buffer. The detail of ComM is shown in Figure 2.

BFSM: in this part, the common functions of embedded file system are provided such as data structure management, allocation management, garbage collection and so on. The BFSM will always reside in main memory. The inode is used to represent a number of data blocks, which could be attached to a file or a directory. Every directory has its own properties such as owner, time information as well as linkage information of its items. The directory item is either directory or file. Because of the block erase feature of NAND flash memory, the blocks are divided into two types: Data Blocks and Pointer Blocks. Data Blocks are used to store the date of files and Pointer Blocks are used to store the pointers which index to the correlative Data Blocks.

Now there are only small SPM provided by the processors. Thus SPM Management must provide finely management for MFSC. Different from common memory management, we divide SPM into different Sections which are allocated to instructions and data. Two Sections are divided: Kernel Section, Data Section as shown in Figure 3. Kernel Section is allocated to the MFSC. MFSC runs in this part of SPM to ensure the security of MFSC data and instructions. Data Section is allocated to the data fetched from buffer of ComM.

Further, different Memory Banks of SRAM are divided into pages to manage as shown in Figure 5.

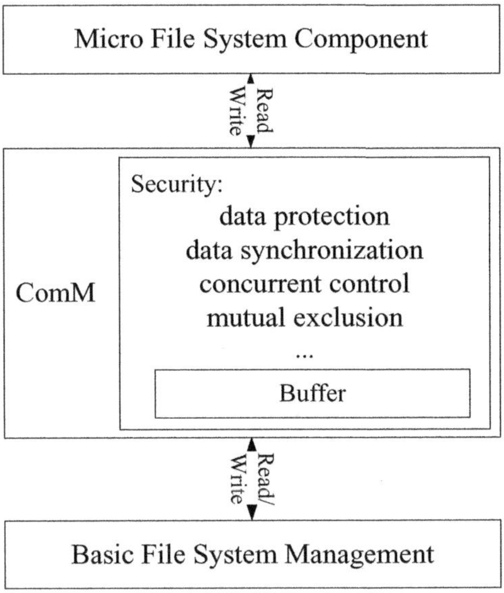

Fig. 2. ComM

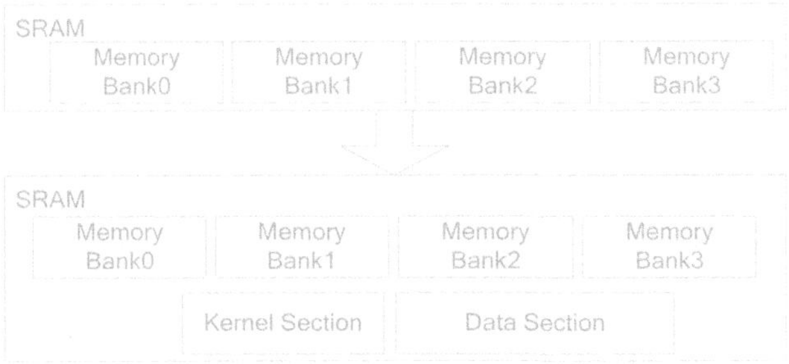

Fig. 3. Section division

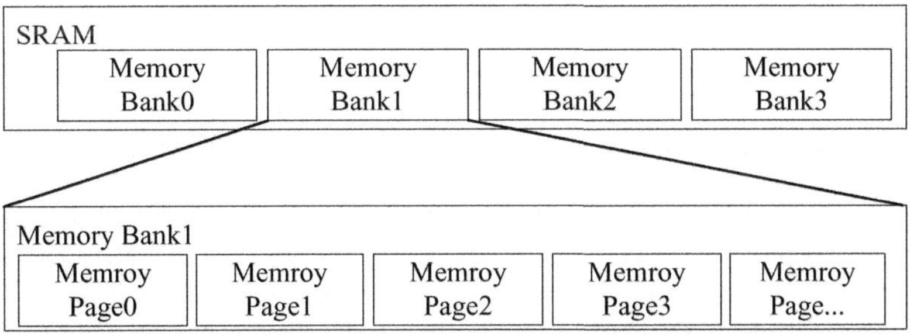

Fig. 4. Divide memory into pages

3 Experimental Results

Now more and more microprocessors support SPM on chip. As an introduction, we will describe the Intel 27x family, which is our experimental hardware. Intel 27x processor is owned by Intel Company and it is an integrated system-on-a-chip microprocessor designed for mobile devices.

High-performance and low-power is the main target for this processor. The architecture is in accordance with ARM 10 but it does not support all of ARM Instructions (V5TE) in which floating point instructions are excluded. The ARM programmer's model is complied by the Intel PXA27x processors. In additional, Intel provides extra supports to PXA27x family which is added by Intel techniques: Intel® Wireless MMX™ integer instructions in applications such as those that accelerate audio and video processing.

PXA27x provides extra 256K cache which is considered as internal memory. This cache is internal memory-mapped SRAM which consists of four banks in which then capacity is 64K. The SRAM array module consists of four banks of 8-K x 64-bit memory arrays. Each memory bank has a dedicated single-entry queue and 8 K x 64 bits for data storage. If a memory bank is in standby mode, the access request is stored in the queue while the memory bank is placed in run mode. The access is completed when the memory bank has entered run mode. If a memory bank is in run mode and the queue does not contain any pending access requests, the queue is bypassed and the memory is accessed normally.

This piece of SRAM is placed on chip and thus PXA27x can provide extra power management which is bank-by-bank management for this cache and thus can reduce the power consumption. In addition, this cache can support Byte Write Operation and are not associated with any I/O signals.

Six parts are consisted of this cache: the four SRAM banks, queues, the system-bus interface, control and status registers, power management block, and memory-bank multiplexing and control.

We used the Linux Trace Toolkit (LTT) and Kernel Function Trace (KFT) to obtain the experimental results. LTT is used to examine the flow of execution (between processes, kernel threads, and interrupts) in a Linux system. This is useful for analyzing where delays occur in the system, and to see how processes interact, especially with regard to scheduling, interrupts, synchronization primitives, etc. The KFT system provides for capturing these callouts and generating a trace of events, with timing details. KFT is excellent at providing a good timing overview of kernel procedures, allowing you to see where time is spent in functions and sub-routines in the kernel. We evaluate the SPMFS file system on an Intel-XScale PXA272 platform running the latest patch version of Linux Kernel2.6, with 64M SDRAM and 64M NAND flash and there are 256K SPM on chip. We run a data access program on both SPMFS and YAFFS2 because they are both file system based on NAND flash. Then we compare our parameters with those of YAFFS2. As a result from Figure 5, SPMFS is more effective than YAFFS2. The results are as follows in Figure 6.

From the performance of file system is improved to some extent especially when the file is small than 256KB. We think this result is correlative to the capacity of SPM on chip of XScale PXA272. If more SPM can be used, such as the Monahans series chipset, on which there will be 768KB SPM at most, the performance should be better than now.

The benchmark is presented in Figure 6 for three configurations: all-DRAM, file data in cache and in SPM with optimization. The optimization means that we modify the kernel of the operating system to adapt to the SPMFS. We gain 26% (cache) and 33% (SPM) speedup. But if we put the data in cache, it will influence the performance of the whole system. It is better to place the file data into SPM.

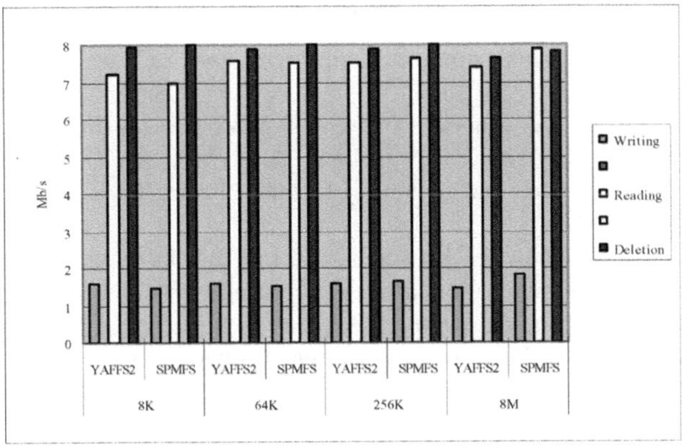

Fig. 5. Performance of SPMFS

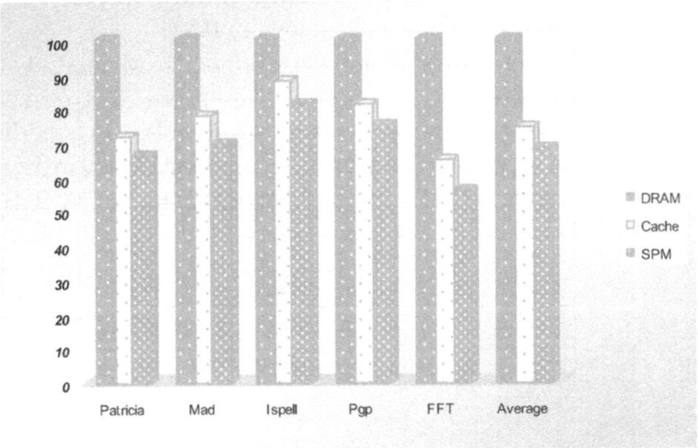

Fig. 6. Comparison of DRAM, Cache and SPM

4 Conclusions and Future Work

In this paper, a new type of embedded file system is presented. This embedded file system, named SPMFS (Scratch-Pad Memory File System), is based on the SPM on chip. It provides a new concept to design embedded file systems. Because the SPM support for embedded file system will be more popular with the advance of hardware of embedded system, it will be more useful for embedded file systems. And there will be also more work to do to satisfy the requirements of embedded systems.

References

[1] J. Hennessy and D. Patterson. Computer Architecture A Quantitative Approach. Morgan Kaufmann, Palo Alto, CA, second edition, 1996.

[2] R. Banakar, S. .Steinke, B.-S. Lee, M. Balakrishnan, and P. Marwedel. Scratchpad Memory: A Design Alternative for Cache On-chip memory in Embedded Systems. In Tenth International Symposium on Hardware/Software Codesign (CODES), Estes Park, Colorado, May 6-8 2002. ACM.

[3] Michael Wu, Willy Zwaenepoel. eNVy: A Non-Volatile, Main Memory Storage System. Proceedings of the sixth international conference on Architectural support for programming languages and operating systems. Pages: 86 – 97, San Jose, California, United States, 1994.

[4] F. Douglis, R. Caceres, F. Kaashoek, K. Li, B. Marsh, and J.A. Tauber, "Storage Alternatives for Mobile Computers", Proceedings of the USENIX Operating System Design and Implementation, 1994.

[5] L. P. Chang and T. W. Kuo,"A Real-time Garbage Collection Mechanism for Flash Memory Storage System in Embedded Systems," The 8th International Conference on Real-Time Computing Systems and Applications, 2002.

[6] L. P. Chang, and T. W. Kuo, "An Adaptive Striping Architecture for Flash Memory Storage Systems of Embedded Systems," The 8th IEEE Real-Time and Embedded Technology and Applications Symposium, 2002.

[7] A. Kawaguchi, S. Nishioka, and H. Motoda,"A flash-memory based File System," Proceedings of the USENIX Technical Conference, 1995.

[8] Intel, Intel® PXA27x Processor Family Developer's Manual, http://www.intel.com/design/pca/prodbref/253820.htm

[9] JoAnn M. Paul, Programmers' views of SoCs, Proceedings of the 1st IEEE/ACM/IFIP international conference on Hardware/software codesign and system synthesis, October 01-03, 2003, Newport Beach, CA, USA

An Efficient Buffer Management Scheme for Implementing a B-Tree on NAND Flash Memory*

Hyun-Seob Lee[1], Sangwon Park[2], Ha-Joo Song[3], and Dong-Ho Lee[4,**]

[1,4] Dept. of Computer Science and Engineering, Hanyang University, Korea
{hyunseob,dhlee72}@cse.hanyang.ac.kr
[2] ICE, Hankuk University of Foreign Studies, Korea
swpark@hufs.ac.kr
[3] Division of Computer, Pukyong National University, Korea
hajusong@pknu.ac.kr

Abstract. Recently, NAND flash memory has been used for a storage device in various mobile computing devices such as MP3 players, mobile phones and laptops because of its shock-resistant, low-power consumption, and none-volatile properties, However, due to the very distinct characteristics of flash memory, disk based systems and applications may result in severe performance degradation when directly adopting them on flash memory storage systems. Especially, when a B-tree is constructed, intensive overwrite operations may be caused by record inserting, deleting, and its reorganizing, This could result in severe performance degradation on NAND flash memory because of its distinct characteristics. In this paper, we propose an efficient buffer management scheme, called IBSF, which eliminates redundant index units in the index buffer and then delays the time that the index buffer is filled up. Consequently, IBSF significantly reduces the number of write operations to a flash memory when constructing a B-tree. We also show that IBSF yields a better performance on a flash memory by comparing it to the related technique called BFTL through various experiments.

Keywords: Flash Memory, BFTL, Index, B-Tree, Buffer Management Scheme.

1 Introduction

In recent years, with the dramatic growth of various mobile computing technologies, embedded systems such as PDAs, MP3 players, and mobile phones have required more efficient and portable storage devices. NAND flash memory is becoming one of the best storage medium for these embedded systems because of its shock-resistant, low-power consumption, and non-volatile properties.

A NAND flash memory chip usually consists of a fixed number of *blocks*, where each blocks typically has 32 *pages*. Each page in turn is composed of 512 bytes of the main area and 16 bytes of the spare area. The main area is usually used for storing

* This work was supported in part by MIC & IITA through IT Leading R&D Support Project.
** Corresponding author.

Y.-H. Lee et al. (Eds.): ICESS 2007, LNCS 4523, pp. 181–192, 2007.

data, while the spare area is often used to store management information and error correction code (ECC) to correct errors when reading and writing[6]. NAND flash memory also provides three basic operations such as *read*, *write* (*program*), and *erase*. The read operation fetches data from a target page, while the write operation writes data to a page. The erase operation resets all values of a target block to 1[6].

The main characteristic of NAND flash memory is that it does not support in-place updates. Once a page is written, it should be erased before the subsequent write operation is performed on the same pages. Moreover, the read/write operations are executed on a page basis, while the erase operation is performed on a block basis. This characteristic is sometimes called *erase-before-write* architecture. Therefore, an intermediate software layer called a *flash translation layer* (FTL) is usually employed to hide the limitation of erase-before-write [5]. FTL achieves this by remapping each write request to an empty location that has been erased in advance, and by maintaining a mapping table to record the mapping information from the logical pages number to the physical location. The other characteristic of NAND flash memory is an asymmetric read/write/erase speed. Unlike a magnetic disk, the write/erase operations require a relatively long latency compared to the read operation. Thus, in order to improve the overall performance, the number of write or erase operations should be minimized. The main role of FTL is to provide an efficient mapping from the logical page number to the physical location to improve the overall performance.

However, although FTL supports the reduction of write/erase operations by an efficient mapping algorithm from the logical page number to the physical location, it could not avoid performance degradation when implementing index structures that tend to generate so many *overwrite* operations at the same logical address.

In order to address problem, C. H. Wu and et. al. proposed BFTL[3] that is a software module for efficiently implementing a B-tree[2] on NAND flash memory. BFTL employs two main data structures such as *reservation buffer* and *node translation table* to handle intensive overwrite operations caused by record inserting, deleting, and B-tree reorganizing. The reservation buffer is only used to hold a fixed amount of records. And, in order to reduce the number of write operations, the records in the buffer are packed into a few pages when flushing them to flash memory. The node translation table is used to map a B-tree node to a collection of logical page numbers where the information of the B-tree index resides. Thus, if a B-tree node is accessed, the node is constructed through the help of the node translation table. However, it has several drawbacks as follows: First, since the data in one node could be scatted over flash memory, it needs so many read when accessing the B-tree. Second, BFTL uses additional overheads to manage the node translation table. Finally, BFTL may have redundant data in the reservation buffer. This may yield performance degradation when committing data from the buffer to flash memory.

In this paper, we propose a buffer management scheme, called IBSF, which efficiently eliminates redundant data in the buffer by new insertion and deletion policies. This leads to the effect of delaying the time that index buffer is filled up. Consequently, the write/erase operations can be significantly reduced in our method. Moreover, since IBSF stores each B-tree node in one page, it needs not the node translation table that is an additional overhead because it has to be maintained in RAM.

The rest of this paper is organized as follows. Section 2 introduces an overview of NAND flash memory and FTL. Section 3 briefly reviews BFTL for B-tree on flash memory and its disadvantages. Section 4 describes the key idea and the detailed buffer management policies of IBSF. Section 5 shows the experimental results. Finally, we conclude our work and discuss our future plan in Section 6.

2 Background

2.1 Overview of NAND Flash Memory and Flash Translation Layer

NAND flash memory usually consists of a number of blocks, where each block typically has 32 pages. Each page is composed of 512 bytes of the main area and 16 bytes of the spare area.

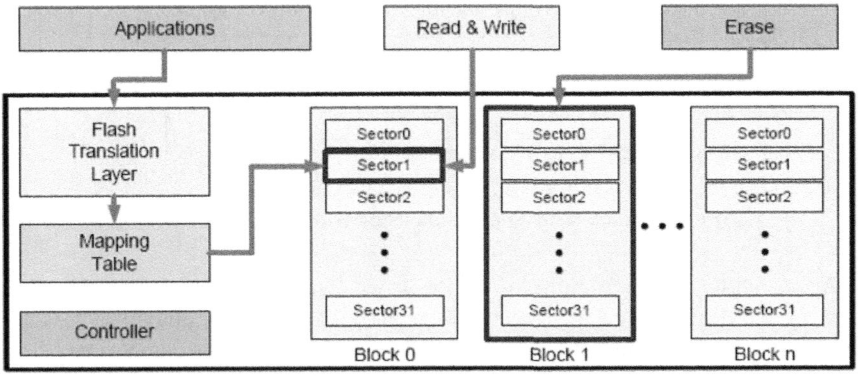

Fig. 1. Structure of NAND Flash Memory

Fig. 1 shows the typical structure of the storage system using FTL on NAND flash memory. As depicted in Fig. 1, the read/write operations are performed on a page basis, but the erase operation is performed on a block basis. Each cost of the read/write/erase operations is about 10μs, 100μs, and 2ms respectively.

FTL is used to directly implement disk based applications on NAND flash memory. It can help to directly implement disk based applications on NAND the flash memory by providing several functions such as logical to physical address mapping, power-off recovery, and wear-leveling. As shown in Fig. 1, NAND flash memory-based storage system usually consists of FTL algorithm, the mapping table, the controller, and the flash memory. The mapping table holds logical/physical address mapping information. The basic scheme for FTL is as follow. By using the logical to physical address mapping table, if the physical address location that being mapped to a logical address is previously written, the input data is written to an empty physical location to which no data have ever been previously written and then the mapping table is updated due to newly changed logical/physical address mapping [1].

2.2 Problem of Index Structure on Flash Memory

The capacity of NAND flash memory has been increased to deal the large data due to the improved technologies. The B-tree is an efficient data structure to speed up data-access in the large storage devices. When accessing the data, the B-tree helps to efficient search the data according to its the index structure and the rule. It is composed by a root node, internal node, and leaf node. The root node is the root of a B-tree. The leaf node is the node of a B-tree that has zero child nodes. The internal node means the node of a B-tree that has child nodes and is thus not a leaf node.

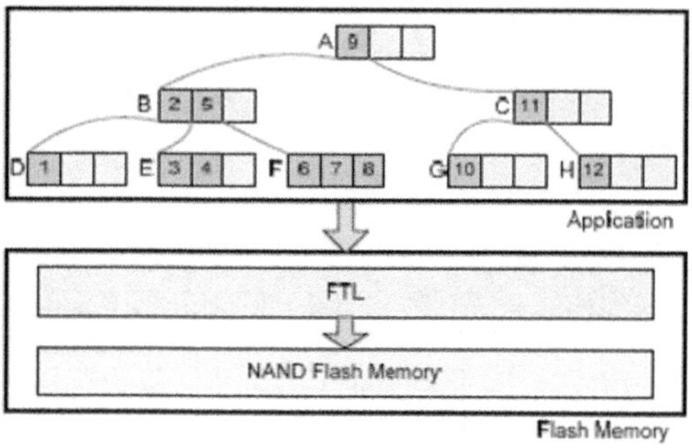

Fig. 2. Structure of Application using B-tree over Flash Memory

Fig. 2 shows the structure of application which adopting a B-tree over flash memory. As depicted in Fig. 2, each node can hold the fixed number of *data* and *link*. The data is called by an entry in B-tree and has a key value or data pointer. The links point left and right child node. Since the size of an entry is smaller than a page, each page can hold a number of entries. For example, if assume the size of a entry is 10 bytes and a node consists of 50 entries, a node is stored to a page in NAND flash memory because the page can hold 512 bytes.

Since the B-tree needs a number of split and redistribution operations as inserting and deleting the records, it tends to generate so many overwrite operations at the same logical address. Although FTL supports an efficient mapping algorithm from the logical page number to the physical location, frequent overwrite operations may degrade the performance of NAND flash memory. For example, as depicted in Fig. 2, if the data having 13 and 14 as the key values are inserted, it will yield overwrite operations to a page which holds node H. If split and redistribution operations are generated, it will yield much more overwrite operations on NAND flash memory.

3 Related Work

3.1 B-Tree Layer on Flash Memory (BFTL)

BFTL is a software module over the original flash translation layer (FTL). Fig. 3 illustrates the architecture of a system which adopts BFTL. BFTL is composed a *reservation buffer* and a *node translation table*. When the applications insert, delete,

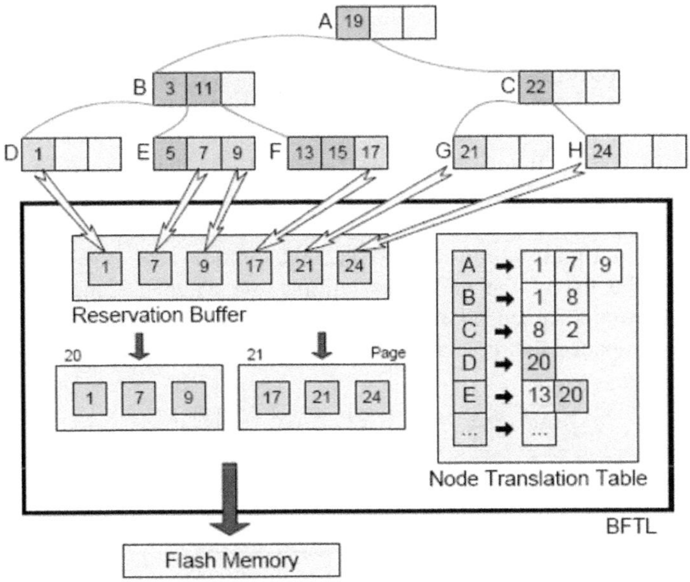

Fig. 3. The architecture of a system which adopts BFTL

or modify a B-tree node, the index unit which contains the information of modified records would be temporarily held by the reservation buffer.

Since the reservation buffer only holds an adequate amount of index units, index units in the buffer should be timely flushed to flash memory. The index unit is relatively smaller than the size of a page. Therefore, many index units are smartly packed into a few pages to reduce the number of pages physically written. As a result, the index units of a B-tree node may exist in different pages over flash memory, and the physical representation of a B-tree node would be different from the original one. Since the index units of a B-tree node might be scattered over flash memory due to the commit policy, a node translation table maintains page numbers which have index units of the corresponding B-tree node to efficiently collect index units. For example, as we see in Fig. 3, the index units are packed in page 20 and 21 when inserting the data which have 1, 7, 9, 17, 21, and 24 as the key value. Like this, since the index units can be stored each other pages for a node, the node translation table is needed. In order to form a correct logical view of a B-tree node, BFTL visit all pages where related index units reside and then construct an up-to-date logical view of the B-tree node. For example, in order to form the logical view of node E in Fig. 3, BFTL has to reference page 13 and 20.

As depicted in Fig. 3, If BFTL has not been adopted, up to six writes might be needed to handle the modification of the index structure when inserting 1, 7, 9, 17, 21, and 24. However, since BFTL packages the index units in page 20 and 21, two write operations are needed when a B-tree is built.

3.2 Disadvantages of BFTL

BFTL has several drawbacks as follows: First, since the data of one node may be scattered in different pages over flash memory, BFTL would visit all pages where the related index units reside to reorganize a B-tree node. It may generate so many read operations to access a B-tree node. For example, BFTL has to read 13 and 20 pages to re-build node E in Fig. 3

Second, the node translation table and its list have to be maintained in RAM and their sizes may rapidly grow. In BFTL, the author also proposed a method for compressing the list of the node translation table when its length grows beyond a threshold. However, since all related index units have to be written back to flash memory to compact a list, it needs additional write operations.

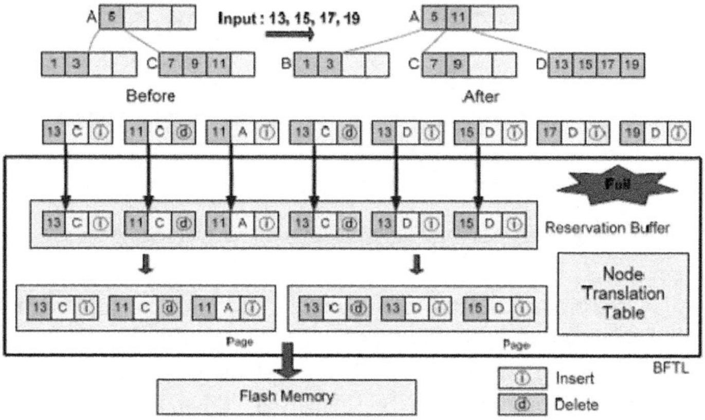

Fig. 4. An Example of BFTL's drawback

Finally, since BFTL stores index units in the buffer by sequential order, the buffer may hold the redundant data when a node in the B-tree is split. Fig. 4 shows the process of the split operation in BFTL. The index units are expressed by [key value, node identifier, operation]. Operation ⓘ and ⓓ mean the insert and delete type of a index unit, respectively. For example, [13, C, ⓘ] means that the data having 13 as the key value must be inserted in node C. As depicted in Fig. 4, we can see redundant index units which have 13 as the key value in the reservation buffer. If redundant data exist in the buffer, than only a latest data is valid. Therefore, these may result in additional write operations when committing index units.

4 The Design and Implementation of IBSF

4.1 Key Idea

As mentioned in section 3, BFTL has several drawbacks. In this section, we introduce a new buffer management scheme, called IBSF. The key ideas of IBSF are as follows: First idea is to store all index units associated with a B-tree node into a page. If do so,

IBSF does not need the node translation table which is an additional overhead. Second idea is to eliminate redundant index units in the index buffer. This leads to the effect of delaying the time that the buffer is full. Consequently, IBSF is able to significantly reduce the number of write operation to a flash memory when constructing a B-tree.

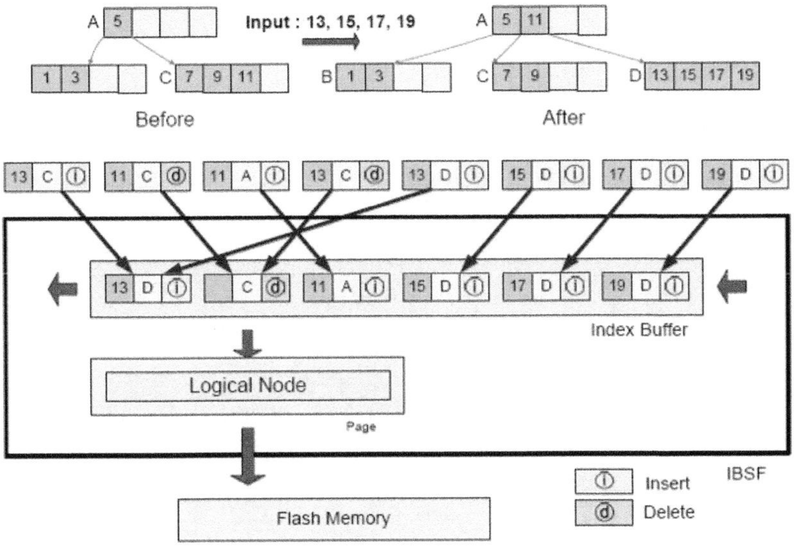

Fig. 5. Overall Architecture of IBSF

Fig. 5 shows the architecture of IBSF which consists of *index buffer*, *insertion policy*, *deletion policy* and *commit policy*. The index buffer keeps index units which reflect modified B-tree nodes when inserting, deleting, or modifying the records. According to the insertion and deletion policies, IBSF handles index units in the index buffer. If the index buffer is filled, it may generate the commit operation by the commit policy. Since IBSF stores the index units for one node of the B-tree in one page, it needs not the node translation table which is an additional overhead. This may improve the read performance of B-tree as compared to BFTL because IBSF visits one page to re-build one node. For example, BFTL has to visit page 1, 7, and 9 to re-build node A in Fig. 3. However, IBSF can re-build node A by one page accessing because the index units related to one node are stored in one page. Moreover, since IBSF eliminates redundant index units in the index buffer, it can delay the commit time. As described in previous section, Fig. 4 shows the process that 13, 15, 17, and 19 are inserted in a B-tree node. Since BFTL does not use any special buffer management scheme, it has to hold all index units without processing of the index unit in the index buffer when records are inserted in a B-tree node. For example, [13, C, ⓘ], [13, C, ⓓ], and [13, D, ⓘ] are redundant index units for a record which has 13 as the key value. If the same index units are existed in the index buffer at the same time, only the latest index unit is valid. Therefore, if we can eliminate the invalid index units in the buffer, we can also delay the time that the buffer is full. Consequently, we can reduce the number of write operations by delaying the commit time.

As depicted in Fig. 4, if the size of the reservation buffer of BFTL is 6, it is not enough to hold all index units when a B-tree node is split by inserting 13, 15, 17, and 19. Therefore, the commit operation is generated. However, IBSF can hold all index units without the commit operation because it eliminates redundant index units when inserting the index units to the index buffer. Therefore, IBSF is able to delay the commit time efficiently.

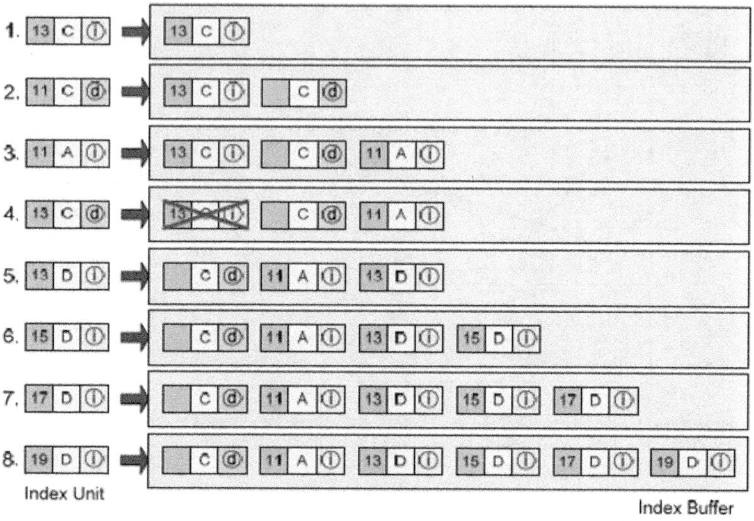

Fig. 6. An Example of the Index Buffer Management in IBSF

Fig. 6 describes an example of the index buffer management in IBSF when inserting index units in Fig. 5. The index units are inserted in the buffer to reflect the split operation in Fig. 5. Namely, [13, C, ⓘ], [11, C, ⓓ], and [11, A, ⓘ] are sequentially inserted in the index buffer without any special processing. However, when [13, C, ⓓ] is inserted, there is already redundant index unit that is [13, C, ⓘ] in the index buffer. If redundant index unit exists in the buffer, only a latest index unit is valid. Therefore, IBSF eliminates the old index unit and replaces it with the latest index unit. IBSF eliminates redundant index units as follows: When [13, C, ⓓ] is inserted in the buffer, it means that the data having 13 as the key value must be deleted in node C. At this time, the index buffer has [13, C, ⓘ] to insert the data in node C. This is redundant index unit for a record which has 13 as the key value. Therefore, IBSF eliminates [13, C, ⓘ]. And then, [13, C, ⓓ] updates [, C, ⓓ] because these are the index units for deleting a record at node C. The detailed policies for insertion and deletion will be explained in the following section.

4.2 The Insertion Policy

In IBSF, newly created index units are inserted into the index buffer to reflect insertion when inserting a record. This processing is done as follows: First, when a record is inserted into a B-tree, IBSF creates the new index unit to reflect it. Then, IBSF inspects the redundant index unit which has the same primary key in the index buffer. If the index unit which has the same key value is already existed in the index buffer, IBSF updates this with the new index unit. On the other hand, if redundant index unit does not exist in the index buffer, IBSF allocates a resource for the new index unit. Namely, IBSF dons not permit the duplicated index units in the buffer. For example, as depicted Fig. 7, if the index unit which has 2 as the key value is newly created to reflect insertion of a B-tree node, IBSF first finds the index unit which has the same primary key in the index buffer. The index buffer has three index units, and each index unit has 2, 9, and 3 as the key value, respectively. Since IBSF can find the index unit which has 2 as the key value at first, it updates the first index unit which has 2 as the key value with the new index unit.

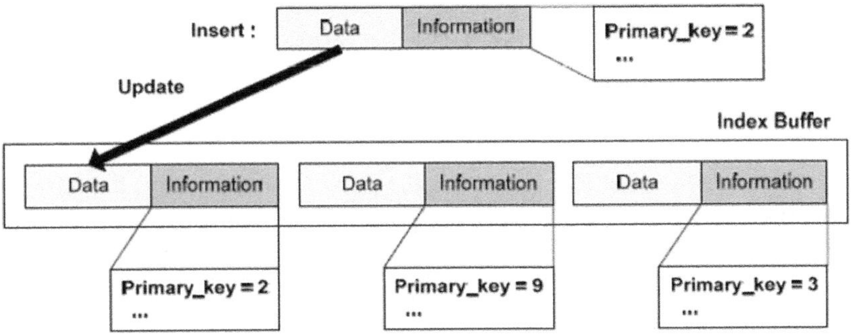

Fig. 7. Insertion Policy

Since IBSF can prevent the index buffer being wasted by eliminating redundant index units, it can delay the commit time. This may lead to the reduction of write operations on NAND flash memory.

4.3 The Deletion Policy

In IBSF, newly created index units are inserted into the index buffer to reflect deletion when a B-tree node is deleted. The deletion policy processing is similar to the insertion policy. However, it has characteristics unlike the insertion policy as follows: First, the index units having a delete-type need only the location of the entry to reflect the deletion of a record in the B-tree node. Since the locations of entries can be expressed as a few bits, the index unit of a delete-type maintains a bit flag set that marks the entries to be deleted. Second, if the index buffer keeps a redundant index unit which is a insert-type as inserting the new index unit of a delete-type, IBSF eliminates it and inserts a new index unit into the buffer. Therefore, IBSF eliminates it and inserts the new index unit into the buffer. Finally, if the index buffer has another index unit of the deletion type which has the same node identifier when it is inserted in the buffer, IBSF updates flag of the new index unit in the existing index unit. On the other hand, if redundant index unit does not exist in the index buffer, IBSF allocates a resource for the new index unit.

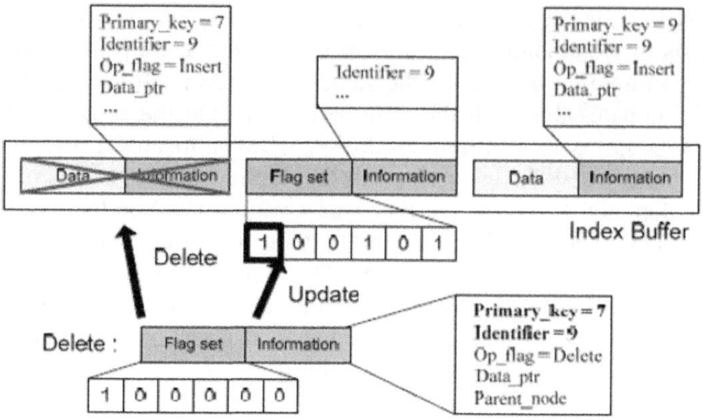

Fig. 8. Deletion Policy

Fig. 8 shows how to use the deletion policy over the index buffer. The newly created index unit has the information that is to delete the record which has 7 as the key value in node 9, and it has flag-set [1, 0, 0, 0, 0, 0] which means the information of the deletion to eliminate entry 0. IBSF finds the index unit which has the same key and identifier in the index buffer to process it. The index buffer has three of the index units in Fig 8. IBSF can find it which has 7 as the key value at first. IBSF eliminates it. And than, it can find a index unit which has delete-information for node 9. Therefore, IBSF updates from [0, 0, 0, 1, 0, 1] to [1, 0, 0, 1, 0, 1] by adding a new flag.

Since the deletion policy could eliminate the redundant index units which have the same key value in the index buffer and maintain a number of the delete-information in the one index unit, IBSF can efficiently reduce the number of index units.

4.4 The Commit Policy

When the index buffer is filled by the fixed number of index units, IBSF has to commit index units from the index buffer to flash memory. The commit policy is processed by FIFO (first in first out) rules. Fig. 9 shows how to use the commit policy in IBSF.

When there is no free space for newly created index unit, IBSF choices the first index unit in the index buffer and collects the index units which have been related to the first index unit. And then, these index units are committed into a page in flash memory. As depicted Fig. 9, when the index buffer is full, the index units are committed according to the commit policy. The first index unit is related with node 1, and the index units which are related the first index unit are second and sixth index units. Therefore, the first, second, and sixth index units are selected as the victim. IBSF writes these index units into a page in the flash memory.

Since IBSF stores all index units which are related to a B-tree node into a page, it needs not the node translation table that is used in BFTL.

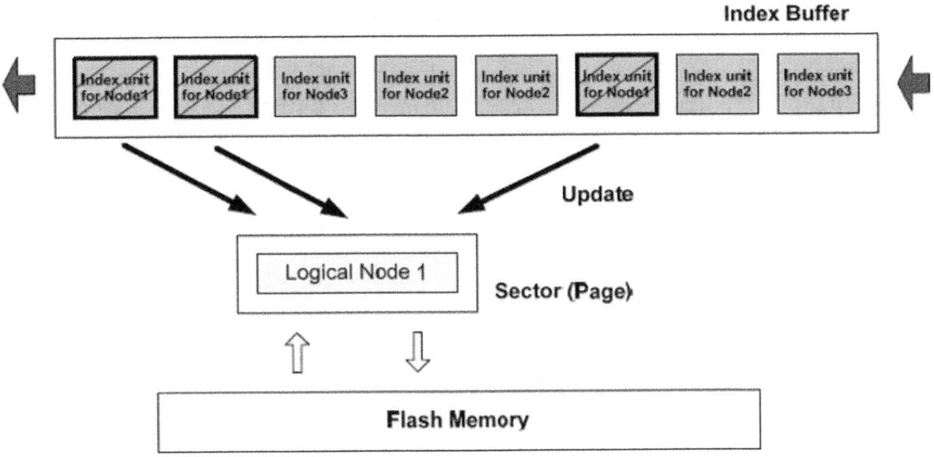

Fig. 9. Commit Policy

5 Experiments

In order to evaluate the performance of IBSF, we developed a simulator for each scheme. In the experiment, the size of NAND flash memory was configured 64 Mbytes and the size of the index buffer is fixed to hold 30 index units. For each experiment, we inserted 24,000 records, and used FAST-FTL [4].

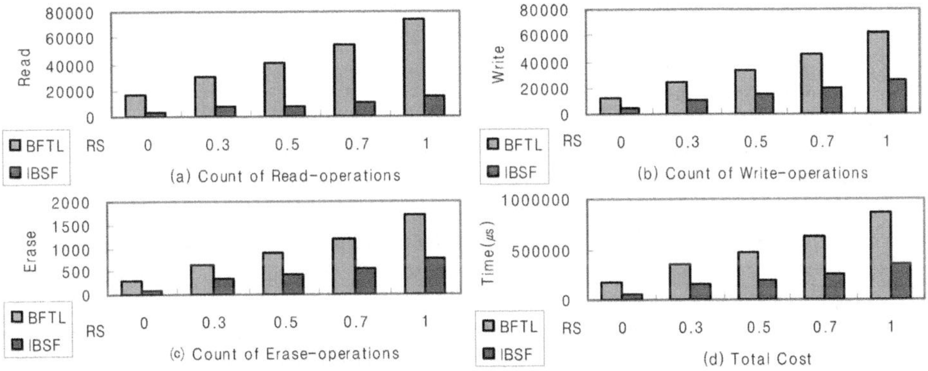

Fig. 10. Performance evaluation: Results

Fig. 10 shows the result of the experiments. In Fig. 10(a) through Fig. 10(d), the Y-axes denote the value of the number of pages read, written, erased, and consumed time, respectively and the X-axes denote the value of *RS* when B-tree was built. The *RS* (ratio of sequence) is used to manipulate the distribution of inserted keys. When *RS* equals to 0, it means that the key values were in ascending order. If *RS* equals to 1, it means that the key values were randomly generated. As shown Fig. 10, regardless the value of *RS*, the performance of IBSF significantly outperforms that of BFTL in all cases. Especially, when the keys were sequentially generated (*RS* = 0), the performance gains of IBSF are increased slightly. When *RS* is 0, the number of the read operations is reduced about 77.76% than that of BFTL and the number of the write operations is reduced about 66.21% than that of BFTL. The number of the erase operations is also reduced about 74.3% than that of BFTL. Finally, the total consumed time is reduced about 68.87% as compared to BFTL. Through the experiments, we can see that IBSF yields a better performance than BFTL in all cases.

6 Conclusion

In this paper we proposed a new index buffer management scheme called IBSF. Since IBSF delays the commit time by eliminating redundant index units in the index buffer, it could efficiently reduce the number of the write/erase operations. Moreover, IBSF eliminates the node translation table which is additional overheard. Therefore, it could reduce the number of the read operations. Finally, though the experiments, we shown that IBSF yields a better performance than BFTL.

In this work, we used FIFO scheme for selecting a victim in the index buffer. In the future, we will exploit an efficient buffer replacement scheme that considers the asymmetric cost of read/write/erase operations on NAND flash memory.

References

1. Tae-Sun Chung, Dong-Joo Park, Sangwon Park, Dong-Ho Lee, Sang-Won Lee, Ha-Joo Song, "System Software for Flash Memory: A Survey.", *International Conference on Embedded and Ubiquitous Computing*, pp394-404, 2006.
2. D. S. Batory, "B+trees and indexed sequential files: a performance comparison", *ACM SIGMOD international conference on Management of data*, pp30 - 39, 1981.
3. Chin-Hsien Wu, Li-Pin Chang, Tei-Wei Kuo, "An Efficient B-Tree Layer for Flash-Memory Storage Systems", *Real-Time and Embedded Computing Systems and Applications (RTCSA)*, pp409-430, 2003.
4. Sang-Won Lee, Dong-Joo Park, Tae-Sun Chung., Dong-Ho Lee, Sangwon Park, Ha-Joo Song, "A Log Buffer based Flash Translation Layer using Fully Associative Sector Translation", *ACM Transactions on Embedded Computing Systems*(accepted for publication).
5. Intel Corporation, "Understanding the Flash Translation Layer(FTL) Specification". Technical report.
6. Jeong-Uk Kang, Heeseung Jo, Jin-Soo Kim, and Joonwon Lee, "A Superblock-based Flash Translation Layer for NAND Flash Memory," *Proceedings of the 6th Annual ACM Conference on Embedded Software (EMSOFT 2006)*, pp161-170, 2006.

A Code Generation Framework for Actor-Oriented Models with Partial Evaluation

Gang Zhou, Man-Kit Leung, and Edward A. Lee

University of California, Berkeley
{zgang,jleung,eal}@eecs.berkeley.edu

Abstract. Embedded software requires concurrency formalisms other than threads and mutexes used in traditional programming languages like C. Actor-oriented design presents a high level abstraction for composing concurrent components. However, high level abstraction often introduces overhead and results in slower system. We address the problem of generating efficient implementation for the systems with such a high level description. We use partial evaluation as an optimized compilation technique for actor-oriented models. We use a helper-based mechanism, which results in flexible and extensible code generation framework. The end result is that the benefit offered by high level abstraction comes with (almost) no performance penalty. The code generation framework has been released in open source form as part of Ptolemy II 6.0.1.

1 Introduction

Embedded software has been traditionally written with assembly language to maximize efficiency and predictability. Programming languages like C are used to improve productivity and portability. These imperative programming languages essentially abstract how a Von Neumann computer operates in a sequential manner. They are good matches for general-purpose software applications, which are essentially a series of data transformations. However, in the embedded world, the computing system constantly engages the physical system. Thus the physical system becomes an integral part of the design and the software must operate concurrently with the physical system. The basic techniques for doing concurrent programming on top of traditional programming languages like C use threads, complemented with synchronization mechanisms like semaphores and mutual exclusion locks. These methods are at best retrofits to the original fundamentally sequential formalism. Therefore they are difficult to reason about and guarantee correctness [1]. In fact, according to a survey [2] conducted by the Microsoft Windows Driver Foundation team, the top reason for driver crashes is concurrency and race conditions. This is not acceptable for embedded applications that are real-time and often safety-critical. We need alternative concurrency formalisms to match the abstractions with the embedded applications.

A number of design frameworks have emerged over the years that offer different concurrency models for the applications they support. For example, StreamIt [3] has a dataflow formalism nicely matched to streaming media applications.

Y.-H. Lee et al. (Eds.): ICESS 2007, LNCS 4523, pp. 193–206, 2007.

Simulink [4] has roots in control system modeling, and time is part of its formal semantics. All these frameworks have formal concurrent models of computation (MoCs) that match their application spaces. They often use block diagram based design environments and the design usually starts with assembling pre-existing components in the library. Such design style has been called domain specific design, model based design or component based design, each emphasizing different aspects of the design. Many of them employ an actor-oriented approach, where actor is an encapsulation of parameterized actions performed on input data and produce output data. Input and output data are communicated through well-defined ports. Ports and parameters form the interface of an actor. Actor-oriented design hides the state of each actor and makes it inaccessible from other actors. The emphasis of data flow over control flow leads to conceptually concurrent execution of actors. Threads and mutexes become implementation mechanism instead of part of programming model.

A good programming model with abstraction properties that match the application space only solves half of the problem. For it to succeed, it is imperative that an efficient implementation be derived from a design described in the programming model. In component based design (we use the terms "actor" and "component" interchangeably in this paper), modular components make systems more flexible and extensible. Different compositions of the same components can implement different functionality. However, component designs are often slower than custom-built code. The cost of inter-component communication through the component interface introduces overhead, and generic components are highly parameterized for the reusability and thus less efficient.

To regain the efficiency for the implementation, the users could write big monolithic components to reduce inter-component communication, and write highly specialized components rather than general ones. Partial evaluation [5] provides an alternative mechanism that automates the whole process. Partial evaluation techniques have recently begun to be used in the embedded world, e.g, see [6]. We use partial evaluation for optimized code generation, transforming an actor-oriented model into target code while preserving the model's semantics. However, compared with traditional compiler optimization, our partial evaluation works at the component level and heavily leverages domain-specific knowledge. Through model analysis, the tool can discover data types, buffer sizes, parameter values, model structures and model execution schedules, and then partially (pre)evaluate all the known information to reach an efficient implementation. The end result is that the benefit offered by the high level abstraction comes with (almost) no performance penalty.

1.1 Related Work

There have been a few design frameworks with code generation functionality. Simulink with Real-Time Workshop (RTW), from the Mathworks, is probably in the most widespread use as a commercial product [4]. It can automatically generate C code from a Simulink model and is quite innovative in leveraging an underlying preemptive priority-driven multitasking operating system to deliver real-time behavior based on rate-monotonic scheduling. However, like most design frameworks, Simulink defines a fixed MoC: continuous time is the underlying MoC for Simulink, with discrete time treated as a special case (discrete time signal is piecewise-constant continuous time signal in Simulink). It can be integrated with another Mathworks product called Stateflow, used to describe complex logic for event-driven systems. The platform we are working on, Ptolemy II, is a software lab for experimenting with multiple concurrency formalisms for embedded system design. It does not have a built-in MoC. The code generation framework built on Ptolemy II is flexible and extensible. It is capable of generating code for multiple MoCs. In particular, we are most interested in generating code for those MoCs for which schedulability is decidable.

Partial evaluation has been in use for many years [5]. The basic idea is that given a program and part of this program's input data, a partial evaluator can execute the given program as far as possible producing a residual program that will perform the rest of computation when the rest of the input data is supplied. It usually involves a binding-time analysis phase to determine the static parts and the dynamic parts of a program, followed by an evaluation phase. The derived program is usually much more efficient by removing computation overhead resulting from the static parts. Partial evaluation has been applied in a variety of programming languages including functional languages [7], logic languages [8], imperative languages like C [9] and object-oriented languages [10]. Its use in embedded software has been more recent. Click is a component framework for PC router construction [6]. It builds extensible routers from modular components which are fine-grained packet processing modules called elements. Partial evaluations are applied at the level of components using optimization tools called click-fastclassifier, click-devirtualize, click-xform, click-undead, etc. For example, classifiers are generic elements for classifying packets based on a decision tree built from textual specifications. The click-fastclassifier tool would generate new source code for a classifier based on the specific decision tree and replace the generic element with this more specific element. The click-devirtualize tool addresses virtual function call overhead. It changes packet-transfer virtual function calls into conventional function calls by finding the downstream component and explicitly calling the method on that component. Again this involves transforming the source code so that method binding can be done in the compile time. The Koala component model for consumer electronics software is another example of applying partial evaluation for generating more efficient implementation [11]. Compared with previous examples, Ptolemy II does not focus on specific applications. Its emphasis is on choosing appropriate concurrent MoCs for embedded system design and generating efficient code for the chosen MoCs.

There has been previous work on code generation for Ptolemy II [12]. The approach there involves transformation of the existing source code (i.e. Java code) in each actor of a system, which results in simplified and hence more efficient Java code. Then a generic Java-to-C converter is used to produce compilable C code. The generated code is not efficient enough to be useful for embedded application. However, the techniques developed there such as specializing token declarations, assigning static offsets to input and output token buffers, static scheduling of SDF actors are useful and can be equally applied in our context.

1.2 Overview of the Code Generation Framework

Ptolemy II is a graphical software system for modeling, simulation, and design of concurrent, real-time, embedded systems. Ptolemy II focuses on assembly of concurrent components with well-defined MoCs that govern the interaction between components. Many features in Ptolemy II contribute to the ease of its use as a rapid prototyping environment. For example, domain polymorphism allows one to use the same component in multiple MoCs. Data polymorphism and type inference mechanisms automatically take care of type resolution, type checking and type conversion, and make users unaware of their existence most of the time. A rich expression language makes it easy to parameterize many aspects of a model statically or dynamically. However, these mechanisms add much indirection overhead and therefore cannot be used directly in an implementation.

The code generation framework takes a model shown to meet certain design specifications through simulation and/or verification. Through model analysis—the counterpart of binding-time analysis in traditional use of partial evaluation for general purpose software, it can discover the execution context for the model and the components (called actors in Ptolemy terminology) contained within. It then generates the target code specific to the execution context while preserving the semantics of the original model. See Fig. 1, which follows notions used in [5].

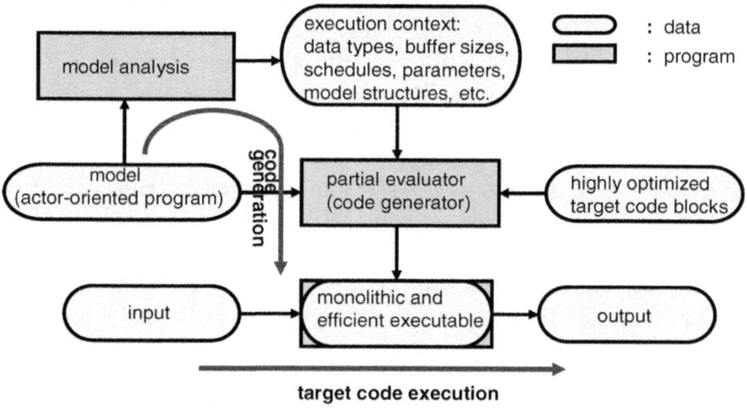

Fig. 1. Code generation with partial evaluation for actor-oriented programs

In this paper, C is our primary target language. In the generated target code, the variables representing the buffers in the input ports of each actor are defined with the data types discovered through type resolution. At the same time, if the model has a static schedule, then buffer sizes can be predetermined and defined too (as arrays), thus eliminating the overhead of dynamic memory allocation. Through model analysis, the framework can also classify parameters into either static or dynamic. Static parameters have their values configured by users and stay constant during execution. Therefore there is no need to allocate memory for them and every time a static parameter gets used in the generated code, the associated constant gets substituted in. On the other hand, dynamic parameters change their values during execution. Therefore a corresponding variable is defined for each of them in the generated code. Most of models have static structures. The code generation framework takes advantage of this and eliminates the interfaces between components. In the generated code, instead of using a dozen or so indirection function calls to transfer data between components, a simple assignment is used, resulting in very efficient execution. For the MoCs that have static schedules, instead of dispatching actors based on the schedule, the schedule is hard-coded into the generated code, i.e., the code flow directly reflects the execution sequence, thus making it run much faster. Finally, for each actor that supports code generation, there is a corresponding helper which reads in pre-existing code blocks written in the target language. These target code blocks are functionally equivalent to the actor written in Java, the language used for Ptolemy II. The helper mechanism is elaborated in the next section.

2 A Helper-Based Architecture

A helper is responsible for generating target code for a Ptolemy II actor. Each Ptolemy II actor for which code will be generated in a specific language has one associated helper. An actor may have multiple helpers to support multiple target languages (C, VHDL, etc.), although we are concentrating on C in this paper.

To achieve readability and maintainability in the implementation of helpers, the target code blocks (for example, the initialize block, fire block, and wrapup block) of each helper are placed in a separate file under the same directory. So a helper essentially consists of two files: a java class file and a code template file. This not only decouples the writing of Java code and target code, but also allows using a target language specific editor while working on the target code, such as the C/C++ Development Toolkit in Eclipse.

For each helper, the target code blocks contained in the code template file are hand-coded, verified for correctness (i.e., semantically equivalent to the behavior of the corresponding actor written in Java) and optimized for efficiency. They are stored in the library and can be reused to generate code for different models. Hand-coded templates also retain readability in the generated code. The code generation kernel uses the helper java class to harvest code blocks. The helper java class may determine which code blocks to harvest based on actor instance-specific information (e.g., port types, parameter values). The code template file contains macros that are processed by the kernel. These macros allow the kernel to generate customized code based on actor instance-specific information.

2.1 What Is in a C Code Template File?

A C code template file has a .c file extension but is not C-compilable due to its unique structure. We use a CodeStream class to parse and use these files. Below are the C code template files for the Pulse and CountTrues actors (see Fig. 2).

```
// Pulse.c
/***preinitBlock***/
int $actorSymbol(iterationCount) = 0;
int $actorSymbol(indexColCount) = 0;
unsigned char $actorSymbol(match) = 0;
/**/

/***fireBlock***/
if ($actorSymbol(indexColCount) < $size(indexes)
        && $actorSymbol(iterationCount) == $ref(indexes, $actorSymbol(indexColCount))) {
    $ref(output) = $ref(values, $actorSymbol(indexColCount));
    $actorSymbol(match) = 1;
} else {
    $ref(output) = 0;
}
if ($actorSymbol(iterationCount) <= $ref(indexes, $size(indexes) - 1)) {
    $actorSymbol(iterationCount) ++;
}
if ($actorSymbol(match)) {
    $actorSymbol(indexColCount) ++;
    $actorSymbol(match) = 0;
}
if ($actorSymbol(indexColCount) >= $size(indexes) && $val(repeat)) {
    $actorSymbol(iterationCount) = 0;
    $actorSymbol(indexColCount) = 0;
}
/**/

// CountTrues.c
/*** preinitBlock ***/
int $actorSymbol(trueCount);
int $actorSymbol(i);
/**/

/*** fireBlock ***/
$actorSymbol(trueCount) = 0;
for($actorSymbol(i) = 0; $actorSymbol(i) < $val(blockSize); $actorSymbol(i)++) {
    if ($ref(input, $actorSymbol(i))) {
        $actorSymbol(trueCount)++;
    }
}
$ref(output) = $actorSymbol(trueCount);
/**/
```

A C code template file consists of C code blocks. Each code block has a header and a footer. The header and footer tags serve as code block separators. The footer is simply the tag "/**/".The header starts with the tag "/***" and ends with the tag "***/". Between the header tags are the code block name and optionally an argument list. The argument list is enclosed by a pair of parentheses "()" and multiple arguments in the list are separated by commas ",". A code block may have arbitrary number of arguments. Each argument is prefixed by the dollar sign "$" (e.g., $value, $width), which allows easy searching of the argument in the body of code blocks, followed by straight text substitution with the string value of the argument. Formally, the signature of a code block is defined as the pair (N, p) where N is the code block name and p is the number of arguments. A code block (N, p) may be overloaded by another code block (N, p') where $p \neq p'$.[1] Furthermore, different helpers in a class hierarchy may contain code blocks with the same (N, p). So a unique reference to a code block signature is the tuple (H, N, p) where H is the name of the helper.

A code block can also be overridden. A code block (H, N, p) is overridden by a code block $(\tilde{H}, N, p)$ given that $\tilde{H}$ is a child class of H. This gives rise to code block inheritance. Ptolemy II actors have a well-structured class hierarchy. The code generation helpers mirror the same class hierarchy. Since code blocks represent behaviors of actors in the target language, the code blocks are inherited for helpers just as action methods are inherited for actors. Given a request for a code block, a CodeStream instance searches through all code template files of the helper and its ancestors, starting from the bottom of the class hierarchy. This mirrors the behavior of invoking an inherited method for an actor.

2.2 What Is in a Helper Java Class File?

Helper classes are inherited from CodeGeneratorHelper. The CodeGenerator-Helper class implements the default behavior for a set of methods that return code strings for specific parts of the target program (init(), fire(), wrapup(), etc.), using the default code block names (initBlock, fireBlock, wrapupBlock, etc.). Each specific helper class can either inherit the behavior from its parent class or override any method to read code blocks with non-default names, read code blocks with arguments, or do any special processing it deems necessary.

2.3 The Macro Language

The macro language allows helpers to be written once, and then used in a different context where the macros are expanded and resolved. All macros used in code blocks are prefixed with the dollar sign "\$" (as in "\$ref(input)", "\$val(width)", etc.). The arguments to the macros are enclosed in parentheses. Macros can be nested and recursively processed by the code generation helper. The use of the dollar sign as prefix assumes that it is not a valid identifier in the target language. The macro prefix can be configured for different target languages. Different macro names specify different rules for text substitutions. Since the same set of code blocks may be shared by multiple instances of one helper class, the macros mainly serve the purpose of producing unique variable names for different instances and generating instance-specific port and parameter information. The following is a list of macros used in C code generation.

\$ref(name). Returns a unique reference to a parameter or a port in the global scope. For a multiport which contains multiple channels, use \$ref(name#i) where i is the channel number. During macro expansion, the name is replaced by the full name resulting from the model hierarchy.

[1] All arguments in a code block are implicitly strings. So unlike the usual overloaded functions with the same name but different types of arguments, overloaded code blocks need to have different number of arguments.

$ref(name, offset). Returns a unique reference to an element in an array parameter or a port with the indicated offset in the global scope. The offset must not be negative. $ref(name, 0) is equivalent to $ref(name). Similarly, for multiport, use $ref(name#i, offset).

$val(parameter-name). Returns the value of the parameter associated with an actor in the simulation model. The advantage of using $val() macro instead of $ref() macro is that no additional memory needs to be allocated. $val() macro is usually used when the parameter is constant during the execution.

$actorSymbol(name). Returns a unique reference to a user-defined variable in the global scope. This macro is used to define additional variables, for example, to hold internal states of actors between firings. The helper writer is responsible for declaring these variables.

$size(name). If the given name represents an ArrayType parameter, it returns the size of the array. If the given name represents a port of an actor, it returns the width of that port.

2.4 The CountTrues Example

Fig. 2 shows a very simple model named CountTrues (notice it has the same name as one actor used in the model) in the synchronous dataflow (SDF) domain (In Ptolemy II, a domain realizes an MoC). In the model the Pulse actor produces "true" or "false" token and the CountTrues actor counts the "true" tokens. The CountTrues actor has its "blockSize" parameter set to 2, which means in each firing it reads 2 tokens from its input port and sends out a token recording the number of "true" tokens. When the model is simulated in the Ptolemy II framework, the produced result is shown on the right hand side of the figure (the model is fired 4 times because the SDFDirector's "iterations" parameter is set to 4). Below is the main function of the generated stand-alone C program.

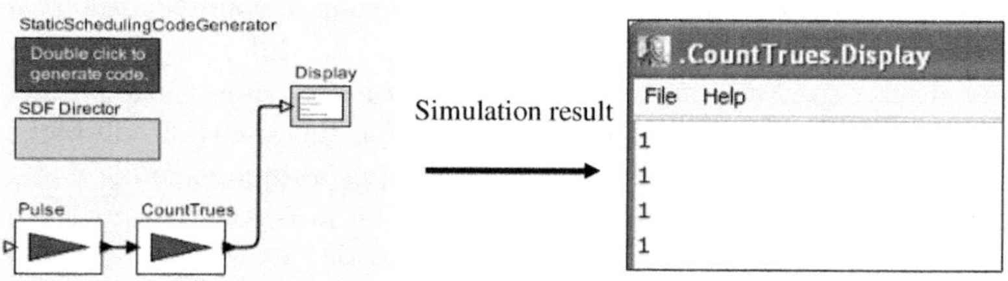

Fig. 2. The CountTrues model and its simulation result

```
......
static int iteration = 0;
main(int argc, char *argv[]) {
    init();
    /* Static schedule: */
    for (iteration = 0; iteration < 4; iteration ++) {
```

```
        /* fire Composite Actor CountTrues */
        /* fire Pulse */
        if (_CountTrues_Pulse_indexColCount < 2
                && _CountTrues_Pulse_iterationCount == Array_get(_CountTrues_Pulse_indexes_ ,
                _CountTrues_Pulse_indexColCount).payload.Int) {
            _CountTrues_CountTrues_input[0] = Array_get(_CountTrues_Pulse_values_ ,
                _CountTrues_Pulse_indexColCount).payload.Boolean;
            _CountTrues_Pulse_match = 1;
        } else {
            _CountTrues_CountTrues_input[0] = 0;
        }
        if (_CountTrues_Pulse_iterationCount
                <= Array_get(_CountTrues_Pulse_indexes_ ,2 - 1).payload.Int) {
            _CountTrues_Pulse_iterationCount ++;
        }
        if (_CountTrues_Pulse_match) {
            _CountTrues_Pulse_indexColCount ++;
            _CountTrues_Pulse_match = 0;
        }
        if (_CountTrues_Pulse_indexColCount >= 2 && true) {
            _CountTrues_Pulse_iterationCount = 0;
            _CountTrues_Pulse_indexColCount = 0;
        }
        /* fire Pulse */
        // The code for the second firing of the Pulse actor is omitted here.
        .....
        /* fire CountTrues */
        _CountTrues_CountTrues_trueCount = 0;
        for(_CountTrues_CountTrues_i = 0; _CountTrues_CountTrues_i < 2;
                _CountTrues_CountTrues_i++){
            if (_CountTrues_CountTrues_input[(0 + _CountTrues_CountTrues_i)%2]) {
                _CountTrues_CountTrues_trueCount++;
            }
        }
        _CountTrues_Display_input[0] = _CountTrues_CountTrues_trueCount;
        /* fire Display */
        printf("Display: %d\n", _CountTrues_Display_input[0]);
    }
    wrapup();
    exit(0);
}
```

In the code the $ref() and $actorSymbol() macros are replaced with unique variable references. The $val() macro in the CountTrues actor's code block is replaced by the parameter value of the CountTrue instance in the model. When the generated C program is compiled and executed, the same result is produced as from the Ptolemy II simulation.

3 Software Infrastructure

Our code generation framework has the flavor of code generation domains in Ptolemy Classic [13]. However, in Ptolemy Classic, code generation domains and simulation domains are separate and so are the actors (called stars in Ptolemy Classic terminology) used in these domains. In Ptolemy Classic, the actors in the simulation domains participate in simulation whereas the corresponding actors in the code generation domains participate in code generation. Separate domains (simulation vs. code generation) make it inconvenient to integrate the model design phase with the code generation phase and streamline the whole process.

Separate actor libraries make it difficult to maintain a consistent interface for a simulation actor and the corresponding code generation actor.

In Ptolemy II, there are no separate code generations domains. Once a model has been designed, simulated and verified to satisfy the given specification in the simulation domain, code can be directly generated from the model. Each helper does not have its own interface. Instead, it interrogates the associated actor to find its interface (ports and parameters) during the code generation. Thus the interface consistency is maintained naturally. The generated code, when executed, should present the same behavior as the original model. Compared with the Ptolemy Classic approach, this new approach allows the seamless integration between the model design phase and the code generation phase.

In addition, our code generation framework takes advantage of new technologies developed in Ptolemy II such as the polymorphic type system, richer variety of MoCs including hierarchical concurrent finite-state machines [14] which are well suited for embedded system design and discussed in Sect. 4.

To gain an insight into the code generation software infrastructure, it is worthwhile to take a look at how actors are implemented for simulation purposes. In Ptolemy II, the Executable interface defines how an actor can be invoked. The preinitialize() method is assumed to be invoked exactly once during the lifetime of an execution of a model and before the type resolution. The initialize() method is assumed to be invoked once after the type resolution. The prefire(), fire(), and postfire() methods will usually be invoked many times, with each sequence of method invocations defined as one iteration. The wrapup() method will be invoked exactly once per execution at the end of the execution.

The Executable interface is implemented by two types of actors: AtomicActor, which is a single entity, and CompositeActor, which is an aggregation of actors. The Executable interface is also implemented by the Director class. A Director class implements an MoC and governs the execution of actors contained by an (opaque) CompositeActor.

The classes to support code generation are located in the subpackages under ptolemy.codegen (In Ptolemy II architecture, all the package paths start with "ptolemy"). The helper class hierarchy and package structure mimic those of regular Ptolemy II actors. The counterpart of the Executable interface is the ActorCodeGenerator interface. This interface defines the methods for generating target code in different stages corresponding to what happens in the simulation. These methods include generatePreinitializeCode(), generateInitializeCode(), generateFireCode(), generateWrapupCode(), etc.

CodeGeneratorHelper, the counterpart of AtomicActor, is the base class implementing the ActorCodeGenerator interface. It provides common functions for all actor helpers. Actors and their helpers have the same names so that the Java reflection mechanism can be used to load the helper for the corresponding actor during code generation. For example, there is a Ramp actor in the package ptolemy.actor.lib. Correspondingly, there is a Ramp helper in the package ptolemy.codegen.c.actor.lib. Here c represents the fact that all the helpers under ptolemy.codegen.c generate C code. Assume we would like to generate code for another target language X, the helpers could be implemented under ptolemy.codegen.x. This results in an extensible code generation framework. Developers can not only contribute their own actors and helpers, but also extend the framework to generate code for a new target language.

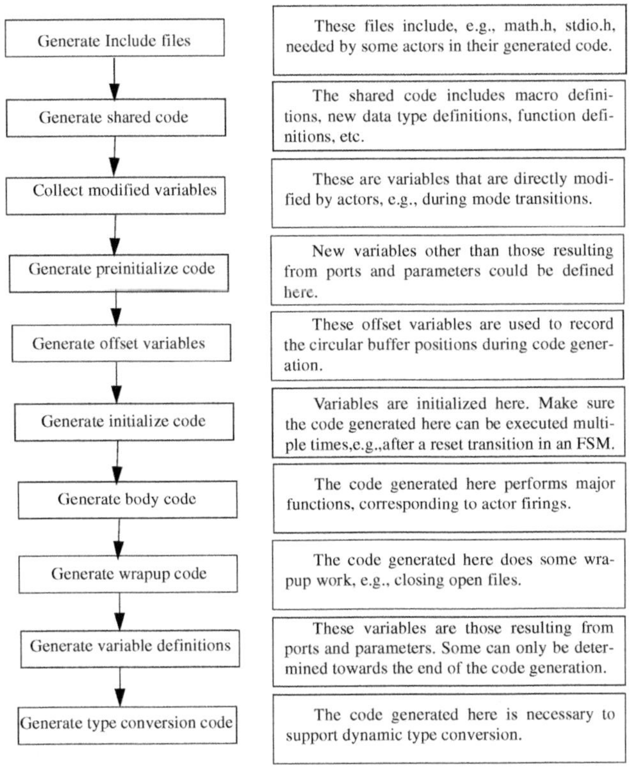

Fig. 3. The flow chart of the code generation process

To generate code for hierarchically composed models, helpers for composite actors are also created. For example, the most commonly used composite actor is TypedCompositeActor in the package ptolemy.actor. A helper with the same name is created in the package ptolemy.codegen.c.actor. The main function of this helper is to generate code for the data transfer through the composite actor's interface and delegate the code generation for the composite actor to the helper for the local director or the helpers for the actors contained by the composite actor. Since a director implements an MoC (called a domain in Ptolemy terminology), a helper is created for each director that supports code generation. These director helpers generate target code that preserves the semantics of MoCs. Currently, the synchronous dataflow domain (SDF), finite state machines (FSM), and heterochronous dataflow domain (HDF) support code generation (see Sect. 4 for more details).

Finally the StaticSchedulingCodeGenerator class is used to orchestrate the whole code generation process. An instance of this class is contained by the top level composite actor (represented by the blue rectangle in Fig. 2). The code generation starts at the top level and the code for the whole model is generated hierarchically, much similar to how a model is simulated in Ptolemy II.

The flow chart in Fig. 3 shows the whole code generation process step by step. The details of some steps are MoC-specific. Notice that the steps outlined in the figure do not necessarily follow the order the generated codes are assembled together. For example, only those parameters that change values during the execution need to be defined as variables. Therefore those definitions are generated last after all the code blocks have been processed, but placed at the beginning of the generated code. Our helper based code generation framework actually serves as a coordination language for the target code. It not only leverages the huge legacy code repository, but also takes advantage of many years and many researchers' work on compiler optimization techniques for the target language, such as C. It is accessible to a huge base of programmers. Often new language fails to catch on not because it is technically inferior, but because it is very difficult to penetrate the barrier established by the languages already in widespread use. With the use of the helper class combined with target code template written in a language programmers are familiar with, there is much less of a learning curve to use our design and code generation environment.

4 Domains

SDF: The synchronous dataflow (SDF) domain [15] is a mature domain in Ptolemy II. Under SDF, the execution order of actors is statically determined prior to execution. This opens the door for generating some very efficient code. In fact, the SDF software synthesis has been studied extensively. Many optimization techniques have been designed according to different criteria such as minimization of program size, buffer size, or actor activation rate. We built the support for SDF code generation to test our framework and use it as a starting point to explore code generation for other domains.

FSM: Finite state machines (FSMs) have a long history. We use hierarchical concurrent finite state machines [14]. In Ptolemy II, an FSM actor can do traditional FSM modeling or specify modal models. In traditional FSM modeling, an FSM actor reacts to the inputs by making state transitions and sending data to the output ports like an ordinary Ptolemy actor. The FSM domain also supports the *charts formalism with modal models. In Fig. 4, M is a modal model with two modes. Modes are represented by states (rendered as circles in the figure) of an FSM actor that controls mode switching. Each mode has one or more refinements that specify the behavior of the mode. A modal model is constructed in a ModalModel actor having the FSMDirector as the local director. The ModalModel actor contains a ModalController (inherited from FSMActor) and a set of Refinement actors that model the refinements associated with states and possibly a set of transition refinements. The FSMDirector mediates the interaction with the outside domain, and coordinates the execution of the refinements with the ModalController. We created helpers for FSMDirector, FSMActor, ModalController, ModalModel, Refinement and TransitionRefinement and are capable of generating C code for both traditional FSM modeling and modeling with modal models.

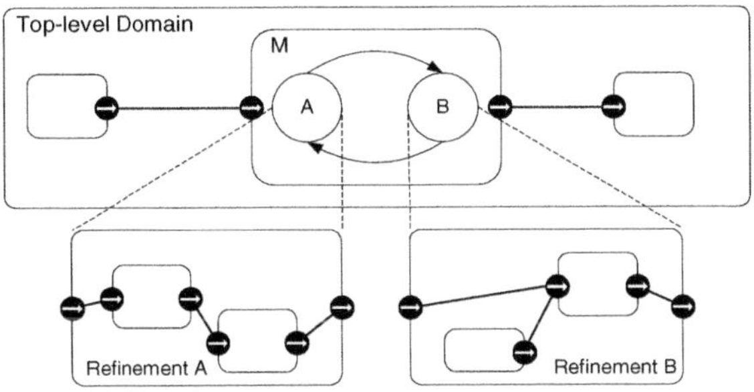

Fig. 4. A modal model example

HDF: In Fig. 4, if the top level domain and the domains inside the refinements are all SDF, then we get the very interesting heterochronous dataflow (HDF) domain. An HDF model allows changes in port rates (called rate signatures) between iterations of the whole model. Within each iteration, rate signatures are fixed and an HDF model behaves like an SDF model. This guarantees that a schedule can be completely executed. Between iterations, any modal model can make a state transition and therefore derives its rate signature from the refinement associated with the new state. The HDF domain recomputes the schedule when necessary. Since it is expensive to compute the schedule during the run time, all possible schedules are precomputed during code generation.

The HDF domain can be used to model a variety of applications that SDF cannot easily model. For example, in control application, the controlled plant can be in a number of operation states, requiring a number of control modes. In communication and signal processing, adaptive algorithms are used to achieve optimal performance with varying channel conditions. In all these applications, the HDF domain can be used to model their modal behaviors, leading to implementations that can adjust operation modes according to the received inputs, while still yielding static analyzability due to finite number of schedules.

5 Conclusion

This paper describes a code generation framework for actor-oriented models using partial evaluation. It uses a helper-based mechanism to achieve modularity, maintainability, portability and efficiency in code generation. It demonstrates design using high level abstraction can be achieved without sacrificing performance. The code generation framework is part of Ptolemy II 6.0.1 release. It can be downloaded from the Ptolemy project website at EECS, UC Berkeley. The software release includes various demos to highlight the features of the code generation framework. We are currently exploring code generation for other MoCs suited to embedded system design. We are also testing the capabilities of the code generation framework with more complicated applications.

Acknowledgements. This paper describes work that is part of the Ptolemy project, which is supported by the National Science Foundation (NSF award number CCR-00225610), and Chess (the Center for Hybrid and Embedded Software Systems), which receives support from NSF, the State of California Micro Program, and the following companies: Agilent, Bosch, DGIST, General Motors, Hewlett Packard, Microsoft, National Instruments and Toyota.

References

1. E. A. Lee. The Problem with Threads. *IEEE Computer*, 39(5):33-42, May 2006.
2. http://www.microsoft.com/whdc/driver/wdf/WDF_facts.mspx
3. W. Thies, M. Karczmarek, and S. Amarasinghe. StreamIt: A Language for Streaming Applications. In *Proceedings of the 2002 International Conference on Compiler Construction*, 2002 Springer-Verlag LNCS, Grenoble, France, April, 2002.
4. http://www.mathworks.com/products/simulink/
5. N. D. Jones, C. K. Gomard, and P. Sestoft. Partial Evaluation and Automatic Program Generation. Prentice-Hall, June 1993.
6. E. Kohler, R. Morris, and B. Chen. Programming language optimizations for modular router configurations. In *Proceedings of the Architectural Support for Programming Languages and Operating Systems (ASPLOS)*, pages 251-263, October 2002.
7. C. K. Gomard and N. D. Jones. A partial evaluator for the untyped lambda-calculus. *Journal of Functional Programming*, vol.1, no.1, Jan. 1991, pp. 21-69.
8. J. W. Lloyd and J. C. Shepherdson. Partial evaluation in logic programming. *Journal of Logic Programming*, vol.11, no.3-4, Oct.-Nov. 1991, pp. 217-42.
9. L. O. Andersen. Partial evaluation of C and automatic compiler generation. In *4th International Conference CC'92 Proceedings.* Springer-Verlag. 1992, pp. 251-7.
10. U. Schultz. Partial evaluation for class-based object-oriented languages. In *Proceedings of Symposium on Programs as Data Objects (PADO)*, number 2053 in Lecture Notes in Computer Science. Springer-Verlag, May 2001.
11. R. V. Ommerling. The Koala component model for consumer electronics software. *IEEE Computer*, 33(3):7885, March 2000.
12. J. Tsay. A Code Generation Framework for Ptolemy II. ERL Technical Memorandum UCB/ERL No. M00/25, Dept. EECS, University of California, Berkeley, CA 94720, May 19, 2000.
13. J. L. Pino, S. Ha, E. A. Lee, and J. T. Buck. Software Synthesis for DSP Using Ptolemy. *Journal on VLSI Signal Processing*, vol. 9, no. 1, pp. 7-21, Jan., 1995.
14. A. Girault, B. Lee, and E. A. Lee. Hierarchical Finite State Machines with Multiple Concurrency Models. *IEEE Transactions On Computer-aided Design Of Integrated Circuits And Systems*, Vol. 18, No. 6, June 1999.
15. E. A. Lee and D. G. Messerschmitt. Synchronous Data Flow. *Proc. of the IEEE*, September, 1987.

Power-Aware Software Prefetching*

Juan Chen, Yong Dong, Huizhan Yi, and Xuejun Yang

School of Computer, National University of Defense Technology, P.R. China
{juanchen,yongdong,huizhanyi,xjyang}@nudt.edu.cn

Abstract. Some traditional optimizations improve the performance of processors, but consume the higher power dissipation. We study this trade-off using software prefetching as performance-oriented optimization technique. We first demonstrate that software prefetching provides a significant performance boost with the higher power on several memory-intensive benchmarks. However, when we combine software prefetching with dynamic voltage/frequency scaling (DVFS), the performance gain can be achieved without power increase, which is called a power-aware approach. Besides reducing power dissipation through DVFS, we also improve the performance through adjusting the prefetch distance. A modified SimpleScalar/Wattch is used to evaluate our power-aware software prefetching. Experimental results show this optimization approach is effective to guarantee no power increase due to prefetching and improve the performance of software prefetching.

1 Introduction

Power/energy consumption has already started to dominate the execution time as the critical metric in system design. In the portable and embedded devices, power is restricted by the limited battery life [1][9]. Unfortunately, some traditional compiler optimization techniques bring the power increase when improving program performance. One natural question is *whether we can improve the performance without power increase through combining traditional performance-oriented optimization and low-power technique*. In other word, it is significant to transfer the original performance-oriented optimization to a power-aware optimization, where "power-aware" means significant performance boost is achieved with no power increase.

Although dynamic voltage/frequency scaling (DVFS) can greatly reduce power dissipation, the performance degradation is inevitable. We explore the opportunities to obtain further performance boost, so it can obtain better performance than simple DVFS. In this paper, we study this using software prefetching as the performance-oriented optimization. We call it power-aware software prefetching.

Prefetching is a latency tolerance technique, which is generally used to reduce the gap between processor speed and memory access speed. In prefetching, cache miss

* This work was supported by the Program of Nature Science Fund under Grant No. 60633050 and was supported by the National High Technology Development 863 Program of China under Grant No. 2002AA1Z2101 and No. 2004AA1Z2210.

Y.-H. Lee et al. (Eds.): ICESS 2007, LNCS 4523, pp. 207–218, 2007.

penalty is eliminated by generating prefetch requests to the memory system to bring the data into the cache before the data is actually used. It can be triggered either by a hardware mechanism, or by a software instruction or by a combination of both. Several prefetching techniques [5][6][10] have been proposed in the past solely to increase the performance. Hardware prefetching needs the extra hardware resource; software prefetching approaches rely on data access pattern, which can be determined by static program analysis so that prefetching can be done selectively and effectively.

Dynamic voltage/frequency scaling (DVFS) has become an important power-management technique to save power or energy consumption. DVFS can obtain significant power reduction by varying the supply voltage and clock frequency of one processor: $Power \propto CV_{dd}^{2} f$, where C is the load capacitance, V_{dd} is the supply voltage and f is the clock frequency. The "dynamic" in DVFS means it allows supply voltage and clock frequency to be adjusted during the execution.

However, in CMOS technology the circuit delay increases as the supply voltage decreases [14]: $delay \propto V_{dd} / (V_{dd} - V_t)^{\alpha}$, where V_t is the threshold voltage, and α is a technology-dependent factor (between 1 and 2). Thus, reducing voltage will result in performance degradation because the clock frequency f needs to be decreased to account for the increased circuit delay [9].

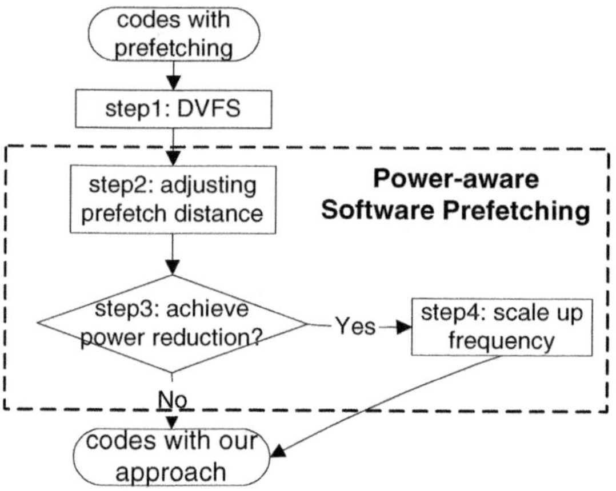

Fig. 1. The framework of our power-aware software prefetching

To reduce such performance degradation due to DVFS, we explore performance improvement opportunities through readjusting prefetch distance. Furthermore, such adjustment probably can achieve further power and performance gain. If it is, we can transfer this power reduction to performance boost through scaling up frequency. Here frequency scaling represents voltage scaling because the frequency and voltage are adjusted together. Figure 1 gives the whole framework, which is divided into four steps. In the first step, DVFS is applied to eliminate power increase due to prefetching. But clock frequency reduction results in performance degradation. In the second step, we exploit performance boost through readjusting prefetch distance because we observe the original prefetch distance is no longer accurate under new clock frequency.

Furthermore, if such a re-adjustment achieves some power reduction, we will scale up clock frequency again to get the more performance improvement with no power increase. That is what step 3 and step 4 do.

For any DVFS algorithm, it focuses only DVFS but not analyzing the detailed optimization method. We feel it is more significant to do the tradeoff between power and performance. Our power-aware software prefetching combines prefetching algorithm with voltage/frequency scaling and explores the performance improvement opportunities even after DVFS.

The remainder of this paper is organized as follows. In section 2, we analyze the power increase due to software prefetching. Section 3 illustrates our power-aware software prefetching approach. Section 4 shows the experimental methodology and experimental results in detail. Section 5 shows the related works. Section 6 gives the conclusions.

2 Power Increase Due to Software Prefetching

2.1 Software Prefetching

Software prefetching relies on the programmer or compiler to insert the explicit prefetch instructions into the codes for memory references that are likely to miss in the cache. At run time, the inserted prefetch instructions bring the data into the processor's cache in advance of its use, thus overlapping the memory access with the processor computation. Software prefetching has been shown to be effective in reducing memory stalls for both sequential and parallel applications, particularly for scientific programs making regular memory access [5][6].

```
// 3D Jacobi Kernel
A(N,N,N), B(N,N,N)
do k=1, N-2
 do j=1, N-2
  do i=1, N-2
    B[k][j][i]=0.167*(A[k][j][i-1]+
                      A[k][j-1][i]+
                      A[k][j][i+1]+
                      A[k][j+1][i]+
                      A[k-1][j][i]+
                      A[k+1][j][i]);
```

(a) Original codes for 3D Jacobi kernel

```
A(N,N,N), B(N,N,N)
do k=1, N-2
 do j=1, N-2
  do i=1, PD, step=4                                   // Prologue Loop
    prefetch(&A[k][j][i]);
    prefetch(&A[k][j+1][i]);
    prefetch(&A[k][j-1][i]);
    prefetch(&A[k-1][j][i]);
    prefetch(&A[k+1][j][i]);
    prefetch(&B[k][j][i]);
  end do
  do i=1, N-PD-2, step=4                               // Unrolled Loop
    prefetch(&A[k][j][i+4+D]);
    prefetch(&A[k][j+1][i+4+D]);
    prefetch(&A[k][j-1][i+4+D]);
    prefetch(&A[k-1][j][i+4+D]);
    prefetch(&A[k+1][j][i+4+D]);
    prefetch(&B[k][j][i+4+D]);
    B[k][j][i]=0.167*(A[k][j][i-1]+A[k][j-1][i]+A[k][j][i+1]+A[k][j+1][i]+A[k-1][j][i]+A[k+1][j][i]);
    B[k][j][i+1]=0.167*(A[k][j][i]+A[k][j-1][i+1]+A[k][j][i+2]+A[k][j+1][i+1]+A[k-1][j][i+1]+A[k+1][j][i+1]);
    B[k][j][i+2]=0.167*(A[k][j][i+1]+A[k][j-1][i+2]+A[k][j][i+3]+A[k][j+1][i+2]+A[k-1][j][i+2]+A[k+1][j][i+2]);
    B[k][j][i+3]=0.167*(A[k][j][i+2]+A[k][j-1][i+3]+A[k][j][i+4]+A[k][j+1][i+3]+A[k-1][j][i+3]+A[k+1][j][i+3]);
  end do
  do i=N-PD-1,N-2                                      // Epilogue Loop
    B[k][j][i]=0.167*(A[k][j][i-1]+A[k][j-1][i]+A[k][j][i+1]+A[k][j+1][i]+A[k-1][j][i]+A[k+1][j][i]);
 end do
end do
```

(b) Affine array perfetching for 3D Jacobi kernel using Mowry algorithm [6]

Fig. 2. Code examples for 3D Jacobi kernel before and after using Mowry's prefetching algorithm

In this paper, we use software prefetching algorithm proposed by Todd Mowry. Mowry's algorithm [6] exploits the precise access pattern information available through static analysis of array references to insert prefetches for only the data needed by the processor. Mowry's prefetch algorithm involves three steps. More details can be found in [6]. To illustrate, Figure 2(a) and Figure 2(b) show the 3D Jacobi kernel before and after prefetch algorithm is applied, respectively. Software prefetching requires computing a prefetch distance, *PD*, to properly schedule prefetches. Recall that $PD = \left\lceil \frac{l}{w} \right\rceil$, where w is the work (the latency) per loop iteration, and l is the memory latency. Hence, *PD* must be calculated for every loop. In this example, *PD* is equal to 16. Locality analysis is performed to determine where to insert perfetch instructions. Prefetching is usually combined with loop unrolling.

2.2 Power Increase Due to Prefetching

Figure 3 compares the power and performance before and after software prefetching. Although software prefetching improves program performance effectively (Figure 3(b)), power dissipation is greatly increased due to prefetching (Figure 3(a)). The description about these memory-intensive benchmarks is given in the later experimental section. Each group of bars include the original version without prefetching and the version optimized with software prefetching. This simulation results use Wattch power model [4], and applying aggressive, non-ideal clock gating, where power dissipation of active units is scaled linearly with the port or unit usage. And the unused units dissipate 10% of their maximum power rather than zero.

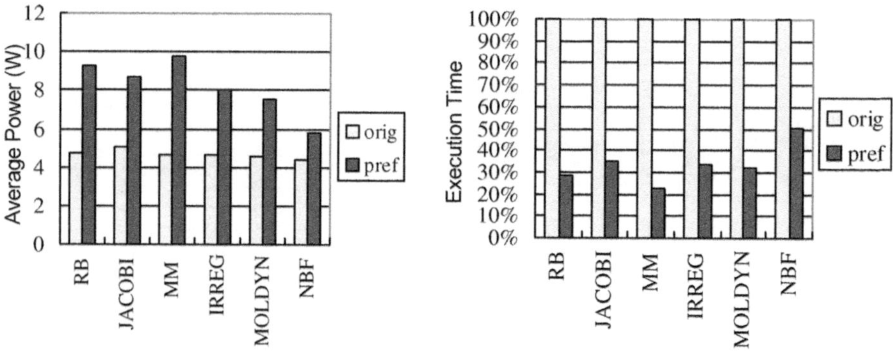

(a) Power dissipation (b) execution time

Fig. 3. Power increase and performance improvement due to software prefetching

To illustrate each unit attribution for power increase, the power dissipation for MM bar is broken down into the following eleven parts: Rename Logic Power (rename), Branch Predictor Power (bpred), Instruction Window Power (window), Load/Store Queue Power (lsq), Register File Power (regfile), Instruction Cache Power (icache),

Data Cache Power (dcache), Level 2 Cache Power (dcache2), Integer ALU Power (alu), Result Bus Power (resultbus), Write Buffers Power (write_buffers). Note that the average clock power increases to 5.1165W from 2.2848W due to software prefetching, which is not plotted in the Figure 4 because this figure is too big to show together with other power values.

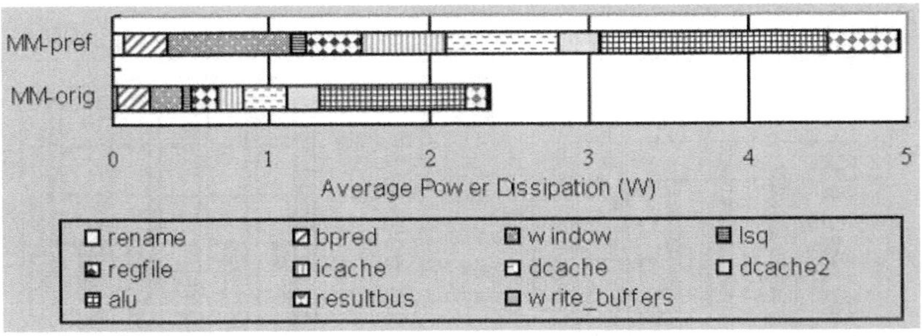

Fig. 4. Power dissipation breakdown for MM (or MATMULT) benchmark

From the above statistics, nearly all the function units show the power increase due to software prefetching. Specially for instruction window, instruction cache, register file and ALU, power increases are more obvious. The major causes about power increase probably are: (1) a number of prefetch instructions are inserted, which increases the number of instructions; (2) The overlap of memory access and CPU computation increases the density of instruction execution, which leads to power increase.

3 Power-Aware Software Prefetching

First, we make the following assumptions about the program, microarchitecture, and circuit implementation:

(1) The program's logical behavior does not change with the frequency.

(2) The relationship between the frequency and voltage is $f \propto (V_{dd} - V_t)^{\alpha} / V_{dd}$ where V_{dd} is the supply voltage, V_t is the threshold voltage, and α is a technology-dependent factor (≈ 2).

(3) There are the energy and delay penalties associated with switching between different (V_{dd}, f) pairs.

(4) Computation can be assigned to different frequencies at an arbitrarily fine grain. That is, a continuous partitioning of the computation and its assignment to different voltage/frequency levels are possible. Also an instruction can run at different frequency.

While the first three assumptions are realistic, the last one is optimistic in the sense that allows for higher energy savings than may be achievable in practice.

With DVFS, we can obtain the results as Figure 5 shows. Figure 5(a) shows the power increase due to prefetching and power reduction by DVFS. In the original version, all the benchmarks run at 1GHz. Prefetching greatly increases the power dissipation. Using simulation-based profiling execution, we adopt the optimal clock frequency level for each benchmark. So, power dissipation is reduced to less than the original level. Specially, frequency scaling instructions are only inserted at the entry and exit of prefetching loop nests. From the left to right in Figure 5, the optimal clock frequencies are 686MHz, 720MHz, 664MHz, 722MHz, 750MHz and 848MHz. Figure 5(b) gives the performance penalty due to DVFS.

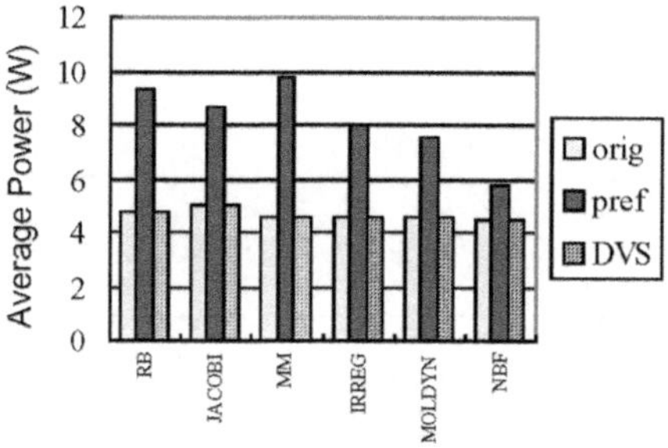

(a) Power dissipation comparison

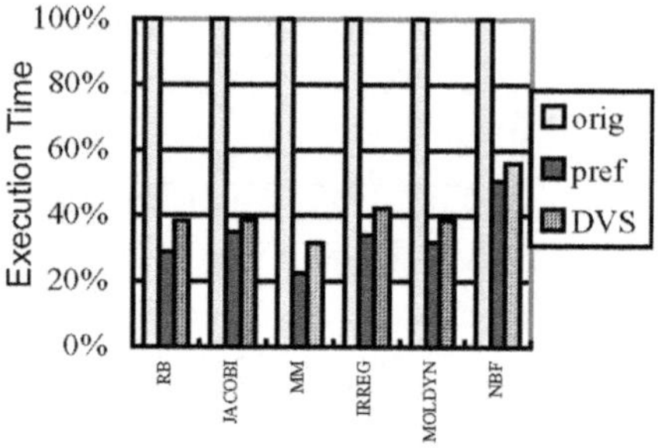

(b) execution time comparison

Fig. 5. Power reduction due to dynamic voltage/frequency scaling (DVFS) and performance penalty

```
X1(M), X2(M), index(N)
setfreq(700);
do i=1, PD, step=2                    // Prologue Loop
   prefetch(&index(i));
do i=1, PD, step=2
   prefetch(&index(i+PD));
   prefetch(&X1(index(i))) ;
   ...
do i=1, N-2*PD-1, step=2              // Unrolled Loop
   prefetch(&index(i+2*PD));
   prefetch(&X1(index(i+PD))) ;
   ...
   d=X1(index(i))-X2(index(i));
   force=d**(-7)-d**(-4);
   X1(index(i+1))+=force;
   X2(index(i+1))+=-force;
   ...
do i=N-2*PD-1,N-PD-1                  // Epilogue Loop
   prefetch(&X1(index(i+PD)));
   d=X1(index(i))-X2(index(i));
   force=d**(-7)-d**(-4);
   X1(index(i+1))+=force;
do i=N-PD-1, N
   d=X1(index(i))-X2(index(i));
   force=d**(-7)-d**(-4);
   X1(index(i+1))+=force;
   X2(index(i+1))+=-force;
setfreq(1000);
...
```

Fig. 6. Illustration of frequency scaling instruction setfreq()

Since power increase is mainly from the loop nests including prefetch instructions, our DVFS policy is to scale down the frequency of these loop nests. Our implementation approach is to add frequency scaling instruction, setfreq(), at the entry of these loop nests in the C program. It is also necessary to scale frequency back to the original level at the end of these loop nests so that the later program execution runs at the normal clock frequency. Figure 6 gives the clear illustration.

During the codes in Figure 6, at first program keeps running at 1GHz clock frequency until meeting setfreq(700). Then clock frequency is changed to 700MHz. After setfreq(1000) the program runs at 1GHz again.

As Figure 1 illustrates, our approach exploits further performance boost opportunities. We use RB benchmark as our example to illustrate our approach. Using DVFS, loop nests including prefetch instructions runs at 686MHz instead of 1GHz. At this time, average power dissipation is 4.7285W (less than the original level) while remaining 1.62 performance speedup. Compared with no DVFS, power reduces 49%.

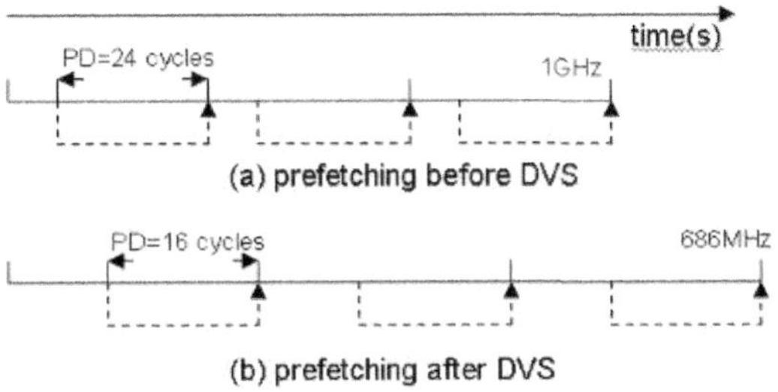

Fig. 7. Prefetch distance adjustment illustration for RB benchmark

Figure 7 explains why the prefetch distance must be adjusted. Reducing the clock frequency prolongs the time of each cycle. To maintain memory access latency as a fixed time in second, prefetch distance must be reduced. In Figure 7, solid line represents CPU computation and dash line is memory access operation due to prefetching. *PD* is prefetch distance.

With the clock frequency 686MHz, prefetch distance for RB is changed to 16 from 24. Table 1 gives some detailed profiling data about prefetch distance adjustment.

Table 1. Result comparisions between DVFS and ours for RB bechmark

Items	original	prefetch	DVFS(686MHz), PD=24	686MHz, PD=16	700MHz, PD=16
Power (W)	4.7408	9.2768	4.7285	4.5218	4.7315
Time (ms)	13.9911	4.0332	5.3377	5.0708	4.9798

In Table 1, the fourth column shows simple DVFS results. According to the analysis of prefetch distance, we adjust *PD* (prefetch distance) to 16 and get the fifth column data. That shows the prefetch distance adjustment obtains performance boost and power reduction. Recall that our objective is to limit the power dissipation under the original level (for RB, that is 4.7408W), so that this part of power savings can be completely transferred to the further performance boost through scaling clock frequency a little up as the last column shows. Although power dissipation is a little larger than 4.7285W, but still lower than the demand level (4.7408W). And performance is better. Our approach achieves 6.7% better performance than simple DVFS.

4 Experimental Methodology and Results

We use software prefetching to improve application performance. All the benchmarks are instrumented with our power-aware software prefetching. The performance and power of these optimized codes are then meansured on a detailed architectural simulator.

4.1 Experimental Methodology

As shown in Figure 1, our approach is based on the DVFS in step 1. This optimal frequency setting is done by simulation-based program profiling. First we estimate a suitable frequency level to profile performance result and later scale up or down frequency so as to guarantee no power increase. We use SimpleScalar sim-outorder, a detailed simulator supporting out-of-order issue and execution [3], and Wattch, an architectural level power analysis tool [4], to track different units accessed per cycle, record the power of each unit and the total power consumed for a given application. Some necessary modifications are made for our simulation.

SimpleScalar tool set [3] models a 1GHz 4-way issue dynamic-scheduled processor. The simulator models all aspects of the processor including the instruction fetch unit, the branch predictor, register renaming, the functional unit pipelines, the reorder buffer, and write buffers. It also models the memory system in detail. We assume a split 8-Kbyte direct-mapped L1 cache with 32-byte cache blocks, and a unified 256-Kbyte 4-way set-associative L2 cache with 64-byte cache blocks. SimpleScalar simulator is modified to accurately model bus contention across the L2-memory bus. For 1GHz clock frequency, L2-memory latency is 160 cycles and the L2-memory bus width is 8 bytes/cycle. That is, memory access time overhead is 160ns. To fix memory access time overhead as 160ns even after DVFS, the number of memory access cycles is adjusted in terms of DVFS. In addition, to enable software prefetching, a perfetch instruction has been added to the ISA of the processor model [7].

Wattch [4] power model is based on 0.1 μ m (instead of default 0.35 μ m) process technology parameter, which is closer to the current embedded systems process technology. Aggressive, non-ideal clock gating is used. In this kind of clock gating, power of active units is scaled linearly with the port or unit usage, and the unused units consume 10% of their maximum power rather than zero. We also add the write buffers energy model to Wattch. We use 1GHz as the baseline processor frequency. Wattch has been modified to support DVFS by inserting one clause "setfreq(900)" in the original C program. This clause scales the clock frequency to 900MHz. This frequency scaling instruction is implemented using "inline asm". With this directive clause, the later program runs under this new voltage/frequency level until meeting another new frequency scaling instruction.

During the voltage switching from V_1 to V_2, there are time and energy overhead. We use the formula (1) and formula (2) to calculate them [2].

$$t_{switch}(V_1, V_2) = \frac{2c}{I_{MAX}} \cdot |V_1 - V_2| \quad (1)$$

$$E_{switch}(V_1, V_2) = (1-u) \cdot c \cdot |V_1^2 - V_2^2| \quad (2)$$

where c is the voltage regulator capacitance and u is the energy-efficiency of the voltage regulator. I_{MAX} is the maximum allowed current. Here we use c=10 μf , I_{MAX}=1A, u=90%.

To drive our simulations, our experimental evaluation employs six benchmarks, representing two classes of data-intensive applications. Table 2 lists the benchmarks along with their problem sizes and memory access patterns. The first three applications in Table 2 perform affine array accesses. MM (or MATMULT) represents the multiply of two matrices. RB performs a 3D red-black successive-over-relaxation, and JACOBI performs a 3D Jacobi relaxation. Both JACOBI and RB are frequently found in multigrid PDE solvers, such as MGRID from the SPEC/NAS benchmark suite. The next three applications perform indexed array accesses. IRREG is an iterative PDE solver for an irregular mesh, MOLDYN is abstracted from the non-bonded force calculation in CHARMM, a key molecular dynamics application used at NIH to model macro-molecular systems, and NBF (Non Bonded Force kernel), is a molecular dynamics simulation. NBF is taken from the GROMOS benchmark [11].

Table 2. Summary of benchmark applications

Application	Problem Size	Access Pattern
RB	200*200*8 grid	Affine array
JACOBI	200*200*8 grid	Affine array
MM	200*200 matrics	Affine array
IRREG	141K node mesh	Indexed array
MOLDYN	128K molecules	Indexed array
NBF	141K nodes	Indexed array

4.2 Experimental Results

For each application, we apply software prefetching by hand. We follow the approach described in Section 3, then measure the performance and power of the optimized codes on our detailed architectural simulator. Here, all the programs are built with –O2 option.

Table 3 reports the computed prefetch distances for all the benchmarks. Here we fix memory access latency as $0.16\ \mu s$ (160 cycle when 1GHz) and memory bandwidth is 8GBytes/sec. The second line "Original" shows the prefetch distances without DVFS;

Table 3. Prefetch distances for loops in all benchmarks versus different approaches

Approaches	RB	JACOBI	MM	IRREG	MOLDYN	NBF
Original	24	16, 68	44	12, 40, 40, 80	2, 2, 3	4
Our approach	16	12, 52	32	10, 38, 30, 68	2, 2, 3	3

the third line "Our approach" gives the new prefetch distances after using our power-aware prefetching approach.

Table 4 lists the detailed power and performance results for all the benchmarks. The fourth column shows the significant power increases due to prefetching. In average, power dissipation increases by 75.43% due to prefetching! DVFS can achieve significant power reduction shown in the fifth column. Applied with our power-aware prefetching, the performance is better than simple DVFS as the last column shows.

Table 4. Power and performance comparisons versus different approaches

Benchmark	Items	original	prefetch	DVFS	Power-aware Prefetching
RB	Power (W)	4.7408	9.2768	4.7285 (686MHz, PD=24)	4.7315 (700MHz, PD=16)
	Time (ms)	13.9911	4.0332	5.3377	4.9798
JACOBI	Power (W)	5.0432	8.6812	5.0416 (720MHz,PD=16,PD1=68)	5.0365 (735MHz, PD=12,PD1=52)
	Time (ms)	13.4944	4.6895	5.1922	4.9326
MM	Power (W)	4.6012	9.8058	4.5920 (664MHz, PD=44)	4.6003 (680MHz, PD=32)
	Time (ms)	178.7044	40.0004	56.1918	54.6336
IRREG	Power (W)	4.5936	8.0231	4.5889 (722MHz, PD=12,PD1=40,PD2=40,PD3=80)	4.5930 (735MHz, PD=10,PD1=38,PD2=30,PD3=68)
	Time (ms)	114.5986	38.6705	48.2146	46.2860
MOLDYN	Power (W)	4.5380	7.5423	4.5287 (750MHz, PD=2,PD1=2,PD2=3)	4.5287 (750MHz, PD=2,PD1=2,PD2=3)
	Time (ms)	465.9938	148.4808	178.4281	178.4281
NBF	Power (W)	4.4246	5.7879	4.4207 (848MHz, PD=4)	4.4200 (861MHz, PD=3)
	Time (ms)	126.8474	64.0246	71.2434	69.8190

DVFS effectively reduce nearly half of power dissipation from the above results. And our power-aware prefetching can obtain the average 4.09% performance improvement compared with simple DVFS except for MOLDYN. MOLDYN can not obtain the gain from re-adjusting prefetch distance is that because three prefetch distances in MOLDYN benchmark is too small.

In the future work, we also can do the tradeoffs between performance and power from the following three aspects:

(1) Considering reducing the number of prefetch instructions to reduce part of power consumption.

(2) Allow power increase no more than an upper, such as allowing 5% power increase. This can increase the performance boost opportunities while power increase is acceptable.

(3) Build an accurate analytical model to do the tradeoff between power and performance.

5 Related Works

In the previous work, we presented an energy-constrained prefetching optimization approach [12]. This approach can limit the energy consumption under a given energy budget through reducing main memory or CPU stalls. We evaluated this approach using an analytical model. We also extent this energy-constrained prefetching optimization to meet two performance objectives [13]. In this article, our optimization objective is to obtain the performance boost as much as possible without any power increase. The main difference of this work and the previous works is that the previous works are mainly based on analysis model, and consider the whole energy consumption of both CPU and main memory. While this current work tries to find the suitable voltage value through simulation experiments and only refers to CPU power dissipation. During the voltage/frequency scaling, we also consider the impact of voltage/frequency scaling on prefetch distance.

Deepak et al. transferred the performance gain from software prefetching to energy reduction through combining prefetching with a dynamic voltage/frequency scaling technique [8]. Experiments approved that their dynamic DVFS algorithm achieves a 38% energy saving without any performance loss. There are two major differences between their work and ours. (1) One difference is that optimization objective is different. Deepak's objective is to reduce energy consumption without performance loss. But many high-performance computing systems and portable systems, "fast enough" is still end user's desire. We cannot sacrifice the whole optimization performance gain to obtain energy reduction. So our objective is to improve the performance as much as possible without power increase; (2) The other difference is that the DVFS algorithm is different. Deepak's online DVFS algorithm periodically conducts real time profiling to estimate the performance gain by prefetching, then this DVFS algorithm can guide the selection of voltage to simultaneously achieve low power and performance guarantee. While our approach improves the performance through readjusting prefetch distance after DVFS.

6 Conclusions

In this paper, we study a power-aware software prefetching approach. We first demonstrate software prefetching provides a significant performance boost with the higher power on several memory-intensive benchmarks. However, when we combine prefetching with DVFS technique, performance gain can be achieved with no power increase. Our approach is different from simple DVFS, which improves the performance through adjusting prefetch distance after DVFS. A modified SimpleScalar/Wattch is used to evaluate our power-aware software prefetching. Experimental results show our optimization can obtain the better performance than the simple DVFS with the same power dissipation.

Acknowledgements

The authors are grateful to Dr. Abdel-Hameed Badawy (at Electrical and Computer Engineering Dept., University of Maryland, College Park, USA) for providing much assistance on this paper, including simulator and most of the benchmarks.

References

[1] Vivek Tiwari, Sharad Malik, and Andrew Wolfe. Compilation Techniques for Low Energy: An Overview. In *the Proceedings of the 1994 Symposium on Low-Power Electronics*, San Diego, CA, October 1994.

[2] T. Burd and R. Brodersen. Design issues for dynamic voltage scaling. In the *Proceedings of International Symposium on Low Power Electronics and Design (ISLPED-00)*, June 2000.

[3] Doug Burger, and Todd M. Austin. The SimpleScalar Tool Set, Version 2.0.

[4] David Brooks, Vivek Tiwari and Margaret Martonosi. Wattch: A Framework for Architectural-Level Power Analysis and Optimizations. In the *Proceedings of the 27th International Symposium on Computer Architecture (ISCA 00)*, pages 83-94, June 2000.

[5] D. Callahan, K. Kennedy, and A. Porterfield. Software Prefetching. In the Proceedings of the 4th International Conference on Architectural Support for Programming Languages and Operating Systems, Santa Clara, CA, April 1991.

[6] Todd C. Mowry. Tolerating Latency through Software-Controlled Data Prefetching. Doctor dissertation. Stanford University, March 1994.

[7] Abdel-Hameed Badawy, Aneesh Aggarwal, Donald Yeung, and Chau-Wen Tseng. The Efficacy of Software Prefetching and Locality Optimizations on Future Memory Systems. Journal of Instruction-Level Parallelism. Vol 6, 2004.

[8] Deepak N. Agarwal, Sumitkumar N. Pamnani, Gang Qu, and Donald Yeung. Transferring Performance Gain from Software Prefetching to Energy Reduction. In *Proceedings of the 2004 International Symposium on Circuits and Systems (ISCAS2004).* Vancouver, Canada. May 2004.

[9] Fen Xie, Margaret Martonosi and Sharad Malik. Intraprogram Dynamic Voltage Scaling: Bounding Opportunities with Analytic Modeling. ACM Transactions on Architecture and Code Optimization. Vol.1, No.3, September 2004. pages 323-367.

[10] T. Chen and J. Baer. Effective Hardware-Based Data Prefetching for High-Performance Processors. Transactions on Computers, Vol.44, No. 5, pages 609-623, May 1995.

[11] W. F. van Gunsteren and H. J. C. Berendsen. GROMOS: GROningen MOlecular Simulation software. tech. rep., Laboratory of Physical Chemistry, University of Groningen, Netherlands, 1988.

[12] Juan Chen, Yong Dong, Huizhan Yi and Xuejun Yang. Energy-Constrained Prefetching Optimization in Embedded Applications. In *Proceedings of International Conference of Embedded and Ubiquitous Computing (EUC 2005).* Nagasaki, Japan, December 2005.

[13] Juan Chen, Huizhan Yi, Yong Dong and Xuejun Yang. Study on Energy-Constrained Software Prefetching Optimization. In *Journal of Software*, ISSN 1000-9825, Vol. 17, No. 7, July 2006, p.1650-1660.

[14] Sakurai T. and Newton A. Alpha-power model, and its application to CMOS inverter delay and other formulas. IEEE Journal Solid-State Circ. Vol. 25, 1990. p.584-594.

Fast Initialization and Memory Management Techniques for Log-Based Flash Memory File Systems

Junkil Ryu and Chanik Park

Department of Computer Science and Engineering
Pohang University of Science and Technology (POSTECH), Republic of Korea
{lancer,cipark}@postech.ac.kr

Abstract. Flash memory's adoption in the mobile devices is increasing for various multimedia services such as audios, videos, and games. The traditional research issues such as out-place update, garbage collection, and wear-leveling are important, the fast initialization and response time issues of flash memory file system are becoming much more important than ever because flash memory capacity is rapidly increasing. In this paper, we propose a fast initialization technique and an efficient memory management technique for fast response time in log-based flash memory file systems. Our prototype is implemented based on a well-known log-based flash memory file system YAFFS2 and the performance tests were conducted by comparing our prototype with YAFFS2. The experimental results show that the proposed initialization technique reduced the initialization time of the log-based flash memory file system regardless of unmounting the file system properly. Moreover our prototype outperforms YAFFS2 in the read I/O operations and the forward/backward seek I/O operations by way of our proposed memory management technique. This technique is also able to be used to control the memory size required for address mapping in flash memory file systems.

Keywords: flash memory, log-based file system, file system initialization, high performance, efficient memory management.

1 Introduction

Flash memory has been widely adopted as a storage media in the mobile devices because it is non-volitle, shock-resident, and power-economic. However the data page in the flash memory cannot be re-used without a block erase operation and the flash memory's page size is not equal to its block size. Note that I/O operations are performed on a page in the flash memory. Thus, additional functions must be implemented to store files in the flash memory. There are two major approaches to provide the file service in flash memory. One is the native file system approach ([1], [2]) which is aware of the characteristics of the flash memory, that the native file system applies to provide efficient file system service. The other is the block-device emulation approach ([3], [4]) and it creates generic block device environments (translation layer) for the existing file systems to use the flash

Y.-H. Lee et al. (Eds.): ICESS 2007, LNCS 4523, pp. 219–228, 2007.

memory. The two approaches' goal is to have applications accessing data on the flash memory transparently using standard file system APIs. In its early stages, most of the research topics on the flash memory focused on harnessing the flash memory such as out-place update, garbage collection, and wear-leveling. But the performance, reliability, and low power comsumption have become much interested research topics on the flash memory in recent years.

In this paper, the initialization time, performance, and efficient memory management for the flash memory file systems will be handled. When a log-based flash memory file system is mounted, any data areas and all spare areas of the used pages in the flash memory must be scanned to reconstruct its house-keeping data structures (meta-data and data address mapping) in the system memory. This procedure is time consuming while maintaining the stored files' house-keeping data (meta data and data address mapping) in the system memory is memory consuming and impractical because the size of the flash memory is becoming larger and the system memory size in the mobile device does not follow the trend of the flash memory size. [Fig. 1]'s experiment shows that the initialization time of the log-based flash memory file system (YAFFS2) increases linearly as the data stored in the flash memory is increased. [Fig. 2]'s experiment shows that the system memory used for data address mapping and meta-data in YAFFS2 increases as the data stored in the flash memory increases. The experimental setup is as follows: Processor is Intel Burlverde PXA270 (520Mhz), system memory is SAMSUNG SDRAM 64MB, and flash Memory is SAMSUNG 1GB NAND flash memory. Hence, the issues of the initialization time and memory management for the flash memory are very important.

The growth of quality and quantity in the multimedia data has cause the mobile device to store many multimedia data and process the multimedia data encoded in high quality. The existing log-based flash memory file system (ex, YAFFS2) has been focusing on applying the physical characteristics of the flash memory to

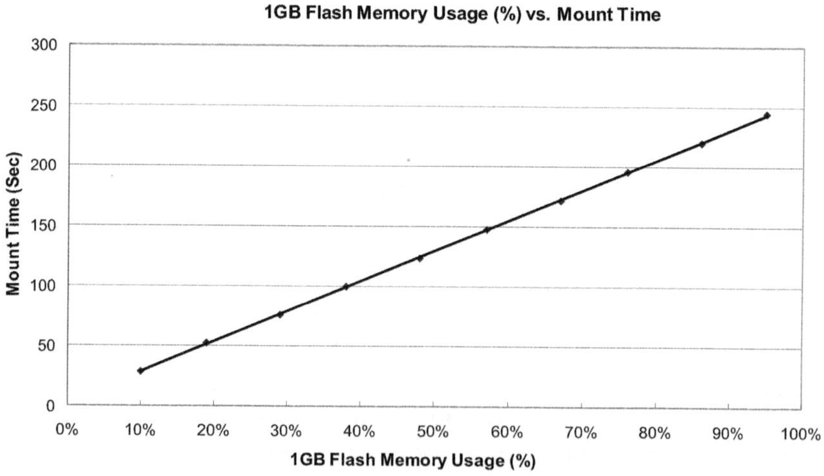

Fig. 1. YAFFS2 Mount Time

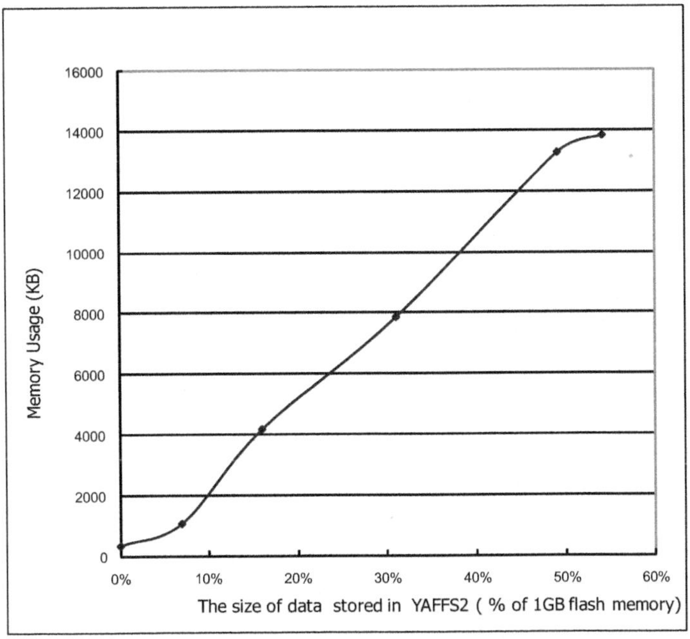

Fig. 2. System Memory used for YAFFS2

provide the file system service. Currently, the high performance flash memory file system is needed to process many high quality and quantity multimedia files.

In this paper, a method for fast initialization, high performance and memory management is proposed for flash memory log-based file systems. For the fast initialization, we allocated the startup area seperately in the flash memory, which is managed by SyncManager. For high performance, a page in the flash memory is addressed directly. For the memory management, the B-Tree technique is used instead of Tnode Tree in YAFFS2 and the data addressing mapping can be unloaded in the system memory when it is unused.

The remainder of this paper is organized as follows: Section 2 introduces the related work and motivations. Section 3 introduces the proposed methods and section 4 provices the performance evaluation of the proposed method over YAFFS2. Finally, section 5 draws conclusion.

2 Related Work

There are two approaches in the file system implementation to provide data accessing transparently in the flash memory. One is the native flash memory file system and the other is the block device emulation. The existing disk file systems can be used with these block device emulations. This paper discusses the flash memory file system, which manages raw flash memory directly (ex, JAFFS2 and YAFFS/YAFFS2). These flash memory file systems are closely related to log-structured file system ([7]) because a page in the flash memory cannot be done in-place updates. When updating the data in a page, the data is moved from a page to another page. Unlike disks, we cannot know where the data is. Hence, the data-stored pages must be tracked and managed in the flash memory file system. In order to resolve this problem, the mapping concept of logical address space and physical addresss space is adopted, where the logical address space is indexed by logical page address (chunkId in YAFFS2) and the physical address space is indexed by physical page address in the flash memory. This mapping can be either one-to-one mapping or one-to-many mapping. The former is used under the block device emulation and the latter is used mainly under the native flash memory file system. However, the YAFFS2 flash memory file system uses one-to-one mapping. A page in the flash memory contains a user data area and a spare area, where the user data area is for the storage of user data in a logical page and the spare area is for ECC, the corresponding logical page address, and other house-keeping data. When flash memory systems (flash memory file systems or block device emulations) are mounted, these mappings are constructed in the system memory to provide efficient file service. If these mappings are not constructed in the system memory when mounting the flash memory file system, then all pages in the flash memory must be scanned whenever accessing data. The log scanning proceduere conducted by a native file system will become a serious issue in the near future because flash memory's size is becoming larger. If the flash memory's size is becoming larger (2GB, 3GB,...), then the existing flash memory file systems (YAFFS2 and JFFS2) will be impractical. To reduce the initialization time of the log-based flash memory file systems, [5]'s and [6]'s method were proposed. [5]'s method is to commit the snapshot of the data structure for the flash memory when the file system is unmounted. This method does not operate well when the file system is not unmounted properly. The old snapshots are not useful in the reconstruction of the file system image in the system memory for the flash memory management and the updated areas are not addressed easily. Snapshotting a file system image when unmounting, elongates the shutdown time regardless of unmounting improperly. To resolve [5]'s problems, [6]'s method was proposed. [6]'s method records the changes of the file system image in the runtime. But when the system crashes, the changed portions in the flash memory cannot be addressed easily because their method records READ/WRITE I/O operations to track the change of the file system image. In this paper, we propose our method to reduce the log-based flash memory file system's initialization time and recovery time and to provide efficient file system service (high performance and small system memory usage) for the multimedia files.

3 The Proposed Method for Log-Based Flash Memory File Systems

To reduce the log-based flash memory file system initialization time and the recovery time, our proposed method introduces the startup area. The startup area is allocated separately from the data area (YAFFS2) and it is managed by SyncManager. The startup area's size must be determined according to usage of the embedded systems using this method. the startup area's size is determined in proportion to the number (not capacity) of the files stored in Flash memory. For example, the startup area need small size relatively for the embedded systems using large-size files (mp3, movies). [Fig. 3] shows the overview of our proposed method. We implemented the prototype based on YAFFS2 but our proposed method can be applied in other log-based flash memory file systems. To track the changes of the file system image, [6] records the changes of I/O operations in a log-segment but the number of log-segments increase as the I/O operations increase. It increases the crash recovery time. [6]'s method focused on I/O operations but our propsed method focuses on the changed files. To track the change of the file system image, we introduced the filter function in the YAFFS2 to confirm which file is changed. The filter functions are inserted in YAFFS2's low-level I/O functions. The changed file is recorded by SyncManager. A log page in the startup area is made for a file, which contains the data address mapping for the corressponding file. When a file is updated, the corresponding log page in the startup area is marked as DIRTY in the tag and the SynManager holds the pointer of the file object. During idle time, the SyncManager writes the changed files' data address mappings into the re-allocated log pages. If the system crash occurs in the state where the startup area is not syncronized with the YAFFS2 data-area, then the updated portions in the flash memory will be tracked by finding the DIRTY-marked log pages in the startup area, allowing fast crash recovery. The startup area is fixed in flash memory. To prevent the startup area from aging quickly, SyncManager reduces I/Os onto the startup area by lazy-updating the changes of a file when the file has been unused for the expected time. When SyncManager does garbage-collection in the startup area and the large portion of the blocks in the startup area is used, the cold blocks are selected as the garbage-collection's victims.

For high performance, our proposed method uses a different page addressing technique from that of YAFFS2. Each Tnode's entry in the YAFFS2 contains a group address, which is not a page address. In YAFFS2, the wanted page is

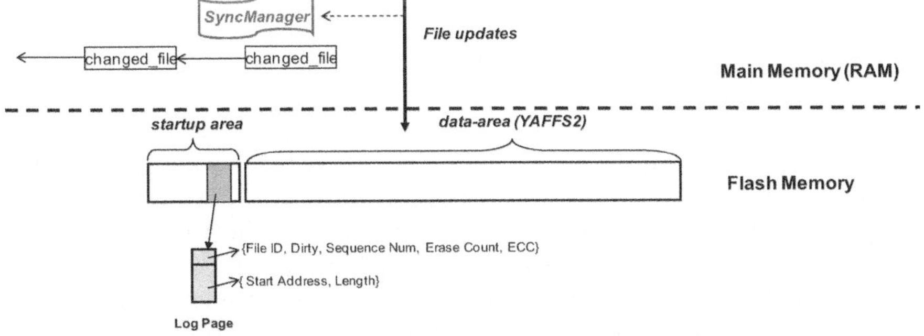

Fig. 3. Overview of the proposed method

found by searching pages in the group containg the wanted page sequentially. To remove this overhead, our proposed method does not use the group address mapping but instead uses the direct page address mapping. However, this method consumes more system memory for directly addressing a physical page. Our proposed method uses the B-Tree technique for the data address mapping instead of YAFFS2's Tnode Tree, which allocates a Tnode with 16 entries for using a page but a node in our B-Tree has a entry and it can represent many pages if the pages is stored continuously in the flash memory. A node in our B-Tree represents a logical address, a physical address, and the length of the continuous pages in the flash memory. A node in our B-Tree uses the more system memory than the YAFFS2's Tnode. But the B-Tree node represents the more information than the YAFFS2's Tnode and our B-Tree node is more effective in the multimedia data, which mainly is stored continuously in the flash memory. To control the usage of the system memory, our proposed method unloads the data address mappings of the unused files from the system memory. When a file is unused for 5 minutes or the number of the used files exceed the guideline, the unused and old loaded files are unloaded. If a file, which does not has its data mapping in the system memory, is requested by the file system, then our proposed system loads the corresponding file's data address mapping from the startup area in the flash memory, whose address is contained in the file object. [Fig. 4] shows our proposed data mapping in the system memory.

4 Performance Evaluation

The experiments were conducted with YAFFS2 and our prototype, which was implemented based on YAFFS2. Our experimental setup is shown in [Fig. 5].

YAFFS2 runs with the "Erasure Check mode", which confirms whether each block in the flash memory has been erased on the mount time or not. Our prototype runs with the "Erasure Check mode" as well. If we do not use the "Erasure Check mode", then our proposed method's initializaton time will be shorter. [Fig. 6] and [Fig. 7] show the flash memory file system initialization time of our prototype and YAFFS2, using small-sized files (average size: 359.5 KB). [Fig. 6] and [Fig. 7] show that our prototype's initialization time is shorter than that of YAFFS2, since the startup area and eachblock's first page are scanned in our proposed method. [Fig. 8] and [Fig. 9] show the flash memory file system initialization time of our prototype and YAFFS2, using mp3 files, whose average file size is 5.9 MB. In [Fig. 8] and [Fig. 9], our prototype's initialization time is under 9 seconds but YAFFS2's initialization time increases linearly while the size of the data stored in the flash memory increases. It is because YAFFS2 scans the used pages and each block's first page. In the mobile device, our proposed method is efficient and practical because multimedia data mainly are stored, their size is large, and the number of the stored multimedia data is limited. Our proposed method records the changed files to track the changes of the file system image and writes the changed files' mappings into the startup area periodically.

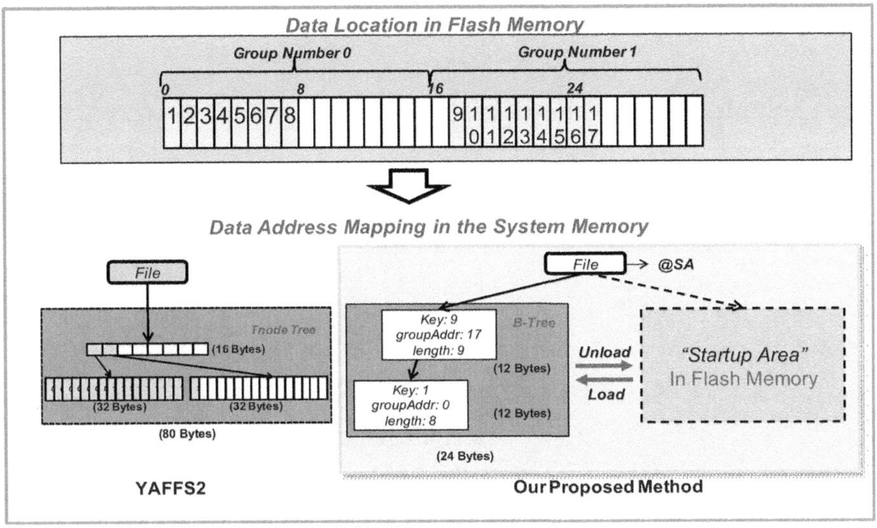

Fig. 4. Our Memory Management

Item	Description
Processor	Intel Bulverde PXA270 (520Mhz)
SDRAM/Flash	Samsung SDRAM 64MB/Intel strata flash 32MB
Ethernet	CS8900A 10 Base T
USB	USB Host 1.1 & Slave 1.1
NAND6EA	1GB NAND Flash Memory x 6

Fig. 5. Experimental Setup

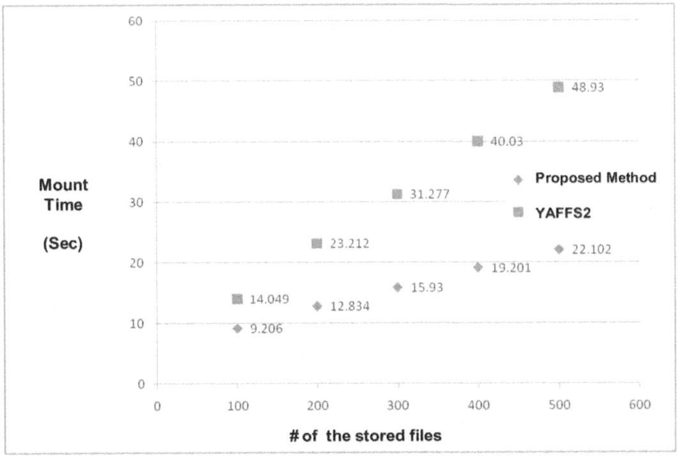

Fig. 6. Mount Time vs. Number of the stored files (average size of the stored files: 359.5KB)

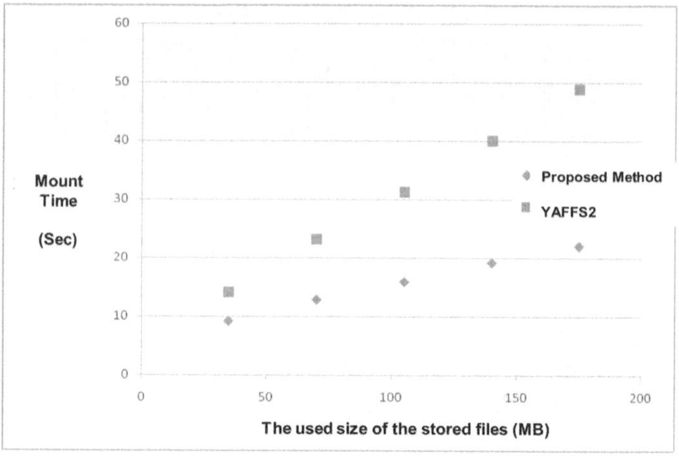

Fig. 7. Mount Time vs. The used size of the stored files (average size of the stored files: 359.5KB)

Fig. 8. Mount Time vs. Number of the stored files (average size of the stored files: 5.9 MB)

Therefore crash recovery time is very short because the updated portions in the flash memory can be addressed exactly.

To compare the performance of YAFFS2 and our prototype, we used iozone benchmark tool. [Fig. 10] showes that our proposed method outperforms YAFFS2, since our method uses the direct page mapping. When playing a movie encoded in MPEG4, 640x480, 24bits Per Pixel, 20fps by using a mplayer without a frame drop, our prototype is average 120.03 seconds faster than YAFFS2 as well. To measure the random seek performance in the large-sized multimedia

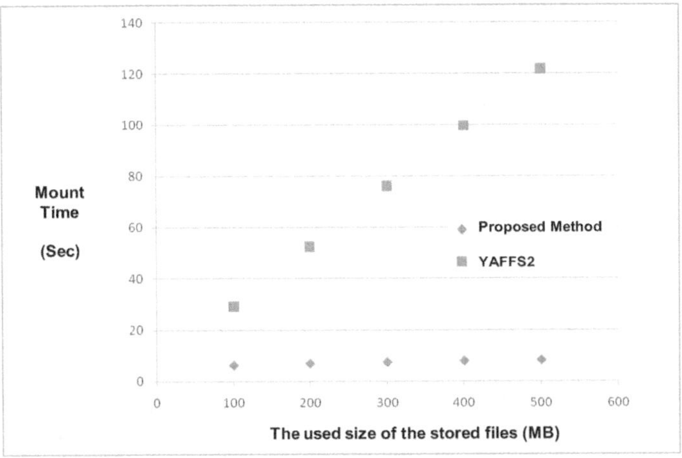

Fig. 9. Mount Time vs. The used size of the stored files (average size of the stored files: 5.9 MB)

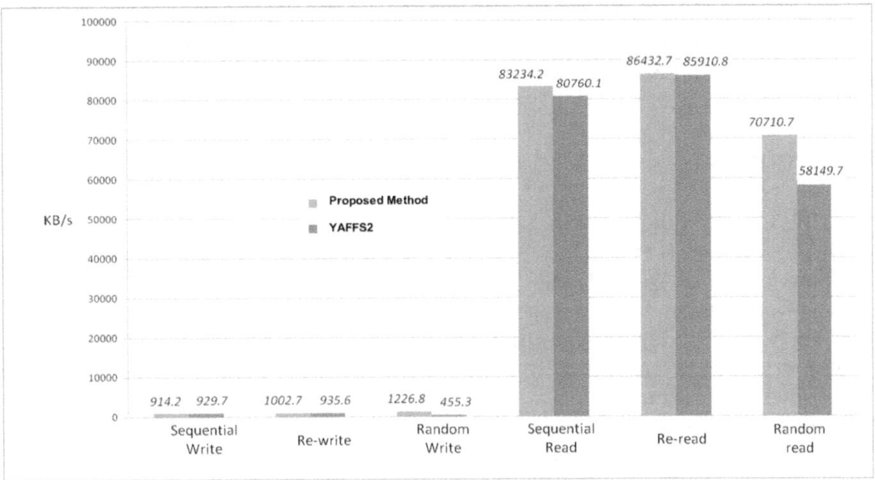

Fig. 10. Performance Test(iozone: transfer size - 4KB)

file, our test used a 321MB sized multimedia file and read 1 byte data at the the relative positions (0%, 90%, 20%, 70%, 40%, 50%, 60%, 30%, 80%, 10%, 100%) from the start of the file. When completing this test, YAFFS2 takes 0.211 seconds while our propopsed method takes 0.112 seconds when the data address mapping is unloaded and 0.012 seconds when the data address mapping is loaded previously. When the data address mapping is unloaded, the overhead is introduced to load the data address mapping.

5 Conclusion

We proposed a method for fast initialization and memory management for the log-based flash memory file systems. This method introduces the start up area allocated separately from the existing file system data area. The startup area is managed by SyncManager and contains log-pages. A log page has the corresponding file in the existing file system (YAFFS2) and the file's mapping data in the flash memory. When a system crash occurs, the unsyncronized files are detected easily by confirming the starup area. So the file system initialization and crash recovery are fast. The mapping address in a log page is a physical page address in the flash memory, hence the proposed method outperforms YAFFS2, which has group address mapping. Our proposed method may not use the system memory to maintain the files' address mappings because when it is needed, it can be loaded from the startup area.

Acknowledgment

This research was supported by the MIC(Ministry of Information and Communication), Korea, under the ITRC(Information Technology Research Center) support program supervised by the IITA(Institute of Information Technology Assessment)(IITA-2006-C1090-0603-0045).

References

1. Aleph One Company, " Yet Another Flash File System".
2. D. Woodhouse, Redhat, Inc., "JFFS: The Journalling Flash File System".
3. Compact Flash Association, " CompactFlash 1.4 Specification," 1998
4. Intel Corporation, "Understanding the Flash Translation Layer (FTL) Specification".
5. Keun Soo Yim, Jihong Kim, and Kern Koh, "A Fast Start-Up Technique for Flash Memory Based Computing Systems," Proceedings of the 2005 ACM Symposium on Applied Computing
6. Chin-Hsien Wu, Tei-Wei Kuo, and Li-Pin Chang, " Efficient Initialization and Crash Recovery for Log-based File Systems over Flash Memory," Proceedings of the 2005 ACM Symposium on Applied Computing
7. M. Rosenblum, and J.K. Ousterhout, " The Design and Implementation of a Log-Structured File System," ACM Transactions on Computer Systems 10(1) (1992)

An Efficient Implementation Method of Arbiter for the ML-AHB Busmatrix

Soo Yun Hwang[1], Hyeong Jun Park[1], and Kyoung Son Jhang[2]

[1] Mobile Telecommunication Research Division, ETRI, Taejon, Korea
{syhwang, parkhj}@etri.re.kr
[2] Department of Computer Engineering, Chungnam National University, Taejon, Korea
sun@cnu.ac.kr

Abstract. The multi-layer AHB busmatrix (ML-AHB busmatrix) proposed by ARM is a highly efficient on chip bus that allows parallel access paths between multiple masters and slaves in a system. In this paper, we present one way to improve the arbiter implementation of the ML-AHB busmatrix. We employ the masking mechanism which does not impose any restrictions on arbitration scheme. Therefore, the proposed scheme is applied to the implementation of busmatrixes to support the transaction based arbitrations as well as the transfer based arbitrations. In addition, we could not only enhance the throughput of bus system but also reduce the total area, clock period and power consumption. Experimental results show that the throughput of our busmatrix based on the transfer based fixed priority (round robin) arbitration scheme is increased by 41% (18%) compared with that of the equivalent busmatrix of ARM. Moreover, we could reduce the total area, clock period and power consumption by 22%, 28% and 19% (12%, 15% and 13%) respectively, compared with the busmatrix employing the transfer based fixed priority (round robin) arbitration scheme of ARM.

1 Introduction

Today's deep submicron fabrication technologies enable design engineers to place billions of transistors on a single chip. These high-integrated circuit technologies make it possible for designers to integrate a number of function blocks such as processors, memories, interfaces and custom logic on a single chip. As the number of intellectual property (IP) blocks increases, the communication among function blocks becomes the new system performance bottleneck [1, 2, 3]. The simplest way of connecting the multiple function blocks on a single chip is to employ the on chip bus.

The on chip buses have been the preferred interconnection in most of the processor-based systems in the past thirty years. They have also been the basic building blocks of almost all implemented system on a chip (SoC). The traditional single bus is a good choice for many systems when the number of connected components is small. However, in the future SoCs, the complexity of a single component is not likely to significantly increase since only relatively simple components can be scaled with technology [4, 5]. Moreover the existing buses may not be the solution to the bandwidth problems because only one pair of master and slave blocks can send and receive the data at a

Y.-H. Lee et al. (Eds.): ICESS 2007, LNCS 4523, pp. 229–240, 2007.

particular time. There are several types of high performance on chip bus proposals like ML-AHB busmatrix from ARM [6, 7], PLB crossbar switch from IBM [8], CONMAX from Silicore [9], Silicon Backplane from Sonics Inc. [10] and so on to solve the bandwidth problems. In particular, the ML-AHB busmatrix of ARM has been widely used in many SoC designs. The reasons are that the AMBA bus has a good architecture for applying embedded systems with low power [11] and the simplicity of AMBA bus is one of the motives that attract a number of IP designers [12].

The ML-AHB busmatrix is an interconnection scheme based on the AMBA AHB protocol, which enables parallel access paths between multiple masters and slaves in a system. This is achieved by using a more complex interconnection matrix called busmatrix and gives the benefit of increased overall bus bandwidth, and more flexible system structure [7]. Especially, the ML-AHB busmatrix employs the slave-side arbitration. The slave-side arbitration is different from the master-side arbitration based on the request and grant signals. The slave-side arbitration uses the response signal of the slave for arbitration, i.e. the master just starts a transaction and waits for the slave response to proceed to the next transfer. Thus, the unit of arbitration can be a transaction or a transfer.

A design method to improve the ML-AHB busmatrix structure of ARM has been proposed [13]. With the removal of the input stage and some restrictions on the arbitration scheme, it is possible to decrease the total area, clock period and power consumption of busmatrix of ARM [13]. However though the unit of arbitration can be a transaction or a transfer in the ML-AHB busmatrix based on the slave-side arbitration, the approach cannot implement the transfer based arbitration scheme because the input stages are removed in the approach [13]. In addition, the transaction based arbitration scheme of the approach requires that the granted master has to insert one or more IDLE transfer after each transaction to avoid starvation of other masters. In this paper, we propose one way to ameliorate the arbiter implementation of busmatrix of ARM. Our approach does not take away the input stages and does not impose any restrictions on arbitration scheme. Therefore, the proposed scheme is applied to the implementation of busmatrixes to support the transaction based arbitrations as well as the transfer based arbitrations. Moreover, we could not only increase the throughput of bus system but also decrease the total area, clock period and power consumption with masking mechanism employed to implement arbiter. In the next section, we introduce the arbitration schemes of the ML-AHB busmatrix of ARM. Section 3 describes an implementation method of our arbiters based on masking mechanism. We present the experimental results in section 4 and the summary and a note on future works in section 5.

2 The Arbitration Schemes of the ML-AHB Busmatrix of ARM

The ML-AHB busmatrix employs the slave-side arbitration scheme. In the slave-side arbitration, the arbiters are located in front of each slave port and the master just starts a transaction and waits for the slave response to progress to the next transfer. Therefore, the unit of arbitration can be a transaction or a transfer; whereas, the transfer based arbitration is impossible in the traditional shared on chip buses since they use the master-side arbitration based on the request and grant signals.

There are two types of arbitration schemes in the ML-AHB busmatrix of ARM: transfer based fixed priority and round robin arbitration schemes (abbreviated FT and RT). Fig. 1 shows an example timing diagram of the FT and RT arbitration schemes.

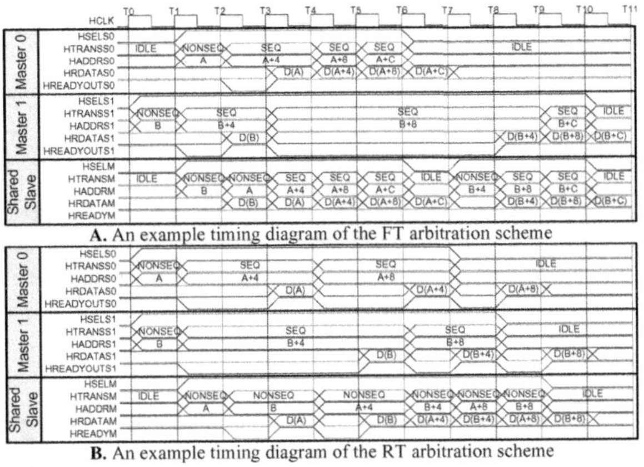

Fig. 1. An example timing diagram of the FT and RT arbitration schemes

In Fig. 1.A, master1 starts a transaction at T1 and master0 requests a transaction at T2. At this point in time, master0 preempts the right to use the bus at T3 when master1 completes only one transfer since the priority of master0 is higher than that of master1. Master1 has to wait until master0 completes a transaction. This is controlled by sending a delay response to master1. Master1 can restart the remained three transfers from T8. In Fig. 1.B, master0 and master1 simultaneously start a transaction at T1 and the arbiter multiplexes the data transfer based on single transfer in round robin fashion. The shared slave inserts a wait state on the first transfer from each port (at T3 and T5), but all subsequent transfers are zero wait state. In a word, the FT (RT) arbiter multiplexes the data transfer based on single transfer at every clock cycle as a fixed priority (round robin) manner. Fig. 2 shows the arbiter logic of the busmatrix of ARM. All the Request signals are combined within the arbitration block to work out which master must be used for the next transfer.

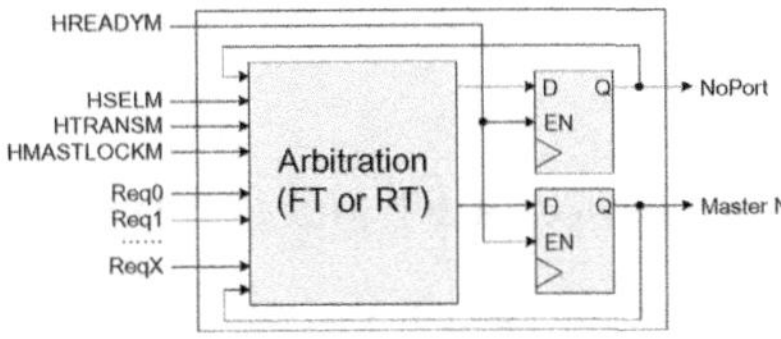

Fig. 2. The arbiter logic of the busmatrix of ARM

The arbitration process of Fig. 2 follows four steps:

1. If HMASTLOCK is asserted, the same master remains selected.
2. If HMASTLOCK is not asserted, all the different requests are examined and the highest priority master is selected. The arbitration algorithm that is used to choose among the masters can be a fixed priority or a round robin.
3. If no master is requesting access and the currently selected master is performing IDLE transfers to the shared slave, i.e., the Sel signal is still asserted, then the same master is selected.
4. If none of the above conditions is met, the NoPort signal is asserted, that is, none of the masters must be selected and the address/control signals to the shared slave must be driven to an inactive state.

In the ML-AHB busmatrix of ARM, the FT algorithm is implemented through a heavy priority encoder and the RT algorithm is realized by the combinations of a de-multiplexer, multiple priority encoders and an OR-ing function. We analyzed the internal parts of the busmatrix of ARM on area overhead. Table 1 shows the analysis results.

Table 1. The analysis results of the internal parts of the busmatrix

	Input Stage	Decoder	Output Stage
Area Overhead	38 %	19 %	43 %

With the analysis of the internal parts of the busmatrix of ARM, we observed that the output stage including arbiter occupies the largest fraction of total area among three components and the arbiter takes most of the area in output stage. We could reduce the total area and clock period of the busmatrix of ARM by the enhanced arbiter implementation elaborated on the next section.

3 Implementation Method of Arbiter Based on Masking Mechanism

We adapt the masking mechanism to improve the arbiter implementation of the ML-AHB busmatrix of ARM. Our approach does not require any restrictions on arbitration scheme. Thus, the proposed approach is applied to the implementation of busmatrixes to support the transaction based arbitrations, i.e. transaction based fixed priority and round robin arbitrations (abbreviated FR and RR), as well as the transfer based arbitrations, i.e. FT and RT arbitrations.

3.1 The Implementation Method of FT and RT Arbitration Schemes

The sequence of our FT arbitration is as follows:

1. If HMASTLOCK is asserted, the same master remains selected.
2. If HMASTLOCK is not asserted and the Sel and Htrans signals of the currently selected master are ‘0’ and IDLE respectively, the next master with the highest

priority is selected by the FT arbitration algorithm. At this point in time, if no master is requesting access, the NoPort signal is asserted.

3. If none of the above applies, the FT arbitration algorithm is performed to select the next master with the highest priority.

Fig. 3 shows the arbitration algorithm of our FT arbiter.

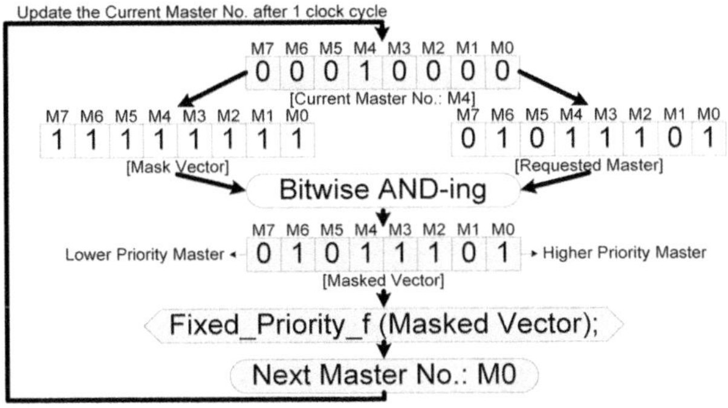

Fig. 3. The arbitration algorithm of our FT arbiter

In the fixed priority policy, each master is assigned a fixed priority, regardless of the currently selected master. Therefore, the masked vector generated by bitwise AND-ing operation between mask vector and requested master vector is inserted to the input parameter of the fixed priority function. And then, the next master with the highest priority is selected through the fixed priority function and the current master is updated after 1 clock cycle. The fixed priority arbitration scheme based on single transfer is performed by the repetition of the arbitration algorithm in Fig. 3. Fig. 4 shows the VHDL code of the fixed priority function at the behavioral level.

```
1: function Fixed_Priority_f (Masked_Vector: std_logic_vector)
2: return integer is
3: variable Next_Master_No : integer;
4: begin
5:     Next_Master_No := 0;
6:     for i in Masked_Vector'left downto 0 loop
7:         if (Masked_Vector (i) = '1') then
8:             Next_Master_No := i;
9:         end if;
10:    end loop;
11:    return Next_Master_No;
12: end;
```

Fig. 4. VHDL code of the fixed priority function

In Fig. 4, a master with the highest priority is selected through the for-statements in line 6 and the priority level of LSB in Masked_Vector is the highest. If we modified the range of the Masked_Vector in line 6 as "0 to Masked_Vector'left", the priority level of MSB is the highest.

The process of our RT arbitration scheme is as follows:

1. If HMASTLOCK is asserted, the same master remains selected.
2. If HMASTLOCK is not asserted and the currently selected master does not exist, a new master with the highest priority is initially selected by the FT arbitration algorithm of Fig. 3. If no master is requesting access, i.e. the currently requested maters do not exist, the NoPort signal is asserted.
3. If none of the above applies, the RT arbitration algorithm is carried out to choose the next master. At the moment, if the requested masters do not exist and Sel signal of the currently selected master is '1', the same master remains selected. Otherwise, the NoPort signal is asserted.

Fig. 5 shows the arbitration algorithm of our RT arbiter that is used in above step 3. Especially, we reuse the fixed priority function of Fig. 4.

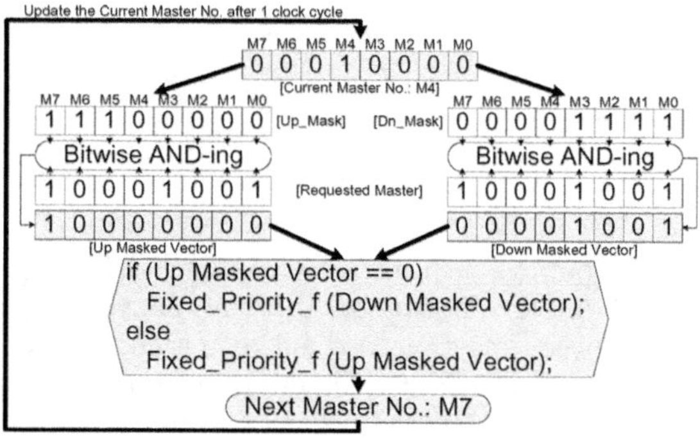

Fig. 5. The arbitration algorithm of our RT arbiter

First of all, we make the up and down mask vectors based on the number of currently selected master as shown in Fig. 5. And then we generate the up (down) masked vector that is created through bitwise AND-ing operation between up (down) mask vector and requested master vector. After the generation of up and down masked vectors, we examine each masked vector if they are zero or not. If the up masked vector is zero (is not zero), the down (up) masked vector is inserted to the input parameter of the fixed priority function. A master for the next transfer is chosen by the fixed priority function and the current master is updated after 1 clock cycle. Through the repetition of aforementioned process, we could establish the single transfer based round robin arbitration scheme.

3.2 The Implementation Method of FR and RR Arbitration Schemes

The FR (RR) arbiter switches the data transfer based on burst transaction as a fixed priority (round robin) fashion; whereas, the FT (RT) arbiter multiplexes the data transfer based on single transfer as a fixed priority (round robin) manner. Therefore, the basic arbitration algorithm of the FR (RR) arbiter is similar to that of the FT (RT) arbiter, except the unit of data multiplexing.

The arbitration process of our FR arbiter follows three steps:

1. Step1 is equal to step1 of FT arbiter.
2. Step2 is equal to step2 of FT arbiter.
3. If none of the above applies, the same master remains selected because the unit of data multiplexing of the FR arbiter is a burst transaction.

The FR arbitration scheme is achieved by the iteration of above process. Fig. 6 illustrates an example timing diagram of our FR arbitration scheme. The transaction type of Fig. 6 is similar to that of Fig. 1.A.

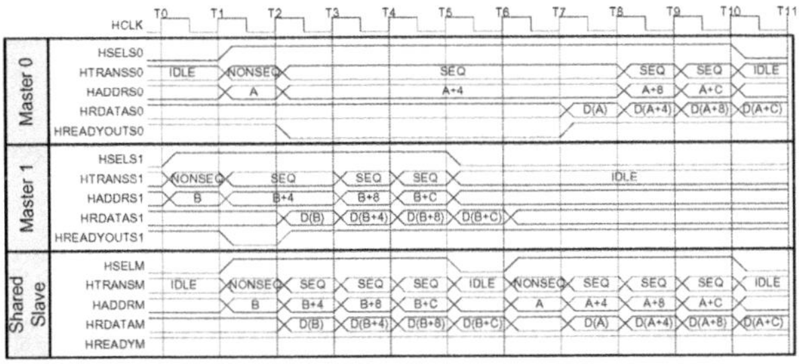

Fig. 6. An example timing diagram of our FR arbitration scheme

In Fig. 6, master1 starts a transaction at T1 and master0 requests a transaction at T2. Master0 does not preempt the right to use the bus at T3 and waits until master1 completes a transaction since although the priority of master0 is higher than that of master1, the unit of arbitration is a burst transaction. Hence, master0 can start a transaction from T7.

The sequence of our RR arbitration is as follows:

1. If HMASTLOCK is asserted, the same master remains selected.
2. If HMASTLOCK is not asserted and the Sel and Htrans signals of the currently selected master are '0' and IDLE respectively, a master for the next transaction is selected by the RT arbitration algorithm of Fig. 5. However, the down mask vector of Fig. 5 is modified as shown in Fig. 7 because if the currently selected master just wants a new transaction after the completion of the previous transaction, the master becomes the lowest priority master to avoid starvation of other masters. At this point in time, if no master is requesting access, the NoPort signal is asserted.
3. If none of the above conditions is met, the same master remains selected since the unit of data multiplexing of the RR arbiter is a burst transaction.

	M7	M6	M5	M4	M3	M2	M1	M0
[Dn_Mask]	0	0	0	1	1	1	1	1

Fig. 7. The changed down mask vector for the RR arbiter

With the repetition of above process, we could accomplish the RR arbitration scheme. Fig. 8 shows an example timing diagram of our RR arbitration scheme. The transaction type of Fig. 8 is also similar to that of Fig. 1.B.

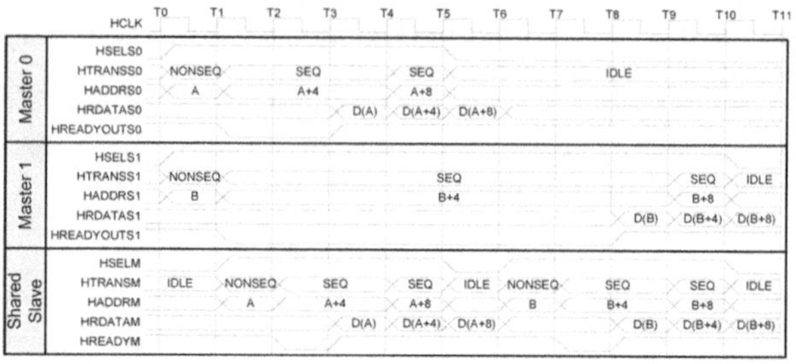

Fig. 8. An example timing diagram of our RR arbitration scheme

In Fig. 8, master0 and master1 concurrently initiate a transaction at T1 and the arbiter multiplexes the data transfer based on burst transaction in round robin fashion. In this case, the burst type is an incrementing burst of unspecified length with 3 transfer length. The shared slave inserts a wait state on the first transfer from each port (at T3 and T8), but all subsequent transfers are zero wait state.

4 Experimental Results

4.1 Implementation Results

The proposed scheme is applied to the implementation of busmatrixes to support the FT, RT, FR and RR arbitration schemes. Our busmatrixes were implemented with synthesizable RTL VHDL targeting XILINX FPGA (XC2V3000-4ff1152) and we used the XILINX design tool (ISE 7.1i) to measure the total area and clock period.

The ML-AHB busmatrix of ARM provides only two arbitration schemes (FT and RT). Therefore, we compared the busmatrixes of ARM (FT and RT) with our busmatrixes (FT and RT) in total area and clock period to show the effectiveness of the proposed scheme. Table 2 shows the comparison results.

Table 2. Comparisons of our busmatrixes with those of ARM in total area and clock period

	MxS	Busmatrix of ARM		Our Busmatrix	
		FT based	RT based	FT based	RT based
Total Area (# of Slices)	2x2	248	248	233	233
	4x4	1045	1046	675	740
	6x6	2474	2505	1965	2233
	8x8	3495	3653	2826	3363

	MxS	Busmatrix of ARM		Our Busmatrix	
		FT based	RT based	FT based	RT based
Clock Period (ns)	2x2	6.77	6.38	5.74	6.35
	4x4	9.16	10.16	6.57	9.39
	6x6	11.18	12.39	7.60	9.91
	8x8	11.56	13.76	7.80	10.65

In Table 2, M x S indicates the number of masters x the number of slaves. The total area and clock period of our FT (RT) based busmatrix are decreased by 22% and 28% (12% and 15%) respectively, compared with those of the FT (RT) based busmatrix of ARM. Table 3 additionally shows the synthesis results of our FR and RR based busmatrixes.

Table 3. Synthesis results of our FR and RR based busmatrixes

MxS	Total Area (# of Slices)		Clock Period (ns)	
	FR based	RR based	FR based	RR based
2x2	241	242	6.19	6.19
4x4	708	715	8.37	9.07
6x6	2044	2149	9.82	10.89
8x8	2975	3100	9.48	11.00

Note that the total area and clock period of our FR (RR) based busmatrix are reduced by 18% and 12% (17% and 13%) respectively, compared with those of the FT (RT) based busmatrix of ARM.

4.2 Power Estimation and Performance Analysis

We used the XPower of XILINX to estimate the power consumption and the Modelsim II simulator to measure the throughput of the ML-AHB bus system. Fig. 9 shows our ML-AHB bus system for simulations.

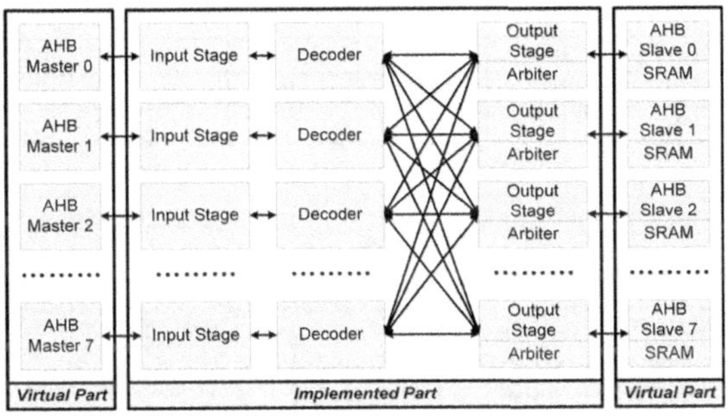

Fig. 9. The ML-AHB bus system for simulations

The ML-AHB busmatrix has a 32-bit address bus, a 32-bit write data bus, a 32-bit read data bus, a 15-bit control bus and a 3-bit response bus. The simulation environment consists of two parts: (1) an implemented part and (2) a virtual part. The implemented part corresponds to the ML-AHB busmatrixes with the FT and RT arbitration schemes and consists of two-masters and two-slaves, four-masters and four-slaves, six-masters and six-slaves and eight-masters and eight-slaves. The virtual part is composed of AHB masters and AHB slaves. AHB master generates the bus transactions and the bus transactions of the masters have the same length as 8-beat wrapping burst type. AHB slaves response to the transfers of the AHB masters and include a SRAM. Both AHB masters and AHB slaves are fully compatible with AMBA AHB protocol [6] and modeled with VHDL at the behavioral level. We also constructed the protocol checker and the performance monitor modules with VHDL and foreign language interface to check the protocol violation.

Before performing the simulation, the workloads should be determined since workloads affect simulation results. However, it is difficult to find appropriate workloads of real applications because real workloads can be obtained when all applications with real input data are modeled exactly. Instead, the workloads for simulations are simply obtained by synthetic workload generation with following parameters:

- The clock period of each ML-AHB bus system, where the ML-AHB bus system consists of the ML-AHB busmatrix, AHB masters and AHB slaves.
- The distribution of bus transactions, which indicates how many portion of total bus transactions each master is responsible for.
- The distribution of accessed slaves by each master.

Through the simple synthetic workload generation, we were able to estimate the power consumption and measure the throughput of the ML-AHB busmatrixes with each arbitration scheme. Table 4 and Table 5 show the simulation parameters.

Table 4. Simulation parameters: distribution of bus transactions

MxS	master 0	master 1	master 2	master 3	master 4	master 5	master 6	master 7	Total transaction #
2x2	1/2	1/2	0	0	0	0	0	0	200
4x4	1/4	1/4	1/4	1/4	0	0	0	0	400
6x6	1/6	1/6	1/6	1/6	1/6	1/6	0	0	600
8x8	1/8	1/8	1/8	1/8	1/8	1/8	1/8	1/8	800

Table 5. Simulation parameters: distribution of accessed slaves by each master

MxS	master0	master1	master2	master3	master4	master5	master6	master7
2x2	slave0,1	slave0,1	0	0	0	0	0	0
4x4	slave0~3	slave0~3	slave0~3	slave0~3	0	0	0	0
6x6	slave0~5	slave0~5	slave0~5	slave0~5	slave0~5	slave0~5	0	0
8x8	slave0~7	slave0~7	slave0~7	slave0~7	slave0~7	slave0~7	slave0~7	slave0~7

- The clock period of each bus system is the estimated minimum clock period of the ML-AHB busmatrix. The estimated minimum clock periods are illustrated in Table 2.
- For the distribution of bus transaction, four cases are made as shown in Table 4. Master0 and master1 are enabled for 2x2, and master0, master1, master2 and master3 are enabled for 4x4, and so on.
- Table 5 shows the distribution of accessed slaves by each master. The target addresses are generated based on uniform distribution random number function. Therefore, each master communicates with the slaves with the same probability.

Table 6. Comparisons of our busmatrixes with those of ARM in power consumption

	MxS	Busmatrix of ARM		Our Busmatrix	
		FT based	RT based	FT based	RT based
Power Consumption (mW)	2x2	590.98	595.96	458.34	502.36
	4x4	608.87	610.87	481.23	522.34
	6x6	630.18	632.76	532.08	568.09
	8x8	674.32	678.49	558.36	588.18

After the achievement of simulations based on aforementioned simulation environments, we could estimate the power consumption of the ML-AHB busmatrixes through the XPower of XILINX. Table 6 shows the experimental results.

As a result, the power consumption of our FT (RT) based busmatrix is decreased by 19% (13%), compared with that of the FT (RT) based busmatrix of ARM.

We also could measure the throughput of each bus system through the simulations. Fig. 10 and Fig. 11 show the experimental results.

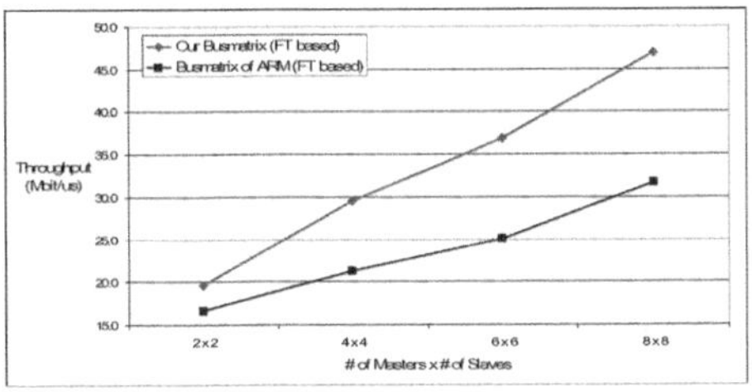

Fig. 10. Comparison of FT Arbitrations

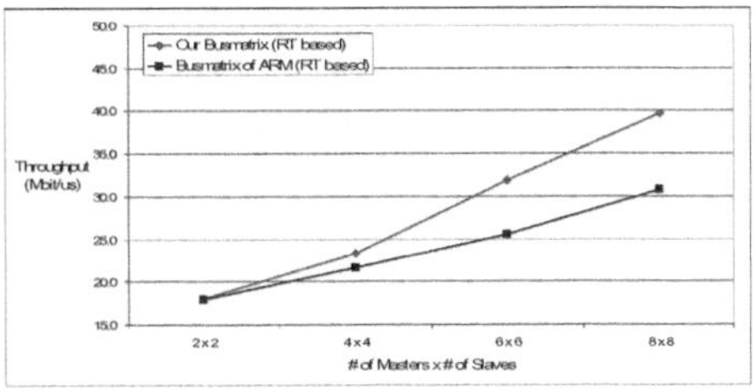

Fig. 11. Comparison of RT Arbitrations

Here, throughput is defined by

$$Throughput = N_{transactions} * N_{transfers} * N_{bit} / (N_{clock\_cycle} * T_{clock\_period})$$

Where $N_{transactions}$ is the total number of bus transactions, $N_{transfers}$ the number of transfers per transaction, N_{bit} the data bit width, N_{clock_cycle} the number of clock cycle during the data transmission and T_{clock_period} the estimated minimum clock period. With the simulation results, we observed that the throughput of our busmatrix based on FT (RT) is increased by 41% (18%) compared with that of the FT (RT) based busmatrix of ARM. The reason is that the estimated minimum clock period of our busmatrix is smaller than that of the busmatrix of ARM. Also, the throughput of the fixed priority scheme is higher than that of the round robin scheme since though the number of clock cycle of the round robin scheme is smaller than that of the fixed priority scheme, the estimated minimum clock period of the round robin scheme is remarkably larger than that of the fixed priority scheme.

5 Summary and Future works

In this paper, we have presented one way to improve the arbiter implementation of the busmatrix of ARM. By virtue of the masking mechanism employed to design the arbiter of the busmatrix, we could not only enhance the throughput of bus system but also reduce the total area, clock period and power consumption. In addition, we applied our proposed mechanism to the implementation of busmatrixes with transaction based arbitrations as well as with transfer based arbitrations since our approach does not require any restrictions on arbitration scheme.

Experimental results show that the throughput of our busmatrix based on the FT (RT) is increased by 41% (18%) compared with that of the FT (RT) based busmatrix of ARM. Moreover, we could reduce the total area, clock period and power consumption by 22%, 28% and 19% (12%, 15% and 13%) respectively, compared with the busmatrix employing the FT (RT) arbitration scheme of ARM.

Currently, we are adapting our busmatrixes to the multimedia applications such as a video phone, MPEG-4 and H.264 codec. In addition, we are looking for the applicability of the proposed scheme to the AMBA 3.0 AXI.

References

1. Kyoung-Sun Jhang, Kang Yi, and Soo Yun Hwang : A Two-level On-Chip Bus System Based on Multiplexers. LNCS-3189, 2004, 09, SPRINGER-VERLAG, pp.363-372.
2. Jian Liang, Swaminathan, S., Tessier, R. : ASOC: a scalable, single chip communications architecture. Parallel Architectures and Compilation Techniques, 15-19 Oct. 2000, Page(s):37-46.
3. D. Langen, A. Brinkmann, and U. Ruckert : High Level Estimation of the Area and Power Consumption of On-Chip Interconnects. Proc. of the 13th Annual IEEE International ASIC/SOC Conference, Sep. 2000. pp. 297-301.
4. D. Sylvester and K. Keutzer : Impact of small process geometries on microarchitectures in systems on a chip. Proceedings of the IEEE, Vol.89, No.4, Apr.2001, pp.467-489.
5. P. Wielage and K. Goossens : Networks on silicon: blessing or nightmare?. Symp. Digital system design, Dortmund, Germany, 4-6 Sep.2002, pp.196-200.
6. ARM, AMBA Specification Rev 2.0, ARM Limited, 1999.
7. AMBA AHB BusMatrix Specification. Document Number ARM DUI 0092C.
8. IBM, 32-bit Processor local bus architecture specification, Version 2.9, IBM Corporation, 2001.
9. Silicore, Wishbone system-on-chip (SoC) interconnection architecture for portable IP cores, Revision: B.1, Silicore corporation, 2001.
10. Sonics, Sonics uNetworks technical overview, Sonics inc., June 2000.
11. D, Flynn : AMBA: Enabling Reusable On-chip Designs. IEEE Micro, vol. 17, issue 4, July-Aug. 1997, pp. 20-27.
12. Nam-Joon Kim and Hyuk-Jae Lee : Design of AMBA™ Wrappers for Multiple-Clock Operations. ICCCAS 2004. International Conference on, June 2004, Volume: 2, pp.1438-1442.
13. Soo Yun Hwang et al. : An Ameliorated Design Method of ML-AHB BusMatrix. ETRI Journal, Vol.28, no.3, June 2006, pp.397-400.

Modeling and Implementation of an Output-Queuing Router for Networks-on-Chips

Haytham Elmiligi[1], M. Watheq El-Kharashi[2], and Fayez Gebali[1]

[1] Department of Electrical and Computer Engineering
University of Victoria, P.O. Box 3055 STN CSC
BC, Canada V8W 3P6
[2] Department of Computer and Systems Engineering
Ain Shams University, Cairo, Egypt
{haytham,watheq,fayez}@ece.uvic.ca

Abstract. Routers are pivotal modules in any networks-on-chip (NoC)-based design. In order to achieve an efficient router design, the size of the queue must be optimally chosen. The choice of queue size affects packet loss probability and impacts the silicon area of the overall NoC-based design. For these reasons, a modeling process is needed to obtain an early estimation of the optimum queue size that matches packet arrival rate, number of traffic sources, and the permissable loss probability. In this paper, we use Markov chain analysis to model an M/D/1/B queue for an NoC output-queuing router. We explain how to optimally chose the queue size using pre-defined design parameters that match different target applications. Our model is validated with a prototype router implementation on FPGA.

1 Introduction

Queuing analysis is a vital process in designing NoC-based routers [1]. The queue size impacts not only the router efficiency, but also the silicon area of a design [2]. A mismatch between the queue size and packet arrival rate could lead to a poor router performance or excessive use of the silicon area [3]. Poor router performance happens when the incoming traffic burstiness ratio exceeds the queue capacity, whereas excessive use of the silicon area takes place if the queue size is over estimated. For these reasons, the choice of the optimum queue size is a critical aspect in any NoC design.

In this paper, we address the queue size problem by proposing a queue model using Markov chain analysis. Our model can be used to acquire the optimum queue size based on three design parameters: number of ports, packet arrival rate, and the required packet loss probability. The advantage of our model is that it helps the designer get the queue size early in the design process and the corresponding packet loss probability on higher levels of abstraction. As a proof of concept, an implementation of an output-queuing router based on our model is done on an FPGA chip to evaluate its performance.

The rest of this paper is organized as follows. Section 2 presents related work in NoC-based router design and modeling. Section 3 describes the output-queuing

Y.-H. Lee et al. (Eds.): ICESS 2007, LNCS 4523, pp. 241–248, 2007.

router architecture. Our Markovian M/D/1/B model is presented in Section 4. Section 5 discusses the experimental results. Router implementation is presented in Section 6. Finally in Section 7, we draw some conclusions and future works.

2 Related Work

Recently, NoC router design, modeling, and implementation have been addressed from different perspectives [4, 5]. Some researchers addressed the trade-off between guaranteed and best-effort services in the router design like [6] and [7]. Another perspective is the analysis of power consumption in the router. Ye et al. [8] analyzed the switch fabric power consumption in NoC routers. FPGA-based implementations have been the focus of many researchers [9,10]. However, only few researchers focused on the router modeling problem [11, 12]. These models were either based on results from experiments - so they are case-based models - or targeted only fixed network topologies. The model we present here addresses this problem.

3 Output-Queuing Router Architecture

Fig. 1 shows the main blocks of an n-port output-queuing router. Packets arrive at the input of the router asynchronously with a packet ready signal indicator (PR). The packet arrival rate depends on the target application [13, 14]. The switch fabric controller reads the packet header, then directs the packet to the corresponding output queue. The configuration commands are generated based

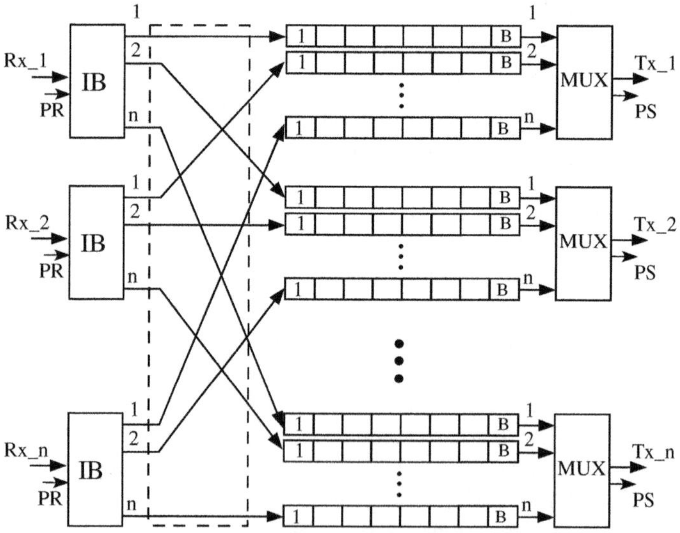

Fig. 1. Output-queuing router architecture details

on routing tables in the controller. There are n queues for each output port serving as FIFO buffers. Finally, a round robin scheduler algorithm serves backlogged queues one after another in a fixed order in the output. Packets are sent with a Packet Sent (PS) signal indicator to the next hop. In output-queuing routers, packet loss may occur because of destination statistics. In other words, bursty behavior - which means two or more packets arrive in adjacent clock cycles from one source, targeting the same output port - could take place and cause packet loss. Based on the distribution of the burstiness of the source, we could chose a proper queue size to reduce the packet loss probability.

4 $M/D/1/B$ Queue Modeling

In this section, we derive an $M/D/1/B$ model for an output queue, which matches routers that have deterministic service rate. The model is driven for a size B queue as a function of packet arrival rate, departure rate, and packet loss probability.

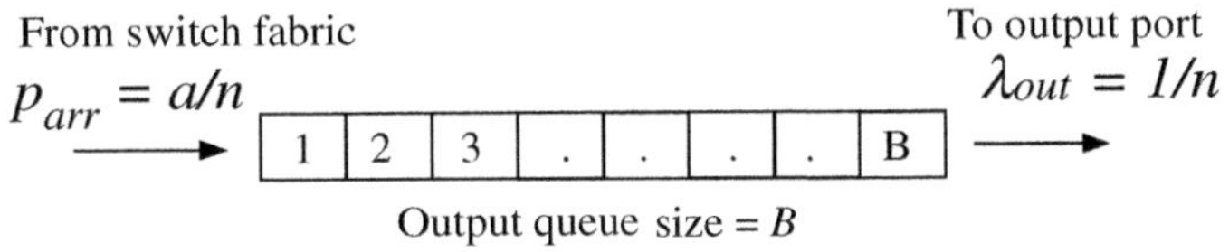

Fig. 2. The arrival probability and departure rate for one output queue of an output-queuing router

Fig. 2 shows one output queue of size B at an output port but associated with one input port. For a fixed packet length, the probability of packet arrival is $p_{in} = a$ and the probability of choosing a port is p_p, which - in our model - equals the packet departure rate λ_{out}. The departure rate in our model is based on round-robin schedular and equals a deterministic value of *1/n*. The probability that a packet arrives and requests an output port can be expressed as:

$$p_{arr} = p_{in}\, p_p = a\left(\frac{1}{n}\right) = \frac{a}{n} \tag{1}$$

Using Markov chain analysis to model our $M/D/1/B$ queue, where changes in the queue size occur by at most one per time step, and assuming $b = 1 - p_{arr}$ and $d = 1 - \lambda_{out}$, the state transition diagram for the queue is shown in Fig. 3, where:

$$\alpha = p_{in}\, p_p\, d = \frac{a}{n}\left(1 - \frac{1}{n}\right) = \frac{a(n-1)}{n^2} \tag{2}$$

$$\beta = (1 - p_{in} p_p)\lambda_{out} = \frac{(n - a)}{n^2} \tag{3}$$

$$f = p_{in}\, p_p\, \lambda_{out} + b\, d = \frac{2a}{n^2} - \frac{1 + a}{n} + 1 \tag{4}$$

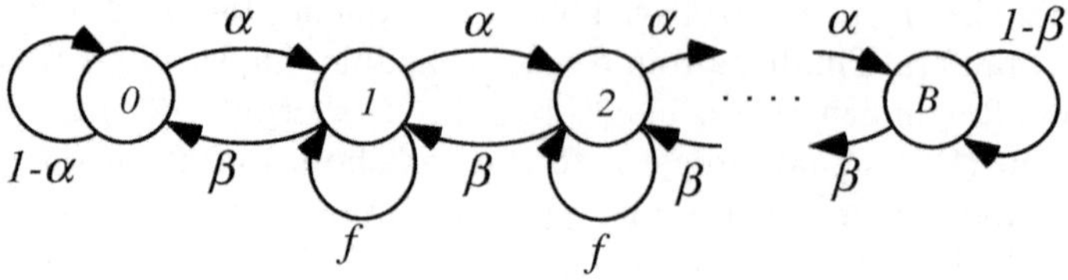

Fig. 3. State transition diagram for M/D/1/B queue

Since the packet arrival rate is independent from the packet departure rate, and based on the assumption that packets can be served at the same time step with a packet departure rate of λ_{out}, the transition matrix can be written as:

$$\mathbf{M} = \begin{bmatrix} \alpha_0 & \beta & 0 & \cdots & 0 & 0 & 0 \\ \alpha & f & \beta & \cdots & 0 & 0 & 0 \\ 0 & \alpha & f & \cdots & 0 & 0 & 0 \\ \vdots & \vdots & \vdots & \ddots & \vdots & \vdots & \vdots \\ 0 & 0 & 0 & \cdots & f & \beta & 0 \\ 0 & 0 & 0 & \cdots & \alpha & f & \beta \\ 0 & 0 & 0 & \cdots & 0 & \alpha & \beta_B \end{bmatrix} \tag{5}$$

where $\alpha_0 = 1 - \alpha$, and $\beta_B = 1 - \beta$.

Using the transition matrix $\boldsymbol{M}$, we can drive an expression for the equilibrium distribution vector (s):

$$\mathbf{s} = \begin{bmatrix} s_0 \; s_1 \; s_2 \; \cdots \; s_B \end{bmatrix}^t, \text{ where } \sum_{i=0}^{B} s_i = 1 \tag{6}$$

s_0 is the probability that the queue is empty and s_B is the probability that it is full. The difference equations for the state probability vector are given by:

$$\alpha s_0 - \beta s_1 = 0 \tag{7}$$

$$\alpha s_0 - g s_1 + \beta s_2 = 0 \tag{8}$$

$$\alpha s_{i-1} - g s_i + \beta s_{i+1} = 0, \qquad 0 < i < B \tag{9}$$

where $g = \alpha + \beta$ and s_i is the component of the distribution vector corresponding to state i. The solution to the above equations can be written in its general form as:

$$s_i = \left(\frac{\alpha}{\beta}\right)^i s_0, \qquad 0 \le i \le B \tag{10}$$

The magnitude of the distribution vector components can be dictated by a distribution index expression [1]. From Equations 2, 3, and 10, we can write an expression for the distribution index for the $M/D/1/B$ queue as:

$$\rho = \frac{\alpha}{\beta} = \frac{a(n-1)}{n-a} \tag{11}$$

From Equation 10, we can write a complete solution as:

$$\sum_{i=0}^{B} s_i = s_0 \sum_{i=0}^{B} \rho_i = 1 \tag{12}$$

From Equations 10 and 12, we obtain an expression for the probability that the queue is empty (s_0):

$$s_0 = \frac{1-\rho}{1-\rho^{B+1}} \tag{13}$$

The output traffic from the $M/D/1/B$ queue is given by:

$$N_0 = p_{in} p_p \lambda_{out} s_0 + \sum_{i=1}^{B} \lambda_{out} s_i = \lambda_{out} \left(1 - \frac{b(1-\rho)}{1-\rho^{B+1}}\right) \tag{14}$$

and the input traffic to the queue is given by:

$$N_i = p_{in}\ p_p = a\ \frac{1}{n} = \frac{a}{n} \tag{15}$$

The efficiency of the $M/D/1/B$ queue is

$$\eta = \frac{N_o}{N_i} = \frac{1}{a}\left(1 - \frac{b\,(1-\rho)}{1-\rho^{B+1}}\right) \tag{16}$$

and the loss probability is given by:

$$L = 1 - \eta = 1 - \frac{1}{a}\left(1 - \frac{b\,(1-\rho)}{1-\rho^{B+1}}\right) \tag{17}$$

and the queue size B can be calculated from the equation:

$$B = \frac{1}{\log(\rho)} \left[\log\left(1 - \frac{b(1-\rho)}{a(L-1)+1}\right)\right] - 1 \tag{18}$$

From Equation 17, we can calculate the loss probability when packets arrive with inter-arrival rate probability of a and use a service rate of *1/n*. Equation 18 gives an indication of the optimum queue size when certain value of the loss probability is required in the design process. In other words, Equation 17 can be used in the performance evaluation process while Equation 18 is derived to be used in the design process.

5 Simulation Results

We used Equations 17 and 18 to study the dependency relation between the loss probability, packet inter-arrival rate, number of ports, and buffer size. Our

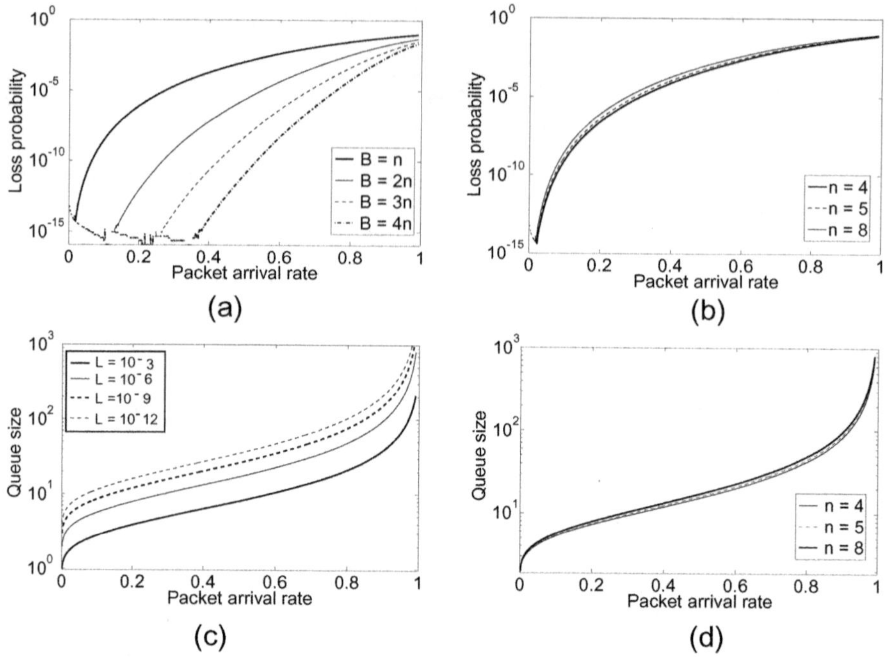

Fig. 4. Simulation results: (a) Loss probability versus packet arrival rate for different queue sizes when number of ports = 8. (b) Loss probability versus packet arrival rate for different number of ports when queue size = 8. (c) Queue size versus packet arrival rate for different loss probabilities for number of ports = 8. (d) Queue size versus packet arrival rate for different number of ports when loss probability = 10^{-6}.

choices for the values of the number of ports are in the range from 4 to 8 to match the requirements of various NoC topologies [15].

The experimental results, shown in Fig. 4, show that the change of the queue size impacts the values of the loss probability significantly. For example, for $n = 8$ in Fig. 4.a, a packet arrival rate of 0.5 has a loss probability of 10^{-3} when using queue size $B = n$, whereas it improves to 10^{-11} when using queue size $B = 4n$. However, this difference decreases gradually as the packet arrival rate reaches its maximum value. For a fixed queue size $B = 8$, changing the number of ports from 5 to 8 does not have a major impact on the corresponding loss probability as can be seen in Fig. 4.b. On the other hand, Fig. 4.c and Fig. 4.d give an early estimation for the optimum queue size when a specific loss probability order of magnitude is required. Fig. 4.c shows the change of the queue size versus the packet arrival rate for an 8-port router, when a pre-designed loss probability values of 10^{-3}, 10^{-6}, 10^{-9}, and 10^{-12} are used. This curve helps the designers choose appropriate queue size according to various application requirements. For example, for a packet arrival rate of 0.7, a queue size of 32 packets is required to achieve a loss probability of 10^{-6}, whereas it has to be changed to a 67 if a loss probability of 10^{-12} is required.

6 FPGA Prototype

We used our model to design and implement an output-queuing router on FPGA. The main three design parameters that must be pre-defined to know the optimum queue size are: the estimated packet arrival rate, the target loss probability, and the required number of ports. As a case study we assumed a packet arrival rate of 0.2, 10^{-6} loss probability, and an 8-port router. From the previous curves, an 8-packet queue size is the optimum choice based on these design parameters. Eight traffic sources/sinks VHDL modules have been designed to implement a star network topology. The traffic sources are designed to generate fixed packets of 16-bit length, while the traffic sinks are used to monitor and analyze the network traffic, and output the needed parameters to calculate the efficiency. We implemented our design on a Xilinx FPGA Vertix II Pro family 100K chip.

The synthesis report shows that equivalent gate costs for the input buffers and switch fabric, queues and control unit, and output multiplexers are 4,787, 38,595, and 1,356 equivalent gates, respectively. The queues and control unit occupy the main area of the router - 86.2% - while the switch fabric occupies only 10.7%, and the output multiplexer unit - which is implemented using LUTs - occupies only 3.1%. The implementation shows the significant effect of the queue size design on the overall router silicon area. Also, the maximum propagation delay between internal gates is found to be 4.778 ns. This value limits the maximum frequency, which can be used in our router as a master clock frequency, to 209.293 MHz. We ran these experiments until 20,107 packets have been received. Our choice of the queue size based on our model results in an 99.12% average efficiency, which is almost the same efficiency obtained theoretically (99.45%) using Equation 16 and this validates our model.

7 Conclusion and Future Work

In this paper, we used Markov chain analysis to drive a queue model for NoC output-queuing router. The proposed model explains the impact of the packet arrival rate, number of ports, and queue size on the router performance. The experimental results show that for low packet arrival rates, increasing the queue size relative to the number of ports improves the router efficiency significantly. However, this improvement is reduced with the increase in the packet arrival rate. We validated our model by implementing an FPGA prototype for output-queuing router. We are planning to apply this design methodology to various real-time applications and address the network congestion problem by modifying the current communication protocol.

References

1. Gebali, F.: Computer Communications Networks: Analysis and Design. 3rd edn. Northstar Digital Design, inc., Victoria, B.C., Canada (2005)
2. Ogras, U.Y., Hu, J., Marculescu, R.: Key research problems in NoC design: A holistic perspective. In: Proceedings of the 3rd IEEE/ACM/IFIP International Conference on Hardware/Software Codesign and System Synthesis (CODES+ISSS'05), Jersey City, NJ (2005) 69–74
3. Hu, J., Marculescu, R.: Application-specific buffer space allocation for networks-on-chip router design. In: Proceedings of the IEEE/ACM International Conference on Computer-Aided Design (ICCAD'04), San Jose, CA (2004) 354–361
4. Kim, J., Park, D., Theocharides, T., Vijaykrishnan, N., Das, C.R.: A low latency router supporting adaptivity for on-chip interconnects. In: Proceedings of the 42nd Annual Conference on Design automation (DAC'05), Anaheim, CA (2005) 559–564
5. Mullins, R., West, A., Moore, S.: Low-latency virtual-channel routers for on-chip networks. In: Proceedings of the 31st Annual International Symposium on Computer Architecture (ISCA'04), Munich, Germany (2004) 188–197
6. Rijpkema, E., Goossens, K., Rădulescu, A., Dielissen, J., Meerbergen, J., Wielage, P., Waterlander, E.: Trade offs in the design of a router with both guaranteed and best-effort services for networks on chip. IEE Proceedings of Computers and Digital Techniques **150**(5) (2003) 294–302
7. Rijpkema, E., Goossens, K., Wielage, P.: A router architecture for networks on silicon (2006) Proceedings of Progress 2001, 2nd Workshop on Embedded Systems, Veldhoven, the Netherlands, October 2001.
8. Ye, T.T., Micheli, G.D., Benini, L.: Analysis of power consumption on switch fabrics in network routers. In: Proceedings of the 39th Conference on Design automation (DAC'02), New Orleans, LA (2002) 524–529
9. Ehliar, A., Liu, D.: A network on chip based gigabit ethernet router implemented on an FPGA (2006) Proceedings of the Swedish System-on-Chip Conference (SSoCC'06), Kolmrden, Sweden, May 4-5, 2006.
10. Zeferino, C., Kreutz, M., Susin, A.: RASoC: A router soft-core for networks-on-chip. In: Proceedings of Design, Automation and Test in Europe Conference and Exhibition (DATE'04), Paris, France (2004) 198–203
11. Lee, I.G., Lee, J., Park, S.: Adaptive routing scheme for NoC communication architecture. In: Proceedings of the 7th International Conference on Advanced Communication Technology (ICACT'05), Park, Korea (2005) 1180–1184
12. Andreasson, D., Kumar, S.: Improving BE traffic QoS using GT slack in NoC systems. In: Proceedings of the 23rd NORCHIP Conference, Oulu, Finland (2005) 44–47
13. Tedesco, L., Mello, A., Giacomet, L., Calazans, N., Moraes, F.: Application driven traffic modeling for NoCs. In: Proceedings of the 19th Annual Symposium on Integrated Circuits and Systems Design (SBCCI'06), Ouro Preto, MG, Brazil (2006) 62–67
14. Lahiri, K., Raghunathan, A., Dey, S.: Evaluation of the traffic-performance characteristics of system-on-chip communication architectures. In: Proceedings of the 14th International Conference on VLSI Design (VLSID'01), Bangalore, India (2001) 29–35
15. Bjerregaard, T., Mahadevan, K.: A survey of research and practices of network-on-chip. ACM Computing Surveys **38** (2006) 1–51

Handling Control Data Flow Graphs for a Tightly Coupled Reconfigurable Accelerator

Hamid Noori[1], Farhad Mehdipour[1], Morteza Saheb Zamani[2], Koji Inoue[1], and Kazuaki Murakami[1]

[1] Department of Informatics,
Graduate School of Information Science and Electrical Engineering,
Kyushu University, Fukuoka, Japan
{noori,farhad}@c.csce.kysuhu-u.ac.jp,
{inoue,murakami}@i.kyushu-u.ac.jp
[2] Department of IT and Computer Engineering, Amirkabir University of Technology,
Tehran, Iran
szamani@aut.ac.ir

Abstract. In an embedded system including a base processor integrated with a tightly coupled accelerator, extracting frequently executed portions of the code (hot portion) and executing their corresponding data flow graph (DFG) on the accelerator brings about more speedup. In this paper, we intend to present our motivations for handling control instructions in DFGs and extending them to Control DFGs (CDFGs). In addition, basic requirements for an accelerator with conditional execution support are proposed. Moreover, some algorithms are presented for temporal partitioning of CDFGs considering the target accelerator architectural specifications. To show the effectiveness of the proposed ideas, we applied them to the accelerator of an extensible processor called AMBER. Experimental results represent the effectiveness of covering control instructions and using CDFGs versus DFGs.

1 Introduction

Using an accelerator for accelerating the execution of frequently executed portions of applications is an effective technique to enhance the performance of a processor in embedded systems. In this technique, data flow graphs (DFGs) extracted from critical portions of an application are executed on an accelerator. Similar technique has been presented in [3, 4, 9, 13, 15, 22, 2, 5, 17, 21]. The accelerator can be implemented as a reconfigurable hardware with fine or coarse granularity or as a custom hardware (such as Application Specific Instruction-set Processors or extensible processors) [7]. The integration of accelerator and the processor can be tightly or loosely coupled [7, 13]. For loosely-coupled systems, there is an overhead for transferring data between the base processor and the accelerator. When an accelerator is tightly coupled [9, 2, 5, 17, 21], data is read and written directly to and from the processor's register file, making the accelerator an additional functional unit in the processor pipeline. This makes the control logic simple, as almost no overhead is required in transferring data to the

Y.-H. Lee et al. (Eds.): ICESS 2007, LNCS 4523, pp. 249–260, 2007.

programmable hardware unit, however, it increases the read/write ports of the register file. Our main focus in this paper is on a tightly coupled reconfigurable accelerator.

DFG extraction can be done at high level or binary level of the source code. In our analysis, we focus on the latter one which means that the DFG nodes are the primitive instructions of the base processor. The DFG containing control instructions (e.g. branch instruction) are called Control Dataflow Graphs (CDFGs). Handling branches (conditional execution) is a challenge in CDFG acceleration, because, due to the result of a branch instruction, the sequence of execution changes. We consider two types of CDFGs:

1. CDFGs which contain at most one branch instruction as its last instruction. In this case the accelerator does not need to support conditional execution.
2. CDFGs containing more than one branch instructions. Accelerators used for executing CDFGs should have conditional execution support.

As mentioned before, accelerators are used for executing hot portions of applications. Therefore, while generating CDFG we only follow hot directions of branches. For a control instruction, the only taken, or not-taken might be hot which means that they have a considerable execution frequency (more than a specified threshold). In some other cases, both directions can be hot. We propose adding only hot directions of branches into the CDFG without being limited to selecting just one or all of the directions. This brings about more instruction level parallelism (ILP) and can hide branch misprediction penalty.

In this work, we intend to answer these two following questions.

a) Does acceleration based on CDFG vs. DFG obtain higher performance?
b) How can the conditional execution be supported on an accelerator?

To answer the first question, we investigate the effect of extending DFGs and covering control instructions on the speedup and present some important motivations for extending DFGs over basic blocks (using CDFGs instead of DFGs). Moreover, as an answer to the second question, we introduce basic requirements for an accelerator with conditional execution support.

Due to the limitations of hardware resources of the accelerator (e.g. the number of inputs, outputs, logics, connections and etc) and different size of extracted CDFGs from various applications, in most cases the whole CDFG can not be mapped on the accelerator. As another contribution in this paper, we present CDFG temporal partitioning algorithms to partition large CDFGs to smaller and mappable ones. Mappable CDFGs satisfy the accelerator architectural constraints, hence, can be mapped and executed on the accelerator.

2 Motivations

In this section, basic arguments to extend DFGs over control instructions and supporting CDFGs are investigated. We follow a quantitative analysis approach and use some applications of Mibench [14] for these analyses. As mentioned above, DFGs are extracted from the frequently executed portions of an application and a control instruction (e.g. branch instruction) may cause the DFG generation to be stopped.

Therefore, short distance control instructions may result in generation of small size DFGs (SSDFG). In fact, SSDFGs are not suitable for improving performance in application execution and have to be run on the base processor [11] because they do not offer any more speedup.

In Fig. 1, a piece of a main loop of *adpcm(enc)* has been shown. *adpcm(enc)* is an application program which includes a loop which consumes 98% of total execution time. The critical portion of application contains 3 loads and 12 branch instructions. According the location of branch instructions, 4 DFGs can be extracted from the piece of loop that has been shown in Fig 1. Three DFGs from four depicted DFGs in Fig. 1 are SSDFGs (have the length less than or equal to 5 (we only execute DFGs which have more than 5 nodes on the accelerator). These SSDFGs do not bring about more speedup and have to be run on the base processor.

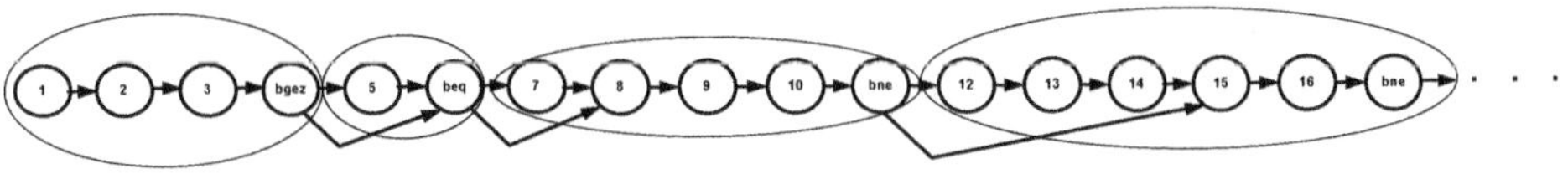

Fig. 1. Control data flow graph of hot portion of *adpcmc(enc)*

This kind of analysis was accomplished for 17 applications of Mibench [14]. Results of analysis motivate us to use CDFGs instead of DFGs for acceleration. Fig. 2 shows the overall percentage of frequently executed (hot) potion of each application. In addition, this figure shows the fraction of applications that can not be accelerated due to SSDFGs. For example, for *bitcount* application, almost 92% of application is hot. On the other hand, 32% out of 92% of hot portions do not worth to be accelerated due to the SSDFGs, therefore, they are dismissed from execution on the accelerator. However, analyses show for some applications like *fft*, *fft(inv)* and *sha* which includes few branch instructions, supporting conditional execution results in no considerable speedup, because a small portion of generated DFGs are removed due to SSDFGs.

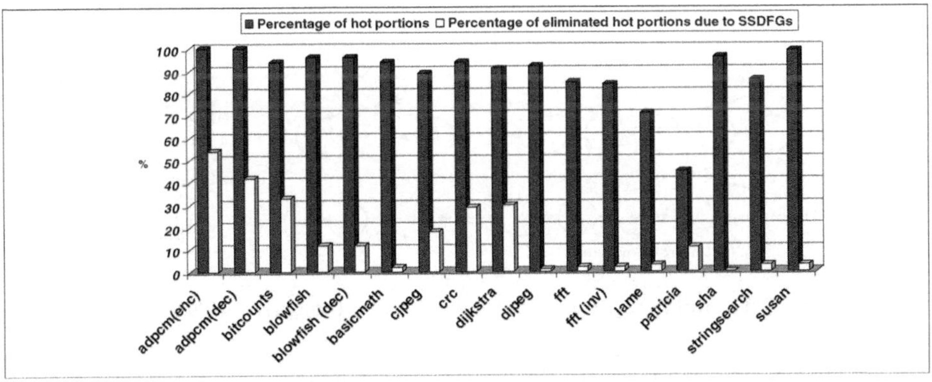

Fig. 2. Fraction of hot portions and eliminated hot portions in applications

Extending DFGs to contain more than one branch instruction and generate the CDFGs vs. DFGs is one solution to prevent many SSDFGs generation. For a control instruction, in some cases only taken or not-taken might be hot and for some others both directions are hot. In latter case, covering both directions may help to the generation of larger CDFGs, hence more parallelism and elimination of branch misprediction penalties. In addition, architecture of the accelerator should be modified to execute the CDFGs. Indeed, appropriate algorithms are required to generate CDFGs considering the specifications of the accelerator.

3 Basic Requirements for Architecture with Conditional Execution Support

To support conditional execution in an accelerator, the capability of branch instruction execution should be added to the accelerator. It is assumed that the proposed accelerator is a coarse grain reconfigurable hardware which is a matrix of functional units (FUs) with specific connections between the FUs. Moreover, each FU like the processor's ALUs can execute an instruction level operation.

In a DFG, the nodes (instructions) receive their input from a single source whereas, in the CDFG, nodes can have multiple sources with respect to the different paths generated by branches. The correct source is selected at run time according to the results of branches. Fig. 3 shows the CFG (contains only control flow of instructions) and DFG for a section of an *adpcm(enc)* loop. Node 8 may receive one of its inputs from nodes 5 or 7. The result of the branch that located in node 6 determines which one should be selected. The nodes that generate output data of a CDFG are altered according to the results of branches as well. Therefore, the accelerator should have some facilities to support conditional execution and generate valid output data. Predicated execution is one technique [16].

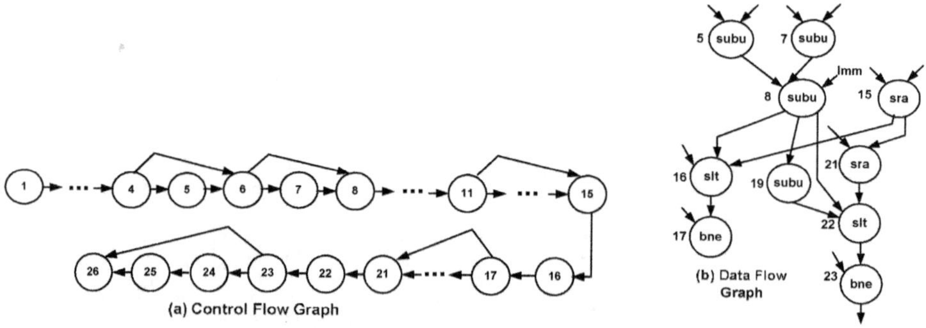

Fig. 3. Control flow (a) and data flow graphs (b) for a part of *adpcm(enc)* loop

Predicated execution is an effective technique to remove control dependency of programs running on ILP (Instruction level parallelism) processors. Proposed architecture in [8] uses predicated instructions. With predicated execution, control dependency is essentially turned into data dependency using predicates. A predicate is a Boolean variable used to represent the control information of a control instruction and to nullify the following instructions associated with it. The following instructions become no-ops if the predicated variable is evaluated to be false. The architecture featuring predicated execution should have radical changes, since every instruction can be predicated and a separated predicated register file is needed. Also, partial architectural support has also been studied [10]. In [10], Mahlke et al. proposed architecture with two new instructions added to the original instruction set to support predicated execution.

In this section, we propose basic requirements of an architecture which can support conditional execution. In the general architecture with conditional execution features, following items are considered to support conditional execution:

a) An FU in the accelerator can receive its inputs directly from accelerator primary inputs or from output of the other FUs.

b) According to the condition of branch instructions, output of each node can be directed to the other nodes from different paths. For example, in Fig. 3 output of node 8 can be routed to nodes 16, 19 or 22. Node 19 will receive the output of node 7 if branch instruction in node 7 is not-taken, otherwise it will be obtained by node 22. Therefore, there may be several outputs for a CDFG and some of them may be valid as its output accelerator final outputs.

According to above mentioned properties, the accelerator architecture must have these following requirements:

a) Capability of selective receiving of inputs from both accelerator primary inputs and output of other instructions (FUs) for each node.
b) Possibility of selecting the valid outputs from several outputs generated by accelerator according to conditions made by branch instructions. In this case, no need to modify the FUs.
c) Accelerator should be equipped by control path besides to data path which provides the correct selection of inputs and outputs for each FU and entire accelerator.

We will give more details on the architecture specifically proposed for an extensible processor in Section 5.

4 Algorithms for CDFG Temporal Partitioning

CDFG extracted from various applications are in different sizes and for some of the CDFGs the whole of it can not be mapped on the accelerator due to the limitations of hardware resources of the accelerator (e.g. number of inputs, outputs, logics and specifically routing resource constraints). Even if the logic resource limitations are considered, some constraints like the routing resource constraints are not applicable in

CDFG generation phase. Satisfying or violating routing resource constraints can be specified after trying to map a CDFG on the accelerator. Therefore, we investigate some algorithms for partitioning CDFGs under the different hardware resources constraints of the accelerator and introduce a mapping-aware framework which considers the routing resource constraints in CDFG generation process. Temporal partitioning can be stated as partitioning a data flow graph (DFG) into a number of partitions such that each partition can fit into the target hardware and also, dependencies among the nodes are not violated [6].

Integrated Framework presented in [11] (based on design flow proposed in [12]) performs an integrated temporal partitioning and mapping process to generate mappable DFGs. This framework takes *rejected* DFGs and attempts to partition them to appropriate ones with the capability of being mapped on the accelerator. The DFGs which are called *rejected* (vs. *mappable*) DFGs are ones that are not mappable on the accelerator due to hardware constraints [11]. Moreover, the partitions obtained from the integrated temporal partitioning process are the same appropriate DFGs which are *mappable* on the accelerator.

Extending the CDFGs to cover hot directions of branch instructions will result in larger CDFGs. Using temporal partitioning algorithms considering the accelerator constraints is a solution to this issue. As the authors knowledge there are small number of algorithms for CDFG partitioning, though a lot of works have been done around the DFG temporal partitioning [1, 6, 12].

In [1] a temporal portioning algorithm has been presented that partitions a CDFG considering target hardware with non-homogenous architecture. Setting control signal values determines a specific path of the data and converts a CDFG to sub-graphs that do not include control instructions. This algorithm considers all states of the control instructions in application to convert corresponding CDFG to a set of DFGs and then it tries to reduce the number of generated DFGs. Using this algorithm the large number of DFGs may be obtained during CDFG to DFG conversion. In addition, the knowledge to different states in application is required to reduce the number of DFGs. In this section, we propose some CDFG temporal partitioning algorithms. The proposed algorithms can also be used as general CDFG temporal partitioning algorithms.

4.1 TP Based on Not-Taken Paths (NTPT)

This algorithm adds instructions from not-taken path of a control instruction to a partition until violating the target hardware architectural constraints (e.g. the number of logic resources, inputs and outputs) or reaching to a terminator control instruction. A terminator instruction is an instruction which changes execution direction of the program, e.g. procedure or function call instructions and also backward branches (to prevent cycles in CDFG). In fact, a terminator instruction is an exit point for a CDFG. Therefore, in our methodology a CDFG can include one or more exit-points according the different paths achieved based on control instructions conditions. Generating a new partition is started with branch instructions which at least one of their taken or not-taken instructions has not been located in the current partition.

4.2 Execution Frequency-Based Algorithms

In NTPT algorithm, instructions were selected only from not-taken paths of branches, whereas execution frequency of taken and not-taken instructions may be different. Our second temporal partitioning algorithm considers the execution frequency (obtained through profiling) of taken and not-taken instructions as an effective factor for selecting the instruction and adding them to the current partition. A frequency threshold is defined to determine that whether instruction is critical or not. Critical instruction means an instruction with a frequency more than the defined threshold. For a branch instruction one of its taken or not-taken instructions or both of them can be critical.

In our frequency-based temporal partitioning algorithm, instructions are added one after another until observing a terminator or a branch instruction. For each instruction, list of all instructions located on its taken and not-taken paths stopping at a terminator are created. All instructions of two lists are added to the current partition if enough space is available. Otherwise the list with higher execution frequency is selected. In this case, the other list is used to create a new partition. If two lists are terminating in a unique instruction, it is attempted to add them to the current partition, so, there is no need to reconfiguration during execution of the current partition instructions.

4.3 Evaluating Proposed Algorithms

The proposed algorithms were compared according to a) the number of generated partitions and b) efficiency factor. The former is a factor that determines the number of reconfigurations required during run-time. The latter has been defined as a factor to show the efficiency of executing CDFGs on the accelerator. Efficiency factor is ratio of the number of clock cycles spent for DFG execution on the base processor to the number of clock cycles on the accelerator. Because of the space limitation we omitted the details of efficiency factor calculation. Larger amount of this factor means lower delay and correspondingly higher speedup. Six applications of Mibench [14] were selected for evaluation of the two proposed algorithms. These applications have considerable number of branch instructions and high potential to get enhanced performance using the conditional execution supporting features (Fig. 2). In addition, in these applications the large numbers of SSDFGs are generated due to the many short distance branch instructions. Comparison of two NTPT and execution frequency-based temporal partitioning algorithms was accomplished with respect to the average number of partitions (CDFGs) generated and the efficiency factor. According to Fig. 4, using NTPT algorithm, small number of partitions is obtained for all of the benchmark applications. We removed all small length CDFGs (SSDFGs) from the CDFG set generated by the temporal partitioning algorithms.

On the other hand, results obtained show that the NTPT algorithm has more or equivalent efficiency in comparing with frequency-based algorithm (Fig. 5). Though, the NTPT algorithm is a simpler approach for temporal partitioning, but it may bring about more efficiency comparing with the frequency-based algorithm which is more complicated. Some compilers which are used for VLIW processors move hot instructions to the not-taken part of branch instructions to avoid the pipeline flushing [9, 19]. For the applications have been modified by this kind of compliers, using NTPT algorithm is suggested. However, we do not claim that the NTPT algorithm does better for all critical portions of applications.

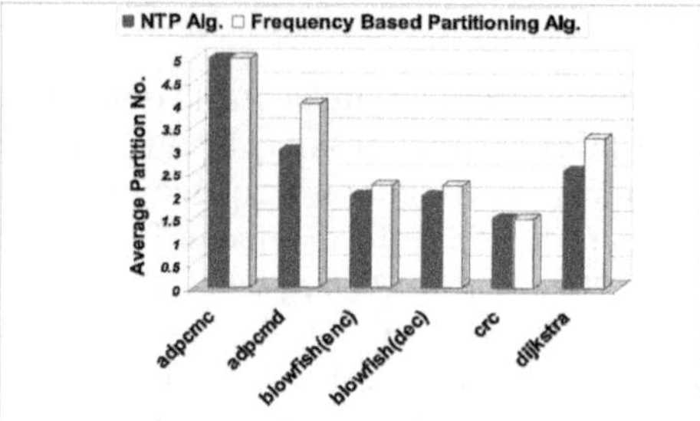

Fig. 4. Comparison of the number of partitions

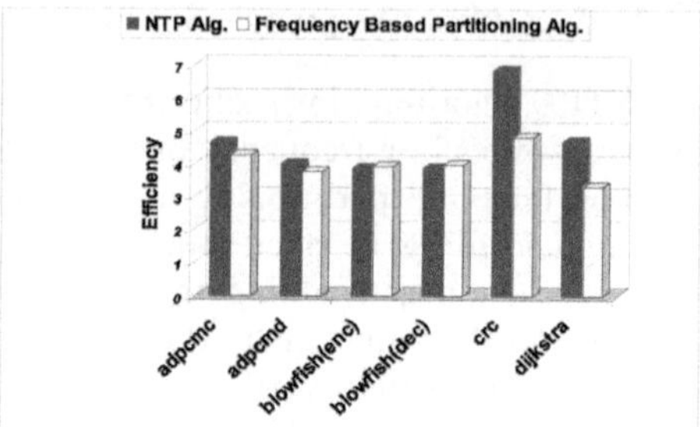

Fig. 5. Comparison of the efficiency factor

5 Case Study: Extending an Extensible Processor to Support Conditional Execution

AMBER is an extensible processor introduced in [15] targeted for embedded systems with the aim of accelerating application execution. Other tightly coupled accelerators have been proposed in [3, 4, 13, 19, 21]. The reconfigurable functional unit (RFU) in AMBER acts as an accelerator and can not support conditional execution. The basic requirements represented in Section 3 are applied for extending the AMBER's RFU to support conditional execution.

5.1 General Overview of AMBER

AMBER has been developed by integrating a base processor with three other main components [15]. The base processor is a general RISC processor and the other three components are: profiler, sequencer and a coarse grain reconfigurable functional unit (RFU). Fig. 6(a) illustrates the integration of different components in AMBER.

The *base processor* is an in-order RISC processor that supports MIPS instruction set. The *profiler* does the profiling for running applications through looking for hot portions which are usually in loops and functions. The *sequencer* mainly determines the microcode execution sequence by selecting between the RFU and the processor functional unit. The *RFU* is based on array of 16 functional units (FUs) with 8 input and 6 output ports. It is used in parallel with other processor's functional units (Fig. 6(b)). RFU reads (write) from (to) register file. In the RFU, the output of each FU in a row can be used by all FUs in the subsequent row [15].

AMBER has two operational modes: the *training* and the *normal mode*. The training mode is done offline. In this phase, target applications are run on an instruction set simulator (ISS) and profiled. AMBER enters the training mode once and after detecting start addresses of the hot portions, generating configuration bit-streams for extracted DFGs and initiating sequencer tables it switches to the normal mode. In the normal mode, using the RFU, its configuration data (from configuration memory) and sequencer DFGs are executed on the RFU. More details on AMBER and its components are out of scope of this paper and can be found in [15].

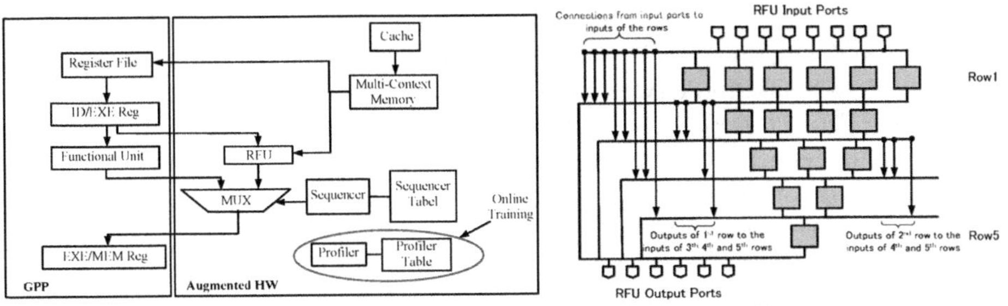

(a) (b)

Fig. 6. Integration of main components in AMBER (a) RFU general architecture (b)

5.2 Extending AMBER RFU to Support Conditional Execution

In this section, we apply the basic requirements introduced in Section 3 to RFU used in AMBER. First, we propose conditional data selection muxes for controlling selectors of muxes used for FU inputs and outputs of the RFU. Fig. 7 shows an example of a RFU (with 5 FUs) without supporting conditional execution. On the other hand, the hardware has been modified as shown in bottom part of Fig. 7 to support conditional data selection.

In the proposed architecture, the selector signals of muxes used for choosing data for FU inputs (the Data-Selection-Mux), along with the RFU output and exit point (not shown in the figure) are each controlled by another mux (the Selector-Mux). The inputs of Selector-Mux (one-bit width) originate from the FUs (which execute branches) of the upper rows and the configuration memory in order to control the selector signals conditionally, as well as unconditionally. The selectors of Selector-Mux are controlled by configuration bits. It should be noted the outputs of FUs are only applied to the Selector-Muxes in the lower-level rows, not in the same or upper rows. A similar structure is used for selecting the valid output data of the RFU.

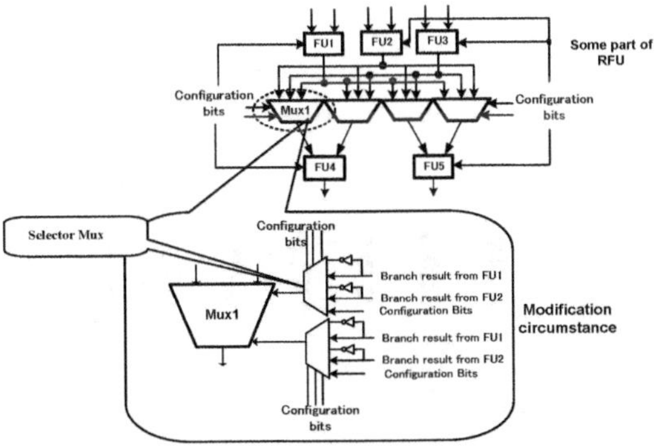

Fig. 7. Equipping the RFU to support conditional execution

For example, suppose a CDFG containing nodes 5, 6, 7, and 8 (Fig. 3) is to be mapped on the modified RFU. The second input of node 8 uses the output of node 5 when node 6 is taken otherwise uses the output of node 7. Nodes 5, 7, 6, and 8 are mapped to FU1, FU2, FU3, and FU5, respectively. Assuming that outputs of FU1, FU2, FU3, and the immediate value have been assigned to inputs 1, 2, 3, and 0 of the *Data Selection Mux* for the second input of FU5. The selector signals of *Selector-Mux* i.e. *Sel1* and *Sel0* are configured to be driven by *Not Branch result from FU3* and *Branch result from FU3*, respectively, using configuration bits. When FU3 (node 6) is taken, *Sel1* is 0 and *Sel0* is 1, therefore the output of FU1 (node 5) is selected. When FU3 is not-taken *Sel1* is 1 and *Sel0* is 0, therefore the output of FU2 (node 7) is selected.

5.3 Performance Evaluation

The extended RFU was developed and synthesized using Synopsys tools [20] and Hitachi 0.18μm. The area of the extended RFU is 2.1 mm^2. Each CDFG needs 615 bits in total for its configuration on the RFU. 375 out of 615 bits is used for control signals. Profiling data was provided by executing applications on the Simplescalar as ISS [18]. Integrated Framework based on NTPT temporal partitioning algorithm is used to generate mappable CDFGs. The required number of clock cycles for executing each CDFG is determined according to depth of CDFG and base processor clock frequency.

We compared the effectiveness of CDFGs versus DFGs. The average number of instructions included in DFGs is 6.39 instructions and for CDFGs is 7.85 instructions. Fig. 8 shows the speedups obtained based on CDFG and DFG compared to the base processor for some applications. The reason for the high speedup obtained by *adpcm* is that it has a main loop with 56 instructions, including 12 branches. For 7 of these branches, both taken and not-taken instructions are hot, so that 27% of branches are mispredicted. Therefore, a big part of executed clock cycles belongs to penalty of the mispredicted branches (18%). For those branches with both directions being hot, the CDFGs include both directions, and hence, the extended RFU architecture eliminates cycles of mispredicted branches. Also, since CDFGs are longer than DFGs, more ILP can be extracted.

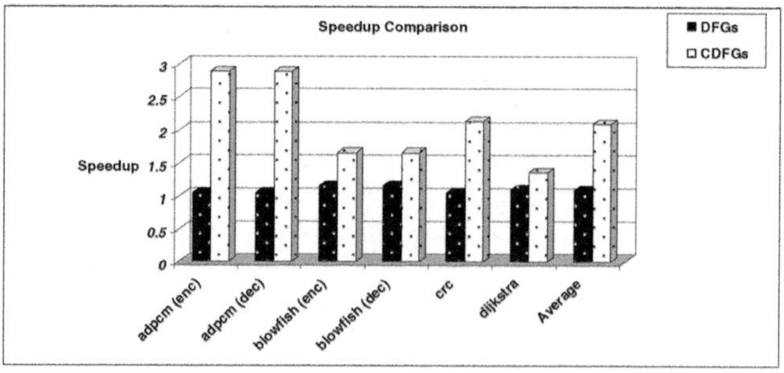

Fig. 8. Speedup comparison of acceleration approaches based on DFGs and CDFGs

6 Conclusion

In this paper, we presented motivation for handling branch instruction in DFGs and extending them to CDFGs. In addition, basic requirements for developing an accelerator featuring conditional execution were presented and some algorithms for CDFG temporal partitioning and generating executable CDFGs on the accelerator were proposed. NTPT is a temporal partitioning algorithm which tries to traverse not-taken path of the branch instructions and partitions the input CDFG. On the other hand, frequency-based temporal partitioning algorithm considers the taken and not-taken frequencies to partition input CDFG. Using this approach it is possible to add both taken and not-taken paths of a branch instruction to a partition. Comparison of these algorithms shows that though NTPT is a simple partitioning algorithm but it generates small number of CDFGs which bring about a comparable and even higher speedup.

To show the effectiveness of supporting conditional execution in hardware, we applied our proposals to the accelerator of an extensible processor called AMBER. RFU was a matrix of functional units which was extended to support the conditional execution. We used an integrated framework based on NTPT algorithm to generated mappable CDFGs on the RFU. These CDFGs are executed on the RFU to accelerate the application execution. Experimental results show the effectiveness of covering branch instructions and using CDFGs versus DFGs.

Acknowledgement

This research was supported in part by the Grant-in-Aid for Creative Basic Research, 14GS0218, Encouragement of Young Scientists (A), 17680005, and the 21st Century COE Program.

References

[1] Auguin, M, Bianco, L, Capella, L, Gresset, E. Partitioning conditional data flow graphs for embedded system design, Proc. of ASAP 2000 (2000) 339-348

[2] Carrillo, J. E, Chow, P. The effect of reconfigurable units in superscalar processors, Proc. of the ACM/SIGDA FPGA (2001) 141-150

[3] Clark, N, Blome, J, Chu, M, Mahlke, S, Biles, S, Flautner, K. An architecture framework for transparent instruction set customization in embedded processors, Proc. ISCA (2005) 272-283

[4] Clark, N, Zhong, H, Mahlke, S. Processor acceleration through automated instruction set customization, MICRO-36 (2003)

[5] Hauck, S, Fry, T, Hosler, M, Kao, J. The Chimaera reconfigurable functional unit, IEEE Symp. on FPGAs for Custom Computing Machines (1997) 206-217

[6] Karthikeya M and Gajjala P and Bhatia D, Temporal partitioning and scheduling data flow graphs for reconfigurable computers, IEEE Transactions on Computers, 48 (6) (1999) 579-590

[7] Kastner, R, Kaplan, A, Sarrafzadeh, M. Synthesis techniques and optimizations for reconfigurable systems, Kluwer-Academic Publishers (2004)

[8] Lee, J.E, Kim, Y, Jung, J, Choi, K. Reconfigurable ALU array architecture with conditional execution, International SoC Design Conference (2004) 222-226
[9] Lodi, A, Toma, M, Campi, F, Cappelli, A, Canegallo, R, Guerrieri, R. A VLIW processor with reconfigurable instruction set for embedded applications, IEEE Journal of Solid-State Circuits, Vol. 38, No. 11 (2003) 1876–1886
[10] Mahlke, S. A, Hank, R. E, McCormick, J.E, August, D. I, Hwu, W. W. A comparison of full and partial predicated execution support for ILP processors. In Proc. ISCA (1995) 138-150
[11] Mehdipour, F, Noori, H, Saheb Zamani, M, Murakami, K, Sedighi, K, Inoue, K. Custom instruction generation using temporal partitioning techniques for a reconfigurable functional unit, Int. Conference on Embedded and Ubiquitous Computing (2006)
[12] Mehdipour, F, Saheb Zamani, M, Sedighi, M. An integrated temporal partitioning and physical design framework for static compilation of reconfigurable computing systems, Int. J. of Microprocessors and Microsystems, Elsevier, Vol. 30, No. 1 (2006) 52-62
[13] Mei, B, Vernalde, S, Verkest, D, Lauwereins, R. Design methodology for a tightly coupled VLIW/Reconfigurable matrix architecture, DATE (2004) 1224-1129
[14] Mibench, www.eecs.umich.edu/mibench
[15] Noori, H, Mehdipour, F, Murakami, K, Inoue, K, Saheb Zamani, M. A reconfigurable functional unit for an adaptive dynamic extensible processor, Proc. of IEEE International Conference on Field Programmable Logic and Applications (2006) 781-784
[16] Park, J.C, Schlansker, M.S. On predicated execution. Technical Report HPL-91-58. Hewlett Packard Laboratories (1991)
[17] Razdan, R, Smith, M.D. A high-performance microarchitecture with hardware-programmable functional units, MICRO-27 (1994)
[18] Simplescalar, www.simplescalar.com
[19] Smith J.E, Sohi, G.S. The microarchitecture of superscalar P. In Proc. IEEE, Vol. 83, (1995) 1609- 1624
[20] Synopsys Inc. http://www.synopsys.com/products/logic/design_compiler.html
[21] Vassiliadis, S, Gaydadjiev, G, Kuzmanov, G. The MOLEN polymorphic processor, IEEE Transactions on Computers, Vol. 53, No. 11 (2004) 1363-1375
[22] P. Yu and T. Mitra, Characterizing embedded applications for instruction-set extensible processors, In Proc. Design Automation Conference (2004) 723-728

Behavioral Synthesis of Double-Precision Floating-Point Adders with Function-Level Transformations: A Case Study

Yuko Hara[1], Hiroyuki Tomiyama[1], Shinya Honda[1], Hiroaki Takada[1], and Katsuya Ishii[2]

[1] Graduate School of Information Science, Nagoya University,
{hara,tomiyama,honda,hiro}@ertl.jp
[2] Information Technology Center, Nagoya University,
Furo-cho, Chikusa-ku, Nagoya, 464-8603, Japan
ishii@itc.nagoya-u.ac.jp

Abstract. Recently, the continuously growing capacity of FPGAs has enabled us to place floating-point arithmetic IPs on FPGAs. The required area for floating-point computations, however, is still high. This paper presents a case study on behavioral synthesis of double-precision floating-point adders and adder/subtracters for FPGAs. With function-level transformations, we design totally 15 adders and 21 adder/subtracters from addition and subtraction functions written in C. Our experimental results show that the circuit area is reduced by 58%, the execution time is shortened by 47% and the area-delay product is improved by 69%. Through the case study, we show the effectiveness of behavioral synthesis with function-level transformations for designing complex arithmetic circuits.

1 Introduction

Traditionally, floating-point arithmetic units have rarely been used in FPGAs due to their high cost. A designer had to convert floating-point numbers in system-level specification into fixed-point ones before starting hardware design. However, the conversion from floating-point numbers into fixed-point ones is very time-consuming and error-prone.

Recently, the continuously growing capacity of FPGAs has enabled us to place single-precision floating-point arithmetic IPs, or even double-precision ones, on FPGAs. In most cases, floating-point arithmetic IPs are provided in the form of gate-level netlist or register-transfer level description in HDL. With such gate- or RT-level IPs, it is often impossible to satisfy application-specific design requirements such as area, clock frequency, latency, and so on. Although RT-level IPs are customizable or modifiable to some extent, it is not easy to significantly change their latency or area.

One of the solution approaches to the design of application-specific complex arithmetic units is the use of behavioral synthesis. Behavioral synthesis is a technology which automatically generates an RT-level circuit from a sequential program [1]. Using behavioral synthesis, various circuits with different area and

Y.-H. Lee et al. (Eds.): ICESS 2007, LNCS 4523, pp. 261–270, 2007.

performance can be generated from the same sequential program by specifying different synthesis options and constraints. Behavioral synthesis techniques have extensively been studied for more than two decades, and behavioral synthesis tools are now being used in practice, particularly in Japanese industry [2] [3].

In this case study, we have designed totally 15 adders and 21 adder/subtracters for double-precision floating-point numbers for FPGAs with using a behavioral synthesis tool. Specifically, we have focused on function-level transformations in order to generate area- and/or performance-efficient designs. Through the case study, we show the effectiveness of behavioral synthesis with function-level transformations for designing complex arithmetic circuits.

The rest of this paper is organized as follows. Section 2 explains experimental environments used in Sections 3 and 4. Section 3 shows a case study on behavioral synthesis of adders. Section 4 studies synthesis of adder/subtracters. Section 5 concludes this paper with a summary.

2 Design Environment

This section describes the design environments used in the experiments of Section 3 and 4.

2.1 Design Tools

We use a commercial behavioral synthesis tool eXCite from YXI [4]. A C program is input to eXCite with several optimization options and design constraints. Then, an RT-level description in VHDL or Verilog-HDL is generated. The optimization options and design constraints include clock frequency, the number of functional units, and so on. For logic synthesis and place-and-route, we use Synplify Pro from Synplicity [5] and XST from Xilinx [6], respectively. Logic synthesis and place-and-route are optimized for performance. Xilinx Spartan 3 is specified as a target device.

2.2 Double-Precision Floating-Point Addition Program in C

We use a double-precision floating-point addition function *double_add* from the SoftFloat suite [7]. The SoftFloat suite is an open-source software implementation of the IEC/IEEE Standard for binary floating-point arithmetic. It includes several fundamental arithmetic operations such as addition, subtraction, multiplication, division, and so on, supporting both single-precision and double-precision floating-point formats. In this paper, we select double-precision floating-point addition due to its high computational complexity and importance.

Note that the size of the double-precision floating-point addition program is relatively large compared with DSP kernels which were often used in the past literature on behavioral synthesis. The addition program consists of more than 600 lines of C code. After behavioral level optimization such as common subexpression elimination and dead code elimination, there exist 298 arithmetic and logic operations, 307 assignments, 77 *if* statements, 26 *goto/return* statements, and so on.

Table 1. Experimental results for adders

Clock const. (MHz)	25		50		100	
Design goal	Perf.	Area	Perf.	Area	Perf.	Area
States	3	21	5	22	10	25
Area (slices)	6,039	5,654	4,913	5,875	3,667	6,121
Clock freq. (MHz)	23.6	29.0	29.4	26.3	49.6	37.3
Exec. Cycles	3	21	5	22	10	25
Exec. time (ns)	127.3	723.2	169.9	835.4	201.6	671.0
Area-delay ($\times 10^3$)	768.7	4,088.7	834.9	4,908.0	739.3	4,107.0

2.3 Evaluation Metrics

We evaluate the quality of designs with three metrics, i.e., *area*, *execution time* and *area-delay product*. Area is measured by the number of slices occupied for the designs. Execution time is defined as the product of clock period and execution cycles. Area-delay product is defined as the product of area and execution time. Since in general area and execution time are in trade-off relation, area-delay product is useful to evaluate the overall quality of the designs.

3 Synthesis of Adders

In this section, we first show a case study on synthesizing adders for double-precision floating numbers. Then, we employ three techniques to improve the quality of adders.

3.1 Simple Synthesis of Adders

First, we synthesized adders from the double-precision floating-point addition function explained in Section 2.2. The clock frequency constraint was set to be 25, 50 and 100 MHz. For each clock frequency, we specified two types of synthesis goal to behavioral synthesis tool eXCite: one is the performance maximization and the other is the area minimization by sharing components as much as possible.

Then, we executed logic synthesis and place-and-route to evaluate area and clock frequency of the designs. The results are shown in Table 1. The row "Design goal" of Table 1 represents the synthesis goal.

When the synthesis goal is the area minimization, the number of required components is smaller than that for performance maximization since several components are temporally shared [1]. The total area, however, is larger as imposing a more severe constraint on clock frequency. This is because more multiplexers and registers are required, and this area overhead is larger than the area saving obtained by reduced components. As a severe clock constraint is given, the control path becomes compilicated and its area is increased. Moreover, the execution time becomes longer, which results in severe performance degradation. In terms of the area-delay product, the synthesis goal for performance yields better designs than that for area.

[1] Information on the types and the numbers of components requried by each design are omitted due to the limited space.

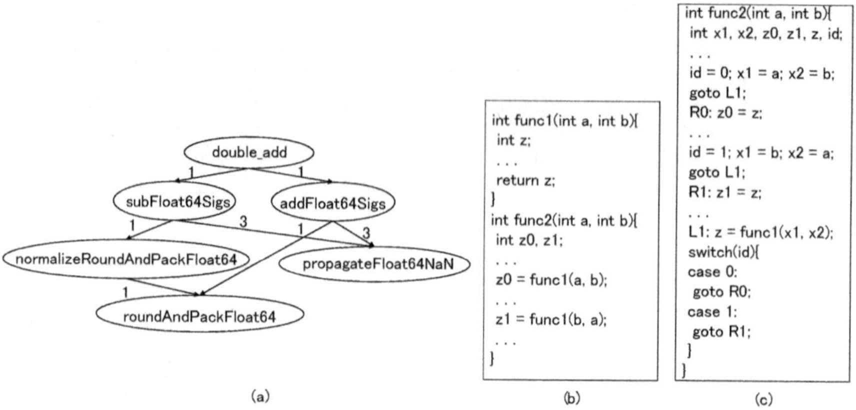

Fig. 1. (a)A call graph of double-precision floating-point addition function, (b)An emample of an original program, (c)The rewritten program with goto conversion

3.2 Synthesis of Adders with Goto Conversion

The double-precision floating-point addition function *double_add* from the Soft-Float suite consists of multi-level function calls. A call graph for *double_add* is shown in Fig. 1 (a). In Fig. 1 (a), *addFloat64Sigs* directly calls *propagate-Float64NaN* three times and *roundAndPackFloat64* once. *subFloat64Sigs* directly calls *propagateFloat64NaN* three times, while it indirectly calls *roundAndPackFloat64* once via *normalizeRoundAndPackFloat64*. *double_add* has two arguments *a* and *b*. If both of their signs are same, *double_add* calls *addFloat64Sigs*, otherwise *double_add* calls *subFloat64Sigs*. In addition to the functions shown in Fig. 1 (a), there exist more than ten functions, but they are omitted here since they are small and to be inlined.

Unless specific options are given, eXCite inlines all callee functions and generates one large function. When synthesizing *double_add* in Fig. 1 (a), for example, all the functions are inlined into *double_add*. In general, functional units can be shared among the inlined functions, which leads to a small circuit area. When large functions which are called multiple times are inlined, however, the number of states is increased. This makes its control path complicated, leading to inefficient designs. This problem is avoided by applying *goto conversion* to such functions. Goto conversion is a transformation to replace function calls with goto statements, and has been used in some behavioral synthesis tools such as [2] [3].

An example of goto conversion is shown in Figs. 1 (b) and (c). Fig. 1 (b) is an original C source code. In this example, there exist two function calls to *func1* in *func2*. Without goto conversion, the body of *func1* is inlined twice. This might lead to large number of states, which results in the complicated control logic. In Fig. 1 (c), only *func2* is rewritten with goto conversion. First, when a goto statement for label *L1* is executed above label *R0*, the control flow jumps to label *L1* and calls *func1*. After executing *func1*, the control flow jumps back to label *R0* from a *switch* statement described below label *L1* since *id* is zero. When the control flow executes a goto statement for label *L1* above label *R1*, it behaves as same as above. In the program in Fig. 1 (c), the body of *fun c1* is inlined only once in spite of being executed at two locations in the C source code. In addition, the components required by *func1* can be shared with other operations as same as inlining.

In this section, goto conversion is applied to synthesis of double-precision floating-point adders. The candidate functions for goto conversion are *propagateFloat64NaN* and *roundAndPackFloat64* since they are relatively large and called several times. Using goto conversion, we have designed three adders as follows, for each clock constraint.

RG: goto conversion is applied to *roundAndPackFloat64* with inlining *propagateFloat64NaN*

PG: goto conversion is applied to *propagateFloat64NaN* with inlining *roundAndPackFloat64*

RPG: goto conversion is applied to both *roundAndPackFloat64* and *propagateFloat64NaN*

We set three constraints on clock frequency, i.e., 25, 50 and 100 MHz. Based on the results in Section 3.1, we specified performance maximization as our synthesis goal. The experimental results are shown in Table 2. Numbers in parentheses in Table 2 are normalized values where baseline is "Perf." in Table 1.

When the clock constraint is 25 or 100 MHz, it is the best to apply goto conversion only to *roundAndPackFloat64* in terms of area-delay product. When the clock constraint is 50 MHz, applying goto conversion only to *propagateFloat64NaN* is the best. When employing RPG on 50 MHz, PG on 100 MHz or RPG on 100 MHz, the areas are larger than those without goto conversion. This is mainly because, with use of goto conversion, the number of registers is largely increased by gate-level retiming. Particularly as more severe clock constraint is given, larger numbers of registers are required. Then, the total area was also increased due to the increase of registers.

In terms of area-delay product, the best design is generated with RG on 25 MHz clock constraint among all the results in Table 2.

Table 2. Experimental results for adders with goto conversion

Clock const. (MHz)	25			50			100		
Technique	RG	PG	RPG	RG	PG	RPG	RG	PG	RPG
States	3	3	3	5	5	5	10	10	10
Area (slices)	5,503	4,799	5,854	4,541	4,614	5,158	3,578	5,468	5,034
	(0.91)	(0.80)	(0.97)	(0.92)	(0.94)	(1.05)	(0.98)	(1.49)	(1.37)
Clock freq. (MHz)	27.6	21.7	28.7	26.7	29.2	27.1	50.1	43.9	49.2
	(1.03)	(0.72)	(1.19)	(1.10)	(1.01)	(1.09)	(0.99)	(1.13)	(1.01)
Exec. Cycles	3	3	3	5	5	5	10	10	10
Exec. time (ns)	108.5	138.4	104.7	187.5	171.4	184.5	199.8	227.9	203.3
	(0.83)	(1.09)	(0.82)	(1.10)	(1.01)	(1.09)	(0.99)	(1.13)	(1.01)
Area-delay ($\times 10^3$)	597.3	664.2	613.0	851.2	791.0	951.9	715.0	1,246.2	1,023.5
	(0.78)	(0.86)	(0.80)	(1.02)	(0.95)	(1.14)	(0.97)	(1.69)	(1.38)

4 Synthesis of Adder/Subtracters

In this section, we design adder/subtracters from an addition and subtraction functions which supports the double-precision floating-point format. Adder/subtracter is an arithmetic circuit which computes both addition and subtraction. In Section 4.1, we show the results with a simple method to merge these two functions. Then, in Section 4.2, we employ goto conversion to generate improved designs compared to the simple design.

4.1 Simple Synthesis of Adder/Subtracters

The double-precision floating-point subtraction function *double_sub* from the SoftFloat suite has a similar structure as addition function *double_add*. *double_sub* takes two arguments *a* and *b*. If both the signs of *a* and *b* are same, *subFloat64Sigs* is called, otherwise *addFloat64Sigs* is called. A call graph of *double_add* and *double_sub* is shown in Fig. 2 (a). *double_addsub* is a new function which is defined to merge *double_add* and *double_sub*. An adder/subtracter for double-precision floating-point format can be generated from *double_addsub*.

First, in this section, *double_sub* was singly synthesized, and then, the new function *double_addsub* was synthesized. *double_addsub* has three input values; two arguments *a* and *b*, and a 1-bit *id*. This program is partially shown in Fig. 2 (b). The bodies of *double_add* and *double_sub* are omitted here. Variables defined as *double* type are automatically converted to *float64* type, which is in actual *unsigned long long* type. The bitwidth of *id* is reduced to one by an option of eXCite although it is originally defined as eight bits in the C source code. If *id* is equal to zero, *double_add* is called, otherwise *double_sub* is called. The experimental results for *double_sub* and a function which merges *double_add* and *double_sub* are shown in Table 3.

For adder/subtracters, the area is almost same as the sum of areas of *double_add* and *double_sub*. The number of components required by an adder/subtracter is also same as the sum of those of *double_add* and *double_sub*. This is because *double_add* and *double_sub* were speculatively executed even though

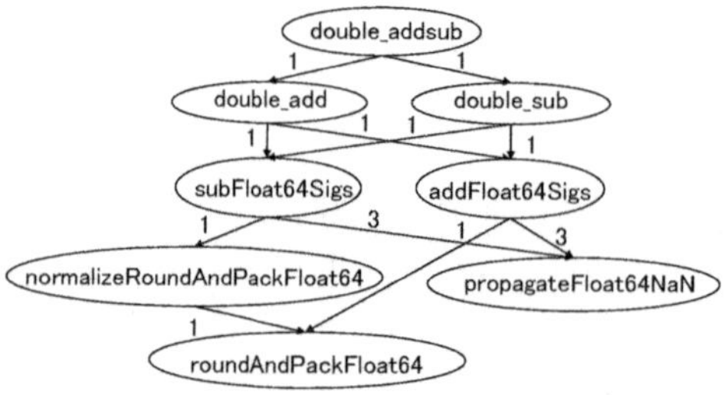


```
typedef unsigned long long float64;

float64 double_addsub (float64 a, float64 b, char id){
  float64 z;    /* output */

  if(id == 0){
    z = double_add(a, b);
  }else{
    z = double_sub(a, b);
  }
  return z;
}
```

(a) (b)

Fig. 2. (a)A call graph of double-precision floating-point addition and subtraction functions, (b)A new function which is defined to merge *double_add* and *double_sub*

Table 3. Experimental results for subtracters and adder/subtracters

Function	Subtracters			Adder/subtracters		
Clock const. (MHz)	25	50	100	25	50	100
States	3	5	10	3	5	10
Area (slices)	5,041	5,184	3,737	8,145	7,381	9,696
Clock freq. (MHz)	21.0	19.6	50.4	16.1	20.5	32.6
Exec. Cycles	3	5	10	3	5	10
Exec. time (ns)	142.6	254.5	198.5	186.6	244.2	306.5
Area-delay ($\times 10^3$)	718.8	1,319.3	741.9	1,519.8	1,802.6	2,971.4

Table 4. Experimental results for adder/subtracters with components sharing

Clock const. (MHz)	25	50	100
States	7	11	21
Area (slices)	8,998 (1.11)	8,264 (1.12)	5,943 (0.61)
Clock freq. (MHz)	15.4 (1.04)	20.9 (0.98)	45.4 (0.72)
Exec. Cycles	4	6	11
Exec. time (ns)	259.9 (1.39)	287.3 (1.18)	242.1 (0.79)
Area-delay ($\times 10^3$)	2,338.2 (1.54)	2,374.0 (1.32)	1,439.0 (0.48)

execution of *double_add* and *double_sub* must be exclusive. Therefore, the components are hardly shared between the two functions.

Next, in order to prevent from the speculative execution of *double_add* and *double_sub*, we explicitly inserted a clock boundary after the condition test in Fig. 2 (b) so that *double_add* and *double_sub* are mutually executed. This helps components be shared. The experimental results are shown in Table 4. Values in parentheses in Table 4 are normalized by "Adder/subtracters" in Table 3.

In terms of area in Table 4, when the clock constraint is 25 or 50 MHz, the areas are increased compared to the results in Table 3. This is mainly because the number of multiplexers is increased to share the components. When the clock constraint is 100 MHz, on the other hand, the area is reduced since the number of registers is significantly reduced. Note that, in general, the speculative execution requires more registers.

4.2 Synthesis of Adder/Subtracters with Goto Conversion

As explained above, *double_add* and *double_sub* have very similar structures. Fig. 2 (a) shows that both *double_add* and *double_sub* call *addFloat64Sigs* and *subFloat64Sigs*. In the experiments in Table 3, both *addFloat64Sigs* and *subFloat64Sigs* are inlined twice since the functions are called by both *double_add* and *double_sub*. This makes designs large. To avoid inlining large functions such as *addFloat64Sigs* and *subFloat64Sigs*, firstly, we employ goto conversion to *addFloat64Sigs* and *subFloat64Sigs*. This design is denoted as **ASG**.

The C source code of *double_add* and *double_sub* are shown in Fig. 3 (a) and (b), respectively. Fig. 3 (a) and (b) have little differences except a condition in the *if* statement to determine a function to be called. Note that *extract64Sign* is a small function which gets a sign bit of an argument, and *aSign* and *bSign* represents the

```
float64 double_add( float64 a, float64 b ){
  int aSign, bSign;

  aSign = extractFloat64Sign(a);
  bSign = extractFloat64Sign(b);
  if ( aSign == bSign ) {
      return addFloat64Sigs(a, b, aSign);
  }else {
      return subFloat64Sigs(a, b, aSign);
  }
}
```

(a)

```
float64 double_sub( float64 a, float64 b ){
  int aSign, bSign;

  aSign = extractFloat64Sign(a);
  bSign = extractFloat64Sign(b);
  if ( aSign == bSign ) {
      return subFloat64Sigs(a, b, aSign);
  }else {
      return addFloat64Sigs(a, b, aSign);
  }
}
```

(b)

```
float64 double_addsub
          (float64 a, float64 b, char id){
  float64 z;    /* output */
  int aSign, bSign;

  aSign = extractFloat64Sign(a);
  bSign = extractFloat64Sign(b);
  if((aSign == bSign && id == 0)
        || (aSign != bSign && id != 0)){
    z = addFloat64Sigs(a, b, aSign);
  }else{
    z = subFloat64Sigs(a, b, aSign);
  }
  return z;
}
```

(c)

Fig. 3. A new function which is defined to merge *double_add* and *double_sub*

signs of a and b, respectively. Then, we define a new function whose condition of *if* statement is rewritten from *if* statements of *double_add* and *double_sub* in order to directly call *addFloat64Sigs* and *subFloat64Sigs* from the new function as shown in Fig. 3 (c). In this function, *addFloat64Sigs* is called when the signs of a and b are same and *id* is zero or when *double_add* and *double_sub* are not same and *id* is not zero, i.e., *id* is one, otherwise *subFloat64Sigs* is called. Goto conversion is not applied to any functions. This design is denoted as **NGT**.

Next, goto conversion is applied to *roundAndPackFloat64* and *propagateFloat64NaN* for *double_addsub* described in Fig. 3 (c). Then, we obtain three designs **NRG**, **NPG** and **NRPG**. The five designs are summarized as follows.

ASG: goto conversion is applied to *addFloat64Sigs* and *subFloat64Sigs*
NGT: *addFloat64Sigs* and *subFloat64Sigs* are directly called in a new function without goto conversion
NRG: goto conversion is applied to *roundAndPackFloat64* in addition to a technique **NGT**
NPG: goto conversion is applied to *propagateFloat64NaN* in addition to a technique **NGT**
NRPG: goto conversion is applied to *roundAndPackFloat64* and *propagateFloat64NaN* in addition to a technique **NGT**

The experimental results are shown in Table 5. Values in parentheses in Table 5 are normalized by "Adder/subtracters" in Table 3. in Table 3. All the results with ASG have better results than the results in Table 3. These results, however, were the worst among with five techniques in Table 5. When the clock constraint is 25 MHz, NRG has the best result. In this case, all the techniques with goto conversion, i.e., NRG, NPG and NRPG have better results than the one with NGT. When the clock constraint is 50 or 100 MHz, NGT which does not employ goto conversion has the best results. This is mainly because of gate-level retiming during logic synthesis. With goto conversion, gate-level retiming easily increases registers, which results in an increase in the circuit area.

Table 5. Experimental results for adder/subtracters with goto conversion

Clock const. (MHz)	25				
Technique	ASG	NGT	NRG	NPG	NRPG
States	3	3	3	3	3
Area (slices)	7,937 (0.97)	6,049 (0.74)	5,446 (0.67)	4,865 (0.60)	5,787 (0.71)
Clock freq. (MHz)	21.1 (0.76)	23.7 (0.68)	30.3 (0.53)	23.0 (0.70)	23.2 (0.69)
Exec. Cycles	3	3	3	3	3
Exec. time (ns)	142.4 (0.76)	126.8 (0.68)	99.1 (0.53)	130.6 (0.70)	129.4 (0.69)
Area-delay ($\times 10^3$)	1,130.3 (0.74)	766.8 (0.51)	539.9 (0.36)	635.4 (0.42)	748.6 (0.49)
Clock const. (MHz)	50				
Technique	ASG	NGT	NRG	NPG	NRPG
States	5	5	5	5	5
Area (slices)	7,190 (0.97)	4,408 (0.60)	4,702 (0.64)	4,732 (0.64)	4,691 (0.64)
Clock freq. (MHz)	22.3 (0.92)	28.7 (0.71)	27.4 (0.75)	30.6 (0.67)	26.7 (0.77)
Exec. Cycles	5	5	5	5	5
Exec. time (ns)	224.5 (0.92)	174.0 (0.71)	182.7 (0.75)	163.4 (0.67)	187.4 (0.77)
Area-delay ($\times 10^3$)	1,613.9 (0.90)	766.8 (0.43)	858.8 (0.48)	773.4 (0.43)	879.0 (0.49)
Clock const. (MHz)	100				
Technique	ASG	NGT	NRG	NPG	NRPG
States	10	10	10	10	10
Area (slices)	5,382 (0.56)	4,054 (0.42)	4,393 (0.45)	5,823 (0.60)	5,227 (0.54)
Clock freq. (MHz)	38.5 (0.85)	44.3 (0.74)	47.9 (0.68)	47.9 (0.68)	47.0 (0.69)
Exec. Cycles	10	10	10	10	10
Exec. time (ns)	259.5 (0.85)	225.9 (0.74)	208.7 (0.68)	208.9 (0.68)	212.6 (0.69)
Area-delay ($\times 10^3$)	1,396.8 (0.47)	915.9 (0.31)	916.8 (0.31)	1,216.4 (0.41)	1,111.5 (0.37)

4.3 Discussion

Through the case study, we have found the following observations.

- Reducing the number of components does not always lead to area reduction because of the increased multiplexers and registers.
- Goto conversion is useful in order to reduce the area.
- However, goto conversion does not always lead to area reduction because of the increased registers through gate-level retiming.

We have seen so far that the quality of designs obtained by behavioral synthesis is affected by a number of factors such as clock constraint, resource constraint, optimization options and so on. Therefore, it is not easy but very important to establish a systematic methodology for behavioral synthesis.

5 Conclusions

In this paper, we have presented several techniques on behavioral synthesis of double-precision floating-point adders and adder/subtracters. We have generated totally 15 adders and 21 adder/subtracters with function-level transformations such as goto conversion.

The future works are considered in two directions. One is to develop other arithmetic IPs for double-precision floating-point computations. The other is to establish a systematic methodology for behavioral synthesis of complex arithmetic circuits.

References

1. D. D. Gajski, N. D. Dutt, A. C.-H. Wu, and S. Y.-L. Lin, *High-Level Synthesis: Introduction to Chip and System Design*, Kluwer Academic Publishers, 1992.
2. K. Wakabayashi and T. Okamoto, "C-based SoC Design Flow and EDA Tools: An ASIC and System Bendor Perspective," *IEEE Trans. CAD*, vol. 19, no. 12, Dec. 2000.
3. K. Wakabayashi, "CyberWorkBench: Integrated Design Environment Based on C-based Behavior Synthesis and Verification," *Int. Symp. VLSI Design, Automation and Test*, 2005.
4. Y Explorations, Inc., http://www.yxi.com/.
5. Synplicity Inc., http://www.synplicity.com/.
6. Xilinx Inc., http://www.xilinx.com/.
7. SoftFloat, http://www.jhauser.us/arithmetic/SoftFloat.html.

NISD: A Framework for Automatic Narrow Instruction Set Design

Xianhua Liu, Jiyu Zhang, and Xu Cheng

Microprocessor Research and Development Center,
Peking University, Beijing, P.R. China, 100871
{liuxianhua,zhangjiyu,chengxu}@mprc.pku.edu.cn

Abstract. Code size is becoming an important design factor in the embedded domain. To deal with this problem, many embedded RISC processors support a dual-width instruction set. Mixed code generation is also introduced in expectation of achieving both higher code density from the narrow instruction set (usually 16 bits) and good performance from the normal one (usually 32 bits), with little extra cost. To a certain application domain, processors can combine an efficient general purpose instruction set and a narrow instruction set tailored to the particular applications. Since the design of instruction set is highly related to the compiler and the application programs, a feedback driven technique will be a good choice.

In this paper, we introduce a framework of automatic narrow instruction set design. The instructions are described in our Instruction Set Description Template (ISDT). Given a set of application programs, the design tool will iteratively use the suggested narrow instruction set represented in ISDT to do mixed-code generation and to update the narrow instruction set according to the evaluation feedback, thus to get an ultimate fine narrow instruction set without human designer's involvement. We describe our method in detail by example of designing narrow instruction set for UniCore with the mediabench as the application set, and show its usefulness through the experiments.

Keywords: dual-width instruction set, narrow instruction set design, automatic instruction set design.

1 Introduction

Embedded systems are more and more important in people's daily life. According to [1], the market size of embedded systems is 100 times bigger than the desktop market and it is estimated that with current growth rates the number of embedded systems will reach 16 billion by 2010. Meanwhile, in the embedded domain, applications must be stored and executed under constraints of limited memory and energy, with a clear and important trend of continuous increase in complexity. In this situation, many RICS processors provide dual width ISA and a way of mixed coding to provide a smaller code size, such as ARM with Thumb, MIPS with MIPS16e, UniCore32 with UniCore16, and etc.. These dual width instruction set processors support both a normal instruction set (usually 32-bit) and a narrow one (usually 16-bit). The narrow

Y.-H. Lee et al. (Eds.): ICESS 2007, LNCS 4523, pp. 271–282, 2007.

instruction set leads to smaller code and lower instruction cache energy consumption [2]. However, because of the limitation of encoding space, the narrow IS often can only encode a subset of the normal instructions and can access only a subset of registers, so some functions can not be easily encoded into the narrow one. Thus it may take more instructions to represent the same program fragments by narrow ISA than the normal one. This brings a difficulty to design of the narrow IS. Besides performance, code size, energy consumption and some other features of the final system, Time to Market is also one of the important factors which determine the profits of the product. Thus, a convenient tool is needed to help to design a proper narrow IS for the particular application sets.

For embedded computer systems, the applications are often fixed in comparison with general purpose computer systems. To a certain application domain, processors can combine an efficient general purpose instruction set and a narrow instruction set tailored to the particular applications. Since the design of instruction set is highly related to the compiler and the application programs, a feedback driven technique will be a good choice. The problem is mainly on how to automatically perform an iterative feedback driven process to free the designers from the repeated work to some extend.

This paper makes the following contributions. First, we present an automatic narrow IS design framework aiming at generating instruction set tailored to particular applications for embedded systems. This framework takes compiler in the design loop. The core part is mainly based on a post-process optimizer in the compiler tool-chain, which can directly deal with a low-level intermediate representation. Based on this intermediate representation, we design our Instruction Set Description Template (ISDT) to guide compilation and simulation. Further more, we present our experimental study of a narrow instruction set design for UniCore, a RISC microprocessor to show details of the design process and its usefulness.

This paper is organized as follows. In section 2, we review some related work in dual width ISA design and automatic ISA design. Section 3 presents the workflow of our framework. The detail of the method is shown in Section 4 and the experimental results are given in Section 5. Section 6 concludes and gives the future work.

2 Related Works

2.1 Dual-Width IS Design and Mixed Code Generation

Several works have already been done in the dual-width instruction set design [3][4][5] and mixed code generation field. In the current dual-width IS design, most of work is done by experts with deep human analysis on the original IS and compiled applications. A typical work is described in [8] by Krishnaswamy and Gupta. They introduced a set of AX (Augmenting eXtensions) to Thumb instruction set and the task of the compiler is to identify and replace proper pairs of Thumb instructions with AX + Thumb instruction pairs. The aim of this method is to improve performance of Thumb code. Because of the limited opcodes width and access to limited registers in the original Thumb code, the performance is generally not as good as ARM code. Some architectures support 32-bit and 16-bit mixed instructions without mode changing, such as Thumb-2 [9]. Thumb-2 is a carefully designed ISA which can provide both 16-bit and 32-bit instructions in Thumb-2 mode. Although Thumb-2 is a big improvement over Thumb and can be seen as a separate instruction set, it still needs more instructions than ARM to finish some work.

Mixed code generation domain is also widely studied. Krishnaswamy and Gupta presented several coarse-grained heuristics with varying costs to make the decisions between using ARM and Thumb code at module level [1]. Each module of the program is either compiled entirely into Thumb code or entirely into ARM code. They use heuristic algorithm to choose between ARM and Thumb code for each of the frequently executed functions which are picked out by profiling. These heuristic algorithms all need to generate both ARM and Thumb codes for all of the frequently executed functions and the compiler misses the opportunity to achieve greater code size reduction by encoding parts of a function into 16-bit code.

A fine-grained method is also given and evaluated in [1]. The authors began with the coarse-grained mixed code and identified patterns of Thumb instruction sequences that are better executed using ARM instructions for each function and replaced these patterns with equivalent ARM code. However, the cycle counts are usually increased due to the cost of using two BX instructions per pattern and thus it exhibits no advantage over their coarse grained method.

Several other fine-grained mixed code generation methods are suggested in [6][7]. These methods usually used explicit mode-changing instructions to switch between the 32-bit and 16-bit modes. The extra mode-changing instructions in mixed code also lead to extra program execution cycles. The method in [10] proposed several Mode-Changing instructions that can switch the processor mode while performing a normal operation. These Mode-Changing instructions should be the ones frequently occurring in the programs so as to provide a mode-changing instruction when needed. In this method, the program is firstly compiled into the normal IS (32-bit), and then the compiler tool-chain will identify the proper instruction sequences and re-encode them with narrow IS. A narrow instruction sequence always begins with an MC instruction which performs the same functional operation as its corresponding instruction in normal IS, as well as telling the processor to change its execution mode into narrow mode. It ends with such an MC instruction, too, which tells the processor to change its execution mode back to the normal one. Each of the instructions between the two MC instructions has a corresponding instruction in the narrow IS. They are changed into narrow mode one by one, so as to reduce the code size and to avoid loss of performance. Our mixed-code generation method is based on this method.

2.2 Instruction Set Extension Design Tools

As embedded systems often aim at certain domain and have relative fixed applications, several works have been done on ways to extend an initial instruction set to adapt to a specific application domain. A number of publications propose to either statically analyze data flow graphs to find chances for new instructions or taking execution frequency into account [14][15]. Most of these publications rely on a specification language to generate compilers and simulators. The main difference between designing a narrow IS and a normal one is that the former often requires a one-to-one mapping relation from a narrow instruction to a normal one. This brings some new features into the design requirements.

The work presented in [11] on narrow IS design uses EXPRESSION Architecture Description Language (ADL) to model the narrow ISA features. The processor architecture with the desired narrow ISA features is described using EXPRESSION ADL and the description is input to the EXPRESS retargetable compiler and SIMPRESS simulator. Then the applications are compiled, simulated and the code size and performance statistics is generated for analysis. However, the several narrow ISAs to be evaluated are given by the authors from profiles, rather than generated by the tool, thus it still needs a lot of human involvement.

3 NISD Overview

In this section, we introduce the framework of our narrow instruction set design tool (NISD). We take the mode-changing mechanism and the fine-grained mixed code generation method presented in [10].

The task of designing a dual-width IS based on the original wide ISA is to design a Mode-Changing Instruction Set and a narrow IS, both of which is a subset of the original wide ISA. Process of automatically selecting instructions for narrow IS is shown in **Fig. 1**.

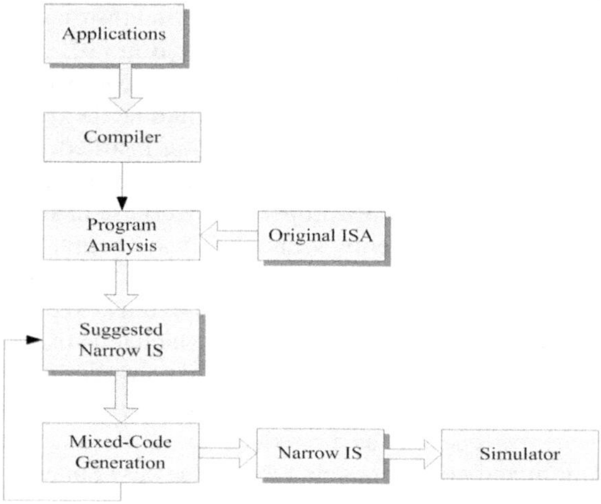

Fig. 1. Narrow IS Design Workflow

We start with the original compiler and simulator with only the normal IS. The MC instruction set and the narrow instruction set are both empty. The original ISA of the processor is described in our Instruction Set Description Template (ISDT). A set of typical application programs on the target embedded system is also given.

Firstly, the application programs are compiled and analyzed. The analyzer records occurrence frequency of each instruction and provides the list of narrow instruction candidates sorted by frequency. The initial narrow IS contains the instructions with the highest frequencies. The details of collecting frequency and generating the initial narrow IS are described in Section 4. We should notice that occurrence frequency is only one heuristic used to design a narrow IS. Whether one instruction in a certain sequence will be encoded into narrow form is determined by the whole narrow instruction set and the compiler tool-chain. Thus the instruction with the highest occurrence frequency is not necessarily the one which will be encoded into the narrow form most, that is, to add this instruction into narrow IS might not provide the highest compression rate. In this consideration, after given the sorted instruction list and the initial narrow IS by the analyzer, the narrow IS will be used in the compiler tool-chain to do mixed-code generation. An iterative process is taken to evaluate the effect of the narrow IS and the IS will be modified according to the feedback.

In the iterative process, the analyzer generates the suggested IS in the form of our ISDT. The compiler compiles all the programs into mixed code and evaluates how much code size reduction can be achieved using each suggested narrow IS. The phase of mixed code generation is taken as a post-processing phase of the compilation. The key idea of the mixed code generation is to identify instructions which can be converted into MC IS and narrow IS, reschedule the code to move such instructions together into contiguous blocks and use MC instructions and narrow instructions to represent them. In the end of an iterative, the effect of each narrow instruction is collected. The weights in the narrow instruction candidate list will be updated and the list will be re-sorted. Details will be presented in Section 4.

Finally, the narrow IS with the highest average compression rate is selected. The simulator is also modified automatically at the same time, in order to check whether there will be any important performance difference.

4 Selecting Instructions Using NISD

In this section, we take UniCore as an example to describe our method. UniCore is a pipelined RISC processor developed by Microprocessor Research and Development Center of Peking University. It has been taped out and used in thin-client systems with small local storages. In UniCore processor, there are two instruction sets of different widths: the 32-bit UniCore32 instruction set and the 16-bit UniCore16 instruction set. The UniCore32 instructions can access all 32 integer registers and have instructions designed aiming at efficiently support digital signal processing and some features in high level languages, such like multiply-accumulate operation, data block translating operations, etc. The Mode-Changing instructions are 16-bit wide and are used to change processor execution mode between 32-bit mode and 16-bit mode as well as performing their normal operations. When executing a UniCore16 instruction, the pre-decoder first turns it into the corresponding UniCore32 instruction and then decodes and executes the UniCore32 instruction. We show the design process of UniCore16 IS in this section. The evaluation is given in the next section.

4.1 Program Analysis and Initial Narrow IS Generation

Our program analysis maps each 32-bit instruction to one or several instruction classes, records the occurrence frequencies and gives the sorted instruction candidate list. The classes are mainly based on the opcode and operand type. The latter includes: how many operands there are in the instruction and how many bits each of them needs. The classes need to be given by experts. The given classes should contain the ones which are convenient to be represented in 16 bits.

Due to the limited encoding space and the requirement of ease to decode, there are many restrictions in narrow IS design. Simplicity prefers regularity. RISC processors often use some set of fixed bits to specify opcodes and several types of operands. In typical narrow IS, such as Thumb, MIPS16 and UniCore16, etc. most of the narrow instructions can only access a fixed set of 8 registers. Each register operand requires 3 bits for specification. In this situation, there will be 7 bits left to specify the opcodes, thus 128 opcodes can be encoded in total. Although this form is popular in many processors, there can be other forms, too. For example, we can use 4 bits to represent each register operand, and there can be 16 opcodes in total. We can also mix these two types of instruction forms. The instruction classes we used are listed in Fig. 2.

3 regs, in r0-r7 / r8-r15 / r16-r23/ r24-r31
3 regs, in r0-r15 / r16-r31
2 regs, in r0-r31
1 reg, in r0-r31
2 regs and 1 imme, regs in r0- r15 / r16-r31, imme: 4 bits
1 reg and 1 imme, imme field: 4bits or 7 bits
1 imme, imme field: 9 bits or 12bits
Other

reg: short for register
imme: short for immediate field

Fig. 2. Instruction operand forms for 16-bit IS

For each instruction in a program, the analyzer finds out which classes it belongs to and increments the occurrence frequency number of relative classes. The classes may have intersections. In some cases, an instruction can belong to several classes. Take "add r0, r2, r3" for example. This instruction can be mapped to both "add, 3 regs, in r0=r7"class and "add, 3 regs, in r0-r15" class. Each frequency number of the two classes will be incremented.

The analyzer maintains an array INST[OP][ARGFORM] to record the occurrence frequency of each instruction class. If an instruction's operands match one of the listed forms, the relative item in INST[OP][ARGFORM] will be incremented. If an instruction's operand form do not belong to any of the listed forms, the item INST[OP][Other] is incremented.

After the frequency statistics of the application programs, the analyzer sorts the items of array INST according to their values, that is, the occurrence frequencies of the instructions. One narrow IS candidate suggested by the analyzer concludes the instructions with the highest frequencies. The analyzer repeats adding the instruction with the highest frequency into the IS and removing it from the sorted array, until the instruction set is full. The number of instructions in the IS is determined by the selected instructions. For example, if the selected instructions are all of "3 regs, all in r0-r15 / r16-r31" operand form, which means each of them needs 12 bits to represent operands, the IS has 16 instructions in total. If the selected instructions are all of "3 regs, in r0-r7 / r8-r15 / r16-r23/ r24-r31" operand form, the IS has 128 instructions in total. The mixed IS' size will be between the two numbers.

Just as the design of any instruction set architecture, the design of narrow IS should also have the compiler tool-chain and application programs in the loop. In this consideration, the suggested narrow IS candidate will be used in the compilation to do mixed-code generation and be evaluated. Our instruction set description template used to guide mixed-code generation is described in Section 4.2 and the iterative design and evaluation process is presented in Section 4.3.

4.2 Instruction Set Description Template

The analyzer generates the narrow IS candidate in the form of our Instruction Set Description Template (ISDT). We take the mixed-code generation phase in a post-processing phase in the tool-chain, which is, a link-time optimization phase, as described in [10]. The intermediate language of the post-processing tool is a low-level language, specifying the opcode, used registers, immediates and so on.

Our ISDT is designed to match its intermediate language, as shown in Fig. 3. It has several fields describing its opcode and operands' requirements. The opcode field identifies the operation of the instruction, e.g. ADD, SUB, etc, which is a subset of the opcode set of the normal IS. The opmask_16 field determines the fixed bits of the instruction, which is used for generating the binary code. The argform field is consistent with instruction operand forms shown in Fig. 2. Some of the instructions is

```
struct inst_template
{
        T_OPCODE        opcode;
        T_INT           opmask_16;
        T_ARGFORM       argform;
        T_CONDITION     cond;
        T_INT           reg_dest_base;
        T_INT           reg_dest_mask;
        T_INT           reg_dest_shift;
        T_INT           reg_source1_base;
        T_INT           reg_source1_mask;
        T_INT           reg_source1_shift;
        T_INT           reg_source2_base;
        T_INT           reg_source2_mask;
        T_INT           reg_source2_shift;
        T_BOOL          is_signed_imme;
        T_INT           imme_mask;
        T_INT           imme_shift;
        T_INT           opmask_32;
        T_INT           reg_dest_shift_32;
        T_INT           reg_source1_shift_32;
        T_INT           reg_source2_shift_32;
        T_INT           reg_imme_shift_32;
};
```

Fig. 3. Instruction Set Description Template for UniCore conditional executed, and the cond field shows which conditions are allowed to be encoded into this instruction. There can be at most 3 register operands in the 16-bit IS for UniCore: one destination register and two source registers, described in our ISDT by reg_dest, reg_source1 and reg_source2 separately. For reg_dest, we take 3 fields to describe its limits. The reg_dest_base field shows the lowest presentable register number for reg_dest of this instruction. The reg_dest_mask field shows the number of bits used for this register operand, and the reg_dest_shift field shows the beginning position of this register operand in the binary representation of this instruction. For example, if the destination register in this instruction ranges from R15 to R23, and bit 6-bit 8 represent this register number, we can define these three fields as follows:

reg_dest_base = 15;   reg_dest_mask = 0x7;   reg_dest_shift = 0x6;

The upper bound of destination register number is the sum of reg_dest_base and reg_dest_mask. When reg_dest_mask is zero, it means this instruction should not contain any destination register. The source registers and the immediate fields are described in the same way. The rest of the fields are used for generating the corresponding 32-bit instruction for simulator. When performing instruction execution simulation, the simulator fetches an instruction and checks if it is in the 32-to-16 Mode-Changing IS table. If so, it converts upper half of it into the relative 32-bit instructions, changes the CPU execution mode and goes on execution. The process of changing CPU mode back to 32-bit mode is almost the same.

4.3 Compiler-in-the-Loop Narrow IS Design and Evaluation

The iterative process of narrow IS design and evaluation phase is illustrated in Fig. 4

After the analyzer generates the sorted narrow instruction candidate list and gives the initial narrow IS in the form of ISDT, the mixed-code generation and narrow instruction evaluation phase is called. This phase contains the following steps:

(1) Narrow instruction table creation

The narrow instruction table is created from the ISDT. It contains three parts: the 32-to-16 Mode-Changing instruction table, the UniCore16 instruction table and the 16-32 Mode-Changing instruction table.

(2) Mixed-code generation and narrow instruction evaluation

I. Mark instructions which are in the current narrow instruction table. The processor scans each instruction and marks all instructions which are in the current

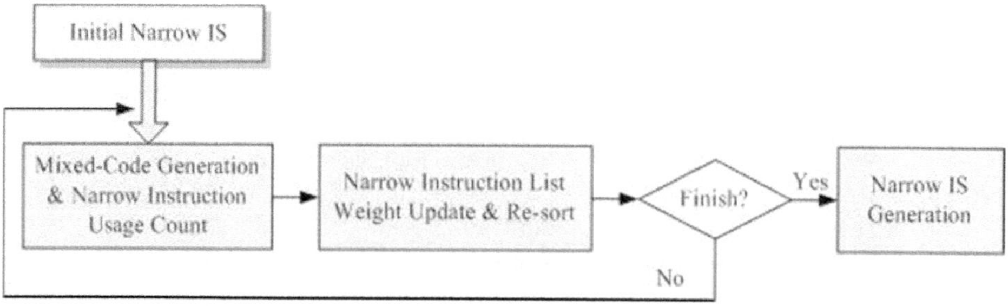

Fig. 4. The Iterative Process of Narrow IS Design and Evaluation

narrow instruction table, that is, which can be encoded into an MC instruction or a general UniCore16 instruction. In the case of branch instructions or load/store instructions, we should calculate the current relative offsets to decide whether one instruction can be coded into one MC instruction or UniCore16 instruction. The actual relative offsets might be smaller after turning some instructions into 16 bits, but it will not be larger than the value calculated now.
2. Instruction schedule. The dependence between each pair of instructions in each basic block is analyzed. The instructions are moved to let more marked instructions be together, thus to generate longer narrow instruction sequence.
3. Mark narrow instruction sequences. The post-processor scans the instructions form the beginning of each basic block. When it meets the first instructions which can be changed to a 32-to-16 MC instruction, it records that the 16-bit instruction sequence begins. After it has scanned the longest narrow instruction sequence ended with a 16-to-32 MC instruction, it changes each instruction to MC or UniCore16. Then it begins a new procedure of scanning until the end of the basic block. The count of each MC or UniCore16 instruction is incremented according to the times it is used.
After all the basic blocks are dealt with, mixed-code generation phase is finished.

(3) Narrow Instruction List Weight Update and Re-sort
The weight of each narrow instruction candidate in the list is updated according to the usage count in the compilation of the application programs. How to update the weight is a matter of question, and we currently use the following method. For each instruction in the list, if the instruction is also in the suggested narrow IS, the usage count of it will be used as its new weight. Thus if an instruction is in the narrow IS and it has seldom be used during the entire compilation process of all the application programs, its weight will get very low, no matter how high its original value is. After the weight update, the narrow instruction candidate list will be re-sorted according to the new weight. If the selected IS has come to a fixed point, or the iterative count is equal to the threshold, the iterative process will be finished, and the narrow IS will be exported.

5 Evaluation

In this section, we illustrate the effect of our technique by presenting the experimental results of the automatic narrow IS design for UniCore. The mixed-code generation phase is implemented as a post pass of GNU tool-chain (gcc 3.2.1). We use mediabench as our benchmark. Each program is compiled with GCC "–O2" level of optimization.

5.1 Code Size Reduction Rate

We compare the code sizes of the programs in a normal IS and the one in mixed-code with our automatically generated narrow IS. The code size reduction rates of the mixed code are shown in Fig. 5. We can see from the figure that the mixed code reduces the program sizes of UniCore32 by 14% to 18%, with an average of 16% code size reduction, and no performance loss. The cycle counts of mixed code are as shown in

Fig. 6, normalized to the normal programs. The experiment shows that the method can work well without human designers and can provide a foundation for further refine. Further more, it generates relatively good results for all the programs. However, the average reduction rate seems to be not as good as some results reported by some fine-tuned narrow instruction set, such as Thumb. This is partly because of the mixed-code generation method we used. As described before and in [10], this fine-grained mixed-code generation method focuses on ensuring no performance loss as well as getting a fine code size reduction rate. The results reported in [3] and [9] both get higher code density at the cost of lower performance. In the future, the performance and code size requires should be added to the framework, to generate instruction set in balance of performance and code density. There are also many details to be adjusted in the framework, e.g., the given instruction oprand types, the way to update instructions' weights, and so on. We are planning to refine these parts in the future.

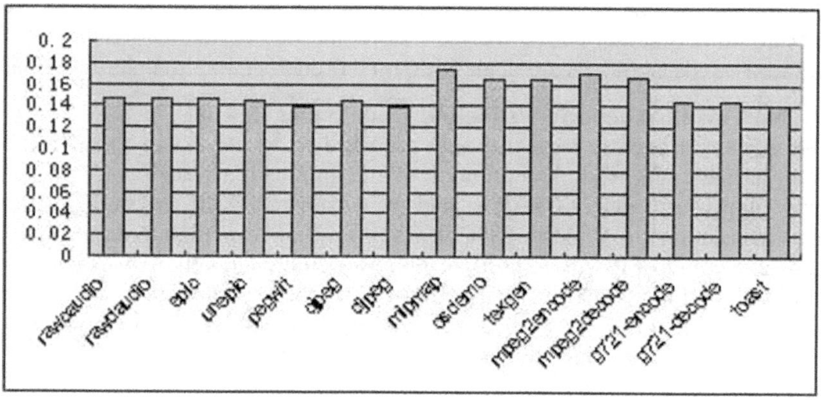

Fig. 5. Code Size Reduction Rate

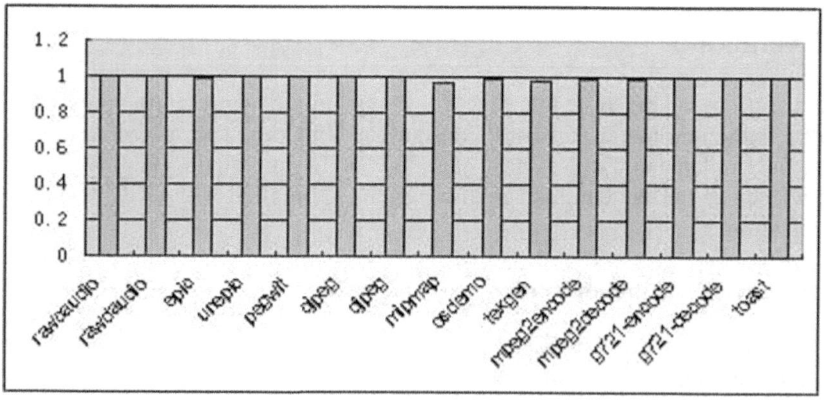

Fig. 6. Normalized Cycle Counts

5.2 Variations of Generated Narrow ISs

Fig. 7 shows the average code size reduction rates of different iterative parse. We can see from the figure that although the initial narrow IS contains the instructions with highest frequencies; the compress rate is relatively low. As NISD iteratively updates the narrow IS, the compress rate gets higher. In our experiments, after the forth iterative, the compress rate begins to grow slowly. This curve and the final IS may be affected by the way of updating the narrow IS. A further study of how to update the narrow IS from the feedback is still desirable.

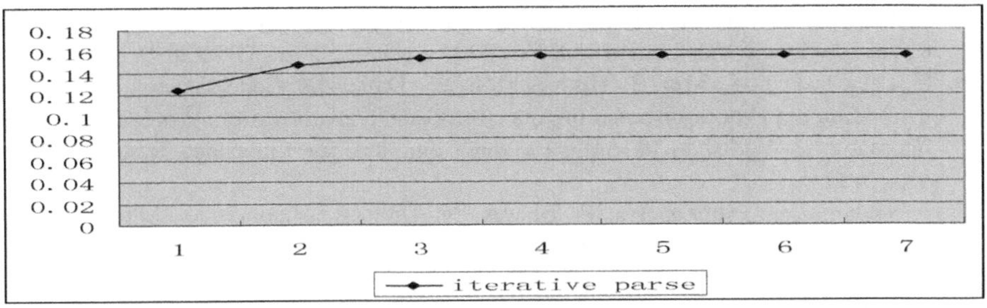

Fig. 7. Average Code Size Reduction Rate of Different Iterative Parse

6 Conclusion and Future Work

In this paper, we present a framework of fast automatic narrow instruction set design. aiming at generating instruction set tailored to particular applications for embedded systems. The set of applications is analyzed and the suggested narrow instruction set is used in the post-process parse of compilation to generate mixed code. Then the effect of each instruction in the set is evaluated and the instruction set is updated according to the feedback. In such an iterative process, when designing a narrow instruction set for a specific application domain, an Instruction Set Description Template (ISDT) is used to describe the current narrow instruction set. The core part of mixed-code generation gets the narrow IS information from the ISDT and the IS is automatically updated through modifying its ISDT representation. Thus it needs no human designers to be involved in.

With the shown experimental results, we can see that this method can work well with out human designers. The code size reduction rates of programs vary between 14% and 18%, with no performance loss. There are also many details to be adjusted in the framework. We are planning to add trade-off of performance and code density in our framework, to let designers add system requirements. Further more, different programs have different code size, and thus they should have different weights, too. We should take this into consideration. The way to update instructions' weights should be studied as well.

References

1. The HiPEAC Roadmap on Embedded Systems.
2. A. Krishnaswamy, R. Gupta. *Profile Guided Selection of ARM and Thumb Instructions.* ACM SIGPLAN Joint Conference on Languages Compilers and Tools for Embedded Systems & Software and Compilers for Embedded Systems, pp. 55-64 June 2002
3. L. Goudge, S. Segars. Thumb: Reducing the Cost of 32-bit RISC Performance in Portable and Consumer Applications. Proceedings of the 41st IEEE International Computer Conference, pp.176, 1996
4. MIPS32 Architecture for Programmers Volume IV-a: The MIPS16 Application Specific Extension to the MIPS32 Architecture. 2001
5. X. Ma, Y. Kwon and H. J. Lee. PARE: Instruction Set Architecture for Efficient Code Size Reduction. Electronics Letters 25th Nov'99 Vol. 35 No. 24 pp. 2098-2099, 1999
6. S. Lee, J. Lee, S. Min, J. Hiser and J. W. Davidson, Code Generation for a Dual Instruction Set Processor based on Selective Code Transformation. Proceedings of the 7th International Workshop on Software and Compilers for Embedded Systems, pp.33-48, Sep. 2003
7. A. Halambi, A. Shrivastava, P. Biswas, N. Dutt, A. Nicolau. *An Efficient Compiler Technique for Code Size Reduction using Reduced Bit-width ISAs.* Design Automation and Test in Europe, March 2002
8. A. Krishnaswamy, R. Gupta. *Enhancing the Performance of 16-bit Code Using Augmenting Instructions.* ACM SIGPLAN Conference on Languages Compilers and Tools for Embedded Systems, June 2003
9. R. Phelan. *Improving ARM Code Density and Performance.* Technical report, ARM Limited, 2003
10. X. Liu, J. Zhang and X. Cheng. *Efficient Code Size Reduction without Performance Loss.* Proceedings of the International Symposium on Applied Computing (SAC), March. 2007. Seoul, Korea.
11. A. Halambi, A. Shrivastava, P. Biswas, N. Dutt and A. Nicolau. *A Design Space Exploration Framework for Reduced Bit-Width Instruction Set Architecture (rISA) Design.* Proceedings of the International Symposium on System Synthesis (ISSS), Oct. 2002. Kyoto, Japan.
12. *UniCore32 ISA and Programming Manual.* Microprocessor Research Center of Peking University, 2002.
13. C. Lee, M. Potkonjak and W. H. Mangion-Smith. *MediaBench: A Tool for Evaluating and Synthesizing Multimedia and Communications Systems.* Proceedings of the 30th Annual International Symposium on Microarchitecture, pp.330-335, Dec. 1997.
14. U. Kastens, D. K. Le, A. Slowik and M. Thies. Feedback Driven Instruction-Set Extension. Proceddings of LCTES, 2004.
15. A. Peymandoust, L. Pozzi, P. Ienne, and G.D. Micheli. Automatic Instruction Set Extension and Utilization for Embedded Processors. Proceedings of 14th International Conference on Application-specific Systems, Architectures and Processors, 2003.

A Hardware/Software Cosimulator with RTOS Supports for Multiprocessor Embedded Systems

Takashi Furukawa, Shinya Honda, Hiroyuki Tomiyama, and Hiroaki Takada

Takada Laboratory, Graduate School of Infomation Science, Nagoya University, Nagoya 464-8603, Japan
{furukawa,honda,tomiyama,hiro}@ertl.jp

Abstract. This paper presents a hardware/software cosimulator for multiprocessor embedded systems. Our cosimulator consists of multiple software simulators each of which simulates a set of application tasks together with an RTOS running on a processor, multiple hardware simulators and a cosimulation backplane. All of the simulators are executed concurrently with communication. Our cosimulator supports two types of communication; one is based on Remote Procedure Call (RPC), and the other is based on a shared memory on a host computer. Using the cosimulator, we successfully performed cosimulation of an MPEG encoder/decoder system with two processors and some peripheral circuits.

Keywords: Cosimulation, RTOS, Multiprocessors, Embedded Systems, ITRON.

1 Introduction

Nowadays, real-time operating systems (RTOSs) have become one of the most important components in embedded systems due to the growing complexity of the system functionalities as well as the pressure to time-to-market. Thus, system designers need a cosimulator which simulates not only application software and hardware but also RTOS.

In our past study, we had developed a hardware/software cosimulator which supports an RTOS [1] [2]. The organization of the cosimulator is shown in Fig. 1. The cosimulator provides an RTOS simulation model which completely conforms to a standardized RTOS API, i.e., the *μITRON* standard [3] [4]. μITRON is one of the most popular RTOSs in Japan for small- to middle-scale embedded systems such as cellular phones and automotive controllers. μITRON is not a specific RTOS product, but is an API standard, so a number of ITRON-compliant RTOSs exist. The RTOS model is compiled and linked with application software tasks to generate a software simulator which is directly executable on a host computer. Due to the native execution, the cosimulator is much faster than traditional cosimulators which use an instruction-set simulator (ISS) of the target processor for software execution. The cosimulator can cooperate with various types of hardware simulators such as HDL simulators, the SystemC reference simulator [5], and functional hardware models written in C or C++. The

Y.-H. Lee et al. (Eds.): ICESS 2007, LNCS 4523, pp. 283–294, 2007.

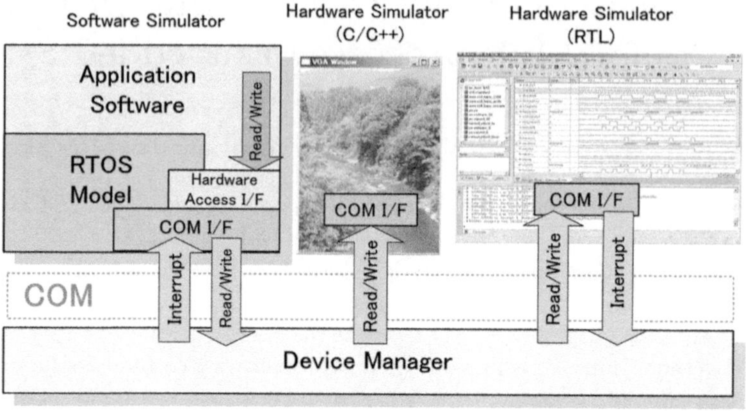

Fig. 1. Cosimulator for single processor systems

software simulator and hardware simulators are executed concurrently, communicating with each other. The communication is enabled by a backplane tool named *Device Manager (DM)*. DM can connect multiple simulators and supports synchronization and communication between them. For connection of the simulators, DM uses *Component Object Model (COM)*, which is standard remote procedure calls (RPCs) on MS-Windows [6]. Therefore, various simulators can be connected with DM easily. However, the cosimulator supports only single processor systems although multiprocessors are increasingly used in embedded systems in order to achieve both high performance and low power consumption. Another drawback of the cosimulator is the large communication overhead due to the COM-based implementation.

In this study, we have significantly improved the cosimulator in two ways. One is support for multiprocessor systems, and the other is support for faster communication based on a shared memory on a host computer. In summary, our new cosimulator features

- cosimulation for multiprocessor systems,
- native (hence fast) simulation of application software,
- complete support of a standard RTOS,
- simulation of various hardware simulators such as HDL simulators, the SystemC simulator and C/C++ functional models, and
- two types of communication; flexible communication based on RPCs and fast communication based on a shared memory on a host computer.

To our knowledge, no other cosimulator supports all of the five features.

This paper is organized as follows. Section 2 presents related work on hardware/software cosimulation with RTOS supports. Section 3 describes the cosimulator which we have developed. A case study with an MPEG encoder/decoder application is presented in Section 4. Section 5 concludes this paper with a summary.

2 Related Work

Due to the increasing importance of RTOSs in embedded systems, several researchers have recently studied cosimulation of not only hardware and application software but also RTOSs.

Generic RTOS simulation models in system-level description languages are developed for cosimulation of hardware and software including RTOS [7] [8]. After cosimulation with the RTOS models, system designers select a real RTOS to obtain a final implementation code. Since most of such generic RTOS models support a minimal set of the service calls, the designer needs to replace the service calls of the generic RTOS in application software with those of the real RTOS. However, replacement of the service calls is time-consuming and may embed errors into application software. Those errors can hardly be found until cosimulation using an ISS. Note that cosimulation with the ISS is very slow, although some advanced techniques (e.g., virtual synchronization [9]) are studied for acceleration.

In our past literature [1] [2], we presented a cosimulator including a simulation model of a standard RTOS which is used in the final implementation. Therefore, the system designer does not have to rewrite the application software. However, the cosimulator does not support multiprocessor systems although they have now become popular.

Another approach to embedded software design is presented in [10], where an application-specific RTOS and its simulation model are automatically generated. In their approach, application software is analyzed first, and then only the RTOS services needed by the application software are included in the final RTOS. The work is similar to ours in that a set of services which can be used in application software is pre-defined. The major difference is that their work puts a special focus on customizing an RTOS while our methodology is based on a standard RTOS.

3 Cosimulation for Multi-processor Systems

3.1 Overview

This section describes the cosimulator which we have developed. The overall structure of the cosimulator is shown in Fig. 2. Our cosimulator consists of multiple software simulators, multiple hardware simulators, and *Device Manager (DM)*. Each of the software simulators simulates a set of application tasks and an RTOS running on a processor. Each software simulator includes a simulation model of the RTOS. The RTOS model is compiled and linked with the application tasks to generate the software simulator which is directly executable on a host computer. Various types of hardware simulators can be executed such as HDL simulators, the SystemC reference simulator [5] and functional hardware models in C/C++.

Each of the components of the cosimulator, i.e., the software simulators, the hardware simulators and DM, is executed as an application on an MS

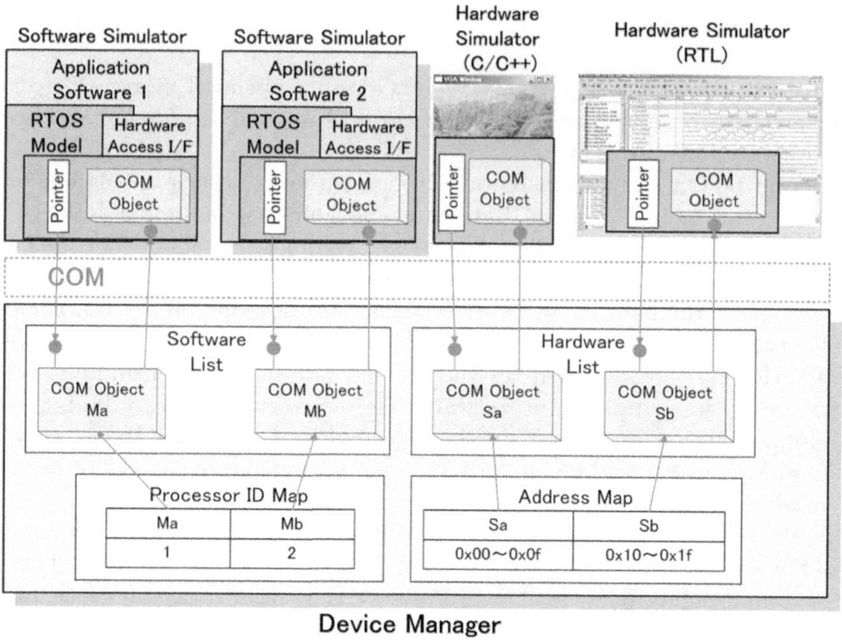

Fig. 2. Improved cosimulator for multiprocessor systems

Windows-based host computer. The simulators are executed concurrently with communication (i.e., read/write accesses from processors to hardware modules) and synchronization (i.e., interrupts from hardware modules to processors or between processors). Our cosimulator features two types of communication mechanism: one is flexible communication based on RPC, and the other is fast communication based on a shared memory on the host computer.

3.2 Flexible Communication by RPC

For communication from software simulators to hardware simulators, our cosimulator supports flexible communication by RPC.

In our cosimulator, memory mapped I/O is assumed. Thus, unique addresses are mapped to hardware simulators. DM manages the map of the addresses and the hardware simulators. When a software simulator needs to perform a read or write access to a hardware simulator, first the software simulator sends an access request with an address, and then DM selects an appropriate hardware simulator with the address map, and transfers the request to the hardware simulator.

The transfers of requests are implemented with a standard RPC on MS-Windows, *COM*. COM is a mechanism for communications between MS-Windows applications. COM enables communication which does not depend on programming language because COM is a binary standard. COM is supported in several languages, e.g., C, C++, Visual BASIC and Java. In order to connect and communicate with each other, software simulators, hardware simulators and DM have their COM objects. In an initial setting phase, each of the simulators connects to DM (which is a server application), and exchanges pointers of the COM objects. Then, they can communicate with each other by RPC with the pointers. The COM communications are used for read/write accesses from processors to hardware modules at cosimulation time.

ITRON project [3] defines a hardware access interface, thus application software on an ITRON-based RTOS can execute reads and writes with the defined interface in final implementation. Since our RTOS simulation model supports the same interface, application software on our cosimulator can execute reads and writes with the same interface at cosimulation phase. Therefore, application software does not have to be modified from the cosimulation phase to the implementation phase.

Application software reads and writes hardware devices using the interface as follows.

```
x = sil_rew_mem(address);  // x = *address;
sil_wrw_mem(address,x+1);  // *address = x+1;
```

These APIs are compiled to RPC calls to DM with our RTOS simulation model at cosimulation phase, and are compiled to accesses to target addresses with a real RTOS at implementation phase.

When the software simulator calls an RPC of DM with an address (and a value to write), DM compares the address and the address map to find a corresponding hardware simulator, and then DM calls an RPC of the hardware simulator. In order to realize this mechanism, the address map consists of addresses and pointers, which point at COM objects for corresponding hardware simulators (Sa and Sb in Fig. 2).

When DM calls an RPC of the hardware simulator, the hardware simulator performs a read or a write. The RPC functions provided by the hardware simulators define detail of behaviors for read and write accesses.

To summarize, the RPC-based communication for read/write accesses is executed in the following way.

- A software simulator calls an RPC of DM with an address.
- DM selects an appropriate hardware simulator with the address map and calls an RPC of the hardware simulator.
- The hardware simulator performs a read or a write.

For the RPC-based communications, some initial settings need to be executed. Each of the software simulators and the hardware simulators connect to DM and exchange their pointers of COM objects immediately after they are invoked. Also, DM sets the address map by RPC calls from hardware simulators.

3.3 Fast Communication by Shared Memory

Although RPC-based communication is flexible, it imposes large overheads of simulation speed. Our cosimulator also supports a fast communication based on

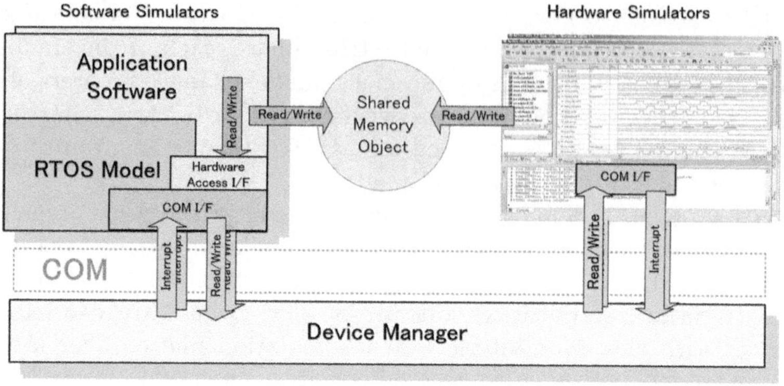

Fig. 3. Shared memory in our cosimulator

shared memory mechanism of MS-Windows. If some of concurrently executed simulators simply access shared memory, however, the memory conflicts may happen. For example, assume that one simulator (named SimA) reads a shared variable (named x), another simulator (named SimB) reads and modifies x, and then SimA modifies x. The final modification by SimA does not take into account the previous modification by SimB. In order to prevent such shared memory conflicts, our cosimulator also supports lock mechanism. Fig. 3 shows the structure of our cosimulator with shared memory. When a software simulator needs to perform a read or write access to a hardware simulator, in the case of the shared memory-based communication, first the software simulator acquires a lock by a lock request, directly accesses to a shared memory not via DM, and releases the lock by an unlock request. Note that the software simulators can perform any number of accesses between the lock and the unlock.

To support the lock mechanism, DM has a lock list which consists of locked address spaces. When a software simulator needs to acquire/release a lock, the software simulator calls an RPC of DM with an address space, and then DM adds/removes the address space to/from the lock list. After the software simulator acquires the lock, it accesses to a shared memory with a pointer of the shared memory.

The shared memory-based communications for read/write accesses are executed as follows.

- A software simulator calls an RPC of DM with an address space to acquire a lock.
- DM adds the address space to the lock list.
- The software simulator directly accesses to the shared memory once or multiple times.
- The software simulator calls an RPC of DM with the address space to release the lock.
- DM removes the address space from the lock list.

In order to acquire and release locks, the shared memory-based communications, as well as the RPC-based communications, need RPC. Thus, if the software simulators acquire and release a lock for each access, the shared memory-based communications also impose large overheads of cosimulation speed. However, as mentioned above, the software simulators can perform any number of accesses between the lock and the unlock, and then the shared memory-based communications can be performed faster than the RPC-based communications.

The lock list is simply initialized to empty. Some other initial settings are needed in order to use shared memory on MS-Windows. Unique addresses are mapped to shared memory objects. Each simulator which accesses to shared memory requests to create shared memory objects by calling an RPC of DM with the addresses and the sizes of the objects. When DM receives the request, DM generates a unique name of the shared memory object from the address, creates shared memory space in virtual memory of MS-Windows, and generates a shared memory object there with the generated name. Then, DM returns the name to the simulator, and the simulator opens the object with the name. Each shared memory object is created or opened as follows.

- A simulator calls an RPC of DM with an address and the size of a shared memory object to create the object.
- DM generates a unique name from given address, creates the shared memory object with the given size and the generated name, and returns the generated name to the simulator. Note that if the shared memory object already exists, DM only increments its reference counter.
- The simulator opens the shared memory object with the returned name.

3.4 Interrupts

Our cosimulator also supports synchronizations, i.e., interrupts from hardware modules to processors or between processors. In order to identify the software simulators, unique processor IDs are mapped to the software simulators. DM manages the map of the processor IDs and the software simulators. In target systems, interrupts are performed immediately by interrupt signals at any time except for when CPU is locked or the interrupts are masked (hence ignored). In our cosimulator, the interrupts are performed immediately by RPC calls. When a simulator needs to interrupt a software simulator, first the simulator calls an RPC of DM for interrupt request, and then DM selects the software simulator where the interrupt request should be transferred, and calls an RPC of the software simulator. The argument of the interrupt request is organized by a processor ID allocated to higher bits and an interrupt number allocated to lower bits as shown in Fig. 4.

In order to generate interrupts by application tasks, our RTOS simulation model supports an interface for interrupt request. The API is compiled to an RPC call of DM with our RTOS simulation model at cosimulation phase, and is compiled to an interrupt generation with a real RTOS at implementation phase. Hardware simulators also can request interrupts by calling RPC of DM.

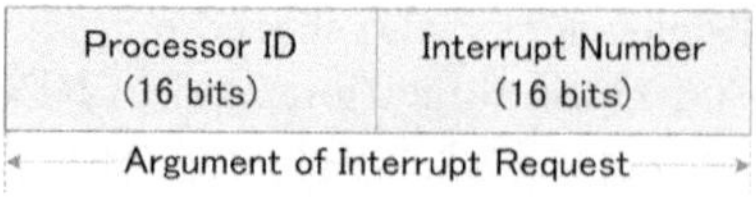

Fig. 4. Structure of argument for interrupt request

When the RPC of DM is called for interrupt, DM compares the processor ID and the processor ID map to find an appropriate software simulator, and calls an RPC of the software simulator. In order to realize this mechanism, the processor ID map consists of the processor IDs and pointers of COM objects for corresponding software simulators. Then, the software simulator suspends a task and calls an interrupt handler with a virtual interrupt mechanism in our RTOS simulation model.

The interrupts are performed as follows.

- A simulator calls an RPC of DM with a processor ID and an interrupt number.
- DM selects an appropriate software simulator by comparing the processor ID map and the given processor ID, and calls an RPC of the software simulator.

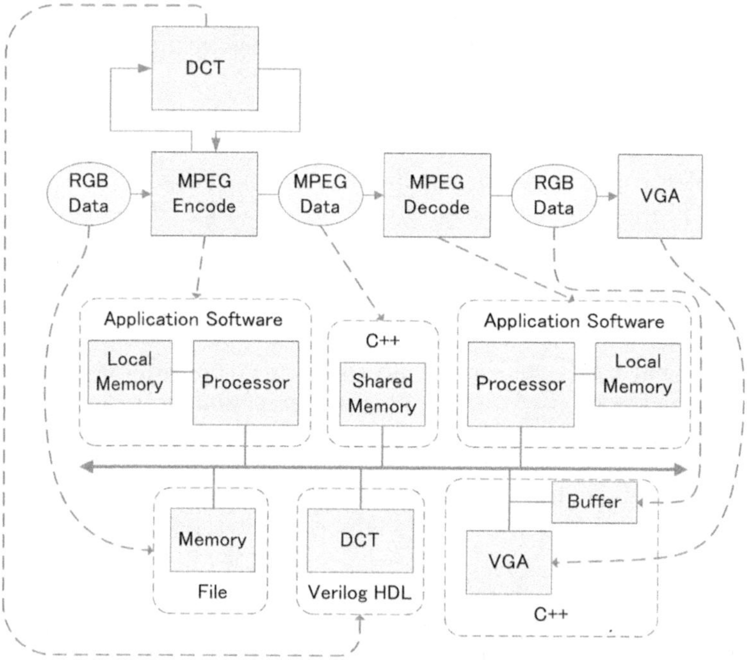

Fig. 5. Flow and hardware organization of the MPEG encoder/decoder

- The software simulator performs the interrupt by suspending a task and calling an interrupt handler.

Our RTOS simulation model also supports an interface for interrupt handler registration. The API is compiled to registration to the virtual interrupt mechanism with our RTOS model at cosimulation phase, and is compiled to registration to real interrupt mechanism with a real RTOS at implementation phase.

As the initial setting, DM sets the processor ID map by RPC calls from software simulators.

4 Design Example

This section evaluates our cosimulator through two case studies with a MPEG encoder/decoder example. This section also compares two types of communication with a simple write example. In these experiments, cosimulation is performed on a dual Xeon 2.8GHz processor system each with dual-threaded execution, running on MS-Windows XP.

4.1 A Case Study with an MPEG Encoder/Decoder

Fig. 5 shows the flow and organization of the MPEG encoder/decoder system. MPEG encoder converts input data in the RGB format into the MPEG2 format, and writes the data to shared memory on the target system. MPEG decoder

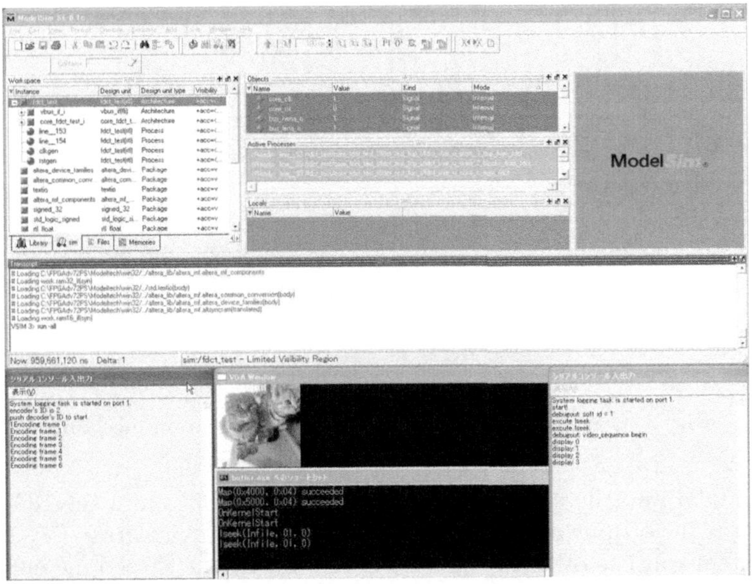

Fig. 6. Screenshot of cosimulation

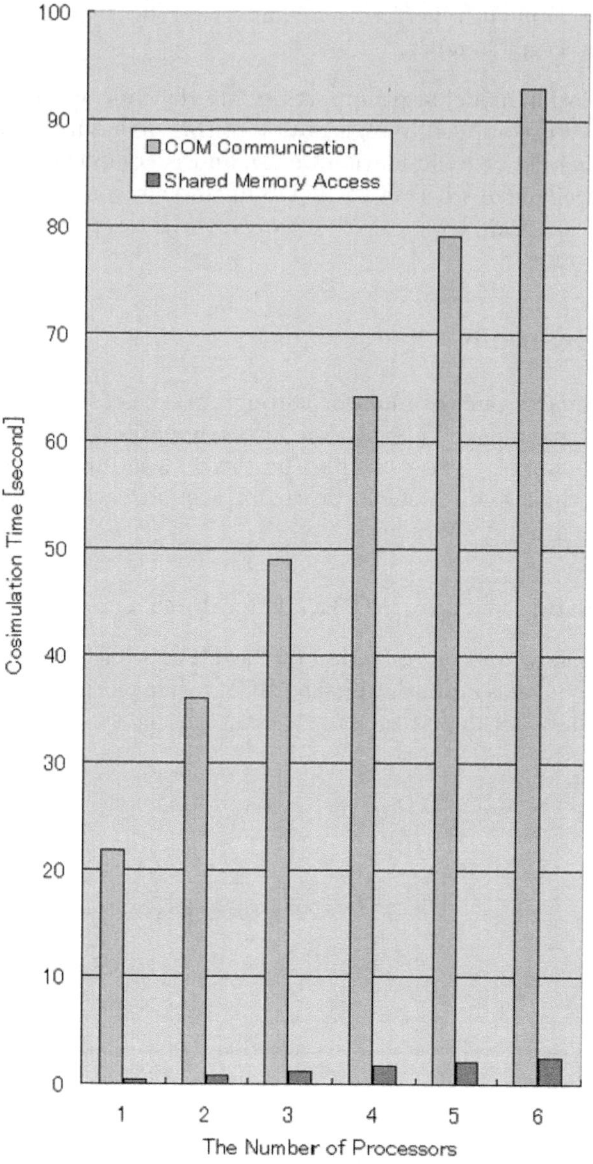

Fig. 7. Cosimulation time with two communication mechanisms

reads the data on the shared memory, converts the data into the RGB format, and writes the output data to a buffer of a video graphics array (VGA) device. The system consists of the VGA device, the buffer, the shared memory, a DCT circuit, and two processors which execute application software each with an RTOS. One processor executes encoding with the DCT circuit, and the other processor executes decoding.

Table 1. Cosimulation time of the MPEG encoder/decoder

System Type	Cosimulation Time
with DCT circuit	262.427 sec/frame
without DCT circuit	0.766 sec/frame

We performed cosimulation of the MPEG encoder/decoder system. The VGA device and the buffer are written in C++ as hardware models and simulated by native execution. The DCT circuit is written in HDL and simulated by HDL simulator *ModelSim*. The two processors are simulated by two software simulators which are generated from our RTOS simulation model with encode/decode applications. A screenshot of the cosimulation is shown in Fig. 6.

We also performed cosimulation of another MPEG encoder/decoder system for comparison, which does not include the DCT circuit.

Table 1 shows cosimulation time of these two systems.

4.2 Comparisons of Communication Mechanisms

In the next experiment, we evaluated communication speed with two types of communication mechanism. The systems for evaluation consist of N processors ($1 \leq N \leq 6$), a VGA device and a buffer. Each processor writes 320×320 pixels to the VGA device.

We performed the cosimulation for 12 cases in total, where the number of processors and communication mechanism are different. Fig. 7 compares the cosimulation time. As the result, the cosimulation with the shared memory-based communication is up to 53 times faster than the cosimulation with the RPC-based communication.

5 Conclusion

RTOSs have become one of necessities in the design of complex embedded systems, and multiprocessors are increasingly used in embedded systems. This paper presented our hardware/software cosimulator for multiprocessor embedded systems, which supports Japanese standard RTOS. Our cosimulator performs cosimulation by concurrent execution of software simulators and hardware simulators with communications. Each of the software simulators is automatically generated from application tasks and an RTOS simulation model included in our cosimulator and directly executable on a host computer. Our cosimulator supports various types of hardware simulator such as HDL simulators, the SystemC reference simulator and functional hardware model written in C/C++. Our cosimulator also supports two types of communication; one is flexible communication based on RPCs, and the other is fast communication based on a host shared memory.

In future, we plan to develop distributed cosimulator running on multiple host computers.

Acknowledgment

This work was partially supported by JSPS Grant-in-Aid for Scientific Research (B) #17300014.

References

1. S. Honda, T. Wakabayashi, H. Tomiyama, and H. Takada. "RTOS-Centric Cosimulator for Embedded System Design". *IEICE Trans. Fundamentals*, vol. E87-A, no. 12:pages 3030–3035, Dec. 2004.
2. S. Chikada, H. Tomiyama, S. Honda, and H. Takada. "Cosimulation of ITRON-Based Embedded Software with SystemC". In *Proc. of International High Level Design Validation and Test Workshop (HLDVT)*, pages 71–76, Nov. 2005.
3. ITRON Project. `http://ertl.jp/ITRON/home-e.html`.
4. H. Takada and K. Sakamura. "μITRON for Small-Scale Embedded Systems". *IEEE Micro*, vol. 15, no. 6:pages 46–54, Dec. 1995.
5. SystemC Open Initiative. `http://www.systemc.org/`.
6. Microsoft Corporation. `http://www.microsoft.com/`.
7. D. Desmet, D. Verkest, and H. D. Man. "Operating System Based Software Generation for Systems-on-Chip". In *Proc. of Conference on Design Automation (DAC)*, pages 396–401, 2000.
8. A. Gerstlauer, H. Yu, and D. D. Gajski . "RTOS Modeling for System Level Design". In *Proc. of the Design, Automation and Test in Europe (DATE)*, pages 130–135, Mar. 2003.
9. Y. Yi, D. Kim, and S. Ha . "Fast and Time-Accurate Cosimulation with OS Scheduler Modeling". *Design Automation for Embedded System*, vol. 8, no. 2:pages 211–228, Aug. 2003.
10. S. Yoo, G. Nicolescu, L. Gauthier, and A. A. Jerraya . "Automatic Generation of Fast Timed Simulation Models for Operating Systems in SoC Design". In *Proc. of the Design, Automation and Test in Europe (DATE)*, pages 620–627, Mar. 2002.

Face Detection on Embedded Systems

Abbas Bigdeli[1], Colin Sim[2], Morteza Biglari-Abhari[2], and Brian C. Lovell[1]

[1] Safeguarding Australia Program,
NICTA, Brisbane, QLD 4000, Australia
{abbas.bigdeli,brian.lovell}@nicta.com.au
[2] Department of Electrical and Computer Engineering
The University of Auckland, Auckland, New Zealand
{csim036,m.abhari}@auckland.ac.nz

Abstract. Over recent years automated face detection and recognition (FDR) have gained significant attention from the commercial and research sectors. This paper presents an embedded face detection solution aimed at addressing the real-time image processing requirements within a wide range of applications. As face detection is a computationally intensive task, an embedded solution would give rise to opportunities for discrete economical devices that could be applied and integrated into a vast majority of applications. This work focuses on the use of FPGAs as the embedded prototyping technology where the thread of execution is carried out on an embedded soft-core processor. Custom instructions have been utilized as a means of applying software/hardware partitioning through which the computational bottlenecks are moved to hardware. A speedup by a factor of 110 was achieved from employing custom instructions and software optimizations.

1 Introduction

The identification and localization of a face or faces from either an image or video stream is a branch of computer vision known as face detection [1, 2]. Face detection has attracted considerable attention over recent years in part due to the wide range of applications in which it forms the preliminary stage. Some of the main application areas include: human-computer interaction, biometrics, content-based image retrieval systems (CBIRS), video conferencing, surveillance systems, and more recently, photography.

The existing visual sensing and computing technologies are at a state where reliable, inexpensive, and accurate solutions for non-intrusive and natural means of human-computer interactions are feasible. Biometrics is an evolving application domain for face detection and is concerned with the use of physiological information to identify and verify a person's identity. In most cases, face recognition algorithms are designed to operate on images assumed to only contain frontal faces [2]. Therefore, face detection is required to first extract faces from an image prior to the recognition step. Examples of commercial biometric systems are BioID [3] and ViiSage[1]. HumanScan is the company that developed BioID; a multimodal system incorporating voice, lip movement and face recognition to authenticate a person. This system implements a model-based face detection algorithm based on the Hausdorff distance [4].

---

[1] www.viisage.com

Y.-H. Lee et al. (Eds.): ICESS 2007, LNCS 4523, pp. 295–308, 2007.

Another application area that can clearly benefit from face detection is surveillance systems that would allow easier identification of criminals in public spaces. Shan *et al* [5] presented a robust face recognition system specifically designed for Intelligent CCTV systems. Another video surveillance system which has the capacity to detect faces is that proposed by Kim *et al* [6]. More recently, FujiFilm[2] and Nikon Corporation[3] have incorporated face detection technologies into some of their camera series to automatically improve pictures taken under poor lighting conditions.

The majority of the research work to date has primarily focused on developing novel face detection algorithms and/or improving the efficiency and accuracy of existing algorithms. As a result, most solutions deployed (similar to the examples given above) are typically high-level software programs targeted for general purpose processors that are expensive and usually non-real-time solutions. Since face detection is typically the first step and frequently a bottleneck in most solutions due to the large search space and extensive amount of computationally intensive operations, it is reasonable to suggest an embedded implementation specifically optimized to detect faces. An embedded solution would entail many advantages including 1) low cost, as only a subset of hardware components are required compared to the general computer based solutions, 2) optimization of the face detection algorithms for real-time operations independent of face recognition or other post-processing concerns and 3) integration with other technologies such as security cameras to create smart devices.

Related Work

Now that reliable, accurate, and efficient face detection algorithms are available coupled with advances in embedded technologies; low-cost implementations of robust real-time face detectors can be explored. The most common target technologies are: pure hardware, embedded microprocessors, and configurable hardware.

Pure hardware systems are typically based on very large scale integrated circuit (VLSI) semiconductor technology implemented as application specific integrated circuits (ASIC). Compared to the other technologies, ASICs have a high operating frequency resulting in better performance, low power consumption, high degree of parallelism, and well established design tools. However, a large amount of development time is required to optimize and implement the designs. Also, due to the fixed nature of this technology the resulting solutions are not flexible and cannot be easily changed, resulting in high development costs and risk. Theocharides *et al* [7] investigated the implementation of a neural network based face detection algorithm in 160 nm VLSI technology based on algorithm proposed by Rowley *et al* in [8, 9], which has a high degree of parallelism.

On the other hand, software programs implemented on general purpose processors (GPP) offer a great deal of flexibility, coupled with very well established design tools that can automatically optimize the designs with little development time and costs. GPPs are ideally suited to applications that are primarily made up of control processing. However, they are disadvantaged because minimal or no special instructions are

---

[2] www.fujifilmusa.com

[3] www.nikonimagings.com

available to assist with data processing [10]. Digital signal processors (DSP) extend GPPs in the direction of increasing parallelism and providing additional support for applications requiring large amounts of data processing. The drawbacks of microprocessors (both GPPs and DSPs) are high power consumption, and inferior performance compared to an ASIC. The performance of the final solution is limited to the selected processor.

Finally, configurable platforms such as field programmable gate arrays (FPGA) combine some of the advantages from both pure hardware and pure software solutions. More specifically, the high parallelism and computational speed of hardware, and the flexibility and short design time of software. By inheriting characteristics from both hardware and software solutions, the design space for FPGAs is extended for better trade-offs between performance and cost. These design trade-offs are far superior to that of pure hardware or software solutions alone. From an efficiency point of view, the performance measures for FPGAs, that is, operating frequency, power consumption, and so on, are generally half way in between the corresponding hardware and software measures.

Several configurable hardware based implementations exist, including that by McCready [11] and Sadri *et al* [12]. McCready specifically designed a novel face detection algorithm for the Transmogrifier-2 (TM-2) configurable platform. The Transmogrifer-2 is a multi-board FPGA based architecture proposed by Lewis *et al* [13]. The algorithm was intentionally designed with minimal mathematical operations that could execute in parallel — engineering effort has been put in to reduce the number of multiplications required. The implemented system required nine boards of the TM-2 system, requiring 31,500 logic cells (LC). The system can process 30 images per second with a detection accuracy of 87%. The hardware implementation is said to be 1,000 times faster than the equivalent software implementation.

On the other hand, Sadri *et al* [12] implemented the neural network based algorithm proposed by Rowley *et al* [8] on the Xilinx Virtex-II Pro XC2VP20 FPGA. Skin color filtering and edge detection is incorporated to reduce the search speed. The solution is partitioned such that all regular operations are implemented in hardware while all irregular control based operations are implemented on Xilinx's embedded hardcore PowerPC processor. This partitioning allows the advantages of both hardware and software to be simultaneously exploited. The system operates at 200 MHz and can process up to nine images per second.

The examples presented illustrate the obvious compromises between accuracy and algorithm robustness versus the amount of resources required. That is, to improve the performance of the face detection algorithms, we must either increase the embedded design complexity, which generally results in higher power consumption and hardware costs, or settle for a lesser solution.

2 PC Based Software Prototype

The initial software prototype of the standard Viola-Jones algorithm was implemented based on the trained classifiers provided in the Open Computer Vision Library

(OpenCV)[4]. The particular classifiers used in this implementation are those trained for a base detection window size of 24x24 pixels. The classifiers are trained to detect upright frontal faces. These classifiers were created and trained by Lienhart *et al* who used a total of 8,000 training samples, of which 5,000 are face images and 3,000 non-face images [14]. The accuracy of the implemented Viola-Jones face detection algorithm was validated using a subset of images from the CMU + MIT face databases, and images retrieved from a random web crawl.

To ensure that the results obtained can be compared with other published sources, detection and false detection events use the definition of Lienhart *et al* [14], as follows. A detection window is said to correctly identify a face if the following criteria are satisfied:

i) The maximum displacement between the centre of the detected window and the actual face do not exceed 30% of the actual face size.
ii) The difference between the detected window and actual face size does not exceed 50% of the actual face size.

At $\Delta = 1.0$ and $s = 1.25$[5], the detection accuracy for the CMU+MIT image set is 80%. This result is consistent with that presented by Lienhart *et al* [14]. On the other hand, the detection accuracy for the web crawl image set is 92%. The slightly better results obtained in the web crawl image set is possibly due to the following factors:

i) The images from the web crawl image set had a higher resolution and better quality
ii) The images' backgrounds were less complex, resulting in less misclassification.

2.1 Implementation Details

In order to standardize the input data for all implementation platforms so that the performance results can be benchmarked, a set of 10 images arbitrarily chosen from a web search is used as input. Each image contains a single frontal face. Multiple images are used so that any variability in the processing time for individual images is better averaged out. All the images are stored as grayscale bitmaps of size 576x720 pixels — image size being arbitrarily chosen. Variability in execution times is primarily attributed to the cascaded nature of the Viola-Jones algorithm. The amount of time required to search an image for a face is closely related to the "complexity" of the image; that is, if an image has large areas that do not contain faces but passes many of the cascaded classifier stages, then more time is required to process the image. Other aspects that contribute to varying the execution times are platform dependent and include: cache and memory access times, pipeline schedule, interrupt mechanisms, and so on.

The software prototype was developed in C and compiled with a GNU GCC compiler under Cygwin. The compiler was set to highest optimization for speed, and the PC was a Pentium 4 processor, 3.20 GHz, with 1.0 GB RAM with Windows XP as the operating system.

---

[4] www.opencv.org

[5] Where s is the scale factor in the search algorithm and, Δ represents the number of pixels to shift the detection window [14].

2.2 Software Implementation Results

All 10 faces within the 10 images were located with two false positives. Due to the small number of images, the ratio between detection and false detection rates may be skewed. The total execution time for the program to process all 10 images is 19.91 seconds. A breakdown of each function and their contribution to the final time are presented in the **Table 1.**

Not all functions used in the program are in **Table 1**; this is because the profiling process is based on samples taken when the program is running. As a result, functions that execute quickly may not be acknowledged. An arrow before a function name indicates that it is called from another function where the function that called it has one less indentation level. As an example, referring to **Table 1**, `InitialiseClassifierStages`, `UpdateClassifierStages`, and so on are all called from the `FaceDetection` function. As seen in the flat profile, the `RunClassifierCascade` function consumes the majority of the execution time. This function is responsible for checking if a sub-window contains a face. The function itself is executed in close to no time; the long processing time is due to the accumulation of over 7.5 million calls. The number of calls to `RunClassifierCascade` is related to the number of search locations which in turn is proportional to the size of the image.

Table 1. Flat profile of the Viola-Jones algorithm

Function Name	Total Time Taken (sec)	Number of Calls	Average Time (sec)	Percentage of Total Time (%)
CalculateIntegralImage	0.35	10	0.04	1.76
CalculateSqIntegralImage	0.03	10	0	0.15
FaceDetection	19.53	10	1.95	98.09
→ InitialiseClassifierStages	0.02	10	0	0.1
→ UpdateClassifierStages	0.02	150	0	0.1
→ RunClassifierCascade	19.46	7,458,250	0	97.74
→ round	0.01	Unknown	N/A	0.05
→ AddSubWindow	0	110	0	0
→ GetFaceWindows	0	10	0	0
FreeIntegralImage	0	20	0	0
FreeFaceWinList	0	10	0	0
FreeSubWinList	0	10	0	0

2.3 Initial Embedded System and Port of Software Code

A fully functional embedded system based on Altera Nios II softcore processor was created on a Stratix FPGA development board. Overall the maximum system operating frequency is 96.42 MHz. However, due to the limitations of the possible frequencies that can be generated by the PLL module, the maximum feasible operating frequency without violating timing constraints is 80 MHz. From this point onwards unless otherwise stated the actual operating frequency for each system is 80 MHz.

Given that the code implemented on the PC is based on GNU libraries which is the same as the software development in the Nios II environment, it was possible to be directly ported across to the Nios II system without many changes.

2.4 Profile of Embedded Code

Initially, the GNU profiler was used to profile the code which was compiled with maximum speed optimization. The original code runs quite slowly. The lengthy processing time is attributed to the extensive number of locations searched within each image. The amount of searching is directly proportional to the input image size and the step size of the detection window. There are several methods available to help reduce the search space, common approaches being, image differencing and skin color modeling. Image differencing as its name suggests involves taking the difference between image frames. Since humans are generally the only objects that move within a scene, searching can be concentrated on the sections that are changing. On the other hand, the skin color modeling method makes use of statistical models of human skin to filter the input image hence the search for faces can then be restricted to those areas. An alternative method is to reduce the size of the input images using an image interpolation algorithm. Once the faces are found in the smaller image, the location and dimension of the detection windows can be rescaled to the size of the original image.

The most popular techniques for enlarging or shrinking images are nearest neighborhood, bilinear, and bicubic down-sampling. Of these methods, bicubic offers the best results in terms of sharpness and preservation of image details. Every point in the resulting image is calculated from a weighted average of 16 pixels adjacent to the corresponding pixel in the original image. The bicubic interpolation algorithm can be expressed as the following set of equations:

$$g(x) = \sum_k c_k u(s_k) \qquad u(s) = \begin{cases} A_1|s|^3 + B_1|s|^2 + C_1|S| + D_1 \\ A_2|s|^3 + B_2|s|^2 + C_2|S| + D_2 \\ 0 \end{cases} \tag{1}$$

Bicubic interpolation function and its kernel [15].

Where g is the interpolation function, c is points in the original image, u is the interpolation kernel, and s is the distance between the pixel of interest and its neighboring pixels. As noted in [15], the accuracy and efficiency of the algorithm lies solely on the interpolation kernel, u. It was empirically found that the smallest possible scale factor without compromising the detection accuracy of the 10 input images is 0.25. All the faces in the original image were detected with no false positives. The performance report after applying bicubic down-sampling is given in **Table 2**.

The down-sampling calculations are carried out in the `Imresize` function. As seen in the performance report, the size reduction of the input image has a positive

Table 2. Performance report after applying bicubic down-sampling

Section	Total Time (sec)	Occurance	Average Time (sec)	Percentage of Total Time (%)
Imresize	84.74	10	8.47	7.46
CalculateIntAndSqIntImages	0.16	10	0.02	0.01
FaceDetection	1050.27	10	105.03	92.52
→ InitialiseClassifierStages	0.19	10	0.02	0.02
→ UpdateClassifierStages	49.14	90	0.55	4.33
→ RunClassifierCascade	1000.78	315,100	0.003	88.16
Average Time Per Image			113.52	

performance affect on all functions that carry out operations on the image. On average, a speedup factor of 16.5 is achieved after down-sampling the input image to a quarter of its original size.

An additional optimization applied was to combine the `Calculate-IntegralImage` and `CalculateSqIntegralImage` functions together. This is a logical step given that these functions have a similar structure and operate on the same data. The resulting function name is `CalculateIntAndSqIntImage`, and completes execution in approximately half the time originally required to calculate the integral and square integral images separately. The reduction in time is a result of not having to fetch the same image data from extended memory (SDRAM) twice.

3 Optimization Using Custom Instructions

Configurable custom processors are becoming an ever more popular implementation technology of choice for addressing the demands of complex embedded applications. Unlike traditional hardwired processors that consist of a fixed instruction set from which application code is mapped; configurable processors can be augmented with application specific instructions, implemented as hardware logic to optimize bottlenecks. This lends towards a method for hardware-software partitioning whereby the efficiency of hardware and the flexibility of software are integrated.

There are a number of benefits in extending a configurable processor with custom instructions. First, transparency; the added custom instructions will improve the performance of the tasks for which they are designed with minor changes to the original code. Second, rapid development; there is a wide variety of off-the-self configurable cores that could be used as a base for development. Additional instructions could be integrated into the processor core as the need to extend its computational capabilities arises. Finally, low-cost access to domain specific processors; generally the fundamental characteristics of an application area is similar. These characteristics can be summarized as a set of instructions and applied to a variety of similar applications, for example, multimedia applications [16].

Unfortunately, there are two minor drawbacks to using custom instructions. For one, additional hardware is required, although this is becoming less of an issue as embedded technologies become more economical. Secondly, as the custom instructions are directly integrated into the processor's pipeline, the maximum operating frequency may be degraded if the instruction is poorly designed. Adding custom instructions is a proven optimization technique that has been applied to a wide range of embedded applications. Some published examples include, embedded real-time operating systems (RTOS) [17], biometrics [18], and multimedia [19].

3.1 Custom Instruction Design Flow

The design flow for identifying and integrating custom instructions into configurable processors is summarized in **Figure 1**. This is a generic framework that could be applied to any application. Firstly, the software code is profiled to reveal bottlenecks that could be alleviated with the introduction of custom instructions. Once the hardware module for the instruction is implemented and tested, it is added to the processor and the whole system is regenerated. Then the software code is updated to make use of the new instructions. Finally, the functionality of the system is verified to ensure bugs are not introduced with the new instruction. This process is repeated until either the performance requirements or resource limits are met.

3.2 Extending Nios II with Custom Instructions

All of the Altera Nios II processor cores are designed to support up to 256 new custom instructions. The logic for the new instructions is directly connected to the arithmetic logic unit (ALU), as illustrated in **Figure 2**. In the face detection application, this comes does to applying the custom instructions to the Viola-Jones algorithm The Viola-Jones application code which includes the initial software optimizations is profiled using performance counters. As expected, the `FaceDetection` function, more specifically, the `RunClassifierCascade` function is the most time consuming. It should be noted that it is not the `RunClassifierCascade` function itself that is time consuming, but due to the large number of times it is called, the accumulated time is large. Hence, the overall processing time could be improved if either the number of calls to `RunClassifierCascade` or its execution time is reduced. Since reducing the number of calls to `RunClassifierCascade` is going to compromise the accuracy of the face detector, the focus is placed on reducing the execution time of the function itself. Any time savings made in each function call will correspond to a large overall saving.

The main operations carried out in the `RunClassifierCascade` function are addition and multiplication of integer values associated with the calculation of indexes into the input image. There are also floating point multiply and addition operations that are required for image normalization and weighting of the classifier features. Since all the integer related instructions are already implemented in hardware, it is believed that there are opportunities to improve the performance of the floating point operations through custom instructions.

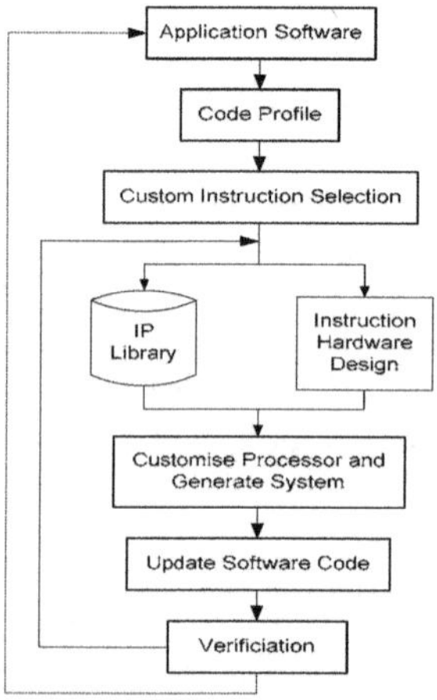

Fig. 1. Custom instructions design flow

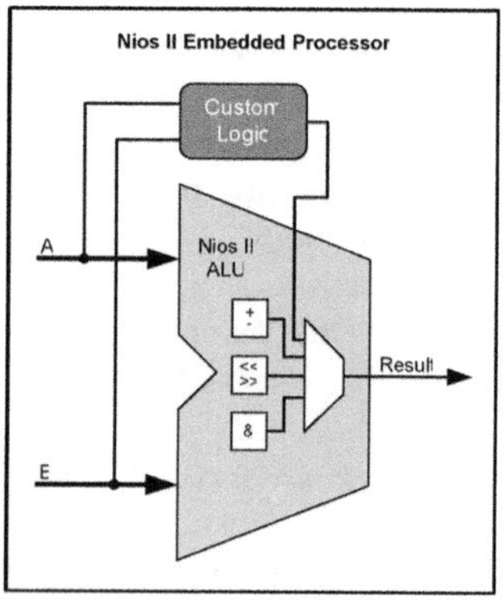

Fig. 2. Connection of custom instruction logic with the Nios II ALU

Floating point multiply is the first operation of interest as it is used most frequently. Further profiling of the `RunClassifierCascade` function indicates that this operation takes up roughly 559 seconds of the total 1135 seconds, approximately 49% of the total processing time. By default all floating point arithmetic are emulated in software. For these reasons the first operation to be implemented as a custom instruction is the floating point multiply. The next instruction that was implemented was floating point add/subtract Instructions. A summary of the performance reported for the face detector after the addition of the floating point multiply instruction and add/subtract Instruction are presented in **Table 3** and **Table 4** respectively.

Table 3. Performance with the use of the floating point multiply custom instruction

Section	Total Time (sec)	Occurance	Average Time (sec)	Percentage of Total Time (%)
Imresize	56.5	10	5.65	9
CalculateIntAndSqIntImages	0.16	10	0.02	0.03
FaceDetection	571.17	10	57.12	90.98
→ InitialiseClassifierStages	0.19	10	0.02	0.03
→ UpdateClassifierStages	36.62	90	0.41	5.83
→ RunClassifierCascade	534.03	315,100	0.002	85.06
Average Time Per Image			62.79	

Table 4. Performance with the use of the floating point addition/subtraction custom instruction

Section	Total Time (sec)	Occurance	Average Time (sec)	Percentage of Total Time (%)
Imresize	57.46	10	5.75	12.73
CalculateIntAndSqIntImages	0.16	10	0.02	0.04
FaceDetection	393.61	10	39.36	87.23
→ InitialiseClassifierStages	0.19	10	0.02	0.04
→ UpdateClassifierStages	34.78	90	0.39	7.71
→ RunClassifierCascade	358.43	315,100	0.001	79.43
Average Time Per Image			45.13	

3.3 Optimization of the `Imresize` Function

The next most time consuming function to focus on is `Imresize`. Since the bicubic resizing algorithm used in the `Imresize` function is not specific to the Viola-Jones algorithm and could also be applied to many other applications, it is an ideal candidate for optimization. As it stands, the `Imresize` function accounts for 13% of the total time.

By examining the bicubic interpolation algorithm more closely, it becomes evident that the coefficients calculated by the interpolation kernel can be fixed constants. More importantly, the exact value of these constants is not essential [20]. A graphical illustration for computing an interpolated value is depicted in **Figure 3**. In essence, the two dimensional convolution like calculations described in Equation 1 can be decomposed to five sets of one dimensional operations. The coefficients, $a0$, $a1$, $a2$, and $a3$, as seen in **Figure 3** all add to one; hence, the intermediate sums will never exceed the largest pixel value of 255. Also, the intermediate results after multiplication are truncated to 8-bit integer values.

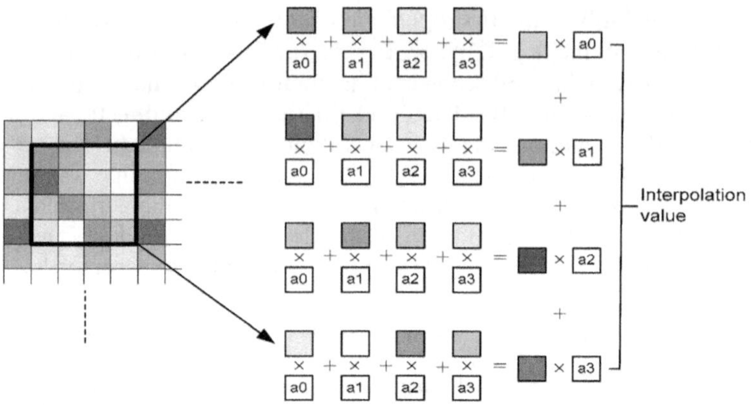

Fig. 3. Graphical description for calculating an interpolation value

A series of experiments were conducted using the original implementation of the bicubic interpolation algorithm to look at the behavior of *a0*, *a1*, *a2* and *a3* for a variety of different scale factors. The following observations were made:

- *a0* and *a3* have the same values
- *a2* is roughly four times larger than *a0* and *a3* while *a1* is roughly two times larger than *a0* and *a3*
- when the coefficients are set to the same value and are close to zero, the resulting image is very dark (basically black)
- when the coefficients are set to the same value and close to one, the resulting image is extremely noisy

Based on these observations, the chosen values for *a0*, *a1*, *a2*, and *a3* are 0.125, 0.5, 0.25, and 0.125, respectively. These coefficients are chosen because they correspond to dividing the pixel values by 2, 4, and 8, that is, shifting of the pixel values to the left by 1, 2, and 3 bits, respectively. The images produced based on the new implementation of the `Imresize` function using these coefficients is identical to the original implementation and that from Matlab — Matlab's implementation is used as an additional confirmation step. The `Imresize` function that utilizes the coefficients, *a0*, *a1*, *a2*, and *a3* is referred to as the "new implementation", while the implementation that makes use of the bicubic kernel is referred to as the "original implementation".

Fig. 4. Examples of images resized to a quarter of their original size. The methods used are: (a) original implementation, (b) new implementation, and (c) Matlab's bicubic resize function.

The performance of the original and new implementation of the `Imresize` function is summarized in **Table 5**; the values obtained are averaged across all 10 face images. The new implementation is 115 times faster than the original implementation.

Table 5. Performance summary of the original and new implementation of the `Imresize`

Section	Average Clock Cycles	Average Time (sec)
Original Imresize	459,693,061	5.75
New Imresize	3,949,404	0.05

4 The Effect of Data and Instruction Caches on Performance

It is also important to investigate what the effects data and instruction caching behavior and size have on performance. Initially, the Nios II processor is configured with the default data cache settings, that is, an on-chip memory size of 16 KB with a data cache line size of 4 bytes. According to the Nios II core documentations, if the line size is greater than 4 bytes, data retrieval from extended memory (SDRAM in our case) is pipelined; hence reducing the impact of data transfer latency. A new system with exactly the same configuration but with the data cache line size increased to 32 bytes is generated. When the face detector and face detector beta programs are ran on this system, the total execution times are 466.23 and 394.18 seconds, respectively – the difference between the two execution times are less. These results give a positive indication that the processor's caches have an influence on performance.

The next experiment is to look at the effects of altering the size of the data cache. A series of eight systems with all the possible data cache sizes are generated. All these systems have a data cache line size of 32 bytes and the instruction cache size is fixed to 4 KB. **Table 6** summarizes these results. The usage of other resources such as DSP blocks, PLLs, and pins remain the same. There are minor fluctuations in the amount of LEs used and operating frequencies, but this is likely due to the variability in optimizations by the synthesis and fitting tools. Logically, the total amount of memory bits utilized linearly scales with the data cache size. As seen in **Table 6**, the size of the data cache does have an affect on the performance of the programs, particularly in the size range from 0.5 to 16 KB. Also, the performance continues to improve with a larger data cache.

A similar system but with data and instruction cache sizes of 64 KB (the largest cache sizes possible) were also generated on a Stratix EP1S40 development board

Table 6. Summary of the resource usage and executions times for varying data cache sizes

Data Cache Size (KB)	LE (%)	Total Memory Bits (%)	Face Detector (sec)	Face Detector Beta (sec)
0.5	66	5.65	589.26	483.07
1	68	6.13	555.3	452.11
2	66	7.07	527.24	433.59
4	66	8.96	507.48	421.03
8	66	12.71	481.64	406.13
16	68	20.19	466.23	394.18
32	68	35.1	458.8	389.05
64	68	64.8	455.79	386.89

(with roughly four times more resources than EP1S10) to confirm that no further improvements were possible with an instruction cache larger than 16 KB. Similarly other computational functions including Divide, Compare, and Round were added as custom instructors and similar speed-ups were observed.

5 Conclusion

This paper investigated the effects of replacing software bottleneck operations of a Face-Detection System based on Viola-Jones algorithm with custom instructions on performance. **Table 7** presents a summary of the new instructions implemented along with a measure of their efficiency — in-order for comparisons to be made fairly, the floating point multiply custom instruction is re-synthesized without the use of DSP blocks.

Table 7. Speedup, resource usage, and efficiency measure for each custom instruction

Floating Point Operation	Resource (LE)	Speedup	Speedup/Area (10^{-3})
Multiply	1,019	18	18
Add/Sub	806	21	26
Divide	1,061	11	10
Compare	77	16	208
Round	354	37	105

These results indicate that the floating point compare custom instruction is by far the most efficient in terms of speedup to area, even though it has a low overall speedup factor when integrated with the face detector application. On the other hand, even though the floating point multiply instruction has a reasonably low speedup to area ratio, when used in the face detector application the speedup for this instruction is high, in part because it is one of the most commonly used operations.

As the Viola-Jones face detection algorithm is primarily dominated by control operations and calculations involving 32-bit integer or floating point numbers, very little benefit is likely to result from the movement of larger functions to hardware.

An inadvertent result revealed through this investigation is that both the size and behavior of the caches, specifically the instruction cache, has a significant affect on the software performance. Experiments have shown that the total execution time may noticeably fluctuate depending on the code or instruction cache size. The implication of this result is that, it is difficult to determine the effectiveness of the optimizations applied — even with custom instructions; since changes to the software code results in a change to the code size and hence caching behavior. Lastly, it has been shown that incremental changes to the software code can add up to substantial reductions in the total execution time. However, the extent and effectiveness of these optimizations is largely attributed to the designer's experience.

Acknowledgement

This project was partly supported by a grant from the Australian Government Department of the Prime Minister and Cabinet. NICTA is funded by the Australian

Government's Backing Australia's Ability initiative and the Queensland Government, in part through the Australian Research Council. However the majority of work was done at The University of Auckland in New Zealand.

References

1. M. H. Yang, D. J. Kriegman, and N. Ahuja: Detecting faces in images: a survey. In IEEE Transactions on Pattern Analysis and Machine Intelligence, vol. 24 (2002) 34-58
2. E. Hjelmas and B. K. Low: Face detection: a survey. In Computer Vision and Image Understanding, vol. 83, (2001) 236-274
3. R. W. Frischholz and U. Dieckmann: BiolD: a multimodal biometric identification system. In Computer, vol. 33 (2000) 64-68
4. D. P. Huttenlocher, G. A. Klanderman, and W. J. Rucklidge: Comparing images using the Hausdorff distance. In IEEE Transactions on Pattern Analysis and Ma-chine Intelligence, vol. 15 (1993) 850-863
5. Ting Shan, Brian C. Lovell, Shaokang, Chen and Abbas Bigdeli: Reliable Face Recognition for Intelligent CCTV. In Proc. of Safeguarding Australia 2006- The 5th Homeland Security Summit & Exposition (2006) 356-364
6. T.-K. Kim, S.-U. Lee, J.-H. Lee, S.-C. Kee, and S.-R. Kim: Integrated approach of multiple face detection for video surveillance. In Proc. of Int. Conf. on Pattern Recognition, vol. 2 (2002) 394-397
7. T. Theocharides, G. Link, N. Vijaykrishnan, M. J. Irwin, and W. Wolf: Embedded hardware face detection. In Proc. of the 17th Int. Conf. on VLSI Design (2004) 133-138
8. H. A. Rowley, S. Baluja, and T. Kanade: Neural network-based face detection. In IEEE Transactions on Pattern Analysis and Machine Intelligence, vol. 20 (1998) 23-38
9. H. A. Rowley, S. Baluja, and T. Kanade: Rotation invariant neural network-based face detection. In IEEE Computer Society Conf. on Computer Vision and Pattern Recognition (1998) 38-44
10. B. D. T. Inc.: Using General-Purpose Processors for Signal Processing. In ARM Developers' Conf. (2004)
11. R. McCready: Real-Time Face Detection on a Configurable Hardware System. In Proc. of The Roadmap to Reconfigurable Computing, 10th International Workshop on Field-Programmable Logic and Applications (2000) 157-162
12. M. S. Sadri, N. Shams, M. Rahmaty, I. Hosseini, R. Changiz, S. Mortazavian, S. Kheradmand, and R. Jafari: An FPGA Based Fast Face Detector. In Global Signal Processing Expo and Conf. (2004)
13. D. M. Lewis, D. R. Galloway, M. Van Ierssel, J. Rose, and P. Chow: The Transmogrifier-2: a 1 million gate rapid-prototyping system. In IEEE Transactions on Very Large Scale Integration (VLSI) Systems, vol. 6 (1997) 188-198
14. R. Lienhart, A. Kuranov, and V. Pisarevsky: Empirical Analysis of Detection Cascades of Boosted Classifiers for Rapid Object Detection. In DAGM, 25th Pattern Recognition Symposium (2003) 297-304
15. R. Keys. Cubic convolution interpolation for digital image processing. In IEEE Transactions on Acoustics, Speech, and Signal Processing, vol. 29 (1981) 1153-1160
16. A. Bigdeli, M. Biglari-Abhari, S. H. S. Leung, and K. I. K. Wang: Multimedia extensions for a reconfigurable processor. In Proc. of 2004 International Symposium on Intelligent Multimedia, Video and Speech Processing, (2004) 426-429

17. T. F. Oliver, S. Mohammed, N. M. Krishna, and D. L. Maskell: Accelerating an embedded RTOS in a SoPC platform. In Proc. of TENCON Conference, vol. 4 (2004) 415-418
18. H. Tsutsui, T. Masuzaki, T. Izumi, T. Onoye, and Y. Nakamura: High speed JPEG2000 encoder by configurable processor. In Proc. of Asia-Pacific Conf. on Circuits and Systems, vol. 1 (2002) 45-50
19. Z. GuangWei and L. Xiang: An efficient approach to custom instruction set generation. In IEEE Int. Conf. on Embedded and Real-Time Computing Systems and Applications (2005) 547-550
20. W. H. Press, W. T. Vetterling, S. A. Teukolsky, and B. P. Flannery: Numerical recipes in C: the art of scientific computing. Second ed. Cambridge University Press, New York (1992)

An Improved Fusion Design of Audio-Gesture for Multi-modal HCI Based on Web and WPS

Jung-Hyun Kim and Kwang-Seok Hong

School of Information and Communication Engineering, Sungkyunkwan University, 300, Chunchun-dong, Jangan-gu, Suwon, KyungKi-do, 440-746, Korea
`kjh0328@skku.edu, kshong@skku.ac.kr`
`http://hci.skku.ac.kr`

Abstract. This paper introduces improved fission rule depending on SNNR (Signal Plus Noise to Noise Ratio) and fuzzy value for simultaneous multi-modality, and suggests the Fusion User Interface (hereinafter, FUI) including a synchronization between audio-gesture modalities, based on the embedded KSSL (Korean Standard Sign Language) recognizer using the WPS (Wearable Personal Station for the next generation PC) and Voice-XML. Our approach fuses and recognizes 62 sentential and 152 word language models that are represented by speech and KSSL, then translates recognition results that is fissioned according to a weight decision rule into synthetic speech and visual illustration (graphical display by HMD-Head Mounted Display) in real-time. The experimental results, average recognition rates of the FUI for 62 sentential and 152 word language models were 94.33% and 96.85% in clean environments (e.g. office space), and 92.29% and 92.91% were shown in noisy environments.

1 Introduction

Multi-modal interaction offers significant ease of use benefits over uni-modal interaction, for instance, when hands-free operation is needed, for mobile devices with limited keypads, and for controlling other devices when a traditional desktop computer is unavailable to host the application user interface. This is being driven by advances in embedded and network-based speech processing, creating opportunities for integrated multi-modal web browsers and solutions that separate the handling of visual and aural modalities [1]. The functionality of a multi-modal interface can be fairly extensive, and applications may be found in a number of fields. To name a few examples, these applications proved to be a viable aid for visually impaired users, an alternative to WIMP (Windows, Icon, Menu, and Pointer based interfaces) interfaces in mobile computing, and an entertaining extension to computer games [2], [3], [4].

However, the desktop PC and wire communications net-based traditional studies on pattern recognition and multimodal interaction generally have some restrictions and problems such as conditionality on the space, limitation of motion, uncertainty of measurement, and necessity of complex computational algorithms according to using the vision technologies for recognition and acquisition of haptic-gesture information. In other words, traditional studies emphasized the fusion of audio-visual or audio-emotion information as integration architecture for multi-modal HCI, and although

Y.-H. Lee et al. (Eds.): ICESS 2007, LNCS 4523, pp. 309–316, 2007.

this fusion was based on speech recognition, a noisy environment as not considered entirely. But, noise and speaker information in speech recognition are very important as benchmark's elements, and can not be ignored.

Consequently, we introduces improved a weight decision rule that fission the handling of haptic and aural modalities by coupling the WPS-based embedded KSSL recognizer with a remote Voice-XML user using SNNR and fuzzy value, for clear language processing in noisy environments, and suggests the FUI including a synchronization between audio-gesture modalities. In contrast to other proposed Multi-Modal interaction approaches, our approach is unique in two aspects: First, because the FUI provides different weight and feed-back function in individual (speech or gesture) recognizer, according to SNNR and fuzzy value, it may select an optimal language processing interface under a given situation or noisy environment, and can allow more interactive (natural) communication functions in noisy environment. Second, according as the FUI fuses and recognizes 62 sentential and 152 word language models that are represented by speech and KSSL, then translates recognition results that is fissioned according to a weight decision rule into synthetic speech and visual illustration (graphical display by Head Mounted Display) in real-time, it provides a wider range of personalized and differentiated information more effectively.

2 Speech Recognition and Synthesis Based on Voice-XML

Voice-XML is the W3C's standard XML format for specifying interactive voice dialogues between a human and a computer. For ASR-engine in architecture [5] of W3C's VXML 2.0, we used the HUVOIS solution that is Voice-XML-based voice software developed by KT Corp. in Korea for those with impaired sight that converts online text into voice and reads out the letters and words punched in through the computer keyboard, thus enabling them to use computers and the internet.

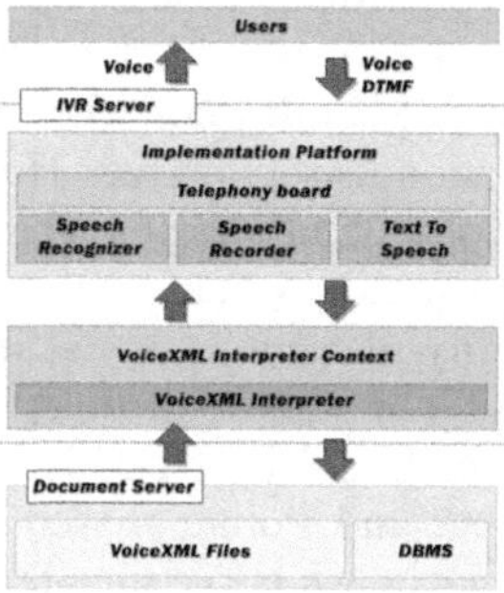

Fig. 1. The Voice-XML's architectural model

The HUVOIS solution consist of HUVOIS-ARS based on HMM, TTS using Triphone unit and HUVOIS Voice-XML, and supports client-sever network, LSS(Load Share Server) and modular structure. The Voice-XML's architectural model is shown in Fig. 1. A document server (e.g. a web server) processes requests from a client application, the Voice-XML interpreter, through the VXML interpreter context. The server produces Voice-XML documents in reply, which are processed by the Voice-XML interpreter. The Voice-XML interpreter context may monitor user inputs in parallel with the Voice-XML interpreter. For example, one Voice-XML interpreter context may always listen for a special escape phrase that takes the user to a high-level personal assistant, and another may listen for escape phrases that alter user preferences like volume or text-to-speech characteristics. The implementation platform is controlled by the Voice-XML interpreter context and by the Voice-XML interpreter.

3 WPS-Based Embedded KSSL Recognizer

For an improved KSSL recognition based on WPS and ubiquitous computing, we used 5DT company's wireless data gloves and Fastrak® which are popular input devices in the haptic application field, and utilized blue-tooth module for the wireless sensor network. Wireless data gloves are basic gesture recognition equipment that can capture various haptic information (e.g. hand or finger's stooping degree, direction) using the fiber-optic flex sensor. In addition, the Fastrak® is a solution for the position/orientation measuring requirements of applications and environments, and is a 3D digitizer and a quad receiver motion tracker, making it correct for a wide range of applications requiring high resolution, accuracy, and range [6], [7].

Statistical classification algorithms such as K-means clustering, Quality Threshold clustering, the fuzzy c-means clustering algorithm and the Self-Organizing Map, have been applied universally in traditional pattern recognition systems with unsupervised training, such as machine training, data mining, pattern recognition, image analysis and bioinformatics [8], [9], [10]. However, such classification algorithms have certain restrictions and problems, such as the necessity of complicated mathematical computation according to multidimensional features, the difficulty of applications in distributed processing systems, relativity of computation costs by pattern size, and minimization of memory swapping and assignment. In this paper, we prescribed 32 basic KSSL motion gestures and 28 hand gestures connected with a travel information scenario, according to "Korean Standard Sign Language Tutor (KSSLT) [11]". KSSL gestures and hand gestures are classified by an arm's movement, hand shape, pitch and roll degree. Consequently, we constructed 62 sentential and 152 word language models according to associability and presentation of hand gestures and basic KSSL motion gestures. In addition, for a clustering method to achieve efficient feature extraction and construction of recognition models based on distributed computing, we suggest and introduce an improved RDBMS (Relational Data-Base Management System) clustering module, to resolve such restrictions and problems.

As the fuzzy logic for KSSL recognition, we applied trapezoidal shaped membership functions for representation of fuzzy numbers-sets, and utilized the fuzzy max-min composition. Two fuzzy relations *R* and *S* are defined in sets *A*, *B* and *C* (we prescribed the accuracy of hand gestures and basic KSSL gestures, object KSSL recognition models as the sets of events that occur in KSSL recognition with the sets

A, B and *C*). That is, $R \subseteq A \times B$, $S \subseteq B \times C$. The composition $S{\cdot}R = SR$ of two relations *R* and *S* is expressed by the relation from *A* to *C*, and this composition is defined in Eq. (1) [12], [13].

$$\begin{aligned} &For\ (x, y) \in A \times B,\ (y, z) \in B \times C, \\ &\mu_{S \bullet R}(x, z) = \underset{y}{Max}\ [Min\ (\mu_R(x, y), \mu_S(y, z))] \end{aligned} \tag{1}$$

4 Simultaneous Multi-Modality-Fusion and Fission Between Modalities

4.1 Fusion Scheme Between Audio-Gesture Modalities

The fusion scheme consists of seven major steps: 1) the user connects to Voice-XML server via PSTN and internet using telephone terminal and WPS based on wireless networks (including middleware), and then inputs prescribed speech and KSSL, 2) the user's speech data, which are inputted into telephone terminal, is transmitted to ASR-engine in Voice-XML, then ASR results are saved to the MMDS (Multi-Modal Database Server; The MMDS is the database responsible for synchronizing data

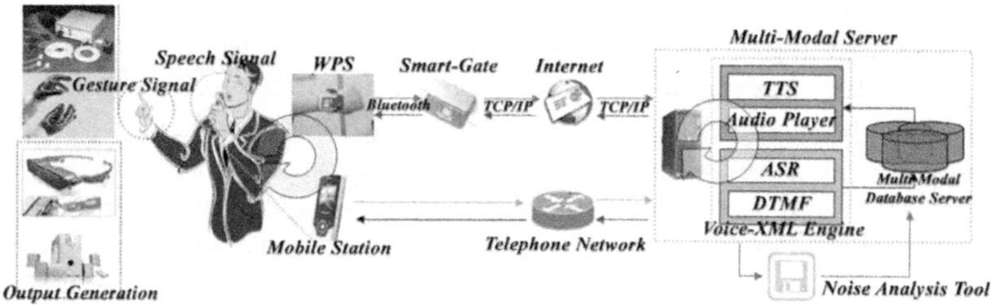

Fig. 2. The components for fusion architecture

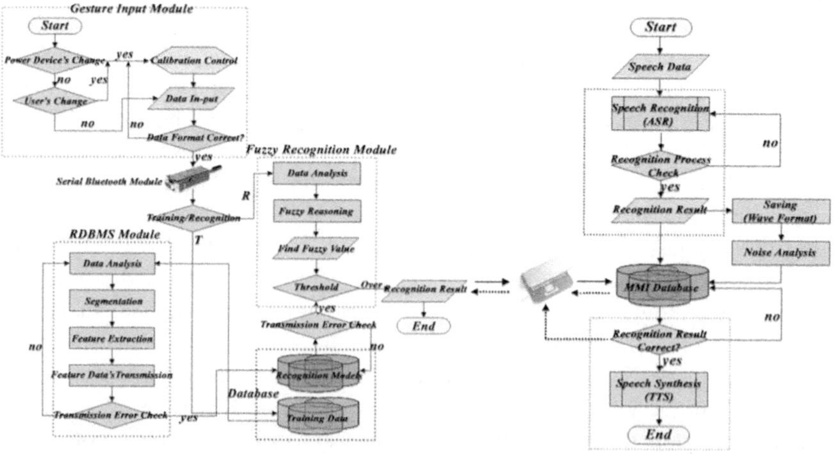

Fig. 3. The flowchart of the FUI integrating 2 sensory channels with speech and gesture

between speech and KSSL gesture), 3) user's KSSL data, which are inputted into WPS, are recognized by embedded KSSL recognizer, then the WPS transmits and saves recognition results to the MMDS, using middleware over TCP/IP protocol and wireless networks, 4) at this point, the user's KSSL and speech data run the synchronization session using internal SQL logic of the MMDS, 5) while suggested the FUI runs a validity check on ASR and KSSL recognition results with pre-scribed language models by internal SQL logic, the NAT(Noise Analysis Tool) analyzes noise for user's speech data which is recorded by Voice-XML, 6) According to analyzed noise and arithmetic result, the FUI gives weight into an individual (gesture or speech) recognizer, 7) finally, user's intention is provided to the user through TTS and visualization. The suggested architecture and flowchart of FUI are shown in Fig. 2 and Fig. 3.

4.2 Synchronization Between Audio-Gesture Modalities and Noise Analysis

This paper solves the asynchronous control problems between speech and gesture signals using a web-logic and word-unit input method based on the database (the MMDS in section 4.1). In other words, for synchronization between speech and gesture signals, after individual speech and KSSL recognizer recognizes inputted speech and the KSSL recognition models, they transmit recognition results into the MMDS for weight application. However, the transmission time of recognition results has some time delay because of asynchronous communication of two input signals. As a result, the speech and KSSL recognition results based on word-unit are recorded sequentially to the MMDS, and while the DB is kept in standby mode via internal web-logic in case one was not input among the two input signals (where, two input signals are the recognition results of speech and KSSL), apply weight according to the degree of SNNR and fuzzy value, in the case where all input values are recorded.

In addition, in noisy environments, speech quality is severely degraded by noises from the surrounding environment and speech recognition systems fail to produce high recognition rates [14]. Consequently, in this paper, we designed and implemented NAT for weight decision in individual (gesture or speech) recognizer. The NAT extracts data samples in mute section as a noise domain, and analysis total sample frames; speech data section from the 'waveformData array' that contains the actual waveform data, then it calculates average energy (mean power; [dB]) for two types of sample frames extracted in the first step, finally, calculate SNNR by Eq. (2), where, P is average power of noise and speech data.

$$SNNR(dB) = 10\log_{10} \frac{P_{signal + noise}}{P_{noise}} \qquad (2)$$

4.3 Fission Depending on SNNR and Fuzzy Value

In this section, we describe a web logic-based a weight decision rule depending on SNNR and fuzzy value for the fission between audio-gesture modalities, in FUI that is an optional language processing interface. We used an average speech recognition rate as speech probability value for weight decision, and to define speech probability value depending on SNNR, we achieved repeatedly speech recognition experiments 10 times with the 20 test speech recognition models in noisy and clean environments, for every 5 reagents. In addition, speech recognition rate does not usually change to a 25 dB SNNR, but if the rate lowers, the speech recognition rate falls rapidly. Therefore, the FUI provides feed-back function according to SNNR value. In case SNNR critical value for weight decision is ambiguous, according as feed-back function requests re-input to user for clear a declaration of intention, more improved language processing is available. The average speech recognition rates as speech probability value are given Table 1, together with weight values that are defined depending on SNNR.

Table 1. Weight value according to the SNNR and critical value for the feed-back function

SNNR Critical value	Weight value (%)		Average speech recognition rate for the 20 test recognition models (%)						
	Speech (W_S)	KSSL(W_G)	Reagent 1	Reagent 2	Reagent 3	Reagent 4	Reagent 5	Average(S)	Differ-ence
more than 40 [dB]	99.0	1.0	98.2	98.4	97.9	98.5	98.2	98.2	0.9
35 [dB] ≤ SNNR < 40 [dB]	98.0	2.0	97.8	97.3	96.6	97.1	97.5	97.3	0.3
30 [dB] ≤ SNNR < 35 [dB]	96.0	4.0	97.5	96.5	96.6	97.0	97.4	97.0	0.2
25 [dB] ≤ SNNR < 30 [dB]	94.0	6.0	97.2	96.5	96.5	96.9	96.9	96.8	0.2
20 [dB] ≤ SNNR < 25 [dB]	92.0	2.0	96.9	95.9	96.4	96.8	96.8	96.6	2.2
15 [dB] ≤ SNNR < 20 [dB]	*Feed-Back*		*92.4*	*96.2*	*93.8*	*95.2*	*94.1*	*94.3*	*11.1*
10 [dB] ≤ SNNR < 15 [dB]	6.0	94.0	83.6	83.4	83.5	82.6	83.2	83.3	8.8
5 [dB] ≤ SNNR < 10 [dB]	4.0	96.0	71.9.	72.5	70.2	79.5	75.6	74.5	22.4
0 [dB] ≤ SNNR < 5 [dB]	2.0	98.0	53.4	51.3	52.6	51.6	51.3	52.0	14.0
less than 0 [dB]	1.0	99.0	38.5	37.6	37.5	38.2	38.5	38.1	-

$$P\_W = W_S \times S + W_G \times G \tag{3}$$

- *P_W : a probability value after weight application*
- *W_S : Defined Weight for Speech recognition mode*
- *W_G : Defined Weight for KSSL recognition mode*
- *S : speech probability (an average speech recognition rate)*
- *G : KSSL probability (the critical value depending on normalized fuzzy value)*

$$G = \frac{Fuzzy\ Value\_Current}{Fuzzy\ Value\_Max} = \frac{Fuzzy\ Value\_Current}{3.5} \tag{4}$$

- *Fuzzy Value_Current : Fuzzy value to recognize current gesture(KSSL)*
- *Fuzzy Value_Max = 3.5 : The maximum fuzzy value for KSSL recognition*

The weight decision processing for fission between modalities consists of three major steps: 1) as speech and KSSL probability value, it calls an average speech recognition rate *(S)* depending on the defined SNNR, and fuzzy value *(G)* for KSSL recognition from the MMDS, then apply weights (W_S and W_G) in called-individual probability value, 2) and then calculate a probability value (P_W) after weight application via by Eq. (3), 3) return the fission result (speech or KSSL recognition result) by calculated the probability value (P_W) to user. Where, the maximum fuzzy value for KSSL recognition is 3.5, and the minimum critical value is 3.2 (in programming). Accordingly, the normalized fuzzy value (*G*) of the embedded KSSL recognizer is defined Eq. (4). Because *KSSL probability (G)* is changed according to *Fuzzy Value_Current*, *P_W* is changed justly.

As a result, if *P_W* value is over than 0.917, the FUI fissions and returns recognition result of speech recognizer based on Voice-XML, while the FUI fissions the embedded KSSL recognizer in case *P_W* value is less than 0.909. The decision rule and SNNR critical value for feed-back function are given in Table 2.

Table 2. In case *Fuzzy Value_Current* is 3.2, a system of measuring of *P_W* values

SNNR	Speech		KSSL		P_W
	W_S	S	W_G	G	
more than 40 [dB]	0.99	0.982	0.01	0.914	0.981
35 [dB] ≤ SNNR < 40 [dB]	0.98	0.973	0.02	0.914	0.972
30 [dB] ≤ SNNR < 35 [dB]	0.96	0.970	0.04	0.914	0.968
25 [dB] ≤ SNNR < 30 [dB]	0.94	0.968	0.06	0.914	0.965
20 [dB] ≤ SNNR < 25 [dB]	0.92	0.966	0.08	0.914	0.917
15 [dB] ≤ SNNR < 20 [dB]			*Feed-Back*		
10 [dB] ≤ SNNR < 15 [dB]	0.06	0.833	0.94	0.914	0.909
5 [dB] ≤ SNNR < 10 [dB]	0.04	0.745	0.96	0.914	0.907
0 [dB] ≤ SNNR < 5 [dB]	0.02	0.520	0.98	0.914	0.906
less than 0 [dB]	0.01	0.381	0.99	0.914	0.909

5 Experiments and Results

The experimental set-up is as follows. The distance between the KSL input module and the WPS with a built-in KSSL recognizer approximates radius 10M's ellipse form. In KSSL gesture and speech, we move the wireless data gloves and the motion tracker to the prescribed position. For every 15 reagents, we repeat this action 10 times in noisy and clean environments. While the user inputs KSSL using data gloves and a motion tracker, and speak using the blue-tooth headset in a telephone terminal. Experimental results, the uni-modal and the FUI's average recognition rate in noisy and clean environment for 62 sentential and 152 word language models, are shown in Table 3, respectively.

Table 3. Language recognition results for the 62 sentential and 152 word language models

Evaluation / Reagent	Uni-modal Language Processing Interface						The FUI			
	KSSL (%)		Speech (%)				KSSL + Speech (%)			
	Noise or Clean (%)		Noise (%)		Clean (%)		Noise (%)		Clean (%)	
	152 models	62 models	152 models	62 models	152 models	62 models	152 models	62 models	152 models	62 models
Reagent 1	92.8	92.7	83.6	85.7	98.1	94.2	92.7	92.5	98.1	94.2
Reagent 2	93.8	91.7	83.5	84.6	95.4	94.9	93.3	91.5	95.5	94.8
Reagent 3	94.1	92.9	82.4	79.8	95.6	93.2	93.7	92.3	95.7	93.2
Reagent 4	92.9	93.2	85.1	82.8	96.3	93.8	92.3	92.9	96.3	93.8
Reagent 5	93.1	93.3	85.6	85.9	96.7	93.9	93.5	92.7	96.9	93.8
Reagent 6	91.8	92.2	84.6	84.2	95.9	95.5	91.1	91.5	96.1	95.5
Reagent 7	92.7	91.7	84.3	79.9	95.7	92.7	92.5	91.2	95.8	92.7
Reagent 8	94.6	91.4	82.6	78.2	96.8	93.2	94.5	90.9	97.1	93.3
Reagent 9	93.4	93.1	83.4	85.3	97.5	94.6	93.3	93.0	97.6	94.6
Reagent10	93.1	93.1	84.9	82.1	97.3	93.8	92.9	92.8	97.4	94.1
Reagent11	93.7	92.2	83.7	84.6	97.8	96.7	93.6	91.8	97.9	96.7
Reagent12	92.4	93.1	82.9	84.1	96.4	93.9	92.2	93.0	96.3	93.7
Reagent13	92.6	92.5	83.6	83.6	96.6	93.4	92.1	92.1	96.9	93.3
Reagent14	93.3	92.8	84.1	82.5	97.1	95.2	92.8	92.5	97.3	95.3
Reagent15	93.3	93.9	84.1	84.7	97.1	94.2	93.4	93.7	97.3	94.2
Average	93.17	92.65	83.85	83.20	96.71	94.21	92.91	92.29	96.85	94.33

6 Conclusions

Wearable and ubiquitous computing-based multi-modal user interfaces have implications for accessibility. A well-designed multi-modal application can be used by people with a wide variety of impairments. Visually impaired users rely on the voice modality with some keypad input. Hearing-impaired users rely on the visual modality with some gesture (and sign language) input. Other users will be "situationally impaired" and simply use the appropriate modalities as desired. In addition, the approaches to Multi-Agent Systems (MAS) varies considerably in many areas, such as computer science, philosophy, mathematics, linguistics, social science, and so on, but even if one limits the analysis to logical systems, one finds that different languages are applied to very similar problems. This study combines natural language and artificial intelligence techniques to allow human computer interaction with an intuitive mix of speech, gesture and sign language based on the WPS and Voice-XML. The FUI's average recognition rates for 62 sentential and 152 word language models were 94.33% and 96.85% in clean environments (e.g. office space), while 92.29% and 92.91% were shown in noisy environments. Finally, we clarify that this study is a fundamental study for implementation of an advanced multi modal recognizer integrating the human's five senses such as sight, hearing, touch, smell, and taste, to take the place of the traditional uni-modal recognizer for natural speech and sign language processing.

Acknowledgement

This research was supported by MIC, Korea under ITRC IITA-2006-(C1090-0603-0046).

References

1. Multimodal Interaction Activity.: Extending the Web to support multiple modes of interaction, http://www .w3.org/2002/mmi/
2. M. Fuchs, P. et al.: Architecture of Multi-modal Dialogue System. TSD2000, Lecture Notes in Artificial Intelligence, Vol. 1902. Springer-Verlag, Berlin Heidelberg New York (2000) 433–438
3. M. J. Wooldridge and N.R. Jennings.: Intelligent agents: Theory and practice, Know. Eng. Review, 10(2):115-152, 1995.
4. R. Fagin, J.Y. Halpern, Y. Moses, and M.Y,Vardi.: Reasoning about Knowledge, MIT Press, (1995).
5. Scott McGlashan et al.: Voice Extensible Markup Language (VoiceXML) Version 2.0. W3C Recommendation, http://www.w3.org (1992).
6. J.-H.Kim. et al.: Hand Gesture Recognition System using Fuzzy Algorithm and RDBMS for Post PC, Proceedings of FSKD2005, Lecture Notes in Artificial Intelligence, Vol. 3614, Springer-Verlag, 2005, pp. 170-175
7. i.MX21 Processor Data-sheet, http://www.freescale.com/
8. Richard O. Duda. et al.: Pattern Classification, 2nd, Wiley, New York (2001)
9. Dietrich Paulus and Joachim Hornegger.:Applied Pattern Recognition, 2nd, Vieweg (1998)
10. J. Schuermann.: Pattern Classification, A Unified View of Statistical and Neural Approaches, Wiley&Sons (1996)
11. S.-G.Kim.:Korean Standard Sign Language Tutor, 1st, Osung, Seoul (2000)
12. C.H.Chen, Fuzzy Logic and Neural Network Handbook. 1st, McGraw-Hill, New York (1992)
13. W. B. Vasantha kandasamy.: Smaranda Fuzzy Algebra. American Research Press, (2003)
14. NIOSH working group.: STRESS...AT WORK NIOSH, Publication No. 99-101,U.S. National Institutes of Occupational Health (2006)

User-Customized Interactive System Using Both Speech and Face Recognition*

Sung-Ill Kim

Department of Electronic Engineering, Kyungnam University,
449 Wolyoung-dong, Masan City, 631-701 Korea
kimstar@kyungnam.ac.kr

Abstract. In this paper, we discuss the user-customized interaction for intelligent home environments. The interactive system is based upon the integrated techniques using both speech and face recognition. For essential modules, the speech recognition and synthesis were basically used for a virtual interaction between user and the proposed system. In experiments, particularly, the real-time speech recognizer based on the HM-Net(Hidden Markov Network) was incorporated into the proposed system. Besides, the face identification was adopted to customize home environments for a specific user. In evaluation, the results showed that the proposed system was useful and easy to use for intelligent home environments, even though the performance of the speech recognizer was not better than the simulation results owing to the ambient noisy environments.

1 Introduction

Currently, there are many methods of biometrical identification such as eye iris, retina, voice, face etc. Among them, the face recognition has been one of the most widely used biometrics for personal verification. Its advantage is that it does not require physical contact as well as any advanced hardware. It can be used with existing image capture devices such as web cam, security cameras etc. The system of face identification matches the given input face image with the one stored in its database and a degree of similarity is finally computed. If such score is higher than a certain acceptance threshold, then the person is classified as a one of the registered users. In the present paper, the face identification can be used for the interface of user-customized system in the intelligent home environments [1,2,3,4,5].

When talking about the intelligent home, it means different things to different people. Figure 1 shows the basic idea of the interaction between user and intelligent home environment where the face identification is used for user-customization. The interactive system using face identification is integrated with the essential components such as speech recognition, and speech synthesis. Assuming that we sit on the sofa that is interconnected with both touch sensor and face identification subsystem, the user-customized interaction is then automatically formed so that the intelligent home can provide you with more convenient and comfortable living environments.

---

* This work is supported by the Kyungnam University Research Fund, 2007.

Y.-H. Lee et al. (Eds.): ICESS 2007, LNCS 4523, pp. 317–327, 2007.

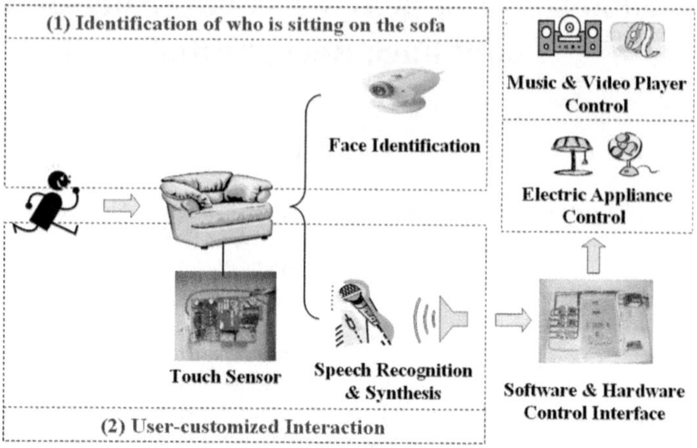

Fig. 1. Concept of the interactive system based on the techniques such as speech recognition, speech synthesis, and fingerprint verification

The basic idea mentioned above is based on the fact that the place we spend most time at home is our living room, particularly on the sofa. The concept is started on the assumption that the interaction between user and system can be built when user sits on the sofa. The proposed system is designed to allow users to converse with their home based on the user-customized interaction where the system puts emphasis on an easy-to-use and user-friendly man-machine interface. As a consequence, the intelligent home, as an aim of this study, makes it possible to lead the living environments to the most suitable condition for users by integrating speech recognition with face identification. For face identification, in this study, it was used to customize the home environments for a specific user. For speech recognition and synthesis, on the other hand, they were used for interaction between user and intelligent home environment.

2 The Interface of Speech Recognition Using HM-Net

HMM(Hidden Markov Model) is a mathematical model which has been widely used in speech recognition systems. In this study, we used HM-Net(Hidden Markov Network) [6,7] which is an efficient representation of context-dependent phonemes for speech recognition. The HM-Net, which has various state lengths and shares their states one another, is automatically generated by SSS(Successive State Splitting) [7,8]. The SSS is an iterative algorithm that progressively grows HM-Net, where each state in the network is associated with a 2-component Gaussian mixture.

In the algorithm, a state is selected to be split according to which has the largest divergence between its two mixtures. The state is then split on the contextual and temporal domains, and the one giving greater likelihood is chosen. The affected states are retrained using the Baum-Welch algorithm [9,10]. The above procedure is iterated until getting to a pre-defined number of states.

The PDT-SSS(Phonetic Decision Tree-Successive State Splitting) [11] based on the SSS algorithm is a powerful technique to design topologies of tied-state models, and is possible to generate highly accurate HM-Net. Each state of HM-Net has the information such as state index, contextual class, lists of preceding and succeeding states, parameters of the output probability density distribution and the state transition probability. If contextual information is given, the model corresponding to the context can be determined by concatenating several associated states within the restriction of the preceding and succeeding state lists.

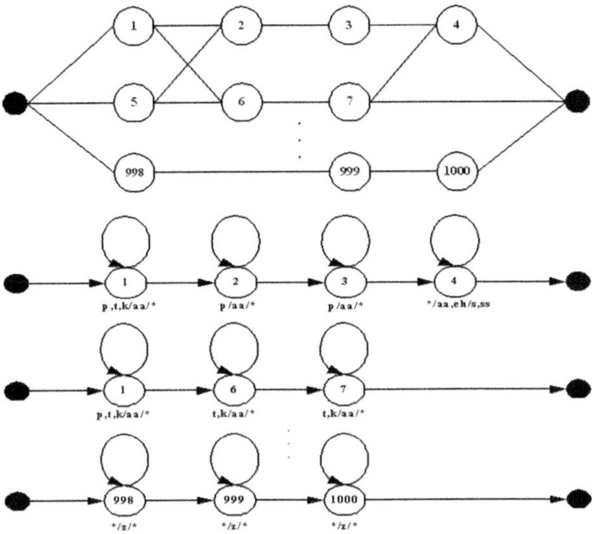

Fig. 2. An example of HM-Net models

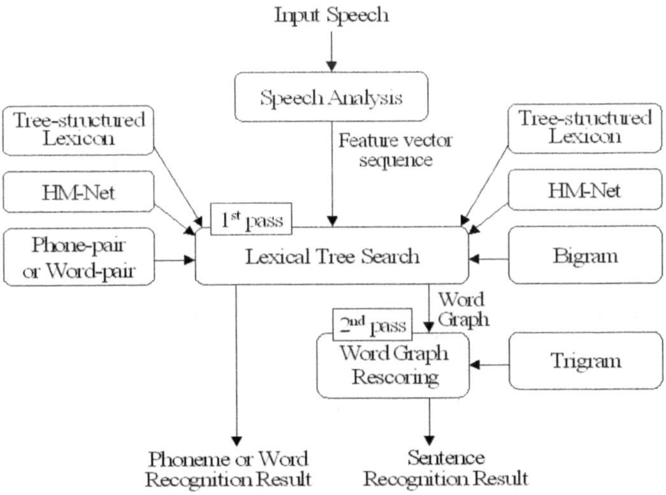

Fig. 3. Overall schematic of HM-Net speech recognition system

The final result of state splitting is a network of states that efficiently represents a collection of context-dependent models, as illustrated in figure 2. In contrast to the training process of the existing HMM, the architecture of the models can be automatically optimized according to the duration of utterances. As a result, the number of states in vowels increases more than that of states in consonants in terms of the architecture.

Figure 3 shows an overall schematic of HM-Net speech recognition system. In case speech signals are given to the system, the acoustic features are first extracted for pre-processing, and then given to the first and the second pass search modules that use tree-structured lexicon, HM-Net Triphones, and semantic grammars. The HM-Net speech recognizer has been proved that it produced better performance than the conventional HMM in the experiments of phoneme, word, and continuous speech recognition [12,13].

3 The Interface of Face Identification

The face identification algorithm implements the advanced face localization, the enrollment and the matching using robust digital image processing algorithms. The interface has two operation modes such as enrollment and matching. It first processes the input face image, extracts features and then writes them to the database. In the mode of face enrollment with features generalization, particularly, it generates the collection of the generalized face features from a number of the face templates of the same person. Each face image is first processed and features are then extracted. In the next step, the collections of features are analyzed and combined into one generalized features collection, which is written to the database. The quality of face recognition increases if faces are enrolled using this mode mentioned above. In the mode of matching, on the other hand, it performs the matching process between the new face image and the face templates stored in the database.

In this study, the interface of face identification was adopted for user-customization of interactive system. In experiments, we used the VeriLook SDK[14] for the interface of face identification. Table 1 shows the technical specification of face identification using a PC with 3GHz Pentium 4 processor.

Figure 4 shows the software interface for face identification module made by VC++. The main application window of the interface has four-pane layout, where two top panes are used for image display and two bottom panes are used for message

Table 1. Technical Specification of Face Identification

Item	Specification
Recommended minimal image size	640 x 480 pixels
Multiple faces detection time(640 x 480 image)	0.1 seconds
Single face processing time	0.15 seconds
Matching speed	100,000 faces/second
Size of one record in the database	2.3 Kbytes
Maximum database size	unlimited

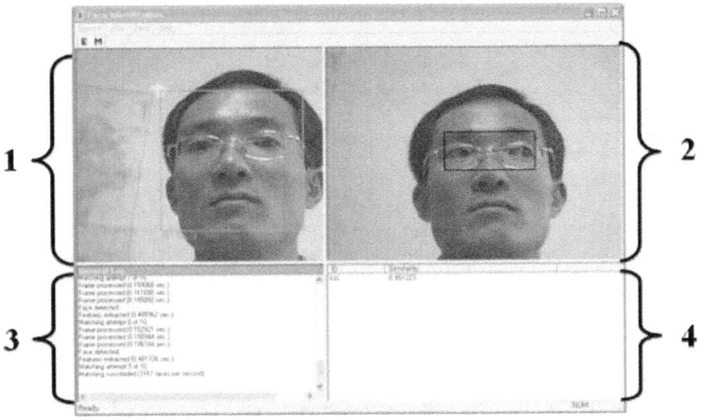

Fig. 4. Interface of face identification (num.1: Face detection pane, num.2: Matching/ enrollment pane, num.3: Application log pane, num.4: Matching results pane)

logging. The face detection pane is used to display the still images, the videos, or the result of face detection algorithm overlaid on image. The matching/enrollment pane is used to display images enrolled to face database or used for matching. The application log pane is used for the system information and the application progress messages. The match results pane is used for listing ID of the subject in the database, most similar to the matched image. Subjects are considered similar if their similarity value exceeds matching threshold set.

4 The Proposed Interactive System

The proposed system can be built by integrating two main module of both HM-Net speech recognition and face identification, mentioned in the previous chapters. Figure 5 shows the flow diagram of the processing based on the proposed system, which is operated in real time. It shows how to build the interaction between user and system.

If user sits on the sofa, the system catches signals from touch sensor and then activates face identification engine to detect face area. If the system recognizes who is sitting on the sofa, it adapts itself to the new circumstances. The system then activates the speech recognition engine where the virtual interaction between user and system is built using speech recognition and synthesis [15]. In case speech recognition is activated, system provides the user-customized services. It can notify user of the necessary information such as important messages or schedules. In the proposed system, the list of the registered recognition candidates can be automatically updated according to the corresponding recognition results.

Figure 6 shows the main window frame of user interface, which was made by VC++, with the modules of both speech recognition and face identification. The system provides several functions. First, it is possible for user to control multimedia application programs such as video, MP3 player, CD player etc. Besides, several kinds

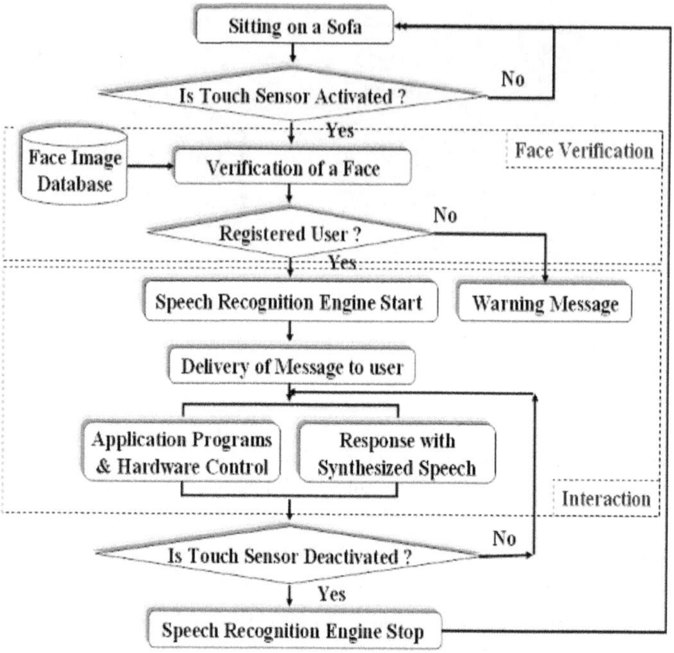

Fig. 5. The flow diagram of building interaction between user and system

of electrical appliances such as electrical fans, lamps can be controlled by the power relay units of print-port interface.

By utilizing the natural human-interfaces such as speech recognition and face identification, the need for a keyboard, mouse, or remote controller can be eliminated in real-world applications. Figure 7 shows the touch sensor, which is one of the

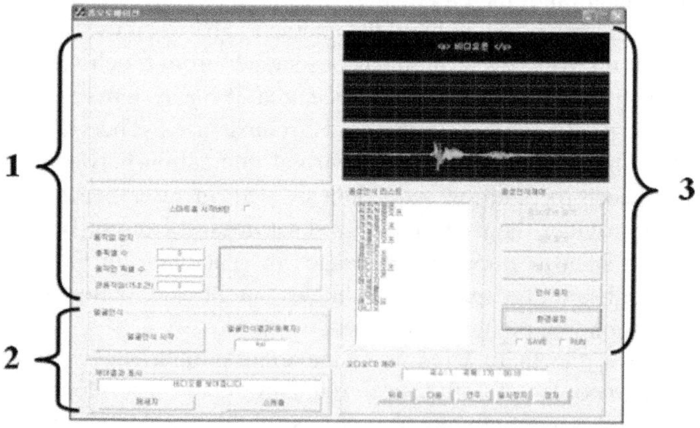

Fig. 6. Main window frame of user interface. (num.1: interface for video processing, num.2: interface of face identification, num 3: interface of speech recognition)

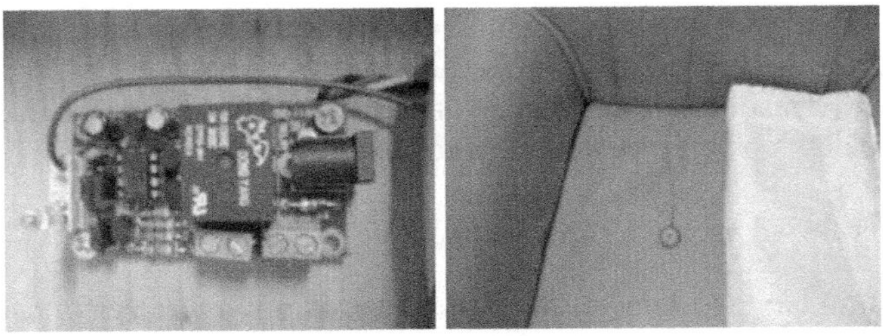

Fig. 7. Touch sensor(left) attached on the sofa(right)

components of hardware interface based on print-port control. It was attached on the sofa so that the input signals from the sensor activate or deactivate the system in case someone sits on the sofa.

5 Experimental Results

5.1 Preprocessing for Speech Recognition

All speech data were sampled at 16kHz, quantized at 16 bits, pre-emphasized with a transfer function of $(1-0.97z^{-1})$, and processed to extract acoustic features using a 25ms Hamming window with a 10ms shift. The feature parameters consisted of total 39th order LPC Mel Cepstrum coefficients including the normalized log-power, the first and the second order delta coefficients. Table 2 shows the analysis of speech signals.

Table 3 shows the speech database and its contents used for both HMM training and recognition process, respectively. For the training process, the database of

Table 2. Analysis of speech signals

Item	Contents
Sampling rate	16kHz , 16bits
Pre-emphasis	0.97
Window	25 ms Hamming window
Frame period	10 ms
Feature Parameter	13th order LPC MEL Cepstrum + 13th order ΔLPC MEL Cepstrum + 13th order ΔΔLPC MEL Cepstrum = Total 39th order LPC MEL Cepstrum

Table 3. Database used in the module of speech recognition

Process	Database	Contents
Training	ETRI	(200 male speakers*280 utterances) + (200 female speakers * 280 utterances) = 112,000 utterances
Word Recognition	KLE	(3 male speakers * 452 words) = 1,356 words
	YNU	4 male speaker * 200 utterances = 800 utterances

ETRI(The Electronics and Telecommunications Research Institute) was used. The database used for the recognition, on the other hand, consists of two kinds of database, one of which is made by KLE(Center for the Korean Language Engineering), and the other is made by YNU(YoungNam University).

5.2 Results Based on the Proposed System

For the preliminary experiments, the speech recognition was performed using a frame synchronous Viterbi beam search algorithm with the phonotactic constraint of Korean

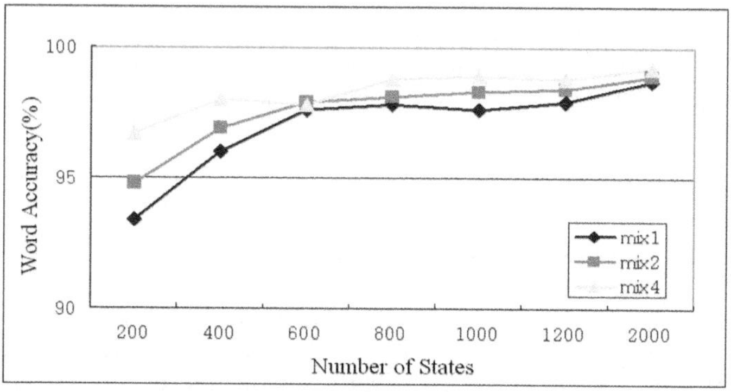

Fig. 8. Speaker and task independent word recognition accuracies according to the number of both mixtures and states using KLE database

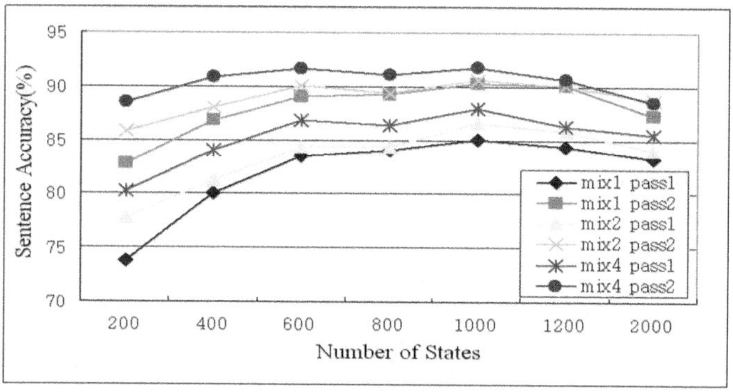

Fig. 9. Speaker and task independent sentence recognition accuracies according to the number of both mixtures and states using YNU database

Table 4. Experimental Conditions for Speech Recognition and Recognition Accuracy

Module	Accuracy(%)
Face Identification	(40/41)*100=97.6
Speech Recognition	(530/738)*100=71.8

language. Figure 8 and 9 shows the recognition accuracies for word and continuous speech, respectively. It is noticed in the recognition results that the accuracies, as a whole, grew gradually with the increase of the number of both mixtures and states.

For experiments, total 41 male college students were participated in the evaluation of the system. For examining the human performance on the accuracies of the proposed system, we first showed them a demonstration of how to use and operate the system, and made them to use it for themselves.

Table 4 shows the average recognition accuracies in each module such as face identification and speech recognition. For the evaluation of speech recognition incorporated into the proposed system, total 738 utterances(41 users * 18 utterances) were used. The evaluation was performed in the laboratory environments with the noises such as computer cooling fan or buzz of voices. In experiments, we adopted speech recognizer with 2,000 states and 4 mixtures per state. For the evaluation of face identification, on the other hand, 41 male college students were first registered in facial image database and the identification test in each user was then conducted.

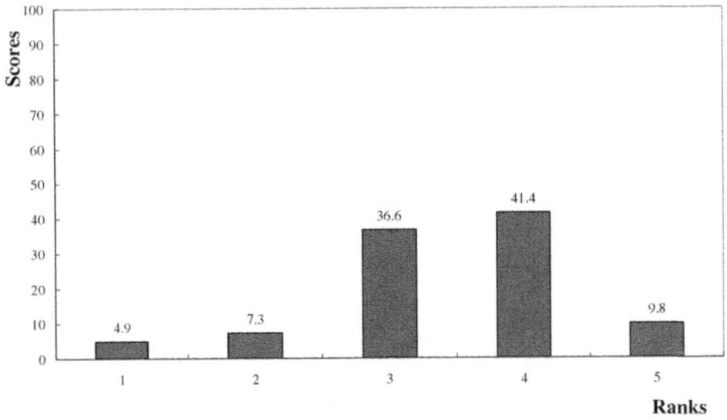

Fig. 10. Evaluation of the system in terms of how easy system was to use

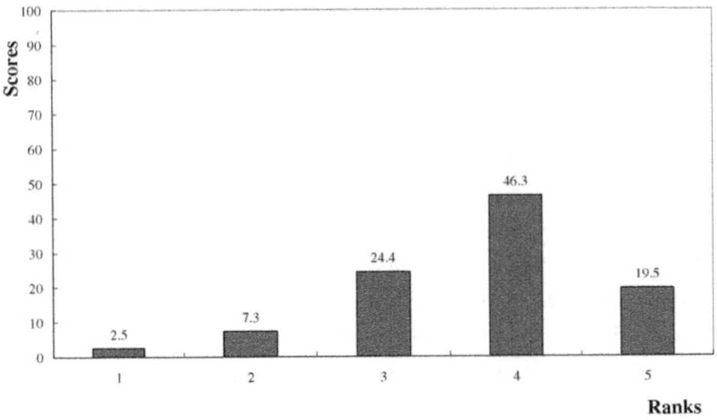

Fig. 11. Evaluation of the system in terms of how useful system would be in real applications

As the evaluation using questionnaire, all participants marked ranks from 1- to 5-point about how easy and how useful they thought the system was to use. We could get the results as shown in figure 10 and 11 that the proposed system was relatively easy to use and would be useful in real applications.

6 Conclusion

This study has described the user-customized interactive system based on the speech and face recognition for intelligent home environments. The results from the experimental evaluation have shown that the proposed system had relatively good performance. This means a possibility for building a virtual interaction using the system that might give us much more convenient and comfortable living environments. However, the accuracy of speech recognition was unsatisfactory owing to the noisy environments, diverse speaking rates, and speaking styles of users. From the evaluation, we could obtain several ideas on the system as future works. Namely, the future works should be conducted on more natural methods of interaction so that the future systems would allow users to feel more natural in virtual interaction for intelligent home environments.

References

1. Machate, J.: Being natural - on the use of multimodal interaction concepts in smart homes, HCI(2) (1999) 937-941, 2. Lee, K.F., Hon, H.W.: Speaker-Independent Phone Recognition Using Hidden Markov Models. IEEE Tran. on Acoustic, Speech and Signal Processing. 37(11) (1989) 1641–1648
2. Kohler, M.: Special Topics of Gesture Recognition Applied in Intelligent Home Environments. Lecture Notes in Computer Science, 1371 (1998) 285-233
3. Mozer, M.: The neural network house: An environment that adapts to its inhabitants. Proc. of the AAAI Spring Symposium on Intelligent Environments (1998) 110-114
4. Cook, D.J., Youngblood, M., Heierman, E., Gopalratnam, K., Rao, S., Litvin, A., and Khawaja, F.: MavHome: An Agent-Based Smart Home. Proc. of the IEEE International Conference on Pervasive Computing and Communications (2003) 521-524
5. Corcoran, P.M., Papai, F., Zoldi, A.: User Interface Technologies for Home Appliances and Networks. IEEE Transactions on Consumer Electronics (1998)
6. Suzuki, M., Makino, S., Ito, A., Aso, H., Shimodaira, H.: A new HMnet construction algorithm requiring no contextual factors. IEICE Trans. Inf. & Syst., E78-D(6) (1995) 662-669
7. Ostendoft, M., Singer, H.: HMM Topology design Using Maximum Likelihood Successive State Splitting. Computer Speech and Language 11 (1997) 17-41
8. Takami, J., Sagayama, S.: A Successive State Splitting Algorithm for Efficient Allophone Modeling. Proc. of ICASSP'92, 1 (1992) 573-576
9. Huang, X., Acero, A., Hon, H.W.: Spoken language processing: a guide to theory, algorithm, and system development, Prentice Hall (2001)
10. Rabiner, L., Juang, B.H.: Fundamentals of speech recognition. Prentice-Hall International, Inc. (1993)
11. Hori, T., Katoh, M., Ito, A., Kohda, M.: A Study on HM-Nets using Decision Tree-based Successive State Splitting. Proc. of ICSP'97, (1997) 383-387

12. Se-Jin, O., Cheol-Jun H., Bum-Koog K., Hyun-Yeol C., Akinori I.: New state clustering of hidden Markov network with Korean phonological rules for speech recognition. IEEE 4th workshop on Multimedia Signal Processing (2001) 39-44
13. Se-Jin, O., Cheol-Jun H., Bum-Koog K., Hyun-Yeol C.: Performance Evaluation of HM-Nets Speech Recognition System using the Large Vocabulary Korean Speech Databases. Proc. of Kyushu-Youngnam Joint Conference on Acoustics (2003) 49-52
14. VeriLook SDK(Software Developer's Kit) version 2.0, Neurotechnologija,. Web Site: http://www.neurotechnologija.com/
15. i-Talk SDK version 2.2, SL2 Corporation. Web Site: http://www. slworld.co.kr/

Visualization of GML Map Using 3-Layer POI on Mobile Device

Eun-Ha Song[1], Laurence T. Yang[2], and Young-Sik Jeong[1,*]

[1] Department of Computer Engineering, Wonkwang University
344-2 Shinyong-Dong, Iksan, 570-749, Korea
{ehsong,ysjeong}@wku.ac.kr
[2] Department of Computer Science, St. Francis Xavier University
Antigonish, NS, B2G 2W5, Canada
lyang@stfx.ca

Abstract. GIS can only be applied to certain areas by storing format, and it is subordinate to a system when displaying geographic information data. It is therefore inevitable for GIS to use GML that supports efficient usage of various geographic information data and interoperability for integration and sharing. The paper constructs *VisualGML* that translates currently-used geographic information such as DXF(Drawing Exchange Format), DWG(DraWinG), or SHP(Shapefile) into GML format to visualize. In order to provide a flexibility of a mobile device, VisualGML constructs integrated map preprocess module which filters geographic information data according to its tag and properties. VisualGML also provides two major GIS services for user and administrator, it can be enable visualizing location search this is applied with 3-Layer POI structure for user. For administrator, it has trace monitoring visualization through moving information of mobile devices.

1 Introduction

Mobile technology is rapidly emerging as a prominent icon representing present days. Due to propagation of wireless PDA, car navigation system, and cell phone, the need for geographic information service is rapidly rising. Current GIS has been developed with multiple methods and forms in order to display, analyze, process, store, gain geographic information data. There exist shortcomings on free usage, integration, application, and sharing due to limited format of GIS; therefore, common interchangeable format is necessary. OGC (Open GIS Consortium) has suggested a GML(Geography Markup Language)[1] specification in order to save and transfer geographic information containing a geographic aspect that has spatial or non-spatial attributes. To provide interoperability of GIS, GML gives a structure to data allowing flexibility of an access to information[2][3][4].

The paper develops VisualGML which visualizes and creates common-format GML that covers heterogeneity of geographic information data, supporting its inter-

* Corresponding Author.

Y.-H. Lee et al. (Eds.): ICESS 2007, LNCS 4523, pp. 328–337, 2007.

operability. VisualGML designs IMP(Integrated Map PreProcessor) in order to overcome insufficient data process memory and low connection speed that is caused by visualizing geographic information data onto a mobile device. IMP makes geographic information data lighter-weighted by extracting unnecessary information of file formats like DXF[5], DWG, or SHP[6], and categorizing those into layers. VisualGML user-centered visualization is based on not just simple GML-based map visualization, but on hierarchical POI information; it also saves, gains, traces, and manages real-time movement information of a mobile device.

2 Related Works

There are number of existing GML-base map visualization system: TatukGIS Viewer 1.4[7] by TatukGIS Inc., FME Universal Viewer[8] by SafeSoftware Inc., Master Map Viewer 2.0[9] by Snowflake Software Ltd., iSMART Explorer 4.4[10] by eSpatial Inc., and GML Viewer by ETRI.

iSMART Explorer 4.4 is very easy to use, has a light-weighted application, and is connected to OCI(Overseas Consultants Incorporated) DB, thus being much easier to be analyzed. It finds GML scheme automatically and reexamine, expand, minimize, and move non-spatial property data; it also allows sufficient spatial editing through web browser, and provides fast response time for low bandwidth connection. There exists almost no file format which TatukGIS Viewer 1.4 supports, which also can process up to 2Gbyte file. It also translates visualized geographic information into PDF file, and measures distance and size between two points. Also with vector property information it displays identical properties of a map with the same color, and when clicking a vector graphic with a mouse it shows a property window. Similarly, FME Universal Viewer 2004 displays identical properties with a same color, shows a property window; additionally, it allows editing properties of geometry.

There exist various map visualization systems besides programs mentioned above; however, the most support simple visualization and cannot provide user-centered map information. Also, they are not every useful in that they are offline single application. VisualGML uses various existing geographic information, extracts core elements for the map display, and converts them into GML; in other words, VisualGML supports heterogeneity and interoperability of geographic information data. During the process of GML conversion, it provides hierarchical location search and map visualization applied with hierarchical POI DB; moreover, VisualGML gains and saves movement coordinates of a mobile device, and provides tracking monitoring visualization.

3 VisualGML System

3.1 VisualGML Architecture and Control Flow

VisualGML is mainly composed of a map server and mobile device. Map server manages in lower weight of geographic information data, generating GML file, and tracking monitoring visualization of a mobile device. Mobile device is user-centered event process and visualization. Fig. 1 shows overview of the architecture of VisualGML.

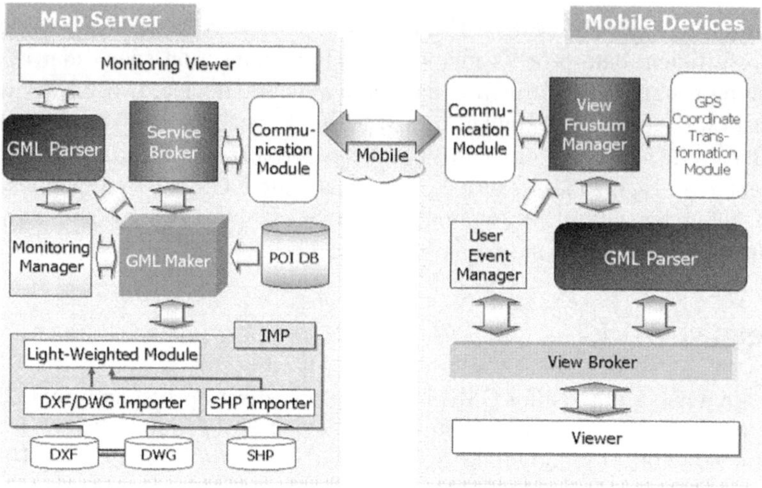

Fig. 1. Architecture of VisualGML

Map server carries on map data process which a mobile device requests mainly through Service Broker. Service Broker receives location coordinates and map area of a mobile device from Communication Module, orders GML generation, and requests monitoring visualization. GML Maker generates GML using IMP, which accepts various map formats and extracts core elements from them for map display, and POI DB which provides location information to the users. Monitoring Manger visualizes GML generated by GML Maker onto Monitoring Viewer. A map is initially visualized without location tracking information of a mobile device; however, tracking monitoring information is visualized when requested by the manager.

Mobile device requests map and mediates visualization are through View Frustum Manager. After mobile device receives location coordinates from GPS, GPS Coordinate Transformation Module converts the coordinates into TM coordinate system. Communication Module transfers location coordinates and map area that is to be requested. View Frustum Manger transfers received GML file through GML Parser. Parsing GML, GML Parser extracts map property, and sends visualization are through View Broker. View Broker mediates real-time map visualization under location coordinates change, and manages event process due to user-altered event such as expand, minimize, or move.

3.2 Integrated Map Preprocessor

Due to massive volume of geographic information data, performance improvement for visualizing the data onto mobile device is required. File formats such as DXF, DWG, and SHP that are currently used widely are visualized onto specific application. This paper constructs IMP that is a part of preprocessing containing expandability of a file format that provides fast access to mobile device and deals with its heterogeneity. IMP categorizes Importer modules by layer according map format, extracts their core elements, and reduces their weight and give them attributes.

DXF/DWG Importer extracts geographic information data property of six sections of DXF and DWG formats. BLOCKS and ENTITIES sections are used when extracting physical information and analyzing through ENTITY Parser. ENTITY Parser makes symbols or marks used in BLOCKS section into groups. Grouped information is used when indicating buildings, farmlands, roads, or rivers, and it is displayed as INSERT in ENTITIES section. INSERT information uses group code layers defined in BOLCKS sections, and save them into Temp Block Data distinguishing from ENTITIES section. INSERT property generates Final Object adding coordinates defined in BLOCKS section onto coordinated defined in ENTITIES section.

SHP brings shape information though File Importer and property information through DBF Importer. Shape information extracts Bounding Box which is maximum and minimum value of coordinates of main header from *.shp file, and defines area of a shape. Shape File Handler approaches to record contents in size of Content Length of record header and opens the contents. Record contents extract the contents according to types of the shapes at Shape Type Importer, and waits in order to match the contents with property information that is to be extracted from *.dbf files. DBF Importer reads *.dbf files and stores its property value into Shape Attribute Table. Shape Attribute Table matches its values with extracted shape information from Shape Type Importer and generates Final Object. Fig. 2 shows structure of DXF/DWG and SHP Importer module.

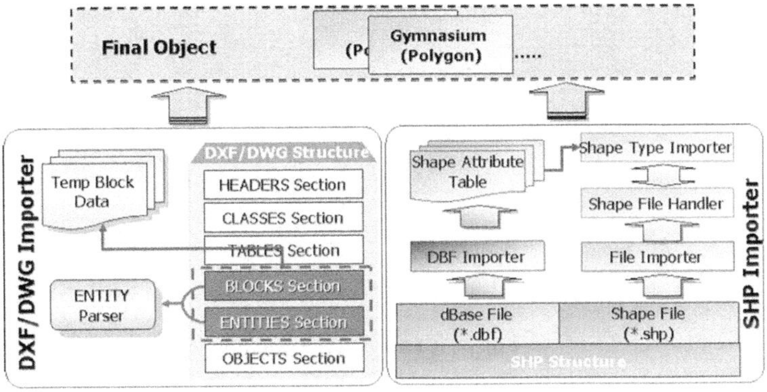

Fig. 2. DXF/DWF and SHP Importer

Light-Weighted Module categorizes Final Object generated by DXF/DWG and SHP Importer into specific layers, thus reducing its weight – it refers to national geographic standard code when categorizing. Extracted layer code is in 4000s (4000 ~ 4637) indicating buildings, 3000s (3000 ~ 3999) indicating roads, and 9000s (9110 ~ 9233) indicating texts. Fig. 3 shows a file extracted from DXF file of “3 Ga, Hanok Village, Pungnam dong, Wansan gu, Jeonju, Jeonbuk, 560-033 Korea” by IMP.

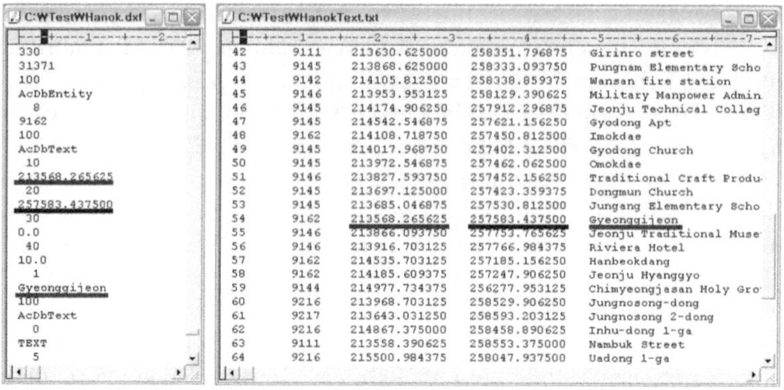

(a) Resource DXF file (b) IMP extract

Fig. 3. Comparison between DXF file and a file extracted by IMP

3.3 Hierarchical POI

VisualGML does not provide simple map visualization but provides POI service which contains location information of individual objects. POI service constructs 3-Layer POI for efficiency of fast search, add, delete, and update of location information. As shown in fig. 4, 3-Lay POI structure refers to DXF standard value map.

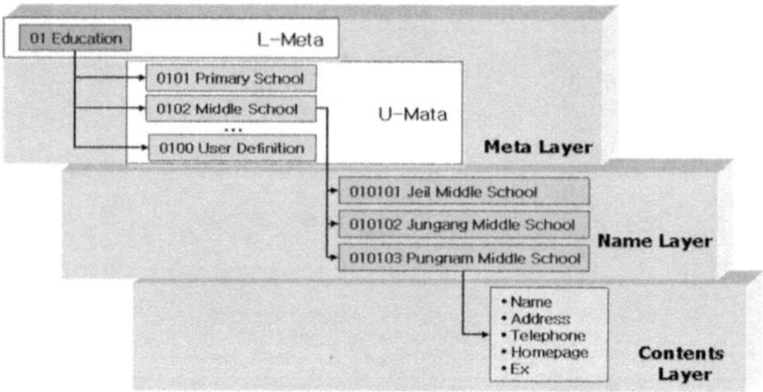

Fig. 4. 3-Layer POI Structure

For buildings with layer code '4' according to DXF standard code, Meta Layer defines user-centered meta code, and gives identical specific key value to the categories that fall into game group so that they can be distinguished from other. Meta code is divided into U-Meta and L-Meta code in order to specialize internally its POI information. U-Meta code is defined as upper group and it is divided into 11 types of codes. Each U-Meta code has L-Meta as a lower code according to its characteristic. Key value is assigned to its names according to Name Layer. Contents Layer is a layer that contains POI information such as name, address, phone number, specifics, or webpage that are to be shown to actual users. POI constructs POI DB defining 14 fields. Table 1 shows major fields of POI DB.

Table 1. POI DB Fields

Filed	Remark
Object ID	ID of geometry
Gu_cd/Dong_cd	Administrative district of geometry
Blg_nm	Name of geometry
X_coord/Y_coord	Location of geometry
Shape_area	Area of geometry
add1	Address of geometry
add2	Detail Address of geometry
Telephone	Telephone number of geometry
EX	Detail information of geometry
URL	Homepage of geometry
Key	Hierarchical code of geometry
O/X	POI presentation of geometry(enabled/disabled)

3.4 GML Maker

GML Maker reconstructs geometry property and property information extracted by IMP into GML file. Fig. 5 shows specific structure of GML Maker.

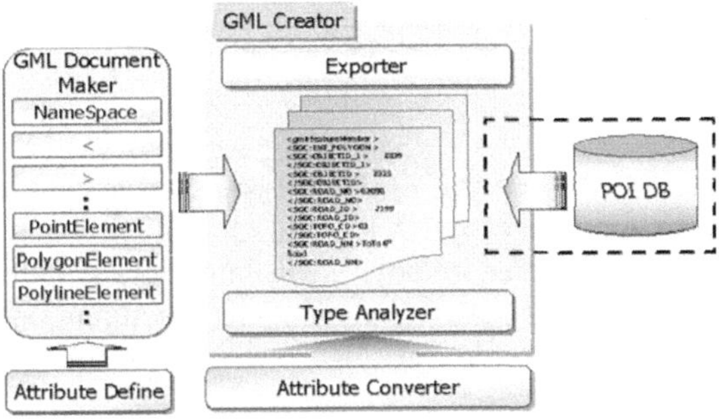

Fig. 5. GML Maker Structure

GML is displayed in different ways according to its map format. Attribute Converter changes data structure of heterogeneous geographic information in order to parse them into common GML format, and matches properties of Final Object and GeoMetricData. Referring to Attribute Define that had defined GML property tags, GML Document Maker provides methods that generate GML schemes and property elements. The generator method is composed of a generator method that deals with basic schemes such as defining NameSpace, generating property, starting tag, ending tag, CDATA configuration, and an element generator method that deals with polygonal properties of Geometry Types such as Polygon, Polyline, or Circle. GML Creator sorts Geometry Types by GeoMetricData, and calls out an element generator method and inserts it to basic scheme. When insertion is complete, GML Creator brings specific field information among information in POI DB. FeatureMember generates GML with Exporter. Fig. 6 shows GML file generated by adding POI information onto DXF file.

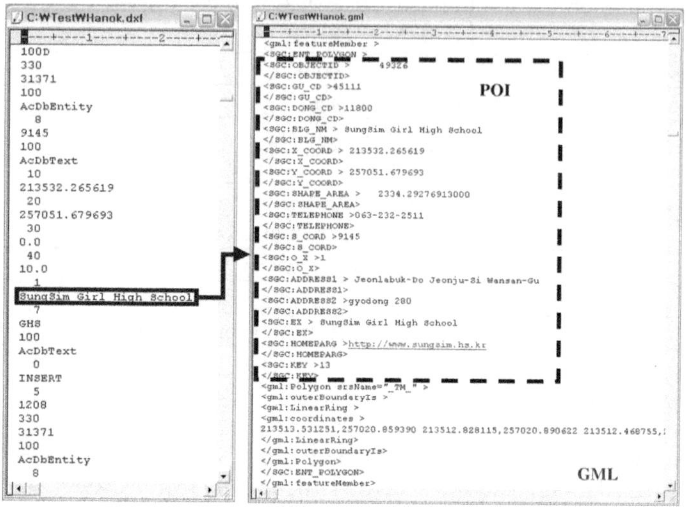

Fig. 6. GML file generated by adding POI information onto DXF file

3.5 GML Parser

GML Parser induced GML parsing through XML Parser, which enhances memory usage and CPU resource usage by SAX method. Among standard library modules provided by SAX, GML Parser inherits XMLParser class and defines GMLParser class. GMLParser class defines individual elements based on GML Schema, and calls out a handler that is defined as event-type form in order to process the individual elements.

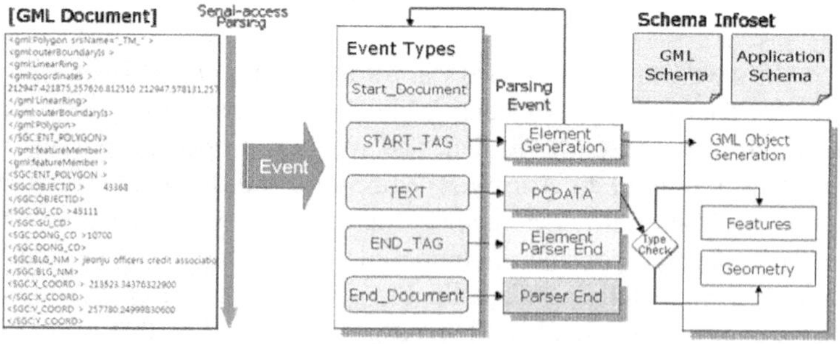

Fig. 7. GML Parsing Process

GMLParser class processes a tag with key and value of an element. The key is name of the tag, and the value is the name of function that will carry on starting and ending tag and is composed of tuple. For example, if the tag is *<vgml id="2" type="simple">*, GMLParser class calls out *vgml_start_tag[{'id':'2', 'type'='simple'}]*. Function is called out in following method: in case of starting tag, handle_starttag function is called out, and in case of ending tag, handle_endtag function is redefined and altered. Fig. 7 shows GML Parsing process.

4 Visualization of VisualGML

Visualization area of VisualGML is "3 Ga, Hanok Village, Pungnam dong, Wansan gu, Jeonju, Jeonbuk, 560-033 Korea". Fig. 8 shows running window that displays map visualization with POI and tracking monitoring of mobile device. The window is composed of a main window that visualizes the map, a hierarchical POI search window, user event window that enables expand, minimize and move. POI visualization emphasizes buildings and its names that were searched under *Education-High School* in hierarchical POI search tree. Also selected 'sungsim girls' high school' is displayed as a pop-up with size of 280*100. Tracking monitoring displays coordinates of mobile devises that are connected to a current server on 800*700 size map. Moving information of three mobile devices were traced and monitored with different colors: red indicates Mobile_Device_1 moved from 'jungang elementary school' to 'cheongsoo pharmacy', green indicates Mobile_Device_2 moved from 'cheonju tradition museum' to 'sungmoon church', and blue indicates Mobile_ Device_3 moved from 'deungyongmoon computer academy' to 'myongji oriental medicine clinic'.

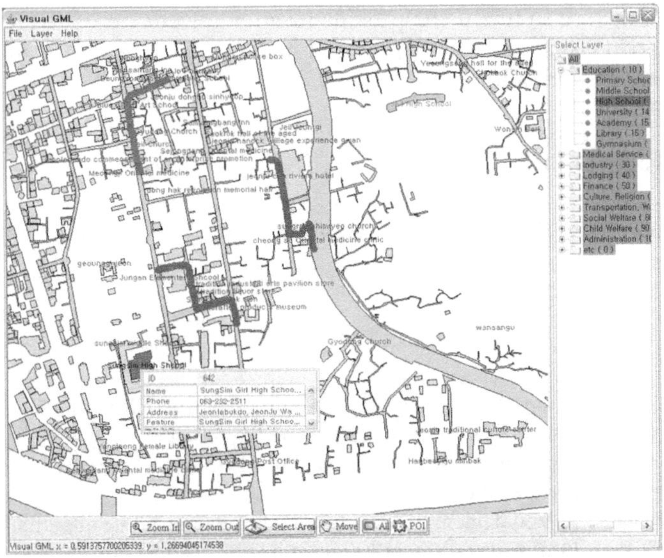

Fig. 8. VisualGML Visualization with POI and Trace Monitoring

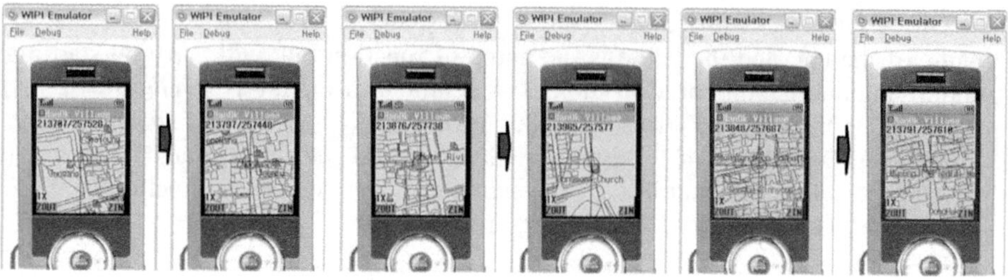

Fig. 9. Movement Visualization of Mobile Devices

Fig. 9 shows that mobile devices with IDs of "1," "2," and "3" are connected to a map server and visualizes GML, having moved certain distance.

5 Conclusions

This paper constructed VisualGML that generates and visualizes map information based on GML which is a standard format of OGC onto a mobile device. Within the process of converting maps such as DXF, DWG, SHP into GML, VisualGML embodied IMP for light-weighted map information data and developed GML Maker and GML Parser for standard map visualization. In order to provide GML-based map with user-centered location information, VisualGML visualized hierarchical POI as well. Specifically, for higher efficiency of data process capacity and data storage volume IMP extracted out unnecessary parts while preserving file's characteristic through DXF/DWG and SHP Importer. Hierarchical POI established POI DB based on 3-Layer POI structure so that it can provide location information as well as hierarchical search method. VisualGML lastly provided monitoring visualization that can gain and save movement information of mobile devices.

Acknowledgement

This work was supported by Ministry of Information & Communication in republic of Korea.

References

1. OpenGIS Consortium, Inc., Geography Markup Language(GML) Implementation Specification, http://www.opengeospatial.org/docs/02-023r4.pdf
2. OpenGIS Consortium, Inc., "OpenGIS Location Service Core Services", http://www.openeospatial.org
3. K. Virrantaus, J. Veijalainen, J. Markkula, "Developing GIS-Supported Location-Based Service", Web Information System Engineering, Proceedings of the Second International Conference on, Vol. 2, 3-6, Dec. 2001.

4. Shashi Shekhar, Ranga Raju Vatsavai, Namita Sahay, Thomas E. Burk, Stephen Lime, "GML, Interoperability, and Standards: WMS and GML based interoperable web mapping system", Proceedings of the 9th ACM international symposium on Advances in geographic information systems, Nov. 2001..
5. Autodesk Drawing eXchange Format, http://www.autodesk.com/techpubs/autocad/acadr14/dxf
6. ESRI, ESRI Shapefile Technical Description. ESRI, INC, http://www.esri.com, 1998.
7. TatukGIS Inc. TatukGIS Viewer 1.4, http://www.tatukgis.com/products/Viewer/viewer.aspx
8. Safe Software Inc. FME Universal Viewer 2003, http://www.safe.com/products/fme
9. Snowflake Software Ltd. OS Master Map Viewer 2.0, http://www.snowflakesoftware.co.uk
10. eSpatial Inc. iSMART Explorer4.4, http:/www.espatial.com

Speaker Recognition Using Temporal Decomposition of LSF for Mobile Environment

Sung-Joo Kim, Min-Seok Kim, and Ha-Jin Yu

School of Computer Science, University of Seoul,
Dongdaemungu Seoul, 130-743, Korea
{sung|mskim|hjyu}@venus.uos.ac.kr

Abstract. A novel approach to speaker recognition in mobile or IP network environment is described. In this approach, we use decoded line spectral frequency (LSF) parameters directly from compressed speech packets instead of using parameters from decompression and analysis procedure. Furthermore, we reduce the number of LSF series based on a restricted temporal decomposition method. Consequently, proposed approach gets more than three times faster than a traditional speaker recognition approach without losing any accuracy according to our experiments.

1 Introduction

Recent communication apparatuses are fast adopting mobile or IP networks, because there are growing needs of mobile and economical communication. Thanks to the wireless mobile network, people can access each others wherever they are, and digital packets transferring speech signal make it possible to share a physical link with others more than ever. Enhanced communication environment detonates new demands for speech applications like speaker recognition in this environment.

Current mobile or IP networks have several characteristics to apply a traditional speech processing approach. Firstly, speech signals are digitally compressed with a coder, mostly code excited linear prediction (CELP) coder [1] for the channel efficiency. Therefore, a traditional speech processing application needs to decompress those packets first to extract required feature vectors. Secondly, the channel error can cause some packet losses. It means feature vectors from decompressed speech signal might have serious distortion comparing with those from original input speech. Thirdly, the compressed packet itself has the parameters for the speech production model, especially LPC or LSF parameters, so the process which decompress it and analyze the decompressed signal to get spectral parameters may be inefficient and redundant.

When porting a speech application on a mobile phone, you may suffer from lack of CPU power and memory, since it is directly connected with the system cost. This is the main obstacle to implementing a speech application on mobile embedded system. In this point of view, the fixed frame rate analysis to extract necessary speech features makes too much overhead. So we need to reduce the feature rate in some way for the mobile embedded system environment.

Y.-H. Lee et al. (Eds.): ICESS 2007, LNCS 4523, pp. 338–346, 2007.

In this research, we try to find and test an efficient feature set for speech processing in mobile or IP network environment. Especially, we focus on the computational efficiency for the future implementation of real world application. We choose the speaker recognition (identification) task as a typical speech processing application in this paper, since it is relatively small task and easy to implement and test, but we hope our result can be applied to other speech processing applications like speech recognition later on.

Here we say the speaker recognition is a technique to determine to whom an input speech signal belongs. More specifically, it is to identify the unknown speaker as one of the previously trained speakers. For this task, using mel-frequency cepstral coefficient (MFCC) [2] feature set and speaker modeling with Gaussian mixture models (GMM) [3] is the most prevalent approach. Besides, several approaches were proposed to overcome the difficulties of implementing speaker recognition task in the mobile or IP network environment. Saastamoinen and et. al. studied on implementation issues during porting a speaker recognition system into a specific mobile phone model [4]. Aggarwal and et. al. proposed compressed speaker recognition (CSR), which uses a feature set directly extracted from compressed speech packet and a micro-clustering technique as a classifier [5]. Although it was for the speech recognition, Alencar and et. al. presented comparison results of several features which are transformed from LPC and LSF parameters of compressed speech packet [6].

In this research, we use LSF parameters decoded from compressed speech packet as a feature set for the speaker recognition task. We exclude the transformation of this parameter into a more discriminative one from this research. However, we do temporal decomposition of LSF series to get concise vector series. According to a previous research, restricted temporal decomposition (RTD) can represent LSF vector series with less number of event vectors and their corresponding event functions almost transparently [4].

The rest of the paper is organized as follows. In the next session, we introduce the RTD of LSF parameters briefly. This is followed by the description of speaker recognition system using RTD. Section 4 then presents the experiment setup we used to show the advantages of the proposed approach and the results. Finally, Section 5 gives the summary and conclusions.

2 Restricted Temporal Decomposition of LSF Parameters

In the area of speech coding, many researchers have studied the efficient quantization of LSF parameters because they have several merits such as local sensitivity, ease of stability checking, and simple synthesis filter [1]. It is the reason why all the CELP coders use LSF parameters as synthesis filter coefficients of speech production model. Besides, the temporal decomposition proposed by B. S. Atal [8] is an efficient method of speech coding which decomposes the given vector trajectory into a set of temporally overlapping event functions and corresponding event vectors. However, the original temporal decomposition method cannot be applied to LSF parameters because of their ordering property.

The original temporal decomposition assumes that each event is a superposed component of a given vector trajectory, so the distribution of the estimated event vectors is different from that of the given vector trajectory. In the case of cepstrum or MFCC parameters, this creates no problem, because each order of those parameters is independent and has no boundary value. However, LSF parameters are dependent to adjacent orders and have the ordering property. Therefore, decomposing LSF into superposed event vectors causes the event vectors not to obtain their respective spectra since they can be unstable, i.e., the event vectors are no longer LSF parameters.

To solve this problem, Kim and et. al. proposed another restriction on event functions so that the sum of all event functions at any time t is always one. As a result, event vectors estimated by RTD method preserve the ordering property of LSF parameters so that they can be quantized efficiently.

Let a given vector trajectory and its corresponding sets of event vectors and functions be $\boldsymbol{X} = [\boldsymbol{x}_1, \boldsymbol{x}_2, ..., \boldsymbol{x}_T]$, $\boldsymbol{A} = [\boldsymbol{a}_1, \boldsymbol{a}_2, ..., \boldsymbol{a}_J]$, and $\boldsymbol{\Phi} = [\boldsymbol{\phi}_1, \boldsymbol{\phi}_2, ..., \boldsymbol{\phi}_J]^T$ respectively, where $\boldsymbol{x}_t = [x_{t,1}, x_{t,2}, ..., x_{t,p}]^T$ is the p-th order LSF vector sampled at time t, $\boldsymbol{a}_j = [a_{j,1}, a_{j,2}, ..., a_{j,p}]^T$ the j-th event vector, and $\boldsymbol{\phi}_j = [\phi_{j,1}, \phi_{j,2}, ..., \phi_{j,T}]^T$ the j-th event function. The temporal decomposition estimates proper event vectors and functions which minimize

$$E = \|\boldsymbol{X} - \boldsymbol{A\Phi}\|^2 = \sum_{t=1}^{T} \|\boldsymbol{x}_t - \boldsymbol{x}'_t\|^2 , \tag{1}$$

where

$$\boldsymbol{x}'_t = \sum_{j=1}^{J} \boldsymbol{a}_j \phi_{j,t} \tag{2}$$

$\phi_{j,t}$ is restricted to the range of [0,1] and to being the maximum value one at its corresponding center $C(j)$. We refer the reader to [7] for details on RTD of LSF algorithm. Here we just describe the brief RTD algorithm as follows.

Step 1. Initialization: Locate the first event at the starting position

Step 2. Segment boundary decision: Find the next local minimum point of spectral transition measure [11], which will be the end of the current segment. Locate an event there.

Step 3. Event function estimation: Estimate the initial event functions $\boldsymbol{\phi}_j$ corresponding to the current set of event vectors. Notice that no iteration is needed to estimate event functions for this step.

Step 4. Event Insertion: If the interpolation error exceeds a given threshold at a certain location, insert an event, set the LSF vector at there to the event vector, then go back to step 3.

Step 5. Event vector re-estimation: Re-estimate the event vectors $\boldsymbol{a}_j$ corresponding to estimated event functions

Step 6. Event function re-estimation: Re-estimate the event functions $\boldsymbol{\phi}_j$ corresponding to estimated event vectors. If the results have been converged or re-estimated a certain number of times, go to step 7. If not, go back to step 5.

Step 7. Going to next segment: Store the events for the current segment. To analyze the next segment, keep last two events as beginning part of the segment. Go back to step 2.

RTD algorithm which was proposed by Kim and et. al. has distinctive features over other temporal decomposition algorithm, since it was designed for a speech coder implementation. First, the way of locating events is simple and definite, so that the procedure converges very fast. Second, the processing buffer is relatively short since it uses spectral transition measure to locate an event. Also user can set the maximum buffer size to prevent too long algorithmic latency. Third, including event insertion mechanism with a threshold argument, the event rate can be controlled with respect to user's need.

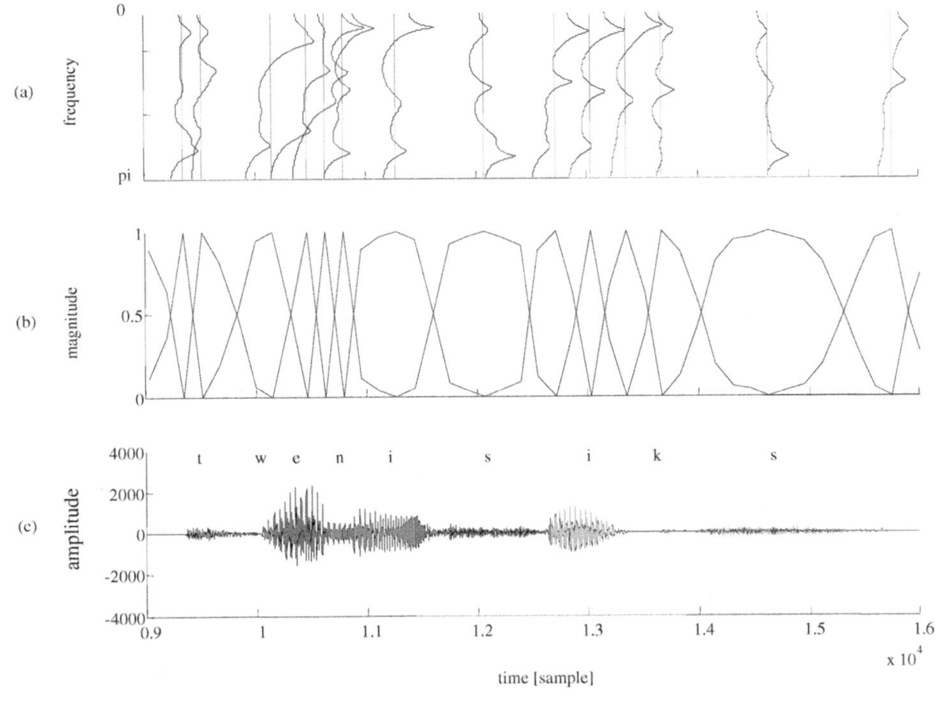

Fig. 1. Example of RTD

Experimental results showed that RTD could interpolate the original vector trajectory of LSF parameters very well and with the event insertion threshold 0.6, the interpolation results was transparent to the original ones [7]. So we set the event insertion threshold to 0.6 from now on in this paper. Figure 1 shows an example of RTD results; (a) is the log spectrums of event vectors, and (b) is the corresponding event function, and (c) is the input speech signal, which is pronouncing '26' in English .

3 Speaker Recognition Using RTD of LSF

We are focusing on the speaker recognition task in mobile or IP network environment and assuming that the speech signal is compressed and packetized before sending.

This unique situation affects the feature extraction module of the speaker recognition, but not recognizer or classifier itself. Therefore, we choose a GMM based speaker recognition as the archetype, which is the most prevalent approach to build a speaker recognition system. GMM is the most prominent approach for modeling in text-independent speaker recognition applications. In GMM, each speaker's acoustic parameter distribution is represented by a speaker dependent mixture of Gaussian distributions,

$$p(\boldsymbol{x} \mid \lambda) = \sum_{i=1}^{M} w_i g_i(\boldsymbol{x}), \qquad \sum_{i=1}^{M} w_i = 1 \tag{3}$$

where M is the number of mixtures, w_i mixture weights and Gaussian densities g_i are,

$$g_i(\boldsymbol{x}) = \frac{1}{(2\pi)^{D/2} \, |\Sigma_i|^{1/2}} \exp\left\{ -\frac{1}{2} (\boldsymbol{x} - \boldsymbol{\mu}_i)^T \boldsymbol{\Sigma}_i^{-1} (\boldsymbol{x} - \boldsymbol{\mu}_i) \right\}. \tag{4}$$

Maximum likelihood parameters are estimated using the EM algorithm. For speaker identification, the log-likelihood of a model given an utterance $\boldsymbol{X} = [\boldsymbol{x}_1, \boldsymbol{x}_2, ..., \boldsymbol{x}_T]$ is computed and the speaker associated with the most likely model for the input utterance is chosen as the recognized speaker $\hat{S}$.

$$\hat{S} = \arg \max_{1 \le k \le S} \sum_{t=1}^{T} \log p(\boldsymbol{x}_t \mid \lambda_k) \tag{5}$$

In mobile or IP networks, speech signal is compressed before transmission mostly with a CELP coder [1], and a CELP coder uses LSF parameters as its synthesis filter coefficients, so we can decode LSF parameters right from the compressed speech packets. Generally a CELP coder uses 20 ms frame buffer for analyzing speech signal, so we can get LSF parameters at the rate of 50 Hz.

Besides the filter parameters, energy of each frame is also an important feature for speaker recognition, but CELP coded packet does not contain the output speech energy value. It only gives us the gains of excitation signals; exactly speaking, gains for an adaptive codeword and a random codeword. Since the output of CELP coder is generated by filtering the sum of those excitation signals, the gains of excitation signals can be a reasonable substitute of energy parameter for speaker recognition.

When we get LSF parameters and an energy substitute from each compressed speech packet, it is possible to run speaker recognition in a traditional way. However, speaker recognition using GMM is very computationally intensive task, so it is burden to implement a real world application. Therefore, we put RTD process in between feature extraction and recognition steps as figure 2.

RTD does not distort the original LSF vector trajectory much, but decompose the whole trajectory into relatively small number of events, which correspond to phonetically meaningful segments. In the previous research, RTD produces events at about the rate of 18 Hz. This means the length of feature vector series can be reduced to almost one third of the origin by using RTD process.

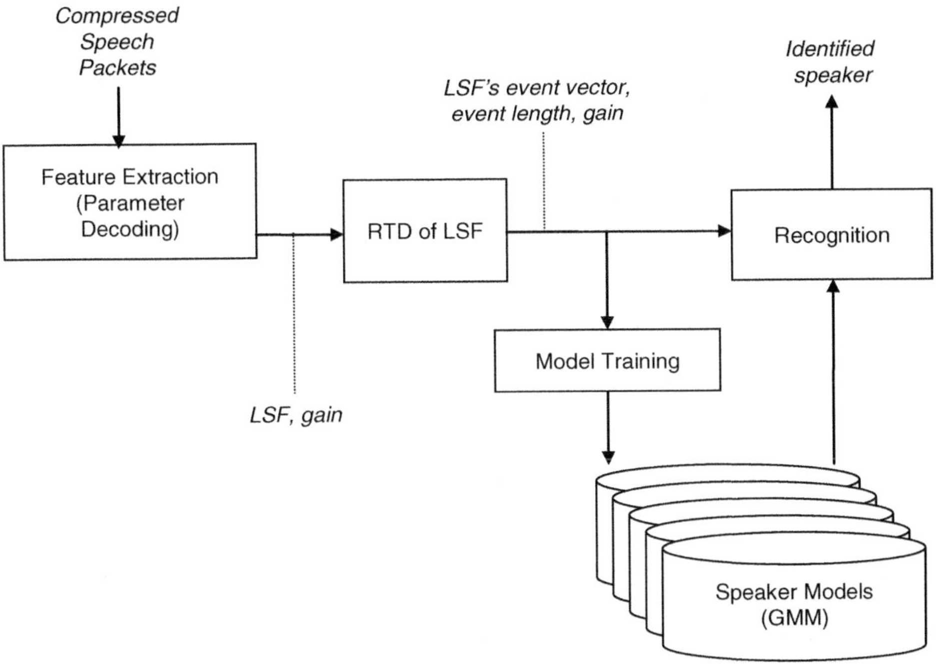

Fig. 2. Proposed System Block Diagram

During adopting RTD in speaker recognition, we should notice that an event has its target vector and weighting function. In RTD, the event vector has the same properties of original vector, so it can substitute for the LSF vector directly. However, we do not know how to handle the information in the event functions properly. In case of speech coding, to re-generate the original vector trajectory at the decoder side, we should send the information in event functions precisely. So we quantize and send each event function by its length and length normalized shape. Nonetheless, in speaker recognition, we do not need to re-generate the original vector trajectory. The point is whether the information in event function is helpful to discriminate speakers or not. After all, we just takes the length of event functions as another dimension of feature vector and feed it to the speaker recognition system in this research.

In summary, proposed speaker recognition system uses 12 dimensional feature vectors which consist of 10 dimensional event vectors, coming from RTD of 10th order LSF parameters, and the lengths of events, and the energies at every event positions.

4 Experiments Setup and Results

We used the YOHO corpus to development, training and testing of our speaker recognition system [9]. This corpus was originally collected for speaker verification systems, but there is no problem to be used for speaker recognition. Actually, this corpus is suitable to check recognition performance over time, since speakers were asked to participate for relatively long period of time in 14 sessions over a 3-month time interval. The particular vocabulary employed in this collection consists of two-digit numbers ("thirty-four," "sixty-one", etc), spoken continuously in sets of three (e.g. "36-45-89"). There are 138 speakers (108 male, 30 female); for each speaker, there are 4 enrollment sessions of 24 utterances each, and 10 verification sessions of four utterances each, for a total of 136 utterances in 14 sessions per speaker [9]. We used total 96 utterances in 4 enrollment sessions of each speaker as the training data and 40 utterances in 10 verification sessions as the test data. Therefore, speaker recognition identified to whom each of total 5,520 utterances belongs during the test stage.

To simulate the speech coder effect in mobile or IP network circumstance, we chose the IS-96a QCELP coder and encoded all the training and test utterances into digital packets at the bit rate of 8 kbps. At this bit rate, ten LSF parameters of each frame are quantized with 4 bits per each and four pitch gains and eight codebook gains are quantized with 3 bits per each. In real situation, the compressed packets are the only inputs for speaker recognition, so LSF parameters and gains mentioned through the experiments below were decoded from the compressed packets by default. For more details about QCELP coder, we refer the reader to IS-96a, wideband spread spectrum standard [10].

At first, the ordinary LSF parameter input was tested as a baseline system. We took every LSF parameters at the rate of 50 Hz from compressed packet and sum of gains as the substitute of energy while varying the number of mixtures from 16 to 128. The recognition accuracy rate of the baseline system with 128 mixtures per each speaker model was 96.79 %. Next, proposed system which uses RTD of LSF parameters was tested. In this case, the input feature vector's dimension was increased by one, since the length of events was added. Although the proposed system used a concise version of feature vector, it gave slightly better accuracy, 97.25% with 128 mixtures. It shows that the RTD is very effective method to remove redundant information from LSF vector trajectory. Finally, to show the clear evidence of RTD effects, we also tested the performance of the baseline system with feature parameters of only every third packets. Consequently, the feature vector rate was almost same to the proposed system, says 16.67 Hz, but the accuracy was dropped to 94.91%. The whole results of speaker recognition tests are shown in Table 1.

Table 1. Experiment Results: Speaker Recognition Accuracies

Num. of Mixtures	Conventional system	Conventional with frame culling	Proposed System
16	91.07 %	87.68 %	90.74 %
32	94.29 %	91.78 %	94.49 %
64	95.96 %	94.02 %	96.45 %
128	96.79 %	94.91 %	97.25 %

Table 2. Comparison of Computational Complexities

	Conventional system	Conventional with frame culling	Proposed System
Parameter Dim.	11	11	12
Data Rate (Hz)	50.00	16.67	16.74
Complexity Factor	550	183	201
Complexity Ratio	100.0%	33.3%	36.5%

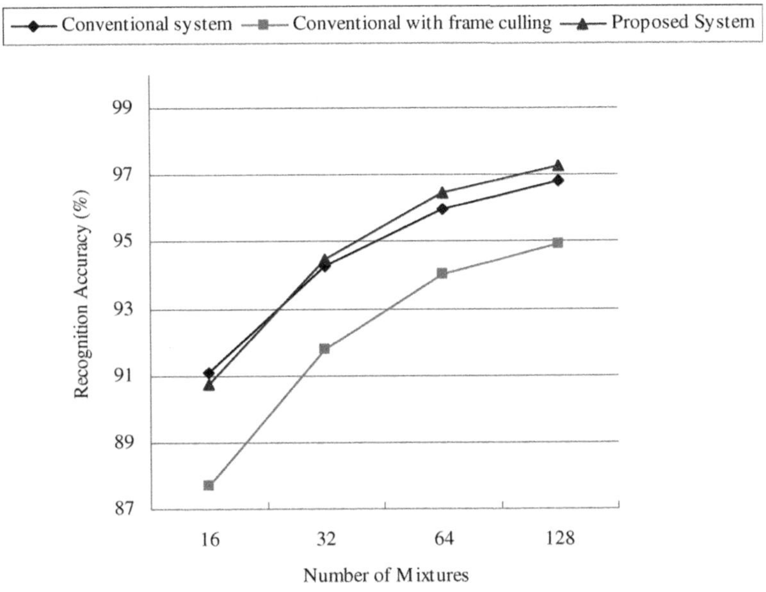

Fig. 3. Tendency of Speaker Recognition Accuracy

Speaker recognition based on GMM requires lots of computations, which are mainly for calculating Gaussian density values. This computational load is very proportional to the number of speakers to identify, the number of mixtures in GMM per speaker, the dimensions of a feature vector, and lastly the number of feature vectors in a test utterance. Therefore, the computational complexity factor can be estimated by the product of these values. We also calculated this complexity factor in Table 2. As you can see in the table, the proposed system requires only 37% of computations of the baseline system. For about the computations for RTD process, since the process runs just once for each utterance and can be implemented as streaming process, it is negligible. In our typical simulation at a PC with Pentium4 3 GHz processor, the proposed system took only 0.19 second to identify each test utterance in average, while the baseline system took 0.59 second. In other words, the proposed system was more than three times faster than the baseline system.

5 Conclusions

This paper has presented a novel approach to speaker recognition in mobile or IP network environment. The proposed approach uses decoded LSF parameters directly from compressed speech packets, so it eliminates decompression and analysis procedures during feature parameters extraction. It is computationally efficient and could be more robust if considering the packet losses. Moreover, we introduced the RTD of LSF process to reduce the number of LSF series without loss of necessary information. Empirically RTD process generated events at around 16 Hz for LSF vector series of YOHO corpus. Experimental results have shown that the proposed approach was over three times faster than a conventional speaker recognition approach, and gave 97.25% identification accuracy, while the conventional one gave 96.79%. We did not analyze whether the performance improvement was confident or not and why the performance was improved using RTD of LSF in this paper, but we guess that the event vector re-estimation might give such an improvement.

References

1. Kondoz, AM.: Digital Speech, Coding for Low Bit Rate Communication Systemss, John Wiley & Sons, (1994)
2. Huang, X., Acero, A., Hon, H.: Spoken Language Processing, A Guide to Theory, Algorithm, and System Development, Prentice Hall, (2001)
3. Reynolds, D.A., Rose, R.C.: Robust Text-Independent Speaker Identification Using Gaussian Mixture Speaker Models, IEEE Transactions on Speech Audio Processing, vol. 3, no. 1, (1995) 72-83
4. Saastamoinen, J., Karpov, E.,Hautamaki, V., Franti, P.: Accuracy of MFCC-Based Speaker Recognition in Series 60 Device, EURASIP Journal on Applied Signal Processing 2005:17, 2816-2827
5. Aggarwal, C., Olshefski, D., Saha, D., Shae, Z.-Y., Yu, P.: CSR: Speaker Recognition from Compressed VoIP Packet Stream, IEEE Int. Conf. on Multimedia & Expo, Amsterdam, The Netherlands, July 2005, 970-973
6. Alencar, VFS., Alcaim, A.: Transformations of LPC and LSF Parameters to Speech Recognition Features, ICAPR 2005, LNCS 3686, 522-528
7. Kim, SJ., Oh, YH.: Efficient quantization method for LSF parameters based on restricted temporal decomposition, Electronics Letters, 10th June 1999, Vol. 35, No. 12, 962-963
8. Atal, B.: Efficient Coding of LPC parameters by temporal decomposition, Proc. ICASSP'83, Boston, MA, (1983) 81-84
9. Campbell, J. Jr.: Testing with the YOHO CD-ROM Voice Verification Corpus, ICASP'95, (1995) 341-345
10. TIA/EIA/IS-96 Speech Service Option Standard for Wideband Spread Spectrum Cellular System
11. Furui, S.: On the Role of Spectral Transition for Speech Perception, Journal of Acoustic Society of America 80(4), (1986) 1016-1025

Voice/Non-Voice Classification Using Reliable Fundamental Frequency Estimator for Voice Activated Powered Wheelchair Control

Soo-Young Suk[1], Hyun-Yeol Chung[2], and Hiroaki Kojima[1]

[1] Information Technology Research Institute, National Institute of Advanced Industrial Science and Technology, AIST Tsukuba Central 2, 1-1-1 Umezono, Tsukuba, Ibaraki, 305-8568, Japan

[2] School of Electrical Engineering and Computer Science, Yeungnam University 214-1, Daedong, Gyungsan, Gyungbuk, 712-749, Korea

{sy.suk,h.kojima}@aist.go.jp, hychung@yu.ac.kr

Abstract. In this paper, we introduce a non-voice rejection method to perform Voice/Non-Voice (V/NV) classification using a fundamental frequency (F0) estimator called YIN. Although current speech recognition technology has achieved high performance, it is insufficient for some applications where high reliability is required, such as voice control of powered wheelchairs for disabled persons. The V/NV classification algorithm, which rejects non-voice input in Voice Activity Detection (VAD), is helpful for realizing a highly reliable system. The proposed V/NV classification adopts the ratio of a reliable F_0 contour to the whole input interval. To evaluate the performance of our proposed method, we used 1567 voice commands and 447 noises in powered wheelchair control in a real environment. These results indicate that the recall rate is 97% when the lowest threshold is selected for noise classification with 99% precision in VAD.

Keywords: Voice non-voice classification, Voice activity detection, YIN, Fundamental frequency estimator, Powered wheelchair.

1 Introduction

Powered wheelchairs provide unique mobility for the disabled and elderly with motor impairments. However, people suffering from severe motor impairments, such as paraplegia and tremors, find it difficult or impossible to control standard powered wheelchairs. Sometimes, the joystick is a useless manipulation tool because the severely disabled cannot operate it smoothly. Using natural voice commands, like "move forward" or "move left" relieves the user from precise motion control of the wheelchair.

The aim of our project is to enable severely disabled persons to move independently; therefore, we develop powered wheelchairs that can be operated by inarticulate speech affected by severe cerebral palsy or quadriplegia, for instance. Although current speech recognition technology has reported high performance,

Y.-H. Lee et al. (Eds.): ICESS 2007, LNCS 4523, pp. 347–357, 2007.

it is not sufficient for safe voice activated powered wheelchair movement. To cope with the pronunciation variation of inarticulate speech, we adopted a lexicon building approach based on intermediate speech coding [1] and data mining [2], in addition to acoustic-modeling-based speaker adaptation [3]. We also developed noise-canceling methods, which reduce mechanical noise and environmental sounds for practical use on the street [4]. However, though our voice command system has improved recognition performance by various methods, the system requires a guarantee of safety for wheelchair users in two additional conditions.

- To move only in response to the disabled person's own voice.
- Do not move to reject non-voice command input.

The first problem is to prevent operation of the powered wheelchair by unauthorized persons near the wheelchair user. A speaker verification method can be applied to solve this problem, but it is difficult to verify when using each short word commands. Therefore, we are now developing a speaker position detection system using a microphone array [5][6]. The second problem is that various non-voice command are inputted when the voice command system is being used in real environment. So, a high-reliability voice application for powered wheelchair is thus necessary to reject noise and non-voice commands such as coughing, and breathing. A general rejection method has achieved a confidence measure using a likelihood ratio in a postprocessing step. However, this confidence measure is hard to use as a non-command rejection method because of the inaccuracy of likelihood when speech recognition deals with unclear voice and non-voice sounds. Thus, the Voice/Non-Voice (V/NV) classification algorithm, which rejects non-voice input in the Voice Activity Detection (VAD) step, can be helpful for realizing a highly reliable system.

Previous V/NV classification algorithms have generally adopted statistical analysis of F_0, the Zero Crossing Rate (ZCR), and the energy of short-time segments. A method for voicing decision within a pitch detection algorithm is presented in [7]. A combination of these methods, a cepstrum-based F_0 extractor, has been proposed [8]. An auditory-based method for voicing decision within a pitch tracking algorithm appears in [9]. In this paper, we propose a V/NV classification using an F_0 estimator called YIN for non-voice rejection. Here, the proposed classification method adopts the ratio of a reliable F_0 contour over the whole input interval.

The paper first presents the voice activated wheelchair system and the disabled person's database in the following section. Next, the F_0 estimator and the proposed V/NV classification algorithm are described in Section 3. In Section 4, we evaluate the performance of YIN and cepstrum-based V/NV classification. Lastly, we offer our conclusions in Section 5.

2 System and Database

Our systems aim to assist physically disabled persons to steer and control powered wheelchairs. Fig. 1 displays a schematic diagram and prototype developed system of the voice activated powered wheelchair control. The proposed system consists of 8 microphones(dual 4 channel), 8 channel analog/digital board, Pentium M 1.2GHz tablet PC, Pentium M 2.0GHz PC and wheelchair controller.

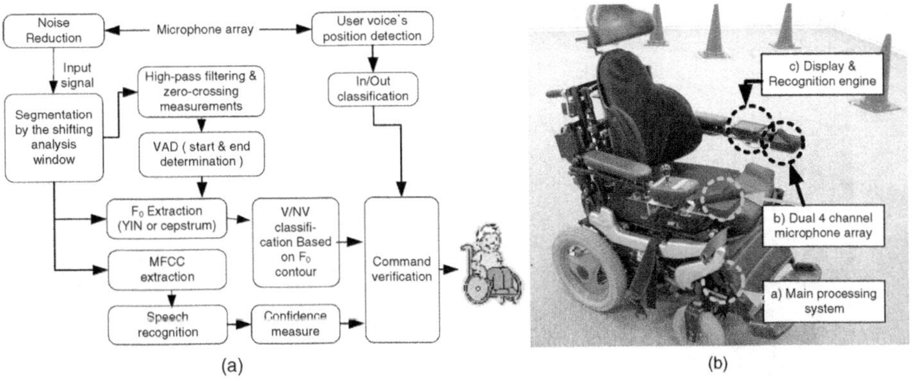

Fig. 1. Voice activated powered wheelchair overview. a) System block diagram. b) Developed powered wheelchair prototype.

First, the microphone array would capture the speech signal. Then, the incoming audio stream would be processed to classify the user's voice or not using the position detection module. Also, stream is sent by input for speech recognition and V/NV classification through noise decrease module. Our recognition engine are employed an Julian decoder [10] with Mel Frequency Cepstral Coefficient (MFCC) feature and adapted speaker dependent acoustic model. Specially, engine are used multiple dictionary for inarticulate speech. Table 1 shows example of multiple dictionary. Finally the recognition result is executed by the powered wheelchair when other result are satisfied with inner voice and voice using in/out classification module and V/NV classification module, respectively.

Table 1. Implemented set and multiple dictionary for inarticulate speech recognition

	command	dictionary
Move Left	hidari hidari hidari	h i d a: r i: d a r i q h i h i i d a: r i ,··· other 25
Move Right	migi	m i g i i ,··· other 15
Move Forward	mae	m a: a e ,··· other 13
Move Backward	koutai	k o u t a i ,··· other 3
Stop	ah	a: ,··· other 5
total		68

Since speech recognition systems are known to demonstrate different results for speech sounds in real usage from speech sounds that have been read, it is important for their evaluation to be based on natural spontaneous speech. To obtain a sample of spontaneous speech affected by disability, which contains specific personal variations, we developed a voice operated toy robot and a graphical simulation demo system that uses the same recognition task such as in powered wheelchair operation.

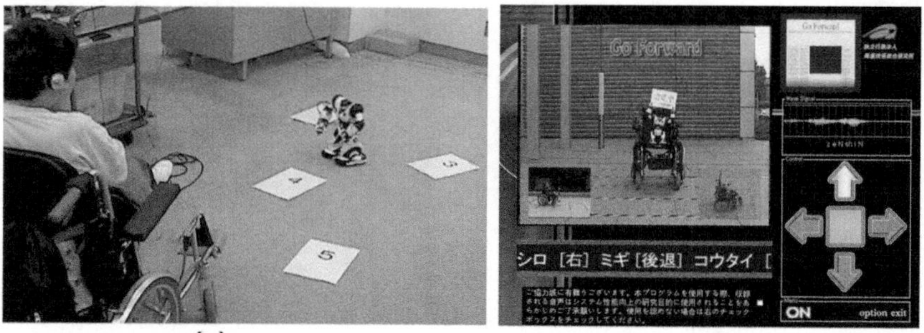

(a) (b)

Fig. 2. Speech recording environment. (a) Voice operated toy robot system. (b) Graphical simulation demo system.

For analysis of the input devices, each input device achieved speech detection through each recognition engine at the same time. Currently, we have collected more than 3000 unclear samples of speech affected by disability, using four types of microphones (Table 2). Bluetooth transmission capacity is limited by an 8 KHz sampling rate.

Table 2. Microphones and their sampling rates

Type	Model	Sampling rate
Headset	Audio-technica: AT810X	16 KHz
Bone conduction	Sony: ECM-TL1	16 KHz
Pin	PAVEC: MC-105	16 KHz
Bluetooth	Sonorix: OBH-0100	8 KHz

Table 3 lists the recorded speech data used for the experimental evaluation. For the headset type, 579 inputs are collected. There are also 426 voice commands, 65 various noises, 76 other utterances that are not commands, and utterances of 12 other people. Therefore, V/NV classification is needed to satisfy voice activated powered wheelchair control requirements while maintaining high speech recognition accuracy.

Table 3. Analysis of the number of recorded data

Type	Voice command	Noise	Other own voice	Other people
Headset	426	65	76	12
Bone conduction	405	339	88	286
Pin	399	21	90	361
Bluetooth	337	22	64	62
Total	1567	447	318	721

3 Voice Activity Detection Using V/NV Classification

The general VAD uses short time energy and/or ZCR for start and end point detection in a real-time voice command system with low complexity. However, VAD has a problem because various sounds are determined as voice sounds. For the purpose of non-voice rejection, we propose a V/NV classification using a reliable F_0 estimator.

3.1 YIN: Fundamental Frequency Estimator

V/NV classification using F_0 information has been strongly tied to the problem of a pitch detection algorithm (PDA). A PDA can be formulated as an average magnitude difference function, average squared difference function, or similar autocorrelation methods in the time domain. In addition, cepstrum analysis is possible in the frequency domain by applying the harmonic product spectrum algorithm. Among these F_0 extraction methods, we use the well known autocorrelation method based on YIN that has a number of modifications to reduce estimation errors [11]. This method has the merit of not requiring fine tuning and uses fewer parameters. The name YIN (from "Yin" and "Yang" of oriental philosophy) alludes to the interplay between autocorrelation and the cancellation that it involves. The autocorrelation function of a discrete signal x_t may be defined as

$$r_t(\tau) = \sum_{j=t+1}^{t+W} x_j x_{j+\tau} \tag{1}$$

where $r_t(\tau)$ is the autocorrelation function of lag τ at time index t, and W is the integration window size. YIN achieves a difference function instead of an autocorrelation function that is influenced in bias value.

$$d_t(\tau) = \sum_{j=t-\tau/2-W/2}^{t-\tau/2+W/2} (x_j - x_{j+\tau})^2 \tag{2}$$

Here, $d_t(\tau)$ is the difference function to search for the values of τ for which the function is zero. The window size shrinks with increasing values of τ, resulting in the envelope of the function decreasing as a function of lag as illustrated in Fig. 3(a). The difference function must choose a minimum dip that is not zero-lag. However, setting the search range is difficult because of imperfect periodicity. To solve this problem, the YIN method replaces the difference function with the cumulative mean normalized difference function of e.q.(3). This function is illustrated in Fig. 3(b).

$$d'_t(\tau) = \begin{cases} 1 & \text{if } \tau = 0, \\ d_t(\tau)/[(1/\tau)\sum_{j=1}^{\tau} d_t(j)] & \text{otherwise.} \end{cases} \tag{3}$$

The cumulative mean normalized difference function not only reduces "too high" errors, but also eliminates the limit of the frequency search range, and no longer needs to avoid the zero-lag dip.

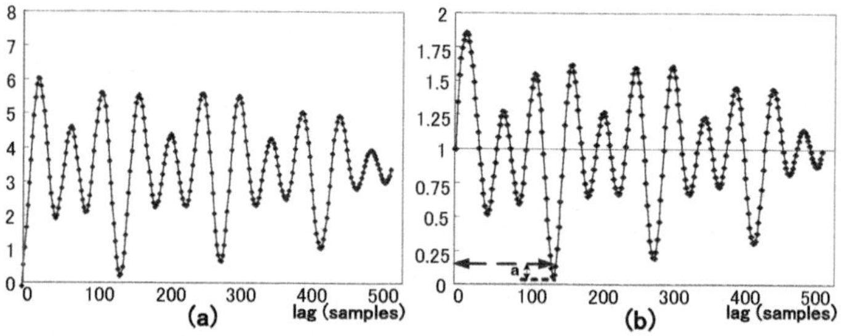

Fig. 3. (a) Example of difference function. (b) Cumulative mean normalized difference function at same waveform.

One of the higher order dips appears often in F_0 extraction, even when using the modified function in e.q.(3). This error is called the subharmonic or octave error. To reduce the sub-harmonic error, the YIN method finds the smallest value of τ that gives a minimum of $d'_t(\tau)$ deeper than the threshold. Here, the threshold is decided by the value that adds a minimum of $d'_t(\tau)$ to the absolute threshold α in Fig. 4 (b). Absolute threshold is possible because of the achieved normalized processing in the previous step. In the final step, F_0 is extracted through the parabolic interpolation and best local estimation process.

3.2 V/NV Classification

The general V/NV classification algorithm participates in the processing of each short-time speech segment. However, classification of a whole input segment is more important in reliable speech recognition in which non-voice rejection is possible. For this classification, the proposed algorithm decides V/NV from the ratio of the reliable F_0 contour over the whole input interval. The function value $d'_t(\tau)$ defined by e.q. (3) is compared with the confidence threshold to decide the reliability of each F_0 frame. Here, the confidence threshold is selected such that the value is 0.05 to 0.2. Figures 2 and 3 depict examples of reliable F_0

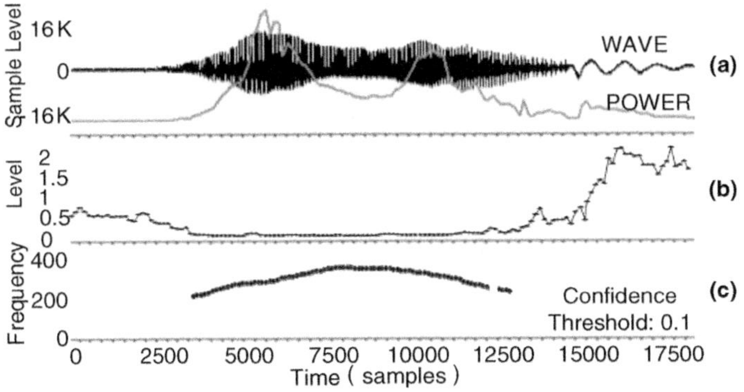

Fig. 4. (a) Example of a voice waveform. (b) Cumulative mean normalized difference function calculated from the waveform in (a). (c) Reliable F_0 contour in which the confidence threshold is applied.

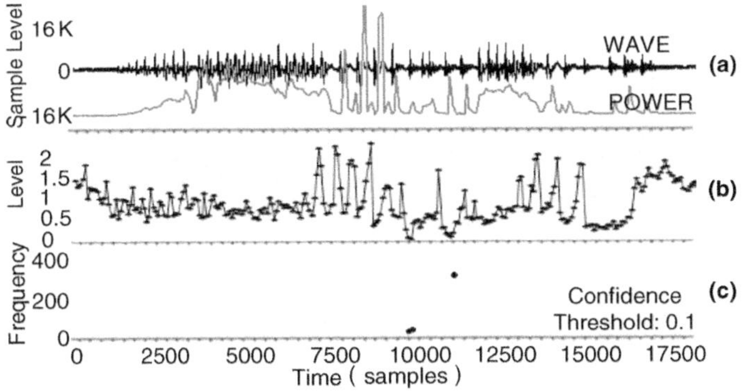

Fig. 5. (a) Example of a noise waveform. (b) Cumulative mean normalized difference function calculated from the waveform in (a). (c) Reliable F_0 contour where the confidence threshold is applied.

contour extraction. A reliable F_0 contour using the cumulative mean normalized difference function is illustrated in Fig. 4 (b). When the confidence threshold of YIN-based F_0 is 0.1, only high reliability areas are selected, as illustrated in Fig. 4 (c).

The conventional VAD method using energy and/or ZCR is detected noise as well as voice in Fig. 5 (a). However, you can see that reliable F_0 appears on only three frames because of the applied confidence threshold 0.1 in Fig. 5 (c). Furthermore, we can prove the performance by the examining that detected frequency is the inner voice frequency area. For V/NV classification from the extracted F_0 contour, we then compute the ratio of frames with the reliable F_0 as follows.

$$d = \frac{1}{M} \sum_{j=1}^{M} P_{th}(i) \tag{4}$$

$$P_{th}(i) = \begin{cases} 1 & \text{if } F_{min} \le F_{0th}(i) \le F_{max}, \\ 0 & \text{otherwise.} \end{cases} \quad (5)$$

Here, M indicates the total number of input frames, and F_{min} =60Hz and F_{max} =800Hz are experimentally chosen for a disabled person's voice. Finally, an input segment is classified as voice if d exceeds the V/NV threshold value. The cepstrum-based algorithm can also be used as the confidence threshold for extraction of the F_0 contour as indicated in Fig. 6. However, the F_0 extraction performance of a cepstrum-based algorithm is inferior to YIN, and it is difficult to determine a suitable threshold in various environments.

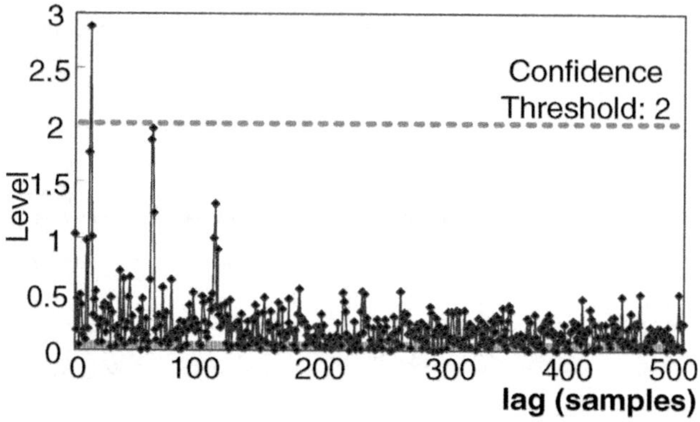

Fig. 6. Example of cepstrum signal to the applied confidence threshold

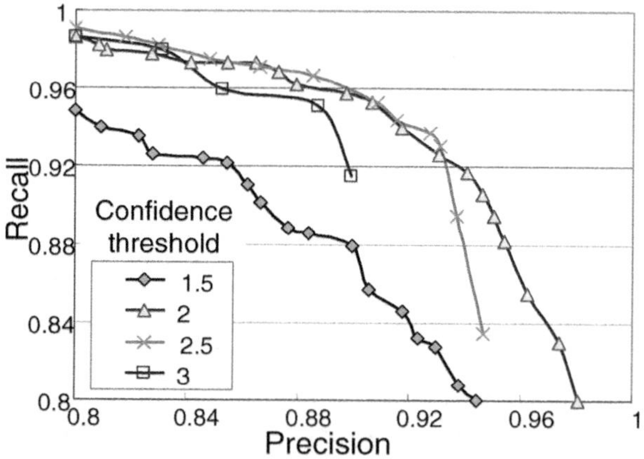

Fig. 7. Recall-precision curve of noise classification using cepstrum

4 Experiment Results

To evaluate the performance of our proposed method, we conducted V/NV classification experiments using YIN or cepstrum. The sampling frequency was 16 kHz, the window size was 25 ms, and the frame shift was 8 ms. All experiments were conducted using the 1567 voice commands and 447 noises in Table 2.

Table 4. Confidence threshold analysis of four types of microphones with the best recall precision

	Headset	Bone conduction	Pin	Bluetooth
Cepstrum	3	2.5	1.5	2
YIN	0.05 0.1	0.06 0.08	0.07 0.1	0.08 0.1

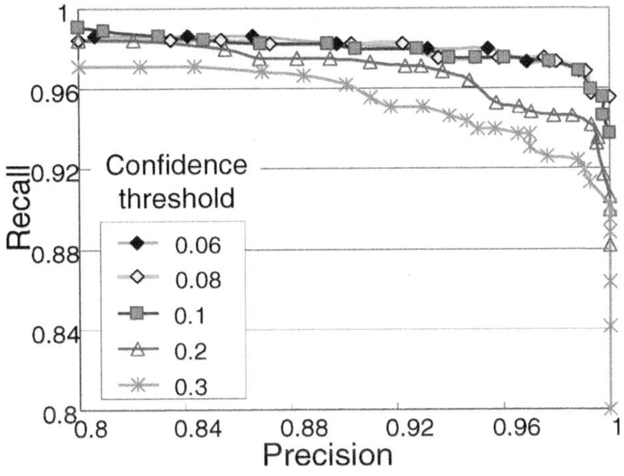

Fig. 8. Recall-precision curve of noise classification using YIN

Figures 7 and 8 depict V/NV classification performance and plot recall-precision curves according to an individual confidence threshold. From the results, the YIN-based algorithm is superior to the cepstrum-based algorithm. When the confidence threshold of YIN is 0.08, the V/NV classification provides the best results with 0.97 and 0.99 rates over recall and precision. In other words, when the smallest threshold was selected for voice detection at a precision rate of 1, the miss-error rate of noise is only 4.9%.

Table 4 lists the best confidence threshold of each microphone with the best recall precision. When YIN uses the F_0 extraction method, the confidence threshold is stable at about 0.08. Although the cepstrum algorithm can use the F_0

extraction method, it is difficult to decide on a suitable confidence threshold in each microphone environment.

5 Conclusions

This paper demonstrates a V/NV classification for reliable VAD in a real environment voice command system with extraneous sounds such as coughing and breathing. The proposed method classifies V/NV from the ratio of reliable F_0 contour over the whole input interval. We adopted the F_0 extraction method where YIN has the best performance among conventional methods. Our experiment results indicate that the false alarm rate is 4.9% with no miss-errors in which voice is determined to be non-voice. Therefore, the proposed VAD, which rejects non-voice input in preprocessing, can be helpful for realizing a highly reliable powered wheelchair control system. In addition, our proposed method can use average F_0 information of input voice without additional computation. This is useful as additional information for a confidence measure of speaker specific systems. Note that the YIN-based VAD entailed only 2% additional computation cost compared to using the ZCR-based method on a Pentium 4 3.2GHz machine.

Acknowledgment

This research is conducted as part of "Development of technologies for supporting safe and comfortable lifestyles for persons with disabilities," funded by the solution oriented research for science and technology (SORST) program of the Japan Science and Technology Agency (JST), Ministry of Education, Culture, Sports, Science and Technology (MEXT) of the Japanese Government.

References

1. Lee SW, Tanaka K and Itoh Y, "Combining Multiple Subword Representations for Open-Vocabulary Spoken Document Retrieval," in Proc. IEEE Int. Conf. Acoustics, Speech, and Signal Processing, pp. 505–508, 2005.
2. Sadohara K, Lee SW and Kojima H, "Topic Segmentation Using Kernel Principal Component Analysis for Sub-Phonetic Segments, " Technical Report of IEICE, AI2004-77, pp. 37–41, 2005.
3. Suk SY, Lee SW, Kojima H and Makino S, "Multi-mixture based PDT-SSS Algorithm for Extension of HM-Net Structure," in Proc. 2005 September Meeting of the Acoustical Society of Japan, 2005.
4. Sasou A, Asano F, Tanaka K and Nakamura S, "HMM-Based Feature Compensation Method: An Evaluation Using the AURORA2," in Proc. Int. Conf. Spoken Language Processing, pp. 121-124, 2004.
5. Jonson DH and Dudgeon DE, *"Array signal processing,"* Prentice Hall, Englewood Cliffs, NJ, 1993.
6. Sasou A and Kojima H, "Multi-channel speech input system for a wheelchair," in Proc. 2006 Mar Meeting of the Acoustical Society of Japan, 2006.

7. J. Rouat, Y. C. Liu, and D. Morrisette, “A pitch determination and voiced/unvoiced decision algorithm for noisy speech,” Speech Communication, vol. 21, 1997.
8. S. Ahmadi and S. S. Andreas, “Cepstrum-based pitch detection using a new statistical V/UV classification algorithm,” in IEEE Trans. Speech Audio Processing, vol 7, no. 3, pp. 333–339, 1999.
9. E. Mousset,W. A. Ainsworth, and J. A. R. Fonollosa, “A comparison of several recent methods of fundamental frequency and voicing decision estimation,” in Proc. Int. Conf. Spoken Language Processing, vol. 2, pp. 1273–1276, 1996.
10. A. Lee, T. Kawahara and K. Shikano, “Julius — an open source real-time large vocabulary recognition engine.” In Proc. European Conference on Speech Communication and Technology, pp. 1691–1694, 2001.
11. de Cheveigne, A., and Kawahara, H., “YIN, a fundamental frequency estimator for speech and music,” *The Journal of the Acoustic Society of the America*, vol 111, 2002.

MPEG-4 Scene Description Optimization for Interactive Terrestrial DMB Content

Kyung-Ae Cha[1] and Kyungdeok Kim[2]

[1] School of Computer and Communication Engineering, Daegu University, Korea
chaka@daegu.ac.kr
[2] Division of Computer Engineering, Uiduk University, Korea
kdkim@uu.ac.kr

Abstract. The Digital Multimedia Broadcasting (DMB) system was developed to provide high-quality multimedia contents in the mobile environment. The system adopts the MPEG-4 standard for its main video, audio and other media formats. It also adopts MPEG-4 scene description for its interactive multimedia contents. Its animated and interactive contents are based on BIFS (Binary Format for Scenes), which refers to the spatio-temporal specifications and behavior of the individual objects. The more interactive contents are, the more high-bitrate the scene description should be. However, the bandwidth for allocating meta-data such as those in scene descriptions is restrictive in the mobile environment. On one hand, the DMB terminal starts demultiplexing contents and decoding individual media with its own decoder. After decoding each medium, the rendering module presents each media stream according to the scene description. Thus, the BIFS stream corresponding to the scene description should be decoded and parsed before the audio or visual object is presented. For these reasons, the transmission delay of the BIFS stream causes the delay in the entire audio-visual scene presentation, although the audio or video streams are en-coded in very low bitrate. This paper presents the effective optimization technique for adapting the BIFS stream into an expected MPEG-2 TS bitrate with-out bandwidth waste and for avoiding delay in the transmission of the initial scene description for interactive DMB contents.

Keywords: T-DMB, BIFS, Scene description Optimization, Interactive Content, MPEG-4 System.

1 Introduction

Digital Multimedia Broadcasting (DMB) provides broadband multimedia information mobile terminals that have limited processing capability and low bandwidth. More-over, in the DMB framework, rich, interactive contents can be further deployed in conjunction with communication channels to access additional or auxiliary information (such as MPEG-4 scene description, JPEG images, etc.) associated with au-dio/video contents[1-4]. With these unique characteristics of MPEG-4, before decoding media stream like video and audio the scene description

Y.-H. Lee et al. (Eds.): ICESS 2007, LNCS 4523, pp. 358–368, 2007.

bitstream must be first received in a user terminal. However, due to the low bandwidth of the wireless net-work, it is difficult to ensure the adequate transmission of the scene description bit-stream. Hence, for interactive DMB content streaming, the data rate of the scene description should be tailored to fit the current available bandwidth.

In this paper, effective techniques in adapting the encoded MPEG-4 scene description(called BInary Format for Scene) into suitable bitrate of the DMB transmission packet size with minimum bandwidth waste are presented. The scene descriptions for the same visible scene and scenario may differ in object ID assignments, node hierarchy organizations, etc., depending on the scene description authors' intentions. So a scene description can be optimized to adopt its encoded bit size into the given re-source constraints. The research focuses on developing an efficient scene description optimization technique that makes it possible to match the expected bit size with the encoded bit stream of the modified scene description without any major loss in the original scene.

Section 2 presents the overview of the scene description for interactive DMB multimedia contents. Section 3 explains the optimization of the proposed method, while section 4 presents the experimental results. In Section 5, conclusions and further re-search direction are discussed.

2 Scene Description for Interactive T-DMB Contents

In the DMB standard, the audio and visual media formats in multimedia contents adopt the MPEG-4 AVC(Advanced Video Coding) and the MPEG-4 BSAC(Bit Sliced Arithmetic Coder), respectively. Moreover, it also adopts MPEG-4 system's object-based coding scheme for scene[1-4]. The scene consists of multiple objects, each of which can be of any type, such as video, audio, text, graphics, etc. as well as scene description refers to the spatio-temporal composition of these objects following the MPEG-4 Core 2D Profile[3,5-8]. The individually encoded contents are multiplexed and encapsulated as MPEG-4 Sync Layer packets. The Sync Layer becomes MPEG-2 TS (Transport Stream)[9] in turn. Finally, the transmission stream is deliv-ered through the Eureka-147 system.

The scene description text is encoded by the BIFS encoder into the BIFS AU (Access Unit). The packetized ES resulting from the SL packetizer becomes the payload of the TS packets.

Figure 1(a) shows an example of the portion of a scene description text, which depicts a rectangular object as geometry. Each text line is numbered for convenience.

The `geometry` node(line number 21) identifies a rectangular object with a width of 100 pixels and a height of 50 pixels. The attributes of the `size` of the rectangular node are mandatory to render the corresponding rectangular object when the scene is presented. On the other hand, the `LineProperties` node(line number 17) is used for describing the linear strokes of the geometry object in its parent `Material2D` node. When the scene description does not define the

```
1) Group {
  2) children [
  3) DEF Switch3000 Switch {
    4) whichChoice 1
    5) choice [
    6) DEF Transform2D3000 Transform2D {
      7) translation -187.00 142.00
      8) scale 1.00 1.00
      9) rotationAngle 0.00
        10) children [
        11) Shape {
          12) appearance Appearance {
          13) material DEF Material2D3000
                Material2D {
          14) emissiveColor 0.75 0.75 0.75
          15) filled TRUE
          16) transparency -1.00
          17) LineProperties {
            18) lineColor 0.00 0.00 0.00
            19) width 1.00
            20) lineStyle 0
            }
    }
          21) geometry Rectangle {
            22) size 100.00 50.00
```

(a)

```
1) Group {
  2) children [
    6) DEF Transform2D3000 Transform2D {
      7) translation -187.00 142.00
        10) children [
        11) Shape {
          12) appearance Appearance {
          13) material DEF Material2D3000
                Material2D {
          15) filled TRUE
          21) geometry Rectangle {
            22) size 100.00 50.00
```

(b)

Fig. 1. A portion of the Scene description text : (a) original scene description;(b) optimized scene description of (a)

node, the presentation draws the real rectangular object with the default value as its line properties. Thus, there is no difference between the original scene and the optimized scene, which removed the `LineProperties` node when the node describes with default values. The scene description text in Figure 1(a) would be optimized as shown in Figure 1(b), where the rectangular object can be presented in the same dimension drawing with the default values for its line stroke and filling attributes.

With this approach of optimization, the removable attributes of the MPEG-4 scene description syntax are categorized. The categorized node type and their field types of the description, based on the characteristics of individual objects, are the criterion from which optimization is made. Moreover, the actual encoded bit size of every node and attribute field are estimated so that the encoded bitrate of a modified scene description text through optimization can be pre-calculated without performing the BIFS encoding process. In order to achieve an accurate estimation value, a practical experiment of the BIFS encoding on every possible case of scene description modification is done. Through the tedious pre-process, detailed information on the encoded bitrate of the scene description node by node and field by field can be obtained. Note that the information is referred to in the Bit-Size Reference Table in Figure 4 and Figure 5.

3 Optimization of Interactive Scene Description

In this section, the optimization process of the scene description for adapting available bitrate is explained in detail.

3.1 Scene Description Parsing

The BIFS parsing is the main part of the proposed system. The modules use the nested loop approach to analyze the scene description text by reading the whole input scene description text.

As mentioned above, object nodes in the scene description are composed of various fields and their assigned values. We categorize three kinds of tokens following with their characteristics.

Reserved Simple Tokens: Simple tokens are already reserved strings in the node parsing table(NODE table) that is constructed on the pre-process stage for scene description parsing. For example, the followings are included this category: "children," "choice," and so on. These tokens should be matched one of the node parsing table elements.

Related tokens: Related tokens should have their actual attribute values so that they can determine the visible attributes of corresponding objects. For example, "emissiveColor," "lineStyle," "size," "radius," "URL," etc. belong to this category. These are also parsed with their assigned values by checking their following numeric, string or boolean type variables.

Combination Tokens: The combination tokens are composed of more than two different tokens that are associated by the dot (.) notation. In this case, each sub token is considered as a *Related Token.* These combination tokens are used in the condition nodes, rout nodes, and time related nodes.

Figure 2 shows the BIFS parser's processing steps. The module gets an original BIFS text and reads strings line by line through the scene description. According to the criterion for splitting tokens such as backspace, parentheses or square brackets, the parser recognizes individual tokens and then compares the NODE table entries and the tokens. The result from token matching process, tokens are classified one of the three types.

In order to detect the interactive scenario of the scene description as well as the spatio-temporal relationship of the objects, the following data structures are defined. The tokens and their related information such as field values are stored in the containers as following their features.

Multimedia object information container: Objects' attribute information and their related sensor information which are used to realize the animated scenario of objects are written in this container. The actual assigned values of `Transform2D`, `Material2D`, `LineProperty`, `TouchSensor`, and other link nodes are in this container.

Rout information container: This has the assigned values of nodes that describe user interactive events and responsible actions. These are source object IDs for route node, action command, and their corresponding destination object ID.

Condition information container: The container is composed of action event types of condition nodes, such as their node ID, action command, destination node ID, and field values to represent the corresponding results of the action.

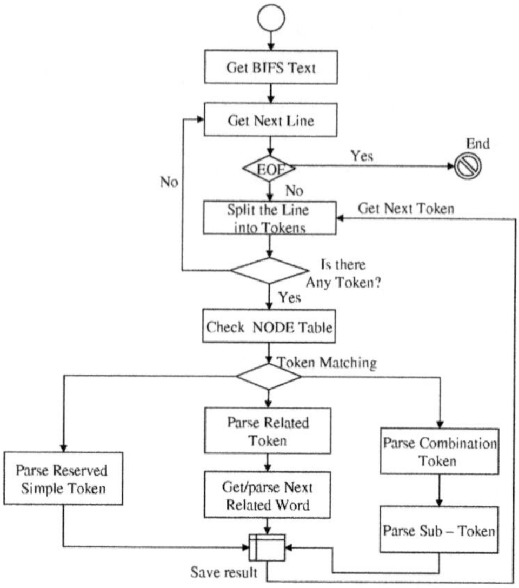

Fig. 2. Processing steps of BIFS Parser

Update OD (Object Descriptor) container: Information used to specify the descriptors of video, image, and audio objects are described in this container.

Figure 3 depicts the relationship between the containers and scene tree attributes. The object nodes and fields are constituted hierarchally so the scene description parsing result can be represented as tree structure. However, the optimization process doesn't need the whole information of the scene tree. Thus the selective values are stored in the related containers as described above. Moreover, information containers provide the prospective view of the scene organization to the optimization process.

3.2 Optimization of Scene Description

The optimal selection process of the objects in an MPEG-4 scene is performed in multiple steps. First, a set of attribute nodes, which affects the visual point of the original scene at a lesser degree, is removed in the sense that the modified scene is under the condition that the sum of the bit rates does not exceed the available bit size. If this condition cannot be met, then the next step removes a set of attributes that can be represented by using some default values without any object dropped under the same constraint. Figure 4 and the following expiations represent the optimization steps.

The Optimization Processor detects and removes the information from the original scene description, the group nodes and switch nodes in turn. And then, IDs of object nodes, rout nodes and conditional nodes are renamed in order to save bits for scene description. Finally, some attribute of object nodes are removed if they are not necessary. These processes are performed with information from containers and Bit-Size Refer Table.

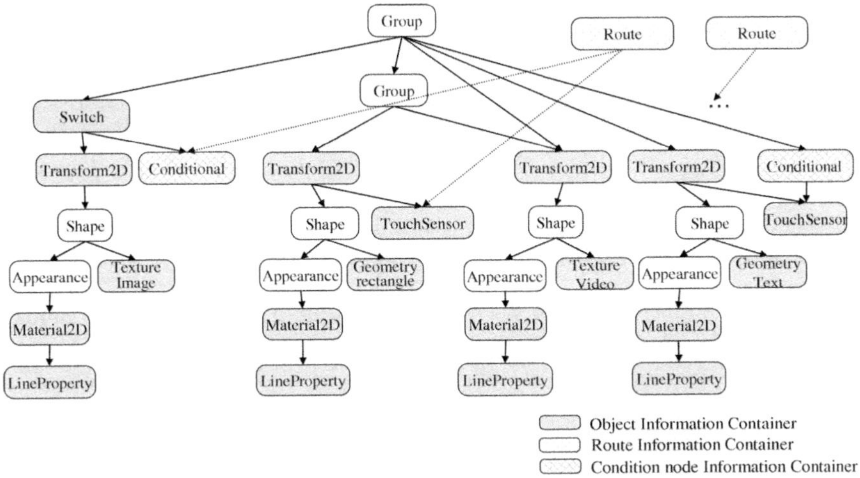

Fig. 3. Scene Tree and related Containers

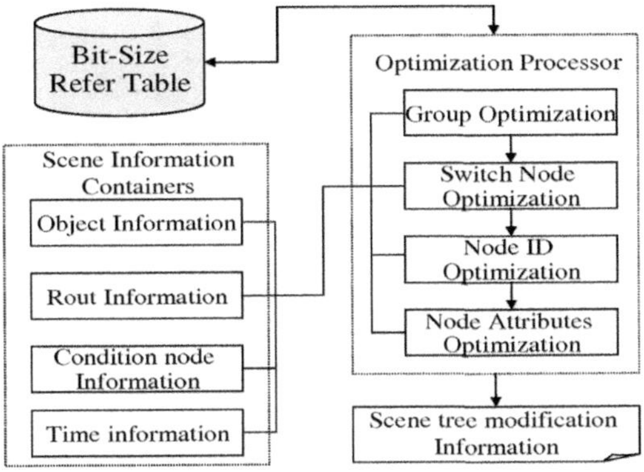

Fig. 4. Optimization processing module

Group Optimization: There are many BIFS visual nodes to manage scenes different ways in grouping and rendering. In scene description, the group concept is used to handle a set of objects more effectively and conveniently on the aspect of authoring. In rendering aspects, the grouping objects do not affect the rendering, thus, grouping information can be removed from the scene description. In this step, it should be checked whether the description contains a sub-group or group ID, and, if contained, it would be deleted from the scene description text.

Switch node filtering: Different from other nodes, the switch node can be deleted from the scene description text even though it has its children nodes, and if the switch node is not used in other condition nodes or time related nodes. If there is a switch node on an object node, this step checks whether the switch node ID is used in the condition node or in the time node. When it is determined that the ID has not been used again, it removes the switch node.

Node ID Optimization: During authoring time, authors can declare their own intentions on the object node IDs, thus every scene description text may have different node ID assignments. Every node ID uses up 1 byte per character, thus it is efficient in reducing the bit size of BIFS to give all node IDs with shorter strings. Based on the rule that the first letter should start as a letter of the alphabet, we give two cipers ID per node, which is composed of one leading alphabet letter and one succeeding digit number. The letter identifies each object, and the digit number identifies the attributes node of the object.

Node Attribute Optimization: As shown in Figure 1, some nodes or fields with default values can be removed. This process detects this kind of attributes from the object information container and removes the related nodes or fields. At this stage, the removal ensures that low level attributes are deleted first. For example, material2D attribute node cannot be removed as long as its line property node exists.

The BIFS parser and Optimization processes, which are explained above, are operating and interacting as seen in Figure 5.

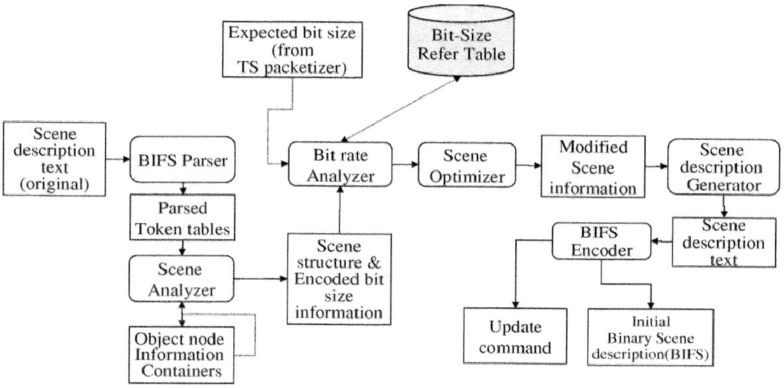

Fig. 5. Scene Description Optimization System Structure

The BIFS parser reads the scene description first, and stores the results of parsing in Token tables. At the same time, the Scene Analyzer module extracts attribute values from the input text and generates Object node Information Containers. In addition, the module constructs the scene structure and bitrate information of the original scene with the generated information. And then, the Scene Optimizer modifies the scene description to adapt an expected bit size by communicating with the Bitrate Analyzer module that predicts accurate BIFS sizes of the modified scene description in previous encoding by referring to the Bit-Size Reference Table. Finally, according to the modified scene information, optimized scene description text is generated and encoded to the BIFS stream.

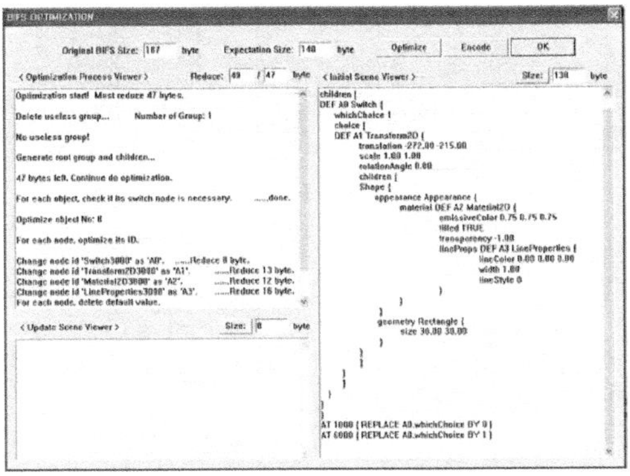

Fig. 6. User interface

4 Experiment Results

The proposed system is implemented by using Microsoft Visual C++ under the Windows platform. Figure 6 depicts the user interface snapshot of our system. The left part of the figure shows the optimization process visually, while the right part shows the modified scene description text when modification occurs. Moreover, the two text boxes at the top represent estimated bitstream sizes of BIFS, in bytes.

The sample contents used in the experiment are composed of various objects and its scene description describes several sub-groups and sensor nodes for interactive scenarios, as seen in Table 1.

Table 1. Sample content specifications

Content No.	Content No.1	Content No.2	Content No.3
Original BIFS Size	3058bytes	4069bytes	2724bytes
Number of Group	8	10	8
Multimedia Object Information	Video: 1	Video: 1	Video: 1
	Audio: 1	Audio: 1	Audio: 1
	Image: 7	Image: 9	Image: 7
	Rectangle: 12	Rectangle:16	Rectangle: 10
	Total:21	Total: 27	Total: 19
Number of Sensor	Touch Sensor: 13	Touch Sensor: 18	Touch Sensor: 11

Each content is composed of one video and one audio object as main audio-visual content. Several image and geometry object that are used to depict menu buttons and hot-spots are specified in the scene description. In addition, the interactive scenario also described using sensor nodes and rout nodes. For example, if user clicks a certain image object(button form) while the presentation, the corresponding text object which shows a products' information appears in the scene.

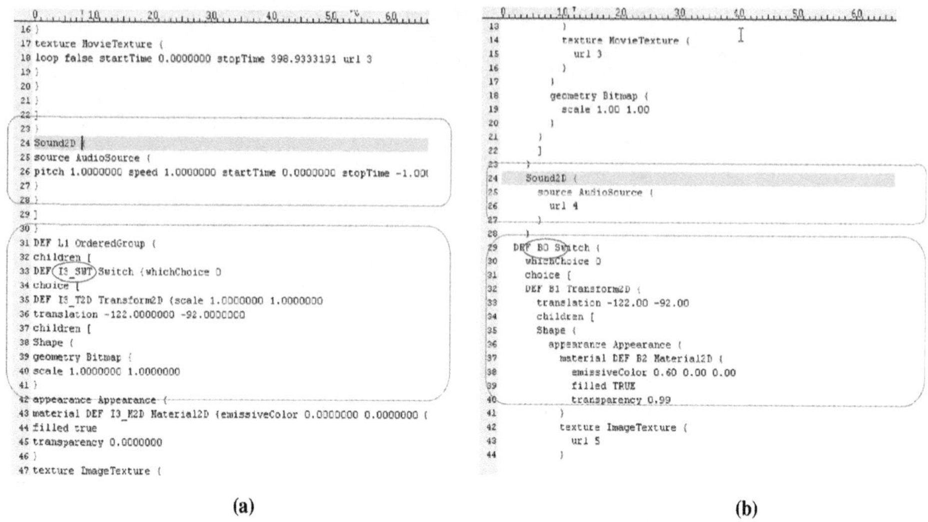

Fig. 7. A portion of the scene description text for Content No.1 : (a) the original scene description; (b) the optimized scene description

The scene descriptions of the sample contents are reconstructed by following the optimization process. At each step, the optimized scene description's bitrate are checked as seen in Table 2. Although the descriptions can be specified as different constitution types, samples followed the generally published scene description specification ways. As a result of the proposed optimization technique, the scene descriptions are reduced in terms of their encoded bit size down to 53.2% at the most, compared to the original descriptions.

Figure 7 shows a portion of the scene description text for content No.1. Figure 7 (a) presents the original description and Figure 7 (b) shows the optimized description for an audio object and an image object. As can seen, the fields that are assigned with default values and the `OrderedGroup` node are removed.Moreover, the node IDs are re-assigned with strings in two ciphers.

Figure 8(a) shows the presentation of content No. 1 at a time instance, while figure 8(b) represents the snapshot of its optimized scene at the same instance.The optimized scene is modified through the three optimization processes resulting from the table 2s Content 1. There is no difference in the two

Table 2. The optimization results of the sample descriptions

Content No.	Content No.1	Content No.2	Content No.3
Original BIFS Size	3058bytes(100%)	4069bytes(100%)	2724bytes(100%)
Group Optimization	3001bytes(98.1%)	4000bytes(98.3%)	2667bytes(97.9%)
Node ID Optimization	2196bytes(71.8%)	2925bytes(71.9%)	1961bytes(72%)
Node Optimization	1664bytes(54.4%)	2251bytes(55.3%)	1450bytes(53.2%)

* Percentage (%) = (Optimized BIFS Size)/(Original BIFS Size)×100

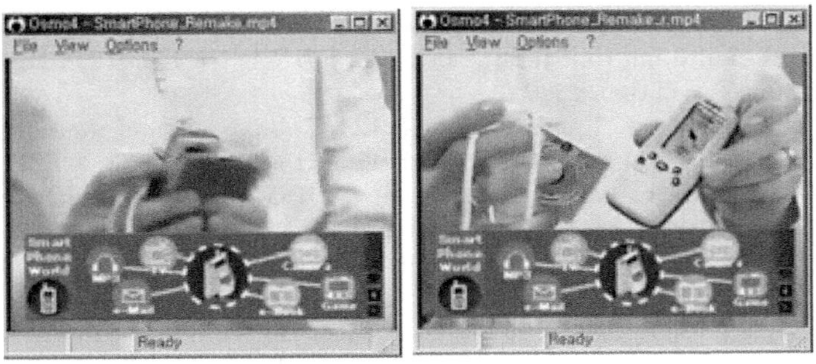

(a) (b)

Fig. 8. Presentation of Content No.1 : (a) original scene; (b) scene using optimized BIFS

scenes, so it can be said that the optimization process was operating properly. In order to verify that the behaviors of the two scenes are same, we compare the parsing results with the original parsing tree of the original scene description. As a result, the number of leaf nodes which means the each object in the scene, is same as that of original scene. Moreover the nodes related with the events such as touchsensors or conditional nodes are same with those of the original one.

5 Conclusions

In this paper, the effective algorithm to the TS bit size of the payload adaptive technique for the scene description of the interactive DMB content is proposed.

The features of the object nodes and their encoded bit size when the scene description text is transformed to the binary format were studied. The adaptive tool, based on optimization rules, was also designed and implemented. The research showed that the proposed optimization method reduced the scene description bitrate efficiently with-out losses in the original information. Basically, optimization should proceed in the scope of not changing the original scene. But if the size of the bitstream becomes bigger than expected after optimization, inevitable losses through optimization should be processed. Thus, when there is a difference between the optimized scene and the original, the scene should be updated in real time by using BIFS commands. Research in utilizing command stream generation is ongoing.

References

1. G. Lee, S. Cho, K. Yang, Y. Hahm and S. Lee: Development of Terrestrial DMB Transmis-sion System based on Eureka-147 DAB System, IEEE Transactions on Consumer Electron-ics, Vol. 51, Issue 1, (2005) 63–68
2. V. Ha, S. Choi, J. Jeon, G. Lee, W. Jang, W. Shim: Real-time Audio/Video Decoders for Digital Multimedia Broadcasting, Proc. of the 4th Int. Workshop on System-on-Chip for Real-Time Applications, (2004)

3. The basic interface between the transmitter and the receiver for video service for Terrestrial digital multimedia broadcasting in the VHF band, Telecommunications Technology Association, (2005)
4. J. Signes, Y. Fisher, A. Eleftheriadis: MPEG-4's binary format for scene description, Signal Processing: Image Communication, vol.15, issues 4-5, (2000) 321–345
5. Olivier Avaro, Alexandros Eleftheriadis: MPEG-4 Systems: Overview, Signal Process-ing: Image Communication 15, (2000) 281–298
6. WG11 (MPEG) MPEG-4 Overview document, ISO/IEC JTC1/SC29/WG11 N4668, (2002)
7. A. Puri, A. Eleftheriadis: MPEG-4: An Object-Based Multimedia Coding Standard Supporting Mobile Applications, Mobile Networks and Applications, vol. 3, (1998) 5–32
8. C. Herpel, A. Eleftheriadis: MPEG-4 Systems: elementary stream management, Signal Processing: Image Communication, Vol. 15 No. 4–5, (2000) 299–320

A Distributed Wearable System Based on Multimodal Fusion

Il-Yeon Cho[1], John Sunwoo[1], Hyun-Tae Jeong[1], Yong-Ki Son[1], Hee-Joong Ahn[1], Dong-Woo Lee[1], Dong-Won Han[1], and Cheol-Hoon Lee[2]

[1] Digital Home Research Division,
Electronics and Telecommunications Research Institute, Daejeon, Korea
{iycho,bistdude,htjeong,handcourage,hjahn,hermes,dwhan}@etri.re.kr

[2] System Software Laboratory, Department of Computer Engineering
Chungnam National University, Daejeon, Korea
clee@cnu.ac.kr

Abstract. Wearable computer can be worn anytime with the support of unrestricted communications and variety of services which provides maximum capability of information use. Key challenges in developing such wearable computers are level of comfort that users do not feel what they wear, easy and intuitive user interface and power management technique. This paper suggests a wearable system that consists of a wristwatch-type gesture recognition device and a personal mobile gateway that functional input/output modules can be freely plugged in and taken out. We describe our techniques implemented during our wearable system development: 1) multimodal fusion engine that recognizes voice and gesture simultaneously, 2) power management technique and 3) gesture recognition engine. Finally, we evaluate the performance of our multimodal fusion engine, and show the power consumption measurement data of our system built with the power management technique.

1 Introduction

People these days do not rely on PCs anymore as wire(less) internet spreads with the trend of computers, communications, and electronics appliances merging together into one. Instead, there is an increasing demand for new information terminal devices which can connect to the network anytime and anywhere with a method that's most familiar and convenient. These information terminal devices enable us to use variety of information freely and conveniently. This phenomenon tells us a factor which influences the success or failure in this digital industry; how many diverse tasks we do is not a factor, instead, it is how easy and simple we do the tasks with a user-friendly and intuitive interface. Computer, fashion and clothing industry are merging together into one in order to satisfy the needs of user interface, and these trials are putting ahead the appearance of new-concept information terminal devices.

Wearable computers provide efficient services with various functions by combining functions of personal devices that are scattered and overlapped [1]. Sony developed GestureWrist that recognizes user's hand gesture as an input [2]. U. Anlinker

Y.-H. Lee et al. (Eds.): ICESS 2007, LNCS 4523, pp. 369–378, 2007.

studied trade-offs between the required computing and the allocation of communication resources during the wearable system design process where the wearable system has input/output module distributed on human body [3].

In this paper we suggest a distributed wearable system that is constructed with the WPGB (Wearable Pointing and Gesture Band) and WPS (Wearable Personal Station). WPGB is a small wristwatch type device loaded with a compact gesture engine supporting a low power operation and WPS is loaded with the multimodal fusion engine that analyzes the gesture recognition result from WPGB and voice recognition result from the WPS itself so that the user's intended command can take place.

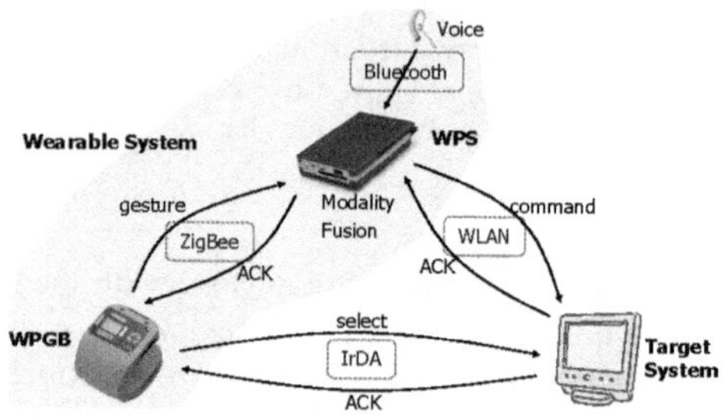

Fig. 1. Design of Wearable System

2 System Architecture

This section describes our proposed system design concept with the structure and functions of hardware and software.

2.1 Design Considerations

Fig. 1 illustrated the construction of suggesting system. As the name stands, the main function of WPGB is to select the object that needs to be controlled and send commands using arm gestures. Default function when not selecting the other objects is to control the wearable system on the user. It is designed to handle applications such as selecting and controlling one of the devices near the user, and transferring current contents or services to other devices freely. Applications such as content and service transfer are possible between the two WPGB users. WPGB communicates to WPS through Zigbee communication and uses IrDA for selecting devices to be controlled.

Multimodal fusion engine runs in WPS so that it can merge a gesture recognition result from WPGB and voice recognition result from the WPS and recognize to one final command. WPS has a Text-To-Speech (TTS) module as well to give user feedbacks according to recognition results.

2.2 WPGB (Wearable Pointing and Gesture Band)

We designed WPGB to have small form factor and power consumption. For the processor we used i.MX21 [4] that supports voltage scaling and frequency scaling.

Multi-Chip Package (MCP) memory and uni-colored OLED are used to build WPGB. We made the power supply circuit that changes the system power level dynamically through our application program.

There is a Kionix KXP84 3-axis accelerometer sensor [5] and a piezo-electronic sensor equipped in the WPGB in order to recognize gestures and distinguish the starting point of each gesture command using finger tapping recognition, respectively. Additionally to give the user feedbacks, there are small-sized vibration motor, buzzer and an OLED. Fig. 2 shows our WPGB prototype.

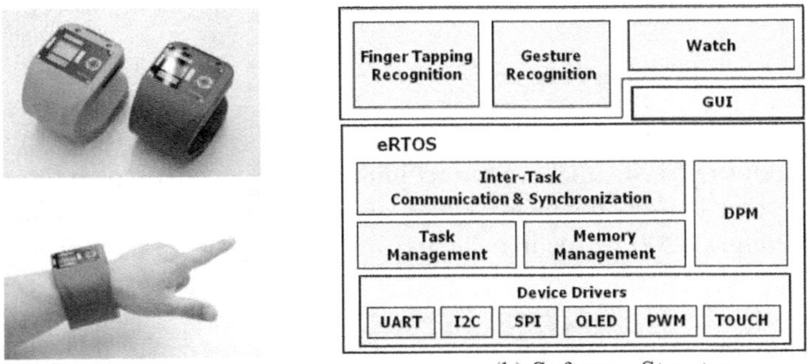

(a) Prototype (b) Software Structure

Fig. 2. Wearable Pointing and Gesture Band

Operating Systems that runs WPGB is ETRI-RTOS (eRTOS). eRTOS (see Fig. 2(b) has basis from the compact, low power operating system called iRTOS [6]. Current kernel size of the eRTOS is around 25KBytes and it operates well in the low capacity RAM/ROM systems.

2.3 WPS (Wearable Personal Station)

WPS is a main platform of our system suggested through this work. It has a performance of an average PDA system with the size and shape that is convenient to carry. It provides functions for a personal mobile gateway. In order to provide such functions, it supports WLAN, Bluetooth, Zigbee communication, and has dimension of 80mm x 54mm x 19mm. It runs on PXA272 [7] processor and supports both embedded Linux and WinCE operating system. It is designed to be geared and used with various

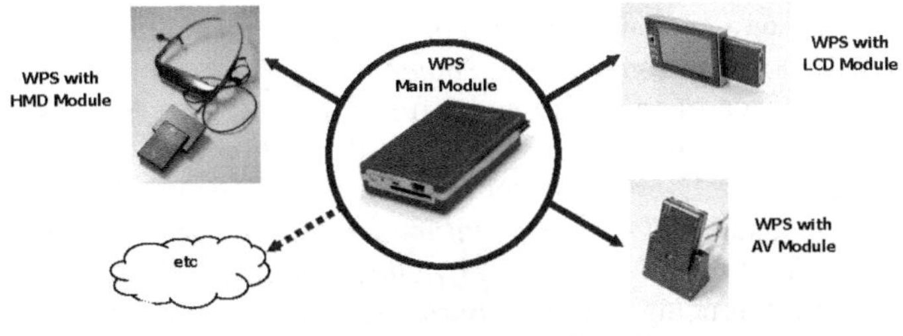

Fig. 3. Expandability of WPS

peripheral modules in a selective way depending on the services. Fig. 3 illustrates the WPS module which can change its functionality and system configuration by pairing with various output modules.

3 Core Technologies

This section describes core technologies that are implemented in our system suggested through this paper. The core technologies are multimodal fusion engine, low power scheme, gesture recognition engine and gesture segmentation cue method.

3.1 Multimodal Fusion Engine

We used PowerASR voice recognition engine from HCILAB for the WPS voice recognition. PowerASR is the voice recognition engine developed for the embedded system use that is user-independent and supports the recognition of variable vocabulary (maximum of 200 words in a database) [8].

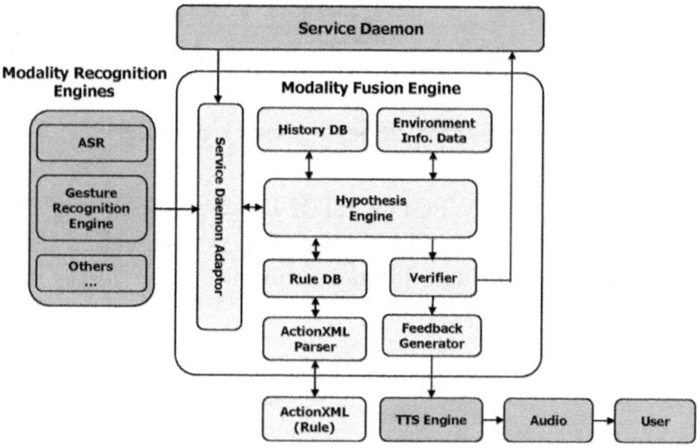

Fig. 4. Structure of Multimodal Fusion Engine

Advantages of the multimodal input system compare to the uni-modal system are known as the reduced uncertainty and improved input accuracy in noisy environment [9]. Methods of multimodal fusion are divided into two in overall: input feature level fusion and semantic level fusion [10]. Our study chose semantic fusion strategy since it is easy to add a new modality, and is convenient in maintaining. Software architecture of our multimodal fusion engine is shown in Fig. 4.

Operation sequence of the multimodal fusion engine is as follows. Fusion engine extracts rules from the *ActionXML* file using the *ActionXML Parser* then saves the rules in *Rule database*. User and system events that are recorded and time-stamped in *Service Daemon* and *Modality recognition engine* are sent to *Hypothesis engine* through the *Service Daemon Adaptor*. *Hypothesis engine* deduces what user intended to command by referencing *System Environment Information Data, History DB and Rule DB* where the past deduced results are recorded. Deduced results in this manner are verified in *Verifier* and are sent to *Service Daemon*. *Verifier* finds an error and notifies user via *Feedback Generator*.

Voice recognizer returns two candidates of recognition result, and gesture recognizer returns one that is the most likely to what the user intended to commend. Combinations of the two (voice + gesture) recognition results are assigned to the commands according to user's needs and registered in *ActionXML* file. The following example shows how the two commands in different modalities are combined into one in order to achieve mutual complementary benefits. We get the mutual complementary benefits when the voice and gesture commands are defined for the same purpose. For instance, both the voice command "NEXT" and gesture command "[RIGHT]" can be mapped to the "→" key in the keyboard. It can be useful in a noisy environment where the voice recognition results are often poor.

Within the mutual complementary policy described above, the following cases will be considered "recognition fail" by the multimodal fusion engine and there will be no resultant action.

- Both the voice and gesture recognizer fail to give recognition results.
- Voice and gesture recognizer give different recognition results.

In contrast, the following are the cases of "recognition success".

- Both the voice and gesture recognizer give same recognition results.
- Only one of the two recognizer gives a successful recognition result.

Excluding the "recognition fail" case shown above, user can define the combinations of voice and gesture in the *ActionXML* file and assign them to the final commands user wants. Or, the user can find the cases of "recognition success" shown above and register them in the *ActionXML* file. Combinations that are not registered in the *ActionXML* file are processed as a recognition failure. However, for the particular combinations of voice and gesture that are often recognized wrong, we can overcome this to a certain level by registering them to *ActionXML* file. The following is an example of overcoming such case.

If the voice recognizer frequently misses to recognize the user's voice command "NEXT" and confuses as "TEXT", then the user can register "TEXT" as same as "NEXT" in ActionXML *file so that the result of "TEXT" is recognized by the fusion engine as "NEXT". In this case, user may not want to assign "TEXT" command.*

Our multimodal fusion engine suggested through this work is designed light enough to be operated together with the voice recognizer, speech synthesizer, and gesture recognizer within an embedded system such as our WPS system. It is implemented to reduce the deduction (reasoning) procedure which takes a considerable amount of time in the fusion engine by letting the user to define multimodal fusion rules into *ActionXML* file directly. Finally it results in the load reduction of our fusion engine so that it can be run on a lower performance embedded system that has small resources.

3.2 Dynamic Power Management (DPM)

WPGB hardware supports the following features for DPM application: WPGB uses Freescale's i.MX21 as CPU. The CPU frequency can be configured as 133MHz and

66MHz. System bus frequency can be changed from 16MHz ~ 66MHz. The CPU core voltage can be changed from 1.4V ~ 1.5V.

DPM and policy in WPGB are implemented based on the methods suggested in [11-13] while considering WPGB hardware and software property.

3.3 Gesture Segmentation Cue

Generally, a hand gesture occurs subsequently after the previous hand movements that maybe meaningless. In order to correctly analyze a user's intended gesture command during such continuous hand movements, recognition engine has to know the starting point and ending point of the gesture. This kind of gesture segmentation issues are being a problem [14]. In our early development stage, we solve this gesture segmentation problem by using a button that can be worn on a finger as illustrated in Fig. 5(a) so that user can press the button only when making a meaningful gesture. However, this system can be inconvenient for everyday life. In order to overcome this inconvenience, we developed *FingerTapButton* that recognizes the bone-conduction sound by touching a thumb and second finger and uses it as a hand gesture segmentation cue, which can avoid the use of mechanical buttons. WPGB only monitors data from the time when the user taps his or her fingers until the user finishes gesture command and stays still. Fig. 5(b) illustrates the basic principle of *FingerTapButton*.

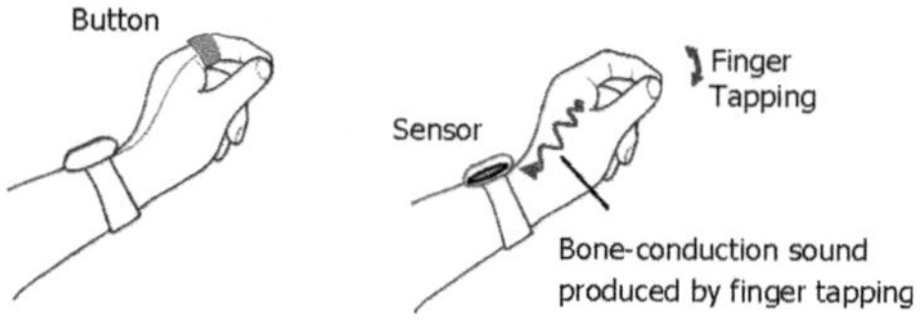

(a) (b)

Fig. 5. Basic principle of *FingerTapButton*

3.4 Gesture Recognition Engine

We define 8 commands that are sufficient to control general multimedia appliances. Each command is mapped to forearm gestures by considering our intuitive gestures used in the real world.

Table 1. Defined gesture table

Commands	Gestures	Commands	Gestures
Device Selection	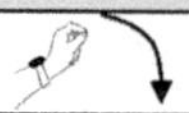	Device Cancel	
Right/Next		Left/Previous	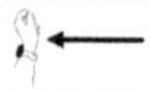
Volume up		Volume down	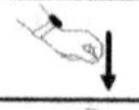
Play		Stop	

The x, y and z sensor data will be sampled only when the user makes meaningful gestures starting with *FingerTapButton*. Each gesture data is normalized to have the fixed height of data range, and sub-sampled to filter out the noise and reduce the data size to lessen the load when the engine analyzes the input. The preprocessed data is analyzed and characterized in terms of 1) the maximum and minimum values of the acceleration along each axis, 2) where they occur in time-vs.-acceleration plots and 3) quantitative comparison of them in order to find parameters for the software recognition engine so that it can recognize each command. In addition, as the command set increased, more geometric characteristics were considered such as the starting/end value and vertex (local maxima/minima) locations of each input vector. This method of extracting characteristic information and classifying them with the rule-based recognition engine is used to distinguish gesture commands [15].

4 System Evaluation

This section describes the use of our multimodal fusion engine that is implemented in our suggesting wearable system.

4.1 Recognition Enhancement Through Multimodal Fusion

As mentioned previously, advantage of multimodal fusion engine is its improved recognition rate compare to that of individual recognition engine. In order to measure the performance of our fusion engine, we used 6 gestures and 66 voice commands. There were 5 test subjects (all males) and each subject was asked to make each combinational voice and gesture command for 10 times.

Fig. 6 shows the comparison of voice only recognition rate, gesture only recognition rate, and voice + gesture recognition. As shown in the Fig. 6, recognition rate using the fusion engine is better than using the voice or gesture recognition engine alone.

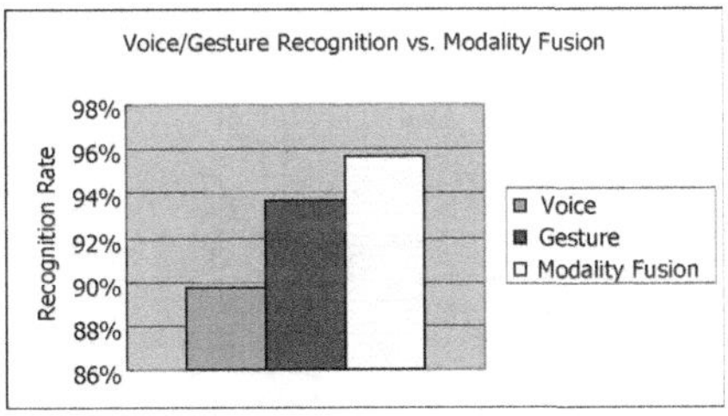

Fig. 6. Recognition rate of Voice/Gesture vs. multimodal fusion

4.2 Power Consumption of WPGB

WPGB hardware is designed to minimize the power consumption, and the operating system runs the WPGB supports a power supply control interface for each component. In order to measure the power consumption, we measured the current of the system using Agilent 34411A digital multi-meter (in 2000 samples/sec) with the supply voltage of 3.7V from Agilent E3648A power supply.

Table 2. DPM Policy

WPGB Task	Operating State	WPGB DPM Policy		
		Default	Idle Scaling	Load Scaling
FINGERTAP	TASK	133/66@1.5V[1]	133/66@1.5V	88/44@1.45V
GESTURE	TASK+1	133/66@1.5V	133/66@1.5V	133/66@1.5V
ICONVIEW[2]	TASK-1	133/66@1.5V	133/66@1.5V	66/33@1.425V
IDLE	IDLE	133/66@1.5V	66/16@1.4V	66/16@1.4V

Considering the CPU requirements of the WPGB tasks, we decided the operating state and applied DPM policy defined in section 3.2. Table 2 shows the WPGB DPM policy of the four tasks.

Fig. 7 shows the measurement data for each policy. Portion noted as ① in the figure is when the WPGB recognizes the starting point of a gesture using the *FingerTapButton* and gives vibration feedbacks through the vibration motor, ② is when it collects the accelerometer sensor data and recognizes the gesture, and ③ is when the gesture results are being displayed on OLED.

Average current and power consumptions are shown in Table 3. As illustrated in the table, we achieved an improvement of 30% in power saving under Idle Scaling policy when compared to non-DPM system where the Idle Scaling policy has a power saving mode only in the system idle state. Under Load Scaling policy which has power saving modes in both the idle state and task operation, there is almost an improvement of 33% in power saving.

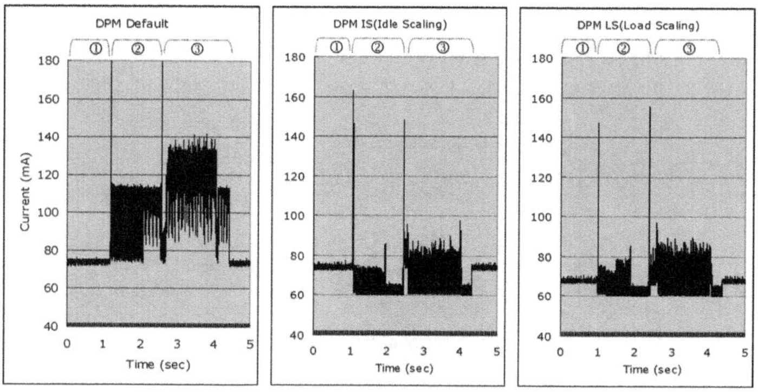

Fig. 7. Current Profile with DPM Policies

When considering the capacity of the battery (300mAh) that powers the WPGB, it has around 3 hours of system run time when DPM default policy is applied, however by applying the DPM Load Scaling policy its run time increases by an hour.

[1] CPU frequency / system bus frequency @ CPU voltage.
[2] Display of recognition results on the OLED.

Table 3. Power Consumption of WPGB

Policy	Average Current Consumption (mA)	Average Power Consumption (mW)	Power Saving (%)[3]
DPM Default	98.50	364.46	-
DPM IS	68.11	252.01	30.85
DPM LS	65.63	242.83	33.37

5 Conclusions

We presented our prototype that consists of a wristwatch type Wearable Pointing and Gesture Band (WPGB) and a small sized Wearable Personal Station (WPS) that the functional input/output modules can be freely plugged in and taken out. WPGB is loaded with a compact low power gesture recognition engine in order to support gesture command based user interface in the wearable computing environment. WPS has a mass storage with a communication gateway and has multimodal fusion capability.

By measuring and analyzing the performance of our multimodal fusion engine, we showed that using both voice and gesture input in a mutual supportive way results in a better recognition rate compared to when using a single input modality. We also showed that using a DPM technique gives us power savings by measuring and analyzing the power consumption rate in our WPGB system where it is operated by the DPM enabled eRTOS.

References

1. T. Starner: The challenges of wearable computing Part 1. IEEE Micro Vol. 21. No. 4. July (2001) 44-52
2. J. Rekimoto: GestureWrist and Gesture Pad: Unobtrusive Wearable Interaction Devices. Proc. IEEE International Symposium on Wearable Computers (2001) 21-27
3. U. Anliker et al.: A systematic approach to the design of distributed wearable systems. IEEE Trans. Computers, Vol.53. No.8. (2004) 1017-1033
4. i.MX21 Applications Processor Reference Manual, MC9238MX21RM, Rev.2 (2005)
5. ±2g Tri-Axis Digital Accelerometer Specifications, Part Number: KXP84-2050, Rev 1, Kionix Inc (2006)
6. H.S. Park, *et al.*: Design of Open Architecture Real-Time OS Kernel. KISS, Vol. 2. (2002) 418-420
7. Intel PXA27x Processor Family Developer's Manual (2006)
8. http://www.hcilab.co.kr
9. A. Corradini, M. Mehta, N.O. Bernsen, and J.C. Martin: Multimodal input fusion in human-computer interaction. Proc. the NATO-ASI Conference on Data Fusion for Situation Monitoring, Incident Detection, Alert and Response Management (2003) 18-29
10. P.R. Cohen, M. Johnston, , D.R. McGee, S.L. Oviatt, J. Pittman, I. Smith, and J. Clow: Quickset: Multimodal Interaction for Distributed Applications. Proc. the 5th International Multimedia Conference, ACM Press (1997) 31-40

[3] Compare to DPM Default.

11. B. Brock and K. Rajamani: Dynamic Power Management for Embedded Systems. Proc. IEEE International SOC Conference (2003) 416-419
12. IBM and MontaVista Software: Dynamic Power Management for Embedded systems. http://www.research.ibm.com/arl/projects/dpm.html (2002)
13. CE linux forum: Power Management Specification _R2", http://tree.celinuxforum.org/CelfPubWiki/Power ManagementSpecification_5fR2 (2004)
14. P.A. Harling and A.D. N. Edwards: Hand tension as a gesture segmentation cue. Proc. Gesture Workshop on Progress in Gestural Interaction (1996) 75-88
15. J. LaViola: A Survey of Hand Posture and Gesture Recognition Techniques and Technology. Technical Report CS99-11. Dept. of Computer Science, Brown University. Providence, Rhode Island (1999)

Randomized Approach for Target Coverage Scheduling in Directional Sensor Network*

Jian Wang, Changyong Niu, and Ruimin Shen

Department of Computer Science and Technology
Shanghai Jiaotong University, Shanghai, China, 200030
{jwang,cyniu,rmshen}@sjtu.edu.cn

Abstract. Recently directional sensors have been widely deployed as they are more practicable under constraints of manufacture, size and cost. One common functionality of networks formed by such directional sensors is to monitor a set of discrete targets continuously. Large scale deployment makes sensor recharge impossible. By abundant deployment, it is reasonable and necessary to select subsets of sensors to operate alternatively so as to prolong the network lifetime. Such problem has been proved to be NP-Complete. This paper approximates network lifetime problem by randomized algorithm. Through constructing *elementary sessions*, which denotes active subset of sensors covering all targets, and linear programming, the approximating solution is derived within extremely less duration comparing to previous works. Simulation results demonstrate the algorithm's performance and sound explanation is also presented.

1 Introduction

Sensor networks consist of large number of sensors that measure their environment. Each sensor is equipped with a sensing module, small processor and wireless communication antenna. The sensors are scattered around a field to collect information specific to applications about targets. The information gathered varies from seismic, acoustic, magnetic, to video data. For example, the sensors can be deployed in a battlefield to monitor enemy troops. When data is gathered by sensors, it is processed if necessary and then transferred to the base station through wireless antenna. Usually the base station has high computation and communication capability, and processes all gathered information according to specific application requirements.

As for manufacture, size and cost, different directional sensors emerge in the real-world. Such sensors have a finite sensing angle. It can not operate as omnidirectional one do. Often such sensor equips with rotation capability to enhance device flexibility. Thus it could operate in different directions so as to cover much larger sensing area. The sensor is usually powered by battery, which makes it very resource constrained. The sensor goes dead quickly if being active continuously, while sensor networks are desirable to last for long period of time, such as

* This work is partially supported by the NFSC under Grant 60672066, China.

Y.-H. Lee et al. (Eds.): ICESS 2007, LNCS 4523, pp. 379–390, 2007.

months or even years. Finding non-disjoint active subsets of sensors and scheduling them alternatively is feasible to prolong the network lifetime [1]. However, such problem is proved to be NP-Complete. The approximating algorithms proposed in [1] have long computation time when sensor network becomes larger. This motivates us to search for faster algorithm.

To be self-contained, we consider the following scenario from [1] in this paper. A target set with known locations are designated in the two-dimensional Euclidean field. A fixed set of directional sensors are randomly scattered within such field to cover these targets. The sensing region of directional sensor is of sector of sensing disk, centered at the sensor with uniform sensing range. If directional sensor faces to a direction, it indicates sensor can sense such direction and such direction is referred as sensing direction. The sensor covers the target only when the target is within sensing region. Usually the sensor network is deployed with abundant sensors guaranteeing network connectivity. Thus it is possible to cover all targets through selecting and scheduling sensor subsets to operate alternatively. The problem now being studied is how to select and schedule subsets to achieve maximum lifetime of directional sensor network.

Our algorithm assumes location information is available to targets and sensors, as well as algorithms running on the powerful base station. It computes the operating schedules and informs sensors when and how long to operate in which direction. Based on location of sensors and targets, sensing angle, and sensing range, *augmented bipartite graph* is constructed for original directional sensor network. Next, *elementary session* is defined as basic scheduling unit. By finding all of them, the optimal lifetime is achieved by linear programming technique. However, the number of all elementary sessions is extremely huge. Thus, Randomized algorithm proposed finds a subset of them and gets approximating solution within much shorter computation time. The remainder is organized as follows: Section 2 discusses related works. The formulation of lifetime problem and randomized algorithm are presented in Sec.3. In Sec.4, simulation results and sound explanation for time reduction are given. We conclude in Sec.5 with future work.

2 Related Work

Sensing coverage is one of common tasks in sensor networks. Usually the sensors are deployed densely so as to achieve high redundancy in coverage and network connectivity. Such coverage is often categorized into two types: One is field coverage, where full field is covered and no coverage hole is tolerated at any time. The other is target coverage, where a set of discrete targets needs to be monitored continuously by at least one sensor during whole lifetime.

For power limitation and recharging difficulty, there have many woks prolonging the network lifetime of omnidirectional sensor networks. In field coverage category, sleeping protocols, such as PEAS [2], PECAS [3], OGDC [4] achieve longer network lifetime through different strategies. Each of them tries to cover the largest area of interesting. [5] introduces k-coverage, where each point in field is monitored by at least k sensors. Thus it improves network fault-tolerance.

[6] utilizes Voronoi diagrams to identify redundant sensors and turns them off. Consequently, it achieves full coverage with minimal sensors. [7] provides a self-scheduling scheme, where differential coverage is provided by adjusting sensor's scheduling parameters, where sensors dynamically schedule themselves while guaranteeing a certain degree of coverage according to parameters more than operating time. [8] organizes sensors into subsets and derive optimal scheduling of these subsets, where lifetime is maximized and all service constraints are satisfied. The problem is formulated as a generalized maximum flow graph and the optimality is found by linear programming.

In target coverage category, a set of discrete targets is designated. Accordingly, lifetime problems are studied intensively. [9] assumes that each sensor only monitor one target at a time, and constructs operating timetable for each sensor. [10] minimizes the breach of coverage and subsets derived upon bandwidth constraints. It organizes sensors into mutually exclusive subsets which are activated properly, and permits that not of all targets need to be covered by one subset. [11] requires that each target must be covered by at least one sensor in each subset, where subsets may overlap with each other. [12] groups sensors into disjoint subsets, each of which covers all the targets, and only one subset is active. The objective is to maximize number of those subsets.

Directional sensor research attracts more attention recently. [13] analyzes the probability of full area coverage, where each node is fixed to one direction. [14] strives to find a minimum set of directions that can cover maximal targets, where each node could rotate to different directions. The resulting subsets of sensors are not allowed to be overlapped. [1] strives to find non-disjoint subsets of sensors covering all targets and schedule them alternatively to achieve optimal lifetime of directional sensor network. This paper considers the lifetime problem in directional sensor network and it belongs to target coverage category. In [14] the subsets are not overlapped and [1] relaxes such constraint. Our work continues to allow overlapped sensing regions, which is not considered in [1]. In the following, sensor and directional sensor will be used interchangeably.

3 Formulation and Randomized Approach

For convenience, the notations and assumptions following [1] are described first. Then the lifetime problem of directional sensor network covering a set of discrete targets is formulated. And *partition* algorithm finding sufficient directions of each sensor is proposed. Further, *augmented bipartite graph* is constructed upon relationships between directions and targets. Finally, *elementary session* is introduced and randomized approach approximates the optimal lifetime. As proved in [1], the NP-Complete feature of lifetime implicates the number of elementary sessions extremely huge. However, most sessions remains dependent to others. Randomized approach finds enough number of them to approximate solution by linear programming technique.

3.1 Notations and Assumptions

- M: the number of targets.
- N: the number of sensors.
- a_m: the mth target, $1 \le m \le M$.
- s_i: the ith sensor, $1 \le i \le N$.
- A: the set of targets, $A = \{a_1, a_2, \cdots, a_M\}$.
- S: the set of sensors, $S = \{s_1, s_2, \cdots, s_N\}$.
- $d_{i,j}$: the jth direction of s_i, $1 \le i \le N$, $1 \le j < \infty$.
- c_i: the number of $d_{i,j}$ for sensor s_i.
- 1: unit lifetime during which sensor could operate actively.
- $xy\,(node)$: coordination function that provides location for *node*.
- ϖ: sensing angle of sensor.
- r: sensing range of sensor.

The target is covered means that it is within sensing direction of at least one sensor. In Fig.1, $a_m, 1 \le m \le 3$ denotes target, $s_i, 1 \le i \le 3$ denotes directional sensor, and $d_{i,j}, 1 \le i, j \le 3$ represents direction of sensor s_i. In addition, $d_{1,1}, d_{2,3}, d_{3,1}$ reflect current sensing directions of sensor s_1, s_2, s_3, respectively. Consequently, a_2, a_3 are covered by sensor s_3 in Fig.1.

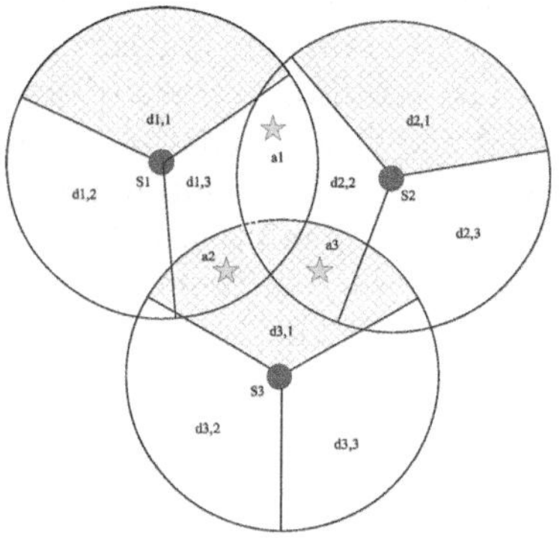

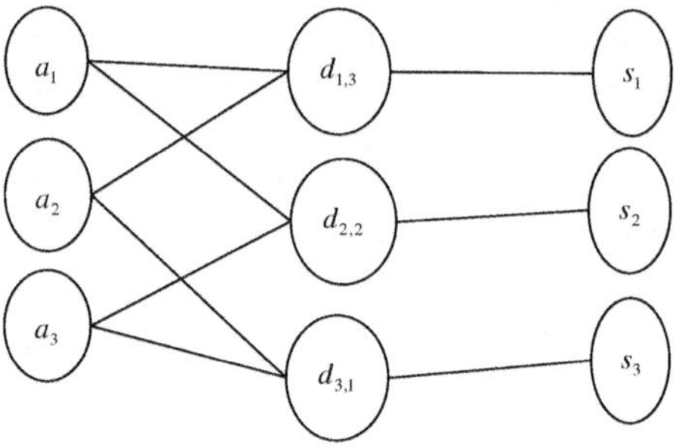

Fig. 1. Directional sensor network [1] **Fig. 2.** Augmented bipartite graph of Fig. 1

The maximum lifetime of directional sensor network in context of target coverage is defined as: Given target set A, sensor set S, coordination function $xy\,(node)$, sensing range r, sensing angle ϖ, and the constraint that each of the targets is covered by at least one sensor, the maximum or optimal network lifetime, during which the constraint is satisfied, and corresponding schedules for each sensors are formalized as following:

$$\text{Maxmize} \sum_k t_k, k \in \{1, \cdots, K\} \tag{1}$$

Subject to

$$S_k \subseteq S, \exists K \in [1, \infty), \forall k \in \{1, \cdots, K\} \tag{2}$$

$$a_m \prec s_i, s_i \in S_k, \forall m \in \{1, \cdots, m\}, \forall k \in \{1, \cdots, K\}, \exists i \in \{1, \cdots, N\} \tag{3}$$

$$\sum_k indicator\,(s_i \subseteq S_k) * t_k \leq 1, \forall i \in \{1, \cdots, N\} \tag{4}$$

$$indicator\,(X) = \begin{cases} 1 & X \text{ is true} \\ 0 & \text{otherwise} \end{cases} \tag{5}$$

The objective function (1) is to maximize sum of lifetime t_k for each sensor subset S_k. Constraint (2) indicates it is desirable to find K of subsets S_k. Constraint (3) guarantees every target a_m is covered by at least one active sensor s_i in each subset S_k, where $a_m \prec s_i$ means target a_m is located in sensing direction of sensor s_i. Constraint (4) ensures that no sensor use more than initial power. The constraint of direction conflict [1] is not explicitly reflected in above formulation because conflict is avoided in the randomized algorithm by defining *elementary sessions*. Note that the power consumption in terms of rotation as well as message transmission is not considered in this paper. Such omission could reveal more insight of sensor scheduling and they will be studied in future works.

3.2 Partition Algorithm for Sensing Directions

As rotation capability compensating for coverage limitation, sensor could rotate to different directions to enhance utility of coverage in context of specific application requirement. Theoretically sensor has infinite directions by rotating continuously. Here *Partition* algorithm is proposed to find all *independent* directions for each sensor, where independent directions represent no equal of their subsets of covered targets.

Algorithm 1: Partition algorithm for sensing directions

Input: sensor s_i, target set A, sensing range r, sensing angle ϖ, coordinate function $xy\,(node)$

Output: collection of target subsets: $cs^i = \{cs^i_1, \cdots, cs^i_j, \cdots\} \subseteq A$, $cs^i_j \neq \varnothing$

Let $B = \varnothing; cs^i = \varnothing$
FOR each $a \in A$
    IF $\|xy\,(a) - xy\,(s_i)\,\|_2 < r$ THEN $B = B \cup \{a\}$ END
END
IF B is $\varnothing$ THEN RETURN $\varnothing$ END
Let $V = \varnothing$
FOR each $a \in B$
    Compute offset angle de with respect to positive axis X, and $V = V \cup de$
END
FOR each $de \in V$

11. Get target set cs^i_j where each target is within angle de and $de - \varpi$. Note comparison is done in context of arithmetic module 2π
12. $cs^i = cs^i_j \cup cs^i$
13. END
14. RETURN cs^i

This algorithm searches for all *independent* directions of sensor s_i, where no direction could be derived by any other ones. $c_i = |cs^i|$. Obviously, such c_i has great impact on complexity of computation.

3.3 Augmented Bipartite Graph and Elementary Sessions

Figure 2 is an instance of augmented bipartite graph, where vertexes consist of targets, directions, and sensors. The left column of vertexes represents all targets A. The middle one is collection of directions of different sensors $\{d_{i,j}\}$. The last denotes sensor set S. With partition algorithm above, each sensor finds set of independent directions, under which target subset is covered. Then augmented bipartite graph is constructed: each target a_m links to each direction $d_{i,j}$, where it is covered. And sensor s_i connects to all its independent directions $\{d_{i,j}\}$. No explicit links between targets and sensors appear in the graph. The graph is well organized for clarity. Furthermore, the links within augmented bipartite graph are labeled with three rules.

Rule 1: the link between target a_m and direction $d_{i,j}$ is represented by $x_{m,i,j} \in \{0,1\}$. As continuous coverage is concerned, at least one direction covers a_m. That means $\sum_{i,j} x_{m,i,j} \geq 1$. $x_{m,i,j} = 1$ here means sensor s_i in direction $d_{i,j}$ covers target a_m.

Rule 2: the link between direction $d_{i,j}$ and sensor s_i is represented by $y_{i,j}$:

$$y_{i,j} = \begin{cases} 1 & x_{m,i,j} = 1 \\ 0 & \text{otherwise} \end{cases} \tag{6}$$

Rule 3: As the sensor s_i is only in one direction at any instant, at most one direction could be selected. That is $\sum_j y_{i,j} \leq 1$

Elementary session is defined as operation state vector of all sensors, where all targets are covered as well as no superfluous sensor is activated. That means if any sensor is removed from elementary session, some target is uncovered absolutely.

Constructs Cartesian tuples for $\{x_{m,i,j}\}$ within above 3 rules and Fig.3 is formed. The collection of $y_{i,j}$ of each row represents an elementary session, while the collection of $x_{m,i,j}$ reflects current sensing direction of each sensors. In Fig.3, same elementary session may correspond to different sets of sensing directions. Thus by removing duplicated elementary sessions, Fig.3 has four rows left: {#1,#2,#3,#7}. Let each row scheduled for periods t_1, t_2, t_3, t_4, respectively. The maximum network lifetime is transferred into linear programming problem:

$$\text{Maximize } t_1 + t_2 + t_3 + t_4 \tag{7}$$

Row \ Var	$x_{1,1,3}$	$x_{1,2,2}$	$x_{2,1,3}$	$x_{2,3,1}$	$x_{3,2,2}$	$x_{3,3,1}$	$y_{1,3}$	$y_{2,2}$	$y_{3,1}$
#1	1	0	1	0	1	0	1	1	0
#2	1	0	1	0	0	1	1	0	1
#3	1	0	0	1	1	0	1	1	1
#4	1	0	0	1	0	1	1	0	1
#5	0	1	1	0	1	0	1	1	0
#6	0	1	1	0	0	1	1	1	1
#7	0	1	0	1	1	0	0	1	1
#9	0	1	0	1	0	1	0	1	1

Fig. 3. All elementary sessions for Fig.2

Subject to

$$\begin{bmatrix} 1\,1\,1\,0 \\ 1\,0\,1\,1 \\ 0\,1\,1\,1 \end{bmatrix} * \begin{bmatrix} t_1 \\ t_2 \\ t_3 \\ t_4 \end{bmatrix} \leq \begin{bmatrix} 1 \\ 1 \\ 1 \end{bmatrix}, \text{ and } 0 \leq t_i \leq 1, i \in \{1,2,3,4\} \tag{8}$$

Resolving the problem and getting the solution: $[t_1, t_2, t_3, t_4]^T = [0.5, 0.5, 0, 0.5]^T$. That means network lifetime $T = \sum_i t_i = 0.5 + 0.5 + 0 + 0.5 = 1.5$. Thus, it indicates that network lifetime T reaches 1.5 times longer than individual sensor lifetime.

3.4 Randomized Approach for Lifetime

Now the randomized approach for lifetime of directional sensor network is proposed. Given target set $A = \{a_1, a_2, \cdots, a_M\}$, sensor set $S = \{s_1, s_2, \cdots, s_N\}$. First, partition algorithm finds direction collection of each sensor. Then they forms large set D=$\{d_{i,j}, 1 \leq i \leq N, 1 \leq j \leq c_i\}$. As every target a_m needs to be covered continuously, thus it must locate within some direction $d_{i,j}$. According to combinatorial theory, it has at most $\xi = P_{|D|}^{M}$ different cases for given targets set A. Obviously, some cases are infeasible because of direction conflicts, while some others may use inexistent link $x_{m,i,j}$. In addition, some feasible choice even use superfluous sensors. Consequently, removing them still guarantees target coverage and prolongs network lifetime. Finally, the maximum lifetime is achieved by finding all *elementary sessions* as well as linear programming technique. However, ξ increasing exponentially makes it impracticable for large scale network. Randomized approach approximates lifetime by reasonable size of *elementary session* set.

Algorithm 2: Random production of elementary session

Input: augmented bipartite graph AG, target set A, sensor set S

Output: random elementary session v

---

1. Let $U = A$; $v = [0]_{1*N}$
2. WHILE U is not $\varnothing$
3. Select target $u \in U$ randomly
4. Select d randomly from directions flowing out from target u in graph AG
5. Set corresponding bit in v to 1 for sensor of direction d
6. $U = U-$ {all targets covered by d simultaneously}
7. Remove d and those directions conflicting with d in AG, as well as corresponding sensor
8. Check AG and remove those links with one vertex left
9. END
10. RETURN v

This algorithm ensures that *elementary session* covers target set A, where no conflicting directions and superfluous sensors are selected.

Algorithm 3: linear programming for elementary session matrix

Input: the matrix V, each column accommodate an elementary session

Output: time period t_j for each elementary session

$$\text{Maximize} \sum_j t_j \tag{9}$$

Subject to

$$V * \begin{bmatrix} t_1 \\ \vdots \\ t_{|V|} \end{bmatrix} \leq \begin{bmatrix} 1 \\ \vdots \\ 1 \end{bmatrix}, t_j \geq 0, j = 1, \cdots, |V| \tag{10}$$

where $|V|$ denotes column number of matrix

This algorithm is effectively implemented by existing linear programming tools, such as *Matlab*.

Algorithm 4: Randomized approach for lifetime of directional sensor network

Input: target set A, sensor set S, direction set D, the minimum difference of lifetime between successive iterations ζ

Output: maximum lifetime T, duration t_j of each elementary session v_j

---

1. Construct augmented bipartite graph AG with direction set D, target set A, and sensor set S
2. Let $T = 0$; $\Delta = 0$; $V = \varnothing$; $\varphi = 200; round = 4$

3. DO
4. round=round-1
5. Get elementary session set $Z = \{v_1, \cdots, v_\varphi\}$ by running **algorithm 2** repeatedly.
6. $V = V \cup Z$
7. Get t_j for each $v_j \subseteq V, j = 1, \cdots, |V|$ by **algorithm 3**
8. $\Delta = \sum_j t_j - T$;
9. $T = \sum_j t_j$
10. IF $\Delta \geq \zeta$ THEN round=4 END
11. WHILE $round > 0$
12. RETURN T and $\{t_j, 1 \leq j \leq |V|\}$

In algorithm 4, the matrix V accommodates elementary session as column, and Δ holds the lifetime difference in successive iterations. In addition, φ is set as 200 as it is used in our simulations. Algorithm 4 introduces elementary session matrix by randomization. Then it determines the lifetime by linear programming. If lifetime difference between successive iterations drops below specified value ζ, the algorithm terminates the loop and returns lifetime T as well as duration set $\{t_j\}$. Obviously, the elementary session $v_j \in V$ is basic scheduling unit denoting each sensor sleeping or working.

In this paper we assume sensors have uniform sensing range, sensing angle, unit lifetime. However, the randomized algorithm proposed in this subsection is independent to them. Heterogeneous sensing range and sensing angle only impact result of algorithm 1, while algorithm 3 adapts heterogeneous initial sensor lifetime by modifying right part of the constraint, i.e. full one vector of column $[1, \cdots, 1]^T$. That means the randomized algorithm is general enough to apply in many other settings.

4 Simulation

We evaluate the randomized algorithm through simulations running on a computer with 1.5 GHz CPU and 512 MB memory. The algorithm is implemented upon the *Matlab*, which provides strong optimization toolboxes. For fair comparisons, the directional sensor network is configured similar to [1] as follows: N sensors with homogeneous sensing radius r and sensing angle ϖ, as well as M targets are scattered randomly in a region of $400m \times 400m$. The directions $\{d_{i,j}\}$ for each sensor s_i are searched by partition algorithm. The minimum lifetime difference between successive iterations ζ is set as 0.0001, the number φ of elementary sessions in bulk is set as 200. In addition, each result is averaged over 10 runs through random scattering sensors and targets.

Network Lifetime. Here the initial lifetime of sensor is set as 1 and sensing angle ϖ is set as $\frac{2\pi}{3}$, while $W = 3$ for feedback and progressive algorithms in [1].

Figure 4 shows the relationship between the network lifetime and number of sensors when $M = 10, r = 100m$. The network lifetime linearly increases as N increases. The randomized algorithm lies between progressive and feedback ones.

When number of sensor is fixed as 50 and that of targets is fixed as 10, we study the relationship between lifetime and sensing range in Fig.5. The lifetime increases as sensing range becomes larger. It is obvious that more targets could be covered with large sensing range. The similar result will appear when sensing angle ϖ becomes large or W in [1] drops down. The randomized algorithm still performs similarly to two others.

Now in Fig.6, we reveal the relationship between lifetime and number of targets when $N = 50, r = 100m, W = 3, \varpi = \frac{2\pi}{3}$. All of three algorithms get similar results and feedback one seems to be better according to network lifetime metric. In these three figures, we conclude that the randomized algorithm performs between progressive and feedback ones according to metric of network lifetime.

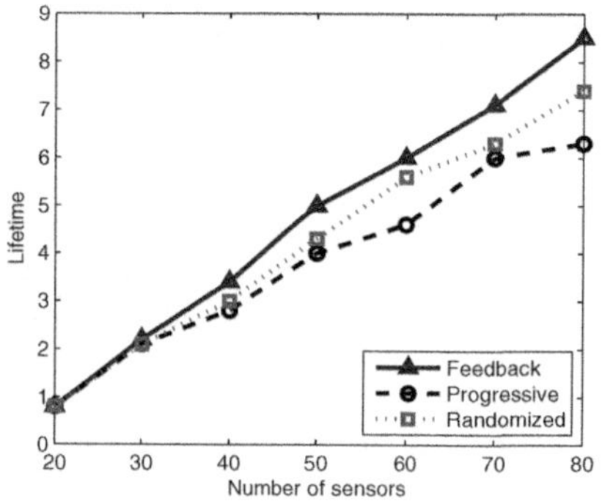

Fig. 4. Lifetime vs. number of sensors

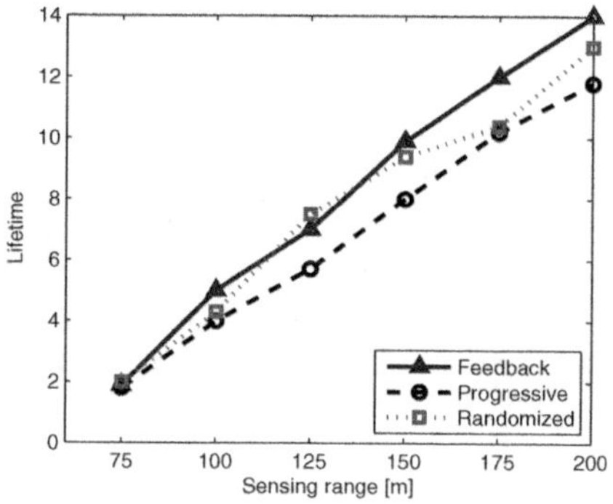

Fig. 5. Lifetime vs. sensing range

Runtime. We fix network with $r = 100m$, $M = 10$ targets. For feedback and progressive algorithm in [1], the W is set as 3, while sensing angle ϖ of randomized algorithm is set as $\frac{2\pi}{3}$. Figure 7 presents the runtime of progressive, feedback, and randomized algorithms. When sensor number N is low, three algorithms complete computation quickly. However, the feedback and progressive ones incurs large computation time when $N = 80$. Note that Fig.7 plot time as logarithmic scales. Feedback one incurs 15600 seconds and progressive requires 1800 seconds. On the contrary, the randomized one only consumes less than 7 seconds. Recall that both feedback and progressive run upon a computer with 3 GHz CPU and 1 GB memory, while randomized algorithm is on 1.5 GHz CPU and 512 MB memory. That is to say, randomized algorithm performs 500 times faster than progressive one, as well as even higher ratio to feedback one with little lifetime loss.

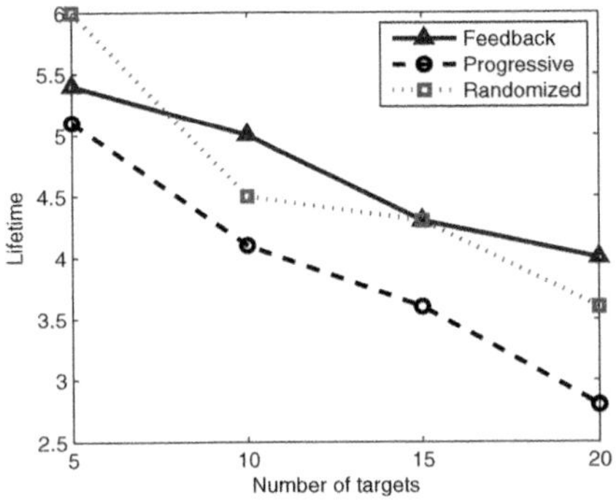

Fig. 6. Lifetime vs. number of targets

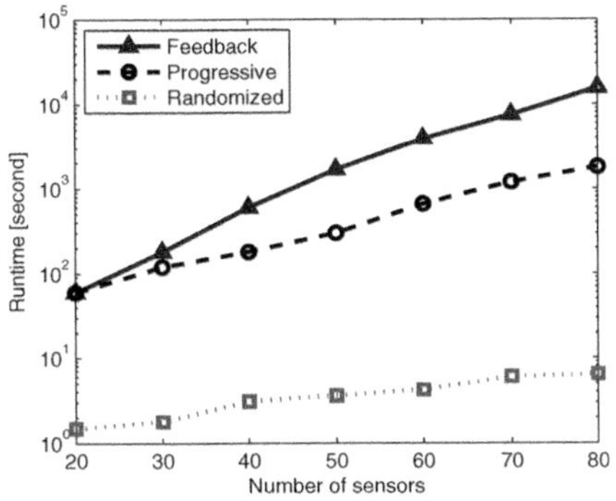

Fig. 7. Runtime vs. number of sensors

Faster ability of randomized algorithm implies that it could apply to larger directional sensor network. Now we give three reasonable explanations:

1. The algorithms in [1] encounter too many conflicts among directions. Each time they get the result of linear programming problem, many of them are useless due to conflicts. Even the large and stable number of variables in linear programming makes the computation harder because the complexity of linear programming is $O(n^3)$, where n is the number of variables. On the contrary, elementary sessions help randomized algorithm avoid direction conflict.
2. Sensor directions are not properly selected. Some of them are unnecessary. The partition algorithm in this paper finds all independent directions of each sensor.
3. Too much duplication makes randomized algorithm effective. In Fig.3, there exists same elementary session corresponding to different direction subsets. When sensor set and target set becomes larger, such phenomena occur even frequently. Thus there is not necessary to exhaust all direction subsets to approximate the optimum lifetime.

5 Conclusion

This paper studies targets coverage in directional sensor network. Due to abundance of sensors and limited sensing angle, there emerges a natural problem for how long the directional sensor network could operate with all targets being covered continuously. The lifetime is proved to be NP-Complete in [1]. Thus the approximating solution is searched for. We propose the randomized algorithm for lifetime, which greatly reduces computation time more than 500 times on average, when directional sensor network becomes larger, with little lifetime loss comparing to algorithms in [1]. Future work includes exploring much faster and more accurate algorithm for lifetime, incorporating power consumption of rotation and communication, and extending such randomized algorithm into decentralized equivalent.

References

1. Yanli Cai, Wei Lou and Minglu Li.: Target-Oriented Scheduling in Directional Sensor Networks. to be appeared in *IEEE INFOCOM 2007*
2. F. Ye, G. Zhong, J. Cheng, S. Lu, and L. Zhang.: PEAS: a robust energy conserving protocol for long-lived sensor networks. in Proceedings of *IEEE International Conference on Network Protocols (ICNP)* 2002.
3. C. Gui and P. Mohapatra.: Power conservation and quality of surveillance in target tracking sensor networks. in Proceedings of *ACM MobiCom 2004*, ,Sept. 2004, Philadelphia, PA, USA.
4. H. Zhang and J. C. Hou.: Maintaining sensing coverage and connectivity in large sensor networks. in *Ad Hoc & Sensor Wireless Networks, An International Journal*, 2005.
5. J. Lu, L. Bao, and T. Suda.: Coverage-aware sensor engagement in dense sensor networks. In Proceedings of *the International Conference on Embedded and Ubiquitous Computing - EUC 2005*, Dec. 2005.
6. K. Shih, Y. Chen, C. Chiang, and B. Liu.: A distributed active sensor selection scheme for wireless sensor networks. in Proceedings of *the IEEE Symposium on Computer Computers and Communications* June 2006.
7. T. Yan, T. He, and J. Stank Stankovic.: Differentiated surveillance for sensor networks. In Proceedings of *1st International Confer Conference on Embedded networked sensor systems*, 2003.
8. M. Perillo and W. Heinzelman.: Optimal sensor management under energy and reliability constraints. In Proceedings of *the IEEE Conference on Wireless Communications and Networking*, March 2003.
9. H. Liu, P. Wan, C. Yi, X. Jia, S. Makki, and P. Niki.: Maximal lifetime scheduling in sensor surveillance networks. in *IEEE INFOCOM 2005*, March 2005, Miami, Florida, USA.
10. M. X. Cheng, L. Ruan, and W. Wu.: Achieving minimum coverage breach under bandwidth constraints in wireless sensor networks. in *IEEE INFOCOM 2005*, March 2005, Miami, Florida, USA.
11. M. Cardei, M. T. Thai, Y. Li, and W. Wu.: Energy-efficient target coverage in wireless sensor networks. in *IEEE INFOCOM 2005*, March 2005, Miami, Florida, USA.
12. M. Cardei an and D. Du.: Improving wireless sensor network lifetime through power-aware organization. in *ACM Wireless Networks*, May 2005.
13. H. Ma and Y. Liu.: On coverage problems of directional sensor networks. in Proceedings of *International Conference on Mobile Ad-hoc and Sensor Networks (MSN)*, 2005.
14. J. Ai and A. A. Abouzeid.: Coverage by directional sensors in randomly deployed wireless sensor networks. *Journal of Combinatorial Optimization*, vol. 11, no. 1, Feb. 2006, pp. 21-41.

Efficient Time Triggered Query Processing in Wireless Sensor Networks

Bernhard Scholz[1], Mohamed Medhat Gaber[2],
Tim Dawborn[1], Raymes Khoury[1], and Edmund Tse[1]

[1] The University of Sydney
Sydney, NSW, Australia
[2] CSIRO
Hobart, TAS, Australia

Abstract. In this paper we introduce a novel system that comprises techniques advancing the query processing in wireless sensor networks. Our system facilitates time triggered queries that are scheduled in a distributed fashion among sensor nodes. Thus, time synchronisation is of paramount importance. Since accurate time synchronisation requires more energy, our system allows a trade off between precision of time and energy according to the user requirements. To minimize the communication overhead for query processing, our system employs new query execution mechanisms.

We have implemented our query processing system on Sun™ Small Programmable Object Technology (SPOT) sensor network platform. The system was entirely programmed in Java enabling an object oriented design and implementation. It provides a friendly graphical user interface for query management and visualisation of results.

Keywords: Wireless communications and ad hoc networks, distributed query processing, communication and energy optimisations, time triggered protocols.

1 Introduction

With the advent of smart sensor devices, wireless sensor networks are an emerging research field [1,2]. Wireless sensor nodes form a wireless ad-hoc network with a large number of nodes which operate without direct human interaction. The applications of wireless sensor networks are diverse and include environment and habitat monitoring [3], traffic control [4], health monitoring [5], supply-chain management [6], security and surveillance systems, and smart homes.

In this work we are concerned with distributed query processing [1,7] in sensor networks. Users are typically interested in continuous streams of sensed data from the physical world. Query processing systems [8,9,10] provide a high-level user interface to collect, process, and display continuous data streams from sensor networks. These systems are high-level tools that allow rapid-prototyping of wireless sensor network applications. In contrast, writing wireless sensor network applications in a systems language such as C is tedious and error-prone.

Y.-H. Lee et al. (Eds.): ICESS 2007, LNCS 4523, pp. 391–402, 2007.

A query processing system abstracts from tasks such as sensing, forming an ad-hoc network, multi-hop data transmission, and data merging and aggregation. A state-of-the-art distributed query system for wireless sensor networks is TinyDB [8] that employs a subset of SQL as an underlying language for queries. In this system the user specifies declarative queries that perform the sensing tasks. For example the query `select avg(temp) from nodes` reports the average temperature of the area covered by the sensor network.

TinyDB forms a routing tree with all sensors in the network. The root of the routing tree is the base station (aka. gateway) that is connected to a PC. Every other node in the wireless sensor network maintains a parent node that is one step closer to the base station. Queries are flooded throughout the network and the query answers are collected and propagated through the routing tree. The query processing consists of three phases: (1) the query preparation phase inputs, parses, and optimises a query at the user's PC, (2) the broad-casting phase injects the sensing and collecting task into the sensor network, and (3) the data collecting phase makes results flowing up and out of the network to the PC where the results are displayed and stored in a disk-based DBMS for later access.

This paper describes a new query processing system for a new wireless sensor network platform Sun SPOT [11,12], that has been developed at Sun Research Labs. This new platform has a 32bit ARM Risc processor, an 11 channel 2.4GHz radio, and approx. 100 times more memory than a state-of-the-art platform such as Berkley Motes [13]. The platform is programmed in Java™ and features a sensor board for I/O and an 802.15.4 radio for wireless communication. The Sun SPOT system runs "Squawk VM" that is a lightweight J2ME™ virtual machine (VM). The VM executes wireless sensor network applications "on the bare metal", i.e., directly on the CPU without any underlying OS, saving overhead and improving performance. With more memory and a faster CPU alternative design decision can be made to minimise energy-costly communication by applying new time-triggered protocols for aggregation.

We have designed and implemented a time-triggered query engine for wireless sensor networks, called SSDQP, which is a distributed query processor that runs on each Sun SPOT. The new platform is programmed in Java. Hence, a clean object-oriented design of the engine was possible.

The contribution of our work is as follows:

- a new design of an acquisitional distributed query (ACQP) system that is time-triggered,
- a time synchronisation mechanism of the nodes that allows a trade-off between cost and accuracy,
- a new communication model for ACQP.

The paper is organised as follows: In Section 2 we survey the related work. In Section 3 we give an overview of our ACQP system. In Section 4 we discuss the trade-off between power consumption and time accuracy of the time synchronisation. In Section 5 we show the advantages of merging results at node level. In Section 6 we draw our conclusion.

2 Related Work

Distributed query processing in wireless sensor networks has been an active research area over the last few years. TinyDB [8] and Cougar [14] represent the first generation of query processing systems in wireless sensor networks. The main objective in these systems has been to preserve the limited power by attempting to reduce the communication overhead. This in turn prolongs the network lifetime.

TinyDB and Cougar [15] provide an SQL-like query language. Sensor data is viewed as a single virtual table. The data is appended at time intervals specified in the query termed as epochs. Results from every sensor find their way to the root node (the node that connects directly to the base station) through a routing protocol. Query lifetime has been introduced for the first time in query processing systems to serve the sensor network applications. The user can specify how long the query should be processed. Pushing computation is used in two forms: partial aggregation and packet merging. In partial aggregation, distributive query operators are used in-network. Intermediate results are then passed to the root to integrate the results. On the other hand, packet merging is used to reduce the communication overhead produced from sending multiple packet headers. Query optimisation is done locally at the central site. Once the query is optimised, the network is flooded through the routing tree to ensure every child node has heard the query. Multiple trees could be formed to allow simultaneous query processing. However, overlay among routing trees can lead to performance decay.

Open issues that have not been addressed in TinyDB and Cougar [15] include multi-query optimisation, storage placement and heterogeneous networks. In multi-query optimisation, the resource utilisation is an open research issue. Storage placement is how to choose nodes that are representative of in-network data and what fault tolerance techniques are required if the storage node fails. TinyDB and Cougar consider only homogeneous networks in which all nodes have the same power. Heterogeneous networks provide new research challenges to the community.

3 Sun SPOT Distributed Query Processing (SSDQP)

The Sun SPOT Distributed Query Processing system consists of two programs: (1) the *query engine* that is executed on the Sun SPOTs and (2) the *control system* on the user's PC that is connected to the base station.

The query engine is implemented as a set of time-triggered tasks. The task scheduler of the query engine executes a task if the start time of the task has been reached. The task scheduler maintains the active tasks in a time queue. Furthermore, tasks can be periodically executed with a fixed time period and the number of repetitions is parameterisable. Tasks can be added and removed from the time queue of the task scheduler. The start time of a task is "global" throughout the network such that sensing and communication can be done in

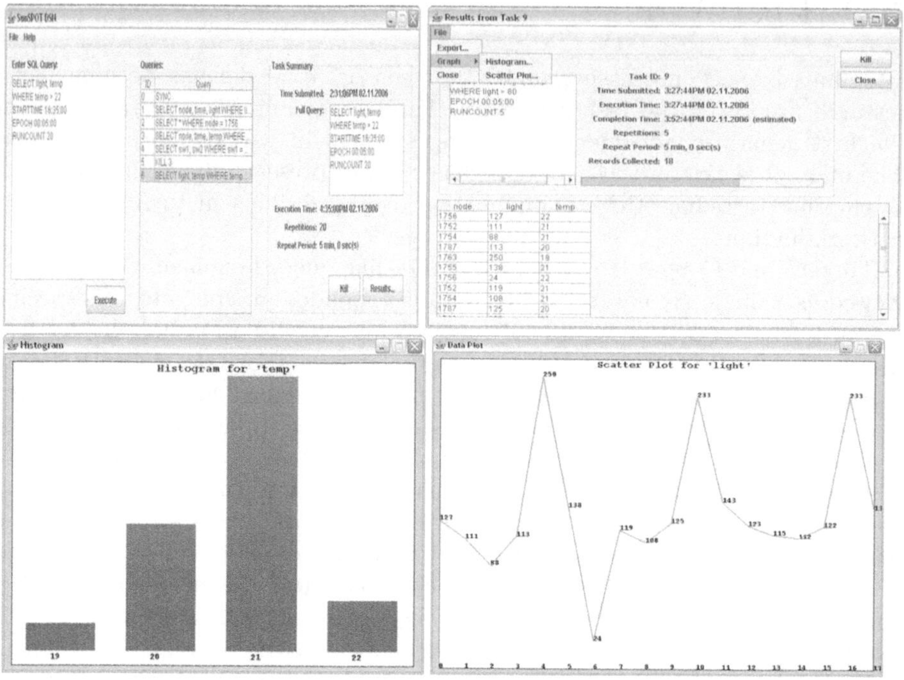

Fig. 1. Screenshots of SSDQP

a synchronised fashion. The query engine has a time synchronisation task that keeps the clocks of the Sun SPOTs in the network in sync.

Query tasks are composed of relational algebra operations that operate on relational tables. Since all sensor readings of the Sun SPOTs are integer values, the system does only support integer attributes in the relational tables. The query engine supports all the fundamental query operators including selection, projection, join and aggregation. In addition to these basic functionalities, there are

- the *sense operation* that reads the values of the sensors and creates a result table with the sensor readings,
- the *forward operation* that takes the input table and forwards the table to the parent node in the routing tree,
- the *merge operation* that receives result tables from the children in the routing tree, merges the tables, and gives as a result the merged tables.

The query operations are represented as expression trees in the query engine. A string representation of the expression tree is used for its contruction, which is sent from the control system to a Sun SPOT node. To minimise the size of

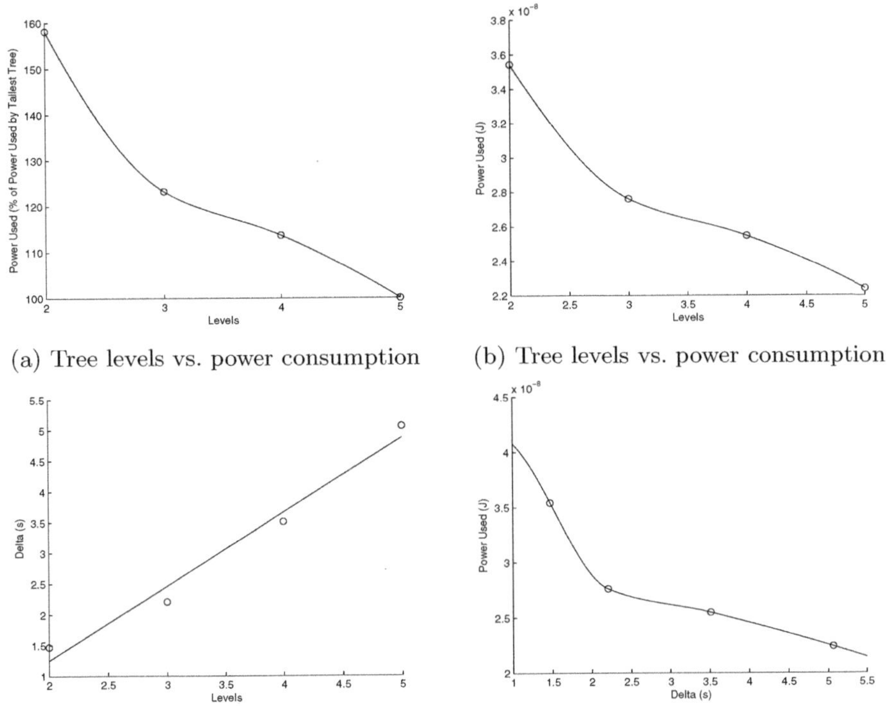

(a) Tree levels vs. power consumption

(b) Tree levels vs. power consumption

(c) Tree levels vs. accuracy

(d) Accuracy vs. power consumption

Fig. 2. Power Consumption

messages (and therefore energy), a basic data compression method is used. The data compression achieves compression rates of about 62% in practice.

The control system runs on the user's PC that is connected to the base station. It is also written in Java. The control system

- inputs and parses SQL queries, optimises the queries, and translates them into distributed relational query operations, which are deployed in the network,
- collects the data from deployed queries,
- manages deployed queries, (i.e., status of deployed queries, termination of deployed queries, etc.),
- provides the global time to all nodes in the network,
- displays and depicts results of queries.

The control system has also a friendly graphical user interface for query input and result visualisation as shown in Figure 1. The system is fully written in Java following true object-oriented software engineering practices. This gives our system the advantage of simple system maintenance and extension.

4 Accuracy Guaranteed Efficient Time Synchronisation

Wireless senor networks are dynamic. New nodes join the network and others die frequently. Static time synchronisation is infeasible in such computing environments. Consequently, time synchronisation techniques run frequently consuming the network energy and shortening its lifetime. Accurate time synchronisation leads to accurate query results due to the low time shifts among network nodes. The performance of time synchronisation techniques degrades with the increase in the network size. This occurs due to the increase in the number of hops to reach distant nodes from the base station. This problem could be overcome by increasing the power level of network nodes. This in turn decreases the number of hops to reach distant nodes. Thus, accurate time synchronisation is achieved at the cost of higher energy consumption. We have developed a parameterised optimiser in our SSDQP system that makes a trade-off between accuracy of time synchronisation and consumed energy. The user inputs an acceptable level of time shift (Δ) between the system time at the base station and the system time at a node in the network. Depending on the application the time shift Δ varies. Our optimiser chooses a network tree topology that minimises the consumed energy (E) and achieves a level of time shift $\Delta' \leq \Delta$. Let us assume that the number of hops of node u to the base station is denoted as h_u and the energy that is consumed for a single hop is e. The total energy E for time synchronisation is given by

$$E = \sum_{u \in T} e \cdot h_u \qquad (1)$$

where T is the topological tree used for time synchronisation. The achieved time accuracy Δ' depends on the maximum h_u in the network, i.e., $\Delta' = \mu \max_{u \in T} h_u$ where μ is the time shift introduced by a single hop. We seek for a topology such that E becomes minimal and $\Delta' < \Delta$.

4.1 Experimental Study

The aim of our experimental study is to provide simulation-based evidence of the significance of our efficient time synchronisation approach described earlier. The experimental setup is described in the following: Considering a full binary tree of height (number of levels)= 5. The radio power setting(I) to reach a parent

- 1 level above is $I = p = p$
- 2 levels above is $I = p + \frac{p}{3} = \frac{4p}{3}$
- 3 levels above is $I = p + \frac{2p}{3} = \frac{5p}{3}$
- 4 levels above is $I = p + p = 2p$

where p is the power setting required to reach a parent one level above. The delta between levels is calculated with a normal distribution, $\mu = 0.4s$. The goal of our first experiment is to show the trade-off between accuracy of time synchronisation and the energy consumed. By varying the number of levels in the routing tree, depending on the accuracy of time synchronisation required, it can be shown that a

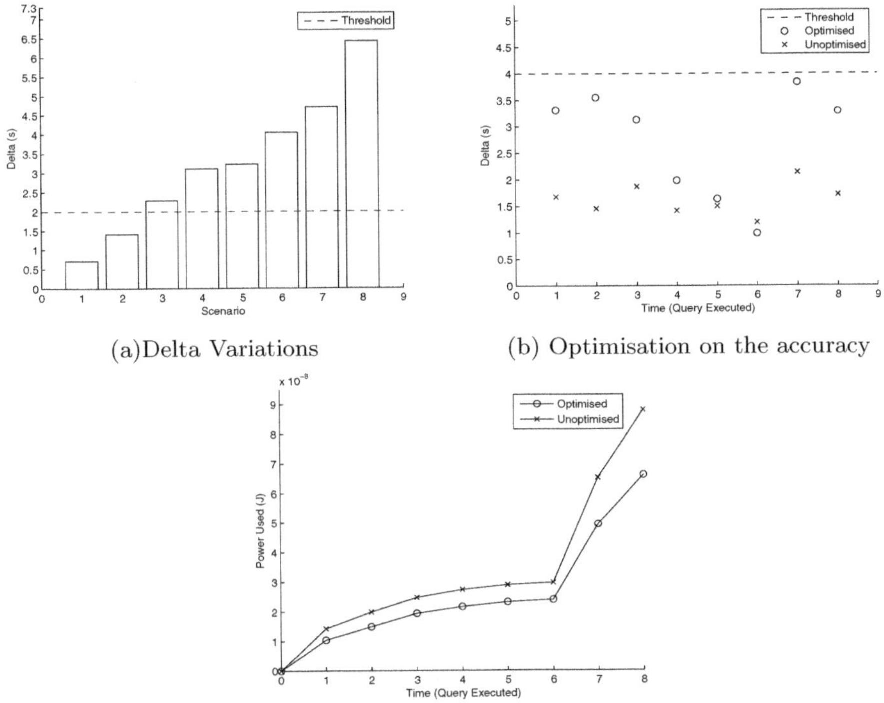

(a)Delta Variations

(b) Optimisation on the accuracy

(c) Power consumption over time

Fig. 3. Accuracy vs. Power Consumption

trade-off between time synchronisation and power consumption of a node can be achieved. A reduction in the number of levels of the tree is accomplished by increasing the radio power level of a node so that it can transmit data to its grandparents, great-grandparents, etc. effectively skipping levels. For a tree with 5 levels, trees with 4, 3 and 2 levels can be constructed from the nodes of the original tree, given that all nodes are able to transmit to one another with a high enough radio power level. For a given delta in time synchronisation required by the users query, one routing tree from these 4 trees can be selected in order to achieve the delta, with a trade off in power. As shown in Figures 2(a)-(d), a reduction in levels of the tree increases power consumption (for one time synchronisation of the entire tree) substantially, however will yield a smaller delta.

In the first experiment we provide evidence that with no optimisation of the routing tree, the accuracy of time synchronisation achieved can exceed the accuracy pre-specified by the user. Assuming a system operating with a fixed routing tree which has been designed to achieve maximum power efficiency, the tree which is being operated on has 5 levels and various subtrees may be synchronised depending on the query scenario executed. Suppose that the user requires a maximum delta in time synchronisation of 2s. As shown in 3(a), although for

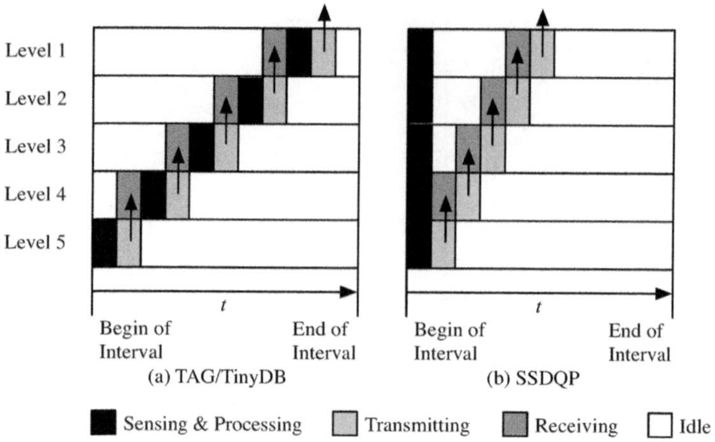

Fig. 4. Communication Model

some small subtrees the accuracy of the synchronisation is achieved, for queries executed over larger subtrees, the delta exceeds the desired threshold delta. This is done at the cost of unnecessary power consumption, which, in time, can substantially reduce the lifetime of the network. Take again a system with a fixed routing tree however this time it has been designed to achieve maximum accuracy in time synchronisation. Assuming that the user requires a maximum delta of 4s, as shown in 3(b), the unoptimised system always achieves a delta substantially below the threshold in all scenarios. Our system, which selects a tree based on the delta, also achieves a delta below the threshold however it is much closer to the threshold. 3(c) shows the power consumption over time of the network as a whole with each system, as various queries are executed. As shown, there is a significant difference in power consumption, particularly when large subtrees are being operated on (queries 7 and 8).

5 Communication Model

In the design of SSDQP we had the choice to either adopt the communication model of TinyDB [8] (and TAG [16] respectively) or to create a new communication model. Since the Sun SPOTs have more memory and more computational power than Berkley Motes; we designed a new communication model. This new communication model is optimised for repetitive queries and has following properties:

- timeliness of sensing, i.e., all nodes in the network sense at the same time, and
- minimised communication overhead achieved by a synchronised merge of results. Therefore, the new communication model uses less energy.

The communication model of TinyDB and TAG [16] is illustrated in Fig. 4(a). The partial information of a query flows up the network toward the root node.

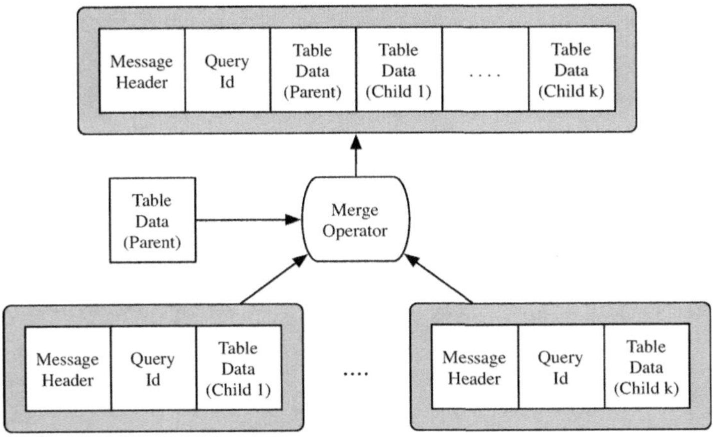

Fig. 5. Merge Operator

In a sensing interval (aka. epoch) a sensor node has four different states: a sensing and processing state, a sending state, a receiving/listening state, and an idle state. If the node is an inner node in the tree, the sequence of states is as follows: (1) receiving state where all the information of the children is gathered, (2) sensing and processing state, (3) sending state in which the information is forwarded to the parent node in the tree network and (4) followed by the idle state. If the node is a leaf node, then the receiving state is omitted because there are no children attached to the sensor node.

The disadvantage of the TinyDB/TAG model is that the point in time when the sensing and processing is performed depends on the tree level in the network. Note that for queries that do *not* have aggregation (e.g. AVG, SUM, etc) the sensed data is directly forwarded to the root node without aggregation. The information is "bubbled up" the network tree. In contrast, the SSDQP communication model de-couples sensing from the aggregation as illustrated in Fig. 4(b). The task scheduler of a sensor node performs two tasks for a single query: the first task performs sensing, and the second task performs the aggregation and the forwarding to the parent node. Both tasks are time-triggered. The second-task needs to be scheduled such that there is enough time for the children to provide their aggregated information. Therefore, the point in time of the second task depends on the child that needs the longest time span to provide the information, i.e. the child whose sub-tree has greatest depth. Even for simple queries without aggregation the partial information of query is merged at all levels before forwarded to the parents in the network tree.

Partial information collected by several sensor nodes is sent in a packet structure consisting of three parts: message header, a query identification, and the actual partial result of a query. The packet structure imposes communication overhead stemming from the message overhead of the Sun SPOT network as well as book-keeping information for the query system. We seek for a communication model that minimises the total number of packets to reduce the communication

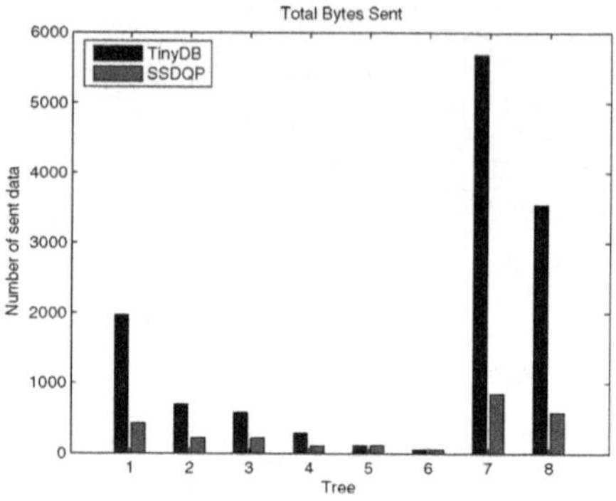

(a) Number of Bytes

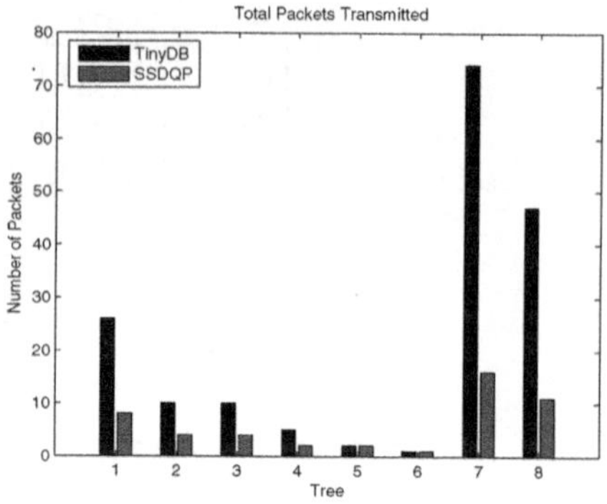

(b) Number of Packets

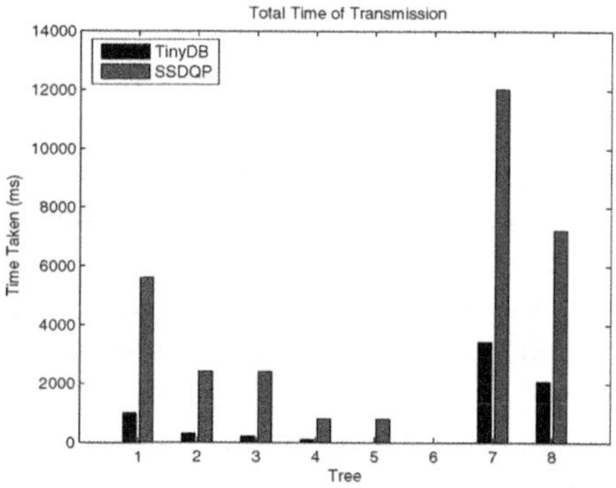

(c) Latency

Fig. 6. Comparison with TinyDB communication model

overhead. We achieve this in our model by a *synchronised merge* operation. This means that a node merges the information of its own data and the data of its children before forwarding it to its parent node. If there are n nodes in the network, we need for one epoch exactly n messages whereas TinyDB/TAG forwards the information without merging the partial information or an on the fly merging in the network layer is used. The consequence is that in the worst case TinyDB has $O(n^2)$ messages for a single query.

The merge operation of a node is depicted in Figure 5. The disadvantage of the merge operation is that more memory is needed in a sensor node and that the latency of a query increases because a time slack for merge operations is to be taking into account for.

A simulation of both communication models was conducted on 8 network trees of various depth and density. For the simulation we used the query `select * from sensors`. The comparison of both communication models is shown in Fig. 6. The first bar-chart in Fig. 6(a) shows the total amount of bytes sent for a single epoch. The information sent in the SSDQP communication model is significant less because there are significant less packets sent in total (cf. Fig. 6(b)).

The total number of sent bytes is proportional to the energy used for the transmitter of the radio and has a great impact on the longevity of the nodes in the network. Especially for trees with larger depth the SSDQP communication model is superior to the communication model of TinyDB because the communication overhead for a single message packet is large in comparison to the data length of a sensor reading.

However, establishing well defined merge points for an inner node increases the latency (cf. 6(c)), i.e. the time span between the begin of an epoch and the point in time when the base station receives the result of a query. Because the information is immediately streamed from the nodes, the TinyDB model is more responsive.

6 Conclusion

In this paper, we have presented our novel distributed query processing system (SSDQP). The system is built on the new Sun SPOT platform from Sun Microsystems. Special considerations in the system design have been paid to preserve energy by minimising the required communication overhead. This paper has proven experimentally that our time synchronisation optimiser can achieve the required accuracy while minimising the required energy. An experimental comparison between our system and TinyDB has shown that our system outperforms TinyDB in terms of communication overhead.

References

1. Zhao, F., Guibas, L.: Wireless Sensor Networks – An Information Processing Approach. Elsevier / Morgan-Kaufman, Amsterdam (2004)
2. Culler, D.E., Hong, W.: Introduction. Commun. ACM **47**(6) (2004) 30–33
3. Szewczyk, R., Osterweil, E., Polastre, J., Hamilton, M., Mainwaring, A., Estrin, D.: Habitat monitoring with sensor networks. Commun. ACM **47**(6) (2004) 34–40
4. Chen, L., Chen, Z., Tu, S.: A realtime dynamic traffic control system based on wireless sensor network. In: ICPPW '05: Proceedings of the 2005 International Conference on Parallel Processing Workshops (ICPPW'05), Washington, DC, USA, IEEE Computer Society (2005) 258–264
5. Lu, K.C., Wang, Y., Lynch, J.P., Lin, P.Y., Loh, C.H., Law, K.H.: Application of wireless sensors for structural health monitoring and control. In: Proceedings of KKCNN Symposium on Civil Engineering, Taiwan (2005)
6. Liu, W., Zhang, Y., Lou, W., Fang, Y.: Managing wireless sensor networks with supply chain strategy. In: QSHINE '04: Proceedings of the First International Conference on Quality of Service in Heterogeneous Wired/Wireless Networks (QSHINE'04), Washington, DC, USA, IEEE Computer Society (2004) 59–66
7. Woo, A., Madden, S., Govindan, R.: Networking support for query processing in sensor networks. Commun. ACM **47**(6) (2004) 47–52
8. Madden, S.R., Franklin, M.J., Hellerstein, J.M., Hong, W.: Tinydb: an acquisitional query processing system for sensor networks. ACM Trans. Database Syst. **30**(1) (2005) 122–173

9. Intanagonwiwat, C., Govindan, R., Estrin, D., Heidemann, J., Silva, F.: Directed diffusion for wireless sensor networking. IEEE/ACM Trans. Netw. **11**(1) (2003) 2–16
10. Demers, A., Gehrke, J., Rajaraman, R., Trigoni, N., Yao, Y.: The cougar project: A work in progress report (2003)
11. Simon, D., Cifuentes, C., Cleal, D., Daniels, J., White, D.: Java on the bare metal of wireless sensor devices: the squawk java virtual machine. In: VEE '06: Proceedings of the 2nd international conference on Virtual execution environments, New York, NY, USA, ACM Press (2006) 78–88
12. Microsystems, S.: (Sun spot world) http://www.sunspotworld.com/.
13. Hill, J., Horton, M., Kling, R., Krishnamurthy, L.: The platforms enabling wireless sensor networks. Commun. ACM **47**(6) (2004) 41–46
14. Yao, Y., Gehrke, J.: The cougar approach to in-network query processing in sensor networks. SIGMOD Rec. **31**(3) (2002) 9–18
15. Gehrke, J., Madden, S.: Query processing in sensor networks. IEEE Pervasive Computing **03**(1) (2004) 46–55
16. Madden, S., Franklin, M.J., Hellerstein, J.M., Hong, W.: Tag: a tiny aggregation service for ad-hoc sensor networks. In: OSDI '02: Proceedings of the 5th symposium on Operating systems design and implementation, New York, NY, USA, ACM Press (2002) 131–146

Dependable Geographical Routing on Wireless Sensor Networks

Yue-Shan Chang[1], Ming-Tsung Hsu[2], Hsu-Hang Liu[3], and Tong-Ying Juang[1]

[1] Dept. of Computer Science and Information Engineering, National Taipei U.
151, University Road, Sanhsia, Taipei County, 237, R.O.C.
{ysc,juang}@mail.ntpu.edu.tw
http://web.ntpu.edu.tw/~ysc/
[2] Institute of Information Management, National Taiwan U.
No. 1, Sec. 4, Roosevelt Road, Taipei, 10617 Taiwan
d94725004@ntu.edu.tw
[3] Institute of Information Management, National Taipei U.
151, University Road, Sanhsia, Taipei County, 237, R.O.C.
hsuhang.liu@gmail.com

Abstract. Geographic routing protocols on Wireless Sensor Network (WSN) had been researched for many years, but they did not concern with the fault problem. In this paper, we propose an approach to enhance dependability of existing geographical routing protocols to deal with the fault problem and consider the routing problem based on the fault map via query-driven models. For query-driven model, a novel algorithm, called Relay Node Selection Algorithm (RNSA) is proposed, which selects a few relay nodes as temporary destinations. Simulation shows that the success rate of data transmission originated from base station can be raised substantially and the hop count is also reduced via the selected relay nodes.

1 Introduction

Most applications of WSNs [1] sensors were deployed over harsh environment such as chemical reactor and battlefield that with high temperature, high noise, and various interferences, which could incur probably sensor nodes work or communication improperly. Of course that will raise invalid respond to seek or requester [2]. A fault estimation model was proposed and based on it to construct fault map [3]. The principle of the model is that the sensor nodes transmitted the detected event to cluster head with some extra sensed data, such as outward temperature and noise. While the desired event sensed by nodes, it transmits the extra sensed data to cluster head. The cluster head will calculate the fault probability according to the extra sensed data and send it back to base station. The fault map can be considered as the information about the location and fault probability of sensor nodes. As the increase of sensed events, the base station can know the distribution of fault nodes in the network gradually.

The development of geographical routing protocols [4, 5] were expanded in WSNs since recent advances in small, low-power and inexpensive Global Positioning System (GPS) receivers and other location services [6, 7]. These routing protocols are

Y.-H. Lee et al. (Eds.): ICESS 2007, LNCS 4523, pp. 403–414, 2007.

concerned with the distance relation among sensor nodes and the remaining energy of sensor nodes. However, when the fault nodes are met in the process of routing, they deal with the problem by retransmitting data. Obviously this behavior is not energy efficient for WSNs. Furthermore, the fault nodes may send the invalid respond to seek or requester. For the reasons, the existing routing protocols can not handle the fault problem. Thus, with the fault information, data retransmission and invalid respond can be avoided by making decision in advance.

The objective of the paper is to develop the strategies that assist the existing geographical routing protocols to deal with the fault problem in WSNs. We consider the routing problem with the fault map via query-driven data delivery models. For query-driven model, a novel algorithm, called Relay Node Selection Algorithm (RNSA) is proposed, which represents the fault regions as convex hull [8] and selects a few of relay nodes as temporary destinations. The advantage of RNSA is low cost, since the base station only need to add the location information of the relay nodes to data packets and exploit existing geographical routing protocols to reach the interesting region. Simulation shows that the success rate of data transmission originated from base station can be raised substantially and the hop count is also reduced via the deployment of relay nodes found by RNSA.

The rest of paper is organized as follows. Section II describes the preliminaries of our research including basic assumption, useful definition, and routing with fault information. The proposed routing algorithms: RNSA is depicted in Section III and Section IV shows numerical performance results. Section V reviews the existing geographical routing protocols in WSNs. Finally, we draw the main conclusion and future work.

2 Preliminaries

2.1 Basic Assumptions

The communication behaviors among sensor nodes are the key function of the sensor networks. The sensor nodes route data between the base station and sensor nodes in a hop-by-hop way by communicating with each other within the communication range r. All sensor nodes inside the communication range r of node x are considered as neighbors of x, as shown in Fig. 1. To sum up, the network model is represented as a unit disk graph (short for UDG) G (V, E), where V is the set of sensor nodes and $E \subseteq V \times V$ is the set of bidirectional communication links between pairs of nodes.

To facilitate the discussion, we make some reasonable assumptions as follows:

1. Sensor nodes are location-aware.
2. Sensor nodes have the location of their neighbors.
3. The deployment of sensor nodes is dense.
4. The generation of fault nodes is with dependency.
5. Sensor nodes have the fault probability of their neighbors.
6. Base station has the fault probability of sensor nodes in the whole network.

For 1 and 2, each node can get the location information of itself via GPS or other location services and then broadcasts to its neighbors. For 3, each sensor node has at

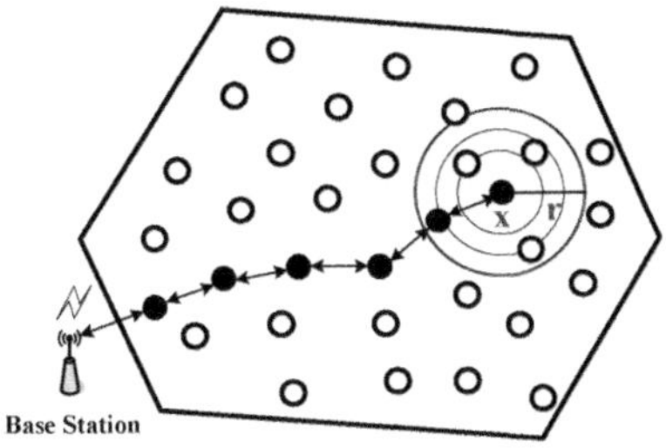

Fig. 1. The network model

least one neighbor. For 4, fault nodes generated by random fault unlikely cause large range of fault region on the terrain, thus they can be bypassed easily by selecting another neighbor. For 5 and 6, these assumptions derive from the process and result of fault map construction.

2.2 Definitions

Before describing proposed approach, we list some definition used in the approach. The convex hull of a geometric object is the smallest convex set containing that object. Because of the characteristic of convex polygon, the adjacent fault nodes are included by minimum number of sensor nodes and redundant paths that get into the fault region are avoided by representing the fault region as convex hull. For example, as shown in Fig. 2, due to the routing path have got into the fault region, it may fail inside the region or increase redundant path. Hence, the computational complexity of finding relay nodes and the failure rate of routing can be reduced using convex hull. Convex set and convex hull are defined as follows:

Definition 1. Convex Set: A set S is convex if whenever two points P and Q are inside S, then the whole line segment PQ is also in S.

Definition 2. Convex Hull: The convex hull of a Convex Set S = {P} is the smallest 2D polygon W that contains S. That is, there is no other polygon L with $S \subset L \subseteq W$.

To define the fault region is the prior assignment before RNSA is introduced. One may notice that the target needed to be avoided is the fault region, neither fault node nor fault line, since they can be bypassed easily by selecting another node. To start with, the fault nodes are decided by whether its fault probability is greater than the threshold. Next, the communication links among those fault nodes are established. Lastly, the fault region represented as convex hull is found by containing all the fault nodes inside the connected graph with cycle. We define the fault/normal node and fault region as follows:

Definition 3. Fault node: A node x in a sensor network graph G (V, E) is a fault node if the probability of $x > \alpha$, where α is the threshold of fault probability.

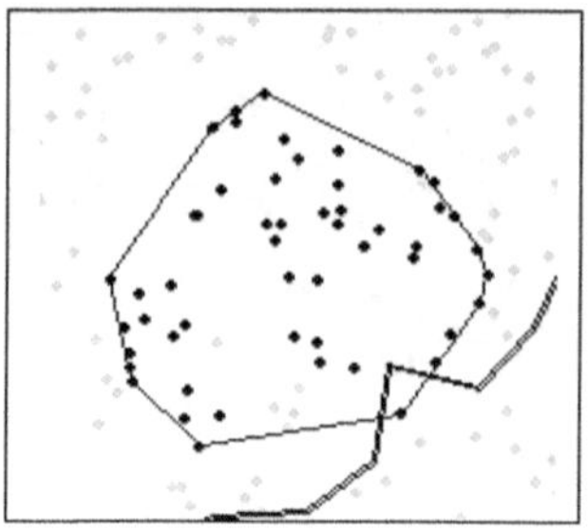

Fig. 2. A fault region is represented by convex hull

Definition 4. Normal node: A node x in a sensor network graph G (V, E) is a normal node if the probability of x <= α, where α is the threshold of fault probability.

Definition 5. Fault region: Given a sensor network graph G (V, E), a fault region (the convex hull in Fig. 3) is represented as convex hull by containing all fault nodes inside the connected cycle sub-graph G_s (V_s, E_s) of G (V, E) that is not included by the same property of sub-graph, where V_s is the vertex set of fault nodes that are connected with each other and $E_s \subseteq V_s$ x V_s is the edge set that consists of communication links between any pair of fault nodes in V_s. Besides, any of two conditions below must be satisfied:

In order to bypass the fault regions, we select a few relay nodes and consider them as temporary destinations. Data packets replace the location of destination on each relay node and the path can be navigated to avoid those fault regions. The definitions of border node and relay node are as follows:

Definition 6. Border node: A node *x* in a sensor network graph G (V, E) is a border node if it is on the border of the fault regions.

Definition 7. Relay node: A node *x* in a sensor network graph G (V, E) is a relay node if it is outside of all the fault regions and be one of the nearest neighbors among the border nodes that are on the shortest path found by RNSA.

2.3 Routing with Fault Information

According to our assumptions, the base station knows the fault probability of sensor nodes in the whole network, thus it finds the path to sensor nodes that locate behind the fault regions in a centralized way when data source is at base station. Conversely, since sensor nodes only know the fault probability of its neighbors due to energy constraint, they find the path to base station or other sensor nodes in a distributed way when data source is on sensor nodes.

Since the base station knows the fault probability of sensor nodes in the whole network, how to exploit them to find the routing path and increase the success rate of routing is our design goal. First of all, a fault region is formed by adjacent fault nodes and be represented as convex hull. Then considering the scenario below, base station wants to make queries in an interesting region, so it must find the path to bypass the fault regions effectively. Although base station has the fault probability of sensor nodes in the whole network, it may not know the position of normal nodes that have never sensed interesting events. Therefore, our idea is to find a few relay nodes around the fault regions and use them as temporary destinations.

In Fig. 3(a), the base station (the large circle in black) wants to query the interesting region (the large square in black) and the fault region (the convex hull) must be avoided on routing path. First, the destination of data packets set to the relay nodes (the middle circles in black). After the packets pass through all relay nodes orderly, the destination of the packets will be replaced with actual destination (the central node of the interesting region). Finally, the routing path (the black line) can be built effectively, since it neither around the fault regions tightly nor get into the fault regions. Similarly, Fig. 3(b) shows the same process of bypassing three fault regions. In addition, it is low cost in the process of routing, since we only need to add the location of the relay nodes to data packets and exploit the existing geographical routing protocols to reach interesting region. In order to focus on routing problem, convex hull, fault region, and relay node are defined below and the details of RNSA are introduced in the next section.

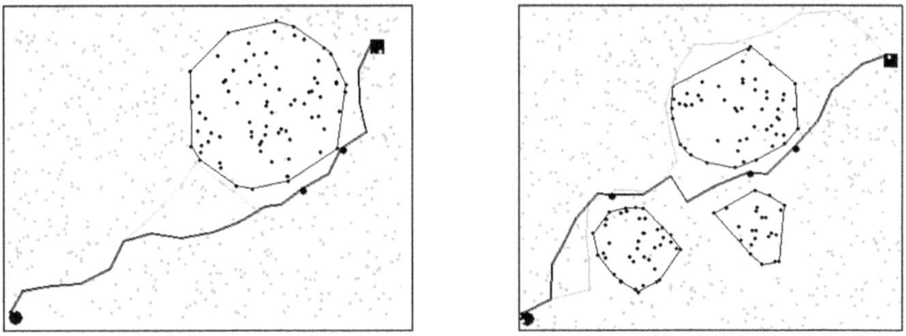

(a) (b)

Fig. 3. Relay nodes for bypassing fault regions: the line in black and gray present the routing path built with relay nodes and without relay nodes respectively. (a). One fault regions (b) three fault regions.

3 Routing Algorithms

We now describe our algorithms, the Relay Nodes Selection Algorithm (RNSA) is for query-driven model, and explain how to integrate them with the existing geographical routing protocols.

3.1 Relay Nodes Selection Algorithm

When there is only one fault region between base station and interesting region, the relay nodes can be simply found in the upper or lower side of it. However, there are possibly more than one fault regions due to the harsh environment of sensor networks.

Therefore, the purpose of RNSA is to find the relay nodes among various fault regions. The steps are shown as Fig. 4.

In the first step, the threshold is set for defining fault nodes, as the black nodes in Fig. 5(a). In step 2, the fault regions are found by connecting the fault nodes within the communication range and represented as convex hulls by containing all fault nodes belong to the connected graph with cycle, as the convex hulls in Fig. 5(b). The algorithm of Graham Scan [8] is applied to find convex hull here. Step 3 is to find the first fault region crossed by the line between base station and interesting region, as shown in Fig. 5(c). However, if there is no fault region between base station and interesting region, RNSA will be terminated since the path can directly reach interesting region. In order to optimize the routing path, all possible fault regions should be considered, thus step 4 is to find the convex hull that includes the first fault region, base station and interesting region, as shown in Fig. 5(d). Next, it is checked if the border node of the convex hull is crossed by any fault regions. If it does, finding the new convex hull that contains the fault regions crossed by the convex hull. It is repeated until that the border of the convex hull is not crossed by any fault regions. This is shown in Fig. 5(e). Step 6 is to find all possible paths among the border nodes that have normal neighbors inside of the minimum convex hull and the paths crossed by any fault regions should be erased, as the lines in Fig. 5(f). Then the shortest path can be found using Dijkstra algorithm [9] in step 7, as the bold line in Fig. 5(g). Eventually, the final step is to find the nearest neighbor of border nodes on the shortest path as relay nodes, as the large circles in black in Fig. 5(h). The order of relay nodes is according to the order of the border nodes on the shortest path from base station to interesting region.

1. Set the threshold for defining fault nodes;
2. Define fault regions and represent them as convex hulls;
3. Find the first fault region crossed by the line between base station and interesting region;
4. Find the convex hull that includes the fault region, base station and interesting region;
5. Find the minimum convex hull whose border do not be crossed by any fault regions;
6. Find all the paths among base station, interesting region and border nodes;
7. Find the shortest path between base station and interesting region;
8. Find the nearest neighbor of the border nodes on the shortest path as relay nodes;

Fig. 4. Steps of RNSA

Then, we analyze the time complexity of RNSA. The time complexity of RNSA is $O(m*nlgn) + O(N^2)$. $O(m*nlgn)$ is for executing step 2, where *nlgn* is for Graham Scan, *m* is the number of fault regions and n is the number of fault nodes. $O(N^2)$ is for executing Dijkstra algorithm in step 7, where *N* is the number of border nodes.

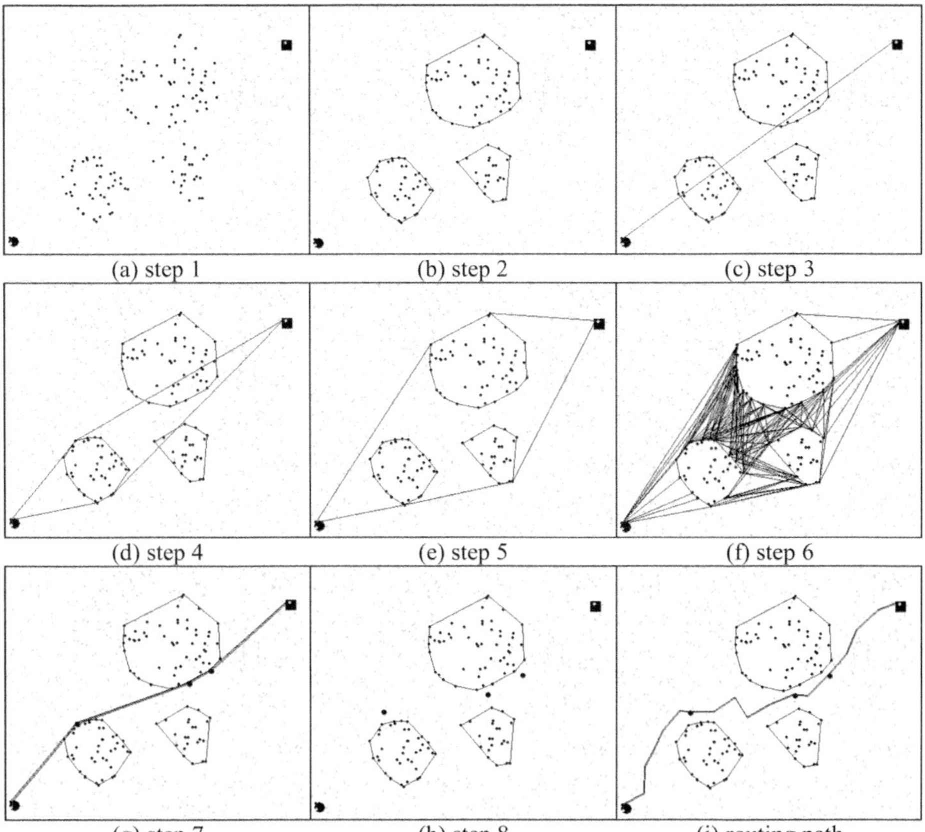

Fig. 5. Result of RNSA algorithm

```
//Initially
Relay node list = arrange the relay nodes from base station to interesting region;
Destination node = the first node in the relay node list;
//When sensor nodes receive data packets
If ( this senor node is the destination node )
  If ( there still have relay nodes in the relay nodes list ){
    Set the next relay node as the destination node;
    Forward to next node using the existing geographical routing protocol;
  }
  Else
    Broadcast the data packets to all nodes inside of the interesting region;
Else
  Forward to next node using the existing geographical routing protocol;
```

Fig. 6. Apply the relay nodes to the existing geographical routing protocols

3.2 Routing Protocol Via Relay Nodes

After the executing above steps, the relay nodes are applied as the temporary destinations and the routing path can be built effectively by integrating with the existing geographical routing protocols, as the bold line in Fig. 5. The algorithm is shown in Fig. 6.

4 Simulation

We first introduce the simulation environment includes its parameters. Then the advantages of our algorithms are presented by comparing with various criteria.

4.1 Simulation Environment

We implement the proposed algorithms to evaluate the performance using Java. The simulation parameters are listed in Table 1. 1000 sensor nodes are deployed in a 500m x 500m area and the transmission range of each node is 35m. The base station is located at (0, 500) and the interesting region along with sensed node are located at (480, 20). In addition, the position of fault region is generated randomly and the fault probability of nodes decreases progressively from the center of fault region. For the effectiveness of the evaluation, the well-known GPSR is chosen as the geographical routing protocol in our simulation.

Table 1. Parameters used for simulations (the parameters with star will vary for evaluating the performance)

Network Size	500m x 500m	*Number of Nodes	1000
*Communication Range	35m	*Number of Fault Regions	4
*Radius of Fault Regions	60m	Location of Base Station	(0,500)
Location of Interesting Region and Sensed Node	(480,20)	Geographical Routing Protocol	GPSR

4.2 Simulation Result

For judging the effect of bypassing fault regions, the criteria of RNSA are considered as success rate and hop count and the following metrics are evaluated: (1) number of fault regions, (2) radius of fault regions, (3) communication range, and (4) density. Besides the success rate and hop count, correct probability of routing is also considered as the criteria of the per-node rule, since its goal is to control the dependability of routing.

In Fig. 7(a), the success rate of GPSR with relay nodes is higher than GPSR about 15 percent even if number of fault regions is increasing. The difference of hop count presented in Fig. 7(b) is unapparent. This is because the fault regions generated randomly are not always located close to the shortest path between base station and interesting region. Furthermore, the hop count is counted only when the routings are successful simultaneously. Fig. 9 shows the impact of radius of fault regions. The success rate of GPSR with relay nodes is still superior and the difference of hop count is raised with the increase in radius of fault regions, as shown in Fig. 8(a) and 8(b) respectively.

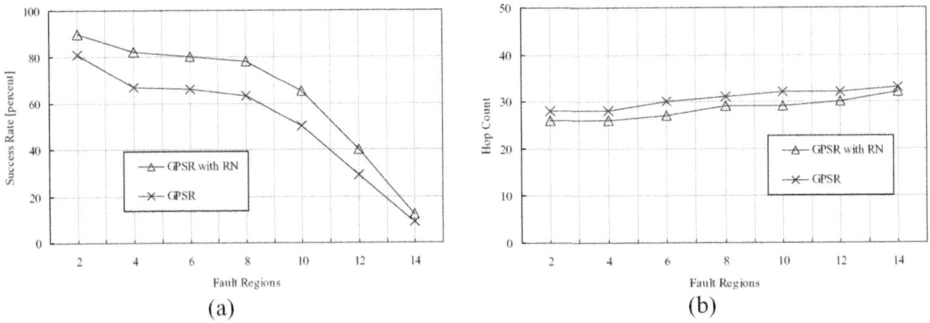

Fig. 7. The impact of number of fault regions (the success rate and hop count of routing without fault regions are 99% and 23 respectively). (a) success rate (b) hop count.

The next two metrics will add a new comparable routing path: GPSR without fault regions. It ignores all fault regions and is referred to the optimal outcome. The impact of communication range is shown as Fig. 9. The success rate of GPSR with relay nodes is close to GPSR without fault regions with the increase of communication range, as shown in Fig. 9(a). The reason is that the routing path could be found easily when the number of neighbors of sensor nodes is raised. Fig. 9(b) shows that the hop count of GPSR with relay nodes is between GPSR without fault regions and GPSR. The same as communication range, the increase of density represents number of neighbors of sensor nodes is raised in Fig. 10, thus the routing path could be found easily. The hop count of GPSR with relay nodes is also between GPSR without fault regions and GPSR.

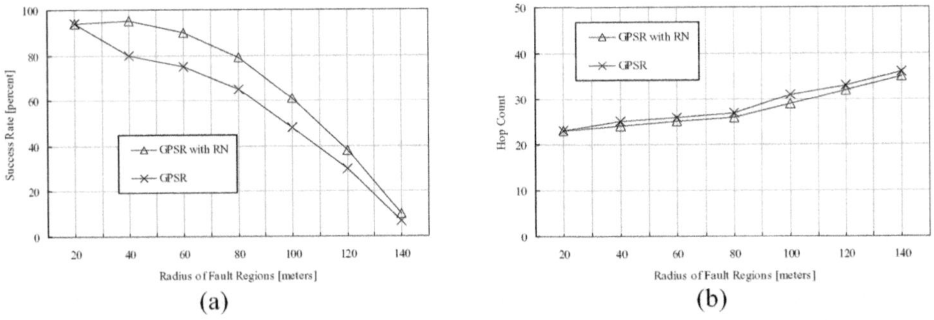

Fig. 8. The impact of radius of fault regions (the success rate and hop count of routing without fault regions are 99% and 23 respectively). (a) success rate (b) hop count.

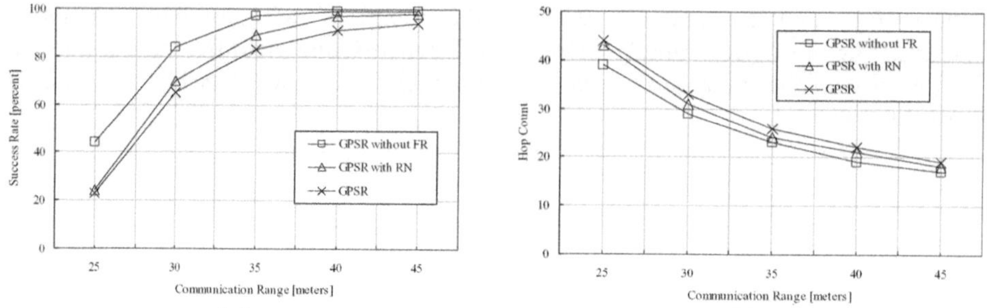

(a) (b)

Fig. 9. The impact of communication range. (a) success rate (b) hop count

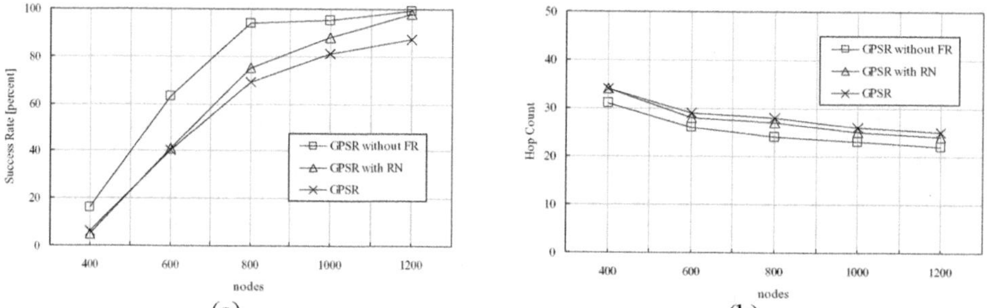

(a) (b)

Fig. 10. The impact of density. (a) success rate (b) hop count

To sum up, the simulation result shows that the success rate of the data transmission originated from base station can be raised substantially and the hop count is also reduced via the deployment of relay nodes.

5 Related Works

Most of the routing protocols for sensor networks require location information for sensor nodes [11]. Also, it has been shown [12] that routing protocols that do not exploit geographical location information are not scalable.

Sensor nodes select the next-hop neighbor within its communication range in various ways. Finn [10] proposed the greedy routing scheme, which selects the closest neighbor to the destination as next-hop. Compass routing scheme [13] selects the neighbor that minimizes the angle between the line to the destination and the line to the neighbors.

Next, we review some geographical routing protocols for WSNs. Greedy perimeter stateless routing (GPSR) [4] uses the positions of routers and a packet destination to make packet forwarding decisions and makes greedy forwarding decisions using only information about a routers' immediate neighbors. When a packet reaches a region where greedy forwarding is impossible, the algorithm recovers by routing around the perimeter of the region. Comparing with GPSR, geographical and energy-aware routing (GEAR) [5] uses extra energy aware neighbor selection to route a packet towards the target region. Each node keeps an estimated cost and a learning cost of reaching the destination through its neighbors. The estimated cost is a combination of remaining energy and distance to destination. The learned cost is a refinement of the estimated cost that accounts for routing around holes in the network. This strategy attempts to balance energy consumption and thereby increase network lifetime. Variable transmission range protocol (VTRP) [14] allows the transmission range to increase in various ways. Thus, data propagation exhibits high fault-tolerance by bypassing obstacles or fault sensor nodes and increases network lifetime since critical sensors close to the base station are not overused.

6 Conclusions and Future Work

In this paper, we have proposed our algorithms based on the fault map: RNSA is for query-driven model, and integrated with the existing geographical routing protocols. The simulation result shows the outperformance of our algorithms. The success rate of the data transmission originated from base station can be raised substantially and the hop count is also reduced via the deployment of relay nodes.

The threshold for defining fault nodes is concerned with the dependability and the success rate of routing. Improper threshold will cause routing with high dependability but low success rate or high success rate but low dependability. Thus, how to dynamic adjust the threshold according to the fault situation of network is the first future work. Similar to the fault nodes, the sensor nodes with low remaining energy may generate invisible obstacles in the terrain. These blocks areas will multiply and grow as time goes on due to the energy constraint of sensor nodes. Therefore, the second future work will consider both the fault probability and remaining energy of sensor nodes.

References

1. Akyildiz, F., Su, W., Sankarasubramaniam, Y., Cayirci E.: Wireless sensor networks: a survey. Computer Networks 38 (2002) 393-422,.
2. Krishnamachari, B., Iyengar, S.: Distributed bayesian algorithms for fault-tolerant event region detection in wireless sensor networks. IEEE Transaction on Computers 53 (2004) 241-250.
3. Chang, Y. S., Juang, T. Y., Lo, C. J., Hsu, M. T., Huang, J. H.: Fault estimation and fault map construction in cluster-based wireless sensor networks. IEEE International Conference on Sensor Networks, Ubiquitous, and Trustworthy Computing, Vol. 2. (2006) 14 – 19.
4. Karp, B., Kung, H. T.: GPSR: Greedy perimeter stateless routing for wireless networks. 6th Annu. Int. Conf. on Mobile Comput. Netw., Boston, MA, (MobiCom 2000), 243–254.
5. Yu, Y., Estrin, D., Govindan, R.: Geographical and energy-aware routing: a recursive data dissemination protocol for wireless sensor networks. UCLA Computer Science Department Technical Report, 2001.
6. Ji, X., Zha, H.: Sensor positioning in wireless ad-hoc sensor networks using multidimensional scaling. INFOCOM 2004. Twenty-third Annual Joint Conference of the IEEE Computer and Communications Societies Vol. 4, (2004) 2652 – 2661.

7. Hongyang, C., Ping, D., Yongjun, X., Xiaowei, L.: A robust location algorithm with biased extended Kalman filtering of TDOA data for wireless sensor networks. International Conference on Wireless Communications, Networking and Mobile Computing, Vol. 2, (2005) 883 – 886.
8. O'Rourke, J.: Computational Geometry in C (Second Edition), Cambridge University Press, 1998.
9. Skiena, S.: Dijkstra Algorithm. §6.1.1 in Implementing Discrete Mathematics: Combinatorics and Graph Theory with Mathematica. Reading, MA: Addison-Wesley, (1990) 225-227.
10. Finn, G. G.: Routing and addressing problems in large metropolitan scale Internetworks. ISI Res. Rep. ISU/RR-87-180, (1987).
11. Al-Karaki, J. N., Kamal, A. E.: Routing techniques in wireless sensor networks: a survey. IEEE Wireless Communications, Vol. 11, No. 6, (2004) 6-28.
12. Jain, R., Puri, A., Sengupta, R.: Geographical routing using partial information for wireless ad hoc networks. IEEE Personal. Communication, Vol. 8, No. 1, (2001) 48–57.
13. Kranakis, E., Singh, H., Urrutia, J.: Compass routing on geometric networks. 11th Canadian Conference Computer Geometry, 1999.
14. Boukerche, A., Chatzigiannakis, I., Nikoletseas, S.: A new energy efficient and fault-tolerant protocol for data propagation in smart dust networks using varying transmission range. Computer Communications, Vol. 29, No. 4, (2006) 477-489.

Minimization of the Redundant Coverage for Dense Wireless Sensor Networks

Dingxing Zhang[1,2], Ming Xu[1], Shulin Wang[1], and Boyun Zhang[1]

[1] School of Computer, National University of Defense Technology, Changsha, China
[2] Computer Department,
Guangdong Technical College of Water Resources & Electric Engineering, Guangzhou, China
green_cordillera@yahoo.com.cn

Abstract. Density control is a promising method to conserve system energy and prolonging lifetime of wireless sensor networks. In this paper, we address the issue of maintaining sensing coverage of surveillance target in large density wireless sensor networks and present an efficient technique for the selection of active sensor nodes. First, the At Most k-Coverage Problem (AM k-Coverage) is defined and modeled as a nonlinear integer programming. Second, Genetic Algorithm which is a quasi-parallel method to construct set cover is designed to solve the multi-objective nonlinear integer programming. And later by using Genetic Algorithm, a central algorithm is designed to organize a sensor network into coverage sets. Finally, Experimental results show that the proposed algorithm can construct the coverage sets reliably and reduce the number of active sensor nodes which is helpful to reduce system energy consumption and prolong the network lifespan.

Keywords: AM k-Coverage, coverage sets, multi-objective optimization, genetic algorithm, Pareto-optimal.

1 Introduction

Tiny and low-cost sensor nodes have made possible the applications of a large number of sensors to accomplish a large sensing task. Since sensor nodes are usually deployed in the ground where access to the area of the objectives to be monitored is difficult or dangerous, it is out of the question to replace or recharge the battery energy. Density control is a promising approach to conserving system energy and extending lifetime of wireless sensor networks. Thus, the coverage problem poses another important issue when controlling density.

Most of previous researches on density control focus on dividing the sensor network into disjoint subsets that every subset completely covers all sensing objects. In [5], [10], for the individual targets coverage, authors designed dominating set algorithms. Cardei and Du [3] address maximum disjoint coverage sets problem and mold the disjoint sets as disjoint coverage sets that every set can completely monitor all the target points. Therefore, they proposed an efficient method to extend the sensor network lifetime by dividing the sensors into a maximal number of disjoint coverage sets. For many sensor network applications, it is preferable to only cover target objects as full as possible while minimizing energy consumption due to the following

Y.-H. Lee et al. (Eds.): ICESS 2007, LNCS 4523, pp. 415–424, 2007.

factors. First, since these coverage subsets are in active mode alternately, the coverage quality can be guaranteed statistically by setting an appropriated subset number even if few blinds occur in coverage subsets. For dense sensor networks, that is, the coverage blinds are not static and can be covered by another subset at another time as long as it is within the sensing range of certain sensor nodes. Second, as the sensing task always correlates with particular application, to improve the coverage quality in practice, the redundant target objects often are set when a target is very important.

Some of previous researches on coverage problems focus on constructing a mathematic model to obtain solution of the problems. Chakrabarty et al [2] adopted the first ILP (Integer Linear Programming) model to study grid sensing field problems in which the ILP model contains quadratic constraints. Cardei et al. [4] improved the network lifetime by further relaxing the constraints of disjoint set covers, i.e., one node can be in multiple set covers.

In the paper, we limit the upper bound of coverage degree on each target to guarantee a lower redundancy. Since we do not limit the lower bound of coverage degree, coverage blinds (i.e., targets are not covered by any sensor nodes in a coverage subset) may occur when a coverage subset is constructed. In the problem, we hope that minimal sensor nodes and blinds occur in coverage subsets. To solve these two problems, one of possible method is to consider the joint optimization on the minimum size of coverage subset and the number of coverage blinds. Thus, an Integer Nonlinear Programming model with $(n+m)$ variables and $2m$ constraints is presented in this paper.

Due to the multiobjective optimality conditions, the resulting optimization problem gives rise to a set of optimal solutions, instead of a single optimal solution. In the parlance of multi-criterion decision-making, multiple optimal solutions are Pareto-optimal [1]. Taking many other Pareto-optimal solutions in the search space into account, we can not think that any of them is optimal besides choosing better solutions from the set of obtained Pareto-optimal solutions according to application requirements. Let us illustrate this aspect with a two-objective optimal problem shown in Figure 1. The figure considers f_1 and f_2 two objectives, both of which are to be minimized. The point A represents a solution which incurs a near-minimal f_2, but is highly accident-prone. On the other hand, the point E represents a solution which is near least f_2. If both objectives are important goals of design, we cannot really say whether solution A is better than solution E, or vice versa. One solution is better than other in one objective, but is worse in the other. In fact, there exist many such solutions (like solution C) which also belongs to the Pareto-optimal set and one cannot conclude about an absolute hierarchy of solutions A, B, D, or any other solution in the set without any further information. All these solutions are known as Pareto-optimal solutions.

Since GA often deals with a population of points, it can capture multiple Pareto optimal in the population. Moreover, GA can encode the solution in a chromosome-like data structure to represent the solution of the problem.

The major contributions of this paper are as follows. First, we propose **At Most *k* Coverage Problem (AM k-Coverage)** to construct the maximal number of cover sets. The degree of coverage is flexible in this framework. Second, the central algorithm is proposed to divide the dense the wireless sensor network into coverage subset based on GA, which is a quasi-parallel method.

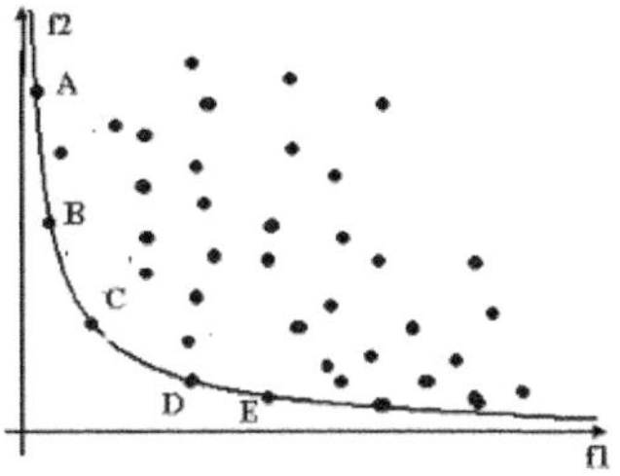

Fig. 1. The concept of Pareto-optimal solutions is illustrated

The rest of the paper is organized as follows. In Section 2, we propose the basic hypothesis and problem definition. Section 3 presents multiobjective optimization using GA to solve the problem raised in the section 2. Section 4 presents the Central algorithm based on GA. Detailed results of performance evaluations are presented in Section 5. Finally in Section 6, we conclude the paper.

2 The Basic Hypothesis and Problem Definition

2.1 Basic Hypothesis and Problem Definition

We consider the wireless sensor network with a large number of sensor nodes which are randomly deployed are close to the target objects which have all known the coordinate. These sensor nodes gather data which are sent to base stations (i.e., central data collector nodes). The sensing data might be processed at the base stations or at the local sensor nodes. Besides, sensor networks can be assumed as follows: (1) all the sensor nodes are static and have the same computation capabilities. (2) Each sensor node has two power states: active and asleep, and energy dissipation is negligible in the sleeping state. (3) Devices can be time-synchronized so that activity decisions can occur in rounds. (4) Like most existing algorithms, sensor nodes know their respective positions since positioning issue has already been addressed [8].

Given a set of sensors, a set of targets and the sensor-target coverage map, we limit the upper bound of coverage degree on each target to guarantee a lower redundancy. We give the definition of the **At Most k Coverage Problem (AM k-Coverage)** as follows:

Definition 1. AM k-Coverage: Given a sensor network with n sensor nodes and a target set $\boldsymbol{T}$ with m targets, we find a family of coverage sets, such that (1) we minimize the number of sensor nodes in coverage sets and the coverage blinds, (2) each target is covered by at most k sensor nodes.

As wireless sensor networks are often deployed randomly by aircrafts, it is difficult to guarantee uniformly distributing sensor nodes in real-world. Thus, a flexible frame to construct coverage sets has to be designed. In **AM k-Coverage** definition, each target object is covered by at most k sensor nodes while differ from the previous work in this field [16].

2.2 Multi-objective Integer Programming Formulation

In this section, we present the Multi-objective Integer Programming Formulation for the **AM *k*-Coverage** problem. We are first given a set of n sensor nodes S={s_1,s_2, … ,s_n}

and a set of targets T={ $t_1, t_2, \ldots, t_m$ }. In addition, a relational matrix $C=(c_{ij})_{n\times m}$ between sensor nodes and targets is given, where c_{ij} is a Boolean variable, for i=1…n, j=1…m, if the target t_j is covered by sensor s_i, then c_{ij}=1, otherwise c_{ij}=0. Let define the Boolean variable x_k (k=1…n) as follows: x_k=1, if the sensor node s_k is selected in a coverage set, otherwise, x_k=0. Using the variables above, we were able to formulate the relational problem.

Definition 2. Total Overlapping Coverage of Single Target (TOC): Let S = $\{s_i| i=1\ldots n\}$ be a wireless sensor network and a target set ***T*** with m targets t_k (k=1…m), the Total Overlapping Coverage of the target t_j is defined as $\sum_{i=1}^{n} c_{ij}x_i$ (j=1…m).

In the definition TOC, the term $\sum_{i=1}^{n} c_{ij}x_i$ is the coverage overlapping of the target t_j. We also define the following Boolean variable y_p(p=1…m) which indicates whether or not target t_p is covered by at least active sensor node(y_p =0, if target t_p is covered by at least an active sensor node, otherwise, y_p =1). Thus, in certain coverage subset, the total cost of coverage blinds is denoted as $\sum_{p=1}^{m} v_p y_p$,where v_p is the weigh of the target point p. According to the above, **AM k-Coverage** can be formally defined as follows: Given a sensor network with n sensor nodes and a target set ***T***, we find a family of sensor nodes to construct a coverage set, to minimize the total cost of coverage blinds $\sum_{p=1}^{m} v_p y_p$ and the total sensor nodes $\sum_{i=1}^{n} w_i x_i$ in the coverage set, **TOC** of each target is at most k, i.e., $\sum_{i=1}^{n} c_{ij}x_i \le k$, j=1…m, where k is some given integer. Without loss of generality, we assume that the cost for keeping a node awake is the same for all sensor nodes. We can further formulate the combinational optimization problem, **AM k-Coverage**, as the following multiobject integer programming problem:

$$
\begin{aligned}
&\textbf{Objective: } \text{Minimize } f_1(x_1\ x_2\ \ldots\ x_n) = \sum_{i=1}^{n} w_i x_i \\
&\qquad\qquad\quad \text{Minimize } f_2(y_1\ y_2\ \ldots\ y_m) = \sum_{j=1}^{m} v_j y_j \\
&\textbf{Subject to } y_j + \sum_{i=1}^{n} c_{ij}x_i \ge 1,\ j = 1\ldots m \\
&\qquad\qquad\quad y_j \sum_{i=1}^{n} c_{ij}x_i = 0,\ j = 1\ldots m \\
&\qquad\qquad\quad \sum_{i=1}^{n} c_{ij}x_i \le k,\ j=1\ldots m \\
&\qquad\qquad\quad x_i, y_j \in \{0,1\},\ i=1\ldots n,\ j=1\ldots m
\end{aligned}
\tag{1}
$$

where w_i , v_k are respectively the weigh of the sensor node i and the target object k. The constraint $y_j + \sum_{i=1}^{n} c_{ij}x_i \ge 1, j = 1\ldots m$ and $y_j \sum_{i=1}^{n} c_{ij}x_i = 0, j = 1\ldots m$ guarantee that y_j =0 is not simultaneous with $\sum_{i=1}^{n} c_{ij}x_i = 0$. That is, if the variable $y_j \neq 0$, then formulate $\sum_{i=1}^{n} c_{ij}x_i = 0$ and vice versa. The constraint, $\sum_{i=1}^{n} x_i c_{ij} \le k$ for all j=1…m, guarantees that each target is covered by at most k active sensors at the working duration of each coverage set.

Obviously, there are 3m constraints in the problem (1), of which 2m is linear and m nonlinear. However, we carefully analyze the constraints $y_j + \sum_{i=1}^{n} c_{ij}x_i \ge 1, j = 1\ldots m$ and $y_j \sum_{i=1}^{n} c_{ij}x_i = 0, j = 1\ldots m$, they only indicate a dependent relation between the vector ***x*** and ***y***. That is, if we obtain the solution vector $\mathbf{x} = (x_1\ x_2\ \ldots\ x_n)$, accordingly, the solution vector $\mathbf{y} = (y_1\ y_2\ \ldots\ y_m)$ can be solved. Thus, we only determine the vector $\boldsymbol{x}$ first, the vector $\boldsymbol{y}$ then is obtained by applying the constraints $y_j + \sum_{i=1}^{n} c_{ij} x_i \geq 1$ and $y_j \sum_{i=1}^{n} c_{ij} x_i = 0, j = 1 \ldots m$. Moreover, it is not complex to solve the vector $\boldsymbol{y}$ from $\boldsymbol{x}$ (i.e., if $\sum_{i=1}^{n} c_{ij} x_i = 0$, then y_j=1, otherwise y_j=0). The constraints in the problem (1) can be reduced by pre-treating constraints $y_j \sum_{i=1}^{n} c_{ij} x_i = 0$ and $y_j + \sum_{i=1}^{n} c_{ij} x_i \geq 1,, j = 1 \ldots m$ .So the key problem is to find the solution vector $(x_1\ x_2\ \cdots\ x_n)$ which is very difficult to obtain its optimal solution. In the next section, we will apply GA to find the approximately optimal solution.

3 Multi-objective Optimization Using Genetic Algorithms

3.1 Individual Representation and Population Sorting

The first step in designing a genetic algorithm is to devise a suitable representation scheme. In the paper, we use a n-bit binary string as the chromosome structure, a value of 1 for the i-th bit implies that sensor node s_i is in the solution. Figure 2 illustrates a typical example of a chromosome.

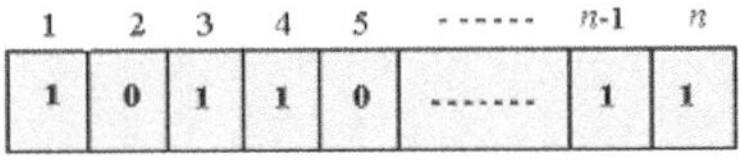

Fig. 2. Binary representation of an individual's chromosome

The paper uses Kalyanmoy Deb.[11] and Srinivas N.[12] proposal to handle the problem (1) . The last solutions are close to the true optimum solution [11], [13]. In this method, the population of GA is composed of different Pareto optimal fronts including unfeasible individuals. Since Pareto optimality defines how to determine the set of optimal solutions, the main idea of our algorithm is to simultaneously find multiple Pareto optimal solutions so that decision maker can choose the most appropriate solution for the current situation. To show our algorithm, we refer to the following terminologies.

Pareto Dominance: A solution **x** is said to dominate the other solution **y** or **x** is non-dominated by **y**, if objective vector **u** = (f_1(**x**), ... , f_k(**x**)) dominates the objective vector **v** = (f_1(**y**), ... , f_k(**y**)). (denoted by $\mathbf{u} \prec \mathbf{v}$). i.e., **u** is partially less than **v**, i.e., $\forall\, i \in \{1, \ldots, k\}$, $f_i(\mathbf{x}) \leq f_i(\mathbf{y}) \wedge \exists\, j \in \{1, \ldots, k\}$: $f_j(\mathbf{x}) < f_j(\mathbf{y})$. For a constrained multiobjective optimal problem, we further define that a solution $\boldsymbol{x}$ is said to constrained-dominate a solution $\boldsymbol{y}$, if any of the following conditions is true: (1)Solution $\boldsymbol{x}$ is feasible and solution $\boldsymbol{y}$ is not. (2) Solution $\boldsymbol{x}$ and $\boldsymbol{y}$ are both infeasible, but solution $\boldsymbol{x}$ has a smaller overall constraint violation. (3) Solutions $\boldsymbol{x}$ and $\boldsymbol{y}$ are feasible and solution $\boldsymbol{x}$ dominates solution $\boldsymbol{y}$.

Pareto Optimality: A solution $\mathbf{x} \in \boldsymbol{\Omega}$ is said to be Pareto optimal with respect to $\boldsymbol{\Omega}$ if and only if there is no **y** that dominates **x**. All Pareto optimal solution consists of a Pareto Optimal Set.

Pareto Front: For a given multiobjective optimal problem F(**x**) and Pareto optimal set P^*, the Pareto front is defined as: $PF^* := \{\mathbf{u} = F(\mathbf{x}) = (f_1(\mathbf{x}), \ldots, f_k(\mathbf{x}))$ so that $\mathbf{x} \in P^*\}$. i.e., a set of Pareto optimal solutions is called the Pareto-optimal front.

In the population, all individuals consist of feasible and unfeasible individuals. We sort all individuals using non-domination-sort way. First, all these non-dominated individuals are assumed to compose the first non-dominated individuals. Then, excluding the first non-dominated individuals temporarily, we process the rest feasible individuals using the same way to classify the second non-dominated individuals. The process is continued until all feasible individuals are classified.

However, the literate [14] does not aim at the constrained multiobjective optimal problems. Moreover, an important issue concerning the use of the binary representation is that the genetic operators may produce infeasible resulting solutions. To handle constraints, we hope that unfeasible individuals evolve towards feasibility guided, and that, feasible individuals have greater probability of selection than unfeasible individuals. After sorting all feasible individuals using non-domination-sort way, the same method is applied to sort all unfeasible individuals in the current population based on overall constraint violation. Thus, all individuals are ascending sort in the current population. Here, an individual **x** is unfeasible, if and only if

$$feasible(\mathbf{x}) = max\left\{\sum_{i=1}^{n} c_{ij}x_i - k, j = 1 \ldots m\right\} \leq 0 \tag{2}$$

Further we define the constraint violation of an individual **x** for the j-th target as follows:

$$violate(x, t_j) = \begin{cases} \sum_{i=1}^{n} c_{ij}x_i - k, \text{ if } \sum_{i=1}^{n} c_{ij}x_i - k > 0 \\ 0, \text{ otherwise} \end{cases} \tag{3}$$

Then an individual x has an overall constraint violations $\sum_{j=1}^{m} violate(x, t_j)$.

Now, we decide each individual rank and the crowding distance corresponding to their position in the front they belong. All the individuals in the first front are given a rank of value 1, the second front individuals are assigned rank 2 and so on. After assigning the rank the crowding distance in each front is calculated based on the literate [13]. So we will not give its description here.

3.3 Selection, Crossover and Mutation

We use tournament selection technique to generate a new population. Although SBC is designed to simulate the operation of a single-point binary crossover directly on real variables, we use (SBX) [14] operator for crossover and polynomial mutation [14]. To aim at binary variables, we slightly modify the genetic crossover and mutation operators from the original.

First, a random number μ that distributes uniformly between 0 and 1 is created. The following probability distribution function is used to create a sample β

$$p(x) = \begin{cases} 0.5(\eta + 1)x^{\eta} & \text{if } 0 \leq x \leq 1 \\ 0.5(\eta + 1)x^{-(\eta+2)} & \text{otherwise} \end{cases} \tag{4}$$

where η is a given crossover distribution index. Then the sample β is chosen such that

$$\int_0^{\beta} p(x)\,dx = \mu \tag{5}$$

After finding β from the above probability distribution, the children solutions c^1, c^2 are calculated as follows:

$$t_i^1 = 0.5\left[(1+\beta)\,p_i^1 + (1-\beta)\,p_i^2\right],\; t_i^2 = 0.5\left[(1-\beta)\,p_i^1 + (1+\beta)\,p_i^2\right] \tag{6}$$

$$c_i^1 = \begin{cases} 1, & \text{if } t_i^1 \geq 1 \\ 0, & \text{otherwise} \end{cases},\qquad c_i^2 = \begin{cases} 1, & \text{if } t_i^2 \geq 1 \\ 0, & \text{otherwise} \end{cases} \tag{7}$$

Choose a sample δ from the following polynomial probability distribution such that $\int_0^{\delta} p(x)dx = \mu$, where φ is a given mutation distribution index.

$$p(x) = 0.5(\varphi+1)(1-x^{\varphi}) \tag{8}$$

After finding δ from the above probability distribution, the children solutions c_i are calculated as follows:

$$y_{ij} = p_{ij} + \delta,\; c_{ij} = \begin{cases} 1, & \text{if } y_{ij} \geq 1 \\ 0, & \text{otherwise} \end{cases} \tag{9}$$

To summarize our modified GA for AM k-Coverage, the following steps are used.

Algorithm 1: Genetic Algorithm Overview

1: Given maximal iterative times *max_gen*, a collection S of sensors, a collection T of targets and the sensor-target coverage map.
2. Generate an initial population P of size *M*. every individual is chosen uniformly at random from the decision space $X=\{0, 1\}^n$.
3. **for** *gen*=1 **to** *max_gen*
4: Sort the population;
5: Individual selection operation using tournament selection technique according to the individual fitness;
6. Make use of SBX operator for crossover and polynomial mutation to obtain offsprings;
7. *gen*=*gen*+1;
8. **end for**
9: **return** Pareto Optimal Set.

4 Central Algorithm Based on GA

Once the wireless sensor network is deployed, the sensors send their coordination and cover information to the central node. The central node divides the sensor network into cover sets by running Algorithm 2 and broadcasts back the sensor schedules.

For a centralized approach, targets must have fixed locations as well as the deployed sensors to work effectively. When the solution is available, it is transmitted to each sensor in form of a coverage set index. The index is used as battery scheduling, that is, a sensor has to be in the sleep mode or in the active mode. Clearly, the disadvantage of centralized algorithms is that they rely on the network's ability to transmit data from every single node to the central node and vice versa. Fortunately, some work has been already done on this subject so we will not consider it here.

Algorithm 2: Central Algorithm for Dividing Coverage Set Based on Algorithm 1
1: Initialize Cover set index, i.e., *cover_index*=1 ;
2: **While** (S≠Φ) **do**
3: Call **Algorithm 1** to obtain Pareto Optimal Set **P={$\mathbf{x}_1 \ldots \mathbf{x}_p$}**
4: Choose a better subset P_s={$\mathbf{x}_{s1} \ldots \mathbf{x}_{sr}$} from the Pareto Optimal Set **P** according to the current application
5: **for** i=1 **to** r
6: each $\mathbf{x}_{si}$ determines a coverage set $S(\text{cover\_}index)$
7: $S \leftarrow S - S(\text{cover\_}index)$.
8: $\text{cover\_}index \leftarrow \text{cover\_}index + 1$.
9: $i \leftarrow i+1$
10: **End for**
11: **End while**
12: **Return** {$S1 \ldots S_{cover\_index}$}.

The idea of algorithm 2 is like this: Call Algorithm 1 to obtain a Pareto Optimal Set. Each element in the set denotes a coverage set, for instance, given a sensor network with 10 nodes, a element X=(1,1,0,0,0,1,0,1,0,0) denotes that s_1, s_2, s_6, s_8 are in the same coverage set. However, a few elements may be in a Pareto Optimal Set, and we have to choose some suitable elements according to current application. It is trivial for the approach so we will not consider it here. The process is continued until all sensor nodes are assigned to at least a coverage set.

5 Implementations and Experiments

In the section, different case studies are presented to show the efficiency of the algorithm. Throughout all these experiments, the average results are given over different problem setting. The deployment problem parameters are randomly generated using a uniform random generator. In all experiments, the crossover distribution index η and mutation distribution index crossover φ set 20.

In the first set of experiments, the convergence of Algorithm 1 is tested in the experiment. We assume that 600 sensor nodes with sensing radius 50*m* and 100 target points is randomly located in a 400*m* ×400*m* area to form a random distributed map. We restrict that each target object is covered by at most 5 sensor nodes. The initial population size is set to 50. We repeated the experiment 50 times with a crossover probability of 0.9.

Figure 3 shows the efficiency of Algorithm 1 with different iterative times. As shown in Figure 3, the Pareto front changes towards the Pareto-optimal front. The experimental results have shown that the algorithm is very robust by searching for the feasible region and better to maintain a representative sampling of solutions along the Pareto-optimal surface.

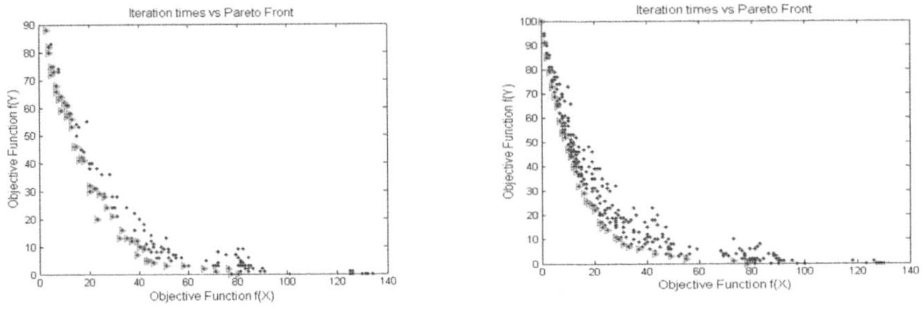

Fig. 3. Comparison of different convergence results is obtained when the number of iterative is 5, and 40 respectively

In the second set of experiments, we consider between 10–50 target points and 90 sensor nodes with a sensing range of 250m randomly distributed in a 500m ×500m area to form a random distributed map. We restrict that each target object is covered by at most 2 sensor nodes and set coverage blinds 0.

Figure 4(a) compares the number of coverage sets output by Algorithm 2 and MC-MIP in [3]. The sensing range of each sensor node in this experiment is 250m. Figure 4(b) shows the comparison of the number of coverage sets output by Algorithm 2 and MC-MIP in [3]. Here we set the sensing range of each sensor node between 100m and 300m with an increment of 20m. The result shows that the algorithm 2 obtains more coverage sets than MC-MIP in [3].

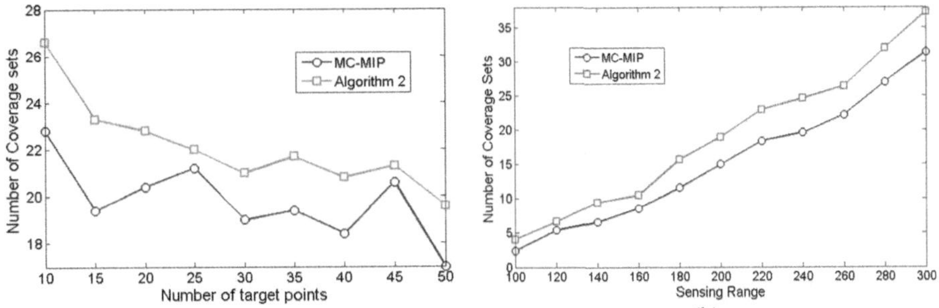

(a) (b)

Fig. 4. Comparison of the number of coverage sets output by Algorithm 2 and MC-MIP

6 Conclusion and Future Works

In this paper we address the issue of constructing a minimal coverage set for a target set and propose **AM k-Coverage** for this problem. We also design a method based on GA to organize a sensor network into coverage sets in parallel. Experimental results show that the proposed algorithm can construct the coverage sets reliably and reduce the number of active sensor nodes which is helpful to reduce system energy consumption and prolong the network lifespan.

However, in large scale sensor networks, the centralized approach obviously consumes a great deal of energy when it collects and issue the coverage information from and to every node. As part of our future work, we will design a distributed and localized algorithm based on the algorithm 2.

References

1. Steuer, R. E.: Multiple criteria optimization: Theory, computation, and application. New York : Wiley(1986)
2. K. Chakrabarty, S. S. Iyengar, H. Qi, and E. Cho.: Grid coverage for surveillance and target location in distributed sensor networks. IEEE Trans. on Comput., 51(12)(2002) :1448–1453
3. M. Cardei, D.Z. Du: Improving wireless sensor network lifetime through power aware organization. ACM Wireless Networks (2005), 11 (3)
4. Cardei M, Thai MT, Li Y, Wu W: Energy-efficient target coverage in wireless sensor networks. in Proceedings of 24th Annual Joint Conference of the IEEE Computer and Communications Societies (INFOCOM), Vol. 3 (2005)1976–1984
5. M. Cardei, J. Wu, M. Lu, and M. O. Pervaiz: Maximum network lifetime in wireless sensor networks with adjustable sensing ranges. Proc. of IEEE International Conference on Wireless and Mobile Computing, Networking and Communications (WiMob) (2005)
6. F. Dai, and J. Wu, An extended localized algorithm for connected dominating set formation in ad hoc wireless networks. IEEE Transactions on Parallel and Distributed Systems Vol. 15, No. 10. (2004) 908–920
7. F. Harary, and T. Haynes: Double domination in graphs. Vol. 55. ARS Combinatoria (2000) 201–213
8. H. Koubaa and E. Fleury: On the performance of double domination in ad hoc networks. Proc. of IFIP Medhoc(2000)
9. J. Shaikh, J. Solano, I. Stojmenovic, and J. Wu: New metrics for dominating set based energy efficient activity scheduling in ad hoc networks. Proc. of the International Workshop on Wireless Local Networks (WLN) (2003)
10. F. Dai and J. Wu: On constructing k-connected k-dominating set in wireless networks. Proc. of IPDPS (2005)
11. Kalyanmoy Deb.: An Efficient Constraint Handling Method for GAs. Computer Methods in Applied Mechanics and Engineering, Vol. 186, No. 2/4(2000)311–338
12. Srinivas N. and Deb K.: Multi-Objective function optimization using non-dominated sorting genetic algorithms.Evolutionary Computation. 2(3) (1994), 221–248.
13. K. Deb, S. Agrawal, A. Pratap, and T. Meyarivan: A Fast Elitist Non-Dominated Sorting Genetic Algorithm for Multi-Objective Optimization:NSGA-II. in Proceedings of Parallel Problem Solving from Nature -PPSN VI. Springer (2000)849–858
14. Kalyanmoy Deb and R. B. Agarwal: Simulated Binary Crossover for Continuous Search Space. Complex Systems (1995) (9)115–148
15. F. Dai and J. Wu: On Constructing K-Connected K-Dominating Set in Wireless Networks. In Proc. of IEEE IPDPS(2005)
16. Abrams Z, Goel A, Plotkin S.: Set k-cover algorithms for energy efficient monitoring in wireless sensor networks. In: Ramchandran K, Sztipanovits J, eds. Proc. of the 3rd Int'l Conf. on Information Processing in Sensor Networks. Berkeley: ACM Press(2004) 424-432

Improved Way Prediction Policy for Low-Energy Instruction Caches

Zhou Hongwei, Zhang Chengyi, and Zhang Mingxuan

School of Computer, National University of Defense Technology, 410073, Changsha, Hunan, P.R. China
forrestzhw@hotmail.com,
{chengyizhang, mxzhang}@nudt.edu.cn

Abstract. In this paper, a multi-way way prediction policy (MWWP) with a two-port Way Predictor (TPWP) is proposed for reducing the dynamic and leakage energy in multi-way set associative drowsy I-Cache without dramatic loss of performance. One port of TPWP is used for predicting the matching way in current set, only the predicted way and not all the ways is accessed to reduce the dynamic energy. The other is used for predicting the matching way in subsequent set, only the cache line in predicted way is pre-woken up from the drowsy mode to reduce the leakage energy. Different with the traditional way prediction policy, the MWWP has the lower performance overhead by selecting multiple ways speculatively for each access to improve way prediction hit ratio (WPHR). The simulation and estimation results show that, in a 4-way set-associative drowsy I-Cache, with 0.98% and 0.4% performance overhead respectively, our proposed 2-way and 3-way way prediction policy with TPWP can reduce 59% and 47% of energy in I-Cache, and save the 6.1% and 5.4% of the whole processor energy. The EDP is improved by 4.5% and 4.1% on average.

1 Introduction

Energy dissipation has become the main restriction on microprocessor design because of the higher density and higher frequency. Especially with the decrease of the transistor's dimension, supply voltage and threshold voltage, leakage energy may be comparable with the dynamic energy in microprocessors. In modern microprocessors, the large capability caches are integrated in chip to improve the processors' performance. They comprise a large portion of chip area and produce large leakage energy. For instance, 60% of the StrongARM and 30% of Alpha 21264 are devoted to cache and memory structures [1, 2]. I-Cache affects total energy consumption particularly due to their high access frequency. For example, ARM920T microprocessor dissipates 25% of its total power in the I-Cache [12].

The main technique to reduce leakage energy in I-Cache is putting those cache lines which are not accessed recently into low-power mode and recovering them when necessary [3, 4, 5, 8, 10]. The *drowsy cache* adopts this technique [5, 10]. The supply voltage of cache lines in drowsy mode is lower than that in active mode and the content in cache lines can be kept yet. When a cache line is accessed, the voltage of this

Y.-H. Lee et al. (Eds.): ICESS 2007, LNCS 4523, pp. 425–436, 2007.

line must be raised from low to high first. A simple policy in drowsy cache is *noaccess* policy [5]. A cache line is put into drowsy mode only if it is not accessed in a time window (decay interval). *PDSR* [7] (Periodically Drowsy Speculatively Recover) adopts a set prediction policy in which the cache lines are recovered speculatively to hide the waking up latency. During the set indexed by current address is being accessed, all the ways in the set indexed by next sequential address are pre-woken up. The dynamic energy in I-Cache is reduced usually by decreasing the unnecessary accesses in tag or data array for each access. The *way prediction* [9] is an effective policy for reducing the dynamic energy by eliminating unnecessary data array access in multi-way set-associative cache.

In this paper, an improved *multi-way way prediction policy with a two-port way predictor* (TPWP) is proposed for more energy saving in I-Cache without dramatic performance overhead. The cache lines are put into drowsy mode according to the noaccess policy and recovered (woken up) speculatively by way predictor. Unlike the traditional policies, way prediction information is used not only for leakage energy saving but also for dynamic energy saving. The way predictor has two ports which are accessed at the same time. One is *pre-access* port for predicting the way that would be hit in current set to reduce the dynamic energy. Only the predicted way is selected to be accessed if way prediction is correct. The other port is *pre-wakeup* port for predicting the matching way that would be accessed in subsequent set. Only one line instead of the whole set is pre-woken up. The leakage energy is reduced because the cache lines in other ways are unnecessary to be woken up if way prediction hits. To reduce the performance overhead, the way prediction hit ratio should be as large as possible. In our multi-way way prediction policy, multiple ways are selected speculatively to be accessed in current access and multiple ways are selected to be pre-woken up for subsequent access.

To evaluate our proposed policy and other policies, we set up an energy and performance estimation model. In this model, not only the normalized energy of I-Cache but also the normalized energy of whole processor is calculated to evaluate the energy saving in different policies. For the performance of processor is more sensitive to the latency of I-Cache, the EDP is also a metric for evaluating the energy efficiency. The rest of this paper is organized as follows. Section 2 introduces the two-port way predictor. Section 3 introduces the multi-way way prediction policy with TPWP. Section 4 introduces the energy and performance estimation model and the experiment framework. The simulation results are analyzed in section 5 and the conclusion and future work are in section 6.

2 Two-Port Way Predictor

In our proposed policy, a two-port way predictor is used. As current set is being accessed, the cache line in subsequent set is selected speculatively to be recovered by pre-wakeup port. Fig.1 shows the difference between the PDSR and our improved recovery policy for pre-waking up. The current access address is VPC_i (Virtual Program Counter), and the next access address predicted by Set Predictor is $SPVPC_i$ (Set Predicted Virtual Program Counter). The SET_i is the set indexed by $VPCi$ and the $SPred\_SET_i$ is the set indexed by $SPVPC_i$. When the SET_i is being accessed, all of the lines in the $SPred\_SET_i$ are pre-woken up in PDSR policy. In our recovery policy, the *WPred_Way* is the way predicted by way predictor. It is generated after the $SPred\_SET_i$ is generated by set predictor. Only the cache line in the *WPred_Way* is pre-woken up by pre-wakeup port and the other cache lines are still in drowsy mode. For example, in 1-way way prediction policy with TPWP, only one cache line is pre-woken up.

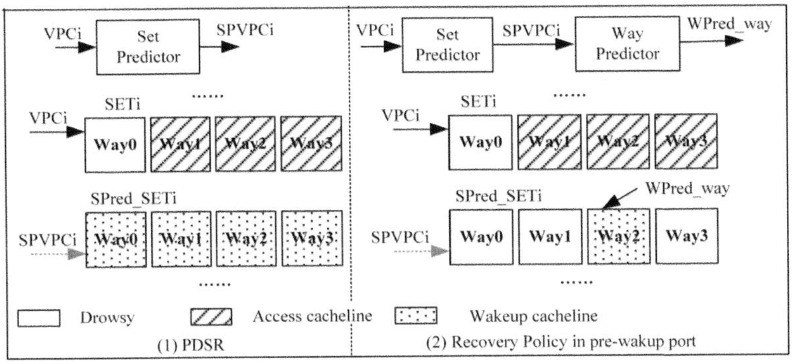

Fig. 1. The difference between PDSR and our improved recovery policy for pre-waking up

By the way prediction information from the pre-access port of TPWP, the predicted way in current set is accessed speculatively. In conventional *way prediction cache* [9], the access energy in tag array and in data array are both reduced because only the predicted tag block and the predicted data block are accessed if way prediction hits. In our improved way prediction policy, to reduce performance overhead caused by incorrect way prediction, all the tag blocks in the set indexed by current access address are accessed at the same time and only the data block in predicted way is accessed speculatively. The reason is that: if way prediction misses, the result of tag comparison in current access must be acquired as soon as possible to ascertain whether the desired data block in matching way need to be woken up. In our improved policy, if the desired data block is in active mode, no extra waking up cycle is incurred. If the desired data block is in drowsy mode, one extra waking up cycle is needed.

Fig.2 shows the improved 4-way set-associative I-Cache with TPWP. The TPWP includes a Way Prediction Table (WPT) with two ports and a Way Prediction Determiner (WPD). The WPT contains a two-bit flag for each set. The two-bit flag is used for speculatively choosing one way from the corresponding set. The WPD determines the value of each way-prediction flag according to the MRU (most-recently used) algorithm. The flags in WPT are modified by WPD when cache misses or way prediction misses. The two ports of WPT are used for way prediction. The solid line represents the way prediction operation by pre-access port. The matching way in current set indexed by *VPC* is predicted to be accessed. The broken line represents the way prediction operation by pre-wakeup port. The matching way in subsequent set indexed by *SPVPC* is predicted to be woken up. To control the performance overhead, the tag array is in active mode all the time. The tag arrays and data arrays also need two ports for two different operations. For high-performance I-Cache, there are two read ports normally: one is for normal fetch, the other is for pre-fetch. We can use the pre-fetch port to realize the pre-wakeup operation.

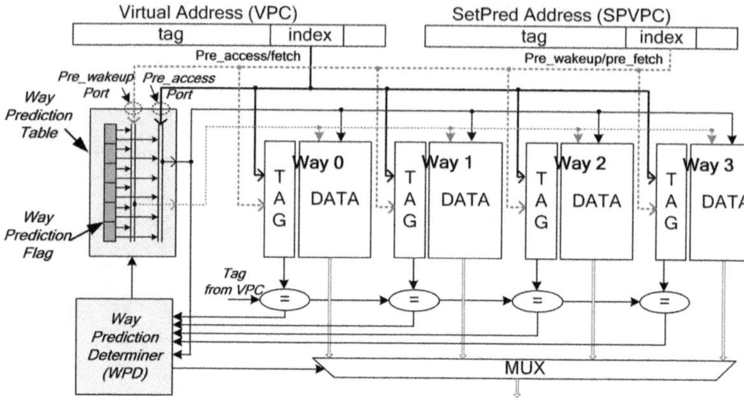

Fig. 2. The 4-way set-associative I-Cache with TPWP

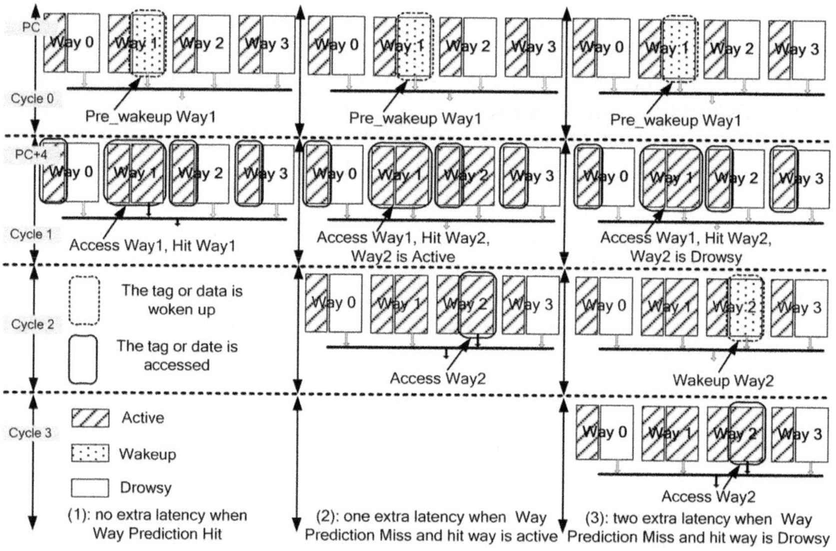

Fig. 3. The access to I-Cache in 1-way way prediction policy with TPWP

Fig.3 shows the access to I-Cache in 1-way way prediction policy with TPWP. Assuming the fetch width is 4 instructions pre cycle. Fig.3.1 is the case of way prediction hits. In Cycle 0, the access address is PC and set predicted address is PC+4. By the pre-wakeup port of TPWP, the predicted way for PC+4 is the way 1 and only the line in this way is pre-woken up. In Cycle1, no branch is taken, so the access address is just PC+4. The cache line in way1 is accessed speculatively according to the way prediction information by the pre-access port. The cache line in way1 is matched by tag comparison, so desired data is acquired in this cycle. The latency of waking up is hidden. Fig.3.2 and Fig.3.3 show the cases of way prediction misses. InFig.3.2, though the cache line in way1 has been pre-woken up in Cycle 0 and accessed speculatively in Cycle 1, the cache line in way2 is matched. If the matched line is in active mode, it can be accessed in Cycle 2 to acquire desired data. Only one-cycle extra latency is incurred. As shown in Fig.3.3, if the matched line is in drowsy mode, then it should be woken up first in Cycle 2 and accessed in Cycle 3. There is a two-cycle extra latency.

3 Multi-way Way Prediction Policy with TPWP

In traditional *way prediction cache* [9], only one predicted way is accessed speculatively. The way prediction hit ratio will be decreased with the associativity of cache increase. The performance overhead is affected by the WPHR. To reduce the loss of performance in way prediction policy, the way prediction hit ratio should be as large as possible. So, we improve our proposed 1-way way prediction policy with TPWP. The *multi-way way prediction policy with TPWP* is proposed. Multiple ways in one set are selected speculatively at the same time for each cache access. For example, in 2-way way prediction policy with TPWP, the WPT contains a pair of two-bit flag for each set, as shown in Fig.4. These paired flags indicate the first and secondary most recently used way according to MRU policy. For each access, two ways in the set indexed by VPC are selected speculatively to be accessed by two pre-access controllers. At the same time, two cache lines in the set indexed by SPVPC are pre-woken up by two pre-wakeup controllers. Each controller sends the wakeup signals or the access

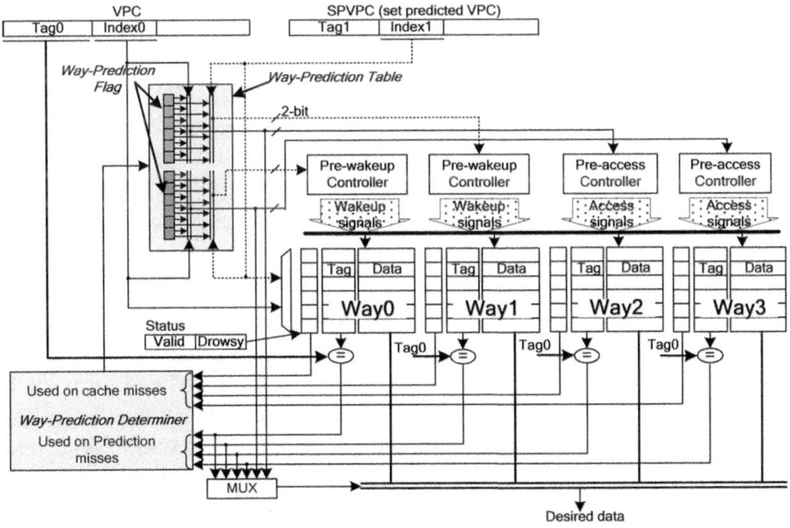

Fig. 4. The 4-way set-associative I-Cache with 2-way way prediction policy

signals to tag and data array according to the way prediction information from corresponding Way Prediction Flag in Way Prediction Table. More two-bit flags are needed if more ways are predicted concurrently. The PDSR policy is a particular case of MWWP. All cache lines in one set are predicted, just like a *full-way way prediction policy*.

4 Methodology

This section describes the energy and performance estimation model and our simulation environment.

4.1 Energy and Performance Estimation Model

The base model is a conventional cache that does not perform energy control. Assuming the average proportion between energy of I-Cache (E_{icache}) and energy of whole processor (E) is α. The energy of processor except I-Cache is E_{else}. E_d and E_s are the baseline dynamic energy and leakage energy respectively, and E'_d and E'_s are the corresponding dynamic and leakage energy with energy controlling policy. The ratio of dynamic energy to leakage energy in E_{icache} and E_{else} are n_1 and n_2 respectively. The ratio of energy in tag array (E_{icache_tag}) to data array (E_{icache_data}) is m. Then,

$$E_{icache} / E = \alpha,\ E_{d\_icache} / E_{s\_icache} = n_1,\ E_{d\_else} / E_{s\_else} = n_2,\ E_{icache\_tag} / E_{icache\_data} = m$$

IPC' and *IPC* are the number of instructions committed per-cycle with and without energy controlling policy. The program execution time is *T'* or *T* when energy controlling policy is used or not. The normalized execution time to base model is *s* and can be calculated as following formula:

$$s = T' / T = IPC / IPC' \tag{1}$$

e_{active} and e_{drowsy} are the leakage energy of one bit memory unit during one cycle in active mode and in drowsy mode respectively and e_{drowsy} are q times of e_{active}. The proportion between the number of cache lines in drowsy mode and the number of all cache lines is $R_{turnoff}$. N_{data} and N_{tag} are the number of bits in all tag array and data array in I-Cache. In data array of I-Cache without energy controlling policy, the leakage energy is $e_{active} N_{data} T$. When energy control policy is used, the leakage energy consumed by drowsy data blocks is $e_{drowsy} R_{turnoff} N_{data} T'$ and the leakage energy consumed by active data blocks is $e_{active}(1 - R_{turnoff}) N_{data} T'$. The energy caused by mode switching between the drowsy and active mode is negligible. Formula (2) shows the normalized leakage to base model in data array of I-Cache. Tag array of I-Cache is active at all the time in our proposed policy. Formula (3) shows the leakage energy consumed by active tag blocks is increased due to longer execution time. The normalized leakage energy to base model in I-Cache is μ and calculated as shown in formula (4).

$$\frac{E'_{s\_icache\_data}}{E_{s\_icache\_data}} = \frac{\left[(1-R_{turnoff})e_{active}N_{data} + R_{turnoff}e_{drowsy}N_{data}\right]T'}{e_{active}N_{data}T} = \left[(1-R_{turnoff}) + R_{turnoff}q\right]s \quad (2)$$

$$\frac{E'_{s\_icache\_tag}}{E_{s\_icache\_tag}} = \frac{e_{active}N_{tag}T'}{e_{active}N_{tag}T} = s \quad (3)$$

$$\mu = \frac{E'_{s\_icache}}{E_{s\_icache}} = \frac{E'_{s\_icache\_tag} + E'_{s\_icache\_data}}{E_{d\_icache\_tag} + E_{s\_icache\_data}} = \left[\frac{m+(1-R_{turnoff})+R_{turnoff}q}{m+1}\right]s \quad (4)$$

N_{way_pred} is the number of ways predicted in one cache access. The cache associativity is N_{assoc}, the cache hit ratio is *CHR* and the way prediction hit ratio is *WPHR*. In our proposed policy, except one access to the data block in the predicted way, one extra access to the data block in matched way is needed when cache hits but way prediction misses. All tag blocks in current accessed set are accessed at the same time. The normalized dynamic energy to base model to I-Cache is v and can be calculated as formula (5) shows.

$$v = \frac{E'_{d\_icache}}{E_{d\_icache}} = \frac{E'_{d\_icache\_tag} + E'_{d\_icache\_data}}{E_{d\_icache\_tag} + E_{d\_icache\_data}} = \frac{N_{assoc}m + N_{way\_pred} + CHR(1-WPHR)}{N_{assoc}(m+1)} \quad (5)$$

The change in the number of instructions issued can be ignored, dynamic energy in Eelse is regard changeless, so $E'_{d\_else} \approx E_{d\_else} = n_2 E_{s\_else}$. The leakage energy in E_{else} is increased as the increasing execution time, so $E'_{s\_else} = sE_{s\_else}$. The normalized energy of I-Cache is γ and the normalized energy of whole processor is η as formula (6) and (7) show respectively.

$$\gamma = \frac{E'_{icache}}{E_{icache}} = \frac{E'_{d\_icache} + E'_{s\_icache}}{E_{d\_icache} + E_{s\_icache}} = \frac{vn_1 + \mu}{(n_1+1)} \quad (6)$$

$$\eta = \frac{E'}{E} = \frac{E'_{d\_else} + E'_{s\_else} + E'_{icache}}{E_{else} + E_{icache}} = \frac{(n_2+s)E_{s\_else} + E'_{icache}}{E_{icache}/\alpha} \quad (7)$$

For $E_{d\_else} + E_{s\_else} = (1-\alpha)E_{icache}/\alpha$ and $E_{d\_else} = n_2 E_{s\_else}$,

So: $E_{s\_else} = \left[(1-\alpha)/\alpha(n_2+1)\right]E_{icache}$

η is calculated finally as formula (8) shows. The EDP is a metric to evaluate the energy efficiency in different policies. Formula (9) shows the normalized of EDP to base model in whole processor.

$$\eta = \frac{(n_2+s)(1-\alpha)}{(n_2+1)} + \gamma\alpha \quad (8)$$

$$\frac{EDP'}{EDP} = \frac{E'}{E} \bullet \frac{IPC}{IPC'} = \eta s \quad (9)$$

4.2 Simulation Environment

We extended *Hotleakage* [6] simulator to estimate energy and performance. As shown in Table 1, the processor parameters model a high-performance microprocessor similar to Alpha 21264 [1]. The energy parameters are based on the 70nm/0.9V technology. Benchmarks are chosen from SPEC CPU2000. Each benchmark is first fast-forwarded a billion instructions and then simulated the 300 millions instructions. We selected three traditional policies (*noaccess*, *PDSR* and the *simple way prediction* (*simple WP*, only dynamic energy is reduced)) to compare with our proposed multi-way way prediction policy with TPWP. The 1-way, 2-way, 3-way way prediction policy with TPWP (*1-way WP*, *2-way WP*, *3-way WP*) are simulated.

Table 1. Architecture/Circuit parameters

Processor parameters	
Fetch/Decode/Issue/Commit width	4 instructions/cycle
L1 I-Cache	64KB, 4-way, 32B block, 1 cycle latency
The switch latency between different mode	1 cycle latency
Energy parameters	
Process Technology	70nm
Temperature	353K
Supply Voltage	0.9V in active mode; 0.3V in drowsy mode
Threshold Voltage	NMOS: 0.1902V; PMOS: 0.2130V
Leakage energy of I-Cache in drowsy mode	0.019142 J
Leakage energy of I-Cache in active mode	0.441827 J

5 Simulation Results

Assuming the decay interval is 32K cycles and the average proportion of I-Cache's energy to whole processor's energy is 10% (α=10%). The parameter m and q can be calculated according to the processor parameters and energy parameters: m=0.14, q=0.04. According to the prediction from ITRS [11], the leakage energy will be equal to dynamic energy in microprocessors when the process technology is 70nm, so we assumes the $n_1 = n_2$=1. Fig.5 shows the WPHR in simple way prediction policy and with our proposed multi-way way prediction policy. When the number of the ways predicted in each access increases, the WPHR is improved. The 3-way WP policy has the highest WPHR. The WPHR in *gcc*, *gzip*, *twolf* and *mesa* are smaller than others especially in 1-way WP policy. Fig.6 shows the normalized execution time in different policies. The performance overhead in *gcc*, *gzip*, *twolf* and *mesa* are higher for less WPHR in these benchmarks. The performance overhead in 1-way WP policy is the worst, about 2.36% on average. The 2-way and 3-way WP policies have the slight loss of performance about 0.98% and 0.4%.

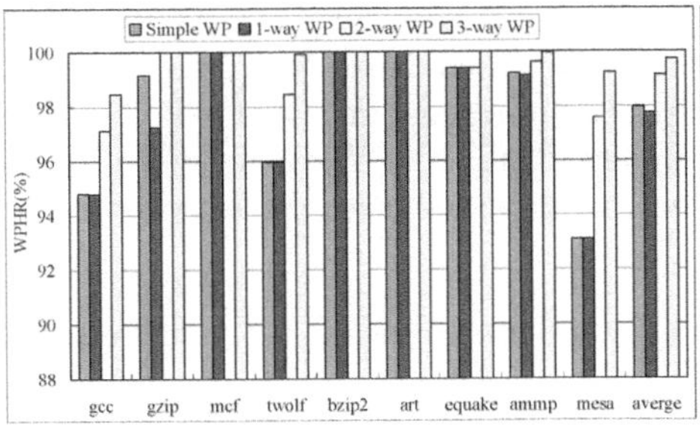

Fig. 5. The way prediction hit ratio

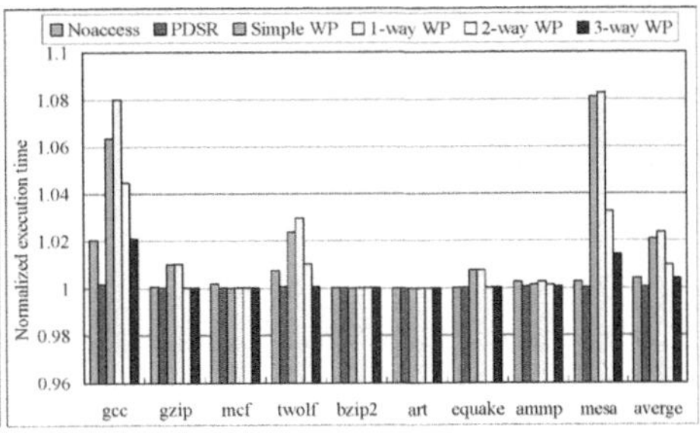

Fig. 6. Normalized execution time

Fig.7 shows the normalized leakage and dynamic energy of I-Cache with different policies. The histogram presents the normalized leakage energy and the line chart presents the normalized dynamic energy. More leakage energy is saved in our proposed policy than in PDSR policy because fewer cache lines are pre-woken up. The noaccess policy has the most leakage energy saving because no cache line is pre-woken up. The simple way prediction policy has a negative leakage energy saving because the execution time of each benchmark is increased. The dynamic energy of I-Cache with Simple WP, 1-way WP, 2-way WP and 3-way WP policies is only 26.6%, 31.7%, 54.32% and 77.12% of dynamic energy in normal I-Cache respectively. No dynamic energy is saved in the noaccess and PDSR policy. The simple WP policy has the lowest dynamic energy of I-Cache because the access energy to tag blocks is also saved when way prediction hits.

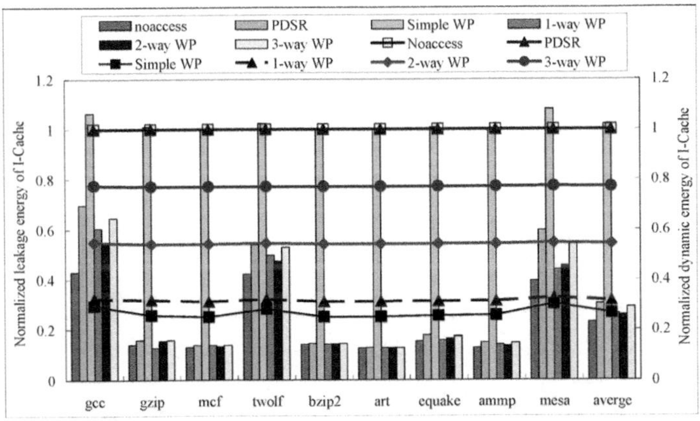

Fig. 7. Normalized leakage and dynamic energy of I-Cache

As shown in Fig.8, the best policy for total energy saving in I-Cache is our proposed multi-way way prediction policy. The 70% of energy in I-Cache is reduced on average in 1-way WP. The 59% and 47% of energy in I-Cache are reduced in 2-way WP and 3-way WP. Fig.9 shows the normalized energy of whole processor with different policies. Our proposed policy can reduce the energy of whole processor obviously for most benchmarks except the gcc and mesa. In gcc and mesa, the energy saved in our proposed policy is counteracted partly by the energy increased due to extra execution time. The energy in whole processor is reduced by 6% on average in 1-way WP. The 5.4% and 4.5% of energy in whole processor is reduced in 2-way WP and the 3-way WP respectively. Our proposed policies are better than traditional policies for energy saving.

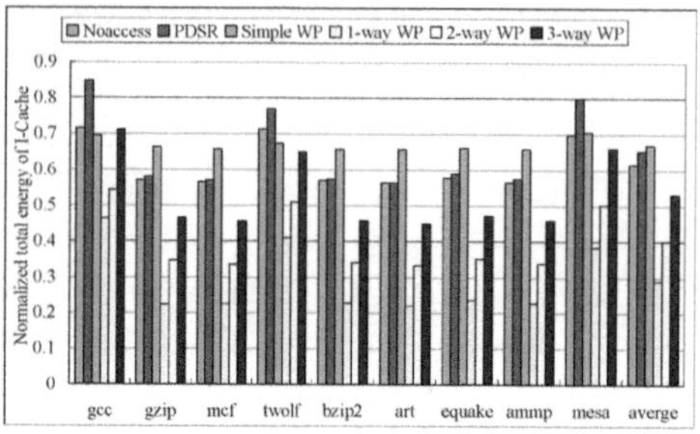

Fig. 8. Normalized total energy of I-Cache

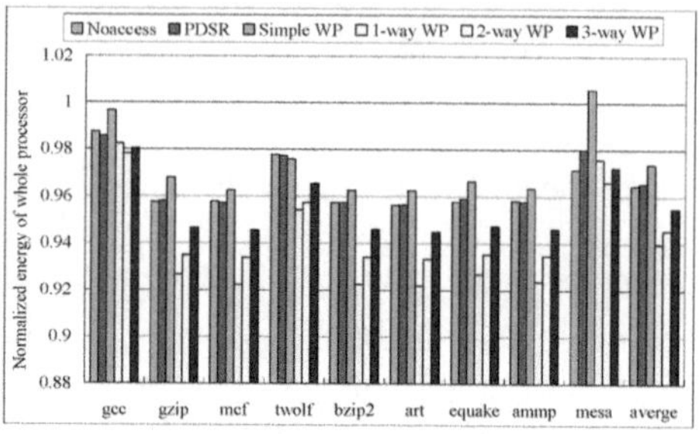

Fig. 9. Normalized energy of whole processor

Then we change the decay interval from 32K to 4K cycles. As shown in Fig.10 and Fig.11, the normalized energy of whole processor and the EDP are both increased with the increasing execution time. The noaccess policy is more sensitive to the change of decay interval and the PDSR policy is less sensitive. Our proposed policy is intervenient and the 32K is the optimum decay interval. With the optimum decay interval, in 1-way WP policy, 6% of energy of whole processor is reduced and the EDP is improved by 3.7%. The 5.4% and 4.5% of energy of whole processor is saved in 2-way WP and 3-way WP policy. The EDP is improved by 4.5% and 4.1% respectively. The energy saving and EDP improvement in our proposed policy with 32K or 16K decay interval are both better than that in traditional policies. When the decay interval is less than 4K, in our proposed policies especially in 1-way WP, the EDP improved by energy saving is almost counteracted by the EDP worsened by increasing execution time.

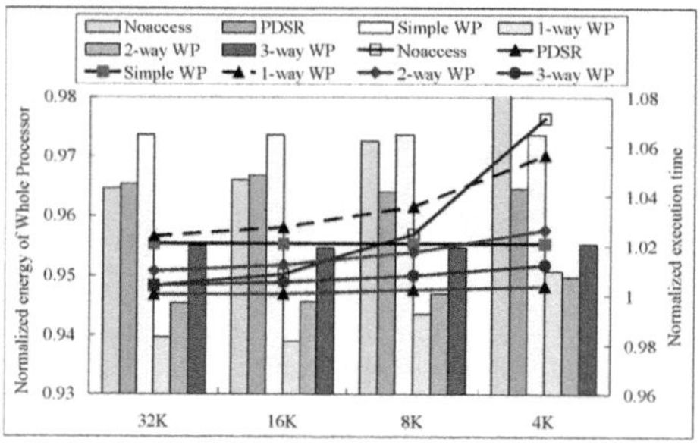

Fig. 10. Normalized Energy of Processor and Normalized Execution Time with different decay interval (α=10%)

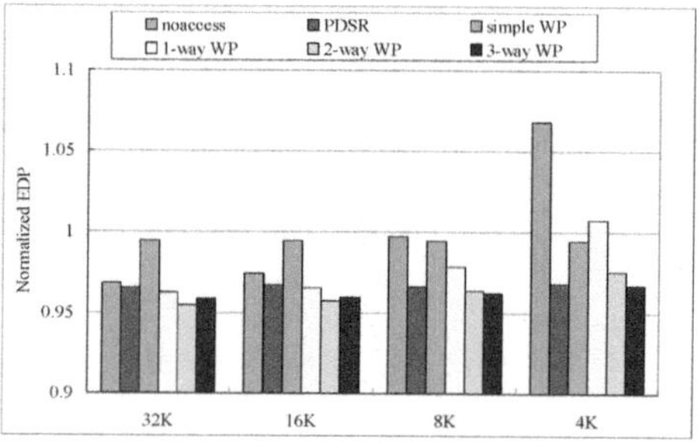

Fig. 11. Normalized EDP(α=10%)

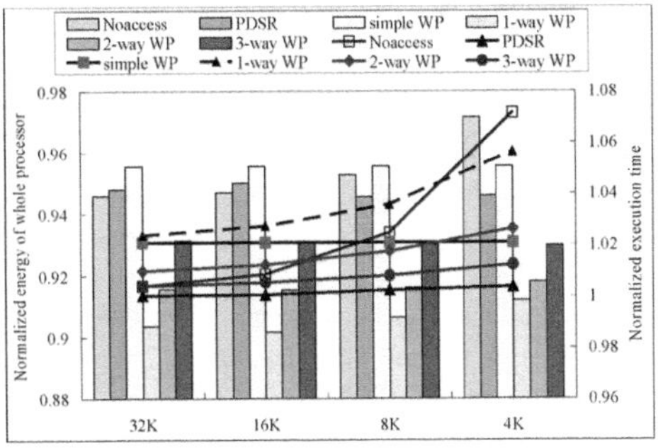

Fig. 12. Normalized Energy of Processor and Normalized Execution Time with different decay interval (α=15%)

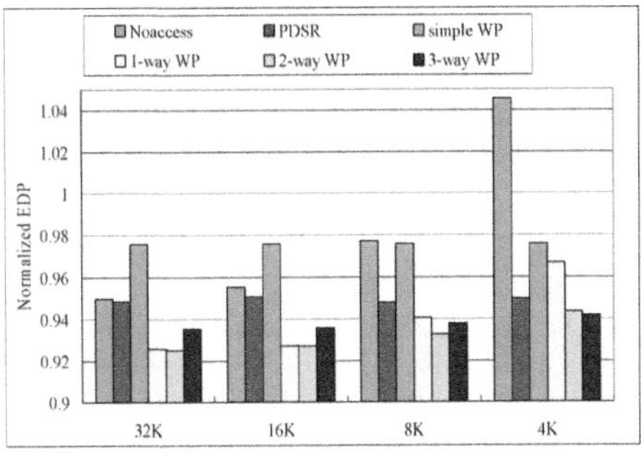

Fig. 13. Normalized EDP(α=15%)

As Fig.12 and Fig.13 shown, if α is increased from 10% to 15%, the energy saving of whole processor and the EDP are both improved. The 1-way WP policy has the most obvious energy saving which is 9.6% and the 2-way WP policy has the optimum EDP which is improved by 7.5% at most. With the proportion of I-Cache's energy to whole processor's energy increases, our proposed multi-way way prediction policy will be more effective than others.

6 Conclusions

This work presents a multi-way way prediction policy with a two-port way predictor to reduce the energy consumption in instruction cache without dramatic loss of performance. An energy and performance estimation model is also set up for evaluating our proposed policy and other policies. The multi-way way prediction policy with TPWP can reduce the energy consumption of I-Cache obviously and save the energy of whole processor effectively. The 1-way way prediction policy with TPWP is very suitable to be used in the domain that low energy is principal such as embedded processors design. With 2.36% performance overhead on average, the 70% of energy in I-Cache is reduced and the 6% of energy of whole processor is saved. The EDP is improved by 3.7%. If the performance is the most important factor such as for high-performance processors design, the 3-way way prediction policy with TPWP is a good choice. With only 0.4% performance overhead on average, the 47% of energy in I-Cache is reduced and the 5.4% of energy of whole processor is saved. The EDP is improved by 4.1%. In future work, branch information will be used in TPWP to reduce the performance loss caused by taken branch instructions.

References

1. Gowan M K, Biro L L and Jackson D B: Power Considerations in the Design of the Alpha 21264 Microprocessor, DAC'98, Los Alamitos, California, U.S. (1998) 26-31
2. S. Manne, A. Klauser, and D. Grunwald: Pipeline Gating: Speculation Control for Energy Reduction, Proc. Of Int. Symp. on Computer Architecture (1998) 132-141

3. M. D. Powell et al.: Gated-Vdd: A Circuit Technique to Reduce Leakage in Deep- Submicron Cache Memories, ISLPED2000, (2000) 90-95
4. S. Kaxiras, Z. Hu and M. Martonosi: Cache Decay: Exploiting Generational Behavior to Reduce Cache Leakage Power. ISCA2001 (2001) 240-251
5. N. S. Kim, K Flautner, D. Blaauw, and T. Mudge: Circuit and Microarchitectural Techniques for Reducing CacheLeakage Power, IEEE Transaction on VLSI Systems, vol.12, no. 2 (2004) 167-184
6. Y. Zhang, D. Parikh, K. Sankaranarayanan, K. Skadron and M. R. Stan.: Hotleakage: An Architectural, Temperature-aware Model of Subthreshold and Gate Leakage, Tech. Report CS-2003-05, Department of Computer Sciences, University of Virginia (2003)
7. Chengyi Zhang, Hongwei Zhou, Minxuan Zhang, and Zuocheng Xing: An architectural leakage power reduction method for instruction cache in ultra deep submicron microprocessors, The 11th Asia-Pacific Conference, ACSAC (2006) 588-594
8. Sung Woo Chung and Kevin Skadron: Using branch prediction information for near-optimal I-Cache leakage, The 11th Asia-Pacific Conference, ACSAC (2006) 24-37
9. Inoue, K., Ishihara, T., and Murakami, K.: Way-predicting Set-Associative Cache for High performance and Low Energy Consumption, Proc. Of 1999 International Symposium on low power Electronics and Design (ISLPED1999) (1999) 273-275
10. K. Flautner, N.S.Kim, S.Martin, D.Blaauw, and T.Mudge: Drowsy Caches: Simple Techniques for Reducing Leakage Power. ISCA2002 (2002) 147-157
11. SIA: International Technology Roadmap for Semiconductors (2004)
12. S. Segars: Low Power Design Techniques for Microprocessors, ISSCC Tutorial, (2001)

Sleep Nodes Scheduling in Cluster-Based Heterogeneous Sensor Networks Using AHP

Xiaoling Wu, Jinsung Cho*, Brian J. d'Auriol, and Sungyoung Lee

Department of Computer Engineering, Kyung Hee University, Korea
{xiaoling,dauriol,sylee}@oslab.khu.ac.kr,
chojs@khu.ac.kr

Abstract. Wireless sensor networks (WSNs) are comprised of energy constrained nodes. This limitation has led to the crucial need for energy-aware protocols to produce an efficient network. The concept of heterogeneity has been introduced in a WSN by deploying a large number of low power sensor nodes and a small number of more powerful nodes to serve as cluster heads (CHs). We propose a sleep scheduling scheme for balancing energy consumption rates in low power sensor nodes based on Analytical Hierarchy Process (AHP). We consider three factors contributing to the optimal nodes scheduling decision and they are the distance to CH, residual energy, and sensing coverage overlapping, respectively. We evaluate the efficiency of our proposed scheme in terms of important network parameters and compare with traditional random sleep scheduling in heterogeneous sensor networks. The proposed scheme is observed to improve network lifetime and conserve energy without compromising desired coverage.

Keywords: Sensor networks, AHP, sleep scheduling, lifetime, coverage.

1 Introduction

Wireless sensor networks (WSNs) are expected to be widely employed in various applications such as medical care, military and environmental monitoring. A typical WSN could contain thousands of small sensors. If these sensors are managed by the base station directly, communication overhead and management complexity could make such a network less energy-efficient. Clustering has been proposed by researchers to group a number of sensors, usually within a geographic neighborhood, to form a cluster. In such a cluster based topology, sensors can be managed locally by a cluster head (CH). Thus the concept of heterogeneity has been introduced in a WSN by deploying a large number of low power sensor nodes and a small number of more powerful nodes to serve as CHs.

The sleeping technique has been used to conserve energy of battery powered sensors. Rotating active and inactive sensors in the cluster, some of which provide redundant data, is an intelligent way to manage sensors to extend its network lifetime.

* Corresponding author.

Y.-H. Lee et al. (Eds.): ICESS 2007, LNCS 4523, pp. 437–444, 2007.

When a sensor node is put into the sleep state, it is completely shut down, leaving only one extremely low power timer on to wake itself up at a later time. This leads to the following sleep scheduling problem: How does the CH select which sensor nodes to be put into sleep, without compromising the sensing coverage of the cluster?

Sleep scheduling which aims to conserve the energy of the sensor nodes has been studied in the literature. In [1], nodes are allowed to sleep based on routing information, and nodes switch between sleep and active state based on the traffic of the network. In [2], a few nodes are selected as coordinators which would then decide the sleep/awake schedule of the other nodes in the network. In [3] nodes are randomly selected to go to the sleep mode and in [4] a linear distance based scheduling has been used to define the sleep schedule of the nodes in a cluster based homogenous network. In [5], the authors release the single hop communication assumption of [4] and introduce a hop-based sleeping scheduling algorithm in a circular sensor network divided by a number of levels. The overall result of these sleep schedules is a considerable reduction in the energy consumption of WSNs.

In this paper, we also investigate this problem and propose a sleeping scheduling scheme based on Analytical Hierarchy Process (AHP). Three factors contributing to the optimal nodes scheduling decision are considered and they are 1) distance to CH, 2) residual energy, and 3) sensing coverage overlapping, respectively. We evaluate the efficiency of our proposed scheme in terms of energy consumption, lifetime and coverage in heterogeneous sensor networks (HSNs).

The rest of the paper is organized as follows. We define the basic assumptions and state the problems in Section 2. The third section presents our sleep nodes scheduling scheme. Section 4 evaluates and analyzes the performance of the proposed method. Finally, we draw the conclusion in Section 5.

2 Problem Statements

We aim to enhance the efficiency of the given sensor network by enabling a balanced usage of energy across the nodes and an improved network lifetime without deteriorating network coverage. Fig. 1 is the illustration of cluster based HSN topology in which our proposed node scheduling scheme will be designed. We focus on energy consumption at the cluster level.

A. Assumptions

We consider the sleep node scheduling problem under several assumptions:

- The target sensor network is heterogeneous with a large number of low power nodes to serve as member nodes and a small number of more powerful nodes to serve as CHs;
- A large number of sensor nodes are deployed over a sensing field, such that at least some sensor nodes can be put into the sleep state without degrading the sensing coverage of the network;
- The CHs can communicate directly with sink and vice- versa. Furthermore, the CH can reach all the sensor members in the cluster in one hop and vice-versa;

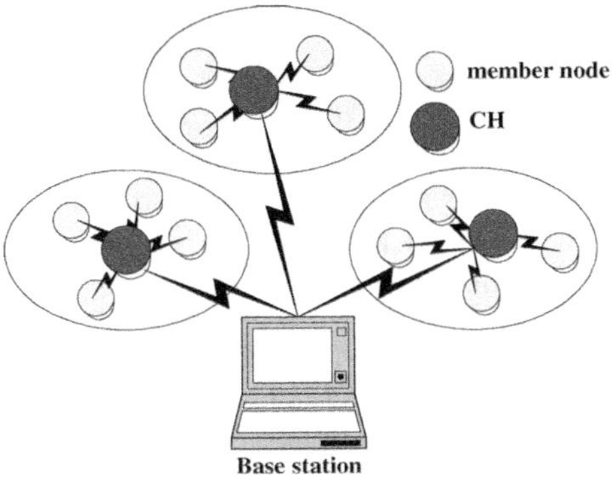

Fig. 1. Cluster based heterogeneous sensor network topology

B. Network Parameters and Energy Model

The user-defined parameters used in defining the network are listed below:

1) Fraction of sleeping nodes in a given round, '*r*': This is the fraction of the total number of nodes in the network that are selected to sleep in each *round*.
2) Threshold limit, 'θ': This denotes the fraction of nodes in the network, which, when dead, determines the lifetime of the network.

We adopt the same radio model as stated in [6] with ε_{fs}=10*pJ/bit/m*^{2} as amplifier constant, E_{elec}=50*nJ/bit* as the energy being dissipated to run the transmitter or receiver circuitry. It is assumed that the transmission between the nodes and their CHs follows a second-order power loss model. The energy cost of transmission for common sensor nodes at distance *d* from its CH in transmitting an *l*-bit data to the CH is calculated as:

$$E_T(l,d) = lE_{elec} + l\varepsilon_{fs}d^2 \quad (1)$$

C. Objectives

To enable load balancing while ensure desired coverage, we put some appropriate nodes to sleep in every cluster. In real WSNs, three factors influence the load balance and coverage directly, that is:

1) Distance to CH: Distance of a node to its CH. It can be approximated by the signal strength of radio transmission. The node with longest distance to the CH is preferred to be put into sleep.
2) Residual energy: Remaining battery of the sensor node. The initial energy is predefined. In addition, the energy consumption for transmission is calculated using Eq. (1) by CH.
3) Sensing coverage overlapping: Overlapped sensing range of a node by neighbor nodes. The node with the largest overlapping degree, i.e., the node with higher redundancy, is desired to be selected as sleeping node.

The optimized sleep nodes scheduling process is a multiple factors optimization problem and can be achieved using AHP which is introduced in the next section.

3 Sleep Nodes Scheduling Scheme by AHP

The Analytical Hierarchy Process (AHP) is a multiple criteria decision-making method which decomposes a complex problem into a hierarchy of simple sub problems (or factors), synthesizes their importance to the problem, and finds the best solution. In this paper, AHP is used to determine the nodes which are eligible to sleep in one cluster. It is carried out in three steps:

1) Collect information and formulate the sleeping nodes selection problem as a decision hierarchy of independent factors.
2) Calculate the relative local weights of decision factors or alternatives of each level.
3) Synthesize the above results to achieve the overall weight of each alternative nodes and choose the one with largest weight as the eligible sleeping node.

A. Structuring Hierarchy

The goal of the decision "select a node eligible to sleep" is at the top level of the hierarchy as shown in Fig. 2. The next level consists of the decision factors which are called criteria for this goal. At the bottom level there exist the *m* alternative sensor nodes to be evaluated.

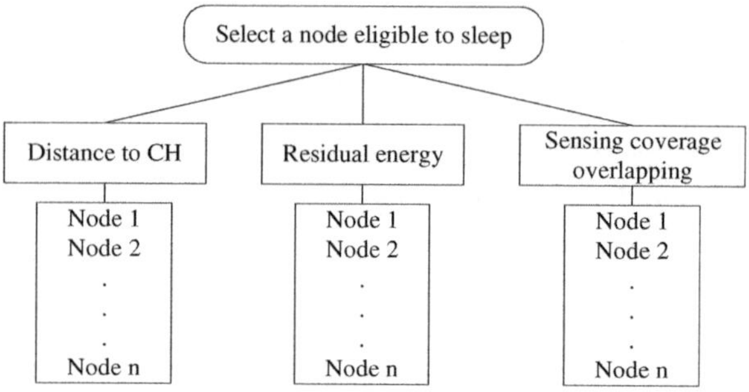

Fig. 2. AHP hierarchy for sleeping nodes selection

B. Calculating Local Weights

Local weights consist of two parts: the weight of each decision factor to the goal and the weight of each nominee to each factor. Both of them are calculated with the same procedure. Taking the former as an example, we describe the procedure as the following three steps.

1) Making Pairwise Comparison

The evaluation matrices are built up through pairwise comparing each decision factor under the topmost goal. The comparison results are implemented by asking the questions: "Which is more important? How much?" and they may be presented in square matrix A as

$$A = \left(a_{ij}\right)_{n \times n} = \begin{pmatrix} a_{11} & a_{12} & \cdots & a_{1n} \\ a_{21} & a_{22} & \cdots & a_{2n} \\ \cdots & \cdots & \cdots & \cdots \\ a_{n1} & a_{n2} & \cdots & a_{nn} \end{pmatrix}, \tag{2}$$

where a_{ij} denotes the ratio of the ith factor weight to the jth factor weight, and n is the number of factors. The fundamental 1 to 9 scale can be used to rank the judgments as shown in Table 1.

Table 1. A fundamental scale of 1 to 9

Number Rating	Verbal Judgment of Preferences
1	Equally
3	Moderately
5	Strongly
7	Very
9	Extremely

2, 4, 6, 8 indicate the medium value of above pairwise comparison.

2) Calculating Weight Vector

For the given matrix A in Eq. (2), we calculate its eigenvalue equation written as AW = $\lambda_{\max}$W, where W is non-zero vector called eigenvector, and $\lambda_{\max}$ is a scalar called eigenvalue. After standardizing the eigenvector W, we regard the vector element of W as the local weight of each decision factor approximately, denoted as:

$$\mathbf{w}_j^T = \{w_1, w_2, \cdots, w_n\} \tag{3}$$

3) Checking for Consistency

If every element in Eq. (2) satisfies the equations $a_{ij}=1/a_{ji}$ and $a_{ik} \cdot a_{kj}=a_{ij}$, the matrix A is the consistency matrix. The evaluation matrices are often not perfectly consistent due to people's random judgments. These judgment errors can be detected by a consistency ratio (CR), which is defined as the ratio of consistency index (CI) to random index (RI). CI can be achieved by

$$CI = (\lambda_{\max} - n)/(n-1), \tag{4}$$

where

$$\lambda_{\max} = (1/n)\sum_{i=1}^{n}(AW)_i / W_i \,. \tag{5}$$

The RI is given in Table 2 [7]. When $CR \le 0.1$, the judgment errors are tolerable and the weight coefficients of the global weight matrix W_j are the weights of decision factor under the topmost goal. Otherwise, the pairwise comparisons should be adjusted until matrix A satisfies the consistency check.

Table 2. Random index

n	1	2	3	4	5	6	7	8	9	10	11
RI	0	0	0.58	0.90	1.12	1.24	1.32	1.41	1.45	1.49	1.51

C. Calculating Global Weights

From above steps, we can obtain not merely the weights of decision factors towards the topmost goal from W_j but also the weights of alternative nodes towards each factor. If there are eight candidate nodes in each cluster, all the eight weight matrixes of alternatives under three factors construct a 8×3 matrix, denoted as $W_{n_i/j}$, i=1, 2, … 8, j=1, 2, 3. The global weight of each senor node can be achieved through multiplying the local weight by its corresponding parent. So the final weight matrix in the symbol of W_{n_i} is calculated as

$$W_{n_i} = W_{n_i/j} \cdot W_j, \tag{6}$$

where the final weight of each alternative is calculated as

$$W_{n_i} = \sum_{j=1}^{3} W_{n_i/j} \cdot W_j. \tag{7}$$

The larger the final weight of node, the higher the probability of node which is eligible to be put into sleep. Thus, the r fraction of nodes with the largest weight are selected as the sleeping nodes in the current *round*.

4 Performance Evaluations

In order to evaluate the sleep scheduling scheme by AHP, we compare it with random scheduling scheme. We don't compare with other existing work because of our different assumptions. In our simulation, the 50*m* × 50*m* square monitored area is assumed. The sensing and communication range is equal to 8*m* and *16m* respectively. Initial energy in each node is 2*J*. We set the total number of nodes N=50 and number of static clusters to be 2. Thus the number of nodes in each cluster is 25 by assuming a uniform distribution of nodes.

In AHP modeling, the matrix A is determined as follows according to Section 3:

$$A = \begin{array}{c} \\ \alpha \\ \beta \\ \gamma \end{array} \begin{array}{c} \begin{array}{ccc} \alpha & \beta & \gamma \end{array} \\ \begin{bmatrix} 1 & 2/1 & 3/1 \\ 1/2 & 1 & 2/1 \\ 1/3 & 1/2 & 1 \end{bmatrix} \end{array}$$

where the three criteria (distance to CH, residual energy and sensing range overlapping) are denoted by α, β and γ respectively.

The computed eigenvector W = [0.5396 0.2970 0.1634]. It indicates the local weight of the distance to CH, residual energy, and sensing coverage overlapping respectively so that we can see that the distance to CH is the most important criterion.

Based on Eq. (5), we get the eigenvalue $\lambda_{max} = 3.0093$. Consistency ratio can then be calculated as $CR = 0.0047 < 0.1$, thus matrix A satisfies the consistency check.

Each sensor node determines the weight matrixes of alternatives under three factors and then gets global weight based on its specific situation. Its eligibility as a sleeping node can be finally decided by the AHP hierarchy model.

Assume the CH plans to allow $25r$ nodes in its cluster to sleep in each cycle. In the random scheduling scheme, the CH randomly selects r fraction sensor nodes to sleep. Fig. 3 provides the energy consumption verses the fraction of sleeping nodes of the two sleep scheduling schemes. It shows that the energy consumption in case of the proposed scheme is less than that of the random scheme. The energy savings can be enhanced with an increasing value of r. For an r value of "0.7", the energy consumed is 49.3% less by the proposed scheme than by random scheme.

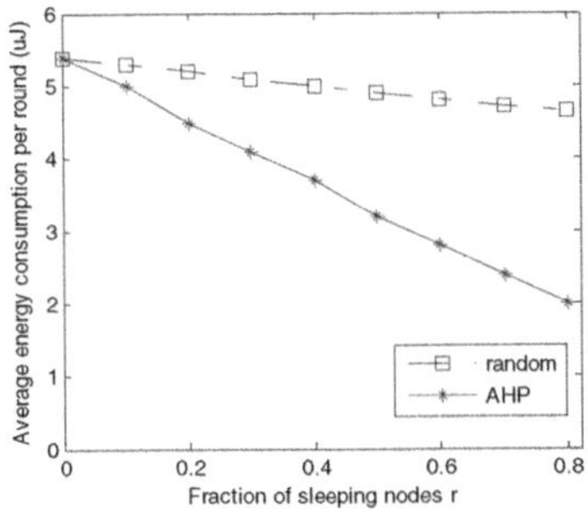

Fig. 3. Energy Consumption in the cluster per round

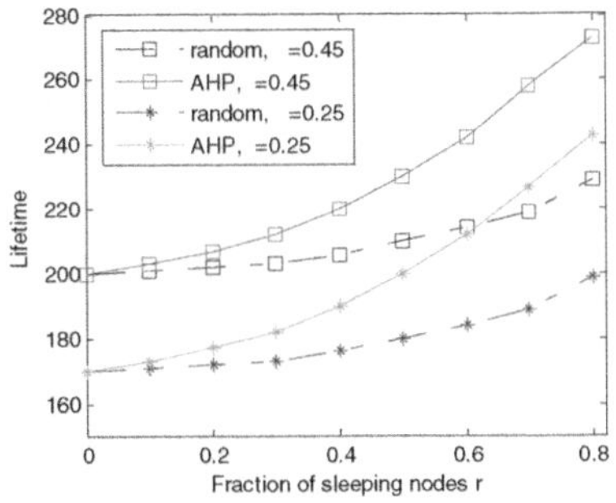

Fig. 4. Lifetime comparison

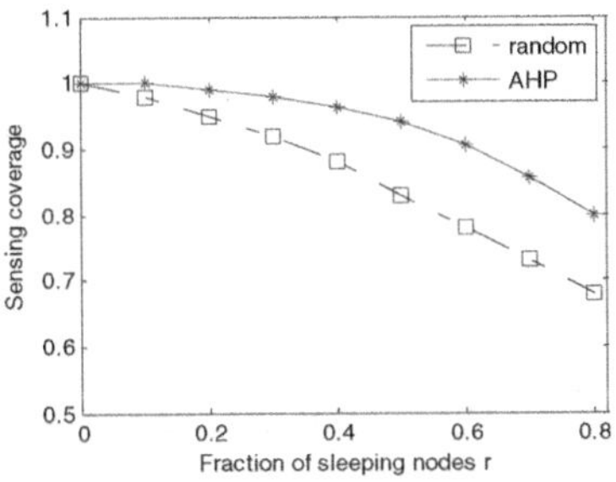

Fig. 5. Coverage verses the fraction of sleeping nodes

Network lifetime can be defined as the time when a fraction of nodes, θ, run out of energy. In Fig. 4, we evaluate the lifetime for various values of r and θ. The length of each round is $5s$. We can see that the lifetime of both schemes is prolonged with the increase of r and the proposed scheme greatly outperforms the random scheme. This is in line with the analysis that the proposed scheme can balance the energy consumption among all the member nodes. It also shows that the lifetime of both schemes increases with an increase of θ. This is because the network can be alive up to the time when θ fraction of nodes are drained of their energy.

Fig. 5 provides the comparison of coverage ratio verses the fraction of sleeping nodes *r*. The coverage here is defined as the ratio of the union of all sensor nodes' sensing areas to the whole monitored environment. For the detailed explanation of coverage ratio calculation, please refer to [8]. Fig. 5 shows that for both schemes the coverage ratio decreases with the increase of *r*. However, in case of the proposed AHP based sleeping scheme, the coverage ratio still can maintain above the desired value of 0.98 when up to 30% nodes are put into sleep. It indicates that the tradeoff in terms of coverage is not very critical by using the AHP based scheme.

5 Conclusion

In this paper, we proposed a sleep scheduling scheme for balancing energy consumption rates in HSNs based on AHP. Three factors contributing to the optimal nodes scheduling decision are considered and they are the distance to CH, residual energy, and sensing coverage overlapping, respectively. We evaluated the efficiency of our proposed scheme in terms of energy consumption, lifetime and coverage ratio, and compared with traditional random sleep scheduling scheme in heterogeneous WSNs. The proposed scheme was observed to improve network lifetime and conserve energy without compromising the sensing coverage of the cluster.

Acknowledgments. This research was supported by the MIC (Ministry of Information and Communication), Korea, under the ITRC (Information Technology Research Center) support program supervised by the IITA (Institute of Information Technology Advancement) (IITA-2006-C1090-0602-0002).

References

1. Y. Xu, J.Heidemann and D. Estrin: Adaptive Energy-conserving Routing for Multihop ad hoc Networks. Research report 527, USC/Information Sciences Institute (2000).
2. B. Chen, and et al.: Span: An Energy-Efficient Coordination Algorithm for Topology Maintenance in Ad Hoc Wireless Networks. ACM Wireless Networks, Vol. 8, No. 5 (2002).
3. W. Ye, J. Heidemann, and D. Estrin: An Energy-Efficient MAC Protocol for Wireless Sensor Networks. Proc of the 21st INFOCOM, New York, NY (2002).
4. J. Deng, Y. S. Han, W. B. Heinzelman, and P. K. Varshney: Scheduling Sleeping Nodes in High Density Cluster-based Sensor Networks. ACM/Kluwer MONET, Special Issue (2005).
5. Yun Wang, Demin Wang, and et al.: Hops-based Sleep Scheduling Algorithm for Enhancing Lifetime of Wireless Sensor Networks. Proc. of MASS, Canada (2006) 709-714
6. Wendi B. Heinzelman, et al: An Application-Specific Protocol Architecture for Wireless Microsensor Networks. IEEE Tran. on Wireless Communications, Vol. 1 (2002) 660 – 670
7. Q. Y. Song and A. Jamalipour: A Network Selection Mechanism for Next Generation Networks. IEEE Int. Conf. Communication (ICC), Vol. 2 (2005) 1418- 1422
8. Xiaoling Wu, et al: Swarm Based Sensor Deployment Optimization in Ad hoc Sensor Networks. . Proc. of ICESS' 05 (LNCS), Xi'an, China (2005) 533-541

Energy-Efficient Medium Access Control for Wireless Sensor Networks

Po-Jen Chuang and Chih-Shin Lin

Department of Electrical Engineering, Tamkang University,
Tamsui, Taipei County, Taiwan 25137, R.O.C.
pjchuang@ee.tku.edu.tw

Abstract. Energy efficiency is a primary issue for the performance of a wireless sensor network. This paper works on both communication and transmission to reduce unnecessary energy waste, i.e., to conserve energy consumption, for a wireless sensor network. To improve idle listening, for example, we allow sensor nodes to activate or sleep periodically; to improve collision and overhearing, we use an algorithm to alternate the wakeup time of neighboring sensor nodes and thus reduce transmission latency.

1 Introduction

A wireless sensor network consists of hundreds or thousands of sensor nodes and is usually deployed in an unprotected environment to collect the needed information. As sensor nodes are battery-powered and are difficult to get recharged after distribution, energy efficiency thus becomes a basic and critical issue. The limited energy resources of sensor nodes are usually wasted through overhearing, idle listening and collision.

Overhearing: When a node sends data, all neighboring nodes within the transmission range, including those which are not the destination of this transmission, will receive the data, unnecessarily consuming the restricted energy.

Idle listening: Despite the fact that each node in the topology will send or receive data only occasionally, it needs to "listen" to the channels all the time for any possible transmission, wasting additional energy.

Collision: If more than two nodes attempt to send data to the same destination at the same time, the destination node may fail to receive the data. In such a case, each of the source nodes will try to resend data and thus consumes extra energy.

Energy efficiency is important and so is transmission efficiency which can be attained through improvement on latency, throughput and load fairness.

Latency: Some applications of the wireless sensor network can be very time-critical. In such time-critical applications, transmission latency should be shortened as much as possible because when a node detect something, it has to report immediately to the base station (BS) which will then take instant and appropriate actions.

Y.-H. Lee et al. (Eds.): ICESS 2007, LNCS 4523, pp. 445–452, 2007.

Throughput: Desirable throughput is especially needed when a wireless sensor network must transmit all of the data collected in a certain period of time.

Fairness: If routing channels are constantly occupied by a certain number of nodes, the other nodes will lose transmission chances and be forced to wait and hold, thus degrading network performance. For improvement, all nodes should be given the same probability to use transmission channels.

Based on the above observation, this paper presents a new medium access control (MAC) protocol which utilizes the special features of the wireless sensor network to achieve power efficiency and low latency. The proposed protocol lets the base station start an initial process in which the height of all sensor nodes are set when the network is first deployed. The height of a node refers to its hop counts to the base station. The active time of nodes whose height difference = 1 is set to be continuous to reduce transmission latency, while the active time of nodes with the same height will stagger to avoid collision, i.e., to reduce the probability of simultaneous transmission.

2 Related Works

S-MAC [1] puts sensor nodes into periodic sleep to reduce power consumption due to idle listening and to decrease the probability of collision. It also works to solve the overhearing problem: When receiving a packet, a sensor node will be forced into sleep -- if it is not the destination node. Putting a sensor node into sleep may solve the overhearing problem; it may also increase transmission latency (due to transmission interruption) and reduce throughput (because the interrupted data must wait until the sensor node wakes up to resume the transmission). **D-MAC [2]** attempts to improve the transmission interruption problem in S-MAC by alternating the wakeup period of sensor nodes. Employing the data gathering tree (e.g. GIT [4]), D-MAC allows nodes on different tree levels to have different but continuous wakeup periods to solve the problem of transmission interruption. **T-MAC [3]** is proposed to reduce energy consumption due to idle listening. It puts nodes into periodic sleep like S-MAC, with a different design -- the dynamic duty cycle (S-MAC adopts the fixed duty cycle). In T-MAC, when a node is in the wakeup mode but sends or receives no data for a certain period of time, it will switch to the sleep mode to avoid wasting energy.

3 The Proposed New Protocol

To reduce idle listening: As nodes in a sensor network are not always sending or receiving data, it is unnecessary for them to listen to routing channels at all times. To reduce idle listening, our new protocol puts sensor nodes into "sleep" periodically (as most established protocols) but adopts the dynamic duty cycle (instead of the fixed duty cycle) to reserve the energy of the nodes.

To reduce latency: Putting sensor nodes into the sleep mode periodically may interrupt data forwarding and as a result increase transmission latency. To solve the problem, our new protocol employs the alternative wakeup schedule in D-MAC, as shown in Fig. 1. The alternative wakeup schedule allows sensor nodes on different levels to wake up **sequentially.** Such a design helps avoid transmission latency -- because when data are being transmitted to the BS, packet routing on all levels will not be interrupted by a sleeping node, as the transmission process in Fig. 2 demonstrates.

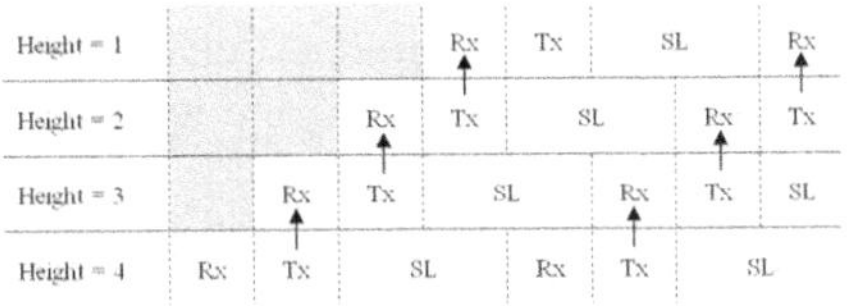

Fig. 1. The alternative wakeup schedule (RX/TX indicates the sensor node is ready to receive/transmit data, SL = the sensor node is put into the sleep mode)

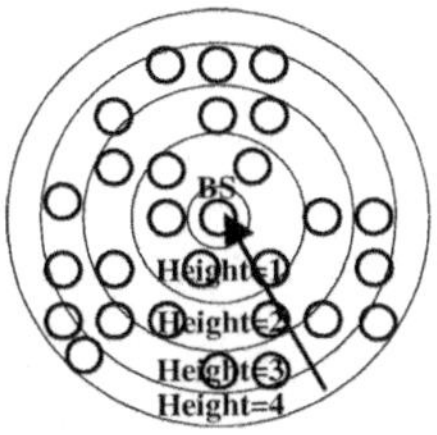

Fig. 2. The transmission process

To avoid collision: The proposed protocol adopts the alternative wakeup schedule in Fig. 1 to reduce transmission latency and also the probability of collision. Collision happens when neighbor nodes attempt to transmit data at the same time. Thus to reduce the probability of collision means to keep neighbor nodes from waking up at the same time. Interchanging the wakeup schedule of neighbor nodes can reduce not only the probability of transmission collision but also energy consumption caused by overhearing. To alternate the wakeup schedule of neighbor nodes, our algorithm (to appear in later sections) will assign a number -- 0 or 1 -- to each node of the same height and the assignment should vary as much as possible to achieve the best effect of collision avoidance. Fig. 3 shows our modified alternative wakeup schedule of nodes with the same height but different numbers (0 or 1). Based on such a schedule, transmission collision can be avoided because the wakeup time of nodes at the same height is staggered (under different numbers).

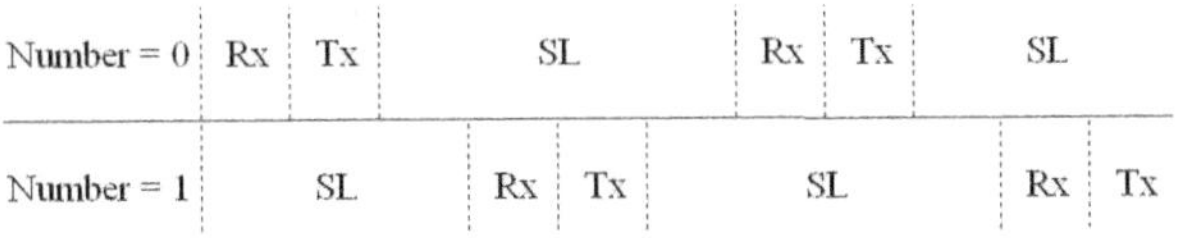

Fig. 3. Our modified alternative wakeup schedule (the schedule difference between nodes of the same height with different numbers -- 0 or 1)

4 The Algorithm for Calculating the Schedule

In our protocol, each sensor node is assigned with h and n. h refers to the node's height (the tree level); n is the number decided by coordination between neighbor nodes to interchange their wakeup time. Each node also needs to record an update time t to indicate its most recent update time. After distribution, sensor nodes first go through the initial process to initialize h and n, and to calculate the wakeup schedule.

To initialize the number: Before node distribution, h and n for each node is set as infinite and t is set to 0. After node distribution, the BS will broadcast an update packet whose number (n_{update}) = 0 and ***whose update time (t_{update}) = the time to send the packet***. After receiving such an update packet, a sensor node faces two situations:

$t < t_{update}$: indicating the sensor node is not yet updated and hence needs to update its number n to (n_{update} + 1) mod 2 and set its update time t to t_{update}. The node then broadcasts the newly updated number and the most recent update time.

$t = t_{update}$: indicating the node is already updated. However, to avoid neighbor nodes getting the same number, a sensor node needs to check if n and n_{update} are the same. If they are, the node will request all of its neighbor nodes to broadcast their numbers and then based on the number distribution choose a most appropriate number.

To initialize the height: When number initialization for all nodes is finished, the BS once again broadcasts an update packet with height (h_{update}) = 0. A node receiving the update packet also faces two situations:

$h - h_{update} \leqq 1$: Indicating the node receives the update packet from a node with bigger height and may ignore this update packet without doing anything.

$h - h_{update} > 1$: Indicating the node receives the update packet from a node with lower height and has to update its own height h to h_{update} + 1 and meanwhile broadcasts the updated data.

To calculate the schedule: After the numbers and heights of all nodes are initialized, nodes move on to calculate the wakeup time according to their heights and numbers. Sensor nodes first divide the cycle time into m parts; each part is taken as a time slot. The schedule for a sensor node in Fig. 4 shows that a sensor node wakes up only at two time slots and is put into the sleep mode at the other time slots.

1 slot	1 slot	(m−2) slots
Receive(RX)	Transmit(TX)	Sleep(SL)

Fig. 4. The schedule of sensor nodes

m will be calculated by the duty cycle as follows:

$$\text{Duty Cycle} = \frac{Active\ \ Time}{Cycle\ \ Time} \times 100\% = \frac{2\mu}{m\mu} \times 100\% = \frac{2}{m} \times 100\% \tag{1}$$

μ : the slot time

Cycle Time = $m\mu$ $(m > 5)$

Active Time = 2μ (RX and TX)

Sleep Time = $(m-2)\mu$

We can now move to calculate the time for each node to start working. Assume each node has different delay time τ . When calculating the delay time, we must take the height (h) and the number (n) of each node into consideration to reduce transmission latency and to decrease the probability of transmission collision. Based on the above discussion, we can set the formula for calculating the delay time as follows.

$$\tau(m,h,n) = [m - (h \bmod m)] + [3 \times n] \tag{2}$$

If the duty cycle is assumed to be 10%, we can obtain m by the above formula.

$$\text{Duty cycle} = \frac{active\ \ time}{cycle\ \ time} \times 100\% = \frac{2\mu}{m\mu} \times 100\% = \frac{2}{m} \times 100\% = 10\%$$

$$\Rightarrow \frac{200}{m} = 10 \Rightarrow m = 20$$

After m is attained, a node can calculate the delay time by its h and n, and start its wakeup schedule. Fig. 5 shows the operation steps of the sensor nodes. The gray zone indicates the delay time during which the nodes are kept under the sleep mode. After the delay time, each node wakes up periodically according to the wakeup schedule. As observed, nodes with n = 1 can construct a route from a higher level to a lower level, and so can nodes with n = 0. Transmission latency is thus reduced. Meanwhile, as nodes with the same height but different numbers will not ***translate*** into the wakeup mode at the same time, the probability of collision can be definitely decreased.

	τ	14	15	16	17	18	19	20	21	22	23	24	25	26	27	28	29	30	31	32	33	34	35	36	37	38	39	40	41
$h=1,n=1$	22									RX	TX	SL	SL	SL	SL	SL	SL	SL	SL	SL	SL	SL	SL	SL	SL	SL	SL	SL	SL
$h=1,n=0$	19						RX	TX	SL	SL	SL	SL	SL	SL	SL	SL	SL	SL	SL	SL	SL	SL	SL	SL	SL	SL	RX	TX	SL
$h=2,n=1$	21								RX	TX	SL	SL	SL	SL	SL	SL	SL	SL	SL	SL	SL	SL	SL	SL	SL	SL	SL	SL	RX
$h=2,n=0$	18					RX	TX	SL	SL	SL	SL	SL	SL	SL	SL	SL	SL	SL	SL	SL	SL	SL	SL	SL	SL	RX	TX	SL	SL
$h=3,n=1$	20							RX	TX	SL	SL	SL	SL	SL	SL	SL	SL	SL	SL	SL	SL	SL	SL	SL	SL	SL	SL	RX	TX
$h=3,n=0$	17				RX	TX	SL	SL	SL	SL	SL	SL	SL	SL	SL	SL	SL	SL	SL	SL	SL	SL	SL	SL	RX	TX	SL	SL	SL
$h=4,n=1$	19						RX	TX	SL	SL	SL	SL	SL	SL	SL	SL	SL	SL	SL	SL	SL	SL	SL	SL	SL	SL	RX	TX	SL
$h=4,n=0$	16			RX	TX	SL	SL	SL	SL	SL	SL	SL	SL	SL	SL	SL	SL	SL	SL	SL	SL	SL	SL	RX	TX	SL	SL	SL	SL
$h=5,n=1$	18					RX	TX	SL	SL	SL	SL	SL	SL	SL	SL	SL	SL	SL	SL	SL	SL	SL	SL	SL	SL	RX	TX	SL	SL
$h=5,n=0$	15		RX	TX	SL	SL	SL	SL	SL	SL	SL	SL	SL	SL	SL	SL	SL	SL	SL	SL	SL	SL	RX	TX	SL	SL	SL	SL	SL
$h=6,n=1$	17				RX	TX	SL	SL	SL	SL	SL	SL	SL	SL	SL	SL	SL	SL	SL	SL	SL	SL	SL	SL	RX	TX	SL	SL	SL
$h=6,n=0$	14	RX	TX	SL	SL	SL	SL	SL	SL	SL	SL	SL	SL	SL	SL	SL	SL	SL	SL	SL	SL	RX	TX	SL	SL	SL	SL	SL	SL

Fig. 5. The operation steps from the 14th to the 41st time slot

To reschedule: After a sensor network performs for a period of time, network topology may change due to such factors as the death of nodes (running out of battery power), the earthquake attack in the observed zone or the distribution of newly added nodes. Sensor nodes affected by these factors must be rescheduled to maintain good function of the network. The BS is in charge of such periodical rescheduling and the rescheduling cycles varies with different applications. The rescheduling runs as follows. The BS first broadcasts a rescheduling packet to each node which then resets its h and n to the initial state and again broadcasts the rescheduling packet out. After all nodes in the network receive the packet and reset their h and n to the initial state, the whole network is re-initialized. To complete rescheduling, simply repeat the above steps (initializing the number and the height of nodes) and calculate the schedule.

5 Performance Evaluation

Experimental evaluation is conducted to compare the performance of different MAC protocols, including S-MAC, D-MAC and our new protocol. S-MAC and D-MAC are included because the former uses the same approach as our protocol to save energy consumed by idle listening and the latter, like our approach, attempts to reduce transmission latency by allowing sensor nodes different delay times. In this simulation, the time slot of each protocol is 10ms; the duty cycle is 10%. Both the sending and receiving slots for D-MAC and our protocol are 10ms, the active time for S-MAC is 20ms, and the sleep time for all three protocols is 180ms. The performance of the three protocols will be measured and compared in terms of their ability to reduce latency and to avoid collision. The collected result of latency refers to the average delay of each transmission and collision indicates the total number of collisions after certain packet transmissions.

The average transmission latency under the straight-line transmission: A simple straight-line transmission with 11 nodes is simulated to evaluate the low latency of our MAC protocol. The distance between two nodes is 50 meters. The first node will send out a packet per 0.5 sec to the last node. Fig. 6 shows the average transmission latency of each packet. The latency pattern of S-MAC is apparently different from that of the other two protocols. The "jumping" latency status of the S-MAC is caused by its interrupted data transmission (mentioned in Section 2). D-MAC and our protocol are free of this problem because of the alternative wakeup schedule which helps transmit data packets from the source node to the destination without interruption.

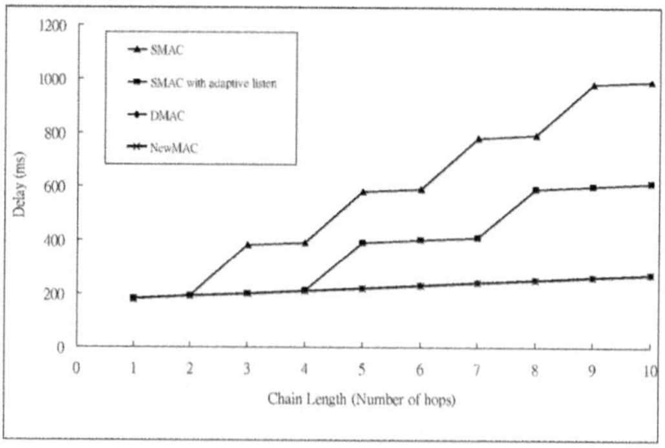

Fig. 6. The average packet transmission latency

The average transmission latency under the random distribution topology: The simulation randomly distributes 100 sensor nodes over a 100m × 500m area. Fig. 7 displays such a random distribution topology. Assume the center node (the triangle in the figure) is the base station. Randomly choose 5 sensor nodes at the outskirt of the topology (the dark dots) as the source nodes to transmit packets. The 5 source nodes will send data packets to the BS with fixed rates. Fig. 8 shows the average transmission latency of each packet for the three protocols. As the result shows, S-MAC depicts bigger latency under the random distribution topology than under the straight-line transmission. This is because more than one source node is transmitting data at the same time under the random distribution topology, resulting in "channel competition". The performance of D-MAC and our protocol, on the other hand, remains relatively stable because both protocols can transmit data to the BS without interruption even when sensor nodes contend for routing channels.

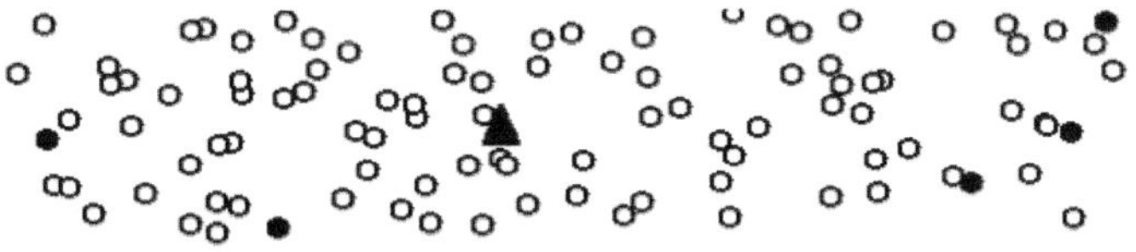

Fig. 7. The random distribution topology

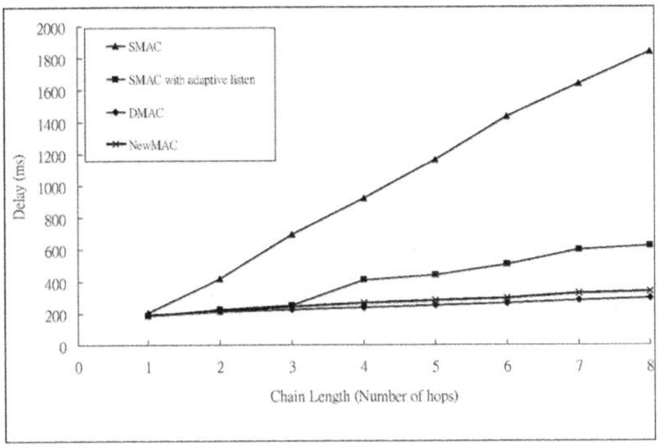

Fig. 8. The average transmission latency of each packet under the random distribution topology

The number of collision under the random distribution topology: The simulation is conducted under the random distribution topology with different numbers of source nodes. It is clear that when the number of source nodes increase, packets under transmission will also increase and so will the probability of collision. As the result in Fig. 9 demonstrates, S-MAC generates the largest number of collision among the three protocols. This is understandable because S-MAC has the longest transmission latency in our simulation and thus will result in the largest number of on-going packet transmissions in the network when increasing source nodes send out more packets at the same time. Our protocol outperforms even the D-MAC. It displays the least collisions due to its mechanism to alternate the wakeup schedule of neighbor nodes by assigning different numbers (0 or 1) to the nodes.

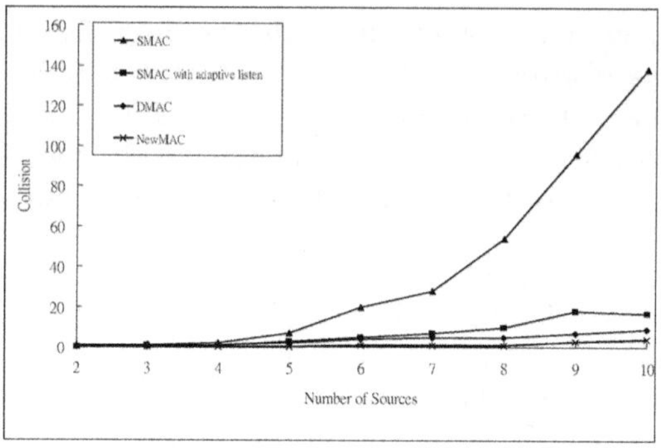

Fig. 9. The number of collisions

6 Conclusion

As the nodes in a wireless sensor network are battery-powered and are difficult to get recharged after distribution, energy efficiency becomes a basic and critical issue. Based on the special features of a wireless sensor network, this paper presents a new and efficient MAC protocol to achieve power efficiency and to reduce transmission latency and collision. When a sensor network is deployed, the proposed protocol starts an initial process to assign a height (hop counts to the BS) and a number (0 or 1) to each node. With such a specific design and function, our protocol is able to arrange favorable job schedules of all sensor nodes and thus facilitate data transmission by reduced transmission latency and collision probability.

References

1. Y. Wei, J. Heidemann, and D. Estrin, "Medium access control with coordinated adaptive sleeping for wireless sensor networks," *IEEE/ACM Trans. on Networking*, Vol. 12, No. 3, pp. 493-506, June 2004.
2. G. Lu, B. Krishnamachari, and C. S. Raghavendra, "An adaptive energy-efficient and low-latency MAC for data gathering in wireless sensor networks," *Proc. 18th Parallel and Distributed Processing Symp.*, Apr. 2004, pp. 224-231.
3. T. van Dam and K. Langendoen, "An adaptive energy-efficient MAC protocol for wireless sensor networks," *Proc. 1st Int'l Conf. on Embedded Networked Sensor Systems*, Nov. 2003, pp. 171-180.
4. T. Aonishi, T. Matsuda, S. Mikami, H. Kawaguchi, C. Ohta, and M. Yoshimoto, "Impact of aggregation efficiency on GIT routing for wireless sensor networks," *Proc. 2006 Int'l Conf. on Parallel Processing Workshops*, Aug. 2006, pp. 151-158.

Automatic Power Model Generation for Sensor Network Simulator

Jaebok Park[1], Hyunwoo Joe[2], and Hyungshin Kim[2,*]

[1] Division of Electronics and Information Engineering,
Chonbuk National University, Joenju, Korea
[2] Department of Computer Science and Engineering,
Chungnam National University, Daejeon, Korea
Tel.:+82-42-821-5446
{parkjaebok,jhwzero,hyungshin}@cnu.ac.kr
http://eslab.cnu.ac.kr

Abstract. Energy consumption estimation in sensor network is a critical process for network lifetime estimation before actual deployment. Energy consumption can be estimated by simulating the sensor network with a power model. Power model is the key component for the accurate estimation. However, the power model is not publicly accessible and it is not easy to generate accurate fine-grain power model. In this paper we proposed a simplified but yet accurate power model for AVR-based sensor nodes. Also, we developed an automated power model generation tool. The tool generates an instruction-level power model that can be connected to sensor network simulators. We model the current consumption of ATmega128 instruction set which is the most widely used processor in sensor node. Loading, execution, and control of the measurement framework are managed by the tool. Using the tool, we can generate power models of various sensor nodes using ATmega128 as their processor. Experimental result shows that our tool successfully generated accurate power models of various sensor nodes including Mica2.

Keywords: sensor network, power model, energy consumption estimation, embedded system, ubiquitous computing.

1 Introduction

Sensor network consists of large number of small sensor nodes called mote. A mote is a tiny computer with wireless communication interface. Most of the case, they are operated with batteries and once they are deployed it becomes infeasible to replace batteries. Hence, estimating operation lifetime of each mote of the planned network topology is a critical process before actual deployment. Identification of hot spots and balancing duties among the motes can be performed from this estimation result.

Energy consumption of general embedded system can be measured in an indoor measurement setup. This measurement-based energy estimation provides very accurate

[*] Corresponding author.

Y.-H. Lee et al. (Eds.): ICESS 2007, LNCS 4523, pp. 453–463, 2007.

result since it is acquired from the actual hardware. Sensor network is a deeply networked embedded system and the measurement-based estimation is infeasible as it consists of hundreds of motes. Hence, energy estimation by simulation is more suitable in sensor network design procedure[1].

Such simulators estimate energy consumption using a power model. The accuracy of the estimation largely depends on that of the power model they use. The power model should be simple because complex power model slows down the energy profiling and estimation process of the simulator. However, for accurate energy estimation, it requires a detailed-enough power model so that it can accurately estimate energy consumption with little overhead to the simulator.

Though there have been a few researches in energy estimation in sensor network field recently, works on power model generation are scarcely reported in the literature. They are using either numerical values from the data book or power model from the chipset manufacturer as their power model. Numerical values of data books are simplified figures and they do not represent dynamic behavior of the component. Power models using these values result to inaccurate energy estimation because of that. Power models from manufacturers are very accurate but it is not open for public access in most of the case. Even though we have accurate power model of a chipset, it is difficult to estimate energy consumption of a complete board until we have power models of all the components on the board. Hence, it will be useful to have a tool that can generate accurate power model of a complete board.

In this paper, we propose a simple yet accurate power model for ATmega128-based[2] motes. Also, we developed an automatic power model generation tool. The proposed power model is instruction-based and the current consumption of the mote is modeled into the instruction set of the mote's processor. ATmega128 is the most widely used processor on sensor nodes including U.C. Berkeley's Mica series[3]. Our power model is simple and that simplifies the model generation process. However, necessary dynamic behaviors of the tested boards are modeled and hence we achieve very accurate model of the mote.

For evaluation, we have generated four power models of four different sensor motes using our automatic power model generation tool. Once the power model is generated, we connect the model to our sensor network energy estimator called MIPS(Machine Instruction level Power estimator for Sensor network)[4]. Using MIPS, we have verified the generated power models are very accurate with accuracy of above 95%. This proves that our automation tool is applicable to many different ATmega128-based motes with great accuracy. This accuracy is attributed to our power modeling method. Our work is unique in that there has been no research on automatic power model generation for sensor node and yet with very accurate power model.

The organization of this paper is as follows. In section 2, related works on power modeling in sensor network are reviewed. Our power modeling method is explained in section 3 and automatic power model generation tool is described in section 4. In section 5, experimental results to verify usability and accuracy of our method is explained and we conclude in section 6.

2 Related Work

Simulator-based methods estimate energy consumption using power model for estimation. In general embedded system, instruction-level simulation methods are proposed in [5] and [6]. They model current consumption of processor's instruction set and compute energy consumption of a program from the model. This model is fine-grained since it can be used for analyzing instruction-level operation of a processor. Macro modeling method[7] was proposed. This method models power consumption of system into software modules and estimates parameters relating the modules to the power model. This approach has faster estimation time and larger estimation error than instruction-based method.

SimplePower[8] and Wattch[9] are RTL-level architecture-based power estimation methods. SimplePower simulates SimpleScalar[10] instruction set and offers capacitor switching statistics of each module to relate each cycle energy. Wattch is implemented in SimpleScalar simulator using power model of microprocessor's functional unit. However, they must have accurate processor's architectural power model which is difficult to acquire.

In sensor network, PowerTossim[1] is the representative tool for energy estimation. This tool is an extension to TOSSIM, a sensor network simulator. PowerTossim's estimation accuracy is relatively poor as it uses current consumption values from data book or limited measured values. In addition to that, PowerTossim can be used only for Mica mote series with TinyOS as its operating system. Other sensor nodes using different operating system cannot use PowerTossim.

In embedded system and sensor network literature, we could not find researches on power model generation. Probably the work in [6] is the closest work to ours. In [6] authors proposed instruction-based energy estimation method. Our method also uses instruction-based method but we focus more on the power model than the estimation procedure. We simplified the power model but yet maintaining good accuracy. We are not generating the power model of a processor. Instead, we generate the power model of the tested board using the processor's instruction set. In overall, our work is unique in that we proposed a power modeling method for sensor node and an automatic model generation tool.

3 Sensor Node Power Modeling Method

In this section, we explain our power modeling method. We used the similar approach as [6] in that we measure current consumption of single instruction while running a program on a sensor node. In this method, each instruction in the instruction set is assigned a fixed energy cost called instruction energy cost. The instruction energy costs of the instruction set become the power model of the given sensor node. The energy cost of an instruction is modeled with base energy cost and overhead cost. The base energy cost is obtained from the measurement framework as shown in Figure 1. We design a number of assembly program that has an infinite loop consisted of single testing instruction. We download the binary image onto the sensor node and measure consumed current during the execution of the program. The measured current value is the base energy cost of the instruction.

However, this simple modeling framework does not generate accurate power model of the tested instruction as explained in [6]. It is due to the dynamic switching behavior of the circuits on the tested hardware. The instruction energy cost should represent not only the energy consumption of the processor but also other dynamic factors induced by peripherals, bus activities, and the manufactured PCB. Instead of trying to model all the factors separately, we simplified the model considering only the two dominant factors. The first factor is known as inter-instruction overhead. It is the current fluctuation induced by the instruction switch between the two neighboring instructions. The other factor is the current fluctuation induced by the operand variation.

The inter-instruction overhead is determined by using a test program that contains an infinite loop with two different instructions in series. For the accurate modeling of the inter-instruction overhead, all combinations of the instruction pairs are needed to be tested. However, we only used one nominal value for all the combinations of instructions. This decision was made to speed up the energy profiling process during simulation while trading-off accuracy. The nominal value is determined by averaging the current variation measured from the limited number of instruction pairs.

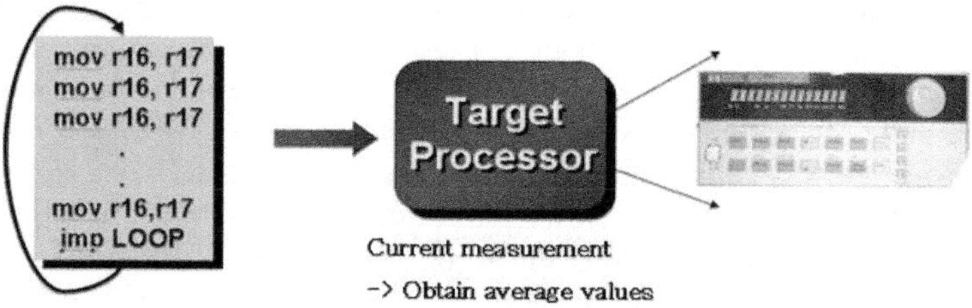

Fig. 1. Energy cost measurement framework

The current variation by different operands can be modeled by measuring all the current consumptions from test programs with varying operands. This approach takes long time to get the correct power model. Instead, we only measure for two extreme cases. The maximum current fluctuation due to the operand variation within the board can be emulated by alternating operands of the test program with 0x00 and 0xff. The minimum case can be achieved with a test program of operand 0x00 only. Then, we average the values from the two measurements. This procedure greatly reduces modeling time with little reduction in accuracy. This method is shown in Figure 2. For branch instructions, we measure power consumption of branch taken for maximum case and branch not taken for minimum case. We developed the power model of 133 instructions of ATmega128 in this method. Other peripherals such as communication chip, LED, and sensors are also modeled in similar way.

Notice that our power model includes energy costs of other components on the sensor nodes. When we measure current consumption of the sensor node, the processor's power line is not separated from other components on the board. Capacitors, resistors, and power level converters affect the power model of given board. Though some motes use the same AVR processor, board layout is different board by board.

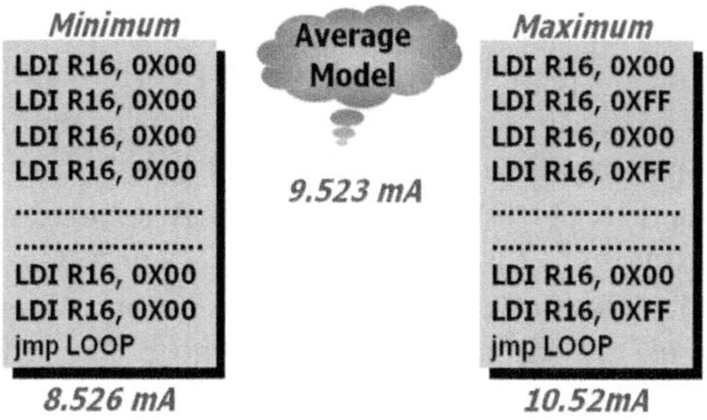

Fig. 2. Operand variation modeling

Hence, the power model of one instruction of a sensor node is different from that of the other nodes. In that sense, our power model includes other unknown current variations due to the board layout and hence, our model can be used to model subtle differences between similar sensor nodes.

4 Automatic Power Model Generation

Power model is created with a host PC, power supply and target sensor node as shown in Fig.3(a). The power supply provides power to the tested board and measures current consumption on the power line. The host PC is connected to the power supply using a RS-232 serial port to control current sampling and power supply.

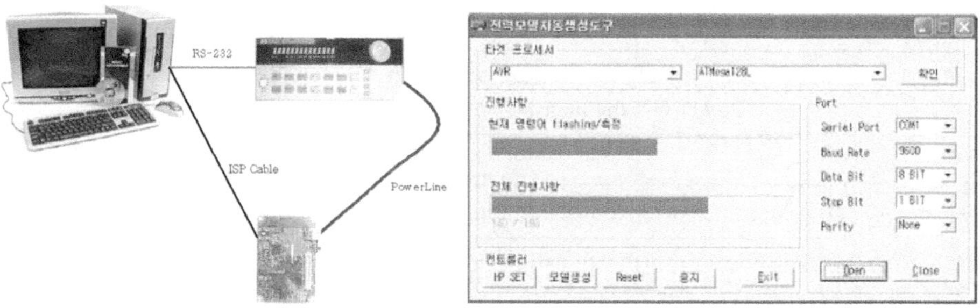

Fig. 3. (a) Power model development environment (b) Automatic power model generation tool

The host PC and the tested board are connected using the ISP(In System Programming) interface on the board. Binary program images are downloaded to the tested board through this ISP interface.

The automatic power model generation tool is executed on the PC and it controls whole model generation process. Fig.3 (b) shows the implemented tool running on the PC.The power model generation procedure is explained as follows. Before model generation, assembly test programs designed as described in section 3 should be assembled and stored on the host PC. When the power generation tool is executed on the host PC, it first configures the power supply through RS-232 serial port. The voltage level and sampling frequency is set. Then, it provides power to the tested board and the board is now ready to download binary code through ISP port. We used routines from Avrdude[11] for ISP download/unload, verify and reset control. The test program is downloaded to the board's on-chip FLASH memory. The host PC sends commands to power supply to turn OFF and ON. Then, the board starts executing the first test program and at the same time, the power supply starts sampling current consumption and transmits the sampled data to the host PC. After sampling for a few seconds, the host PC stops measuring and repeat this measurement cycle with next test program. This modeling procedure continues until all the test programs are executed and measured. Fig.4 shows the modeling procedure.

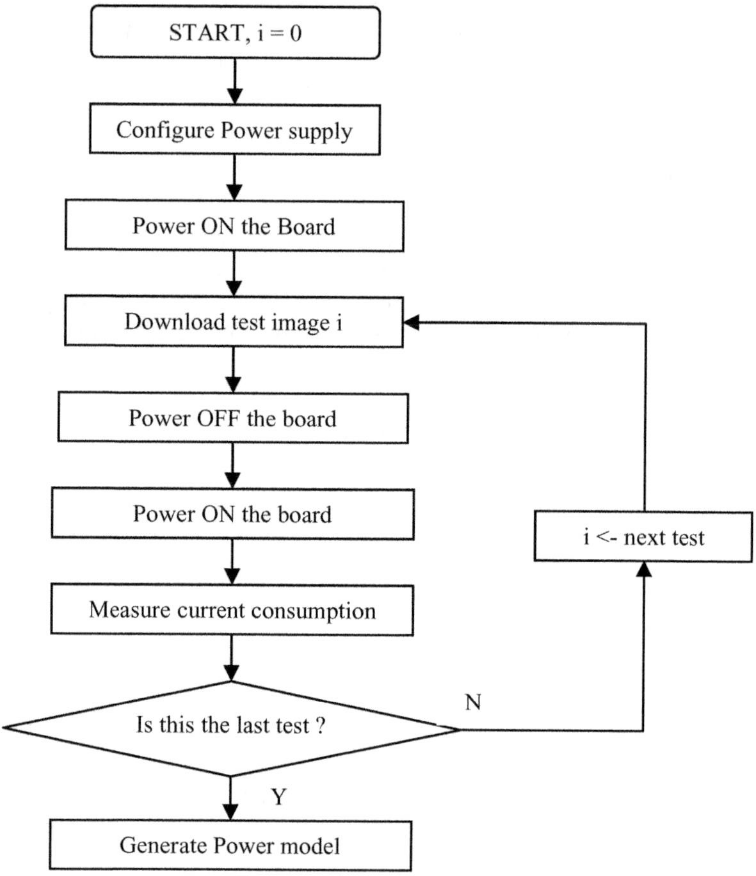

Fig. 4. Automatic power model generation procedure

Proposed procedure develops instruction-based power model of AVR ATmega128-based sensor node using 196 test programs. They are designed to measure base energy cost and inter-instruction overhead of each instruction. Automatic power model generation tool loads test programs into target sensor node according to the measurement list and records average current while the program is running.

The final power model is constructed as instruction name, number of execution cycles and current consumption of each instruction after the overhead compensation. In this way, we can accurately model AVR-based sensor node's power consumption and eventually, the sensor network simulator using our power model can accurately estimate energy consumption during simulation with little run-time overhead. Fig.5 shows the partial result of the generated power model.

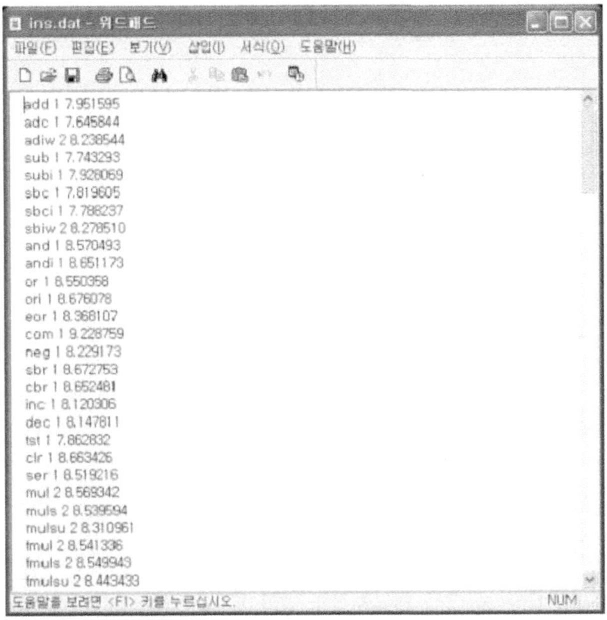

Fig. 5. Generated power model

5 Experiments and Evaluation

Four different AVR-based sensor nodes are selected to verify the applicability of our modeling tool and accuracy of the generated power model. Table 1 shows the specification of the selected nodes. Nano-24[12] and Zigbex[14] are commercial sensor node using ATmega128L microcontroller with CC2420 Zigbee communication module. CESL mote[13] is the sensor node developed in our laboratory. Mica2[3] is the well-known sensor node developed by U.C. Berkeley. It is different from the other sensor boards in that it is using CC1000 as its wireless interface. The number of sensors on-board and the power line design affects the total energy consumption of the board and hence its power model.

We have generated four power models using our modeling framework. It took 3.5 hours to generate the power model of one sensor board. Figure 6 shows the generated power models respect to each instruction. Current consumptions of sensor nodes show

Table 1. Selected AVR-based Sensor nodes

Platform	Nano24	Zigbex	CESL	Mica2
figure				
MCU	ATmega128L	ATmega128L	ATmega128L	ATmega128L
MCU freq.	8MHz	7.37MHz	8MHz	8MHz
Comm	CC2420	CC2420	CC2420	CC1000
Comm freq.	2.4GHz	2.4GHz	2.4GHz	900MHz
Extension Memory	512Kbyte flash	512Kbyte flash	X	512Kbyte flash
LED count	4	4	3	3
Sensor count	0	4	0	0
Battery line feature	Resistor use	Regulator use	Resistor use	directly connection
power supply	AA X 2 3V	AA X 2 3V	AA X 2 3V	AA X 2 3V

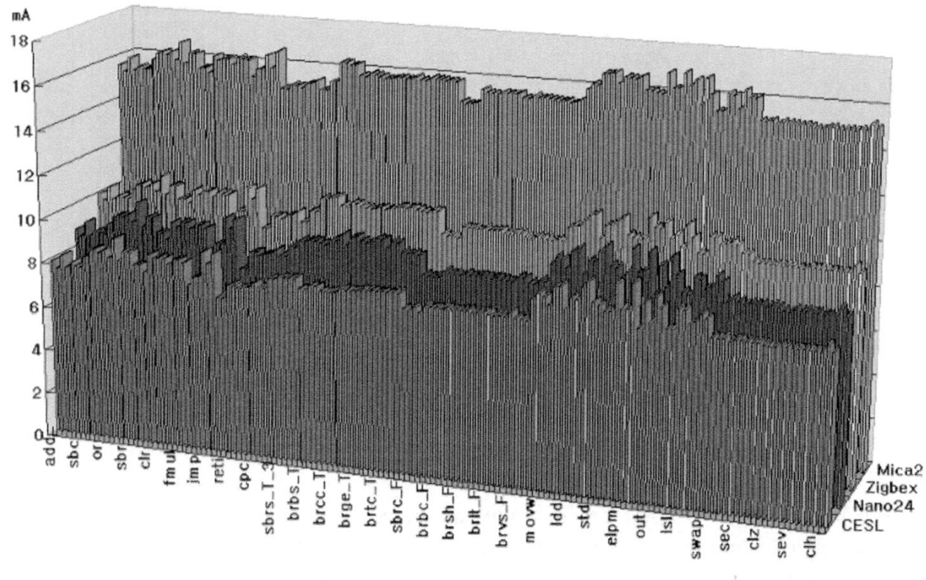

Fig. 6 Generated power models of four sensor nodes. CESL, Nano-24, Zigbex, and Mica2 from the front row to back row respectively.

wide variation though they use the same ATmega128L. The CESL mote consumes the least current among the tested nodes. Nano-24 consumes 1mA more than CESL, which is almost 15% more than CESL. It is because the CESL mote further reduces power consumption by using resistors on the power line. The Zigbex mote consumes 25% more current than the CESL mote and it is because the Zigbex mote has a LED that is ON all the time. Without this LED, the Zigbex shows the smallest current consumption due to its slowest operating frequency. The use of regulator on the Zigbex mote is another reason of this extra current consumption. Regulators cannot convert the input power with 100% efficiency and hence, this is the source of extra current consumption.

The Mica2 consumes 90% more current than the CESL mote. Mica2 uses CC1000 instead of CC2420 and CC1000 requires additional circuits on board. Hence, these additional circuits consume additional power that does not exist on other boards.

Table 2. Nano-24 Power model verification result

Benchmark	Measured (mJ)	simulated (mJ)	Accuracy (%)
illuminance	1317,905	1261,924	95,75
Temperature	1209,958	1182,892	97,76
Humidity	1129,397	1097,113	97,14
Gas	18701,47	18683,02	99,91
Led	1165,738	1151,249	98,75
Sink(RF)	5810,112	5736,206	98,72
Sensor(RF)	2216,61	2215,517	99,95

Table 3. CESL Mote Power model verification result

Benchmark	Simulated(mJ)			Measured (mJ)	Accuracy (%)
	MCU	LED/RF	Sum		
Blink1(2sec)	54,56289	39,99176	94,55465	98,16774429	96,32
Blink2(5sec)	136,4071	97,10657	233,51368	241,7679913	96,59
Blink3(10sec)	272,8141	193,2867	466,10086	482,8300199	96,54
Blink4(15sec)	409,2212	286,5967	695,81785	722,1201182	96,36
Blink5(20sec)	545,6282	381,7654	927,39356	959,5253313	96,65
CPU operating1	272,182	-	272,18202	273,0619106	99,68
CPU operating2	276,5153	-	276,51526	278,8975451	99,15
CPU operating3	269,6815	-	269,68148	277,87337	97,05
CPU operating4	276,2975	-	276,29749	282,0006608	97,98
CPU operating5	279,3753	-	279,37532	286,1951321	97,62
ADCToLeds	158,5284	619,6876	778,21597	805,5238789	96,61
RfmToLeds	153,5254	600,372	753,8974	782,6679789	96,32
CntToLedsAndRfm	158,9944	618,6992	777,69351	792,032182	98,19

Table 4. Zigbex Power model verification result

Benchmark	Simulated(mJ)			Measured (mJ)	Accuracy (%)
	MCU	LED/RF	SUM		
Blink1(2sec)	68,80215	7,25863	76,06078	75,243663	98,93
Blink2(5sec)	172,0053	17,62533	189,63059	187,8987099	99,09
Blink3(10sec)	344,0104	35,08263	379,09305	376,0360494	99,19
Blink4(15sec)	516,0156	52,01898	568,03457	564,2461935	99,33
Blink5(20sec)	688,0208	69,2927	757,31346	752,2754778	99,33
CPU operating1	346,1375	-	346,13751	350,6559342	98,71
CPU operating2	352,7322	-	352,73216	355,5713271	99,20
CPU operating3	345,188	-	345,18795	356,7770217	96,75
CPU operating4	350,6066	-	350,60655	356,9174763	98,23
CPU operating5	346,1375	-	346,13751	350,6976561	98,70
ADCToLeds	228,4879	619,6876	848,17541	837,137573	98,70
RfmToLeds	221,3042	600,372	821,67619	831,6671377	98,80
CntToLedsAndRfm	228,9637	618,6992	847,66289	841,7745489	99,31

Also, the Mica2 does not use resistors on the power line and this direct connection of the board to the battery pack draws more power than the other boards where they use resistors.

We evaluated accuracy of the generated power models using a sensor network simulator called MIPS. Our power model is read by the MIPS during the simulation. The simulator computes consumed energy during execution of a test program on AVR-based sensor nodes.

Table 5. Mica2 Power model verification result

Benchmark	Simulated(mJ)			Measured (mJ)	Accuracy (%)
	MCU	LED	SUM		
Blink1(2sec)	105,397	9.97746	115,37441	113,2057905	98,12
Blink2(5sec)	263,4922	24,22716	287,71937	282,7844928	98,28
Blink3(10sec)	526,9843	48,22336	575,20768	566,8507115	98,55
Blink4(15sec)	790,4764	71,50347	861,97989	851,0574481	98,73
Blink5(20sec)	1053,969	95,24732	1149,21584	1134,433124	98,71
CPU operating1	565,7249	-	565,72491	557,6943305	98,58
CPU operating2	566,8009	-	566,80086	559,1576627	98,65
CPU operating3	524,4255	-	524,42549	528,1850094	99,29
CPU operating4	532,9529	-	532,95289	540,5136759	98,60
CPU operating5	537,9974	-	537,99738	539,9655657	99,64

For the test program, we have selected a number of benchmark programs provided by the manufacturers. Nano-24 has QPlus[15] as its operating system and all the other sensor nodes are using TinyOS. For comparison, we execute the same benchmark programs on the test board and measured current consumption using our measurement framework. Then, we compared the measured energy consumption with the simulator's energy consumption estimation result. All four sensor boards are used for this experiment.

Table 2 shows the experiment result for Nano-24 power model. Seven benchmark programs are used. Five of them are simple sensor read out programs and two of them are communication programs. For the measurement, we have installed two nodes and actual RF communication was performed. All the benchmark programs show good accuracy above 95%.

Table 3, 4 and 5 show the power model verification results of the other three sensor nodes. All the TinyOS applications have shown more than 96% accuracy in all three occasions. From these experimental results, we can conclude that our power model is highly accurate.

6 Conclusion

Recently, there have been a few works reported on energy consumption estimation for sensor network. The accuracy of the estimation relies on the accuracy of the power model they use. However, research on generating accurate power model is rarely reported. In this paper we reported an automated power model generation tool for AVR ATmega128-based sensor nodes. Our tool generates instruction-level power model and it can be used by the sensor network energy estimator. We have performed experiments to verify applicability of our tool and accuracy of the generated power model. From the experiment, we have shown that our tool can generate power model of a sensor board in about 3.5 hours without user's intervention. Also, the generated power model was verified through the comparison between the measured value and simulator out value. The verification results show that the accuracy of the power model is above 95% in all the four test sensor boards.

Using our automatic power model generation tool, users can quickly generate accurate power model for any AVR-based sensor node. Hence, we can estimate energy consumption of AVR-based sensor network using our power model.

Acknowledgement

This study was financially supported by research fund of Chungnam National University in 2005.

References

1. V. Shnayder et al, "Simulating the power consumption of large-scale sensor network applications", SenSys04, pp.188-200, 2004
2. ATmega128, http://www.atmel.com
3. Crossbow Technology, Inc. Mica2 http://www.xbow.com
4. ETRI, Research on low power measurement for sensor network, Project report, 2005
5. A. Sinha et al, "JouleTrack – A Web based tool for software energy profiling", DAC 2001
6. V.Tiwari, S.Malik, and A. Wolfe. "Power analysis of embedded software:A first step towards software power minimization", IEEE Transactions on VLSI system, 2(4):437-445, December 1994
7. A. Muttreja et al, "Automated energy/performance macromodeling of embedded software", DAC2004, pp.99-102, 2004
8. W. Ye et al, "The design and use of SimplePower", in Proc. ACM/IEEE Design Automation Conf., pp.340-345, 2000
9. D. Brooks, et al, "Wattch: A framework for architectural-level power analysis and optimization", ISCA, pp.83-94, 2000
10. D.burger and T. Austin. The simplescalar tool set, version 2.0 Technical report, Computer Sciences Department, University of Wisconsin, June, 1997
11. Avrdude Manual, http://www.cs.ou.edu/~fagg/classes/general/atmel/avrude.pdf
12. Octacomm Corp. Nano-24 Http://www.octacomm.net
13. CESL Laboratory, CESL Mote http://eslab.cnu.ac.kr
14. Hanback Corp. Zigbex Http://www.hanback.co.kr
15. Electronics telecommunication Research Institute. Nano-qplus http://qplus.or.kr/english/jsp/transfer/transfer_03_1.jsp

Situation-Aware Based Self-adaptive Architecture for Mission Critical Systems

Sangsoo Kim, Jiyong Park, Heeseo Chae, and Hoh Peter In*

College of Information & Communications, Korea University,
5-ga, Anam-dong, Seogbuk-gu, Seoul 136-701, Korea
{sookim,jayyp,royalhs,hoh_in}@korea.ac.kr

Abstract. Conventional mission-critical systems cannot prevent mission failure in dynamic battlefield environments in which the execution situations or missions change abruptly. To solve this problem, self-adaptive systems have been proposed in the literature. However, the previous studies do not offer specifics on how to identify changes in a system situation or to transform situation information into the actions the systems must take in dynamic environments. This paper proposes a situation-awareness based self-adaptive system architecture (SASA) to support more efficient adaptation and, hence, achieve more accurate and successful missions, even in dynamic execution environments. A case study for air defense systems (ADS) using tests in a HLA/TRI-based real-time distributed simulation environment was implemented.

Keywords: Situation-Awareness, Self-Adaptation, Mission Critical System, HLA/RTI, Real-Time Distributed Simulation.

1 Introduction

Mission critical systems are somewhat limited in certain fields, as the name implies [1]. Therefore, their applications are also usually limited and fixed to the early assumptions of their operating circumstances and goals. To solve this problem, self-adaptive middleware concepts in designing system architecture have been proposed in the literature [2][3]. However, previous studies have not addressed specific ways to recognize changes in system environments and situations or to transform the situation information into the response actions the systems must execute.

In the real world, mission-critical real-time systems are often exposed to complex, dynamic situations, especially in ubiquitous battlefield environments. Therefore, it is inevitable that much information is generated about the systems and this information affects how efficiently the systems run. Thus, an adaptive architecture is required to reflect the dynamically generated, specific information in the systems. In particular, systems in the military domain can be affected by such dynamic environments more than systems in other domains. Battlefield

* Corresponding author.

Y.-H. Lee et al. (Eds.): ICESS 2007, LNCS 4523, pp. 464–475, 2007.

environments have changed dynamically in the past and will continue to change dynamically in the future.

In the future, even the near term, new designs in aircraft and missiles that can render air defense systems (ADS) useless will be developed for use on the battlefield. Therefore, to guarantee and maintain the defense capability of ADS from this threat, ADS should be able to understand the actions and situation of an enemy aircraft or missile and destroy it by adjusting a weapon system's search and track algorithm to each situation. Determining a strategy suitable to each situation and changing the guidance algorithm for missile control should be achieved in a very short time to allow immediate response actions. It is difficult for ADS to respond quickly if control commands must go through a ground control center (GCC). Common air defense systems use the conditional expression method, one of the self-adaptive categories, for defense. Nevertheless, this method is still relatively inadequate for bringing threats under control. Therefore, a system that automatically recognizes any changes in environment, evaluates its functional situation awareness, establishes a suitable strategy, verifies the strategy's effectiveness, and executes the mission in real time would be indispensable.

In this paper, self-adaptive system architecture (SASA) for supporting ADS which is now being testing for enhanced future ADS systems is proposed. For better adaptation, situation-aware middleware is applied to our proposed software architecture. The proposed SASA consists of three parts: situation-aware middleware, self-adaptive software, and real-time systems. To verify the effectiveness of the proposed architecture, we tested it in the HLA/RTI based real-time distributed simulation environment now widely used for various domains, including the testing and evaluation of Department of Defense (DoD) weapons systems [4].

The related works which are the basis of our proposed architecture are introduced briefly in chapter 2, and the self-adaptive system architecture (SASA) for mission critical real-time systems, especially ADS, are presented in chapter 3. In chapter 4, the results of implementing the HLA/RTI-based real-time distributed simulation for ADS-adapted SASA are presented, and chapter 5 describes the testing by simulation federation implemented to verify the effectiveness of the self-adaptive requirements. Finally, we present our conclusions and discuss future work.

2 Related Work

The research in air defense systems (ADS) in the military domain is conducted on an ongoing basis. ADS are composed of distributed real-time systems because they collect information and manage numerous communication systems. The problems of scheduling, load balancing, and coordination among the nodes of distributed real-time systems are studied in [5]. ADS can reduce inconsistent, unintegrated, and inexact information and actively deal with a mission if a knowledge-based database is composed because a knowledge system can more efficiently cope with emergencies. The system in [6] offers a decision-making system that uses a war control center. In addition, the research in [7] develops a situation analysis system and estimates a danger state using fuzzy logic technologies. However, it is difficult to adapt for mission change that occurred during the mission time, though those methods are aptitude to ascendant initial target.

Various types of research have been done about self-adaptive systems, such as an architecture-based approach [3], rainbow [2], self-optimization [8], a self-adaptation genetic algorithm [9], and self-adaptive for robotics [10]. Most of this research focused not on real-time systems but on everyday systems and non-mission critical systems. Self-adaptive systems for real-time methods were studied by [11]. However, most researchers focused on the adaptive methodology and algorithm.

In a ubiquitous environment, situation-aware middleware and language for specifying situation awareness is researched. In [12], reconfigurable context-sensitive middleware is extended in ubiquitous computing environments to simplify the development of Situation-Awareness (SA) application software and achieve reusability and runtime reconfigurability.

In this paper, we apply situation-aware middleware, which is briefly introduced in the next section, to our proposed situation-aware based self-adaptive system architecture (SASA) for accurate information analysis about mission environments. Situation awareness can significantly improve the performance of ADS. Typical real-time systems and knowledge-based systems have insufficient flexibility and treating capacity because of lack of data. In an unpredictable situation, the systems will have difficultly managing emergencies and will demonstrate inferior agility because they must communicate through a centralized system and process large amounts of general data. System-based situation awareness can overcome these defects.

3 Situation-Aware Self-Adaptive System

3.1 SASA for ADS

A self-adaptive system architecture (SASA) for ADS has the form of a missile system complemented by self-adaptive systems properties. SASA has been adapted to guided missiles among ADS subsystems. As Fig. 1 shows, the missile-adapted SASA consists of three parts.

Situation-Awareness Expresser (SAE): Analyzes situations and derives actions from radar, seeker, GPS, and other external information. It collects situation data in a database and receives the required context acquisition. The situation analysis feature determines the present state based on the data collected, then assigns and schedules action tuples.

Adaptive Engagement Manager (AEM): If a new strategy is required after the extracted actions are compared with an existing engagement strategy, the new strategy is produced by the adaptation engine.

Guidance and Control Unit (GCU): The new strategy is passed through a self-adaptation executer to the weapons system's guidance and control unit (GCU).

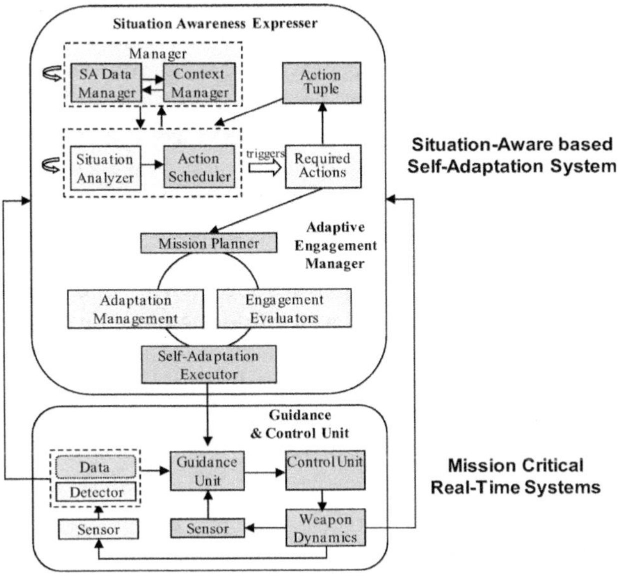

Fig. 1. SASA for Air Defense Systems (for a Guided Missile)

A typical GCU consists of a guidance unit, control unit, and air frame. For guided missiles, GCUs play the most important role during engagement with a target. The guidance unit communicates with the AEM and the control unit sends and receives situational information about the mission environment and the target by communicating with the SAE. The SAE and AEM are loaded in the GCU, implemented with middleware.

3.2 Situation-Aware Expresser

The SAE plays a role in recognizing dynamic changes in operating environments and extracting proper responses to meet those changes [13]. The SAE is composed of the following:

- *SA Data Manager*: Manages the situation awareness data and mission data from mission critical real-time systems. The context tuple is <*t, c1, c2, ..., cn*>. t is the time stamp and *c1, c2, ..., cn* is a set of context attributes.
- *Context Manager*: Receives context acquisition from the SA Data Manager and sends the collected context data to it. The context data is composed of target information, priority and correspondence methods for the situation, mission results, and so on.
- *Situation Analyzer*: Recognizes situations based on situation-awareness criteria, and communicates reciprocally with the SA Data Manager.
- *Action Scheduler*: Identifies the actions to be triggered by the recognized situations, approves permitted actions, and schedules these actions.

- *Action Scheduler*: Identifies the actions to be triggered by the recognized situations, approves permitted actions, and schedules these actions.
- *Action Tuple*: <*t, a1, a2, ..., an*>, where t is the time the action is performed and *a1, a2, ..., an* is a set of attributes of the action. Attributes can be name, parameter types, parameter values, and the like. When an action is taken, information about the action is recorded using an action tuple value.
- *Situation Expression*: Has the format: $[\forall, \exists]$ t in <*time range*> [*context, derivative, action, situation*]<*compare*><*value*>.

We can form new situations by performing "*not*," "*and*," or "*or*" operations in defined situations. To specify an event-handling plan, i.e., what actions should be taken to respond to different situations, we define related rules to associate actions to situations as follows: [*activate at situation x*] *action y*.... A list of such "*situation x*" and "*action y*" forms a plan. The event handler monitors the situation-match events, and activates the actions associated to them according to the plan.

3.3 Situation-Aware IDL

In a mission situation, SASA decides new missions that change the original targets based on the priority of the target type and distance between the target and missile. In order to suggest the development method which can describe the situation and make the situation-aware service, SA-IDL is used. The SA-IDL model such a tuple format is essential to justify the collaborative relation and conflict. Thus SA-IDL model has the component which are Context Tuple, Action Tuple and Derived Context as follows:

Action := (*Time, Target, State, StateValue*)
Context := (*Timestamp, Target, State, StateValue*)
A := {x | *x* is an Action}
C := {x | *x* is a Context}
DerivedContext := P(C) $\longrightarrow$ {*true, false*}
Situation := (*DerivedContext, P(C), A*)

In action tuple, an action is used in two manners: one is to change attribute values of target, and the other is to give orders to target. The context has information of target each time, and the situation constitutes the "*Derived Context*" that accumulated the information of the context. Especially, the state of action tuple and context tuple have attributes of attitude, speed, coordinates, priority of target, and the "*StateValue*" is the real value of the states.

The system operates situation awareness in a target with the knapsack algorithm [14], which is the one of dynamic programming and mathematical models that defined the successful condition of ADS. The system can reduce total mission time by situation awareness.

Fig. 2 shows a portion of the SA-IDL specification for the application software based on the identified situation-awareness requirements. For example, the action

```
SASAApplication SA {
Class Time {int year; int month; int day; int hour; int minute; int second; int milisecond; int microsecond;}
Class Location {String loc;}
Class History {Time beginTime; Time endTime; List string idList;}
Class Mission {String ID; Time beginTime; Time endTime; List string enemyList;}
Class Enemy {String ID; String priority; String type; String speed; String altitude;}
                    Context Collection Rate = 0.1;
                    ...
                    CompositeSituation readyToMission (Mission m, Enemy en, Histroy h)
                                    collectSituation(m, t, loc) && allowToMission(m, en, h)
                    CompositeSituation emergencyState (Mission m, Enemy en, Histroy h)
                                    immediateState(m, t, h) && alarm(m) && checkMission(m, en, loc)
                    ...
                    Rule missionState ActiveAt readyToMission(Mission m, Enemy en, Histroy h) {[local]
void missionState();
                    Rule emergency ActiveAt emergencyState(Mission m, Enemy en, Histroy h) {[local]
void emergency();
                    ...
}
```

Fig. 2. Partial SA-IDL Specification

'*missionState*' is triggered when 'the system collects the start of mission caused by enemy' (*collectionSituation*) and '*the center system is allowed to start the mission*' (*allowToMission*). The action '*emergency*' is triggered by '*the mission starts with unpredictable situation*' (*emergencyState*).

Definition of success and selection of new definition of SA-IDL through modeling is presented as shown in Fig. 3.

Success:= (*C*, *Action*, *Action*) { $\exists$ (*c*, *x*, *y*): Sucess; $\forall$ *a*, *b*: Situation | *c* $\in$ *a*.P(*C*) $\cap$ *b*.P(*C*) and *c* $\neq \emptyset$ and *a*.*DerivedContext* (*c*) = true and *b*.*DerivedContext* (*c*) = true and *x* $\in$ *a*.A and *y* $\in$ *b*.A and *x*.Time = *y*.Time and *x*.Target = *y*.Target and *x*.State = *y*.State and *x*.NewState $\neq$ *y*.NewState }	Select:= (*C*, *Action*, *Action*) { $\exists$ (*c*, *x*, *y*): Select; $\forall$ *a*, *b*: Situation | *c* $\in$ *a*.P(*C*) $\cap$ *b*.P(*C*) and *c* $\neq \emptyset$ and *a*.DerivedContext (*c*) = true and *b*.DerivedContext (*c*) = true and *x* $\in$ *a*.A and *y* $\in$ *b*.A and *x*.State = *y*.State and *x*.Priority > *y*. Priority and *x*.Target $\neq$ *y*.Target and *x*.NewState $\neq$ *y*.NewState then Success(*C*, *Action*, *Action*)}

Fig. 3. Definition of Success and Select

There exists a conflict (c, x, y) for any two situations, a and b. The above constraint defines the context set c that triggers successful action. The intersection of $\mathrm{P}(a.C)$ and $\mathrm{P}(b.C)$ denotes a set of context sets that is shared between two situations, a and b. The context set c should be an element of this intersected set. Also, it is an input element of the Derived Context functions, and it satisfies both requirements of the two situations. Additionally, the c should not be an empty set. The above constraint defines two actions, x and y, that are same as each other. X is an element of a's action set, and y is of b's. The two actions change the same state of the same target at the same time with different values.

However, the mechanism of target selection with the success of ADS has different forms in the priority. The priority of a new target is different from that of the original target; and then the missile selects a new target to define of a successful situation.

4 Implementing the SASA

4.1 ADS Simulation

We implemented ADS to verify the effectiveness of our SASA. To implement and test it in conditions most similar to real systems, we implemented the HLA/RTI-based real-time distributed simulation. HLA/RTI is now applied by the DoD Defense Modeling and Simulation Office (DMSO) for simulation-based weapons systems testing and evaluation. Thus, it is an infrastructure suitable for virtual experiments under the circumstances of real-time systems.

ADS have been developed to assess the performance of runtime infrastructure (RTI) for high-level architecture (HLA) and to test or evaluate surface-to-air missiles now under construction [4][15]. Through this paper, we present our remodeled ADS, which has SASA applied, and verify its effectiveness. ADS simulation has seven components: Simulation control center (SMCC), air target simulator (ATS), multifunction radar (MFR), engagement control simulator (ECS), launcher (LAU), missile (MSL), and runtime infrastructure (RTI).

The SMCC monitors and controls the real-time distributed simulation for air defense systems. The ATS creates the air targets and transmits their information. The MFR searches out the position of airborne targets and missiles. The ECS evaluates the threat degree of any airborne targets and assigns threat priority to the missiles. The LAU transfers information from the ECS to the MSL and simulates the launcher function. MSL represents the missile and traces the airborne targets by threat evaluation. These six components interact with each other, guided by the RTI.

4.2 Algorithm for Engagements

To achieve a mission in a various and changeable situation, SASA needs an algorithm that can perceive a situation and threat it actively. The algorithm for engagements in mission-critical situations is given below:

- Step 1. The ADS scans the situation in the radar capable region and updates the situation data. It checks for changes in the general situation or allocation mission and sends the data to the SA Data Manager.
- Step 2. The mission must be check-and-change adaptable in the present situation in the mission state if new mission data about the number of targets and acquisition of new targets is not to coincide with the general situation.

(a) The situation that finds unpredictable target.
(b) The situation that makes a change in a target.

- Step 3. The ADS terminates the mission situation and updates the situation data in the database.

In Step 2(a), the system needs a priority algorithm for each situation. Military aircraft allocation algorithms are applied to the field of large-scale allocation problems in which a collection of resources (assets) must be mapped in an optimal or near-optimal manner to a number of objectives (targets), as measured by an objective function [16].

$$\Pi_j = 1 - \prod_{i=1}^{m}(1 - x_{i,j}p_{i,j}) \tag{1}$$

$$U(X) = \sum_{j=1}^{n} P_j \Pi_j \tag{2}$$

$$U(X) = \sum_{i_1=1}^{m}\sum_{i_2=1}^{m}\sum_{j=1}^{n} \varepsilon_{i_1,i_2,j}x_{i_1,j}x_{i_2,j} \tag{3}$$

$$Y(X) = \sum_{i} v_i \sum_{j} \gamma_{i,j}x_{i,j} \tag{4}$$

If the efficiency $p_{i,j}$ is interpreted as the probability of the event "*elementary asset i will achieve elementary objective j if so allocated*," and if these events are statistically independent, then the probability of elementary objective j being achieved by allocation strategy X is (2). The degree to which the events fail to be independent is captured by $V(X)$, which quantifies the additional benefit of allocating multiple assets to the same objective. $Y(X)$ measures the cost of the strategy X. This cost includes deterministic costs, such as fuel and ordnance, as well as statistical costs, such as risk of asset damage or loss. Combining these terms (2), (3), (4), gives us the final algorithm in (5):

$$J(X) = AU(X) + BV(X) - rY(X) \tag{5}$$

where, the efficiency $p_{i,j}$ of asset B_i in achieving objective T_j, the value v_i of asset B_i, the risk i,j associated with allocating B_i to T_j , and the joint efficiency $\varepsilon_{i1,i2,j}$ added by simultaneously assigning assets B_{i1} and B_{i2} to objective T_j.

The SASA system controls an objective with a high-priority target using the algorithm in each situation. After the mission, it updates the situation data in the database and refers to it in next mission.

5 Evaluation

5.1 Test Environments

The test results, which include performance measurements, gave us information about the mission elapsed time and the hit rate for missiles. We validated the usefulness of the systems having self-adaptation capability as a result, then compared systems having this capability with systems without it.

The mission elapsed time is the period of time from missile launch to target shoot-down to accomplish a mission. It is calculated as follow:

$$T_{mission} = T_{hit} - T_{launch} \tag{6}$$

Where $T_{mission}$ is the mission time, T_{hit} is a time when the missile hits the target or explodes by itself, T_{launch} is when the missile is launched to engage the target.

The hit rate of missiles measures the success rate in shooting down targets. The probability of single shot kill (P_{ssk}) is used as the hit rate. Assume, if given one shot,

$$P_{ssk} = \int_{-\infty}^{\infty} f(x) \cdot l(x) \cdot d(x) \tag{7}$$

Where *f(x)* is hit probability, *l(x)* is lethality function. The Gaussian lethality function is:

$$l(r) = P_0 \cdot e^{\frac{-x^2}{2a^2}} \tag{8}$$

Where P_0 is kill probability at x*=0* (x is the distance from the target) and lethality constant a is predefined as weapon characteristics. It is assumed that our missile's lethality constant is 7 meters.

In the execution environments, we changed the number of targets and missiles to represent dynamic mission situations. The test outputs allowed us to distinguish between the results for systems having self-adaptation capability and systems without it.

5.2 Test Results

As Table 1 shows, we obtained average values by comparing the systems having situation-aware based self-adaptation capability with the systems without it, judged according to the number of targets. Systems 1 and system 2 are, respectively, the first and second targets in the mission simulation.

According to the test results, the mission time of the systems having situation-aware based self-adaptation capability shows moderate reduction over the elapsed time of systems without this capability. Within a 10ms error rate, the results reveal

Table 1. Mission Time of non-SASA and SASA

Number of Target	Non SASA System 1	System 2	SASA System 1	System 2
4	36804.91	38920.95	36736.03	38846.31
6	46504.26	49170.48	46469.68	49035.68
8	48927.71	51800.27	48422.40	51621.94
10	57340.85	60808.92	56773.07	60120.36

a gap in elapsed time between the situation-aware self-adaptive systems and the other systems as the number of targets increases. The results also show a maximum term of 680ms. The reason for this is that a missile target has changed without commands from the GCC.

Table 2. Accuracy Rate of SASA and Non-SASA

Number of Target	Non SASA	SASA
4	87	90
6	86	88
8	84	88
10	84	88
Average	85.25	88.5

Table 2 shows the accuracy rate of the SASA applied system and the non-SASA applied system in conditions in which the targets are changed. Because ADS have demonstrated an 85% mission success rate in real-world situations, we can assume that the non-SASA systems in this paper also have an 85.25% success rate. The approximately 15% mission failure rate is caused by defects in a missile, incorrect radar commands, missile control errors, and tracking faults caused by changes in targets. In the SASA applied systems, the systems estimate an 88.5% mission success rate in the simulation because SASA can reduce the mission elapsed time to shoot down and destroy targets while continuing to track the most threatful and dynamic targets in the absence of commands from the MFR.

6 Conclusions

This paper presents a self-adaptive system architecture (SASA) for surface-to-air missile guidance. To achieve a more sophisticated adaptation capability, we applied situation-aware middleware to our work. The SASA presented in this paper includes compositions of concepts such as situation awareness, self-adaptation, verification, and real-time systems. To verify the proposed architecture, we implemented a HLA/RTI-based real-time distributed simulation, tested it, and compared the systems having self-adaptation capability with systems lacking that capability. According to the test results, the time consumed in processing self-adaptation during a mission did not influence mission success.

On the contrary, the total mission execution time was shortened by saving the communication time between the missile and the GCC, a conventional situation. The self-adaptive system determined the mission properly by referring to changes in the surrounding situation and finally processed the mission in valid time. Although the communication delay time between subsystems eventually increased, we could confirm that the mission success rate was considerably increased. Consequently, the SASA adapted system not only saved on total mission execution time but also increased the hit rate of missiles. It is expected that our proposed architecture will output equivalent performance in real systems because the simulation and test environments are based on HLA/RTI, which is basically used for weapons systems testing and evaluation by the DoD.

As future work, we plan a study to verify the self-adaptive systems of real surface-to-air missile systems and check the effectiveness of an engagement strategy automatically determined by these self-adaptive systems through a model checking approach. In addition, situation awareness expression language is necessary for hard, real-time systems in a mission critical case.

Acknowledgments. This work was supported by the 2nd Brain Korea 21 Project in 2006.

References

1. Krishna, C. M., Shin, K. G.: Real-Time Systems, McGraw Hill, New York (1999)
2. Garlan, D., Cheng, S., Huang, A., Schmerl, B., Steenkiste, P.: Rainbow: Architecture-Based Self-Adaptation with Reusable Infrastructure,IEEE Computer. October (2004) 46–54
3. Oreizy P., Gorlick, M. M., Taylor, R. N., Heimbigner, D., Johnson, G., Medvidovic, N., Quilici, A., Rosenblum, D. S., and Wolf, A. L.: An Architecture-Based Approach to Self-Adaptive Software, IEEE Intelligent Systems. May/June (1999) 54–62
4. Lee, T. D., Jeon, B. J., and Choi, S. Y.: RISA: Object-oriented Modeling and Simulation of Real-time dIstributed Systems for Air defense, Lecture Notes in Computer Science, OOIS'03. September (2003) 346–355
5. Choi, S. Y., Wijesekera, D.:The DADSim: Air Defense Simulation Environment, High Assurance Systems Engineering, Fifth IEEE International Symposim on. HASE (2000) 75–82
6. Lin, C. E., Chen, K. L.: Automated Air Defense System Using Knowledge-Based System, IEEE transactions on aerospace and electronic systems. v.27 no.1 (1991) 118–124
7. Hua, X. Q., Jie, L. Y., Xian, L. F.: Study on Knowledge Processing Techniques in Air Defense Operation Intelligent Aid Decision, Computational Intelligence and Multimedia Applications, ICCIMA 2003. Proceedings. Fifth International Conference (2003) 114–119
8. Ganak, A. G., Corbi, T. A.: The Drawing Automatic Computing era. IBM System Journal v.42 no.1 (2003) 5–18
9. Wang , Z., Cui, D., Huang, D., and Zhou, H.: A Self-Adaptation Genetic Algorithm Based on Knowledge and Its Application, Proceedings of the 5'World Congress on Intelligent Control, and Automation. June 15-19, Hangzhou, P.R. China (2004) 2082-2085
10. Kim, J., Park, S.: Self Adaptive Software Technology for Robotics, Proceedings of the 11th Asia-Pacific Software Engineering Conference (APSEC'04) (2004)
11. Shetty, S., Neema, S., Bapty, T.: Model Based Self Adaptive Behavior Language for Large Scale Real Time Embedded Systems, IEEE Conference on the Engineering of Computer Based Systems (ECBS), Brno. Czech Republic. May (2004)
12. Yau, S., Huang, D., Gong, H., Seth, S.: Development and Runtime Support for Situation-Aware Application Software in Ubiquitous Computing Environments, COMPSAC -NEW YORK-, v.28 (2004) 452–457

13. Yau, S., Wang, Y., and Huang, D., In, H.: Situation-Aware Contract Specification Language for Middleware for Ubiquitous Computing, The Ninth IEEE Workshop on Future Trends of Distributed Computing Systems (FTDCS'03) (2003) 93–99
14. Martello, S., Toth, P.: Knapsack Problems: Algorithms and Computer Implementations, John Wiley & Sons, New York (1990)
15. Jeong, C. S., and Choi, S. Y.: An Object-oriented Simulation Systems for Air Defense, Lecture Notes in Computer Science. May (2003) 674–683
16. Abrahams, P., Balart, R., Byrnes, J. S., Cochran, D., Larkin, M. J., Moran, W., Ostheimer, G.: MAAP: the Military Aircraft Allocation Planner", Evolutionary Computation Proceedings, IEEE World Congress on Computational Intelligence, The 1998 IEEE International Conference (1998) 336-341

Micromobility Management Enhancement for Fast Handover in HMIPv6-Based Real-Time Applications*

Sungkuen Lee, Eallae Kim, Taehyung Lim, Seokjong Jeong, and Jinwoo Park

Korea University, Anam-dong Seongbuk-ku, Seoul 136-713, S. Korea
{food2131,eallae,stonebell,jwpark}@korea.ac.kr

Abstract. In this paper, we propose a fast handoff algorithm for micromobility management enhancement in HMIPv6 networks, which eliminates the DAD procedure involved in the regular HMIPv6 in order to decrease handoff latency and increase the resource utilization efficiency. In the proposed scheme, the MAP is designed to guarantee the uniqueness of MN's interface identifier within a MAP domain as long as the MN moves in a MAP domain, so that the MN configures the new address without the DAD procedure resulting in the decreased handoff latency significantly. When the MN resides in a subnet, MIPv6 is used adaptively as a mobility management protocol, which is to reduce bandwidth waste from the IP packet header overhead of IP-in-IP tunneling from the regular HMIPv6. Thru various computer simulation results, we verified the superior performance of the proposed scheme by comparing with the results of other schemes, MIPv6 and HMIPv6.

1 Introduction

Next-generation broadband wireless/mobile networks, such as WLAN, WiBro and WiMAX, are envisioned to have IPv6-based infrastructure. One of the research challenges for next-generation all IPv6-based networks is the design of intelligent IP mobility management protocol which has a seamless mobility and minimal signaling overhead. Considering a rapidly increasing demands of real-time services recently, it is more essential to develop the fast handoff protocol in order to support real-time services like VoIP in wireless/mobile networks [1] and [2].

Internet Engineering Task Force (IETF) has proposed the Mobile IPv6 (MIP v6) as the basic mobility management protocol for IPv6-based wireless/mobile networks [3]. MIPv6, however, suffers from several shortcomings, such as high handoff latency, large signaling overhead because it is considered to be a macromobility management protocol. Therefore, it is insufficient to support real-time IP services. In other words, when the mobile node (MN) detects that it has moved to a new subnet, the MN first needs to perform duplication address detection (DAD) to verify

* This work was supported by University IT Research Center Project at Korea University.

Y.-H. Lee et al. (Eds.): ICESS 2007, LNCS 4523, pp. 476–487, 2007.

the uniqueness of its link-local address on the new link, as specified in IPv6 [4]. In addition, after forming the new care-of-address (CoA) with stateless address autoconfiguration [5], the MN must update the binding cache its home agent (HA) and correspondent node (CN) by sending a binding update (BU). Consequently, two procedures of the address resolution and (home) network registration in MIPv6 are primarily elements in long handoff latency, which can heavily deteriorate the delay-sensitive IP real-time services.

To enhance the performance of the basic MIPv6, researchers have been actively working on a fast handoff protocol such as hierarchical mobile IPv6 (HMIPv6) [7], fast handover for mobile IPv6 (FMIPv6) [8] and so on. Particularly, there have been numerous extension proposals, based on HMIPv6 [9]-[12]. HMIPv6 are designed to minimize handoff latency and the amount of signaling to HA and CN by allowing the MN to locally register in a mobile anchor point (MAP) domain. However, HMIPv6 is also insufficient to support real-time IP services, which is the same as MIPv6, because of long address resolution time of the DAD procedure to verify the uniqueness of the new CoA. In addition, for the local mobility management in HMIPv6, it uses the IP-in-IP packet tunneling approach using IPv6 encapsulation to deliver data packets to an MN. However, bandwidth waste from the IP packet header overhead of IP-in-IP tunneling is occurred especially for the MN with low mobility. And this is more severe to small packets, such as voice packets. Moreover, considering bandwidth-limited wireless link, this inefficiency of resource utilization is also more severe.

In this paper, we propose a fast handoff algorithm for micromobility management enhancement in HMIPv6 networks, which eliminates the DAD procedure for the fast micromobility handoff and utilizes MIPv6 scheme adaptively based on the HMIPv6 for the efficient resource utilization. In the proposed scheme, the MAP guarantees the uniqueness of MN's interface identifier within a MAP domain as long as the MN moves in a MAP domain. Therefore, the MN configures the new address without any DAD procedures, so that handoff latency and signaling is decreased significantly. And also the proposed scheme utilizes HMIPv6 as a mobility management protocol only when the MN moves from one subnet to another, while it utilizes MIPv6 as a mobility management protocol when the MN resides in a subnet. Therefore, it reduces bandwidth waste from the IP packet header overhead of IP-in-IP tunneling, which results in an efficient resource utilization.

The rest of paper is organized as the following: We describe the proposed mobility management scheme in section 2. Section 3 presents some simulation results comparing the proposed scheme to MIPv6 and HMIPv6. After that we provide some concluding remarks in section 4.

2 The Proposed Handoff Algorithm

2.1 Principle

We propose a fast handoff algorithm for micromobility management enhancement in HMIPv6 networks, which eliminates the DAD procedure for the fast micromobility handoff and utilizes MIPv6 scheme adaptively based on HMIPv6 for the efficient resource utilization.

The DAD time for a new address takes quite a long time with respect to the handoff latency. If the DAD time is reduced or eliminated, handoff latency will be quite low, so that the protocol can meet the requirement for traffic that is delay sensitive such as VoIP. In the proposed scheme, the MAP guarantees the uniqueness of MN's interface identifier within a MAP domain as long as the MN moves in a MAP domain. Therefore, the MN configures the new address without any DAD procedures, so that handoff latency and signaling is decreased significantly.

For the local mobility management in HMIPv6, it uses the IP-in-IP packet tunneling approach using IPv6 encapsulation to deliver data packets to an MN. However, if the MN does not move between subnets frequently and resides in a subnet for a long time, bandwidth waste from the IP packet header overhead of IP-in-IP tunneling can be occurred. Considering 40 bytes of IP packet header, this is more severe to small packets, such as voice. And considering bandwidth-limited wireless link, this inefficiency of resource utilization is also more severe. Therefore, the proposed scheme utilizes MIPv6 scheme adaptively based on HMIPv6 for the efficient resource utilization. In other words, when the MN resides in a subnet, MIPv6 scheme is utilized for mobility management to decrease the bandwidth waste from IP-in-IP tunneling. On the contrary, when the MN moves from one subnet to another, the mobility management protocol is changed to HMIPv6 scheme to support fast handoff.

2.2 Initialization (Power Up)

When an MN is powered up in a MAP domain, the procedure of the initialization in the proposed mobility management scheme is similar to that of MIPv6, except that the proposed scheme has an additional procedure for the registration of MN's interface identifier to MAP. The initialization procedure for the proposed scheme is described as follow (Fig. 1).

- Step 1: The MN forms link-local address with link-local prefix and MN's interface identifier and, then, it verifies the uniqueness of its link-local address on the new link through the DAD procedure [4].
- Step 2: The MN sends a router solicitation (RS) message to new access router (nAR) and waits for a router advertisement (RA) message from nAR.
- Step 3: When a RA message from nAR is received, the MN forms its new CoA (nCoA) with the network information contained in a RA message through stateless address autoconfiguration [5].
- Step 4: Once the nCoA construction is done, the MN sends a interface identifier registration (IIR) message to MAP through the nAR in order to register and guarantee the uniqueness of MN's interface identifier in a MAP domain.
- Step 5: The MAP verifies the uniqueness of MN's interface identifier in a domain. And if the check is successful, the MAP registers MN's interface identifier and guarantees the uniqueness of MN's interface identifier as long

as the MN moves in a MAP domain. Then, the MAP sends an interface identifier registration acknowledgment (IIRA) message to MN in response to a IIR message.

- Step 6: After registering MN's interface identifier with the MAP, the MN registers MN's current nCoA with HA by sending a binding update (BU) message, which specifies the binding (nCoA, home address).

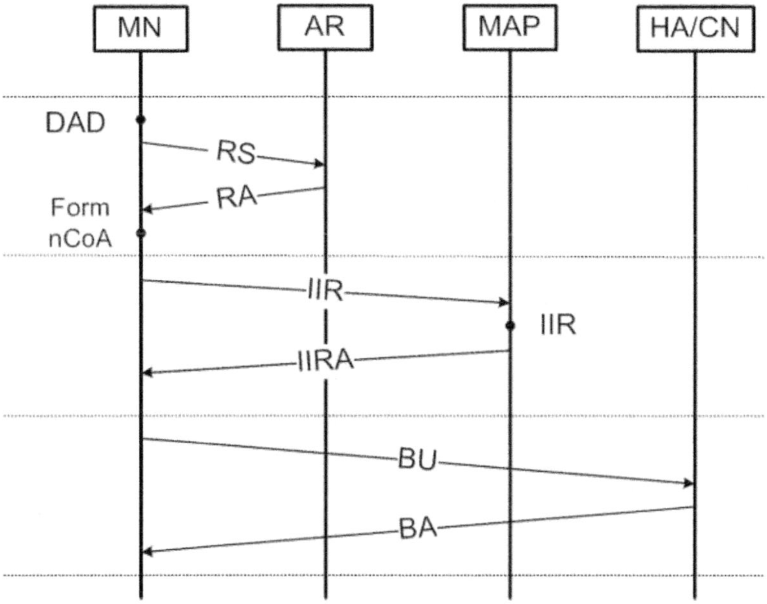

Fig. 1. The procedure of the initialization

2.3 Micromobility Handoff (Intra-domain Handoff)

When the MN moves from one subnet to another in a MAP domain, the procedure of micromobility handoff in the proposed mobility management scheme is described as follow (Fig. 2)

- Step 1: Before layer2 handoff (L2HO), the MN sends a RS message to old access router (oAR) to request the network information on the new access router (nAR) and waits for a RA message from oAR.
- Step 2: With the network information in a RA message from oAR, the MN forms its new CoA (nCoA), based on MN's interface identifier, without the DAD procedure.
- Step 3: The MN sends a local binding update (LBU) message to MAP that specifies the binding (oCoA, nCoA). And then, the MAP returns a local binding acknowledgement (LBA) message to the MN and starts tunneling data packets to the nCoA using IPv6 encapsulation. The nAR buffers MN's data packets until it receives a fast neighbor advertisement (FNA) message

from the MN. Therefore, after local binding update, mobility management protocol is changed from MIPv6 scheme to HMIPv6.

- Step 4: On receiving a LBA message from the MAP via the oAR, the MN performs L2 handoff from the oAR to the nAR. After L2 handoff complete, the MN sends a fast neighbor advertisement (FNA) message to the nAR.
- Step 5: When the nAR receives a FNA message, it returns a neighbor advertisement acknowledgement (NAACK) message to the MN and also starts forwarding the buffered data packets.
- Step 6: After receiving a NAACK message, the MN updates MN's current nCoA with HA and CN by sending a BU message which specifies the binding (nCoA, home address). Therefore, after micromobility handoff, mobility management protocol is changed from HMIPv6 scheme to MIPv6.

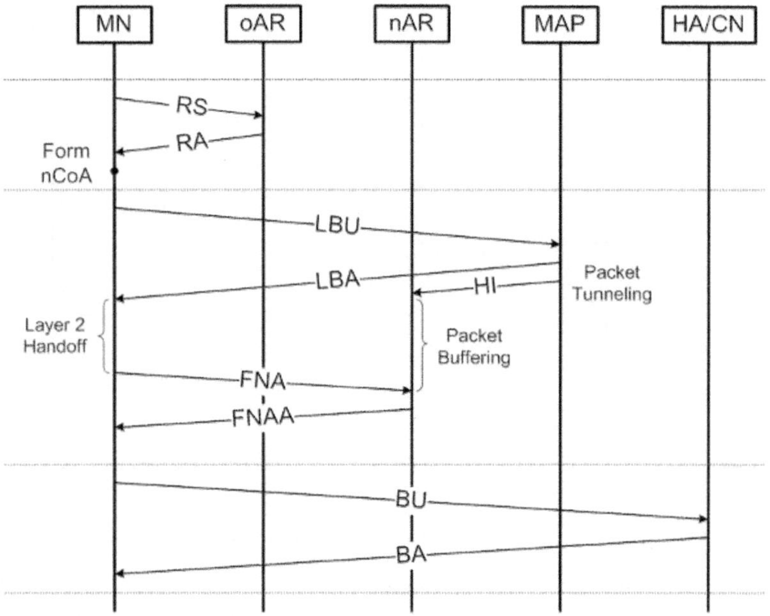

Fig. 2. The procedure of micromobility handoff

There is a binding cache in the MAP for recording the association between the MN's oCoA and nCoA. When the MAP receives MN's data packets, it checks its binding cache firstly. If not in its binding cache, it forwards data packets by normal route rule. Otherwise, it intercepts these packets, and tunnels them to the nCoA of the MN using IPv6 encapsulation.

2.4 Analysis and Discussions

We further explain the proposed mobility management scheme with handoff timing, as shown in Fig. 3. We assume that the time for step (1) and (2) of the

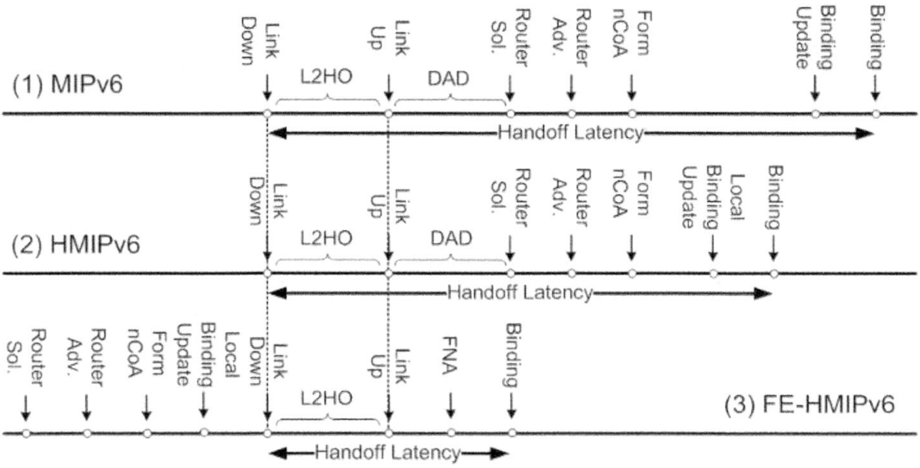

Fig. 3. Handoff timing in MIPv6, HMIPv6 and the proposed scheme

proposed scheme is T_R, which is the time of a RS from the MN to the oAR and a RA from the oAR to the MN. The time for step (2) is assumed to be zero, because the proposed scheme does not perform the DAD. The time for step (3) is T_{LBU}, which is the time of LBU from the MN to the MAP and LBA from the MAP to the MN. T_{L2HO} is the time for layer2 handoff (L2HO) in step (4) and T_{FNA} is the time of FNA from the MN to the nAR and FAACK from the nAR to the MN in step (5). For the proposed scheme, total time of signaling for micromobility handoff is expressed as:

$$T_{Proposed-scheme} = T_R + T_{LBU} + T_{L2HO} + T_{FNA} \tag{1}$$

However, because the proposed scheme anticipates MN's movement based on L2 triggers, the MN can receive the network information for the nAR via oAR and form the new address before layer2 handoff. Therefore, we can ignore the time of T_R and T_{LBU} and total real time of handoff signaling is as follow:

$$T_{Proposed-scheme} = T_{L2HO} + T_{FNA} \tag{2}$$

Equation (3) expresses total time of signaling for micromobility handoff in MIPv6, and HMIPv6 [3], [7]. In this equation T_{DAD} is the time taken for the DAD procedure and T_{BU} is the time taken for binding update to HA and CN.

$$\begin{aligned} T_{MIPv6} &= T_{L2HO} + T_R + T_{DAD} + T_{BU} \\ T_{HMIPv6} &= T_{L2HO} + T_R + T_{DAD} + T_{LBU} \end{aligned} \tag{3}$$

If we compare the total time of signaling to MIPv6 and HMIPv6 by subtracting (3) by (2), we have the following:

$$\begin{aligned} T_{MIPv6} - T_{Proposed-scheme} &= T_R + T_{DAD} + T_{BU} - T_{FNA} = T_{DAD} + T_{BU} \\ T_{HMIPv6} - T_{Proposed-scheme} &= T_R + T_{DAD} + T_{LBU} - T_{FNA} = T_{DAD} + T_{LBU} \end{aligned} \tag{4}$$

Equation (4) shows that the total time of signaling in the proposed scheme is considerably lower than any other schemes, such as MIPv6 and HMIPv6. This is because the MN can configure the new address without any DAD procedures under the government of the MAP in a domain. Therefore, the proposed scheme can support fast handoff mobility management with very few packet loss.

Table 1. Simulation parameters

Parameters	Values
L2 handoff delay	150 ms
DAD time for LCoA	500 – 1300 ms
Wired link bandwidth	100 Mbps
Wireless link bandwidth	20 Mbps
Packet rate	20 – 100 pps
Wired link delay between MAP and AR	10 ms
Wired link delay between AR and BS	10 ms
Wired link delay through the Internet	50 ms
Wireless link delay between BS and MN	10 – 50 ms
UDP packet length	200 bytes

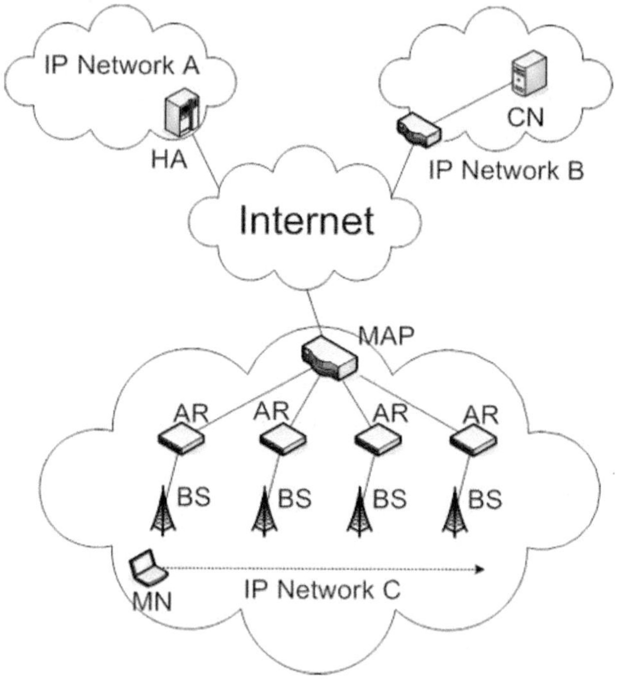

Fig. 4. Simulation architecture topology

3 Simulation Results and Analysis

In this section, we attempt to investigate into the micromobility handoff performances of the proposed scheme and compare to those of two conventional mobility management schemes, MIPv6 and MIPv6, through the computer simulation.

3.1 Simulation Environment

Simulation model is developed using OPNET^{TM} and performance metrics are micromobility handoff delay and packet losses. Fig. 4 shows the simulation

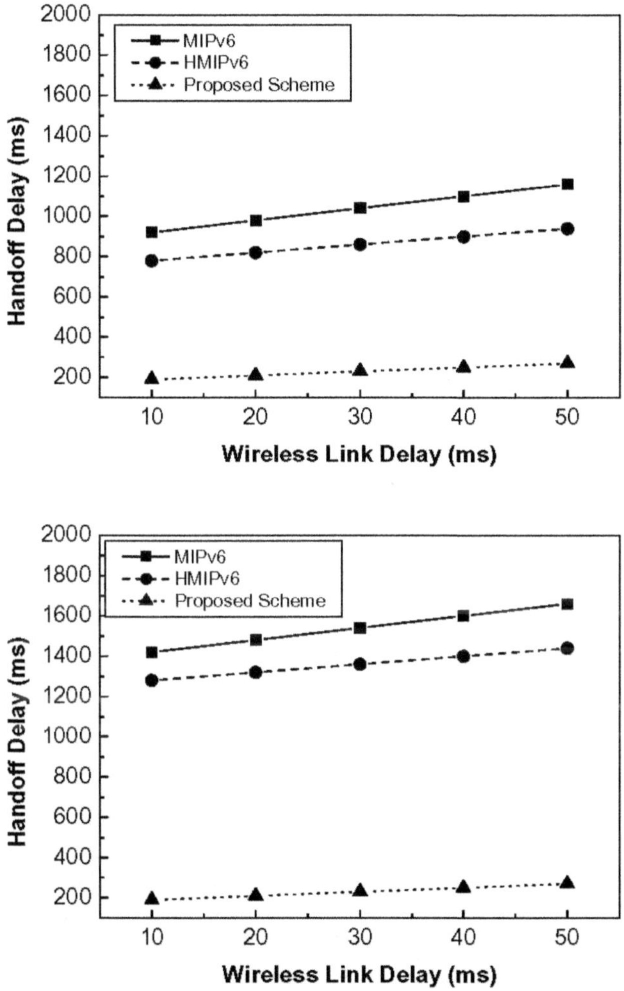

Fig. 5. Comparison of micromobility handoff delay versus wireless link delay: (a) In case of 500 ms DAD time (up), (b) In case of 1 s DAD time (down)

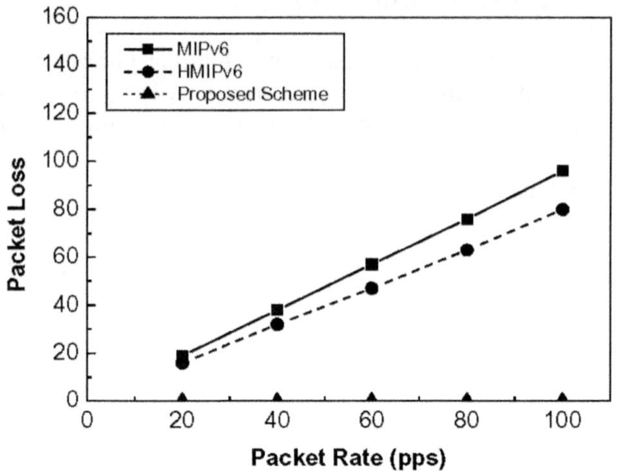

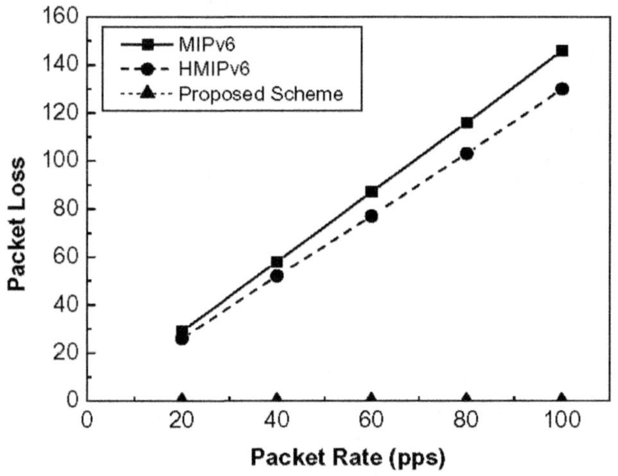

Fig. 6. Comparison of micromobility packet losses versus data generation rates: (a) In case of 500 ms DAD time (up), (b) In case of 1 s DAD time (down)

architecture topology. IP network A, B and C are connected to each other through the Internet. The MN in IP network C is assumed to move following the path of the arrow, as shown in Fig. 4. In order to simulate the real traffic, the CN generates constant bit rate (CBR) traffic over a user datagram protocol (UDP). Network parameters of simulation are summarized in Table 1.

3.2 Simulation Results

Fig. 5 presents comparison of micromobility handoff delay for the proposed scheme versus MIPv6 and HMIPv6 as a function of wireless link delay. The

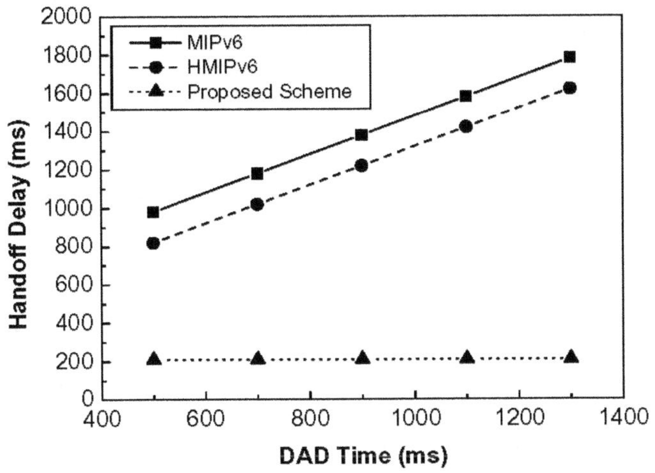

Fig. 7. Comparison of micromobility handoff delay versus DAD time

typical wireless link delay between the MN and base station (BS) is between 10 and 50 ms, depending on the channel condition and their distance. In this simulation, we consider two cases for DAD time, which are (a) 500 ms and (b) 1 s. As shown in Fig. 5, we can see that MIPv6 and HMIPv6 have high handoff delay due to the influence of the DAD time. It also shows that handoff delay of these two schemes increases as the DAD time increases. Although HMIPv6 improves the handoff performance, it is not sufficient to support IP real-time services. However, of particular significance from these simulations are that the proposed scheme shows considerably low and stable handoff latency regardless of the DAD time. This is because the proposed scheme can eliminate the DAD procedures by guaranteeing the uniqueness of MN's interface identifier in a MAP domain.

Fig. 6 presents comparison of micromobility packet loss for the proposed scheme versus MIPv6 and HMIPv6 as a function of data generation rates of the CN. In this simulation, wireless link delay is assumed to be 20 ms and we also consider two cases for DAD time, which are (a) 500 ms and (b) 1 s. Simulation results show that the proposed scheme has no packet loss by using no DAD procedures and buffering mechanism for MN's packet in the new access router. However, we can see that MIPv6 and HMIPv6 have lots of packet losses and these are more severe as data generation rates increase in CN.

Fig. 7 shows the micromobility handoff delay between the proposed scheme and others, MIPv6 and HMIPv6, for various DAD times. Wireless link delay is also assumed to be 20 ms. Simulation results show that the proposed scheme demonstrates a considerable performance improvement in terms of handoff delay over other schemes, which has high handoff delay due to the influence of the DAD time. Therefore, the proposed scheme is more suitable for larger network, which has lots of IPv6 addresses and might take a longer time to perform the DAD.

4 Conclusion

We propose a fast handoff algorithm for micromobility management enhancement in HMIPv6 networks, which eliminates the DAD procedure for the fast micromobility handoff and utilizes MIPv6 scheme adaptively based on HMIPv6 for the efficient resource utilization.

For analyzing the performance evaluation, we attempt to investigate into the micromobility handoff performances of the proposed scheme and compare to those of two conventional mobility management schemes, MIPv6 and MIPv6, through the computer simulation. Simulation results show that the proposed scheme shows considerably low and stable handoff latency and has no packet losses in a micromobility handoff. Therefore, we believe that the proposed scheme can lay the foundation for the prototype of a fast and efficient mobility management scheme to support real-time services, such as VoIP, in a larger network.

References

1. P. Marques, H. Castro and M. Ricardo, "Monitoring Emerging IPv6 Wireless Access Networks," *IEEE Wireless Commun.*, pp.47-53, Feb. 2005
2. N. Montavont and T. Noel, "Handover management for mobile nodes in IPv6 networks," *IEEE Commu. Mag.*, vol. 40, issue 8, pp.38-43, Aug. 2002
3. D. Jonhnson and C. Perskins, "Mobility Support in IPv6," IETF RFC 3775, 2004
4. T. Narten, E. Nordmark and W. Simpson, "Neighbor Discovery for IPv6," IETF RFC 2461, 1998
5. S. Thomson and T. Narten, "IPv6 Stateless Address Autoconfiguration," IETF RFC 2462, 1998
6. J. Bound, B. Volz, T. Lemon, C. Perkins and M. Carney, "Dynamic Host Configuration Protocol for IPv6 (DHCPv6)," IETF RFC 3315, July 2003
7. H. Soliman, C. Castelluccia, K. El Malki and L. Bellier, "Hierarchical Mobile IPv6 Mobility Management (HMIPv6)," IETF RFC 4140, Aug. 2005
8. R. Koodli, "Fast Handovers for Mobile IPv6," IETF RFC 4068, July 2005
9. K. Omae, M. Inoue, I. Okajima and N. Umeda, "Handoff Performance of Mobile Host and Mobile Router Employing HMIP extension," *in proc. IEEE Wireless Commun.*, Netw., vol. 2, pp.1218-1223, Mar. 2003
10. R. Hsieh, W. G. Zhou and A. Seneviratne, "S-MIP: A Seamless Handoff Architecture for Mobile IP," *in proc. IEEE 22nd Annu. Joint Conf. IEEE Comput. Commun. Soc.*, vol.3, pp.1774-1784, May 2003
11. T. E. Klein and S. J. Han, "Assignment Strategies for Mobile Data Users in Hierarchical Overlay Networks: Performance of Optimal and Adaptive Strategies," *IEEE J. Sel. Areas Commun.*, vol. 22, no. 5, pp.849-861, June 2004
12. W. Ma and Y. Fang, "Dynamic Hierarchical Mobility Management Strategy for Mobile IP Networks," *IEEE J. Sel. Areas Commun.*, vol. 22, issue 4, pp.664-676, May 2004

13. S. Deering and R. Hinden, "Internet Protocol version 6 (IPv6) Specification," IETF RFC 2461, 1998
14. G. Daley, B. Pentland, and R. Nelson, "Effects of Fast Router Advertisement on Mobile IPv6 Handovers," *in proc. 8th IEEE Int. Symp. Comput. Commun.*, pp. 557-562, 2003
15. W. K. Lai and J. C. Chiu, "Improving handoff performance in wireless overlay networks by switching between two-layer IPv6 and one-layer IPv6 addressing," *IEEE J. Sel. Areas Commun.*, vol. 23, issue 11, pp.2129-2137, Nov. 2005

DVSMT: Dynamic Voltage Scaling for Scheduling Mixed Real-Time Tasks

Min-Sik Gong[1], Myoung-Jo Jung[1], Yong-Hee Kim[1], Moon-Haeng Cho[1], Joo-Man Kim[2], and Cheol-Hoon Lee[1]

[1] System Software Lab., Dept. of Computer Engineering, Chungnam National University, Daejeon 305-764, Korea
{msgong,mjjung,yonghee,root4567,clee}@cnu.ac.kr
[2] Dept. of Bioinformation & Electronics, Pusan National University, Pusan 609-735, Korea
joomkim@pusan.ac.kr

Abstract. In this paper, we address a power-aware scheduling algorithm for mixed real-time tasks. A mixed-task system consists of periodic and sporadic tasks, each of which is characterized by its worst-case execution requirements and a deadline. We propose a dynamic voltage scaling algorithm called DVSMT, which dynamically scales down the supplying voltage (and thus the operating frequency) using on-line slack distribution when jobs complete earlier while still meeting their deadlines. Simulation results show that DVSMT saves up to 60% more than the existing algorithms both in the periodic and mixed task systems.

1 Introduction

In recent years, computation and communication have been steadily moving toward battery-operated mobile and portable platforms/devices, such as cellular phones, unmanned robots, and ubiquitous sensor network nodes. In these applications, the energy savings is very important to extend the lifetime of devices.

In the last decade, significant research and development efforts have been made on Dynamic Voltage Scaling (DVS) for real-time systems to make energy savings by scaling the voltage and frequency while maintaining real-time deadline guarantees [1-7]. This is possible because the energy dissipated per cycle with CMOS circuitry scales quadratically to the supply voltage ($E \propto V^2$) [8]. Although real-time tasks are specified with worst-case computation requirements, they generally use much less than the worst-case values for most invocations [9]. Most DVS algorithms make use of these unused slack times when scaling down the supply voltage (and hence, frequency) while still meeting all deadline requirements. Phillai and Shin[2] proposed a novel DVS algorithm called cycle-conserving EDF (called ccEDF) along with some improvements for the periodic-task systems. It calculates the scaling factor upon release or completion of a job of each task by distributing the slack to all the tasks in the system.

Aydin *et al.* suggested a dynamic reclaiming algorithm, called DRA, which attempts to allocate the maximum amount of unused CPU time to the first task at the appropriate priority level[6].

Y.-H. Lee et al. (Eds.): ICESS 2007, LNCS 4523, pp. 488–497, 2007.

For sporadic-task systems, Qadi, *et al.* [4] suggested the DVSST algorithm which scales the processor frequency up and down depending solely when jobs are released without making use of the slack time.

Recently Lee and Shin[5] proposed an on-line dynamic voltage scaling algorithm, called OLDVS, for a general task model. OLDVS does not assume task periodicity, and thus, nor requires any a priori information on the task set to schedule.

In this paper, we propose a DVS algorithm called DVSMT for a mixed-task system which consists of both periodic and sporadic tasks. When calculating the scaling factor, the DVSMT algorithm distributes the slack time to all ready tasks. With this scheme, we could reduce the variation of voltage levels, resulting in a more energy savings. The proposed algorithm requires only $O(1)$ computation on release and completion of a job of each task, so it is fairly easy to incorporate it into a real-time operating system. Simulation results show that DVSMT saves up to 60% more than the existing algorithms both in the periodic-task and mixed-task systems.

The paper is organized as follows. In the next chapter, we present the system model and basic concepts of the proposed algorithm considered in this paper. Chapter 3 presents details of the proposed algorithm and illustrates how it works. The simulation results are presented in Chapter 4 and Chapter 5 concludes the paper with a summary.

2 The DVS Algorithm for the Mixed Tasks

2.1 System Model

We consider a preemptive hard real-time system in which real-time tasks are scheduled under the EDF scheduling policy. The application considered in this paper is a mixed-task system $\mathbf{T} = \{T_1, T_2, ..., T_n\}$ of which each task $T_{i,j} = (p_i, e_i)$ is a periodic task or a sporadic task with the period of p_i and the worst-case execution time($WCET$) of e_i . Also, each task has the relative deadline of D_i and we assume that $D_i = p_i$. All tasks are independent and preemptive. Each task T_i invokes an infinite series of jobs $J_{i,j} = (r_{i,j}, d_{i,j})$, for $j \geq 1$, with the release time of $r_{i,j}$ and the deadline $d_{i,j}$. If T_i is a periodic task, $r_{i,j+1} = r_{i,j} + p_i$. Otherwise, if T_i is a sporadic task, $r_{i,j+1} \geq r_{i,j} + p_i$. In other words, the minimum inter-arrival time of jobs of a sporadic task is its period. In both types of task, we assume that $d_{i,j} = r_{i,j} + p_i = r_{i,j} + D_i$. The utilization u_i of task T_i is the ratio of the execution requirement to its period(*i.e.*, $u_{i,j} = e_i/p_i$). The total utilization u_{tot} is the sum of utilizations of all tasks (*i.e.*, $u_{tot} = \sum_{i=1}^{n} u_i$). The target variable voltage processor is assumed to be able to scale its supply voltage and clock speed within its operational ranges $[f_{min}, f_{max}]$ and $[v_{min}, v_{max}]$. Each operating frequency is associated with one minimum supply voltage, *i.e.*, (f_i, v_i). Real-time systems that use DVS-based scheduling scale the $WCET$ assuming that the worst-case execution cycle($WCEC$) remains constant even with a change in the frequency.

To reduce energy consumption of CPU, we may well decrease the operating frequency and voltage level. The scaling factor to adjust the operating frequency of the processor may be determined by the current total utilization u_{tot} of all the released tasks under EDF. Let $\alpha = f_i/f_{max}$ denote the scaling factor that represents the fraction of the current processor frequency f_i over the maximum processor frequency f_{max}. As we consider a power-aware algorithm for a mixed task set under EDF scheduling, a schedule is feasible for the task set if and only if $\sum_{i=1}^{n} \frac{e_i}{p_i} \leq \alpha$.

2.2 Basic Concepts

We propose a dynamic voltage scaling algorithm called DVSMT, which dynamically scales down the supplying voltage (and thus the operating frequency) using the on-line slack distribution scheme explained so far in the case that jobs complete earlier while still meeting their deadlines. The slack of a finished task is expressed by its borrowed cycles.

We will illustrate the concept of the proposed algorithm as follows. Consider a set **T** real-time tasks whose worst case total utilization is equal to or less than 1 (for example, $u_i + u_j + u_k \leq 1$ in Fig. 1). That consists of three tasks T_i, T_j, and T_k where each task is denoted by three-tuple $T_i(p_i, d_i, e_i)$. When a task T_i is released, the worst-case execution requirements e_i of T_i can be distributed to its deadline, *i.e.*, from the arrival time to the deadline of each its jobs, as shown in Fig. 1(b).

Suppose that, for any time interval, the CPU cycles are allocated to each task proportionally to their utilizations(see Fig. 1(b)). In this case, each job completes exactly at its deadline with the scaling factor $\alpha = u_i + u_j + u_k (\leq 1)$. For any time interval $[t_1, t_2)$, let $c_{i,[t_1,t_2)}$ denote the CPU cycles allocated to T_i with its utilization u_i in the interval. Then, $c_{i,[t_1,t_2)} = u_i \cdot (t_2 - t_1)$. With the condition that $r_i \leq t_1 < t_2 \leq d_i$, $c_{i,[t_1,t_2)}$ is equal to or less than the worst-case execution requirements e_i, *i.e.*, $c_{i,[t_1,t_2)} \leq e_i$.

Definition 1. *For a time interval $[t_1, t_2)$ during which job $J_{i,j}$ executes, the total amount $c_{tot,[t_1,t_2)}$ of CPU cycles allocated in this interval is as follows:*

$$c_{tot,[t_1,t_2)} = \sum_{k=1}^{n} c_{k,[t_1,t_2)}. \tag{1}$$

To guarantee the feasible execution of T_i under the worst-case scenario with the condition that $r_i \leq t_1 < t_2 \leq d_i$, $c_{tot,[t_1,t_2)}$ must be greater than or equal to the worst-case execution requirements e_i, *i.e.*, $c_{tot,[t_1,t_2)} \geq e_i$.

Definition 2. *For any time interval $[t_1, t_2)$ during which job $J_{i,j}$ executes, the borrowed cycles $B_{i,j}$ of $J_{i,j}$ is as follows:*

$$B_{i,j} = \sum_{k \neq i} c_{k,[t_1,t_2)}. \tag{2}$$

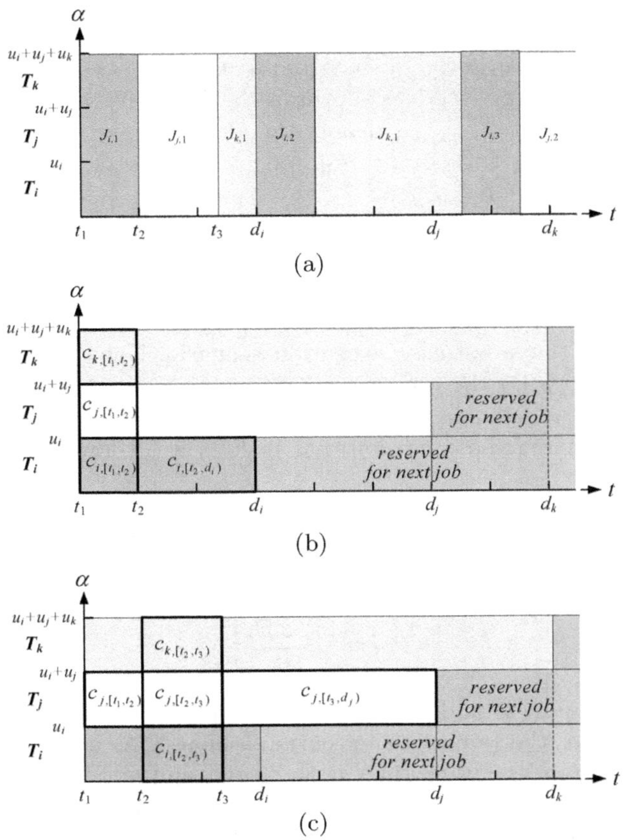

Fig. 1. Figures to illustrate the concept of the DVSMT

Corollary 1. *For given a set of real-time tasks whose worst case total utilization is equal to or less than 1, the borrowed cycles $B_{i,j}$ of job $J_{i,j}$ which started at time t_1 and completed without preemption at time t_2 is equal to $u_i \cdot \{D_i - (t_2 - t_1)\}$ under the worst-case execution scenario. That is,*

$$B_{i,j} = u_i \cdot \{D_i - (t_2 - t_1)\}. \tag{3}$$

If the equation (3) does not hold, deadline misses may occur under the worst case scenario because the execution requirements are not conserved for ready tasks preempted by job $J_{i,j}$. Therefore the borrowed cycles must be given back to the ready tasks from which task T_i borrowed CPU cycles.

For example, in Fig. 1(b), $J_{i,1}$ starts execution immediately upon release at time t_1 and it is the highest priority task during $[t_1, d_i)$. Thus, job $J_{i,1}$ consumes a portion of the execution requirements of T_j and T_k, as the amount of $c_{j,[t_1,t_2)}$ and $c_{k,[t_1,t_2)}$, respectively, during its execution. Under the worst-case execution scenario, it is obvious that $c_{i,[t_1,t_2)} + c_{i,[t_2,d_i)} = c_{i,[t_1,t_2)} + c_{j,[t_1,t_2)} + c_{k,[t_1,t_2)}$ to conserve the execution requirements of $J_{i,1}$. Then, $c_{i,[t_2,d_i)} = c_{j,[t_1,t_2)} + c_{k,[t_1,t_2)}$. By definition, the borrowed cycles $B_{i,1}$ are equal to $c_{j,[t_1,t_2)} + c_{k,[t_1,t_2)}$, hence $B_{i,1} = c_{i,[t_2,d_i)}$. Because $c_{i,[t_2,d_i)}$ is equal to $u_i \cdot (d_i - t_2)$, $B_{i,1}$ are consequently equal to $u_i \cdot \{D_i - (t_2 - t_1)\}$ as shown in the Corollary 1.

For simplicity, let $E_{i,j,[t_1,t_2)}$ denote the elapsed time $t_2 - t_1$ of $J_{i,j}$. In other words, $J_{i,j}$ executes without preemption by other task in the interval $[t_1, t_2)$. Hence, $c_{i,[t_2,d_i)} = u_i \cdot E_{i,j,[t_1,t_2)}$.

On the contrary, as for task T_j, its job $J_{j,1}$ releases at time $r_j(= t_1)$ and starts execution at time $t_2(> t_1)$ as shown in Fig. 1(c). In other words, task T_j was preempted by the higher priority task T_i in the interval $[t_1, t_2)$. Then, task T_j completes at time t_3. Therefore, $c_{j,[t_1,t_2)} + c_{j,[t_2,t_3)} + c_{j,[t_3,d_j)} = c_{i,[t_2,t_3)} + c_{j,[t_2,t_3)} + c_{k,[t_2,t_3)}$ under the worst-case execution scenario. Thus, $c_{j,[t_1,t_2)} + c_{j,[t_3,d_j)} = c_{i,[t_2,t_3)} + c_{k,[t_2,t_3)}$. By the way, $c_{j,[t_1,t_2)} + c_{j,[t_3,d_j)} = u_j \cdot \{(d_j - t_1) - (t_3 - t_2)\} = u_j \cdot (D_j - E_{j,1,[t_2,t_3)})$, where D_j is $d_j - t_1$. From this, we can see that the Corollary 1 is also valid under the condition that task T_j is preempted by higher-priority tasks.

From the equation (3), on the completion time of any job $J_{i,j}$, the borrowed cycles $B_{i,j}$ can be distributed in the interval of $D_i - E_{i,j}$. We denote the current utilization $u_{i,j}$ of the completed job $J_{i,j}$ as the following equation:

$$u_{i,j} = \frac{B_{i,j}}{D_i - E_{i,j}}. \tag{4}$$

From equations (3) and (4), $u_{i,j}$ always equals to the worst-case utilization $u_i = e_i/p_i$ under the worst-case execution scenario. As a task completes earlier than its worst-case execution time, both its $B_{i,j}$ and $E_{i,j}$ become smaller. Hence, $u_{i,j}$ of a task is smaller than or equal to its worst-case utilization $u_i (i.e., u_{i,j} \leq u_i)$. Consequently, we can scale down the CPU speed by re-calculating the current utilization using the borrowed cycles consumed by the just finished task. Also, as for sporadic tasks, if the finished task is not released again at its deadline, from that time the current utilization can be set to zero until its next release. These concepts can be applied to the DVS-based real time system with the periodic and sporadic tasks.

3 The Algorithm DVSMT

To guarantee the feasible execution of all the upcoming tasks under the worst-case scenario, we must make a conservative algorithm. For this, DVSMT gives back the borrowed cycles of the just finished task to all ready tasks until its deadline.

When the job $J_{i,j}$ is released, we cannot know its actual execution requirements, so we must make a conservative assumption that it will need its specified worst-case execution requirements. DVSMT starts with a minimum possible frequency level using the worst-case utilization u_i of the released jobs rather than using the static voltage algorithm of [2] to set the initial frequency level which is theoretically zero.

We introduce a deadline queue, denoted by dQ, which consists of jobs which are released but their deadlines are not elapsed. The deadline queue $dQ = \{J_{i,j}\}$ is sorted by the deadlines of jobs where the k-th job has the k-th nearest deadline. It is updated on the arrival, deadline, and completion times of each job. When a job $J_{i,j}$ is released, if its previous job $J_{i,j-1}$ does not exist in dQ, $J_{i,j}$ is inserted into the queue. Otherwise, $J_{i,j}$ replaces $J_{i,j-1}$ in dQ. If a sporadic task T_i does not release a next job $J_{i,j+1}$ at its deadline $d_{i,j}$, the algorithm removes $J_{i,j}$ from dQ.

The DVSMT is simple and works as shown in Fig. 2. It should be fairly easy to incorporate into a real-time operating system, and does not require a significant processing cost. The dynamic schemes require $O(1)$ computation, and should not require significant processing over the scheduler. The most significant overheads may come from the hardware voltage switching times. However, no more than three switches can occur per task, so there overheads can easily be accounted for, and added to, the worst-case task execution times.

```
on initial or IDLE state:
    α = 0.0;    // scaling factor
    Empty dQ;

on arrival time of J_{i,j}:
    // update B_{k,j} and E_{k,j}
    //          for the current task T_k
    B_{k,j} = B_{k,j} + (t − l) · (α − u_{k,j});
    E_{k,j} = E_{k,j} + (t − l);

    l = t; // set the context switch time l
           // to the current time t
    E_{i,j} = 0; // reset the elapsed time
    B_{i,j} = 0; // reset the borrowed cycles

    if J_{i,j−1} exists in dQ then
        replace J_{i,j−1} with J_{i,j};
    else
        insert J_{i,j} into dQ;
    endif;
    sort dQ by the deadline under EDF;
    set u_{i,j} to e_i/p_i;
    scale_voltage_and_frequency();

on completion time of J_{i,j}:
    B_{i,j} = B_{i,j} + (t − l) · (α − u_{i,j});
    E_{i,j} = E_{i,j} + (t − l);

    update u_{i,j} = B_{i,j}/(D_i − E_{i,j});
    scale_voltage_and_frequency();

on deadline d_{i,j} of J_{i,j}:
    extract J_{i,j} from dQ;
    scale_voltage_and_frequency();

scale_voltage_and_frequency():
    select the next higher frequency
    f_i ∈ { f_min, ..., f_max | f_min < ... < f_max }

    such that Σ_{i=1}^{m} u_i ≤ f_i/f_max,
                                   for {J_{i,j}} in dQ
    select the supply voltage
                              associated with f_i;
```

Fig. 2. Pseudo-code for the algorithm DVSMT

As mentioned above, the DVSMT algorithm adjusts the supply voltage and operating frequency of the processor on the release, deadline, and completion times of each job. Each set **T** of real-time tasks with the total utilization less than or equal to 1 is feasibly schedulable by DVSMT. This is proved in the following lemma and theorem.

Lemma 1. *Given a set of real-time tasks whose worst case total utilization is equal to or less than 1, the total sum of the executed cycles of a task T_i, which is preempted n times during its execution under the DVSMT algorithm satisfy the following equation, where $[t_{s,j}, t_{e,j})$ is the j-th preemption interval and the scaling factor α_j is equal to or less than 1.*

$$\sum_{j=1}^{n} \alpha_j E_{[t_{s,j}, t_{e,j})} \leq e_i \tag{5}$$

Proof. The higher priority task consumes the borrowed cycles for its lower priority tasks and then those are given back on its completion until its deadline (see Corollary 1). Therefore, all the cycles allocated during execution of the higher tasks are given back to each preempted task T_i. Consequently, $\sum_{j=1}^{n} \alpha_j E_{[t_{s,j}, t_{e,j})}$ is equal to e_i under the worst-case execution scenario and less than e_i in other cases. □

If $\sum_{j=1}^{n} \alpha_j E_{[t_{s,j}, t_{e,j})}$ is greater than e_i, then task T_i misses its deadline. However, every job is given back its CPU cycles borrowed by higher-priority tasks until its deadline. This means that each job completes at or before its deadline. Therefore, for a real-time task set **T**, if its total utilization is less than or equal to 1, the DVSMT algorithm always finds a feasible schedule. This is formally stated in the following theorem.

Theorem 1. *Each set* **T** *of real-time tasks with the total utilization less than or equal to 1 is feasibly schedulable by DVSMT.*

Proof. It is obvious from Lemma 1. □

4 Experimental Results

To evaluate the potential energy savings from voltage scaling in a real-time scheduled system, we performed some simulations by using RTSIM [10] which is a real-time system simulator. We show some simulation results and provide insight into the most significant system parameters affecting energy consumption.

The simulation assumes that a constant amount of energy is required for each cycle of operation at a given voltage. Only the energy consumed by the processor is computed, and variations as different types of instructions executed are not taken into account. The simulation also assumes a perfect machine in that a perfect software-controlled halt feature is provided by the processor, so idle time consumes no energy. In particular, we do not consider preemption overhead, task switch overheads, and the required time to switch operating frequency or voltages. The real-time task sets are specified with a pair of numbers for each task indicating its period and worst case computation time. The task set is composed of 20 tasks and it is generated randomly as follows. Each task has an equal probability of having a short (1-10ms), medium (10-100ms), or long (100-1000ms) period. Within each range, task periods are uniformly distributed. This simulates the varied mix of short and long period tasks commonly found in real-time systems. Finally, the task computation requirements of the sporadic tasks are chosen such that the total processor utilization of all mixed tasks becomes 1. Due to the variability of execution times of the real-time applications, we performed experiments where the actual execution time follows a normal probability distribution function.

We compared our DVSMT to ccEDF, DVSST, and non-DVS. To evaluate the effectiveness of the variability of the target variable voltage processors, we simulate for both ideal processor and the practical processors. Ideal processor is able to scale its supply voltage and clock speed continuously within its operational ranges $[f_{min}, f_{max}]$ and $[v_{min}, v_{max}]$. The practical processors considered are Intel PXA250[11] and Transmeta TM5800[12] which have discrete voltage and frequency levels. The following summarizes the hardware voltage and frequency settings, where each tuple consists of the frequency and the corresponding processor voltage :

Ideal CPU : $[f_{min}, f_{max}]$=[0, 1] and $[v_{min}, v_{max}]$=[0, 1]
PXA250 : {(100, 0.85), (200, 1.0), (300, 1.1), (400, 1.3)}
TM5800 : {(300, 0.8), (433, 0.875) (533, 0.95) (667, 1.05), (800, 1.15), (900, 1.25), (1000, 1.3)}.

First of all, to evaluate the effectiveness of the load ratio for periodic task sets with 20 tasks and the worst-case total utilization $u_{tot} = 1$, we performed simulations and compared with others for energy consumption as shown in Fig. 3. The load ratio is the ratio of the actual execution time $\hat{e}_i$ to the worst case execution time. The mean and standard deviations are set to $\hat{e}_i/WCET$ and $(0.1 \cdot WCET)/3$, respectively. These choices ensure that, on the average, 99.7% of the execution times fall in the interval [load-$0.1 \cdot WCET$, load+$0.1 \cdot WCET$]. The simulation results show that the proposed algorithm, DVSMT, outperforms ccEDF up to 25% and DVSST up to 55% for ideal processor. Also, both for PXA 250 and TM5800, DVSMT outperforms them up to 15%. The energy savings increase as the load ratio decreases and the difference of the energy consumption between DVSMT and the others decreases as the load ratio increases.

We also performed simulations for mixed tasks that consist of five sporadic tasks and fifteen periodic tasks. The sum of the utilizations of all sporadic task are set to be around 0.3 of the total utilization. Fig. 4 shows the effect of the inter-arrival times of sporadic tasks on energy savings under the load ratio of 0.5. The inter-arrival time of the sporadic tasks is characterized by an exponential distribution with mean set to integer multiples of their relative deadlines. The result shows that the energy savings is not affected by the inter-arrival times of sporadic tasks. For ideal processors, DVSMT outperforms DVSST up to 60%

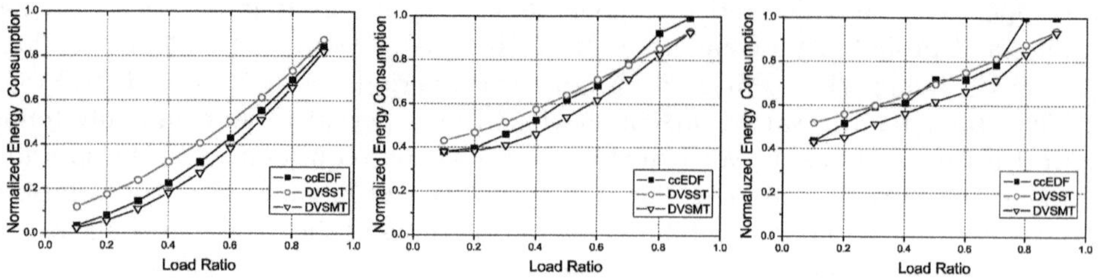

(a) Ideal CPU (b) TM5800 (c) PXA250

Fig. 3. Normalized energy consumption to evaluate the effect of the variation of the load ratio for periodic task set

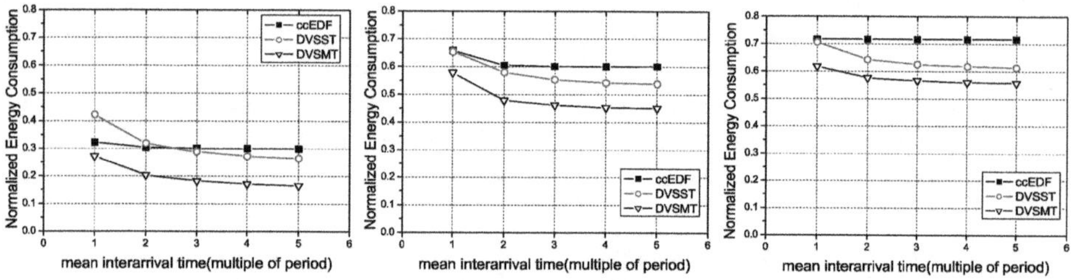

(a) Ideal CPU (b) TM5800 (c) PXA250

Fig. 4. Normalized energy consumption to evaluate the effect of the inter-arrival of the sporadic with load ratio=0.5 for mixed task set

and ccEDF up to 45%. For PXA250 and TM5800, DVSMT outperforms DVSST and ccEDF up to 20% and 25%, respectively.

5 Conclusions

In this paper, we present a power-aware scheduling algorithm called DVSMT for mixed hard real-time tasks, which consist of periodic and sporadic tasks, using dynamic voltage scaling. This algorithm is based on on-line slack distribution to improve energy savings while still meeting all deadlines.

The DVSMT algorithm adjusts the supply voltage and operating frequency of the processor on the release, deadline, and completion times of each job, so it is fairly easy to incorporate into a real-time operating system.

We have shown that the proposed DVS algorithm can effectively be applied for the mixed task set. Our simulation results show that DVSMT saves energy up to 60% more than DVSST in the mixed task sets.

In the future, we will also introduce the temporal locality for the mobile devices under ubiquitous environments.

Acknowledgments. This work was supported by the R&D Support Project of MIC, Korea. Cheol-Hoon Lee is the corresponding author.

References

1. F. Gruian: Hard real-time scheduling for low energy using stochastic data and DVS processors. Proc. Int'l Symposium on Low-Power Electronics and Design. (2001) 46-51.
2. P. Pillai and K. G. Shin: Real-time dynamic voltage scaling forlow-power embedded operating systems. Proc. 18th ACM Symposium on Operating System Principles. (2001) 89-102.
3. A. Dudani, F. Mueller, and Y. Zhu: Energy-Conserving Feedback EDF Scheduling for Embedded Systems with Real-Time Constraints. Proc. of the joint conf. on Languages, compilers and tools for embedded systems: software and compilers for embedded systems. (2002) 213-222.
4. A. Qadi, S. Goddard, and S. Farritor: A dynamic voltage scaling algorithm for sporadic tasks. Proc. of the 24th IEEE Int'l Real-Time Systems Symposium. (2003) 52-62.
5. C.-H. Lee and K. G. Shin: On-line dynamic voltage scaling for hard real-time systems using the EDF algorithm. Proc. of the 25th IEEE Int'l Real-Time System Symposium. (2004) 319-327.
6. H. Aydin, R. Melhem, D. Mosse and P. Mejia-Alvarez: Power-aware scheduling for periodic real-time tasks. IEEE Trans. on Computers. Vol. 53. (2004) 584-600.
7. Xiliang Zhong and Cheng-Zhong Xu: Energy-Aware Modeling and Scheduling of Real-Time Tasks for Dynamic Voltage Scaling. Proc. of the 26th IEEE Int'l Real-Time Systems Symposium. (2005) 366-375.
8. T. D. Burd and R. W. Brodersen: Energy efficient CMOS microprocessor design. Proc. 28th Hawaii Int'l Conf. on System Sciences. (1995) 288-297.
9. R. Ernst and W. Ye: Embedded Program Timing Analysis Based on Path Clustering and Architecture Classification. Proc. Int'l Conf. Computer-Aided Design. (1997) 598-604.
10. RTSIM:Real-time system simulator. http://rtsim.sssup.it.
11. INTEL Corporation. http://developer.intel.com/design/intelxscale.
12. TRANSMETA Corporation. http://www.transmeta.com.

Real-Time Communications on an Integrated Fieldbus Network Based on a Switched Ethernet in Industrial Environment

Dao Manh Cuong and Myung Kyun Kim

School of Computer Engineering and Information Communication,
University of Ulsan, Nam-Gu, 680749 Ulsan, Republic of Korea
mkkim@ulsan.ac.kr

Abstract. In recent years, fieldbuses have been more widely used in real-time distributed control systems. There are many international fieldbus protocol standards, but they are not interoperable among themselves. This paper proposes an integrated fieldbus network architecture based on a switched Ethernet which provides real-time communication features to the nodes in different fieldbuses. This paper also analyzes the schedulability conditions for real-time periodic messages on the switched Ethernet and an EDF (Earliest Deadline First)-based scheduling algorithm to support the real-time communication requirements of the periodic messages without any change in the principles of the switch.

1 Introduction

Real-time distributed control systems are becoming more widely used in industrial environment. They are used to support a broad range of applications such as process control, factory automation, automotive, and so on. Fieldbuses are used in real-time communications among field devices such as sensors and actuators in the distributed control systems. There are many international fieldbus protocol standards such as CAN [1], Profibus, WorldFIP, Foundation Fieldbus [2], etc., but they are not interoperable among themselves. Nowadays, the need to communicate seamlessly among nodes in heterogeneous fieldbuses has increased, and several standards bodies and research groups have proposed frameworks for interoprability among heterogeneous fieldbus systems [3], [4]. However, those interoperability frameworks do not provide end-to-end real-time communication features among nodes in different fieldbus systems. To satisfy the real-time communication features end to end, we propose an integrated fieldbus network based on a switched Ethernet, which integrates heterogeneous fieldbuses at the data link level.

The switched Ethernet can provide real-time message delivery to the communicating nodes by eliminating message collisions on the network. Thus, the use of switches to offer real-time guarantees in industrial communications has been suggested and analyzed by a number of authors [7], [8]. Hoai Hoang *et al.* [9] proposed the real-time switched Ethernet where the switch and and the

Y.-H. Lee et al. (Eds.): ICESS 2007, LNCS 4523, pp. 498–509, 2007.

end nodes control the real-time traffic with EDF scheduling. However, their approach requires the changes (adding the real-time protocol) to the switch. M. K. Kim *et al.* [10] proposed a distributed scheduling algorithm of periodic messages for hard real-time communications on a switched Ethernet without modifying the operation of the standard switch. However, they did not show the feasibility condition of periodic messages on the switched Ethernet.

In this paper, we propose an integrated fieldbus network based on a switched Ethernet which provides the real-time communication features to the nodes in different fieldbuses. This paper also analyzes the schedulability conditions for real-time periodic messages on the switched Ethernet and an EDF-based scheduling algorithm to support the real-time communication requirements of the periodic traffic over the switched Ethernet without any change in the switch. The integrated fieldbus network operates in a master-slave mode and the periodic traffic is handled by a master node to enhance the real-time performance of the switched Ethernet

The rest of this paper is organized as follows. In section 2, the integrated fieldbus network based on the switched Ethernet and a logical fieldbus protocol for seamless communications among nodes in different fieldbuses are discussed. In section 3, we describe the schedulability conditions for periodic messages and the EDF-based message scheduling algorithm to satisfy the real-time communication requirements of the periodic messages on the switched Ethernet. Finally, we conclude and discuss about the future work in the last section.

2 Integrated Fieldbus Network

The integrated fieldbus network consists of an Ethernet switch and logical fieldbus bridges, each of which connects a fieldbus to the switched Ethernet, as shown in Fig. 1. Each logical fieldbus bridge performs a frame conversion between a fieldbus and an Ethernet, and checks the schedulability conditions for each real-time message and makes a transmission schedule for a set of schedulable messages on the switched Ethernet.

2.1 Logical Fieldbus Protocol

For seamless communication among nodes on different fieldbuses, we define a logical fieldbus protocol as shown in Fig. 2. The convergence layer provides a logical fieldbus addressing scheme and a frame conversion function between a fieldbus and an Ethernet. Each node that needs a remote communication (a communication between two nodes that are on different fieldbuses) is assigned a logical fieldbus address (LF address), which consists of ($FieldbusID$, $DeviceID$). $FieldbusID$ uniquely identifies a specific fieldbus and $DeviceID$ identifies a node on the fieldbus. A node sends its data to the remote node in a LF frame which is defined in Fig. 3. The admission control layer is used to check the schedulability of a real-time message on the integrated fieldbus network.

The header of a logical fieldbus frame consists of 4 fields (*FRType, FRLen, SrcLFAddr, DstLFAddr*). $FRType$ specifies the type of frame that is transmitted

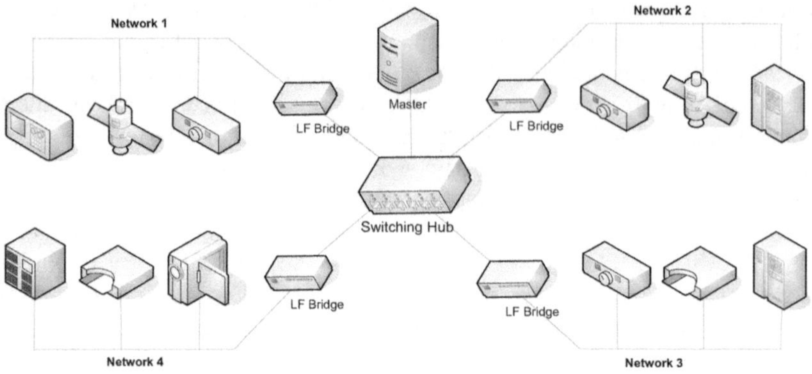

Fig. 1. Integrated Fieldbus Network Architecture

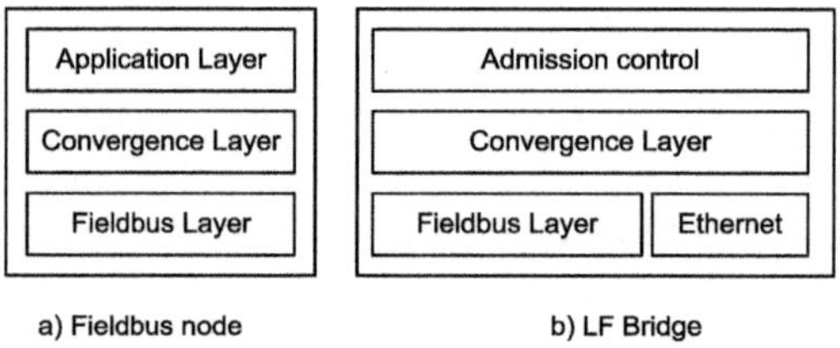

Fig. 2. Logical Fieldbus Protocol Architecture

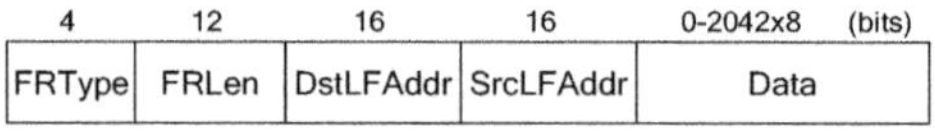

Fig. 3. Logical Fieldbus Frame Format

in the LF frame and *FRLen* denotes the length of the LF frame. *SrcLFAddr* and *DstLFAddr* denotes the LF addresses of the source and the destination nodes, respectively.

2.2 Data Transmission on the Integrated Fieldbus Network

The LF frame is transmitted by being encapsulated in a physical fieldbus frame. The source fieldbus frame is converted to an Ethernet frame by the source LF bridge and transmitted to the destination LF bridge. The destination LF bridge converts the Ethernet frame to the destination fieldbus frame and sends it to the destination node. Data transmission on the switched Ethernet is based on a master-slave protocol. One of the LF bridges acts as a master node. Each link between each LF bridge and the switched Ethernet consists of a transmission link (*TL*), which is a link from the LF bridge to the switch, and a reception link (*RL*), which is a link from the switch to the LF bridge. Both *TL* and *RL* links consist of successive elementary cycles (ECs), which is similar to FTT-CAN [6]. The source or destination LF bridges perform frame format conversion between a fieldbus frame and an Ethernet frame.

3 Real-Time Message Scheduling Algorithm

In this section, we propose the real-time message scheduling algorithm based on EDF scheduling algorithm that was first introduced by Liu and Layland [5]. The switched Ethernet operates in master-slave mode and uses synchronized model. The master node handles the transmission of periodic message to guarantee the timeliness of all the periodic messages.

3.1 Network Architecture

One of the nodes in the switched Ethernet acts as a master to handle the real-time communication of periodic messages. The real-time layer is added to all end nodes to enhance the real-time performance of switched Ethernet(Fig. 4). Moreover, we assume that the switch operates in cut-through mode to minimize the switch latency of the messages when they are transmitted over switched Ethernet (for further details see subsection 3.2).

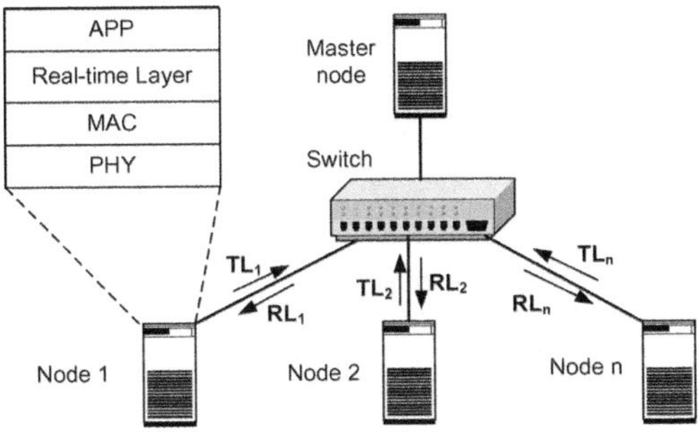

Fig. 4. Network Architecture

The operation of real-time communication network can be described as follows. Firstly, all the slave nodes send the real-time requirements to the master node. After receiving all the request frames from slaves, the master node checks the feasibility of the synchronous messages (admission control) and broadcasts the result to all the slaves to indicate which messages can be transmitted over the switched Ethernet and meet their deadline. The real-time periodic messages, when arriving at slave nodes, are sorted in the increasing order of their deadline at the real-time layer. Then a master node periodically broadcasts a trigger message(TM) to all slave nodes to synchronize the communication system and to indicate a set of messages to be transmitted.

3.2 Message Transmission Model

In this paper, we assume that all nodes operate in the synchronized model, which is similar to that of FTT-CAN [6]. All the transmission and reception links are slotted into a sequence of fundamental time units, called Elementary Cycles (ECs). An EC consists of a TM, a SMP (Synchronous Message Period) and a AMP (Asynchronous Message Period) as shown in Fig. 5-(a). The TM (Trigger Message) is used to synchronize all nodes and contains a schedule for the periodic messages that can be transmitted on the respective EC. The SMP and the AMP are the time durations for transmitting real-time periodic messages and aperiodic messages on the EC, respectively. In this paper, we only consider the scheduling of periodic messages, so for the simplicity of the analysis, we assume there is no AMP in each EC as shown in Fig. 5-(b). In Fig. 5, L_{TM} is the length of TM, T_L is a transmission delay of a frame from a source node to a destination node without queuing delay and $E' = E - 2 * T_L - L_{TM}$ is the available time for transmitting messages on an EC. The transmission delay without queuing delay T_L can be computed as follows:

$$T_L = 2 * t_p + t_{sw}$$

where t_p is a propagation delay between a node and a switch and t_{sw} is the switching latency (destination port look-up and switch fabric set-up time)that depend on the switch vendor. With a 100Mbps switch using cut-through mode, t_{sw} is about $11\mu s$.

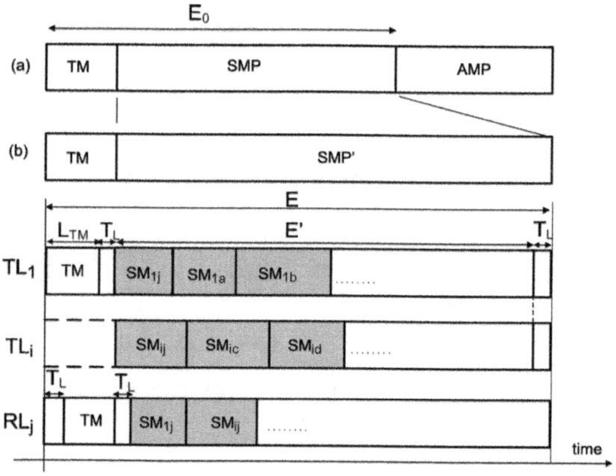

Fig. 5. Message Transmission Model

The real-time requirements of periodic messages are characterized by SM_{ij} $(D_{ij}, P_{ij}, O_{ij}, C_{ij})$ where SM_{ij} is the synchronous(periodic) message from node i to node j and D_{ij}, P_{ij}, O_{ij}, C_{ij} are the deadline, period, initial offset and amount of data of SM_{ij}, respectively. Moreover, we assume that all the D_{ij}, P_{ij} and O_{ij} are the multiple integers of E and $P_{ij} = D_{ij}$.

3.3 Scheduability Analysis

Now we analyze the schedulability condition for the periodic messages to support hard real-time communication over switched Ethernet under EDF-based scheduling algorithm. Besides using the above message transmission model, we assume that $T_L = 0$ for simple analysis and define some following notations:

(1) UT_i and UR_j are the utilization of TL_i and RL_j:

$$UT_i = \sum_{j \in ST_i} \frac{C_{ij}}{P_{ij}} \tag{1}$$

$$UR_j = \sum_{i \in SR_j} \frac{C_{ij}}{P_{ij}} \tag{2}$$

where ST_i is a set of nodes to which node i sends the messages and SR_j is a set of nodes from which node j receives the messages.

(2) $UT_{max,j}$ is the maximum utilization of a set of transmission links that transmit messages to node j, such that:

$$UT_{max,j} = \max_{i \in SR_j}(UT_i) \tag{3}$$

(3) $T_{i,n}$ is the total time for transmitting messages on TL_i in n^{th} EC.

Theorem 1. *A given set of messages SM_{ij} from node i to node j are scheduable if, for all i and j,*

$$UT_i + UR_j \leq \frac{E' - 2 * max(C_{ij}) + min(C_{ij})}{E} \tag{4}$$

Proof. According to basic theory of EDF scheduling algorithm [5], the schedulability condition for a set of preemption tasks is:

$$U = \sum_i \frac{C_i}{P_i} \leq 1 \tag{5}$$

where U is the utilization factor of real-time traffic, C_i and P_i are the execution time and the period of task i, respectively. Because the transmission of a set of periodic messages is non-preemptive, Pedreira *et al.* [6] showed that the schedulability condition is:

$$U = \sum_i \frac{C_i}{P_i} \leq \frac{E' - max(C_i)}{E} \tag{6}$$

where E' is the available time to transmit periodic messages on a shared medium.

The main idea of our scheduling algorithm is that the periodic messages which are transmitted at each EC of transmission link must be able to be delivered completely at the respective EC on reception links, which means meeting their deadline. From the schedulability condition (6), we can make a schedule for the periodic messages that satisfies the following condition:

$$T_{i,n} \leq UT_i * E + \mathbf{max}(C_{ij}) \leq E' \tag{7}$$

We call $T_{max,i} = UT_i * E + max(C_{ij})$ the maximum total time to transmit messages on TL_i at every EC.

For hard real-time communication, all the periodic messages have to meet their deadline in the worst-case scenario. In our message transmission model, if we restrict $T_{i,n}$ to be less than or equal to $T_{max,i}$ for every TL_i, all the periodic messages can be transmitted on TLs within the respective ECs. So, the worst-case situation occurs on RL_j and when:(i) all the periodic messages arrive at a reception link at the same time, and (ii) the arrival time of the first message on an EC on RL_j is latest, which means there is a shortest amount of time for transmitting messages on the current EC.

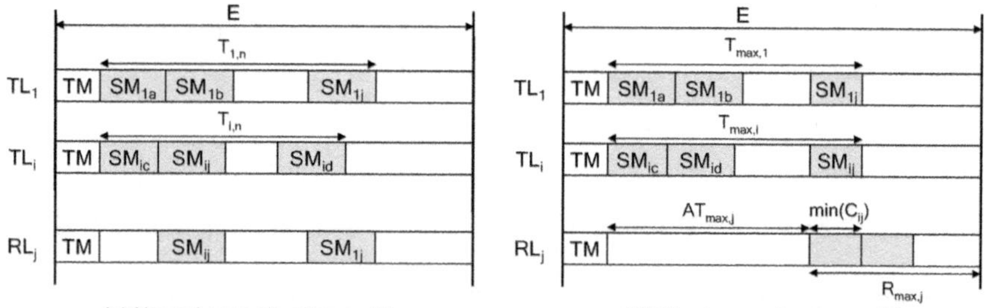

(a) Normal case situation on RL_j (b) Worst-case situation on RL_j

Fig. 6. Normal case and worst-case situations on RL_j

Fig. 6 shows the normal and worst-case situations on RL_j when the messages are transmitted over switched Ethernet. The figure also shows that by limiting the total time of TL_i to $T_{max,i}$, the temporal constraints of periodic messages can be satisfied if we bound the total time to transmit messages on reception link RL_j not to exceed the remaining amount of time in the EC (which is denoted by $R_{max,j}$ in Fig. 6) and they are not affected by the FIFO queue.

Now we can express the worst-case situation occurring on RL_j when: (i) the utilizations of all transmission links that are transmitting messages to RL_j are equal, and (ii) all the messages arrive at RL_j on the nth EC at the latest time. From the condition (i), we can see that, for all i such that $i \in SR_j$:

$$UT_i = UT_{max,j} \tag{8}$$

which leads to

$$T_{max,i} = UT_{max,j} * E + max(C_{ij}) \tag{9}$$

As shown in Fig. 6, the latest finishing time of periodic messages on TL_i is $T_{max,i}$ where $\forall i \in SR_j$. So the latest arrival time of messages on RL_j, $AT_{max,j}$, is

$$AT_{max,j} = T_{max,i} - min(C_{ij}) = UT_{max,j} * E + max(C_{ij}) - min(C_{ij}) \quad (10)$$

when the size of messages SM_{ij}, $\forall i \in SR_j$, is the smallest. If this worst-case situation happens, the available time to transmit messages on RL_j, $R_{max,j}$, is

$$R_{max,j} = E' - AT_{max,j} = E' - UT_{max,j} * E - max(C_{ij}) + min(C_{ij}). \quad (11)$$

We can use again the schedulability condition (6) to analyze the schedulability of periodic messages on the reception links. Thus, a set of periodic messages on RL_j is scheduable if

$$UR_j \leq \frac{R_{max,j} - max(C_{ij})}{E} \quad (12)$$

Replacing $R_{max,j}$ by (11), we have

$$UR_j \leq \frac{E' - UT_{max,j} * E - max(C_{ij}) + min(C_{ij}) - max(C_{ij})}{E} \quad (13)$$

which leads to

$$UR_j + UT_{max,j} \leq \frac{E' - 2 * max(C_{ij}) + min(C_{ij})}{E} \quad (14)$$

Combining (3) and (14), finally we have the schedulability condition (4) for supporting hard real-time communication of periodic messages over switched Ethernet under EDF-based scheduling algorithm. This is the end of the proof of **Theorem 1**.

3.4 EDF-Based Scheduling Algorithm

After checking the schedulability condition for a given set of periodic messages, the master node nakes a schedule for transmitting periodic messages in each EC according to the EDF-based scheduling algorithm. The following algorithm is an EDF-based scheduling algorithm which makes a schedule for a set of periodic messages which satisfies the feasibility condition of **Theorem 1**. For describing our scheduling algorithm, we use the following additional notations that some of them were already shown in Fig. 6.

$T_{i,n}$: the time to transmit messages on TL_i at n^{th} EC
$R_{j,n}$: the time to transmit messages on RL_j at n^{th} EC
$NT_{i,n}$: the number of messages that node i can transmit at n^{th} EC
$T_{max,i} = UT_i * E + max(C_{ij})$
$R_{max,j} = E' - UT_{max,j} * E - max(C_{ij}) + min(C_{ij})$
$r_{k,n}$: 1 if k^{th} message is ready to transmit at n^{th} EC

```
// EDF-based message scheduling algorithm
1. for (k = 1; k ≤ N; k++) {r_{k,1} = 0;}      // N : the number of messages
2. for(n = 0; n ≤ LCM(P_ij); n++) {    // LCM : Least Common Multiple
3.     T_{i,n} = 0, NT_{i,n} = 0 for all i; R_{j,n} = 0 for all j;
4.     {sort messages in increasing order of deadline};
5.     for (k = 1; k ≤ N; k++) {
6.         r_{k,n+1} = r_{k,n};
7.         if (r_{k,n} = 1) {
8.             read SM_ij;
9.             if((T_{i,n} + C_ij ≤ T_{max,i} ) and (R_{j,n} + C_ij) ≤ R_{max,j})) {
10.                T_{i,n} = T_{i,n} + C_ij;
11.                R_{j,n} = R_{j,n} + C_ij;
12.                NT_{i,n}++;
13.                r_{k,n+1} = 0;
14.            }
15.        }
16.        if ((n-1) mod P_ij/E = O_ij) r_{k,n+1} = 1;
17.    }
18. }
```

The master node goes through all ECs in line 2, and sorting at line 4 is carried out when new messages enter the system. The master checks whether a ready message can be transmitted or not by checking the total time to transmit message in the transmission and reception links (line 9) on the current EC. If the conditions are not satisfied, the message is delayed to the next EC. Finally, the master node considers the initial offset O_{ij} of message SM_{ij} at line 16.

By the following theorem, we can prove that each message in a feasible message set satisfying the condition of **Theorem 1** can be delivered within its deadline if we schedule those messages according to the proposed EDF-based scheduling algorithm.

Theorem 2. *The proposed EDF-based scheduling algorithm guarantees the timely delivery of messages for a message set satisfying the feasibility condition of* ***Theorem 1****.*

Proof. Assume that there is a new message SM_{ij} satisfies the condition (4) and is scheduled by EDF-based scheduling algorithm. Then the latest finishing time of SM_{ij} on TL_i (line 9) is:

$$T_{max,i} = UT_i * E + max(C_{ij}) \tag{15}$$

so the latest arrival time of SM_{ij} on RL_j is

$$L_{max,j} = UT_i * E + max(C_{ij}) - min(C_{ij}) \tag{16}$$

When arriving at RL_j, in the worst-case situation, SM_{ij} has to wait for other messages in the switch buffer. But this delay, according to scheduling algorithm, is bounded by:

$$R_{max,j} = E' - UT_{max,j} * E - max(C_{ij}) + min(C_{ij}) \tag{17}$$

so the finishing time $F_{ij,n}$ of SM_{ij} on n^{th}(current) EC will be :

$$F_{ij,n} \leq \ L_{max,j} + R_{max,j} \tag{18}$$

which leads to

$$F_{ij,n} \leq \ E' - (UT_{max,j} - UT_i) \tag{19}$$

Because $UT_i \leq \ UT_{max,j}$:

$$F_{ij,n} \leq \ E' \tag{20}$$

so SM_{ij} is transmitted on the same EC on both TL_i and RL_j, that means it meets its deadline. This is the end of the proof of **Theorem 2**.

4 Message Scheduling Example

In this section, we describe our message scheduling algorithm by a simple example as shown in Table. 1. The network consist of 5 slave nodes and a master node. At the beginning, these slaves send the request message that contain their real-time requirements of periodic message to master node.

Table 1. Requirement Table

Source \ Destination	N_1	N_2	N_3	N_4	N_5
N_1	-	0.15/3	0.2/2	-	0.1/1
N_2	0.2/2	-	0.1/1	0.15/3	-
N_3	0.1/1	0.15/3	-	-	0.2/2
N_4	-	0.15/1	0.2/2	-	0.15/3
N_5	0.1/2	0.2/3	0.2/2	0.2/1	-

cf. Each entry specifies C_{ij}/P_{ij} of SM_{ij}

We assume that $E = 1$ and $E' = 0.9$. When the master node checks the schedulability condition of messages, the messages are sorted according to their deadline as follows: SM_{15}, SM_{23}, SM_{31}, SM_{42}, SM_{54}, SM_{13}, SM_{21}, SM_{35}, SM_{43}, SM_{51}, SM_{53}, SM_{12}, SM_{24}, SM_{32}, SM_{45}, SM_{52}.

By using the schedulability condition (4), the master node rejects the requests of two periodic messages SM_{53} and SM_{52}. After establishing a set of schedulable

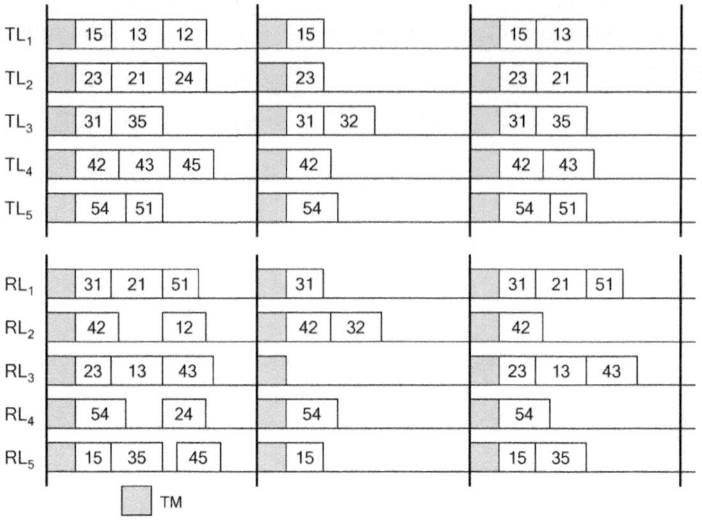

Fig. 7. Message Scheduling Example

messages, the schedule for transmission of periodic messages is made as shown in Fig. 7. This figure shows the message scheduling on the first 3 ECs when all the periodic messages are ready at time t=0 (that is, O_{ij}=0 for all i and j).

The values of $UT_{max,j}$, $T_{max,i}$ and $R_{max,j}$ for this example are shown on Table. 2. In our scheduling algorithm, the total time for transmitting messages on TL_i and RL_j is bounded by $T_{max,i}$ and $R_{max,j}$, so the message SM_{32} is delayed to the second EC (see Fig. 7).

Table 2. Variable Values

Variable \ Node	1	2	3	4	5
$UT_{max,j}$	0.25	0.3	0.3	0.25	0.3
$T_{max,i}$	0.45	0.45	0.45	0.5	0.45
$R_{max,j}$	0.55	0.5	0.5	0.55	0.5

5 Conclusions and Future Works

In this paper, we have proposed an integrated fieldbus network based on the switched Ethernet for seamless and transparent real-time communications among heterogeneous fieldbuses. To guarantee the real-time transmission requirement of periodic messages, we also have proposed an EDF-based scheduling algorithm for periodic messages over the switched Ethernet in the integrated fieldbus network and analyzed the schedulability condition for real-time periodic messages. The proposed periodic message scheduling algorithm is dynamic, which means that a new periodic message can be added if the message satisfies the schedulability condition.

We have assumed that the changes in synchronous requirements is carried on the aperiodic message cycle. We will analyze the schedulability of aperiodic message as well as the level of flexibility of the scheduling algorithm in the future.

Acknowledgment

The authors would like to thank Ministry of Commerce, Industry and Energy and Ulsan Metropolitan City which partly supported this research through the Network-based Automation Research Center (NARC) at University of Ulsan.

References

1. CAN Specification 2.0, Parts A and B, Robert Bosch, September (1991).
2. General Purpose Fieldbus: Vol. 1: P-Net; Vol. 2: PROFIBUS; Vol. 3: WorldFIP, Amend. 1: Foundation Fieldbus'H1, European Standard EN 50170 (2000).
3. IEC 65/240/CD (61499): Function blocks for industrial process management and control systems Part 1: Architecture.
4. IEC Commitee No. 65C, "IEC61804 general requirements specification", IEC Draft (2000).
5. C. L. Liu and J. W. Layland, Scheduling algorithms for multiprogramming in a hard real-time environment, J. ACM, vol. 20, no. 1, pp. 4661, 1973.
6. L. Almeida, P. Pedreiras, and J. A. Fonseca, The FTT-CAN protocol: Why and how, IEEE Trans. Ind. Electron., vol. 49, no. 6, pp. 11891201, Dec. 2002.
7. Lee K. and Lee S.: Performance evaluation of switched Ethernet for real-time industrial communications. In Comput. Stand. Interfaces, Vol. 24, No. 5 (2002).
8. Jasperneit J., and Neumann P.: Switched ethernet for factory communication. In Proc. of ETFA - 8th IEEE Int'l Conf. on Emerging Technologies and Factory Automation, Antibes, France (2001).
9. Hoang H., Jonsson M., Hagstrom U., and Kallerdahl A.: Switched real-time ethernet with earliest deadline first scheduling- protocols and traffic handling. In Proc. of Int'l Workshop on Parallel and Distributed Real-Time Systems, Fort Lauderdale, FL, USA (2002).
10. M. K. Kim and H. C. Lee "Periodic message scheduling on a switched Ethernet for hard real-time communication" HPCC'2006, Munich, Germany, Sep. 2006.

On Scheduling Exception Handlers in Dynamic, Embedded Real-Time Systems

Binoy Ravindran[1], Edward Curley[1], and E. Douglas Jensen[2]

[1] ECE Dept., Virginia Tech, Blacksburg, VA 24061, USA
binoy@vt.edu, alias@vt.edu
[2] The MITRE Corporation, Bedford, MA 01730, USA
jensen@mitre.org

Abstract. We consider the problem of scheduling exception handlers in real-time systems that operate under run-time uncertainties including those on execution times, activity arrivals, and failure occurrences. The application/scheduling model includes activities and their exception handlers that are subject to time/utility function (TUF) time constraints and an utility accrual (UA) optimality criterion. A key underpinning of the TUF/UA scheduling paradigm is the notion of "best-effort" where high importance activities are always favored over low importance ones, irrespective of activity urgency. (This is in contrast to classical admission control models which favor feasible completion of admitted activities over admitting new ones, irrespective of activity importance.) We consider a transactional style activity execution paradigm, where handlers that are released when their activities fail (e.g., due to time constraint violations) abort the failed activities after performing recovery actions. We present a scheduling algorithm called *Handler-assured Utility accrual Algorithm* (or HUA) for scheduling activities and their handlers. We show that HUA's properties include bounded-time completion for handlers and bounded loss of the best-effort property. Our implementation on a Real-Time Java Virtual Machine demonstrates the algorithm's effectiveness.

1 Introduction

Embedded real-time systems that are emerging in many domains such as robotic systems in the space domain (e.g., NASA/JPL's Mars Rover [1]) and control systems in the defense domain (e.g., airborne trackers [2]) are fundamentally distinguished by the fact that they operate in environments with dynamically uncertain properties. These uncertainties include transient and sustained resource overloads due to context-dependent activity execution times, and non-deterministically distributed activity arrivals and failure occurrences (which may also cause overloads). Nevertheless, such systems require the strongest possible assurances on activity timeliness behavior. Another important distinguishing feature of most of these systems that are of interest to us is their relatively long activity execution time magnitudes, compared to conventional real-time subsystems—e.g., from milliseconds to minutes.

Y.-H. Lee et al. (Eds.): ICESS 2007, LNCS 4523, pp. 510–529, 2007.

When resource overloads occur, meeting time constraints of all activities is impossible as the demand exceeds the supply. The urgency of an activity is sometimes orthogonal to the relative importance of the activity—e.g., the most urgent activity may be the least important, and vice versa; the most urgent may be the most important, and vice versa. Hence when overloads occur, completing the most important activities irrespective of activity urgency is often desirable. Thus, a clear distinction has to be made between urgency and importance during overloads. (During underloads, such a distinction generally need not be made, especially if all time constraints are deadlines, as algorithms that can meet all deadlines exist for those situations—e.g., EDF [3].)

Deadlines by themselves cannot express both urgency and importance. Thus, we consider the abstraction of *time/utility functions* (or TUFs) [5] that express the utility of completing an activity as a function of that activity's completion time. We specify a deadline as a binary-valued, downward "step" shaped TUF; Figure 1(a) shows examples. Note that a TUF decouples importance and urgency—i.e., urgency is measured on the X-axis, and importance is denoted (by utility) on the Y-axis. TUFs usually have a *termination time* — the latest time after which the function is not defined. For downward step TUFs, this time generally is the function's discontinuity point.

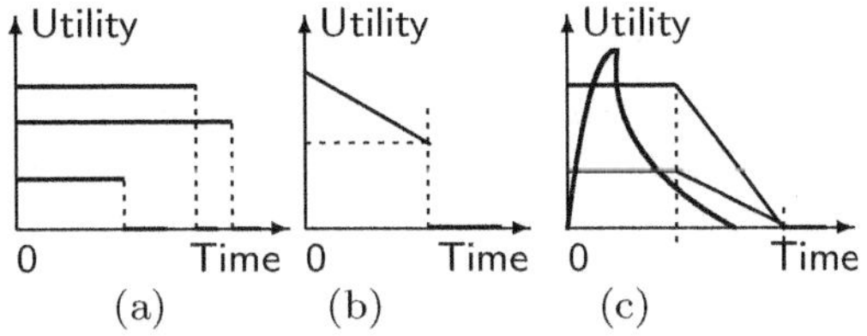

Fig. 1. Example TUF Time Constraints: (a) Step TUFs; (b) TUF of an AWACS [2]; and (c) TUFs of a Coastal Air defense System [4].

Some real-time systems also have activities with *non-deadline* time constraints, such as those where the utility attained for activity completion *varies* (e.g., decreases, increases) with completion time. Figures 1(b)–1(c) show examples from two defense applications [2, 4].

When activity time constraints are expressed with TUFs, the scheduling optimality criteria are based on maximizing accrued activity utility—e.g., maximizing the total activity accrued utility. Such criteria are called *utility accrual* (or UA) criteria, and sequencing (scheduling, dispatching) algorithms that optimize UA criteria are called UA sequencing algorithms (see [6] for example algorithms). UA criteria may also include other factors—e.g., dependencies that may arise between activities due to synchronization.

UA algorithms that maximize total utility under downward step TUFs (e.g., [7, 8]) default to EDF during underloads, since EDF satisfies all deadlines during underloads. Consequently, they obtain the optimum total utility during underloads. During overloads, they inherently favor more important activities over less important ones (since more utility can be attained from the former), irrespective of activity urgency, and thus exhibit adaptive behavior and graceful timeliness degradation. This behavior of UA algorithms is called "best-effort" [7] in the sense that the algorithms strive their best to feasibly complete as many high importance activities — as specified by the application through TUFs — as possible.[1] Consequently, high importance activities that arrive at any time always have a very high likelihood for successful completion (irrespective of their urgency). Note also that EDF's optimal timeliness behavior is a special-case of UA scheduling.

1.1 Contributions: Scheduling Exception Handlers with Timing Assurances

When a failure (e.g., a time constraint violation) occurs to an activity in such dynamic, best-effort real-time systems [9], control of the activity is immediately transferred to the (application-defined) exception handler block associated with the type of that failure. Such handler blocks (or handlers) may have time constraints and will compete for the processor along with other activities. Under a termination model, when a handler executes (not necessarily when control is transferred to it), it will abort the failed activity after performing recovery actions that are necessary to avoid inconsistencies. After a handler completes its execution, the application may desire to resume the execution of the failed activity's logic—e.g., the parent activity (or another activity that was waiting for the completion) of the failed activity creates a new child activity to resuscitate the failed activity's logic.

Scheduling of the handlers (along with their activities) must contribute to system-wide timeliness optimality. Untimely handler execution can degrade timeliness optimality—e.g.: high urgency handlers are delayed by low urgency non-failed activities, thereby delaying the resumption of high urgency failed activities; high urgency, non-failed activities are delayed by low urgency handlers.

A straightforward approach for scheduling handlers is to conceptually model them as normal activities, insert them into the ready queue when activities arrive, and schedule them along with the normal activities, according to a discipline that provides acceptably optimal system-wide timeliness. However, constructing a schedule that includes an activity and its handler implies that the activity *and* the handler will be dispatched for execution according to their order in the schedule. This is not true, as the handler needs to be dispatched only if and when the activity fails. Furthermore, an activity is released for execution, which is a scheduling event, it is immediately ready for execution. However, its handler is ready for execution only if and when the activity fails. Thus, constructing a schedule at an activity's release time such that it also includes the activity's handler will require a prediction of when the handler will be ready for execution in the future — a potentially impossible problem as there is no way to know if an activity will fail (in dynamic systems).

These problems can possibly be alleviated by considering an activity's failure time as a scheduling event and constructing a schedule that includes the activity's

[1] Note that the term "best effort" as used in the context of networks actually is intended to mean "least effort."

handler at that time. Doing so means that there is no way to know whether or not the handler can feasibly complete, satisfying its time constraint, until the activity fails. In fact, it is quite possible that when the activity fails, the scheduler may discover that the handler is infeasible due to an overload — e.g., there are more activities than can be feasibly scheduled, and there exists a schedule of activities excluding the handler from which more utility can be attained than from one including the handler.

Another strategy that avoids this predicament and has been very often considered in the past (e.g., [10,11]) is classical *admission control*: When an activity arrives, check whether a feasible schedule can be constructed that includes all the previously admitted activities and their handlers, besides the newly arrived one and its handler. If so, admit the activity and its handler; otherwise, reject. But this will cause the very fundamental problem that is solved by UA schedulers through its best-effort decision making—i.e., a newly arriving activity is rejected because it is infeasible, despite that activity being the most important. In contrast, UA schedulers will feasibly complete the high importance newly arriving activity (with high likelihood), at the expense of not completing some previously arrived ones, since they are now less important than the newly arrived.

Note that this problem does not occur in hard real-time systems (i.e., those that are assured to meet all deadlines) because the arrival and execution behaviors of activities are statically known. Thus, activities and their handlers are statically scheduled to ensure that all deadlines are met; if no feasible schedule exists, the application is redesigned until one exists [12].

Thus, scheduling handlers to ensure their system-wide timely execution in dynamic, best-effort real-time systems involves an apparently paradoxical situation: an activity may arrive at any (unknown) time; in the event of its failure, which is unknown until the failure occurs, a handler is immediately activated, and as strong assurances as possible must be provided for the handler's feasible completion.

We precisely address this problem in this paper. We consider real-time activities that are subject to TUF time constraints. Activities may have arbitrary arrival behaviors and failure occurrences. Activities may synchronize their execution for serially sharing non-processor resources, causing dependencies. For such a model, we consider the scheduling objective of maximizing the total utility accrued by all activities on one processor. This problem is $\mathcal{NP}$-hard. We present a polynomial-time heuristic algorithm called the *Handler-assured Utility accrual Algorithm* (or HUA).

We show that HUA ensures that handlers of activities that encounter failures during their execution will complete within a bounded time. Yet, the algorithm retains the fundamental best-effort property of UA algorithms with bounded loss—i.e., a high importance activity that may arrive at any time has a very high likelihood for successful completion. HUA also exhibits other properties including optimal total utility for a special case, deadlock-freedom, and correctness. Our implementation experience of HUA on a RTSJ (Real-Time Specification for Java) Virtual Machine demonstrates the algorithm's effectiveness.

Thus, the contribution of the paper is the HUA algorithm. To the best of our knowledge, we are not aware of any other efforts that solve the problem solved by HUA.

The rest of the paper is organized as follows: Section 2 outlines our activity model and state the scheduling objectives. We present HUA in Section 3 and establish the algorithm's properties in Section 4. Section 5 reports our implementation experience. We conclude the paper in Section 6.

2 Models and Objectives

Threads and Scheduling Segments. Our basic scheduling entity is the thread abstraction. Thus, the application consists of a set of threads, denoted $T_i, i \in \{1, 2, ..., n\}$. Threads can arrive arbitrarily and be preempted arbitrarily.

A thread can be subject to time constraints. A time constraint usually has a "scope"—a segment of the thread control flow that is associated with a time constraint [13]. We call such a scope, a "scheduling segment." A thread presents an execution time estimate of its scheduling segment to the scheduler when it enters that segment. This time estimate is not the worst-case; it can be violated at run-time (e.g., due to context dependence) and can cause processor overloads.

Resource Model. Threads can access non-processor resources including physical (e.g., disks) and logical (e.g., locks) resources. Resources can be shared, and can be subject to mutual exclusion constraints.

We consider a single-unit resource model. Thus, only a single instance is present for each resource and a thread must explicitly specify the resource that it needs.

A thread may request multiple shared resources during its lifetime. The requested time intervals for holding resources may be nested or disjoint.

Timeliness Model. A thread's time constraints are specified using TUFs. A TUF is always associated with a thread scheduling segment and is presented by the thread to the scheduler when the thread enters that segment. We focus on *non-increasing* unimodal TUFs, as they encompass the majority of the time constraints of interest to us. Figures 1(a), 1(b), and two TUFs in Figure 1(c) show examples.

Each TUF has an *initial* time and a *termination* time, which are the earliest and the latest times for which the TUF is defined, respectively. We assume that the initial time is the thread release time; thus a thread's absolute and relative termination times are the same. In this paper, we also assume that the termination time of a downward step TUF is its discontinuity point.

Exceptions and Abort Model. An exception handler block — simply referred to as a *handler* — is assumed to be associated with each scheduling segment of a thread. We consider a termination model for failures that are encountered during thread executions including time-constraint violations and logical errors. When a thread segment encounters such a failure during its execution, an exception is raised, and the segment's execution control is immediately transferred to the handler.

When the handler executes (not necessarily when control is transferred to it), it will abort the thread after performing compensations and recovery actions that are necessary to avoid inconsistencies—e.g., rolling back, rolling forward, or making other compensations to logical and physical resources that are held by the failed thread to safe states. The handler will also perform actions that are required to ensure the safety and stability of the external state.

A handler also has a time constraint, which is specified using a TUF. The handler's TUF's initial time is the time of failure of the handler's thread. The handler's TUF's termination time is relative to its initial time. Thus, a handler's absolute and relative termination times are *not* the same.

A handler also specifies an execution time estimate. This estimate along with the handler's TUF are described by the handler's thread when the thread enters the corresponding scheduling segment.

To summarize, when a thread enters a scheduling segment, it presents the following scheduling parameters to the scheduler: (1) execution time estimate of the scheduling segment; (2) time constraint of the segment (described using a TUF); (3) execution time estimate of the segment's exception handler; and (4) time constraint of the handler (described using a TUF).

A thread is assumed to present these scheduling parameters to the scheduler through a scheduling API that it invokes when entering a scheduling segment. Example such scheduling APIs include Real-Time CORBA 1.2's [13] `begin_scheduling_segment` API and [14]'s `REQ_CPU` API that are invoked by distributable threads and normal threads to enter a scheduling segment, respectively.

Handlers are not allowed to mutually exclusively access non-processor resources. Violation of a handler's absolute termination time will cause the immediate execution of system recovery code, which will recover thread's held resources and return the system to a consistent and safe state.

Scheduling Objectives. Our goal is to design a scheduling algorithm that maximizes the sum of the utility accrued by all the threads as much as possible. For downward step TUFs, maximizing the total utility subsumes meeting all TUF termination times as a special case. For non-step TUFs, this is not the case, as different utilities can be accrued depending upon the thread completion time, even when the TUF termination time is met. When all termination times are met for downward step TUFs (possible during underloads), the total accrued utility is the optimum possible. During overloads, for step and non-step TUFs, the goal is to maximize the total utility as much as possible.

Further, the completion time of handlers must be bounded. Moreover, the algorithm must exhibit the best-effort property of UA algorithms (described in Section 1) to the extent possible.

This problem is $\mathcal{NP}$-hard because it subsumes the problem of scheduling dependent threads with step-shaped TUFs, which has been shown to be $\mathcal{NP}$-hard in [8].

3 HUA Scheduling Algorithm

3.1 Basic Rationale

Since the task model is dynamic—i.e., when threads will arrive, how long they will execute, which set of resources will be needed by which threads, the length of time for which those resources will be needed, the order of accessing the resources are all statically unknown, future scheduling events such as new thread arrivals and new resource requests cannot be considered at a scheduling event. Thus, a schedule must be constructed solely exploiting the current system knowledge.

Since the primary scheduling objective is to maximize the total utility, a reasonable heuristic is a "greedy" strategy: Favor "high return" threads over low return ones, and complete as many of them as possible before thread termination times, as early as possible (since TUFs are non-increasing).

The potential utility that can be accrued by executing a thread defines a measure of its "return on investment." We measure this using a metric called the *Potential Utility Density* (or PUD). A thread's PUD measures the utility that can be accrued per unit time by immediately executing the thread and those thread(s) that it (directly or transitively) depends upon for locked resources.

Since the best-case failure scenario is the absence of failure for the thread and all of its dependents, the corresponding PUD can be obtained as the total utility accrued by executing the thread and its dependents divided by the aggregate execution time spent for executing the thread and its dependents. The PUD for the worst-case failure scenario (one where the thread and all of its dependents fail) can be obtained as the total utility accrued by executing the handler of the thread and that of its dependents divided by the aggregate execution time spent for executing the thread, its handler, the thread's dependents, and the handlers of the dependents.[2] The thread PUD can now be measured as the minimum of these two PUDs, as that represents the worst-case.

Thus, HUA examines threads for potential inclusion in a feasible schedule in the order of decreasing PUDs. For each thread, the algorithm examines whether the thread and its handler, along with the thread's dependents and their handlers, can be feasibly completed. If infeasible, the thread, its handler, the dependents, and their handlers are rejected. The process is repeated until all threads are examined, and the schedule's first thread is dispatched. Rejected threads are reconsidered for scheduling at subsequent scheduling events, until their termination times expire.

This process ensures that the threads included in the schedule at any given time have feasible handlers, thereby ensuring that when those threads encounter

[2] In the worst-case failure scenario, utility is accrued only for executing the thread handlers; no utility is gained for executing the threads themselves, though execution time is spent for executing the threads and the handlers.

failures *during* execution, their handlers are assured to complete. Note that no such assurances are afforded to thread failures that are encountered otherwise—e.g., when termination times of threads that are rejected at a scheduling event eventually expire. Handlers for those failures are executed in a best-effort manner —i.e., in accordance with their potential contribution to the total utility (at termination time expirations).

Handler Feasibility. Feasibility of a thread can be tested by verifying whether the thread can complete before its termination time. For a handler, feasibility means whether it can complete before its *absolute* termination time, which is the time of thread failure plus the handler's termination time. Since the thread failure time is impossible to predict, possible choices for the handler's absolute termination time include: (A) predicted thread completion time (in the current schedule) plus the handler's termination time; and (B) thread's termination time plus the handler's termination time.

The difference between A and B is in the delay suffered by the handler before its execution begins (A incurs less delay than B). Delaying the handler's start time (until its latest start time) potentially allows threads that may arrive later but with an earlier termination time than that of the handler to be feasibly scheduled. Thus, B is more appropriate from the standpoint of maximizing total utility.

There is always the possibility that a new thread T_i may arrive after the failure of another thread T_j but before the completion of T_j's handler. As per the best-effort philosophy, T_i must immediately be afforded the opportunity for feasible execution, in accordance with its potential contribution to the total utility. However it is possible that a schedule that includes T_i may not include T_j's handler. Since T_j's handler cannot be rejected, as that will violate the commitment made to T_j, the only option left is to not consider T_i for execution until T_j's handler completes, consequently degrading the best-effort property. In Section 4, we quantify this loss, and thereby establish the tradeoff between bounding handler completion times and the loss of the best-effort property.

We now overview the algorithm, and subsequently describe each of its components in detail.

3.2 Overview

HUA's scheduling events include the arrival of a thread, completion of a thread or a handler, a resource request, a resource release, and the expiration of a TUF termination time. To describe HUA, we define the following variables and auxiliary functions:

- $\mathcal{T}_r$ is the current set of unscheduled threads. $T_i \in \mathcal{T}_r$ is a thread. T_i^h denotes T_i's handler.
- σ is the ordered schedule. $\sigma(i)$ denotes the thread occupying the ith position in schedule σ.
- $U_i(t)$ denotes T_i's TUF; $U_i^h(t)$ denotes T_i^h's TUF.

- $T_i.X$ is T_i's termination time. $T_i.ExecTime$ is T_i's estimated remaining execution time. $T_i.Dep$ is T_i's dependency list.
- H is the set of handlers that are *released* for execution, ordered by non-decreasing handler termination times. A handler is said to be released for execution (i.e., activated for execution by transferring control to it) when the handler's thread fails. $H = \emptyset$ if all released handlers have completed.
- Function `updateReleaseHandlerSet()` inserts a handler T_i^h into H if the scheduler is invoked due to a thread T_i's failure; deletes a handler T_i^h from H if the scheduler is invoked due to T_i^h's completion. Insertion of T_i^h into H is at the position corresponding to T_i^h's termination time.
- `Owner(`R`)` denotes the threads that are currently holding resource R; `reqRes (`T`)` returns the resource requested by T.
- `headOf(`σ`)` returns the first thread in σ.
- `sortByPUD(`σ`)` returns a schedule ordered by non-increasing thread PUDs. If two or more threads have the same PUD, then the thread(s) with the largest $ExecTime$ will appear before any others with the same PUD.
- `Insert(`T`,`σ`,`I`)` inserts T in the ordered list σ at the position indicated by index I; if entries in σ exists with the index I, T is inserted before them. After insertion, T's index in σ is I.
- `Remove(`T`,`σ`,`I`)` removes T from ordered list σ at the position indicated by index I; if T is not present at the position in σ, the function takes no action.
- `lookup(`T`,`σ`)` returns the index value of the first occurrence of T in the ordered list σ.
- `feasible(`σ`)` returns a boolean value indicating schedule σ's feasibility. σ is feasible, if the predicted completion time of each thread T in σ, denoted $T.C$, does not exceed T's termination time. $T.C$ is the time at which the scheduler is invoked plus the sum of the $ExecTime$'s of all threads that occur before T in σ and $T.ExecTime$.

Algorithm 1 describes HUA at a high level of abstraction. When invoked at time t_{cur}, HUA first updates the set H (line 3) and checks the feasibility of the threads. If a thread's earliest predicted completion time exceeds its termination time, it is rejected (line 6). Otherwise, HUA calculates the thread's *Local Utility Density* (or LUD) (line 7), and builds its dependency list (line 8).

Each thread's PUD is computed by `calculatePUD()`, and the threads are then sorted by their PUDs (lines 10–11). In each step of the *for*-loop from line 12 to 15, the thread with the largest PUD, its handler, the thread's dependents, and their handlers are inserted into σ, if it can produce a positive PUD. The output schedule σ is then sorted by the threads' termination times by the procedure `insertByETF()`.

If one or more handlers have been released but have not completed their execution (i.e., $H \neq \emptyset$; line 17), the algorithm checks whether any of those handlers are missing in the schedule σ (lines 18– 21). If any handler is missing, the handler at the head of H is selected for execution (line 23). If all handlers in H have been included in σ, the thread at the head of σ is selected (line 24).

```
input: T_r, H; output: selected thread T_exe;
Initialization: t := t_cur; σ := ∅;
updateReleaseHandlerSet ();
for each thread T_i ∈ T_r do
    if feasible(T_i)=false then
        reject(T_i);
    else
        T_i.LUD = min( U_i(t+T_i.ExecTime) / T_i.ExecTime , U_i^h(t+T_i.ExecTime+T_i^h.ExecTime) / (T_i.ExecTime+T_i^h.ExecTime) );
        T_i.Dep := buildDep(T_i);
for each thread T_i ∈ T_r do
    T_i.PUD:=calculatePUD(T_i, t);
σ_tmp :=sortByPUD(T_r);
for each thread T_i ∈ σ_tmp from head to tail do
    if T_i.PUD > 0 then
        σ := insertByETF(σ, T_i);
    else break;
HandlerIsMissed := false ;
if H ≠ ∅ then
    for each thread T^h ∈ H do
        if T^h ∉ σ then
            HandlerIsMissed := true;
            break;
if HandlerIsMissed := true then
    T_exe :=headOf(H);
else
    T_exe:=headOf(σ);
return T_exe;
```

Algorithm 1. HUA: High Level Description

3.3 Computing Dependency Lists

HUA builds the *dependency list* of each thread—that arises due to mutually exclusive resource sharing—by following the chain of resource request and ownership.

Algorithm 2 shows this procedure for a thread T_k. For convenience, the thread T_k is also included in its own dependency list. Each thread T_l other than T_k in the dependency list has a successor job that needs a resource which is currently held by T_l. Algorithm 2 stops either because a predecessor thread does not need any resource or the requested resource is free. Note that "**·**" denotes an append operation. Thus, the dependency list starts with T_k's farthest predecessor and ends with T_k.

```
input: Thread T_k; output: T_k.Dep ;
Initialization : T_k.Dep := T_k; Prev := T_k;
while reqRes(Prev) ≠ ∅ ∧
Owner(reqRes(Prev)) ≠ ∅ do
    T_k.Dep :=Owner(reqRes(Prev)) ·T_k.Dep;
    Prev := Owner(reqRes(Prev));
```

Algorithm 2. `buildDep(`T_k`)`: Building Dependency List for a Thread T_k

3.4 Resource and Deadlock Handling

To handle deadlocks, we consider a deadlock detection and resolution strategy, instead of a deadlock prevention or avoidance strategy precisely due to the dynamic nature of the systems of interest — which resources will be needed by which threads, for how long, and in what order are all unknown to the scheduler. Under a single-unit resource request model, the presence of a cycle in the resource graph is the necessary and sufficient condition for a deadlock to occur. Thus, a deadlock can be detected by a straightforward cycle-detection algorithm. Such an algorithm is invoked by the scheduler whenever a thread requests a resource. A deadlock is detected if the new edge resulting from the thread's resource request produces a cycle in the resource graph. To resolve the deadlock, some thread needs to be aborted, which will result in some utility loss. To minimize this loss, we compute the utility that a thread can potentially accrue by itself if it were to continue its execution, which is measured by its LUD (line 7, Algorithm 1). HUA aborts that thread in the cycle with the lowest LUD.

3.5 Computing Thread PUD

Procedure `calculatePUD()` (Algorithm 3) accepts a thread T_i (with its dependency list) and the current time t_{cur}. It determines T_i's PUD, by assuming that threads in $T_i.Dep$ and their handlers are executed from the current position (at t_{cur}) in the schedule, while following the dependencies.

To compute T_i's PUD at time t_{cur}, HUA computes the PUDs for the best-case and worst-case failure scenarios and determines the minimum of the two.

For determining T_i's total accrued utility for the best-case failure-scenario, HUA considers each thread T_j that is in T_i's dependency chain, which needs to be completed before executing T_i. The total expected execution time upon completing T_j is counted using the variable t_c of line 4. With the known expected completion time of each thread, we can derive the expected utility for each thread, and thus obtain the total accrued utility U (line 5) for T_i's best-case failure-scenario.

For determining T_i's total accrued utility for the worst-case failure-scenario, the algorithm counts the total expected execution time upon completing T_j's handler using the variable t_c^h of line 6. The total accrued utility for the worst-case failure

1: **input:** T_i, t_{cur}; **output:** $T_i.PUD$;
2: *Initialization* : $t_c := 0$, $t_c^h := 0$, $U := 0$, $U^h := 0$;
3: **for** *each thread* $T_j \in T_i.Dep$, *from tail to head* **do**
4: $\quad t_c := t_c + T_j.ExecTime$;
5: $\quad U := U + U_j(t_{cur} + t_c)$;
6: $\quad t_c^h := t_c^h + T_j^h.ExecTime$;
7: $\quad U^h := U^h + U_j^h(t_{cur} + t_c + t_c^h)$;
8: $T_i.PUD := \min\left(U/t_c, U^h/(t_c + t_c^h)\right)$;
9: **return** $T_i.PUD$;

Algorithm 3. `calculatePUD(`T_i`,`t_{cur}`)`: Calculating the PUD of a Thread T_i

scenario U^h can be determined once the thread's completion time followed by its handler's completion time is known (line 7).

The best-case and worst-case failure scenario PUDs can be determined as U and U^h divided by t_c and $t_c + t_c^h$, respectively, and the minimum of the two PUDs is determined as T_i's PUD (line 8).

Note that the total execution time of T_i and its dependents consists of two parts: (1) the time needed to execute the threads that directly or transitively block T_i; and (2) T_i's remaining execution time. According to the process of `buildDep()`, all the dependent threads are included in $T_i.Dep$.

Note that each thread's PUD is calculated assuming that they are executed at the current position in the schedule. This would not be true in the output schedule σ, and thus affects the accuracy of the PUDs calculated. Actually, we are calculating the highest possible PUD of each thread by assuming that it is executed at the current position. Intuitively, this would benefit the final PUD, since `insertByETF()` always selects the thread with the highest PUD at each insertion on σ. Also, the PUD calculated for the dispatched thread at the head of σ is always accurate.

3.6 Constructing Termination Time-Ordered Feasible Schedules

Algorithm 4 describes `insertByETF()` (invoked in Algorithm 1, line 14). `insertByETF()` updates the tentative schedule σ by attempting to insert each thread, along with its handler, all of the thread's dependent threads, and their handlers into σ. The updated schedule σ is an ordered list of threads, where each thread is placed according to the termination time that it *should* meet.

Note that the time constraint that a thread should meet is not necessarily its termination time. In fact, the index value of each thread in σ is the actual time constraint that the thread should meet.

A thread may need to meet an earlier termination time in order to enable another thread to meet its termination time. Whenever a thread is considered for insertion in σ, it is scheduled to meet its own termination time. However, all of the threads in its dependency list must execute before it can execute, and

```
1: input  : T_i and an ordered thread list σ
2: output: the updated list σ
3: if T_i ∉ σ then
4:     Copy σ into σ_tmp: σ_tmp :=σ;
5:     Insert(T_i, σ_tmp, T_i.X);
6:     Insert(T_i^h, σ_tmp, T_i.X + T_i^h.X);
7:     CuTT = T_i.X;
8:     for each thread T_j ∈ {T_i.Dep − T_i} from head to tail do
9:         if T_j ∈ σ_tmp then
10:            TT=lookup(T_j, σ_tmp);
11:            if TT < CuTT then
                   continue;
12:            else
13:                Remove(T_j, σ_tmp, TT);
14:                TTh=lookup(T_j^h, σ_tmp);
15:                Remove(T_j^h, σ_tmp, TTh);
16:        CuTT:=min(CuTT, T_j.X);
17:        Insert(T_j, σ_tmp, CuTT);
18:        Insert(T_j^h, σ_tmp, T_j.X + T_j^h.X);
19:    if feasible(σ_tmp) then
20:        σ := σ_tmp;
21: return σ;
```

Algorithm 4. insertByETF(σ, T_i): Inserting a Thread T_i, T_i's Handler, T_i's Dependents, and their Handlers into a Termination Time-Ordered Feasible Schedule σ

therefore, must precede it in the schedule. The index values of the dependent threads may be changed with Insert()in line 17 of Algorithm 4.

The variable $CuTT$ keeps track of this information. It is initialized with the termination time of thread T_i, which is tentatively added to the schedule (line 7). Thereafter, any thread in $T_i.Dep$ with a later termination time than $CuTT$ is required to meet $CuTT$ (lines 13; 16–17). If, however, a thread has a tighter termination time than $CuTT$, then it is scheduled to meet that time (line 11), and $CuTT$ is advanced to that time since all threads left in $T_i.Dep$ must complete by then (lines 16–17).

When T_i (or any thread $T_j \in T_i.Dep$) is inserted in σ, its handler T_i^h is immediately inserted to meet a termination time that is equal to T_i's termination time plus T_i^h's (relative) termination time (lines 6, 18). When a thread in $T_i.Dep$ with a later termination time than $CuTT$ is advanced to meet $CuTT$, the thread's handler is also correspondingly advanced (lines 14–15; 18).

Finally, if this insertion (of T_i, its handler, threads in $T_i.Dep$, and their handlers) produces a feasible schedule, then the threads are included in this schedule; otherwise, not (lines 19–20).

Computational Complexity. With n threads, HUA's asymptotic cost is $O(n^2 \log n)$ (for brevity, we skip the analysis). Though this cost is higher than that of many traditional real-time scheduling algorithms, it is justified for applications with longer execution time magnitudes such as those that we focus on here. (Of course, this high cost cannot be justified for every application.)

4 Algorithm Properties

We first describe HUA's bounded-time completion property for exception handlers:

Theorem 1. *If a thread T_i encounters a failure during its execution, then under HUA with zero overhead, its handler T_i^h will complete no later than $T_i.X + T_i^h.X$ time units (barring T_i^h's failure).*

Proof. If T_i fails at a time t during its execution, then T_i was included in HUA's schedule constructed at the scheduling event that occurred nearest to t, say at t', since only threads in the schedule are executed (lines 23–25, Algorithm 1). If T_i was in HUA's schedule at t', then both T_i and T_i^h (besides T_i's dependents and their handlers) were feasible at t', since infeasible threads and their handlers (along with their dependents) are rejected by HUA (lines 19–20, Algorithm 4). Thus, T_i^h was scheduled to complete no later than $T_i.X + T_i^h.X$ (lines 6, 18, Algorithm 4).

When a thread T_i arrives after the failure of a thread T_j but before the completion of T_j^h, HUA *may* exclude T_i from a schedule until T_j^h completes, resulting in some loss of the best-effort property. To quantify this loss, we define the concept of a *Non Best-effort time Interval* (or NBI):

Definition 1. *Consider a scheduling algorithm $\mathcal{A}$. Let a thread T_i arrive at a time t with the following properties: (a) T_i and its handler together with all threads in $\mathcal{A}$'s schedule at time t are not feasible at t, but T_i and its handler are feasible just by themselves;*[3] *(b) One or more handlers (which were released due to thread failures before t) have not completed their execution at t; and (c) T_i has the highest PUD among all threads in $\mathcal{A}$'s schedule at time t. Now, $\mathcal{A}$'s NBI, denoted $NBI_{\mathcal{A}}$, is defined as the duration of time that T_i will have to wait after t, before it is included in $\mathcal{A}$'s feasible schedule. Thus, T_i is assumed to be feasible together with its handler at $t + NBI_{\mathcal{A}}$.*

We now describe the NBI of HUA and other UA algorithms including DASA [8], LBESA [7], and AUA [15] (under zero overhead):

Theorem 2. *HUA's worst-case NBI is $t + \max_{\forall T_j \in \sigma_t} \left(T_j.X + T_j^h.X\right)$, where σ_t denotes HUA's schedule at time t. DASA's and LBESA's worst-case NBI is zero; AUA's is $+\infty$.*

[3] If $\mathcal{A}$ does not consider a thread's handler for feasibility (e.g., [7,8]), then the handler's execution time is regarded as zero.

Proof. The time t that will result in the worst-case NBI for HUA is when $\sigma_t = H \neq \emptyset$. By NBI's definition, T_i has the highest PUD and is feasible. Thus, T_i will be included in the feasible schedule σ, resulting in the rejection of some handlers in H. Consequently, the algorithm will discard σ and select the first handler in H for execution. In the worst-case, this process repeats for each of the scheduling events that occur until all the handlers in σ_t complete (i.e., at handler completion times), as T_i and its handler may be infeasible with the remaining handlers in σ_t at each of those events. Since each handler in σ_t is scheduled to complete by $\max_{\forall T_j \in \sigma_t}\left(T_j.X + T_j^h.X\right)$, the earliest time that T_i becomes feasible is $t + \max_{\forall T_j \in \sigma_t}\left(T_j.X + T_j^h.X\right)$.

DASA and LBESA will examine T_i at t, since a task arrival is always a scheduling event for them. Further, since T_i has the highest PUD and is feasible, they will include T_i in their feasible schedules at t (before including any other tasks), yielding a zero worst-case NBI.

AUA will examine T_i at t, since a thread arrival at any time is a scheduling event under it. However, AUA is a TUF/UA algorithm in the classical admission control mould and will reject T_i in favor of previously admitted threads, yielding a worst-case NBI of $+\infty$.

Theorem 3. *The best-case NBI of HUA, DASA, and LBESA is zero; AUA's is* $+\infty$.

Proof. HUA's best-case NBI occurs when T_i arrives at t and the algorithm includes T_i and all handlers in H in the feasible schedule σ (thus the algorithm only rejects some *threads* in σ_t to construct σ). Thus, T_i is included in a feasible schedule at time t, resulting in zero best-case NBI.

The best-case NBI scenario for DASA, LBESA, and AUA is the same as their worst-case.

Thus, HUA's NBI interval $[0, \max_{\forall T_j \in \sigma_t} T_j.X + T_j^h.X]$ lies in between that of DASA/LBESA's $[0]$ and AUA's $[+\infty]$. Note that HUA and AUA bound handler completions; DASA/LBESA do not.

HUA produces optimum total utility for a special case:

Theorem 4. *Consider a set of independent threads subject to step TUFs. Suppose there is sufficient processor time for meeting the termination-times of all threads and their handlers. Now, a schedule produced by EDF [3] is also produced by HUA, yielding equal totaly utility.*

Proof. For a thread T_i without dependencies, $T_i.Dep$ only contains T_i. During underloads, σ from line 14 of Algorithm 1 is termination time-ordered. The TUF termination time that we consider is analogous to the deadline in [3]. From [3], an EDF schedule is optimal (with respect to meeting all deadlines) during underloads. Thus, σ yields the same total utility as EDF.

HUA also exhibits non-timeliness properties including freedom from deadlocks, correctness (i.e., the resource requested by a thread selected for execution by HUA is free), and mutual exclusion. These properties are self-evident from the algorithm description. For brevity, we omit their proofs.

5 Implementation Experience

We implemented HUA in a real-time Java platform. This platform consisted of the *meta-scheduler* middleware scheduling framework in [14] implemented atop Apogee's Aphelion Real-Time Java Virtual Machine that is compliant with the Real-Time Specification for Java (RTSJ). This RTSJ platform ran atop the Debian Linux OS (kernel version 2.6.16-2-686) on a 800MHz, Pentium-III processor.

Besides HUA, we implemented DASA and a simplified variant of HUA called HUA-Non-Preemptive (or HUA-NP), for a comparative study. DASA does not consider handlers for scheduling until failures occur. When a thread fails, DASA then considers its handler for scheduling just like a regular thread, resulting in zero NBI. Similar to DASA, HUA-NP also does not consider handlers for scheduling until failures occur. However, when a thread fails, unlike DASA, HUA-NP immediately runs the thread handler non-preemptively till completion, resulting in a worst-case and best-case NBI of one handler execution time. In this way, HUA-NP seeks to accrue as much utility as possible by excluding handlers from schedule construction (and thus is more greedy than HUA), while maintaining an upper bound on handler completion. Thus, DASA and HUA-NP are good candidates for a comparative study as they represent two interesting end points of the NBI-versus-handler-completion-time tradeoff space.

Our test application created several periodic threads that consume a certain amount of processor time, request a shared resource, and periodically check for abort exceptions. Each thread created had a unique execution time, period, and maximum utility. These parameters were assigned based on three PUD-based thread classes that were used: *high*, *medium*, and *low*. The classes differed in thread execution times, thread periods, and threads PUDs by one order of magnitude. The classes, however, differed in handler execution times, handler periods, and handler PUDs only by a small factor. Within each class, thread execution times and thread PUDs were higher than that of their handler execution times and handler PUDs, respectively, by one order of magnitude. For all the experiments, an even number of threads from each of the three classes were used. Thus, the three classes give the algorithms a rich mixture of thread properties to exhibit their NBI and handler completion behaviors.

Our metrics to evaluate HUA included the NBI, Handler Completion Time (HCT), Accrued Utility Ratio (AUR), and Deadline Miss Ratio (DMR). HCT is the duration between a handler's completion time and it's release time. AUR is the ratio of the total accrued utility to the maximum possible total utility (possible if every released thread completes before its termination time). DMR is the ratio of the number of threads that missed their termination times to the number of released threads.

We manipulated five variables during our experiments: (1) the percentage of failed threads, (2) system load caused by normal tasks, (3) system load caused by handlers, (4) the ratio of handler execution time to normal task execution time, and (5) the number of shared resources within the system. The variables affect the system's "stress factor" and influence the four metrics.

We measured the four metrics under a constant value for these variables, except for the failure percentage, which was varied between 0% and 95%. To vary the failure percentage, the set of threads that must fail for a given percentage must be repeatable. However, to have a repeatable set of discrete failures (i.e., not a random distribution), the actual percentage of failures may be slightly off from the predicted value—e.g., if an experiment had 50 threads and 25% of them needed to be failed, it is impossible to fail 12.5 threads; thus the failure percentage would be 24% or 26%.

Normal task load was 150%, handler load was 90%, and the ratio of handler execution to normal execution was 50%. We first focused on zero shared resources and then considered shared resources.

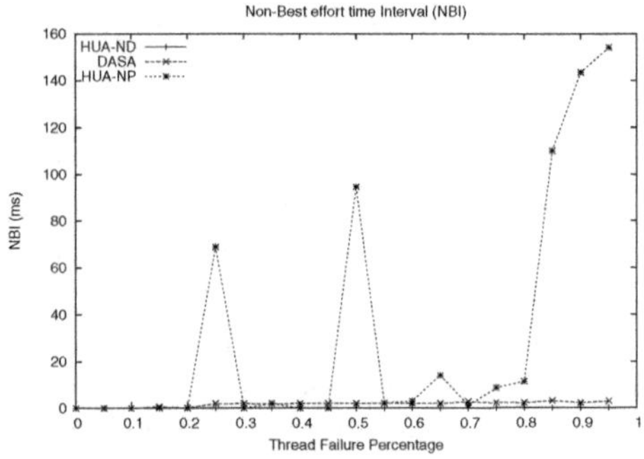

Fig. 2. Non-Best effort time Interval (NBI)

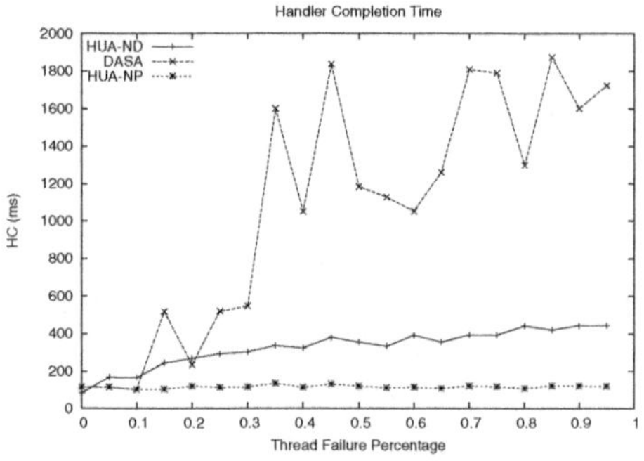

Fig. 3. Handler Completion Time

Figure 2 shows the measured NBI of DASA, HUA-NP, and HUA under increasing number of failures. We observe that HUA provides a smaller NBI than DASA and HUA-NP. HUA has a smaller NBI than DASA because DASA is unlikely to execute low-PUD threads like handlers. Thus, it is likely to keep them pending and incur a non-zero NBI due to scheduler overhead when a high PUD thread arrives. HUA has a smaller NBI than HUA-NP because HUA-NP will always have a non-zero NBI when a high PUD thread arrives during its non-preemptive handler execution. However, the only time HUA will have a non-zero NBI is when a high PUD thread arrives with such little slack that the pending handlers cannot fit within that slack.

Figure 3 shows the average HCTs for HUA, DASA, and HUA-NP. In general, DASA's HCTs are highest and rather inconsistent, HUA-NP's are smallest and very consistent, and HUA's are somewhat consistent, but always within a certain bound. As DASA was not designed to bound HCTs, it makes sense that its HCTs would be larger than the other two algorithms. Likewise, it makes sense that HUA-NP would have the least average HCT as the handler is run to completion when it is released. To allow more threads to be scheduled, HUA does not immediately run the handler when it is released. This delay in running the handler causes HUA's average HCT to be higher than HUA-NP's. However, as

HUA is designed to provide a finite bound on HCT, it will generally be smaller than DASA's.

Figures 2 and 3 also indicate that the trends acquired from our experiments display a less than smooth response to changes in failure percentage. (Figures 4 and 5 also display this behavior.) This is likely due to the way the failure percentage is varied. Since the set of threads that fail for a given failure percentage is not a strict subset of the set of threads that fail for a larger failure percentage, it is possible that lower-PUD threads may fail at higher failure percentages. Thus, algorithms like DASA and HUA-NP may find a more beneficial schedule at higher failure percentages.

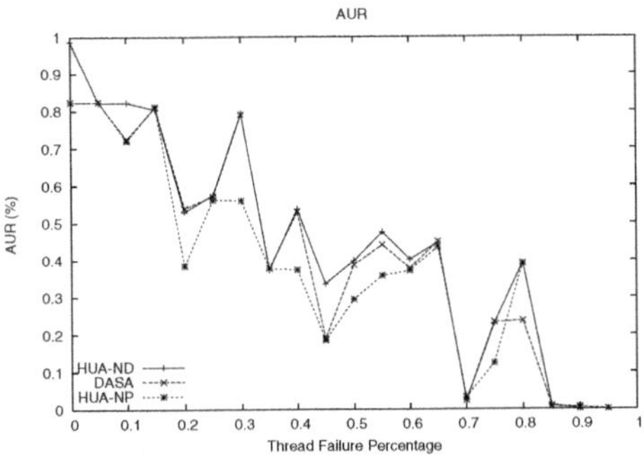

Fig. 4. Accrued Utility Ratio

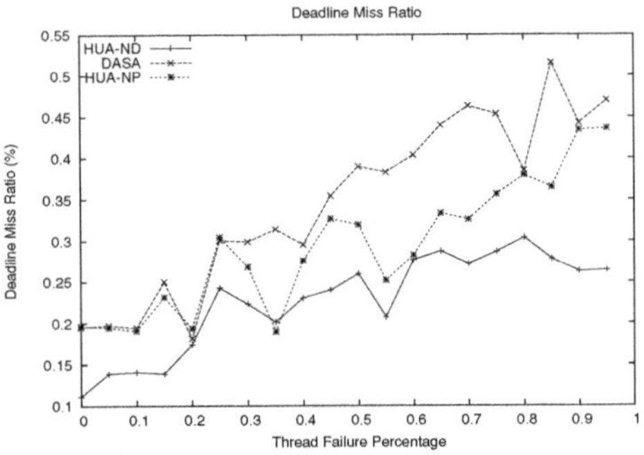

Fig. 5. Deadline Miss Ratio

Figure 4 shows how the AUR of each algorithm is affected under increasing failures. In general, HUA will have a lower AUR as it reserves a portion of its schedule for handlers which generally have lower PUDs or may not even execute. However, as can be seen from the figure, HUA has an AUR that is comparable to, if not better than that of DASA and HUA-NP for this thread set. This is because DASA only analyzes handlers that have been released. This limits DASA's ability to discern whether it would be more beneficial to abort the thread and run its handler instead. As HUA has no such limitation, it can better decide whether to run the thread or abort the thread and run its handler.

Figure 5 displays the measured DMR under increasing failures. As the number of failures increases, the number of termination times (or deadlines) missed also increases. This is due to the added load that handlers put on the system. In the case of DASA, this load is completely unforeseen and as the handlers have less PUD than most normal threads, DASA may never schedule them causing their termination times to be missed. Thus, DASA is affected most by increased failures. While the handler load is also unanticipated for HUA-NP, the effects are mitigated somewhat due to HUA-NP's non-preemptive handler execution property. Because HUA takes the handler load into consideration when forming a schedule, the extra load on the system affects HUA the least.

Figure 6 and Figure 7 show the average HCT and average NBI of HUA under increasing number of shared resources. From the figures, we observe that HUA's

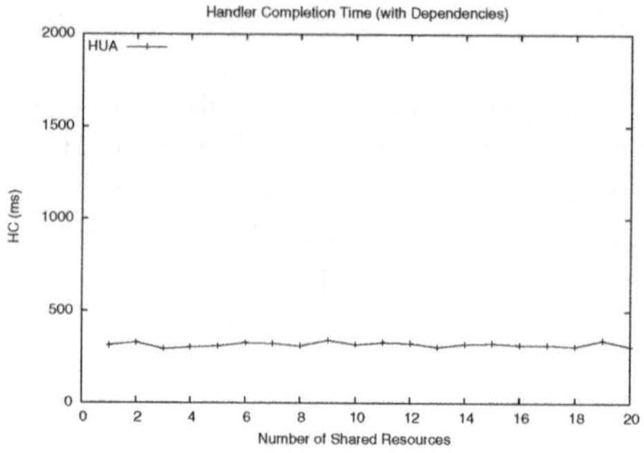

Fig. 6. Handler Completion Time with Dependencies

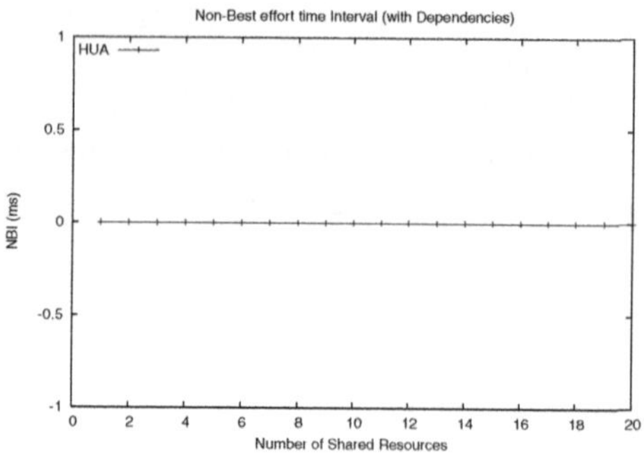

Fig. 7. NBI with Dependencies

HCT and NBI are unaffected by dependencies that arise between threads due to shared resources.

6 Conclusions and Future Work

We presented a real-time scheduling algorithm called HUA. The algorithm's application model includes threads and their exception handlers with TUF time constraints, and a transactional-style execution paradigm where handlers abort the failed threads after performing recovery actions. Threads may serially share non-processor resources. We showed that HUA bounds (A) the completion times of handlers that are released for threads which fail during execution, and (B) the time interval for which a high importance thread arriving during overloads has to wait to be included in a feasible schedule. Our implementation on a RTSJ Virtual Machine demonstrated HUA's effectiveness.

Property (A) is potentially unbounded for best-effort algorithms, and property (B) is potentially unbounded for admission control algorithms. By bounding (A) and (B), HUA conceptually places itself between these two models, allowing for applications to exploit the tradeoff space.

Directions for future work include extending the results to [16]'s variable cost function model for thread/handler execution times, multiprocessor scheduling, and scheduling [13]'s distributable threads.

References

1. Clark, R.K., et al.: Software organization to facilitate dynamic processor scheduling. In: IEEE WPDRTS. (2004)
2. Clark, R., et al.: An adaptive, distributed airborne tracking system. In: IEEE WPDRTS. (1999) 353–362
3. Horn, W.: Some simple scheduling algorithms. Naval Research Logistics Quaterly **21** (1974) 177–185

4. Maynard, D.P., Shipman, S.E., et al.: An example real-time command, control, and battle management application for alpha. Technical report, CMU CS Dept. (1988) Archons Project TR 88121.
5. Jensen, E.D., et al.: A time-driven scheduling model for real-time systems. In: IEEE RTSS. (1985) 112–122
6. Ravindran, B., Jensen, E.D., Li, P.: On recent advances in time/utility function real-time scheduling and resource management. In: IEEE ISORC. (2005) 55 – 60
7. Locke, C.D.: Best-Effort Decision Making for Real-Time Scheduling. PhD thesis, Carnegie Mellon University (1986)
8. Clark, R.K.: Scheduling Dependent Real-Time Activities. PhD thesis, Carnegie Mellon University (1990)
9. Northcutt, J.D.: Mechanisms for Reliable Distributed Real-Time Operating Systems - The Alpha Kernel. Academic Press (1987)
10. Bestavros, A., Nagy, S.: Admission control and overload management for real-time databases. In: Real-Time Database Systems: Issues and Applications. Kluwer Academic Publishers (1997)
11. Streich, H.: Taskpair-scheduling: An approach for dynamic real-time systems. Mini and Microcomputers **17** (1995) 77–83
12. Kandasamy, N., et al.: Scheduling algorithms for fault tolerance in real-time embedded systems. In Avresky, D.R., ed.: Dependable Network Computing. Kluwer Academic Publishers, Norwell, MA, USA (2000)
13. OMG: Real-time corba 2.0: Dynamic scheduling specification. Technical report, Object Management Group (2001)
14. Li, P., Ravindran, B., et al.: A formally verified application-level framework for real-time scheduling on posix real-time operating systems. IEEE Transactions on Software Engineering **30** (2004) 613 – 629
15. Curley, E., Anderson, J.S., Ravindran, B., Jensen, E.D.: Recovering from distributable thread failures with assured timeliness in real-time distributed systems. In: IEEE SRDS. (2006) 267–276
16. Wu, H., et al.: Utility accrual real-time scheduling under variable cost functions. In: IEEE RTCSA. (2005) 213–219

PR-MAC: Path-Oriented Real-Time MAC Protocol for Wireless Sensor Network

Jianrong Chen, Peidong Zhu, and Zhichang Qi

College of Computer Science, National University of Defense Technology, Changsha, Hunan, China, 410073
{Jrchen,Pdzhu,zcq}@nudt.edu.cn

Abstract. This paper proposes a Path-oriented Real-time Medium Access Control (PR-MAC) protocol for sensor networks to guarantee the bounded delay of data transmission. PR-MAC removes sleep delay with a Bidirectional Pipelining Schedule (BPS) algorithm, and reduces communication delay caused by contention with a multi-channel communication mechanism. BPS enables a node to wake twice during a work cycle so as to support bidirectional data transmission. In either direction, the nodes along a path wake up sequentially. The multi-channel mechanism allocates a special channel for each communication path so that multiple simultaneous events will not interfere with one another. The data delay and energy consumption of PR-MAC is compared with those of S-MAC and DMAC. We implement the prototype of PR-MAC on the ns-2 simulator. Experiments showed PR-MAC performs better than S-MAC in reducing the transmission delay of both data and control message.

Keywords: Sensor network, real time, MAC, schedule, channel.

1 Introduction

A Wireless Sensor Network (WSN) deploys a large number of sensors with processing and communication capabilities for collecting information from and responding to the physical world. A typical WSN consists of a set of nodes and one common sink. The nodes collect information and deliver messages to the sink. The sink is capable of processing the messages and controlling the working state of the WSN accordingly. There are two directions of data transmission in WSNs: *data report* from a source to the sink, and *network control* from the sink to a source.

Maximizing the network lifetime is a common objective of sensor network research, since sensor nodes are assumed to be disposed when they are out of battery. However, a great number of WSN applications, such as battlefield surveillance, disaster and emergency response, are required of real time properties, which constrain the delay of end-to-end data transmission [1]. For example, a WSN for environment surveillance may require a sensor node to detect a fast moving target and to send the information to the sink within one second. The sink is supposed to react by commanding a node before the target moves out of the sensing range of the WSN. However, to guarantee real time properties of sensor networks is challenging due to

Y.-H. Lee et al. (Eds.): ICESS 2007, LNCS 4523, pp. 530–539, 2007.

the following two reasons. First, the nodes in a WSN communicate through one channel by contention, which leads to undeterministic communication delay. Second, the sleep/wakeup mechanism for saving energy consumption results in *sleep latency*, which means an intermediate node may have to wait until the receiver wakes up before it can forward a packet received from its previous hop [3].

To achieve a bounded delay of end-to-end data transmission without much sacrifice on energy, this paper proposes a new medium access control protocol, named Path-oriented Real-time Media Access Control (PR-MAC). The protocol addresses the two causes of data transmission delay with a schedule algorithm called Bidirectional Pipelining Schedule (BPS) and a multi-channel communication mechanism, respectively. The BPS schedule algorithm is devised to reduce sleep latency in both directions of data transmission. BPS enables a node to wake up twice during a work cycle, each for data transmission in one direction. The time interval of two wakes of a node within one work cycle depends upon the number of hops between the node and the sink. In either direction, the nodes along a path wake up sequentially in the way of pipelining. PR-MAC replaces one channel mechanism in traditional WSN protocols with the multi-channel communication mechanism to reduce the data transmission delay due to the contention. The multi-channel mechanism is only used on paths where data transmission occurs. BPS together with the multi-channel mechanism enables a WSN to construct a quick bidirectional path for each event. With the quick paths, the WSN can quickly adapt to changing real time requirements in an application by changing its information sampling frequency and waking up offset of nodes.

The remainder of the paper is organized as follows. Section 2 overviews the existing delay-reducing solutions. In Section 3, we elaborate the design of the PR-MAC protocol. In Section 4, the transmission delay and energy consumption of PR-MAC are theoretically analyzed and compared with those of the most often cited protocols S-MAC [2][3] and DMAC [4]. Section 5 presents the implementation of PR-MAC on the ns-2 simulator. The experiments we conducted showed that PR-MAC is able to satisfy real time constraints on applications featured by simultaneous events. Section 6 concludes the paper with a discussion of future work.

2 Related Work

A number of protocols have been proposed to reduce sleep latency resulted from the sleep/wakeup schedule, including S-MAC, T-MAC and LE-MAC. In S-MAC [3], the time frame is divided into the listen and sleep periods. In order to reduce the sleep latency, *adaptive listen* uses the RTS-CTS mechanism to wake up neighbors of the sender and the receiver after a packet is delivered. The adaptive listen can avoid schedule miss and half the latency. T-MAC [4] is another contention-based low duty cycle MAC protocol. In contrast to S-MAC where nodes listen passively, T-MAC uses an active future request-to-send (FRTS) scheme, which notices the third hop node with a future-request-to-send packet. LE-MAC [8] exploits the feature of physical carrier sensing in CSMA/CA. When nodes in the routing path between a source and a sink are signaled of the traffic, they wake sometime later during the sleep period for transmitting data. In comparison with S-MAC, LE-MAC is similar in employing the overhearing mechanism, but performs better in energy saving.

With the above protocols, sleep latency in WSNs can be reduced to some extent but cannot be totally removed, because the scope of either overhearing or FRTS is limited to a number of hops and not able to cover the whole paths in a WSN.

Schedule algorithms for avoiding sleep latency have also been researched. Among them, DMAC [5] is closely related to BPS proposed in this paper. As a schedule algorithm specifically designed for data gathering tree applications, where multiple sources and a single sink in the network construct a data forwarding tree, DMAC staggers the activity schedule of nodes on the multihop path to wake up sequentially like a chain reaction. Sleep latency is eliminated if there is no packet loss due to channel error or collision. In [6], a schedule algorithm similar to DMAC called FPA is demonstrated with an implementation based on S-MAC.

DMAC and FPA can confine data transmisstion delay to about 100ms per hop. However, they are still incapable of satisfying real time requirements on WSNs. The inadequacy of them lies in three aspects. First, the delay bound of 100ms is unacceptable in most real time applications. Second, the presumption of DMAC that no packet loss occurs cannot generally hold because sensor networks usually run in complex environment. Most importantly, the sleep latency of control messages delivered from the sink is not addressed.

Among the researches about multi-channel communication, a protocol called MMSN is proposed in [7]. MMSN takes advantage of multi-frequency availability of communication hardware, and also takes into account the restrictions in wireless sensor networks. Although MMSN provides four frequency assignment options, it reduces rather than avoids communication collision. To our knowledge, none of the existing protocols can ensure a bounded delay of data transmission.

3 The PR-MAC Protocol

We design a protocol called PR-MAC to ensure a bounded delay of data transmission in sleep/wakeup sensor networks. Our work targets persistent applications where a communication path can work for some time. PR-MAC aims to obtain a bounded and minimal end-to-end delay of data transmission, fast adaptation to changing real-time requirements, as well as low energy consumption.

3.1 Bidirectional Pipelining Schedule

Each node in PR-MAC wakes up periodically for listening. Fig.1 shows the schedule of a set of nodes on a data delivery path, where $Node_n$ denotes a node whose distance to the sink is n hops. During one work cycle, a node wakes up twice: $Listen_{up}$ for transmitting data messages from source nodes to the sink, and $Listen_{down}$ for transmitting control message from the sink to source nodes. In Fig.1, the fuscous and gray panes respectively denote the time moment of $Listen_{up}$ and $Listen_{down}$ for each node. In either direction between sources and the sink, nodes on a multi-hop path wake up sequentially like pipelining with offset σ, which is long enough for transmitting or receiving a packet. The moment $Node_n$ wakes depends on its depth n in the path. The following equation (1) defines $T_{up}(i)$, the relative time of $Node_i$'s

$Listen_{up}$ ahead of the sink In the following equations, T_{frame} is the length of a work cycle and x % y derives the remainder of x modules y.

$$T_{up}(i)=|T_{frame}-i*\sigma| \% T_{frame} \tag{1}$$

The interval of two wakes of a same node is:

$$T_{inter}(i)=(2*i*\sigma) \% T_{frame} \tag{2}$$

The time of $Listen_{down}$ of the node is

$$T_{down}(i)=(T_{up}(i)+ T_{inter}(i)) \% T_{frame} \tag{3}$$

The above equations may lead to an interval less than σ between two wakes of a same node, as shown by $Node_5$ in Fig.1. Such an interval is too small for $Listen_{down}$ to occur if a data message is delivered during $Listen_{up}$. In order to ensure the occurrence of $Listen_{down}$ in each work cycle on each node, the equation (4) practically replaces the equation (2) to enlarge the interval.

$$T_{inter}(i)=2*\sigma*(i \% (N-1)) \tag{4}$$

where is the integer in $[(T_{frame}-\sigma)/(2*\sigma), T_{frame}/(2*\sigma)]$.

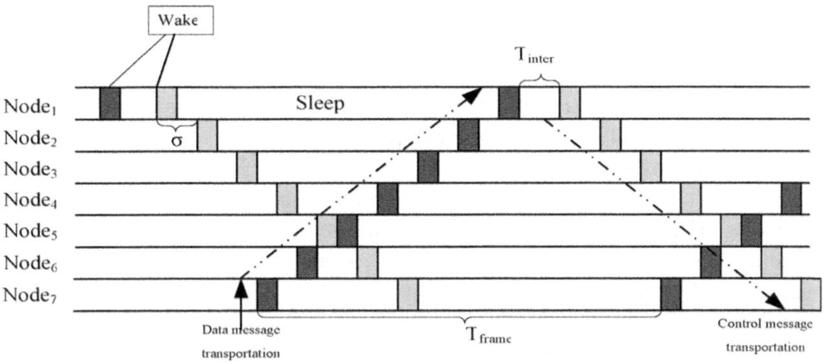

Fig. 1. Bidirectional Pipelining Schedule

Since the waking time of each node depends on its local clock, synchronization is needed. Local synchronization is enough because a node only needs to be aware of its neighbors' schedule. The following discussions assume that synchronization is available.

In PR-MAC, the sink is responsible for obtaining real time requirements of the task through analyzing the messages it receives. According to the real time requirements, the sink calculates the sampling frequency and transmission latency for the source nodes. For example, on receiving a message that represents a moving target with the velocity of 1m/s, the sink is supposed to assign the sampling frequency as one message per second and the transmission latency as less than 0.4 second. The sampling frequency decides the T_{frame} for the nodes on the communication path. The transmission latency is used to set the waking interval (**σ**) of two neighbor nodes. By sending the nodes a control message containing T_{frame} and σ, the sink is able to tune the frequency and latency of the nodes. A node that receives the control message changes its working pattern till the next work cycle. Despite that the waking offset of a pair of neighbor nodes can vary in different tasks, it must be greater than scores of ms to deal with communication collision. The limitation on offset prevents WSNs from satisfying real time requirements of certain applications. In order to avoid the communication collision, PR-MAC uses multi-channel communication.

3.2 Multi-channel Communication

Current WSN hardware, such as Micaz and Telos that use CC2420 radio [9], supports multiple frequencies [10]. It is feasible for WSNs to use multi-frequency MAC protocols to improve the network throughput with parallel transmission. IEEE standard 802.15.4 regulates that there is a single channel between 868 and 868.6MHz, 10 channels between 902.0 and 928.0MHz, and 16 channels between 2.4 and 2.4835GHz. The standard also allows dynamic channel selection. Our protocol PR-MAC exploits multiple channels by allocating one as the common channel and the others as special channels. When the sink in a WSN receives a message from a path and estimates that the path will be working for some time, it informs all nodes on the path to use a special channel. Then all nodes on the path will use the special channel in their next Listenup. The sink will still use the common channel to send control messages.

In PR-MAC, each node maintains a table to record the channels used by and the waking moments of its neighbor nodes. A node *A* sends a message to its neighbor *B* at the waking moment of *B* through the channel *B* uses.

The mechanism of using the common channel differs from that of the special channels. Nodes compete for using the common channel. To reduce collision, every node backs off for a period (BP) plus a random time within a contention window at the beginning of a sending slot. The window increases exponentially in the case of contention. When the channel is available, the node exchanges RTS/CTS to avoid the hidden node problem. When a node receives a packet, it transmits the ACK packet back to sender after a short period (SP). In summary, the offset for the common channel, denoted as σ_c is calculated as follows:

$$\sigma_c = BP + RTS + SP + CTS + DATA + SP + ACK$$

where RTS, CTS, DATA and ACK respectively represent the time periods of transmitting the corresponding packets. In special channels, because T_{frame} is much greater than σ, it is impossible for neighbor nodes to simultaneously send packets. There is no hidden node problem, so RTS/CTS exchange is unnecessary and a node sends data immediately after a backoff once the channel is available. Therefore, the offset for the special channels, denoted as σ_s, is calculated as follows:

$$\sigma_s = BP + DATA + SP + ACK$$

When the monitored event finishes or the sink does not get message for some work cycles, the sink sends the nodes a control packet to restore their work pattern to the original.

3.3 Working of the Sink

The sink in a WSN is the destination of data transmission. It works as the coordinator and controller of the other nodes. In PR-MAC, the sink has three tasks, namely path channel selection, data receive and network control.

For channel selection, the sink maintains a event table recording event location, sampling frequency, channel frequency, wake offset and message arrival time. When the sink receives some data that has been recorded in the event table, it updates the corresponding item in the event table. If it receives some data that represents a new event, the sink executes a procedure of channel selection as follows.

Step 1: If the sink has unoccupied special channels, it randomly selects a channel for the event. Otherwise, it selects the channel of the existing event that is farthest to the upcoming event in polar coordinate.

Step 2: Compute the event sampling frequency and waking offset.

Step 3: record the event in the event table.

After a channel is selected, the sink sends a control message including T_{frame} and σ to all nodes on the path.

To receive data, the sink listens to the channels according to the channel frequency recorded in its event table. When no event is to listen from the special channels, the sink listens to the common channel.

The sink performs network control through analyzing the features of the received events, or the working state of the network, or the requirement from the outside terminals. Control messages in the whole network share the common channel. The number of control messages is much less than that of data messages. Therefore no much collision will happen on the common channel.

4 Performance Analysis

If there is no packet loss due to channel error, the delay of every hop is σ_s as defined in the Section 3.3. The transmission delay of data message delivered by $Node_i$ is $i*\sigma_s$. The transmission delay of control message sent by $Node_i$ is $i*\sigma_c\%(N-1) + i*T_{frame}/(N-1)$.

In the following, we compare the performance of PR-MAC with S-MAC and DMAC with respect to transmission delays of the two types of messages. In S-MAC, the two types of data have the same delay, of which the average is $(i*T_{frame}/2+2\ (BP+DATA+SP+ACK)-T_{frame}/2)$. DMAC does not consider the delay of control messages. The average delay of data messages in DMAC is $(i*\mu\ (\mu=BP+DATA+SP+ACK)$.

Fig. 2. shows the data delay on a set of nodes in a WSN with 10% duty cycle. The interference between multiple events is disregarded. With any of the three protocols, data delay on a node is linear to the distance between the node and the sink. PR-MAC is better than DMAC because the backoff period is much less than that in DMAC.

Fig. 3 shows the data delays on the node whose distance to the sink is 5 hops in WSNs with different duty cycles. Using either PR-MAC or DMAC, the delay is independent of the duty cycle. It shows that the network does not consume more energy for satisfying higher real time requirements.

Fig. 4 shows the delays of control messages of various nodes using PR-MAC and S-MAC, respectively. With PR-MAC, the control delay of a node is approximately

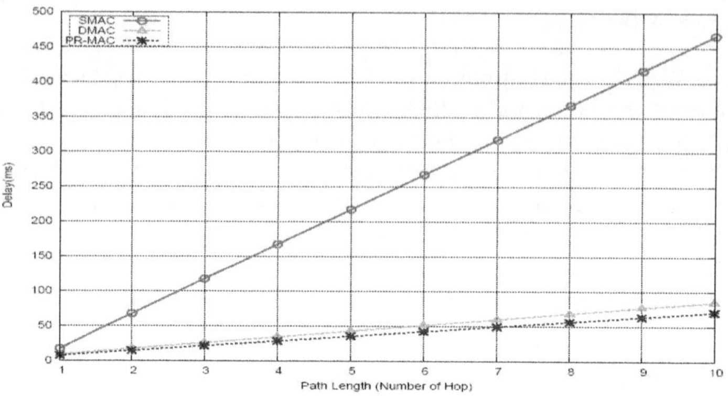

Fig. 2. Data delay on various nodes

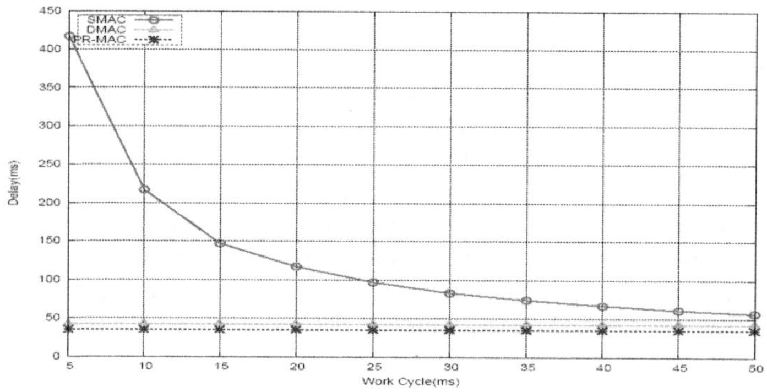

Fig. 3. Data delay of $Node_5$ in WSNs with different duty cycles

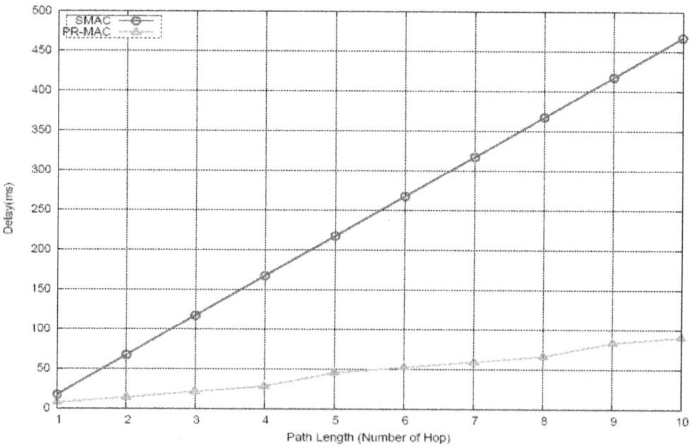

Fig. 4. Control delay using PR-MAC and S-MAC

linear to the distance between the node and the sink. The minor variations to the linear relation are caused by the intentional extention to the waking offset between neighbor nodes. The control delay is little enough for the network to quickly adapt to different types of events by changing its working pattern.

Besides the above advantages, PR-MAC needs an initialization period to construct a special channel for an event. During the initialization period, data messages are transmitted through the common channel. Data transmission of the initializing event will not interfere with those of the events that have special channels. So the delay of data transmission in the initialization period is acceptable and less than the average data delay in DMAC. The working process of PR-MAC with an initialization period matches the characteristics of general real time applications. Take the application that monitors moving targets as an example. During the time span between the moments that a target enters and leaves the sensing range, the sensor nodes detect the target periodically. During the initialization period of the event, the purpose of the WSN is just to detect the target. After the initialization, the WSN is supposed to react to the event, which is required of stricter real time constraints. Meanwhile, the execution of the protocol comes to a stable status.

Concerning energy consumption, PR-MAC needs one more waking in each work cycle than traditional protocols. A wake for low power listen costs the time of 3 ms and the power of 5.75 mW [11]. If the work cycle is 50s, PR-MAC consumes at most 0.4% more power than other protocols when there is no data transmission in the network. When there is data transmission, the excessive power consumption is negligible because RTS/CTS exchange is saved.

5 Experimentation

We implemented the prototype of PR-MAC on ns-2 simulator. The routing protocol in ns-2 simulator is modified to support the execution of PR-MAC. We conducted an experiment to compare the performance of PR-MAC to that of S-MAC with adaptive listen. In the experiment, the work cycle of the WSN is set to 100 ms, and the duty

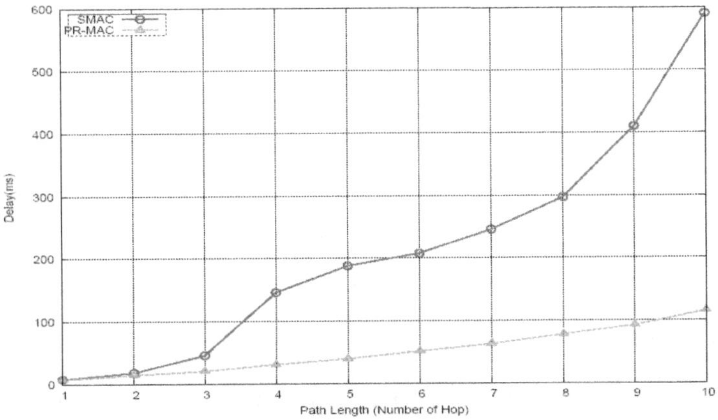

Fig. 5. Data delay of PR-MAC and S-MAC

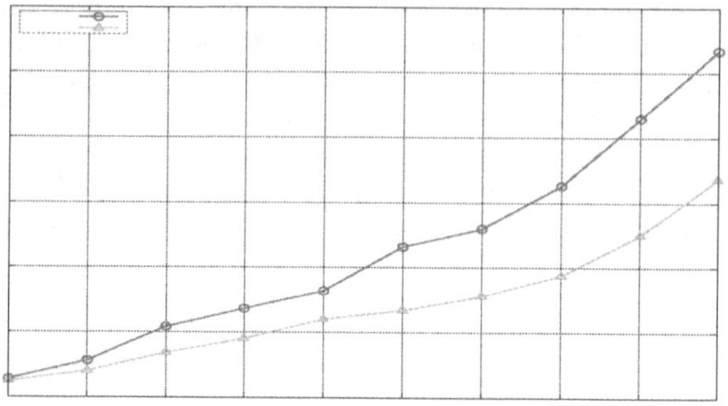

Fig. 6. Energy consumption of PR-MAC and S-MAC

cycle is 10%. Three interfering paths are used to send independent random packet sequences. The average interval between two sequential packets is 100 ms. The radio bandwidth is 250 kbps and radio energy character as table 1 in [11]. Fig. 5 shows the data delay of the two protocols. When there are multiple interfering events, PR-MAC keeps a bounded data delay which is decided just by the distance of the node. Fig. 6 shows the energy consumption of the two protocols. The multi-channel mechanism of PR-MAC can reduce the energy consumption.

6 Conclusion

The paper proposed a protocol named Path-oriented Real-time MAC (PR-MAC) to ensure bounded data transmission latency in multi-hop WSNs. PR-MAC employs Bidirectional Pipelining Schedule (BPS) to remove sleep latency, and multi-channel communication to reduce data latency. PR-MAC provides a soft real time service for WSN applications. Experiments showed that our protocol has advantages in data latency and energy consumption over existing protocols in the case of simultaneous multiple events. The proposed protocol is suitable for applications which accepts slow initialization and requires periodical data collection or query. The shortage of PR-MAC is it needs the support of route layer and requires the sink to take more operations, which complicates the implementation of the protocol. One of the future working directions is to support the data fusion and the cross of multiple paths. Another direction is to conduct more experiments on the real platform such as Micaz.

References

[1] Tian He, Pascal Vicaire, Ting Yan et al. *Achieving Real-Time Target Tracking Using Wireless Sensor Networks*. In 12th IEEE Real-Time and Embedded Technology and Applications Symposium (RTAS). 2006.

[2] W. Ye, J. Heidemann, and D. Estrin, *An Energy-efficient MAC Protocol for Wireless Sensor Networks*, in 21st Conference of the IEEE Computer and Communications Societies (INFOCOM). 2002. p. 1567--1576.

[3] W. Ye, J. Heidemann, and D. Estrin, *Medium access control with coordinated adaptive sleeping for wireless sensor networks*. IEEE/ACM Transactions on Networking, 2004. **12**(3): p. 493-506
[4] T.v. Dam and K. Langendoen, *An Adaptive Energy-Efficient MAC Protocol for Wireless Sensor Networks*, in The First ACM Conference on Embedded Networked Sensor Systems (SenSys'03). 2003, ACM Press: Los Angeles, California, USA. p. 171--180.
[5] G. Lu, B. Krishnamachari, and C.S. Raghavendra. *An Adaptive Energy-Efficient and Low-Latency MAC for Data Gathering in Sensor Networks*. in Four Workshop on Algorithms for Wireless, Mobile, Ad Hoc and Sensor Networks (WMAN). 2004. Santa Fe, NM.
[6] Y. Li, W. Ye, and J. Heidemann, *Energy and Latency Control in Low Duty Cycle MAC Protocols*, in Proceedings of the IEEE Wireless Communications and Networking Conference. 2005,New Orleans, LA, USA.
[7] Z. Gang, et al., *MMSN: Multi-Frequency Media Access Control for Wireless Sensor Networks*. 2006.
[8] http://dx.doi.org/10.1007/11807964_45Changsu Suh, Deepesh Man Shrestha, Young-Bae Ko. *An Energy-Efficient MAC Protocol for Delay-Sensitive Wireless Sensor Networks*. EUC Workshops 2006: 445-454
[9] "CC2420 2.4 GHz IEEE 802.15.4 / ZigBee-ready RF Transceiver," http://www.chipcon.com.
[10] "XBOW MICA2 Mote Specifications," http://www.xbow.com.
[11] Ye, W. and J. Heidemann, *Ultra-Low Duty Cycle MAC with Scheduled Channel Polling*, in The 4th ACM Conference on Embedded Networked Sensor Systems. 2006: Boulder, Colorado, USA.

Real-Time Traffic Packet Scheduling Algorithm in HSDPA System Considering the Maximum Tolerable Delay and Channel Assignment

Xiaodong Yu, Sung Won Kim, and Yong Wan Park

Department of Information & Communication Engineering, Yeungnam University, Gyeongsan-si, Korea
silenceyu@hotmail.com, ksw@ieee.org, ywpark@yu.ac.kr

Abstract. In this paper, we consider a new packet scheduling algorithm for real time traffic in the high speed downlink packet access system that has been introduced for WCDMA system to providing high transmission rates. The objective of the design is to meet the maximum tolerable delay and consider the channel assigning based on the received SIR for real-time traffic users. The proposed scheduling algorithm shows that the users are ranked by the ratios of the bits in the buffer to the residual time for transmission, the ranked users are assigned channels based on the SIR value table and get service one by one. The simulation results show that the proposed algorithm can provide the lower packet drop rate for real time quality of service (QoS) requirement.

1 Introduction

Wideband Code Division Multiple Access (WCDMA) is the most widely adopted air interface for Third Generation system. One of these technologies is the High Speed Downlink Packet Access (HSDPA), which permits to increase user peak data rates up to 10Mbps, reduce the service response time, and improve the spectral efficiency for downlink packet data service. Its concept consists of a fast scheduling that supports per 2-ms transmission time interval (TTI), adaptive modulation and coding scheme (AMC), fast cell selection (FCS) and multiple input multiple output (MIMO) antenna technology for higher performance.

In HSDPA, fast scheduling is the mechanism determining which user transmits in a given time interval. Maximum system throughput is obtained by assigning all available radio resources to the user with the currently best radio-channel conditions, while a practical scheduler should include some degree of fairness.

In this paper, we propose a QoS guarantee of packet scheduling algorithm considering requirement maximum tolerable delay and backlogged packet in the buffer to decrease the packet drop of real-time service users. In this scheme we get the priority users ranking by the ratio of maximum tolerable delay to backlogged packet in the buffer, after that we assign different number of HS-PDSCH to the service user by the received SIR that can provide the system throughput at the same time.

Y.-H. Lee et al. (Eds.): ICESS 2007, LNCS 4523, pp. 540–547, 2007.

2 Related Works

Many wireless packet scheduling algorithms have been designed to support data traffic in the Third Generation Partnership Project (3GPP). Three schemes of packet scheduling are introduced in the HSDPA specification such as Max CIR (maximum carrier to interference), Round robin and Proportional Fairness.

The Max CIR scheduler directs transmission to the user with the momentarily best channel conditions, allowing for the highest possible data rate at each instant and thus maximizing the overall throughput. This serving principle has obvious benefits in terms of cell throughput, although it is at the cost of lacking throughput fairness.

The round robin scheduler cycles through the list of active users and thus is fair in the average sense. As the round robin scheduler is not based on the varying channel quality, the throughput performance however suffers.

The proportional fairness scheduler schedules the user with the currently highest ratio between instantaneous C/I and average transmission rate. It serves in every TTI the user with largest priority:

$$P_i(t) = \arg\max(R_i(t) / r_i(t)), \tag{1}$$

where $P_i(t)$ denotes the user priority, $R_i(t)$ is the instantaneous supportable data rate experienced by user i, and $r_i(t)$ is the user throughput. In the current investigation, the user throughput $r_i(t)$ is simply computed as the number of bits correctly received by user i during the period (t_i, t) divided by such a period, where t_i denotes the instant when the user starts his downlink transmission. This scheme is introduced to compensate the disadvantage of Max CIR and Round robin.

Above schemes are very well suited for non-real time traffic, that only considering the throughput and fairness as QoS requirement, but the transport of real-time traffic over HSDPA is an important challenges in order to guarantee its quality of service (QoS) requirement. Providing QoS, in particular meeting the data rate and packet drop constraints of real-time traffic users, is one of the requirements in emerging high-speed data network.

3 Proposed Algorithm

In this section, we present some basic concepts and definitions, and then described in detail the steps to operate our proposed algorithm.

3.1 Minimum Requirement of Bit Rate for Maximum Tolerable Delay

For each user i with the total length of $L_i(t)$ bits for the backlogged packet in the buffer at time slot t, $T_{\max}$ is the maximum tolerable delay for real-time traffic waiting in the buffer, $W_i(t)$ is the waiting time for a head of line (HOL) packet for user i in each buffer. A minimum requirement bit rate at slot time t is defined as

$$P_i(t) = \frac{L_i(t)}{T_{\max} - W_i(t)} \tag{2}$$

From a conceptual perspective, the minimum requirement of bit rate can guarantee the transmission of the backlogged packets in buffer transmitted without packet drop. That is, if a user wants to transmit packets without packets drop, the user must conduct in accordance with the minimum requirement of bit rate of transmission in next several time slots.

3.2 Channel Assignment in HSDPA

Scheduler in HSDPA system uses HS-DSCH for high transmission rate in downlink case. HS-DSCH is consisting of 15 the real channels (HS-PDSCH) that can be assigned to the service users in one time slot.

In previous scheduling algorithm, 15 channels could be assigned to a service user selected by the scheduler in each time slot. Here we assign different number of channels to multi-users depending on the SIR table. Scheduler collects all SIR values of each user in CPICH to select service users for the next time slot. Table 1, is the assigned channel number based on received SIR. In this case, even highest-priority user in a poor channel state can still guarantee the transmission of information. When the channel state changes better, the user will get more channels to complete the information transmission.

Table 1. SIR table for number of assigning channe

SIR level	Assigned channel numbers
SIR ≥27dB	15
27dB> SIR≥22dB	9
22dB> SIR≥16dB	6
16dB> SIR	4

3.3 Proposed Scheme Procedure

In this paper, we consider the real-time traffic in HSDPA system. Our design is to decrease the packet drop of real-time service users ranking by the minimum requirement of bit rate transmission. For providing the system throughput at the same time, we assign different numbers of HS-PDSCH to the service users by the received SIR value. Figure 1 shows the proposed scheme process.

Step1: We need to calculate the minimum requirement on bit rate as a priority ranking standards. In this process, if greater the amount of data storage in the buffer, the

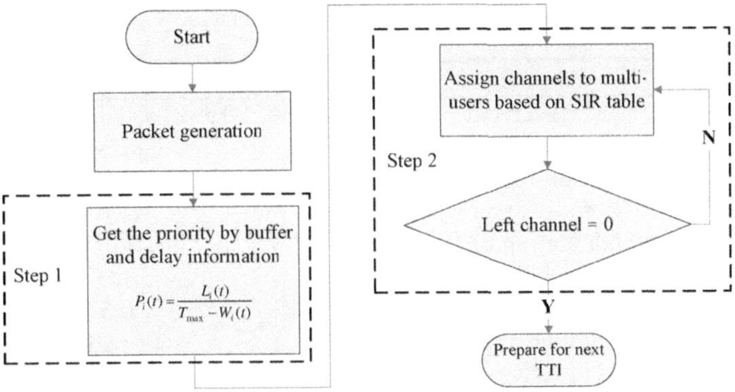

Fig. 1. Proposed scheme flow chart

remaining service time is shorter; the user will be in a higher priority in the ranking. Otherwise, the user would get service later.

Step2: Scheduler defines the SIR level using the table for the assigning channel number of the highest priority user. When the highest priority user gets service with the defined number of channels, the residual channels will be assigned to the secondary priority user based on the table. Step2 will be repeated until the residual amount of channel is 0.

This scheme guarantees the higher priority and SIR value user transmitted with more number of channels, the difference with previous schemes is the user with lower SIR value but higher priority also could get channels for service, thus avoiding packet drop by the long time delay and buffer overflow.

4 Performance Analysis and Evaluation

4.1 Simulation Environment

In this paper, the simulation system is based on the 3GPP standards. Table 2 gives the major simulation parameters.

This subsection describes the configuration of the system level simulation. We employed a 3-sectored 19-cell model. In each sector, the distribution of topography and constriction is basically the same. The correlation coefficient between cells sites and that between sectors were 0.5 and 1.0. The location of each user was randomly assigned with a uniform distribution within each cell. Once the simulation begins, the location of all users is fixed. The propagation model between the base station and mobile station is $128.1 + 37.6\log(R)$, here $R(Km)$ is the distance between base station and mobile station, lognormal shadowing with a standard deviation of 8dB and instantaneous 12 multi-paths fading.

Table 2. Simulation Parameters

Parameter	Value
Cell layout	19 cells, 3sector/cell
User distribution	Uniform
Cell radius	1Km
BS total Tx power	17W
Standard deviation of shadowing	8dB
Correlation between sectors	1.0
Correlation between cells	0.5
Number of paths	12 paths
Hybrid ARQ scheme	Chase combing
Carrier frequency	2000MHz
The number of users	Fixed (100 to 500 real-time traffic user)

Table 3. Modulation and Coding Scheme

MCS level	Coding rate	Modulation	Data rate
1	1/4	QPSK	1.2Mbps
2	1/2	QPSK	2.4Mbps
3	3/4	QPSK	3.6Mbps
4	3/4	8PSK	5.4Mbps
5	1/2	16QAM	4.8Mbps
6	3/4	16QAM	7.2Mbps
7	3/4	64QAM	10.8Mbps

Meanwhile, we applied AMC in the radio link level simulation, which controls the MCS according to the average received SIR over one TTI. In the 7 MCS levels, in table 3, the MCS used in this paper is mcs2, mcs5, mcs6 and mcs7. For FCS case, the user will chose 3 cells with the most SIR values as the active set; the most one of the 3 cells will get service. In each cell, the number of the service provider is same.

To implement the HSDPA feature, the HS-DSCH (High Speed Downlink Shard Channel) is introduced in the physical layer specification. HS-DSCH consists of 15 HS-PDSCH (High Speed Physical Downlink Shard Channel) which are the real channels, and can be assigned to the service users in one time slot. The Transmission Time Interval (TTI) or interleaving period has been defined to be 2ms for the operation between the base station and mobile station.

4.2 Traffic Model

In the paper it is assumed that the modified streaming traffic model is real-time traffic model. Traffic model parameters of an RT streaming traffic are show in table 4.

The size of each packet call is distributed based on the Pareto distribution with the maximum size of m. This probability density function $f_p(x)$ is expressed by using the minimum value of the distribution k,

$$f_p(x) = \begin{cases} \frac{\alpha \times k}{x^{\alpha+1}}, k \le x < m \\ \beta, x = m \end{cases}, \beta = \left(\frac{k}{m}\right)^{\alpha}, \quad (3)$$

where α = 1.1, k = 4.5 Kbytes and m = 2 Mbytes. Based on these parameters, the average value of the packet call size becomes 25 Kbytes. The reading time is approximated as a geometrical distribution with the average value of 5 sec. The maximum tolerable delay for each packet is fixed as 72ms; the maximum buffer capacity is 450000 bits.

Table 4. Major Traffic Model Parameters

	Distribution	Parameters
Packet calls size	Pareto with cutoff	α=1.1, k=4.5Kbytes m=2Mbytes Average packet call size 25Kbytes
Reading time	Geometric	Average 5 sec
Packet size		12Kbit
Packet inter-arrival time	Geometric	Average 6 ms
Maximum tolerable delay ($T_{\max}$)	Fixed	72ms

4.3 Definition of Performance Indicators

We introduce the concept of the service throughput and packet loss rate for evaluation of system performance.

Service throughput is a ratio between the transmission good bits and the total number of the cell:

$$Service\_throughput = \frac{1}{N_{cell}} \sum_{k=1}^{N_{cell}} Service(k), \quad (3)$$

in the above function, $Service(k)$ are the successful transmission bits per TTI in cell k. It is calculated as follows:

$$Service(k) = \frac{1}{N_{second}} \sum_{i=1}^{N_{second}} N_{good\_bits}(i), \quad (4)$$

here $N_{good\_bits}(i)$ is a successful transmission bit at time slot i and N_{second} is total simulation time.

The real-time traffic packet drop rate is measured as the number of drop packets divided to the total transmission packets

$$packet\_drop\_rate = \frac{drop\_packet}{total\_trans\_packet}, \tag{5}$$

where $drop\_packet$ consists of two parts. One is the packet loss caused by exceeding the maximum tolerable delay and the other is total packet of the user exceeding its buffer capacity.

4.4 Numerical Result and Evaluation

We compare the service throughput and packet drop rate among the proposed algorithm and previous two schemes. An obviously improvement in packet drop rate as well as high throughput can be obtained

Figure 2 shows the HSDPA service throughput versus the number of users. The service throughput of the proposed scheme is increasing with the number of users in the system. The proposed scheme is not much different from the Max C/I and PF schemes.

Figure 3 shows the relationship between number of users and the packet loss rate. The packet loss rate means the ratio of packet exceeding the maximum tolerance delay to the total transmission packets. Considering the 72ms requirement delay, the proposed scheme packet loss rate is lower than the MCI and PF schemes. More number of users is, the higher the performances are.

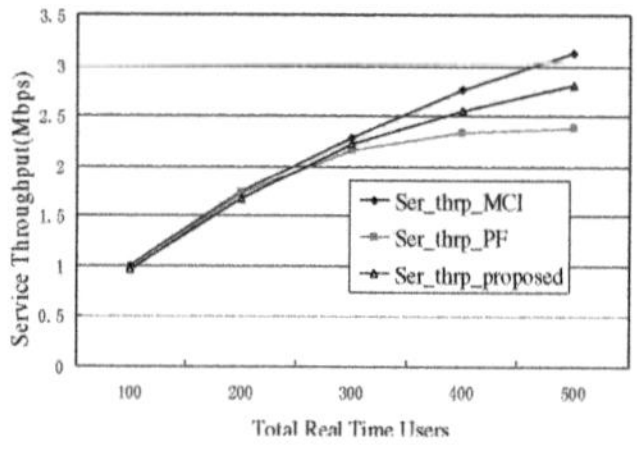

Fig. 2. Throughput performances

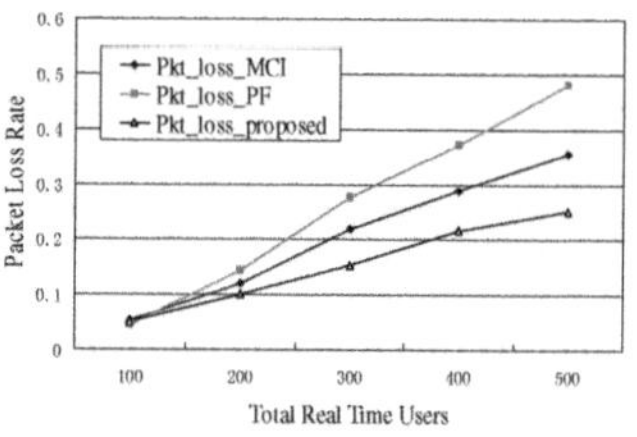

Fig. 3. Packet loss performances

Figure 4 shows the buffer overflow performances. When the buffers of users exceed the maximum buffer capacity, the packets will be lost. In this simulation, the buffer capacity is set 450000bits. In the packet drop statistic, the buffer overflow rate is less influenced than the packet loss rate caused by exceeding the requirement delay, but still need to be considered for real time traffic. The proposed scheme decreases by 0.5% as compared with the MCI scheme and 2% as compared with PF scheme.

Figure 5 shows the packet drop rate as the number of real-time traffic users increases. It is obvious that the proposed scheme outperforms in packet drop rate performance over the other two schemes, especially when the number of users increases.

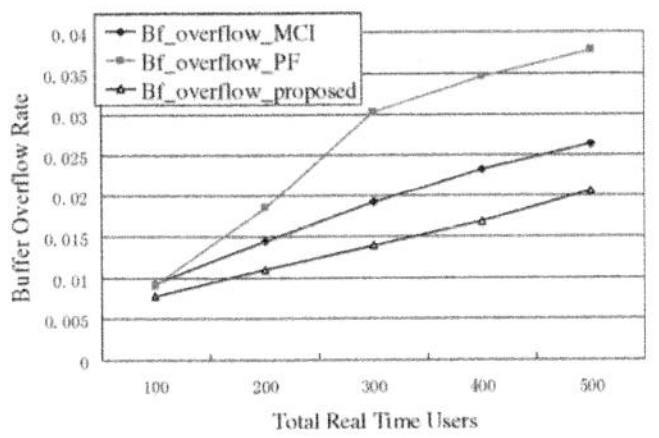

Fig. 4. Buffer overflow performances

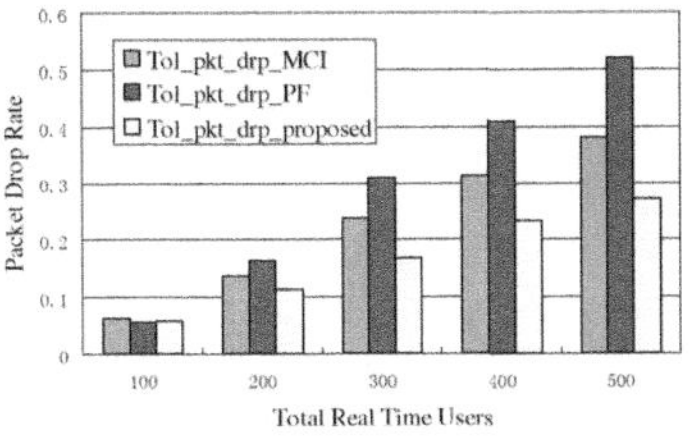

Fig. 5. Packet drop performances

For the 72ms maximum tolerable delay, 450000 bits buffer capacity and 500 users, the packet drop decrease of the proposed scheme is 10% as compared with Max C/I. This improvement is more obvious with the PF schemes.

5 Conclusions

In this paper, we propose a scheduling algorithm for the real-time traffic in HSDPA system for WCDMA downlink case. The proposed scheme can satisfy the QoS guarantee of the real-time traffic for both throughput and packet drop. The simulation results elucidate that although the proposed scheme throughput is between the Max C/I and PF method, it is advantageous in reduction of user packet loss rate and buffer overflow. The last simulation in Fig. 5 is shown the packet drop rate of proposed scheme is reduced by approximately 10% compared to Max C/I method and 15% to PF method.

References

1. 3GPP, 3G TR 25.848. Physical Layer Aspects of UTRA High Speed Downlink Packet Access.
2. H. Holma, and A.Toskala. WCDMA for UMTS Radio Access for Third Generation Mobile Communication. John Wiley & Sons, Ltd. (2004)
3. Y.Ofuji, A.Morimoto, S.Abeta, and M.Sawahashi. Comparison of packet scheduling algorithms focusing on user throughput in high speed downlink packet access. in Proc. Of IEEE PRMRC'02. (2002) vol.3, pp.1462-1466.
4. K.Ramanan, A.Stolyar, P.Whiting, M.Andrews, K.Kumaran, and R.Vijayakumar. Providing quality of service over a shard wireless link. IEEE communication Magazine, (2001) vol.39, no.2 , pp.150-154.
5. D.H.Kim, B.H.Ryu, and C.G.Kang. Packet Scheduling Algorithm Considering a Minimum Bit Rate for Non-realtime Traffic in an OFDMA/FDD-Based Mobile Internet Access System. ETRI Journal. (2004) Volume 26, Number1, pp.48-52.
6. M.Adamou, S.Khanna,I.Lee,I,Shin, and S,Zhou. Fair Real-time Traffic Scheduling over A Wireless LAN. (2001) IEEE, 0-7695-1420-0/01, pp.279-288.
7. C.J.Ong, Peter H.J.Chong, and Raymond Kwan. Effect of Various Packet Scheduling Algorithms on the Performance of High Speed Downlink Shared Channel in a WCDMA Network. (2003) IEEE, 0-7803/-7978-0/03, pp. 935-937.

L4oprof: A System-Wide Profiler Using Hardware PMU in L4 Environment

Jugwan Eom, Dohun Kim, and Chanik Park

Department of Computer Science and Engineering
Pohang University of Science and Technology
Pohang, Gyungbuk 790-784, Republic of Korea
{zugwan,hunkim,cipark}@postech.ac.kr

Abstract. The recent advance of L4 microkernel technology enables building a secure embedded system with comparable performance to a traditional monolithic kernel-based system. According to the different system software architecture, the execution behavior of an application in microkernel environment differs greatly from that in traditional monolithic environment. Therefore, we need a performance profiler to improve performance of the application in microkernel environment. Currently, L4's profiling tools provides only program-level information such as the number of function calls, IPCs, context switches, etc. In this paper, we present L4oprof, a system-wide statistical profiler in L4 microkernel environment. L4oprof leverages the hardware performance counters of PMU on a CPU to enable profiling of a wide variety of hardware events such as clock cycles and cache and TLB misses. Our evaluation shows that L4oprof incurs 0~3% higher overhead than Linux OProfile. Moreover, the main cause of performance loss in L4Linux applications is shown compared with Linux applications.

Keywords: L4 microkernel, performance analysis, performance measures, performance monitoring, statistical profiling, hardware PMU.

1 Introduction

To analyze a program's performance, its execution behavior is investigated by monitoring runtime information. Monitoring program execution is important, because it can find the bottlenecks and determine which parts of a program should be optimized. The type of collected information depends on the level at which it is collected. It is divided into the following two levels.

1. The program level: the program is instrumented by adding calls to routines which gather desired information such as the number of time a function is called, the number of time a basic block is entered, a call graph, and an internal program state like queue length changes in the kernel block layer.

2. The hardware level: the program does not need to be modified. CPU architecture like caches, pipelines, superscalar, out-of-order execution, branch prediction, and speculative execution can lead to large differences between the best-case and the

Y.-H. Lee et al. (Eds.): ICESS 2007, LNCS 4523, pp. 548–559, 2007.

worst-case performances, which must be considered to increase program performance. Most of current CPUs have a hardware component called PMU (Performance Monitoring Unit) for programmers to exploit the information on CPU. The PMU measures the micro architectural behavior of the program such as the number of clock cycles, how many cache stalls, how many TLB misses, which is stored in performance counters.

The goal of performance analysis is to find where time is spent and why it is spent there. Program-level monitoring can detect performance bottlenecks, but finding their cause is best solved with hardware-level monitoring, which may result from function calls, algorithmic problems, or CPU stalls. Therefore, the two levels of monitoring must be used complementarily for proper performance analysis.

The recent advance of L4 microkernel technology enables building a secure embedded system with comparable performance to a traditional monolithic kernel-based system. Industry such as QUALCOMM sees L4 microkernel's potential as a solution to the security problems of embedded systems. In a microkernel-based system, the basic kernel functions such as communication, scheduling, and memory mapping are provided by the microkernel and most of OS services are implemented as multiple user level servers on top of the microkernel, in which the execution behavior of an L4 application differs greatly from that in traditional monolithic environment. Therefore, we need a performance profiler to improve performance of the application in microkernel environment. However, L4 microkernel provides only program-level profiling tools which do not utilize the PMU information that is also valuable for fine-grained performance profiling, which enables to locate the cause of performance inefficiency in an application.

In this paper, we present L4oprof, a system-wide statistical profiler in L4 microkernel environment. L4oprof leverages the hardware performance counters of PMU on a CPU to enable profiling of a wide variety of hardware events such as clock cycles and cache and TLB misses without program modification. L4oprof can profile applications in the system and the L4 microkernel itself. This paper also shows the main cause of performance loss in L4Linux applications compared that in Linux applications. L4oprof has been modeled after the OProfile [5] profiling tool available on Linux systems.

The remainder of the paper is organized as follows. Section 2 describes related work. We describe the aspects of L4 and OProfile as background for our work in Section 3. Section 4 describes the design and implementation of L4oprof. Then, we present L4oprof's performance in Section 5. Finally, we summarize the paper and discuss the future work in Section 6.

2 Related Work

Several hardware monitoring interfaces [8, 9] and tools [6, 7, 10, 15] have been defined for using hardware performance monitoring on different architectures and platforms. Xenoprof [15] is a profiling toolkit for the Xen virtual machine environment, which has inspired the current L4oprof's approach.

In L4 microkernel-based environment, a few performance monitoring tools are available. Fiasco Trace Buffer [11] collects the kernel internal events such as context switches, inter process communications, and page faults. It is attached with the kernel and configured via L4/Fiasco kernel debugger. rt_mon [14], GRTMon [12] and Ferret [13] are user-space monitoring tools, which provide a monitoring library and sensors that store the collected information. Currently, existing monitoring tools in L4 environment only use program level information via instrumentation and cannot help pinpoint problems in how software uses the hardware features. L4oprof extends the profiling abilities of L4, allowing hardware level performance events to be counted across all system activities. Utilizing the information collected from the PMU enables any application to be profiled without any modification.

3 Background

In this section, we briefly describe the L4 microkernel based environment and the OProfile for statistical profiling on Linux.

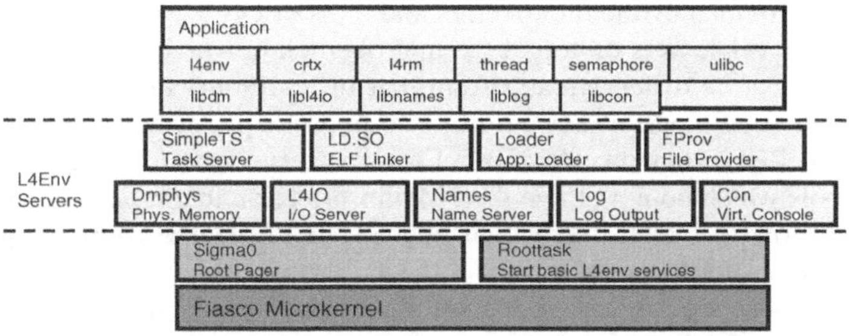

Fig. 1. L4 microkernel-based Environment

3.1 L4 Microkernel-Based Environment

L4 is a second generation microkernel ABI [2]. Our work uses the Fiasco [17] microkernel-based environment. As shown in Figure 1, this environment consists of a set of cooperating servers running on top of the microkernel. All servers use the kernel-provided synchronous interprocess communication mechanism for communication.

L4Env [4] is a programming environment for application development on top of the L4 microkernel family. It provides a number of servers and libraries for OS services such as thread management, global naming, synchronization, loading tasks, and resource management. L4Linux [3] is a para-virtualized Linux running on top of the microkernel using L4Env, which is binary-compatible with the normal Linux kernel. The Linux kernel and its applications run as a server in user mode and system calls from Linux applications are translated into IPC to the L4Linux server. Current L4Linux is unable to configure some features such as ACPI, SMP, preemption, APIC/IOAPIC, HPET, highmem, MTRR, MCE, power management and other similar options in the Linux.

3.2 OProfile

OProfile [5] is a low-overhead system-wide statistical profiler for Linux included in the 2.6 version of the kernel. The Linux kernel supports OProfile for a number of different processor architectures. OProfile can profile code executing at any privilege level, including kernel code, kernel modules, user level applications and user level libraries.

OProfile can be configured to periodically take samples to obtain time-based information for indicating which sections of code are executed on the computer system. Many processors include a dedicated performance monitoring hardware component called PMU (Performance Monitoring Unit), which allows to detect when certain events happen such as clock cycles, instruction retirements, TLB misses, cache misses, branch mispredictions, etc. The hardware normally takes the form of one or more counters that are incremented each time an event takes place. When the counter value "rolls over," an interrupt is generated, making it possible to control the amount of detail (and therefore, overhead) produced by performance monitoring. OProfile uses this hardware to collect samples of performance-related data each time a counter generates an interrupt. These samples are periodically written out to disk; later, the statistical data contained in these samples can be used to generate reports on system-level and application-level performance.

OProfile can be divided into three sections: the kernel support, the daemon, and the sample database with analysis programs. The kernel has a driver which controls the PMU and collects the samples. The daemon reads data from the driver and converts it into a sample database. The analysis programs read data from the sample database and present meaningful information to the user.

4 L4oprof

In this section, we describe the design and implementation of L4oprof which we have developed for the L4 microkernel based environment. The L4oprof has similar capabilities to OProfile. It uses the hardware PMU to collect periodic samples of performance data. The performance of applications running in L4 environment depends on interactions among the servers for OS services, for example, the L4Linux server in case of the Linux application, and the L4 microkernel. In order to achieve a proper performance analysis, the profiling tool must be able to determine the distribution of performance events across all system activities.

Figure 2 shows an overview of the L4oprof. At an abstract level, the L4oprof consists of a L4 microkernel layer which services performance-counter interrupts and an OProfile server layer which associates samples with executable images, and merges them into a nonvolatile profile database and a modified system loader and other mechanisms for identifying executable images. As shown in Figure 2, the L4oprof reuses the OProfile code and extends its capabilities to be used in the L4 environment instead of starting from scratch. The remainder of this section describes these pieces in more detail, beginning with the L4 microkernel layer.

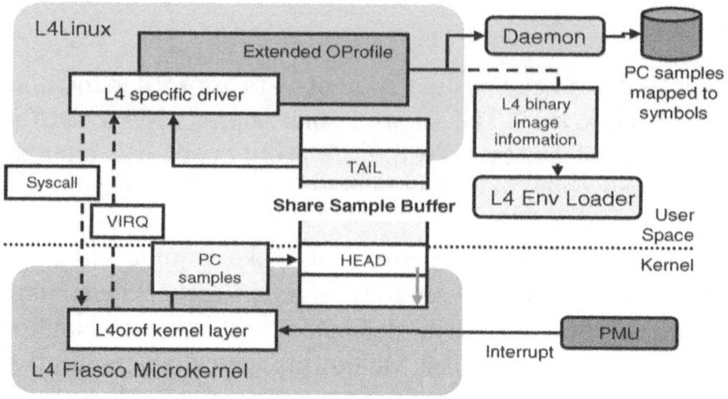

Fig. 2. L4oprof overview

4.1 L4 Microkernel Layer

The L4 microkernel layer of the L4oprof uses the same hardware counter based sampling mechanism as used in OProfile. It defines a user interface which maps performance events to the physical hardware counters, and provides a system call for OProfile server layer to setup profiling parameters, start and stop profiling. L4oprof can be configured to monitor the same events supported by OProfile.

When a performance counter overflows, it generates a high-priority interrupt that delivers the PC of the next instruction to be executed and the identity of the overflowing counter. When the interrupt handler in the L4 kernel layer handles this interrupt, it records the sample that consists of the task identifier (L4 Task ID) of the interrupted process, the PC delivered by the interrupt, and the event type that caused the interrupt. The L4 kernel layer hands over the PC samples collected on counter overflow to the OProfile server layer for further processing. PC samples are delivered via a shared sample buffer synchronized with a lock-free method in order to support high-frequency performance counter overflow interrupt and reduce profiling overhead. Next, the L4 kernel layer notifies the OProfile server layer of generating a sample via a virtual interrupt. However, if current user process is not the Oprofile server, it delays executing the virtual interrupt handler in OProfile server layer, resulting in L4oprof's poor performance. Therefore, we separated actual data delivering from counter overflow notification.

4.2 OProfile Server Layer

The OProfile server layer extracts samples from the shared sample buffer and associates them with their corresponding images. The data for each image is periodically merged into compact profiles stored as separate files on disk.

The OProfile server layer operates in a manner mostly similar to its operation in OProfile on Linux. For low level operations, such as accessing and programming performance counters, and collecting PC samples, it is modified to interface with the L4 microkernel layer of L4oprof. The high level operations of the OProfile server in the layer remain mostly unchanged.

Architecture-specific components in OProfile are newly implemented to use the L4 kernel layer virtual event interface. The interrupt thread in L4Linux waits until the L4 kernel layer signals a generating sample. After copying PC samples from the shared sample buffer, the OProfile server layer determines the routine and executable image corresponding to the program counter on each sample in the buffer. In case of Linux kernel and applications, this is determined by consulting the virtual memory layout of the Linux process and Linux kernel, which is maintained in the L4Linux kernel server. Since PC samples may also include samples from the L4 kernel address space, the OProfile server layer is extended to recognize and correctly attribute L4 kernel's PC samples. In order to determine where the images of other L4 applications including the L4Env servers are loaded, the L4Env loaders are modified. There are two loaders in L4Env: the Roottask server starts applications using boot loader scripts according to Multi Boot Information [18] and the Loader server supports dynamic loading. A modified version of each loader handles requests from the OProfile server layer. The response from the loader contains the L4 task ID, the address at which it was loaded, and its file system pathname.

The OProfile server layer stores samples in an on-disk profile database. This database structure is the same as the Linux OProfile's database structure. Thus, post-profiling tools in OProfile can be used without any modification.

5 Evaluation

The profiling tools must collect many thousands of samples per second yet incur sufficiently low overhead so that their benefits outweigh their costs. Profiling incurs performance slowdown of applications compared to the performance of applications without profiling. In this section, we summarize the results of experiments designed to measure the performance of our profiler. The hardware used for evaluation was a Pentium 4 1.6GHz processor with 512MB of RAM, and Intel E100 Ethernet controller. For the comparison, OProfile in Linux 2.6.18.1 is used. Table 1 shows the workloads used.

Table 1. Description of Workloads

Workload	Description
Multiply	Multiplies two numbers by using two different methods in the loop, CPU-bound
Tar	Extracts Linux kernel source, Real workload
Iperf [16]	Measures network bandwidth, IO-bound

5.1 Profiling Test and Verification

Prior to presenting the performance overhead, we demonstrate that L4oprof works correctly. We tested and verified our profiling tool under time-biased configuration, i.e. GLOBAL POWER EVENTS event that is the time during which the processor is not stopped, in which L4oprof monitors the clock cycles by running the Multiply workload. This configuration generates the distribution of time spent in various routines in Multiply workload. We compared the profiling result of L4oprof to that of OProfile and GNU gprof. GNU gprof enables us to know the exact number of times a function is called using the instrumentation; it is enabled using the `-pg` option of GNU cc. Figure 3 shows the result which each profiler has produced. All profilers have a similar distribution of time spent in three functions, `main`, `slow_multiply`, and `fast_multiply`.

```
Each sample counts as 0.01 seconds.
  %   cumulative   self              self     total
 time   seconds   seconds    calls  ns/call  ns/call  name
 99.05      3.14     3.14  4000000   785.00   785.00  slow_multiply
  0.63      3.16     0.02                             main
  0.32      3.17     0.01  4000000     2.50     2.50  fast_multiply
```

(a)

```
CPU: P4 / Xeon, speed 1513.55 MHz (estimated)
Counted GLOBAL_POWER_EVENTS events (time during which processor is
not stopped) with a unit mask of 0x01 (mandatory) count 100000
samples  %        image name               symbol name
824571   99.3596  multiply                 slow_multiply
4920      0.5929  multiply                 main
395       0.0476  multiply                 fast_multiply
```

(b)

```
CPU: P4 / Xeon, speed 1513.55 MHz (estimated)
Counted GLOBAL_POWER_EVENTS events (time during which processor is
not stopped) with a unit mask of 0x01 (mandatory) count 100000
samples  %        image name               symbol name
827170   99.4093  multiply                 slow_multiply
4533      0.5448  multiply                 main
391       0.0458  multiply                 fast_multiply
```

(c)

Fig. 3. Comparison of profiling result from the three profiles (a) GNU gprof (b) OProfile (c) L4oprof

5.2 Profiling Performance

The accuracy and overhead of the profiling can be controlled by adjusting the sampling interval (i.e., the count when notifications are generated). We evaluated our profiling tool's performance in terms of profiling overhead caused by handling overflow interrupts. To measure the overhead, we ran each workload at least 10 times varying the frequency of overflow interrupts. The PMU was programmed to monitor GLOBAL POWER EVENTS event, because it basic event type. We compared the profiling overhead of L4oprof to that of OProfile. OProfile is well known for its low overhead and is one of the most popular profilers for Linux.

Figures 4, 5, and 6 show the profiling overhead of L4oprof and OProfile under running Multiply, Tar, Iperf workload respectively. L4oprof incurs 0~3% higher profiling overhead than OProfile under the default settings which cause around 15000, 13050, and 750 interrupts per seconds with Multiply, Tar, and Iperf workload respectively. These figures also indicate that the performance of L4oprof is more sensitive than that of OProfile to the frequency of the generated interrupts since the overhead gap between L4oprof and OProfile is increasing as the interrupt frequency increases.

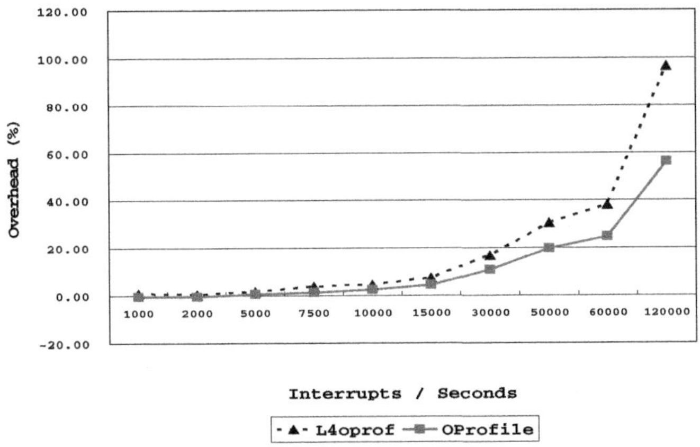

Fig. 4. Profiling overhead, L4oprof vs. OProfile (Multiply)

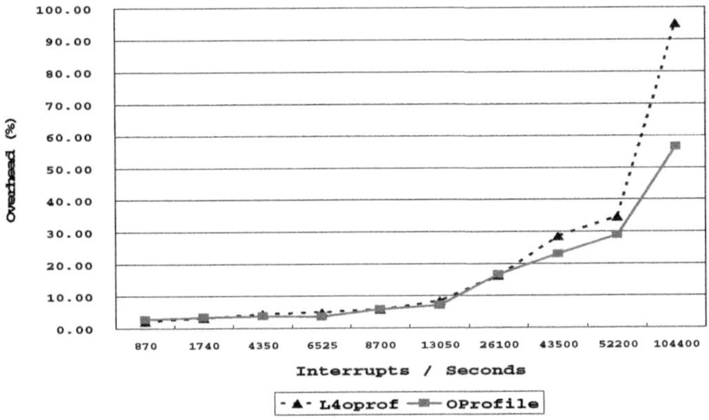

Fig. 5. Profiling overhead, L4oprof vs. OProfile (Tar)

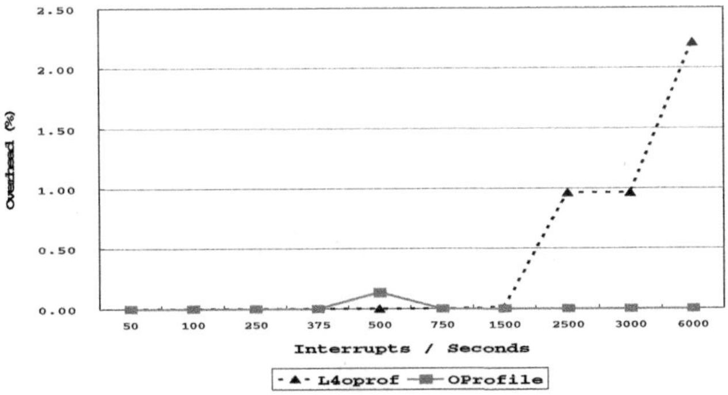

Fig. 6. Profiling overhead, L4oprof vs. OProfile (Iperf)

5.3 The Cause of Profiling Overhead

There are two main components to L4oprof's overhead. First is the time to service performance-counter interrupts. Second is the time to read samples and merge the samples into the on-disk profiles for the appropriate images. To investigate the cost of the first component, we gathered the number of cycles spent in the interrupt handlers of L4oprof and OProfile. We believe that the second component does not contribute to the overhead gap between L4orpof and OProfile, since the operation of the second component in L4oprof was not changed greatly from that in OProfile. In order to optimize performance, however, it must be fine-tuned, which will be our future work. During handling performance-counter interrupts, OProfile directly accesses the performance counters and collects the PC samples itself. But in the case of L4oprof, this operation is divided into the interrupt handler in the L4 microkernel and the virtual interrupt handler in the L4Linux kernel server of the OProfile server layer. Therefore, we read the Time Stamp Counter (TSC) values increased each clock signal at the beginning and the end of each interrupt handler and used the difference as the elapsed cycles for the interrupt service. We collected a total of 2327 samples.

Figure 7 shows that L4oprof's interrupt service time and its variance are larger than OProfile. As Figure 8 shows, the virtual interrupt handler in the L4Linux kernel server causes large variance of time to interrupt service in L4oprof, which is why L4oprof has lower performance than OProfile when the interrupt is generated more frequently. If the interrupt frequency is becoming higher and higher, L4oprof can become more easily overloaded with counter interrupts than OProfile.

Finally, we must answer the question, "why this happen in L4oprof?" This is mainly caused by running Linux in user mode on top of the microkernel. For L4Linux to receive a virtual interrupt IPC, context switching may be needed. And, in the middle of handling an interrupt, the L4Linux kernel server can be preempted. This phenomenon cannot occur in normal Linux. In other words, the current performance overhead gap between L4oprof and OProfile is neither caused by L4oprof'design nor its implementation being defective.

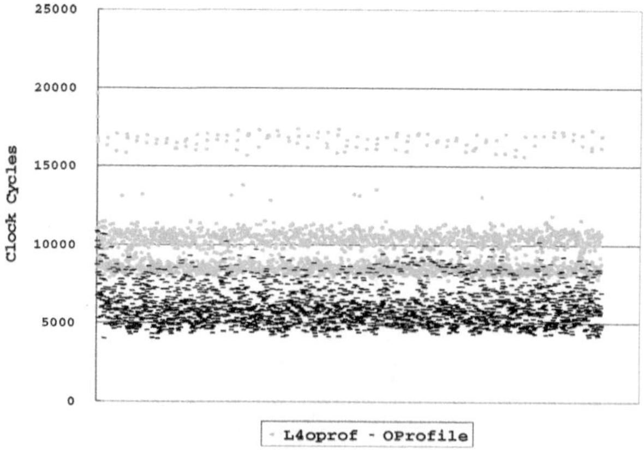

Fig. 7. The clock cycle distribution for interrupt service, L4oprof vs. OProfile

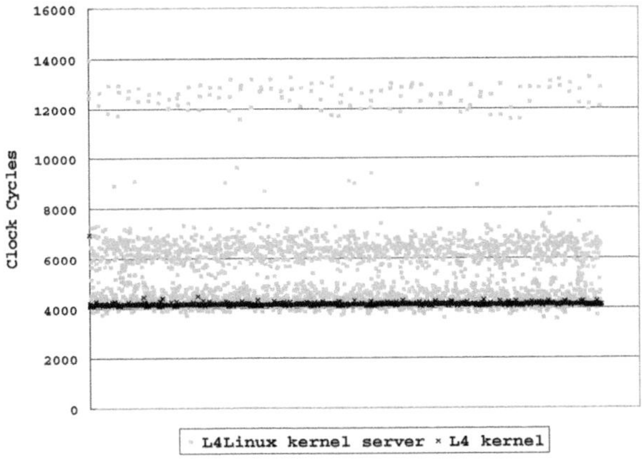

Fig. 8. The components of clock cycle distribution for interrupt service in L4oprof

5.4 Performance Analysis of L4Linux Applications Using L4oprof

An application's performance in L4linux differs from its performance in normal Linux. Figure 9 compares the performance of the L4Linux and Linux for Multiply and Tar workloads.

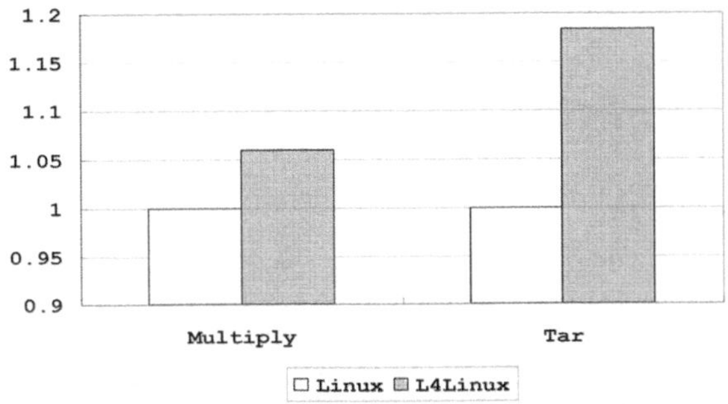

Fig. 9. Relative user application's performance on L4linux and Linux

In L4linux, an application's performance is about 5~17% slower than Linux. We profile the Linux and L4linux, and compare the aggregate hardware event counts in the two configurations for the following hardware events: instruction counts, L2 cache misses, data TLB misses, and instruction TLB misses. Figure 10 and 11 show the normalized values for these events relative to the Linux numbers.

Figures 10 and 11 show that L4linux has higher cache and TLB miss rates compared to Linux. Because the L4 kernel considers L4Linux's applications as user process, each L4Linux system call leads to at least two context switches, i.e., one context switch from the application to the L4Linux server and the other context switch back to the application, resulting in more TLB flushes and performance degrade. It is the main cause of performance degrades in L4Linux.

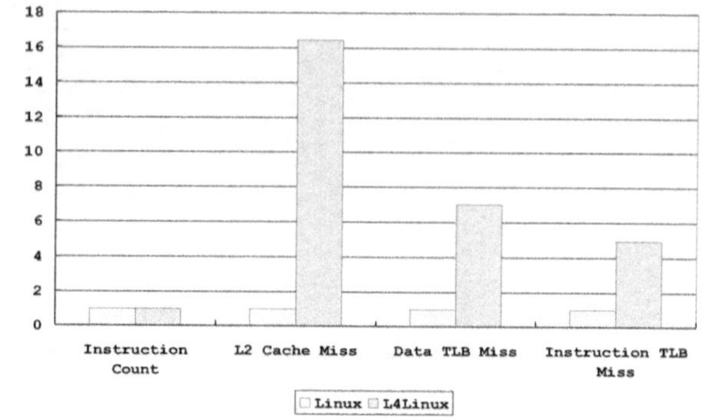

Fig. 10. Relative hardware event counts in L4Linux and Linux for Multiply workload

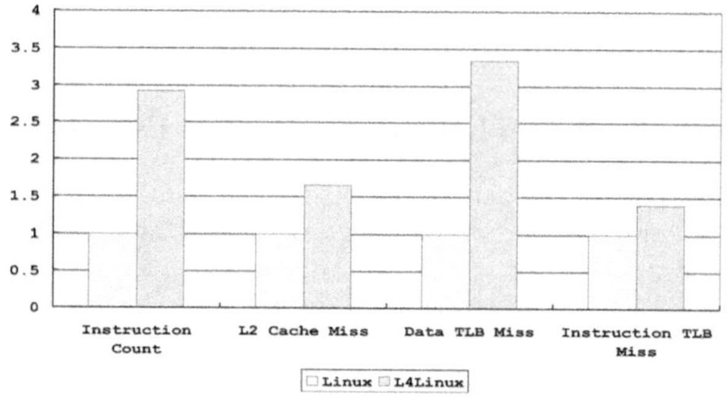

Fig. 11. Relative hardware event counts in L4Linux and Linux for Tar workload

6 Conclusions

In this paper, we presented L4oprof, a system-wide statistical profiler in the L4 microkernel environment. L4oprof leverages the hardware performance counters of PMU on a CPU to enable profiling of a wide variety of hardware events such as clock cycles and cache and TLB misses. It is the first performance monitoring tool using the hardware PMU in an L4 microkernel based environment. We reused the OProfile in Linux and extended its capabilities to be used in the L4 environment instead of starting from scratch. L4oprof can help in building a L4 microkernel-based secure embedded system with good performance.

Our evaluation shows that L4oprof incurs 0~3% higher overhead than Linux OProfile, depending on sampling frequency and workload. We discovered that the major overhead of L4oprof is caused by running Linux in user mode on top of the microkernel. Moreover, it is also shown that profiling user applications running on L4Linux by L4oprof allows locating the main cause of performance loss compared to the same applications running on Linux.

Currently, L4oprof only supports Intel Pentium 4 CPU. We will port it to additional CPU modes such as ARM/Xscale and AMD64. Supporting multiple

L4Linux instances is also part of our future work. To reduce the performance overhead gap compared to OProfile, we will find an alternative structure, for example, moving the operations in the current OProfile server layer into the L4 microkernel layer, to eliminate the user-mode running effects.

Acknowledgement

This research was supported by the MIC(Ministry of Information and Communication), Korea, under the ITRC(Information Technology Research Center) support program supervised by the IITA(Institute of Information Technology Assessment) (HY-SDR Research Center).

References

1. Intel. IA-32 Architecture Software Developer's Manual. Vol 3. System Programming Guide, 2003
2. J. Liedtke. L4 reference manual (486, Pentium, PPro). Research Report RC 20549, IBM T. J. Watson Research Center, Yorktown Heights, NY, September 1996.
3. Adam Lackorzynski. L4Linux Porting Optimizations. Master's thesis, TU Dresden, March 2004.
4. Operating Systems Group Technische Universitat Dresden. The l4 environment. http://www.tudos.org/l4env.
5. J. Levon. OProfile. http://oprofile.sourceforge.net.
6. J. M. Anderson, W. E. Weihl, L. M. Berc, J. Dean, S. Ghemawat. Continuous profiling: where have all the cycles gone? In ACM Transactions on Computer Systems, 1997
7. Intel. The VTuneTM Performance Analyzers. http://www.intel.com/software/products/vtune.
8. S. Eranian. The perfmon2 interface speciation. Technical Report HPL-2004-200(R.1), HP Labs, Feb 2005.
9. M. Pettersson. The Perfctr interface. http://user.it.uu.se/mikpe/linux/perfctr
10. ICL Team University of Tennessee. PAPI: The Performance API.,http://icl.cs.utk.edu/papi/index.html.
11. A. Weigand. Tracing unter L4/Fiasco. Grober BelegTechnische Universitat Dresden, Lehrstuhl fur Betriebssysteme, 2003.
12. T. Riegel. A generalized approach to runtime monitoring for real-time systems. Diploma thesis, Technische Universitat Dresden, Lehrstuhl fur Betriebssysteme, 2005.
13. M. Pohlack, B. Dobel, and A. Lackorzynsiki. Towards Runtime Monitoring in Real-Time Systems. In Eighth Real-Time Linux Workshop, October 2006
14. M. Pohlack. The rt_mon monitoring framework, 2004.
15. A. Menon, J. R. Santos, Y. Turner, G. Janakiraman, and W. Zwaenepoel. Diagnosing Performance Overheads in the Xen Virtual Machine Environment. In First ACM/USENIX Conference on Virtual Execution Environments, June 2005
16. The University of Illinois. Iperf. http://dast.nlanr.net/Projects/Iperf.
17. Michael Hohmuth. The Fiasco kernel: System architecture. Technical Report TUD-FI02-06-Juli-2002, TU Dresden, 2002. I, 2
18. Free Software Foundation, Multiboot Specification, http://www.gnu.org/software/grub/manual/multiboot/multiboot.html

An Adaptive DVS Checkpointing Scheme for Fixed-Priority Tasks with Reliability Constraints in Dependable Real-Time Embedded Systems

Kyong Hoon Kim[1] and Jong Kim[2]

[1] Department of Computer Science and Software Engineering
The University of Melbourne, Carlton, VIC, Australia
jysh@csse.unimelb.edu.au
[2] Department of Computer Science and Engineering
Pohang University of Science and Technology (POSTECH), Pohang, Korea
jkim@postech.ac.kr

Abstract. Recent research on embedded real-time systems has focused on dynamic power management for fault-tolerance or dependability. In this paper, we provide an adaptive checkpointing scheme for fixed priority-based DVS scheduling in dependable real-time systems. Since there are some trade-offs in selection of dynamic processor scaling in terms of energy consumption and task reliability, we provide an adaptive energy-aware scaling assignment scheme with the feasibility test for fixed-priority scheduling with checkpointing. In the provided scheme, we analyze the number of tolerable faults of a task and the optimal checkpointing interval in order to meet the deadline and guarantee its specified reliability. The feasibility analysis of the fixed priority-based scheduling algorithm in dependable real-time systems is provided as well.

1 Introduction

The rapid growth of computer and communication technologies has induced the significant development of embedded devices, such as PDAs. The performance of embedded processors keeps increasing, which enables to execute various recent real-time applications. However, these embedded systems have power-constraints due to the battery lifetime. In order to overcome the power consumption, much research has focused on power reduction using dynamic voltage scaling (DVS) technique [1,2,3]. The DVS scheme reduces dynamic energy consumption by lowering the supply voltage at the cost of performance degradation. Recent embedded processors support such ability to adjust the supply voltage dynamically.

In embedded real-time systems, DVS technique is useful to reduce the energy consumption. The slowdown of the processor performance with low supply voltage results in tardiness of a task result. This late completion of the task execution can be allowed as long as the task meets its deadline. Therefore, much recent research has been done on DVS scheduling in real-time systems [4,5]

Another issue of embedded devices is reliability or fault-tolerance. Better portability and less power of embedded devices may decrease system reliability.

Y.-H. Lee et al. (Eds.): ICESS 2007, LNCS 4523, pp. 560–571, 2007.

Therefore, fault-tolerant techniques need to be applied in embedded real-time systems to provide the required reliability. Checkpointing and rollback recovery scheme is an efficient way of overcoming transient faults. In checkpointing scheme, a task stores its status to a stable device and re-executes from the most recent status in case of fault.

A few recent studies have been conducted on power management in checkpointing of real-time tasks [6,9,10,11]. In [6,10], they investigate an integrated approach for achieving fault tolerance and energy reduction under the assumption of fixed number of faults. EDF scheduling strategy is used in [6] in order to analyze the effect of checkpointing to task slack time. In [9], they analyze the adaptive checkpointing based on fixed-priority scheduling. Reliability-awareness of checkpointing is first taken into consideration as well as energy savings in [10]. The task reliability is defined as the probability of being executed correctly at the maximum processor speed without any fault. It does not consider fixed-priority scheduling, but focuses on energy-efficient use of a task slack time. In [11], an adaptive checkpointing for double modular redundancy (DMR) with two processors is provided.

In this paper, we consider an energy-efficient DVS checkpointing for real-time tasks which require their minimum reliabilities for fixed-priority scheduling. Tasks have different reliabilities according to significance and criticality. The task reliability in [10] is determined by the system fault rate and the task execution time. This paper generalizes it more so that a task can be specified with the reliability value that a user wants to be guaranteed. In addition, the proposed scheme gradually increases the supply voltage as faults occur. Since it is based on fixed priority-based scheduling, this paper includes the feasibility analysis of a task set while taking energy savings into consideration.

The rest of this paper is organized as follows. Section 2 describes system model and problem definition dealt with in this paper. In Section 3, the proposed scheduling and checkpointing scheme is provided. Analysis of reliability and feasibility with checkpointing is given in Section 4, and this paper concludes with Section 5.

2 System Model and Problem Definition

2.1 Energy Model

The main power consumption in CMOS circuits is composed of dynamic and static power. We only consider the dynamic power dissipation because it is more dominating factor in the total power consumption. The dynamic energy consumption by a task is proportional to V_{dd}^2 and N_{cycl}, where V_{dd} is the supply voltage and N_{cycl} is the number of clock cycles of the task [3]. The DVS scheme reduces the dynamic energy consumption by decreasing the supplying voltage, which results in slowdown of the execution time.

Another approach to model the dynamic energy consumption is based on the normalized processor speed and the task execution time. Since the clock speed or processor frequency is in proportion to the supply voltage, the dynamic power consumption can be represented by a function of the normalized speed. For a normalized processor speed S ($S_{min} \leq S \leq S_{max} = 1$), the total energy consumed during the time interval $[t_1, t_2]$ is $\mathcal{E} = \int_{t_1}^{t_2} P(S(t))dt$, where $P(S)$ is a power consumption function of the speed S. $P(S)$ is usually a increasing convex function and represented by a polynomial of at least the second degree [1,6]. In this paper, we assume the dynamic energy consumption under the normalized processor speed S during time interval t is defined as following, where α is a proportional constant [6].

$$\mathcal{E} = \alpha S^2 t \tag{1}$$

We assume that the processor can adjust its supply voltage from V_1 to V_m discretely. The associated processor speed, S_i, with each supply voltage V_i is normalized by the maximum speed S_m with the voltage V_m ($S_m = 1, 0 < S_i \leq 1$). Without loss of generality, S_{i+1} is assumed to be larger than S_i ($i = 1, \ldots, m-1$).

2.2 Task Model

A task set $T = \{\tau_1, \tau_2, \cdots, \tau_N\}$ is given in the system. Each task τ_i is defined by (P_i, E_i, D_i, C_i, R_i) and each parameter is described as followings.

- P_i: The period of released jobs. Each task releases jobs periodically so that a job of task τ_i is released at every P_i unit times.
- E_i: The execution time requirement of a job. The worst-case execution time of τ_i's job is assumed to be E_i under the maximum speed (S_m) of the system. E_i is the execution time requirement in fault-free condition.
- D_i: The relative deadline of each job. A job of task τ_i should be finished before D_i time units from its released time ($D_i \leq P_i$).
- C_i: The checkpointing cost. It is given by C_i time units under the maximum speed of the system.
- R_i: The reliability of task τ_i. It is defined as the probability that a job of task τ_i is finished by the deadline regardless of several transient faults.

A task set is composed of N periodic tasks with their own parameters. The task set is assumed to be schedulable by a fixed priority-based scheduling algorithm such as RM (Rate Monotonic) under fault-free condition. Tasks are sorted by the priority so that task τ_i has higher priority than τ_{i+1} ($1 \leq i \leq N-1$).

Since tasks have different size of execution codes and require various amount of memory, we define each task τ_i's checkpointing cost as C_i time units including the checkpointing latency and overhead [12]. Both E_i and C_i are defined under the maximum processor speed in fault-free condition. If a job of task τ_i is executed on the processor with speed S in fault-free condition, its execution time and checkpointing cost are defined as E_i/S and C_i/S, respectively.

Our system model differentiates each task's fault-tolerance or reliability with R_i, so that a task requiring higher reliability can be specified with larger R_i. In [10], a task's reliability is defined by the probability of executing the task correctly on the maximum speed processor without any fault. Thus, it is defined by $e^{-\lambda E_i}$ under the assumption of the fault rate λ. However, mission-critical tasks may require higher reliabilities than $e^{-\lambda E_i}$ so that they should meet their deadlines in spite of several faults. In [9], all tasks can tolerate k faults regardless of each task's required reliability. This paper generalizes these previous models [9,10] in a way that each task can be specified by its own reliability.

2.3 Fault and Recovery Models

We assume that a transient fault may occur at the system and it causes the fault of the task that is running at the instance of the fault arrival. The transient fault is generally recovered by re-executing the task that affected by the fault. It is also assumed that the system can detect the fault immediately at each checkpointing point.

The fault arrivals are modeled by Poisson process with a rate λ. The probability of k fault arrivals during time interval t is defined by $\frac{(\lambda t)^k e^{-\lambda t}}{k!}$ and the mean number of faults during time interval t is λt. In DVS-processor systems, transient faults can be affected by voltage scaling according to each supply voltage and processor frequency [10,13,14]. Thus, the fault rate at processor speed S is generally modeled as following [10].

$$\lambda(S) = \lambda_m \cdot g(S)$$

where λ_m is the average fault rate at the processor speed S_m. Transient fault rates are generally exponentially-related to the supply voltage [10]. For example, $g(S)$ is modeled as $10^{\frac{d(1-S)}{1-S_1}}$ in [10], where d is a constant. Hereafter, the fault rate for each processor speed S_j is denoted as λ_j $(1 \leq j \leq m)$. Since the fault rate is generally increasing in a low speed processor, it follows that $\lambda_j \geq \lambda_{j+1}$ $(1 \leq j \leq m-1)$.

The fault recovery scheme in this paper is based on checkpointing strategy. Each job stores its job status occasionally to a stable storage for the purpose of restarting it from the most recent checkpointing point in case of a fault occurrence. The checkpointing scheme reduces the average execution time by avoiding restarting from the beginning when a fault occurs. Figure 1 shows examples of checkpointing and rollback recovery with three checkpointings during task execution. We assume there is no fault during task checkpointing.

The dynamic power management scheme can be applied to checkpointing in order to reduce the energy consumption. Figure 1 shows examples of executing the same task on two different speed processors. On a high-speed processor (Figure 1(a)), the task completes earlier but may consume much energy due to the high supply voltage. As long as the task meets the deadline, it can be executed on a low-speed processor, as shown in Figure 1(b).

2.4 Research Motivations

In our system model, we consider DVS checkpointing for reducing energy consumption as well as meeting task deadlines and reliabilities. There are some trade-offs in selection of processor speed. Executing a task on a high-speed processor generally provides high reliability because of two main reasons. First, the

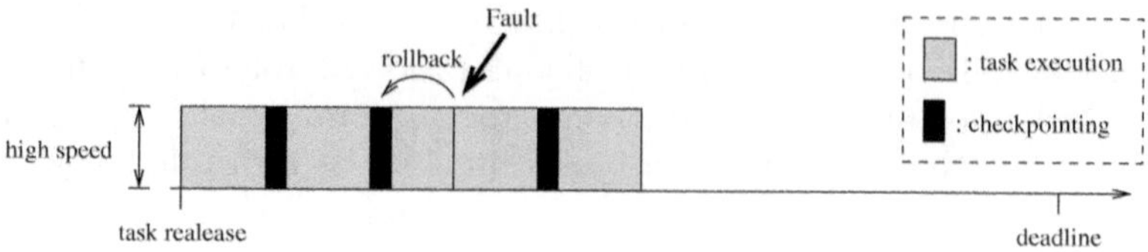

(a) Checkpointing and rollback recovery on a high–speed processor

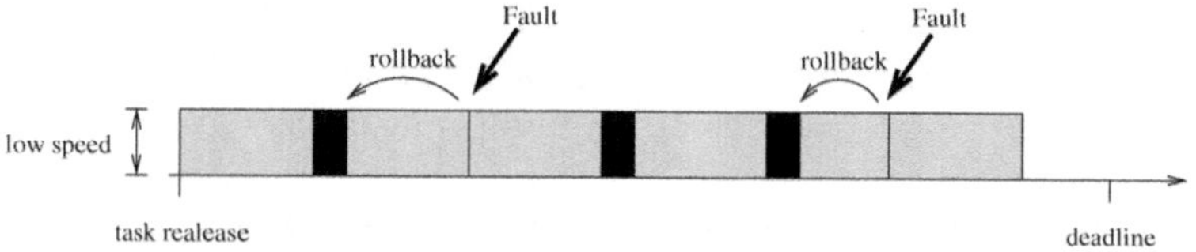

(b) Checkpointing and rollback recovery on a low–speed processor

Fig. 1. DVS checkpointing and rollback technique

possibility of meeting the deadline is higher by executing it fast and reducing the exposure time to possible faults. Second, if we run a processor at very low voltages for low-power operation, then the processor is more prone to timing errors [13,14]. However, it consumes much energy as indicated in Equation (1).

On the contrary, running a task on a low-speed processor tends to reduce the energy consumption at the cost of reliability, which comes from the opposite reasons of high speed case: low possibility of meeting the deadline and fault-prone property of low processors. Moreover, occasional rollbacks from transient faults may consume more energy because the consumed energy is also in proportional to the execution time, as shown in Equation (1). Thus, this paper deals with an appropriate selection of speed scaling with consideration of checkpointing.

The problem in this paper is to provide an energy-aware checkpointing scheme for fixed-priority scheduling in fault-tolerant real-time systems. The m different normalized speed levels $\{S_1, \ldots, S_m\}$ and corresponding fault rates $\{\lambda_1, \ldots, \lambda_m\}$ are given. So, the problem is to assign appropriate speed scalings to tasks in $T = \{\tau_i(P_i, E_i, D_i, C_i, R_i) \mid i = 1, \ldots, N\}$ for the purpose of minimizing the total energy consumption, under the constraints of guaranteeing their specified reliabilities and meeting their deadlines based on fixed-priority scheduling.

3 An Adaptive DVS Scheduling with Checkpointing

The scheduling approach in this paper is based on fixed-priority scheduling, such as Rate Monotonic (RM) and Deadline Monotonic (DM). It is also possible to give higher priorities to tasks of which reliability requirement is higher. Thus, the scheduler always executes the highest-priority job among available jobs. As shown in Figure 2(a), tasks periodically generate their jobs which are inserted to the waiting queue. The dispatcher selects the highest-priority job in the waiting queue and executes it. At the same time, it controls the supply voltage level

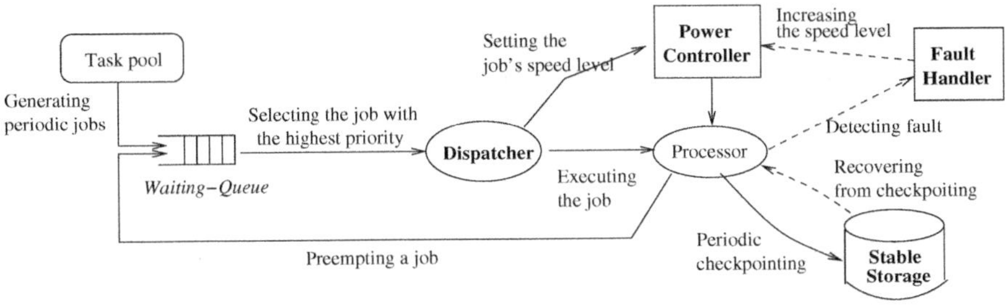

(a) DVS scheduling and checkpointing scheme

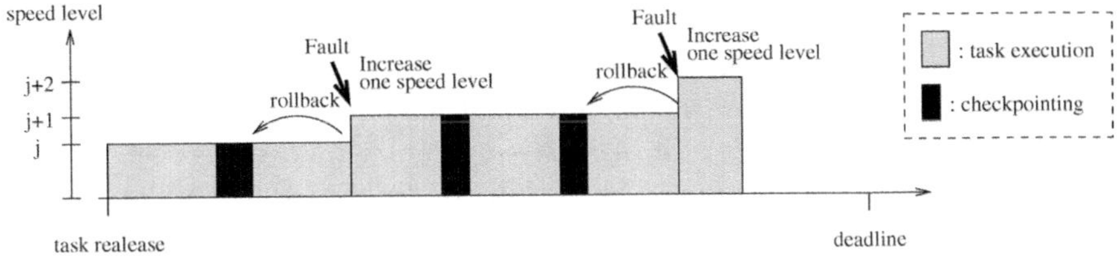

(b) Adaptive checkpointing and rollback recovery

Fig. 2. DVS scheduling and checkpointing scheme

of the processor as the pre-defined one for each task. We will discuss how to determine the speed level of each task in Section 4.3.

The fault handler in Figure 2(a) plays a role in checkpointing and recovery from fault. It periodically checkpoints the current executing job to a stable storage for the case of fault. If a fault is detected, the job is recovered from the recent checkpointed data. In addition, the proposed DVS checkpointing scheme can control the speed level of task τ_i adaptively according to fault arrival. Let us consider that a job is executed under the speed level j $(1 \leq j < m)$. As long as no fault occurs, the voltage level is kept at the same level as j. However, once a fault arrives, the speed level is raised to $j+1$ in order to enhance the job's reliability. When a fault occurs at the maximum speed level m, the processor is operated at the same level. Figure 2(b) shows an example of adjusting the speed level of a job according to fault arrivals.

The proposed scheme considers both inter-task and intra-task Dynamic Power Management (DPM). Since each task has its own speed level σ_i, the scheduler differentiate the speed level between tasks (*Inter-task DPM*). The DVS checkpointing scheme can change the speed level of a task if faults occur during its execution (*Intra-task DPM*).

In order to provide energy-efficiency and reliability, several key issues should be solved. The followings are main problems based on the proposed DVS scheme and will be discussed in the next section.

- *The number of tolerable faults (in Section 4.1):* The number of tolerable faults of a task means how many faults the task can overcome during its execution. Since the scheduling algorithm is based on fixed-priority, the worst-case execution time of each task should be clarified for feasibility analysis. Moreover, in order to meet the task's reliability requirement, a certain number of tolerable faults are to be guaranteed.
- *The optimal number of checkpointing (in Section 4.2):* The checkpointing interval indicates how often a job should be checkpointed. A short checkpointing interval causes much overhead in case of no fault, while a long interval increases the re-execution time after recovery. The optimal number of checkpointing is critical to system performance.
- *The speed level of a task (in Section 4.3):* The objective of dynamic power management is to reduce the energy consumption. There are some trade-offs between high speed level and low one. An appropriate choice of a task's speed level is important for energy-efficiency.
- *The feasibility analysis of a task set (in Section 4.3):* A task set is said to be *feasible* if all tasks in the set is guaranteed to meet the deadline under their reliability constraints. Feasibility analysis of the proposed DVS scheduling shows the condition of feasibility of a given task set.

4 Analysis of the Proposed DVS Scheduling and Checkpointing

4.1 The Number of Tolerable Faults for Guaranteeing Task Reliability

In order to meet the reliability requirement of a task, the proposed scheme defines the number of faults that the task's job can tolerate. As long as the number of faults does not exceed this value, the job can recover from faults. It is obvious that the more number of tolerable faults implies the higher reliability guaranteed. In this subsection, we derive the least number of tolerable faults to guarantee a task's reliability.

Let us define $PF(\lambda, t, k)$ as the probability of at most k-fault arrivals during t unit times when the fault arrival rate is λ. Then, $PF(\lambda, t, k)$ is given by Equation (2) according to Poisson distribution.

$$PF(\lambda, t, k) = \sum_{i=0}^{k} \frac{(\lambda t)^i e^{-\lambda t}}{i!}, \quad k = 0, 1, \ldots \tag{2}$$

When the task can tolerate maximum k faults, the reliability of the task is given by $PF(\lambda, t, k)$. Let us assume that a task's reliability is r, the execution time is t, and a fault rate is λ. Then, the least number of tolerable faults, k, should satisfy $PF(\lambda, t, k) \geq r$ in order to guarantee the required reliability r, as in Equation (3).

$$k = \text{the least } i \text{ such that } PF(\lambda, t, i) \geq r, \quad \text{where } i = 0, 1, \ldots \tag{3}$$

Now, we define the number of tolerable faults of a task for each speed level. For a given task τ_i, the minimum number of tolerable faults under the processor speed S_j is denoted as $K_{i,j}$. The task execution time is E_i/S_j on the S_j-speed processor. The fault rate of the S_j speed is defined by λ_j. Therefore, Equation (4) tells the least number of tolerable faults in order to meet the reliability of task τ_i under the processor speed S_j.

$$K_{i,j} = \text{the least } k \text{ such that} PF(\lambda_j, E_i/S_j, k) \geq R_i, \quad \text{where } k = 0, 1, \ldots \tag{4}$$

For example, let us consider a DVS-enabled processor with six different supply voltage levels, as shown in Table 1. Fault rates are also assumed to be given as the second column in Table 1. For a given reliability requirement of task τ_i, we can obtain the number of tolerable faults to meet $R_{i,j}$. Table 1 shows those values ($K_{i,j}$) for each reliability (R_i) according to Equation (4). In Table 1, E_i is assumed to be 25.

Table 1. An example of the number of tolerable faults ($K_{i,j}$)

Speed level	Fault rate	Reliability requirement (R_i)					
(S_j)	(λ_j)	0.7	0.8	0.9	0.95	0.99	0.999
0.5	0.1	6	7	8	9	11	13
0.6	0.0398	2	3	3	4	5	7
0.7	0.0158	1	1	2	2	3	4
0.8	0.0063	0	0	1	1	2	3
0.9	0.0025	0	0	0	1	1	2
1.0	0.001	0	0	0	0	1	1

4.2 The Optimal Number of Checkpointing

One important issue in checkpointing scheme is to determine the optimal checkpointing interval. If the interval is too short, the checkpointing itself leads to overhead in case of no fault. On the contrary, if the checkpointing interval is too long, the amount of restarting time at a fault arrival becomes large. Thus, the optimal checkpointing interval needs to be analyzed.

Suppose that $(n-1)$ checkpoints are placed during a task τ_i's execution under the maximum speed S_m $(n > 0)$. The worst-case execution time $W_{i,m}(n)$ for $K_{i,m}$-fault tolerance is given by Equation (5). The term $(n-1) \cdot C_i$ corresponds to the total checkpointing overhead, while $K_{i,m} \cdot \frac{E_i}{n}$ is the worst-case re-execution time in case of $K_{i,m}$ fault arrivals.

$$W_{i,m}(n) = E_i + (n-1) \cdot C_i + K_{i,m} \cdot \frac{E_i}{n} \tag{5}$$

In case of the speed level $S_j < S_m$, the worst-case execution time is the maximum value among worst-case execution times for each fault occurrence.

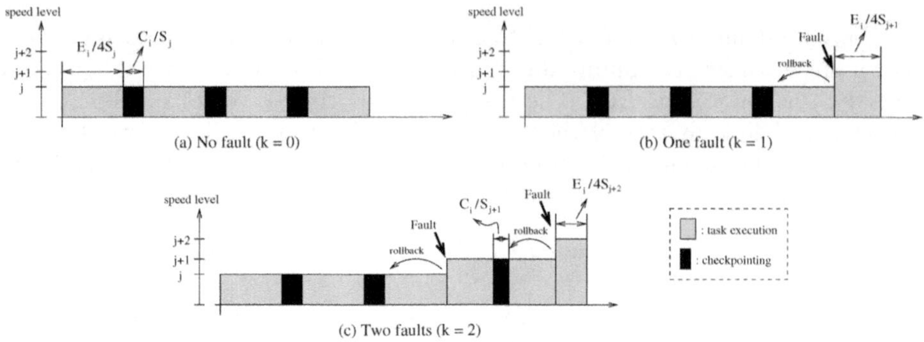

Fig. 3. Worst-case execution times *vs.* the number of faults ($n = 4$)

For example, let us consider task τ_i with $K_{i,j} = 2$ and $n = 4$. Figure 3 shows the worst-case execution time of each number of fault occurrences. Thus, the generalized form of $W_{i,j}(n)$ is given by Equation (6).

$$W_{i,j}(n) = \max_{k=0}^{K_{i,j}} \left\{ \left(\frac{E_i}{n \cdot S_j} + \frac{C_i}{S_j} \right)(n-k) + \sum_{m=1}^{k} \left(\frac{E_i}{n \cdot S_{j+m}} + \frac{C_i}{S_{j+m}} \right) + \sum_{m=0}^{k-1} \frac{E_i}{n \cdot S_{j+m}} - \frac{C_i}{S_{j+k}} \right\} \quad (6)$$

$$\text{where} \quad S_{m+j} = S_m \ \text{ if } \ j \geq 1$$

In Equation (6), $\frac{E_i}{S_j}$ and $\frac{C_i}{S_j}$ are greater than $\frac{E_i}{S_{j+1}}$ and $\frac{C_i}{S_{j+1}}$, respectively. Since we consider the worst-case execution time, $W^*_{i,j}(n)$ is used for deriving the optimal checkpointing number.

$$W^*_{i,j}(n) = \frac{E_i}{S_j} + (n-1) \cdot \frac{C_i}{S_j} + K_{i,j} \cdot \frac{E_i}{n \cdot S_j} \quad (7)$$

The optimal checkpointing number $n_{i,j}$ of task τ_i under the speed S_j is obtained by minimizing $W^*_{i,j}(n)$. Such optimal value is $\sqrt{K_{i,j} \cdot E_i / C_i}$. Since $n_{i,j}$ is a integer value, it is either $\lfloor \sqrt{K_{i,j} \cdot E_i / C_i} \rfloor$ or $\lceil \sqrt{K_{i,j} \cdot E_i / C_i} \rceil$. Thus, the optimal checkpointing interval under the S_j speed is given by $\frac{E_{i,j}}{S_j \cdot n_{i,j}}$.

For example, Table 2 shows the optimal number of checkpointing for each checkpointing overhead based on the same system model as in Table 1. The checkpointing overhead is defined by $\frac{C_i}{E_i}$. As the checkpointing overheard becomes larger, the number of checkpointing decreases. In addition, the processor under higher-speed level requires less checkpointing because it is more reliable.

4.3 Assignment of Speed Level and Feasibility Analysis

Fixed priority-based scheduling algorithms in DVS should consider both energy minimization and feasibility of tasks. For a given task set $T = \{\tau_1, \tau_2, \ldots, \tau_N\}$

Table 2. The optimal number of checkpointing ($n_{i,j}$) of Table 1 when $R_i = 0.99$

Speed level (S_j)	Fault rate (λ_j)	Tolerable Faults ($K_{i,j}$)	Checkpointing overhead (C_i/E_i)				
			2.5%	5%	10%	15%	20%
0.5	0.1	11	20	14	10	8	7
0.6	0.0398	5	14	10	7	5	5
0.7	0.0158	3	10	7	5	4	3
0.8	0.0063	2	8	6	4	3	3
0.9	0.0025	1	6	4	3	2	2
1.0	0.001	1	6	4	3	2	2

Algorithm Feasibility_Test_with_Speed_Assignment (T)
/* - $T = \{\tau_i(P_i, E_i, D_i, C_i, R_i) | i = 1, \dots, N\}$: a task set
*/
for i **from** 1 **to** N **do**
  $\sigma_i \leftarrow 0$;
  $\mathcal{E}_i \leftarrow LARGE\_VALUE$;
  for j **from** 1 **to** m **do**
    Calculate $n_{i,j}$ as described in Section 4.2.
    $\mathcal{E}_{i,j} \leftarrow \alpha S_j^2 W_{i,j}(n_{i,j})$;
    if ($\exists t \leq D_i$ such that $RT_{i,j}(t) \leq t$) **then**
      if ($\mathcal{E}_{i,j} < \mathcal{E}_i$) **then**
        $\sigma_i \leftarrow j$;
        $\mathcal{E}_i \leftarrow \mathcal{E}_{i,j}$;
      endif
    endif
  endfor
  if ($\sigma_i == 0$) **then return** *Non-Feasible*
endfor
return *Feasible*

Fig. 4. Feasibility test and speed level assignment

and a set of processor speed levels $\{S_1, S_2, \dots, S_m\}$, the optimal solution can be found by the exhaustive search of $O(N^m)$. This paper provides an algorithm that assigns the speed level of each task and tests the schedulability at the same time from higher-priority tasks first.

Figure 4 shows the pseudo-algorithm of feasibility test and speed level assignment. In Figure 4, the speed level assignment of task τ_i is denoted by σ_i. Also, we define the response time of task τ_i under the speed S_j by Equation (8). The feasibility test in fixed priority-based scheduling algorithms can be obtained by worst-case response time analysis [16]. Equation (8) shows τ_i's response time function of t considering the worst-case time of $K_{i,j}$-fault occurrence which is given by $W_{i,j}(n_{i,j})$. The speed assignment of higher-priority tasks than τ_i is already done at the time of τ_i's test so that σ_h is used in Equation (8). If there exists a specific $t \le D_i$ such that $RT_{i,j}(t) \le t$, then τ_i is schedulable [16].

$$RT_{i,j}(t) = W_{i,j}(n_{i,j}) + \sum_{h=1}^{i-1} \lceil \frac{t}{P_h} \rceil \cdot W_{h,\sigma_h}(n_{h,\sigma_h}) \tag{8}$$

The algorithm in Figure 4 tests higher-priority tasks first (line 1). For each speed level S_j, the optimal checkpointing number ($n_{i,j}$), and the expected energy consumption ($\mathcal{E}_{i,j}$) are calculated (line 5 and 6). If the feasibility test is successfully passed under the speed S_j (line 7), the assignment of the speed level is set to S_j if $\mathcal{E}_{i,j}$ is the minimum energy consumption which is less than $\mathcal{E}_i$ (line 8-11). Throughout the algorithm in Figure 4, the feasibility test is done and the assignment of speed level to each task is obtained as a result.

5 Conclusions

This paper considers a problem on checkpointing of reliability-aware real-time tasks on DVS-enabled embedded systems based on fixed-priority scheduling algorithms. We proposed an adaptive DVS scheduling and checkpointing scheme which gradually increases the supply voltage as faults occur to the system. In order to guarantee the task reliability, the number of tolerable faults is analyzed and guaranteed. For each scaling speed, the optimal checkpointing number and the expected energy consumption is analyzed. The proposed scheme reduces the energy consumption by testing the feasibility from the speed level with lower expected energy consumption.

We plan to study other issues related on the proposed scheme, such as global optimization of assigning tasks' speed levels. The global optimization of energy reduction requires the exhaustive search of $O(N^m)$, where N is the number of tasks and m is the number of available speed levels. It can be improved by applying other techniques such as branch-and-bound scheme or genetic algorithms.

Acknowledgement

This research was supported by the MIC (Ministry of Information and Communication), Korea, under the ITRC (Information Technology Research Center) support program supervised by the IITA (Institute of Information Technology Assessment) (IITA-2005-C1090-0501-0018).

References

1. Hong, I., Qu, G., Potkonjak, M., Srivastava, M.B.: Synthesis techniques for low-power hard real-time systems on variable voltage processors. Proceedings of 19th IEEE Real-Time Systems Symposium (1998) 178–187

2. Hong, I., Kirovski, D., Qu, G., Potkonjak, M., Srivastava, M.B.: Power optimization of variable-voltage core-based systems. IEEE Transactions on Computer-Aided Design of Integrated Circuits and Systems (1999) **18(12)** 1702–1714
3. Burd, T.D., Brodersen, R.W.: Energy efficient CMOS microprocessor design. Proceedings of the 28th Annual Hawaii International Conference on System Sciences (1995) 288–297
4. Krishna, C.M., Lee, Y.H.: Voltage-clock-scaling techniques for low power in hard real-time systems. Proceedings of IEEE Real-Time Technology and Applications Symposium (2000) 156–165
5. Pillai, P., Shin, K.: Real-time dynamic voltage scaling for low-power embedded operating systems. Proceedings of 18th ACM Symposium on Operating System Principles (2001) 89–102
6. Melhem, R., Mosse, D., Elnozahy, E.N.: The interplay of power management and fault recovery in real-time systems. IEEE Transactions on Computers **53(2)** (2004) 217–231
7. Zhang, Y., Chakrabarty, K.: Energy-aware adaptive checkpointing in embedded real-time systems. Proceedings of IEEE/ACM Design, Automation and Test in Europe Conference (2003) 10918–10925
8. Zhang, Y., Chakrabarty, K.: Task feasibility analysis and dynamic voltage scaling in fault-tolerant real-time embedded systems. Proceedings of IEEE/ACM Design, Automation and Test in Europe Conference (2004) 1170–1175
9. Zhang, Y., Chakrabarty, K.: A unified approach for fault tolerance and dynamic power management in fixed-priority real-time embedded systems. IEEE Transactions on Computer-Aided Design of Integrated Circuits and Systems **25(1)** (2006) 111–125
10. Zhu, D.: Reliability-aware dynamic energy management in dependable embedded real-time systems. Proceedings of 21th IEEE Real-Time and Embedded Technologies and Applications Symposium (2006) 397–407
11. Li, Z., Chen, H., Yu, S.: Performance optimization for energy-aware adaptive checkpointing in embedded real-time systems. Proceedings of Design, Automation and Test in Europe (2006) 678–683
12. Vaidya, N.H.: Impact of checkpoint latency on overhead ratio of a checkpointing scheme. IEEE Transactions on Computers **46(8)** (1997) 942–947
13. Ernst, D., Das, S., Lee, S., Blaauw, D., Austin, T., Mudge, T., Kim, N.S., Flautner, K.: Razor: circuit-level correction of timing errors for low-power operation. IEEE Micro **24(6)** (2004) 10–20
14. Zhu, D., Melhem, R., Mosse, D.: The effects of energy management on reliability in real-time embedded systems. Proceedings of the International Conference on Computer Aided Design (2004) 35–40
15. Punnekkat, S., Burns, A., Davis, R.: Analysis of checkpointing for real-time systems. Journal of Real-Time Systems **20** (2001) 83–102
16. Liu, J.W.: Real-Time Systems. Upper Saddle River, NJ: Prentice-Hall (2000)

Energy-Efficient Fixed-Priority Scheduling for Periodic Real-Time Tasks with Multi-priority Subtasks

Zhigang Gao[1], Zhaohui Wu[1], and Man Lin[2]

[1] College of Computer Science, Zhejiang University, Hangzhou, Zhejiang, P.R. China, 310027
{gaozhigang,wzh}@zju.edu.cn
[2] Department of Mathematics, Statistics and Computer Science, St. Francis Xavier University
Antigonish, NS, B2G2W5, Canada
mlin@stfx.ca

Abstract. With the rapid development of embedded systems, battery life becomes a critical restriction factor. Dynamic voltage scaling (DVS) has been proven to be an effective method for reducing energy consumption of processors. This paper proposes an energy-saving algorithm under a task model (the MSPR model) where a task consists of multiple subtasks with different fixed priorities. This algorithm includes two parts. The first part is a static algorithm, which exploits the relationship among tasks to set the slowdown factors of subtasks. The second part is an algorithm that dynamically reclaims and reuses the slack time of precedent subtasks during the execution of tasks. To the best of our knowledge, this is the first work for energy-efficient scheduling under the complex periodic real-time task model where a task consists of multiple subtasks with different fixed priorities. Experimental results show this method can reduce energy consumption by 20%-80%, while guaranteeing the real-time requirements of systems.

1 Introduction

Many of embedded real-time systems are powered by rechargeable batteries in order to provide autonomy and/or mobility. Among components in embedded systems, processors are one of the most energy-consuming components. Because the current advances in battery technology fall far behind those in processor technology, battery life becomes a critical restriction factor.

DVS technology, which uses the energy characteristics of modern processors made by CMOS (Complementary Metal-Oxide-Semiconductor Transistor) technology and the fact that tasks usually have some slack time, can reduce energy consumption at the cost of increasing the execution time of tasks.

In hard real-time systems, the extension of a task's execution time must respect its timing requirements, i.e., its deadline must be met. Although many research works have been carried out on hard real-time DVS [2-8], most of them only consider regular fixed-priority task sets where a task is the smallest unit in a system and has only a single priority. In this paper, we focus on DVS for periodic task sets where

Y.-H. Lee et al. (Eds.): ICESS 2007, LNCS 4523, pp. 572–583, 2007.

each task consists of a sequence of subtasks with different fixed priorities. We call this task model the MSPR model (multiple subtasks with precedence relationship), which is an extension to regular fixed-priority task model. With the statically assigned multi-priorities for the subtasks, the MSPR model allows a task to run at different priority level at runtime without requiring OS (operating system) support for dynamic priority adjustment.

There have been some research efforts on the energy-saving problem under precedent task model [10, 11]. However, they are aimed at multiple processors using list scheduling [13], and complex priority-assigning mechanism and dynamic dispatch of tasks are needed. The method presented in this paper uses fixed priority scheduling and fixed task set on a single processor, and aims at the systems with restricted resources and critical hard real-time requirements.

In this paper, we propose an energy-saving scheduling algorithm under the MSPR model. This algorithm includes two parts. The first part calculates the slowdown factor of each subtask by analyzing the relationship among tasks. And the second part reclaims and reuses the slack time of precedent subtasks during runtime. The algorithm aims at energy savings while at the same time guaranteeing all the tasks to meet their deadlines.

The rest of this paper is organized as follows. Section 2 describes the task model, processor model, and timing analysis technique used in this paper. Section 3 proposes the energy-saving algorithm. Section 4 gives the evaluation of this algorithm. We conclude this paper in Section 5.

2 System Model and Timing Analysis Technique

In this section, we introduce the task model, processor model, and timing analysis technique that will be used throughout this paper.

This paper uses the MSPR task model. In this task model, a system is composed of n periodic tasks, represented as $\Gamma=\{\tau_1,\cdots,\tau_n\}$. A task τ_i is represented as a three-tuple $\{T_i, D_i, C_i\}$, where T_i is the period, D_i is the relative deadline, and C_i is the worst-case execution time (WCET). One instance of τ_i is generated every T_i intervals, called a *job* of τ_i. The task τ_i consists of m subtasks, $\tau_{(i,1)},\cdots,\tau_{(i,m)}$. The subtask $\tau_{(i,k)}$ is characterized by a WCET $C_{(i,k)}$ and a priority $P_{(i,k)}$. $\tau_{(i,k)}$ has the same period as that of τ_i, and the WCET of τ_i is equal to the sum of the WCET of all τ_i's subtasks. After a job of τ_i is released, its subtasks are executed sequentially. We assume no subtask can be included in more than one task; there is no blocking time caused by resource sharing among subtasks of different tasks; and system overheads, such as scheduler and context-switching overheads, are ignored. In this paper, we only consider the energy-saving problem on a single processor. And we also assume that there is no energy consumption difference among different instruction types.

We assume processors can run at a sequence of discrete operating frequencies with corresponding supply voltages. That is, a processor Pr_i has the parameters of $\{(f_1,V_1),\cdots, (f_{max},V_{max})\}$, where f is the operating frequency, and V is the supply voltage. In this paper, subtasks are the fundamental entities that apply DVS technology. We apply a suitable voltage for a subtask to achieve the purpose of energy savings. We are only interested in the relative energy consumption of subtasks when they run on different supply voltages. Therefore, we normalize the energy to the maximum energy consumption. If Pr_i is running on V_i, its unit energy consumption W_i is defined as $V_i^2f_i/(V_{max}^2f_{max})$. Note that the WCET and the actual execution time (AET) of a subtask $\tau_{(i,j)}$ are all measured at the full speed of the processor where $\tau_{(i,j)}$ resides.

Timing analysis algorithm is the foundation of guaranteeing the real-time requirements of tasks. This paper uses the timing analysis algorithm for MSPR model under fixed priority scheduling policy presented by Harbour, Klein, and Lehoczky [1] (We call it the HKL algorithm). Because of the limitation of space, we only introduce some notations used in this paper.

For a task τ_k, $P_{min(k)}$ refers to the minimum priority of all τ_k's subtasks. If $P_{min(k)} \geq P_{(i,j)}$, τ_k has *multiply preemptive effect* on $\tau_{(i,j)}$. We use $MP(\tau_i)$ to denote the task set that has multiply preemptive effect on τ_i. If its initial multiple continuous subtasks' priorities is higher than $P_{(i,j)}$, and can preempt $\tau_{(i,j)}$ once, τ_k has *singly preemptive effect* on $\tau_{(i,j)}$. If its internal multiple subtasks' priorities is higher than $P_{(i,j)}$, and can block $\tau_{(i,j)}$ once, τ_k has *blocking effect* on $\tau_{(i,j)}$.

The canonical form of a task τ_i is a task τ_i' whose subtasks maintain the same order, but have monotonically increasing priorities. The HKL algorithm has proven that the response time of a task is equal to that of its canonical form. A subtask in the canonical form is called a *canonical form subtask*. When we analyze the completion time of $\tau_{(i,j)}'$, an *H segment* stands for multiple continuous subtasks whose priorities are not lower than $P_{(i,j)}'$; an *L segment* stands for multiple continuous subtasks whose priorities are lower than $P_{(i,j)}'$. C_i^h denotes the execution time of the initial H segment of τ_i; B_i denotes the blocked time that τ_i suffers. The response time of τ_i can be analyzed as follows: first, convert τ_i into τ_i'. Second, classify other tasks into five types (from type1 to type 5) according to the priority of $\tau_{(i,1)}'$, and calculate the busy period of τ_i'. Third, calculate the response time of every job of τ_i' in its busy period in order of subtasks. The longest response time of all τ_i''s jobs is the worst-case response time (WCRT) of τ_i. When we analyze the completion time of $\tau_{(i,j)}'$, the type-1 tasks only have multiply preemptive effect on $\tau_{(i,j)}'$; the type-2 and type-3 tasks have singly effect or blocking effect on $\tau_{(i,j)}'$; the type-4 tasks only have blocking effect on $\tau_{(i,j)}'$; the type-5 tasks have no influence on $\tau_{(i,j)}'$.

3 Voltage Assignment Algorithm

In this section, we present an energy-saving scheduling algorithm—HDVS algorithm. The HDVS algorithm includes two parts. First, it sets slowdown factors of subtasks using a hierarchical method. Second, it reclaims and reuses the slack time of runtime subtasks, and dynamically sets voltages of subtasks.

3.1 Static Slowdown Factor

In this subsection, we first introduce the Time Scaling Factors for a Single task/subtask (TSFS) and its calculation method in the MSPR model, and then present the method for setting static slowdown factors of subtasks.

TSFS and its Calculation Method. Lehoczky et al. [9] presented the notion of Critical Scaling Factor (CSF), which is a metric of the time sensitivity of a task set. For a system with the CSF of α, if we multiply all tasks' WCET by a factor of α, the system will still be schedulable. In this paper, we borrow the idea of CSF, and propose the notion of TSFS. For a task τ_i with the TSFS of α, if we multiply all tasks' WCET by a factor which is no more than α, τ_i is still schedulable (Note that the schedulability of other tasks is not considered in the notion of TSFS for a task. It is obvious that the CSF of a system is equal to the least TSFS of all its tasks). If a task τ_i has the TSFS of α, all the subtasks of τ_i have the default TSFS of α. In the following subsection, we will see a subtask of τ_i can also have a different TSFS of β (obviously, $\beta \le \alpha$).

Algorithm Find_TSFS (i, TS)

```
/* i is the task number; TS is the task set in the
system; TH_h is the biggest threshold of the TSFS of τ_i; TH_l
is the least threshold of the TSFS of τ_i; R_i is the WCRT of
the task τ_i.*/
Begin
  Calculate the WCRT of τ_i;
  if (R_i>D_i) return -1;
  TH_h= D_i/R_i;
  TH_l=1;
  while (abs(TH_h-TH_l)>=0.000001)
  {
      Calculate R_i when all tasks' WCET is multiplied by a
      factor of (TH_h+TH_l)/2;
      if (R_i>D_i)
        TH_h=(TH_h+TH_l)/2;
      else
        TH_l=(TH_h+TH_l)/2;
  }
  return (TH_h+TH_l)/2;
End
```

Fig. 1. Find_TSFS algorithm

Under the MSPR model, a task's WCRT is obtained by calculating all subtasks' completion time subsequently. Scaling the WCET of a task may change the singly preemptive time, multiply preemptive time, or blocking time for other tasks, which increases the computation complexity of TSFS. In this paper, we develop a binary search algorithm named Find_TSFS algorithm to calculate the TSFS of an arbitrary task τ_i. In the Find_TSFS algorithm, we first calculate the WCRT of τ_i, R_i. Then set the threshold of the TSFS of τ_i as follows: if $R_i \le D_i$, we set its maximum TSFS to be D_i/R_i, least TSFS to be 1. If $R_i > D_i$, the Find_TSFS returns –1 to denotes the TS is unschedulable. After the TH_h and Th_l of τ_i have been set, we can use binary search to determine the TSFS of τ_i.

The Method of Hierarchical Setting Static Slowdown Factor. When $\tau_{(i,k)}$'s execution speed is slowed down, we call its maximum allowable execution time *maximum time extension*, and (the maximum time extension)/$C_{(i,k)}$ the *maximum time extension factor*. From the definition of TSFS, we know that TSFS(τ_i) only denotes the possible maximum time extension factor of τ_i. In fact, τ_i may have multiply preemptive effect, singly preemptive effect, or blocking effect on other tasks. In order to guarantee the schedulability of other tasks, the time extension of the subtasks of τ_i must be restricted, and no more than TSFS(τ_i). The HDVS algorithm sets supply voltages on the base of subtasks. For a subtask, its slowdown factor is equal to its TSFS. So the slowdown factor and TSFS are interchangeable for subtasks. For a task τ_j, its first canonical form subtask has the least priority. In the following sections, when we say τ_i can singly preempt, or block τ_j, it means τ_i can singly preempt, or block $\tau_{(j,1)}$'.

Based on the timing analysis theory of the HKL algorithm and the definition of TSFS, when changing the execution speeds of the task τ_i, three rules must be followed:

A. If τ_i is a multiply preemptive task of $\tau_{(j,1)}$, the maximum time extension factor of all τ_i's subtasks can not exceed TSFS(τ_j);
B. If τ_i is a type-2 or type-3 task of τ_j, the maximum time extension factor of τ_i's initial H segment can not exceed TSFS(τ_j); the maximum time extension of τ_i's internal H segments can not exceed TSFS(τ_j)*(C_i^h+ B_j). If τ_i is a type-3 task of τ_j, the maximum time extension of τ_i's final H segments can not exceed TSFS(τ_j)*B_j.
C. If τ_i is a type-4 task of τ_j, the maximum time extension of the internal H segments of τ_i can not exceed TSFS(τ_j)*B_j.

It must be noted that the rules A, B, and C are sufficient conditions for the schedulability of task sets, but not necessary conditions. Under fixed priority scheduling and discrete voltage levels, assigning the optimal slowdown factors is an NP-hard problem [12]. In this paper, we do not try to find the optimal slowdown factors of subtasks, but to find feasible slowdown factors of subtasks.

For all tasks in systems, we must guarantee the rules A, B, and C are met when setting their static slowdown factors. We present a method of hierarchical setting slowdown factors (HSSF). HSSF first calculates the TSFSes of all the tasks in systems, and then sets the slowdown factors of subtasks.

The HSSF algorithm can be divided into two parts.

The first step is classifying tasks into different levels, as shown in Figure 2, and sets subtasks' slowdown factors. The original task set is TS, which contains all the tasks in a system. Assume τ_k is the task with the least TSFS in TS. In the level L_1, TS is divided into two parts where the left node is MP(L_1) (note that MP(L_1)= τ_k+ MP(τ_k)); the right node, OT(L_1), is equal to TS-MP(L_1). For each task τ_m in MP(τ_k)-τ_k, the TSFSes of all the subtasks is set to be TSFS(τ_k) in order to avoid the multiply preemptive time from τ_m being too long. If a task τ_m is a type-2 or type-3 task in OT(L_1), the slowdown factors of the subtasks in the initial H segment of τ_m is set to be TSFS(τ_k). Then we find the task with the least TSFS in OT(L_1), classify OT(L_1) into MP(L_2) and OT(L_2) and set the TSFSes of subtasks. This process is iterated until no task is left. For a task τ_m, because the changes of the TSFSes of the subtasks in τ_m will

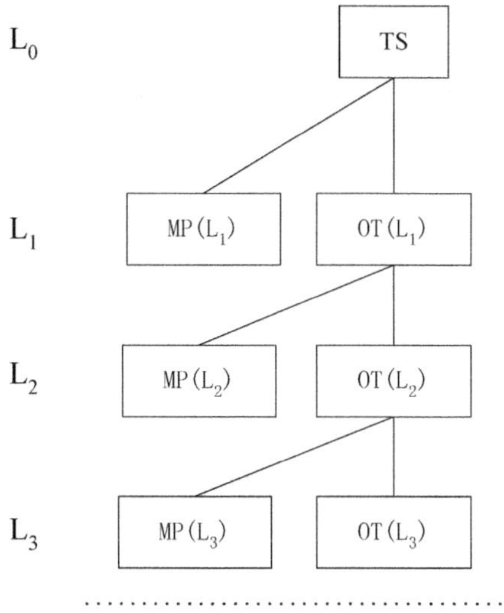

Fig. 2. Task level tree

influence the maximum time extension of τ_m's internal H segments and final H segment, we do not set the TSFSes of all internal and final H segments of τ_m, and deal with them in the second step.

The second step is to perform TSFS adjustment. For each task τ_j in TS, find the type-2, type-3, and type-4 tasks of τ_j. If τ_k is a type-2 or type-3 task of τ_j, calculate the maximum time extension TM of each internal H segment H_b of τ_k. TM is defined as $\sum_{\tau_{(k,p)} \in H_b} TSFS(\tau_{(k,p)}) \cdot C_{(k,p)}$. If TM is larger than TSFS(τ_j)*(B_j+C_k^h), it means H_b may block τ_j longer than expected. We adjust the TSFSes of the subtasks in H_b, and multiply their TSFSes by a factor of TSFS(τ_j)*(B_j+C_k^h)/TM. If τ_k is a type-3 task of τ_j, except the internal H segments of τ_k, we should also calculate the maximum time extension TM of its final H segment H_f. If TM is larger than TSFS(τ_j)*B_j, it means H_f may block τ_j longer than expected. We multiply the TSFSes of all subtask in H_f by a factor of TSFS(τ_j)*B_j/ TM. If τ_k is a type-4 task, calculate the maximum time extension TM of each internal H segment H_b in τ_k. If TM is larger than TSFS(τ_j)*B_j, multiply the TSFSes of all subtasks in H_b by a factor of TSFS(τ_j)*B_j/ TM to avoid too long blocking time from τ_k.

3.2 Dynamic Reclamation and Reuse of Slack Time

Section 3.1 uses WCET as the time parameter of a task to set it subtasks' slowdown factor. WCET is a pessimistic estimation of the execution time of a task. In the runtime of tasks, their actual execution time is usually shorter than their WCET. When executing a task τ_i, we can use the slack time caused by the difference between its AET and WCET to lower the operating frequency further while guaranteeing τ_i's deadline.

Under the MSPR model, a task is composed of multiple subtasks. In this paper, our slack time reclamation algorithm only reclaims the slack time in the identical job of a task. Before running a subtask $\tau_{(i,j)}$, the slack time of the completed subtasks of τ_i, together with the WCET of $\tau_{(i,j)}$ is used to determine the lowest operating frequency of $\tau_{(i,j)}$. Changing the operating frequency of $\tau_{(i,j)}$ not only influence the WCRT of τ_i but also influence the WCRT of other tasks.

From the HKL algorithm, we know that, if we do not consider the blocking effect from τ_j, then all subtasks of τ_j can reuse the slack time from its precedent subtasks, and do not influence the response time of other tasks. Similarly, we can prove the reuse of the slack time intra a task will not increase its WCRT.

Reclamation and Reuse of Slack Time. Although any subtask $\tau_{(i,k)}$ reuses the slack time from its precedent subtasks in the same job does not increase the response time of τ_i, it may increase other tasks' response time when $\tau_{(i,k)}$ belongs to an internal or final H segment for other tasks, while its precedent subtasks do not.

In order to restrict the maximum slack time that the subtasks in the non-initial H segments of the type-2, type-3, and type-4 tasks can reuse, we use the STA algorithm to set the reclamation tags of subtasks and their maximum slack time available.

Algorithm STA (TS)
```
/* TS is the task set in the system; Bi is the maximum
blocking time of τi; MST is the maximum slack time that a
subtask can reuse. MTE(Hi) is the maximum time extension
of all subtasks in Hi.*/
Begin
  for (each task τi in TS)
  {
    Set the reclamation flag of the first subtask of τi to
    be false, and the reclamation flag of the other
    subtasks of τi to be true;
    Set the MST of each subtask of τi to be 0;
  }
  for (each task τi in TS)
  {
    Convert τi into its canonical form τi';
    Use P(i,1)` to classify other tasks;
    for (each task τk in TS- τi)
    {
      if (τk is a type-2 or a type-3 task of τ(i,1)`)
      {
        for (each internal H segment Hi of τk)
        {
          TM= MTE(Hi) + the maximum reclaimed slack time;
          ti=TSFS(τi)*(Bi+Ck^h);
          if (TM> ti)
```

Fig. 3. STA algorithm

```
          {
            Set the reclamation tag of the first subtask in
            Hi to be false.
            if (the MST of the first subtask in Hi is
                  larger than ti -MTE(Hi))
              Set the MST of the first subtask in Hi to be
              ti -MTE(Hi);
          }
        }
        if (τk is a type-3 task of τ(i,1)`)
        {
          TM = the maximum time extension of all subtasks
               in τk's final H segment Hi + the maximum
               reclaimed slack time;
          ti=TSFS(τi)*Bi;
          if (TM> ti)
          {
            Set the reclamation tag of the first subtask in
            Hi to be false.
            if (the MST of the first subtask in Hi is
                  larger than ti -MTE(Hi))
            Set the MST of the first subtask in Hi to be ti
            -MTE(Hi);
          }
        }
      }
      else if (τk is a type-4 task for τ(i,1)`)
      {
        for (each internal H segment Hi of τk)
        {
          TM = MTE(Hi) + the maximum reclaimed slack time;
          ti=TSFS(τi)*Bi;
          if (TM> ti)
          {
            Set the reclamation tag of the first subtask in
            Hi to be false.
            if (the MST of the first subtask in Hi is
                  larger than ti -MTE(Hi))
              Set the MST of the first subtask in Hi to be
              ti -MTE(Hi);
          }
        }
      }
    }
  }
End.
```

Fig. 3. (*continued*)

Because most of the STA algorithm is similar to the second part of the HSSF algorithm, we do not explain it in detail. It should be noted that the maximum reclaimed slack time of H_i refers to the maximum time extension of all the subtasks in τ_i before H_i. We use the $MST(\tau_{(i,j)})$ to restrict the maximum slack time that $\tau_{(i,j)}$ can reuse in order to avoid too long blocking time for other tasks. A reclamation tag denotes whether we should consider the MST of a subtask. If the reclamation tag of a subtask is *false*, the maximum slack time that it can reuse should be no more than its MST. If a subtask belongs to the first subtask of multiple H segments, its MST is the least one.

STA algorithm sets all subtasks' reclamation tags before the task set is admitted to be executed. After a task τ_i is released, its subtasks are executed one by one. We use the DSTR algorithm to set the dynamic operating voltage of a subtask $\tau_{(i,j)}$. If $\tau_{(i,j)}$ is a subtask whose reclamation tag is *false*, we use MST($\tau_{(i,j)}$) to restrict the maximum slack time that $\tau_{(i,j)}$ can reuse. Then the maximum time extension of $\tau_{(i,j)}$ is set to be TSFS($\tau_{(i,j)}$)`=( TSFS($\tau_{(i,j)}$)*$C_{(i,j)}$+ TST($\tau_i$))/ $C_{(i,j)}$ in order to reuse the slack time. Assuming $V_i$ is the lowest voltage that makes $f_i/f_{max}$ equal to or larger than 1/ TSFS($\tau_{(i,j)}$)`, the operating voltage of the processor, $V_{(i,j)}$`, is set to be $V_i$ before $\tau_{(i,j)}$ is released. The total slack time of $\tau_i$, TST($\tau_i$), is set to be TST($\tau_i$)+TSFS($\tau_{(i,j)}$)*$C_{(i,j)}$ - fmax/f($V_{(i,j)}$`)*$AET_{(i,j)}$ at the end of τ_i's execution. This process is repeated until τ_i ends.

DSTR ($\tau_{(i,j)}$)

```
/* τ(i,j) is the subtask to be executed. CTA is the current
time available. TST(τi) is the current slack time of τi.
f(V(i,j)) is the operating frequency corresponding to V(i,j);
f(V(i,j)`) is the operating frequency corresponding to
V(i,j)`; AET(i,j) is the actual execution time of τ(i,j). */
Before task release:
CTA = TST(τi);
if (the reclamation flag of τ(i,j) is false)
{
  if (TST(τi)> MST(τ(i,j)))
    CTA = MST(τ(i,j));
}
TSFS(τ(i,j))`=( TSFS(τ(i,j))*C(i,j)+ CTA)/ C(i,j);
if (Vi is the least voltage that makes fi/fmax equal to or
    larger than 1/ TSFS(τ(i,j))`);
  Set the operating voltage V(i,j)` to be Vi;
Upon task completion:
TST(τi) = TST(τi)+TSFS(τ(i,j))*C(i,j) -fmax/f(V(i,j)`)*AET(i,j);
```

Fig. 4. DSTR algorithm

4 Experiment and Analysis

Because the task model and scheduling policy in this paper is different from the existing work in energy-saving research, we are not able to compare our method to other known DVS algorithm, such as the RT-DVS algorithm [4], the DRA algorithm [7], and the DVSST algorithm [8]. We developed a simulator to test the algorithm presented in this paper. In the following experiments, we use the method presented in

[4] to generate test task sets. The WCET of tasks are assigned using the product of the system utilization and the task periods with a maximum deviation of 20%. We use a uniformly distribution function to generate the AET of tasks. The TSFS range of task set refers to the TSFSes under the utilization of 0.9. With the decrease of the utilization, the TSFSes of tasks will increase correspondingly. Every data point is an average value of ten experiments. The total energy of the task set is measured in [0, LCM], where LCM is the least common multiple of all tasks' periods.

Different speed/voltage function

In this experiment, we use three processors with different speed/voltage functions to investigate their effect on energy consumption. Their speed/voltage functions are listed as follows.

Processor 1 (P1): { (1, 1.35), (0.9, 1.3), (0.8, 1.2), (0.667, 1.1), (0.533, 1), (0.433, 0.925), (0.3, 0.8) }

Processor 2 (P2): { (1, 1.3), (0.75, 1.1), (0.5, 1), (0.25, 0.85) }

Processor 3 (P3): { (1, 1.3), (0.75, 1.2), (0.5, 1.1) }

We use a task set generated randomly with the following parameters: task number: 6; subtask number in each task: 2-5; TSFS: 1.01-6.11. The experiment results are shown in Figure 5(a).

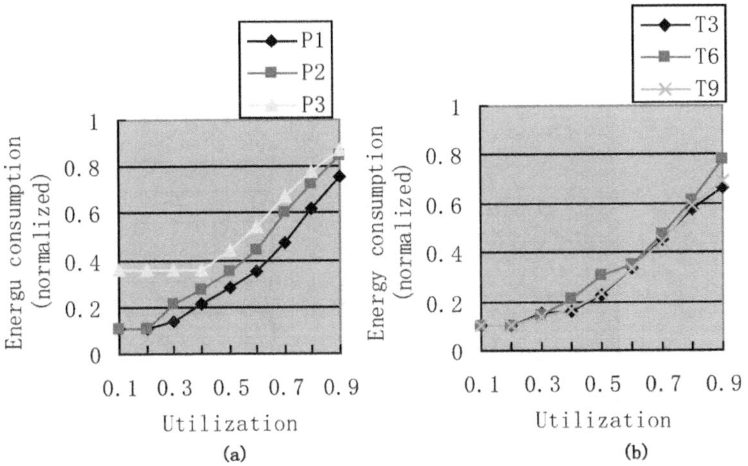

Fig. 5. (a) Energy consumption on P1, P2, and P3 (b) Energy consumption with different task number

Figure 5(a) shows that, the finer the granularity of speed/voltage adjustment, the less the energy consumption of task set is. It also shows that the energy consumption under low utilization is restricted by the lowest energy consumption of a processor, while under high utilization (above 0.7), the energy consumption depends on the bigger values of the speed/voltage function.

In the following experiments, we use processor 1 as the processor platform.

Different task number
In this experiment, we use three task sets with task number of 3 (T3), 6 (T6), and 9 (T9) to investigate their effect on energy consumption. They have the following parameters: subtask number in each task: 2-5; TSFS: 1.01-7.25. The experiment results are shown in Figure 5(b).

Figure 5(b) shows the HDVS algorithm is not sensitive to task number. But under the high utilization (above 0.7) and the medium utilization (0.3-0.6), the energy consumption of T6 is higher than that of T3 and T9 because its moderate task number cannot make good use of static slowdown factor and dynamic slack reuse.

Different subtask number
In this experiment, we use three task sets, the task set 1 (TS1), the task set 2 (TS2), and the task set 3 (TS3). Each task in TS1 has 2-4 subtasks; there are 5-7 subtasks in a task in TS2, 8-10 subtasks in a task in TS3. Except the subtask number, TS1, TS2, and TS3 have the same task parameter. The experiment results are shown in Figure 6(a).

Figure 6(a) shows under the low utilization (0.1-0.3), the energy consumption of TS1, TS2, and TS3 has no notable difference because they are all restricted by the lowest energy consumption of the processor P1. When the utilization is larger than 0.3, the larger the utilization is, the larger the difference of the energy consumption is; the more the average subtask number is, the least the energy consumption is.

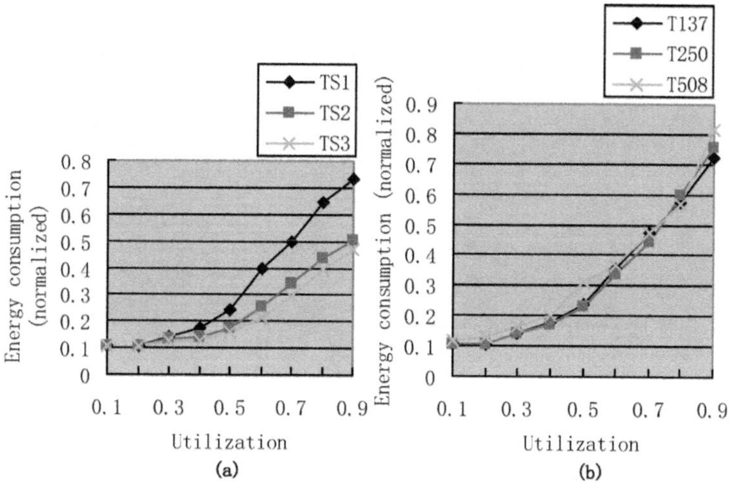

Fig. 6. (a) Energy consumption with different subtask number (b) Energy consumption with different TSFS range

Different TSFS range
In this experiment, we investigate the influence of different TSFS range, but with the similar CSF. We use a task set with the following parameters: task number: 6; subtask number in each task: 2-5. We adjust the priorities of subtasks in order to change the range of TSFSes of the task set, and obtained three TSFS ranges: 1.06-1.37 (T137), 1.05-2.5 (T250), 1.03-5.08 (T508). The experiment results are shown in Figure 6(b).

The experiment results show the energy consumption of a task set is mainly restricted by its least TSFS (i.e. the CSF of the task set). The HDVS algorithm is not sensitive to the TSFS distribution because the static slowdown factors and dynamic slack reuse mechanism can work efficiently. From Figure 6(b), we can see the least the TSFS range is, the more smooth the curve line of energy consumption is. It means the less TSFS distribution has the advantage of more predictable energy consumption.

5 Conclusions and Future Work

Aimed at the MSPR task model, we present an energy-saving method called the HDVS algorithm. The HDVS algorithm uses TSFSes of subtasks to decide slowdown factors of subtasks, and reclaims and reuses slack time in the runtime of tasks. Our future work will focus on how to assign the priorities of subtasks in order to obtain better energy-saving effect.

References

1. Harbour, M., Klein, M.H., Lehoczky, J.: Timing analysis for fixed-priority scheduling of hard real-time systems. IEEE Trans. Software Eng.. Vol. 20, no. 2. (1994) 13-28
2. Yao, F., Demers, A.J., Shenker, S.: A scheduling model for reduced CPU energy. Proc. IEEE Symp. Foundations Computer Science. (1995) 374–382
3. Saewong, S., Rajkumar, R.: Practical Voltage-Scaling for Fixed-Priority RT-Systems. Proc. Ninth IEEE Real-Time and Embedded Technology and Applications Symp. (RTAS). (2003)
4. Pillai, P., Shin, K.G.: Real-Time Dynamic Voltage Scaling for Low-Power Embedded Operating Systems. Proc. 18th ACM Symp. Operating Systems Principles. (2001)
5. Gruian, F.: Hard real-time scheduling using stochastic data and DVS processors. In International Symposium on Low Power Electronic and Design. (2001)
6. Liu, Y., Mok, A.K.: An Integrated Approach for Applying Dynamic Voltage Scaling to Hard Real-Time Systems. Proc. Ninth IEEE Real-Time and Embedded Technology and Applications Symp.. (2003) 116-123
7. Aydin, H., Melhem, R., Mosse´, D., Mejı´a-Alvarez, P.: Power-Aware Scheduling for Periodic Real-Time Tasks. IEEE Trans. Computers. Vol. 53, no. 5. (2004) 584-600
8. Qadi, A., Goddard, S., Farritor, S.: A Dynamic Voltage Scaling Algorithm for Sporadic Tasks. Proc. 24th Real-Time Systems Symp.. (2003) 52-62
9. Lehoczky, J., Sha, L., Ding, Y.: The rate monotonic scheduling algorithm: exact characterization and average case behavior. Proc. IEEE Real-Time Systems Symposium. (1989) 166–171
10. Gruian, F., Kuchcinski, K.: LEneS: task scheduling for low-energy systems using variable voltage processors. Proc. 2001 conference on Asia South Pacific design automation (ASP-DAC). (2001) 449-455
11. Zhu, D., Mossé, D., Melhem, R.G.: Power-Aware Scheduling for AND/OR Graphs in Real-Time Systems. IEEE Trans. Parallel Distrib. Syst.. Vol 15, no. 9. (2004) 849-864
12. Yun, H., Kim, J.: On energy-optimal voltage scheduling for fixed priority hard real-time systems. Trans. Embed. Comput. Syst., Vol. 2, no. 3. (2003) 393–430
13. Dertouzos, M.L., Mok, A.K.: Multiprocessor On-Line Scheduling of Hard-Real-Time Tasks. IEEE Trans. Software Eng.. Vol. 15, no. 12. (1989) 1497-1505

A C-Language Binding for PSL

Ping Hang Cheung and Alessandro Forin

Microsoft Research, One Microsoft Way, Redmond, WA, USA
cheung@cecs.pdx.edu, sandrof@microsoft.com

Abstract. In recent years we have seen an increase in the complexity of embedded system design and in the difficulties of their verification. As a result, engineers have been trying to verify the specifications at a higher level of abstraction. In this paper we present an automated tool which is able to perform runtime verification of a programs logical properties asserted by the programmer. The idea is to leverage the Assertion Based Verification language PSL, which is widely used by hardware engineers, extending it to the software verification of C language programs. The properties expressed in a simple subset of PSL are evaluated by the tool during full system simulation. Like in hardware Assertion Based Verification, the tool can handle both safety properties (absence of bad events) and liveness properties (good events eventually happen). The liveness property is not widely supported in existing verification tools.

Keywords: Property Specification Language, C, Assertion Based Verification.

1 Introduction

Assertions Based Verification (ABV) is an approach that is used by hardware design engineers to specify the functional properties of logic designs. Two popular languages based on ABV are the Property Specification Language PSL and the SystemVerilog Assertion system SVA [1]. PSL is now an IEEE standard P1850 [2]. PSL specifications can be used both for the design and for the verification processes. A single language can be used first for the functional specification of the design and later on as an input to the tools that verify the implementation. The backbone of PSL is Temporal Logic [3], [4]. Temporal Logic can describe the execution of systems in terms of logic formulas augmented by time sequencing operators.

In this paper, we introduce a binding of PSL to the C programming language. A programmer can write PSL statements about her C program and the properties are verified during execution. Our initial work has shown that the approach is feasible; we have defined a simple subset of PSL (sPSL) and realized a few tools with which we can perform ABV of C programs using Linear Temporal Logic (LTL). The sPSL LTL operators are provided for describing events along a single computation path.

sPSL is implemented using the Giano simulator [5] as the execution platform. Giano is a dual headed hardware software simulator. It is capable of performing

Y.-H. Lee et al. (Eds.): ICESS 2007, LNCS 4523, pp. 584–591, 2007.

the full system simulations of CPUs and hardware peripherals as well as the behavioral simulation of hardware designs written in Verilog. The sPSL engine is realized modifying an existing ARM CPU simulation module from Giano.

The rest of the paper is structured as follows. Related work in the verification field is discussed in Section 2. Section 3 introduces the sPSL language. The architecture of the sPSL execution engine is described in Section 4 and Section 5 provides some simple examples. Section 6 concludes with a discussion of improvements we have planned for further assessments of the sPSL capabilities.

2 Related Work

LTL properties can be translated into code that is added to the target program to monitor it during execution, as with the Temporal Rover and DBRover tools [6], [7]. Temporal Rover is a code generator which accepts source code from Java, C, C++, Verilog or VHDL. The LTL assertions are expressed as comments embedded in the source code. With the aid of a parser, the assertions are inserted in the source code that is then compiled and executed.

Roşu [8] suggests re-writing techniques to evaluate LTL formulas. The execution of an instrumented program creates traces of interesting events and the rewriter operates on such traces. Some algorithms assume the entire trace is available for (backward) analysis, others can process each event as it arrives. Roşus algorithms make it possible to generate very efficient monitors that can be used by practical tools such as the Java PathExplorer (JPaX) [9].

In Design by Contract [15], a class specification is augmented with behavioral specifications. The user (client) must agree both to the syntactic requirements and to the behavioral requirements in order to invoke a method specified by such a class. One instance is the Java Modeling Language (JML) [10]. JML is a behavioral interface specification language for Java modules. The JML Compiler (jmlc) compiles JML code into runtime checks of the class contracts. In [11], the jmlc compiler is used in conjunction with an Extended Static Checker for Java version2 (ESC/Java2). In [12] this approach is used to perform verification of a full compiler. ESC/Java2 makes additional use of static analysis, a technique that does not require actually executing the program for fault detection. Another instance is Spec# [13]. The Spec# programming language is a superset of C# which provides method contracts in the form of pre-conditions and post-conditions, as well as object invariants. The Spec# compiler provides runtime checking for method contracts and object invariants. A Spec# static program verifier generates the logical verification for Spec# program and an automated theorem prover analyzes the verification directives to prove the programs correctness.

All of these systems insert instrumentation code into the executing program to monitor and check events and therefore introduce some execution overhead that can potentially modify the programs temporal behavior. This is not acceptable for real-time programs and even a limited overhead is poorly received by developers. In our approach the program binary is not modified in any way, the monitoring is performed entirely by the execution engine (the Giano simulator).

3 sPSL

Properties in the sPSL are expressed as declarations in the PSL language. In order to validate the system we need to use verification directives *vunit* that specify how/when those properties hold true. Since we are considering simulation based verification, formal verification flavored units like *assume* are not currently covered. *Assume* statements specify the values of input variables for use by a formal verification tool.

3.1 Declarations

Each sPSL property declaration is introduced by an identifier for that property. The property is then followed by an expression involving one or more operators. Time advances monotonically along a single path, left to right through the expression. Only a subset of the PSL operators is included in sPSL, taken from the Foundational Language (FL) subset. Valid sPSL operators are *always, never, eventually, until, before* and *next.* Each operator belongs to an operator class. For instance, *always* and *never* are the FL invariance operators, eventually and until are the FL occurrence operators, *before* and *next* are the bounding operators. In order to express the liveness properties we also support the operators *eventually!*, *until!*, *before!* and *next!*.

3.2 Operators

always - The operator *always* guarantees that a temporal expression will hold true. If the expression is a global variable, *always* in this case means for the entire life of the program. If the expression instead refers to local variables then the property will be checked only while those variables are in scope, meaning for the duration of the function call.

never - guarantees that the expression will never become true.

until - guarantees that an expression is true until a second expression becomes true.

before - guarantees that an expression is true before a second expression becomes true. There are two variations of this operator - *before* and *before!*. The strong operator *before!* requires that the expression will eventually become true and it is an error if this never happens. This is not an error instead for the operator *before.*

next - guarantees that an expression will hold true in the next execution cycle. The existing prototype supports the use of the *next* and *next!* variants. This operator is slightly different from the original PSL definition, which referred to a concept of system clocks and cycle counts that is not directly applicable to software. In sPSL the "next execution cycle" means rather "the next event". We use next to require that if left operand becomes true then in next assignment that affects any of the logic properties it will be right operand that becomes true. The operator *next!* is used in the same way as PSL, to require that if left operand becomes true then right operand will eventually become true as well. This operator can be useful when dealing with critical sections of code where the processor cannot be interrupted.

eventually! - guarantees that "something good" eventually happens. If the expression left operand becomes true then there must be an execution path which leads to right operand also becoming true sometimes in the future. It is indeed a violation of the property if right operand never becomes true.

4 Evaluation

There are two separate components that make up our implementation, namely the data model generator and the evaluation engine. The data model generator is responsible for processing data from the sPSL source, C source file, and from a textual dump of the debugging information contained-in/related-to the executable image and collect it into a single file for later use by the evaluation engine.

The evaluation engine has two interfaces, one to the execution processor and one to the data model. It retrieves from the execution processor such information as memory addresses, instructions, and register contents. It uses the data generated by the data model generator to realize the desired property checking. Figure 1 depicts the architecture of the prototype.

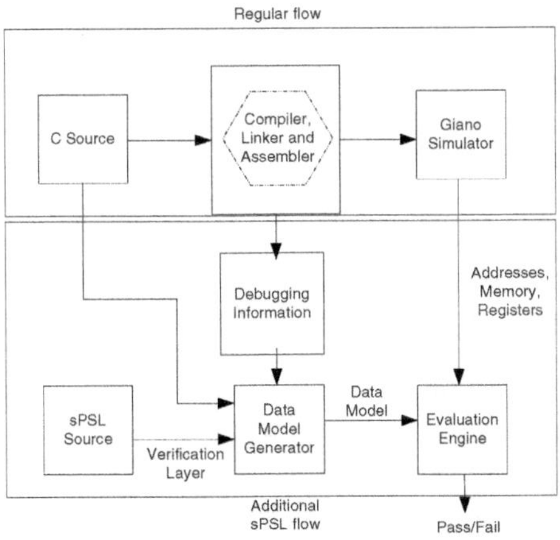

Fig. 1. Architecture of the Prototype

4.1 Data Model Generation

The sPSL source is processed first by a script to create one entry for each property declared in the sPSL source file. After processing the C source file the model will also contain a tag for each of the variables and functions found in the C source. The C source is compiled and the compiler is instructed to generate maximum debugging information. This information is extracted into a text file by compiler tools such as OBJDUMP or similar. The data model generator reads that information and adds to the data model the addressees and offsets of functions and variables, register allocation information and the values of some individual instructions. The data model also contains the start and end addresses of the basic blocks, which are needed to recognize the entering and exiting of the scope of local variables. If the image is actually executed at a different load address (runtime relocation) an offset is added to the statically identified information.

4.2 Evaluation Engine

The sPSL evaluation engine is a module that is physically part of the Giano simulator and monitors the instruction addresses, memory references, and registers accesses during program execution. Every time a new program is launched during execution, the runtime system notifies the Giano simulator of the program name and the address at which it was loaded. The evaluation engine uses the program name to look for a corresponding data model file, if it finds it, it parses it and creates the corresponding PTree. When a specific property is live, the engine creates and initializes an evaluation tree for that individual property (ETree) and the monitoring task is started.

4.3 Tree Evaluation

The evaluation of the ETree is performed with a depth-first, left-first traversal. Each branch/sub-branch corresponds up to 2 leaves. These leaves contain either a value or an operator. We use ternary logic during the evaluation, with the values true (T), false (F) and undefined (Z).

Let us illustrate this with an example property:
$always(a = 1\ next\ b = 1) \rightarrow until\ (c = 1)$ where the node a=1 is the first node of the property. The parent node is a next operator, we need to wait until the next event to be able to decide whether the operator is satisfied or not, therefore we return Z. If the next event is indeed an assignment of "1" to the variable b the next operator can return T. If instead the variable is "0" an F is returned. Either way the operator next can now return a defined value. Once the parent node until receives a "T" from the left-side subtree it can monitor the release point for the right-hand subtree, namely c=1. Until the c=1 is satisfied we return Z. Once c=1 and provided that a=1 next b=1 still hold, the until can return T to the parent node always.

The invariance operator always cannot return a definite value until termination, which is either the exiting of the scope or program termination. The event of its operand becoming true does have an effect though, logically the property is satisfied and immediately re-instated. Evaluation restarts then from the initial state. Notice that when a subtree reports an F this is not cause for failure, only if this happens at the top of the tree. A simple counter-example is "not (a=1)".

5 Examples

```
1 : int main()
2 : {
3 : UINT32 addr1 = 1;
4 : UINT32 addr2 = 2;
5 : UINT32 INTR = 0;
6 : UINT32 op = 0;
7 :
8 : send_to_HW(addr2, 0x0, 0x3);
9 :
10 : while(1)
11 : {
12 :     INTR = TheBCTRL → GCTRL_out;
13 :     if(INTR == 1)
14 :     {
15 :         op = 5;
16 :         send_to_HW(addr1, addr2, op);
17 :         break;
18 :     }
19 : }
20 : return(0);
21 : }
```

The partial code shown above is a real-time C program with two simple steps. On line 8 the function call to send_to_HW($addr2, 0x0, 0x3$) affects a certain peripheral hardware, which is expected to trigger an interrupt in return. On line 13, if INTR is 1 it means that the interrupt has indeed happened.

```
vunit check_intr(example.c :: main)
property intr_event =
    always(send_to_HW(addr2, 0x0, 0x3) → eventually! INTR = 1)
    assert intr_event;
```

In the above code, we create a property intr_event to monitor that INTR eventually happens. The left operand send_to_HW(addr2,0x0,0x3) is the insertion point for the tree and INTR=1 is marked as release point. When the insertion point is satisfied, the evaluation engine will monitor the release point. Before the release point holds, the eventually! node returns a "Z". It returns a T only once the right operand holds. Iff the right operand does not hold until the scope exits the property fails.

```
int i = 0;
charbuffer[10];

intmain()
{
    while(1)
```

```
7:    {
8:       i++;
9:       buffer[i] = 1;
10:   }
11:   return(0);
12: }
```

The partial code shown above is a general purpose C program. On line 9, a buffer overflow error will occur if the index into the buffer exceeds 10.

```
vunit check_overflow(example.c)
  property overflow = never((i > 10) OR (i < 0));
  assert overflow;
```

The above sPSL code shown the property "overflow" monitors the increment of i. The operator never holds the value "T" if 0¡i¡10. Otherwise, "F" is returned.

6 Conclusion and Future Work

The first prototype of sPSL shows that it is possible to use a simple subset of the Property Specification Language PSL to perform assertion based verification of C language programs. To our knowledge, this is the first time that PSL, an IEEE-standard language widely used for hardware verification, has been applied to software programs.

The approach we used, namely to use a modified full-system simulator to execute the program, has not been used before for the verification of software programs. The main advantage of this approach is that no modifications are made to the executable program and no additional instrumentation code is required, thereby increasing the confidence in the verification process itself.

The prototype generates execution traces in terms of function calls and variable changes that are useful to the programmer to understand the reason for the erroneous behavior. The traces could also be used by other tools for further analysis, such as performance analysis and assessment of execution time boundaries. The tool already supports real-time specification and this could be used for performance verification as well.

The sPSL language and the evaluation engine do not depend on the particular programming language we used, they would apply just as well to any block-structured language implemented by a stack-register architecture. It should therefore be possible to extend sPSL to other languages like C# or even FORTRAN simply by creating the corresponding programming language parser. Similarly for a different processor like the PowerPC or the MIPS.

The current prototype does not provide support for the Sequential Extended Regular Expressions (SERE). Within the FL operators, suffix implication and partial logical implication will be implemented for the next prototype. The current prototype supports only the equality operator in Boolean expressions, and furthermore expressions can only refer to a single variable.

We have made no attempt at this point to quantify and/or minimize the overhead in execution time due to the sPSL engine. One possible extension of this work is to attack the problem of mixed software-hardware verification. Giano would appear to be a promising tool in this regard. [14] component based co-verification is one project that is trying to find a unified solution to the problem.

References

1. Accellera, "SystemVerilog."
2. Accellera, "IEEE P1850 PSL."
3. Past, Present and Future: Oxford University Press, 1967.
4. "The temporal logic of programs," *Proceedings of the 18th IEEE Symposium on the Foundations of Computer Science (FOCS-77)*, pp. 46-57, 1977.
5. A. Forin, B. Neekzad, and N. L. Lynch, "Giano: The Two-Headed System Simulator," *Microsoft Research Technical Report*, vol. MSR-TR-2006-130, 2006.
6. D. Drusinsky, "The Temporal Rover and the ATG Rover," *Proceedings of SPIN'00: SPIN Model Checking and Software Verification*, vol. 1885, pp. 323-330, 2000.
7. D. Drusinsky, "Monitoring Temporal Rules Combined with Time Series.," *Proceedings of CAV'03: Computer Aided Verification*, vol. 2725, pp. 114-118, 2003.
8. G. Roşu and K. Havelund, "Rewriting-based Techniques for Runtime Verification," J. of ASE, vol. 12, pp. 151-197, 2005.
9. K. Havelund and G. Roşu, "Java PathExplorer — A runtime verification tool," *Proceedings 6th International Symposium on Artificial Intelligence, Robotics and Automation in Space*, ISAIRAS'01, Montreal, Canada, 2001.
10. G. T. Leavens, E. Poll, C. Clifton, Y. Cheon, C. Ruby, D. Cok, P. Muller, J. Kiniry, and P. Chalin, "JML Reference Manual," 2006.
11. P. Chalin and P. James, "Cross-Verification of JML Tools: An ESC/Java2 Case Study," *Microsoft Research Technical Report*, vol. MSR-TR-2006-117,2006.
12. P. Chalin, C. Hurlin, and J. Kiniry, "Integrating Static Checking and Interactive Verification: Supporting Multiple Theories and Provers in Verification," in VSTTE 2005, 2005.
13. K. R. M. L. Mike Barnett, Wolfram Schulte, "The Spec# programming system: An over-view," *CASSIS 2004*, LNCS vol. 3362, 2004.
14. F. Xie, X. Song, H. Chung, and R. Nandi, "Translation-based co-verification," *3rd ACM IEEE International Conference on Formal Methods and Models for Co-Design (MEMOCODE 2005)*, pp. 111-120, 2005.
15. B. Meyer, "Object-Oriented Software Construction, Second Edition", *Prentice Hall Professional Technical Reference*, 1997.

Cut Sequence Set Generation for Fault Tree Analysis

Dong Liu[1], Weiyan Xing[2], Chunyuan Zhang[1], Rui Li[1], and Haiyan Li[1]

[1] Department of Computer, National University of Defense Technology,
Changsha, Hunan 410073, China
windleaf1980@163.com
[2] China Huayin Ordnance Test Center, Huayin 714200, China

Abstract: For a fault tree, especially for a dynamic fault tree, the occurrence of top event depends on not only the combination of basic events, but also on the occurrence order of basic events. Cut sequence is a set of basic events that fail in a particular order that can induce top event. Cut sequence set (CSS) is the aggregate of all cut sequences in a fault tree. The paper puts forward an algorithm, named CSSA (CSS Algorithm), to generate the CSS of a fault tree. CSSA uses sequential failure symbol (SFS) to describe the sequential failure relationship between two events. And then, cut sequence can be expressed by sequential failure expression (SFE), which is a chain of basic events connected by SFSs. In order to get the CSS, SFS transformation is applied to static gates and dynamic gates, the result of which is reconstructed to the standard form of CSS according to the inference rules of SFE. At length, an example is used to illustrate the detailed processes of the approach. CSSA provides a new qualitative method that extends the existing fault tree analysis models.

Keywords: fault tree analysis; cut sequence set; sequential failure expression.

1 Introduction

In the field of dependability analysis, fault tree model is well accepted by reliability engineers and researchers for its advantages of compact structure and integrated analyzing methods. There have been many methods developed for the evaluation of fault trees [1] [2]. With the development of computer technology, former static fault tree analysis is not suitable for some new situations, since static fault trees can not deal with the systems that characterize dynamic behaviors, such as sequential failure or redundancy. Hence, dynamic fault trees, which contain some new dynamic gates, such as FDEP (Functional Dependency), CSP (Cold Spare), PAND(Priority AND) and SEQ (Sequence Enforcing), was put forward to analyze the systems that characterize function dependency, redundancy, sequential failure and so on [3].

Markov model and Monte-Carlo simulation are two primary methods to analyze dynamic fault trees [4]. If there is only a little part of dynamic fault trees containing dynamic gates, modular solutions [5] [6] can be used to decompose dynamic fault trees, which are widely adopted in commercial software [7] [8]. Even though the use of modular solutions, if the subtree under top event is a large dynamic tree, we still have to tend to Markov model, Monte-Carlo simulation or other approximate

Y.-H. Lee et al. (Eds.): ICESS 2007, LNCS 4523, pp. 592–603, 2007.

methods, and traditional methods, such as cut set and BDD (Binary Decision Diagram) analysis, are not applicable any more. However, both Markov model and Monte-Carlo simulation have to confront the exponential complexity of time and space.

For a dynamic fault tree, the occurrence of top event relies on not only the combination of basic events (namely cut set), but also on the occurrence order of basic events. The dynamic behaviors such as sequential failure bring the difficulty to analyze dynamic fault trees.

[9] is the first one that analyzed the sequential logic of PAND gate, where Fussell et al. provided a quantitive method for PAND gate with no repair mechanism.

Tang et al. introduced sequential failure to the traditional minimal cut set for dynamic fault tree analysis, and provided the concept of minimal cut sequence [10]. Minimal cut sequence is the minimal failure sequence that causes the occurrence of the top event in a dynamic fault tree. In the generation of minimal cut sequence, dynamic gates are replaced with the static gates corresponding to their logic constraints, firstly; then, minimal cut set of the new static fault tree is generated using ZBDD (Zero-suppressed BDD) algorithm [11]; finally, each minimal cut set is expanded to minimal cut sequence by considering the timing constraints. However, [10] does not provide the detailed processes that indicate how to expand minimal cut set to minimal cut sequence.

Assaf et al. provided a method to diagnose failed system using diagnostic decision tree (DDT) [12] [13]. DDT is created based on minimal cut set and component sensitivity. If DDT method is used to diagnose dynamic system, it has to construct the minimal cut sequence of dynamic fault trees.

Besides the above methods, Distefano et al. introduced a new approach to modeling the system reliability, i.e., dynamic reliability block diagrams, DRBD [14], attempting to offer an effective and flexible solution to dynamics, dependencies, redundancy and load sharing. Boudali et al. presented a Bayesian network approach to solve dynamic fault trees, and has applied the method to the Galileo tool [15].

From the above investigation, we figure that cut sequence provides a powerful modeling to express the dynamic behavior of components in a system. Therefore, it is an applicable way to analyze cut sequence for dynamic fault trees. This paper focuses on the generation of cut sequence and cut sequence set (CSS), the aggregate of cut sequences, to provide a new method to study the reliability of dynamic system.

Section 2 of this paper provides the background and assumptions of cut sequence. Section 3 presents an integrated method to generate CSS. In section 4, an example is used to illustrate the processes of our method. And the conclusion is made in section 5.

2 Background and Assumptions

Using dynamic gates, dynamic fault trees attain the ability to describe dynamic systems in a more feasible and flexible way. The top event of dynamic fault trees not only depends on the combination of basic events (namely cut set), but also on the failure sequence of basic events. Rauzy et al. provided an integrated algorithm that generates the minimal cut set of static fault trees using ZBDD in [11]. And Tang et al. expended the concept of minimal cut set for static fault trees on the base of Rauzy's research, and provided the concept of minimal cut sequence for dynamic fault trees. Cut sequence is a basic event sequence that can result in the occurrence of top event in a dynamic fault tree, whereas cut set does not consider the sequential failure relation among basic events. For example, cut sequence $\{A\text{->}B\}$ means that top event will occur if basic event A fails before event B; otherwise, if B fails before A, top event will not occur.

In this paper, we use the following assumptions for a system:

- The failure time of components is random, and components are s-independent;
- There is no common cause failure;
- Components or system can not be repaired;

3 Generation of Cut Sequence Set

3.1 Cut Sequence Set

Since top event has a close relation to the sequential failure of basic events, it should be described in a manner that is composed of basic events and their sequential failure relation. Thus, in this paper, we define a new symbol, sequential failure symbol (SFS) "→" to express the failure sequence of events (the events need not to be basic events).

SFS connects two events, which indicates that the left event fails before the right event. SFS and its two events constitute sequential failure expression, SFE, such as $A \rightarrow B$, where A and B may be basic events. Several events can be chained by SFS. For example, $A \rightarrow B \rightarrow C$ indicates that A, B and C fail according to their positions in the expression, namely, A fails first, B fails next and C fails last.

Using SFS, top event of dynamic fault trees can be expressed by SFEs, i.e. cut sequences. And all the cut sequences of a dynamic fault tree constitute the cut sequence set, CSS. If there are not less than two cut sequences, CSS can be expressed by the OR conjunction of some SFEs.

In fact, cut set of static fault trees can also be translated into CSS. For example, for cut set $\{AB\}$, its corresponding CSS is $\{(A \rightarrow B) \cup (B \rightarrow A)\}$. Therefore, in this paper, we will integrate cut set of static fault trees and CSS of dynamic fault trees, and use CSS to express the top event of general fault trees.

Several SFEs can be assembled in a form that contains OR or AND gates, such as $\text{CSS} = \{(A \rightarrow (B \cup C)) \cup (C \rightarrow (A \cup B))\}$. We call this type of anomalous form as the elementary form of CSS. In order to clarify the expression of CSS, we present some other concepts about CSS.

- Standard SFE (SSFE): the SFE that only contains "¬", "→" and basic events, where logic NOT symbol "¬" only acts on a basic event.
- Standard Cut Sequence (SCS): the cut sequence that is expressed by a SSFE.
- Standard CSS (SCSS): the CSS that is expressed by SCSs.

SCSS reflects all the sequential failure modes that incur the occurrence of top event. In order to generate the CSS that is composed of SFEs, we should decompose static gates and dynamic gates into SFEs. We call the processes of decomposition as SFS transformation.

3.2 SFS Transformation of Static Gates and Dynamic Gates

3.2.1 AND Gate

For an AND gate that has n inputs, $n!$ SFEs can be obtained. For example, if the structure function of a fault tree is $\Phi = ABC$, it has $3! = 6$ SFEs, namely

$$CSS = \{(A \to B \to C) \cup (A \to C \to B) \cup (B \to A \to C) \cup \\ (B \to C \to A) \cup (C \to A \to B) \cup (C \to B \to A)\} \quad (1)$$

Generally, the CSS of a fault tree has more than one cut sequence and is expressed by the OR-structure of several SFEs, so there is no need to transform OR gate. Furthermore, since k/n gate can be reconstructed by AND and OR gates, we will not consider the SFS transformation of k/n gate.

Since the SFS transformation of AND gate will generate a great deal of SFEs, and AND gate has no restraints on the sequence of its inputs, we can sometimes remain $\cap$ in SFE and neglect the decomposition of AND gate. We call the CSS that contains $\cap$ as the simplified form of CSS.

3.2.2 PAND Gate

PAND gate is an extension of AND gate. Its input events must occur in a specific order. For example, if a PAND gate has two inputs, A and B, the gate output is true if:

- Both A and B have occurred, and
- A occurred before B.

If A or B has not occurred, or if B occurred before A, PAND gate does not fire. Since we assume that there is no common cause failure, the output of PAND gate only relates to the occurrence sequence of inputs. In the SFS transformation of PAND gate, we use SFSs to connect its inputs according to their positions. For example, if a fault tree has the structure function $\Phi = A$ PAND B PAND C, the CSS of it will be CSS = $\{A \to B \to C\}$.

3.2.3 FDEP Gate

FDEP gate has tree types of events:

- A trigger event: it is either a basic event or the output of another gate in the tree.
- A non-dependent output: it reflects the status of the trigger event.
- One or more dependent events: they functionally rely on the trigger event, which means that they will become inaccessible or unusable if the trigger event occurs.

FDEP gate reflects the occurrence relation among inner events in a fault tree, but, in fact, it is equivalent to a combination of other logic gates, just like k/n gate. For example, in the dynamic fault tree that shown in Fig. 1(a), A is the trigger event, and B is a dependent event. The failure of A will result in the failure of B, and the top event will occur if both B and C fail. The fault tree can be transformed to the fault tree shown in Fig. 1(b), where the top event will occur if both A and C, or both B and C fail. Then, the CSS of the fault tree is CSS = $\{(A \to C) \cup (C \to A) \cup (C \to B) \cup (B \to C)\}$.

In the SFS transformation of FDEP gate, the gate should be transformed to its equivalent static gates firstly. Then, the SFS transformation of the static gates is used to get the CSS of the new generated fault tree. The following describes the detailed processes that transform FDEP gate into its equivalent static gates.

1. The trigger event is denoted by E_1;
2. Suppose that E_1 has occurred. In this condition, all dependent events become inaccessible and should be neglected. Analyze the residual fault tree, and the result is denoted by E_2;
3. Suppose that E_1 do not occur. Analyze the residual fault tree in the new condition, and the result is denoted by E_3;
4. Then, the equivalent fault tree is: $(E_1 \cap E_2) \cup E_3$.

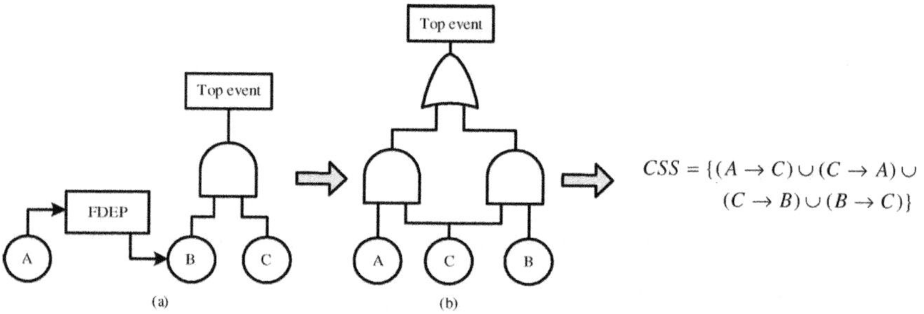

Fig. 1. The processes that generate the CSS of FDEP gate

3.2.4 CSP Gate

CSP gate has a primary input and one or more alternate inputs. All inputs are basic events. The primary input is initially powered on, and the alternate input(s) specify the components that are used as the cold spare unit. The output of CSP gate becomes true if all inputs occur. The basic event representing the cold spare unit has inputs to more than one CSP gates depending on which of the primary units fails first.

Concept 1: ${}_A^0B$

${}_A^0B$ has a left superscript 0 and a left subscript A. It means that B is a cold spare unit of A, and that B starts to work after A fails. The failure rate of B is zero before A fails.

Since the failure rate of cold spare units is zero, we can use $A \rightarrow {}_A^0B$ to show the failure relation between A and B, where B is a cold spare unit of A. Notice that, ${}_A^0B$ must occur after A fails.

Concept 2: $A >> B$

The symbol >> means that A fails before B.

>> is different from →. For $A >> B$, there maybe exist some other events between A and B. However, $A \rightarrow B$ means that it is B that fails just after A, and that there is no event between A and B. Thereby, if B is a cold spare unit of A, there must be $A >> {}_A^0B$.

The SFS transformation of CSP gate is described below:

1. The primary unit of CSP gate is denoted by E_1;
2. Suppose that E_1 has occurred. The residual fault tree is analyzed in this condition, and the result is denoted by E_2;
3. If there are more than one alternate, 1) - 2) are executed recursively;
4. Then, a part of the CSS is $CSS_1 = \{E_1 \rightarrow E_2\}$;
5. If there exist alternates that are shared by several CSP gates, 1) - 4) are executed recursively for each CSP gate. The result are denoted by CSS_2, CSS_3, ..., CSS_n respectively;
6. Then, the final result of SFS transformation is $CSS = \{CSS_1 \cup CSS_2 \cup \ldots \cup CSS_n\}$. An example is used in Fig. 2 to show the processes of getting the CSS of CSP gates, where *B* and *C* are cold spare units that are shared by *A* and *D*.

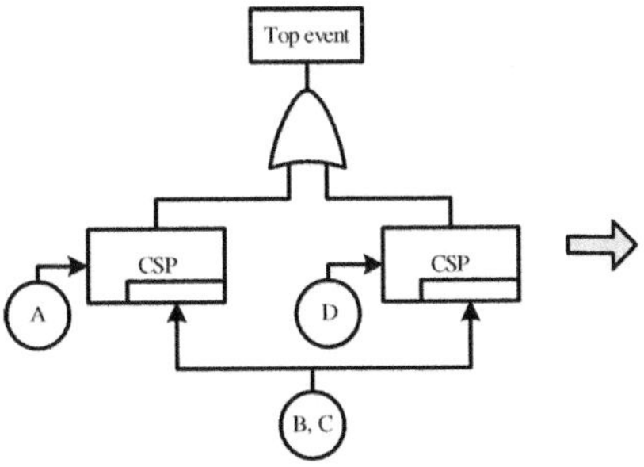

$$\begin{aligned} CSS = &\{A \rightarrow [({}^0_A B \rightarrow ({}^0_B C \cup D)) \cup (D \rightarrow ({}^0_D C \cup {}^0_A B))]\} \cup \\ &\{A \rightarrow [({}^0_A C \rightarrow ({}^0_C B \cup D)) \cup (D \rightarrow ({}^0_D B \cup {}^0_A C))]\} \cup \\ &\{D \rightarrow [({}^0_D B \rightarrow ({}^0_B C \cup A)) \cup (A \rightarrow ({}^0_A C \cup {}^0_D B))]\} \cup \\ &\{D \rightarrow [({}^0_D C \rightarrow ({}^0_C B \cup A)) \cup (A \rightarrow ({}^0_A B \cup {}^0_D C))]\} \end{aligned}$$

Fig. 2. The processes that generate the CSS of CSP gates

3.2.5 WSP Gate

WSP gate is similar to CSP gate except that the alternate units in a WSP gate can fail independently before primary active unit. In order to show this kind of relation, we will define additional two concepts.

Concept 3: ${}^{\alpha}_{A}B$, (0<α<1)

${}^{\alpha}_{A}B$ has a left superscript α and a left subscript *A*. It means that *B* is a warm spare unit of *A*, and that *B* goes into operation state after *A* fails. The dormancy factor of *B* is α, which means that the failure rate of *B* is α times to its normal failure rate before *A* fails.

Concept 4: ${}^{\alpha}B$, (0<α<1)

${}^{\alpha}B$ has only one left superscript. It means that *B* fails independently and its dormancy factor is α before *B* fails.

For events *A* and *B*, ${}^{\alpha}_{A}B$ can not occur after ${}^{\beta}A$, where β is the dormancy factor of *A*. The legitimate relationship is $A >> {}^{\alpha}_{A}B$ or ${}^{\beta}_{C}A >> {}^{\alpha}_{A}B$, where *C* is the event that leads *A* to start to work.

Suppose that the primary input of a WSP gate is E, and x_1, x_2, …, x_n are the alternate units, there are more than one failure modes of the WSP gate, since x_i ($1 \le i \le n$) can fail independently in warm standby state or fail in operation state. For example, for a WSP gate that has a primary input E and two alternate inputs, x_1 and x_2, if x_1 fails before x_2, all the possible failure modes are:

$$E \rightarrow {}^{\alpha_{x1}}_{E}x_1 \rightarrow {}^{\alpha_{x2}}_{x_1}x_2 \tag{2}$$

$$E \rightarrow {}^{\alpha_{x1}}x_1 \rightarrow {}^{\alpha_{x2}}_{E}x_2 \tag{3}$$

We designed the function WSP-AddScript(E, X) to generate the SFE like formula (2), where $X=\{x_1, x_2, \ldots, x_n\}$ are the alternate units of E, and x_1, x_2, …, x_n have the time relationship $x_1 >> x_2 >> \ldots >> x_n$. WSP-AddScript($E$, X) adds left superscripts and left subscripts for x_i, and the result is $\{ {}^{\alpha_{x1}}_{E}x_1, {}^{\alpha_{x2}}_{x_1}x_2, \ldots, {}^{\alpha_{xn}}_{x_{n-1}}x_n \}$.

We designed the function WSP-FindIndependent(E, X) to find all the possible failures modes that contain independent failures (the SFEs like formula (3)). The function is described below:

```
//there are i events failed independently in {x1, x2, …,
xn}, where 1<=i<n.
for (i=1; i<n; i++) {
  Choose i events in {x1, x2, …, xn},
    and denote the chosen events as {x1', x2', …, xn'}.
  Add left superscripts for these events,
    the result of which is {αx1' x1', αx2' x2', …, αxi' xi'}.
 The left events are denoted by Y={x1", x2", …, xn-i-1"}.
    Call WSP-AddScript(E, Y).
}
```

The SFS transformation of WSP gate is described below:

1. The primary unit of WSP gate is denoted by E;
2. The WSP gate is considered to be a CSP gate. The SFS transformation of CSP gate is used to generate a set of SFEs. In all the generated SFEs, if event x_i has a left superscript 0, the superscript is changed to the dormancy factor. The result of this step is denoted by CSS_1.
3. The WSP gate is considered to be an AND gate. The SFS transformation of AND gate is used to generate a set of SFEs. In all the generated SFEs, if one SFE has the form like $E >> x_1 >> x_2 \ldots >> x_n$, call WSP-FindIndependent(E, X), where $X=\{ x_1, x_2, \ldots, x_n\}$. The result of this step is denoted by CSS_2.
4. The final result of SFS transformation is $CSS = \{CSS_1 \cup CSS_2\}$.

An example is used in Fig. 3 to show the processes that generate the CSS of WSP gates.

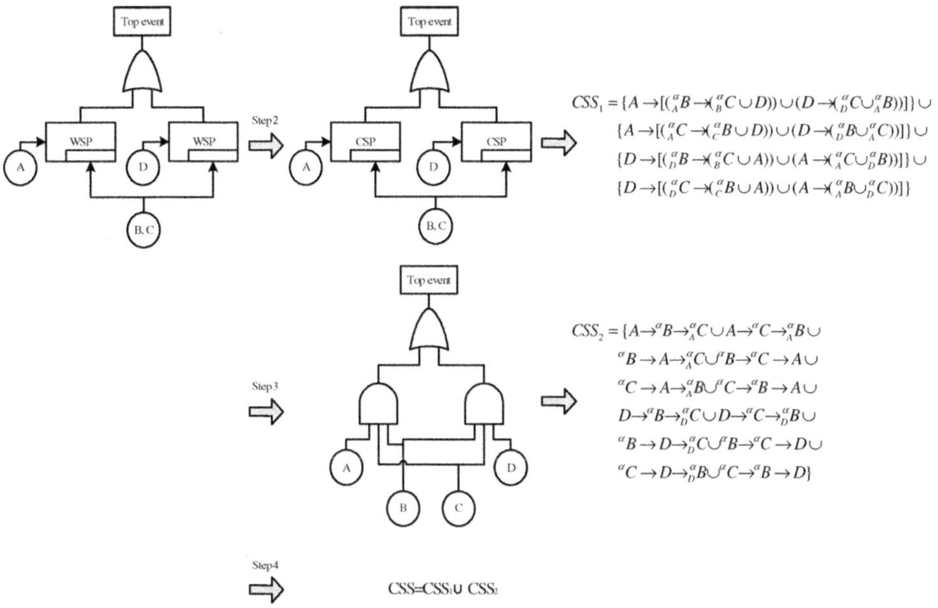

Fig. 3. The processes that generate the CSS of WSP gates

3.2.6 SEQ Gate

SEQ gate forces events to occur in a particular order. The output of SEQ gate does not occur until all its inputs has occurred in the left-to-right order. All the inputs, except the first one, of SEQ gate must be basic events, so, if the first input is a basic event, SEQ gate is the same to CSP gate. Therefore, in this subsection, we only consider the condition where the first input is not a basic input.

Let E, x_1, x_2, …, and x_n be the inputs of SEQ gate, where x_i ($1 \leq i \leq n$) is a basic event and E is not a basic event. E is the first input, and x_1, x_2, …, x_n are the 2nd, 3rd, .., (n+1)th input, respectively. Then, the failure process of x_1, x_2, …, x_n is almost the same to that of the alternates in CSP gate, except that the time when x_1 goes into operation state depends on the last basic event in E. For example, if the inputs of a SEQ gate are E, x_1, x_2 respectively, where $E=\{y_1 \cap y_2\}$ can be rewritten to the standard form $E=\{(y_1 \rightarrow y_2) \cup (y_2 \rightarrow y_1)\}$, the final SFS transformation result of the SEQ gate will be

$$(y_1 \rightarrow y_2 \rightarrow {}_{y_2}^{0}x_1 \rightarrow {}_{x_1}^{0}x_2) \cup (y_2 \rightarrow y_1 \rightarrow {}_{y_1}^{0}x_1 \rightarrow {}_{x_1}^{0}x_2) \tag{4}$$

3.3 Inference Rules of SFE

The elementary form of CSS is the combination of several SFEs. In order to get the final SCSS from the elementary form, we will use some inference rules of SFE, which are described in table 1 and table 2.

Similar expressions can also be deduced from the above inferences. The inferences can be proved according to the occurrence relations among events. For example, $x \rightarrow (y \cup z)$ means that x occurs before y or z, which has the same meaning to

Table 1. The inference rules of normal SFEs

Distributive Law	$x \to (y \cup z)$	$\Leftrightarrow$	$(x \to y) \cup (x \to z)$
	$x \to (y \cap z)$	$\Leftrightarrow$	$(x \to y) \cap (x \to z)$
	$(x \cup y) \to z$	$\Leftrightarrow$	$(x \to z) \cup (y \to z)$
	$(x \cap y) \to z$	$\Leftrightarrow$	$(x \to z) \cap (y \to z)$
Associative Law	$x \to (y \to z)$	$\Leftrightarrow$	$(x \to y) \to z \quad \Leftrightarrow \quad x \to y \to z$
Absorptive Law	$x \to x$ or $(x \to y) \cup x$	$\Leftrightarrow$	X
	$(x \to y) \cup y$	$\Leftrightarrow$	Y
	$(x \to y) \cap x$ or $(x \to y) \cap y$	$\Leftrightarrow$	$x \to y$
OR distributive law	$(x_1 \to x_2 \to \ldots \to x_m) \cap (y_1 \to y_2 \to \ldots \to y_n)$ where $m \le n$, and $x_i \ne y_j$ $(1 \le i \le m,\ 1 \le j \le n)$	$\Leftrightarrow$	$(x_1 \to x_2 \ldots \to x_m \to y_1 \to y_2 \ldots \to y_n) \cup (x_1 \to x_2 \ldots \to x_{m-1} \to y_1 \to x_m \to y_2 \ldots \to y_n) \cup \ldots (y_1 \to y_2 \ldots \to y_n \to x_1 \to x_2 \ldots \to x_m)$
Illegal SFEs	$x \to y_1 \to y_2 \to \ldots \to y_n \to x,\ x \to \neg x$		

Table 2. The inference rules of SFEs of CSP and WSP gates

Inference rules bout CSP gate	$(x >>{}_{x}^{0} y) \cup y$ or $(x >>{}_{x}^{0} y) \cap y$	$\Leftrightarrow$	$x >>{}_{x}^{0} y$
Inference rules bout WSP gate	$(x >>{}_{x}^{\alpha} y) \cup y$	$\Leftrightarrow$	$(x >>{}_{x}^{\alpha} y) \cup {}^{\alpha} y$
	$(x >>{}_{x}^{\alpha} y) \cap y$	$\Leftrightarrow$	$(x >>{}_{x}^{\alpha} y)$
Illegal SFEs	${}_{x}^{0} y >> x,\ {}_{x}^{\alpha} y >> x,\ {}_{x_1}^{\alpha_y} y >>{}_{x_1}^{\alpha_z} z$		

$(x \to y) \cup (x \to z)$. OR distributive law is used to decompose $\cap$ and get the final SCSS. Absorptive law is used to simplify SFEs in CSS.

In the real world, the SFEs, like $x \to y_1 \to y_2 \to \ldots \to y_n \to x$, $x \to \neg x$ and so on, do not exist, so we should cancel these illegal SFEs.

3.4 CSS Generation Algorithm

According to the above study, we summarize the CSS generation algorithm in this subsection. The flow chart of the algorithm, named CSSA, is show in Fig. 4.

In order to get the CSS of a fault tree, static gates and dynamic gates should be transformed to SFEs firstly. The result is the elementary form of CSS. Then, inference rules of SFEs are used to get the SCSS of the fault tree.

In CSS, a cut sequence is similar to a failure chain in Markov model. It is known that Markov model will confront the problem of combination explosion with the increment of events. It is the same to CSSA. But there are differences between two models. Cut sequence does not contain the events that do not influence the occurrence of top event, and the events can either be in operation state or in failed state, so, in this point, it is similar to ZBDD [11]. Furthermore, the simplified form of CSS, containing $\cap$, is equivalent to the modular approach of Markov model, so it has less computation complex to figure out the CSS of a fault tree.

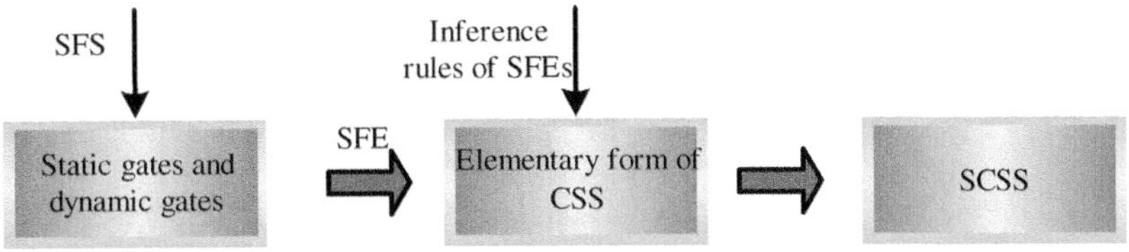

Fig. 4. 0Flow chart of CSSA

4 Case Study

In this section, we will present the detailed processes about the generation of CSS using a case system. The system is referred in [6], and named HDS, Hypothetical Dynamic System.

HDS has four components, namely *A*, *B*, *C* and *S*. We would like to suppose that *A*, *B* and *C* are power supports of an equipment, and *S* is a switch that controls *C*. *C* is a cold spare unit that will take over *A* or *B* depending on which one fails first. If *S* fails before *A* or *B*, it will affect *C* that *C* can not switch into the system and thus can be thought failed. However, if *S* fails after it switches *C* into the system, it will no longer influence *C*. HDS requires at least two power supplies for operation. The fault tree of HDS is shown in Fig.5, where FDEP gate indicates that its trigger event, the output of a PAND gate, will suspend *C*. The output of PAND gate becomes true if *S* fails before *A* or *B*.

1. SFS transformation of dynamic gates

   HDS contains dynamic gates, i.e. CSP, PAND and FDEP gates, and two static OR gates. The SFS transformation of dynamic gates is listed below:

- CSP gate

  Two CSP gates are transformed into $E_1 = \{(A \to (B \cup {}_{A}^{0}C)) \cup (B \to ({}_{B}^{0}C \cup A))\}$.

- PAND gate

  The PAND gate can be transformed into $E_2 = \{S \to (A \cup B)\}$.

- FDEP gate

  The FDEP gate can be transformed into $E_3 = \{E_2 \cap (A \cup B)\}$.

2. Generate the elementary form of CSS

   The elementary form of CSS is

$$\begin{aligned} CSS &= \{E_1 \cup E_3\} \\ &= \{((A \to (B \cup {}_{A}^{0}C)) \cup (B \to ({}_{B}^{0}C \cup A))) \cup ((S \to (A \cup B)) \cap (A \cup B))\} \end{aligned} \quad (5)$$

3. Get the SCSS

$$
\begin{aligned}
SCSS &= \{((A \to (B \cup {}_{A}^{0}C)) \cup (B \to ({}_{B}^{0}C \cup A))) \cup \\
&\quad ((S \to (A \cup B)) \cap (A \cup B))\} \\
&= \{(A \to B) \cup (A \to {}_{A}^{0}C) \cup (B \to {}_{B}^{0}C) \cup \\
&\quad (B \to A) \cup ((S \to (A \cup B)) \cap (A \cup B))\} && \text{distributive law} \\
&= \{(A \to B) \cup (A \to {}_{A}^{0}C) \cup (B \to {}_{B}^{0}C) \cup \\
&\quad (B \to A) \cup (S \to (A \cup B))\} && \text{absorptive law} \\
&= \{(A \to B) \cup (A \to {}_{A}^{0}C) \cup (B \to {}_{B}^{0}C) \cup \\
&\quad (B \to A) \cup (S \to A) \cup (S \to B)\} && \text{distributive law}
\end{aligned}
$$

The SCSS of HDS is

$$
\begin{aligned}
SCSS = \{&(A \to B) \cup (A \to {}_{A}^{0}C) \cup (B \to {}_{B}^{0}C) \cup \\
&(B \to A) \cup (S \to A) \cup (S \to B)\}
\end{aligned} \tag{6}
$$

From the above SCSS, we can figure out all the possible failure modes of HDS: *A* fails before *B*, or *A* fails before *C*, or *B* fails before *C*, or *B* fails before *A*, or *S* fails before *A*, or *S* fails before *B*.

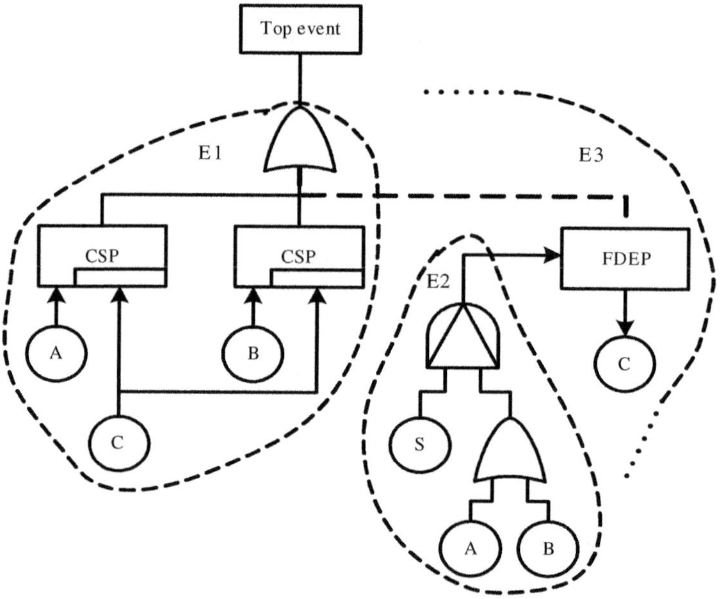

Fig. 5. The fault tree of HDS

5 Conclusion

This paper presents a new method to analyze fault trees using cut sequence set. The method is a new qualitative way that extends the existing fault tree analysis models.

Based on the generation of CSS, further quantitive analysis can be done to get the occurrence probability of top event in a fault tree.

Acknowledgements. This work was supported by National Natural Science Foundation of China (No. 60573103).

References

1. Coudert O, Madre J. C.: Fault tree analysis: 10^{20} prime implicants and beyond. Reliability and Maintainability Symposium, (1993) 240-245
2. Amari, S. V., Akers, J. B.: Reliability analysis of large fault trees using the Vesely failure rate. RAMS'04, (2004) 391-396
3. Dugan, J. B., Bavuso, S., and Boyd, M.: Dynamic fault tree models for fault tolerant computer systems. IEEE Transactions on Reliability, vol.41, (1992) 363-377
4. Manian, R., Coppit, D. W., Sullivan, K. J., et al.: Bridging the gap between systems and dynamic fault tree models. In Annual Reliability and Maintainability Symposium 1999 Proceedings, Washington, DC, USA, (1999) 105-111
5. Gulati, R., Dugan, J. B.: A Modular Approach for Analyzing Static and Dynamic Fault Trees. Philadelphia: RAMS'97, January, (1997) 57-63
6. Ou Yong, Dugan, J. B.: Modular solution of dynamic multi-phase systems. IEEE Transactions on Reliability, vol.53, (2004) 499–508
7. Joanne Bechta Dugan, Bharath Venkataraman, and Rohit Gulati: DIFTree: A software package for the analysis of dynamic fault tree models. RAMS'97, Philadelphia, PA, (1997) 13-16
8. Kevin J. Sullivan, Joanne Bechta Dugan, and David Coppit: The Galileo fault tree analysis tool. In Proceedings of the 29th Annual International Symposium on Fault-Tolerant Computing, Madison, Wisconsin, (1999) 232-235
9. Fussell, J.B., Aber, E.F., Rahl, R.G.: On the quantitative analysis of priority-AND failure logic. IEEE Transactions on Reliability, (1976) 324–326
10. Tang Zhihua, Dugan, J. B.: Minimal Cut Set/Sequence Generation for Dynamic Fault Trees. In Annual Reliability and Maintainability Symposium 2004 Proceedings, LA, (2004)
11. Rauzy A.: Mathematical foundations of minimal cut sets. IEEE Transactions on Reliability, vol.50, (2001) 389-396
12. Assaf T., Dugan, J. B.: Diagnostic Expert Systems from Dynamic Fault Trees. Proceedings of 2004 Annual Reliability and Maintainability Symposium, LA, (2004)
13. Assaf T. and Dugan, J. B.: Automatic generation of Diagnostic Expert Systems from Fault Trees. RAMS'03, Tampa, FL, (2003)
14. Distefano S., Xing Liudong. A New Approach to Modeling the System Reliability: Dynamic Reliability Block Diagrams. RAMS '06, (2006) 189-195
15. Boudali H., Dugan, J. B.: A new bayesian network approach to solve dynamic fault trees. RAMS'05, (2005) 451-456

Multilevel Pattern Matching Architecture for Network Intrusion Detection and Prevention System

Tian Song, Zhizhong Tang, and Dongsheng Wang

Department of Computer Science and Technology
Tsinghua University, Beijing, P.R. China
songt02@mails.tsinghua.edu.cn,
{tzz-dcs,wds}@tsinghua.edu.cn

Abstract. Pattern matching is one of the most performance critical components in network intrusion detection and prevention system, which needs to be accelerated by carefully designed architectures. In this paper, we present a highly parameterized multilevel pattern matching architecture (MPM), which is implemented on FPGA by exploiting redundant resources among patterns for less chip area. In practice, MPM can be partitioned to several pipelines for high frequency. This paper also presents a pattern set compiler that can generate RTL codes of MPM with the given pattern set and predefined parameters. One MPM architecture is generated by our compiler based on Snort rules on Xilinx FPGA. The results show that MPM can achieve 4.3Gbps throughput with only 0.22 slices per character, about one half chip area than the most area-efficient architecture in literature. MPM can be parameterized potential for more than 100 Gbps throughput.

1 Introduction

With the development of networking applications, network security becomes more and more important against a larger number of system hacks, worms, viruses and et al. To protect computer and network from these attacks, applications of network security require much more efficient inspections on the payload of packets. Network Intrusion detection and prevention systems (NIDS/NIPS) are well-suited to this purpose not only for packet header checking, but also for packet payload scanning.

The widely used NIDS/NIPS are misused based, which scan every incoming byte to look for patterns that would indicate intrusions. In practice, there are thousands of patterns with various formats and it is hard for software-based systems to keep up with gigabit line rate. The Snort system [1], for example, can handle link rates only up to 100Mbps under normal traffic conditions and worst case performance is even less. The software solutions can not meet the needs of modern network applications.

At the same time, experimental results on Snort show that up to 80% of total processing is due to pattern matching, which is the most computationally intensive parts and the performance bottleneck.[3] Therefore, seeking for hardware-based solutions, especially using FPGA for pattern matching is a better way to increase performance of related systems for gigabit rate speed.

Y.-H. Lee et al. (Eds.): ICESS 2007, LNCS 4523, pp. 604–614, 2007.

Besides NIDS/NIPS, other systems based on the payload checking require pattern matching architecture. These systems include spam filter, content filter, anti-virus systems, uniform threat management (UTM) and et al.

FPGAs are flexible, reconfigurable with high frequency. They can be programmed for fast pattern matching by taking advantages of their internal logics and on-chip memory. In this paper, we take advantage of FPGAs and design a highly parameterized pattern matching architecture, named MPM (multilevel pattern matching).

The remainder of this paper is organized as follows. Section 2 provides an overview of related works on pattern matching architecture. Section 3 begins our method by giving symbols and definitions used in this paper. Then our multilevel pattern matching architecture is proposed in details in section 4. In section 5, the parameterized pattern set compiler which can generate RTL code from parameters and given pattern set is presented. The example MPM architecture is generated and results are shown in section 6. Finally some conclusions are drawn.

2 Related Works

Pattern matching is not a new issue to be focused in network security. The traditional method is to optimize algorithms for higher efficiency. New method based on hardware design is proposed from 2001. All the related works can be classified to two categories: the ones based on FPGA and others based on ASIC (application specific integrated circuit) [16,17].

The difference between the two categories is the method to store the pattern set. ASIC designs store pattern set in the memory (RAM or CAM) with proper format, such as DFA model, while FPGA designs convert pattern set to logics and present them inside FPGA. Although some ASIC designs may use FPGAs as the prototype, we classify them into the category of ASIC.

In this paper, we mainly focus on the architectures based on FPGA, which convert pattern set to logics. This model can take advantage of high parallelism and distributed internal memory of FPGA.

S.Dharmapurikar presented a multiple-pattern matching solution by using the algorithm of parallel bloom filters [4]. The proposed scheme builds a bloom filter for each possible pattern length. This could conquer parallelism limits in some virus databases because pattern lengths may vary from tens to thousands of bytes.

I. Sourdis [7] proposed a pattern matching architecture on FPGA using the idea of decoding. It can achieve area efficient by using character pre-decoding CAM and efficient shift register implementation. At the same time, it can achieve high operating frequencies by using fine grain pipelining and decoupling the data distribution network from the processing components.

Later Christopher R. Clark and David E. Schimmel [8] present an efficient and scalable FPGA design scheme for pattern matching at network speed from 1 Gbps to 100 Gbps and beyond. It uses multi-character decoder NFA technique to produce high-performance circuits over a wide range of pattern set sizes.

Peter Sutton[10] introduces the idea of partial character decoding in which the character matching units are shared so that the number of signals needed to be routed is reduced.

Tian Song [15] furthers the research by proposing a select character decoding (SCD) scheme, which results in the most area efficient.

There are also several pattern matching architectures based on NFA.[5-15]. For example, Sidhu and Prasanna mapped NFA for regular expression onto FPGA to implement fast pattern matching [5]. In this paper, our MPM architecture will continue the research of the same topic and improve the performance a lot.

3 Some Definitions of Pattern Set

Rules are the essential elements in network intrusion detection and prevention systems (NIDS/NIPS). Each rule consists of rule header and body. Patterns are part of rule body, which are matched to discover the malicious codes.

In this section, some symbols and definitions of pattern and pattern related conceptions are addressed, which may be used as the basis of our highly parameterized multi-level pattern match architecture throughout this paper.

Definition 1. *Pattern* is represented as a vector, signed as $p=(c_1c_2\cdots c_l)$, where l is the length and $c_i\,(i=1,2,\cdots,l)$ are the corresponding characters.

Definition 2. *Pattern set* includes all patterns existed in the rules, signed as P_n, in which n is the number of elements in the pattern set.

Definition 3. *Length of pattern set* is defined as the maximal length of all patterns in P_n, signed as l^{max}, and the corresponding pattern is signed as p^{max}.

Characters can be explained as any width of binary format in NIDS. For example, the character c_i with 8 bit width can be represented as two characters c^1_i and c^2_i with 4 bit width each. Here we give a definition for this circumstance.

Definition 4. *Width of Characters* is defined as the number of bits to represent each character under some understanding, signed as *WoC*.

In this paper, the default value of *WoC* is 8 bit except specific explanation.

Definition 5. *Full alphabet* (*f*A) is defined as the set of all possible characters with some *WoC*, signed as $\sum^{WoC}$. $\sum^8$ is signed as $\sum$ for simplification.

Definition 6. *Alphabet of pattern set* (A*ps*) includes all the characters existing in pattern set P_n, signed as $\sum_\mathrm{P}$. To each pattern $p_i=(c_{i1}c_{i2}\cdots c_{il})\in\mathrm{P}_n$, there is $c_{ij}\in\sum_\mathrm{P}$.

Definition 7. *Alphabet of vertical left alignment* (A*vla*) is constructed by vertical arrangement of all the patterns in the set of P_n with the manner of left alignment, as figure 1 shows.

Alphabets of vertical left alignment are the sets of characters in columns of figure 1. For example, $\sum_j\,(j=1,2,\cdots,l^{max})$ stands for the set of characters in jth column. For a given P_n, the number of alphabets of vertical left alignment equals with the length of P_n (l^{max}). Obviously, $\sum_\mathrm{P}=\sum_1\cup\sum_2\cup\cdots\cup\sum_{l^{max}}$.

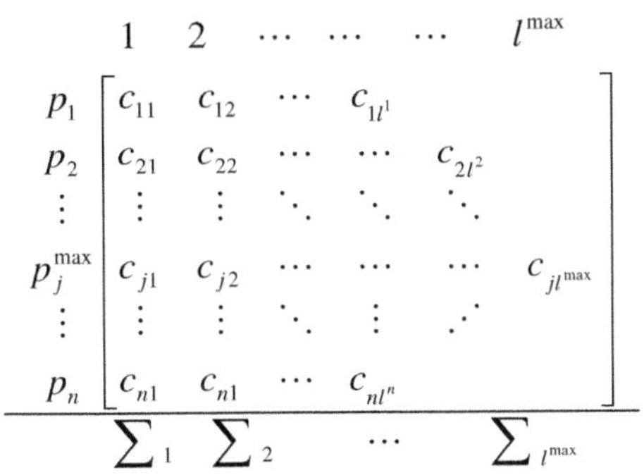

Fig. 1. The construction of Alphabet of Vertical left alignment

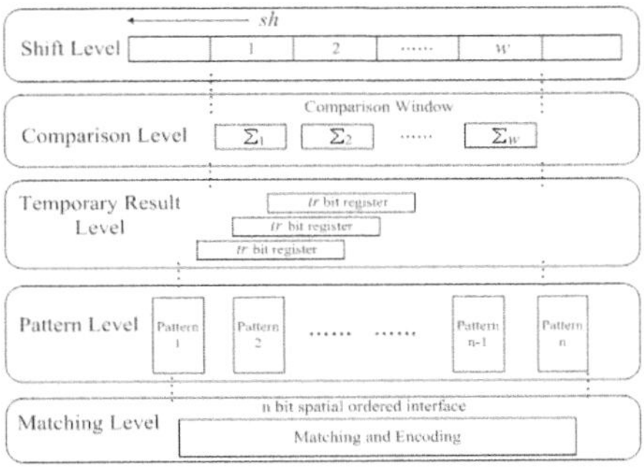

Fig. 2. Overview of multilevel pattern matching architecture

4 Multilevel Pattern Matching Architecture

4.1 Our Ideas

For pattern matching architecture on FPGA, the most important issue is to minimize the chip area and to maximize the matching speed. In this paper, a parameterized multilevel pattern match architecture (MPM) is proposed. The methods of MPM are to reduce the chip area by partitioning the whole architecture to several parts and reusing the resources within each part. Our idea is a kind of *pattern set based* implementation that exploits common resources within the whole pattern set.

To achieve better performance for hardware implementation, we choose an easy algorithm for MPM, named brute force. There are several algorithms for pattern matching or string matching, such as Boyer-Moore [18], Knuth-Morris-Pratt (KMP) [19], Aho-Corasick [20], et al. Some are very efficient in the view of mathematics. However, for hardware implementation, the easy and elegant algorithm is preferred.

MPM consists of five levels: shift level (SL), comparison level (CL), temporary result level (TL), pattern level (PL) and matching level (ML), as figure 2 shows. The detail structures of these five levels are mentioned in the next section. It should note that the partition of different levels is not original used for more pipelines, though it can assist the construction of pipelining for higher frequency.

4.2 The Five Levels

Shift level (SL) is the first level of MPM. This level fetches the payload from the previous component into shift registers and shifts left *sh* bytes every cycle. To transfer characters to the next level (comparison level), shift registers have a comparison window with *w* bytes, as figure 3 shows. The two parameters of *sh* and *w* are used to define the structure of this level.

Comparison level (CL) receives inputs from SL by using comparison window. For each byte in the comparison window, there is a suit of comparison logic in CL correspondingly. These logics will determine (decode) what the characters in comparison window are and output spatial arranged physical signals to identify characters in each place of comparison window.

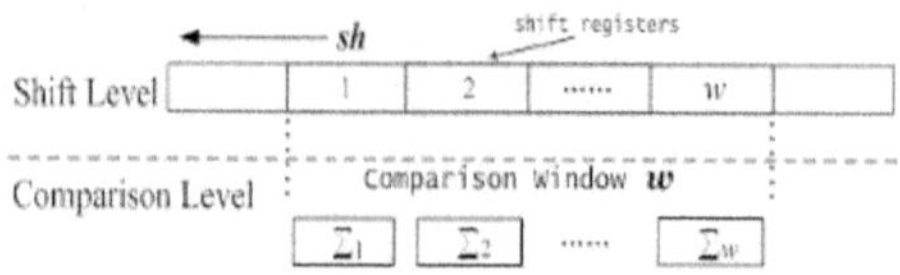

Fig. 3. Details of shift level in MPM

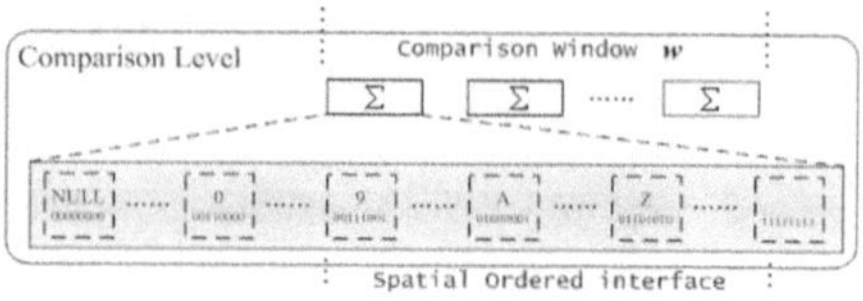

Fig. 4. CL based on *f*A in MPM

Figure 4 shows the details of comparison level based on full alphabet. Full alphabet (*f*A) logic has *WoC* bit input and 2^{WoC} bit output.

The *f*A Logic is implemented with 256 comparison units. Each comparison unit can match one definite character. The *f*A logic is the same as a 8 bit width decoder, which is widely used in pattern match architectures [6-10,15].

With full alphabet logic, CL can implement comparison for any pattern set. However, this kind of architecture consumes much more comparison units and increases chip area and energy, because some of the characters may be never uses in P_n. If reconfigurable hardware is considered, we can relate CL with pattern set and condense the architecture by using alphabet of pattern set (A*ps*) for saving chip area and energy, as figure 5 shows. The dark areas stand for the cancellation from full alphabet logic.

The chip area of CL based on A*ps* can represent as follows:

$$AreaCL_{Aps} = w \times \left|\Sigma_{\mathrm{P}}\right| \times Area_{CmpUnit} \tag{1}$$

A*ps* based CL can result less chip area than the *f*A based one. However, it is not the best one since there are still some redundant comparison units. The redundancy comes from the sameness of all the *w* suits of comparison units corresponding to the comparison window. For example, suppose that MPM shifts left one byte each cycle and the first character of all the patterns will never be “A” but the other characters may be “A”. That means, “A” is in the alphabet of pattern set (A*ps*), while there will be never used for the comparison unit of “A” in the first suit of comparison units.

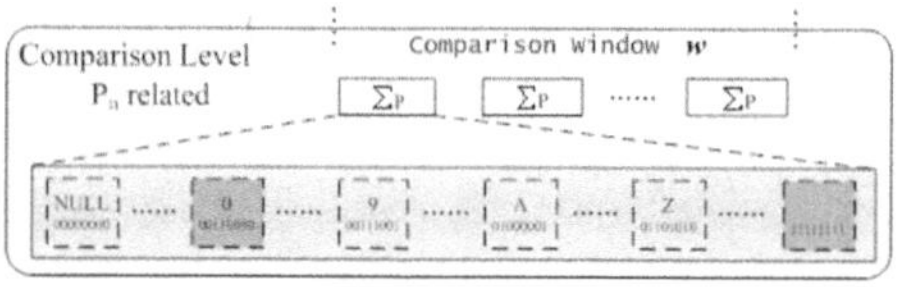

Fig. 5. Comparison level based on alphabet of pattern set in MPM

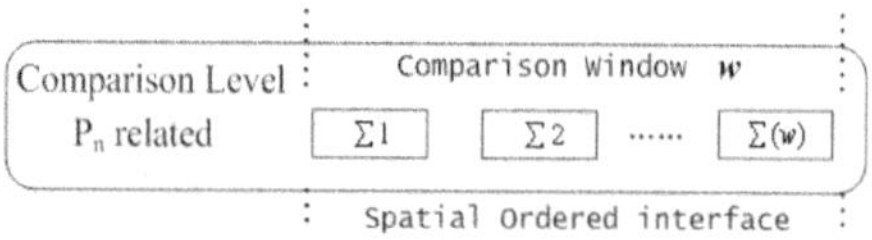

Fig. 6. Comparison level based on alphabet of vertical left alignment

To further condense the chip area of MPM, the sameness of all suits of comparison units should be modified first. We relate each character in comparison window with a separate suit of comparison units, signed as $\sum(j)(j=1,2,\cdots,w)$. That is, the *j*th character in comparison window is related with the suits of comparison units based on $\sum(j)$, as figure 6.

In figure 6, we face the problem how to calculate the alphabets of $\sum(j)$. In this paper, we use the method of *selected character decoding* based on definition 7, named SCD, to do the calculation. The details of SCD are discussed in [15]. In this paper, only conclusions are given. The alphabets of $\sum(j)$ is as equation 2.

$$\Sigma(j) = \begin{cases} \Sigma_1 \cup \Sigma_2 \cup \cdots \cup \Sigma_j & 1 \le j \le sh \\ \Sigma_j \cup \Sigma_{j-1} \cup \cdots \cup \Sigma_{j-sh+1} & sh < j \le w - sh + 1 \\ \Sigma_{j-sh+1} \cup \Sigma_{j-sh+2} \cup \cdots \cup \Sigma_{w-sh+1} & w - sh + 1 < j \le w \end{cases} \tag{2}$$

Based on the figure 6 and equation 2, the chip area of CL based on A*vla* can represent as follows:

$$AreaCL_{Avla} = \sum_{j=1}^{w} |\Sigma(j)| \times Area_{CmpUnit} \tag{3}$$

Temporary result level is used for storing comparison results of comparison level. It can save the results of current leftmost *sh* characters in comparison window and the results of previous $dp_{TL} \times sh$ characters. At the same time other comparison results from the comparison level are directly sent to next level, as figure 7 shows.

dp_{TL} is the depth of the registers, and the value of upper stage registers can be passed to the near lower stage each cycle. As a whole, the registers of these dp_{TL} stages can save the results of $dp_{TL} \times sh$ characters.

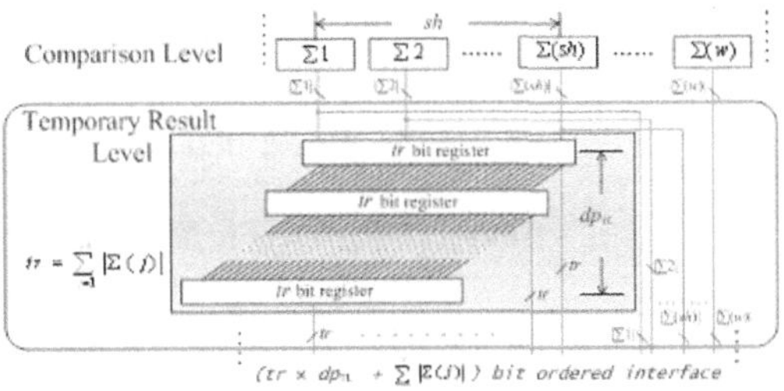

Fig. 7. Details of temporary result level in MPM

The output interface is composed by the outputs of registers and outputs of comparison level in this current cycle. The interface is spatial ordered, so more information can be represented rather than implicit express. Actually, this level is not the necessary one in MPM.

Pattern level (PL) is the level that patterns are really matched with the input. PL consists of all pattern logics in P_n. For each pattern, there are *sh* AND logics that match the selected *l* inputs from the above level. Each AND logic matches one alignment from 0 to *sh*-1, as figure 8 shows. The *l* inputs to each AND logic are correspondingly the ones that this pattern stands for with a certain alignment.

For example, if there is a pattern with content "ABCDE", the first AND logic selects the wire of "A" from the first group of wires in the interface, the wire "B" from the second group, …, the wire "E" from the fifth group. The AND of the five results can match pattern "ABCDE" with alignment of zero.

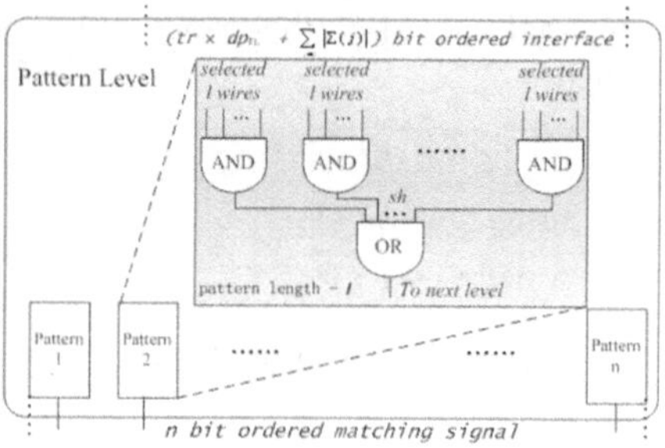

Fig. 8. Details of pattern level in MPM

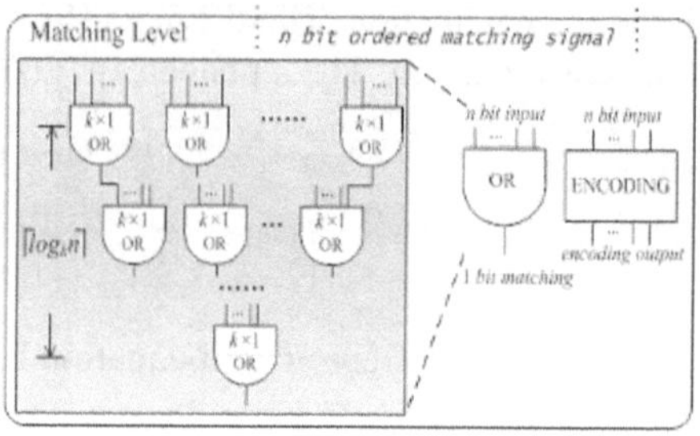

Fig. 9. Details of matching level in MPM

Matching level is the last one in MPM which outputs matching signals. Matching signals are the result of OR logic with n bit input, as figure 9 shows.

In fact, the size of pattern set is several thousand, relatively large, that is, n is big. The OR logic may result in $\lceil \log_k n \rceil$ stage. Here k is the input of each basic OR logic and $\lceil \# \rceil$ means the ceiling of the number.

4.3 Basic Theory About MPM

From the description of previous parts, we know that MPM can be parameterized by some parameters, as table 1 shows. The different combination of values can result in different MPM architectures with various performances.

Table 1. Parameters in MPM

Parameters	Belongings	Comments
WoC	ALL Levels	The width of character
sh	Shift Level	The bytes shifting left in one cycle
w	Shift Level	Width of comparison window
Type of Alphabet	Comp Level	*fA*, *Aps* or *Avla*
dp_{TL}	Temp Result	The depth of registers; value 0 means no temporary result level.
n	Pattern Level	The size of pattern set
h	Pattern Level	The input of basic AND and OR LOGIC using in this Level
k	Matching Level	The input of basic OR LOGIC using in this level

The maximal payload speed of network can be determined by MPM. Here we suppose that $Frequency_{MPM}$ is the typical frequency of MPM and $Speed_{payload}$ is the maximum speed for payload matching in network intrusion detection system. Then the following equation is obvious.

$$Speed_{payload} = sh \times WoC \times Frequency_{MPM} \tag{4}$$

Equation 4 comes from shift level of MPM. In this level, *sh* characters are shifting left every cycle, and each character is with the width of *WoC*. The cycle time is determined by frequency of MPM, $Frequency_{MPM}$.

From the figure 7, we know that only *w*-*sh*+1 alphabets can be placed in *w* width of comparison window. That is, the maximum length of pattern can be matched in MPM is *w*-*sh*+1 characters in the view of comparison level. Temporary result level is the level for temporarily storing the results of comparison level. Each stage of registers can save the results of *sh* characters and the dp_{TL} stages can save the results of $dp_{TL} \times sh$. This level is the important reinforce for characters' comparison. Based on these two levels, to P_n in MPM, the following should be satisfied.

$$(w - sh + 1 + dp_{TL} \times sh) \geq l^{max} \tag{5}$$

Equation 5 gives the restriction of MPM that implements a given pattern set. It means that the maximal width of comparison characters should be no less than the length of pattern set. Otherwise, some longer pattern cannot be matched.

5 Pattern Set Compiler

Pattern set compiler is a software that can convert a given pattern set to a proper format of codes which is later used in MPM architecture.

In this paper, pattern set compiler generates RTL (register transfer level) codes from a given pattern set and predefined parameters. The output codes are formatted in verilog language and are later synthesized by Xilinx ISE or other EDA tools. Figure 10 shows the procedure from given pattern set to MPM implementation. Together with Xilinx ISE, the routes can be regarded as a MPM generator.

Pattern set compiler also supports the updating of patterns. The output updated codes are also RTL ones with some instructions for reconfiguration.

6 Analyses and Results

Previous sections address many details about our MPM architecture and related theory. In this section, some analyses about MPM and results for real patterns of Snort are given to evaluate our design.

Snort[1,2] is a widely used open source NIDS system, and its patterns are very valuable for the research of pattern match architecture. Here, we choose the one release of Snort rules with version 2.3.3. After eliminating the redundant ones, we get a pattern set with 1785 different patterns, signed as pattern set P_{1785}.

For P_{1785}, there are 107(l^{max}) alphabets of vertical left alignment (A*vla*). Figure 11 shows the relationship between the size of each A*vla* and the length of pattern. We can find that the size of A*vla* is decreasing rapidly with the increasing of the length of patterns. The reason is that they are fewer patterns with longer length.

Three types of alphabets (*f*A, A*ps* and A*vla*) are used for the construction of comparison levels. They may result in different chip areas.

Here suppose that dp_{TL}=0, w-sh+1=l^{max} and $WoC = 8$, that is, there is no temporary result level and the patterns in P_{1785} can be compared in one cycle.

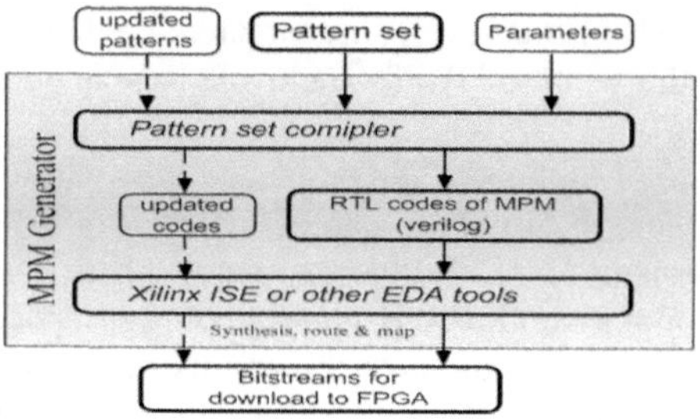

Fig. 10. MPM generator and pattern set compiler

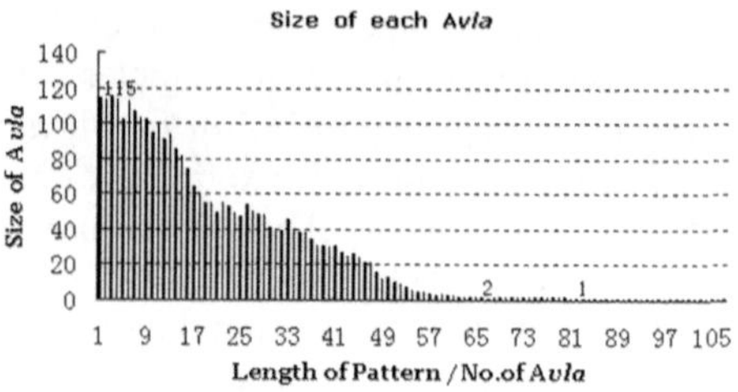

Fig. 11. Size of Avla and length of pattern

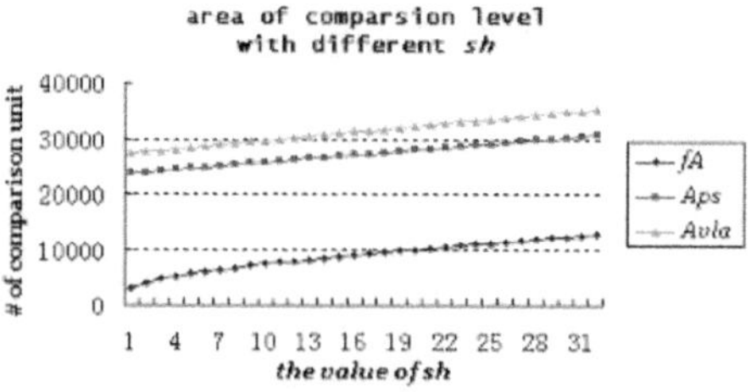

Fig. 12. Area of comparison level with different *sh*

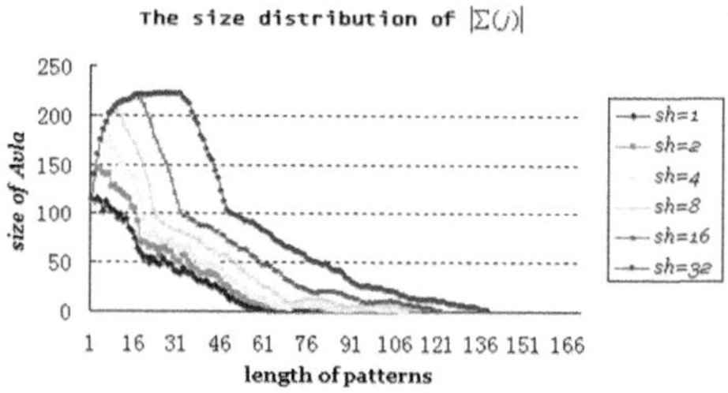

Fig. 13. The size distribution with different *sh*

According to the figure 4 and 5, the areas based on *f*A and A*ps* are as follows:

$$AreaCL_{fA} = (107 + sh - 1) \times 256 \times Area_{CmpUnit} \tag{6}$$

$$AreaCL_{Aps} = (107 + sh - 1) \times 222 \times Area_{CmpUnit} \tag{7}$$

Because equation 2 is heavily related with *sh*, the result of $AreaCL_{Avla}$ is hardly to be represented as a formula. However $AreaCL_{Avla}$ can be calculated by equation 2&3.

Figure 12 shows the areas of comparison level based on *f*A, A*ps* and A*vla* with different value of *sh* from 1 to 32. The area of comparison level is calculated as the number of basic comparison units. The upper line is the $AreaCL_{fA}$ with different *sh*. The middle line is $AreaCL_{Aps}$ and the bottom one is the $AreaCL_{Avla}$ with different *sh*.

The distribution of A*vlas*' size is the key for the insight analysis of the reason why area using A*vla* is efficient. Figure 13 shows this distribution with different value of *sh*. In this figure, the curves of upper and left are with the bigger value of *sh*.

Taking consideration of speed and chip area, results of our MPM architecture are drawn from the synthesis tools, as table 2 shows.

Table 2 shows the comparison with other architectures on FPGA, which use logics of FPGA to do the matching other than the DFA based architectures. We can find that MPM uses about one half chip area than the most area efficient architecture. At the same time, its performance with 5 pipelines is the highest among all the architectures. More pipelines do not increase the chip area of MPM architecture.

Table 2. Comparisons with other architectures on FPGA

Architectures	slice/char	speed(Gbps)	Notes
MPM in this paper	0.22	4.3 or more	Virtex-2
Cho-MSmith [9]	5.2	2.8	Virtex-E
Pre-decoded CAMs [10]	0.64	2.68	Virtex-2
Bloom Filter [14]	8.9	0.5	Virtex-E
Decoder NFA [8]	~0.55	2.0	Virtex-2
USC Unary [22]	0.46	2.1	Virtex-2

7 Conclusions

This paper has presented a highly parameterized multilevel pattern matching architecture on FPGA, named MPM, for less chip area and higher performance. MPM can be embedded into network intrusion detection or prevention systems to achieve higher performance. The parameterized MPM can fit for many circumstances, such as UTM, spam filter, and et al.

In this paper, MPM is in-depth analyzed and designed. Then a pattern set compiler is presented that can convert pattern set to RTL code of MPM architecture. That is, for a given pattern set, a pattern matching architecture can be generated by some definitions of parameters.

For Snort patterns, a prototype system is generated. The experimental results show that the example MPM can achieve 4.3Gbps matching speed with 5 stages of pipelines. The chip area is about half of the best one that is known in literature. With the different parameters, the performance of MPM can be scalable near linearly, potential for more than 100Gbps throughput if chip area is not concerned.

References

1. M. Roesch, "Snort - Lightweight Intrusion Detection for Networks," *USENIX LISA Conference*, 1999
2. Xilinx : www.xilinx.com
3. M. Fisk and G. Varghese. An analysis of fast string matching applied to content-based forwarding and intrusion detection. In *Techical Report CS2001- 0670*, University of California -San Diego, 2002.
4. S. Dharmapurikar, et al.: Implementation of a Deep Packet Inspection Circuit using Parallel Bloom Filters in Reconfigurable Hardware; In *Hot Interconnects*, 2003.
5. R. Sidhu, V. K. Prasanna: Fast Regular Expression Matching using FPGAs. In *Proceedings of 9th IEEE Symposium on Field-Programmable Custom Computing Machines*, April 2001
6. I. Sourdis, D. Pnevmatikatos: Pre-decoded CAMs for Efficient and High-Speed NIDS Pattern Matching. In *IEEE Symposium on Field- Programmable Custom Computing Machines*, 2004
7. I. Sourdis, D. Pnevmatikatos: Fast, Large-Scale string matching for a 10Gbps FPGA-based network intrusion detection system. In *Proceedings of 13th International Conference on Field Programmable Logic and Applications*, Lisbon, Portugal, 2003.

8. C. R. Clark, D. E. Schimmel: Scalable Pattern Matching for High Speed Networks; In *IEEE Symposium on Field-Programmable Custom Computing Machines*, April 2004. Napa, CA, USA.
9. Young H. Cho, William H. Mangione-Smith: Deep packet filter with dedicated logic and read only memories. In *IEEE Symposium on Field-Programmable Custom Computing Machines*, 2004 USA.
10. Peter Sutton: Partial Character Decoding for Improved Regular Expression Matching in FPGAs; In *Proceedings of International Conference on Field-Programmable Technology*, 2004
11. Chris Clark, Wenke Lee, et al: A Hardware Platform for Network Intrusion Detection and Prevention. In *Proceedings of 3rd Workshop on Network Processors and Applications*, Spain, February 2004.
12. S. Dharmapurikar, P. Krishnamurthy, et al: Deep packet inspection using bloom filters. In *Hot Interconnects*, August 2003. Stanford.
13. R. Sidhu and V. K. Prasanna. Fast Regular Expression Matching using FPGAs. In *IEEE Symposium on Field-Programmable Custom Computing Machines*, Napa Valley, CA, April 2001. IEEE.
14. James Moscola, John Lockwood, Ronald P. Loui, and Michael Pachos. *Implementation of a content-scanning module for an internet firewall.* In *IEEE Symposium on Field- Programmable Custom Computing Machines*, April 2003. Napa, CA, USA
15. Tian Song, Wei Zhang, Zhizhong Tang, Dongsheng Wang: "Alphabet Based Selected Character Decoding for Area Efficient Pattern Matching Architecture on FPGAs"; the 2nd International Conference on Embedded Software and Systems (ICESS-05), Xian, P.R.China
16. Jan van Lunteren. High-Performance Pattern-Matching for Intrusion Detection. In *25th Conference of IEEE INFOCOM,* Apr. 2006
17. Lin Tan, T. Sherwood. A High Throughput String Matching Architecture for Intrusion Detection and Prevention. In *32nd Annual ISCA*, June, 2005
18. R.S. Boyer, J.S. Moore: A Fast String Searching Algorithm; Communications of the ACM 20, 10, 762-772 (1977).
19. Knuth D.E., Morris J.H., Pratt V.R.: Fast pattern matching in strings; SIAM Journal on Computing. 1977,6(1): 323-350
20. A. Aho and M. Corasick: Efficient string matching: An aid to bibliographic search; Communications of the ACM, vol. 18, no. 6, June 1975, pp. 333-343.
21. Sun Wu and Udi Manber: A fast algorithm for multi-pattern searching; Tech. Rep. TR94-17, Department of Computer Science, University of Arizona, May 1994
22. Z. K. Baker, V. K. Prasanna. High-throughput linked-pattern matching for intrusion detection systems. In *symposium on Architecture for Networking and Communications Systems* (ANCS), Oct. 2005

Smart Actuator-Based Fault-Tolerant Control for Networked Safety-Critical Embedded Systems

Inseok Yang[1], Donggil Kim[2], Kyungmin Kang[2], Dongik Lee[2], and Kyungsik Yoon[3]

[1] Dept. Industrial Applied Mathematics, Kyungpook National University, 1370, Sankyug-dong, Buk-gu, Daegu, 702-701, Korea
jewill@hanmail.net

[2] School of Electrical Engineering & Computer Science, Kyungpook National University, 1370, Sankyug-dong, Buk-gu, Daegu, 702-701, Korea
{eastroad,rapdk,dilee}@ee.knu.ac.kr

[3] Dept. Digital Information Media, Gimcheon College, 754, Samrak-dong, Gimcheon, 740-704, Korea
kyungsy@gimcheon.ac.kr

Abstract. In this paper, a fault-tolerant control method is presented with an application to steer-by-wire (SBW) system. SBW is a network-based vehicle steering system in which the mechanical linkage and hydraulics are replaced by electrical motors and fieldbus networks. Since failure of a steering system may result in a catastrophic accident, SBW can be considered as a safety-critical embedded system for which very high level of dependability must be satisfied. This paper proposes an effective control strategy to tolerate faulty actuators. The proposed method has a simple structure to be implemented on low cost embedded processors. The reconfiguration strategy consists of two fold: i) a smart actuator of which embedded microprocessor provides the fast and accurate diagnostic information through a time-triggered fieldbus, and ii) an IMC-PID controller which is capable of tolerating the effect of faults based on the diagnostic information being sent from the smart actuator. Simulation results with a SBW model show that the proposed method can enhance the system dependability in the presence of faults without using any redundant actuators.

1 Introduction

Recent advances in microelectronics have made the application of networked architectures, based on smart components and fieldbuses, to safety-critical embedded systems, such as "steer-by-wire (SBW)" system for automobiles. SBW is a networked steering system for next-generation vehicles, in which the mechanical linkage and hydraulics are replaced by electric motors and fieldbus networks. Since failure of a steering system may result in a catastrophic accident, SBW has to meet the strict requirements on system dependability. That is, a SBW system must be able to continue its function even in the presence of fault with subcomponents, such as fieldbuses, sensors and actuators.

Y.-H. Lee et al. (Eds.): ICESS 2007, LNCS 4523, pp. 615–626, 2007.

To satisfy the required level of dependability for a networked safety-critical embedded system at a reasonable cost, Lee highlighted that the system should be in a time-triggered architecture with a fault-tolerant controller and smart devices that are interconnected through a deterministic fieldbus in [9]. The importance of fieldbus is of paramount as a SBW system is built on the basis of communication networks. Over the last two decades automotive industry has paid significant effort to develop highly reliable and deterministic fieldbus technologies, so called time-triggered protocols, such as TTP/C [17] and FlexRay [3]. TTP/C or FlexRay offers many advantages that can enhance the network performance in terms of fault-tolerance and deterministic temporal behaviour.

Apart from the fieldbus protocols, a survey reveals that actuator problems are the most common cause for the deterioration of a controlled system [7]. In response to this concern, control engineers have paid a great deal of attention to fault-tolerant control techniques. Fault-tolerant control is a set of techniques to provide the system with the ability of graceful degradation; that is, to maintain the desired performance of the system in case of faults with sensors or actuators [1], [14]. While sensor faults can be tolerated by applying a model-based estimation technique, compensating actuator faults requires controller reconfiguration and/or redundant actuators. However, employing redundant actuators often leads to extra costs, more power consumptions and complexity in the resulting system. Therefore, reconfigurable control techniques have been exploited as an effective solution to deal with actuator faults. A reconfigurable controller can change its parameters and/or structure to maintain the desired performance when a fault occurs. See [1] and [14] for a survey on the previous work.

In general a reconfigurable controller consists of a Fault Detection and Isolation (FDI) module and a reconfiguration mechanism. When a fault occurs the reconfiguration mechanism redesigns the control system on-line based on the diagnostic information provided by the FDI module. However, most of the previous work has only focused on the systems with a centralized architecture for which the design of an FDI module is very difficult and limited. FDI with a centralized system can be inaccurate and slow due to the limitations with measured data and the accuracy of mathematical model used. Consequently, the reconfigured system often leads to an unsatisfactory or even an unstable system.

This paper presents a reconfigurable control method for safety-critical embedded systems with a networked architecture in which smart actuators are interconnected through a time-triggered fieldbus. The proposed method utilizes the benefits of deterministic fieldbus and local diagnosis being performed by the smart actuator. The reconfiguration mechanism consists of two fold:

- An accurate and fast FDI module, which is independent of actuator types and calculated by the local processor of smart actuator; and
- An IMC-PID controller, of which parameter can be readjusted based on the diagnostic information being sent from the smart actuator through a fieldbus.

The IMC (Internal Model Control) technique is adopted for the online tuning of PID parameters in the event of fault with actuators. The proposed method is applied to a SBW system, and its effectiveness is analysed using computer simulations.

2 Networked System Architectures

Networked embedded systems, as shown in Fig. 1, can be found across wide range of industry, including process automation and automobiles. Not only does a networked control system offer reduced wiring and simplified maintenance, it also provides the opportunity to implement more sophisticated control laws. However, incorporating a real-time communication network presents significant challenges to the system designers. Design requirements are no longer justified simply by 'system and control', but the networked nature of systems are drawing greater attention. One of the most significant difficulties induced by a communication network is the randomly varying delays in delivering messages. These delays can cause the system performance degraded or even unstable [13]. In response to this concern, many researchers in the control society have developed a number of techniques to overcome the problems. For examples, Luck & Ray [11] applied an observer based compensator, while Chan & Ozguner [2] proposed a solution based on the queues. For latest outcomes, refer to [16] and [19]. However, many of these approaches only try to solve the problem without using a deterministic communication protocol. Consequently, the resulting approaches are often too complicated or non-deterministic to be used in embedded systems such as SBW.

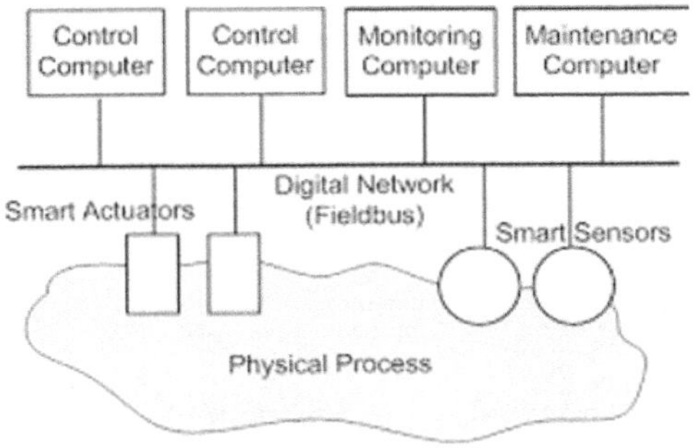

Fig. 1. A networked control system

Meanwhile, automotive industry has focused on the development of deterministic communication protocols to overcome the network related problems. Time-triggered protocols, such as TTP/C and FlexRay, are the outcome from such effort by automotive industry. By adopting a time-triggered protocol based on a precise and accurate global time reference, it is possible to achieve deterministic temporal behaviour of a networked system. In addition, such deterministic behaviour helps to enhance the system dependability in a great deal, while minimizing the system complexity.

In this paper, it is assumed that the controlled system is implemented on the basis of a time-triggered protocol. This assumption leads to the development of a fault-tolerant control method which is efficient, simple, and reliable. Further discussions about the needs for the integration of time-triggered approaches with fault-tolerant control techniques in safety-critical applications can be found in [9].

3 Smart Actuator

3.1 Fault Accommodation Using Smart Actuator

A smart actuator is an actuator system that can offer additional functionality achieved by the built-in processor and fieldbus network. By utilizing a built- in processor it is possible to implement advanced control techniques, such as fault diagnosis and nonlinearity compensation. Key features of the smart actuators are classified into four categories:

- Self diagnosis;
- Self compensation;
- Validation data; and
- Fieldbus interfaces.

In addition to the capability of self diagnosis, the smart actuator can also offer the opportunity for self compensation of the fault, for example, using a nonlinearity inverse method [10]. As shown in Fig. 2, the extra information or condition data is transmitted to the higher level supervisor module by which the loop controller can be reconfigured to accommodate the fault with an actuator. For this strategy to be realistic, it is necessary to develop not only an accurate and fast FDI module, but also an efficient and reliable reconfiguration mechanism. Since they must be implemented in real-time on low-cost embedded microprocessors, it is crucial to design both modules using simple techniques.

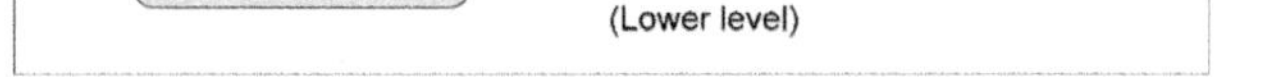

Fig. 2. Reconfiguration structure with smart actuator

To comply with the above requirements, this paper aims to develop:

- An FDI module requiring no sophisticated mathematical models;
- A PID type reconfigurable control method requiring no hardware redundancy.

In general the embedded processors for smart actuators have very limited computing resources. Therefore, any fault diagnosis algorithms requiring a sophisticated mathematical model are unrealistic. Meanwhile, PID type controllers are chosen because of the fact that they are most commonly used in industry, and have the simplest structure to be implemented on a low cost processor. The constraint with the use of redundant actuators is introduced by the fact that redundant actuators are often not available due to the limitation of cost, space, power consumptions, etc.

3.2 Modeling of Smart Actuator

By assuming that the actuator is only operating within the attainable range, the dynamics of smart actuators can be represented by a first order model [8]:

$$G = \frac{K}{\tau s + 1} \tag{1}$$

Note that the structure of the model is virtually independent of the type of actuators because it only represents the relationship between the input and the output of actuator.

Any faults with the actuator may result in a change of actuator dynamics. For example, increased friction caused by a faulty bearing of electric motor can lead to a sluggish angular velocity. Degraded actuator dynamics degraded affect the performance of the controlled system. For compensating the actuator fault, therefore, it is very useful to estimate the parameters τ and K from Eq (1) in the event of fault. The estimates of these parameters can be transmitted through a fieldbus network to the supervisor module by which the loop controller can be reconfigured so as to compensate for the loss of actuation force due to the fault.

3.3 Estimation Method

In this paper, an analytical estimation algorithm proposed by Yang *et al.* [18] is employed to determine the new parameters of τ and K when a fault occurs. The estimation is performed locally inside the smart actuator. Details of the algorithm are presented in [18], and this paper only gives a brief summary.

The estimation method requires no recursive calculations, but the parameters are calculated based on the performance index $\gamma(t)$ which is defined by the ratio between the actual and desired performance of the actuator as follow:

$$\gamma(t) = \frac{\text{actual performance}}{\text{desired performance}} = \frac{\int_0^t u_a(\sigma)d\sigma}{\int_0^t u_d(\sigma)d\sigma} \tag{2}$$

where, u_a is the actual output of the actuator and u_d is the desired input. Using this index the actuator performance can be uniquely represented. Based on the performance index, the rate factor $\alpha(t)$ for the demand input $u_d(t) = t^n$ can be written as follow:

$$\alpha(t) = \frac{u_a(t)}{\gamma(t)}$$

$$= \frac{\dfrac{1}{n+1} t^{n+1} kn! \left\{ \sum_{p=0}^{n} \dfrac{(-\tau)^{n-p} t^p}{p!} + \dfrac{(-\tau)^{n+1} e^{-\frac{t}{\tau}}}{\tau} \right\}}{kn! \left\{ \sum_{p=0}^{n} \dfrac{(-\tau)^{n-p} t^{p+1}}{(p+1)!} - (-\tau)^{n+1} \left(e^{-\frac{t}{\tau}} - 1 \right) \right\}} \tag{3}$$

For a step input, Eq (3) can be reduced to:

$$\alpha(t)=\frac{t\left\{1-e^{-\frac{t}{\tau}}\right\}}{t+\tau e^{-\frac{t}{\tau}}-\tau} \tag{4}$$

It is clear that α(t) is a continuous decreasing function which satisfies $\lim_{t\to 0}\alpha(t)=2$ and $\lim_{t\to\infty}\alpha(t)=1$. And, when $t=\tau$, it holds that $\alpha(\tau)=e-1$. Thus, by the theorem of intermediate value, τ is the unique value which satisfies $\alpha(\tau)=e-1$. Since $u_a(t)$ and $\gamma(t)$ are known, it is possible to calculate α(t) and determine whether α(t) is equal to $(e-1)$ or not for every time t. Conversely, for an arbitrary point of time t, if $\alpha(t)=e-1$, then it is true that $t=\tau$. Once the parameter τ is determined, the parameter K is calculated as follow:

$$K=\frac{e}{\gamma(\tau)} \tag{5}$$

For the calculation of the parameters in a discrete system, refer to [18].

4 Design of Reconfigurable IMC-PID Controller

4.1 Basic Concept of IMC

The Internal Model Control (IMC) structure in Fig. 3 is a well-known technique mainly developed by Morari and his co-workers [4], [5], [6], [12], [15].

The estimation method requires no recursive calculations, but the parameters are calculated based on the performance index γ(t) which is defined by the ratio between the actual and desired performance of the actuator as follow:

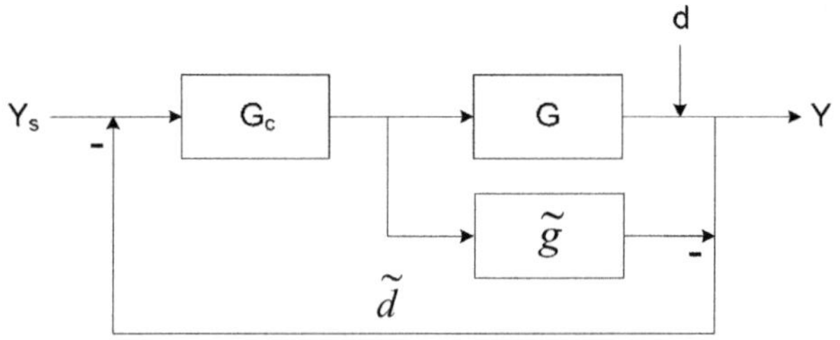

Fig. 3. The IMC structure. G and $\tilde{g}$ denote the transfer functions of actual plant and model.

Some important properties of the IMC structure are as follow:

Property 1 - Dual Stability. Assume perfect match ($\tilde{g}=G$). Then the system is effectively open-loop, and closed-loop stability is implied by the stability of G and

G_C. The IMC structure guarantees the closed-loop stability for all stable controller G_C and G.

Property 2 - Perfect Control. Assume IMC controller G_C is given by reciprocal of the model $\tilde{g}$, i.e., $G_C = \tilde{g}^{-1}$, and the system is stable. Then perfect control is archived for all t and disturbance d, i.e., $Y = Y_S \quad \forall t > 0$.

Note that Property 2 cannot be realized for a system with right-half plane zeros and time delay. However, despite these limitations, the IMC structure can be realized through the following steps.

Firstly, factorizing the process model yields to

$$\tilde{g} = \tilde{g}_+ \cdot \tilde{g}_- \tag{6}$$

Note that, in Eq. (6), all the time delays and right-half plane zeros are included in the term $\tilde{g}_+$, and thus $\tilde{g}_-$ is always stable. Now $\tilde{g}_+$ is factorized such that the integrated absolute error (IAE) can be minimized:

$$\tilde{g}_+ = e^{-\theta s} \prod_i (-\beta_i s + 1), \quad \text{where } \mathrm{Re}(\beta_i) > 0 \tag{7}$$

The second step is to define the IMC controller as the form of:

$$G_C = \tilde{g}_-^{-1} \cdot f \tag{8}$$

where, f is a low pass filter with a unit steady state gain. It is straightforward that the simplest form for f can be given as below:

$$f = \frac{1}{(\varepsilon s + 1)^r} \tag{9}$$

where, r denotes the order of filter, which should be sufficiently large to guarantee that the resulting IMC controller G_C is proper. By defining G_C it is possible to determine a PID controller c that can be applied to virtually all types of processes in industry. The resulting PID controller is given in the form of:

$$c = \frac{G_c}{1 - \tilde{g} \cdot G_c} = \frac{\tilde{g}_-^{-1}}{f^{-1} - \tilde{g}_+} \tag{10}$$

4.2 Reconfiguration in Case of Actuator Fault

The closed-loop dynamics of an actuator, represented by Eq (1), may change in the event of fault with any components of the actuator. Since the parameters for modified actuator dynamics are estimated and provided by the smart actuator, the reconfiguration mechanism can determine $\tilde{g}_-$ which is then applied to the calculation of a new control parameter. If a minimum phase model ($\tilde{g}_+ = 1$) and a first-order filter are used, then the closed-loop transfer function with a feedback controller c can be given:

$$c = \frac{1}{\varepsilon} \cdot \frac{\tilde{g}_-^{-1}}{s} \tag{11}$$

$$\frac{Y}{Y_S} = \frac{1}{\varepsilon s + 1} \tag{12}$$

Note that there is only one adjustable design parameter, ε, which could be chosen by the designer. This fact is a significant benefit in terms of designing a controller. For designing a reconfigurable IMC-PID controller, the actuator can be considered as a minimum phase model. Once $\tilde{g}_-$ is obtained from the local diagnostic module of the smart actuator, ε can be then determined to place the pole at the desired location which is chosen by the designer.

5 Simulation Results and Discussion

5.1 Modeling of SBW System

The effectiveness of the proposed control method is analysed with a rack-pinion type SBW system shown in Fig. 4. The measured angular position of the steering wheel is converted to the corresponding displacement of the pinion, which is then transmitted to the SBW controller via a FlexRay network. The SBW controller then determines the required control signal for driving the BLDC motor so that the desired direction of each road wheel can be achieved. The proposed IMC-PID method is applied to the design of a reconfigurable controller for the given SBW system.

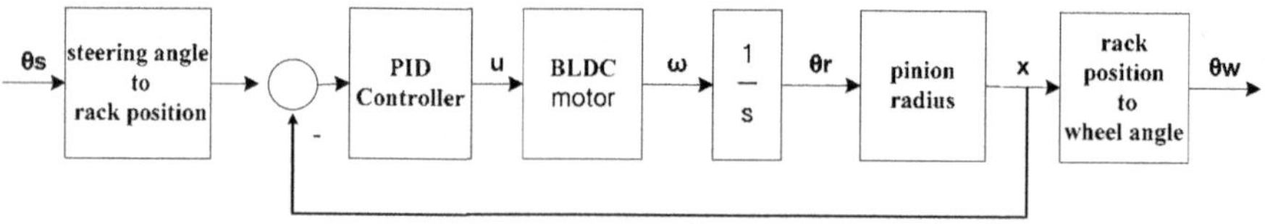

Fig. 4. Block diagram for the SBW control system

The mathematical model of the BLDC motor used in the design of IMC-PID is represented by a first-order model:

$$\frac{\omega(s)}{V(s)} = \frac{K}{\tau s + 1} \tag{13}$$

where, V and w represent the input voltage and angular velocity, respectively, and K and τ are given as follows:

$$K = \frac{1}{k_E} \tag{14}$$

$$\tau = \frac{R \cdot J}{k_E \cdot k_T} \tag{15}$$

Details of the parameters used in the simulation are summarized in table 1.

Table 1. BLDC motor specifications used for the computer simulations

Parameter	Definition	Value
R	Stator resistance	$21.2[\Omega]$
k_E	Back emf constant	$0.1433[V \cdot s / rad]$
k_T	Torque constant	$0.1433[Kg \cdot m / A]$
J	Inertia of rotor	$1 \cdot 10^{-5}[Kg \cdot m \cdot s^2 / rad]$

Using the specifications shown in table 1, the transfer function, Eq (13), of the BLDC motor during normal operation is represented by:

$$G(s) = \frac{6.978}{0.01s + 1} \tag{16}$$

The filter coefficient of the IMC controller is set to 0.5, and the PD controller is given by:

$$C(s) = 0.0001s + 0.009 \tag{17}$$

The sampling period is chosen as T=0.001sec.

5.2 Simulation Results

Estimating the actuator parameters: In order to verify the effectiveness of the proposed method, a fault with the BLDC motor is injected. It is assumed that the stator resistance R is changed abruptly at t=30sec, resulting in the change of the actuator time constant from τ=0.01sec to τ=0.4sec, or the actuator dynamics with fault is modified to: The filter coefficient of the IMC controller is set to 0.5, and the PD controller is given by:

$$G(s) = \frac{6.978}{0.4s + 1} \tag{18}$$

Fig. 5 shows the trajectory of the rate factor $\alpha(t)$ which will be used for estimating the actuator parameters τ and K. From Fig. 6 it is clear that the time at which $\alpha(t)$ is equal to (e-1) is around t=0.4sec. Accurate calculations identify that $\alpha(0.401)$

<e-1<α(0.402), indicating that T_l is given by 0.402sec. Applying T_l=0.402sec to the estimation method by [18] yields to $\hat{\tau} = 0.4012$ and $\hat{K} = 6.9881$, which are very close to the true values.

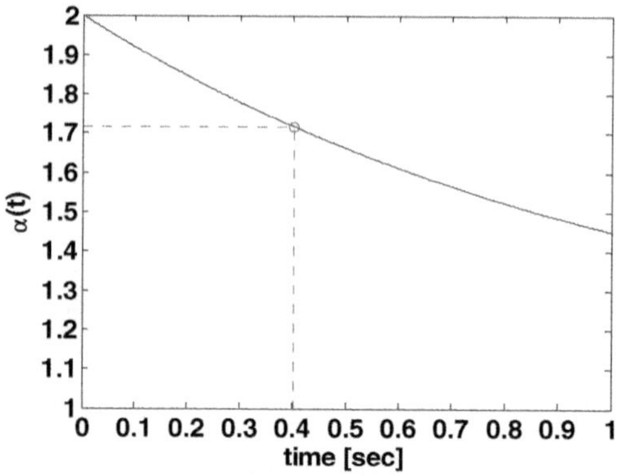

Fig. 5. Trajectory of the rate factor α(t) used for diagnosing the actuator fault

Controller reconfiguration:_Fig. 6 shows the response of the SBW system in the event of fault after t=30sec. Since the BLDC motor has become sluggish due to the fault, the SBW system output shows a large overshoot which may result in a dangerous driving situation.

On the other hand, by reconfiguring the controller based on the diagnostic information on the modified actuator dynamics, the control system can tolerate the fault without using a redundant actuator, as shown in Fig. 7. It is seen that about 0.5sec was taken to diagnose and compensate for the fault. Note that the reconfigured system has a larger settling time compared as the normal condition. However, by giving a warning signal to the driver about the fault it may still be possible to control the vehicle with care.

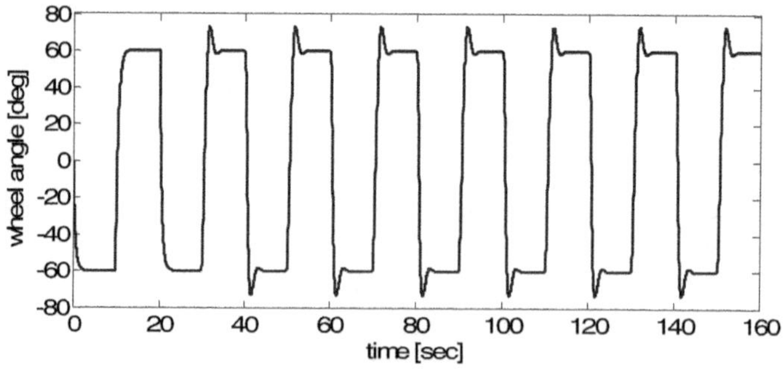

Fig. 6. Output trajectory of SBW system without reconfiguration

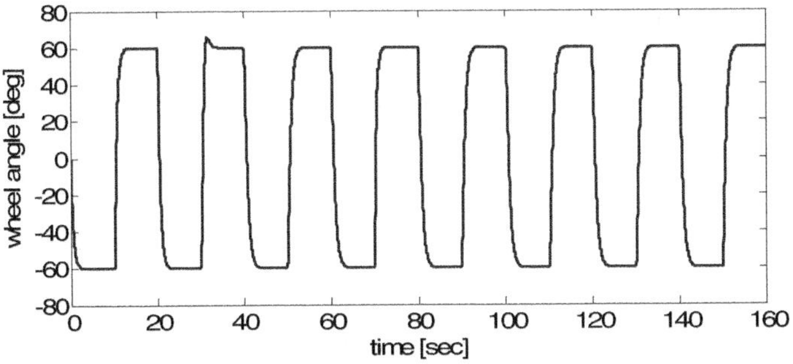

Fig. 7. Output trajectory of SBW system with reconfiguration using the estimated parameters

6 Concluding Remarks

In this paper a reconfigurable control method for safety-critical embedded systems with a time-triggered network has been presented. The proposed method utilizes the benefits of deterministic fieldbus and local diagnosis carried out inside the smart actuator. The reconfiguration mechanism consists of a fault diagnosis module and an IMC-PID controller. By assuming that the actuator dynamics can be represented by a first order model independent of the actuator types, it is possible to obtain fast and accurate diagnostic information on the actuator characteristics with fault. This information is now exploited by the IMC-PID controller so as to compensate for the effect of fault. The proposed IMC-PID control technique is applied to a SBW system. Simulation results with the SBW system indicate that the proposed method can tolerate the fault without using any redundant actuators. For the future work, it is planned to implement the proposed method in real-time with a real SBW system incorporating a FlexRay network.

References

1. Blanke, M., Kinnaert, M., Lunze, J., Staroswiecki, M.: Diagnosis and Fault-Tolerant Control. Springer (2003)
2. Chan, H., Ozguner, U.: Closed-loop Control of Systems over a Communication Network with Queues. International J. Control. Vol. 62, No. 3 (1995) 493-510
3. FlexRay Consortium.: FlexRay Communications System Specifications (ver 2.1). Available http://www.flexray.com (2005)
4. Garcia, C.E., Morari, M.: Internal Model Control 1. A Unifying Review and Some New Results. Ind. Eng. Process Des. Dev. Vol. 21 (1982) 308-323
5. Garcia, C.E., Morari, M.: Internal Model Control 2. Design Procedure for Multivariable Systems. Ind. Eng. Process Des. Dev. Vol. 24 (1985) 472-484
6. Garcia, C.E., Morari, M.: Internal Model Control 3. Multivariable Control Law Computation and Tuning Guidelines. Ind. Eng. Process Des. Dev. Vol. 24 (1985) 484-494
7. Harrold, D.: Select and Size Control Valves Properly to Save Money. Control Engineering. October (1999) 55-60

8. Isermann, R., Raab, U.: Intelligent Actuators-ways to Autonomous Actuating Systems. Automatica. Vol. 19, No. 5 (1993) 1315–1331
9. Lee, D.: Distributed Real-Time Fault-Tolerant Control Using Smart Actuators and Time-Triggered Communication. PhD Thesis, Dept. Auto. Contr. & Syst. Eng., Sheffield University, U.K
10. Lee, D., Allan, J., Thompson, H.A., Bennett, S.: PID Control for a Distributed System with a Smart Actuator. Cont. Eng. Prac. Vol. 9 (2001) 1235–1244
11. Luck, R., Ray, A.: An Observer-based Compensator for Distributed Delays. Automatica. Vol. 26, No. 5 (1990) 903-908
12. Morari, M., Zafiriou, E.: Robust Process Control. Prentice-Hall (1989)
13. Nilsson, J.: Real-time Control Systems with Delays. PhD Thesis, Lund Institute of Technology, Sweden (1998)
14. Patton, R.J.: Fault-tolerant control: the 1997 situation (survey). Proceedings of the IFAC SAFEPROCESS, U.K. (1997) 1033-1055
15. Rivera, D.E., Morari, M., Skogestad, S.: Internal Model Control 4. PID Controller Design. Ind. Eng. Process Des. Dev. Vol. 25 (1986) 252-265
16. Tipsuwan, Y., Chow, M.Y.: Control methodologies in networked control systems. Cont. Eng. Prac. Vol. 11 (2003) 1099-1111
17. TTP/C.: TTP/C Specifications. Available http://www.ttagroup.org (1993)
18. Yang, I., Kim, D., Kang, K., Lee, D., Yoon, K.: Estimating actuator characteristics with faults. To be appeared on Proc. IFAC Workshop on Dependable Control of Discrete Systems (DCDS07), Paris, France, June (2007)
19. Yang, T.C.: Networked control system a brief survey. IEE Proc. Control Theory Appl. Vol. 153, No. 4 (2006) 403-412

KCT-Based Group Key Management Scheme in Clustered Wireless Sensor Networks

Huifang Chen[1,2], Hiroshi Mineno[2], Yoshitsugu Obashi[3], Tomohiro Kokogawa[3], and Tadanori Mizuno[2]

[1] Dept. of Information Science and Electronic Engineering, Zhejiang University
No. 38, Zheda Road, Hangzhou 310027, P.R. China
chenhf@zju.edu.cn
[2] Dept. of Computer Science, Shizuoka University
3-5-1 Johoku, Hamamatsu, Shizuoka 432-8011, Japan
{mineno,mizuno}@inf.shizuoka.ac.jp
[3] NTT Service Integration Lab., NTT Corporation
3-9-11 Midori, Musashino, Tokyo 180-8585, Japan
{obashi.yoshitsugu,tomohiro.kokogawa}@lab.ntt.co.jp

Abstract. Confidentiality, integrity, and authentication services are critical to preventing an adversary from compromising the security of a Wireless Sensor Network (WSN). An essential component of any key-based security solution is managing the encryption keys to providing this protection. Hence, we propose a novel group key management scheme based on the key-chain tree mechanism for the clustered WSNs in this paper. In this scheme, the functions of key management are decoupled and distributed among multiple network elements of the clustered WSNs for providing compromise/failure resistance. This scheme also supports rekeying to enhance network security and survivability against the node capture. Analysis results show that the scheme does provide a secure encryption of the messages even if the revoked sensor nodes collude with each other or the cluster head is compromised.

1 Introduction

Wireless Sensor Networks (WSNs), which consist of many inexpensive sensor nodes, are stimulating toward diverse deployments for a wide range of applications [1]. Sensor nodes are significantly constrained in the amount of resources in term of computing and communication capabilities, storage capacity, battery-powered energy. Furthermore, WSNs may be deployed in the hostile and unattended environments where communication is monitored and sensor nodes are subject to capture and surreptitious use by an adversary. However, many applications are dependent on the secure operation of WSNs, and have serious consequences if the network is compromised. Therefore, WSNs require secure communications, sensor capture detection, key revocation and sensor nodes disabling, etc.

Confidentiality, integrity, and authentication services are critical to preventing an adversary from compromising the security of a WSN. Perrig et al. gave an overview

Y.-H. Lee et al. (Eds.): ICESS 2007, LNCS 4523, pp. 627–640, 2007.

of security related issues and services required for WSNs in [2]. Most prior work has focused on the energy-efficient key management [3], authentication [4], routing [5] and Denial-of-Service (DoS) resistance [6]. In WSN security, a very important challenge is the design of key management schemes. The objective of key management schemes is to establish and maintain secure channels among communication parties. Typically, key management schemes use administrative keys for the secure distribution, generation of the communication keys to the communication parties. Communication keys may be pair-wise keys used to secure a communication channel between two sensor nodes, or they may be group keys shared by numerous sensor nodes.

Moreover, to ensure the scalability and increase the efficiency of network operations, clustering approaches have become an emerging technology for building scalable, robust, energy-efficient WSN applications. Operations in a WSN are inherently collaborative, where sensor nodes forming the WSN collectively perform a task. Thus, secure group communication should be utilized to support efficient operations in the clustered WSNs. Secure group communication requires that each authorized member of a secure network has knowledge of one or more communication key(s) shared by a group(s) of sensor nodes. When a sensor node is compromised and performs anomalous behaviors [7], it is necessary to exclude this sensor node and revoke the communication key(s) known by it in order to guarantee the security. Based on a key management scheme, the new communication keys are generated and distributed to the remaining group members in the secure mode, and these new keys should not be obtained by the excluded member. Therefore, group key management scheme is a core component in any secure group communication.

In this paper, we present a new solution for the group key management problem in clustered WSNs, which is based on a Dual Directional Key Chains (DDKC) structure that two one-way key chains to facilitate node(s) revocation. This scheme decouples the responsibilities of key management and distributes them among multiple network components in clustered WSNs for providing attack/failure resistance. The scheme also employs the Key-Chain Tree (KCT) mechanism to provide efficient rekeying in a large cluster and simplify the addition and exclusion of sensor nodes. Analysis results show that this scheme provides a secure encryption of the messages even if the revoked sensor nodes collude with each other or the Cluster Head (CH) is compromised. In addition, to update a secure group communication key in a cluster of size N with R revoked sensor nodes, the scheme requires $2\log_2 N$ keys storage, a single decryption operation and at most (N-1) one-way function operation at each cluster member, at most $2R$ encryption broadcasting from CH.

The remainder of this paper is organized as follows. Section 2 introduces the system setting and threat model. Section 3 presents the details of our schemes. Section 4 analyzes the security and performance of the proposed scheme. The related work is reviewed in section 5. Finally, section 6 concludes this paper.

2 Model Statement

2.1 System Model

We assume that there are three kinds of nodes in the deployed WSN, sink node, specific sensor node acting as Cluster Head (CH) and general sensor node acting as Cluster

Member (CM). The general sensor nodes are grouped into clusters, which can be formed based on various criteria [8]. Each cluster is controlled by a CH, which can broadcast messages to all sensor nodes (i.e. CMs) in its cluster. We assume that CMs and CHs are stationary and their communication range is known. Each CH is assumed to be reachable to CMs in its cluster, either directly (in one-hop) or indirectly (in multi-hop). Each CM performs three main functions: sensing, computing and communicating. The sensing component is responsible for detecting the environment to track a target/event. The collected data is processed simply and transmitted to the CH. If a CM is more than one hop away from the CH, its transmitted data is relayed by other CMs. Hence, CMs communicate only using short-haul radio communication. The CH aggregates data from different sensor nodes and transmits it to the sink node via long-haul radio communication. The architecture of the clustered WSN is depicted in Fig. 1.

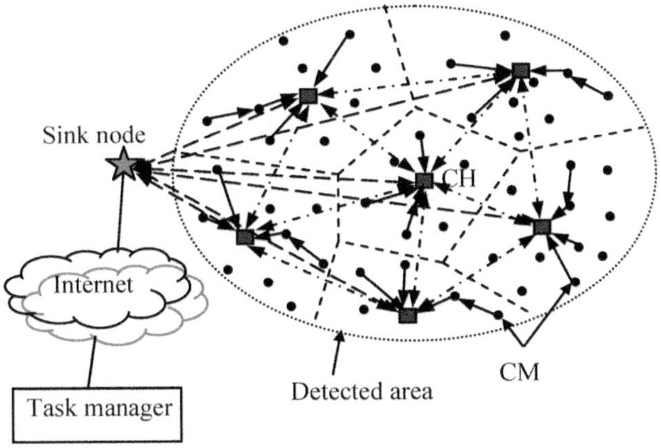

Fig. 1. The architecture of clustered WSN

The capability of each type of nodes is different. The sink node is resource-rich, and is located at a considerable distance from the detected region. The CHs are moderately powerful with sufficient energy to transmit with the sink node as well as perform the required key management functions. The CMs are resource-constrained.

2.2 Threat Model

The objective of an adversary is that tries to manipulate the system through capturing and compromising some network nodes. No trust assumptions are made on the CMs, which means that the memory of the captured sensor nodes can be read, tampered or erased. Hence, an adversary would know the keys of a compromised sensor node. The CHs are also not assumed to be tamper-proof, and can be compromised by an adversary. However, we assume that the compromise of a CH is more difficult than that of a CM. The compromise of CH includes the uncovering of the keys, the physical damaging of the computing and communication capabilities, and the controlling of its operation after being compromised by an adversary. Thus, the consequence caused by the compromise of a CH is more serious than that of a CM's.

3 Group Key Management Scheme

In this section, we develop a group key management scheme for clustered WSNs with the objective of enhancing network survivability against node capture. We assume that the sink node is secure while the CHs and the CMs can be compromised by an adversary. All network nodes have unique identifiers.

3.1 Key-Chain Tree Scheme

Since our group key management scheme is based on the KCT mechanism proposed in [9], we first introduce it in this section.

3.1.1 Dual Directional Key Chain (DDKC)

A DDKC is composed of two one-way key chains with equal length, a forward key chain (K^F) and a backward key chain (K^B). Each one-way key chain is a chain of cryptographic keys generated by repeatedly applying a one-way hash function H to a random number (i.e. key seed). To construct a key chain of size N, the Key Generator (KG) first randomly chooses a key seed S, and then computes $K_1=\mathsf{H}(S)$, $K_2=\mathsf{H}(K_1)$, …, $K_N=\mathsf{H}(K_{N-1})$. Because of the one-way property of H, given K_i, it is computationally infeasible to compute K_j for $j<i$. However, a user can compute any K_j for $j>i$ ($K_j=\mathsf{H}^{j-i}(K_i)$).

A DDKC with 8 keys in each key chain and 8 users is shown in Fig. 2, and each user u_i gets K_i^F in the forward key chain and K_{8-i+1}^B in the backward key chain. Obviously, u_i can compute all the keys K_j^F for $j>i$ in the forward key chain and K_j^B for $j>8$-i+1 in the backward key chain, and this property can be used to revoke a user or a set of users having consecutive IDs efficiently. For example, if the set of revoked users is $\mathcal{R}=\{u_3, u_4, u_5\}$, the non-revoked users can be departed into two subsets $S_1=\{u_1, u_2\}$ and $S_2=\{u_6, u_7, u_8\}$. According to the property of the DDKC, K_2^F is only known by the users in subset S_1 and K_3^B is only known by the users in subset S_2. These two keys are named as *subset cover keys*. Hence, if we use the subset cover keys to encrypt the new group key separately and broadcast the encrypted information to the group. All users except for users in $\mathcal{R}$ can derive at least one of the subset cover keys and then decrypt the new group keys.

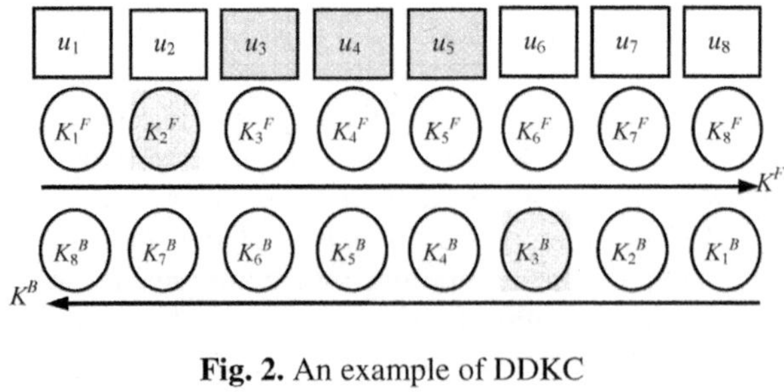

Fig. 2. An example of DDKC

3.1.2 KCT Scheme

In order to revoke multiple users which may not be adjacent to each other, [9] proposed the KCT scheme, which allows revoking any number of users regardless of their positions and works very well even when the excluded users collude with each other in an arbitrary way.

System Setup: Given a maximum group size N, the KCT schemes maps the users to the leaves of a binary tree. Without loss of the generality, we assume $N=2^d$, where d is an integer. Fig. 3 shows an example of a KCT. A subgroup G_i is defined as the collection of users in the subtree rooted at an internal node i. Each G_i is associated with a DDKC. Thus, each user u_i is associated with $\log_2(N)$ DDKCs along the path from the root to leaf i, and corresponding forward/backward keys are assigned to u_i as its personal secrets [1]. For example, the personal secrets of u_4 is $\{K_{0,4}^F, K_{0,5}^B, K_{1,4}^F, K_{1,1}^B, K_{4,2}^F, K_{4,1}^B\}$ in Fig. 3, where $K_{i,j}^F$ and $K_{i,j}^B$ denote the keys at position j in the forward key chain and the backward key chain with G_i respectively.

User Revocation: Obviously, the R revoked users partition the remaining set of users into at most (R+1) blocks, which are called as contiguous subsets. Formally, there has a contiguous subset $S_{m\text{-}n}=\{u_i| m<i<n, m=0 \text{ or } u_m\in \mathcal{R}, n=N+1 \text{ or } u_n\in \mathcal{R}, u_i\notin \mathcal{R} \text{ for all } i\}$. It is necessary to find the set of encryption keys to cover every $u_i\in \mathcal{M}\backslash\mathcal{R}$. For example, the set of subset cover keys in Fig. 3 is $\{K_{0,3}^F, K_{0,2}^B, K_{2,1}^F\}$ to revoke $\mathcal{R}=\{u_4, u_6\}$.

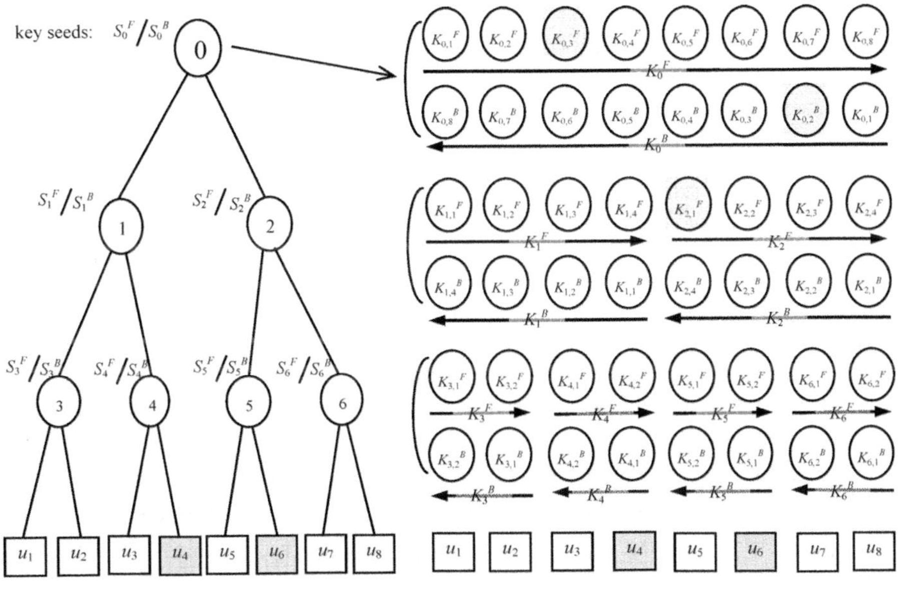

Fig. 3. An example of KCT

[1] The personal secrets are named as the administrative keys in the group key management schemes.

3.2 System Components and Capabilities

3.2.1 Sink Node

The sink node is assumed to be a trusted entity and resource-rich node, and it cannot be compromised by an adversary. The responsibilities of the sink node are follows:

- It preloaded keys (K_d, K_{KG}, K_i) of all sensor nodes in the detected region.
- It can detect the compromise/failure of any CH.
- It also triggers renewal of the communication keys and the administrative keys in order to prevent potential on-going spoofing.

3.2.2 Cluster Head

Each CH can directly communicate with the sink node. The keys owned by each CH are:

- $K_{CH,SN}$: a preloaded key used for secure communication between CH and the sink node.
- $K_{CH,CH}$: the inter-CH key distributed by the sink node is used for secure inter-CH communication.
- K_d: a CM discovery key distributed by the sink node.

Each CH controls a cluster consisting of a number of CMs. Each cluster will be assigned a set of distinct communication keys for data encryption. The responsibilities of each CH are follows:

- Assigning a logical identifier to each CM in its cluster.
- Generating the communication keys for its cluster.
- Forming KTC, generating and distributing administrative keys for other clusters in which it acts as a KG.
- Refreshing communication keys of its cluster after secure network sets up.
- Detecting and excluding the compromised sensor nodes in its cluster.

3.2.3 Cluster Member

Each sensor node belongs to a cluster controlled by a CH. The keys and functions preloaded are follows:

- K_d: a preloaded CM discovery key.
- K_{KG}: a preloaded key for initial key distribution shared with the KG of its cluster.
- K_i: a preloaded individual key shared with the sink node for providing individual secure communication.
- H_1: a preloaded one-way hash function to recomputed K_d, and K_i.
- H_2: a preloaded one-way hash function to computed administrative keys.

Furthermore, each CM should have enough memory for storing the administrative keys and communication keys.

3.3 System Initialization and Normal Operation

In this section, we present the procedures for system initialization and normal operation.

3.3.1 Network Initialization

Network initialization involves the CH registration and cluster formation.

CH registration. After deployment, each CH, CH[i], establishes communication with the sink node. CH[i] broadcasts a registration announcement with ID and position information encrypted with $K_{CH[i],SN}$. Upon receiving the announcements from all CHs, the sink node establishes link-specific keys for inter-CH communication (i.e. for each pair of CH[i] and CH[j], the sink node establishes $K_{CH[i],CH[j]} \neq K_{CH[j],CH[i]}$). The sink node sends the inter-CH communication keys encrypted with $K_{CH[i],SN}$ to each CH[i]. And then CHs use the inter-CH communication keys to establish secure contact with each other. The sink node also distributes each CH the key K_d for establishing the initial communication with sensor nodes.

Cluster formation. After setting up the sink node to CHs and inter-CH links, CM discovery procedure starts. Each CH broadcasts a CM discovery request with its ID and position information encrypted using K_d. In the detected area, the number of the deployed CHs is large enough to guarantee the area coverage. Upon receiving one or more CM discovery requests, a sensor node decrypts the messages and selects one of CHs as its CH according to a criterion, and then it broadcasts a CM discovery response containing its ID and the ID of the selected CH encrypted with K_d. Once receiving the CM discovery responses from sensor nodes, every CH assigns a logical ID to each sensor node in its cluster, tabulates the ID and logical ID of all CMs in its cluster, and informs its CMs with their cluster association in encryption mode. The logical ID of sensor node is unique in the cluster and is randomly selected from [1, CM_{max}], where CM_{max} is the maximum number of the CMs in a cluster and it is a system parameter whose value may depend on the network density, the number of CHs, the hostility of the operating environment, etc. How to decide the value of CM_{max} is beyond the scope of this paper and is a part of our future research plan. CH[i] also forwards the table of its CMs to the sink node encrypted with $K_{CH[i],SN}$. When the cluster formation is finished, all CMs recompute K_d using H_1 in order that CHs do not know the K_d used next time.

3.3.2 Initial Key Distribution

KG assignment. For each cluster CH_i, the sink node designates a CH other than CH[i] as the KG, KG[i], whose responsibility is to generate the administrative keys for CH_i. And then the sink node informs CH[i] and KG[i] that KG[i] is the KG of CH_i. According to the table of CMs of CH_i, the sink node forwards KG[i] the keys K_{KG} of all CMs of CH_i, where each K_{KG} corresponds with the CM's logical ID. Subsequently, CH[i] sends $CM_{max}[i]$ to KG[i]. On receiving this information, KG[i] establishes the KCT and generates the administrative keys for CMs in CH_i, where the key seeds of the administrative keys are also generated by KG[i]. Therefore, CH[i] would know the ID and logical ID of each CM in CH_i without generating the administrative keys themselves. On the other hand, KG[i] would know the logical ID and K_{KG} of each CM in CH_i, and generate the administrative keys for each CM in CH_i.

Key distribution. For the administrative keys generated by KG[i] are distributed to the CMs of CH_i, the following steps are repeated for each cluster CH_i.

1. KG[i] constructs a message including individual administrative keys for each CM, $CM_j \in CH_i$, which is supposed to know these keys. The message is first encrypted with $K_{KG}[CM_j]$, and then is encrypted using $K_{KG[i],CH[i]}$ before being transmitted to CH[i].
2. CH[i] receives and decrypts the message. Since CH[i] does not know $K_{KG}[CM_j]$, it cannot reveal the administrative keys that KG[i] had included in the message. And then CH[i] broadcasts the contents to its cluster.
3. CM_j uses its preloaded key $K_{KG}[CM_j]$ to uncover its administrative keys.
4. After KG[i] distributes the administrative keys to all CMs in CH_i, CH[i] generates a group communication key $K_g[CH_i]$ and informs KG[i] about it. Subsequently, KG[i] generates a message which contains $K_g[CH_i]$ encrypted with the administrative key known by all CMs of CH_i directly or indirectly (by computing), and then returns it to CH[i] encrypted with $K_{KG[i],CH[i]}$. CH[i] decrypts and broadcasts the contents to its cluster.
5. All CMs in CH_i use the distributed administrative key to uncover the $K_g[CH_i]$.

Obviously, CH[i] can also generate a communication key which is only known by a part of CMs of CH_i. Under this condition, KG[i] will generates messages containing the communication key encrypted separately with the administrative keys known by the recipient CMs of the communication key. Without loss of the generality, we only consider the communication key for the all CMs except for the revoked ones of each cluster in this paper.

3.3.3 Normal Network Operation

During normal network operation, the group key management scheme will be activated in case of rekeying or the addition of new sensor nodes.

Rekeying. The communication keys used in the network are periodically refreshed in order to prevent on-going cryptanalytic attacks. To refresh the communication key, CH[i] generates and sends the new communication key to KG[i] encrypted with $K_{CH[i],KG[i]}$. And then KG[i] separately encrypts it using the administrative key known by the legitimate CMs of CH_i and returns it/them to CH[i] encrypted with $K_{KG[i],CH[i]}$. CH[i] decrypts and broadcasts the contents to its cluster, and then legitimate CMs uncover the new communication key.

The administrative keys of the cluster can also be refreshed periodically. KG[i] generates the new administrative keys and encrypts them with their respective older ones. The messages are encrypted with $K_{KG[i],CH[i]}$ and sent to CH[i]. CH[i] decrypts them and broadcasts the contents to its cluster, and CMs of CH_i uncover the new individual administrative keys using older counterpart. Obviously, CH[i] cannot uncover the new administrative keys since it does not know the current ones.

Addition of new sensor nodes. New sensor nodes will be deployed in the detected area for replacing the older ones or extending the sensing area. In order to include the new sensor nodes, the sink node first notifies the CHs that new sensor nodes are being deploying and informs the CHs of K_d to be used. Each CH broadcasts a CM discovery request containing its ID and position information encrypted using K_d. Upon receiving one or more requests, a new sensor node decrypts the message(s) and selects one of CHs as its own CH, and then it broadcasts a CM discovery response including its ID and the selected CH's ID in encryption mode. Once receiving the CM discovery responses from new sensor nodes, CH assigns an unused logical ID to each new CM, tabulates ID and logical ID of the new CMs, and informs its new CMs with their cluster association encrypted using K_d. And CH[i] also forwards the table of its new added CMs to the sink node encrypted with $K_{CH[i],SN}$. The sink node informs KG[i] about K_{KG} of new added CMs in every cluster which has new sensor nodes. CH[i] and KG[i] then performs the key distribution steps in Section 3.3.2 for the new added sensor nodes.

3.4 Node Revocation

Node revocation procedures are invoked in case of detecting compromised or faulty sensor nodes. We assume that the sink node and CHs are responsible to monitoring the CHs' and sensor nodes' behavior/health and detecting their compromise/failure, respectively. As a key management scheme, it is needless to distinguish the compromise and failure and can deal with them in the same way.

3.4.1 CM Compromise/Failure

On identifying a compromised/faulty CM in CH_i, CH[i] generates a new communication key $K_g[CH_i]$ and informs $K_g[CH_i]$ and the logical ID of the compromised/faulty CM to the KG[i] encrypted using $K_{CH[i],KG[i]}$. Based on the informed logical ID, KG[i] decides the subset cover keys for revoking the compromised/faulty CM, and then separately encrypts $K_g[CH_i]$ with the subset cover keys and sends them to CH[i] encrypted with $K_{KG[i],CH[i]}$. CH[i] decrypts and broadcasts the contents to its cluster. All CMs except for the compromised/faulty CM can uncover the $K_g[CH_i]$ using one of their administrative keys. Therefore, the compromised/faulty CM cannot decrypt future data encrypted with $K_g[CH_i]$.

As two or more CMs are compromised/faulty at the same time, the node revocation method is same as mentioned above but the subset cover keys may be different.

During the period between two administrative keys rekeying process, the number of the compromised/faulty CMs in CH_i is incremental. Thus, the KG[i] needs to store the logical IDs of the compromised/faulty CMs until the administrative keys of CH_i are refreshed.

3.4.2 CH Compromise/Failure

Upon identifying a compromised/faulty CH, the sink node notifies other CHs to delete the inter-CH keys shared with the compromised/faulty CH. Recovery from a compromised/faulty CH can be handled by either deploying a new CH or re-clustering the CMs controlled by the compromised/faulty CH among the uncompromised/ healthy CHs.

New CH replacing. If it is possible to replace the compromised/faulty CH, $CH[i]_{revoked}$, with a new CH, $CH[i]_{new}$, which has compatible capabilities, the existing CMs-to-clusters association is not impacted, and the recovery operation would be a regeneration and redistribution of the group communication keys of CH_i.

Once the new CH is deployed, the sink node sets up keys for communication between existing uncompromised/ healthy CHs and $CH[i]_{new}$. And then the sink node informs $CH[i]_{new}$ the table with IDs and logical IDs of the CMs in CH_i, and the logical

ID and the keys K_{KG} of CMs of each CH_j in which $CH[i]_{new}$ acts as a KG, where $j \neq i$. And then the group communication key of CH_i is regenerated and redistributed. $CH[i]_{new}$ also generates and distributes the set of administrative keys for other clusters in which it acts as a KG.

CMs re-clustering. When replacing a new CH for the compromised/faulty one is infeasible, the CMs of CH_i need to be re-clustered to other uncompromised/healthy CHs. The sink node generates and informs the uncompromised/healthy CHs about the new K_d Since $CH[i]_{revoked}$ does not know the new K_d, it cannot interference with the re-clustering process. The uncompromised/healthy CHs starts up a CM discovery process and each CM of the CH_i will be associated to a new CH. The CHs with newly added CMs perform the procedure of the addition of new sensor nodes in Section 3.3.3.

Although the compromised/faulty CH knows the ID and the logical ID of CMs of its cluster, it cannot manipulate them since it does not know the set of administrative keys. Similarly, while $CH[i]_{revoked}$ knows the logical ID and the keys K_{KG} of the CMs of other clusters in which it acts as the KG, it cannot manipulate these CMs because it does not know the ID and the group communication key of the CMs. Furthermore, because the inter-CH keys are changed to exclude the compromised/faulty CH, $CH[i]_{revoked}$ cannot interference with the recovery process. $K_g[CH_i]$ and K_d known by $CH[i]_{revoked}$ are made obsolete by the recovery process.

4 Security and Performance Analysis

4.1 Security Analysis

According to the LEMMA 1 in [9], the encryption keys for the contiguous subset in KCT is key indistinguishable for users are not in this subset if assume H_2 is a perfect cryptographic hash function.

Theorem 1. The KCT-based group key management scheme does provide a secure encryption of the messages even if the revoked sensor nodes collude with each other or the CH is compromised.

Proof: The goal of the scheme is secure against the collusion of the revoked sensor nodes and the compromise of CH, we give a proof as follow:

Group key distribution: For a cluster, when multiple CMs of a cluster are compromised by an adversary, the KG searches the subset cover keys of the remaining uncompromised CMs, and the group communication key is regenerated by CH and distributed to the remaining uncompromised CMs encrypted with the subset cover keys separately. Since the remaining uncompromised CMs know one of the subset cover keys, they can uncover the new group communication key. On the other hand, the subset cover keys is indistinguishable for the compromised CMs, the new communication key encrypted with one of the subset cover keys cannot be decrypted by the compromised CMs. Therefore, the proposed scheme provides a secure encryption of the messages even if there are multiple compromised sensor nodes that can collude with each other.

CH revocation: When a CH is compromised by an adversary, attacker cannot pretend as a CH to distribute the faked group communication key since it does not know the administrative keys used for the communication key distribution. In proposed scheme, the functions of key management are decoupled and distributed them among multiple CHs. Therefore, although the compromised CH knows some secret information, such as the ID or the key K_{KG}, it cannot manipulate the CMs of its cluster or the CMs of the other cluster(s) in which it acts as the KG.

4.2 Performance Analysis

The storage requirement for the proposed scheme is coming from three parts. First, each CM is required to store two preloaded keys (K_d and K_{KG}), $2\log_2(CM_{max})$ administrative keys, a group communication key (K_g) and an individual key (K_i). Second, each CH is required to store a table with ID and logical ID of all CMs in its cluster, a preloaded CH-to-sink node key ($K_{CH\text{-}SN}$), several inter-CH keys ($K_{CH,CH}$), a discovery key (K_d) and a group communication key (K_g). Third, the KG of a cluster is required to store the KG-to-CM keys (K_{KG}) and logical ID of all CMs, the logical ID of the revoked CMs, $2CM_{max}\log_2(CM_{max})$ administrative keys or ($2CM_{max}$-2) key seeds.

The computational overhead of the scheme for a group communication key update can be divided into three parts. First, each CH performs a new group communication key generation operation, an encryption operation and a decryption operation. Second, each KG performs a decryption operation, two encryption operations for each update message. Third, each CM needs a single decryption operation and at most (CM_{max}-1) one-way function operations. The number of the update message is decided by the set of the revoked CMs.

The communication cost of the scheme for a group communication key update includes an encryption message containing new group communication key from CH to KG, at most $2R$ encryption message from KG and CH, and at most $2R$ encryption broadcasting from CH to its cluster, where R is the number of revoked CMs in the corresponding cluster.

5 Related Work

There are many group key management schemes for wire and wireless networks presented in the literature, which can be classified as centralized, decentralized, or distributed. In [10], a survey on the secure group communication is given. Group Key Management Protocol (GKMP) [11], Logical Key Hierarchy (LKH) [12], One-way Function Chain Tree (OFCT) [13], and Efficient Large-group Key distribution (ELK) [14] are the typical examples of the centralized schemes. Examples of the decentralized schemes are MARKS [15] and Kronos [16], and examples of the distributed schemes are Conference Key Agreement (CKA) [17] and Distributed LKH [18]. The objective of most of these schemes is to balance communication cost with memory cost. The main drawback of using most of these group key management schemes for WSNs is the lack of support for faulty and misbehaving sensor nodes, and the overhead incurred to support key management activities including setup and rekeying.

Among existing group key distribution techniques, three approaches are potential candidates for large wireless networks: self-healing key distribution [19], stateless key distribution [20] and EBS-based key distribution [21]. Recently, the Hybrid Key Tree (HKT) scheme is proposed in [22] to balance security and efficiency using a two level hybrid key tree. HKT has a sublinear storage complexity at the controller with cluster architecture. These schemes are also presented for the traditional wireless networks, and cannot use for WSNs directly. Our scheme is based on the KCT mechanism that is one of the stateless key distribution techniques. KCT-based group key management scheme splits the functions of group communication key's generation, administrative keys' generation and distribution into different CHs, which provides scalability and prevents the manipulation of the whole cluster due to the CH's compromise.

In the last few years, a lot of key predistribution management schemes have been proposed for WSNs. Eschenauer and Gligor proposed a probabilistic key predistribution scheme for pair-wise key establishment [3]. Chan et al. extended the idea in [3] and developed three key predistribution schemes, the q-composite key predistribution scheme, the multi-path key reinforcement scheme and the random pair-wise keys scheme [23]. In [24], Liu and Ning proposed two pair-wise key predistribution schemes, a random subset assignment scheme and a hypercube-based scheme. A low energy key management scheme based on key clusters for WSNs is proposed in [25]. And in [26], we proposed an energy-aware key predistribution management scheme for WSNs. However, key predistibution management schemes do not provide rekeying capability, and they may impede in-network processing, which is widely accepted as an essential paradigm for enhancing the energy-efficiency in WSNs. Our proposed scheme provides rekeying and supports the secure data aggregation protocol.

An EBS-based group key management scheme for WSNs is proposed in [27]. In order to address the collusion problem in EBS, Younis et al. proposed the SHELL, an EBS-based scheme that performs location-aware key assignment to minimize the number of keys revealed by capturing collocated sensor nodes, in [29]. However, the collusion attack still exists in EBS-based key management schemes. Our proposed scheme provides a secure encryption of the messages even if the revoked sensor nodes collude with each other or the CH is compromised.

6 Conclusions

Since many applications are dependent on the secure operations, and network compromise may be induce the serious consequences, security is not a trivial issue for these WSN scenarios. An essential component of any key-based security solution is managing the encryption keys in the system. Hence, we propose a KCT-based group key management scheme for the clustered WSNs in this paper. This scheme decouples the functions of key management and distributes them to different CHs in order to provide attack/failure resilient solutions. And it also provides rekeying process to enhance network security and survivability against node capture, simplify the addition and exclusion of sensor nodes. Security analysis results show that the scheme provides a secure encryption of the messages even if the revoked sensor nodes collude with each other or the CH is compromised. Moreover, for a secure group communication key update, the scheme requires $2\log_2 CM_{max}$ keys storage, a single decryption operation and at most (CM_{max}-1) one-way function operation at each CM, at most $2R$ encryption broadcasting at CH.

References

1. Akyildiz, I.F., Su, W., Sankarasubramaniam, Y., Cayirci, E.: Wireless Sensor Networks: A Survey, Computer Networks, Vol. 38, No. 4, (2002) 393-422
2. Perrig, A., Stankovic, J.A., Wagner, D.: Security in Wireless Sensor Networks, Communications of the ACM, Vol. 47, (2004) 53-57
3. Eschenauer, L., Gligor, V.D.: A Key Management Scheme for Distributed Sensor Networks, Proc. of CCS'02, (2000) 41-47
4. Zhu, S., Setia, S., Jajodia, S., Ning, P.: An Interleaved Hop-by-Hop Authentication Scheme for Filtering False Data in Sensor Networks, Security and Privacy, (2004)
5. Karlof, C., Wagner, D.: Secure Routing in Wireless Sensor Networks: Attacks and Countermeasures, Proc. of SNPA'03, (2003) 113-127
6. Wood, A.D., Stankovic, J.A.: Denial of Service in Sensor Networks, IEEE Computer, Vol. 35, (2002) 54-62
7. Rafaeli, S., Hutchison, D.: A Survey of Key Management for Secure Group Communication, ACM Computing Surveys, Vol. 35, No. 3, (2003) 309-329
8. Gober, P., Ziviani, A., Todorova, P., Amorim, M.D., Hunerberg, P., Fdida, S.: Topology Control and Localization in Wireless Ad Hoc and Sensor Networks, Ad Hoc & Sensor Networks, Vol.1, (2005) 301-322
9. Wang, P., Ning, P., Reeves, D.S.: Storage-Efficient Stateless Group Key Revocation, LNCS, Vol. 3225, (2004) 25-38
10. Harney, H., Muckenhirn, C.: Group Key Management Protocol (GKMP) Specification, RFC 2093, Internet Soc., (1997)
11. Wallner, D., Harder, E, Agee, R.: Key Management for Multicast: Issues and Architectures, RFC 2627, Internet Soc., (1999)
12. Wong, K., Gouda, M., Lam, S.: Secure Group Communications Using Key Graphs, IEEE/ACM Trans. Networking, Vol. 8, No. 1, (2000) 16-30
13. Canetti, R., Malkin, T., Nissim, K.: Efficient Communication-Storage Tradeoffs for Multicast Encryption, Proc. of EUROCRYPT'99, (1999) 459-474
14. Perrig, A., Song, D., Tygar, J.: ELK, A New Protocol for Efficient Large-Group Key Distribution, Proc. of Security and Privacy, (2001)
15. Brisco, B.: MARKS: Multicast Key Management Using Arbitrarily Revealed Key Sequences, Proc. of WNGC'99, (1999)
16. Setia, S., Koussih, S., Jajodia, S.: Kronos: A Scalable Group Rekeying Approach for Secure Multicast, Proc. of Security and Privacy, (2001)
17. Boyd, C.: On Key Agreement and Conference Key Agreement, Proc. of Information Security and Privacy, (1997)
18. Rodeh, O., Birman, K., Dolev, D.: Optimized Group Rekey for Group Communication Systems, Proc. of NDSS'00, (2000)
19. Staddon, J., Miner, S., Franklin, M., Balfanz, D., Malkin, M., Dean, D.: Self-healing Key Distribution with Revocation, Proc. of ISSP'02, (2002) 224-240
20. Naor, D., Naor, M., Lotspiech, J.: Revocation and Tracing Schemes for Stateless Receivers, LNCS, Vol. 2139, (2001) 41-62

21. Eltoweissy, M., Heydari, H., Morales, L., Sadborough, H.: Combinatorial Optimization of Key Management in Group Communications, J. Network and Systems Management, Vol. 12, No. 1, (2004) 33-50
22. Duma, D., Shahmehri, N., Lambrix, P.: A Hybrid Key Tree Scheme for Multicast to Balance Security and Efficiency Requirements, Proc. of WETICE'03, (2003)
23. Chan, H., Perrig, A., Song, D.: Random Key Pre-distribution Schemes for Sensor Networks, Proc. of ISRSP'03, (2003) 197-213
24. Liu, D., Ning, P., Li, R.: Establishing Pairwise Keys in Distributed Sensor Networks, ACM Trans. on Information and System Security, Vol.8, No.1, (2005) 41-77
25. Chen, H., Ying, B., Chen, B., Mineno, H., Mizuno, T.: A Low Energy Key Management Scheme in Wireless Sensor Networks, Proc. of CHINACOM2006, (2006)
26. Ying, B., Chen, H., Zhao, W., Qiu, P.: An Energy-Aware Key Management Scheme in Wireless Sensor Networks, Proc. of ICICIC2006, (2006)
27. Eltoweissy, M., Younis. M.F., Ghumman. K.: Group Key Management Scheme for Large-Scale Wireless Sensor Network, Ad Hoc Networks, (2005) 796-802
28. Younis, M.F., Ghumman, K., Eltoweissy, M.: Location-Aware Combinatorial Key Management Scheme for Clustered Sensor Networks, IEEE Trans. On Parallel and Distributed Systems, Vol. 17, No. 8, (2006) 865-882

A Secure Packet Filtering Mechanism for Tunneling over Internet

Wan-Jik Lee[1], Seok-Yeol Heo[2], Tae-Young Byun[3,*], Young-Ho Sohn[4], and Ki-Jun Han[5]

[1,2] Department of Bio-Electronics
Pusan National University of Pusan, Korea
[3] School of Computer and Information Communications Engineering
Catholic University of Daegu, Gyeongsan, Gyeongbuk, Korea
[4] School of Electrical Engineering and Computer Science
Yeungnam University of Daegu, Korea
[5] Department of Computer Engineering
Kyungpook National University of Daegu, Korea
{wjlee,syheo}@pusan.ac.kr, tybyun@cu.ac.kr, ysohn@yu.ac.kr, kjhan@bh.knu.ac.kr

Abstract. Unlike Internet design policies of early stage, various types of tunneling are currently used in Internet for IPv4/IPv6 transition, IP multicasting and IP mobility. As tunneled packets have dual IP headers, general firewall systems apply the filtering rules only to the outer header but not to the inner header when these packets pass the firewall. Thus, many present firewall systems may have serious security problems to packet filtering for tunneled packets. To resolve this issue, a new packet filtering mechanism to filter tunneled packets is proposed in this paper. We design and implement the packet filtering mechanism by using Linux Netfilter. Through this study, the packet filtering system was also found operating correctly in the IPv6-in-IPv4/IP-in-IP tunneling.

Keywords: Packet Filtering, Tunneling, Firewall, Netfilter, Security.

1 Introduction

Still these days, various protocols coexisting in the Internet environment are not compatible with each other. For example, IPv6, the next generation Internet protocol, is not compatible with IPv4. Thus, various types of IP-based tunneling are used for interworking those incompatible protocols, and more employments of tunneling in the Internet are expected due to IPv6 deployment and extension of MBONE etc. These tunneled packets can be generated in various forms such as IPv4-in-IPv4, IPv6-in-IPv4, IPv4-in-IPv6, IPv6-in-IPv6 depending upon supporting protocols and network environments.

* Correspondent Author.

Y.-H. Lee et al. (Eds.): ICESS 2007, LNCS 4523, pp. 641–652, 2007.

In case of inflow of these tunneled packets into firewalls, the possibility that a firewall may recognize only the outer header and process it is fairly high. A Filtering system hooks the packet and filters it, it is impossible to recognize the inner header and filter this packet in case of a software based firewall.

In this paper, we propose a new packet filtering mechanism to solve the security problem, and also design and implement the packet filtering mechanism based on Linux Netfilter. Our proposed packet filtering mechanism recognizes dual headers of incoming packets and filters the outer headers and inner header properly. We also see if the packet filtering mechanism operates correctly in the IPv4/IPv6 transition and IPv4-in-IPv4 encapsulation environments.

The rest of the paper is consists of followings. Section 2 discusses the security issues of current packet filtering mechanism for tunneled packets. In Section 3, the proposed mechanism and implementation are described. The correct operation of implementation is described in section 4. Finally, we explain our conclusions in section 5.

2 Security Issues Due to Tunneled Packets

Tunneling over Internet is used for supporting IPv4/IPv6 transition, multicasting, VPN(Virtual Private Network) and mobile IP. Among these, a VPN fundamentally uses tunneling for security, and a mobile IP mandatorily employs IPsec, so security problems by these tunneling are hardly occurred. However, tunneling for IPv4/IPv6 transition and IP multicasting may bring about security problems such as packet filtering avoidance at a firewall.

Figure 1 shows a procedure of tunneling, where an IPv6 packet runs through non-IPv6 networks, and a structure of tunneled packet that is encapsulated as a form of IPv6-in-IPv4.

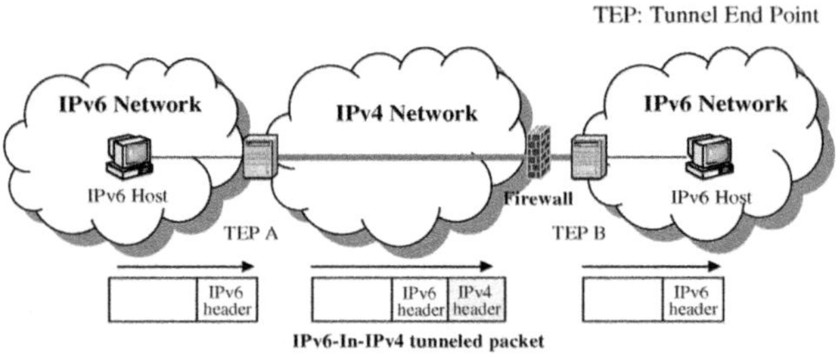

Fig. 1. An example of tunneling using IPv6-in-IPv4 encapsulation

Outer IPv4 header has the IPv4 address of TEP A as a source address, also the IPv4 address of TEP B as a destination address and it is generated while a packet goes through an IPv4 area. A firewall in figure 1 recognizes only outer IPv4 header, thus, though filtering rules for IPv6 packet are set, a firewall can not apply filtering rules to inner IPv6 header. Due to these problems, if tunneling is intentionally used to detour filtering function of firewall, it can be a severe threat to network. Also, IP multicast packet has the same problem as above except for using IPv4-in-IPv4 encapsulation.

Tunneling for IPv4/IPv6 transition roughly can be categorized as configured tunneling and automatic tunneling[4]. In a configured tunneling, a network administrator statically sets both of TEP addresses for tunnel. So, we can use IPsec in this case, and the use of IPsec is recommended in standard documents. However, some standardized automatic tunneling mechanisms are devised for user convenience. Because these automatic tunnels are dynamically created and removed and also both of end addresses are changed, we can not adopt IPsec to automatic tunnel. Currently, standardization for some automatic tunneling including 6to4[5], ISATAP[6], Teredo[7], DSTM[8] are finished or work in progress in IETF. Among them, 6to4 and Teredo are already standardized, and implemented in general operating system including Microsoft Windows and Linux. In addition, IPv6 related organizations provide tunneling services such as 6to4 and TEREDO to not only authorized organizations, but also client hosts of normal users to promote IPv6 deployment. Figure 2 shows an example of threat on the tunneling environment.

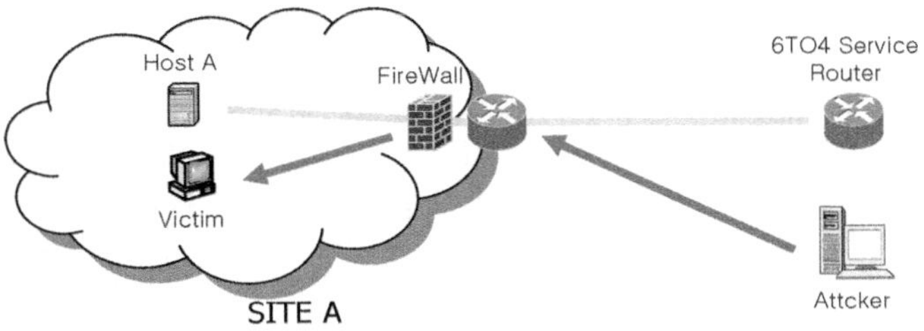

Fig. 2. An example of malicious use of tunneling

In figure 2, an attacker can generate a malicious IPv6-in-IPv4 packet, which disguises 6to4 packet from a fair 6to4 router, encapsulates the source address of IPv4, then may attack a victim host in site A. In this case, because a firewall in site A can not recognize inner malicious IPv6 packet within tunneled packet, a firewall can not distinguish fabricated packets attacking a victim host from normal packets to host A.

What firewall does know is only an information that IPv6 packet is within IPv4 payload, therefore, a firewall can not apply IPv6 packet filtering rules to inner IPv6 packet. That is, firewall in figure 2 performs packet filtering after routing ingress packets. While a procedure of routing is going on, IPv4 packets and IPv6 packets are separately proceeded along to different routines. Therefore, packets in an IPv4 routing procedure can not be delivered to an IPv6 routing procedure. A conceptual processing procedure of a packet is illustrated in figure 3.

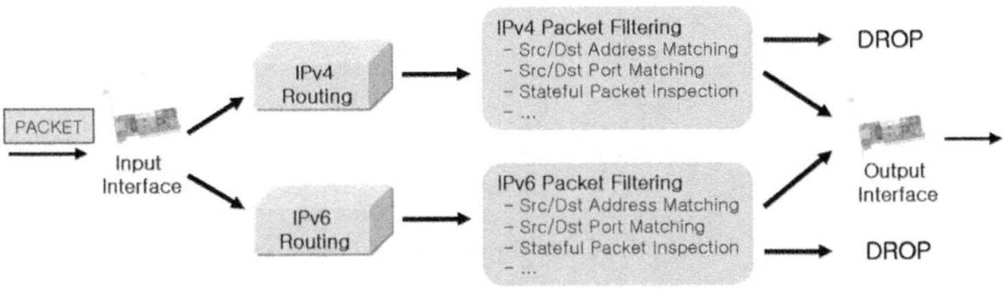

Fig. 3. A packet processing procedure in firewall

The security problem like this is due to tunneling itself. Because a packet of layer 3 is embedded in a packet payload of layer 3, tunneling disobeys protocol layering concept. Accordingly, it is necessary to apply filtering rules to inner header of tunneled packet.

Currently, security problems related to IPv6 have been studied in several research organizations, and some network manufacturers and security providers already released common firewall products that deal with IPv6 packets. Additionally, firewall framework such like Netfilter provides filtering capability to IPv6 basic header and extension header. Nevertheless, the studies for security problems due to tunneling for IPv4/IPv6 transition are comparably poor.

The v6ops working group of the IETF classifies these security problems into security threat caused to IPv4/IPv6 transition and recommends countermeasures to these [10, 11]. Also, [12] has proposed a packet filtering mechanism to a variety of IPv4/IPv6 transitions. This paper proposed only a filtering scheme using relationship between outer IPv4 address and inner IPv6 packet, provided a simple filtering function to only inner IPv6 address. Nevertheless, this scheme has a limitation that IPv6 filtering rules already set in a firewall can not be applied into inner IPv6 packet.

Tunneling for IP multicasting is similar to previous IPv4/IPv6 tunneling except for using IPv4-in-IPv4 encapsulation instead of IPv6-in-IPv4 encapsulation, so the same security problems as tunneling for IPv4/IPv6 transition can occur in tunneling for IP multicasting. The multicast security working group of the IETF also deals with security issues of IP multicasting, but intensively studies authentication methods for group membership of IP multicast[14]. They only recommend the use of IPsec in establishing tunnel for multicasting.

3 Design and Implementation of Netfilter-Based Packet Filtering for Tunneling

3.1 Packet Filtering Based on Netfilter

Netfilter is a kind of framework of Linux kernel that supports packet filtering, NAT (Network Address Translation) and a packet mangling function with user interface tool of iptables. Netfilter provides a development environment for filtering and

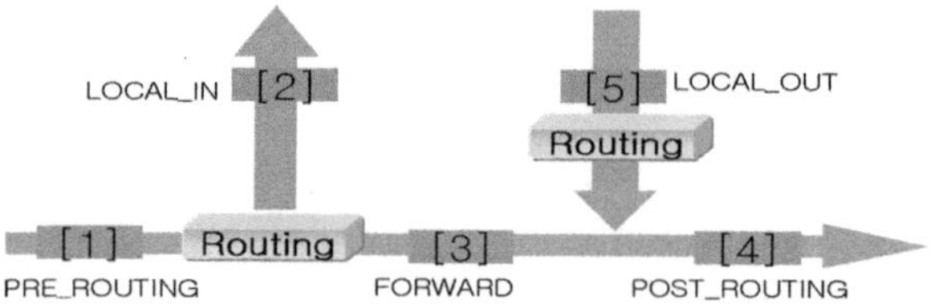

Fig. 4. Hooking points of Netfilter

address translation where it hooks the traversing packet on a specific point of internal system. Figure 4 shows hooking points of Netfilter.

In figure 4, three hooking points such as LOCAL_IN, FORWARD, and LOCAL_OUT are available for packet filtering. Hooking points of PRE_ROUTING and POST_ROUTING are used in NAT and packet mangling. Packet filtering rules are applied to a point of receiving the packet (LOCAL_IN), forwarding the packet (FORWARDING) and sending the packet (LOCAL_OUT) respectively by hooking the traversing packet. At this time, the rules applied to each hooking point are assigned independently and a network firewall(not a personal firewall) applies this packet filtering rules to a forwarding hooking point.

The filtering rules applied to the hooking point are set by iptables or ip6tables command and commands are divided into two parts of Match and Target. Match commands set the conditions, then decide if each packet satisfies this rule and Target commands direct processing of the matched packet. For example, when an user applies the rule *'iptables –A FORWARD –s 200.1.1.0/24 –j DROP'*, this command indicates several means of followings.

- This command should be applied to FORWARD hooking point.
- Source address of packet is in '200.1.1.0/255.255.255.0'.
- Option *DROP*, which follows option *–j(JUMP)* means that matched packet should be discarded.

Netfilter stores this rules in filtering table of internal kernel. When a packet flows into the kernel, Netfilter filters this packet by using the filtering table. Figure 5 illustrates the procedure as follows in detail.

- NF_HOOK in IPv4 packet processing code delivers the packet to forward hooking point in figure 5.
- Packet handling routine in hooking point processes the packet according to predefined rules in packet filtering table, ip_tables.

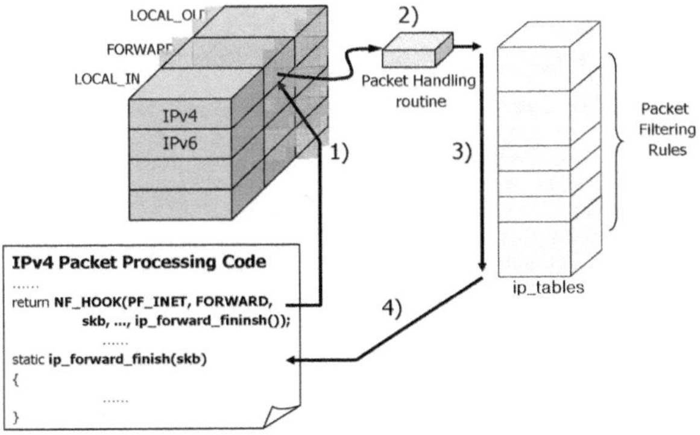

Fig. 5. Existing Netfilter packet filtering procedure

3.2 Design and Implementation of Filtering Mechanism for Tunneling

It is necessary to augment the following functions of processing to apply packet filtering rules to tunneled packets properly.

- To recognize tunneled packet
- To deliver the packet to proper filtering table for inner IP header

In this paper, we modified packet-processing code in figure 5 and designed a new filtering mechanism for tunneled packet as shown in figure 6.

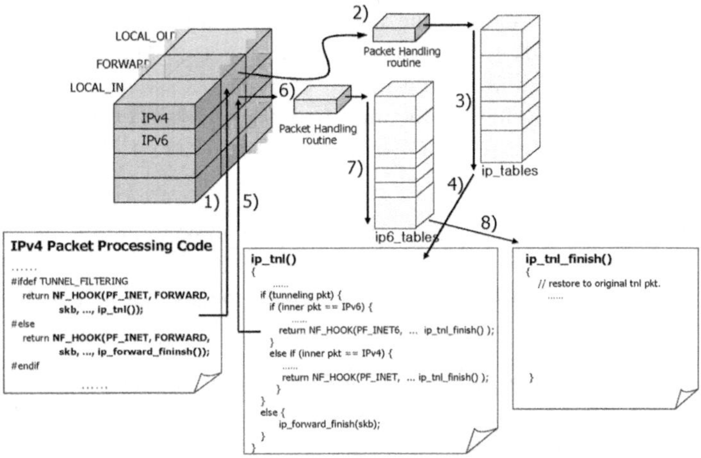

Fig. 6. Our proposed tunneled packet filtering procedure

ip_tnl() function

- *Check the packet is a tunneled packet.*
- *if not a tunneling packet, return to ip_forward_finish().*
- *if the packet is a IPv6-in-IPv4 tunneling packet*
  - skb->prehdr_offset = iph->ihl*4;
  - skb->nh. ipv6h = (skb->data + iph->ihl*4);
  - skb->data += iph->ihl*4;
  - skb->len -= iph->ihl*4;
  - return NF_HOOK(PF_INET6, FORWARD, …, ip_tnl_filter());
- *else if the packet is a IPv4-in-IPv4 tunneling packet*
  - skb->prehdr_offset = iph->ihl*4;
  - skb->nh. iph = (skb->data + iph->ihl*4);
  - skb->data += iph->ihl*4;
  - skb->len -= iph->ihl*4;
  - return NF_HOOK(PF_INET6, FORWARD, …, ip_tnl_filter());

ip_tnl_finish() function

- *Restore the packet to original tunneled packet*
  - skb->len += skb->prehdr_offset;
  - skb->data -= skb->prehdr_offset;
  - skb->nh.iph = skb->data;
- *return to ip_forward_finish()*

Fig. 7. Function ip_tnl() and ip_tnl_finish()

IPv4 packet processing code in figure 6 was modified so that the packet which passed outer IPv4 packet filtering table executes ip_tnl() function if kernel compile option TUNNEL_FILTERING is set. Function ip_tnl() investigate packets whether it is tunneled or not. If it is tunneled packet, function ip_tnl() reenter this packet to ip6_tables or ip_tables filtering tables. Figure 7 shows function ip_tnl() and function ip_tnl_finish() which process the packet passed second filtering table.

To reenter tunneled packet to the second filtering table as explained above, it is necessary to modify some fields of skb which is data structure of packet in Linux kernel. By performing packet modification, the tunneled packet can be processed as the independent packet by the second filtering table. After the packet passed the second filtering table, the additional procedure, which restores the packet to original tunneled packet format, is required. This skb change and restoration are accomplished in function ip_tnl() and ip_tnl_finish() as shown in figure 7.

An IPv6 packet filtering procedure can be applied the same as an IPv4 packet processing procedure. That is, in case of processing IPv6 packet the recognition of tunneled packet and reentering the packet to filtering table according to inner packet can be performed.

We implemented our packet filtering processing mechanism for tunneling on Linux kernel 2.6.10 with iptables-1.3.5. The details of operation are explained in section 4.

4 Behavior Test and Experimental Evaluation

To show the correct operation of our implementation, we performed the behavior test on cases of two network configurations, an IPv6-in-IPv4 network configuration and an IPv4-in-IPv4 network configuration.

4.1 Behavior Test of Our Implementation

4.1.1 IPv6-in-IPv4 Network Configuration

Figure 8 illustrates our simple IPv6-in-IPv4 network environment. Here, we use three linux systems, a net-fw that serves as a firewall, an in-host plays a role of host in the network which the firewall protects and an out-host plays a role of host outside the network respectively.

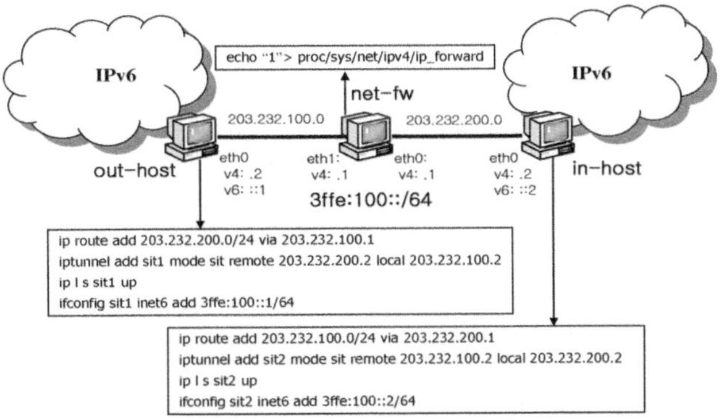

Fig. 8. IPv6-in-IPv4 tunneling testbed

Figure 8 also shows IPv6-in-IPv4 tunnel configuration, both out-host and in-host have IPv4/IPv6 dual protocol stacks and we assume that the network between two systems supports only IPv4. The details of commands for tunnel configuration are shown in square boxes of figure 8 respectively. We make TEP interface called sit1 in the out-host and assign it with 3ffe:100::1/64 address. Also, we set TEP interface called sits2 in the in-host with 3ffe:100::2/64 address.

To emphasize the advantages of our implementation, we performed behavior test on two cases.

(1) Behavior test of packet filtering without our proposed filtering mechanism

We test existing filtering functions for tunneled packets of firewall without our filtering mechanism in figure 8(IPv6-in-IPv4 tunneling environments) and figure 9 presents the result of filtering test. Although we command "drop all icmpv6 packets and drop all packets sent from 3ffe:100::1" in a terminal window of the firewall(net-fw) in figure 9, ping6 packets that travels from out-host(3ffe:100::1) to in-host(3ffe:100::2) can not be dropped, thus, ping6 commands in a terminal window of out-host works well. This indicates that the filtering functions of firewall(net-fw) for inner header of tunneled packets not works at all.

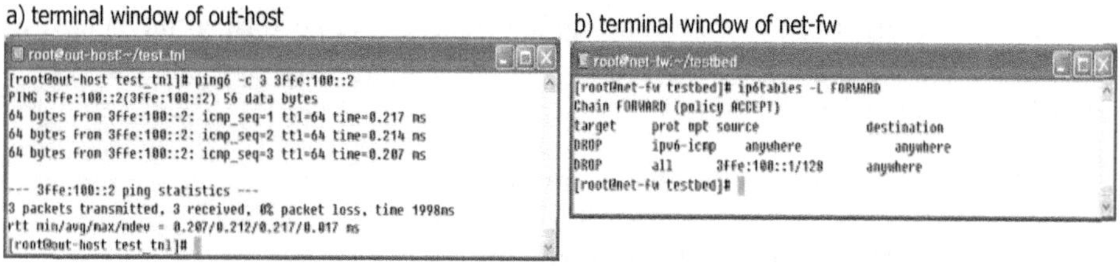

Fig. 9. Filtering test for IPv6-in-IPv4 tunneled packets without our filtering mechanism

(2) Behavior test of packet filtering with our proposed filtering mechanism

Next, we performed the same tests after enabling our mechanism on the firewall. Figure 10 shows the test results of filtering for tunneled packets on the same IPv6-in-IPv4 environments in figure 8.

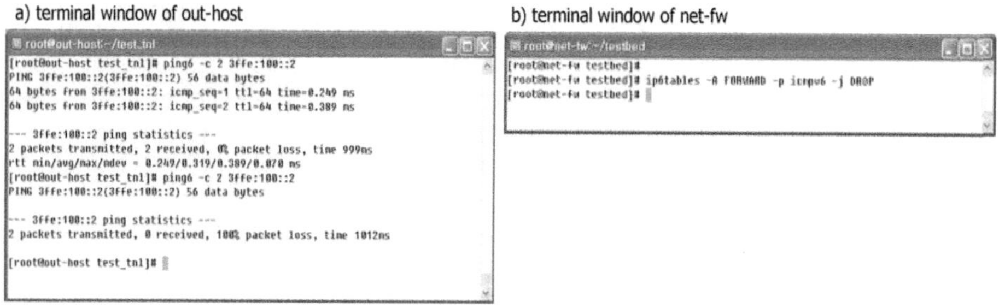

Fig. 10. Filtering test for IPv6-in-IPv4 tunneled packets with our filtering mechanism

In figure 10, the first ping6 command works well as shown in a terminal window of the out-host, but the second ping6 command does not work after setting a packet filtering command(Drop all icmpv6 packets) in a terminal window of net-fw. These behavior test results verify that filtering functions of our implementation are applied to inner header of tunneled packets, drop packets that match to filtering rules.

4.1.2 IPv4-in-IPv4 Network Configuration

Figure 11 shows an IPv4-in-IPv4 tunnel configuration. Systems in testbed are the same as the figure 8, but tunnel and network configurations are changed to establish IPv4-in-IPv4 tunnel from out-host to in-host. We assign IP address 100.1.1.1 to TEP interface(tnl1) of the out-host, IP address 100.1.1.2 to TEP interface(tnl1) of the in-host.

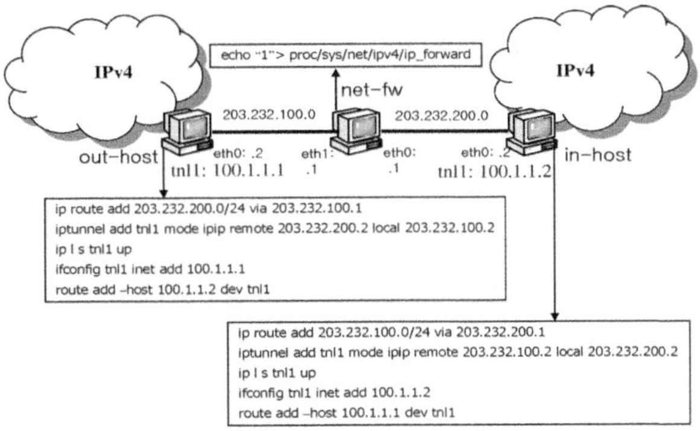

Fig. 11. IPv4-in-IPv4 tunneling testbed

(1) Behavior test of packet filtering without our proposed filtering mechanism

In figure 12, we can also see that the filtering functions for inner header of tunneled packets do not work properly in the absence of our filtering mechanism like as figure 9.

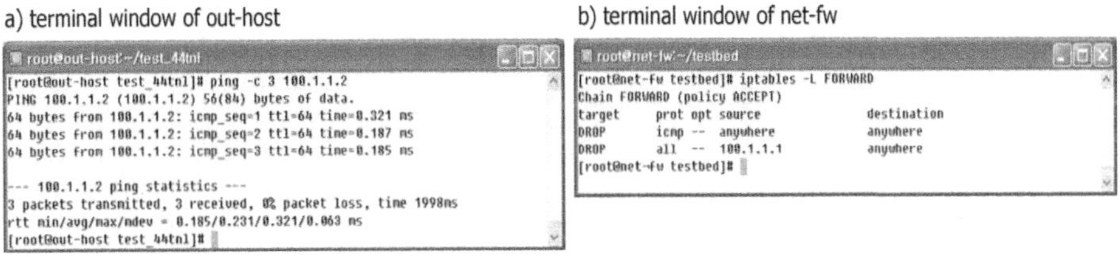

Fig. 12. Filtering test for IPv4-in-IPv4 tunneled packets without our filtering mechanism

(2) Behavior test of packet filtering with our proposed filtering mechanism

IPv4-in-IPv4 packet filtering tests in figure 13 show the same result as figure 10. These test results verify that filtering functions of our implementation are applied to inner header of tunneled packets, drop packets that match to filtering rules.

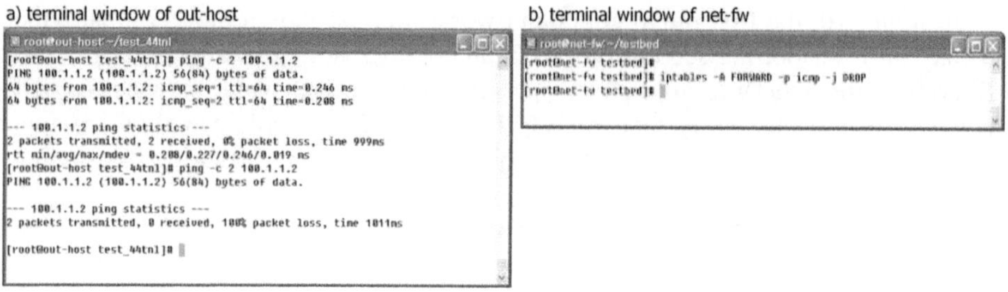

Fig. 13. Results of filtering test for IPv4-in-IPv4 tunneled packets with our filtering mechanism

Besides above tests, we test many filtering rules for inner header in tunneled packets, also test for IPv6-in-IPv6, IPv4-in-IPv6 tunneled packets with Libnet[20] and ethereal tools which provide packet generation and packet capturing. In addition, we check functions of our implementation with these tests.

4.2 Experimental Evaluation

We simply evaluate experimental performance of our filtering mechanism by using ping6 program. In the IPv6-in-IPv4 environment such as figure 8, we measure ping6 packet latencies from out-host to in-host with varying packet size 100 bytes to 1000 bytes. The number of ping6 packets per packet size is 500 and we average latencies of 500 packets per packet size.

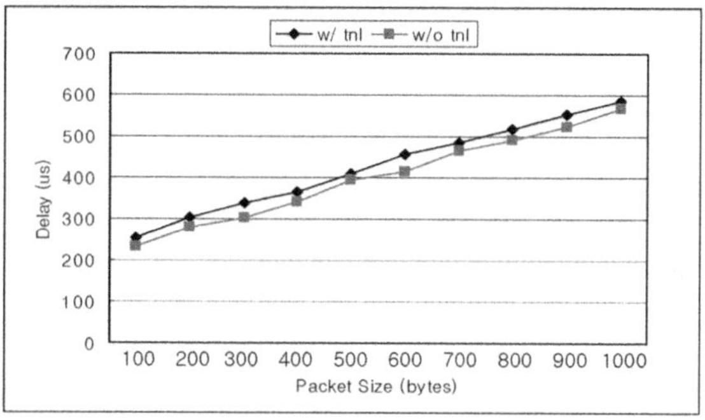

Fig. 14. Ping6 latencies with our filtering mechanism and without our filtering mechanism (no filtering rules in the firewall)

Figure 14 shows two curves of ping6 latencies on the IPv6-in-IPv4 tunneling environment, the one is ping6 latencies while our filtering mechanism is enabled and the other is that of ping6 latencies while our filtering mechanism is disabled. Label "w/ tnl" in figure 14 means that our filtering mechanism is enabled, on the other hand, label "w/o tnl" indicates our filtering mechanism is disabled. When we compare with

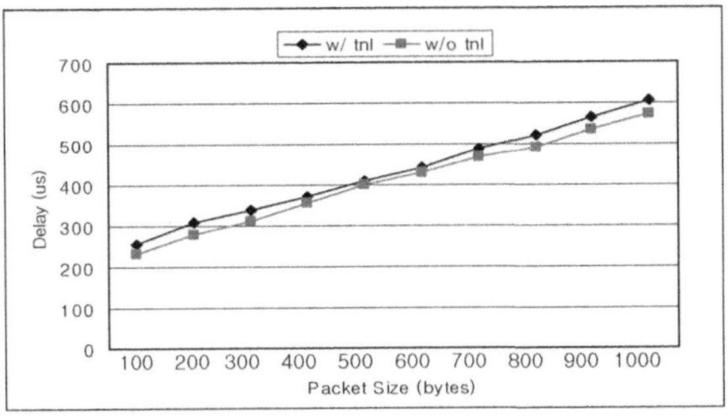

Fig. 15. Ping6 latencies with our filtering mechanism and without our filtering mechanism (20 filtering rules for IPv4 packets and 20 filtering rules for IPv6 packets in the firewall)

two curves, the difference is caused to additional operations that consist of inner header decision, packet's structure modification and filtering hooking function call. Average value of difference is about 30 micro-second, which is not a large value, so it's negligible. This justify that adoption of our mechanism does not severely affect system performance for packet filtering and improve the security against network threat.

Figure 15 shows ping6 packet latencies on the same condition as Figure 14 except for setting 20 filtering rules for IPv4 packet and 20 filtering rules for IPv6 packet in firewall. In case of our filtering mechanism enabled, total of 40 filtering rules are applied to tunneled packets, however, only 20 filtering rules are applied to tunneled packets in case of our filtering mechanism disabled. Comparing with figure 14, we know that latencies in figure 15 increase a little due to matching operations for additional filtering rules.

5 Conclusions

Many firewall systems used in present provide filtering capabilities to only outer header of incoming tunneled packets, but these systems have a drawback of not providing filtering to inner header of the packet. As the use of tunneling over Internet increases, a drawback of not supporting filtering functions to inner header of tunneled packets will be a great threat to network security.

To solve this problem, we proposed a new packet filtering mechanism which distinguishes various types of inner packet in tunneled packet, and performs packet filtering to inner header of the packet. Also, we implemented our proposed packet filtering mechanism on basis of Linux Netfilter, showed correct behavior of packet filtering over various tunneling environments including IPv6-in-IPv4 and IPv4-in-IPv4.

We expect that our proposed mechanism, in this paper, can be contributed to improve security of firewall system for dealing with tunneled packets that would be frequently used in the future. Especially, our implementation based on Netfilter can be easily portable to software-based firewall system, router and NATs running over embedded Linux.

References

1. Rusty Russell, "Linux 2.4 Packet Filtering HOWTO," www.netfilter.org
2. Rusty Russell, "Linux Netfilter Hacking HOWTO," www.netfilter.org
3. The 6NET Consortium, "6net: An IPv6 Deployment Guide," September 2005
4. R. Gilligan and E. Nordmark, "Transition Mechanisms for IPv6 Hosts and Routers," RFC 2893, August 2000
5. B. Carpenter and K. Moore, "Connection of IPv6 Domains via IPv4 Clouds," RFC 3056, February 2001
6. F. Templin et al., "Intra-Site Automatic Tunnel Addressing Protocol (ISATAP)," draft-ietf-ngtrans-isatap-24.txt(work in progress), January 2005
7. C. Huitema, "Teredo: Tunneling IPv6 over UDP through Network Address Translation (NATs)," RFC 4380, February 2006
8. J. Bound, L. Toutain and H. Affifi, "Dual Stack Transition Mechanism (DSTM)," Internet Draft, August 2003, work in progress
9. Christian Benvenuti, "Understanding LINUX Networking Internals," O'REILLY Press, pp. 466-473, 2006
10. E. Davies and et al., "IPv6 Transition/Co-existence Security Considerations," draft-ietf-v6ops-security-overview-06.txt, May 2005, work in progress
11. P. Savola, "Firewalling Considerations for IPv6," draft-savola-v6ops-firewalling-01.txt, March 2003, work in progress
12. Seok-Yeol Heo and et al., "Design and Implementation of Packet Filtering Systems for IPv4/IPv6 Tunneling Environment," Journal of KISS: Information Networking, Vol. 33, December 2006
13. R. Finlayson, "IP Multicast and Firewalls," RFC 2588, May 1999
14. Tsunemass Hayashi and et al., "Requirements for Accounting, Authentication and Authorization in Well Managed IP Multicasting Services," draft-ietf-mboned-maccnt-req-04.txt, February 2006, work in progress
15. P. Savola, "Security of IPv6 Routing Header and Home Address Options,"draft-savola-ipv6-rh-ha-security-03.txt, December 2002, work in progress
16. E. Davies and J. Mohacsi, "Recommendations for Filtering ICMPv6 Messages in Firewalls," draft-ietf-v6ops-icmpv6-filtering-recs-02.txt, January 2007, work in progress
17. P. Savola, "Security Considerations for 6to4," RFC 3964, December 2004
18. R. Graveman and et al., "Using IPsec to Secure IPv6-in-IPv4 Tunnels," draft-ietf-v6ops-ipsec-tunnels-02.txt, March 2006, work in progress
19. IANA, "Special-Use IPv4 Addresses," RFC 3330, September 2002
20. Libnet Homepage, http://libnet.sourceforge.net

An End-to-End Packet Delay Optimization for QoS in a MANET

Sang-Chul Kim

School of Computer Science, Kookmin University,
861-1, Chongnung-dong, Songbuk-gu, Seoul, 136-702 Korea
sckim7@kookmin.ac.kr

Abstract. This paper[1] focuses on calculating an end-to-end packet delay optimization for Quality of Service (QoS) in a mobile ad hoc network (MANET). Each intermediate node in an active path can achieve the optimized data rate which is obtained by using Lagrangian function and the end-to-end packet delay constraint. It is shown that the amount of data rate compared to the one which is not optimized can be saved in the proposed algorithm.

1 Introduction

Wireless communications systems continue to use exponentially expand bandwidth with the recent fast growth in wireless communication technologies as a result of advances in digital communications, commercial laptop computers and semiconductor technologies. The most popular networks of the traditional wireless model are cellular and mobile IP networks, which have been configured with a wired backbone and one last wireless hop, which is a point-to-point channel between the base station and the mobile user. In the wireless cell domain, the base station provides centralized control for the mobile users to access the medium. IS-54 (The first generation of the digital standard with TDMA technology), IS-95 (The standard for CDMA), cdma2000, W-CDMA, and IMT-2000 are currently standardized in cellular communication systems.

For the past few years, MANETs have been emphasized as an emerging research area due to the growing demands for mobile computing, where the dynamic topology for the rapid deployment of independent mobile users becomes a new considering factor. For instance, mobile users across a campus can transmit data files to each other, group members of a search and disaster rescue and recovery team or military solders in automated battlefield can communicate in order to coordinate their actions, without using a base station. These example networks are called ad hoc wireless networks where centralized and organized connectivity may not be possible. The examples show that MANETs need to have the abilities to provide for establishing survivable, efficient, dynamic communication for emergency/ search-and-rescue operations, disaster relief efforts, law enforcement in crowd control and military networks. One of the outstanding features

[1] This research was supported by the Seoul R&BD program of Korea.

Y.-H. Lee et al. (Eds.): ICESS 2007, LNCS 4523, pp. 653–663, 2007.

of MANETs could be the self-creating, self-administrating, self-organizing and self-configuring multihop wireless network characteristic.

Addressing the QoS in MANETs has recently gained increased attention. Future high speed wireless packet-switching networks are expected to provide traffic engineering (TE), guaranteed QoS and differentiated services (DS) for a variety of different traffic. The QoS is a broadly used term, which is the guarantee by the network to satisfy a set of predetermined service performance constraints for the user traffic flows in terms of an available bandwidth, end-to-end delay statistics, a jitter, a probability of packet loss rate, a received bit-energy-to-noise-density, etc. The QoS in a wired network is well specified in Integrated Service (InteServ) and Differentiated Service (DiffServ). IntServ focuses on per-flow resource reservation. DiffServ is the mechanism to ensure per-class service differentiation. The application requiring fixed delay bound service and the application requiring reliable and enhanced best effort service are provided by the Guaranteed Service and the Controlled Load Service in IntServ respectively. The Type Of Service (TOS) bits in the IP header, which is called the DS field and a set of packet forwarding rules, which is called Per-Hop-behavior (PHB) are the main components to implement DiffServ. QoS in a MANET has been widely recognized as a challenging problem. Due to the node mobility, dynamic topology and time-varying link capacity, the provisioning of QoS guarantees is one of the difficult issues to be implemented in MANET. The performance metrics for evaluating the MANET QoS can be adaptively defined based on one of the wired networks or newly defined according to the MANET properties.

2 Related Work

This paper studies a situation that when a node asks an end-to-end packet delay towards a destination in MANET networks, each intermediate node needs to select the optimized data rate so as to meet some delay constraint while minimizing costs of network resources. In IEEE 802.11a and 802.11g, multiple data payload transfer rate capabilities such as 1, 2, 5.5, 6, 9, 11, 12, 18, 24, 36, 48, and 54 Mbps are allowed. However, the algorithm to perform rate switching is beyond the scope of the IEEE 802.11a and 802.11g standards [1], [2], [3]. Toumpis proposed the capacity regions for wireless ad hoc networks, which describes the set of achievable rate at intermediate nodes between all source destination pairs under various transmission strategies. Changing algorithm of the transmission rate at a node has not been studied in [4] and it is assumed that the transmitter node varies the transmission rate based on the value of SINR to satisfy a given performance metric [4]. Gupta [5] calculates the capacity of wireless networks. When each node uses a fixed power and each node sends data to a randomly chosen destination, each node can get a throughput of $\Theta^2(W/\sqrt{nlogn})\ bit/s$ in the protocol model, and $c_1W/\sqrt{nlogn}$ and $c_2W/\sqrt{n}\ bit/s$ are lower and upper bounds of the throughput in the physical model. While each node uses an optimally chosen power and an optimally distributed traffic, then each node can get a transport capacity of $\Theta(W\sqrt{n})\ bit - meters/s$ in the protocol model, and $c_3 W\sqrt{n}$ and $c_4 W n^{\frac{\alpha-1}{\alpha}}$ $bit - meters/s$ are lower and upper bounds of the transport capacity in the physical model. To calculate the wireless network capacity at each node, it is essential for nodes to know the total number of nodes represented by n in the MANET area with mechanisms of exchanging control messages or data packets which piggyback control messages. [5] does not give any mechanism for each node to choose an optimized data rate. As compared to [1], [4] and [5], the benefit of our approach shows a mechanism to choose an optimal data rate in an on-demand MANET networks. Ju used an discrete time M/M/1 queueing traffic model to evaluate the average packet delay in multi-hop packet radio TDMA network [6]. In [7], throughput-delay analysis is studied in ad-hoc network with Kleinrock independence approximation by using TDMA. A disadvantage of [5] and [7] which use contention-free multiple access protocol is that the increasing complexity of TDMA or dynamic assignment of frequency bands of FDMA due to the non-centralized control in MANETs could not be the best solution. As a contention-based protocol, Carrier Sensing Multiple Access with Collision Avoidance (CSMA/CA) has been standardized in the IEEE 802.11 (IEEE stands for Institute of Electronics and Electrical Engineering) and can be one of the possible MAC protocols for MANETs. Kleinrock calculated the throughput-delay characteristics in ALOHA and CSMA protocols. In [8], the traffic source is also modeled as an independent Poisson source with an average mean packet generation rate of λ packets/sec. As a one of the application of Little's theorem, the end-to-end network delay for a packet described in [9] can be used to network topology design in order to minimize network costs, capacity planning so as to guarantee the required traffic performance, and delay minimization by choosing a path which gives minimum end-to-end delay. IEEE 802.11 wireless local area network (LAN) is called a cut-through routing-free (CTRF) network where each medium access control (MAC) packet is transmitted completely over one link before starting transmission to the next compared to the concept of a cut-through routing (CTR) kind of network [3], [9]. Therefore, a long packet in the first queue gives more processing time to the second queue in a tandem queue [9] can not be applied in the MANET due to the property of the wireless channel where only one node can send or receive a packet among its neighbor nodes during a certain time. In a wired network, a link can permit several packet streams, however, in a wireless network, a link permits only a single packet stream during a given time interval. Since the traffic processing time in the first queue does not affect to the arrival of traffic of the second queue in an on-demand MANET network, it is appropriate to adopt an $M/M/1$ queueing model for each on-demand link regardless of traffic on this link with traffic on other links. It implies that packet arrivals to each link are independent from the delay and queue process over the previous relaying wireless link [7]. Therefore, Kleinrock independence approximation can be used to analysis the average packet delay time in on-demand MANET networks.

[2] Based on Knuth's notation, $f(x) = \Theta(g(x))$ denotes that $f(x) = O(g(x))$ and $g(x) = O(f(x))$, where $f(x) = O(g(x))$ denotes that $\frac{f(x)}{g(x)} \leq c$ for some constant c and for all sufficiently large x.

The remainder of this paper is organized as follows: Chapters 3 and 4 define the system model and an optimization procedure for the end-to-end packet delay respectively. Chapter 5 introduces a mechanism to implement the optimization in on-demand MANET networks. Chapter 6 contains simulation results and performance analysis. Chapter 7 presents the conclusions.

3 System Model

In a MANET with N nodes, each node has a transmitter, a receiver and an infinite buffer, and communicates with the other nodes by multi-hop routing. Node t_j transmits at a fixed power P_{t_j} and all transmissions occupy a system bandwidth (W[Hz]) in a wireless channel. When t_j transmits, r_j which composes a pair of nodes with t_j receives the signal with power $G_{t_j,r_j}P_{t_j}$ where G_{t_j,r_j} is a channel gain between the transmitter node t_j and the receiver node r_j. A *transmission scheme* S is a complete description of the information flow between different nodes in the network at a given time instant and it consists of all transmit-receive node pairs at that time, the transmission rate and the original source node of the transmitted information [4]. For a specific transmission scheme, which can be described as a triple $\mathcal{S}^\rho = \{\mathcal{T}^\rho, \mathcal{R}^\rho, \mathbf{P}^\rho\}$, a set of transmitting nodes is represented as $\mathcal{T}^\rho = \{t_1, \ldots, t_n\} \in \{1, \ldots, N\}$ and a set of their intended receivers is $\mathcal{R}^\rho = \{r_1, \ldots, r_n\} \in \{1, \ldots, N\}$. Let transmit powers of the nodes be $\mathbf{P}^\rho = \{P_{t_1}, \ldots, P_{t_n}\}, (P_{t_i} = 0 \; for \; t_i \notin \mathcal{T})$. Together with channel gain values, this determines achievable rates between the transmitter and receiver pairs. For a specific transmission scheme $\mathcal{S}^\rho$, a signal to interference and noise ratio (SINR) between the active pair of nodes (t_j, r_j) is given by

$$\xi^\rho_{t_j,r_j} = \frac{P^\rho_{t_j} G^\rho_{t_j,r_j}}{\eta_{r_j} W + \sum_{k:t_k \in \mathcal{T}_\rho, t_k \neq t_j} P^\rho_{t_k} G^\rho_{t_k,r_j}} \tag{1}$$

where η_{r_j} is a thermal noise and a background noise power spectral density specified at node r_j. It is assumed that nodes cannot transmit and receive data packet at the same time and nodes have a perfect knowledge of the channel gain matrix (G), the noise (η) and the power (P) vectors. Nodes t_j and r_j can have a maximum data rate R^ρ_j, which can be represented as a function of $\xi^\rho_{t_j,r_j}$. For example, based on Shannon capacity, the maximum data rate under a specific digital modulation at a BER requirement can be calculated as [4]

$$f(\xi^\rho_{t_j,r_j}) = \begin{cases} W\log_2\left(1 + \xi^\rho_{t_j,r_j}\right), (t_j, r_j) \in (\mathcal{T}^\rho, \mathcal{R}^\rho) \\ 0 \qquad\qquad\qquad\quad , otherwise. \end{cases} \tag{2}$$

$f(\cdot)$ is a function that reflects the quality of the receiver. The data rate vector $\mathcal{R}^\rho = \left[R^\rho_1 \cdots R^\rho_n\right]^T$ represents simultaneously achievable data rates between the active transmitter and receiver pairs at the transmission scheme $\mathcal{S}^\rho$.

4 End to End Packet Delay Optimization

The problem is to choose a data rate at the node t_j for its wireless link of a path α so as to minimize a linear cost function of the path α [9]

$$\sum_{t^{\rho}_{j=1}}^{n} p^{\rho}_{j} R^{\rho}_{j} \tag{3}$$

where p^{ρ}_{j} is a known positive price per unit data rate, subject to the constraint that the average delay per packet at the path α should not exceed a given constant T which is the QoS end-to-end packet delay requirement. The implementation of the T is described in Section V. An arrival rate on the node t_j for the path α during a time interval $(\mathcal{S}^{\sigma}, \mathcal{S}^{\rho}]$, where a time difference between $\mathcal{S}^{\rho}$ and $\mathcal{S}^{\sigma}$ is always greater than zero, can be denoted λ^{ρ}_{j} and is expressed in the same unit as the departure rate (R^{ρ}_{j}) which is serviced at the node t_j as the maximum achievable data rate at the $\mathcal{S}^{\rho}$. The $M/M/1$ queueing model is adopted based on the Kleinrock independence approximation for serial wireless links in tandem to form a path, where serial wireless links through the network make a virtual wireless packet stream in the MANET, therefore the average end-to-end packet delay constraint for the path α can be expressed as

$$\frac{1}{\gamma^{\rho}} \sum_{t^{\rho}_{j=1}}^{n} \frac{\lambda^{\rho}_{j}}{R^{\rho}_{j} - \lambda^{\rho}_{j}} \leq T \tag{4}$$

where γ^{ρ} is the total arrival rate, which is the summed arrival rate at active nodes in the tagged path α during the time interval $(\mathcal{S}^{\sigma}, \mathcal{S}^{\rho}]$. The arrival rate vector $\Lambda^{\rho} = [\lambda^{\rho}_{1} \cdots \lambda^{\rho}_{n}]^{T}$ during the interval $(\mathcal{S}^{\sigma}, \mathcal{S}^{\rho}]$ at the active nodes depends on the known input arrival rates and the routing policy. It is assumed that routing and the input arrival rates are known.

When an arrival rate (λ^{ρ}_{j}) at the node t_j is known, the problem is to minimize the linear cost $\sum_{t^{\rho}_{j=1}}^{n} p^{\rho}_{j} R^{\rho}_{j}$ over the maximum data rate R^{ρ}_{j}, which is subject to the above end-to-end packet delay constraint. In addition, it is clear that the constraint will be satisfied as an equality of the optimum. A Lagrange multiplier δ is introduced and the Lagrangian function can be formed as

$$L = \sum_{t^{\rho}_{j=1}}^{n} \left(p^{\rho}_{j} R^{\rho}_{j} + \frac{\delta}{\gamma^{\rho}} \frac{\lambda^{\rho}_{j}}{R^{\rho}_{j} - \lambda^{\rho}_{j}} \right) \tag{5}$$

The partial derivative $\partial L / \partial R^{\rho}_{j}$ is set to zero in accordance with the Lagrange multiplier technique:

$$\frac{\partial L}{\partial R^{\rho}_{j}} = p^{\rho}_{j} - \frac{\delta \lambda^{\rho}_{j}}{\gamma^{\rho} (R^{\rho}_{j} - \lambda^{\rho}_{j})^{2}} = 0 \tag{6}$$

Solving for R_j^ρ yields

$$R_j^\rho = \lambda_j^\rho + \sqrt{\frac{\delta \lambda_j^\rho}{\gamma^\rho p_j^\rho}} \tag{7}$$

and substituting into the constraint equation, T is given as

$$T = \frac{1}{\gamma^\rho} \sum_{t_{j=1}^\rho}^{n} \frac{\lambda_j^\rho}{R_j^\rho - \lambda_j^\rho} = \sum_{t_{j=1}^\rho}^{n} \sqrt{\frac{\lambda_j^\rho p_j^\rho}{\gamma^\rho \delta}} \tag{8}$$

From the above equation,

$$\sqrt{\delta} = \frac{1}{T} \sum_{t_{j=1}^\rho}^{n} \sqrt{\frac{\lambda_j^\rho p_j^\rho}{\gamma^\rho}} \tag{9}$$

which when substituted in $R_{\rho,j}$ gives the optimal solution

$$R_j^{\rho,*} = \lambda_j^\rho + \frac{1}{T} \sqrt{\frac{\lambda_j^\rho}{\gamma^\rho p_j^\rho}} \sum_{t_{l=1}^\rho}^{n} \sqrt{\frac{\lambda_l^\rho p_l^\rho}{\gamma^\rho}} \tag{10}$$

The solution can also be written as

$$R_j^{\rho,*} = \lambda_j^\rho \left(1 + \frac{1}{\gamma^\rho T} \frac{\sum_{t_{l=1}^\rho}^{n} \sqrt{p_l^\rho \lambda_l^\rho}}{\sqrt{p_j^\rho \lambda_j^\rho}} \right) \tag{11}$$

Finally, based on the cost function for the path α which is $\sum_{t_{j=1}^\rho}^{n} p_j^\rho R_j^\rho$, the optimal cost can be expressed as

$$\begin{aligned} optimal\ cost &= \sum_{t_{j=1}^\rho}^{n} p_j^\rho R_j^{\rho,*} \\ &= \sum_{t_{j=1}^\rho}^{n} p_j^\rho \lambda_j^\rho + \frac{1}{\gamma^\rho T} \left(\sum_{t_{j=1}^\rho}^{n} \sqrt{p_j^\rho \lambda_j^\rho} \right)^2 \end{aligned} \tag{12}$$

5 Observation

In QoS applied MANET routing protocols, a node can require an end-to-end packet delay (T) by issuing routing messages (or fields, which are included in the messages) such as a *resource request* and a *resource reply* for the path α. For example, in on-demand MANET routing protocols, when a source node initiates the *resource request* field in the route discovery mechanism, which transfers the required end-to-end packet delay (T) for the path α towards a destination, traffic negotiation and resource reservation are accomplished at each intermediate node. For responding the *resource request*, the destination needs to reply the *resource reply* field back to the source. While each intermediate node backwards the *resource reply*, the end-to-end packet delay constraint (T) at each intermediate node, which, for example, can be confirmed as

$$f(T,n) = \Theta\big(g(T,n)\big) \tag{13}$$

where n is the number of the MANET nodes in the path α and $\Theta(\cdot)$ is used to compensate the variable number of MANET node in the path α. From the equations (1) and (2), each intermediate node can calculate its maximum data rate at the transmission scheme $\mathcal{S}^\rho$. In the case when the R_j^ρ, which is the maximum data rate for the node t_j at the transmission scheme $\mathcal{S}^\rho$ is less than the minimum QoS optimized data rate ($R_j^{\rho,*}$) calculated from the equation (11) for the required QoS end-to-end delay, the QoS mode of the node t_j turns into best effort where the maximum data rate R_j^ρ is serviced for the required QoS data rate. Since the best effort cannot guarantee the QoS end-to-end packet delay requirement, it is counted as a violation of the QoS service. As another case, when the R_j^ρ is higher than the optimized QoS data rate $R_j^{\rho,*}$ at the transmission scheme $\mathcal{S}^\rho$, instead of using the maximum R_j^ρ, the node t_j can select the optimized QoS data rate $R_j^{\rho,*}$, and save the cost of using node and network resources whose amount can be represented by $p_j^\rho R_j^\rho - p_j^\rho R_j^{\rho,*}$. The selection of the data rate of the node t_j for the required QoS end-to-end packet delay at the transmission scheme $\mathcal{S}^\rho$ can be represented as

$$\begin{aligned} R_j^{q,*} &= min\big(R_j^\rho, R_j^{\rho,*}\big) \\ &= \begin{cases} R_j^\rho &, \text{use } R_j^\rho \text{ for best effort} \\ R_j^{\rho,*} &, \text{use optimized } R_j^{\rho,*} \end{cases} \end{aligned} \tag{14}$$

The optimal cost for the path α for the required QoS end-to-end packet delay at the transmission scheme $\mathcal{S}^\rho$ can be represented as

$$optimal\ cost = \sum_{t_j^\rho=1}^{n} p_j^\rho R_j^{q,*} \tag{15}$$

Therefore, the total cost saved at the path α can be represented by $\sum_{t_j^\rho=1}^{n} p_j^\rho R_j^\rho - \sum_{t_j^\rho=1}^{n} p_j^\rho R_j^{q,*}$.

6 Numerical Results

To provide multi-hop routing, a MANET operates different transmission schemes at different times. It is assumed that the MANET operation is organized in a frame of a given fixed duration. To service each frame, the network operates using successive schemes $\mathcal{S}_1, \cdots, \mathcal{S}_k$, with scheme $\mathcal{S}_i$ operating during a fraction of w_i, where $\sum_{i=1}^{k} w_i = 1$. Therefore, the network uses the time-division routing schedule for a path α which can be represented as $\mathcal{H}_\alpha = \sum_{i=1}^{k} w_i \mathcal{S}_i$, where w_i is referred as weights of the time-division routing schedule [4]. Based on successive transmission scheme, nodes in an active path send data frames to their neighbors and data frames are delivered toward a randomly selected destination. Monte Carlo computer simulations are performed to evaluate the transmission schemes and to calculate the optimal data rate for the tagged path. It is assumed that relay nodes have infinite queue capacity, the channel is an ideal channel without errors at any transmission cycle of distributed coordination function (DCF) [10], there is no packet error while data packet is transmitted and the maximum achievable data rate is used in the case of no-optimization.

Table 1. Parameters for IEEE 802.11 A [**:bytes]

Parameter	Value	Parameter	Value	Parameter	Value
CW_{min}	15μsec	T_{slot}	9μsec	T_{difs}	34μsec
T_{sifs}	16μsec	T_{sym}	4μsec	τ	1μsec
T_p	16μsec	T_{sig}	4μsec	L_{data}^{max}	2312B**
L_{data}^{h}	34B	L_{ack}	14B	N_{dbps}	216bits

In the simulation, thirty nodes are movable in the network area 1000m×1000m and IEEE 802.11a technology [1] is considered where some of the parameters are defined in Table I. To calculate the achievable maximum data rate (R_j^ρ) for 54 Mbps in IEEE 802.11a, a transmission cycle of DCF is composed of distributed inter-frame space (DIFS) deferral, backoff, data transmission, short inter-frame space (SIFS) deferral and ACK transmission [11]. Therefore, R_j^ρ is calculated as

$$R_j^\rho = \frac{8L_{data,j}^\rho}{T_{data} + T_{ack} + 2\tau + T_{difs} + T_{sifs} + \overline{CW}} \tag{16}$$

where τ is a propagation delay, the average backoff time, $\overline{CW} = (CW_{min}/2) \times T_{slot}$, is used to model the packet error-free channel. The equation of R_j^ρ is used to simulate the arrival rate (λ_j^ρ) and to simulate the maximum departure data rate (R_j^ρ) which is not optimized data rate in a transmission scheme $\mathcal{S}^\rho$ at the node t_j. The data transmission delay T_{data} and the transmission delay ACK T_{ack} are expressed as follows:

$$T_{data} = T_p + T_{sig} + T_{sym} \cdot \left\lceil \frac{16 + 6 + 8L_{data}^h + 8L_{data,j}^\rho}{N_{dbps}} \right\rceil$$

$$T_{ack} = T_p + T_{sig} + T_{sym} \cdot \left\lceil \frac{16 + 6 + 8L_{ack}}{N_{dbps}} \right\rceil \tag{17}$$

where T_p is physical layer convergence procedure (PLCP) preamble duration, T_{sig} is duration of the signal BPSK-OFDM symbol, T_{sym} is symbol interval, N_{dbps} is the number of data bits per OFDM symbol. When PHY layer bit rate goes to infinity, N_{dbps} goes to infinity as well. The throughput upper limit (TUL) [10] is existed as $TUL = 8L^{\rho}_{data,j}/\left(2T_p + 2T_{sig} + 2\tau + T_{difs} + T_{sifs} + \overline{CW}\right)$.

Fig. 1 shows the cumulative distribution function (CDF) of the simulated data rate. The end-to-end packet delay constraints are selected as $10,000ms$, $800ms$, $100ms$, $70ms$, and $50ms$ for the tagged path [11]. To show the case of a loose (a tight) end-to-end packet delay constraint, $10,000ms$ ($50ms$) is selected.

Lemma 1. *When active MANET nodes do not have any constraint on end-to-end packet delay for a path α, the nodes turn into a mode of not-optimized which only services arrival data rate at a specific transmission scheme S^{ρ} of the nodes.*

Proof. The numerical expression of no-constraint situation can be extracted from the equation (11) by letting T go to infinity. Therefore, $R^{\rho,*}_j$ converges to λ^{ρ}_j, which can be represented as

$$\begin{aligned}\lim_{T\to\infty} R^{\rho,*}_j &= \lim_{T\to\infty}\left[\lambda^{\rho}_j\left(1 + \frac{1}{\gamma^{\rho}T}\frac{\sum_{t^{\rho}_{l=1}}^{n}\sqrt{p^{\rho}_l\lambda^{\rho}_l}}{\sqrt{p^{\rho}_j\lambda^{\rho}_j}}\right)\right]\\ &= \lambda^{\rho}_j. \end{aligned} \tag{18}$$

Lemma 2. *When active MANET nodes do not permit any end-to-end packet delay for a path α, the nodes should have a data rate of infinity.*

Proof. The numerical representation of this situation can be seen from the equation (11) when the T goes to zero, $R^{\rho,*}_j$ converges to ∞, which can be represented as

$$\begin{aligned}\lim_{T\to 0} R^{\rho,*}_j &= \lim_{T\to 0}\left[\lambda^{\rho}_j\left(1 + \frac{1}{\gamma^{\rho}T}\frac{\sum_{t^{\rho}_{l=1}}^{n}\sqrt{p^{\rho}_l\lambda^{\rho}_l}}{\sqrt{p^{\rho}_j\lambda^{\rho}_j}}\right)\right]\\ &= \infty. \end{aligned} \tag{19}$$

When the end-to-end packet delay time constraint is restricted in the optimized cases illustrated in Fig. 1, the probability required to use higher data rate in MANET nodes is increased to satisfy the end-to-end packet delay time constraint. To compare the required data rate used at different end-to-end packet delay constraints in a MANET node, $100ms$ and $50ms$ are chosen as an example. At a probability of 10% of $50ms$, the MANET node used more 5Mbps data rate than a probability of 10% of $100ms$. Therefore, the optimal data rate at each MANET node strongly depends on the end-to-end packet delay constraint.

In addition, it is shown that MANET nodes can select the optimized data rate at each transmission scheme and save the amount of data rate compared to the one which is not optimized. For example, in the case of not-optimized, a usage probability using 25 Mbps data rate is around 45%. However, in the optimized

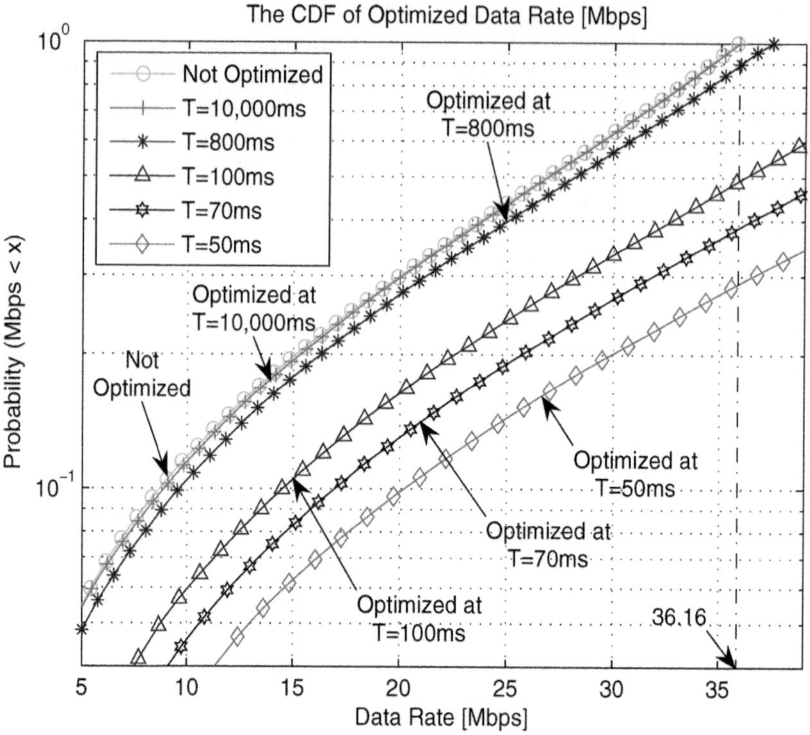

Fig. 1. Effect of optimized data rate

case of 100*ms*, the usage probability using 25 Mbps data rate is around 23%. Therefore, the MANET nodes optimized at 100*ms* can save 22% amount of data rate at 25 Mbps compared to the not-optimized MANET nodes.

7 Conclusion

This paper introduces a novel method to obtain an optimized data rate subject to an end-to-end packet delay constraint in a MANET. By using Lagrangian function and the end-to-end packet delay constraint, each intermediate node in an active path can achieve the optimized data rate. When the required QoS data rate is higher than the maximum achievable data rate at each intermediate node, the maximum achievable data rate is used, which is counted as the violation of the guaranteed QoS service. Due to the use of the optimized QoS data rate when the achievable maximum data rate is higher than the optimized QoS data rate, each intermediate node in the path can save the cost of using node and network resources. Moreover, this paper proposes several metrics for measuring the QoS performance of the end-to-end packet delay. The total degraded QoS throughput shows the result of the QoS throughput not having any QoS service on the path.

References

1. *Wireless LAN medium access control (MAC) and physical layer (PHY) specifications: High-Speed Physical Layer in the 5GHz Band*, IEEE Standard 802.11a-1999, IEEE Computer Society LAN MAN Standards Committee, 1999.
2. *Wireless LAN medium access control (MAC) and physical layer (PHY) specifications: Amendment 4: Further Higher Data Rate Extension in 2.4GHz Band*, IEEE Standard 802.11g-2003, IEEE Computer Society LAN MAN Standards Committee, 2003.
3. V. Mitlin, "Optimal MAC packet size in netwroks without cut-throuth routing,", *IEEE Trans. Commun.*, vol 2, pp. 901-910, Nov. 2003.
4. S. Toumpis and A. J. Goldsmith, "Capacity regions for wireless ad hoc networks," *IEEE Trans. Commun.*, vol. 2, no.4, pp. 736- 748, July. 2003.
5. P. Gupta and P. R. Kumar, "The capacity of wireless networks," *IEEE Transaction on information theory*, vol. IT-46, No. 2, pp. 388-404, March 2000.
6. J-H. Ju and V. O. K. Li, "TDMA scheduling design of multihop packet radio networks based on Latin Squares," *IEEE Journal on Selected Areas in Communications*, vol.17, no.8, August 1999, pp.1345-1352.
7. B. Shrader, M. Sánchez, and T.C. Giles, "Throughput-delay Analysis of Conflict-free Scheduling in Multihop Ad-hoc Networks," *Proceedings of the 3rd Swedish Workshop on Wireless Ad-hoc Networks*, Stockholm, Johannesbergs Slott,6-7 May 2003.
8. L. Kleinrock and F. A. Tobagi, "Packet switching in radio channels: Part I - carrier sense multiple access modes and their throughput-delay characteristics," *IEEE Transactions on Communications*, COM-23, pp. 1400-1416, December 1975.
9. D. Bertsekas and R. Gallager, *Data Networks, Upper Saddle River.* Englewood Cliffs, NJ: Prentice-Hall, 1992.
10. Y. Xiao and J. Rosdahl, "Throughput and Delay Limits of IEEE 802.11," *IEEE Commun. Lett.*, vol. 6, no. 8, Aug. 2002, pp. 355-357.
11. M. Baldi and Y. Ofek, "End-to-end delay analysis of videoconferencing over packet-switched networks," *IEEE Transactions on Networking.*, vol 8, no. 4, pp. 479-492, August 2003.

Power Efficient Relaying MAC Protocol for Rate Adaptive Wireless LANs*

Jaeeun Na, Yeonkwon Jeong, and Joongsoo Ma

School of Engineering, Information and Communications University
Daejeon, 305-732, Korea
{davini02,ykwjeong,jsma}@icu.ac.kr

Abstract. To exploit multi-rate capability as well as improve performance in wireless networks, many relaying mechanisms are proposed on IEEE 802.11 media access control (MAC) layer. However, no effort has been invested to exploit the multi-rate capability for power saving mechanism in MAC. In this paper, we propose a Power Efficient Relaying MAC Protocol, called PERP, to achieve both performance improvement and power saving by leveraging the multi-rate capability. In proposed relaying scheme, if a node can support low rate node's packet at higher rate and has sufficient power, after voluntarily helping data transmission at higher rate, all nodes go into sleep mode as quickly as possible to reduce power consumption. Simulation results show that the PERP improves throughput by 30∼50% as well as reduces power consumption and transmission delay by 10∼55% than the legacy mechanism.

Keywords: Multi-rate Adaptation, Relaying, IEEE 802.11 MAC, Power Saving Mechanism, Wireless Networks.

1 Introduction

As the portable devices exponentially increase in wireless networks, the development of power efficient and fast transmission mechanisms become more important recently. In the last few years, there have been many researches about efficient power conserving mechanisms at various layers. Among them, [5] suggested that power saving mechanism of medium access control (MAC) layer could significantly reduce the power consumption by putting the wireless interface in the doze mode. Hence, this paper focuses on power conserving of MAC protocol. In [6, 7], they proposed the adaptive power saving MAC protocols that allow mobile nodes to keep doze mode as much as possible to reduce unnecessary idle power consumption. However, those protocols only consider power consumption of nodes and do not improve overall network throughput. Therefore, this paper

* This research was supported by MIC (Ministry of Information and Communication), Korea, under the ITRC (Information Technology Research Center) support program supervised by the IITA (Institute of Information Technology Assessment). (IITA-2006-C1090-0603-0015).

Y.-H. Lee et al. (Eds.): ICESS 2007, LNCS 4523, pp. 664–675, 2007.

proposes the power efficient MAC protocol with multi-rate capability to improve performance as well as save power for wireless local area networks (WLANs).

IEEE 802.11 standard for WLAN [1] provides a multi-rate capability on physical layer (PHY) to support higher bandwidth by using different modulation schemes. For example, IEEE 802.11b supports data rates of 1, 2, 5.5, 11Mbps, which are inversely proportional with the transmission distance between sender and receiver. To further exploit multi-rate capability and improve performance, several relaying protocols [3,4] have been proposed on MAC layer. This approach makes that low rate transmission is replaced with two higher rate transmissions by using intermediate node as relay node. When sender transmits data at low data rate due to long distance between sender and receiver, it selects a suitable relay node of neighbor nodes that supports higher data rate. Instead of direct transmission at low rate, sender transmits indirectly data packet to a selected relay node and then a relay node just transmits it to receiver at higher rate without additional contention.

By using this relaying approach and power saving mechanism of MAC layer, we propose a Power Efficient Relaying MAC Protocol (PERP). The purpose of this protocol is to achieve both performance improvement and power saving by leveraging the multi-rate capability. During only fixed period, called ATIM (Announcement Traffic Indication Message) window, a node decides direct transmission rate and announces it to neighbor nodes by piggybacking rate information into legacy ATIM frames. If a node can relay low rate node's packet at higher rate and has sufficient power, it records low rate transmission in table. After ATIM window, nodes that have records of low rate nodes in table help relevant nodes to transmit data at higher rate through voluntary notification prior to their low rate data transmission. Moreover, nodes can go into sleep mode as quickly as possible through cooperatively sending data packet at higher rate.

The remaining of this paper is organized as follows. In section 2, we present the details of PERP and analyze the performance. Section 3 evaluates the performance of PERP by means of simulations. Section 4 concludes the paper.

2 The Power Efficient Relaying MAC Protocol

2.1 PERP Operation

In this section, we propose the Power Efficient Relaying MAC protocol that is based on power saving mechanism (PSM) of DCF (Distributed Coordination Function). The basic concept of PERP is that every awake node quickly enters doze mode through cooperatively helping transmit data at higher rate. By using control packets, nodes can decide suitable data rate without additional rate adaptation procedure during ATIM window. All control packets are transmitted at base rate (2Mbps) and can be overheard by other nodes. In our proposed scheme, the period following ATIM window in beacon interval is called DATA window. To save unnecessary idle power during DATA window of legacy PSM, sender or receiver can go into doze mode when they have no more sending or

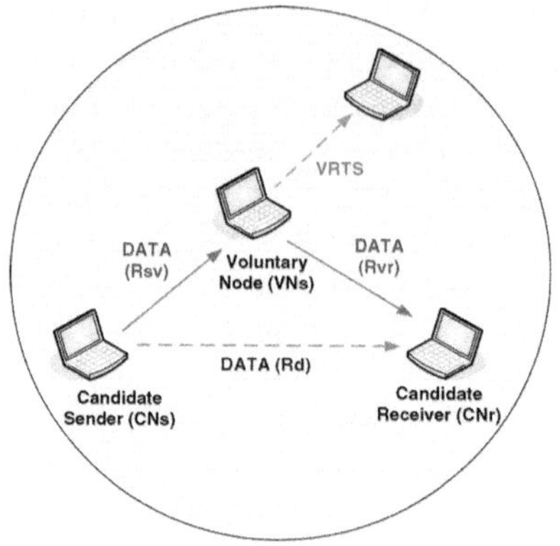

Fig. 1. Voluntary Relaying Procedure of PERP (solid line: relaying transmission, dotted line: direct transmission)

receiving data, including other node's relaying data. Receivers can know whether receiving packets are remaining or not through the 'more data bit' field in MAC header of data packet [1]. Each node also maintains the *candidate table* only for current beacon interval to assist low rate transmission of other node. And we restrict that a node can assist only one neighbor node to avoid much power consumption by relaying many other packets.

The PERP operation is illustrated in Figure 1 and 2, and is explained in detail by the following steps:

1) In ATIM window, sender having data packet transmits ATIM frame to receiver. On receiving ATIM frame, receiver measures received signal strength (RSS) to decide direct data rate (R_d, as shown Figure 1). And then, receiver notifies R_d to sender and neighbor nodes via ACK (Acknowledgement) frame with piggybacked rate information. Every nodes overhears all ongoing ATIM/ACK frames and determines two indirect data rates (R_{sv}, R_{vr}) between sender (or receiver) and itself respectively through measurement of RSS. In addition, by extracting the piggybacked rate information in ACK frame, they can also find out R_d. If R_d is lower than 2Mbps, nodes compare it with R_{sv} and R_{vr}. If a node supports higher rate than direct data rate ($L/R_{sv} + L/R_{vr} < L/R_d$, L : packet length), it add the new *candidate node* (CN_s) information in candidate table. This table is consisted of sender (CN_s) address of low rate transmission, R_{sv}, R_{vr}, and total RSS of ATIM/ACK frames.

The senders, which can transmit its data at high rate (5.5 or 11 Mbps) and have more than one CN_s in table, have high priority for data transmission with smaller contention window size. Since these nodes have to notify their CN_s that they will relay low rate packet at higher rate, before CN_s sends out its data packet at low rate. Moreover, they will consume more transmission power as a result of relaying other packets, so priority scheme makes their power consumption be reduced by shorter contention time.

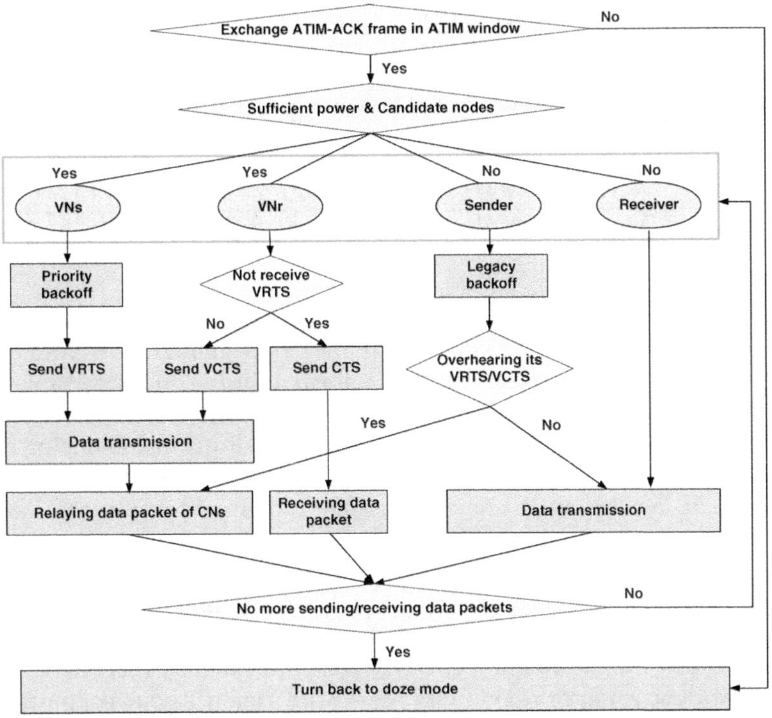

Fig. 2. The Flow Diagram of PERP Algorithm During One Beacon Interval

2) After ATIM window is over, awake nodes follow DCF scheme to send data packet with priority backoff scheme.

a) Sender first senses the idle channel for a DIFS time and its backoff time.

b) Sender checks whether it has sufficient power and any CN_s in candidate table.

c) In case two conditions of (b) are not satisfied, sender transmits RTS (Request To Send) frame to receiver. Otherwise, sender enables to relay other node's packets in table, which is called the voluntary sender (VN_s). VN_s selects an optimal CN_s which has the highest total R_{sr} and R_{vr} in candidate table. If there are several optimal candidate nodes, they select CN_s having the highest total RSS. After that, VN_s transmits the Voluntary RTS (VRTS) that piggybacks CN_s's address and supporting R_{sv} and R_{vr} in RTS frame.

3) When receiver receives VRTS, it just sends out CTS to sender after SIFS time to avoid collision with sender's relaying data transmission. On the other hands, if receiver receive RTS, then it repeats (2.b) and (2.c) procedures; checking status, selection of CN_s, sending CTS (Clear To Send) or VCTS (Voluntary CTS) frame after SIFS time. Receiver sending VCTS is called the voluntary receiver (VN_r). At this time, neighbor nodes having same CN_s's information of VRTS or VCTS in own candidate table deletes the relevant CN_s's information.

Table 1. Duration of Control Frames for NAV

Control Frames	Duration (NAV)
RTS	$3 \times SIFS + T_{CTS} + L/R_d + T_{ACK}$
RTS_{CN_s}	$4 \times SIFS + T_{CTS} + L/R_{sv} + L/R_{vr} + T_{ACK}$
VRTS	$NAV_{RTS} + 2 \times SIFS$
CTS	$NAV_{RTS(VRTS)} - SIFS - T_{CTS}$
VCTS	$NAV_{CTS} + 2 \times SIFS$

4) Once receiving CTS or VCTS, sender transmits data packet at R_d. If receiver receives data successfully, it replies by sending ACK frame. At this time, nodes that have current sender's information in candidate table delete it. After data transmission is completed, sender and receiver go into sleep mode, except for VN_s or VN_r, if there is no remaining data transmission or reception. However, if remaining DATA window time is shorter than transition time from doze state to awake state, they maintains awake mode to avoid more power consumption by frequent transitions. VN_s and VN_r continuously keep awake mode until relaying data transmission is finished.

5) If selected CN_s overhears VRTS or VCTS, it prepares data transmission regardless of its remaining backoff time. After data transmission of voluntary node (VN_s or VN_r) is completed, CN_s starts immediately relaying transmission of own data via voluntary node just after SIFS time without contention.

When CN_s and its receiver (CN_r) sends out RTS/CTS, they repeats from (2.b) to (3) procedures because they can also relay other low rate node's data at higher rate according to location. After that, CN_s transmits data to voluntary node at dedicated rate R_{sv}. If voluntary node receives data of CN_s, it sends data to CN_r at rate R_{vr}. Finally, CN_r sends ACK frame to CN_s directly and voluntary node goes into doze mode. (If CN_s or CN_r has no relaying data packet, they also enter doze mode.)

At this time, to maintain backward compatibility with IEEE 802.11 MAC protocol, we adopt the data relaying scheme that uses Address 4 field of MAC header in [3]. Subtype denotes the relaying data packet as the specific value and Address 4 field stores the address of voluntary node. In addition, CN_s and voluntary node enable to set exact duration for NAV because they know indirect data rates of relaying packet as shown Table 1. Note that the voluntary nodes set the additional duration for relaying data to only 2 × SIFS time in case CN_s moves to another place or does not overhear VRTS (or VCTS) due to worse channel status. If CN_s does not send RTS within 2 × SIFS time, voluntary node turns back to sleep mode promptly and other nodes restart their backoff timer.

2.2 Throughput Analysis

In this section, we will derive the throughput of legacy PSM and PERP within beacon interval. We assume that all nodes are uniformly distributed in the coverage area. Let the distance thresholds for data rate 11, 5.5, 2 Mbps ($R_{11}, R_{5.5}, R_{base}$)

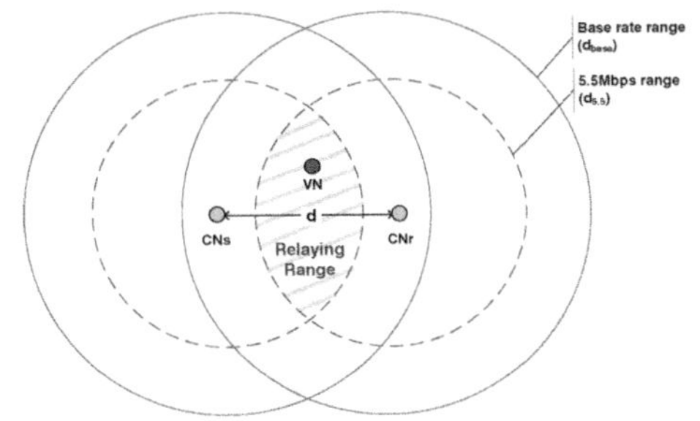

Fig. 3. The Probability of Finding Relay Node

are d_{11}, $d_{5.5}$, d_{base} meters respectively. (Assume that a node transmits only one fixed size data packet at least 2Mbps.)

First of all, we express the number of nodes sending ATIM frame when N_{node}^{cont} nodes contend in ATIM window (Th_{ATIM}).

$$N_{node}^{ATIM} = \min(N_{node}^{cont}, N_{node}^{nego}) \tag{1}$$

$$N_{node}^{nego} = \left\lfloor \frac{Th_{ATIM}}{T_{tx} + T_{rx} + T_{over} + T_{cont}^{N_{node}^{cont}}} \right\rfloor$$

where N_{node}^{nego} is the maximum number of nodes that can negotiate by sending ATIM/ACK frames until ATIM window is saturated. $T_{tx}, T_{rx}, T_{over}, T_{cont}$ are ATIM/ACK transmission, reception, overhead (SIFS, DIFS) and contention time. If multiple nodes attempt to send packet at the same time, packet will collide and be retransmitted. As the number of nodes (N) increases, the contention time increases. Here we use a simple approximation proposed in [2]:

$$T_{cont}^{N} = T_{slot} \cdot \frac{CW_{min}}{2} \cdot \frac{1 + Pro_{coll}^{N}}{2 \cdot N} \tag{2}$$

where collision probability is $Pro_{coll}^{N} = 1 - (1 - 1/\ CW_{min})^{N-1}$ and one slot time is T_{slot}.

Next, in case of legacy PSM, we can express the number of sending data packet in DATA window (Th_{DATA}) when data packet is transmitted at 2Mbps.

$$N_{legacy} = \min(N_{tx}^{legacy}, N_{ATIM})$$

$$N_{tx}^{legacy} = \left\lfloor \frac{Th_{DATA}}{L/R_{base} + T_{over} + T_{cont}^{N_{node}^{ATIM}}} \right\rfloor \tag{3}$$

where N_{ATIM} is the total number of data packets that N_{node}^{ATIM} nodes will transmit, L is data packet length and N_{tx}^{legacy} is the maximum number of sending data packets until DATA window is saturated.

In case of PERP, we must consider different transmission time based on data rate and voluntary relaying procedure. When voluntary node relays data packet of CN_s at higher rate, it has to locate within at least common $d_{5.5}$ range of CN_s and CN_r, that is *Relaying Range* as depicted Figure 3. Thus, voluntary relaying probability for CN_s can be defined following equation:

$$\begin{aligned} x &= \sqrt{d_{5.5}^2 - (d/2)^2}, (d_{5.5} \le d \le 2 \cdot d_{5.5}) \\ angle &= \arcsin(x/d_{5.5}) \\ Pro_{vol} &= \frac{4 \cdot \{angle/(2 \cdot \pi) \cdot d_{5.5}^2 \cdot \pi - (d/2) \cdot x \cdot 0.5\}}{d_{base}^2 \cdot \pi} \end{aligned} \tag{4}$$

where d is the distance between CN_s and CN_r.

Let us denote the fraction of nodes of direct data rate iMbps among awake nodes by F_i and the fraction of selected CN_s among low rate nodes by F_{relay}.

$$\begin{aligned} F_{11} &= d_{11}/d_{base} \\ F_{5.5} &= (d_{5.5} - d_{11})/d_{base} \\ F_{base} &= (d_{base} - d_{5.5})/d_{base} \\ F_{relay} &= Pro_{vol} \cdot F_{base} \end{aligned} \tag{5}$$

Finally, we may express the maximum number of sending data packets in DATA window similar to equation (3).

$$N_{PERP} = \min(N_{tx}^{PERP}, N_{ATIM}) \tag{6}$$

$$\begin{aligned} T_{dir} &= L \cdot \left\{ \frac{F_{11}}{R_{11}} + \frac{F_{5.5}}{R_{5.5}} + \frac{(F_{base} - F_{relay})}{R_{base}} \right\} \\ T_{relay} &= L \cdot F_{relay} \cdot 2/R_{5.5} \\ T_{data}^{avg} &= (T_{dir} + T_{relay})/(F_{11} + F_{5.5} + F_{base}) \\ N_{tx}^{PERP} &= \left\lfloor \frac{Th_{DATA}}{T_{data}^{avg} + T_{over} + T_{cont}^{N_{node}^{ATIM} \cdot (1 - F_{relay})}} \right\rfloor \end{aligned} \tag{7}$$

where T_{dir} and T_{relay} and T_{data}^{avg} are direct data transmission time, voluntary relaying time, and average data transmission time.

Therefore, the throughput of two protocols (legacy PSM and PERP) during beacon interval (Th_{beacon}) is given by the following equation:

$$Throughput = \frac{N_{protocol} \cdot L}{Th_{beacon}} \tag{8}$$

2.3 Power Consumption Analysis

In this subsection, we analyze mathematically the average power consumption of a node within one beacon interval based on the aggregate throughput analysis in previous subsection.

First of all, the average power consumed by a node is expressed as following equation:

$$Power_{node} = \frac{E_{node}^{ATIM} + E_{node}^{DATA}}{Th_{beacon}} \tag{9}$$

where E_{ATIM} and E_{DATA} is the energy consumption of a node during ATIM window and DATA window period.

In ATIM window, the operations for both PERP and legacy PSM are the same. Hence, equation(10) shows the average energy consumption during the ATIM window in more detail. In this equation, E_{ATIM} is divided two part; one for total energy consumption of the N_{ATIM} nodes exchanging ATIM/ACK frames successfully within ATIM window (E^{succ}_{ATIM}) and the other for that of the remaining nodes (E^{fail}_{ATIM}) when N^{cont}_{node} nodes contend for channel access.

$$E^{ATIM}_{node} = \frac{E^{succ}_{ATIM} + E^{fail}_{ATIM}}{N^{cont}_{node}} \tag{10}$$

$$E^{succ}_{ATIM} = N^{ATIM}_{node} \cdot \{P_{tx} \cdot T_{tx} + P_{rx} \cdot T_{rx} + P_{idle} \cdot (Th_{ATIM} - T_{tx} - T_{rx})\}$$

$$E^{fail}_{ATIM} = (N^{cont}_{node} - N^{ATIM}_{node}) \cdot (P_{idle} \cdot Th_{ATIM})$$

where T_{tx} and T_{rx} are the transmission and reception time of ATIM/ACK frames. P_{tx}, P_{rx} and P_{idle} are transmission, receiving, and idle power consumed by MAC layer respectively.

E^{succ}_{ATIM} is a combination of the transmitted and received power for exchanging ATIM/ACK frames. During the remaining ATIM window time, except for T_{tx} and T_{rx}, a node stays in idle mode. The nodes that does not exchange ATIM-ACK frames waste the unnecessary idle power for entire ATIM window (E^{fail}_{ATIM}). In addition, these nodes turn back into doze mode until DATA window is over, whose energy consumption is expressed as equation (11).

$$E^{sleepnode}_{DATA} = (N^{cont}_{node} - N^{ATIM}_{node}) \cdot (P_{doze} \cdot Th_{DATA}) \tag{11}$$

In next DATA window, both schemes have different operations and accordingly different energy consumption. Legacy PSM's average energy consumption is given by (12). In this equation, the energy consumption during DATA window is also classified into three parts; one for successful data transmission nodes (N_{legacy}), second one for not transmitting nodes, last one for sleep nodes.

$$E^{DATA-legacy}_{node} = \frac{E^{succ}_{l-DATA} + E^{fail}_{l-DATA} + E^{sleepnode}_{DATA}}{N^{cont}_{node}} \tag{12}$$

$$E^{succ}_{l-DATA} = N_{legacy} \cdot \{P_{tx} \cdot T_{tx-data} + P_{rx} \cdot T_{rx-data} + P_{idle} \cdot (Th_{DATA} - T_{tx-data} - T_{rx-data})\}$$

$$E^{fail}_{l-DATA} = (N_{ATIM} - N_{legacy}) \cdot (P_{idle} \cdot Th_{DATA})$$

where $T_{tx-data}$ and $T_{rx-data}$ are data transmission and reception time. In case successful transmission nodes, they consume idle power during the remaining time except for transmission and receiving time. On the other hand, failure nodes deeps the idle state until the end of DATA window.

In case of PERP, the nodes that its all data transmission and reception is over go into sleep mode. Hence, successful transmitting nodes have idle time until own data transmission starts and enter into sleep mode after all transmission is finished. The idle time is computed by T_{end}^{DATA} that all N_{PERP} nodes transmit their data packets. These nodes have the half of T_{end}^{DATA} averagely, except for data transmission time. Therefore, the average energy consumption is expressed as following equation :

$$\begin{aligned}
E_{node}^{DATA-PERP} &= \frac{E_{p-DATA}^{succ} + E_{p-DATA}^{fail} + E_{DATA}^{sleepnode}}{N_{node}^{cont}} \qquad (13)\\
E_{p-DATA}^{succ} &= N_{PERP} \cdot \{P_{tx} \cdot T_{tx-data} + P_{rx} \cdot T_{rx-data} \\
&\quad + P_{idle} \cdot T_{idle} + P_{doze} \cdot T_{sleep}\} \\
E_{p-DATA}^{fail} &= (N_{ATIM} - N_{PERP}) \cdot (P_{idle} \cdot Th_{DATA}) \\
T_{end}^{DATA} &= N_{PERP} \cdot \{T_{data}^{avg} + T_{over} + T_{cont}^{N_{node}^{ATIM} \cdot (1-F_{relay})}\} \\
T_{idle} &= \frac{T_{end}^{DATA} - (T_{data}^{avg} + T_{over})}{2} \\
T_{sleep} &= Th_{DATA} - (T_{idle} + T_{data}^{avg} + T_{over})
\end{aligned}$$

where the $T_{tx-data}$ and $T_{rx-data}$ are data transmission and reception time according to various data rate which can be calculated by T_{data}^{avg}.

3 Performance Evaluation

In this section, we evaluate the performance of PERP through simulation. Similar to [4], the distance threshold for 11, 5.5, 2Mbps are 100m, 200m, and 250m respectively. The data packet length is fixed at 512 bytes. Other basic parameters follows IEEE 802.11b MAC standard. The nodes are randomly distributed in $250m \times 250m$. The number of nodes chosen to be from 10 to 60 and the step is 10. In each case, half of the nodes are senders and the rest are receivers. For calculating power consumption, we use 1.65W, 1.4W, 1.15W and 0.045W as value of power consumed by MAC layer in transmit, receive, and idle modes and doze state respectively. We have 4 performance metrics, i.e. aggregate throughput (Kbps), average power consumption (mW), energy efficiency (Bytes/Joule), and transmission delay (ms).

One of the important issues in our scheme is to decide the optimal ATIM window size. If ATIM window size is too large, many nodes cannot send data during short DATA window time. In addition, it leads to unnecessary idle power consumption and longer transmission delay. Otherwise, if ATIM window is too small, nodes sending packet cannot negotiate sufficiently and remaining DATA window time is wasted. Hence, we first simulate aggregate throughput according to ATIM window size. As you can see Figure 4, legacy PSM shows the maximum throughput when ATIM window is 20ms. On the contrary, PERP has maximum throughput when ATIM window is 30ms. In other words, utilization of DATA window is maximized without unnecessary idle time when ATIM window is 30ms. Thus, we will compare legacy PSM with 20ms, PERP with 20 and 30ms ATIM window.

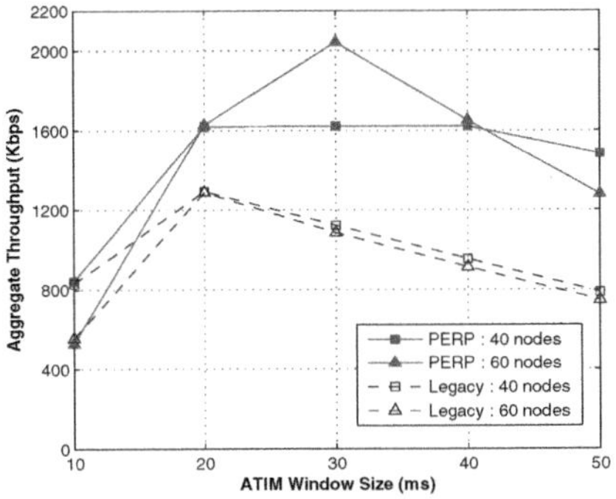

Fig. 4. ATIM Window size vs Aggregate Throughput

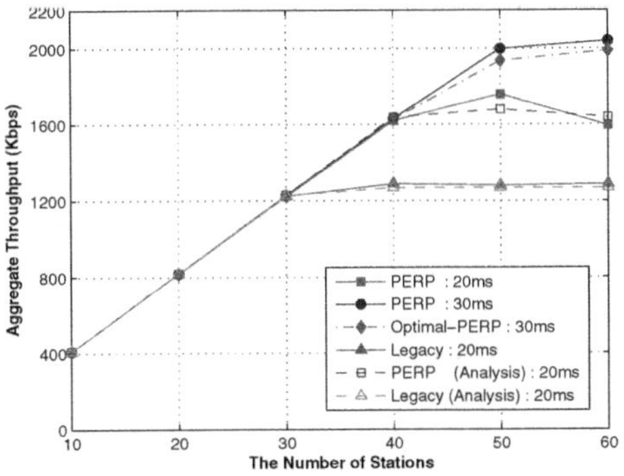

Fig. 5. Aggregate Throughput

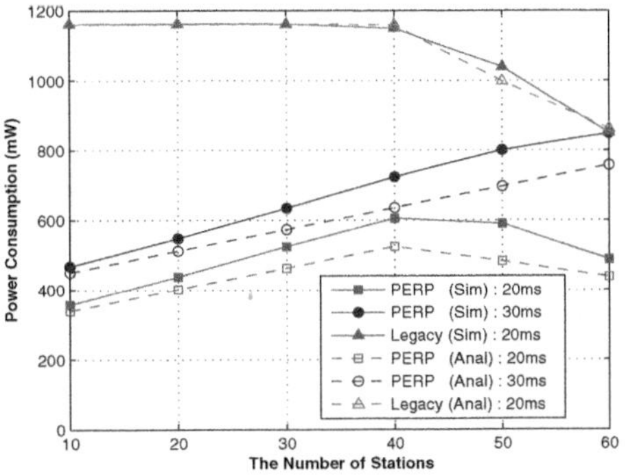

Fig. 6. Power Consumption

Figure 5 shows the aggregate throughput during one beacon interval when using legacy PSM, PERP and Optimal-PERP. First of all, we can see that our throughput analysis is similar to simulation results. In PERP, sometimes there are several potential relay nodes that want to help data packet of a low rate node. Among them, the optimal node is defined by a potential relay node supporting the highest indirect data rates. Due to using the priority backoff scheme and the existence of multiple candidate nodes, PERP is hard to guarantee that the voluntary node actually helping a low rate node always will be selected as the optimal relay node. Hence, we compare PERP with Optimal-PERP using the optimal relay node. The simulation result shows that there is a little difference of the aggregate throughput between them. It means that voluntary node provides the nearly optimal data rate to low rate nodes and that our priority based backoff scheme can well retrieve the small throughput gap of two protocols. Next, comparing PERP with legacy PSM, they have same throughput due to enough DATA window time to transmit all data of senders when the number of nodes is small. Otherwise, PERP outperforms legacy PSM (30% $\sim$ 60%) when

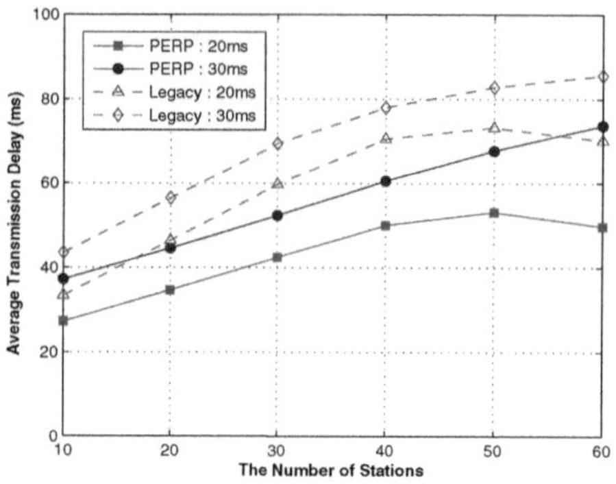

Fig. 7. Average Transmission Delay

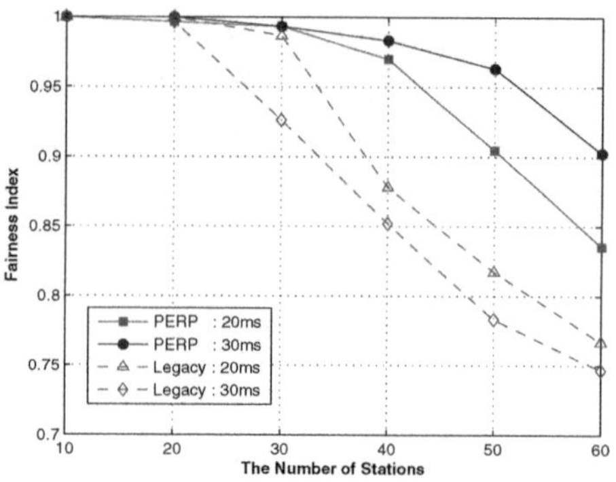

Fig. 8. Fairness Index

the number of nodes is more than 30 due to higher data rate transmission and voluntary relaying procedure.

Figure 6 compares the average power consumption of a node by using simulation (Sim) and analysis (Anal). The analysis results is similar to simulation results. In case of PERP, the small gap between simulation and analysis is due to no consideration of priority backoff scheme in analysis. Next, PERP saves power at almost 10% $\sim$ 55% than PSM because nodes enter into sleep mode rapidly once they transmit or receive all packets and relaying packet. On the contrary, in PSM, all nodes must awake to transmit data during entire beacon interval. At PERP with 20ms, power consumption is reduced when there is more than 50 nodes. Since many nodes cannot send ATIM frame during short ATIM window, so most of them go to sleep mode until next beacon interval. However, it may lead to longer transmission delay. In case of PERP with 30ms, it results the higher power consumption than 20ms because all nodes must maintain awake state for longer duration of ATIM window.

Figure 7 shows the average packet transmission delay. The delay is the time interval from the packet entering the sender's queue to the time being delivered to receiver. As you can see, the multi-rate capability and relaying data transmission of PERP reduce significantly average transmission delay than legacy PSM. Comparing with the cases of different ATIM window size, transmission delay increases as approximately the difference ATIM window size (10ms) due to waiting time of longer ATIM window. However, when the number of nodes is 60, the transmission delay is more increase than 10ms because many awake nodes cannot sends out data packet within shorter DATA window.

Figure 8 shows the fairness index [8] of two mechanisms. The purpose of this figure is to prove fairness of PERP as comparison with PSM. PERP use priority based backoff scheme and slow node transmits data packet quickly regardless of its remaining backoff time by negotiation procedure. Hence, other nodes may suffer from starvation by unfair backoff scheme. However, as you can see this figure, the fairness index of PERP is rather higher than legacy PSM. This is due to the fact that more nodes can acquire the channel access opportunity through faster data transmission. Thus, PERP also has additional advantages to give the fair medium access to all nodes rrespective of transmission rate and relaying procedure.

4 Conclusions

In this paper, we propose the PERP that exploits the multi-rate capability with power saving mechanism for WLANs. In multi-rate wireless network, low data rate nodes consume proportionally more channel access time and transmission power than high rate nodes, resulting in degradation of performance and power efficiency.

However, in PERP, the neighbor nodes help voluntarily low rate node to be delivered data faster through indirect transmission. It also makes that all nodes can enter quickly into doze mode through voluntarily helping transmit data packet. Simulation results show that the proposed scheme outperforms the legacy PSM in terms of throughput, transmission delay, fairness, and power efficiency. The proposed mechanism does not need a complex procedure for relaying data transmission and can be applied to mobile environments and 802.11 a/b/g.

References

1. "IEEE Std. 802.11b-1999, Part 11: Wireless LAN Medium Access Control (MAC) and Physical Layer (PHY) Specifications: High-Speed Physical Layer Extension in the 2.4GHz Band," 1999.
2. M. Heusse, F. Rousseau, G. Berger-Sabbatel, and A. Duda, "Performance anomaly of 802.11b," *in Proc. of IEEE INFOCOM*, San Francisco, USA, March 2003.
3. P. Liu, Z. Tao, and S. S. Panwar, "A Cooperative MAC Protocol for Wireless Local Area Networks," *in Proceedings of the 2005 IEEE International Conference on Communications (ICC)*, Seoul, Korea, May 2005.
4. H. Zhu and G. Cao, "rDCF: A relay-enabled medium access control protocol for wireless ad hoc networks," *in Proc. of IEEE INFOCOM*, Miami, FL, Mar. 2005.
5. H. Woesner, J. P. Ebert, M. Schlager, and A. Wolisz, "Power-saving mechanisms in emerging standards for wireless LANs: The MAC level perspective," *IEEE Personal Communications*, Jun 1998.
6. E. S. Jung and N. H. Vaidya, "An Energy Efficient MAC Protocol for Wireless LANs," *IEEE INFOCOM02*, New York, June 2002.
7. S.-L. Wu and P.-C. Tseng, "An Energy Efficient MAC Protocol for IEEE 802.11 WLANs," *IEEE CNSR04*, Canada, May 2004.
8. Z. Fang, B. Bensaou, and YuWang, "Performance evaluation of a fair backoff algorithm for IEEE 802.11 DFWMAC," *In Mobile Computing and Networking*, pp. 48-57, Atlanta, Georgia, USA, September 2002.

PHY-MAC Cross-Layer Design of Reliable Wireless Multicast Protocol with a Case Study of MB-OFDM WPAN*

Jaeeun Na, Cheolgi Kim, and Joongsoo Ma

School of Engineering, Information and Communications University
Daejeon, 305-732, Korea
{davini02,cheolgi,jsma}@icu.ac.kr

Abstract. Wireless Multimedia Broadcastings have been being promising applications. Recently, the multimedia multicastings have started to be embedded into the legacy wireless networks. To provide high quality multimedia with multicast, wireless multicast ARQ (Automatic Repeat reQuest) scheme is required. In multicast ARQ, multiple receivers may return feedback control packets, such as ACK (Acknowledgement) or NAK (Negative ACK), simultaneously to the transmitter. In this paper, we show that the multiple feedback control packets can be successfully decoded in transmitter without additional hardware cost. Based on the proposition, we described a conceptual flow of wireless multicast algorithm, and then proposed multimedia multicast protocol on Multiband-OFDM Wireless Personal Area Network (MB-OFDM WPAN) specifications. In simulation, we showed that the proposed mechanism reduces the power consumption and achieves improved performance.

Keywords: Multicast, ARQ, UWB, Multi-band OFDM (MB-OFDM), WPAN, Wireless Communications.

1 Introduction

Media broadcasting services, such as radio and TV broadcastings have been some of the most promising applications in wireless communications area. In early years, its success is because of its entertainment provision with low initial investment for a coverage, a hundred miles per TV station. As computing technology grows up, wireless media broadcasting services are moving to portable entertainment devices. For example, DMB (Digital Multimedia Broadcasting) and DVB-H (Digital Video Broadcasting for Handhelds), are being actively developed, these days.

Another potential movement related to wireless multimedia, is combining broadcasting, in another word *streaming*, with legend wireless communications.

* This research was supported by MIC (Ministry of Information and Communication), Korea, under the ITRC (Information Technology Research Center) support program supervised by the IITA (Institute of Information Technology Assessment). (IITA-2006-C1090-0603-0015).

Y.-H. Lee et al. (Eds.): ICESS 2007, LNCS 4523, pp. 676–685, 2007.

Some cellular companies try to exploit their surplus bandwidth to extend the coverage of DMB or DVB-H for the in-building and subway environments. Internet broadcastings or cyber lectures are already being delivered via WLANs. Moreover, WPAN protocols, such as MB-OFDM (Multi-Band Orthogonal Frequency Division Modulation) [1, 2] by WiMedia Alliance or DS-UWB (Direct Sequence Ultra-Wideband), mainly target multimedia communications with the data communications as extra services. Embedded streaming enables plenty of multimedia applications, such as cyber lectures, internet broadcastings, wireless private headphones in a transportation not to interfere other people, and iPod music sharing with buddies in a cafe via multiple wireless headphones dedicated to each person, as well as extended coverage of legend media broadcasting services.

Legacy wireless communications, such as cell phones and WLAN, do not have clean communication environment like TV broadcasting, such that an ARQ (Automatic Repeat reQuest) kind of packet recovery scheme is required. Achieving high SINR (Signal to Interference plus Noise Ratio) with low data rate is still valid, but not appropriate because it consumes too much radio resources, which could have been allocated to other communications. However, the dilemma is that provision of ARQ in multicast is not easy and straight forward like unicast. Feedback packets, such as CTSs (Clear To Send) and ACKs (Acknowledgement), from multiple receivers have been supposed hard to maintain because of a collision with each other. Thus, most communication standards do not allow multicast ARQ in their specifications.

There have been several approaches to adapt ARQ mechanism proposing multicast ARQ. [3] and [4] allow receivers to send NAK (Negative ACK) packets at the same instance to the same channel altogether, and regard any collisions or broken packets as a NAK at that instance to handle multiple ARQ packets. As they rely on the communication model based on MAC perspective, their model is not well matched with the real radio environment. They are covered in Section 2.

In Section 3, we show a proposition that the feedback packets from multiple receivers can be decoded not making a collision without any additional circuits by multi-path fading resolution scheme. Based on this proposition, we propose a simple conceptual protocol of wireless multicast algorithm with ARQ in order to how it works.

We designed wireless multicast protocol for MB-OFDM, which is described in Section 4. We adapt Hybrid ARQ (HARQ) for energy efficiency and reliability. The performance of our protocol is described in Section 5. Section 6 concludes this paper.

2 Related Work

To go around the inherent difficulty of multicast ARQ, so called, layering approaches have been proposed for multimedia multicast. They divide the content into several layers by gradations of importance, and cope with the layers in a selective manner [5, 6, 7]. Nodes with bad channel quality subscribe the only layers with high priority, while ones with good channel quality deserve the whole layers. As a result, the only nodes with high channel quality can enjoy high quality media and others must suffer from the low quality.

One of the approaches adapting feedback in multicast is the rate control mechanism. SNR-based Auto Rate for Multicast [8], which is influenced by Rate-Adaptive Multicast for wired networks [9], adapts transmission rate based on the SNR (Signal to Noise Ratio) values given by receivers through beacon packets. Since SNR values are embedded in beacons, it cannot handle individual errors occurred in each packet. Thus the rate must be conservatively controlled for robust communication.

In wired network area, some works have proposed feedback aggregation protocols [10, 11] to relieve the feedback overhead. The ACK/NAK messages are combined by receiver nodes in a distributed manner making a tree aggregation graph. Even it reduces the overhead of transmitter node in a wired network, it is hardly useful in wireless environment because of its common shared channel property rather than individual wires between nodes.

J. Kuri et al. proposed wireless multicast ARQ mechanism using RTS/CTS/NCTS and ACK/NAK together [3]. Suppose that multiple receivers send feedback packets (CTS/ACK) simultaneously to the transmitter. The packets may collide with each other such that neither CTS nor ACK from each receiver will properly delivered to the transmitter. To handle this problem in [3], only one node is allowed to send positive feedbacks (CTS/ACK) not to make collisions, while no restriction is given to the negative feedbacks (NCTS/NAK). Thus, there may be multiple NCTS/NACK, while only one CTS/ACK is permitted at a given instance. If CTS/ACK is safely delivered to the transmitter, the transmitter regards the former process succeeded. Otherwise, for example NCTS/NAK delivery or any kind of collisions of packets, it stops the procedure and retries the transmission if needed. The authors assumed any simultaneous transmissions of packets make collisions. To avoid collision incurred by simultaneous positive feedbacks, they have proposed three alternatives of policies, expecting single positive feedback reception on the successful occasions.

However, simultaneous packet transmissions may not make a collision in the real world. Here is an example. Assume that the receiver having sent ACK is very close to the transmitter with distance d_1 and the receiver having failed to receive a packet so having sent NAK is fairly far from the transmitter with distance d_2 eventually. It is likely to happen because closer nodes commonly have higher SINR. The SINR of the signal from the node at d_1 against interference by the node at d_2 is given by

$$\text{SINR} = \left(\frac{d^2}{d^1}\right)^{\alpha} \tag{1}$$

where pathloss exponent is α. If $d_1 = 1m$, $d_2 = 10m$, and $\alpha = 4$, SINR is 40 dB, high enough for successful communication without making collision.

Gupta et al. proposed multicast protocol with only negative feedbacks based on tones, instead of conventional packets for feedbacks [4]. Since the tones are assumed to be sinusoidal wave out of communication band, their protocol requires additional tone detector circuits and bandwidth. Moreover, the channel environment of communication and tones will be different with each other.

3 Proposition of Wireless Multicast with Collision-Proof Feedbacks

Previous work is developed based on the assumption that multiple simultaneous packet transmissions make a collision. However, as long as the packets convey the same signature of signal, they can be added in a constructive manner similar to multi-path fading. Let's assume that all feedback packets from multiple receivers for each multicast packet are identical. As long as the receivers are synchronized with the transmitter altogether, their transmissions will be delivered in an identical manner with multipath reflections of a single signal, which can be decoded with multi-path fading resolution scheme without any additional circuit!

Our conceptual protocol is as follows:

1. **Transmitter** senses carrier and waits for quiet enough to transmit a packet.
2. **Transmitter** transmits packet after a certain random backoff delay if channel is idle.
3. **Receiver** listens to and decodes the packet.
4. **Receiver** returns NAK after a certain time, for example SIFS (Short Inter Frame Space) in 802.11, if the decoding has failed. Otherwise, it stays silent.
5. **Transmitter** listens to NAK and decodes it with the multi-path fading resolution circuit. If NAK is recognized, transmitter retransmits the packet for conventional ARQ or additional FEC (Forward Error Correction) of HARQ.
6. Step 4, 5 are repeated for the nodes that have not succeeded their reception as long as there are the nodes, and the number of trials has not exceeded a certain limit.

The first step of protocol is carrier sense. Although there have been arguments whether carrier sense without RTS/CTS is enough to avoid the hidden terminal problem, some work has shown that CSMA wholly relying on carrier sense level has quite competitive performance or outperforms RTS/CTS scheme [12,13,14]. It can be easily extended to multicast environment without modifications.

After transmission, the transmitter needs to decode the NAK from multiple receivers. Since the receivers are all synchronized to the transmitter for communication, they will transmit NAK at the same time after some specified interval such as SIFS. The time difference of NAK transmissions between receivers are about the difference between their propagation delays. Therefore, the time difference between NAK arrival time at the transmitter will be about twice longer than the difference between the propagation delays if we assume that the delays incurred by the internal circuits of receivers are negligible. It is quite acceptable assumption. Note that we can measure the distance between devices by UWB turn-around time [15]. Its accuracy is a several centimeters.

Let's assume that there is a communication system whose modulation is OFDM. A transmitter has transmitted multicast packet to several receivers and

N of them have failed decoding the packet. a_i denotes i-th node among those N receivers that need to transmit NAK. A single frame of NAK signal can be denoted as $X(k)$ in frequency domain, where k denotes each carrier. Then, the expected received signal function of a single NAK from a_i to the transmitter is given by

$$Y_i(k) = X(k)H_i(k) + \omega_i(k) \tag{2}$$

where $H_i(k)$ is a complex channel function due to the fading and ω_i is white gaussian noise. The channel estimator is to estimate $H_i(k)$. In multiple NAK situation from N failed receivers, the total receiving signal is given as

$$Y(k) = X(k)\left[\sum_{i=1}^{N} H_i(k)\right] + \omega(k) \tag{3}$$

where $\omega(k)$ is white gaussian noise. Finally, we have

$$Y(k) = X(k)H(k) + \omega(k) \tag{4}$$

where $H(k) = \sum_i H_i(k)$. Therefore, the NAK from multiple receivers can be decoded with multi-path fading resolution scheme at the transmitter as long as the time synchronization error among receivers are negligible.

4 Multicast Protocol for MB-OFDM

In this section, we introduce the multicast protocol for MB-OFDM based on the proposition discussed in Section 3. To accomplish both reliability and power efficiency, proposed protocol uses the punctured convolutional code and packet aggregation scheme.

In conventional approaches, transmitter sends multicast data at lowest data rate out of supported rates. It allows that all receivers decode data successfully, since data with lower rate has more redundancy bits and longer transmission time. However, this approach is inefficient in point of power and delay. Although several receivers are able to decode data without redundancy bits, all receivers have to decode the longer data stream with many redundancy bits. Consequently, transmitter and several receivers waste power due to lowest data rate. Hence, we use the punctured convolutional code to meet suitable rate of each receivers. Recall that the puncturing scheme supports higher data rate by omitting transmitted data [1]. It leads to reduce transmission time, receiving time, and power consumption. On the other hand, puncturing scheme leads to the higher bit error rate (BER). To improve reliability of punctured multicast data and reduce overhead caused by many retransmission, transmitter sends the aggregated data and only several receivers send NAK if the decoding is failed.

4.1 Multicast Transmission Frame

Transmitter does not send full data packet at a time, only sends a partial packet selectively. The our proposed multicast packet is divided into four parts by using

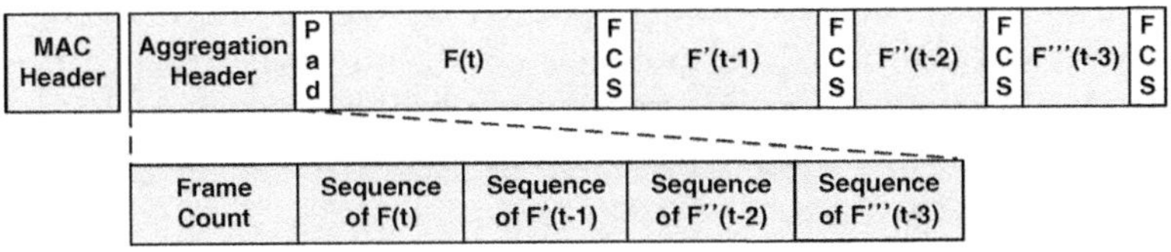

Fig. 1. Proposed Aggregated Multicast frame format

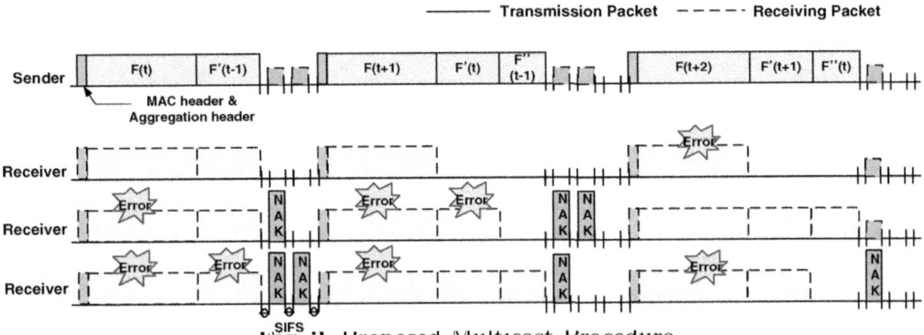

Fig. 2. Proposed Multicast Procedure

punctured convolutional code; one mandatory data frame and three optional retransmission frames. These four frames are encoded at different coding rate [1]. The first part is transmitting data frame that is encoded at 3/4 coding rate. The remaining three parts are retransmission frames that are encoded by 5/8, 1/2, 1/3 coding rate respectively, however, excludes the redundant bits with previous part. In actuality, the number of retransmitted bits become gradually decrease than one of previous part. Since retransmitted bits is much small, the attached header is big overhead and repetitive retransmission brings long transmission delay. Hence, the retransmission frame is aggregated to next transmitting packet without additional overhead. As you see Figure 1, $F(t)$ is data frame which transmitted at time t and $F'(t-1)$ is first retransmission frame of $F(t-1)$. $F''(t-2)$ is second retransmission frame of $F(t-2)$ and $F'''(t-3)$ is third retransmission frame of $F(t-3)$. In addition, aggregation header is attached with a common MAC header holding the sequence information of each aggregated frames. The FCS (Frame Check Sequence) field is also inserted between two different frames to distinguish them respectively.

4.2 Multicast Protocol Description

The proposed multicast procedure is described in Figure 2. We assume that power proportionates directly to receiving and transmission time. To reduce unnecessary power consumption and receiving time of receivers, transmitter has to decide the optimal data rate before it send out the multicast packet. The data rate of each transmission is based on estimated BER through distance to receivers and the history of previous successful transmission through NAK information. With equation (5), transmitter is able to change the data rate of each frames in order to adapt optimally the condition of receivers.

$$\min_{r} RRT \tag{5}$$

$$\begin{aligned} \text{subject to} \quad RRT &= \sum_{i=1}^{n} RT_r(i) \\ RT_r(i) &= \sum_{j=1}^{l} PER_r(j-1) \cdot Len_r(j) \cdot r \\ PER_r(j) &\geq Threshold_j \\ RT_r(i) &\leq t \end{aligned}$$

When receivers receive multicast packet, they become aware of sequence numbers of aggregated frames through aggregation header. At this time, they decide which retransmission frames must be received. If receiver decodes earlier receiving data frame or retransmission frame successfully, it doesn't receive relevant retransmission frame to reduce power consumption. Otherwise, it decodes retransmission frame in combination with earlier receiving frame. In different way of conventional approach, although decoding has failed, receiver stores error frame instead of dropping it. And then, receiver transmits NAK at relevant slot time that delayed based on consisted frame order in multicast packet. Although multiple receivers simultaneously transmit NAK, collision is not occurred by proof in Section 3. If transmitter receive NAK, it retransmits selectively the only relevant frame.

Table 1. Symbol and definition of equation (5)

Symbol	Definition
RRT	Total receiving time of all receivers when packet is transmitted at data rate r including retransmission
$RT_r(i)$	Receiving time of ith receiver when packet is transmitted at data rate r
Len_r	Encoded packet length at data rate r
$PER_r(j-1)$	Packet error ratio of earlier transmission or retransmission at data rate r
$Threshold_j$	Threshold of PER when counts of retransmission is j
r	Data rate : It depends on coding rate
n	The number of receivers
l	The number of retransmissions, $l = 0, 1, 2, 3$
t	The limited transmission time of a packet including retransmission

5 Simulation Results

In this section, we provide simulation results demonstrating performance enhancement of the proposed multicast protocol.

The estimated value of power consumption is referred to IEEE 802.11b at 11 Mbps [16]; sleep mode is 47mW, idle mode is 739mW, receive mode is 900mW and transmit mode is 1346mW. (Because we have not referenced power value of MB-OFDM.) The simulation settings are as follows: the network size is 10m*10m; maximum 20 nodes are randomly deployed into this area; the lowest data rate is 53.3 Mbps; all the points in our performance figures are computed from 10 trials and each trial transmits 1000 packets.

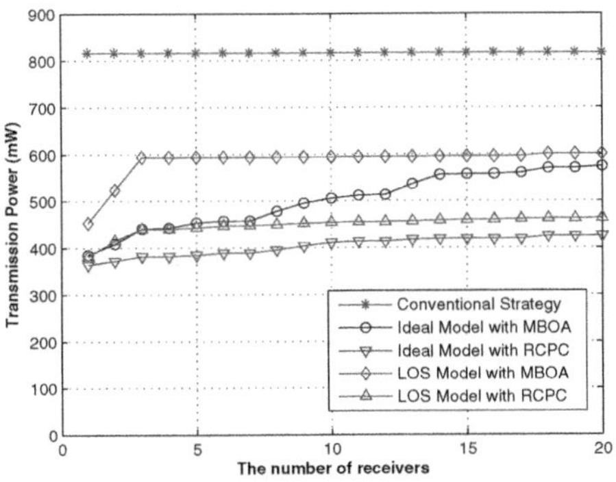

Fig. 3. Transmission Power

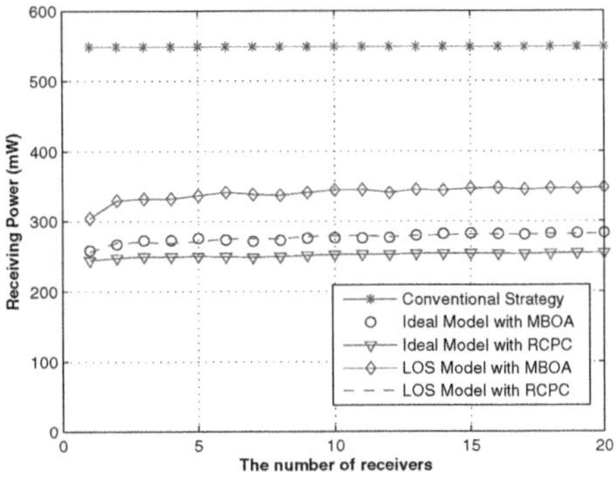

Fig. 4. Receiving Power

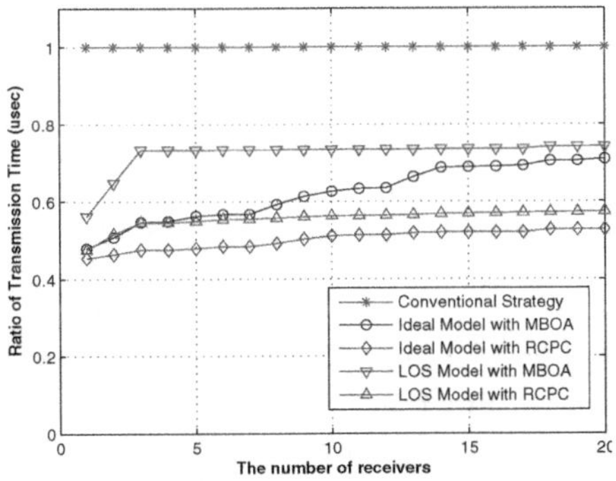

Fig. 5. The Ratio of the Transmission Time

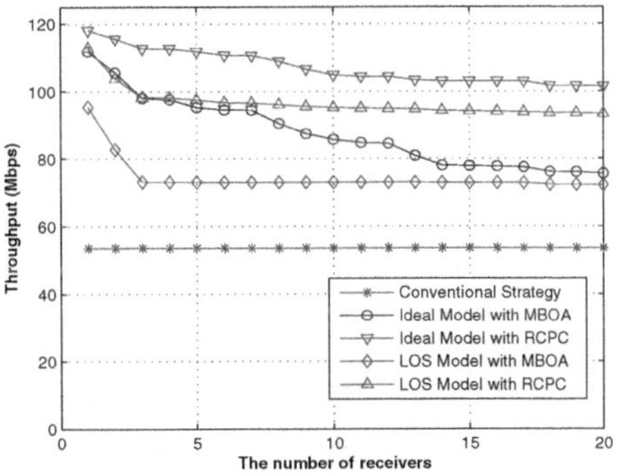

Fig. 6. Throughput

We use the following three metrics to evaluate the performance of proposed protocol: 1) Power consumption at transmitter and receivers. 2) The ratio of transmission delay. 3) Aggregate throughput. Furthermore, we compare the 5 models for performance evaluation; The first model is conventional strategy, which multicast data is transmitted at lowest data rate without retransmission and acknowledgement. The remaining four models are based on our proposed scheme. They use different punctured coding scheme and UWB models. The coding schemes use punctured patterns of MB-OFDM code (MBOA) [1] or rate-compatible punctured code (RCPC code) [17] which is the optimal punctured convolutional code. The RCPC code requires that lower rate codes use the same coded bits as the higher rate codes plus one or more additional bits. To compare with similar coding rates of MB-OFDM, we choice RCPC code with 4/5, 2/3, 1/2, and 1/3 coding rate. In addition, UWB models are Ideal model or LOS (Line of Sight) model whose SNR is calculated by equations in [18].

Figure 3 and 4 show transmission power of transmitter and average receiving power of one receiver as the number of receivers increase, when transmitter sends 1000 packets. As illustrated in the figure, transmission power of proposed protocol is much lower than conventional strategy from 25% to 50% according to punctured code and UWB model. The RCPC code has lower power consumption than MB-OFDM code because it has the optimal pattern to decode successfully packet. In addition, the LOS model is higher power consumption than Ideal model because it has higher BER. As the number of receivers increase, transmission power become gradually higher due to increment of the number of distant receiver from transmitter. Moreover, the receiving power is also reduced from 37% to 55% through selective reception of aggregated frames based on previous failed frame reception.

Figure 5 shows the ratio of average transmission delay of different schemes. The proposed scheme reduces transmission delay as compared with conventional strategy from 25% to 50%. The main reason is that, data transmits at higher data rate and retransmission also transmits much higher data rate without additional overhead. Further, Figure 6 illustrates the the aggregated throughput, which also improves from 10% to 50% according to puncturing and UWB models.

6 Conclusion

In this paper, we show that the multiple feedback control packets can be successfully decoded in transmitter without additional hardware cost. Based on the proposition, we described a conceptual flow of wireless multicast algorithm.

Moreover, we proposed multimedia multicast scheme on MB-OFDM WPAN specifications. We addressed the topic of optimizing power consumption and delay of multicast traffic in WPAN. We presented a new approach for power efficient multicast protocol. It uses the punctured convolutional coding to reduce power consumption and aggregation scheme to retransmit without overhead for reliability. Moreover, proposed protocol use NAK mechanism to get feedback information. From the simulation study, we verify that the proposed scheme reduces power consumption as well as delay, and achieves the improved performance.

References

1. anonymous, Ed., *MBOA - PHY Layer Technical Specification, MBOA PHY Specification.* WiMedia Alliance PHY Subcommittee, Jan. 2005, vol. Final Draft 1.0.
2. J. O'Conor and R. Brown, Eds., *MBOA - Distributed Medium Access Control (MAC) for Wireless Networks.* WiMedia Alliance MAC Subcommittee, Jan. 2005, vol. Draft 0.93.
3. J. Kuri and S. K. Kasera, "Reliable multicast in multi-access wireless lans," *Wireless Networks*, vol. 7, no. 4, pp. 359–369, July 2001.
4. S. Gupta, V. Shankar, and S. Lalwani, "Reliable Multicast MAC Protocol for Wireless LANs," in *Proc. of IEEE ICC '03*, May 2003.
5. S. McCanne, V. Jacobson, and M. Vetterli, "Receiver-driven Layered Multicast," in *Proc. of ACM SIGCOMM '96*, Aug. 1996, pp. 117–130.
6. P. A. Chou, A. E. Mour, A. Wang, and S. Mehrotra, "FEC and pseudo-ARQ for receiver-driven layered multicast of audio and video," in *Proc. of IEEE Data Compression Conference 2000*, Mar. 2000, pp. 440–449.
7. W. Tan and A. Zakhor, "Video multicast using layered FEC and scalable compression," *IEEE Trans. on Circuits and Systems for Video Technology*, vol. 11, no. 3, pp. 373–387, Mar. 2001.
8. Y. Park, Y. Seok, N. Choi, Y. Choi, and J.-M. Bonnin, "Rate-Adaptive Multimedia Multicasting over IEEE 802.11 Wireless LANs," in *IEEE CCNC '06 Special Sessions on Multimedia and QoS in Wireless Networks*, Jan. 2006.
9. U. Nguyen and X. Xiong, "Rate-adaptive multicast in mobile ad-hoc networks," in *Proc. of IEEE Int'l Conf. on WiMob '05*, Aug. 2005.
10. W. T. Strayer and B. J. Dempsey, *XTP–The Xpress Transfer Protocol.* Addison-Wesley Pub. Co., 1992.
11. S. Floyd, V. Jacobsen, S. McCanne, C.-G. Liu, and L. Zhang, "A Reliable Multicast Framework for Light-weight Sessions and Application Level Framing," in *Proc. of ACM SIGCOMM '95*, vol. 25, Oct. 1995, pp. 342–356.
12. T.-S. Kim, H. Lim, and J. C. Hou, "Improving Spatial Reuse through Tuning Transmit Power, Carrier Sense Threshold and Data Rate in Multihop Wireless Networks," in *ACM MobiCom '06*, Sept. 2006.
13. J. Zhu, X. Guo, L. L. Yang, W. S. Conner, S. Roy, and M. M. Hazra, "Adapting physical carrier sensing to maximize spatial reuse in 802.11 mesh networks," *Wireless Communications and Mobile Computing*, vol. 4, no. 8, pp. 933–946, Nov. 2004.
14. H. Zhai and Y. Fang, "Physical Carrier Sensing and Spatial Reuse in Multirate and Multihop Wireless Ad Hoc Networks," in *Proc. of IEEE INFOCOM '06*, 2006.
15. J.-Y. Lee and R. A. Scholtz, "Ranging in a Dense Multipath Environment Using an UWB Radio Link," *IEEE Journal on Selected Areas in Communications*, vol. 20, no. 9, pp. 1677–1683, Dec. 2002.
16. L. Feeney and M. Nilsson, "Investigating the Energy Consumption of a Wireless Network Interface in an Ad Hoc Networking Environment," in *Proc. of IEEE INFOCOM 2001*, Apr. 2001.
17. J. Hagenauer, "Rate-Compatible Punctured Convolutional Codes (RCPC Codes) and their Applications," *IEEE Trans. on Communications*, vol. 36, no. 4, Apr. 1998.
18. L. Williams, D. Wu, E. Staggs, and A. Yen, "Ultra-wideband radio design for multi-band ofdm 480 mb/s wireless usb," in *Proc. of DesignCon 2005*, 2005.

An Adaptive Multi-paths Algorithm for Wireless Sensor Networks*

Zhendong Wu and Shanping Li

College of Computer Science, Zhejiang University, Hangzhou, China
zhendongwu@hotmail.com, shan@cs.zju.edu.cn

Abstract. Multi-path strategy is one of the favorable choices to transmit data efficiently and flexibly in sensor networks. Due to various applications, it is hard to devise a generic WSN routing strategy to meet all requirements of various applications and environments at the same time. Therefore, a novel routing strategy should provide flexible schemes which adjusts forwarding schemes dynamically according to the different requirements. In this paper, we proposed an adaptive multi-path routing algorithm (AMPRA), which could provide convenient client-interface for flexible switching between various routing strategies. Through studying the *local minimum phenomenon*, a new method *Clockwise-Rule* is proposed to overcome the *local minimum phenomenon*. Based on the *Clockwise-Rule*, AMPRA provides flexible transmission schemes. Simulations show that AMPRA can significantly improve the performance of networks.

Keywords: Sensor Networks, Adaptive Multi-paths, Local Minimum Phenomenon, Right hand rule.

1 Introduction

Recent advanced in micro electromechanical systems (MEMS) has fostered the development of low-power, inexpensive, data relaying micro-sensors. Thousands of sensors can be quickly deployed to monitor different environments, capture various physical properties and react with all sorts of users. Many applications emerged with the development of sensor networks. Due to application diversity, it is hard to devise a generic WSN routing strategy to meet all requirements of various applications and environments at the same time. Therefore, a novel routing strategy should provide flexible schemes which adjusts forwarding schemes dynamically according to the different requirements. Multi-paths is one of the choices to provide flexible forwarding schemes for various applications.

Recent empirical studies ([1] [2] [3]) have shown that wireless links in real sensor networks may be unreliable. In order to overcome the unreliable links in network layer, some new metrics over unreliable links are proposed by ([4] [5] [6]). These forwarding schemes all focus on single path optimization. Multi-paths have the potential to provide

* This paper is supported by National Natural Science Foundation of China (No. 60473052).

Y.-H. Lee et al. (Eds.): ICESS 2007, LNCS 4523, pp. 686–698, 2007.

robust and high-throughput data transmitting over unreliable links in sensor networks. Swades *et al* [7], Ye *et al* [8] proposed different multi-path routing algorithms respectively. Swades *et al* [7] don't consider the local minimum phenomenon. Ye *et al* [8] use flooding mechanism to get each node's "cost" value which indicates the distance from local node to destination node. However flooding mechanism is not suitable for large-scale sensor networks. Obviously, suitable forwarding schemes over unreliable and reliable links are different. In this paper, we focus on how to choose adaptive multi-paths without flooding mechanism and provide flexible forwarding schemes.

The physical nature of sensor network's deployment makes geographically scoped queries natural ([9] [10]). If nodes know their locations, geographic queries can reduce control overhead evidently. Many geographic routing protocols including single-path ([11] [12]) and multi-paths ([13] [14]) have been proposed. The multi-path algorithms that have been proposed need flooding mechanism and require central processing at the source or destination node in normal. Geographic forwarding has to face a fundamental difficulty: the *local minimum phenomenon* ([11] [15]). Specifically, a packet could get stuck at the closest 1-hop neighborhood to the destination. Message will be sent reiteratively between two nodes. To help packets get out of the local minima, strategies proposed previously use the long-known *right-hand rule* which requires the graph planar (no crossing edges). But, planarizing graph may make the graph lost many links which could be used in multi-path and increase the overhead of routing protocols. It seems that *right-hand rule* is not suitable for multi-path in sensor networks. Qing Fang *et al* [15] studied the local minimum phenomenon and introduced a distributed algorithm, BOUNDHOLE, to forward around holes which local minimum phenomenon occurs. In this paper, we think of restricting greedy forwarding in one region which makes the reiteration-sending not occur. Based on the assumption that the boundary is a Convex Polygon, we proposed a new method *Clockwise-Rule* that helping packets get out of the local minima instead of using the *right-hand rule*. Using *Clockwise-Rule* and an overhearing mechanism, a multi-path routing algorithm (AMPRA) is proposed, which can get multi-paths in parallel while eliminate flooding mechanism completely.

The paper is organized as follows. In section 2, *Clockwise-Rule* is described. Adaptive multi-paths algorithm AMPRA is proposed in section 3. Simulations and conclusions are presented in section 4, 5.

2 The *Clockwise-Rule* Algorithm

In this section, based on Convex Polygon assumption, a new method *Clockwise-Rule* to deal with the local minimum phenomenon is proposed. First the Convex Polygon assumption is described and justified. And then the *Clockwise-Rule* is proposed.

As introduced above, geographic greed forwarding suffers from so-called local minimum phenomenon. To help packets get out of the local minima, strategies proposed previously use the long-known *right hand rule* which requires the graph planar (a graph in which no two edges cross is known as planar, see [11]). But, according to ([11] [16] [17]), each neighborhood change will affect the result of the graph planarizing. It is necessary to replanarize the graph as soon as the neighborhood varied. It result in one node can not choose two or more next-hop nodes simultaneously. So *right hand rule* is not suitable for adaptive multi-path choosing.

Moreover, planarizing graph will make the graph lost many links which could be used in multi-path. Fig.1, for example, shows two planar graphs well-known in varied disciplines ([16] [17]): Relative Neighborhood Graph (RNG) and Gabriel Graph (GG). It can be concluded that planarized graphs lost many links, which could be used in multi-paths.

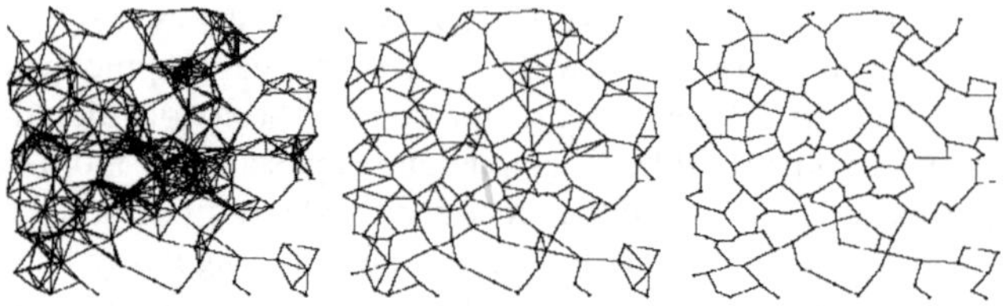

Fig. 1. Left: the full graph of a radio network. 200 nodes, uniformly randomly placed on a 2000 x 2000 meter region, with a radio range of 250 m. Center: the GG subset of the full graph. Right: the RNG subset of the full and GG graphs.

As discussion above, it is required to propose a new method to deal with the local minimum phenomenon in multi-path environment. *Clockwise-Rule* is proposed to help packets to get out of the local minima without using the *right-hand rule* based on the assumption that the boundary is a Convex Polygon.

2.1 The Convex Polygon Assumption

It is proved by Qing Fang *et al* [15] that when a node encounters the local minima, it must be on the boundary of a hole. The whole boundary can be divided into two or more partitions by the beeline defined by local node and destination node. Here, the Convex Polygon assumption means that the beeline divides whole boundary into two Convex

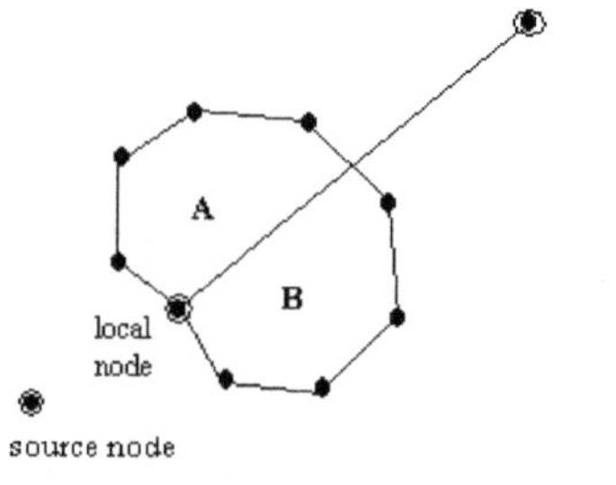

Fig. 2. Convex Polygon Assumption

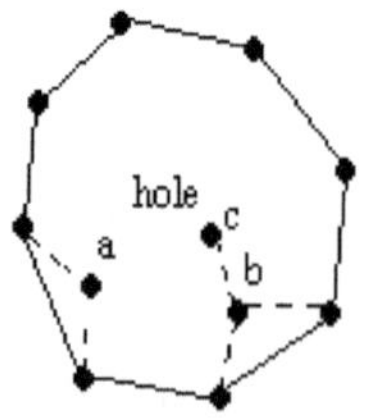

Fig. 3. Convert to Convex Polygon

Polygon partitions. For example, as Fig.2 shows, local node encounters the local minima when it using geographic greed forwarding strategy. Then, it faces to a hole which is enclosed by a closed boundary, as shown in Fig.2. The beeline defined by local node and destination node divides the boundary into two partitions A and B. The Convex Polygon assumption means that A and B are both Convex Polygons. Convex Polygon has such a property that any beeline through its boundary divides it into two independent partitions.

First, it is simple that convert the graphs which do not accord with the Convex Polygon assumption to the graphs that the Convex Polygon assumption always holds. If the neighborhoods of one node C are all in its *half communication region*, it should inform its neighborhoods (if we assume one node's communication region is a disk, then *half communication region* is half-disk). The neighborhoods received this information will mark this node C and continue checking whether itself belongs to *half communication region* after it omitted node C. After all nodes inform their neighborhoods, the convex polygon assumption can hold. When encountering local minima, the marked nodes should be avoided to be chosen as the next-hop nodes, doing like this, the convex polygon assumption is hold. For example, as Fig.3 shows, the neighborhoods of node *a, c* are all in its *half communication region*; and omit node *a c*; then *b* is in *half communication region*, omit *b;* the Convex Polygon assumption is hold.

Second, we studied 40 stochastic scenarios produced by ns2 where 200 nodes are randomly distributed in a 2000×2000 meter region. The boundaries in all scenarios accord with the Convex Polygon assumption. Specifically, in ([11] [15]), there are some scenarios for sensor networks, which are all accord with the Convex Polygon assumption. It seems that the Convex Polygon assumption is reasonable. In fact, in real sensor networks environment, holes usually happen when there are some obstacles in the way. If using some sensor nodes enclosing the obstacle, the boundary comprised by these sensor nodes could be thought a Convex Polygon in normal.

From above discussion, it can be concluded that the Convex Polygon assumption always holds in generally, and if the assumption does not hold, the graph can be converted simply to accord with the assumption.

2.2 *Clockwise*-Rule

The *Clockwise-Rule* is based on the following assumptions.

- The Convex Polygon assumption.
- All nodes in communication range are reachable.

A. CLOCKWISE_REGION and ANTICLOCKWISE_REGION

The beeline defined by local node and destination node divides the communication region of local node into two parts, as shown in Fig.4. The region that is passed by local node clockwise forwarding is called CLOCKWISE_REGION, and the other region is called ANTICLOCKWISE_REGION. Neither of them includes the beeline.

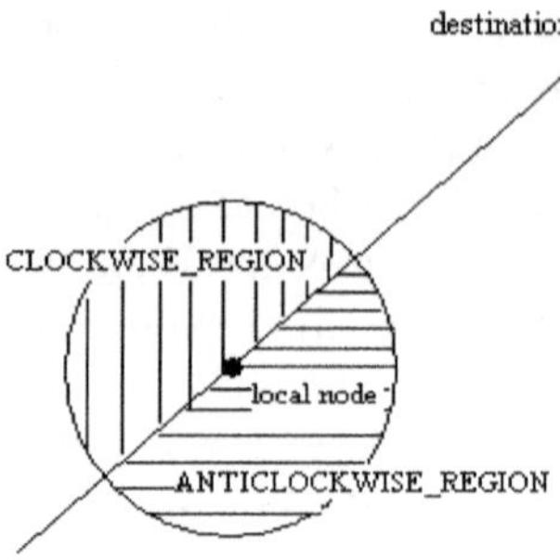

Fig. 4. CLOCKWISE_REGION and ANTICLOCKWISE_REGION

B. ***Clockwise-Rule*****:** Using greedy forwarding in CLOCKWISE_REGION (or ANTICLOCKWISE_REGION).

At the beginning of the forwarding, the CLOCKWISE_REGION or ANTICLOCKWISE_REGION forwarding is chosen. If the rule is chosen, it can't be changed until the forwarding get out of the local minima. For example, it is not allowed to apply CLOCKWISE_REGION in the first node and ANTICLOCKWISE_REGION in the second node.

Theorem 1. If the boundary accords with the Convex Polygon assumption, forwarding can get out of the local minima using *Clockwise-Rule*. Here, the boundary encloses a hole where local minimum phenomenon occurs.

Proof. It is proved by Q. Fang et al [13] that wherever local minimum phenomenon occurs, it will be enclosed by a close boundary. According to Convex Polygon assumption, any beeline through the boundary divides it into two partitions. If the beeline gets through the hold, the CLOCKWISE_REGION or ANTICLOCKWISE_REGION will not be empty; otherwise, local node is not in the local minima. Because all nodes in communication range are reachable, choosing a new node will always be successful using greedy forwarding in CLOCKWISE_REGION or ANTICLOCKWISE_REGION. It can be deduced from the definition of CLOCKWISE_REGION and ANTICLOCKWISE_REGION that if one node is in local node CLOCKWISE_REGION or ANTICLOCKWISE_REGION, the node CLOCKWISE_REGION or ANTICLOCKWISE_REGION will not cover the local node. This property guarantees that the reiteration will not occur in *Clockwise-Rule*. In addition, loop (the next hop has been chosen before) will not occur unless the chosen nodes compose a close curve around the hole. But that case will not happen since there must be a node that is not in the local minima around the hole. Finally, loop will not occur. *Clockwise-Rule* will forward the packet to a new node that hasn't been visited. This process will continue until packets reach the node that is not in the local minima (nodes around the hole is limited), namely getting out of the local minima.

According to theorem.1 and the definition of *Clockwise-Rule*, *Clockwise-Rule* can hold many links for multi-paths and change the choosing-numbers flexibly since it does not need planarizing graphs. So *Clockwise-Rule* is more suitable for adaptive multi-paths than *right-hand rule*.

3 Adaptive Multi-Path Routing Algorithm: AMPRA

3.1 The AMPRA Algorithm

The AMPRA algorithm consists of three steps: *neighbors set adjusting*, *route discovery* and *route confirm*.

Neighbors set adjusting: Once deployed and localized, each active node will acquire its neighbor's location and link quality information through exchanging information with its neighbors. According to link quality information, each node could *blacklist some neighbors which link's reliability is too low*. According to researches ([1] [2] [3] [18]), the longer the distance between two nodes is, the higher the probability of unreliable links is. Since greed forwarding strategy intends to choose longer links, blacklisting mechanism can make greed forwarding avoid choosing too bad links.

Route discovery: This step starts from the source node and stops at the destination node. First, if source node does not encounter local minimum phenomenon, it chooses m nodes as next-hop pending nodes using greedy forwarding strategy, otherwise, it chooses m nodes using *Clockwise-Rule*. After choosing m next-hop pending nodes, source node sends ROUTE_REQUEST packets to these nodes. Each node that receives the ROUTE_REQUEST packet will repeat the same actions as source node does until the ROUTE_REQUEST packet arrives at the destination node. Here the m can be adjusted according to the environment parameters, 2 or 3 is enough in normal.

```
switch(Forward_State)
{
    case NORMAL_STATE:
       forwarding using greedy forward;
       if(encounter the local minimum)
          Forward_State = CLOCKWISE_STATE;
       else break;
    case CLOCKWISE_STATE:
       forwarding using Clockwise-Rule;
       if(get out of the local minimum)
          Forward_State = NORMAL_STATE;
}
```

Route confirm: There is a simple but useful observation on communications in sensor networks: the broadcast nature of the wireless medium allows sensor nodes detecting their neighbor's transmission. It means that one node can determine whether the packets are relayed by next-hop nodes through detecting the next-hop node's transmission. After sending ROUTE_REQUEST packets to next-hop pending nodes, one node detects whether these nodes relaying the same ROUTE_REQUEST packets. If the packet is relayed successfully, the pending node will be confirmed as one next-hop node. Those pending nodes that don't be detected will be deleted from the set of next-hop nodes.

Fig.5 shows a multi-path using AMPRA algorithm with $m = 2$. The width of the routing network can be adjusted through increasing or decreasing the m value. Furthermore different relaying nodes can use different m values.

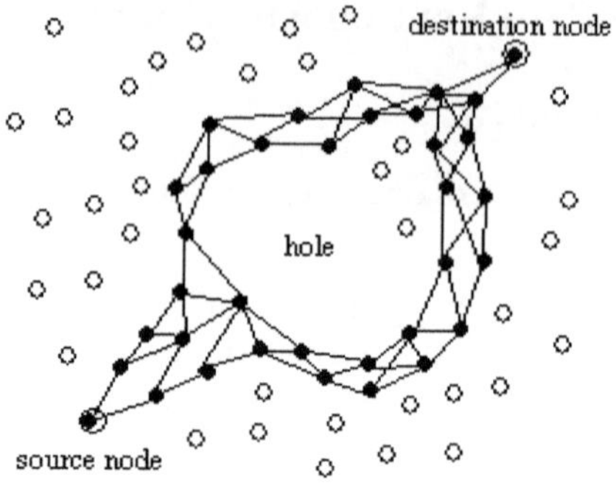

Fig. 5. Pictorial views of multi-path, *m*=2

3.2 Adaptive Routing with AMPRA

AMPRA allows various forwarding schemes realized over multi-paths according to different applications and environments. Moreover, different forwarding schemes can switch each other at any relaying-node. It is useful for providing adaptive routing scheme in a large sensor network with changed environments. Table.1 is an adaptive routing-function class, which provides function interface to adjust routing-schemes flexibly.

Table 1. Adaptive Routing Interface

```
class RouteInterface {
public:
    status_t get_Status();
     /* the node_info includes: link-quality, node-location, and so on*/
    int get_NeighborsInfo(node_t **node_info);
    /*route_strategy =Auto, Disjoint Routing, Select Routing, Direct Routing*/
    int get_RouteStrategy();
    int set_AutoAction(status_t local_status, node_t **node_info);
    /* this function can be rewritten by users*/
    virtual int compute_RouteStrategy(node_t **node_info) { return Auto; }
   /* m_ is used to adjust the width of the route*/
    int appoint_RouteStrategy(int route_strategy, int m_);
    /* there are two tables nodes_info_tab and route_tab in **node_info */
     int adjust_RouteTab(node_t **node_info, int route_strategy);
private:
    status_t local_status;
    node_t **node_info;
    int route_strategy;
    int m_;
   };
```

Depend on this interface, we could conveniently change routing-strategy (appoint_RouteStrategy( )), or adjust routing-tab (adjust_RouteTab( )) at any nodes. Here three forwarding schemes are proposed for adaptive routing-function class.

Disjoint parallel: *multi-path forwarding*: In order to realize disjoint forwarding, AMPRA algorithm need do some improvement in *Route discovery* and R*oute confirm*. In R*oute discovery*, source node chooses *m* next-hop nodes as *m* disjoint paths starting nodes (each node is assigned a serial number 1~*m*). Then each relaying node has its own serial number. It chooses a main node from *m* next-hop nodes and assigns its own serial number to it. If the main node has been occupied by other path, it sends PATH_OCCUPIED packet to upstream node. In *route confirm* step, if one node receives the PATH_OCCUPIED packet, it chooses another node as the main node from *m* next-hop nodes. From above improvement, AMPRA can provide a disjoint multi-path net in which each relaying node has a main next-hop node and *m*-1 assistant next-hop nodes. If the wireless links are fairly reliable and disjoint multi-paths can use efficient multiple access control protocol, etc. CDMA system, *disjoint forwarding* will improve the network's throughput and load balance significantly. It is difficult for some multi-path algorithms, such as GRAB [8], to switch meshed multi-paths to disjoint multi-paths at any routing-node since flooding mechanism and centralized process are needed.

Selective forwarding: Each relaying node just chooses one next-hop node to forward the packets based on local conditions (e.g. health of the next-hop nodes). If the wireless links in sensor networks are not so reliable, *selective forwarding* can improve the transmission's reliability fairly.

Direct forwarding: Omitted *route confirm*, the data packets can be delivered directly through replacing ROUTE_REQUEST packets appeared in the step of *route discovery*. Using *direct forwarding*, a packet from a source is copied along some possible paths to its destination. Although consuming more energy than other two forwarding schemes, it guarantees and speeds up the arrival of data packets. If there are some emergency data packets need to be transferred, *direct forwarding* is a suitable choice.

If one relaying-node detects that environments has changed and another forwarding scheme is more suitable for the packets forwarding, it can switch to the new forwarding scheme using routing interface immediately. The function compute_RouteStrategy( ) can be used to judge which forwarding scheme should be used.

4 Simulations and Comparisons

The algorithm AMPRA is simulated on a variety of static network topologies. With *disjoint parallel multi-path forwarding* scheme, the network's load balance, energy consumption and traffic efficiency are measured. With *selective forwarding* scheme, the probability of successful arrival of a packet to the destination is studied. A high probability of successful transmission could result in good energy efficiency and throughput. With *direct forwarding* scheme, the average delay time is measured because it is the main parameter when transmitting emergency data in networks if the correct transmission can be guaranteed. We evaluate how AMPRA through comparing with GPSR [11], ETX metric [6], Lazy loss detection [4], GRAB [8] and M-MPR-SF [7]. It can be concluded from these measurements that AMPRA is a good choice for efficient and reliable transmission.

4.1 Simulation Environment

We use ns2.28 to simulate AMPRA algorithm. A route agent is installed to ns2. In ns2 simulations, Shared Media interface is initialized with parameters to make it work like the 914MHz Lucent WaveLAN DSSS radio interface. Simulations are for networks of 50 nodes with 802.11 WaveLAN radios, with a nominal 250-meter range, 2Mbps bandwidth. The nodes are initially placed at random in a rectangular region. Through adjusting the size of the region, different node density got.

Numerical experiments are used to evaluate the probability of successful arrival of a packet to the destination.

To evaluate the load balance of a network, the metric Energy Variance (Evar) is used. When the value is lower, the load balance is better. If the value is very high, it means some nodes will exhaust their energy soon, and result in useful system lifetime decline. *N* is the sum of nodes.

$$\text{Evar} = \frac{1}{N}[(E_1 - \text{Emean})^2 + (E_2 - \text{Emean})^2 + \ldots + (E_N - \text{Emean})^2] \quad (1)$$

$$\text{Emean} = \frac{\text{the sum of the energy spent}}{N} \quad (2)$$

4.2 Simulation Results

A. Using *disjoint parallel multi-path forwarding* scheme

In this part, we assume the wireless links are reliable. Then the GPSR, ETX metric, Lazy loss detection can be seen the same in normal. Three disjoint multi-paths are chosen using AMPRA, and its performance is compared with GPSR, GRAB using ns2 with 2 CBR flows in 1kByte/s. GRAB is a multi-path routing algorithm which needs a flooding mechanism – cost field building to establish the multi-paths route table. The energy overhead of GRAB consists of two parts, forwarding and cost field building. Because the cost value of each node will change with the packets forwarding, cost field building should be carried out periodically.

For evaluating the network's Evar, we modify the energy consumption simulation code of CMU slightly in wireless-phy.cc. Fig.6 shows the Energy Variance (Evar) at different densities (Neighbors/Range). Obviously, AMPRA has better load balance than GPSR and GRAB. It is mainly because AMPRA can provide parallel disjoint multi-paths. Although GRAB also provides multi-paths, it forwards the packets along with one route not parallel routes selected from the routes. In fact, GRAB is not suitable for reliable links because it is designed to forward packets over unreliable links. It can be found out from Fig.6 that lower density has higher Energy Variance. It mainly because the lower density means fewer neighborhood's interference, namely, more energy could be conserved by those not-routing nodes.

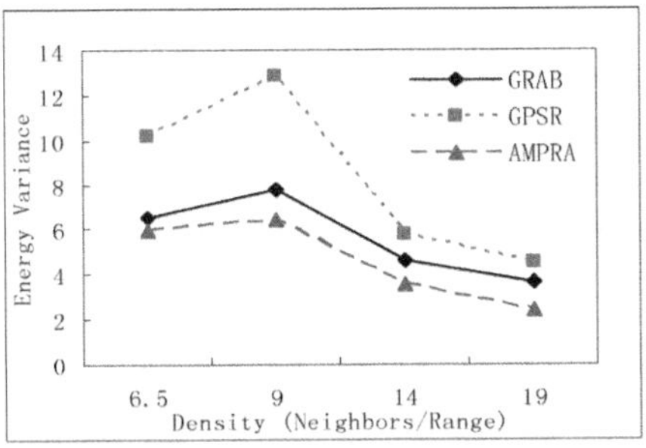

Fig. 6. Energy Variance (Evar)

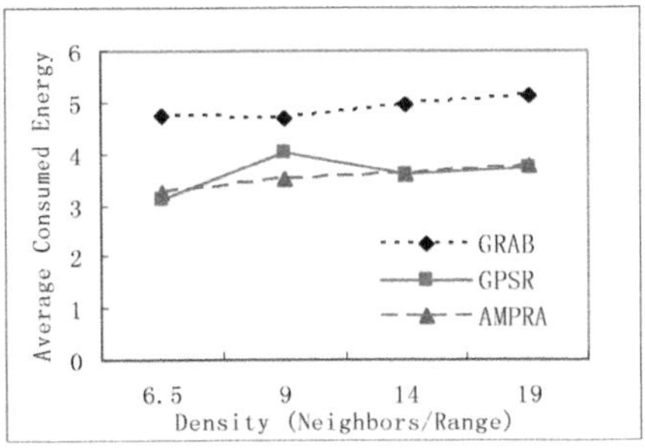

Fig. 7. Average Consumed Energy (Emean)

Fig.7 shows the Average Consumed Energy (Emean) at different densities (Neighbors/Range). GRAB consumes more energy than GPSR and AMPRA because of the periodical flooding mechanism. It can be concluded that AMPRA in general has the same average consumed energy as GPSR. It does not increase much amount of overhead traffic due to multiple paths. Moreover, it consumes energy more smoothly (See Fig.7, Density 9). In density 9, the forwarding encounters some local minimum phenomenon. GPSR lost some "good" links and need more hops, so it consumes more energy than AMPRA. It's evidence that *Clockwise-Rule* consumes lower energy than *right hand rule*. The highest Evar in Fig.6 Density 9 also based on this reason.

The metric Average Delay Time is used to evaluate the network's traffic efficiency. As shown in Table.2, the Average Delay Time (point to point) of AMPRA is lower than GPSR and GRAB. Before forwarding packets, GRAB need establish the route table first through flooding mechanism, which consumes much time. AMPRA can provide 2*3Mbps bandwidth in-between source and destination, but GPSR and GRAB have only 2Mbps bandwidth. Although GRAB has multi-path, it only chooses one next-hop node from multi next-hop nodes to forward the packets in one transmission. AMPRA can carry large data through 3 routes in parallel. The traffic efficiency is improved significantly. Low density means large rectangular region which result in large hops, so the Average Delay Time decreases with the increase of the density.

Table 2. Average Delay Time (point to point)

Density	6.5	9	14	19
GRAB	91ms	79ms	63ms	49ms
GPSR	43ms	37ms	30ms	25ms
AMPRA	24ms	19ms	13ms	12ms

B. using *Selective forwarding* scheme

In this part, we assume the wireless links are not so reliable, and the packet receive rate of each link is distributed in 0.85~0.99 randomly. Using AMPRA algorithm ($m = 2$), ETX metric and Lazy loss detection, the probability of successful arrival of a packet to the destination is evaluated using numerical experiments.

Fig.8 shows the change of the successful arrival probability with different distance between source and destination. Because multi-paths can choose more reliable links at each relaying node according to current conditions, as Fig.8 shows, it (e.g. AMPRA) gets more reliable transmission than single path strategy (e.g. ETX metric, Lazy loss detection). Due to enhance the reliability of reverse links, Lazy loss detection gets some better performance than ETX metric. As proved by [4] (section II.B), no ACK transmission will decrease the packet receive rate to 0 as the hops increase. So retransmission over unreliable wireless sensor links is needed. It implicates that high probability of successful transmission will result in high energy efficiency and throughput because of the retransmission's decrease. Since AMPRA can provide more reliable transmission, it has higher energy efficiency and throughput than ETX metric and Lazy loss detection.

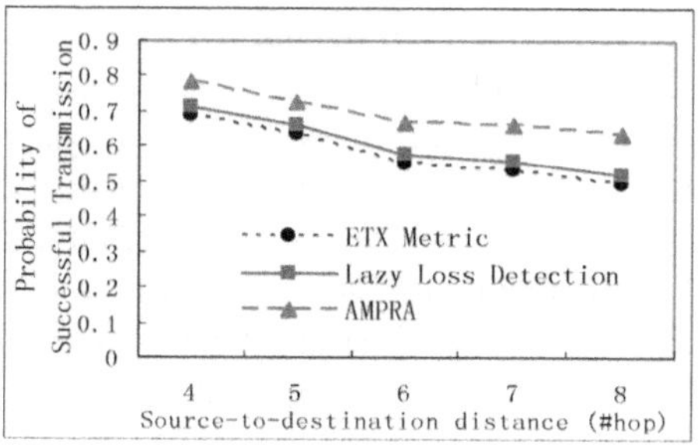

Fig. 8. The packets arrival rate

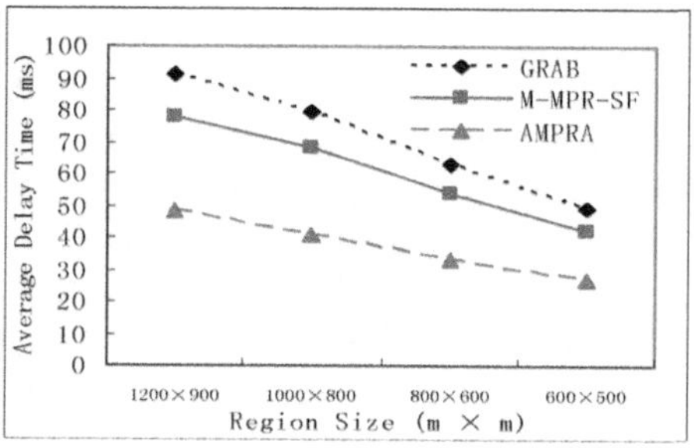

Fig. 9. The transmission speed of emergency data

C. using *direct forwarding* scheme

As mentioned in subsection 3.2, *direct forwarding* using all links in the multi-paths to transfer the same packets sent from source node. It guarantees the correct of packets transmission as high probability even if there are errors in some links. For emergency data, rapid and correct transmission is the most important thing. In this part, the speed of *direct forwarding* is studied using ns2 with 1kbyte data packet and 64byte route packet.

GRAB and M-MPR-SF are two multi-paths routing algorithms which are all need establish the multi-paths route table before transmitting data packets. During the multi-paths establishment, GRAB use flooding and destination reply mechanisms and M-MPR-SF use greedy forwarding and destination reply mechanisms. Fig.9 shows the average delay time of AMPRA, GRAB and M-MPR-SF with different region size. As mentioned above, large region size means large hops. The average delay time decreases with the decrease of region size. Compared with GRAB and M-MPR-SF, AMPRA decreases the average delay time of emergency data transmission evidently. It mainly derives from that AMPRA do not need the process of multi-paths establishment which consumes much time. Due to flooding mechanism will bring interference, GRAB consumes more time than M-MPR-SF in transmitting emergency data. It can be concluded that AMPRA with *direct forwarding* has quick speed in emergency data transmission. *Direct forwarding* is suitable for emergency data transmission.

5 Conclusions

Through adjusting the forwarding schemes, Multi-paths can provide more efficient transmission in sensor networks. After deeply studying the local minima, we proposed an adaptive multi-path algorithm (AMPRA) for sensor networks. AMPRA can provide flexible forwarding schemes satisfying different transmission requirement. It can balance energy load and extend network's bandwidth through using *disjoint parallel multi-path forwarding* scheme, or speed up the emergency data transmission through using *direct forwarding* scheme, or improve the reliability of the transmission over unreliable links through using *selective forwarding* scheme. Simulation results confirm the effectiveness of the AMPRA.

References

1. Ganesan, D., Krishnamachari, B., Woo, A., Culler, D., Estrin D., Wicker, S., 2002. Complex Behavior at Scale: An Experimental Study of Low-Power Wireless Sensor Networks. UCLA CS Technical Report UCLA/CSD-TR 02-0013.
2. Zhao, J., Govindan, R., 2003. Understanding Packet Delivery Performance in Dense Wireless Sensor Networks. Proceedings of the 1st international conference on Embedded networked sensor systems (SenSys'03), p. 1 – 13.
3. Woo, A., Tong, T., Culler, D., 2003. Taming the Underlying Issues for Reliable Multhop Routing in Sensor Networks. Proceedings of ACM Sensys 2003, Los Angeles, California, 2003.
4. Qing Cao, Tian He, Fang Lei, Abdelzaher, T., Stankovic, J., 2006. Efficiency Centric Communication Model for Wireless Sensor Networks. IEEE INFOCOM'06.
5. Seada, K., Zuniga, M., Helmy, A., Krishnamachari, B., 2004. Energy Efficient Forwarding Strategies for Geographic Routing in Lossy Wireless Sensor Networks. Proceedings of the 2nd international conference on Embedded networked sensor systems (SenSys'04), p. 108 - 121.
6. de Couto, D.S.J., Aguayo, D., Bicket, J., Morris, R., 2003. A High-Throughput Path Metric for Multi-Hop Wireless Routing. Proc. ACM Ninth International Conference on Mobile Computing and Networking (Mobicom'03).
7. Swades De, Chunming Qiao, Hongyi Wu, 2003. Meshed multipath routing with selective forwarding: an efficient strategy in wireless sensor networks. Computer Networks 43 (2003) 481-497.
8. Ye, F., Zhong, G., Lu, S., Zhang, L., 2005. GRAdient Broadcast: A Robust Data Delivery Protocol for Large Scale Sensor Networks. ACM Wireless Networks (WINET), Vol. 11, No. 2, p. 285-298.
9. Savarese, C., Langendoen, K., Rabaey, J., 2002. Robust Positioning Algorithms for Distributed Ad-Hoc Wireless Sensor Networks. Proc. Usenix Annual Technical Conference, Monterey, CA, June 2002.

10. Chintalapudi, K., Govindan, R., Sukhatme, G., Dhariwal, A., 2004. Ad-Hoc Localization Using Ranging and Sectoring. Proc. IEEE INFOCOM'04, Vol. 4, p. 2662 – 2672.
11. Karp, B., Kung, H., 2000. Greedy Perimeter Stateless Routing. Proceedings of the 6th annual international conference on Mobile computing and networking (Mobicom 2000), p. 243 - 254.
12. Yan Yu, Govindan, R., Estrin, D., 2001. Geographical and energy aware routing: A recursive data dissemination protocol for wireless sensor networks. UCLA Computer Science Department Technical Report UCLA/CSD-TR-01-0023.
13. Nasipuri, A., Castaneda, R., DAS, S., 2001. Performance of Multipath Routing for On-Demand Protocols in Mobile Ad Hoc Networks. ACM/Kluwer Mobile Networks and Applications(MONET) Journal, 2001,6(4): 339-349.
14. Papadimitratos, P., Hass, Z. J., Sirer, E. G., 2002. Path set selection in mobile Ad hoc networks. Proc. of the 3rd ACM Int'l Symp. on Mobile Ad Hoc Networking & Computing. New York: ACM Press, p. 1~11.
15. Qing Fang, Jie Gao, Guibas, L., 2004. Locating and Bypassing Routing Holes in Sensor Networks. Proc. The 23th Conference on Computer Communications (IEEE INFOCOM'04). Vol. 4, p. 2458 – 2468.
16. Gabriel, K., Sokal, R., 1969. A new statistical approach to geographic variation analysis. Systematic Zoology *18*, p. 259–278.
17. Toussaint, G., 1980. The relative neighborhood graph of a finite planar set. Pattern Recognition *12*, 4 (1980), 261–268.
18. Zuniga, M., Krishnamachari, B., 2004. Analyzing the Transitional Region in Low Power Wireless Links. Proceedings of IEEE SECON 2004, p. 517-526.

Distributed Self-Pruning(DSP) Algorithm for Bridges in Clustered Ad Hoc Networks*

Seok Yeol Yun[1] and Hoon Oh[2,**]

[1] Kangwon National University, Chuncheon, Kangwon-do, Korea
kw477@hanmail.net
[2] University of Ulsan, Ulsan, Korea

Abstract. In clustered ad hoc networks, it is often required that a clusterhead, a leader of cluster, send a message to all its neighbor clusterheads. One simple approach is to use a flooding scheme in which every bridge node receiving a message simply relays it only if it receives the message for the first time. However, the flooding tends to degrade network efficiency severely because many bridges relay the message unnecessarily, causing neighbor clusterheads to receive multiple copies of the same message along different paths. A distributed self-pruning algorithm proposed in this paper attacks this problem.

1 Introduction

In a variety of applications, nodes are often required to send a message to all other nodes of a mobile ad hoc network. The brute-force approach to this problem has been known as flooding, in which every node relays a message only if the message has been received for the first time. Flooding causes nodes to receive multiple copies of the same message along different paths, degrading network efficiency severely. In this paper, assuming that nodes in ad hoc network forms a number of disjoint clusters, we devise an efficient algorithm to handle the case that a clusterhead, the leader of a particular cluster, sends a message to all of its neighboring clusterheads.

Some previous researches have been performed as part of the proposed routing protocols [2] [3] or independent protocols aimed at improving efficiency [1] [7] [9] [10]. Key broadcasting protocols are discussed for their advantages and disadvantages.

SBA [7], a self pruning protocol, uses a neighbor elimination scheme to reduce the number of retransmissions. A node sends a broadcast message (BMSG) after piggybacking a set consisting of its one-hop neighbors. The receiving node retransmits the BMSG only if it has at least one neighbor node not covered by the forwarding node. However, the effectiveness of SBA is often limited because

* This research was supported by the MIC(Ministry of Information and Communication), Korea, under the ITRC(Information Technology Research Center) support program supervised by the IITA(Institute of Information Technology Assessment).
** corresponding author.

Y.-H. Lee et al. (Eds.): ICESS 2007, LNCS 4523, pp. 699–707, 2007.

a receiving node usually has a node in the opposite side of the forwarding node, except for the nodes positioned at the edges of a network.

In OLSR [2], every node selects a Multipoint Relay (MPR) set that is a minimal subset of neighboring nodes such that their combined radio range covers all nodes located within 2-hops. Thus, only the nodes that belong to the MPR set are allowed to retransmit a received BMSG. It reduces a lot of overhead, but suffers from a high level of computational complexity required to select the minimal subset. Their proposed heuristic algorithm still takes on a high degree of computation in relatively dense networks.

The FNSB [10] protocol was devised for use in clustered networks to promote efficient message exchange among the clusterheads of neighboring clusters (hereafter referred to as *neighbor clusterhead*). In this protocol, every clusterhead selects a minimum number of bridges, known as the forward set, such that it can cover all neighboring clusterheads; the forward set is relayed separately to its neighbors. FNSB is similar to the OLSR protocol in that only the nodes that belong to the forward set retransmit the BMSG. Unlike OLSR, however, FNSB does not suffer from a computational overhead as the number of neighboring clusterheads are typically not very large. In addition, this algorithm is also not a distributed type.

In the Neighbor Dependent Cluster (NDC) [1], a source node forms a cluster prior to the initiation of route discovery. A route is explored by a limited flooding, rather than a simple flooding, by exploiting the cluster structure, in which initial nodes (nodes before a cluster is formed), clusterheads, and selected bridges take part in forwarding. A clusterhead selects a set of forwarding bridges such that the more clusterheads a bridge passes through, the higher the chance of selection becomes. A tie is broken by the number of non-clusterheads connected by a particular bridge. However, the problem with NDC is that the bridge selection is done by a clusterhead. Furthermore, the set of bridges selected according to the proposed algorithm may not cover all neighboring clusterheads.

In Passive Clustering(PC) [3], each bridge declares its connecting pair of clusterheads by sending a declaration message if it has not yet received such a message. The receiving bridge subsequently gives up its forwarding role unless it does not have another distinct connecting pair of clusterheads. If two bridges declare the same connecting pair of clusterheads, the bridge with the lowest ID is given priority. In this protocol, an extra message is needed to claim the forwarding role. Moreover, even though a given bridge is capable of covering more than one clusterhead, it is forbidden to do so. The end result of PC is a reduction of superfluous forwardings, especially in dense networks.

The approach used in this paper does not determine the forwarding bridge set *a priori*. Instead, all the bridges that receive a BMSG make an independent judgment regarding whether or not to forward or relay by parsing some tiny information piggybacked in the message. Accordingly, the additional overhead required to perform this algorithm is almost negligible. The computational complexity for judgment is $O(n)$ where n is the number of neighboring clusterheads.

In Section 2, we identify the problem and overview our approach. Section 3 gives the detailed description of the proposed algorithm. We evaluate the algorithm by applying it to the existing protocols PCDV (Proactive Cluster-based Distance Vector) [5] and GDSR (Group Dynamic Source Routing) [4] in Section 4. Lastly, the contributions of the new algorithm and future research directions are discussed in Section 5.

2 Problem Identification

In clustered ad hoc networks it is common for a clusterhead to send messages to its neighboring clusterheads (the clusterheads of its neighboring clusters). Such examples are shown in the PCDV routing protocol or in a protocol where a node broadcasts a network-wide message [4] [6]. In this case, a message is delivered via some intermediate bridges to the sender's neighbor clusterheads by flooding. However, in a mesh network with multiple routes between a pair of neighboring clusterheads, flooding causes multiple copies of the identical message to be delivered to the neighboring clusterheads. This overhead is a serious factor in the degradation of network performance.

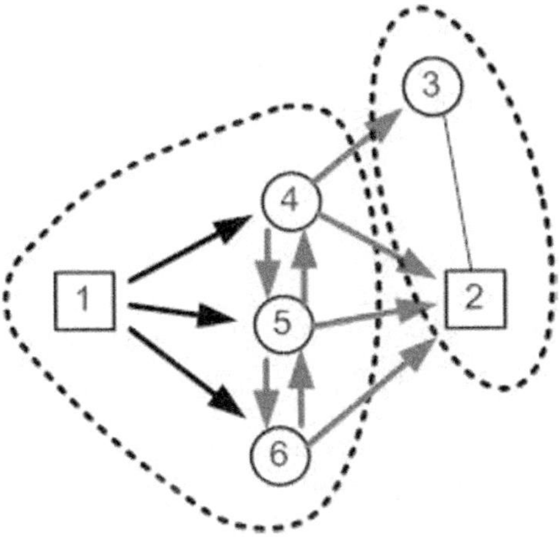

Fig. 1. On-the-fly route optimization

For example, Fig. 1 shows a small wireless network consisting of two clusters, each of which is encircled by a dashed line. The clusterheads are denoted by rectangles, which are connected to each other by four bridges (circles 3, 4, 5, and 6). We do not discuss the clustering method here since it is beyond the scope of the paper. To demonstrate how flooding works, one can envision a message transmitted by clusterhead 1 toward its neighboring clusterhead 2 that is first delivered to bridges 4, 5, and 6. The receiving node adjacent to a bridge relays the message immediately. However, bridge 3, which receives the message from bridge 4, will also forward the message. In the end, clusterhead 2 receives four identical messages. This is far from the optimal case in which only one bridge would relay the received message.

One method to solve the problem discussed above would be to have a bridge detect that one of its neighboring bridges has already sent the identical message, and to abort sending the message if that is the case. For instance, referring again to Fig. 1, if one assumes that node 5 sent the message *prior to* two neighboring bridges and bridges 4 and 6 were able to overhear the transmission, if bridge 5 can mark the fact that the message was delivered to clusterhead 2 within the message, bridges 4 and 6 (which overheard the message) can give up sending the message.

3 Algorithm Description

Consider the case of an arbitrary clusterhead that sends a message to all the neighboring clusterheads that are at most three hops away (if the considered network is not partitioned). In a dense network, numerous identical messages can be delivered to each neighboring clusterhead along the different paths, which is due to the fact that a bridge does not know that its neighboring bridges have already relayed a message to the clusterheads to which it is about to send the same message.

Let C(b) be a set of clusterheads that bridge *b* can cover directly (by one hop) or indirectly (by two hops) by forwarding the message. Let N(b) be a set of *b*' neighbor bridges. Let N(b-) be a set of bridges that belongs to N(b), but sent the message prior to bridge *b*. Bridge *b* need not relay the message if the following condition holds: $C(b) \subseteq \{x | x \in C(v), v \in N(b-)\}$.

If bridge *b* can maintain the covered set information C(b) for the clusterheads that it can cover directly or indirectly against node mobility, each node becomes capable of making a judgment regarding the sending of a message according to the Relay Rule, which hereby is denoted as the Distributed Self-Pruning (DSP) algorithm. Fortunately, we can maintain the covered set of each bridge easily by resorting to the Hello messages without using additional control messages. In this paper, the Hello messages are utilized for exchanging the cluster structure information, detecting link connectivity, and building the covered sets. Consequently, a node relays a received message only if the following two conditions are satisfied simultaneously:

(1) The receiving node is a bridge; and

(2) $Not(C(b) \subseteq \{x | x \in C(v), v \in N(b-)\})$.

Let $BMSG_i$ denote a broadcast message initiated by clusterhead *i*. We define two notations - $coverableSet_i$ and $BMSG_i.coveredSet$. $coverableSet_i$ is the set of bridge *i*'s neighboring clusterheads and the clusterheads of bridge *i*'s neighboring bridges that belong to another cluster. The element of the set (clusterhead, distance) that consists of clusterhead and distance to the corresponding clusterhead.

Note that all the clusterheads in the set are at the most within two hops, and therefore such information can be generated with ease by exchanging Hello messages. $BMSG_i$. coveredSet is a set of clusterheads to which $BMSG_i$ has been delivered directly before or at the same time the message arrives at a certain bridge. Every bridge piggybacks the coveredSet upon relaying a received message. The result is that all of the receiving bridges know which neighboring clusterheads have already received the message. A detailed description of the DSP algorithm is given in Fig. 2.

```
//BMSG_i = (msg, coveredSet).
//BMSG_i.msg: a message initiated by clusterhead i.
//BMSG_i.coveredSet: a set of clusterheads to which
//BMSG_i has been delivered directly before or at
//the same time the message arrives at a certain bridge.
//coverableSet_i : the set of bridge i's neighbor
//clusterheads and the clusterheads of bridge i's
//neighbor bridges that belong to bridge another cluster.
o sending clusterhead i:
  send BMSG_i = (msg, coveredSet);
o clusterhead j that receives BMSG_i:
  Process BMSG_i;
  free(BMSG_i);
o ordinary node l that receives BMSG_i:
  free(BMSG_i);
o bridge k that receives a BMSG_i
  S = coverableSet_i - {(src, d)| d = 1 or 2};
  // α is delay coefficient
  // randomDelay is a random delay
  delay-jitter = α * (|S| - |S|_{d=1}) * randomDelay;
  set BMSG_i's transmission delay to delay-jitter;
  put the BMSG_i into the queue and execute the timer;
o bridge k whose timer expires
  // S includes all covered sets received along different
  //routes
  for each coveredSet v in the queue that belongs to BMSG_i do
    S = S ∪ v;
  endfor;
  // i is the source node that initiated BMSG
  S = coverableSet_k − {(i,d)} − {(x,1), (x,2) | (x,d)∈ S};
  if (S != ∅ ) then
    S' = {(x, d)| (x, d) ∈ S, d = 1};
    resend BMSG_i = (msg, S');
  elseif;
  delete all queued messages with respect to BMSG_i;
```

Fig. 2. DSP Algorithm

Fig. 3 illustrates the application example of the DSP algorithm. Each bridge maintains its coverableSet. For example, node 13 can cover 0 and 1 directly. However, bridge 13 cannot cover clusterhead 6, even though it is two hops away, since their respective clusters are not neighbor. Suppose that clusterhead 1 sends

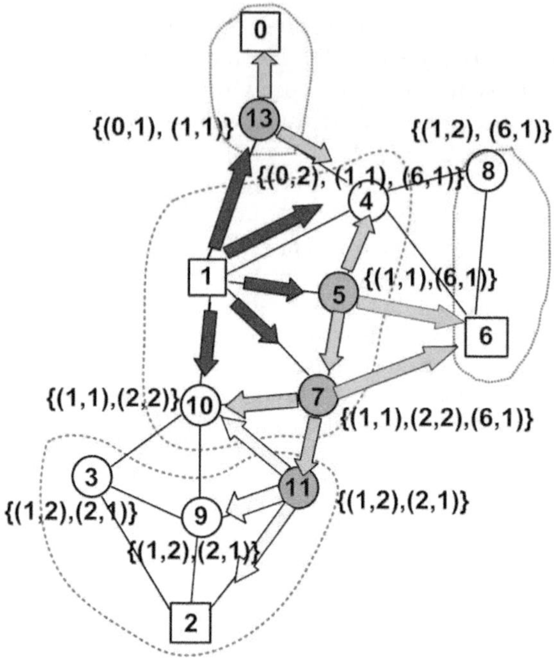

Fig. 3. Optimized Retransmission of Messages

a message $BMSG_1$ to its neighbor clusterheads 0, 2, and 6. Because the source clusterhead does not have any clusterhead to cover directly, it sends a message with coveredSet = $\emptyset$, and bridges 4, 5, 7, 10, and 13 subsequently receive the message with coveredSet = $\emptyset$. Assume that node 5 considers the judgment first without loss of generality. Then, $coverableSet_5 = \{(1, 1), (6, 1)\}$. Bridge 5 can cover clusterheads 1 and 6 directly, and since node 1 is the originator, it is neglected. Bridge 5 sends a message with coveredSet = $\{6\}$ which is received by bridges 4 and 7. Now, suppose that nodes 7 and 13 make a relay judgment (note that nodes 4 and 13 cannot send a message at the same time because of collision). Node 13 can cover clusterhead 0, and thus relays the message with coveredSet = $\{0\}$. Bridge 4 knows that all clusterheads in its $coverableSet_4$ have been covered by both bridge 13 and bridge 5, and gives up relaying $BMSG_1$. Bridge 7 relays the message with coveredSet = $\{6\}$ where clusterhead 6 can be directly covered. Among the receiving bridges 10 and 11, suppose that bridge 11 makes a judgment first. Bridge 11 sends the message with coveredSet = $\{2\}$. Upon receiving the message, Bridge 10 knows that clusterhead 2 has already been covered by bridge 11. In this way, almost 50% of bridges give up relaying the message.

4 Performance Analysis

To analyze the effectiveness of the DSP algorithm, we applied the proposed DSP algorithm to two cluster-based protocols, PCDV [5] and GDSR [4] to which the algorithm can be easily adapted with a slight modification. GlomoSim 2.03 [8] was used for simulation study. The parameter values are given in Table 1.

Table 1. Simulation parameters

Parameter	value
Node mobility pattern	Random WayPoint
Node Mobility	5 (m/sec)
Pause time	30 (sec)
Number of Nodes	50, 75, 100, 150, 200, 250
Dimension size	1500 x 300
Transmission Range	250 (m)
Bandwidth	2 (Mbps)
Traffic type	CBR
Simulation Time	300 (sec)

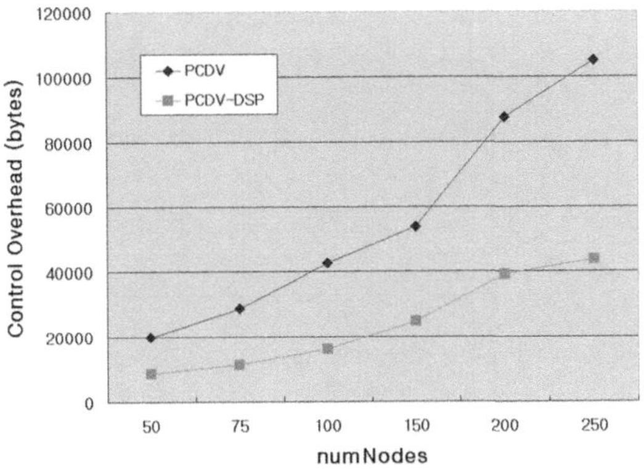

Fig. 4. Comparison of Control Overhead between PCDV and PCDV-DSP

Fig. 4 shows the variation of control overhead (as measured in bytes) according to varying number of nodes. The PCDV-DSP, which employs the DSP algorithm, was able to reduce overhead by approximately 50% compared to the PCDV alone, regardless of node density. Fig. 5 shows a gain of performance similar to that observed in the application of DSP to PCDV. However, the overhead of the GDSR employing DSP decreases with the higher node density, since nodes issue RREQs less frequently due to the increased connectivity between groups. The overall effect increased the stability of the group route.

Fig. 5 shows a gain of performance to that observed in the application of DSP to GDSR. However, the overhead of the GDSR employing DSP decreases with the higher node density, since nodes issue RREQs less frequently due to the increased connectivity between groups. The overall effect increased the stability of the group route.

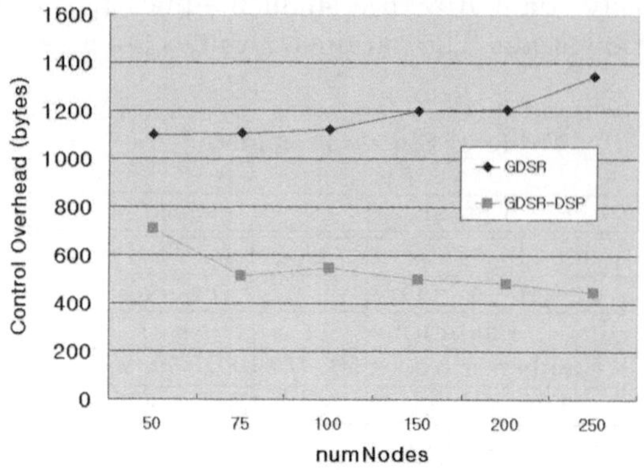

Fig. 5. Comparison of Control Overhead between GDSR and GDSR-DSP

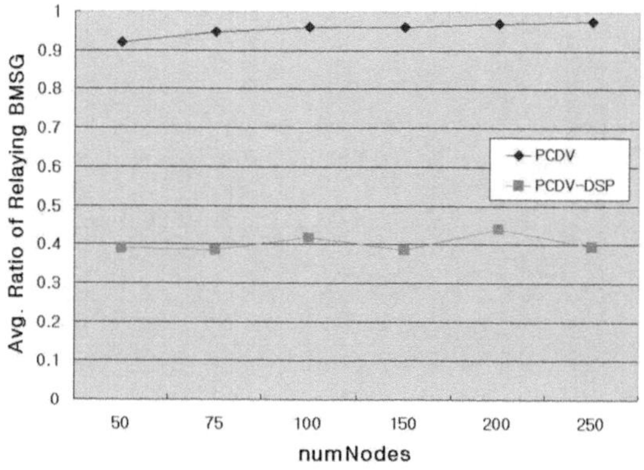

Fig. 6. Avg. Ratio of Relaying BMSG in PCDV and PCDV-DSP

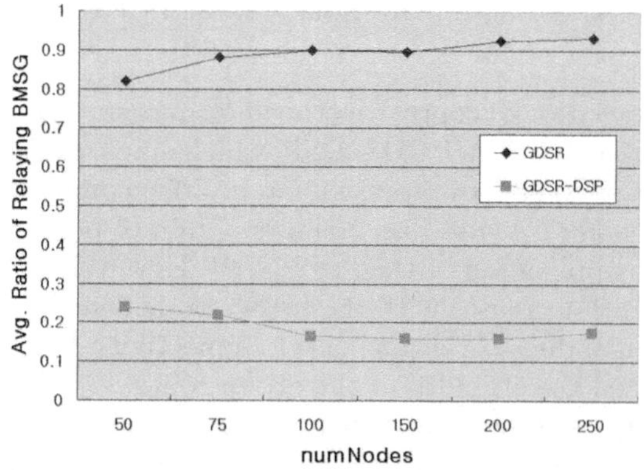

Fig. 7. Avg. Ratio of Relaying BMSG in GDSR and GDSR-DSP

Note that the DSP algorithm increases the size of a BMSG by piggybacking a coveredSet. Here, we analyze how many nodes participate in relaying a BMSG without considering the size of a BMSG. This analysis is meaningful, as multiple transmissions of a message with a small payload are more harmful than a single transmission of a message with a large payload. According to the simulation results shown in Fig. 6 and Fig. 7, the performance gain obtained was up to 60% or 80%, depending on which protocol was applied.

5 Conclusion

In this paper, we presented a new algorithm that reduces the number of bridges required to participate in relay activity. Unlike other methods, this algorithm does not set the bridges that need not relay the message *a priori*. Rather, each bridge makes an on-the-fly relay judgment by checking small information piggybacked in the received message. The high efficiency of this algorithm was demonstrated by simulation.

References

1. Tzu-Chiang Chiiang, Po-Yi Wu, Yueh-Min Huang, "A limited flooding schmeme for mobile ad hoc networks," Wireless And Mobile Computing, Networking And Communications, 2005. (WiMob'2005), IEEE International Conference, vol.3, Aug. (2005) pp.473-478.
2. Philippe Jacquet, Paul Muhlethaler, Thomas Clausen, Anis Laouiti, Amir Qayyum, Laurent Viennot: "Optimized link state routing protocol for ad hoc networks." In IEEE International Multi Topic Conference, (2001).
3. Taek Jin Kwon, Mario Gerla: "Efficient flooding with passive clustering(PC) in ad hoc networks," ACM Computer Communication Review, vol.32, no.1, Jan.(2002) pp.44-56.
4. D. M. Ngoc, H. Oh,"A Group Dynamic Source Routing Protocol for Ad Hoc Networks," Proc. 1st IFOST 2006, Oct. (2006) pp.134-137.
5. Hoon Oh, Seok-Yeol Yun: "Proactive cluster-based distance-vector(PCDV) routing protocol in mobile ad hoc networks", To be published, IEICE Trans. On Communications.
6. Hoon Oh, Hong Seong Park: "Communication architecture and protocols for broadcast-type mobile multimedia ad hoc networks," MILCOM 2002. Proceedings, vol.1, 7-10, Oct. (2002) pp.442-447.
7. Wei Peng, Xi-Cheng Lu: "On the Reduction of Broadcast Redundancy in Mobile Ad Hoc Networks," Proc. First Ann. Workshop Mobile and Ad Hoc Networking and Computing, Aug. (2000) pp.129-130.
8. UCLA Parallel Computing Laboratory and Wireless Adaptive Mobility Laboratory. GloMoSim: A Scalable Simulation Environment for Wireless and Wired Network Systems, http://pcl.cs.ucla.edu/projects/glomosim
9. Ivan Stojmenovic, Mahtab Seddigh, Jovisa Zunic: "Dominating Sets and Neighbor Elimination-Based Broadcasting Algorithms in Wireless Networks," IEEE Transactions on Parallel and Distributed Systems, vol.13, no.1, Jan. (2002) pp.14-25.
10. Jie Wu, Wei Lou: "Forward-Node-Set-Based Broadcast in Clustered Mobile Ad Hoc Networks," Wireless Networks and Mobile Computing, special issue on Algorithmic, Geometric, Graph, Combinational, and Vector, vol.3, no.2, (2003) pp.155-173.

Chaotic Communications in MIMO Systems

Karuna Thapaliya[1], Qinghai Yang[1], and Kyung Sup Kwak[1]

UWB Wireless Communications Research Center (INHA UWB-ITRC),
Inha University, 402-751, Incheon, Korea
karunaa2@yahoo.com

Abstract. In wireless communications, chaotic communications have been a field of interest due to its low complexity in hardware implementation and low power consumption in chaotic signal generation. Among the modulation schemes using the chaotic signal, Differential Chaos Shift Keying (DCSK) is a robust noncoherent technique. Multiple-input multiple-output (MIMO) system is a technology that uses multiple transmit and/or multiple receive antennas in order to improve the system performance in wireless systems. In our paper, we have proposed a new scheme of MIMO-DCSK which utilizes the benefits of MIMO system into the chaotic communication system by transmitting and receiving DCSK modulated signals through multiple antennas. Our analysis and simulation results show how the chaotic communications in the new MIMO-DCSK benefits over the single input single output (SISO) system and the BER performance of DCSK in additive white Gaussian noise (AWGN) channels using Alamouti space-time code and the maximum likelihood decoding is analyzed.[1]

1 Introduction

Chaotic communications have been a subject of major interest in the field of wireless communications due to the wideband spectrum, random like signals, non-repetition of the signals, easiness of generating the chaotic signals, low power consumption property and less complex system. In chaotic communications, the information is directly mapped to some property of a chaotic signal thus avoiding the need of additional spectrum spreading. Other significant advantages of chaotic communications are no use of carriers and the possibility of highly secured communications.

Many chaos based communication systems have been proposed as chaos shift keying (CSK), chaos frequency modulation (CFM), chaos pulse position modulation (CPPM) [1].For our analysis, differential chaos shift keying (DCSK) modulation scheme has been considered.

Multiple-input multiple-output (MIMO) system is a technology using multiple antennas for transmission and reception thus increasing the channel capacity and

[1] This research was supported by the MIC (Ministry of Information and Communication), Korea, under the ITRC (Information Technology Research Center) support program supervised by the IITA (Institute of Information Technology Advancement). (IITA-2006-(C1090-0603-0019)).

Y.-H. Lee et al. (Eds.): ICESS 2007, LNCS 4523, pp. 708–717, 2007.

reliability in wireless communications. Alamouti code is an ingenious transmit diversity technique in MIMO technology. It is the first technique that utilizes the space time block codes. Basically Alamouti space time is a simple scheme of 2x2 system that achieves a full diversity gain with a simple maximum likelihood decoding algorithm.

To our best knowledge, DCSK in MIMO system has not been exploited yet. In this paper, a novel MIMO-DCSK scheme is proposed for chaotic communications. Our simulations show how the MIMO system improves the system performance as compared to SISO system. In addition to this advantage, the proposed scheme reduces the signal generation complexity by the use of a smaller signal spreading factor.

2 System Description

In DCSK two chaotic signals are sent for each symbol period which corresponds to one bit of information. The first signal is used as a reference signal whereas the second signal is the information bearing signal. The information bit is extracted at the receiver by differentially coherent demodulation.

Transmission of reference chip via the same channel is generally considered as loss in transmitted energy per bit. This may be valid for the AWGN channel only. But real channels have linear or non-linear distortion and the modulated carrier has to be correlated with a reference signal distorted in the same manner as the modulated carrier to get the best system performance. And correlation with original distortion free reference results in performance degradation. Since in chaotic communication both the reference and information bearing signals undergo the same channel distortion, it offers a better system performance. In other words we can say that reference signal can be considered as a test signal used to measure the channel characteristics.

In our proposed system of DCSK with Alamouti space time code, the information bits are first DCSK modulated and then the encoder takes a block of two modulated symbols s_1 and s_2 in each encoding operation and gives it to the transmitting antennas according to the code matrix. At the receiver, combiner combines the received signal and gives it to the maximum likelihood (ML) detector for signal detection and then to the DCSK demodulator for the information bits recovery.

Fig.1 shows the structure of conventional DCSK transceiver [3]. Fig.3 and Fig.4 show the block diagram of the Alamouti space-time encoder and the Alamouti's two antenna transmit diversity scheme respectively.

2.1 DCSK Modulation

The discrete chaotic sequence s_i for one bit is represented as:

$$s_i = \begin{cases} x_i & 0<\text{i}\leq M \\ b_l x_{i-m} & M<\text{i}\leq 2M, \end{cases} \tag{1}$$

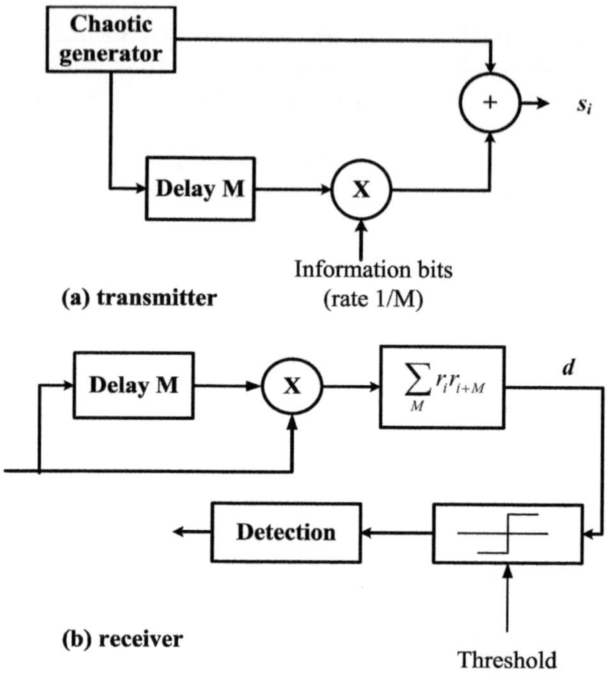

Fig. 1. DCSK Transceiver

where $b_l = +1$ for information bit=1 and b_l=-1 for information bit=0. For bit 1 the modulator as shown in Fig.1(a) transmits the same chaotic signal twice in succession, while for bit 0 the message signal, which is the chaotic signal delayed by M time period as compared to the reference signal, is an inverted copy of the reference signal.

The chaotic signal represented by (1) is shown in Fig.2 for both bit 1 and bit 0 transmissions. A certain guard interval is also inserted between reference and message signals so as to avoid the overlapping between these two signals as shown in Fig.2.

2.2 DCSK Demodulation

Signal recovery is done in the receiver side by multiplying the received reference and message signals, i.e., signal r_i and the received signal delayed by M, r_{i+M} [3]. The output of the correlator is given as:

$$d = \sum_M r_i r_{i+M}, \tag{2}$$

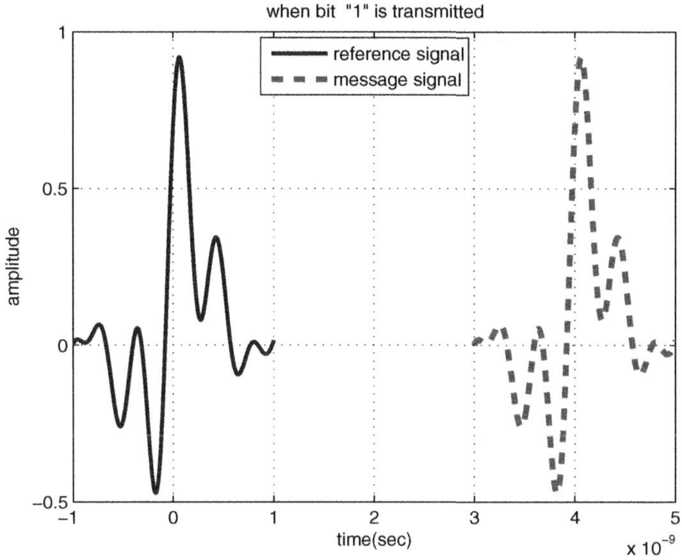

(a) DCSK modulation - when bit 1 is transmitted

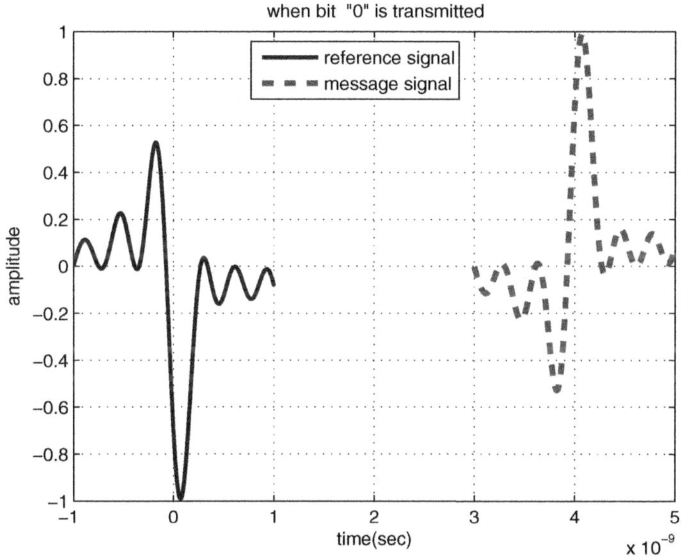

(b) DCSK modulation - when bit 0 is transmitted

Fig. 2. DCSK Modulation

making assumptions as received signal $r_i = s_i + \xi_i$, where ξ_i is a stationary random process with $\prec \xi_i \succ = 0$ such that for any $i \neq j$, ξ_i and ξ_j are statistically independent. Thus the output of the correlator becomes [1]:

$$\begin{aligned} d &= \sum_{i=1}^{M} (s_i + \xi_i)(s_{i+M} + \xi_{i+M}) \\ &= \sum_{i=1}^{M} (b_l x_i^2 + x_i(\xi_{i+M} + b_l \xi_i) + \xi_i \xi_{i+M}) \\ &= b_l \sum_{i=1}^{M} x_i^2 + \sum_{i=1}^{M} (x_i(\xi_{i+M} + b_l \xi_i) + \xi_i \xi_{i+M}). \end{aligned} \quad (3)$$

In (3) the first term is the important signal for the correlator and the second term is a zero mean random quantity.

The positive correlation output from equation (3) indicates that the receiving bit is 1 else the negative result of correlation indicates bit 0. In a noise free case, the magnitude of correlator output at the decision time instant is equal to the transmitted energy per bit.

2.3 Alamouti Space Time Code

As mentioned earlier Alamouti code is the transmit diversity technique in MIMO technology. Two DCSK modulated symbols s_1 and s_2 are taken by the encoder and supplied to the transmit antennas according to the code matrix [7],

$$S = \begin{bmatrix} s_1 & -s_2^* \\ s_2 & s_1^* \end{bmatrix}, \quad (4)$$

where the first column represents the first transmission period and the second column represents the second transmission period. The first row represents the

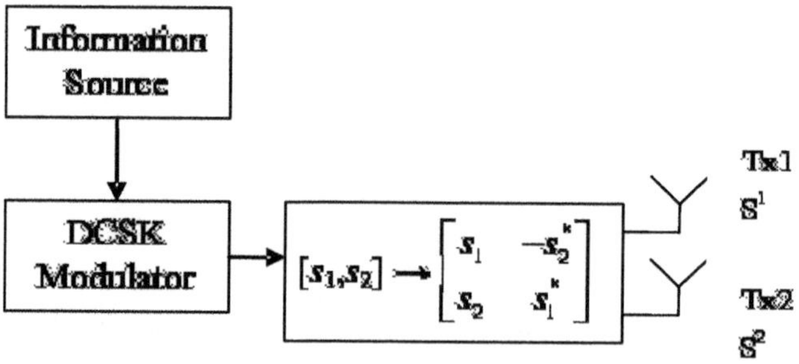

Fig. 3. Block diagram of Alamouti space-time encoder

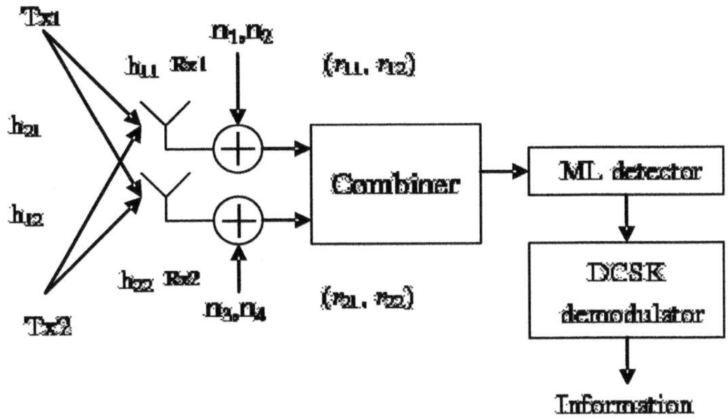

Fig. 4. Alamouti's two-antenna transmit diversity

signal transmitted by the first antenna while the second row represents the second antenna as:

$$S^1 = \left[s_1, -s_2^*\right],$$
$$S^2 = \left[s_2, s_1^*\right], \tag{5}$$

where S^1 is information transmitted by the first antenna and S^2 is the information transmitted by the second antenna. Thus from (5), it is observed that the inner product of S^1 and S^2 equals to zero thus making the sequences orthogonal. From (5), it is also observed that the transmission is done in space, i.e., two antennas and in time with two transmission intervals.

Let H be the fading channel defined as:

$$H = \begin{bmatrix} h_{11} \; h_{12} \\ h_{21} \; h_{22} \end{bmatrix}, \tag{6}$$

where h_{ij} denotes the fading channel coefficients, and the subscripts i and j denotes the receiving antenna index and the transmitting antenna index respectively.

Then the received signal R is,

$$R = H * S + N,$$
$$R = \begin{bmatrix} h_{11} \; h_{12} \\ h_{21} \; h_{22} \end{bmatrix} \cdot \begin{bmatrix} s_1 & -s_2^* \\ s_2 & s_1^* \end{bmatrix} + \begin{bmatrix} n_1 \; n_2 \\ n_3 \; n_4 \end{bmatrix},$$
$$R = \begin{bmatrix} r_{11} \; r_{12} \\ r_{21} \; r_{22} \end{bmatrix}, \tag{7}$$

where N, n_1, n_2, n_3, and n_4 represent the additive white Gaussian noise. Then the combiner combines this received signal as follows:

$$S_c^1 = h_{11}^* r_{11} + h_{12} r_{12}^* + h_{21}^* r_{21} + h_{22} r_{22}^*,$$
$$S_c^2 = h_{12}^* r_{11} - h_{11} r_{12}^* + h_{22}^* r_{21} - h_{21} r_{22}^*. \tag{8}$$

The combiner then sends these combined signals to the ML detector [7] wherein the decision is made. From (7) we get,

$$r_{11} = h_{11}s_1 + h_{12}s_2 + n_1, \tag{9}$$

$$r_{12} = -h_{11}s_2^* + h_{21}s_1^* + n_2, \tag{10}$$

$$r_{21} = h_{21}s_1 + h_{22}s_2 + n_3, \tag{11}$$

$$r_{22} = -h_{21}s_2^* + h_{22}s_1^* + n_4. \tag{12}$$

And (10) and (12) can be also be modified as:

$$r_{12}^* = -h_{11}s_2 + h_{21}s_1 + n_2, \tag{13}$$

$$r_{22}^* = -h_{21}s_2 + h_{22}s_1 + n_4. \tag{14}$$

(9), (11), (13) and (14) can be represented in a simpler form as follows:

$$\begin{bmatrix} r_{11} \\ r_{12}^* \\ r_{21} \\ r_{22}^* \end{bmatrix} = \begin{bmatrix} h_{11} & h_{12} \\ h_{21} & -h_{11} \\ h_{21} & h_{22} \\ h_{22} & -h_{21} \end{bmatrix} \cdot \begin{bmatrix} s_1 \\ s_2 \end{bmatrix} + \begin{bmatrix} n_1 \; n_2 \\ n_3 \; n_4 \end{bmatrix},$$

$$R^{'} = H^{'}.S^{'} + N, \tag{15}$$

The ML detector gives:

$$\hat{S} = \arg\min_{S'} \left\| R' - H'.S' \right\|_2 . \tag{16}$$

Hence the decision is made by the ML detector.

3 Simulation Results

In this paper, we have evaluated the performance of DCSK in MIMO systems under the additive white Gaussian noise (AWGN) channel. Simulations are done under several conditions as different values of spreading factor, comparison of the single input single output (SISO) and MIMO systems. The results of our simulations are presented in terms of BER versus the ratio E_b/N_o expressed in dB, where E_b is the energy per bit, and N_o is the single-sided spectral noise density.

3.1 Conventional DCSK Simulation

In this part DCSK modulation is performed under the AWGN channel for different values of spreading factor M (3) to show the significance of M in the single input single output (SISO) system.

Our simulation results in Fig.5 compare the system performance for different values of M under the AWGN channel. And it is observed that the larger the value of the spreading factor M, the better the system performance. As for example, from Fig.5 we can see a gain of about 3.5 dB at BER= 10^{-2} with the increase of M from 40 to 80.

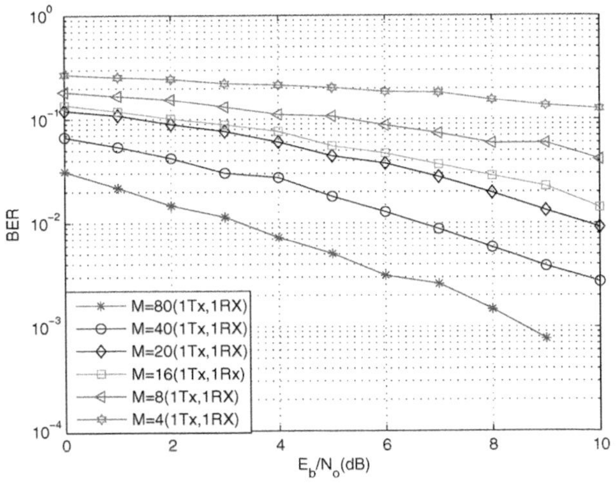

Fig. 5. BER performance of DCSK modulation for different values of M in SISO system under the AWGN channel

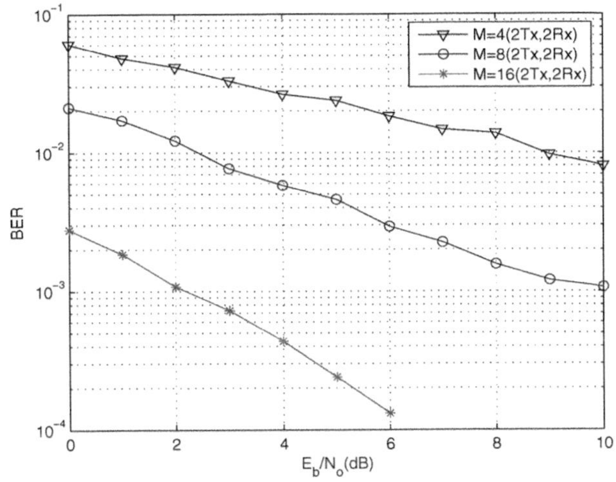

Fig. 6. BER performance of DCSK modulation for different values of M in a 2x2 MIMO system under the AWGN channel

3.2 DCSK in MIMO System

In this part we analysed the MIMO-DCSK performance. As mentioned earlier the MIMO system used in our simulations is Alamouti space time code. Fig.6 shows our simulation results for DCSK modulation in MIMO system with two transmitting antennas and two receiving antennas for different values of spreading factors. Comparing the results of Fig.5 and Fig.6, we can observe that for

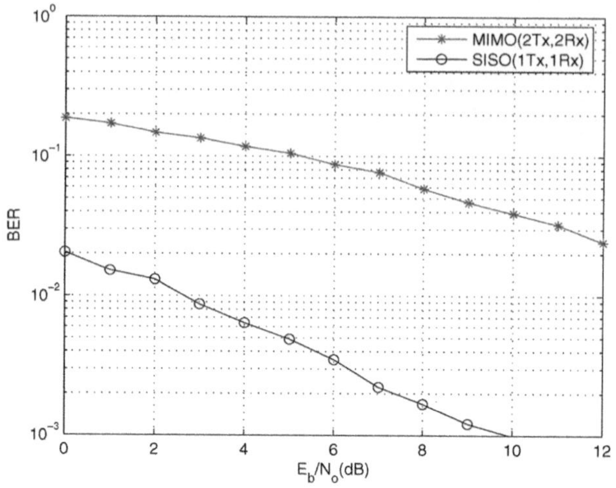

Fig. 7. Comparison of BER performance of SISO (1x1) and MIMO (2x2) with DCSK modulation for M=8

smaller values of spreading factor we can achieve a better performance in MIMO system than in the SISO system. From our simulation results in Fig.6, it is observed that the performance is much better giving the BER value of 10^{-3} at about $E_b/N_o = 2.25dB$ for the case of M=16. But in case of SISO, we get the BER value of 10^{-3} at about $E_b/N_o = 8.5dB$ even at M=80 as shown by our simulation results in Fig.5. From Fig.5, it can also be observed that the system performance is poor in SISO-DCSK for M=4, 8, 16 but for the same values of M, a better performance is obtained for the MIMO-DCSK as in Fig.6.So, we don't have to consider the complex cases with higher values of M as 40, 80 for the case of MIMO-DCSK. Our analysis illustrates that the MIMO-DCSK offers the improved system performance along with the reduced complexity in chaotic signal generation by the use of smaller values of spreading factor M thus proving to be a new improved chaotic communication system.
Our simulation results in Fig.7 is a comparison between SISO-DCSK and MIMO-DCSK under the AWGN channel for M=8 which shows a remarkably improved performance in MIMO system than in the general SISO system.

4 Conclusions

In this paper, we analysed the system performance of the conventional DCSK system under the AWGN. The analysis is done for different values of spreading factor M. Our results show that the larger the value of the spreading factor M, the better the system performance.

The major part of the paper is the analysis of a new scheme of combining DCSK with MIMO system. As for the MIMO system, we considered the Alamouti space time code for our simulation. Our simulation results show an improved performance with MIMO-DCSK as compared to SISO-DCSK. Also with a reasonable small value of spreading factor, we can obtain a much improved system performance hence reducing the complexity in chaotic signal generation.

The new MIMO-DCSK makes chaotic communications more effective and attractive along with the advantages of MIMO. For future analysis, MIMO-DCSK under multipath environment should be studied.

References

1. Ben Farah, M.A., Kachouri, A., Samet, M.; "Design of secure digital communication systems using DCSK chaotic modulation", Design and Test of Integrated Systems in Nanoscale Technology, 2006. Publication Date: Sept. 5-7, 2006, pp. 200 - 204.
2. Galias, Z., Maggio, G.M., "Quadrature chaos-shift keying: theory and performance analysis", IEEE Transactions on Circuits and Systems-I: Fundamental Theory and Applications, Vol. 48, NO. 12, Dec 2001, pp. 1510-1519.
3. Yungil Kim, Jaehwan Kim, Jae-Hyon Kim, Joonhyuk Kang, "Comparison of DCSK Receiver and Enhanced DCSK Receiver with Synchronization Error", VTC 2006-spring IEEE 63rd ,volume 5,2006, pp. 2261 - 2265.
4. Geza Kolumban, Tamas Krebesx, "UWB Radio: A Real Chance for Application of Chaotic Communications", NOLTA 2006, 11-14 September, 2006, pp. 475-478.
5. A.S. Dmitriev, A.I. Panas, K.V. Zakharchenko, "Basic Principles of Direct Chaotic Communications", Nonlinear Phenomena in Complex Systems. 2003. vol. 6. no. 1, pp. 1-14.
6. Kennedy, M.P., Kolumban, G.; Kis, G., Jako, Z., "Performance evaluation of FM-DCSK modulation in multipath environments", IEEE Transactions on Circuits and Systems-I: Fundamental Theory and Applications, Vol. 47, NO. 12, Dec 2000, pp. 1702 - 1711.
7. Mohinder Jankiraman, "Space-time codes and MIMO systems", Artech house, 2004.

A QoS Provisioning MAC Protocol for IEEE 802.11 WLANs

Hu Zhengbing[1,2] and Han Xiaomin[2]

[1] HuaZhong Normal University, Department of Information Technology
430073, Wuhan, China
kievpastor@yahoo.com
[2] Wuhan Institute of Technology, College of Computer Science,
430073, Wuhan, China
hanxmn@163.com

Abstract. In this paper we present extended age dependent backoff protocol (EADB), an extension of the age dependent backoff (ADB) proposed to alleviate the delay and jitter of real-time packets. The proposed retransmission scheme considers not only the persistence factors but also the contention window (CW) to reduce collision rate. The persistence factor (PF) is based on the ages of the real-time packets in the transmission queue and the lifetimes of real-time packets. Moreover, we also consider the collision rate that stations experience to adjust the CW. The proposed scheme is able to prevent the degradation the performance of the network caused by setting the CW as the minimum value after successful transmission. Simulation results indicate that the EADB provides the delay, jitter, and drop rate better than ADB.

1 Introduction

The wireless access network makes people enjoy the convenience of accessing the network and supports the mobility for people getting the information in the moving. Cellular network is the well-known wireless access network. However, the bandwidth of the cellular network is the bottleneck to provide multimedia services that need a great amount of bandwidth. In the early years, Cellular network provides only voice transmissions, and now it can provide simple multimedia data, such as images. The transmissions of multimedia data should be further worried about because of the scarce bandwidth. Nowadays, the wireless local area network (WLAN) have become popularity. In addition, the easy installation of the WLAN is an attractive reason to use it. The main reason is that WLAN technologies have become mature and can provide much larger bandwidth than cellular network.

With the growing popularity and acceptance of 802.11 WLANs, it is essential to focus on service differentiation support at the 802.11 medium access control layer. The current 802.11 MAC protocol does not support application with quality of service (QoS) requirements. The QoS support is critical to multimedia applications. Time-bounded services require some specified bandwidth, the delay, and the jitter guarantee. The distributed coordination function (DCF) is the basic medium access mechanism of 802.11 WLANs, which uses CSMA/CA (Carrier Sense Multiple

Y.-H. Lee et al. (Eds.): ICESS 2007, LNCS 4523, pp. 718–727, 2007.

Access With Collision Avoidance) protocol. In DCF, all stations competes the resources and channels with the same priority. The DCF does not have any mechanism to guarantee packet delay and jitter to stations for differentiation services.

The IEEE 802.11 task group E is currently working on the support of QoS in a new standard, called IEEE 802.11e. The 802.11e draft introduced enhanced distributed coordination function (EDCF) and hybrid coordination function (HCF), which are currently under discussion [1,2]. The EDCF is the contention-based channel access mechanism. The goal of this scheme is to enhance the DCF access mechanism of IEEE 802.11. The EDCF can provide a distributed access approach that can support the service differentiation.

Recently, several schemes [3,4,7] are proposed to enhance the IEEE 802.11 MAC protocol and to support service differentiation. These schemes proposed scaling the backoff contention window, assigning different interframe spaces (IFS), and assigning different frame sizes according to the traffic priorities. There are four major strategies for IEEE 802.11 DCF, including the CW strategy, the priority strategy, the real time strategy, and the handshaking mechanism. In this paper, the main factors considered are consisting of collision number, packet delay, packet drop rate, and packet jitter.

The EDCF mechanism improves the QoS of real-time traffic, but the performance obtained is not optimal since EDCF parameters (CWmin, PF) can not be adapted according to the network conditions. Thus, the proposed scheme in advance considers the collision rate and age of real-time packet to dynamic adjust EDCF parameters to achieve the better performance of throughput, the low delay, and the low collisions.

In this paper, we present two schemes: One scheme updates the CW after each successful transmission; the other scheme updates the persistence factor after each unsuccessful transmission.

2 Age Dependent Backoff Scheme

The age dependent backoff scheme improves the QoS performance of EDCF in IEEE 802.11e WLANs. It proposes the ADB for high priority real-time packet. The ADB dynamically adjusts PF according to the age of real-time packet and the lifetime of the real-time packet [5]. After a collision, the new CW is redefined as:

$$newCW[TC] = ((oldCW[TC]+1) * PF[TC]) - 1 \tag{1}$$

where

$$PF[TC] = 2(1 - \frac{AGE}{LT[TC]})$$

The newCW[TC] never exceeds the parameter CWmax[TC], but can be less than CWmin [TC]. Packet with queuing delay longer than the lifetime (Age > LT[TC]) will be discarded. It can be seen in formula (1) and (2) that in the first half of the packet lifetime, the new CW is expanded by a factor PF between 1 and 2. The first half increase the backoff time to avoid high collision probability. In the second half of the packet lifetime, PF is compressed by a factor between 0 to 1. The second half decrease the backoff time to raise transmission probability preventing packets from dropped due to Age > LT[TC].

3 The Proposed Scheme

The proposed scheme is based on the ADB scheme. The ADB always sends packet starting with the minimum CW after each successful transmission. However, the proposed scheme does not send the packet with the minimum CW, but adapts the Adaptive EDCF backoff algorithm to dynamic adjust its CW according to the network condition [6]. Thus the performance of the network will not be degraded. In the following, we describe the propose scheme in detail. There are two update strategies. One strategy is adapted after each successful transmission and the other is adapted after each collision. The scheme is introduced in Fig. 1.

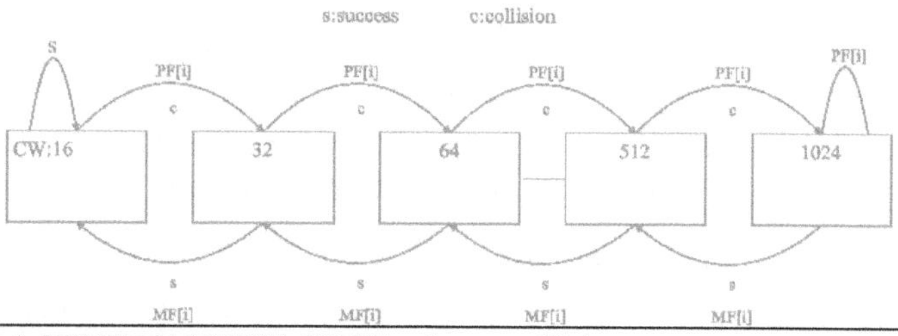

$CW[i]=\min[PF[i]*OldCW[i],CW[i]_{max}]$ on a collision
$CW[i]=\max[CW[i]_{min},MF[i]*OldCW[i]]$ on a success

$PF[i] = s(1-\frac{Age}{LT[i]})$,

Age is the real time packet's age in the transmission queue.
LT is the lifetime of the real packet.
PF is S/2 and S in the first half of the packet's lifetime,
PF is 0 and S/2 in the second half of the packet's lifetime.

$R(i,j) = \frac{Nc(i,j)}{Np(i,j)}$, $R(i,j)$ is the estimated collision rate.

$R(i,j)$ is always in the range [0,1].

$\mathrm{Re}(i,j) = (1-\alpha) * R(i,j) + \alpha * \mathrm{Re}(i,j-1)$, $\mathrm{Re}(i,j)$ is the average collision rate in step j, α is a smoothing factor.

$MF[i] = \min(((1+(i*2))\,\mathrm{Re}(i,j), 0.8)$.

$CW = \max[CW[i]]_{\min}, MF[i] * OldCW[i]]$ on success.

Fig. 1. The proposed backoff scheme

3.1 Update Strategy After Each Successful Transmission

A dynamic procedure is adopted to change the CW value after each successful transmission. This scheme will increase much more the total goodput of traffic than the basic EDCF. In the basic EDCF scheme, after the transmission is successfully complete, the CW[i] values are reset to CWmin[i]. The proposed scheme resets the CW[i] values more slowly to adaptive values.

Since the EDCF mechanism reset the CW of the corresponding class to its minimum CW, it does not take into account the network conditions. The proposed scheme defines a new estimated collision rate R(i,j) for each queue in each station, which is defined in formula (3).

$$R(i,j) = \frac{Nc(i,j)}{Np(i,j)} \tag{2}$$

where

Nc: Total number of collisions.
Np: The total number of packets that has been sent.
Nc(i, j): The number of collisions in the period j and in the queue i.
Np(i, j): The number of packets sent in the period j and in the queue i.
R(i,j): The collision rate in the period j and in the queue i.

Note the R(i,j) is always in the range of [0,1].

Next, the busty collisions are considered, in which Re(i,j-1) indicates the average collision rate at each update period j. Re(i,j) is the average collision rate in the period j and in the queue I, as defined in formula (4).

$$\mathrm{Re}(i,j) = (1-\alpha) * R(i,j) + \alpha * \mathrm{Re}(i,j-1) \tag{3}$$

where α is the weight and the smoothing factor. After the successful transmission, the proposed scheme takes the average collision rate Re(i,j) to estimate the next CW, $NewCW[i]$.

$$MF[i] = \min(((1+(i*2))\,\mathrm{Re}(i,j),0.8) \tag{4}$$

In order to keep the CW less than the previous CW, β should be less than 1.

$$CW = \max[CW[i]]_{\min}, MF[i] * OldCW[i]] \tag{5}$$

The NewCW[i] is always greater than or equal to CWmin[i], and the priority relationship is always maintained.

3.2 Update Strategy After Each Collision

In the 802.11 DCF protocol, after a collision the CW will be doubled in order to reduce collision probability. But the doubing process will cause a large delay and jitter. This is a big problem for time-sensitive application.

In the 802.11 EDCF protocol, after a collision the new size of CW is determined by expanding the size of the old CW by a factor of a PF. The PF is dynamically adjusted according to the age of a real-time packet in the transmission queue and the lifetime of the real-time packet. The relationship between the newCW[i], and the oldCW[i] after a collision is shown in formula (7).

$$newCW[i] = ((oldCW[i]+1) * PF[i]) - 1 \tag{6}$$

where *PF[i]* is given as:

$$PF[i] = s(1 - \frac{Age}{LT[i]}) \quad (7)$$

Age: The age of packet in the transmission queue.
LT[i]: The lifetime time of the packet.
Then, we choose the minimum CW parameter from the NewCW[i] and the maximum CW[i].

4 Simulation Results and Analyses

In this paper, to evaluate the performance of the proposed EADB scheme, we use the SMPL to simulate EADB on a wireless network.

4.1 Simulation Environment

The proposed simulation model has n wireless stations. All mobile stations compete to each other for accessing shared wireless medium. They are all active in an independent Basic Service Set (BSS) and there are no hidden stations are present in the independent BSS. Each wireless station transmits three kinds of different traffic, including voice, video, and data. The parameters of the traffic used in the simulation is provided in table 1.

Table 1. Parameters of the proposed simulation

Parameters	Value
Channel rate	11Mbps
SIFS	10us
Slot time	20us
DIFS	10us+2 *20us=50 us
AIFS[1] (voice)	10us+2 *20us=50 us
AIFS[2] (video)	10us+3 *20us=70us
AIFS[3] (data)	10us+4 *20us=90us
[CWmin,CWmax](DCF)	[31,1023]
[CWmin[1],CWmax[1]](voice)	[7,31]
[CWmin[2],CWmax[2]](video)	[15,63]
[CWmin[3],CWmax[3]](data)	[15,255]

4.2 Traffic Sources

It is assumed that the voice frame rate is 12 frames/sec, and the voice frame length is exponentially distributed with mean 500 bytes. The video frame rate is 16 frames/sec, and the video frame length is exponentially distributed with mean 800 bytes. The best-effort traffic frame rate is 28 frames/sec, and the video frame length is exponentially distributed with mean 1024 bytes.

4.3 Performance Evaluation

The packet delay, jitter and loss for voice traffic are main performance parameters. We conceived our network as an independent BSS with n voice stations, n video stations, and n FTP client and server stations. We define the jitter as the variance of the delay and the drop rate as the percentage of packet with delay longer than their lifetime. For voice and video packet, the maximum acceptable value are assumed to be

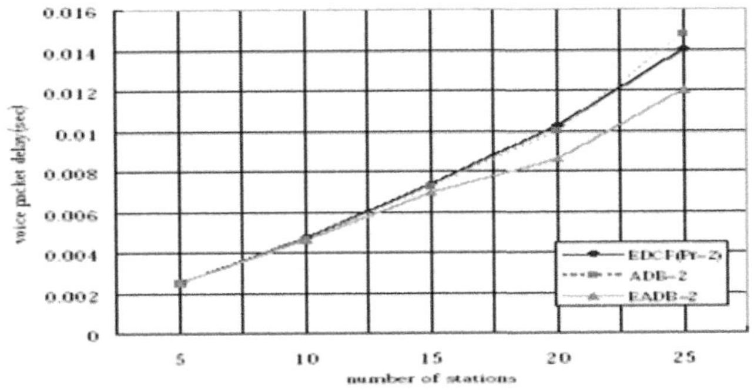

Fig. 2. Illustrates the packet delay versus number of station for voice traffic. Evidently, the packet delay increases with the number of station, which is due to more traffic volume will be attended to contend the limited bandwidth. The results show that the proposed scheme is much better than other two schemes, especially when the number of station become large. This is because the proposed scheme takes into account the ages of voice packet as well as the collision rate. Thus, it could more precisely estimate the suitable backoff time.

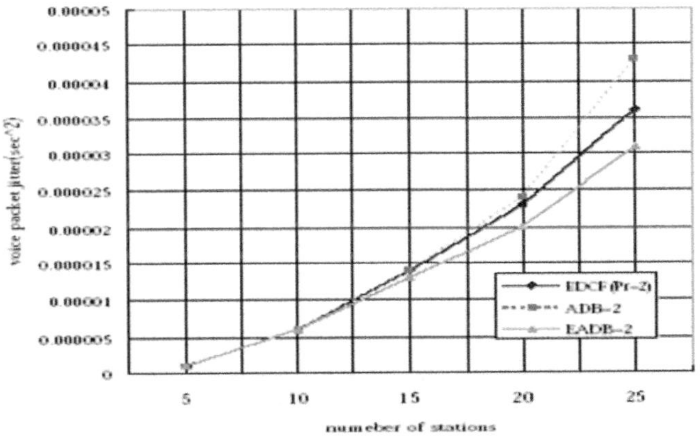

Fig. 3. Illustrates the packet jitter versus number of stations for voice traffic. The packet jitter increases with the number of stations due to that more traffic volume will be attended to content the limited bandwidth. The results show that the proposed scheme is much better than other two schemes, especially when the number of station is from 15 to 25. The variation of jitter of the proposed scheme is lower than other two schemes. When the traffic load is heavy, the proposed scheme takes into account the collision rate. Thus, it could degrade the variation of the jitter.

25ms and 75ms. Namely, LT(Life Time) for voice and video are 25ms and 75ms. Voice packet delay, jitter, drop, and throughput are shown in Fig. 2, 3, 4, and 5 respectively. The EADB not only adjust the value of the PF based on the ages of voice packet but also consider the collision rate that stations experience to transmission new packet, rather than always adapt the minimum contention for the new packet. Therefore, the voice packet delay, the jitter, the drop rate, and the throughput are improved. Fig. 6, 7, 8, 9 and 10 show that the EADB provides the significant improvement in video delay, jitter, drop, and throughput.

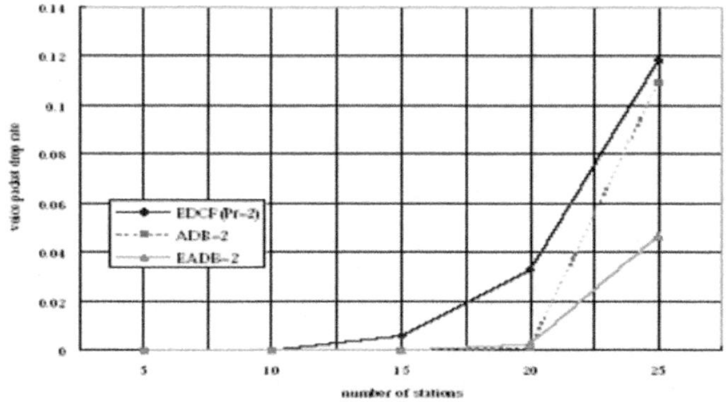

Fig. 4. Shows the packet drop rate versus number of stations for voice traffic. The voice packet lifetime is 25ms. The packet drop rate increases with the number of stations, in which more stations brings more traffic volume. The results show that the proposed scheme is much better than other two schemes, especially when the number of station become larger. This is because the proposed scheme takes into account the ages of voice packet as well as the collision rate. Thus, it is able to decrease the delay of voice packets. As a result, the dropping rate of voice packet will be reduced.

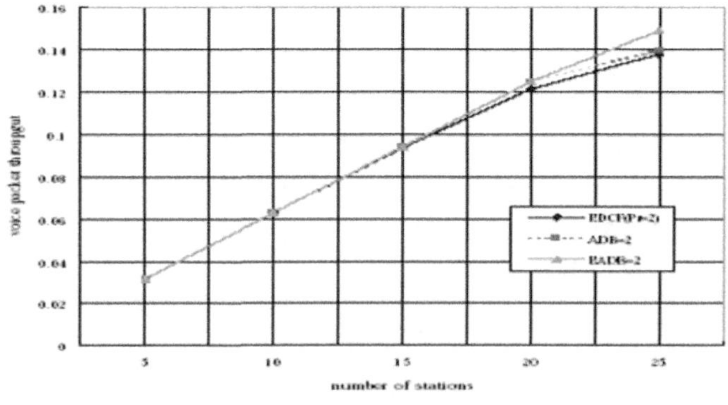

Fig. 5. Demonstrates packet throughput versus number of stations for voice traffic. Evidently, the voice packet throughput increases with the number of stations. This is due to that the priority of voice packet is the highest and so they will be transmitted at the largest opportunity. The results show that the proposed scheme is much better than other two schemes, especially when the number of station become larger. This is because the proposed scheme decreases the delay time and dropping rate of voice packet. Thus, it is capable of enhancing the throughput of voice packet.

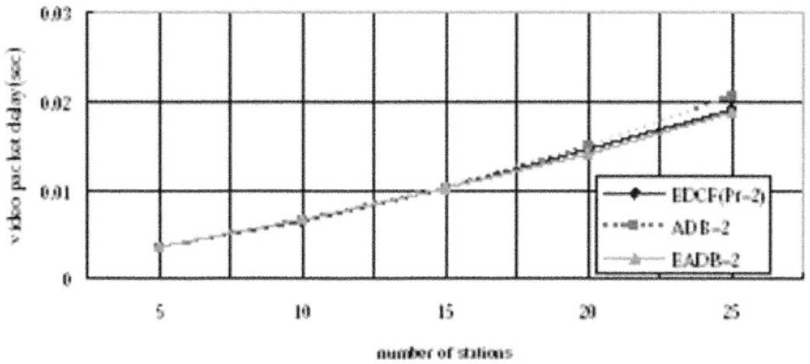

Fig. 6. Illustrates the packet delay versus number of station for video traffic. Evidently, the packet delay increases with the number of station, which is due to that more traffic volume will be attended to contend the limited bandwidth. But the difference among these three schemes is not distinguishable. That is because the proposed scheme is much better than other scheme for voice traffic. For the video packets, the performance is similar to other schemes.

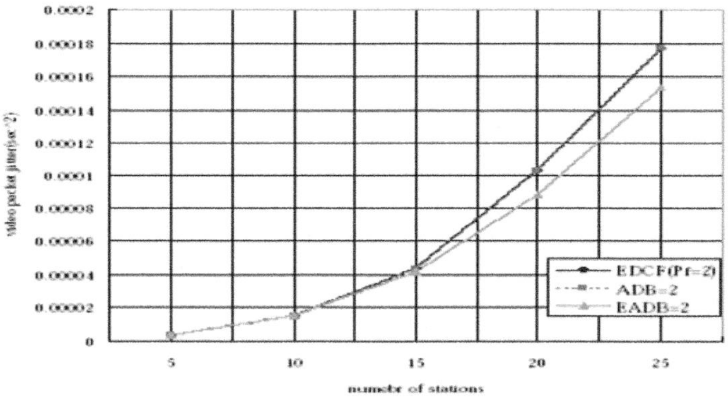

Fig. 7. Illustrates the packet jitter versus number of stations for video traffic. When the number of station gets larger, the packet jitter will also increase since the total traffic volume contenting the shared medium increases. The simulation results show that the proposed scheme is much better than other two schemes, especially when the number of station is between 15 and 25. The variation of jitter of the proposed scheme is lower than other two schemes. This is due to the fact that the proposed scheme takes into account the collision rate when the traffic load becomes heavy. Therefore, it could apparently degrade the variation of the jitter.

We simulate two different scheme EDCF, and ADB to compare with the proposed scheme EADB, in which EDCF indicates the scheme with PF equal to 2, ADB 2 indicates the age dependent backoff scheme with adaptive PF between 0 and 2, and EADB indicates the proposed scheme that is the modified dependent backoff scheme. Delay is the duration from queue to successful transmission. Jitter is the variation of the Delay according to the statistics, as shown in formula (9). Drop rate is the

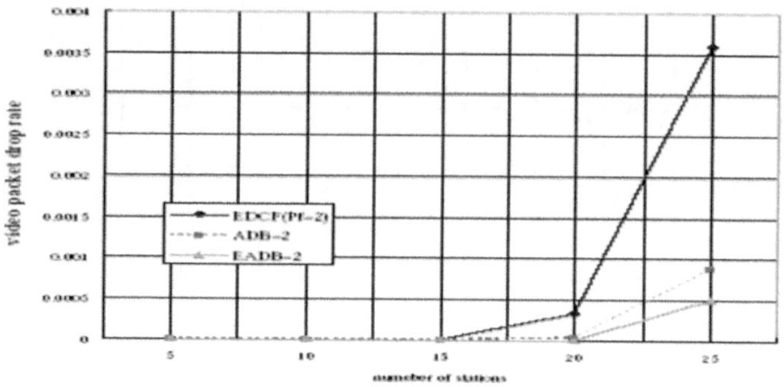

Fig. 8. Illustrates the packet drop rate versus the number of stations for video traffic. The video packet lifetime is assumed to be 75ms. Evidently, the packet drop rate increases with the number of stations due to the increment of traffic volume. The simulation results show that the proposed scheme is much better than other two schemes, especially when the number of station become large. This is because the proposed scheme takes into account the ages of video packet as well as the collision rate. Therefore, it could decrease video packets delay much more and also reduce the dropping rate of video packet.

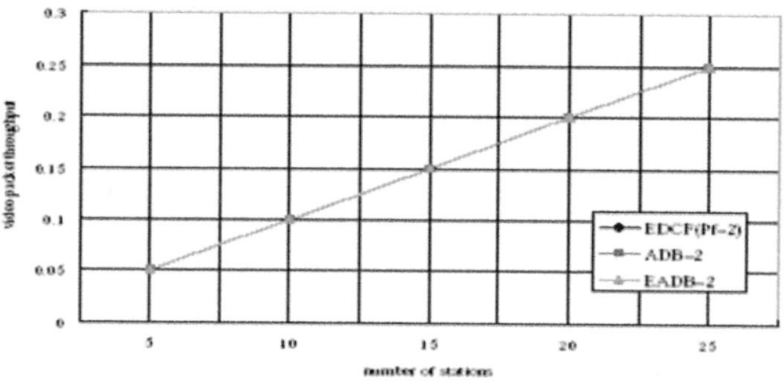

Fig. 9. Illustrates the throughput versus number of stations for video traffic. Evidently, the video packet throughput increases with the number of stations. The simulation results show that the differentiation between these three schemes seem little. This is due to that our proposed scheme gives higher priority on voice traffic rather than video traffic. Therefores, the throughput of video packet cannot be improved significantly.

percentage of packets with delay longer than their lifetime. Throughput is number of packets successful transmission in total simulation time.

$$Jitter = \frac{\sum_{k=1}^{N} (x_k - u)^2}{N} \tag{8}$$

Xk: The packet delay.
u: The average packet delay.
N: Total number of the packets.

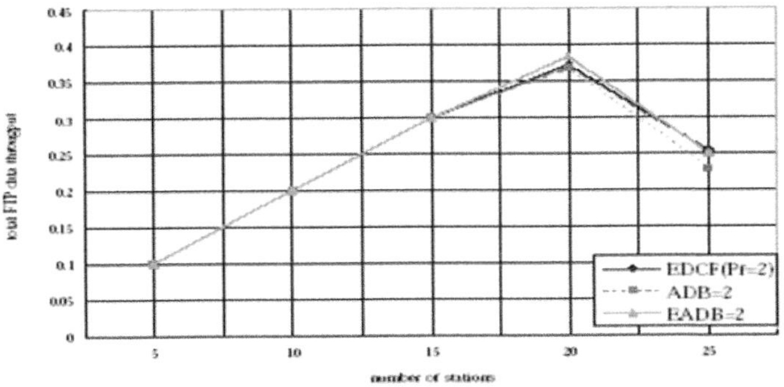

Fig. 10. Illustrates the packet throughput versus number of stations for data traffic.The data packet throughput increases with the number of stations at the beginning.When the number of stations higher than 20, the throughput will go down evidently due to the congestion and collision. Although the data packet priority is the lowest, the proposed scheme does not cause the data packet starvations. The simulation results show that the proposed scheme offers the higher priority to voice and video packet, but at the same time the data traffic do not suffer starvation.

5 Conclusions

The ADB scheme does not work well when the traffic load is heavy. That is because when a packet is successfully transmitted, the CW is reset to the minimum value. Thus, it leads to more collisions, more packet delay, and less throughput for real-time packets. Moreover, the EDCF scheme generate the unnecessary delay when the traffic load is light. That is because the longer backoff time is produced from the CW size which is doubled after each unsuccessfully packet transmission. In this paper, the proposed EADB scheme control the CW based on the ages in the transmission queue, as well as the collision rate. The simulation results indicate that EADB has apparent improvements in delay, jitter, drop rate, and throughput of real-time packets. Furthermore, there is no starvation for the best effort traffic.

References

1. IEEE 802.11e/D4.0,"Draft Supplement to Part 11: Wireless Medium Access Control (MAC) and Physical layer (PHY) specifications: Medium Access Control(MAC) Enhancements for Quality of Service (QoS)", November 2002.
2. S. Mangold, S. Choi, P. May, O. Klein, G. Hiertz, L. Stibor," IEEE 802.11e Wireless LAN for Quality of Service", In Proc. European Wireless '02,Florence,Italy,February 2002.
3. Aad and C. Castelluccia, "Differentiation mechanisms for IEEE 802.11 ", IEEE Procs. INFOCOM 2001. Volume:1, 2001 Page(s): 209 -218
4. IEEE P802.11 TASK GROUP E, http://www.ieee802.org/11/
5. Wong, G.W, Donaldson, R.W.," Improving the QoS performance of EDCF in IEEE 802.11e wireless LANs", IEEE 2003
6. Romdhani, L., Qiang Ni, Turletti, T.," Adaptive edcf: enhanced service differentiation for IEEE 802.11 wireless ad-hoc networks", IEEE 2003
7. Su Jun, Hu Zhengbing, "A Bandwidth Degradation QoS Scheme for 4G Mobile Networks", Proceedings of IEEE ICI' 2006, Tashkent, Uzbekistan, 19-21 September, 2006. IEEE.

A Leader Election Algorithm Within Candidates on Ad Hoc Mobile Networks*

SungSoo Lee, Rahman M. Muhammad, and ChongGun Kim**

Department of Computer Engineering, Yeungnam University, Korea
lssung@chol.com, rahman_742@hotmail.com, cgkim@yu.ac.kr

Abstract. Leader election is an extensively studied problem in Ad hoc networks. In our study, an extended idea of leader election algorithms for energy saving on arbitrary changing topological environment is derived. Our focus is to reduce the number of leader election processes, to make it more energy efficient. The proposed algorithm shows that each node maintains a list of candidates to minimize the total number of leader elections. Simulation results show that the leader election algorithm using candidates has less leader elections process and generates less message than those of the existing leader election algorithms.

1 Introduction

A mobile Ad hoc network (MANET) is a collection of mobile nodes that can communicate via message passing over wireless links. The nodes communicate via other nodes if they are not within a specified transmission range.

Leader election is a fundamental control problem in both wired and wireless systems (e.g. MANET, Sensor networks) [1]. For example, in group-communication protocols, a leader election is necessary when a group leader crashes or departs from the system [1]. Leader election has a large number of applications such as key distribution [4], routing coordination [5], sensor coordination [6] and general control [3, 7]. It can serve for creating particular tree communication structures [2] and other standard problems in distributed systems.

The algorithm of the leader election problem [8] elects a unique leader from a fixed set of nodes. To accommodate frequent topology changes, leader election in MANET have to be adaptive. The elected leader should be the *most-valued-node* among all the nodes of the network. The value for the leader node selection is a performance-related characteristic such as remaining battery life, minimum average distance from other nodes or computation capabilities [1].

Many solutions are proposed for leader election, but most of them are not fit perfectly to dynamic nature of mobile networks. Leader election algorithm provided in [7], maintains a directed acyclic graph with a single sink, which is the leader.

* This research was supported by the Yeungnam University EmTEC and SAMSUNG research grants in 2006.

** Corresponding Author.

Y.-H. Lee et al. (Eds.): ICESS 2007, LNCS 4523, pp. 728–738, 2007.

However this algorithm [7] is proved correct for a completely synchronous system with a single link change. The algorithms proposed in [9, 10] work only if the topology remains static and hence cannot be used in mobile networks. Self-stabilizing spanning tree algorithms [12, 13] assume a shared-memory model and are not suitable for an Ad hoc mobile network. Besides, several clustering and hierarchy-construction schemes [11, 14] may be adopted to perform leader election, but they cannot be used in an asynchronous mobile system. Leader election algorithm presented in [1], manage the election process very efficiently. But the method requires a large number of leader elections, which is not very supportive to energy conservation. To solve this problem, we implements an algorithm which is based on Leader election algorithm presented in [1], but every node keeps a leader list instead of a single leader. This algorithm is mainly emphasized for lower power consumption.

2 Existing Algorithms for Leader Election

We describe an existing leader election algorithm [1] that is based on diffusing computations by Dijkstra and Scholten [15]. First we describe the algorithm for static networks and then for mobile environments.

2.1 Leader Election in a Static Network

This algorithm acts under the assumption that nodes and links never fails. It uses three types of messages, viz. Election, Ack and Leader. The algorithm works as follows:

Election: If a leader node doesn't exist in the network, an initiator node transmits *Election* message to immediate neighbor nodes. The neighbor nodes propagate the messages to their neighbors (except the parent).This process is continued until all leaf nodes get the *Election* messages. This phase is referred as the growing phase of the spanning tree.

Ack: When any node receives an *Election* message from a neighbor (not parent), it immediately responds with an *Ack* message. Instead of sending *Ack* message to its parent, a node waits until it receives *Acks* from all its children. On receipt of the *Election* message, every leaf node sends an *Ack* message along with its own ID, to its parent. The parent node compares its own ID with these incoming IDs from all its children. Then it selects the highest one and sends it through the *Ack* message to its parent. This process is continued until the initiator node gets all *Acks* from all children. This phase is referred as the shrinking phase of the spanning tree.

Leader: When the initiator node gets *Ack* messages from all its children, it selects the highest ID as the leader node. It then broadcasts this ID in the *Leader* message to all nodes of the network.

Figure 1 shows an example of leader election. In figure 1(a), node 3 is the initiator that sends *Election* (E) message to its neighbor. In figure 1(b), nodes 2 and 5 set their pointers to point to parent node 3. They get *Election* messages from each other and immediately acknowledged. In figure 1(c), a complete spanning tree is created. In figure 1(d), nodes 7 and 9 send their *Ack* messages (A) to their parents with their own IDs. In figure 1(e), nodes 2 and 5 compare their own IDs with the incoming ones and send the higher IDs in *Acks* to node 3. In figure 1(f), node 3 selects 9 as the leader ID and broadcasts it via the *Leader* message (L).

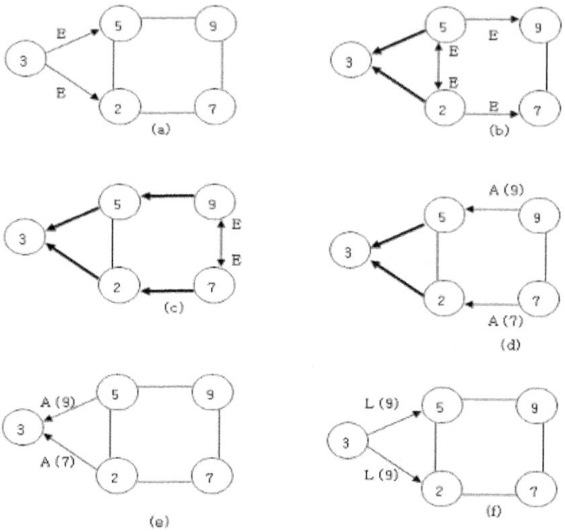

Fig. 1. An execution of leader election algorithm based on Dijkstra-Scholten termination detection algorithm

2.2 Leader Election in Mobile Environment

In this section we briefly describe the leader election algorithm proposed in [1] for mobile Ad hoc networks.

The leader node of a connected network periodically (after each 20 seconds) sends heartbeat messages to other nodes. The absence of heartbeat messages from its leader for a predefined timeout period (3 times) triggers a fresh leader election process at a node. Then the election proceeds as mentioned in the previous section. But when node mobility, node crashes, link failures, network partitions and merging of partitions are introduced during the leader election process. To solve this problem, two extra messages, *Probe* and *Reply* are used.

In the dynamic environment, the algorithm [1] applies the following techniques in the leader election process.

Handling Multiple, Concurrent Computations: More than one node may concurrently detect leader departure. These nodes initiate separate leader election independently that leads to concurrent leader elections. To handle this situation, the algorithm [1] requires each node participates in only one diffusing computation at a time. To achieve each diffusing computation is identified by a *computation-index*.

This *computation-index* is a pair, viz. $\langle num, ID\rangle$, where *ID* represents the identifier of the node that initiates this computation and num is an integer as described below.

$$\langle num_1, ID_1\rangle > \langle num_2, ID_2\rangle \Leftrightarrow ((\, num_1 > num_2) \vee ((num_1 = num_2) \wedge (ID_1 > ID_2)))$$

A leader election with higher *computation-index* has higher priority than another leader election. When a node participates in a leader election, the node hears another leader election with a higher *computation-index*. Eventually a node with highest *computation-index* initiates the leader election process.

Handling Network Partition: Once a node joins in a leader election, it must receive *Ack* messages from all of its children, before it send the *Ack* message to its parent. However, during the shrinking phase of the spanning tree, some nodes may go out of the network. To detect such events, each node sends periodic *Probe* messages to the neighbors of the spanning tree. A node which receives the *Probe* message, responds with a *Reply* message. If a node fails to get *Reply* message from a node for a certain timeout period, removes that node from its neighbor list of the spanning tree. A node must detect this event; otherwise it never reports an *Ack* to its parent.

Handling Networks Merge: Node mobility can merge network partitions, when at least two nodes from different partitions, come in the communication range of each other. Both nodes exchange each other's leader information. The node having lower leader ID accepts the other leader as the new leader of its partition and propagates the message to other nodes of the partition.

Node Crashes and Restarts: If a node failure creates network partitions, appropriate actions are taken as described earlier. When a node recovers from a crash, a node without leader starts a new election to find its leader.

3 Leader Election Within Candidates

The proposed algorithm is based on the leader election algorithm [1]. In this algorithm, we propose a list of leaders instead of just one leader to be maintained in every node. Each node contains a leader list of five nodes (in descending order), where the first node is considered as the active leader of the network. If the first one is absent for a specified period, the second becomes the active leader and so on.

We follow the assumptions and constraints that are mentioned in [1]. We assume MANET is an undirected graph. Here vertices represent the mobile node and an edge represents the communication link between any two nodes within communication range. Thin arrows represent the direction of flow of messages and thick arrows indicate pointer of child node to parent. We apply the following constraints:

- ✓ All nodes have unique identifiers
- ✓ We consider the node's ID (identifier) as the key value for leader election (for simplicity to describe and simulate), i.e. the node having the highest ID in a network is considered as the *most-valued-node* (leader).
- ✓ Links are bidirectional and FIFO (First in First out).

- ✓ Node mobility can change topology arbitrarily, including network portioning/merging. Furthermore, node can crash and come back to its original network at any time.
- ✓ Each node has a large buffer to avoid buffer overflow at any point in its lifetime.

3.1 Leader Election Algorithm Within Candidates

We implement candidates based leader election. Every node maintains leader list (L) and set the size of L to 5. Empty ID is denoted by -1 in L.

Check the existence of the leader in the network during several heart-beats interval.

1. If Leader doesn't exist in the network after the specified period (Six heart-beat interval)
   A. Select an initiator node
   B. Initiator node sends the election message to all of its children. This process is continued until these messages reach to all leaf nodes.
   C. For the leaf nodes, l, in the network
      i. Add l to its own leader list, L.
      ii. Send L to its parent within Ack message.
      iii. Parent node sorts (in descending order) its ID with the contents of L. The node propagates L to its parent. Repeat this process until the initiator node gets all the leader lists from each branch.
      iv. In this shrinkage phase of the spanning tree, each node sends periodic Probe message and waits for Reply message from the neighbors, to maintain the connectivity among the nodes.
   D. Initiator node selects the highest-valued-L from the collected Leader lists, and broadcast it to the network, by Leader message.

2. If at least one leader exists in kth (position in L) level of the leader list
   A. Send Require message to the corresponding candidate leader node and receive Ack message.
   B. Update leader list by setting the active kth level of L to the proper position by shifting the invalid leaders of L for future rejoin operation.
   C. Broadcast this to the network.

3. If several active leaders of different networks exist in the same network
   A. Multiple leader lists are combined and new five candidate nodes are selected by selecting the active leaders (in descending order) in the front positions of the list. The first position node of the list becomes the active leader node.

3.2 Leader Election in Mobile Environment

We now describe how this algorithm accommodates arbitrary changes in topology induced by node mobility. Our algorithm shares the idea of multiple concurrent computation, network partioning and merging, node crashes and restarts during the leader election process [1].

Leader Election Process: Figure 2(a) to 2(c) show the growing phases of the spanning tree. Every node maintains a Leader list. In our example we use the size of the *Leader* list to 5. Figure 2(d) shows that the leaf nodes 7 and 9 add their IDs in the list and send these to their parents in the *Ack* messages. Figure 2(e) shows that the initiator receives two lists from its two branches and they are A (7, 2, -1, -1,-1) and A (9, 5, -1, -1,-1). From these two lists the initiator node selects the Leader list L (9, 7, 5, 3, 2) and broadcasts to all nodes of the network. Like the previous algorithm [1], here all nodes send periodic *Probe* messages and wait for the *Reply* from the neighbors of the spanning tree, to maintain the connectivity.

Unlike the algorithm [1], this algorithm manages network partitions and merges.

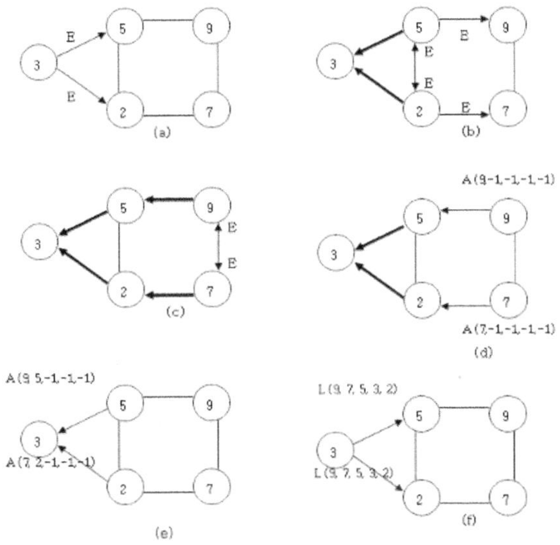

Fig. 2. The leader election process within candidates

Handling Network Partitions: In figure 3, the advantage of having multiple candidates are shown. In figure 3(a), all nodes of the network maintain the same Leader list, where the active leader is 50. But as node 3 disappears, two networks are created. In figure 3(b), on the right network, nodes 50, 20, 17 exist. This network does not modify the Leader list. But on the left network, the first three candidate IDs are absent in the leader list. So after the time out of three levels of leader nodes checking, node 10 becomes initiator and sends the heartbeat message to all nodes of the network. To reduce the waiting time, all nodes update their Leader lists by shifting the invalid IDs to the end of the Leader lists. But we shouldn't delete these nodes from the Leader lists for a while, for future rejoin.

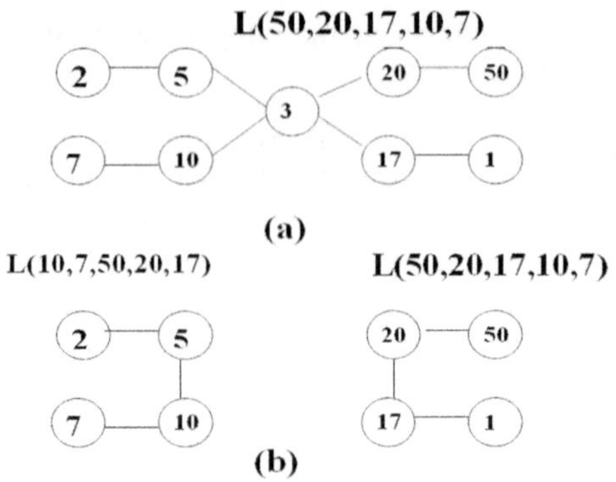

Fig. 3. Handling network partitions by the Leader Election algorithm using candidates

Handling networks Merge: Network merging can be managed efficiently by this method. In figure 4(a), there are three networks and they maintain the Leader lists L (10, 7, 5, 2, and 1), L (25, -1, -1, -1, -1) and L (50, 20, 17, 1, -1). According to our algorithm every node in the merged network has finally L (50, 25, 10, 20, 17), where nodes 50, 25 and 10 were the active leaders. After the merging operation in figure 4(b) node 50 becomes the active leader.

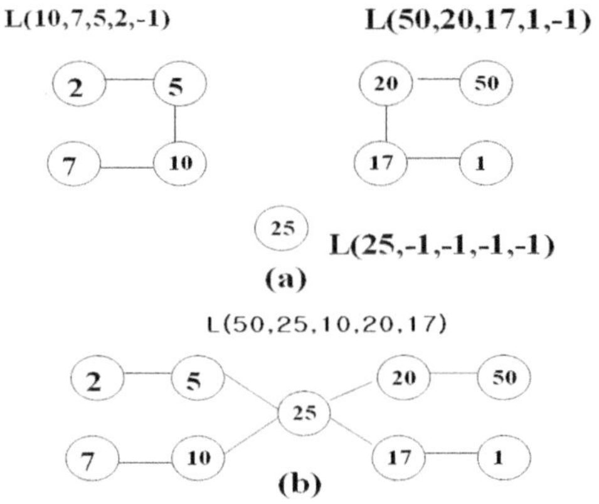

Fig. 4. Handling networks merge by the Leader election algorithm using candidates

4 Simulation Results

We compare the performance between the existing [1] and the proposed leader election algorithm through simulations. Both leader election algorithms are implemented in C++. Here MANET size is 2000*2000 square meters. In the simulation, nodes can move from 1 m/sec (Vmin) to maximum 19 m/sec (Vmax). To see the effect of transmission range over the algorithms, we use transmission ranges of 200, 250 and 300 meters. We set message traversal time between the two nodes to 0.03 second as default value. We allow the number of nodes (N) up to 200 in the simulation area. Due to the node mobility, several nodes can go out of the simulation area and can enter into the simulation area at any time. As the requirement of the existing algorithm, each simulation is run for duration of 200 minutes. Finally the simulation results are taken from the averaged values of 20 simulations run times.

Impact of Node Density: The graphs in figure 5 show the Election Rate for three different values of Vmax viz. 3m/s, 9m/s and 19m/s. The election rate means 숙 number of leader election process. In these graphs, we see the Election Rate of node first increases with node density (N), and then start decreasing with any further increase in N. This is because when N = 20, most of nodes are expected to be isolated. But as N increases, there are few networks with few nodes. Node mobility causes frequent leader departures and hence Election Rate increases. But after a certain threshold, the node density becomes very high and most of the nodes belong to large networks. As networks remain connected for long duration, Election Rate drops.

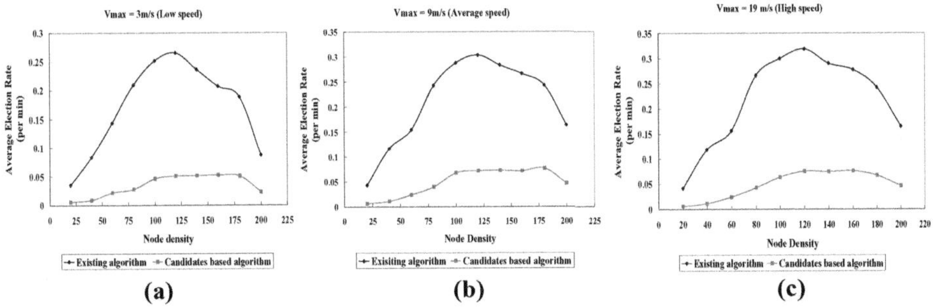

Fig. 5. Average Election Rate Vs Vmax. Here Vmin = 1 m/sec and transmission range of each node is 300 meter.

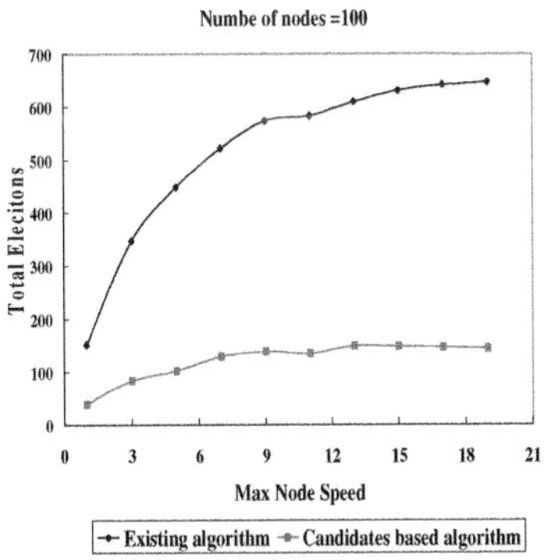

Fig. 6. Total Elections Vs moderate node density (100). Here Vmin = 1 m/sec and transmission range of each node is 300 meter.

Impact of Node Speed: Figure 6 shows the total number of Elections for moderate node density (here it is 100). In this graph, we see the Leader election increases with the increase of node speed. This is because in the low speed most of the nodes exists in the large networks, and remain there for long. So leader election is also lower in node's low speed. But as node speed increases, there are many networks with few nodes. Node mobility causes frequent leader departures and hence Election Rate increases.

Impact of Transmission Range: We study the impact of Transmission range (Tx) on Election Rate for three different choices of Tx, viz. 200m, 250m and 300m. From the graphs of figure 7, we see increased transmission range of nodes leads to a higher Election Rate when N is small (i.e. N = 20). This is because, for large value of Tx, there are fewer isolated nodes, but each network has few nodes. But for large values of N, the Election Rate becomes smaller with increase in Tx. The reason is the network sizes are larger for large values of Tx and partition occurs less frequently. For all values of Tx, Election Rate by the candidate based method is much smaller than that of the existing method.

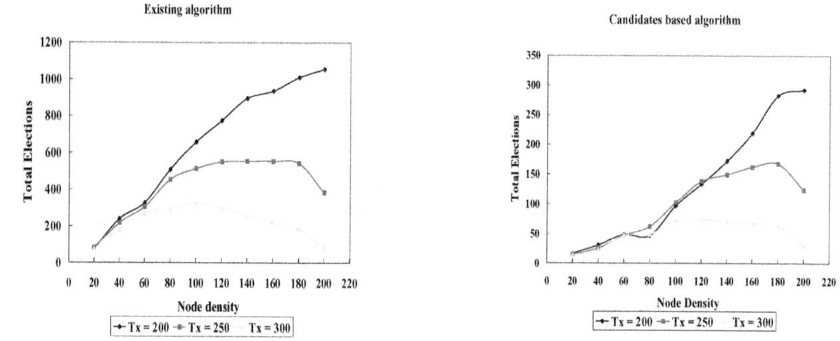

(a) (b)

Fig. 7. Average Election Rate Vs Tx. Here Vmin = 1 m/sec and Vmax = 3m/s.

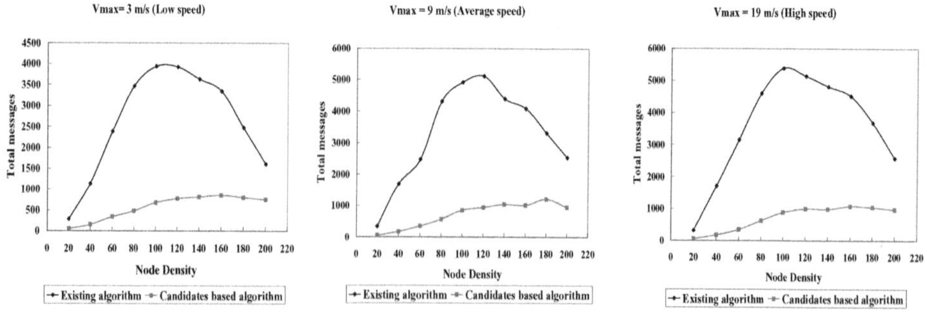

(a) (b) (c)

Fig. 8. Total generated messages Vs Vmax. Here Vmin = 1 m/sec and Tx = 300 meter.

Impact on Message Generation: The graphs of figure 8 show the total number of messages that are generated for leader election. In every graph, we see the leader election algorithm using candidates has significant performance advantages over that of the existing algorithm. This leads to an assumption that the candidates based algorithm has energy saving feature than that of the existing algorithm.

5 Conclusions and Future Work

Energy saving is an important research area for Ad hoc mobile and Sensor networks. To achieve this purpose, we derive an efficient leader election algorithm, which successfully guarantees that every node must have leader in every situation and save energy in Ad hoc mobile networks. Our focus for saving energy is to reduce the number of leader election processes. Because leader election needs three phases of transmissions and receptions of messages that use a lot of energy. Our simulation results show that the candidate-based algorithm has significant energy saving feature than that of the other. Another good fact is that proposed candidate based algorithm is particularly simple and straightforward. Our future plan is to implement the practical protocols.

References

1. Vasudevan, S., Kurose, J, Towsley, D. Design and Analysis of a Leader Election Algorithm for Mobile Ad Hoc Networks. Proceedings of the 12th IEEE International Conference on Network Protocols (ICNP) (2004) 350-360
2. Y. Afek and A. Bremler. Self-stabilizing unidirectional network algorithms by power supply. Chicago Journal of Theoretical Computer Science, December 1998.
3. Bayazit, J. Lien, and N. Amato. Better group behaviors in complex environments using global roadmaps. 8th International Conference on the Simulation and Synthesis of living systems (Alife '02), Sydney, NSW, Australia, pp. 362-370, December 2002.
4. DeCleene et al. Secure group communication for Wireless Networks. In proceedings of MILCOM 2001, VA, October 2001
5. Perkins and E. Royer. Ad-hoc On-Demand Distance Vector Routing. In proceedings of the 2nd IEEE Workshop on Mobile Computing Systems and Applications, New Orleans, LA, February 1999,pp. 90-100
6. W. Heinzelman, A. Chandrakasan and H. Balakrishnan. Energy-Efficient Communication Protocol for Wireless Micro sensor networks. In proceedings of Hawaiian International Conference on Systems Science, January 2000.
7. N. Malpani, J. Welch and N. Vaidya. Leader election Algorithms for Mobile Ad Hoc Networks. In fourth International Workshop on Discrete Algorithms and Methods for Mobile Computing and Communications, Boston, MA, August 2000.
8. N. Lynch. Distributed Algorithms. 1996, Morgan Kaufmann Publishers, Inc.
9. R. Gallager, P. Humblet and P. Humblet and P. Spira. A Distributed Algorithm for Minimum Weight Spanning Trees. In ACM Transactions on Programming Languages and Systems, vol.4, no.1, pages 66-77, January 1983.
10. Peleg. Time Optimal Leader Election in General Networks . In journal of Parallel and Distributed Computing, vol.8, no.1, pages 96-99, January 1990.

11. Coore, R. Nagpal and R. Weiss. Paradigms for Structure in an Amorphous Computer. Technical report 1614, Massachussetts Institute of Technology Artificial Intelligence Laboratory, October 1997.
12. Y. Afek, S. Kutten and M.Yung. Local Detection for Global Self Stabilization. In Theoretical Computer Science, Vol 186, No. 1-2, 339 pp. 199-230, October 1997.
13. S. Dolev, A. Israeli and S. Moran. Uniform dynamic self-stabilizing leader election part 1: Complete graph protocols. Preliminary version appeared in proceedings of 6th International Workshop on Distributed Algorithms (S. Toueg et.al., eds.), LNCS 579, 167-180,1992),1993.
14. C. Lin and M. Gerla. Adaptive Clustering for Mobile Wireless Networks. In IEEE journal on selected areas in communications,15(7): 1265-75, Sep 1997.
15. E.W. Dijkstra and C.S. Scholten. Termination detection for diffusing computations. In Information Processing Letters, vol. 11, no. 1, pp. 1-4, August 1980.

An Improvement of TCP Downstream Between Heterogeneous Terminals in an Infrastructure Network

Yong-Hyun Kim, Ji-Hong Kim, Youn-Sik Hong, and Ki-Young Lee

University of Incheon,
177 Dowha-dong Nam-gu,
402-749, Incheon, Korea
{riot999,yh-kim,yshong,kylee}@incheon.ac.kr

Abstract. We measured a performance of data transmission between a desktop PC and a PDA in an infrastructure network based on IEEE 802.11x wireless LAN. Assuming that a PDA is mainly used for downloading data from its stationary server, i.e., a desktop PC, a PC and a PDA acts as a fast sender and a slow receiver, respectively, due to substantial differences in their computational capabilities. With data transmission between these heterogeneous terminals a transmission time during downstream is slower than that during upstream by 20% at maximum. To mitigate this, we present two distinct approaches. First, by increasing the size of a receive buffer for a PDA the congestion window size of TCP becomes more stable. Thus, an approximate 32% increase in throughput can be obtained by increasing its size from 512 bytes to 32768 bytes. Second, a pre-determined delay between packets to be transmitted at the sender should be given. By assigning the inter-packet delay of 5 ms during downstream achieves a best performance which improves by 7% compared to that without such a delay. Besides, such a delay reduces the number of erroneous packets remarkably.

Keywords: PDA, TCP downstream, wireless LAN, congestion window, inter-packet delay.

1 Introduction

The transmission of multimedia over wireless networks using mobile devices is becoming a research topic of growing interest. With the emergence of small wireless handheld devices such as PDAs (Personal Digital Assistants), it is expected that interactive multimedia will be a major source of traffic to these handheld devices [5], [6].

Different types of terminals such as desktop PCs as fixed hosts (FHs) and PDAs as mobile hosts (MHs) can be connected to an infrastructure network. Assuming that a PDA is currently used for downloading data from its stationary server such as a desktop PC, a desktop PC and a PDA acts as a fast sender and a slow receiver, respectively, due to substantial differences in their computational capabilities.

Y.-H. Lee et al. (Eds.): ICESS 2007, LNCS 4523, pp. 739–746, 2007.

Actually, a PDA has a lower performance, less memories and poor user interfaces compared to a desktop PC. Most of the works deal with measurements and analysis of their performance with emphasis on laptop PCs [2], [3]. In that case, a desktop PC and a laptop PC are considered as a fast sender and a fast receiver, respectively, or vice versa.

This work provides a performance characterization of three types of transmissions: upstream, downstream and wireless-to-wireless. Measures were carried out on a test-bed which reproduces (on a small scale) a real prototype of an infrastructure network. Particularly, during the downstream from a desktop PC as a FH to a PDA as a MH, transmissions between these heterogeneous hosts may result in the degradation of an overall performance. Experimental analysis of the traffic profiles during the downstream has been done. In addition, we propose methods for improving the performance of such multimedia downstream.

This paper consists of the following; we discuss the related works in Chapter 2. In Chapter 3, we show experimental analysis of TCP downstream and then present our proposed methods to improve performance. The experimental results are shown in Chapter 4. Finally, we conclude our works in Chapter 5.

2 Related Works

Data transmission protocol adopted in this paper is TCP. TCP uses what it calls the congestion window to determine how many packets can be sent at one time. The larger the congestion window size becomes, the higher the throughput becomes [4]. Typically, the congestion window size in a wired network remains constant after short delay. However, it over a WLAN oscillates too rapidly. If the congestion window size increases rapidly, it can add to network traffic before the network has completely recovered from congestion. If congestion is experienced again, the congestion window size will shrink rapidly. This alternating increase and decrease in congestion window size causes the performance of data transmission over a WLAN to reduce remarkably [2]. Besides, we consider a manipulation of the send buffer and the receive buffer at the transport layer as well as an application buffer at the application layer to enhance the performance of a PDA by tuning TCP [7].

According to operating systems, the socket buffer size is different [7]. For each socket, there is a default value for the buffer size, which can be changed by the program using a system library call just before opening the socket. There is also a kernel enforced maximum buffer size. The buffer size can be adjusted for both the send and receive ends of the socket [4]. It varies with the operating systems. FreeBSD gives 16384 bytes of default TCP socket buffer size, whereas Windows 2000 and XP give 8192 bytes.

To achieve maximal throughput it is critical to use the optimal sizes of the TCP send and receive socket buffer for the link we are using. If the buffers are too small, the TCP congestion window will never fully open up. If the buffers are too large, the sender can overrun the receiver, and the TCP window will shut down [4].

It is important to improve the TCP performance in wireless networks without any modifications of TCP syntax. The Snoop protocol of *Balakrishan* et al. [2] modified network-layer software at a base station to improved TCP performance in wireless networks. It used a split mode that a base station connected a fixed host and a mobile host. In split mode, a base station has to reveal data before it reaches the destination, thus violating the end-to-end semantics of the original TCP.

3 Experimental Analysis of TCP Downstream

3.1 A Test-Bed Infrastructure Network

There are several simulation and analytical studies on a wired and wireless network, whereas in this work, we test a real system to measure the performance of multimedia transmission. Thus, we have designed and implemented VMS (*Voice Messenger Systems*). VMS is an infrastructure network that integrates a wired LAN based on Ethernet with a WLAN based on the IEEE 802.11 standard. In our test-bed network, BS (*Base Station*) is simply AP (*Access Point*). A desktop PC and a PDA represents FH and MH, respectively. The hardware specification of the hosts used in the VMS is listed in Table 1.

VMS is a kind of file transfer system. It is similar to short message services (SMS) available on digital mobile phones. Let us briefly explain how it works: a VMS client records one's voice and then sends it to the VMS server after converting it into a wave file format. The server receives this voice message and stores it in its hard disk. It transfers the message to the authenticated client that requests it.

Table 1. The hardware specification of the hosts used in the VMS

Host type		CPU	RAM	NIC
MH	PDA	Samsung S3C2440 (400MHz)	128MB	PCMCIA (11Mbps)
FH	PC	Pentium 4 (2.4~3.0GHz)	1GB	PCI (100Mbps)

Before we discuss about performance metrics, we should define the terminology to be used: ***Upstream*** is a process of transmitting data from a PDA as a MH to its server as a FH. On the contrary, we call ***downstream*** a process of receiving data for a PDA from its server. It moves in an opposite direction to the upstream.

3.2 An Analysis of Three Types of Transmissions

We have analyzed three types of transmissions: upstream, downstream and wireless-to-wireless (PDA-to-PDA). Notice that when measuring the performance of such transmission, we located MH, i.e. PDA, within a 5-meter radius of an AP to maintain both good signal quality and strength.

In the first traffic profile, we use a file size dimension up to 4688 Kbytes. These files are generated by recording one's voice for 60 to 600 seconds. In Fig. 1(a) the behavior of the transmission time with respect to the file size is shown when the packet size is 1460 bytes. The elapsed time to complete the downstream is slower than that to complete the upstream by 20% at maximum. Such difference becomes greater as the file size becomes larger. In addition, the transmission time of the PDA-to-PDA transmission is approximately equal to the sum of these two figures.

In the second traffic profile, we use an application buffer size dimension of the sender up to 7168 bytes. In Fig. 1(b), the throughputs for the three types of transmissions are shown when we use both the file size of 2344 Kbytes and the packet size of 1500 bytes. One of the particular interests is the case of more than 1500 bytes of data, where it exceeds MTU (*maximum transfer unit*). In this test, fragmentation can take place at the sending host by varying the buffer size of the sender. If the buffer size is less than the MTU, the throughput in the downstream is superior to the upstream as depicted in Fig. 1(b).

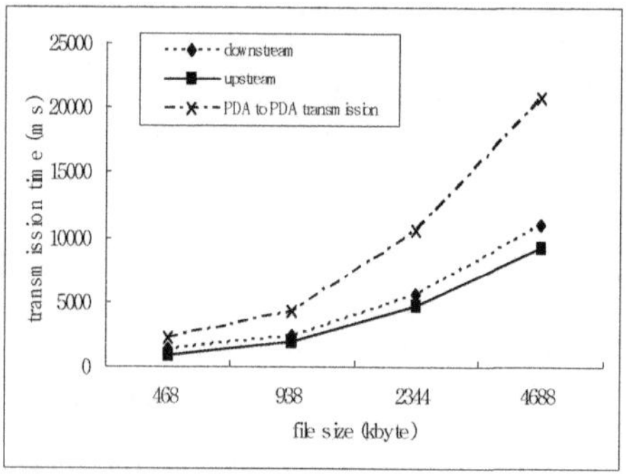

(a) The transmission times with respect to file size

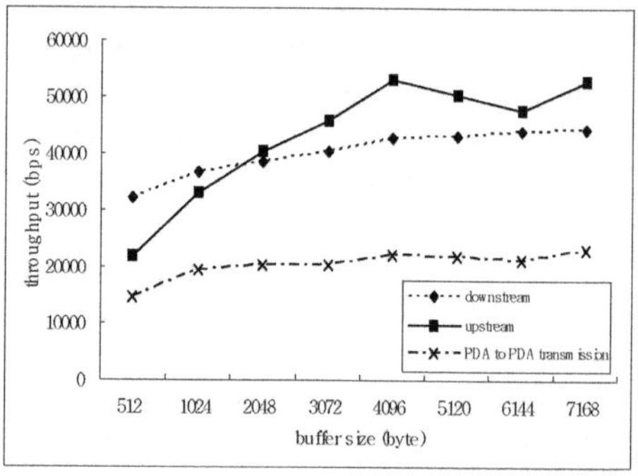

(b) The throughputs with respect to buffer size

Fig. 1. The traffic profiles for three types of transmissions

In that case, the possibility of fragmentation is very low and thus the transmission rate is moderate due to the relatively low traffic. We think that as the size of the application buffer at the sender increases it heightens the possibility of burst traffic and thus causes a high traffic. If the size of the buffer is larger, the throughput in the upstream is better. For the downstream, the degradation of the performance is due to the substantial differences in their computational complexities between these two heterogeneous hosts, a desktop PC and a PDA.

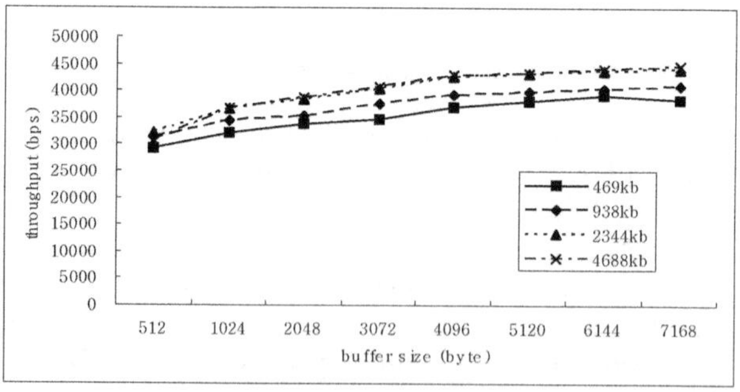

Fig. 2. The throughputs with respect to both file size and buffer size

In Fig. 2, we show the comparative analysis on 4 different file sizes during the downstream. As expected, the throughput increases as both the file size and the size of the buffer size at the sender increase.

To see more details above, the traces for both the upstream and the downstream have been done by using the Network Analyzer [9]. Each arrival time of the first 11 packets during the downstream and the upstream is depicted in Fig 3. During the upstream, the VMS server as a FH receives 7 packets within 4.3ms. However, during the downstream a PDA as a VMS client receives only 6 packets within 7.1ms.

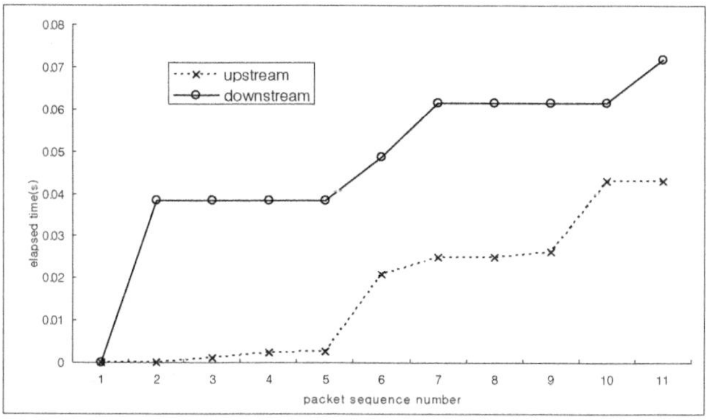

Fig. 3. The arrival time of the first 11 packets during the downstream and the upstream (with the buffer size of 4096 bytes)

3.3 A Proposed Method of Improving the TCP Downstream

From the analysis of the traffic profiles during the downstream, two aspects are clearly depicted: During the downstream (i) the window update is occurred frequently and (ii) the delayed ACK is generated very often compared to the upstream. This phenomenon causes the performance to reduce remarkably.

First, the size of the window offered by the receiver can usually be controlled by the receiving process. This can affect the TCP performance. The size of the receive buffer is the maximum size of the advertised window for that connection. Thus, during the downstream we can use different receive buffer size dimensions. To be specific, buffers in routers are designed to be larger than the bandwidth-delay product [8]. To compute it, the bandwidth and the round trip time is measured by 426300bps and 19ms, respectively, in the case of both the file size of 2344 Kbytes and the packet size of 1500 bytes. Thus, the lower limit is 810 bytes (approx.). Smaller buffers mean a higher packet drop rate [8]. Notice that the maximum allowable TCP window advertisement is 65535 bytes. However, too large buffer may lead to unacceptable delay of file access due to the smaller computational power of a PDA. So we should measure it to consider its impact.

Second, in an application layer, an inter packet delay (IPD) refers to the time interval between the transmission of two successive packets by any host. In general, the transmission time increases as IPD decreases. However, if there is a clear difference in processing capability between sender and receiver, IPD should be adjusted to give enough time to complete its internal processing for the low-end devices. The proposed method to be taken here is that longer IPD means the lower packet drop rate. In our test, we empirically chose IPD. Theoretically, IPD is chosen judiciously by considering network parameters, such as round trip time, the size of the transmit buffer and the receive buffer, and the capacity of the link, to avoid the degradation of the overall performance.

4 Performance Analysis of TCP Downstream

4.1 The Size of the Receive Buffer

In Fig. 4 the behavior of the transmission time with respect to the size of the receiver buffer during the downstream is depicted. This diagram demonstrates that the large buffer size increases the advertised window for the connection.

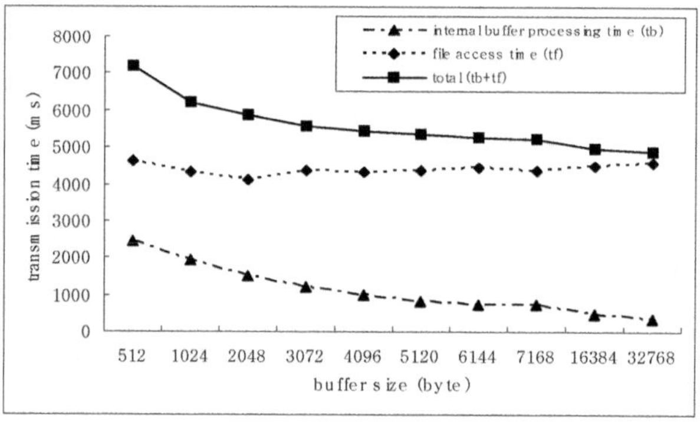

Fig. 4. The transmission time with respect to the size of the receive buffer

An approximate 32% increase in throughput is seen by just increasing the buffer to 32768 bytes from 512 bytes. In our test, the lower bound on the buffer size is approximately 810 bytes as discussed in the Section 3.3. By just increasing the buffer to 1024 bytes from 512 bytes, the remarkable increase in throughput is obtained.

Moreover, the diagram also demonstrates the un-correlation between the transmission time and the file access time. The elapsed time to access its internal files which resides in the memory of PDA can be kept constant with varying sizes of the receive buffer.

4.2 The Time Interval of the Inter-packet Delay

In Fig. 5, the throughputs for two types of settings are measured with varying IPD: one is that IDP is set only at the sending side and the other is that IDP is set both at the sending side and the receiving side. In Fig. 5(a), during the upstream the behaviour of the transmission time with respect to the IDP is depicted. As expected, with no such delay the transmission time is the fastest independent of the transmission type.

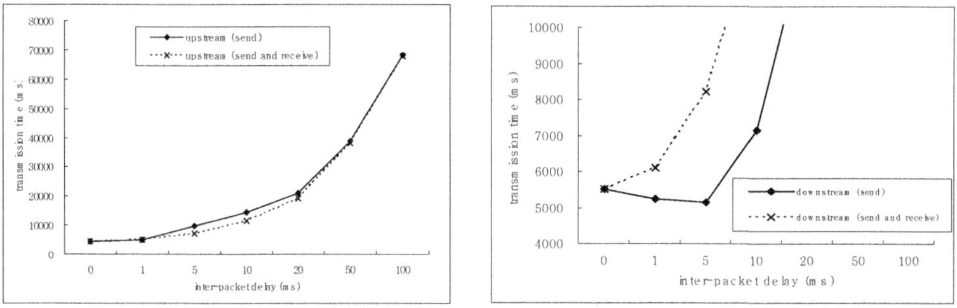

(a) The transmission times with respect to inter-packet delay during the upstream

(b) The transmission times with respect to inter-packet delay during the downstream

Fig. 5. The throughputs for both upstream and downstream with respect to IPD

In the case of the downstream as depicted in Fig. 5(b), by setting the IPD of 5 ms only at the sending side achieves a best performance which improves by 7% compared to that without IPD. From the analysis of these empirical results the possible range of the IPD will be 1ms < IPD < 10ms. In addition, during the downstream we analyzed the packet losses with respect to IPD by using the AiroPeek [10]. Typically, all kinds of packet losses decrease with increases in IDP. In other words, reduces in packet loss cause the throughput to increase.

5 Conclusions

We measured a performance of multimedia transmission between a PDA as a mobile host and a desktop PC as a fixed host in an infrastructure network. To evaluate such a performance more precisely, a test bed system called VMS that adopted TCP as a transmission protocol was built. The elapsed time to complete the downstream is slower than that to complete the upstream by 20% at maximum. During the downstream, the degradation of the performance is due to the substantial differences in their computational capabilities between these two heterogeneous hosts, a desktop PC and a PDA. From the analysis of the traffic profiles, two aspects are clearly depicted: During the downstream (i) the window update is occurred frequently and (ii) the delayed ACK is generated very often compared to the upstream. These cause the performance to reduce remarkably.

First, by increasing the size of the receive buffer for a PDA the congestion window size of TCP becomes more stable. From our experiments, an approximate 32% increase in throughput is seen by just increasing the buffer to 32768 bytes from 512 bytes. In our test, the theoretical lower bound on the buffer size is approximately 810 bytes. Moreover, the results also demonstrate that the elapsed time to access its internal files which resides in the memory of PDA is kept constant with varying sizes for the receive buffer.

Second, the inter-packet delay (IPD) should be needed to give enough time to complete its internal processing for the low-end device (PDA) during the downstream. By setting the inter-packet delay of 5 ms only at the sender achieves a best performance that improves by 7% compared to that with no such delay. From the analysis of the empirical results the possible range of the IPD will be 1ms < IPD < 10ms.

References

1. Stevens, W. R.: TCP/IP Illustrated – Volume 1: The Protocols, Addison-Wesley (1994)
2. Balakrishnan, H., Seshan, S., Amir, E., Katz, H.: Improving TCP/IP Performance over Wireless Networks, ACM MOBICOM (1995)
3. Nguyen, G. T., Katz, R. H., Noble, B., Satyanarayanan, M.: A Trace-Based Approach for Modeling Wireless Channel Behavior, In Proceedings of the Winter Simulation Conference (1996) 597-604
4. Tierney, B. L.: TCP tuning guide for distributed application on wide area networks, ;login: The magazine of USENIX & SAGE, Vol. 26, No. 1 (2001) 33-39
5. Zheng, B. and Atiquzzaman, M.: A Novel Scheme for Streaming Multimedia to Personal Wireless Handheld Devices, IEEE Transcations on Consumer Electronics, Vol. 49, No. 1 (2003)
6. G. Isannello, A. Pescape, G. Ventre, and L. Vollero, Experimental Analysis of Heterogeneous Wireless Networks, WWIC 2004 (2004) 153-164
7. Karadia, D.: Understanding Tuning TCP, Sun Microsystems, Inc., http://www.sun.com/blueprints (2004)
8. Lachlan L. H. Andrew, et al, Buffer Sizing for Non-homogeneous TCP Sources, IEEE Communication Letters, Vol. 9, No. 6 (2005) 567-569
9. Analyzer web site, http://analyzer.polito.it
10. Wildpackets web site, http://wildpackets.com

Intra Routing Protocol with Hierarchical and Distributed Caching in Nested Mobile Networks

Hyemee Park, Moonseong Kim, and Hyunseung Choo*

Intelligent HCI Convergence Research Center
Sungkyunkwan University, Korea
{hyemee,moonseong,choo}@ece.skku.ac.kr

Abstract. We propose a novel route optimization protocol for intra-NEMO communication using a hierarchical and distributed caching scheme. The proposed scheme employs the routing cache of each nested MRs to optimize a route to be taken for traffic between MNNs within nested mobile network. For this goal, it supports an efficient cache design and adaptive mechanism for managing cache. By using tree based routing, it has greater data efficiency with less packet overheads, and improves the latency of the data traffic using an optimal route. To support seamless mobility, we propose a solution that reduces the mass signaling for all nested mobile networks when the nested MR handoff frequently occurs. The proposed scheme has approximately 29% of performance improvements in comparison with previous schemes.

1 Introduction

As the number of wireless networking technologies proliferate, users expect to be connected to the Internet using portable devices such as cell phones, laptops or PDA (personal Digital Assistant) from anywhere at anytime. In order to satisfy such demand, recent research has concentrated on the development of both wireless and mobile computing to provide seamless Internet service in vehicular environments. As a result, network mobility (NEMO) becomes increasingly important in supporting the movement of a mobile network consisting of several mobile nodes. For network mobility, the IETF NEMO working group proposed the NEMO basic support protocol [1] extending host mobility support protocol, Mobile IPv6 [2]. The ultimate objective of this solution is to allow all nodes in the mobile network to be reachable via their permanent IP addresses, as well as to maintain ongoing sessions when the Mobile Router (MR) changes its point of attachment to the Internet. It ensures session continuity by using a bi-directional tunnel between the MR and the Home Agent (HA). By using this MR-HA tunneling, it suffers from the a pinball routing problem, since all packets sent between a source and destination node are forwarded via the HAs of all the MRs. It suffers from increased latency and packet size as an extra IPv6 header is added per level of nesting.

* Corresponding author.

Y.-H. Lee et al. (Eds.): ICESS 2007, LNCS 4523, pp. 747–756, 2007.

Most research focuses on a Route Optimization (RO) solution to allow packets between two end nodes to be routed along the optimal path. Although there are various RO schemes for nested NEMO, most approaches solve the pinball routing problem in inter-NEMO communication between a mobile network (*e.g.* MNN) and external Internet (*e.g.* CN). However, such a problem is generated in intra-NEMO communication between nodes inside the same nested mobile network. The traffic for internal routing within the mobile network should be routed via external Internet, all HAs of nested MRs. This results in undesirable effects, such as longer route leading to increased delay, increased packet overhead and processing delay. In addition, internal routing is affected by the Internet connectivity of root-MR. That is, if AR loses its connection to the global Internet, two nodes within the mobile network can no longer communicate with each other, even though the direct path between them is unaffected. Previous works do not consider such problems in inter-NEMO data commutations. The packet is encapsulated as the nesting levels, since a network node does not know whether the destination node belongs inside the same nested mobile network or not. To provide efficient internal routing, it requires a caching mechanism for sharing the route information of the nested mobile network.

In this paper, we propose a novel route optimization protocol for intra-NEMO communication using a hierarchical and distributed caching scheme. The proposed scheme employs the routing cache of each nested MR to optimize a route to be taken for traffic between MNNs within the nested mobile network. For this goal, it supports an efficient cache design and adaptive mechanism for managing the cache. Each cache entry is composed of simplified routing information by hierarchy architecture of nested mobile networks, enabling scalable and efficient cache maintenance. Routing update procedure is proposed for cache consistency with minimum signaling overhead. Outbound packet from the source node is transmitted based on the prefix delegation method without nested tunneling, and inbound packet to the destination node is forwarded using tree routing. As it does not require many levels of encapsulation, it has greater data efficiency with less packet overhead, and improves the latency of the data traffic using an optimal route. To support seamless mobility, we propose a solution that reduces the mass signaling for all nested mobile networks when the nested MR handoff frequently occurs. Consequently, the proposed scheme minimizes the consumption of overall network resources from the lighter network load.

The rest of this paper is organized as follows. In Section 2, related works are introduced with some discussion. Section 3 presents the proposed scheme for intra-NEMO routing optimization. The performance of the proposed scheme is evaluated in Section 4. Finally, we conclude in Section 5.

2 ROTIO for Intra-NEMO Communication

ROTIO [3] is a routing optimization scheme for intra-NEMO based on the extended tree information option (xTIO) that contains the CoAs of nested MRs. Each MR appends its CoA in the xTIO suboption of the RA message while the

RA is propagated to the overall network. Then, the receiving MR can obtain the information of all ancestors MRs from the RA message with this option. The MR sends two BU messages: a normal BU to its HA, and local BU to the TLMR. The former informs the HoA of the TLMR as its CoA. The latter appends the xTIO option with the list of CoAs of all ancestor MRs to each binding update message. It is to allow the TLMR to learn the topology of the nested mobile networks. The binding cache of the TLMR consists of its HoA and the CoAs of intermediate MRs between TLMR and corresponding MR. In the ROTIO scheme, when the MR receives the packet from the MNN, it encapsulates the packet as the source address of the outer header is set to the TLMR's HoA. When the TLMR receives the packet, it searches its binding cache to find whether the destination address in the HAO belongs itself or not. If it exists, then the TLMR decapsulates and performs source routing using the list of intermediate MRs in its cache entry. Fig. 1 represents the operation of ROTIO protocol.

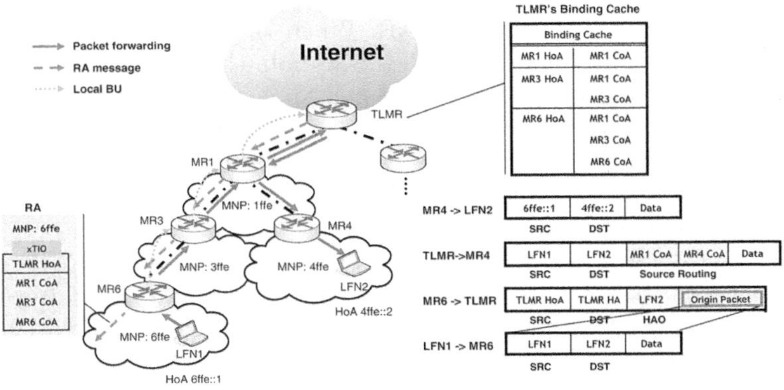

Fig. 1. The operation of ROTIO protocol

Even though ROTIO supports intra-NEMO routing optimization, there are overheads associated with the binding cache formation and maintenance. To maintain the cache in a dynamic large network requires a lot of message exchange between the TLMR and nested MRs. The control message that contains the addresses of intermediate MRs suffers from increasing overhead as the depth of the MR increases. The binding cache demands memory space of large volumes as it should keep all ancestor MRs of each nested mobile network. The more MRs are nested, the more entries need to be made in the cache. In addition, as the number of nested levels increases, it suffers from overhead due to the increased number of packets for source routing between the TLMR and destination node. The packet should pass through the TLMR, since it only keeps the binding cache of entire mobile networks. Although it maintains only one tunnel within nested mobile networks, it does not consider the ingress filtering problem, and may incur nested tunneling in each hop.

3 Proposed Scheme

3.1 Hierarchy Based on Prefix Delegation

Nested mobile networks create a hierarchy architecture using the prefix delegation method. Prefix delegation is a method where MRs of mobile networks share the prefix of the Access Router (AR), to reduce the tunneling overhead according to ingress filtering. Each MR keeps the prefix advertised from AR, called the Delegated Prefix (DP), in addition to its original subnet prefix, called the Mobile Network Prefix (MNP). The DP is disseminated to the entire mobile network through the extended Router Advertisement (RA) message adding the new DP option. Each MR inserts the address of AR received from upstream MR into the DP option and propagates the RA message downwards. The receiving MRs can deduce the DP from this option. If the MR receives the RA message without this option, it recognizes the information contained in the RA message as the prefix of the AR. Then, it relays the RA message after appending the DP option with the address of the AR. When the MRs of each nested mobile network receive the RA message with this option, they additionally allocate the DP to their ingress interface link. They can forward the packet with the source address configured by the MNP and DP, without nested tunneling by ingress filtering. Although the prefix of the AR is propagated to the overall network, all MRs and MNNs configure their address (*e.g.* HoA or CoA) using the MNP advertised by default MR.

Mobile networks form a tree topology from the AR to the MRs of nested mobile networks based on the proposed prefix delegation method. In this paper, we propose to use the MR's Hierarchy ID (HID) as a logical address, other than global IP addresses such as the HoA or CoA. The 64-bit HID is divided into eight nesting levels, each with eight bits. That is, each MR can have at most 255 child MRs. The logical HID indicates the location of nodes on the tree topology. This is a routing information to deliver the packets among MNNs within mobile networks. It enables to optimize the route for intra-NEMO data communication, and to efficiently manage the routing cache with minimum overhead. In order to configure the HID of the tree topology, each MR establishes a parent-child association with the upper MR using a 3-way handshake. After establishing this association, each MR uses the parent as a default route toward the AR. Control packets of the 3-way handshake procedure consist of the RA message disseminated for prefix delegation, ID Request, and Ack. Each MR adds a new ID option with its HID to the RA message.

When the MR receives one or more RA messages from the upper MRs, it obtains their HID and sends ID Request message to the selected node as a parent from among the messages. The receiving MR selects a positive integer which is not yet assigned in its children, and sends it with the Ack message. When the MR receives the Ack message from the parent MR, it concatenates the receiving number and parent's ID, and then propagates the HID with the RA message. For example, if the parent using HID 1.2.1 receives the request message from the child node, it selects a random number (x) from 1 to 255, which is not used by others.

Then, the parent notifies x to child through the Ack message. As the child MR concatenates x and 1.2.1, the HID will be set to 1.2.1.x. The 3-way handshake procedure ensures that all MRs have a unique ID without duplicating and avoid a tree loop caused by multiple associations. This procedure is performed only by MRs when nested mobile networks are organized in the initial phase, or when the parent-child association is reconfigured by mobility.

3.2 Routing Cache Management

The AR and all MRs have a routing cache that consists of MNP and HID pairs of each nested mobile networks for intra-NEMO routing optimization. In order to construct and maintain the routing cache, the MR performs a Routing Update (RU) procedure for exchanging routing information within nested mobile networks. In the proposed scheme, each MR processes two kinds of updating messages: BU and RU. The former is transmitted to the MR's HA to update its CoA newly configured by changing its point of attachment. The latter is to update the routing information (MNP, HID) to cache of MRs within nested mobile networks. The RU is divided into registration and de-registration phases for cache consistency. The MR performs the registration procedure to save new routing information of the mobile network in the upstream MRs' cache. If the MR detects movement, it sends the RU message, which contains its MNP and new HID pair, to the AR through parent-child path. The receiving MR updates its routing cache entry and forwards recursively the RU message to its parent MR. When the MR performs the RU, its upstream MRs along the path toward the AR can obtain new information at a time.

In contrast, the de-registration procedure is to report the invalid routing information, and allows the corresponding cache entry to delete. If mobile network moves to another network, it results in routing error, since the routing information is no longer applicable. Furthermore, it may require additional costs for maintaining the useless information. For these reasons, the MR transmits the RU message for de-registration to upper mobile networks. Each MR periodically monitors its network nodes to perform de-registration on behalf of the MR which does not exist in the subnet. It can detect the loss of its child nodes using RA and Router Solicitation (RS) in the Neighbor Discovery Protocol (NDP) of IPv6 [4]. If the parent MR does not receive the RA message from its child within a predefined time, it assumes that the child MR has moved away. It deletes the cache entry, releases the positive integer assigned to the child, and transmits the de-registration message with the routing information of corresponding mobile network to the AR. Then, the upstream MRs and AR can delete their cache entry. When they perform the de-registration procedure, they delete the cache entry of the MR which is contained in the RU message and that of its downstream mobile networks at the same time. In other words, they delete the HIDs derived from the corresponding MR's ID since the HIDs of downstream mobile networks are no longer valid by changing their location of tree topology.

The RU message for registration and de-registration is carried by the Hop-by-Hop extension header of IPv6. Hop-by-Hop header includes options that need to be processed by every node along the packet's delivery path (include final receiver) [5]. When the MR transmits the RU message with the destination field set to the AR's address by using this option header, it can register and update the routing cache of the all MRs along the path toward the AR. Consequently, AR keeps the routing information of entire mobile networks, and each MR keeps that of its downstream mobile networks in the routing cache. The message of two phases is distinguished by the flag. The registration is set to 'R' flag, on the other hand, the de-registration is set to 'D' flag. The cache entry consists of the MNP and HID of each nested mobile network, and the RU message contains the same information as the cache. By using the hierarchical ID based on tree topology, the routing information required for the mobile network is simplified. Therefore, the routing cache and RU message keep constant size regardless of nesting level of mobile networks. As the volume of them is considerably reduced, the proposed scheme can efficiently manage the routing information for intra-NEMO at minimum cost.

3.3 Routing Operation

We propose the optimal routing protocol using the routing cache based on hierarchical mobile networks for intra-NEMO data communications. When the MR receives the packet, it first searches its cache for the prefix of destination address in the packet. If it finds the corresponding entry in the cache, the packet is then forwarded to the subnet with the destination node. In contrast, if the corresponding entry does not exist, the MR transmits the packet to its parent MR recursively. Finally, if it is not matched in the AR's cache, the destination node does not belong to the mobile network behind the AR. Then, the packet is delivered through the external network (*e.g.* HA).

When the MR receives the packet from the MNN, it replaces the prefix of source address with the DP advertised from the AR to avoid nested tunneling by ingress filtering. That is, the source address configured by <MNP || MNN's ID> is changed to <DP || MNN's ID>. After that, the MR inserts the original MNN's address into the extended slot. The modified packet is directly forwarded to the AR without tunneling overhead since every MRs keeps the DP in its subnet prefix list. Each MR that receives the packet with the source address configured by DP searches its cache to find out whether the destination node belongs to downstream mobile networks or not. If the MNP of destination address exists, it obtains the corresponding HID.

After appending the hop-by-hop option with the HID to the packet header, the MR forwards this packet downwards. Then, intermediate MRs along the route toward the destination mobile network check this option and deliver the packet to the child node selected by the longest prefix matching algorithm. This algorithm is used to determine the next hop node in order to reach the destination by using the HID. When the packet arrives at the MR with the HID of the hop-by-hop option, it removes the additional option with the HID and extension slot with the original source address, and transmits to the destination node.

Since the proposed scheme performs the tree routing based on the hierarchical ID, it can reduce the routing overhead by eliminating unnecessary flooding to the overall network. In addition, it does not need to pass through the top level root node (AR) as every MR keeps the routing information of each nested mobile network. As a result, it can reduce routing delay by optimal path between the source and destination nodes. This results in low packet overhead in comparison with previous work, because it has no tunneling by prefix delegation and source routing by tree path.

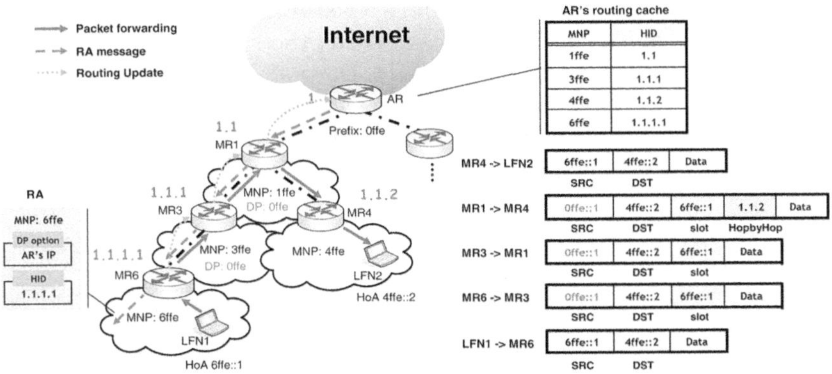

Fig. 2. The operation of the proposed protocol

3.4 Handoff Consideration

Each MR sends a BU message to its HA when the CoA is changed by performing the handoff. In the proposed scheme, the HID of the MR is also affected by changing its point of attachment. The MR performs the 3-way handshake procedure to associate with the new parent node, and configures a new HID. However, a simple change in the point of attachment for the root MR will require every nested MR to change their HID and delegated prefix. These will significantly cause a burst of RUs to the AR whenever the MR changes its point of attachment. We propose an efficient handoff scheme by reducing the signaling overhead.

The handoff leader MR inserts the AR's address received from new parent MR and its new HID into the RA message, and propagates it to the overall network. Its downstream MRs do not need to perform the BU, since their CoAs are not changed by keeping the parent node. The receiving MR adds new DP to prefix list of ingress interface link, and replaces the old HID with the new one. It reconfigures its HID internally without performing the 3-way handshake procedure. It keeps a positive integer assigned from parent MR in previous phase, and the rest is only replaced with the parent's HID. For example, if the MR using HID 1.2.3 receives the RA message with HID 1.4.1 from the parent, it replaces the previous parent's HID 1.2 with that of new parent. That is, the new HID is set to 1.4.1.3. The MR simply concatenates the previous integer and new parent's HID, since it is assumed that it receives a unique integer from the parent. Then, it transmits a new HID via the RA message to its subnet recursively. This procedure reduces the cost required for reconfiguring the ID by network mobility.

All MRs in downstream mobile networks should inform new routing information to upper MRs, as their HIDs are changed. To reduce the overhead for routing update, the handoff leader MR performs on behalf of its subnet. If the MR detects the movement and changes its HID, it updates the routing information of its downstream mobile networks in the cache. It changes all HIDs derived from its previous HID into a new one using its current HID. After updating the cache entry, it sends the RU message collecting the updated information in its cache to the AR. Then, it can update the routing information of the entire network, which moves in the AR's subnet at the same time. The RU message is simplified by using the hierarchical ID. Downstream MRs update their cache entry when they reconfigure the HID like that shown above. Since it guarantees the cache consistency as described in Section 3.2, each MR keeps a valid routing cache, and enables that the MR updates the cache itself.

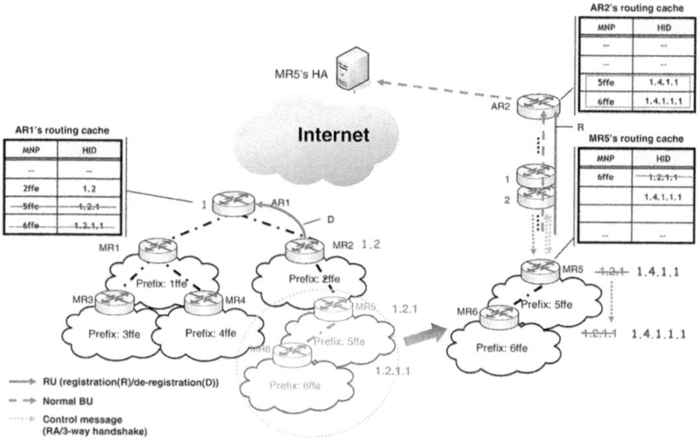

Fig. 3. The handoff procedure of the proposed protocol

In the proposed scheme, the handoff leader MR only performs the BU, ID reconfiguration by 3-way handshake (parent-child association reestablishment), and the RU. On the other hand, the remaining MRs internally update their ID and routing cache without additional RU procedure. The proposed scheme supports seamless mobility with low handoff cost, as the BU and RU storm does not occur due to the mobility of nested mobile networks.

4 Performance Evaluation

4.1 Simulation Environment

In this section, the performance of the proposed scheme is evaluated in comparison with NEMO Basic Support protocol and ROTIO. Simulation implemented in C is conducted. Our simulation models a wireless network of mobile nodes placed randomly. Simulation traffic is generated by Continuous Bit Rate (CBR) sources spreading the traffic randomly. The bandwidth of the wired link is set to 100 Mb/s and that of the wireless link is set to 11 Mb/s. It is assumed that all HAs, which are uniformly distributed in the Internet, have a 10ms delay in wired link and the mobile nodes have a 1ms delay in wireless link.

4.2 Simulation Results

The average routing delay of the proposed and previous schemes is first compared for various nesting level. This simulation varies the depth of the nested mobile networks between 1 and 10. We measure the delay required when the traffic is routed between the source and destination pair belonging to the nested mobile network behind the AR. The routing delay is the summation of transmission, propagation and processing time in each hop.

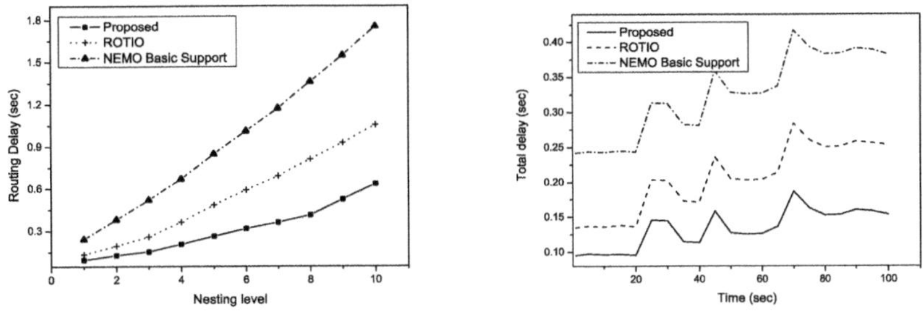

(a) Routing delays according to nesting levels (b) Total delays according to the handoff

Fig. 4. Simulation results of three schemes

As shown in Fig. 4(a), the proposed scheme has better performance than other schemes as the number of nesting levels increases. NEMO Basic Support protocol suffers from overhead due to the increased number of packets and transmission delay as the packets are repeatedly encapsulated by all the HAs of the nested MRs. ROTIO utilizes the shorter delay for communication within nested mobile networks than NEMO Basic Support, however, it has increased delay for intra-NEMO routing in comparison with the proposed scheme. In ROTIO, the size of the packets is consistently increasing for source routing as the number of nested levels increases. The proposed scheme remains constant irrespective of the number of nesting levels. As the packet is delivered via the optimal route, the transmission and propagation delays are smaller than other schemes.

We calculate the total delay by adding the cost required when handoff event occurs randomly during simulation time. The total delay summates the cost of handoff procedure (*e.g.* BU, RU) performed by mobile network after detecting its movement in each scheme. The simulation result is presented in Fig. 4(b). In NEMO Basic Support protocol, the handoff procedure is relatively simple than existing RO schemes as the handoff leader MR performs only BU to its HA. However, as the depth of the nested mobile networks increases, the BU message also suffers the undesirable effects of sub-optimal routing. In ROTIO, control message overhead is much higher than that of the proposed scheme. The message size is increasing according to nesting level of mobile networks, and all nested MRs should perform a local BU to update the TLMR's cache when nested mobile networks move concurrently. Consequently, the result represents that the proposed scheme has less packet overheads and results in lighter network load.

5 Conclusion

In this paper, we propose the intra-NEMO RO scheme to solve the pinball routing problem in internal routing of nested mobile networks. The proposed scheme provides an adaptive mechanism for efficient cache design and management, and optimizes the route using this cache. As the routing operation is based on prefix delegation method and tree routing, it improves overall QoS characteristics such as latency, bandwidth usage, network load, and data efficiency. In our simulation, the proposed scheme has approximately 29% of performance improvements in comparison with previous schemes.

Acknowledgment

This research was supported by MIC, Korea under ITRC IITA-2006-(C1090-0603-0046).

References

1. V. Devarapalli, R. Wakikawa, A. Petrescu, P. Thubert, "Network Mobility (NEMO) Basic Support Protocol," IETF, RFC 3963, January 2005.
2. D. Johnson, C. E. Perkins, and J. Arkko, "Mobility Support in IPv6," IETF, RFC 3775, June 2004.
3. H. Cho, T. Kwon, and Y. Choi, "Route Optimization Using Tree Information Option for Nested Mobile Networks," IEEE JSAC, Vol. 24, Issue. 9, pp. 1717- 1724, September 2006.
4. T. Narten, E. Nordmark, and W. Simpson "Neighbor Discovery for IP Version 6 (IPv6)," IETF, RFC 2461, December 1998.
5. S. Deering, R. Hinden, "Internet Protocol, Version 6 (IPv6) Specification," IETF, RFC 2460, December 1998.

Performance Analysis of 802.11e Burst Transmissions with FEC Codes over Wireless Sensor Networks

Jong-Suk Ahn[1], Jong-Hyuk Yoon[1], and Young-Im Cho[2]

[1] Department of Computer Engineering, Dong-Guk University, Seoul, South Korea*
{jahn,ronaldo}@dongguk.edu
[2] Department of Computer Science, University of Suwon, Suwon, South Korea
ycho@suwon.ac.kr

Abstract. WSNs (Wireless Sensor Network) can employ a burst technique known as 802.11e TXOP (Transmission Opportunity) operation to send sensor data backlogged during the sleep period [1] and FEC (Forward Error Correction) techniques to resist against their high BER (Bit Error Rate) [2]. This paper extends the 802.11e evaluation model [3], [4] to accurately calculate the performance of two TXOP schemes such as BI (Basic Immediate ACK) and BB (Basic Block ACK) with FEC codes. The generalized model accounts for the effect of propagation errors negligible in wireless LANs, the impact of HOB (Head-Of-Block) collision, and the effect of adopting FEC codes. This paper evaluates this extended model over real WSN channels abstracted by Gilbert model. The numerical calculations over real WSN traces confirm that the inclusion of HOB collisions causes the throughput difference of BB by up-to 194 % comparing to [3]. They also predicts a trade-off between the performance improvement and the overhead of FEC codes over WSN channels.

Keywords: 802.11e Burst Transmissions, Wireless Sensor Networks.

1 Introduction

As various applications have been developed for WSNs, WSNs actively adopt several techniques in their protocol stacks to improve their performance and lengthen sensor nodes' life time [2], [5]. Among them, WSNs recently employ data burst techniques to efficiently send a large amount of sensor data accumulated during their long sleep time. During the sleep intervals, they turn off the transceiver of sensor nodes while continuously collecting sensing data all the time. For further enhancements, WSNs can adopt FEC techniques since WSN propagation errors frequently and non-uniformly occur due to their low transmission power, random deployment of sensor nodes, and moving intermediate obstacles.

* This research was supported by Seoul Future Contents Convergence (SFCC) Cluster established by Seoul R&BD Program.

Y.-H. Lee et al. (Eds.): ICESS 2007, LNCS 4523, pp. 757–764, 2007.

This paper proposes an extended evaluation model to compute the accurate throughput of 802.11e burst transmissions with FEC codes. Differently from the previous research [3], [4], our model accounts for WSN propagation errors to accuratly evaluate the effect of noisy wireless channels on the two burst schemes such as BI and BB. In detail, it modifies the 802.11 BEB (Binary Exponential Back-off) performance model [6], [7] by including the channel error probability. It also accounts for the impact of collision and corruption on the first packet sent during a TXOP period named as HOB in the performance calculation. It finally accommodates the impact of FEC codes to predict the tradeoff between the FEC code's amount and the throughput as a function of BER. Note that either the excessive FEC codes or the light FEC ones deteriorate the performance. This model only assumes the block FEC code such as RS (Reed-Solomon) code.

Based on this extended model, this paper calculates the throughput of BI and BB with FEC codes over real WSN channels abstracted with Gilbert model [8] rather than uniform distributions inadequate for burst errors. The analytical computations based on real 3-hour WSN packet traces confirm that BB performs better than BI due to its light ACK overhead like [3]. They also show that the accommodation of HOB behavior and Gilbert model improves the throughput efficiency by up-to 113 % and 194 % respectively comparing to [3]. They finally predict the optimal amount of FEC codes over our experimental WSNs.

This paper is organized as follows. Section 2 illustrates BI and BB to compare and the modified analytical evaluation model for estimating them over erroneous channels. Section 3 explains the extended model when BI and BB adopt FEC codes. Section 4 calculates the throughput efficiency of the two schemes over WSN channels abstracted by Gilbert model. Section 5 finally summarizes this paper's contributions and lists some future research items.

2 A Burst Transmission Model Without FEC Codes

This section builds an evaluation model for comparing two burst techniques abbreviated with BI and BB shown in Figure 1 over WSN channels [4]. They are two possible implementations proposed for burst transmissions known as TXOP in 802.11e. Here, we exclude the burst transmissions with RTS (Request To Send)/CTS (Clear To Send) since the existence of these control packets rarely affect the performance comparison of these two schemes especially over noisy channels. We believe that their sizes are too small to be contaminated by propagation errors contrasting to data packets.

In BI in Figure 1, each packet's arrival is confirmed by an ACK immediately followed after SIFS (Short InterFrame Space) gap during the TXOP period. In BB, data packets are sent back-to-back with SIFS gap and all their arrivals are collectively verified by BACK (Block ACK) requested with BREQ (Block ACK Request). The first packet in these schemes named as HOB is protected by an ACK to minimize the collision overhead. When HOB is not collided, the rest packets are sure to be sent without collisions since each is sent after SIFS gap.

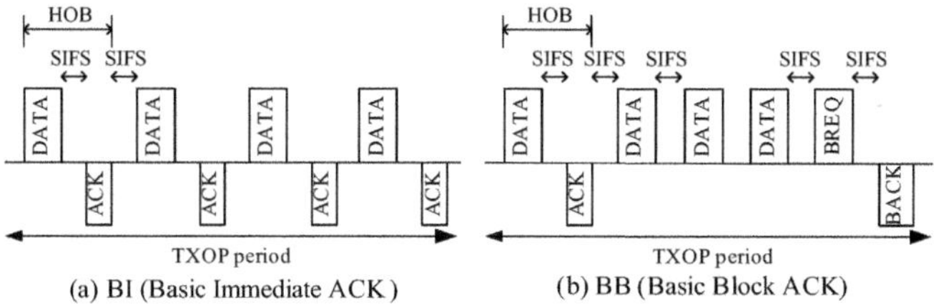

Fig. 1. Two burst transmissions with different ACK policies

As a performance comparison metric, Equation 1 defines throughput efficiency Th_{eff} over noisy channels as like [3]. Th_{eff} is the average data bits successfully transmitted $E[L_{pld}]$ divided by the average slot time $E[T]$ spent for $E[L_{pld}]$ transmission when n nodes constantly try to transmit N_b packets of L_f bits within a TXOP interval. $E[L_{pld}]$ consists of two terms, $P_S * L_f * N_b$ the average amount of data successfully sent without any error and $P_E * E[L]$ the average amount of data successfully sent in the block where some data packets are corrupt. $E[L]$ averages the amount of data survived in an error block when the number of error packets ranges from 1 to N_b where p_e represents the probability of a packet' s corruption.

$$Th_{eff} = \frac{E[L_{pld}]}{E[T]} = \frac{P_S L_f N_b + P_E E[L]}{P_I T_I + P_S T_S + P_E T_E + P_C T_C}$$

$$\text{where } E[L] = \sum_{i=1}^{N_b} \binom{N_b}{i} (p_e)^i (1-p_e)^{N_b-i} (N_b - i) L_f. \quad (1)$$

Equation 2 enumerates the time duration for four states experienced for sending a block of packets as idle period T_I, successful transmission time T_S, collision time T_C, and unsuccessful transmission time T_E due to propagation errors. T_I is equal to one slot time σ. T_S is comprised of N_b packets' transmission time, overhead time T_{OH} for receiving ACKs, and finally a trailing DIFS (Distributed InterFrame Space) before starting a new contention. A packet's transmission time is divided into T_{DATA} of sending L_f payload, T_{PHYhdr} of its physical header, T_{SIFS} for sending a next packet in the block and one-way propagation delay δ. Since the transmission of the physical header adopts different modulation scheme than the following data, T_{PHYhdr} should be computed separately from T_{DATA}. T_{OH} of BI in Equation 2 is the time to send N_b ACKs while T_{OH} of BB is time to send one ACK for HOB, BREQ, and BACK.

T_C is the time summing a HOB packet's transmission and EIFS (Extended InterFrame Space) before initiating a new contention. Different from [3], T_E is equal to either T_C or T_S depending on what packet is corrupted. When HOB is corrupted, the sender will contend for a new TXOP since it can't differentiate corruption from collision. Otherwise, the sender continuously sends packets within the TXOP interval regardless of whether or not packets in the block are in error.

$$
\begin{aligned}
&T_I = \sigma. \\
&T_S = N_b * (T_{PHYhdr} + T_{DATA} + T_{SIFS} + \delta) + T_{OH} + T_{DIFS}. \\
&T_C = T_{PHYhdr} + T_{DATA} + \delta + T_{EIFS}. \\
&T_E = \begin{cases} T_S \text{ when HOB is not in error.} \\ T_C \text{ otherwise.} \end{cases} \\
&\quad \text{where } T_{OH} = \begin{cases} N_b * (T_{ACK} + T_{SIFS} + \delta) & \text{in BI} \\ T_{ACK} + T_{BREQ} + T_{BACK} + 2 * T_{SIFS} + 3 * \delta & \text{in BB} \end{cases}
\end{aligned} \tag{2}
$$

Equation 3 lists the four probabilities in Equation 1 where n is the total number of nodes to compete and τ is the probability of a node's sending a packet during a slot time. P_I is the probability that none sends a packet while P_S is the probability that a node successfully delivers a packet without collision and without error. Note that p_e^{bta} is the probability that any packet out of N_b ones in the TXOP block is corrupted while p_e denote the probability of a packet's corruption. Differently from [3], P_E is also divided into two, one that HOB is corrupt and another that the other packets in the block are in error. P_C finally is the remaining probability subtracting the three probabilities from 1.

$$
\begin{aligned}
&P_I = (1-\tau)^n. \\
&P_S = n(1-\tau)^{n-1}(1-p_e^{bta}) \qquad \text{where } p_e^{bta} = 1-(1-p_e)^{N_b}. \\
&P_E = \begin{cases} n\tau(1-\tau)^{n-1}p_e & \text{when HOB is in error.} \\ n\tau(1-\tau)^{n-1}(p_e^{bta} - p_e) & \text{otherwise.} \end{cases} \\
&P_C = 1 - P_I - P_S - P_E.
\end{aligned} \tag{3}
$$

For computing over noisy channels, we substitute $(1-p)$ [6], the successful transition probability back to the initial window from any state, with $(1-p)*(1-p_e)$ since the contention window resets only when a packet should arrive without both collision and corruption over noisy channels. Here, p stands for the collision probability of a transmitted packet and we assume that ACKs are not collided and not corrupted due to their small size comparing to data packets. Based on this modified Markov chains, we compute both p and τ. Please refer to [6], [7], [9] for these two variables' computation.

For p_e, we abstract WSN channel behavior as Gilbert model, a two-state Markov chain consisted of good state S_g and bad one S_b. Here, p_{bad} and p_{good} represent the transition probability from S_g to S_b and vice versa respectively. Gilbert model is known to be one of the common models to appropriately represent the burstiness of wireless channel errors.

According to this channel model, the probability that any transmission symbol out of c is in error is $(1-(p_{good}/(p_{bad}+p_{good}))(1-p_{bad})^{c-1})$ since the probability of being in S_g and the probability of revisiting c-time consecutively S_g are $p_{good}/(p_{bad}+p_{good})$, $(1-p_{bad})^{c-1}$ respectively. Note that most wireless networks modulate some number of bits as one transmission symbol for speedup. In TIP50CM [10] used for establishing our experimental WSN, for example, the size of one transmission symbol is 2-bit since it employs offset-DQPSK (Differential Quadrature Phase Shift Keying). Equation 4 calculates p_e when a packet's size is L_f/d symbols and one transmission symbol size is d bits. In Equation 4, p_{bad} and p_{good} would be computed by matching CCDF (Complementary Cumulative Distribution Function) of real traces' run lengths with that of Gilbert model in Section 3.

$$p_e = 1 - \frac{p_{good}}{p_{bad} + p_{good}}(1 - p_{bad})^{\frac{L_f}{d}-1}. \quad (4)$$

3 A Burst Transmission Model with FEC Codes

This section explains an evaluation model to include the impact of FEC codes when each data frame in block transmissions attaches some amount of FEC codes at their trailer. The adoption of FEC codes at packets affects throughput efficiency and packet error probability since they increase the packet length while enhancing the error rate. Equation 5 redefines throughput efficiency with FEC codes Th_{eff} over noisy channels as like Equation 1. Equation 5 is equal to Equation 1 except that the amount of data decrements to $L_f(1-\alpha)$ from L_f to subtract the FEC code size where α represents the ratio of the FEC code size to the total payload. Note that these two equations assume the fixed packet size.

$$Th_{eff} = \frac{E[L_{pld}]}{E[T]} = \frac{P_S L_f(1-\alpha)N_b + P_E E[L]}{P_I T_I + P_S T_S + P_E T_E + P_C T_C}$$
$$\text{where } E[L] = \sum_{i=1}^{N_b} \binom{N_b}{i} (p_e)^i (1-p_e)^{N_b-i} (N_b - i) L_f (1-\alpha). \quad (5)$$

For p_e at the existence of FEC codes, we need to compute the FEC symbol error probability p_f shown in Equation 6 and the packet recovery probability $(1-p_e)$ in Equation 7. For p_f, we assume that one FEC symbol consists of some number of transmission symbols where m and l denote the size of one FEC symbol and one transmission symbol. Note that in block FEC algorithms, FEC symbol is a basic unit to recover regardless of how many bits are corrupted in one symbol.

$$p_f = 1 - \frac{p_{good}}{p_{bad} + p_{good}}(1 - p_{bad})^{\frac{m}{l}-1}. \quad (6)$$

Equation 7 [9] computes $(1-p_e)$ of successfully recovering a packet by RS algorithm when the size of one packet, the size of FEC codes, and the size of a FEC symbol are $n(=L_f/m)$, t in the unit of FEC symbols and m-bit respectively. When $n \le (2^m - 1)$, meaning that a packet size is less than that of a FEC codeword, $(1-p_e)$ is the probability that the number of corrupt symbols is less than or equal to $(t/2)$ out of n symbols. In RS algorithm, the FEC symbol size m determines the maximum number of FEC symbols $(2^m - 1)$ to protect called codeword and when one codeword contains t FEC code symbols, this codeword can maximally correct $(t/2)$ error symbols. When $n > (2^m - 1)$, p_{pkt_rec} is the probability that the number of contaminated symbols is not greater than $(t/2d)$ in each codeword since the packet is comprised of $d(= n/(2^m - 1))$ codewords and $(t/2)$ symbols are assumed to be equally distributed over d codewords. When d is not an integer, the remaining FEC code, $t - (d - 1) * \lfloor t/d \rfloor$ is allocated to the last codeword. Note that $\lfloor\rfloor$ is the floor operator truncating fractions.

$$1 - p_e = \begin{cases} \sum_{k=0}^{t/2} \binom{n}{k} (p_f)^k (1 - (p_f)^{n-k}) & \text{when } n \leq (2^m - 1). \\ \left(\sum_{k=0}^{t/2d} \binom{\frac{n}{d}}{k} (p_f)^k (1 - (p_f)^{\frac{n}{d}-k})\right)^d & \text{when } n > (2^m - 1). \end{cases} \quad (7)$$

4 Throughput Efficiency over WSN Channels

This section numerically calculates BI and BB Th_{eff} based on Gilbert model which we determine by matching CCDF of WSN channel run lengths or error burst lengths with that of Gilbert model. Note that burst and run lengths represent the number of successive bits in error and the number of successive bits in no error respectively. For deriving the analytical model, traffic traces are collected from sensor networks where a sender continuously transmits 80-byte packets with the speed of 1.28 kbps to its receiver which is 10-meter apart on line-of-sight. Based on these traces, we determine p_{bad} and p_{good} of Gilbert model to produce its average BER and CCDF of run lengths as close as to those of real traces. The similarity of two CCDF distributions is evaluated by LMS (Least Mean Square) error.

Figure 2 compares four throughput efficiency; BI_{mod} and BB_{mod} evaluated by our model over 15 Gilbert models, and $\text{BB}_{\text{prv-unf}}$ and $\text{BB}_{\text{prv-GM}}$ computed by the previous model [3] over uniform distributions and Gilbert models respectively. In Figure 2, Th_{eff} is normalized by the underlying physical channel spped 256 kbps and BER represents the average BER of 15 traces used for generating 15 Gilbert models. For the throughput computation, we assume a sensor network where 10 nodes constantly contend to send fixed-size packets with operational parameters specified in Table 1.

Table 1. Parameters for TIP50CM's PHY and 802.11e using FHSS

Parameter	value	Parameter	value
PHY data rate	256 kbps	Slot time (σ)	501μs
Frame size	80-byte	SIFS	281μs
PHY header	24-byte	DIFS	1281μs
ACK size	14-byte	EIFS	1.341ms
BREQ size	24-byte	TXOP limit	40ms
BACK size	152-byte	Number of node (n)	10
Propagation delay (δ)	1μs	τ	0.0373

Figure 2 confirms that BB_{mod} outperforms BI_{mod} by 107 % all the time since the BI overhead of sending individual ACKs is much greater than the BB ACK overhead while their recovery costs of packet losses in the block are the same. Note that since BACK distinctly notifies lost packets, BB only needs to send the lost packets not all the packets in the block like BI. It also indicates that $BB_{prv\text{-}unf}$ accomplishs much less by up-to 194 % than BB_{mod} since more packets tend to be contaminated in uniform distributions than bursty distributions at the same average BER. It finally observes that BB_{mod} even achieves slightly more efficiency than $BB_{prv\text{-}GM}$ due to the HOB effect. The collision time of BB_{mod} is much shorter than $BB_{prv\text{-}GM}$ since BB_{mod} stops the remaining packets once HOB is collided.

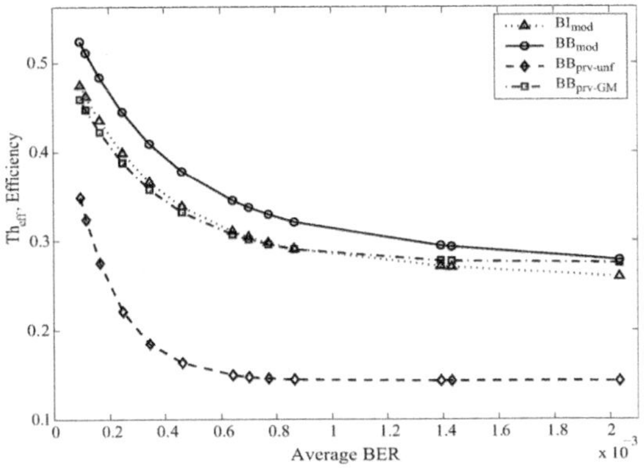

Fig. 2. Throughput efficiency as a function of the average BER

Figure 3 plots BB_{mod} throughput efficiency as a function of the average BER and the FEC code ratio to the total frame size. For Figure 3, FEC symbol size is fixed at 8-bit. It shows that our model predicts the tradeoff between the FEC

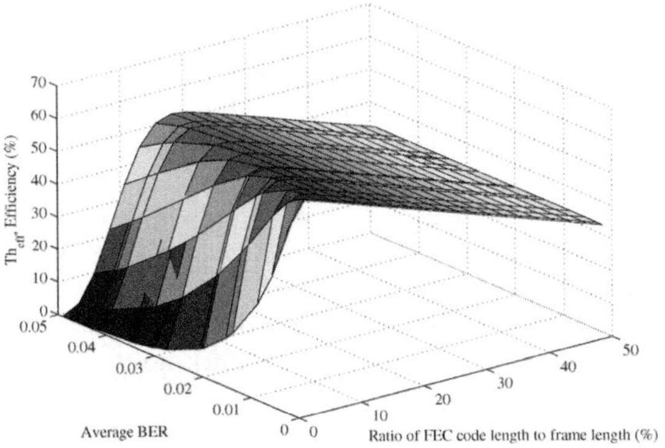

Fig. 3. BB_{mod} throughput efficiency

code size and the throughput efficiency in BB scheme. BB_{mod} Th_{eff} improves as the FEC ratio grows up until BER is equal to around $1.9 * 10^{-3}$ and after the optimal point monotonically deteriorates since the amount of FEC codes becomes excessive. It also indicates that Th_{eff} achieves the best performance of 64 % at $1.9 * 10^{-3}$ BER when the ratio of FEC codes is around 2.5 %.

5 Conclusions

This paper generalizes the evaluation model [3], [4] to evaluate the two basic burst transmission techniques with FEC codes over WSN channels. From comparing the throughput results of our model with the previous ones [3] and [4], we verify our extended model's validity. For the future research, we will validate our performance model's accuracy by implementing these two burst transmissions schemes in sensor nodes and measuring their throughput.

References

1. T. Dam and K. Langendoen, "An Adaptive Energy-Efficient MAC Protocol for Wireless Sensor Networks", ACM SenSys '03, pp. 171-180, Nov. 2003.
2. J. S. Ahn, S. W. Hong, and J. Heidemann, "An adaptive FEC code control algorithm for mobile wireless sensor networks", Journal of Communications and Networks, vol. 7, no. 4, pp. 489-499, Dec. 2005.
3. T. Li, Q. Ni, T. Turletti, and T. Xiao, "Performance Analysis of the IEEE 802.11e Block ACK Scheme in a Noisy Channel", IEEE BroadNets 2005, vol. 1, pp. 511-517, Oct. 2005.
4. I. Tinnirello, and S. Choi, "Efficiency Analysis of Burst Transmissions with Block ACK in Contention-Based 802.11e WLANs", ICC 2005, vol. 5, pp. 3455-3460, May. 2005.
5. W. Ye, J. Heidemann, and D. Estrin, "An Energy-Efficient MAC Protocol for Wireless Sensor Networks", INFOCOM, pp. 1567-1576, Jun. 2002.
6. G. Bianchi, "Performance analysis of the IEEE 802.11 distributed coordination function", IEEE Jounal on Selected Areas in Communications, vol. 18, no. 3, pp. 535-547, Mar. 2000.
7. H. Wu, Y. Peng, K. Long, S. Cheng, and J. Ma, "Performance of Reliable Transport Protocol over IEEE 802.11 Wireless LAN: Analysis and Enhancement", INFOCOM, vol. 2, pp. 599-607, Jun. 2002.
8. E. N. Gilbert. "Capacity of a burst-noise channel", Bell Syst. Tech. J., 39: 1253-1265, Sep. 1960.
9. J. S. Ahn, J. H. Yoon, and K. W. Lee, "Performance and Power Consumption Analysis of 802.11 with Reed-Solomon Code over Wireless Sensor Networks by Varying the FEC Symbol Size", Journal of Communications and Networks, under second revision, http://network.dongguk.ac.kr/publication/JCN-06.pdf
10. MAXFOR Corporation. Wireless sensor network node, http://www.maxfor.co.kr.

Efficient Location Management Scheme for Inter-MAP Movement Using M/G/1 Multi-class Queues in Hierarchical MIPv6*

Jonghyoun Choi, Teail Shin, and Youngsong Mun

School of Computer Science, Soongsil University,
Sangdo 5 Dong, Dongjak Gu, Seoul, Korea
{wide,nullx}@sunny.ssu.ac.kr, mun@comp.ssu.ac.kr

Abstract. Hierarchical Mobile IPv6 (HMIPv6) has been proposed to accommodate frequent mobility of an MN and reduce the signaling load in the Internet. In this paper, we propose hierarchical management scheme for Mobile IPv6 where MAP (Mobility Anchor Point) has priority queues for faster processing location update procedure in HMIPv6 system. The performance analysis and the numerical results presented in this paper show that our proposal has superior performance to the hierarchical Mobile IPv6.

1 Introduction

The Internet users have desire for high quality internet service at anywhere. The number of mobile device users worldwide continues to increase by growth of mobile device and wireless techniques. MIPv6 [1] proposed by IETF (Internet Engineering Task Force) provides a basic host mobility management scheme. In MIPv6, when an MN moves from home network to foreign network, it configures a new Care-of-Address (CoA) and requests the Home Agent (HA) to update its binding. This binding process requires high signaling load. Thus, Hierarchical Mobile IPv6 (HMIPv6) [2] has been proposed to accommodate frequent mobility of MNs and reduce the signaling load in the Internet. In HMIPv6, when an MN moves into new AR domain, MN may perform one or two types of binding update (BU) procedures: both the global binding update and the local binding update (inter-MAP) or only the local binding update (Intra-MAP). However, HMIPv6 focused on the intra-MAP domain handoff, not on the inter-MAP domain handoff [4], [8.] In this paper, we propose hierarchical management scheme for Mobile IPv6 where MAP has priority queues for processing binding procedure fast in HMIPv6 system.

2 Overview of Hierarchical Mobile IPv6 system [2]

The HMIPv6 protocol separates mobility management into intra-MAP domain mobility and inter-MAP domain mobility. A MAP in HMIPv6 treats the mobility

* This research was supported by the MIC(Ministry of Information and Communication), Korea, under the ITRC(Information Technology Research Center) support program supervised by the IITA(Institute of Information Technology Advancement)" (IITA-2006-C1090-0603-0040).

Y.-H. Lee et al. (Eds.): ICESS 2007, LNCS 4523, pp. 765–772, 2007.

management inside a domain. Thus, when an MN moves around the sub-networks within a single domain, the MN sends a BU message only to the current MAP. When the MN moves out of the domain or moves into another domain, Mobile IPv6 is invoked to handle the mobility.

In HMIPv6, when an MN moves into new AR domain, the MN may perform one or two types of BU procedures: either both the global binding update and the local binding update (intra-MAP) or only the local binding update (Inter-MAP). A MAP is a router located in a network visited by the MN. A MAP provides the localized mobility management for the visiting MNs. One or more MAPs can exist within a visited network.

In HMIPv6, the MN has two addresses, a Regional CoA (RCoA) on the MAP's link and an on-link CoA (LCoA). When a MN moves into a new MAP domain, it needs to configure two CoAs: an RCoA and LCoA. After forming the RCoA based on the network prefix in the MAP option received from MAP, the MN sends a local BU to the MAP. This BU procedure will bind the mobile node's RCoA to its LCoA. The MAP then is acting as a HA. Following a successful registration with the MAP, a bi-directional tunnel between the MN and the MAP is established. After registering with the MAP, the MN registers its new RCoA with it's HA by sending a BU that specifies the binding (RCoA, Home Address) as in Mobile IPv6. When the MN moves within the same MAP domain, it should only register its new LCoA with its MAP. In this case, the RCoA remains unchanged.

3 Proposed Scheme

In this paper, the MAP has priority queues for faster processing location update procedure. We give high priority to global binding update procedure which is relatively high cost against local binding update. Thus, we can reduce the cost of global binding update. Fig.2 shows procedure of the proposed scheme.

When an MN moves from AR1 to AR2, the procedure of proposed system is same to HMIPv6's. While, the MN moves into new MAP domain, the MN send new binding update message like Fig.3 with set P bit to "1." When the MAP receives this message, it enqueues this message into high priority queue. Thus the average waiting time of binding update procedure can be reduced. Fig.1 shows queue discipline in MAP. λ and μ denote arrival rate and departure rate, respectively.

Fig.3 shows new binding update message format for the proposed scheme. P bit is set to "1" when an MN moves into new MAP domain.

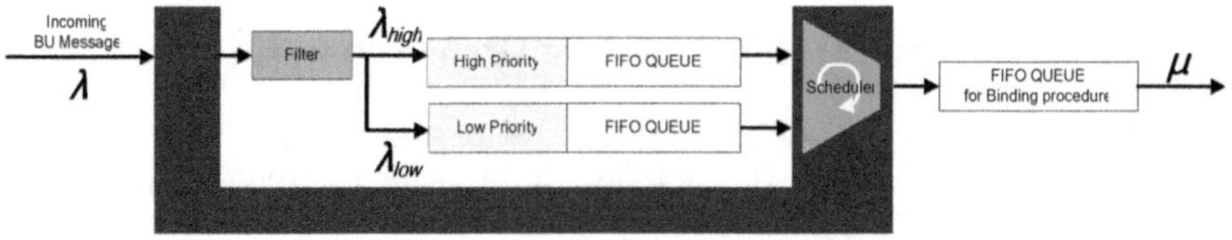

Fig. 1. M/G/1 non-preemptive Multi-class queues in MAP

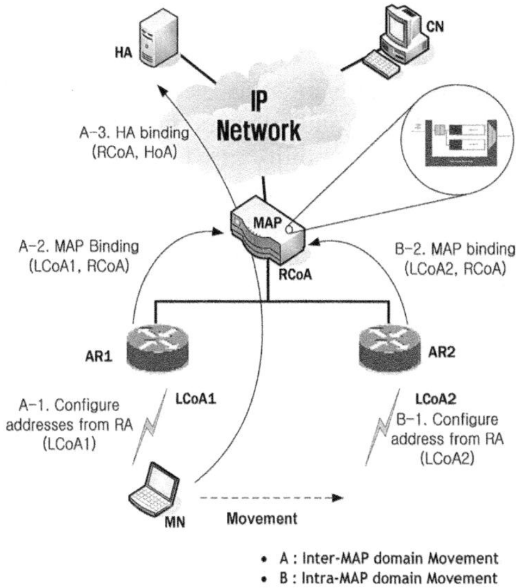

Fig. 2. Procedure of the proposed scheme

Bits 0–15 (0 1 2 3 4 5 6 7 8 9 0 1 2 3 4 5)	Bits 16–31 (6 7 8 9 0 1 2 3 4 5 6 7 8 9 0 1)
	Sequence #
A H L K M P Reserved	Lifetime
Mobility options	
:	

Fig. 3. New binding update message format for the proposed scheme

4 Performance Analysis

4.1 Mobility Model

In this paper, we use hexagonal cellular network model, as shown in Fig. 4. Each MAP domain is assumed to consist of the same number of Range Rings, ***R***. The center cell is innermost cell 0. The cells labeled by 1 form the first Range Ring around cell "0," the cells labeled by 2 formed the second Range Ring around cell 1 and so on.

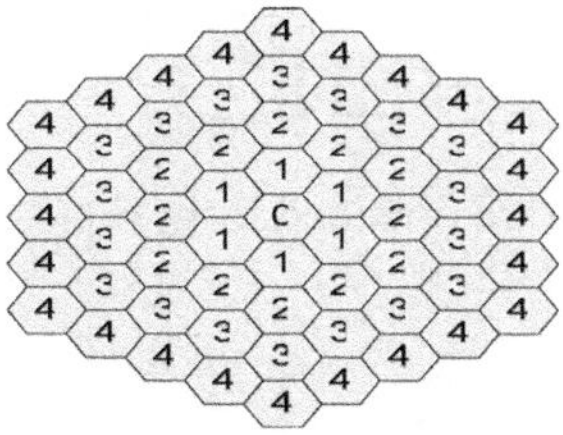

Fig. 4. Hexagonal cellular network architecture

In terms of user mobility model, Random-Walk mobility model is taken into consideration as commonly used mobility model. The Random-Walk model is appropriate for pedestrian movements where mobility is generally confined to a limited geographical area such as residential and business buildings [4].

In terms of Random-Walk mobility model, we consider the two-dimensional Markov chain model used in [5]. In this model, the next position of an MN is equal to the previous position plus a random variable whose value is drawn independently from an arbitrary distribution [5]. In addition, an MN moves to another cell area with a probability of $1-q$ and remains in the current cell with probability q. In the cellular architecture shown in Fig. 4, if an MN is located in a cell of Range Ring r ($r > 0$), the probabilities of movement resulted in an increase or a decrease in the distance from the center cell are given by

$$p^+(r) = \frac{1}{3} + \frac{1}{6r} \text{ and } p^-(r) = \frac{1}{3} - \frac{1}{6r} \tag{1}$$

We define the state r of a Markov chain as the distance between the current cell of the MN and the center cell. This state is equivalent to the index of a Range Ring where the MN is located. As a result, the MN is said to be in state r if it is currently residing in Range Ring r. The transition probabilities $Outer_{r,r+1}$ and $Inner_{r,r-1}$ represent the probabilities of the distance of the MN from the center cell increasing or decreasing, respectively. They are given as follows:

$$Outer_{r,r+1} = \begin{cases} (1-q) & \text{if } r = 0 \\ (1-q)p^+(r) & \text{if } 1 \le r \le R \end{cases} \tag{2}$$

$$Inner_{r,r-1} = (1-q)p^-(r) \quad \text{if } 1 \le r \le R \tag{3}$$

where q is the probability that an MN remains in the current cell.

Let $P_{r,R}$ be the steady-state probability of state r within a MAP domain consisting of R Range Rings. As Eq.(2) and Eq.(3), $P_{r,R}$ can be expressed in terms of the steady state probability $P_{0,R}$ as follows:

$$P_{r,R} = P_{0,R} \prod_{i=0}^{r-1} \frac{Outer_{i,i+1}}{Inner_{i+1,i}} \quad \text{for } 1 \le r \le R \tag{4}$$

With the requirement $\sum_{r=0}^{R} P_{r,R} = 1$, $P_{r,R}$ can be expressed by

$$P_{0,R} = \frac{1}{1 + \sum_{r=1}^{R} \prod_{i=0}^{r-1} \frac{Outer_{i,i+1}}{Inner_{i+1,i}}} \tag{5}$$

where $Outer_{r,r+1}$ and $Inner_{r,r-1}$ are obtained from Eq.(3) and Eq.(4)

4.2 Location Update Cost

Fig.5 shows system model of proposed scheme. Alphabet means hop distance between nodes. In the IP networks, the signaling cost is proportional to the hop distance of two network entities.

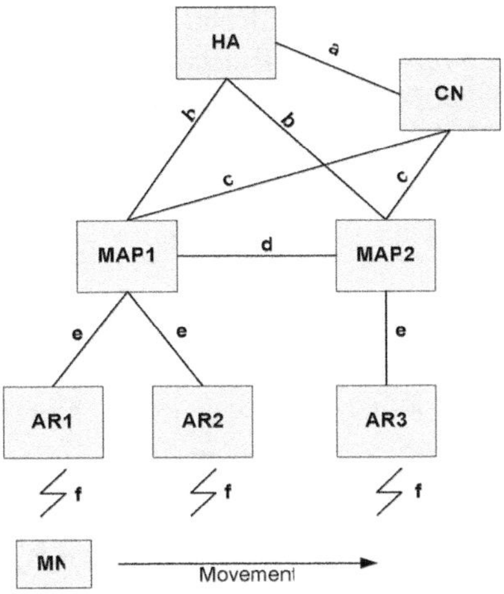

Fig. 5. System model of proposed scheme

In terms of the Random-Walk mobility model, the probability that an MN performs a global binding update is as follows:

$$P_{R,R} \cdot Outer_{r,r+1} \tag{6}$$

Specifically, if a MN is located in Range Ring $\boldsymbol{R}$, the boundary ring of a MAP domain composed of R Range Rings, and performs a movement from Range Ring $\boldsymbol{R}$ to Range Ring $\boldsymbol{R}$ + 1. The MN then performs the global binding update procedure. In other cases, except this movement, the MN only performs a local binding update procedure. Hence, the location update cost ($\boldsymbol{C_{LU}}$) of normal and proposed scheme ($\boldsymbol{C_{newLU}}$) can be expressed as follows:

$$C_{LU} = P_{R,R} \cdot Outer_{r,r+1} \cdot C_{LU-global} + (1 - P_{R,R} \cdot Outer_{r,r+1}) \cdot C_{LU-local} \tag{7}$$

$$C_{newLU} = P_{R,R} \cdot Outer_{r,r+1} \cdot C_{newLU-global} + (1 - P_{R,R} \cdot Outer_{r,r+1}) \cdot C_{newLU-local} \tag{8}$$

In HMIPv6, the MN has two addresses, an RCoA on the MAP's link and an on-link CoA (LCoA). When a MN moves into a new MAP domain, it needs to configure two CoAs: an RCoA on the MAP's link and an on-link CoA (LCoA). After forming the RCoA based on the prefix received in the MAP option, the mobile node sends a local BU to the MAP. This BU procedure will bind the mobile node's RCoA to its LCoA. The MAP then is acting as a HA. Following a successful registration with the MAP, a bi-directional tunnel between the MN and the MAP is established. After registering with the MAP, the MN registers its new RCoA with it's HA by sending a BU that specifies the binding (RCoA, Home Address) as in Mobile IPv6. When the mobile node moves within the same MAP domain, it should only register its new LCoA with its MAP. In this case, the RCoA remains unchanged.

When a MN moves into new AR domain, MN may perform one or two types of binding update procedures: both the global binding update and the local binding update or only the local binding update. $\boldsymbol{C_{LU\text{-}global}}$, $\boldsymbol{C_{LU\text{-}local}}$, $\boldsymbol{C_{newLU\text{-}global}}$ and $\boldsymbol{C_{newLU\text{-}local}}$

denote the signaling costs of the global and local binding update of HMIPv6 and proposed scheme, respectively. In the IP networks, the signaling cost is proportional to the distance of two network entities. $C_{LU\text{-}global}$, $C_{LU\text{-}local}$, $C_{newLU\text{-}global}$ and $C_{newLU\text{-}local}$ can be obtained from the below equations.

$$C_{LU-global} = 2\cdot(\kappa\cdot f+\tau\cdot(b+e))+2\cdot N_{CN}\cdot(\kappa\cdot f+\tau\cdot(c+e)) + (PC_{HA}+W_Q)+N_{CN}\cdot(PC_{CN}+W_Q)+(PC_{MAP}+W_Q)+C_l \tag{9}$$

$$C_{LU-local} = 2\cdot(\kappa\cdot f+\tau\cdot e)+(PC_{MAP}+W_Q) \tag{10}$$

$$C_{newLU-global} = 2\cdot(\kappa\cdot f+\tau\cdot(b+e))+2\cdot N_{CN}\cdot(\kappa\cdot f+\tau\cdot(c+e))+(PC_{HA}+W_Q) + N_{CN}\cdot(PC_{CN}+W_Q)+(PC_{MAP}+W_{Q(high)})+(C_{new-l}-W_{Q(low)}+W_{Q(high)}) \tag{11}$$

$$C_{newLU-local} = 2\cdot(\kappa\cdot f+\tau\cdot e)+PC_{MAP}+W_{Q(Low)} \tag{12}$$

where τ and κ are the unit transmission costs in a wired and a wireless link, respectively. As Fig. 5, ***b***, ***c***, ***e*** and ***f*** are the hop distance between nodes. PC_{HA}, PC_{CN} and PC_{MAP} are the processing costs for binding update procedures at the HA, the CN and the MAP, respectively. N_{CN} denotes the number of CNs which is communicating with the MN. W_Q denotes a waiting time for binding update messages in single-class queuing system. $W_{Q(high)}$ and $W_{Q(low)}$ denote a waiting time for binding update messages in the high class, the low class on multi-class queuing system, respectively. In proposed scheme, as we give high priority to global binding update procedure, we can reduce the cost of global binding update which is relatively high cost against local binding update. We use M/G/1 multi-class queuing system for analyzing the proposed scheme.

In M/G/1 system, we have a single server, an infinite waiting room, exponentially distributed inter-arrival times (with parameter λ) and an arbitrary service time distribution, for which at least the mean value μ and the standard deviation is known. The service discipline is FIFO and non-preemptive. In a non-preemptive system a service in progress is not interrupted. Following equations are about waiting time, W_Q, $W_{Q(high)}$ and $W_{Q(low)}$ [3.]

$$\lambda = \lambda_{high} + \lambda_{low} \tag{13}$$

$$W_Q = \frac{\lambda E(S^2)}{2[1-\lambda E(S)]} \tag{14}$$

$$W_{Q(high)} = \frac{\lambda E(S^2)}{2[1-\lambda_{high}E(S_{high})]} \tag{15}$$

$$W_{Q(low)} = \frac{\lambda E(S^2)}{2[1-\lambda_{high}E(S_{high})][1-\lambda_{high}E(S_{high})-\lambda_{low}E(S_{low})]} \tag{16}$$

where $E(S)$ and $E(S^2)$ are the first two moments of the service distribution.

5 Numerical Results

This section presents performance analysis of proposed scheme as compared with normal HMIPv6. The parameter values for the analysis were referenced from [6], [7] and [8.] They are shown in Table 1.

Table 1. Numerical simulation parameters for performance analysis

parameter	α	β	τ	K	a	b	c
value	0.1	0.2	1	2	6	6	4
parameter	d	e	f	N_{CN}	PC_{HA}	PC_{MAP}	PC_{CN}
Value	1	2	1	2	24	12	6

Fig.6 shows the variation in the global location update cost as the size of Range Ring($\boldsymbol{R}$). The global location update cost becomes less as the size of Range Ring($\boldsymbol{R}$)

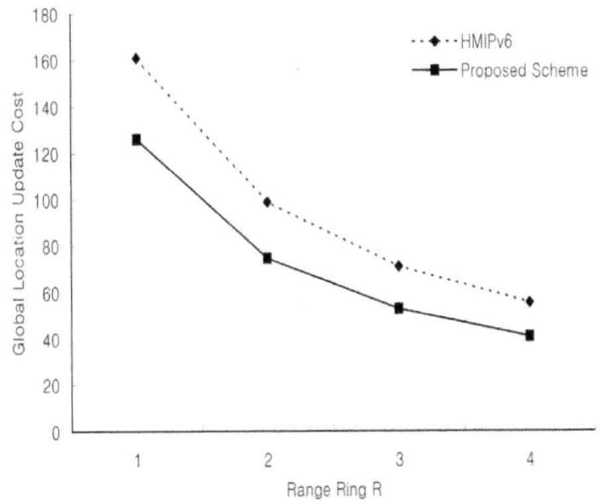

(a) q=0.2, λ=0.8, μ=2

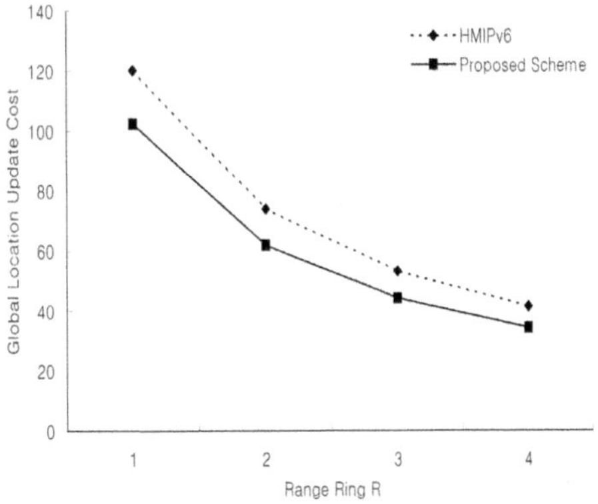

(b) q=0.4, λ=0.6, μ=2

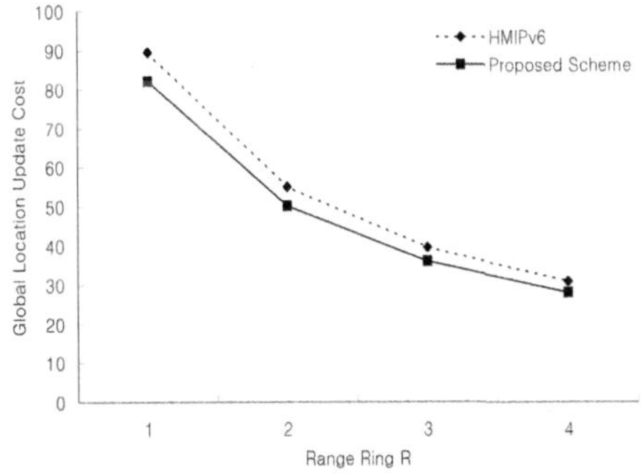

(c) q=0.6, λ=0.4, μ=2

Fig. 6. The Global location update cost as function of the radius of Range Ring ($\boldsymbol{R}$)

increases. The size of Range Ring(***R***) shrinks that means the frequency of global location update is high. Smaller ***q*** means that an MN moves frequently. To compare with other secure HMIPv6, proposed mechanism reduces the global location update cost by from 26% to 5% approximately.

6 Conclusions

HMIPv6 [2] has been proposed to accommodate frequent mobility of the mobile nodes and reduce the signaling load in the Internet. However, HMIPv6 focused on the intra-MAP domain handoff, not on the inter-MAP domain handoff [4]. We propose hierarchical management scheme for Mobile IPv6 where MAP has priority queues for processing location update procedure fast in hierarchical Mobile IPv6 networks. The performance analysis and the numerical results presented in this paper shows that our proposal has superior performance to HMIPv6. The proposed scheme reduces the global location update cost by from 26% to 5% approximately.

References

1. D. B. Johnson and C. E. Perkins, "Mobility support in IPv6," IETF RFC 3775, June, 2004.
2. H. Soliman, C. Castelluccia, K. El Malki, "Hierarchical Mobile IPv6 Mobility Management (HMIPv6)", RFC 4140, Aug. 2005.
3. Sheldon M. Ross, "Introduction to Probability Models," 8th Ed., Academic Press, 2003
4. Sangheon Pack and Yanghee Choi, "A study on performance of hierarchical mobile IPv6 in IP-based cellular networks," IEICE Transactions on Communications, vol. E87-B no. 3 pp.462-469, Mar. 2004
5. I.F. Akyildiz and W. Wang, "A dynamic location management scheme for next-generation multitier PCS systems," IEEE Trans. Wireless Commun., vol.1, no.1, pp.178–189, Jan. 2002.
6. M. Woo, "Performance analysis of mobile IP regional registration," IEICE Trans. Commun., vol.E86-B, no.2, pp.472–478, Feb. 2003.
7. X. Zhang, J.G. Castellanos, and A.T. Capbell, "P-MIP: Paging extensions for mobile IP," ACM Mobile Networks and Applications, vol.7, no.2, pp.127–141, 2002.
8. Jonghyoun choi and Youngsong Mun, "An Efficient Handoff Mechanism with Web Proxy MAP in Hierarchical Mobile IPv6," ICCSA2005, LNCS 3480, pp. 271-280, May 2005

A Scheme to Enhance TEBU Scheme of Fast Handovers for Mobile IPv6*

Seonggeun Ryu and Youngsong Mun

School of Computing, Soongsil University,
Sangdo 5 Dong Dongjak Gu, Seoul, Korea
sgryu@sunny.ssu.ac.kr, mun@computing.ssu.ac.kr

Abstract. In Mobile IPv6, a handover latency is an important issue. To reduce the handover latency, mipshop working group in IETF has studied the fast handovers for Mobile IPv6 (FMIPv6) which creates and verifies a new care-of address (NCoA) in advance before a layer 2 handover resulting in reduced handover latency. Then the paper which reduces delay of a binding update to a home agent (HA) is emerged, called the TEBU (Tentative and Early Binding Update) scheme. This scheme can reduce handover latency, since the NCoA is registered to the HA during the layer 2 handover of FMIPv6. Additionally, if Return Routability (RR) procedure which introduces long delay is performed in advance like the TEBU scheme, the handover latency may be reduced significantly. Therefore, we propose an enhanced TEBU (eTEBU) scheme that the binding update (BU) and RR procedure are started during the layer 2 handover. The BU message and the messages for RR procedure are transferred through a fast binding update message (FBU) of FMIPv6. We perform analysis of handover latency for the performance evaluation. As a result, we found that the eTEBU scheme guarantees lower handover latency than the TEBU scheme and FMIPv6.

1 Introduction

As demand for the wireless Internet access services and mobility support is increasing dramatically, the Internet engineering task force (IETF) has standardized Mobile IPv6 (MIPv6) [1]. MIPv6 supports maintaining an IP address of a mobile node (MN) while changing its point of Internet attachment. Hence, the MN can be reachable and maintain ongoing connections to correspondents. In MIPv6, when the MN changes a point of Internet attachment, it needs a certain process called a handover, which causes a long delay problem. The delay during handover process is called the handover latency. To reduce the handover latency of MIPv6, mipshop working group in IETF has studied fast handovers for Mobile IPv6 (FMIPv6) [2]. The handover latency has been reduced through this new protocol. FMIPv6 creates and verifies a new care-of address (NCoA) in advance before a layer 2 handover. Also, the tentative and early binding update

* This work was supported by grant No. (R01-2004-000-10618-0) from the Basic Research Program of the Korea Science & Engineering Foundation.

Y.-H. Lee et al. (Eds.): ICESS 2007, LNCS 4523, pp. 773–782, 2007.

(TEBU) [3] scheme is emerged. The TEBU scheme reduces the handover latency for registration delay to a home agent (HA).

In FMIPv6, the handover latency is shorter than the one of MIPv6, since address test is performed before the layer 2 handover. Also, packets from a correspondent node (CN) to the MN are not lost during the handover, because a tunnel is established between a previous access router (PAR) and a new access router (NAR) and the NAR buffers packets destined to the MN. However, In FMIPv6, a registration delay of an NCoA is still long. To reduce the registration delay for the MN's IP address, the TEBU scheme is proposed. A binding update (BU) message to the HA is encapsulated in a fast binding update (FBU) message of FMIPv6 and is delivered before the layer 2 handover.

Additionally, if Return Routability (RR) procedure which introduces long delay is performed in advance like the TEBU scheme, the handover latency may be reduced significantly. Therefore, we propose an enhanced TEBU (eTEBU) scheme that the binding update and RR procedure are started before the layer 2 handover in FMIPv6. The BU message and the messages for RR procedure are transferred through the FBU message of FMIPv6. The messages for RR procedure are a home test init (HoTI) and a care-of test init (CoTI) messages. These messages encapsulated in the FBU message are forwarded to the NAR through a handover initiate (HI) message of FMIPv6. The NAR sends the BU and HoTI messages to the HA and sends the CoTI message to the CN, if it verifies the NCoA successfully. The HA receives the BU message and registers the NCoA with a binding cache entry (BCE) in the HA. Then, the HoTI message is forwarded to the CN.

By using the eTEBU scheme, the registration delay to the HA and CN can be reduced, since the registration process with the HA and RR procedure are started before the layer 2 handover.

The rest of this paper is organized as follows: in section 2, FMIPv6 and the TEBU scheme are presented as related works. The eTEBU scheme is proposed in section 3, and in section 4, the eTEBU scheme is evaluated through analysis of the handover latency. Finally, in section 5, we conclude discussion with future study.

2 Related Works

2.1 Fast Handovers for Mobile IPv6 (FMIPv6)

In FMIPv6, there are two modes, such as predictive and reactive mode. In this paper, we only explain and use the predictive mode for simplicity of schemes. In FMIPv6, several portions of the layer 3 handover are performed prior to the layer 2 handover. In other words, the MN performs the layer 3 handover while it is connected to a PAR, and in this case, the PAR must have known information about destined AR. The PAR establishes a tunnel between itself and a NAR, and then verifies the MN's NCoA by exchanging a handover initiate (HI) message and a handover acknowledge (HAck) message. Packets that arrive at previous care-of address (PCoA) are forwarded to the NAR through an established tunnel during the handover. The tunnel is kept until the MN's NCoA is registered to a HA. Fig. 1 shows the message flow of FMIPv6.

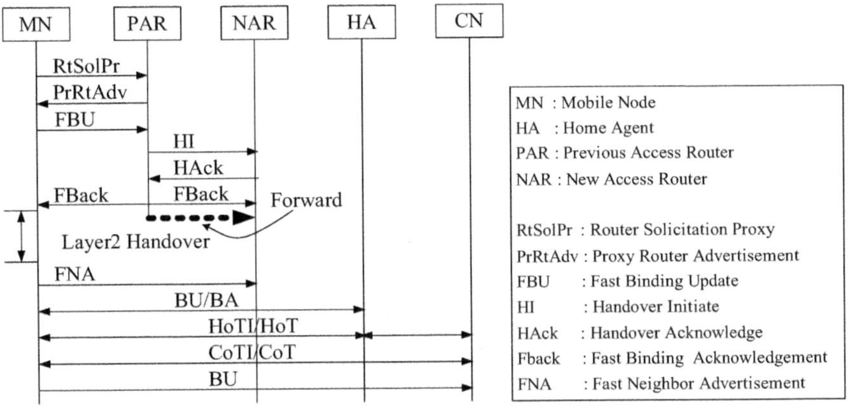

Fig. 1. The message flow of FMIPv6

The MN initiates FMIPv6 when the layer 2 trigger take places. The MN sends a router solicitation for proxy (RtSolPr) message to the PAR and receives a proxy router advertisement (PrRtAdv) messages with information of the NAR. The MN creates the NCoA and sends a FBU message with the NCoA. When the PAR receives the FBU message, it sends a HI message and receives a HAck message in order to verify the NCoA in the NAR and to establish a tunnel between the PAR and the NAR. The PAR sends a fast binding acknowledge (FBack) messages to the MN and the NAR, respectively, after verification of the NCoA. The MN performs the layer 2 handover when it receives the FBack message. The MN sends a fast neighbor advertisement (FNA) message to NAR to inform its movement after the layer 2 handover. Then the MN registers the NCoA to the HA and the CN. To register to the CN, Return Routability (RR) procedure used to establish a security association between the MN and the CN is needed [4]. RR procedure consists of a home test init (HoTI) / a home test (HoT) and a care-of test init (CoTI) / a care-of test (CoT) messages [1]. After the registration, the handover is finished.

2.2 The TEBU Scheme

The TEBU scheme has enhanced FMIPv6 by performing the registration with the HA during the layer 2 handover. In the TEBU, hence, the registration latency of the NCoA is reduced. It is assumed that the BU lifetime is limited by 3 seconds referred to [5] to avoid a false binding, such as a ping-pong condition. This BU message is transferred encapsulated in the FBU message. The BU message is forwarded through the PAR to the NAR. The NAR sends the BU message to the HA after verification of the NCoA.

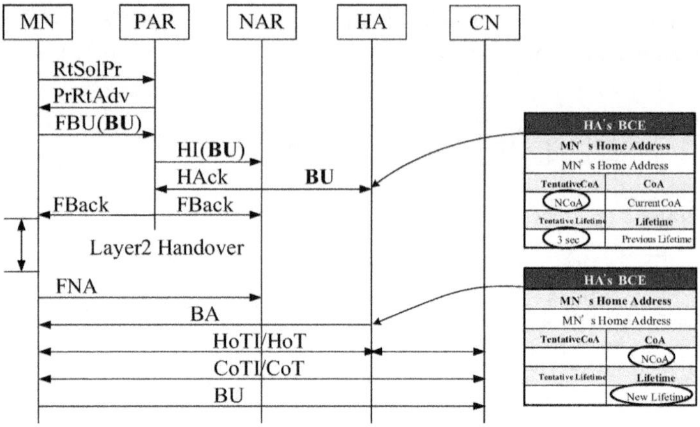

Fig. 2. The message flow of the TEBU scheme

The message flow of the TEBU scheme refers to FMIPv6 except the BU message. In the TEBU scheme, dual CoA fields (CoA and tentative CoA fields) in a binding cache entry (BCE) are defined. If the HA receives the tentative BU message, then it stores the CoA with the tentative CoA field. Also, if the HA receives a general BU message, then it store the CoA with the CoA field and the tentative CoA field is cleared. If the tentative CoA field of the BCE is not empty, then the HA forwards packets to an IP address of tentative CoA field. If is not, then the HA forwards packets to an address of the CoA field.

3 The Proposed Scheme (eTEBU)

During the handover, An MN cannot communicate with the CN directly. This handover latency is a critical problem for delay sensitive real-time applications, such as voice over IP (VoIP) which require seamless handover and short latency. Hence, to reduce the handover latency, FMIPv6 and the TEBU scheme are emerged. Two schemes, however, do not consider the registration delay with the CN which consists of RR procedure. Therefore, we propose a scheme (eTEBU) based on the TEBU scheme. The base of the eTEBU scheme is similar to the TEBU scheme. When the FBU message is transferred, the HoTI and CoTI messages of RR procedure as well as the BU message are encapsulated in it. These messages encapsulated in the FBU message are transferred and processed during the layer 2 handover. After the layer 2 handover, the MN will receive a BA message and HoT and CoT messages. Hence, the MN sends a BU message to the CN for registration. After that, the MN can communicate with the CN directly. Figure 3 shows the message flow of the eTEBU scheme.

In Fig. 3, after the NAR verifies the MN's NCoA, it sends the BU and HoTI messages to the HA and the CoTI message to the CN, respectively. The HA responds to the BU message with the BA message, and forwards the HoTI

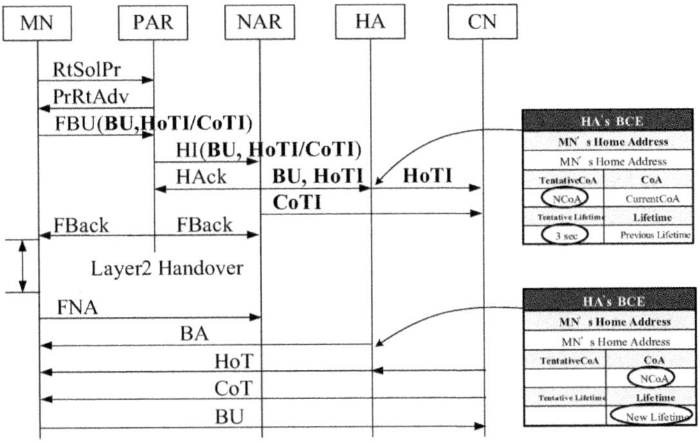

Fig. 3. The message flow of the eTEBU scheme

message to the CN. The CN responds to the HoTI and CoTI messages with the HoT and CoT messages, respectively. The eTEBU scheme can considerably reduce the handover latency compared with FMIPv6 and the TEBU scheme, since the transmission delay of RR procedure decreases.

4 Performance Evaluations

In this section we make a comparison between FMIPv6, TEBU, and eTEBU handover procedures in terms of handover latency. The handover latency consists of the link-layer (L2) switching delay and the layer 3 signaling delay. We define a period of handover latency between the moment the L2 triggers are received (i.e. sending the RtSolPr message) and the moment of completing Route Optimization mode, under various conditions. For simplicity we consider the model illustrated in Fig. 4 referring to [6].

The following notations are used: The delay between the MN and the AR is t_s, which is the time to send a message over the subnet via a wireless link. The delay of layer 2 handover is t_{L2}, which is link layer establishment delay. The delay between the MN and its home network (HA) is assumed to be t_h, which is the time necessary for a message to be delivered to the home network. The delay between the PAR and the NAR is assumed to be t_{pn}. The delay between the MN and the CN is t_{mc}. The delay between the MN's home network and the CN is t_{hc}. In this paper we only consider the scenario where the CN is in its home network, although the CN is an MN.

In general, we can assume $t_s < t_h$ and that the processing and queuing times are negligible, since these times are much shorter than above times [7].

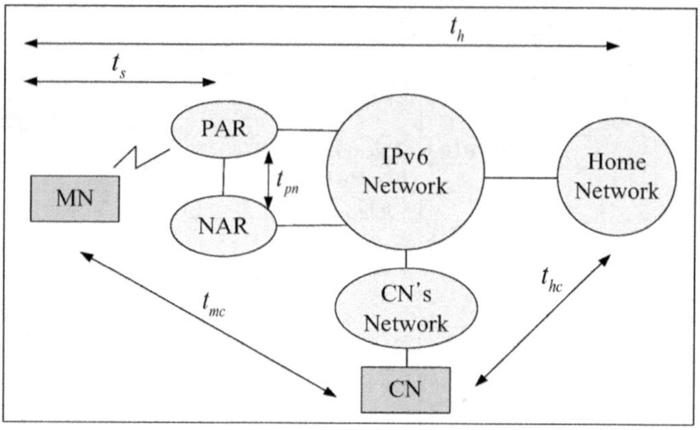

Fig. 4. A simple model for analysis

4.1 Analysis of FMIPv6

We analyze the TEBU scheme referring to Fig. 1. In FIMPv6, several messages are exchanged between the MN, the PAR, and the NAR before the layer 2 handover. This period during transferring the messages is denoted by T_{fast}, which consists of transmission delays for the RtSolPr, PrRtAdv, FBU, HI, Hack, FBack messages. The transmission delay of this period is given by

$$T_{fast} = 2t_s + t_s + 2t_{pn} + t_s. \tag{1}$$

After T_{fast}, the layer 2 handover is performed to establish the link layer connection (t_{L2}). Once the MN attaches the new network, it sends the FNA message. Then the MN perform the registration procedure with the HA and the CN. This period is denoted by $T_{reg.}$, which consists of transmission delays for the FNA, BU/BA messages with the HA, HoTI/HoT, CoTI/CoT, BU messages with the CN. Transmission delay of RR procedure is $max(2(t_h + t_{hc}), 2t_{mc})$, since HoTI/HoT and CoTI/CoT messages are exchanged simultaneously. The transmission delay of the registration procedure is given by

$$T_{reg.} = t_{L2} + t_s + 2t_h + max(2(t_h + t_{hc}), 2t_{mc}) + t_{mc}. \tag{2}$$

Therefore, handover latency of FMIPv6 is the sum of Eq. (1) and (2), and is equal to

$$T_{FMIPv6} = t_{L2} + 5t_s + 2t_{pn} + 2t_h + max(2(t_h + t_{hc}), 2t_{mc}) + t_{mc}. \tag{3}$$

4.2 Analysis of the TEBU Scheme

We analyze the TEBU scheme referring to Fig. 2. Since this scheme is based on FMIPv6, T_{fast} of this scheme is equal to one of FMIPv6. In this scheme, the BU message to HA is transferred encapsulated in the FBU message. The

BU message is sent to the HA, when the NAR verify the NCoA. That is, the registration with the HA is performed during the layer 2 handover. Then, other messages for the registration are exchanged after the layer 2 handover. Hence,

$$T_{reg.} = max(t_{L2}, 2(t_h - t_s)) + t_s + max(2(t_h + t_{hc}), 2t_{mc}) + t_{mc}. \quad (4)$$

Therefore, handover latency of the TEBU scheme is sum of Eq. (1) and (4), and is equal to

$$T_{TEBU} = 5t_s + 2t_{pn} + max(t_{L2}, 2(t_h - t_s)) + max(2(t_h + t_{hc}), 2t_{mc}) + t_{mc}. \quad (5)$$

4.3 Analysis of the Enhanced TEBU (eTEBU) Scheme

We analyze the eTEBU scheme referring to Fig. 3. T_{fast} of this scheme is also equal to one of FMIPv6, since this scheme is based on FMIPv6. In this scheme, the HoTI and CoTI messages of RR procedure as well as the BU message to HA are transferred encapsulated in the FBU message. The BU and HoTI message is sent to the HA and the CoTI message is sent to the CN, when the NAR verify the NCoA. That is the registration with the HA and RR procedure is performed during the layer 2 handover. In this case, the transmission delay of RR procedure is $max(2(t_h - t_s + t_{hc}), 2(t_{mc} - t_s))$. Hence, we calculate $T_{reg.}$ as

$$T_{reg.} = max(t_{L2}, 2(t_h - t_s), max(2(t_h - t_s + t_{hc}), 2(t_{mc} - t_s))) + t_s + t_{mc}. \quad (6)$$

Therefore, handover latency of the eTEBU scheme is sum of Eq. (1) and (6), and is equal to

$$T_{eTEBU} = 5t_s + 2t_{pn} + max(t_{L2}, 2(t_h - t_s + t_{hc}), 2(t_{mc} - t_s))) + t_{mc}. \quad (7)$$

4.4 Numerial Results

In this section we present some results based on the above analysis. In the first two figures (the (a) and (b) in Fig. 5), we assume $t_s = 10ms$, considering relatively low bandwidth in the wireless link [6]. On the other hand, the delay between the wired foreign networks is relatively short due to high bandwidth; thus, t_{pn} is assumed to be 4 ms [8]. Furthermore, we assume that processing time in each entity is negligible since it normally takes less than 1 ms [9]. The layer 2 handover briefly consists of two phase, a search phase and execution phase. In FMIPv6, to reduce handover latency the search phase is performed in advance. Hence, the execution phase is only performed during the layer 2 handover [10], and then $t_{L2} = 7.1$ [11].

We take into consideration four configurations. In the first one, the MN is located in its home network and connected via a wireless link, while the CN's distance from the MN varies. In the second one, the MN and CN are close to each other, while the distance between the MN and its home network varies. In the third and last configuration, we plot the results while we vary the wireless link delay and layer 2 link-switching delay.

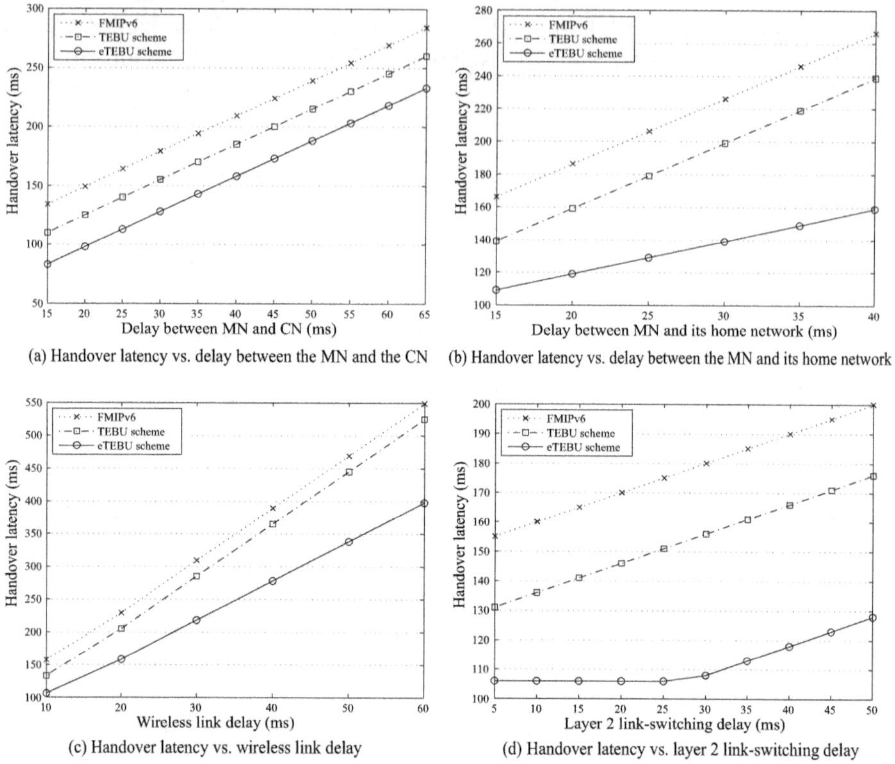

Fig. 5. Numerical results

The (a) in Fig. 5 shows the handover latency as the delay from the MN to the CN, t_{mc}, increases. Here we assume that the MN is located in its home network ($t_h = 12ms$). Obviously, $t_h + t_{hc} = t_{mc}$ in this case.

The (b) in Fig. 5 shows the handover latency as the delay from the MN to the MN's home network, t_h, increases. Here the MN and CN are assumed to be close: $t_{mc} = 17ms$. (Since the wireless link delay is 10 ms, and the MN is connected via wireless links, and the CN is connected to another domain, we believe 17 ms is sufficiently small with this configuration [7].) Also, we assume that the delay between the MN's home network and the CN is fixed, $t_{hc} = 12ms$.

The third experiments show the impact of the low-bit-rate wireless link on the handover latency. The (c) in Fig. 5 shows the handover latency as the message transmission delay over the wireless link increases. Note that this delay also applies to the wireless link to the CN. The basic configuration is the same as that of the first experiment (The (a) in Fig. 5); that is, the MN is in its home network. Also, we assume that the MN and CN are at a moderate distance ($t_{mc} = t_s + 10ms$). As the wireless link delay increases, the overall signaling delay to handle handoff considerably increases.

The last experiments show the impact of the layer 2 link-switching delay. The basic configuration is the same as that of the first experiment. The (d) in Fig. 5 shows the handover latency as the layer 2 link-switching delay increases. In this figure, the handover latency of eTEBU scheme is lower than the others while $t_{L2} <$ delay of RR procedure. This is because RR procedure is performed during layer 2 handover.

Shown in Fig. 5, the eTEBU scheme considerably reduces the handover latency. This is because of performing RR procedure during the layer 2 handover, while RR procedure introduces a long delay.

5 Conclusions

A handover process occurs when an MN moves between networks in MIPv6. This handover process introduce a long delay which the MN cannot send or receive packets. this process is called the handover latency. FMIPv6 has been standardized to reduce the handover latency. Also, the TEBU scheme is emerged to reduce the registration delay with an HA. These schemes reduce the handover latency; however, RR procedure still introduces a long delay. Therefore, we propose an enhanced TEBU (eTEBU) scheme which RR procedure as well as the registration is performed during the layer 2 handover in FMIPv6.

We have evaluated the performance of the eTEBU scheme in terms of handover latency. We have shown that the eTEBU scheme reduces the handover latency more than FMIPv6 and the TEBU scheme through the performance evaluation. That is, the eTEBU scheme may be more appropriate for real-time applications than the existing schemes.

Currently, FMIPv6 was standardized in IETF. The eTEBU scheme can help improve the performance of FMIPv6. Therefore, when eTEBU scheme is used with FMIPv6, a performance of the handover process will be improved.

References

1. Johnson, D., Perkins, C., and Arkko, J.: Mobility Support in IPv6, RFC 3775 (2004)
2. Koodli, R.: Fast Handovers for Mobile IPv6, RFC 4068 (2005)
3. Ryu, S. and Mun, Y.: The Tentative and Early Binding Update for Mobile IPv6 Fast Handover, LNCS 3794, (2005) 825-835
4. Nikander, P., Arkko, J., Aura, T., Montenegro, G., and Nordmark, E.: Mobile IP Version 6 Route Optimization Security Design Background, RFC 4225 (2005)
5. Vogt, C., Bless, R., Doll, M.: Early Binding Updates for Mobile IPv6, work in progress (2004)
6. Kwon, T., Gerla, M., Das, S., and Das, S.: Mobility Management for VoIP Service: Mobile IP vs. SIP, IEEE Wireless Communications (2002) 66-75
7. Fathi, H., Prasad, R., and Chakraborty, S.: Mobility Management for VoIP in 3G Systems: Evaluation of Low-Latency Handoff Schemes, IEEE Wireless Communications (2005) 96-104

8. Hernandez, E. and Helal, A.: Examining Mobile-IP Performance in Rapidly Mobile Environments: The Case of a Commuter Train, 26th Annual IEEE Conf. Local Comp. Net., (2001)
9. Perkins, C. and Wang, Kuang-Yeh: Optimized Smooth Handoffs in Mobile IP, Intl. Symp. Comp. Commun. (1999) 340-346
10. McCann, P.: Mobile IPv6 Fast Handovers for 802.11 Networks, RFC 4260 (2005)
11. Vatn, J.: An experimental study of IEEE 802.11b handover performance and its effect on voice traffic, SE Telecommunication Systems Laboratory Department of Microelectronics and Information Technology (IMIT) (2003)

Network-Adaptive Selection of Transport Error Control (NASTE) for Video Streaming over Embedded Wireless System

SungTae Moon and JongWon Kim

Networked Media Lab., Department of Information and Communications,
Gwangju Institute of Science and Technology (GIST), Gwangju, 500-712, Korea
{stmoon,jongwon}@nm.gist.ac.kr

Abstract. The wireless networking is embedded into a wide variety of common devices. In many embedded networking situations, there have been increasing demands on the embedded wireless system for video streaming. However, it is inherently vulnerable to loss from dynamic wireless channel. In order to alleviate the effect of losses in the transport layer, the error control schemes are used. However, since each error control scheme shows different performance, a suitable scheme should be selected and applied. In this paper, we propose and implement a network-adaptive selection of transport error control (NASTE). To verify the feasibility of the proposed NASTE, we have implemented it in the embedded system which includes IEEE 802.11g WLAN environment. The experimental results indicate that the proposed mechanism can enhance the overall transport performance by recovering packet losses.

1 Introduction

With the advancement of embedded wireless networking technologies, there have been ever-increasing demands on the video streaming. However, video quality at the streaming client is degraded seriously due to losses caused by the unstable wireless channel. In order to offer video streaming with good quality over the hostile WLAN environments, an error control scheme is required. Traditional systems have been using two general error control schemes on the link layer. However, since the schemes cannot recover all packet losses, the error control in an upper layer is essential to recover the residual lost packets. For the residual error recovery, packet-level FEC or delay-constrained ARQ is used. To alleviate the burst packet losses, we can use interleaving with packet-level FEC. However, each error control scheme has different effects according to the application and channel status [1]. To improve the performance of error recovery, the hybrid scheme that combines several schemes has been proposed.

Many researchers have tried to minimize packet losses by using a hybrid error control scheme. This hybrid scheme alleviates disadvantages of ARQ and FEC [2]~ [4]. [2] presents a hybrid ARQ that transmits redundant packets when only receiver requests retransmission after sending original packets. However,

Y.-H. Lee et al. (Eds.): ICESS 2007, LNCS 4523, pp. 783–790, 2007.

since the scheme always waits response from receiver, unnecessary delay is required. [3] presents a switching scheme among ARQ, FEC, and hybrid ARQ. This scheme considers playback buffer status and packet loss rate. However, it does not provide a solution for burst packet losses. [4] proposes a low-delay interleaving scheme which uses the playback buffer as a part of interleaving memory. In this case, the interleaving scheme does not increase the delay significantly and the memory requirement is limited by the amount that is imposed by the video encoder. Although this scheme has a solution of burst packet losses, unnecessary usage of interleaving scheme still causes considerable delay. In addition, most existing schemes prove their performance through simulations. It may be able to provide guideline on the expected performance. However, it is subject to discrepancy when it is applied to real-world environment. In addition, traditional schemes depend on feedback message to measure the channel status. However, the feedback method has limitation that does not exactly represent the wireless channel condition. This is because the feedback message only reflects passive observation of underlying wireless network condition.

This paper proposes and implements network-adaptive selection of transport error control (NASTE) that selects or combines error control mode according to application and channel status. NASTE improves efficiency of mode switching and memory utility by using a shared buffer. In order to measure the status, the proposed mechanism uses end-to-end monitoring (E2EM) and cross-layer monitoring (CLM). To verify the feasibility of the proposed NASTE mechanism in the embedded system, we have implemented it while minimizing memory usage by using VideoLAN [5] and evaluate the transport performance through MPEG-2 video streaming over a real IEEE 802.11g WLAN testbed.

The remaining part of this paper is organized as follows. Section 2 describes the architecture of the proposed NASTE mechanism. Section 3 provides the details of the proposed NASTE mechanism. Section 4 explains how to change error control mode. The experimental results are presented in Section 5 and followed by the conclusion in Section 6.

2 Architecture Overview

The proposed NASTE mechanism focuses on how to increase the packet loss recovery while utilizing bandwidth efficiently and minimizing delay. For this target, various error control schemes, so-called error control modes (e.g., packet-level FEC, delay-constrained ARQ, interleaving, and their hybrid schemes) are used. In order to select a suitable error control mode, the proposed mechanism measures both application and channel status through E2EM and CLM. Before explaining the proposed NASTE mechanism further, let us review several assumptions to make the NASTE implementation feasible. 1) We assume that the proposed NASTE mechanism is used for single hop. 2) The available bandwidth is assumed to be sufficient so that the required capacity for error control can be covered. 3) Packet loss rate is limited by 60%. 4) The de-jittering buffer tolerates delay jitter caused by interleaving whose maximum depth is 10.

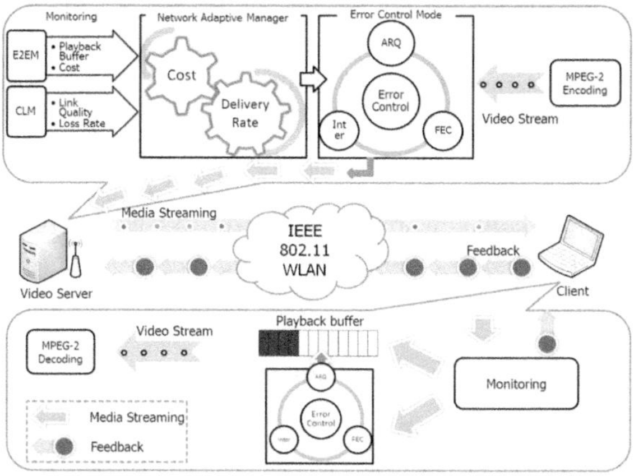

Fig. 1. The proposed NASTE architecture

Fig. 1 illustrates the proposed NASTE architecture. The proposed NASTE mechanism is roughly divided into a monitoring, a network-adaptive manager, and an error control mode parts. Since the mechanism works on transport layer, the proposed NASTE can apply to any application regardless to characteristics of the application. In monitoring part, NASTE monitors the packet loss rate and the playback buffer status through E2EM. For channel status, link quality is monitored through CLM. Since the previous feedback information is applied to select the current error control mode, the period of the feedback is a sensitive factor which affects the performance directly. The network-adaptive manager is designed to select an error control mode after checking available modes based on application and channel status. For the mode switching, packet delivery rate and cost are utilized. Once the error control mode is selected, media packets are encoded and transported in the error control mode part. At the same time, the receiver continually monitors and stores the packets into the playback (also de-jittering) buffer.

3 Embedded Implementation of Error Control Mode with Flexible Mode Switching

3.1 Error Control Mode

For mode switching, the proposed NASTE uses 4 error control modes which are AFEC, DCARQ, AFEC&ARQ, and IFEC&ARQ. Each error control mode has different performance. Therefore, we should know the features of each error control mode and method of mode design. The AFEC mode (`MODE#1`(n, k)) adds h redundant packets to k original source packets in order to recover lost packets (within some bound). For experiments, k and h are set to 18 and 6, respectively. The DCARQ mode (`MODE#2`) detects lost packets at the receiver and automatically requests retransmissions. Each retransmitted packet, if successfully received, can be used for incremental quality improvement [1]. The AFEC&ARQ mode (MODE#3(n, k)) combines the AFEC and DCARQ mode. While improving overall performance, the mode spends much delay and overhead. Thus, if the receiver tolerates resource spending caused by both AFEC and DCARQ, the mode is selected. The IFEC&ARQ mode (MODE#4(n, k, d)) adds interleaving to AFEC&ARQ mode to convert burst packet losses into isolated packet losses. However, it also has same problems with the AFEC&ARQ mode. The mode should tolerate delay jitter caused by interleaving. For find-grained control, the mode select the depth(d) of interleaving. d is limited from 1 to 10.

3.2 Implementation of Error Control Mode

The proposed NASTE mechanism designs and implements the error control modes in order to improve efficiency of mode switching and memory usage. For the hybrid error control mode, it combines several basic error control schemes (i.e., FEC, interleaving, and ARQ). This mechanism helps mode switching without delay, since the basic error control schemes is independent. On the other hand, the embedded systems usually have strict memory limitation that must play a factor in designing an embedded system. In order to improve efficiency of memory usage and reduce overhead, a buffer used for error control is separated from the error control module and is used as a shared buffer for all error control modules. That is so-called NASTE buffer.

The NASTE buffer is designed to manage and collect the packets as a special handling of buffers. Basically, the buffer is used at the receiver in order to store the received packets and reduce delay jitter. With the function, the buffer has different functions which help decoding/encoding for error control. To manage encoded packets easily, the proposed buffer is utilized as a block unit which contains several packets. For encoding/decoding of error control, the buffer checks whether the block can be decoded by error control mode or not. Moreover, the packet buffering has the ability to gather dispersed packets into each adequate block by means of de-interleaving.

4 Mode Switching Algorithm

For mode switching, the proposed NASTE passes through the procedure of error control mode selection. Before mode switching, the mechanism monitors the application and channel status such as PLR (packet loss rate), $D_{playback}$(playback buffer level), LQ (link quality), and $Cost$ at time period $(i * P_{ms})$ where i and P_{ms} are time index and time interval, respectively. In this paper, P_{ms} is set to 1 second. These monitored values are used as parameters of the mode selection function (F_{ms}) which consists of packet delivery rate (PDR) and cost used for error recovery ($Cost$). PDR indicates packet delivery rate after error recovery procedure. The $Cost$ indicates ratio of how many packets are used for error recovery. It is noted that packet delivery rate is more important than cost for overall performance improvement. Once the error control mode is selected, details for mode control are controlled.

4.1 Monitoring

In order to select a suitable error control mode, NASTE measures both the application and channel status. Although most of the information is gathered through receiver's feedback, channel status such as link quality and packet loss rate is gathered through CLM instead of E2EM for fast and precise monitoring. The wireless streaming media is fragile to the delay jitter that causes highly objectionable disruption or stalling in the playback. A typical way to reduce the frequency of the playback disruption is to employ a playback buffer at the receiver. NASTE monitors playback buffer level which means the number of frames stored in the playback buffer. The playback buffer level can be converted to a time domain ($D_{playback}$ (ms)) and approximated by using Eq. (1).

$$D_{playback}(i) = Timestamp_{last}(i-1) - Timestamp_{first}(i-1), \qquad (1)$$

where $Timestamp_{first}$ and $Timestamp_{last}$ indicate timestamp of first and last packet. The wireless interference is measured based on the observed SNR. Even if SNR is not key factor that indicates the reason for packet loss, the burst packet losses are quite related to the SNR [6]. To represent SNR in wireless channel, the link quality (LQ) is commonly used. The packet loss rate can be calculated by measuring the number of lost packets within P_{ms} through the feedback of the receiver. However, the measurement through E2EM may cause wrong decision of NASTE, since the feedback information may be lost and cause delay. Therefore, the proposed NASTE calculates the packet loss rate by using the number of the received ACKs and the transmitted packets in MAC layer through CLM [7]. The estimation of PLR is done using EWMA function and is written by Eq. (2).

$$PLR(i) = \alpha * PLR(i) + (1-\alpha) * PLR(i-1), \qquad (2)$$

where α is set to 0.9.

4.2 Mode Selection

Based on the monitoring, NASTE calculates mode selection function (F_{ms}) which considers packet delivery rate and cost according to the proposed error control mode ($MODE$) as mentioned above. We define $MODE$ as

$$MODE = \{\texttt{MODE\#1, MODE\#2, MODE\#3, MODE\#4}\}. \qquad (3)$$

The mode selection function is approximated by using Eq. (4).

$$F_{ms}(MODE, i) = PDR(MODE, i) + \lambda * (1 - Cost(MODE, i)). \qquad (4)$$

where λ is set to 0.1. PDR of each error control mode has different performance, since the modes have different property according to the application and channel status. In order to calculate PDR of each mode, some papers present mathematical solution [2]. However, the equation of each error control mode is not enough to express all complex network status. Thus, in this paper, packet delivery rate is measured through simulation as shown in Fig. 2. For the simulation, we have modeled the wireless network channel as a packet-erasure channel. The measurement of the erasure channel can be represented as the Gilbert model.

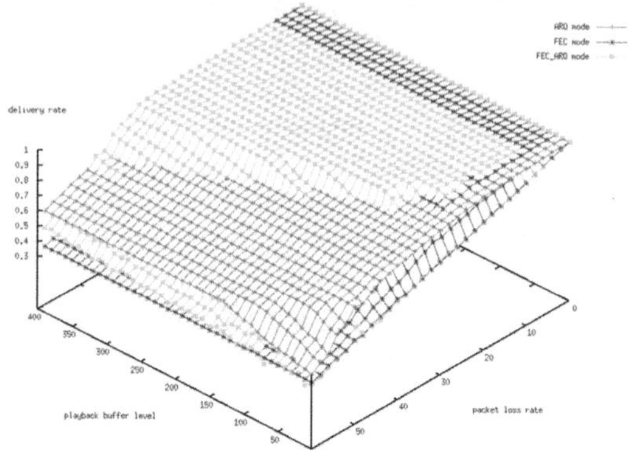

Fig. 2. The *PDR* comparison of error control modes

4.3 Fine-Grained Control of Selected Mode

The simulation cannot show performance of all situations since it is limited to express all properties of network and fine-grained control for the mode. For the fine-grained control of selected mode, NASTE control the number of redundant packets and depth. Before choosing the number of redundant packets for FEC, the throughput of FEC should be calculated like Eq. (5) based on packet loss rate [2]. Then, we select the number of FEC redundant packets (n-k) that maximizes the throughput of FEC assuming that the packet loss happens independently.

$$T_{FEC} = \frac{k}{n} \sum_{j=0}^{n-k} \binom{n}{j} PLR^j (1 - PLR)^{(n-j)}, \tag{5}$$

where X is the random variables that indicate the number of the lost packet in a FEC block. In the implementation, the number of the redundant packets of AFEC derived from the maximum throughput of FEC is stored as the lookup table so that the number of redundant packets can be simply selected according to the estimated packet loss rate. The interleaving depth (d) is calculated as Eq. (6) by comparing with $D_{playback}$ after deciding n of FEC.

$$d = \left\lfloor \frac{D_{playback}}{n \cdot L \cdot \left(\frac{1}{r_{rouce}} + \frac{1}{r_{sending}} + RTT + D_{process,inter} \right)} \right\rfloor, \tag{6}$$

where d_{min}, n, L indicate the minimum depth of interleaving, the size of FEC block and packet length, respectively. Also, r_{source}, $r_{sending}$, and $D_{process,inter}$ indicate media sending rate, transmission rate, and approximate processing delay of the receiver when using interleaving, respectively.

5 Experimental Results

In this section, we evaluate the performance of the proposed NASTE mechanism through experiments over IEEE 802.11g WLAN environment based on the HostAP which allows a WLAN card to perform the functions of an AP. A video streaming server uses a MPEG-2 video content which is CBR (constant bit rate) at about 7.5 Mbps. The target frame rate is 29.97 fps. For the experiments, we configure a testbed for the WLAN SD (standard definition) streaming. To generate an erroneous scenario, we fix the HostAP with streaming server in the room and move the streaming client via a uniform route.

In order to evaluate the performance of each selected mode according to the loss pattern, we measure the loss recovery rate with related factors as shown in Fig. 3. In the case of sparse loss pattern as shown in Fig. 3(a), we just use the DCARQ mode that improves bandwidth efficiency because of no redundant packets. However, if $D_{playback}$ is not enough to use DCARQ mode, we fail to recover packet losses. Fig. 3(b) shows that packet losses are recovered by AFEC mode. In this case, since the packet losses happen frequently, AFEC mode is appropriate. Fig. 3(d) shows that when the burst packet loss happens, the packet losses are recovered by the interleaved AFEC&ARQ mode. Since the burst packet losses are split by interleaving, the mode can recover the split packets efficiently by FEC and ARQ. Lastly, Fig. 3(c) shows that the AFEC&ARQ mode recovers packet losses. Although the IFEC&ARQ mode is more appropriate than this mode, we cannot apply IFEC&ARQ mode since $D_{playback}$ is not sufficient to use interleaving.

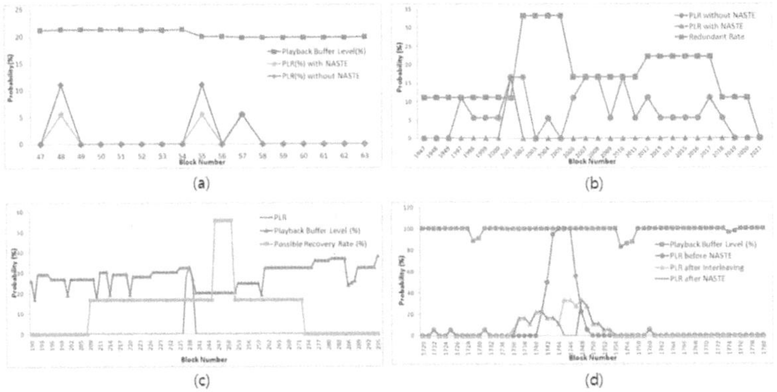

Fig. 3. Performance result of selected error control mode according to application and channel status. (a) DCARQ mode, (b) AFEC mode, (c) AFEC&ARQ mode, and (d) IFEC&ARQ mode.

For the performance comparison, we evaluate the loss rate and overhead caused by redundant packets of no error control (EC), hybrid ARQ, and the proposed NASTE mechanism as shown in Table 1. This result indicates that

Table 1. The proposed NASTE performance comparison

	No EC	hybrid ARQ	NASTE
Total loss rate(%)	4.88	3.28	2.99
Total overhead(%)	0	14.7	14.7

although the total overhead is about the same, the proposed mechanism can reduce more packet losses than hybrid ARQ by selecting a suitable error control mode. In addition, since the burst packet loss is split by interleaving, the probability of error recovery through packet-level FEC increases.

6 Conclusion

We proposed and implemented an error control mechanism in order to apply to MPEG-2 video streaming system in WLAN. The proposed NASTE mechanism can recover the number of packet loss caused by interference, channel fading, and delay via a selected error control mode. For more appropriate measurement of application and channel status, we use CLM and E2EM concurrently. To verify the performance, we have experimented NASTE over IEEE 802.11g WLAN environment. As a result, the NASTE had better capability to recover packet loss.

Acknowledgments

The work reported in this paper was supported by the Basic Research Program of the Korea Science and Engineering Foundation (KOSEF) under Grant No. (R01-2006-000-10556-0).

References

1. S. Chan and X. Zheng, "Video loss recovery with FEC and stream replication," *IEEE Transaction on Multimedia*, vol. 8, no. 2, pp. 370-381, Apr. 2006.
2. D. G. Sachs, I. Kozintsev, and M. Yeung, "Hybrid ARQ for robust video streaming over wireless LANs," in *Proc. ITCC 01*, pp. 317-321, Las vegas, USA, Apr. 2001.
3. F. Hartanto and H. R. Sirisena, "Hybrid error control mechanism for video transmission in the wireless IP networks," *IEEE LANMAN 99*, pp. 126-132, Sydney, Australia, Nov. 1999.
4. S. Aramvith, C.-W. Lin, S. Roy, and M.-T. Sun, "Wireless video transport using conditional retransmission and low-delay interleaving," in *Proc. IEEE Trans. on Circuits and Systems for Video Technology*, vol. 12, no. 6, pp. 558-565, June 2002.
5. VideoLAN, "http://www.videolan.org".
6. D. Aguayo, J. Bicket, S. Biswas, G. Judd, and R. Morris, "Link-level measurements from an 802.11b mesh network," in *Proc. ACM SIGCOMM 2004*, vol. 34, no. 4, pp. 121-132, Newyork, USA, Aug. 2004.
7. S. Park, H. Yoon and J. Kim, "Network-adaptive HD MPEG-2 video streaming with cross-layered channel monitoring in WLAN," in *Proc. International Packet Video Workshop (PV2006)*,vol. 7, no. 5, pp. 885-893, Hangzhou, China, Apr. 2006.

An Energy-Efficient and Traffic-Aware CSMA/CA Algorithm for LR-WPAN

JunKeun Song[1,2], SangCheol Kim[2], HaeYong Kim[2], and PyeongSoo Mah[1,2]

[1] University of Science and Technology, Deajeon, South Korea
[2] Sensor Network OS Research Team,
Embedded Software Research Division,
Electronics and Telecommunications Research Institute (ETRI), Daejeon, South Korea
{jun361,sheart,haekim,pmah}@etri.re.kr

Abstract. In this paper, we propose an energy-efficient and traffic-aware CSMA/CA algorithm, referred to as ETCA, that aims to reduce redundant transmission of IEEE 802.15.4 Standard for Low-Rate Wireless Personal Area Networks (LR-WPAN). In Wireless Sensor Networks (WSNs), reducing energy consumption is one of the most important issues because it makes the network life-time longer. Sensor nodes consume most of energy for computing and transmitting operations [1]. Unlike IEEE 802.11, IEEE 802.15.4 MAC doesn't use Request To Send (RTS) and Clear To Send (CTS) frames, and it still has hidden terminal problems. Thus, if there are some hidden nodes, there are many collisions and retransmissions [2]. To reduce retransmission, we improve the carrier sensing features in MAC layer of IEEE 802.15.4. When the network is busy, the MAC detects it and adaptively chooses parameters of CSMA/CA mechanism to minimize collisions and the number of retransmission based on ETCA. We evaluated the proposed scheme with original 802.15.4 MAC on the ns-2 simulator. The results showed that our scheme outperforms the original by 15% in average when there is a retransmission activity.

Keywords: IEEE 802.15.4 LR-WPAN, back-off algorithm, CSMA/CA, traffic-aware, energy-efficient.

1 Introduction

IEEE 802.15.4 was developed for simple, low-power and low-cost wireless communication. In the past couple of years, it has become a popular technology for wireless sensor networks (WSN) and home networking [3].

The 802.15.4 standard shows that the throughput of 2.4GHz PHY is 250kbps. However it decreases into 164kbps at MAC layer even though it is not concerned collision and retransmission [4]. Furthermore, it can be used only a part of it, because there is no interference preventing mechanism and hereby hidden nodes make collisions frequently.

The 802.15.4 beacon-enabled PAN uses a slotted CSMA/CA algorithm and there is a high probability that collision and retransmission occur. There is no way to detect hidden nodes unlike IEEE 802.11. That's why 802.15.4 beacon-enabled mode makes

Y.-H. Lee et al. (Eds.): ICESS 2007, LNCS 4523, pp. 791–799, 2007.

many collisions. If a collision occurs, CSMA/CA executes retransmission operation. But in WSNs, transmit operations consume high energy. So it's very important to decrease retransmission count.

The proposed algorithm derives the parameters to minimize collision and retransmission through traffic monitoring. As MAC detects the traffic, it can reduce the number of retransmission, and hereby save energy.

We describe the IEEE 802.15.4 CSMA/CA algorithm briefly in Section II and the proposed algorithm in Section III. The section IV describes the simulation results compared with original mechanism using ns-2. Finally, the concluding remarks are drawn in Section V.

2 Preliminaries

2.1 Overview of the MAC Protocol in IEEE 802.15.4

IEEE 802.15.4 is a new standard to address the need for low-rate low-power low-cost wireless networking. The MAC protocol in IEEE 802.15.4 can operate on both beacon-enabled and non-beacon mode. In the beaconless mode, the protocol is essentially a simple CSMA/CA protocol. Since most of the unique features of IEEE 802.15.4 are in the beacon-enabled mode, we will focus our attention on this mode.

In beacon-enabled mode, the 802.15.4 MAC uses a slotted CSMA/CA algorithm and superframe structure. In a single WPAN, the format of the superframe is defined by PAN coordinator. The duration of superframe is described by the values of *macBeaconOrder* and *macSuperFrameOrder*. *macBeaconOrder(BO)* describes the Beacon Interval(BI) at which the coordinator shall transmit its beacon frames. Each superframe starts with the transmission of a beacon, and has active inactive portions. The value of *macSuperFrameOrder(SO)* describes the length of the active portion of the superframe which is refered to as SD (Fig. 1).

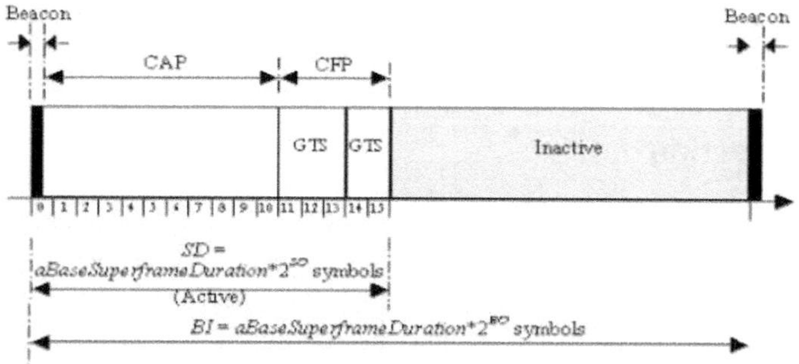

Fig. 1. Superframe Structure in IEEE 802.15.4

The active portion is composed of three parts: beacon, contention access period (CAP), and contention free period (CFP). All frames, except acknowledgement frames and any data frame that immediately follows the acknowledgement of a data request command transmitted in the CAP, must use a slotted CSMA/CA mechanism to access the channel.

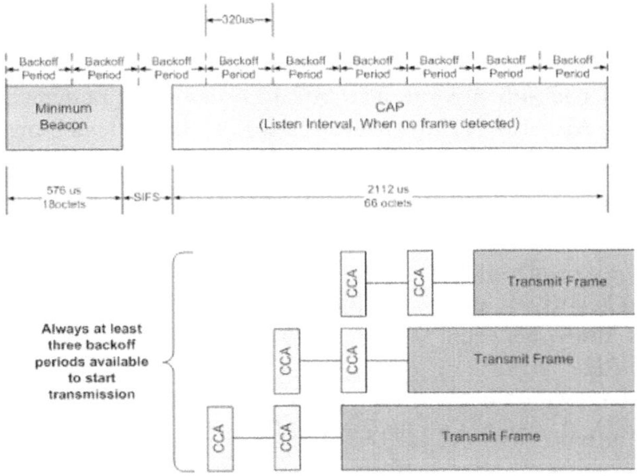

Fig. 2. Backoff period and Transmission mechanism

The CSMA/CA algorithm is implemented using units of time, called *backoff period*, each of length *aUnitBackoffPeriod*(= 20symbol times = 320us in 2.4GHz channel). Note that 10 bytes can be transmitted in one backoff period. Sensing and transmitting must be started at the boundary of each backoff period (Fig. 2).

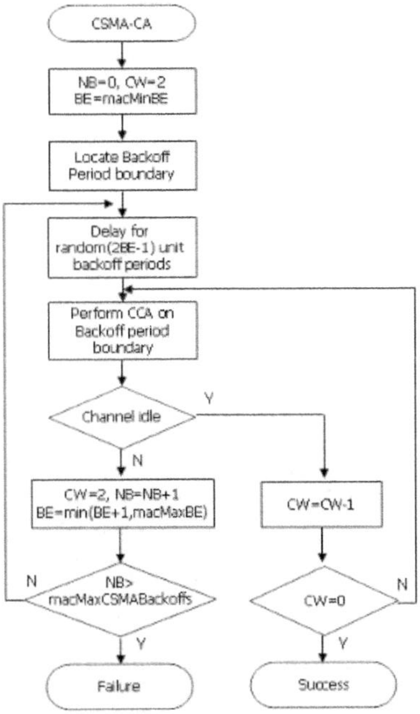

Fig. 3. A slotted CSMA-CA algorithm in IEEE 802.15.4

Comparing with IEEE 802.11 MAC, IEEE 802.15.4 doesn't use RTS/CTS, so it's more difficult to detect other nodes' network traffics, and collision probability will be increased according to the number of nodes.

The original back-off algorithm in 802.15.4 has some parameters (CW, NB, BE) which is set by MIB (MAC information base) [4]. Each device maintains these three variables for each transmission attempt.

- CW is the number of backoff periods, which need to be clear of channel activity before the transmission can commence. MAC ensures this by performing *clear channel assessment*(CCA).
- BE is backoff exponent. Before performing CCA, a node takes backoff of random units between 0 and 2^{BE}-1. BE is initialized to lesser of 2 and *macMinBE.*
- NB is number of backoff. If NB is greater than *macMaxCSMABackoffs*, the CSMA/CA algorithm terminates with Failure Status.

The whole CSMA/CA algorithm is illustrated in Figure 3.

2.2 Collision Tests with Hidden Nodes

In evaluating IEEE 802.15.4 original MAC protocol performance using ns-2, we found that many packets were resent by collision when hidden nodes exist. Figure 4 is one of the simulated test results. It shows the number of retries of CSMA-CA algorithm with hidden terminals. There are 9 nodes in PAN and each node makes 10Kb/s traffics. As a slotted CSMA/CA mechanism, CSMA/CA failed after 3 retries and the packet dropped finally. That makes the channel busy without transmitting, and causes throughput to fall and unnecessary energy consumption. There is no MAC-level congestion control mechanism in IEEE 802.15.4. In next section, we propose an energy-efficient and traffic-adaptive CSMA/CA algorithm by decreasing the number of retransmission.

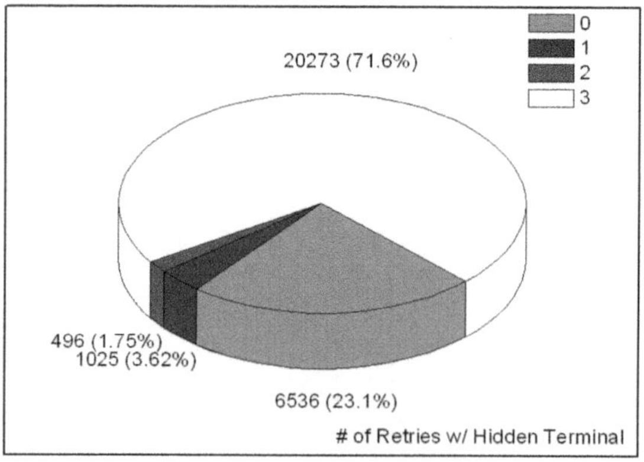

Fig. 4. The number of retires per packet

3 Proposed Algorithm

Our main idea is that changing the MIB parameters suitable for adapting the network traffic information. It's easy to apply previous product because we only change the MIB parameters for each transmission not whole algorithm. The processing steps are follows.

Each node has *the node traffic indication value(NTIV)* which indicates local traffic rate. The NTIV can be adjusted by some events like ACK received, CCA fail or CSMA success. Table 1 shows some parameters using in ETCA. Each node adjust its' NTIV according to that parameters. These parameter values can be changed according to network size or application. The parameters marked with (+) are increasing the NTIV and the parameters marked with (-) represent decreased traffic events.

Table 1. Parameters for adjusting the traffic indication values

	Parameter	Event
Ack	α^-	Receive Ack Completely
	α^+	Don't Receive Ack
CCA	β^-	CCA Success
	β^+	CCA Failure
CSMA	τ^-	CSMA Success
	τ^+	CSMA Failure

Figure 5 shows the modified CSMA/CA algorithm and some other actions according to events. When each node calculates its' own NTIV, and send it to the coordinator. Each node transfers NTIV information within FrameControlField of ACK or Data Frame. There are 5 reserved bits and it's useful to transfer some additional data without changing the MAC header. The PAN coordinator received packet which has NTIV, then figure out *the cluster traffic indication value (CTIV).* CTIV represents the global traffic information of that cluster or PAN. The coordinator broadcast CTIV to other nodes using FrameControlField of beacon frame. Every node in the PAN received the beacon and change NTIV with CTIV as follows

$$NTIV = \lambda NTIV + (1-\lambda)CTIV$$

λ is the local weight value. It can get a different value for node characteristics. For example, end device or RFD(Reduced Function Device) can have lower value than PAN coordinator or FFD(Full Function Device).

As each node gets all information about traffic, the node finally decides the CSMA/CA parameters referencing NTIV and CTIV to minimize the collisions and retransmissions. Referring to NTIV, ETCA can check the channel state more strictly by increasing CW, and it can make lower channel access probability by increasing BE.

Choosing the parameter values in ETCA is a heuristic problem. We can't optimize these parameters because it depends on application type or network size. We'll show some examples how it works in the next section. ETCA will result in good performance of whole network than original one.

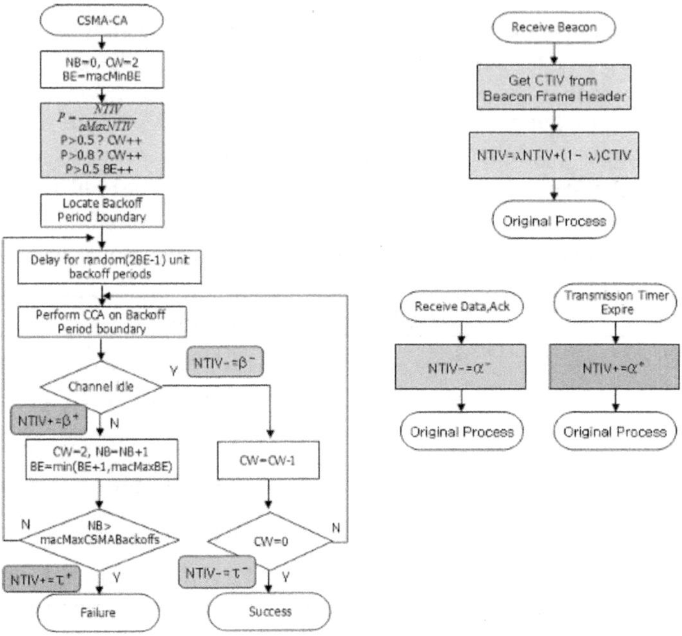

Fig. 5. ETCA

4 Simulation Result

For performance evaluations, we used ns-2.29 and a modified version of the IEEE 802.15.4 MAC implemented by SAIT-CUNY Joint Lab with the ETCA characteristics [3, 5].

We use 2.4 GHz with 20m CS, RX threshold. There are 5 nodes in WPAN and each node generates the 32kbps traffic to PAN coordinator. We used star topology; each node only connected with coordinator. Each device can't listen to neighborhood node except coordinator (Fig. 6). The red circle means the carrier sensing range of a node.

We use two traffic distribution models in simulation, one is poisson and another is CBR (constant bit rate). In addition, we set BO=3, SO=3 for superframe structure. It means there is no inactive portion. And no GTS slot is used.

For ETCA, we set the parameters instinctively as follows:

$$\alpha^{+} = 2,\ \alpha^{-} = \text{-}1,\ \beta^{+} = 3,\ \beta^{-} = \text{-}1,\ \tau^{+} = \text{-}2,\ \tau^{-} = 4.$$

The NTIV is ranged from 0 to 255. If NTIV is larger than 128, initialized value of CW increased. And If NTIV is greater than 192, BE is initialized to less than 3 and *macMinBE*. Local weight rate of NTIV and CTIV is set 6:4 in end-device and 3:7 in PAN coordinator. We set λ of PAN Coordinator as smaller than half, because PAN coordinator always listens every node's traffic indication value and we assumed latest information represent the network state more accurate.

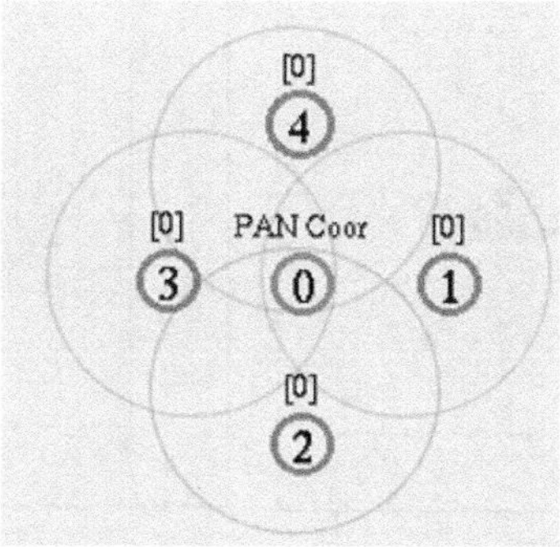

Fig. 6. Simulation Node Setting

Figure 7 shows the number of retransmission trial count in whole network and the number of packets node sent, using poisson traffic. It means MAC has to try 5~6 backoffs to send a packet before adapting ETCA. But it significantly goes down to 2~3 backoff using ETCA. In Fig. 7, the red line shows how ETCA controls the CSMA/CA mechanism adaptively.

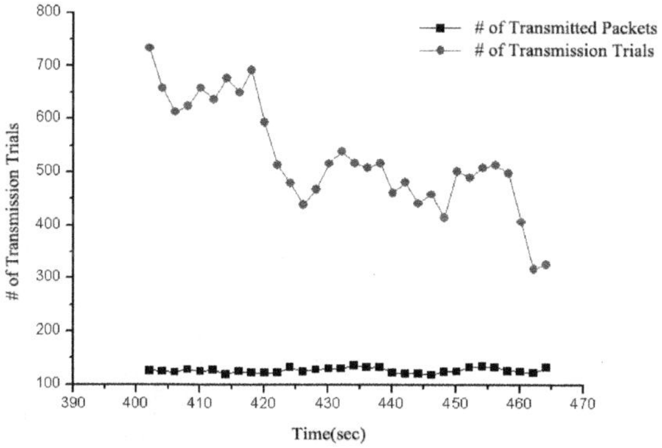

Fig. 7. Packet counts of target flow

Figure 8 shows the results of difference between original CSMA algorithm and ETCA. Because of using CBR traffic, the number of retries is not move dramatically unlike Fig 7. However, using ETCA, it is decreased backoff time and unnecessary transmission than original algorithm. The gap between blue and gray line means the enhancement of re-sent packets in ETCA. It can be saved more than one hundred of tries per second in whole network and hereby it can make the network lifetime 10% longer at least. Using MicaZ sensor node[7], each transmission operation node consumes 17mA in CC2420 transceiver. ETCA reduces retransmissions which include TX, RX and CCA [6]. Figure 9 graph represents how many real transmissions occur to send one packet.

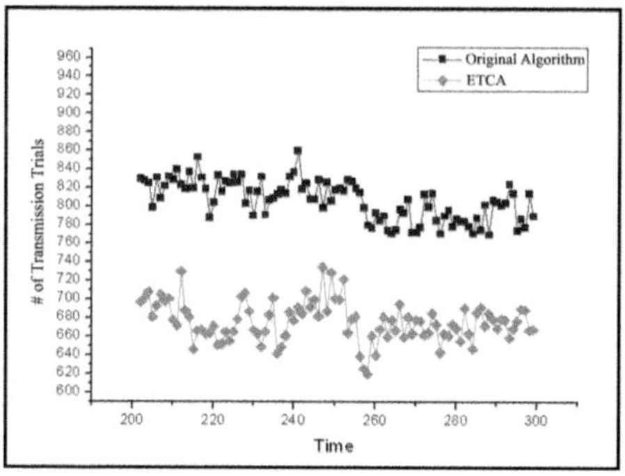

Fig. 8. the number of transmission trials with CBR traffics

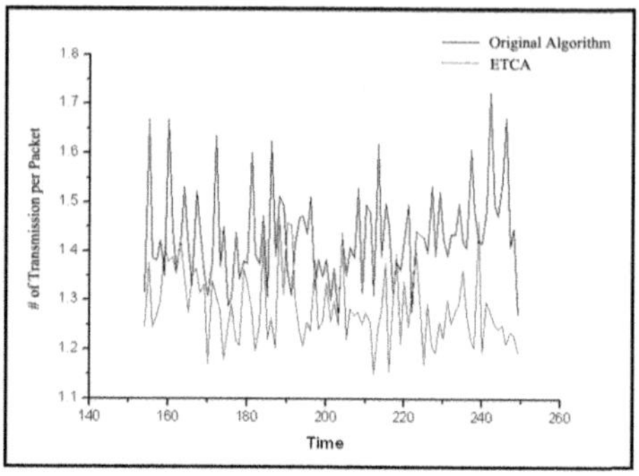

Fig. 9. Transmission Count Per packet

In spite of decreasing transmission count, the drop rate and throughput in ETCA results better than original algorithm. Throughput of whole network using ETCA results 134.2kb/s but only 125kb/s in original one(Fig 10). The data of figure 11 show the drop rate. The Drop rate stands for

$$droprate = \frac{\# \quad of \quad packet \quad received}{\# \quad of \quad packet \quad sent} \tag{1}$$

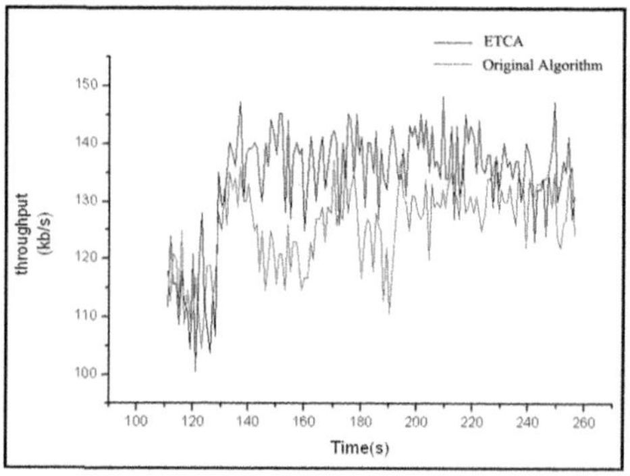

Fig. 10. Throughput

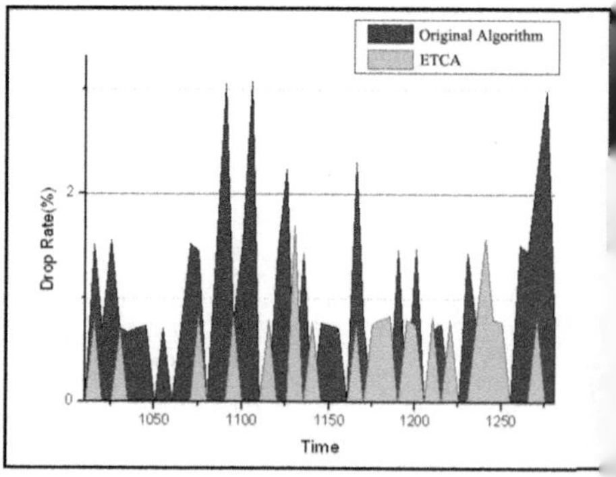

Fig. 11. Drop Rate

It means that ETCA makes CSMA/CA more strictly and it can detect traffic more accuracy. In our scenario, devices only reach the coordinator. But adjacent nodes can make collision. The original CSMA results 4.9% drop rate, but ETCA shows only 2.3% drop rate. It is certain that the transmission probability is improved using ETCA.

5 Conclusion

We designed an energy-efficient and traffic-adaptive CSMA/CA algorithm (ETCA) for IEEE 802.15.4 LR-WPAN and simulated using ns-2. Using dynamic parameters, we evaluated whole network throughput. It is improved by reducing the number of retransmissions. Redundant transmissions cause unnecessary energy consumption and makes network lifetime be short. Thus ETCA can be applied and used in real wireless sensor network environments to extend the lifetime of sensor networks.

References

1. Victor Shanayder, Mark Hempstead, Bor-rong Chen, Geoff W. Allen, and Matt Welsh: "Simulating the Power Consumption of Large-Scale Sensor Network Applications", SenSys (2004).
2. Marina Petrova, Janne Riihijarvi, Petri Mahonen, and Saverio Labella: "Performance Study of IEEE 802.15.4 Using Measurements and Simulations", WCNC (2006).
3. E. Callaway, P. Gorday, L. Hester, J. A. Gutierrez, M. Naeve, B. Heile, and V. Bahl: "Home Networking with IEEE 802.15.4: A Developing Standard for Low-Rate Wireless Personal Area Networks," *IEEE Communications Magazine*, vol. 40, no. 8, pp. 70–77, (2002).
4. IEEE 802.15.4 Standard (2006)
5. Samsung/CUNY: "Ns2 simulator for 802.15.4," http://www-ee.ccny.cuny.edu/zheng/pub.
6. Chipcon CC2420 Radio Datasheet (2004)
7. Crossbow Technology Inc.: "MICAz wireless measurement system", http://www.xbow.com (2004)

Packet Interference and Aggregated Throughput of Bluetooth Piconets in a Ubiquitous Network

Seung-Yeon Kim[1], Se-Jin Kim[2], Ki-Jong Lee[3], Yi-Chul Kang[4],
Hyong-Woo Lee[1], and Choong-Ho Cho[2]

[1] Department of Electronics and Information Engineering, Korea University, Korea
{kimsy8011,hwlee}@korea.ac.kr
[2] Department of Computer and Information Science, Korea University, Korea
{kimsejin,chcho}@korea.ac.kr
[3] KT, Korea
kijong@kt.co.kr
[4] NIA(National Information Society Agency), Korea
kangyc@nia.or.kr

Abstract. In a ubiquitous environment, various sensors and wireless devices communicate with each other. Recently, the number of wireless devices using Bluetooth technology operating in the unlicensed 2.4GHz ISM band is increasing rapidly. Interference among communicating devices sharing the ISM band can cause significant throughput degradation. In this paper, we present an analytical model of packet interference with multi-path fading channel in a cluster of piconets. Through analysis, we obtain the packet collision probability and aggregated throughput assuming capture effect. Numerical examples are given to demonstrate the effect of various parameters such as capture ratio, Rice factor and cluster size on the system performance.

1 Introduction

Bluetooth is the common name for the technology described by the IEEE standard 802.15 for short-range wireless connections. Bluetooth devices are used many applications, such as mobile phones, headsets, keyboards, mice, digital cameras, and other devices. This is because Bluetooth has several advantages, some of which are low cost, low power, and flexibility. In addition, using a globally available unlicensed frequency (2.4GHz Industrial, Scientific and Medical: ISM) band for worldwide compatibility. These features cause rapid increase of Bluetooth devices in the world market. However, this trend towards wide spread deployment of wireless technologies and devices in 2.4GHz causes new problems and necessitates new research areas of collision avoidance or reduction. One of the biggest problems is wireless interference among communicating devices.

A Bluetooth piconet consists of a master, which essentially controls the channel, and maximum of seven slaves. Due to an absence of coordination between independent masters which accessing the common wireless medium, devices can encounter high packet interference if several piconets are simultaneously operating in the same

Y.-H. Lee et al. (Eds.): ICESS 2007, LNCS 4523, pp. 800–809, 2007.

area. Since even a headset and a mobile phone can be connected with a Bluetooth link forming a piconet, it may not be unusual to find tens of independent piconets in crowded places like airports, international conferences, shopping malls, and so on[1].

El-Hoiydi [2] has given a probabilistic model of interference of single-slot packets in a homogeneous cluster of piconets, i.e., all piconets are either of 79-hop type or of 23-hop type. The author also considered a heterogeneous cluster of piconets in which both 79-hop types and 23-hop types share the common radio channel. However, in this paper, we only consider 79-hop for the simplicity and most Bluetooth devices use 79-hop. Naik et al. [3] have given a generalized model of interference of various packets such as 1-, 3-, and 5-slot in a cluster of piconets but the model of Naik et al. [3] uses collision model only. In general, collision and throughput are effected by interfering power of other piconets and the capture effecture a wireless environment.

For this reason, in this paper, we present an analytical model of packet interference in a cluster of piconets using multiple-slot packets, such as 1-slot, 3-slot, and 5-slot in asymmetric mode. The main purpose of our analytic model is to investigate the potential benefits of capture effect in the event of mobile data communications in the environment of Rayleigh and Rician fading channels.

The paper is organized as follows. Multi-path fading channel and collision probability of Bluetooth piconet are described in Section II. The analytical model is in Section III. Numerical examples of the analysis of collision and throughput for our model are presented shown in Section IV. Some concluding remarks are given in Section V.

2 Mathematical Formulation

2.1 Multi-path Fading Channel

Multi-path fading can happen by reflections of the radio waves due to obstacles such as Fig.1, so that radio waves reach the receiver in more than one way. This fading is fast and the distribution of the amplitude can be modeled by the Rayleigh distribution. Rayleigh distribution is

$$f_{Ray}(x) = \frac{x}{\sigma_I^2}\exp\left(-\frac{x^2}{2\sigma_I^2}\right) \tag{1}$$

where x is the signal amplitude and σ_I^2 is the average scattered power.

In a situation where the distance between the base station and the mobile user is small, and the environment is static, there is a fixed spatial pattern of maxima and minima. Mostly there is a line-of-sight path. The fast component can then be modeled by a Rician distribution[4]. Rician distribution is

$$f_{Rice}(x) = \frac{x}{\sigma^2}\exp\left(\frac{-(x^2+\alpha_0^2)}{2\sigma^2}\right)I_0\left(\frac{\alpha_0 x}{\sigma^2}\right),\ x \geq 0 \tag{2}$$

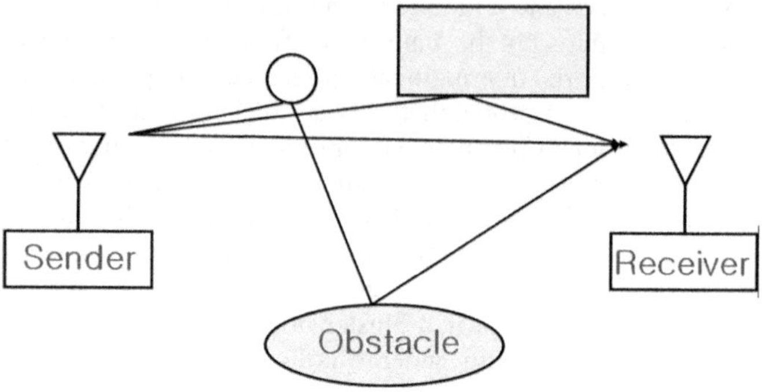

Fig. 1. Multi-path fading in a wireless transmission

where x is the signal amplitude σ^2 is the average fading power, α_0 is the peak value of the directly received signal, and $I_n()$ is the modified *Bessel function* of the first kind and nth order.

$$I_0(x) = \frac{1}{2\pi}\int_0^{2\pi} \exp(x\cos\theta)d\theta \tag{3}$$

The Rician distribution is characterized by the parameter K, the Rice factor, which is defined as the ratio of the average specular power and the average fading power received over specular paths.

$$K = \frac{\alpha_0^2}{2\sigma^2} \tag{4}$$

When the direct signal does not exist, i.e. when α_0 becomes zero ($K=0$), equation (2). reduces to eqn.1. Also, when α_0 is large, then equation (2) is approximately Gaussian. Therefore, Rayleigh statistics is one extreme case of the Rician statistics, while Gaussian is another extreme case of the Rician statistics[5,6].

2.2 The Modeling of Channel Interference Probability

Data traffic in a piconet is said to be symmetric if both the master and a slave transmit at the same rate. This implies that they equally share the channel slots. Let p_{ij} be the interference probability between a piconet transmitting i-slot packets and a piconet transmitting j-slot packet. The variables i and j can take on discrete values from the set {1, 3, 5}. To simplify the discussion, in the calculation of p_{ij}'s, we assume that the packet to slot ratio is one, i.e., the duration occupied by the i-slot packet is exactly the same as the total length of i slot(s) for i = 1, 3, and 5. Also, be informed that the p_{ij}'s in [4] are computed under the assumption that two consecutive transmit(Tx) and receive(Rx) slots will not use the same hop frequency according to the Bluetooth specification[7], which is right for a piconet using single-slot packets, when computing p_{31} or p_{51}, as an example, it is assumed that in any run of three or five consecutive slots in a 1-slot piconet a hop frequency is not repeated[1].

All piconets are either of 79-hop type or of 23-hop type but we only consider the type of 79-hop in our analysis. In addition, for discussion convenience, let Tx(1), Tx(3), and Tx(5) be the Tx slot of 1-slot, 3-slot, and 5-slot, respectively, and let Rx(1), Rx(3), and Rx(5) be the Rx slot of 1-slot, 3-slot, and 5-slot, respectively.

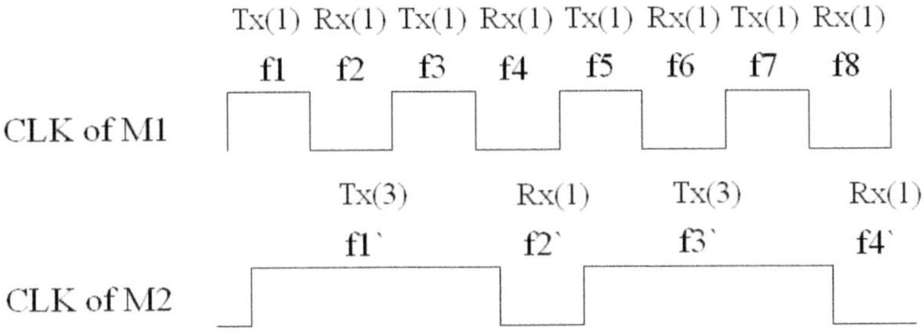

Fig. 2. Interference between two asymmetric, asynchronous piconets(1- and 3-slot packets)

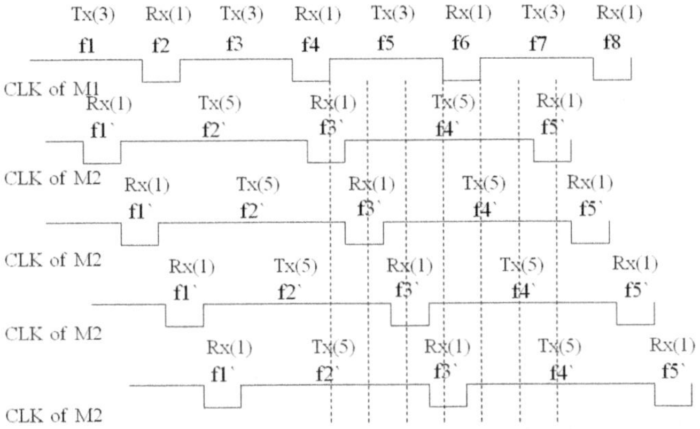

Fig. 3. Interference between two asymmetric, asynchronous piconets(3- and 5-slot packets)

We now use Fig.2 to explain the probability of interference between master 1(*M1*) and master 2(*M2*). When *M2*(which has 3-slot for Tx and 1-slot for Rx) interferes *M1* (which has 1-slot for Tx and Rx), the probability(p_{13}) of interference for *M1* is 2/79 during frequency 1(*f1*). The probability of interfering *M1* by *M2* is the same as p_{13}. Likewise, the probability of interfering *M1* by *M2* is 1/79 during *f2* and *f3* but the probability is 2/79 again during *f4*.

On the contrary, when *M1* interferes *M2*, the probability(P_{31}) of interference for *M2* is 4/79 during *f1`*. The probability of interfering *M2* by *M1* is 2/79 during *f2`*. The

[1] In reality, the probability that a hop frequency is repeated in any run of three or five consecutive slots is extremely low. Thus, to simplify the discussion, we assume that it is 0.

average is (4/79+1/79)/2=3/79 in the two cases. We simply know that P_{35} and P_{53} are 5/237, 5/158 respectively by using the previous way in Fig.3. The rest of the cases are p_{11}=2/79, p_{33}=2/79, p_{55}=2/79, p_{15}=4/237, and p_{51}=4/79[1].

3 The Analytical Model

When piconets exist in a small place, each piconet uses one hop in 79 hops to communicate. If all piconets use symmetric and synchronous modes, the interference probability is 1/79. However, the probability is different in asymmetric and asynchronous modes as discussed in 2.2. Analysis model consists of a main peconet and N-1 sub-piconets. The probability of n piconets using the same channel is Pr[n].

$$\Pr[n] = \binom{N-1}{n} \cdot p^n \cdot (1-p)^{N-1-n} \qquad n = 0,1,2,\cdots,N-1 \tag{5}$$

Here, p is decided by the probability of packet transmit method such 1-, 3-, and 5-slot type.

At first, let the power of main piconet obeys Rician distribution and the power of sub-piconets obey Rayleigh distribution. We, thus, have throughput S given by equation (10) through equation (6), (7), (8), and (9).

$$S = 1 - \left[\sum_{n=1}^{N-1} \Pr[n] F(z_0) \right] \tag{6}$$

$$F(z_0) = \Pr\{P_s / P_n < z_0\} = \int_0^{z_0} dz \int_0^{\infty} f_{P_s}(zw) f_{P_n}(w) w\,dw \tag{7}$$

where z_0 is the capture threshold for the ratio of the main piconet and sub-piconets, P_s is the power of the intended signal and P_n is the power of the interfering signal. The probability density functions of P_s and P_n are, respectively, given as follows.

$$f_{P_s}(P_s) = \frac{1}{\sigma^2} \exp\left[-\frac{2P_s + S_t^{\,2}}{2\sigma^2} \right] I_0\left[\frac{\sqrt{(2P_s)}S_t}{\sigma^2} \right], \quad P_s = (1/2)x^2 \tag{8}$$

where S_t is power of main piconet.

$$f_{P_n}(P_n) = \frac{1}{\sigma^2} \frac{(P_n / \sigma_I^2)^{n-1}}{(n-1)!} \exp\left[-\frac{P_n}{\sigma_I^2} \right], \tag{9}$$

(P_n = Total power of sub-piconets)

where P_n is total power of interfering sub-piconets.

Equation (9) is obtained by convolving $f_{Pw}(P_s) = 1/\sigma^2 \exp\left[-P_s/\sigma_I^2\right]$ with n times and gamma distribution.

$$S = \left(1 - \sum_{n=1}^{N-1} \Pr[n]\left\{1 - \int_0^{\infty} \frac{t^{n-1}}{(n-1)!} \times \exp(-t) Q\left[\varepsilon, \sqrt{(2Mt)}\right] dt\right\}\right) \tag{10}$$

where $\varepsilon \underline{\underline{\Delta}} (2K)^{1/2}$, $M \underline{\underline{\Delta}} z_0 \frac{\sigma_I^2}{\sigma^2}$, and $Q(a,b)$ is the Marcum Q function[4].

Now, let both the main piconet and sub-piconets obey Rician distribution. In this case, we have throughput S by equation (12) through equation (6), (7), (8), and (11).

$$f_{P_n}(P_n) = \frac{1}{2\sigma^2}\left(\frac{P_n}{S_n}\right)^{(n-1)/2} \times \exp\left[-\frac{P_n + S_n}{2\sigma_I^2}\right] I_{n-1}\left[\frac{\sqrt{p_n S_n}}{\sigma_I^2}\right], \tag{11}$$

$$S_n = n^*(\text{ Power of Line-of-sight for sub-piconets })^2$$

$$S = \sum_{n=1}^{N} \Pr[n]\left[1 - \frac{1}{\varepsilon_1^{n-1}} \times \exp\left(-\frac{\varepsilon_1^2}{2}\right) \times \int_0^{\infty} x^n \exp\left(-\frac{x^2}{2}\right) I_{n-1}[\varepsilon_1 x] Q\left[\alpha, \sqrt{z_0} \cdot \frac{\sigma_I}{\sigma} x\right] dx\right] \tag{12}$$

where $K_d = S_t^2 / 2\sigma^2$, $K_u = S_n^2 / 2\sigma_i^2$, $\varepsilon_1 = \sqrt{2nk_u}$, and $\alpha = \sqrt{2K_d}$.

Table 1 is used to calculate the aggregated throughput for a cluster of piconets using multiple-slot packets and for more accurate throughput.

Table 1. Condition of calculating aggregated throughput

Slot	Total duration	Payload
1-slot	625 μs	240 bits (30bytes)
3-slot	1875 (3*625) μs	1464 bits (183bytes)
5-slot	3125 (5*625) μs	2712 bits (339bytes)

The aggregated throughput of the system is

$$S_{th\_put} = N \times S \times payload \text{ bits/sec} \tag{13}$$

For simplicity, we only concern the analysis in asymmetric and asynchronous modes in this paper. Every piconet always transmits and the percentage of 1-, 3-, and 5-slot are each 1/3.

4 Numerical Examples

In this section, we present some results of numerical examples. Throughout this section we used $K = 4\text{dB}$, $K_d = 7\text{dB}$, $\sigma_I^2 / \sigma^2 = 2dB$ and $z_0 = 4\text{dB}$, unless otherwise stated.

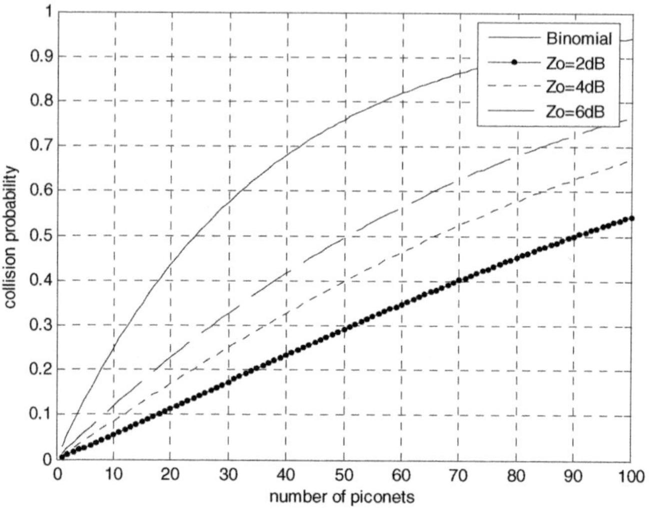

Fig. 4. Collision probability with various interfering power when the main piconet and sub-piconets are Rician and Rayleigh distribution respectively

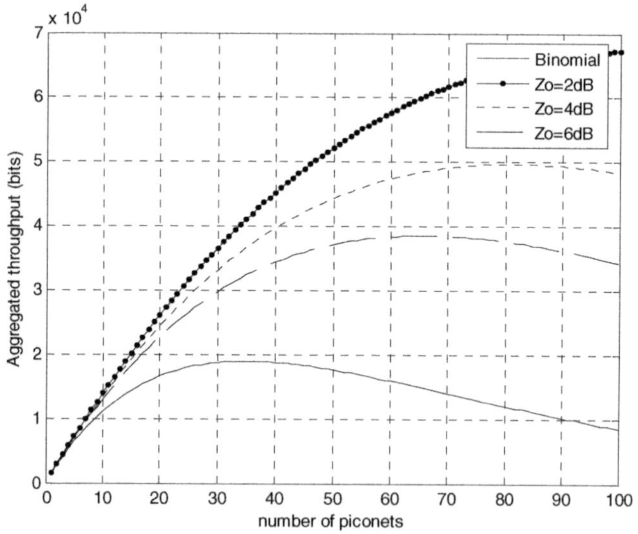

Fig. 5. Aggregated throughput with various interfering power when the main piconet and sub-piconets are Rician and Rayleigh distribution respectively

Fig.4 shows the effect of collision probability with different threshold for capture effect z_0 in a cluster of piconets when the amplitude of the main piconet obeys Rician distribution and those of sub-piconets obey Rayleigh distribution. In other wards, the collision probability is affected by the threshold of power between the main piconet and the sub-piconets. In the figure, 'binomial' means that the threshold of power is not considered so a collision always occurs if piconets use the same channel simultaneously. On the whole, higher threshold(z_0 = 2dB) results in increased collisions more than lower threshold(z_0 = 6dB). The main piconet tends to cause less interference in Rayleigh distribution because there is no line-of-sight.

Fig.5 shows the effect of aggregated throughput with different z_0 in a cluster of piconets when the amplitude of the main piconet obeys Rician distribution and those sub-piconets obey Rayleigh distribution. The results reflect the result shown in Fig.4 because a condition of low collision means higher success probability and throughput increase. The throughput increases as z_o decreases as expected.

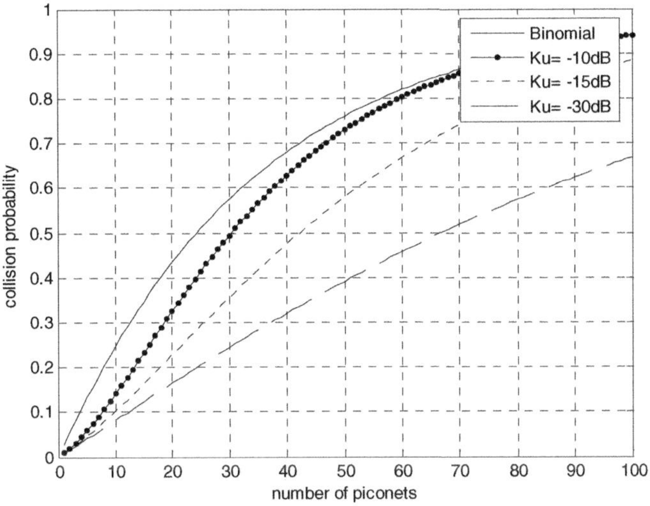

Fig. 6. Collision probability with various interfering power(K_u) when the main piconet and sub-piconets are Rician distribution (z_0 = 4dB)

Fig.6 shows the effect of collision probability with different K_u with fixed K_d = 7dB and z_0 = 4dB in a cluster of piconets when amplitude of both the main piconet and sub-piconets obey Rician distribution.

Collision probability increases as the number of piconets increases. As the level of line-of-sight component of interfering piconet increases, from K_u = –30dB to –10dB, the collision probability increases as well. As shown in Fig.6, when K_u is –30dB, collision probability increases almost linearly with the number of piconets. However, when K_u is –15dB, –10dB and 'binomial', collision probabilities increase rapidly and taper off as the number of piconets increases.

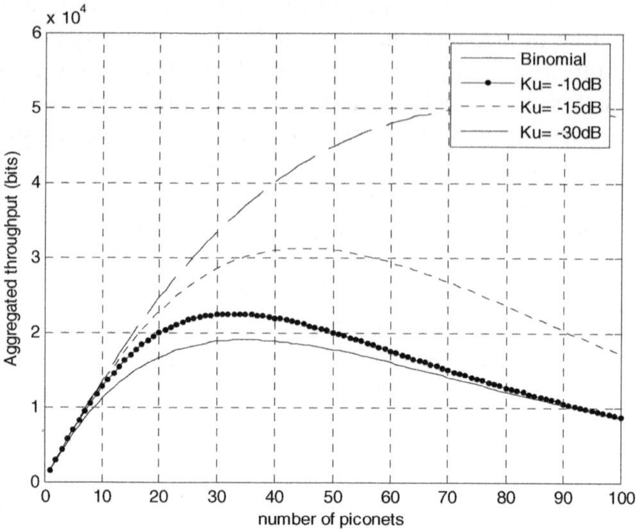

Fig. 7. Aggregated throughput with various interfering power(K_u) when the main piconet and sub-piconets are Rician distribution (z_0= 4dB)

Fig.7 shows the effect on the aggregated throughput of different K_u with K_d = 7dB and z_0 = 4dB in a cluster of piconets where the power from both the main piconet and sub-piconets are Rician distributied. As expected from Fig.6, the aggregated throughput decreases as K_u increases.

5 Conclusion

We have developed a model of packet interference in a cluster of piconets using multi-slot packets and showed how the collision probability and aggregate throughput in a cluster of piconets degrade under various traffic scenarios and under various traffic scenarios, such 1-, 3-, and 5-slot packets in asymmetric and a synchronous condition of master clocks. We have also added the effect of interference power to the analysis model with Rayleigh and Rician distribution for the more realistic analysis. Through numerical results, we observe that if piconets using the same channel are not interfered by line-of-sight interferers, packet collision would decrease compared with 'binomial' model. This does not seem to be the case when there exist line-of-sight interferers. A further investigation is required to include the effect of packet generation rate for more realistic analysis.

Acknowledgement

This research was supported in part by KT in Republic of Korea.

References

1. K. Naik, D. S. L. Wei, Yu T. Su, and N. Shratori, "Analysis of packet interference and aggregated throughput in a cluster of Bluetooth piconets under different traffic conditions", IEEE Journal of Selected Areas in Communications, Vol.23, No.6, pp.1205-1218, June 2005.
2. A. El-Hoiydi, "Interference between Bluetooth networks-upper bound on the packet error rate", IEEE Communication. Letter, Vol.5, No.6, pp.245-247, June 2001.
3. K. Naik, D. S. L. Wei, and Y. T. Su, "Packet interference in a heterogeneous cluster of Bluetooth picondts", IEEE Vehicular Technology, Conference, pp.582-586, Oct. 2003.
4. J. G. Proakis, *Digital Communications*, 2nd ed. McGraw-Hill, New York, 1989.
5. R. Prasad, and C.-Y. Liu, "Throughput analysis of some mobile packet radio protocols in Rician fading channels", IEE PROCEEDINGS-I, Vol. 139, No.3, June 1992.
6. S. Benedetto, E. Biglieri, and V. Castellani, *Digital Transmission Theory*, PRENTICE-HALL, 1987.
7. The Bluetooth Special Interest Group. Baseband Specification Version 1.1 (2001). [Online]. Available: http://www.bluetooth.com.

Jitter Distribution Evaluation and Suppression Method in UWB Systems

Weihua Zhang, Hanbing Shen, Zhiquan Bai, and Kyung Sup Kwak

UWB Wireless Communications Research Center (INHA UWB-ITRC),
Inha University, 402-751, Incheon, Korea
{zhweihua2000}@hotmail.com

Abstract. For the extreme short duration of the baseband Impulse Radio (IR) Ultra-Wideband (UWB) transmission waveforms, even small amounts of timing jitter can bring out considerable system performance degradation. Thus jitter performance evaluation and corresponding suppression methods are very important for UWB high rate transceiver. We analyzed the jitter distribution function in UWB systems, also a jitter suppression method is proposed by modification of template waveforms. Performance of our proposed waveforms and traditional template waveforms are compared by analysis and simulation, and the results verify our jitter suppression method works.[1]

1 Introduction

Ultra-wideband (UWB) is proposed as the primary candidate for the physical layer technology of next high speed short range wireless communication for personal area networks (PAN) [1]. This radio technology is based on the radiation of waveforms formed by a sequence of very short, about nanosecond or below nanosecond, base band pulses [2]. The impulsive nature means that synchronization error (or jitter) influences the correlation of the received waveform and the template waveform generated in the receiver, thus deteriorates the system perform.

Some past researches about this problem have been proposed: The effects of timing jitter on the bit error rate (BER) of UWB have been analyzed [3][4]. To suppressing this degradation system clock with higher stability is proposed which has the capability of precisely positioning the sub-nanosecond pulses with Gaussian distributed root-mean-squared (RMS) jitter of 10ps and within a 50ns time window [5]. However, even if the system clocks are very stable and introduce very little jitter, other issues such as relative velocities between transmitter and receiver introduce additional degradation [6].

[1] This research was supported by the MIC (Ministry of Information and Communication), Korea, under the ITRC (Information Technology Research Center) support program supervised by the IITA (Institute of Information Technology Advancement) (IITA-2006-(C1090-0603-0019)).

Y.-H. Lee et al. (Eds.): ICESS 2007, LNCS 4523, pp. 810–817, 2007.

We offered an approach to suppress the system BER degradation introduced by timing jitter in the paper. This approach is based on modification of the receiver template according to the jitter distribution function to gain more correlation with the jittered received signals. We also offered two evaluation methods of jitter distribution function which can be adopted in our proposed schemes.

2 System Model

2.1 Signal Model of Transmission and Receiving

Generic transmission signal $s(t)$ of BPSK and PPM systems for the n-th bit can be given by:

$$\begin{aligned} &\text{BPSK:} \quad s(t)=\sqrt{\frac{E_b}{N_s}}\sum_{n=-\infty}^{\infty}\sum_{j=0}^{N_s-1} b_n w_t(t-nT_f-jT_h) \\ &\text{PPM:} \quad s(t)=\sqrt{\frac{E_b}{N_s}}\sum_{n=-\infty}^{\infty}\sum_{j=0}^{N_s-1} w_t\left(t-nT_f-jT_h-\frac{\delta}{2}(1-b_n)\right) \end{aligned} , \quad (1)$$

where $b_n \in \{-1,+1\}$ is the n-th transmitted binary data bit. E_b is the energy of one bit signal. $w_t(t)$ is the transmitted waveform with unit energy. N_s is the number of pulses per bit. T_h is the nominal interval between two pulses. $T_f = N_sT_h$, which is the average time duration of one transmission symbol. δ is the modulation index if the modulation is PPM.

The received signals are given by:

$$\begin{aligned} &\text{BPSK:} \quad s(t)=\alpha\sqrt{\frac{E_b}{N_s}}\sum_{n=-\infty}^{\infty}\sum_{j=0}^{N_s-1} b_n w_r(t-nT_f-jT_h-\tau_j(n))+n(t) \\ &\text{PPM:} \quad s(t)=\alpha\sqrt{\frac{E_b}{N_s}}\sum_{n=-\infty}^{\infty}\sum_{j=0}^{N_s-1} w_r\left(t-nT_f-jT_h-\frac{\delta}{2}(1-b_n)-\tau_j(n)\right)+n(t) \end{aligned} \quad (2)$$

where α is attenuation amplitude in the transmission path and $n(t)$ is additive white Gaussian noise (AWGN) with double sided spectrum of $N_0/2$. $w_r(t)$ is the received signal waveform with unit energy corresponding to $w_t(t)$. $\tau_j(n)$ is transmission delay for the j-th pulse of the n-th bit.

2.2 Timing Jitter

Jitter is simply the time difference between when a pre-defined event should have occurred and when it actually did occur [7]. In a UWB correlator receiver, the template signal can be given by:

$$v(t) = \sum_{n=-\infty}^{\infty}\sum_{j=0}^{N_s-1} w_r\left(t-nT_f-jT_h-\hat{\tau}_j(n)\right)+n(t), \quad (3)$$

where $\hat{\tau}_j(n)$ is the estimate value of $\tau_j(n)$. The time offset between these two delays $\epsilon_j(n) = \hat{\tau}_j(n) - \tau_j(n)$ is called timing jitter. The exact value of $\epsilon_j(n)$ can not be easily evaluated, whereas its distribution function can be evaluated. Timing jitter distribution characteristics models the timing jitter $\epsilon_j(n)$ as a sequence of Gaussian random variables with zero means and standard deviation of σ . The probability density function (pdf) can be given by:

$$f_\epsilon(\sigma,\tau) = \frac{1}{\sqrt{2\pi}\sigma}\exp\left(-\frac{\tau^2}{2\sigma^2}\right). \tag{4}$$

σ is also the average timing error of the jitters from the ideal template timing position, and it is the only parameter defining the jitter distribution.

3 Templates with Jitter Suppression Abilities

3.1 Pulse Shape of Proposed Templates

We assume that the template is jitter free and all the jitters come only from the received waveforms in analysis and simulation of this paper. To improve the system perform, higher correlation coefficient is required. Thereby a novel template is proposed to replace the original template waveform $w_r(t)$. We set

$$\hat{w}_r(t) = \int_{-\infty}^{\infty} f_\epsilon(\sigma,\tau)w_r(t-\tau)d\tau \tag{5}$$

as the novel template waveform. The correlation coefficient between timing shifted received waveform and proposed template is given by:

$$\hat{R}_{w_j}(\tau) = \frac{\int_{-\infty}^{\infty} w_r(t-\tau)\hat{w}_r(t)dt}{\sqrt{\int_{-\infty}^{\infty} w_r^2(t-\tau)dt}\sqrt{\int_{-\infty}^{\infty}\hat{w}_r^2(t)dt}} = \frac{\int_{-\infty}^{\infty} w_r(t-\tau)\hat{w}_r(t)dt}{\sqrt{\int_{-\infty}^{\infty}\hat{w}_r^2(t)dt}}. \tag{6}$$

The correlation between the timing shifted received waveform and jitter free template waveform is $R(\tau)$.Thus the integral correlation coefficient between the jitter free template waveform and the jittered received waveform is given by:

$$\rho = \int_{-\infty}^{\infty} f_\epsilon(\sigma,\tau)R(\tau)d\tau = \int_{-\infty}^{\infty} f_\epsilon(\sigma,\tau)\int_{-\infty}^{\infty} w_r(t-\tau)w_r(t)dtd\tau = \int_{-\infty}^{\infty}\hat{w}_r(t)w_r(t)dt. \tag{7}$$

The integral correlation coefficient between the jitter free proposed template waveform and the jittered received waveform is given by:

$$\hat{\rho} = \int_{-\infty}^{\infty} f_\epsilon(\sigma,\tau)\hat{R}(\tau)d\tau = \sqrt{\int_{-\infty}^{\infty}\hat{w}_r^2(t)dt}. \tag{8}$$

Next we will compare the correlation coefficients ρ and $\hat{\rho}$. We have $\hat{\rho} \geq 0$ in (8).

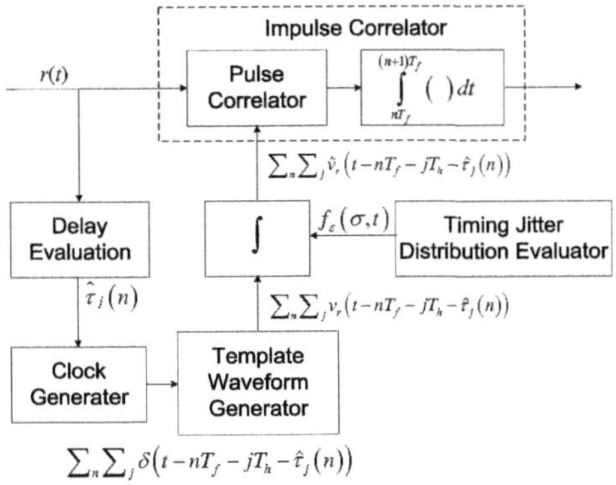

Fig. 1. General structure of proposed jitter suppression UWB correlator receiver

If $\rho < 0$,$\hat{\rho} \geq \rho$ deservedly. If $\rho \geq 0$, we use the method below to compare two correlation coefficients:

$$\left(\frac{\rho}{\hat{\rho}}\right)^2 = \frac{\left(\int_{-\infty}^{\infty} \hat{w}_r(t) w_r(t) dt\right)^2}{\int_{-\infty}^{\infty} \hat{w}_r^2(t) dt}. \tag{9}$$

Applying the Schwartz inequality to (9), we obtain:

$$\left(\int \hat{w}_r(t) w_r(t) dt\right)^2 \leq \int \hat{w}_r^2(t) dt \cdot \int w_r^2(t) dt = \int \hat{w}_r^2(t) dt. \tag{10}$$

So we have $\hat{\rho} \geq \rho$, consequently.

The conclusion is that our proposed template waveform has higher correlation value with the jittered received signal waveform than the original template waveform in any jitter distribution schemes.

3.2 Receiver Structure and Novel Template Waveforms Functions

The structure of the proposed receiver is given in Fig.1, where timing jitter distribution evaluator and an integrator used to realize our proposed template are added to the template waveform generator.

If the jitter free pulse waveform is given by

$$w_r(t) = \left(1 - 4\pi\left(\frac{t}{\tau_m}\right)^2\right) \exp\left(-2\pi\left(\frac{t}{\tau_m}\right)\right), \tag{11}$$

the proposed template waveforms can be deduced as:

$$\hat{w}_r(t) = \int f_\epsilon(\sigma,\tau) w_r(t-\tau) d\tau = \mu\left(\tau_m^2 + 4\pi\sigma^2 - 4\pi t^2\right) \exp\left(\frac{-2\pi t^2}{\tau_m^2 + 4\pi\sigma^2}\right), \tag{12}$$

where μ is attenuation parameters which can be used to adjust the amplitude of the template waveform. Fig.2(a) and Fig.2(b) give out the samples of our proposed jitter robust template waveforms, where the original jitter free waveform is same as (11), and proposed waveforms corresponding to different jitter distribution parameters ($\sigma = 0.1$ns, $\sigma = 0.2$ns and $\sigma = 0.5$ns) are given, respectively.

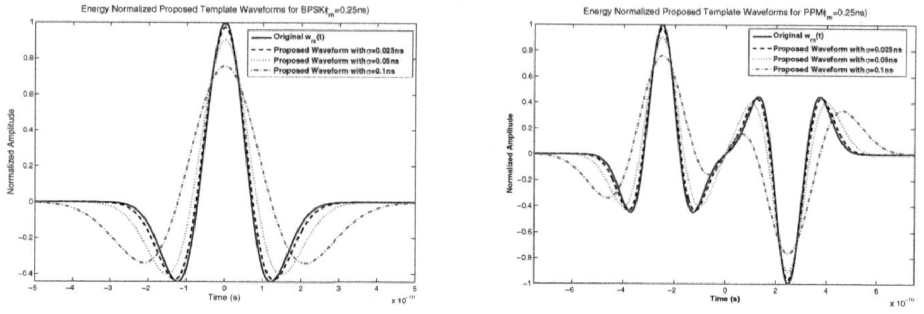

(a) BPSK system (b) PPM system

Fig. 2. Original template and the proposed jitter robust templates

4 Jitter Evaluation Methods

Timing jitter distribution evaluator is the key function module in proposed jitter suppression scheme. As jitter distribution is a Gaussian i.i.d function, the target of jitter distribution evaluation is to achieve the unique Gaussian distribution parameter σ. There are two different schemes to evaluate this parameter σ: pilot impulse sequence (PIS) and waveform parameter evaluation (WPE):

4.1 Pilot Impulse Sequence (PIS) Method

This method depends on such a scheme: the transmitter sends fixed pilot sequence of impulse-like waveforms periodically, which is given by:

$$S_T(t) = \sum_{n=0}^{N_t-1} \delta(t - nT_d), \tag{13}$$

where N_t is the number of impulse-like waveforms, and T_d is the fixed time interval of the waveforms. Received impulses sequence is given by:

$$S_R(t) = \alpha \sum_{n=0}^{N_t-1} \delta(t - nT_d - \tau - \epsilon(n)) + n(t), \tag{14}$$

where α is the amplitude weight of the channel and τ is the time delay which is introduced by channel, $\epsilon(n)$ is timing jitter. $n(t)$ is Gaussian distributed noise.The receiver produces a sequence of same impulse-like waveforms with the same periodic:

$$R_R(t) = \sum_{n=0}^{N_t-1} \delta(t - nT_d - \tau). \tag{15}$$

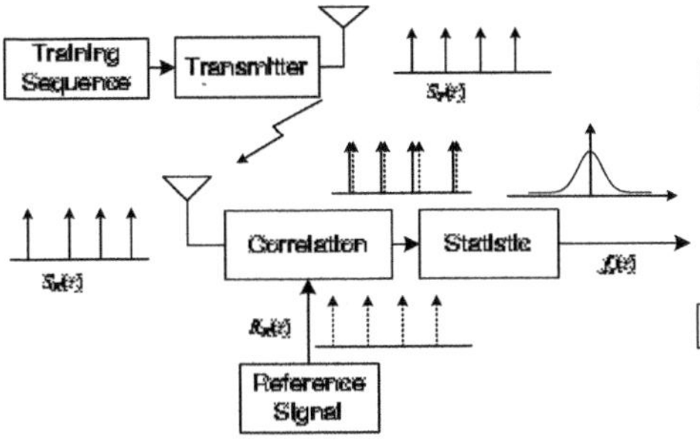

Fig. 3. PIS jitter distribution evaluator

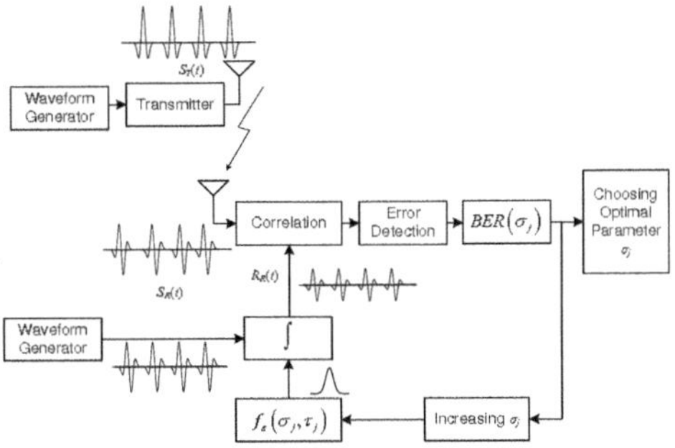

Fig. 4. WPE jitter distribution evaluator

Without considering the noise, the n-th timing jitter $\epsilon_e(n)$ can be evaluated by comparing $R_R(t)$ and $S_R(t)$ in the n-th time slice:

$$\begin{aligned} m(n,\tau_d) = \int_{nT_d+\tau}^{(n+1)T_d+\tau} S_R(n,t)R_R(t+\tau_d)dt \cong R_\delta(\tau_d - \epsilon(n)) \\ \epsilon_e(n) = \arg\max_{\tau_d}\left(m(n,\tau_d)\right) \quad . \end{aligned} \tag{16}$$

After achieving enough statistic of $\epsilon_e(n)$, jitter distribution function can be achieved. The system block is given in Fig.3. The PIS method is suitable for systems with any distribution functions and parameters. The disadvantage rests with request for system clock with high definition and stability. The definition and stability of the system clock confirms the evaluation veracity.

4.2 Waveform Parameter Evaluation(WPE) Method

We can design jitter resist template waveforms of different s. The template achieving the best BER is the optimal template. This method also requires a long WPE duration in which transmitter sends a series of waveforms with predefined information. If this predefined information is all "1", the transmitted waveform can be given by:

$$S_T(t) = \sum_{n=0}^{N_t-1} w_t(t - nT_d). \tag{17}$$

The receiver produces N_s different template waveforms, each is designed with different jitter resist parameter $f_\epsilon(\sigma_j, \tau_j)$ by the proposed method. The j-th template waveform is given by:

$$\hat{w}_r(j,t) = \int_{-\infty}^{\infty} f_\epsilon(\sigma_j,\tau_j) w_r(t-\tau_j) d\tau_j. \tag{18}$$

σ_j increases from 0 to a certain value with a step of $\Delta\sigma_j$, a statistic mechanism will count the corresponding BER, the evaluated distribution parameter σ_e is:

$$\sigma_e = \arg\max_{\tau_j}\left(BER(\sigma_j)\right). \tag{19}$$

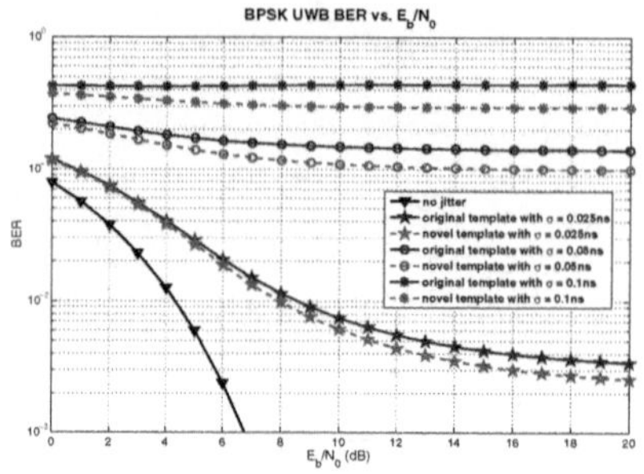

Fig. 5. BER vs. E_b/N_0 of BPSK systems

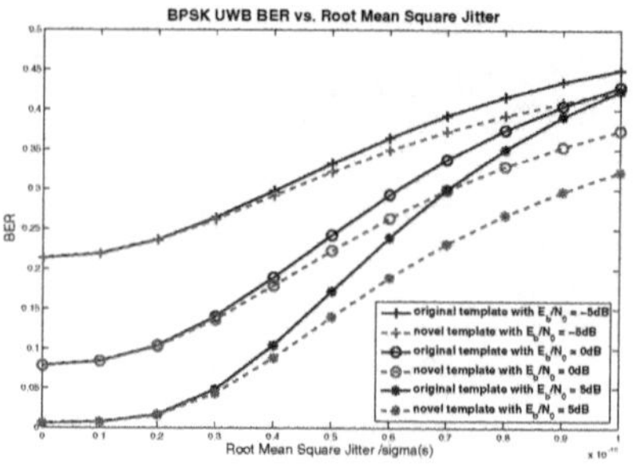

Fig. 6. BER vs. σ of BPSK systems

The system block figure is given in Fig. 4. WPE does not require a firm restriction on definition and stability of system clock. Also impulse-like waveforms are not imperative. However, it can only deal with a pre-known jitter distribution function, e.g. Gaussian distribution.

5 Computer Simulations

Based on the developed framework above, the system performance is evaluated and compared by computer simulations in this section.

Our simulations are categorized into two systems, a BPSK system and an orthogonal PPM system. We utilize the waveform of (11) and setting the time duration of the waveform as 0.5ns, τ_m as 0.25ns and the nominal interval between two pulses T_h as 2ns in both modulation schemes. To realize orthogonal PPM system time shift δ is set to equal to the pulse width 0.5ns.

The pulses are assumed to be transmitted through an AWGN channel for simplification in our analysis and simulation. Multi-user and multi-path are not considered, either.

The preliminary simulation results are presented in Fig.5 $\sim$ 8. Fig.5 and 6 are BER performance of BPSK systems. Fig.7 and 8 are of orthogonal PPM systems. At the same time, performances are compared by different E_b/N_0 and different jitter distribution parameters.

Fig.5 and 7 compare the BER vs. E_b/N_0 performance of conventional and proposed systems in different jitter distribution scenarios. Fig.6 and 8 compare the characteristics of BER vs. RMSJ of conventional and proposed systems in scenarios of different E_b/N_0.

Firstly, all scenarios show that our proposed jitter robust template waveforms outperform the original waveforms. Secondly, as E_b/N_0 increases (Fig.5 and 7), the BER reaches a static value; this is because that in the case of high E_b/N_0, it is the jitter not noise degrades BER. Also we found that as the jitter distribution parameter increases (Fig.6 and 8), more gain can be achieved by proposed schemes. This means that proposed schemes can perform better than the conventional ones when the jitter is severe.

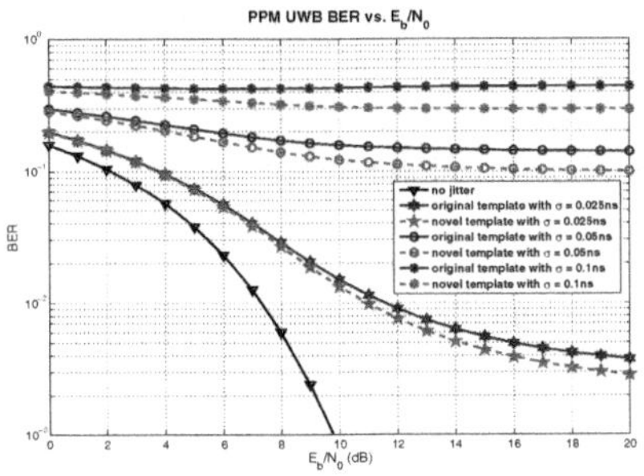

Fig. 7. BER vs. E_b/N_0 of PPM systems

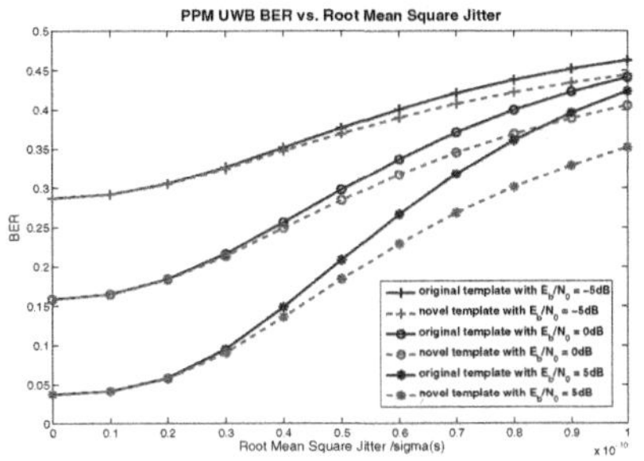

Fig. 8. BER vs. σ of PPM systems

6 Conclusions

We analyzed the properties of timing jitter and offer a novel jitter robust receiver template design method in UWB systems in this paper. Also we propose two jitter evaluation methods to perform proposed schemes. By analysis, we analyzed the performance of proposed waveforms and compared the proposed schemes with the conventional ones by computer simulation. Simulation results verified the proposed waveform with jitter suppression abilities outperform the conventional ones. Proposed template waveform design method can be used in other modulation schemes, for example pulse shape modulation (PSM) and is expected to achieve the same results.

References

1. 1. S. Roy, J. R. Forester, V. S. Somayazulu, and D. G. Leeper: Ultrawideband radio design: The promise of high-speed, short-range wireless connectivity. Proc. IEEE, Vol. 92, (2004) 295–311
2. M. Z. Win and R. A. Scholtz: Impulse radio: How it works. IEEE Communications Letters, Vol. 2, Iss. 2 (1998) 36–38
3. W. M. Lovelace and J. K. Townsend: The effects of timing jitter on the performance of impulse radio. Ultra Wideband Systems and Technologies, 2002. Digest of Papers. (2002) 251–254
4. P. B. Hor, C. C. Ko, and W. Zhi: BER performance of pulsed UWB system in the presence of colored timing jitter. Proc. IEEE Ultra Wideband Syst. Tech., 2004, (2004) 293-297
5. D. Kelly, S. Reinhardt, R. Stanley, and M. Einhorn: PulsON second generation timing chip: enabling UWB through precise timing. Proc. IEEE Conf. UWB Syst. Technol. (2002) 117–121
6. W. M. Lovelace and J. K. Townsend: The effects of timing jitter and tracking on the performance of impulse radio. IEEE J. Select. Areas Commun., Vol. 20, No. 9 (2002) 1646–1651
7. Maxim/Dallas Semiconductor: Jitter in Digital Communication Systems, Part 1. HFAN-04.0.3 Application Note 794 (2001)

An Analyzer of the User Event for Interactive DMB

Hlaing Su Khin and Sangwook Kim

Department of Computer Science, Kyungpook National University
1370 Sankyuk-dong Bukgu, Daegu, 702-701, Korea
{hskhin,swkim}@woorisol.knu.ac.kr

Abstract. The interactive digital multimedia broadcasting stands for a convergence application between digital multimedia broadcasting service and wireless internet service. It develops MPEG-4 BIFS (Binary Format for Scene) technologies which is standard component of associated data service for DMB. In this paper, we propose system architecture of the interactive DMB, called the interaction manager. The interactive DMB facilitates to transmit interactive contents and user can easily use these contents by clicking or typing some additional information. The proposed interactive DMB system can capture and response user interaction information by using the return channel. In this paper, we are mainly focused on extracting the event data of the user interaction on the device. We suggest an analyzer to catch the user event and transform into a specific format for bidirectional DMB service system.

1 Introduction

The interactive DMB is the new trend and interesting research in nowadays. The user will not be a receiver only but also he can interact by using the interactive DMB service system. User can directly interact with the advertisement products or retrieve the additional information. For that reason, the interaction between the user and the server is the important part to think for this kind of bidirectional service.

The earliest research was only emphasized on the whole part of the system and without detail considering about the interaction between the user and the server. They did not explain detail about the steps to develop this system. We imply the system architecture of the bidirectional DMB data service and describe how the user communicates with the DMB server and how the DMB servers can response to the user's requirements.

In this paper, we propose the idea that the interactive DMB service system and discuss each module of this system. Especially, we analyze the user event from the interaction part of the interactive DMB system. This is based on the BIFS of the MPEG-4 contents, which is the system level. In this part, the extraction of the user information is important and basis of the interaction of the DMB.

The rest of this paper is organized as follows. In section 2, we discuss about the related works of the DMB system, we introduce and describe the interactive data service for DMB system in section 3. In section 4, we describe about the user event analyzer, which is the first module in the proposed interactive DMB system. Finally, we conclude the paper and we give a note on our future work.

Y.-H. Lee et al. (Eds.): ICESS 2007, LNCS 4523, pp. 818–825, 2007.

2 Related Works

The current TV broadcasting also provides the interactive service indirectly, such as quiz program and voting based on viewer's feedback over telephone lines. In [4], Jitae Shin and others developed an interactive DMB system based on the MPEG-4 BIFS for bidirectional services. They provide the typical scenarios and corresponding data in detail for interactive DMB services and introduce the current TV broadcasting services to a direct mode by using a BIFS mechanism installed in the DMB terminal. [4] Before that B.Bae and other proposes a T-DMB extended wireless Internet platform for interoperability (WIPI) over a code division multiple access (CDMA) system for the return channel. Some paper focuses on the transmission of the DMB system.

The interactive DMB system can be categorized into three types. The user can interact with the server by the web browser, sending and receiving SMS messages or using return channel, for example CDMA cellular network, a wireless local area network (WLAN) in a hot-spot service area etc. In order to operate these environments, we need to set the protocol of data transfer in the return channel.

For the bidirectional data service via web browser, it needs the additional web server to support and manage the web site, contents and user information. User can be easily linked to the specific web site from the contents received by the server. It is possible to be implemented by ahchor node supported in MPEG-4 BIFS [5]. In the case of the bidirectional DMB system with the web server, the content provider can support lots of complicated services for the users such as, shopping, file downloading, voting online and so on. This kind of interactive service has to provide the site management fee and the web surfing fee. For the SMS service, the system is light weight, simple and easy to be implemented. But the data that can be held by the SMS message is very limited. EMS (Enhanced Messaging Service) was developed to send the rich media contents such as pictures, animation and melodies in original SMS services. It is also less widely supported than SMS on wireless devices. In the case of the return channel, the user can interact with the contents and transmit the user event information to the server directly and response the user event information in real time [7]. To support the bidirectional event, it need the specific protocol between the server (contents authoring tool and streaming server) and the player in user terminal. By using the bidirectional DMB service via a return channel, we proposed to add one main part in the original DMB system to deal with the user interaction.

3 Proposed Interactive DMB System Based on MPEG-4

In this section, we describe the architecture and the operations of the proposed interactive DMB system.

3.1 Architecture

Figure 1 shows the overall structure of the proposed interactive DMB system. In the DMB system, the various multimedia objects composing the contents can be encoded by correspondent encoder separately.

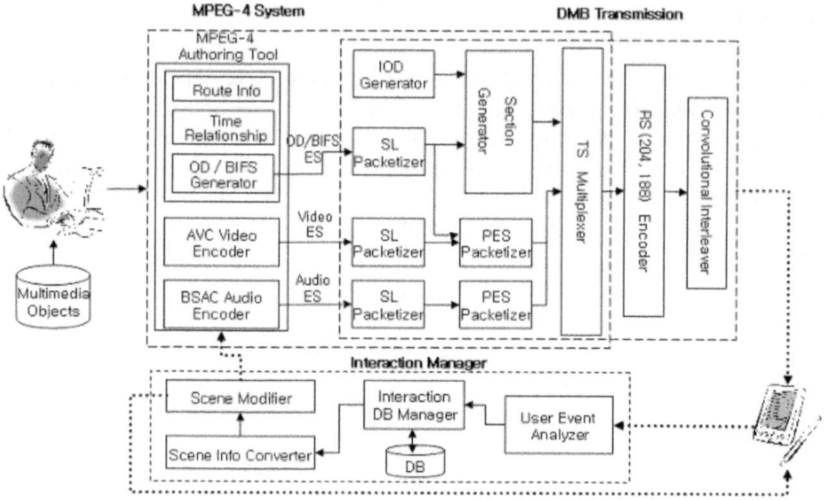

Fig. 1. The User Interactive DMB System with the Interaction Manager

Each elementary stream will go through the synch layer (SL) packetizer, transport stream (TS) multiplexer and it will be multiplexed at one stream. After adding forward error correction code (FEC: RS encoder and convolution interleave), the contents stream finally can be transmitted to the user's terminal [8].

For the bidirectional DMB service via a return channel, we designed a new module, called interaction manager to analyze and transmit user event information to the server. It consists of four modules, user event analyzer, interaction DB manager, scene info converter and scene modifier. The interaction manger can capture and analyze user's interaction from the handheld device and to arrange and return the requested information to the user. In authoring tools side, it needs to add some modification for creating the bidirectional contents. For the player, it needs to parse the scene information to extract the user's interaction information. The user interactions can be performed in two ways, mouse click and the text input. For example, the corresponding scenarios can be secret vote, online vote, commercial information, online quiz, file downloading and so on.

3.2 Operations

3.2.1 User Event Analyzer

In this module, we will extract the user's interaction to transform MPEG-4 BIFS to the requirement data type for the whole system. The user interaction will start when the user interacts with the contents by clicking mouse or type the text. The user interaction can be classified into two types, the interaction between the user and the streaming contents called inner action and the interaction between the user and the server, called bidirectional interaction.

The bidirectional interaction notifier is used to distinguish these two types. We added two fragments to the correspondent nodes ID to identify distinctly. The interaction info extractor will extract the node id of the corresponding object from the use event. If it is a text node, it will also extract the text contents. The information converter will convert the data from the interaction info extractor. It will convert data into the required information such as alternative ID in online quiz program. Information wrapping will bind the converted information with some additional data, such as user ID, content ID, etc. For deciding and defining the user's questions type (i.e., send, retrieve, search), we add one more field named action type. For the detail operation of user event analyzer, we will explain in detail in section 4.

3.2.2 Interaction DB Manager

The main function of the interaction DB manager is to make the decision processes for the user event information.

Simple operation of the Interaction DB Manager

```
begin (Action)
if ActionType= "1" then        RetrieveContents ();
    //Information correspondent to the current streaming contents from the database
  // ActionType, "1" for Retrieving the user requested data from the database , "2"
for Searching user requested information, and "3" for Storing the data into the da-
tabase if the user is answering online quiz or online voting
    elseif ActionType=" 2 " then  Search();
      //Search the user requested information from the database by given key words
    else Store();
endif
        GetData();//get the data from the database
        DecisionProcess();
         //make the decision using rules and the data from the database
         AddField(); //Info
     if  Info= "Important"  then AddFieldTrue(); //Server
         else AddFieldFalse();
     endif
      //Server Reaction Type,true for all users, false for individual user
     if  ActionType='3' then Store();
         else SelectResultInformation();
 SendData(); // send data to next step
end.
```

The example output data of the interaction DB manager will be Server Reaction Type, User ID, Contents ID, Question ID, Answer and Statistics (optional), etc.

3.2.3 Scene Information Converter

The purpose of this sub module is to create scene update plan for the user requested information. From the previous module, we already get the decision for the user's event.

Simple Algorithm for Scene Information Converter

```
begin SceneInfoConverter
    GetOutputData();        //result info from interaction manager
    Select(Decision Info);  // from the info data
repeat
    {
     AddScene();
     DeleteScene();
     ReplaceScene();
    }
until  UpdateInfo Finish
    ConvertInfo();
    UpdateBifs();
    SendData(); //send data to next step scene modifier
end.
```

The example output data for the scene information converter will be Server Reaction Type, User ID, Contents ID, Question ID and BIFS Commands for the Answer.

3.2.4 Scene Modifier

The Scene Modifier has only one main process. The following algorithm shows the processes occurred in the Scene Modifier.

Simple Algorithm for Scene Modifier

```
begin (SceneInfoConverter)
    GetData()
    for ( user from 1 to count)
       {
        Get(Time); //time scheduling
        If (User1Time>User2Time)   then Priority=User2
        Endif
       }
    endfor
    if  ReactionType='true' then TransmitToServer();
       else {
              EncodeData();
              TransmitToClient();    //transmit directly to the user
              }
end.
```

Output data format of the information for the individual person will be User ID, Contents ID, Question ID and the Encoded BIFS Stream data for the Answer. For the information needed to send to the every user will be User ID, Contents ID, Question ID, and Scheduled BIFS Command for the Answer.

4 User Event Analyzer

In this module, we will extract the user's interaction to transform MPEG-4 BIFS to the requirement data type for the whole system. There are five main parts in the user event analyzer.

The user interaction will start when the user interacts with the contents such as commercial advertisement, shopping request, electronic online voting, online quiz program, secret vote, and file downloading by clicking mouse or type the text. The user interaction can be classified into two types, the interaction between the user and the streaming contents called inner action and the interaction between the user and the server, called bidirectional interaction. The bidirectional interaction notifier is used to distinguish these two types. We added two fragments to the correspondent nodes ID to identify distinctly. A sample algorithm for the user event analyzer is as followed. The Example output data for the online quiz will be, User ID, Content ID, Action Type, Question ID and Candidate ID. The algorithm for the user event analyzer is as shown below.

Simple Algorithm for the User Event Analyzer

```
begin User Event
      if (User Click the contents Display)  then Get Node ID
         {
            if  Frag1 = 'bi'   then {
                                       if Frag2='0'
                                       then Select "Node ID, Question
                                               Action Type, Candidate ID, etc..."
                                       else goto Begin};
                                     }
            elseif Check Invoker="1"
                     then  {
                              Select "User ID, Content ID, Action Type..."
                           }
            else goto begin
           endif
         }
     else goto begin
    }
  else waiting user action;
end.
```

There are two ways to create the contents display. The contents consist of normal BIFS code or some specific script code. For the first case, when the user interaction occurs, we can only get node ID of the object correspondent to the user event. For this reason, we need to distinguish the outer action and the inner action by this node ID. Therefore the only way to notify the bidirectional action is adding some fragments to the node ID. For the second case, we need to pick up the value of the parameters in VRML script function. When the user interaction occurs, the event information will be stored into this parameter. Using the VRML scripts can be easy to implement the user event analyzer module. But it is difficult to author the contents in the server side. To notify whether it is outer action or not, we added a fragment to the original node ID. The node ID of the outer action in our system starts from the first fragment. The value of this fragment can be predefined with the authoring tool. The object for the outer action can be divided into two categories. One is the bidirectional start point and the other is the bidirectional interaction invoker. In our system, '0' means invoker and '1' means start point. We used Osmo4 as an open source Mpeg4-player for replaying the MP4 file in the demonstration. This sub system describes capturing the data of the user interaction. We are adding fragment in the normal BIFS data, so we can categorize the bidirectional event or interaction as mentioned above.

And we can also give the example for managing the user requested interaction as follows.

Fig. 2. A Screenshot Example of BouncingRectangle.mp4

This is example of the user interaction. When the user clicks the 'slow' button, the bouncing rectangle will bounce slowest rate as mentioned in the program, 'medium' and 'fast' button will be also working respectively. Additionally, we can see the rectangle translation in there too. This is just we can show that the user event can be captured and we can get the important data from the user event. Our proposed user event analyzer is based on this example and we will extend to develop the second part of the interaction manager.

5 Conclusion and Future Work

In this paper, we designed and added the interaction manager module for bidirectional user interactive DMB system. We explained each sub module of the interaction manager. Moreover, we gave attention on the first module, the user event analyzer and developed the rules to extract the user's interaction. In our example we used the naming technique for checking the inner action or the bidirectional action. We can find out the user's interaction information and also manage the required data for the remaining steps in the interaction manager. For this implementation we used the open sources for the MPEG-4 standards, GPAC Osmo4 player (GPAC Ver 0.4.2) and OSMO4 Client.

In future, we will continue our research on complete user event analyzer and the interaction DB manager, which is especially making an update plan for reaction information of the server and the command scheduling technique.

References

1. G.Lee, S.Cho, K.Yang, Y.Hahm and S.Lee, "Development of Terrestrial DMB Transmission System based on Eureka-147 DAB System," IEEE Transactions on Consumer Electronics, Volume 51, Issue 1, pp.63-68, February 2005.
2. DMB for Mobile Video for Cell Phone System, Radio-Electronic.com, http://www.radio-electronics.com/info/cellulartelecomms/mobile_video/dmb.php#top
3. net&tv Inc., http://www.netntv.co.kr/pdf/idmb_brochure.pdf
4. J. Shin, D.Y. Suh, Y. Jeong, S. H. Park, B. Bae, and C. Ahn, "Demonstration of Bidirectional Services Using MPEG-4 BIFS in Terrestrial DMB Systems," ETRI Journal, Volume 28, No.5, pp. 583-592, October 2006.
5. V.Ha, S.Choi, J.Jeon, G.Lee,W .Jang and W.Shin, "Realtime Audio/Video Decoders for Digital Multimedia Broadcasting," 4th IEEE International Workshop on (IWSOC'04), pp.162-167, July 2004.
6. M. Grube, P. Siepen, C. Mittendorf, M.Boltz and M.Srinivasan, "Applications of MPEG-4: Digital Multimedia Broadcasting," IEEE Transactions on Consumer Electronics, Volume 47, No.3, pp.474-484, August 2001.
7. Y. He, Ahmad, I.,Liou,M.L, "Real-Time Interactive MPEG-4 System Encoder using a Cluster of Workstations," IEEE transactions on Multimedia, Volume 1, Issue 2, pp.217-233, June 1999.
8. O.Avaro, A. Eleftheriadis, "MPEG-4 Systems: Overview" Signal Processing: Image Communication, Tutorial Issue on the MPEG-4 Standard, Volume 15, No.4-5, pp. 281-298, January 2000.
9. WG11 (MPEG) MPEG-4 Overview (V.21-Jeju Version) Document, ISO/IEC JTC1/SC29/WGN4668, March 2002.
10. Puri and A.Elefthriadis, "MPEG-4: An Object-Based Multimedia Coding Standard Supporting Mobile Applications," Mobile Network Applications, Volume 3, pp.5-32, June 1998.
11. Herpel and A.Eleftheriadis, "MPEG-4 Systems: Elementary Stream Management," Signal Processing: Image Communication, Volume 15, No.4-5, pp.299-320, January 2000.
12. K.A.Cha and S.Kim, "MPEG-4 STUDIO: An Object- Based Authoring System for MPEG-4 Contents," MULTIMEDIA TOOLS AND APPLICATIONS, Kluwer Academic Publishers, Volume 25, No.1, pp.111-131, January 2005.
13. Open Source, Developer Connection, http://developer.apple.com//opensource/index.html
14. Telecom Paris,http://www.comelec.enst.fr/osmo4/

Author Index

Lecture Notes in Computer Science

For information about Vols. 1–4389

please contact your bookseller or Springer

Vol. 4523: Y.-H. Lee, H.-N. Kim, J. Kim, Y. Park, L.T. Yang, S.W. Kim (Eds.), Embedded Software and Systems. XIX, 829 pages. 2007.

Vol. 4517: F. Boavida, E. Monteiro, S. Mascolo, Y. Koucheryavy (Eds.), Wired/Wireless Internet Communications. XIV, 382 pages. 2007.

Vol. 4515: M. Naor (Ed.), Advances in Cryptology - EUROCRYPT 2007. XIII, 591 pages. 2007.

Vol. 4510: P. Van Hentenryck, L. Wolsey (Eds.), Integration of AI and OR Techniques in Constraint Programming for Combinatorial Optimization Problems. X, 391 pages. 2007.

Vol. 4509: Z. Kobti, D. Wu (Eds.), Advances in Artificial Intelligence. XII, 552 pages. 2007. (Sublibrary LNAI).

Vol. 4506: D. Zeng, I. Gotham, K. Komatsu, C. Lynch, M. Thurmond, D. Madigan, B. Lober, J. Kvach, H. Chen (Eds.), Intelligence and Security Informatics: Biosurveillance. XI, 234 pages. 2007.

Vol. 4504: J. Huang, R. Kowalczyk, Z. Maamar, D. Martin, I. Müller, S. Stoutenburg, K.P. Sycara (Eds.), Service-Oriented Computing: Agents, Semantics, and Engineering. X, 175 pages. 2007.

Vol. 4493: D. Liu, S. Fei, Z. Hou, H. Zhang, C. Sun (Eds.), Advances in Neural Networks – ISNN 2007, Part III. XXVI, 1215 pages. 2007.

Vol. 4492: D. Liu, S. Fei, Z. Hou, H. Zhang, C. Sun (Eds.), Advances in Neural Networks – ISNN 2007, Part II. XXVII, 1321 pages. 2007.

Vol. 4491: D. Liu, S. Fei, Z.-G. Hou, H. Zhang, C. Sun (Eds.), Advances in Neural Networks – ISNN 2007, Part I. LIV, 1365 pages. 2007.

Vol. 4486: M. Bernardo, J. Hillston (Eds.), Formal Methods for Performance Evaluation. VII, 469 pages. 2007.

Vol. 4484: J.-Y. Cai, S.B. Cooper, H. Zhu (Eds.), Theory and Applications of Models of Computation. XIII, 772 pages. 2007.

Vol. 4483: C. Baral, G. Brewka, J. Schlipf (Eds.), Logic Programming and Nonmonotonic Reasoning. IX, 327 pages. 2007. (Sublibrary LNAI).

Vol. 4482: A. An, J. Stefanowski, S. Ramanna, C.J. Butz, W. Pedrycz, G. Wang (Eds.), Rough Sets, Fuzzy Sets, Data Mining and Granular Computing. XIV, 585 pages. 2007. (Sublibrary LNAI).

Vol. 4481: J. Yao, P. Lingras, W.-Z. Wu, M. Szczuka, N.J. Cercone, D. Ślęzak (Eds.), Rough Sets and Knowledge Technology. XIV, 576 pages. 2007. (Sublibrary LNAI).

Vol. 4480: A. LaMarca, M. Langheinrich, K.N. Truong (Eds.), Pervasive Computing. XIII, 369 pages. 2007.

Vol. 4479: I.F. Akyildiz, R. Sivakumar, E. Ekici, J.C.d. Oliveira, J. McNair (Eds.), NETWORKING 2007. Ad Hoc and Sensor Networks, Wireless Networks, Next Generation Internet. XXVII, 1252 pages. 2007.

Vol. 4472: M. Haindl, J. Kittler, F. Roli (Eds.), Multiple Classifier Systems. XI, 524 pages. 2007.

Vol. 4471: P. Cesar, K. Chorianopoulos, J.F. Jensen (Eds.), Interactive TV: a Shared Experience. XIII, 236 pages. 2007.

Vol. 4470: Q. Wang, D. Pfahl, D.M. Raffo (Eds.), Software Process Dynamics and Agility. XI, 346 pages. 2007.

Vol. 4464: E. Dawson, D.S. Wong (Eds.), Information Security Practice and Experience. XIII, 361 pages. 2007.

Vol. 4463: I. Măndoiu, A. Zelikovsky (Eds.), Bioinformatics Research and Applications. XV, 653 pages. 2007. (Sublibrary LNBI).

Vol. 4462: D. Sauveron, K. Markantonakis, A. Bilas, J.-J. Quisquater (Eds.), Information Security Theory and Practices. XII, 255 pages. 2007.

Vol. 4459: C. Cérin, K.-C. Li (Eds.), Advances in Grid and Pervasive Computing. XVI, 759 pages. 2007.

Vol. 4453: T. Speed, H. Huang (Eds.), Research in Computational Molecular Biology. XVI, 550 pages. 2007. (Sublibrary LNBI).

Vol. 4452: M. Fasli, O. Shehory (Eds.), Agent-Mediated Electronic Commerce. VIII, 249 pages. 2007. (Sublibrary LNAI).

Vol. 4451: T.S. Huang, A. Nijholt, M. Pantic, A. Pentland (Eds.), Artifical Intelligence for Human Computing. XVI, 359 pages. 2007. (Sublibrary LNAI).

Vol. 4450: T. Okamoto, X. Wang (Eds.), Public Key Cryptography – PKC 2007. XIII, 491 pages. 2007.

Vol. 4448: M. Giacobini et al. (Ed.), Applications of Evolutionary Computing. XXIII, 755 pages. 2007.

Vol. 4447: E. Marchiori, J.H. Moore, J.C. Rajapakse (Eds.), Evolutionary Computation,Machine Learning and Data Mining in Bioinformatics. XI, 302 pages. 2007.

Vol. 4446: C. Cotta, J. van Hemert (Eds.), Evolutionary Computation in Combinatorial Optimization. XII, 241 pages. 2007.

Vol. 4445: M. Ebner, M. O'Neill, A. Ekárt, L. Vanneschi, A.I. Esparcia-Alcázar (Eds.), Genetic Programming. XI, 382 pages. 2007.

Vol. 4444: T. Reps, M. Sagiv, J. Bauer (Eds.), Program Analysis and Compilation, Theory and Practice. X, 361 pages. 2007.

Vol. 4443: R. Kotagiri, P.R. Krishna, M. Mohania, E. Nantajeewarawat (Eds.), Advances in Databases: Concepts, Systems and Applications. XXI, 1126 pages. 2007.

Vol. 4440: B. Liblit, Cooperative Bug Isolation. XV, 101 pages. 2007.

Vol. 4439: W. Abramowicz (Ed.), Business Information Systems. XV, 654 pages. 2007.

Vol. 4438: L. Maicher, A. Sigel, L.M. Garshol (Eds.), Leveraging the Semantics of Topic Maps. X, 257 pages. 2007. (Sublibrary LNAI).

Vol. 4433: E. Şahin, W.M. Spears, A.F.T. Winfield (Eds.), Swarm Robotics. XII, 221 pages. 2007.

Vol. 4432: B. Beliczynski, A. Dzielinski, M. Iwanowski, B. Ribeiro (Eds.), Adaptive and Natural Computing Algorithms, Part II. XXVI, 761 pages. 2007.

Vol. 4431: B. Beliczynski, A. Dzielinski, M. Iwanowski, B. Ribeiro (Eds.), Adaptive and Natural Computing Algorithms, Part I. XXV, 851 pages. 2007.

Vol. 4430: C.C. Yang, D. Zeng, M. Chau, K. Chang, Q. Yang, X. Cheng, J. Wang, F.-Y. Wang, H. Chen (Eds.), Intelligence and Security Informatics. XII, 330 pages. 2007.

Vol. 4429: R. Lu, J.H. Siekmann, C. Ullrich (Eds.), Cognitive Systems. X, 161 pages. 2007. (Sublibrary LNAI).

Vol. 4427: S. Uhlig, K. Papagiannaki, O. Bonaventure (Eds.), Passive and Active Network Measurement. XI, 274 pages. 2007.

Vol. 4426: Z.-H. Zhou, H. Li, Q. Yang (Eds.), Advances in Knowledge Discovery and Data Mining. XXV, 1161 pages. 2007. (Sublibrary LNAI).

Vol. 4425: G. Amati, C. Carpineto, G. Romano (Eds.), Advances in Information Retrieval. XIX, 759 pages. 2007.

Vol. 4424: O. Grumberg, M. Huth (Eds.), Tools and Algorithms for the Construction and Analysis of Systems. XX, 738 pages. 2007.

Vol. 4423: H. Seidl (Ed.), Foundations of Software Science and Computational Structures. XVI, 379 pages. 2007.

Vol. 4422: M.B. Dwyer, A. Lopes (Eds.), Fundamental Approaches to Software Engineering. XV, 440 pages. 2007.

Vol. 4421: R. De Nicola (Ed.), Programming Languages and Systems. XVII, 538 pages. 2007.

Vol. 4420: S. Krishnamurthi, M. Odersky (Eds.), Compiler Construction. XIV, 233 pages. 2007.

Vol. 4419: P.C. Diniz, E. Marques, K. Bertels, M.M. Fernandes, J.M.P. Cardoso (Eds.), Reconfigurable Computing: Architectures, Tools and Applications. XIV, 391 pages. 2007.

Vol. 4418: A. Gagalowicz, W. Philips (Eds.), Computer Vision/Computer Graphics Collaboration Techniques. XV, 620 pages. 2007.

Vol. 4416: A. Bemporad, A. Bicchi, G. Buttazzo (Eds.), Hybrid Systems: Computation and Control. XVII, 797 pages. 2007.

Vol. 4415: P. Lukowicz, L. Thiele, G. Tröster (Eds.), Architecture of Computing Systems - ARCS 2007. X, 297 pages. 2007.

Vol. 4414: S. Hochreiter, R. Wagner (Eds.), Bioinformatics Research and Development. XVI, 482 pages. 2007. (Sublibrary LNBI).

Vol. 4412: F. Stajano, H.J. Kim, J.-S. Chae, S.-D. Kim (Eds.), Ubiquitous Convergence Technology. XI, 302 pages. 2007.

Vol. 4411: R.H. Bordini, M. Dastani, J. Dix, A.E.F. Seghrouchni (Eds.), Programming Multi-Agent Systems. XIV, 249 pages. 2007. (Sublibrary LNAI).

Vol. 4410: A. Branco (Ed.), Anaphora: Analysis, Algorithms and Applications. X, 191 pages. 2007. (Sublibrary LNAI).

Vol. 4409: J.L. Fiadeiro, P.-Y. Schobbens (Eds.), Recent Trends in Algebraic Development Techniques. VII, 171 pages. 2007.

Vol. 4407: G. Puebla (Ed.), Logic-Based Program Synthesis and Transformation. VIII, 237 pages. 2007.

Vol. 4406: W. De Meuter (Ed.), Advances in Smalltalk. VII, 157 pages. 2007.

Vol. 4405: L. Padgham, F. Zambonelli (Eds.), Agent-Oriented Software Engineering VII. XII, 225 pages. 2007.

Vol. 4403: S. Obayashi, K. Deb, C. Poloni, T. Hiroyasu, T. Murata (Eds.), Evolutionary Multi-Criterion Optimization. XIX, 954 pages. 2007.

Vol. 4401: N. Guelfi, D. Buchs (Eds.), Rapid Integration of Software Engineering Techniques. IX, 177 pages. 2007.

Vol. 4400: J.F. Peters, A. Skowron, V.W. Marek, E. Orłowska, R. Słowiński, W. Ziarko (Eds.), Transactions on Rough Sets VII, Part II. X, 381 pages. 2007.

Vol. 4399: T. Kovacs, X. Llorà, K. Takadama, P.L. Lanzi, W. Stolzmann, S.W. Wilson (Eds.), Learning Classifier Systems. XII, 345 pages. 2007. (Sublibrary LNAI).

Vol. 4398: S. Marchand-Maillet, E. Bruno, A. Nürnberger, M. Detyniecki (Eds.), Adaptive Multimedia Retrieval: User, Context, and Feedback. XI, 269 pages. 2007.

Vol. 4397: C. Stephanidis, M. Pieper (Eds.), Universal Access in Ambient Intelligence Environments. XV, 467 pages. 2007.

Vol. 4396: J. García-Vidal, L. Cerdà-Alabern (Eds.), Wireless Systems and Mobility in Next Generation Internet. IX, 271 pages. 2007.

Vol. 4395: M. Daydé, J.M.L.M. Palma, Á.L.G.A. Coutinho, E. Pacitti, J.C. Lopes (Eds.), High Performance Computing for Computational Science - VECPAR 2006. XXIV, 721 pages. 2007.

Vol. 4394: A. Gelbukh (Ed.), Computational Linguistics and Intelligent Text Processing. XVI, 648 pages. 2007.

Vol. 4393: W. Thomas, P. Weil (Eds.), STACS 2007. XVIII, 708 pages. 2007.

Vol. 4392: S.P. Vadhan (Ed.), Theory of Cryptography. XI, 595 pages. 2007.

Vol. 4391: Y. Stylianou, M. Faundez-Zanuy, A. Esposito (Eds.), Progress in Nonlinear Speech Processing. XII, 269 pages. 2007.

Vol. 4390: S.O. Kuznetsov, S. Schmidt (Eds.), Formal Concept Analysis. X, 329 pages. 2007. (Sublibrary LNAI).

Batch number: 10844661

Printed by Printforce, the Netherlands